National Parks, Conservation, and Development

The Role of Protected Areas
in Sustaining Society

National Parks, Conservation, and Development

The Role of Protected Areas in Sustaining Society

Edited by **Jeffrey A. McNeely** and **Kenton R. Miller**
IUCN Commission on National Parks and Protected Areas

Proceedings of the World Congress on National Parks
Bali, Indonesia, 11–22 October 1982

International Union for Conservation
of Nature and Natural Resources

in cooperation with

United Nations Environment Programme
United Nations Educational, Scientific and Cultural Organization

World Wildlife Fund–U.S.

PARKS Canada
United States National Park Service

Published by the **Smithsonian Institution Press,** Washington, D.C.

Copyright © 1984 by the Smithsonian Institution.
All rights reserved.

Library of Congress Cataloging-in-Publication Data

World Congress on National Parks (1982 : Bali, Indonesia)
  National parks, conservation, and development.

  Bibliography: p.
  1. National parks and reserves—Congresses.   2. Natural
areas—Congresses.   3. Nature conservation—Congresses.
4. Conservation of natural resources—Congresses.
I. McNeely, Jeffrey A.   II. Miller, Kenton.   III. International Union for Conservation of Nature and Natural
Resources.   IV. Title.
SB481.A2W67   1982   333.78'3   84-600007
ISBN 0-87474-663-9

54,522

The paper in this book meets the guidelines for permanence and
durability of the Committee on Production Guidelines for Book
Longevity of the Council on Library Resources.

This book was edited by Ruth W. Spiegel.
Design by McIver Art.

Cover photograph by James W. Thorsell

Contents

CAMROSE LUTHERAN COLLEGE
LIBRARY

viii

Meeting in Denpasar, Bali, from 11 to 22 October 1982, in response to the generous invitation of the Government of Indonesia, the World National Parks Congress considered principles and policies to guide the establishment and management of national parks and other types of protected areas in light of the broad principles governing the interrelationships among population, resources, environment, and development formulated by the series of intergovernmental conferences that began at Stockholm in 1972. The Congress took particular note of the World Conservation Strategy (1980) and the World Charter for nature (1982) and reaffirmed the fundamental role of national parks and other protected areas in contributing to sustainable development and the spiritual and cultural needs of humankind. Participants included planners, managers, and supporters of protected areas, and scientists from 68 countries.

**Declaration of the World
National Parks Congress
Bali, Indonesia, 11–22 October 1982**

WE, the participants in the World National Parks Congress, BELIEVE that:

People are a part of nature. Their spiritual and material wellbeing depends upon the wisdom applied to the protection and use of living resources. Development needed for the betterment of the human condition requires conservation of living resources for it to be sustainable.

Earth is the only place in the universe known to sustain life, yet as species are lost and ecosystems degraded, its capacity to do so is rapidly reduced, because of rising populations, excessive consumption and misuse of natural resources, pollution, careless development, and failure to establish an appropriate economic order among people and among States. The benefits of nature and living resources that will be enjoyed by future generations will be determined by the decisions of today. Ours may be the last generation able to choose large natural areas to protect.

Experience has shown that protected areas are an indispensable element of living resource conservation because:

they maintain those essential ecological processes that depend on natural ecosystems;

they preserve the diversity of species and the genetic variation within them, thereby preventing irreversible damage to our natural heritage;

they maintain the productive capacities of ecosystems and safeguard habitats critical for the sustainable use of species;

they provide opportunities for scientific research and for education and training.

By so doing, and by providing places for recreation and tourism, protected areas make an essential contribution to sustainable development.

At the same time protected areas serve the spiritual and cultural needs of people by securing the wilderness and sacred areas on which so many draw for aesthetic, emotional, and religious nourishment. They provide a vital link between us, our past, and our future, confirming the oneness of humanity and nature.

To these ends, therefore, WE DECLARE the following actions as fundamental:

1. Expand and strengthen the global and regional networks of national parks and other protected areas to give lasting security to: representative and unique ecosystems; as full a range as possible of Earth's biotic diversity including wild genetic resources; natural areas important for scientific research; natural areas of spiritual and cultural value.

2. Support the establishment and management of protected areas through national commitment and international development assistance.

3. Provide permanent status for protected areas in legislation securing their objectives against compromise.

4. Plan and manage protected areas using the best available scientifc information; increase scientific knowledge through research and monitoring programmes; and make it readily available to scientists, managers, and the general public throughout the world.

5. Recognize the economic, cultural, and political contexts of protected areas; increase local support for protected areas through such measures as education, revenue sharing, participation in decisions, complementary development schemes adjacent to the protected area, and, where compatible with the protected area's objectives, access to resources.

6. Implement fully the existing international conventions concerning protected areas, and adopt such new conventions as may be required.

WE PLEDGE ourselves to these actions as a contribution to sustainable development and hence to the spiritual and material welfare of all people; and

CALL UPON all governments, singly and collectively, to take these actions with due despatch, bearing in mind their responsibility for the whole of life and their accountability to present and future generations.

Acknowledgements

The Bali Congress reflected the spirit of the International Union for Conservation of Nature and Natural Resources. It was an effort of hundreds of people and dozens of institutions, most of them donating their time and efforts voluntarily. While it is impossible to allocate all the credit that is due, the following deserve special mention:

The Steering Committee was comprised of the Director General of IUCN (Lee M. Talbot), the Director General of the host institution, the Indonesian Department of Forestry (Soedjarwo), the Chairman of IUCN's Commission on National Parks and Protected Areas as the lead IUCN Commission responsible for planning the Congress (Kenton R. Miller), representatives of the three UN agencies which served as co-sponsors of the Congress and who make major contributions to protected areas worldwide (Reuben Olembo from UNEP, Javier Prats Llaurado from FAO, and Francesco di Castri from Unesco), representatives from the other three major co-sponsors (Robert Milne from the US National Park Service, Harold Eidsvik from Parks Canada, and Arne Schiotz from World Wildlife Fund), and the Chairmen of IUCN's other five Commissions (Albert Baez from Education, Peter Jacobs from Environmental Planning, Derrick Ovington from Ecology, Grenville Lucas from Species Survival, and Wolfgang Burhenne from Policy, Law, and Administration. The Executive Officer of CNPPA served as Secretary (Jeffrey A. McNeely). P.H.C. Lucas (Deputy Chairman of CNPPA, Department of Lands

and Survey of New Zealand) chaired the original committee appointed by the IUCN Director General to prepare a proposal for the Congress. Opportunities for participation in planning and implementing the event were available through the IUCN Commissions, newsletters, the IUCN Bulletin, and a number of other channels.

In Indonesia, the hosts of the Congress established a very active and hardworking Organizing Committee, as follows: Chairman: Ir. Wartono Kadri; Vice-Chairmen: Ir. Armena Darsidi, Ir. Harsono, and Kepala Kantor Wilayah Departemen Pertanian Dati I; Secretaries: Ir. Uum Somawidjaja, Drs. Samihadji, and Kepala Dinas Kehutanan Dati I Bali; treasurers: Ir. Ben Soedarmo and Agus Trobani; Secretarial Committee: Tarich Chusrani (Chairman), Ir. Mariyanti, Ir. Sunaryo, Ir. Suranto, and Balai Konservasi Sumberdaya Alam VII; funding Committee: Sukandi SH (Chairman), Simandjuntak SH, and Ismadi; Information Committee: Ir. Herman Suwardi (Chairman), Ir. Soemarsono Hardianto, Yuyung Mudjizat, and Hubungan Masyarakat Pemerintah Dati I Bali; Registration, Accommodation and Transportation Committee: Ir. Kardjono Kadarsin (Chairman), Drs. Dibyo Sartono, Drs. Siradjuddin, and Sub-Balai Perlindugan & Pengawetan Alam Bali; Ceremony Committee: Y.B. Widod Sutoyo SH (Chairman), Dra. Tuti Ahem, Protokol Daerah, Daerah Tingkat I Bali, and Kantor Wilayah Dep. P&K Dati I Bali; Sessions Committee: Ir. SL. Tobing (Chairman), S. Prayitno SH, Ir. Soeprato, Ir. Wahyudi Wardoyo, Drs. Sutarto, and Wakil dari Ditjen Protokol

& Konsuler Departemen Luar Negeri; Tours Committee: Ir. Widayat Eddypranoto (Chairman), Ir. Moch. Saleh, Drs. I. Soepadi Rahardjo, Ir. Koesno, and Kantor Wilayah Ditjen Pariwisata Dati I Bali; Exhibitions Committee: Ir. Soeparmo (Chairman), Ir. Dharmono, Kartiko, Hafiz SH, Balai Planologi Kehutanan IV; and Security Committee: Ir. Walter Nadapdap (Chairman), Irs. Satyo Sarono, Unsur Dinas Kehutanan Daerah Tingkat I Bali, and Unsur Kodak XI Nusa Tenggara di Bali. Ir. Effendi Sumardja served very effectively as liaison with Steering Committee and with IUCN.

At the Congress, the Steering Committee established the following organization: Co-Chairmen: Lee M. Talbot and Soedjarwo; Co-Secretaries-General: Kenton R. Miller and Wartono Kadri (responsibilities for directing the operations of the Secretariat); Deputy Secretary-General of Operations, Registration, and Protocol: Harold K. Eidsvik (responsibilities for ensuring that the physical facilities and supplies were appropriate for each session, that all meeting rooms were available as necessary, registration, protocol, finance, translation, and interpretation); Assistants to the Deputy Secretary-General of Operations: Bernardo Zentilli (IUCN Regional Liaison Officer), Richard Herring (Canadian Nature Federation and Parks Canada), and Bill Henwood. Press Relations: Raisa Scriabine, Don Hinrichsen, Paul Wachtel; Interpretation and Translation: Cyrille de Klemm and Catherine Johnston; Deputy Secretary-General of Programme: Jeffrey A. McNeely (responsibilities for organization of the technical dimensions of the Congress, ensuring that each session is organized, that speakers are briefed, that evening *ad hoc* sessions are scheduled, and that the necessary documents are made available). Assistants to the Deputy Secretary-General of Programme: Ken Erdman (Alberta Parks and Wildlife Service), Dawna Jones, John Shores (University of Michigan), and Bradley Cross (University of Michigan). Documentation was handled by Jean Packard, Paula Pritchard and Sue Rallo. Jeremy Harrison of IUCN's Conservation Monitoring Centre was responsible for data handling.

A special thanks for spectacular evening entertainments for the entire Congress go to Professor Sudarsono, Minister of Agriculture, Dr. Ida Bagus Mantra, Governor of Bali, and Soedjarwo, Director General of Forestry. Their efforts made a lasting impression on all participants.

No Congress of this scale can be held without the support of the institutions sending their staff to participate, and most of the individuals at the Congress came under their own steam. Support for the preparation of key papers was provided by the United Nations Environment Programme, who also contributed to the Congress in numerous other ways. The Division of Ecological Sciences of Unesco made important contributions, particularly in connection with the World Heritage Convention. The crucial contributions of Parks Canada were mostly hidden in the organization and preparation of the Congress, but without their help the Congress would have been impossible. The World Wildlife Fund made some of their staff available and supported the attendance of a number of individuals linked from tropical countries. FAO also provided travel support. Finally, a major vote of appreciation goes to the US National Park Service, who provided a grant which enabled the session papers to be prepared for the Congress and to be finalized for subsequent publication. WWF-US generously provided publication support for the proceedings volume.

Introduction:
Protected Areas Are Adapting
to New Realities

Jeffrey A. McNeely
Executive Officer, IUCN Commission on National Parks
and Protected Areas
Gland, Switzerland

ABSTRACT. *National Parks have long been the foundation of the international conservation movement. But with rising human demands on nature, national parks everywhere are coming under increasing pressure. The World Congress on National Parks showed how the increasing pressures are being faced in different parts of the world. Two conclusions were very clear: national parks need to be even better protected in the future; and national parks need to be supplemented by a wide range of other sorts of protected areas which can help meet the social and economic needs of modern human society.*

1. INTRODUCTION

National parks are generally considered to be areas of outstanding natural significance where the influences of humans are minimal. But in a period of increasing human populations, economic uncertainty and social instability, many governments are finding that the traditional national park approach is no longer sufficient to meet their needs for recreation, education, genetic resource management, watershed protection, and the many other goods and services produced by protected area conservation.

Paradoxically, this does not mean a weakening of the national park ideal, but rather a strengthening of it; people and governments around the world still appreciate the values of national parks, but they also realize that the stringent protection required for such areas is not necessarily appropriate for all areas which should be kept in a natural or semi-natural state. National parks must be as carefully protected as ever, but they must be supplemented by a range of other categories of protected areas in order to meet the social and economic development needs of modern society.

What is the role of protected areas in the process of social and economic development? Many diverse and even contradictory answers have been suggested:

- Protected areas must be inviolate nature sanctuaries, "living museums" where all species of plants and animals have the right to exist, free from the influences of man;
- The only hope for protected areas is to open them to compatible human uses—particularly education, research, and tourism—so that people have a vested interest in conserving them;
- Protected areas are a luxury which most countries cannot afford, so land must be devoted primarily to uses more productive for immediate human needs;
- Protected areas must be a compromise between nature conservation ideals and the needs of people for timber, grazing land, game animals, and others of nature's products and services;
- Protected areas are a land-use tool which can be used when, for attaining various human objectives, it is necessary for relatively large expanses of land to be kept in as natural a state as possible.

These options, and many others which could be suggested, all have something to contribute to the definition of how protected areas relate to human welfare. No single answer appears sufficient. What seems clear is that we need diversity in our approaches to protected areas, and we need to develop the scientific, technical, managerial and administrative tools to enable us to adapt to a range of different situations. The World National Parks Congress was designed to illustrate some of the different approaches that are being taken in various

1

parts of the world to integrate nature with human concerns.

The new approach which was agreed upon at the Congress is presented in the Bali Action Plan as the conclusion of these proceedings (Chap. 16). But it is useful to briefly highlight several of the major points:

- In order to meet the needs of both mankind and nature, each nation needs a full range of categories of protected areas, ranging from Category I "strictly protected nature reserves" to Category VIII "multiple-use management areas" (see Fig. 1 and IUCN, this volume, for a complete discussion of categories).
- Even the most stringently-protected categories of reserves serve social and economic needs through scientific research and monitoring, conservation species and genetic resources, conservation of ecological processes such as water cycling, soil formation, carbon cycling, evolution of plants and animals, and many others. Areas which allow visitors under controlled conditions can also meet needs for tourism, recreation, and education.
- Linking nature protection with social and economic requirements is a positive step to ensure the necessary public support for conservation activities, and does not necessarily compromise conservation values. The Congress reaffirmed its strong support for the principle that national parks and nature reserves (IUCN Categories I, II and III) must not contain *any* form of resource exploitation; activities such as hunting, logging, mineral exploitation, and dam construction were seen as inappropriate within these three categories of protected areas.
- At the opposite end of the protected area spectrum, Category VIII multiple-use areas which are managed for sustainable timber production, grazing, hunting, or other extractive use, can also provide conservation benefits such as genetic resource preservation, recreation, environmental education, monitoring, and watershed protection.
- Finally, protected areas must be selected and managed to support the overall fabric of social and economic development; not as islands of anti-development, but rather as critical elements of regionally envisioned harmonious landscapes. Through a planned mix of national parks and other types of reserves, amidst productive forests, agriculture or fisheries, protected areas can serve people today and safeguard the well-being of future generations.

2. SOME ANCIENT HISTORY: THE HUMAN ECOLOGY OF PROTECTED AREAS

There has always been something of a love-hate relationship between man and nature. Early man lived on nature's bounty, but nature also held dangers which could threaten man's very survival. Through the eons, social systems, tools, and customs evolved which allowed humans to live in a sort of balance with their environment, to make a comfortable accommodation with the constraints of natural ecosystems. These "ecosystem people" lived within the limits set by their local environments (Dasmann, 1980).

Once agriculture began to develop some 10,000 years ago, man's relationship with the land began to change at an accelerating rate; the ecological niche of *Homo sapiens* expanded as man began to control the forces of nature for the benefit of his expanding population. While the area of wilderness was reduced, it was still extensive and much of the natural world was still protected from the most disruptive human influences by cultural/ecological factors such as taboos preventing over-exploitation, tribal warfare which kept wide areas as wilderness "buffer zones" between groups, land ownership by ancestors rather than individuals, and many others.

The industrial revolution involved a fundamental ecological change on a global scale. What was once a diverse collection of local ecosystems became a much less diverse and more closely interlinked system which covered the entire world. Most ecosystem people became "biosphere people," who drew their support not from any one local ecosystem but from the entire capital of the world's living matter (Dasmann, 1980). A simplified example will illustrate the point: Oil from Saudi Arabia fuels the machines and makes the fertilizers and pesticides which allow marginal land in West Africa to grow a crop of cocoa for Switzerland to make into chocolate which is flown on American-made airplanes to Singapore for distribution in southeast Asia; the profit made by the West African farmer allows him to purchase a Japanese motorcycle, Ethiopian coffee, and Thai rice. No longer so vulnerable to local ecological factors, the West African farmer is now maintained by a complex of international commodity agreements, market forces, and the many other factors which enable the world to function as a single ecosystem.

The result of this greatly expanded human ecological niche can be seen clearly in the booming population of the species. At least for the time being, biosphere man is able to continue to increase his numbers due ultimately to the energy subsidies provided to the growing and distribution of food by coal and oil, the accumulated capital of ecosystems which disappeared millions of years ago. The dominance of this all-encompassing ecological niche has placed the human species in a position to destroy many living resources and to disrupt the natural ecological processes which sustain all life. For the first time in history, a single species has the capability of driving large numbers of other species to extinction; informed estimates are that as many as a million species may be gone forever by the turn of the century (Myers, 1980).

Whereas species and ecosystems were conserved in simpler times by the low level of technology, cultural controls on over-exploitation, and man's relative ecological humility, other, more explicit, conservation mechanisms became necessary for man's self-control as his technology allowed him to exceed natural ecological controls.

Early in the industrial revolution, a few individuals of vision promoted the concept of man's purposeful responsibility for ensuring the survival of at least representative portions of natural ecosystems through the establishment of national parks. Following the creation of Yellowstone National Park in Wyoming in 1872, protected areas have spread steadily throughout the world as the primary means for conserving natural ecosystems.

3. MORE RECENT HISTORY: IUCN AND PROTECTED AREAS

Since the establishment of Yellowstone a little over a hundred years ago, the ecological niche of man has expanded dramatically, enabling the total population of the species to double over the past generation. What were once marginal habitats have been brought into food production by using new machines, pesticides, fertilizers, and social organizations, often producing for consumers far away; habitats of species which formerly were masters of their niche have been usurped in order to provide for the needs of the expanding human population.

Equally, people have found that it is within their power to ensure that species and ecosystems are maintained as part of the global ecosystem of which man is a part. But since the threat to nature involves global ecological, economic, and technological factors, conservation too must include an international element in order to counter the hazards inherent in the world ecological niche of modern biosphere man. It is therefore no coincidence that IUCN has been deeply involved with national parks from its very beginnings.

Following the 1959 Resolution of the United Nations Economic and Social Council which charged IUCN with the task of maintaining an up-to-date list of the world's national parks and equivalent reserves, IUCN took two important steps to "internationalize" national parks: first, it produced the first edition of the *United Nations List of National Parks and Equivalent Reserves* (1961), which established the principle that parks were a national effort worthy of full international concern; and second, it sponsored in 1962 the First World Conference on National Parks, which summarized current knowledge and provided the foundation for greatly expanded development of national parks in the ensuing years.

Ten years later, the Second World Conference represented the next major step in the process, documenting the progress of the preceding decade and identifying the needs of the future. 1972 was also a milestone year for two other reasons: the holding of the United Nations Conference on the Human Environment at Stockholm, which established the United Nations Environment Programme; and the approval at Unesco's General Conference of the World Heritage Convention. These events set the stage for the 1970s, which saw the greatest expansion of protected areas in history (Harrison, Miller, and McNeely, this volume).

Other IUCN involvement with protected areas has included:

- Establishing the Commission on National Parks in 1960. Now enlarged to become the Commission on National Parks and Protected Areas (CNPPA), the body had a membership of 258 from 89 countries in 1982.
- Publishing lists and directories of protected areas (IUCN, 1961; 1971; 1975a; 1977; 1980a; 1982a; 1982b; and Carp, 1980). The Protected Area Data Unit (PADU) was established in 1981 to computerize data held by IUCN and to promote its wider application.
- Publishing the quarterly PARKS Magazine, now in its seventh year, with a circulation of some 7,000.
- Publishing basic conceptual papers dealing with protected area matters (IUCN, 1978a; 1979; 1980c; Eidsvik, 1980; Lausche, 1981).
- Establishing a system of biogeographic provinces of the world (Udvardy, 1975, this volume; Ray *et al.*, this volume), now widely used for assessing protected area coverage and suggesting regions for priority attention.
- Cooperating closely with United Nations agencies involved in protected area matters (FAO, UNEP, Unesco), at both conceptual and field levels. This includes providing technical evaluations of natural sites nominated for the World Heritage List to Unesco's World Heritage Committee (see IUCN, 1982c) and acting as the Bureau for the Convention on Conservation of Wetlands of International Importance.
- Supporting field projects, especially in developing countries, aimed at establishing and managing national parks and protected areas. Funded primarily by the World Wildlife Fund, some 1500 projects involving the expenditure of over $40 million had been implemented in support of protected areas by the end of 1982. Countries with major programmes have included China, Costa Rica, Ecuador, India, Indonesia, Kenya, Madagascar, Mali, Oman, Tanzania, and Zambia.
- Holding meetings in various parts of the world to promote protected areas. CNPPA holds two working sessions per year, rotating among the biogeographic realms (see, for example, IUCN 1980d and 1981). In addition, IUCN has organized major international meetings on protected areas, including the First World Conference on National Parks in Seattle, Washington in 1962 (Adams, 1964), the Second World Conference on National Parks

in Grand Teton, Wyoming in 1972 (Elliott, 1974), the International Conference on Marine Parks and Reserves in Tokyo in 1975 (IUCN, 1976a) and the World National Parks Congress in Bali, Indonesia, in 1982 (this volume).

However human ecology develops in the future, protected areas must adapt to the changing conditions. Evolving from the national park idea of strict protection and promotion of tourism which had its inception at Yellowstone over 100 years ago, protected areas now must go beyond national parks to contribute to modern social, ecological and economic demands, while still serving the best interests of nature conservation. The Bali Congress showed how this is being done in various parts of the world, and what is required to promote further an appropriate linkage between protected areas and human development.

4. THE PROCEEDINGS

From 11 to 22 October 1982, 450 of the world's leading authorities on national parks and other protected areas from 70 countries met in Bali to attend an experts' meeting to chart a course for the future of protected areas in the world. As experts, they were there to represent their professional opinions, and did not profess to express the viewpoints of governments or other governmental or non-governmental institutions. They presented to case studies, held workshops and symposia, enjoyed outstanding hospitality from the host country, and visited protected areas to see real problems on the ground.

This book comprises the record of the plenary sessions of the Congress. Each author was given the opportunity to make both editorial and substantive changes in his paper at the Congress. The papers were then edited to standardize terminology and to reduce repetition and length, in order to produce as short and inexpensive a volume as possible without any sacrifice in quality. A few of the papers presented in workshop sessions have been included to maintain balance, and the order of the papers has been adjusted in order to make the flow more logical. The result is not just a collection of papers, but a volume with a surprising universality of perspective.

Virtually all authors have taken the view that protected areas must serve human society if they are to survive in a period of increasing demands on nature. This is most definitely not a defeatist approach. Quite the opposite. For with greatly increased responsibilities for helping to ensure that social and economic development meets the real needs of human societies, protected areas can expect to receive a significantly greater amount of support from governments, international development agencies, and local people. Protected area personnel will become recognized professionals, with a status similar to that of other community leaders (doc-

tor, forest manager, teacher, industrial director, etc.). Scientists will have a management focus for some of their research in natural areas. Wildlife will have a secure niche in the world ecosystem. The public will have a range of natural attractions to visit, either in person or vicariously through television, books, or films. And protected areas will become an inseparable part of the modern human society.

I. *Scientific Reserve/Strict Nature Reserve.* To protect nature and maintain natural processes in an undisturbed state in order to have ecologically representative examples of the natural environment available for scientific study, environmental monitoring, education, and for the maintenance of genetic resources in a dynamic and evolutionary state.

II. *National Park.* To protect natural and scenic areas of national or international significance for scientific, educational, and recreational uses.

III. *Natural Monument/Natural Landmark.* To protect and preserve nationally significant natural features because of their specal interest or unique characteristics.

IV. *Managed Nature Reserve/Wildlife Sanctuary.* To assure the natural conditions necessary to protect nationally significant species, groups of species, biotic communities, or physical features of the environment, where these require specific human manipulation for their perpetuation.

V. *Protected Landscape.* To maintain nationally significant natural landscapes which are characteristic of the harmonious interaction of man and land, while providing opportunities for public enjoyment through recreation and tourism within the normal life-style and economic activity of these areas.

VI. *Resource Reserve.* To protect the natural resources of the area for future use, and prevent or contain development activities that could affect the resource pending the establishment of objectives which are based upon appropriate knowledge and planning.

VII. *Natural Biotic Area/Anthropological Reserve.* To allow the way of life of human societies living in harmony with the environment to continue undisturbed by modern technology.

VIII. *Multiple-use Management Area/Managed Resource Area.* To provide for the sustained production of water, timber, wildlife, pasture, and outdoor recreation, with the conservation of nature primarily oriented to the support of the economic activities (although specific zones may also be designated within these areas to achieve specific conservation objectives).

IX. *Biosphere Reserve.* To conserve for present and future use the diversity and integrity of representative biotic communities of plants and animals within natural ecosystems, and to safeguard the genetic diversity of species on which their continuing evolution depends.

X. *World Heritage Site*. To protect the natural features for which the area was considered to be of World Heritage quality, and to provide information for worldwide public enlightenment.

5. THE WORLD CONGRESS ON NATIONAL PARKS: AN OUTLINE

Welcoming addresses at the Bali Congress were given by IUCN's major partners in protected area conservation: FAO, Unesco, UNEP, and WWF. Marco Flores Rodas, Assistant Director General of FAO, drew the attention of the meeting to the importance of people in protected area considerations. "Until and unless the rural people are ensured adequate food and shelter and a dignified standard of life," Flores Rodas stated, "all efforts to establish and manage national parks and protected areas will be nothing else but grandiose projects in futility. I submit to you that this Congress should focus attention on the interests of the rural people in developing countries who live in the vicinity of national parks and protected areas."

Michel Batisse, Deputy Assistant Director General of Unesco, continued on this theme in his welcoming address, pointing out that Unesco has contributed to protected areas on three inter-related fronts: socio-scientific; educational; and ethical. "It is our strong belief that conservation has to be founded on solid scientific grounds and that it must be seen by the populations concerned as an activity of practical value to them and their children," Batisse stated. "As a tool for long-term conservation of ecosystems compatible with their optimal utilization by the population, we advocate the development of an international network of ecologically representative areas within the framework of the applied research programme called Man and the Biosphere."

Peter Thacher, Deputy Executive Director of UNEP, outlined the strong and positive links that have existed between UNEP and protected areas since the time of Stockholm, involving cooperation with countries, regions, FAO, Unesco, and IUCN. The UNEP Regional Seas Programme was also seen as a valuable means for promoting conservation of coastal and marine protected areas as part of regional development.

Charles de Haes, Director General of the World Wildlife Fund, pointed out that by far the majority of WWF's field projects have been carried out to support protected areas, in close collaboration with IUCN. He stated that WWF will be concentrating its efforts in the coming year on tropical rainforests, which would also be expected to contribute to protected areas. He welcomed the advice of the world's protected area managers in helping WWF and IUCN to establish priorities for future international cooperation.

Lee M. Talbot, Director General of IUCN, expressed the deep appreciation of the Congress participants for the warm hospitality and painstaking preparation of the Congress hosts, the Government of Indonesia, its Ministry of Agriculture, and its local Balinese representatives. Talbot pointed out that the preparation of the Congress epitomized the IUCN approach. "The Commission on National Parks and Protected Areas has accepted the lead responsibility in the preparation and organization, but they have done so within the total context of IUCN," he said. "You will note that there are sessions or parts of sessions prepared by all Commissions and other components of IUCN. Equally, significant parts are devoted to the endeavours of our principal collaborators, including WWF, UNEP, Unesco, FAO, the US National Park Service, and Parks Canada. Lacking a special secretariat staff or budget for the Congress, we have relied on volunteer assistance and contributions from a wide variety of sources, including our own global network of major governmental organizations, various governments, and international development agencies."

Following the ceremonial opening, the real work of the Congress began with a review of the world coverage of protected areas, including a slide presentation reviewing the world situation, the unveiling of a revised system of terrestrial biogeographic provinces and a new system of coastal and marine biogeographic provinces, a mapping of all protected areas on the biogeographic map, and an introduction to IUCN's Protected Areas Data Unit.

Addresses by key figures in the major disciplines of conservation—species survival; ecological processes; environmental planning; environmental policy, law and administration; and protected areas—were followed by a series of plenary sessions presenting status reviews, case studies, and analyses of future prospects for each of the world's eight biogeographic realms. Each realm session had as Chairman a senior individual who was responsible for running the session; as Keynote Speaker, a distinguished individual from the realm addressing the historical background and current situation of protected areas in the realm; five to ten Case Studies (depending on the size of the realm) which dealt with the most important current issues in the realm; and a Future Directions Speaker, who looked to the future, identifying the directions that protected areas in the realm may take in the next decade. A special session was devoted to Indonesia as the host country, reviewing its remarkable recent expansion of protected areas.

At the end of the first week, there was a half-day session on "New Directions," a series of thought-provoking papers which aimed at giving the participants another view of their profession. Most speakers were from outside the protected area business, so they were able to look at things with a fresh and stimulating perspective.

The first 3 days of the second week were devoted to workshops on three major topics:

Managing Protected Areas in the Tropics;
Managing Coastal and Marine Protected Areas; and
Training Protected Areas Personnel.

Each of these three topics was addressed by about 12 workshop sessions, each dealing with a specific set of principles and developing guidelines for their application. The workshops distilled the set of principles and guidelines and applied specific illustrations from different parts of the world to the basic principles being addressed. Case studies from the plenary sessions, invited papers for workshop sessions, and voluntary papers provided the raw material for the three workshops, each of which will lead to a handbook dealing with the subject of the workshop.

Thursday of the second week was devoted to international support for protected area management. Following the keynote address by His Excellency Ali Murtopo, Indonesian Minister of Information, there was a series of addresses which outlined some of the steps that are being taken by the United Nations, bi-lateral agencies, development banks, multi-national business, research institutions, and protected area management authorities.

The afternoon discussed two major programmes being carried out under the auspices of Unesco: the Man and the Biosphere Programme; and the World Heritage Convention. The latter reviewed the current status of natural World Heritage Sites, presented a case study from Ethiopia to show how the Convention is being used on the ground, and speculated on where the Convention is going.

The concluding day consisted of several reports from committees which had been established earlier. Key reports and discussions dealt with:

The Bali Declaration. This document is a statement from the protected area professionals of the world to the upper level policy-makers and the public at large, stating in succinct form precisely the new, socially-conscious, role the Congress sees protected areas playing in the future. This document, developed over a period of several months by an IUCN Committee chaired by Dr. David Munro and finalized following further discussions at Bali, provides the broad policy framework to guide future action.

Recommendations. To establish priorities for the coming critical years, the Congress prepared a series of 20 Recommendations. The recommendations were developed by a Committee chaired by Adrian Phillips (UK) and comprising representatives from all eight biogeographic realms: Bing Lucas (New Zealand); Admiral Ibsen de Gusmao Camara (Brazil); Walter Lusigi (Kenya); Mike McCloskey (USA); John

Foster (UK); Arthur Dahl (New Caledonia); Ivan Gavva (USSR); Don Johnstone (Australia); Marc Dourojeanni (Peru); Hemendra Panwar (India); and Barbra Lausche (USA).

World Parks Association. Chaired by Bing Lucas, a working group examined the advisability of starting an association to unify the international protected area profession internationally, based on PARKS Magazine, PADU, the World Congress, and various other existing cooperative mechanisms. The group concluded that while such an association may eventually prove worthwhile, it should not be considered a matter of high priority as it would duplicate many existing efforts.

Awards. In a session under the chairmanship of Dr. Emmanuel Asibey, the IUCN/CNPPA Fred M. Packard International Parks Merit Award was presented by Dr. Harold Jefferson Coolidge, Honorary President of IUCN, to individuals representing each of the world's eight biogeographic realms (Annex II).

The concluding address was given by Dr. Kenton R. Miller, Co-Secretary General of the Congress and Chairman of IUCN's Commission on National Parks and Protected Areas. Based on the discussions at the Congress and on reports on priorities from working groups representing the world's eight biogeographic realms, Miller's address set out a plan of action for the future, outlining what needs to be accomplished by the next World National Parks Congress in 1992. The draft action plan was circulated widely for comment and further work was done at the IUCN secretariat, leading to the "Bali Action Plan," a document for guiding future international activities in support of protected areas (see Chap. 16).

Closing addresses were given by Lee M. Talbot, Director General of IUCN and Prof. Sudarsono, the Minister of Agriculture of the Republic of Indonesia. Dr. Talbot pointed out the importance of maintaining the integrity of protected areas, even while ensuring that they also meet the needs of society. In closing, he stressed the importance of action. "We have laid the foundations for what may be considered a true revolution in the development of protected areas and in the way protected areas are included in the development process," he said. "But if all this is to be accomplished, it is up to us to build on these foundations. The success of this Congress will have been a hollow one, if ten years from now we do not look back on a decade of accomplishment consistent with the aims and aspirations we have expressed here."

Prof. Sudarsono warmly thanked the organizers of the Congress and announced that Indonesia was in the process of submitting an application for sovereign state membership in IUCN. "We are determined to support and to implement the programme of IUCN and the World Conservation Strategy, notwithstanding the many constraints," he said. "However, as stated by the Vice

President in his opening address, the benefits of natural resources are shared by developed and developing countries alike therefore, the responsibility and the expenses of safeguarding natural resources for the future should also be equitably shared. We urge generous financial support and the provision of technical assistance from the developed countries and international organizations to the developing countries where the natural heritage of the world finds its richest expression. Conservation and protected areas are not only for the people of a country or a region, but for the whole of mankind."

Chapter 1
Opening Session

Opening Address:
Protected Areas and Political Reality

Adam Malik
Vice President of the Republic of Indonesia

It gives me great pleasure to welcome all of you to Indonesia and particularly to the island of Bali. We are proud and pleased indeed Bali has been chosen to be the venue of this third World National Parks Congress.

To me, this choice signifies a number of important aspects.

First of all, Indonesia's readiness to host the Congress shows the Government's deep commitment to the cause of the environment, a commitment further underscored by the inauguration of yet another series of national parks during the course of the Congress. Our readiness should also be seen as an acknowledgement of our responsibility toward the task of conserving our natural heritage.

Second, and in a more special sense, Bali represents a culture and a traditional life-style which is rich in ancient and indigenous environmental wisdom and is to be safeguarded as part of our national and the world's cultural heritage.

There is, however, a still deeper significance of holding the Congress here in Bali. It is for the first time that such a congress is being held in the Third World and as such it represents an important milestone. As we all know, the two previous Conferences were held in the United States as was indeed appropriate because American naturalists and environmentalists deserve the greatest of credit for having pioneered and initiated the establishment of national parks.

American scientists must also be credited for having amassed and developed the great body of knowledge relevant to the establishment, maintenance and management of national parks over more than one hundred years. This knowledge is now widely shared.

Although national parks have been established in various countries throughout the world, it was only in the last ten years or so that such parks have become widespread throughout the Third World. In those past ten years, more national parks have been established in the Third World than anywhere else. This signifies that on the part of the developing countries there is a deep and growing commitment to and an awareness of the environment and the responsibility to preserve for the world what is deemed to be the common global natural heritage.

The focus of attention toward national parks has also gradually shifted toward the Third World and holding this meeting here in Bali underscores that shift. In a manner of speaking, with regard to the issue of national parks, the centre of gravity is now here in the Third World. This, then, is the deeper significance of our meeting here today.

Such a shift must necessarily be accompanied by a change in our perceptions regarding national parks and their attendant problems. In the past, a prime motive was a desire to preserve natural beauty, the desire to leave nature undisturbed in its pristine beauty. This motive still exists today but there are additional and perhaps more important reasons for establishing national parks, namely the realization of their intrinsic value and potential to sustain the development processes which Third World countries have begun, and a sense of responsibility towards our future and our natural heritage.

At the same time I am deeply aware of the problems ahead of us should we wish to intensify our efforts to conserve nature or even if we merely wish to stand still and defend the parks that we already have. These problems have arisen partly as a consequence of the conditions of today and partly because of our perception of an increased global significance of the natural heritage that we wish to protect.

The conditions in Indonesia and in most developing

countries are vastly different from those in the west when national parks were first established and when land was still in abundance. At that time, there were no stringent calculations of economic benefits to be gained from the establishment of national parks, nor were there many questions about economic profits foregone because a piece of land had been turned into a national park or a nature reserve; nor was there the pressure of a vast population encroaching upon a park's territory.

The many problems that are faced today can be attributed to three basic issues: poverty; an ever-increasing need for land; and the processes of development. Actually these three basic issues cannot be differentiated or separated from one another; all three are closely interwoven and all three, separately or jointly, are also interconnected to the environment.

Because we are poor, we must proceed with development but our rate of development is hampered by the very poverty we wish to overcome. Poverty and development require land and this in turn leads to pressures upon the environment. All this is further aggravated by a rapidly growing population.

Our economists can tell you the extent of our poverty and the magnitude of the basic needs that have to be fulfilled. Our planners can tell you how much land and what rate of productivity we need. You and other environmental experts can provide us with the environmental considerations.

I would like to urge you, however, to consider the basic issues of poverty, land hunger, development and the environment from a plain human vantage point as well. I would urge you to consider the misery of poverty, what it does to a person, to his expectations of tomorrow and to his dignity as a human being.

We must also consider the problems of a government in the face of poverty; for instance, the problem of how to provide land and a living to millions of people today. These problems won't wait for five or ten years. In the face of poverty and hunger, how does a Government allocate land? How much land for the hungry of today and how much land for genetic resources to be preserved for tomorrow? What value should be placed on genetic resources for tomorrow in comparison to the value of exploiting natural resources for the alleviation of poverty today?

Today we are unable to answer comprehensively such questions. That is why we are turning to experts from within as well as from outside our country to help us formulate the wisest possible policies in the utiliza-

tion and management of our natural resources. We are determined to push forward with development but we are equally determined that such development should not be destructive to the environment and that both development and environment in the end sustain one another.

To do so we need help; we need ideas, concepts, knowledge, technical and management skills—all kinds of capabilities, funds and materials. These will also better enable us to carry out our responsibility to conserve the world's natural heritage found within the boundaries of our nation.

I am convinced that Indonesia and the other developing nations have provided ample evidence of their good faith in assuming their proper share of responsibility over the world's natural resources. While I cannot speak for all developing countries, I know that the ASEAN countries have translated their good intentions into actual action and actual monetary contributions in such joint efforts as the Common Seas Programme.

Another proof of our good intentions is the establishment of national parks throughout the developing world. Efforts to open more national parks continue despite doubts about the appropriateness of our actions, about our capability to maintain both national parks and provide land for other economic endeavours. There are also doubts about who will benefit most from our national efforts.

As the benefits of natural resources are to be equitably shared, the responsibility and expense of safeguarding such resources for the future should also be equitably shared. That responsibility should also be proportionate to the benefits obtained. In the past we have neither received a fair share of the benefits nor have we received a fair share of assistance—other than expensive advice and even more expensive criticism—in the efforts to safeguard the common global natural heritage. Despite all of our good intentions, we can only carry out our responsiblity if others provide us with their fair share of assistance.

We shall do our share and responsibly plan the use of our natural resources, responsibly develop our production and consumption patterns and responsibly manage our population growth. We invite all nations to do so and assist others who up to now have carried the heavier burden of responsibility. Unless such responsibilities are equitably shared, all our good intentions will only lead to global environmental destruction.

Peril and Opportunity:
What It Takes to Make Our Choice

Peter S. Thacher
Executive Director
United Nations Environment Programme
Nairobi, Kenya

I am delighted to have the opportunity on behalf of a co-sponsoring organization to address this Congress at the outset of this key session. I bring you greetings from Dr. Mostafa Tolba and many other of your colleagues at our Headquarters in Nairobi. Enjoying as we do an institutional vantage point in the Third World, we see that it is here, in the developing countries, that the perils and opportunities lie. I believe you, organizers and participants, have an opportunity to help the world make a choice of great significance for the future of all.

The *peril* we face is the accelerating destruction of the living resources of this planet in a way which strips diversity, increases risks of instabilities, and undercuts the basis for sustainable development.

The *opportunity* is to change course and carry out the World Conservation Strategy.

The *choice* is whether we pay now, or later.

It has been said that the day of the "free lunch" is finished. Surely all here know that there never was a "free lunch", or at least not since humankind grew apart from nature and began to manipulate nature for its own benefit; nothing is cost-free. There may, however, be choices as to when, and how much, to pay. While we now recognize that "prevention pays," the calculation needs to be examined in each instance. With good management, prevention can increasingly be made profitable not only for our grandchildren, but today, now, certainly for farmers, as well as bankers; prosperity may not always "trickle down," but surely depression on the farm "trickles up." I believe that if we cannot demonstrate that conservation is profitable *now*, as well as the future, the credibility of the World Conservation Strategy is in doubt, and our monetary and political systems are in for more severe shocks.

It's encouraging to see reason, in the form of good management, practiced in recycling metals and paper, by which non-renewable resources can be converted into something resembling renewable resources.

But mostly we see bad management converting renewable resources into what for all practical purposes are non-renewable. A forest that is ruthlessly exploited like a "mine" of trees will soon be exhausted beyond recovery. Considering the time and energy required to create soil, once it's lost it is for all practical purposes gone forever. Even if the world today enjoyed economic prosperity it would be hard to find a desert that could be made to bloom in the near future. On the contrary, soil loss and aridification and genetic reduction are proceeding at a frightening pace, yet nowhere do we see adequate priorities or resources being applied to arrest these destructive processes. These destructive processes constitute the "peril".

As to the nature of the choice, I believe that most governments of this planet—and certainly most of the richest governments—face a choice that can be seen starkly in terms of "trees now, or tanks later". Let me explain.

Throughout the world there is abundant evidence of systems gone bust so that their productive capabilities for sustaining human life have been overwhelmed. The only option of hope in such cases is flight—no matter what the risk. Hence the boatloads of refugees from Haiti and in the South China Sea. Environmental refugees are evident in many parts of the world and as the productive base erodes, their numbers can be expected to swell. Haiti has given the North American TV viewer a disturbing glimpse of a future which does not work, of the consequences of failure to find the tools to protect forests which until 30 years ago covered fully one half of that country.

But so long as mankind is Earthbound, total escape is not possible and economic, social, and political turmoil become inevitable. With it comes the traditional inclination of politicians to rely on force to restore order. I believe it is precisely this fear of pending disorder in Spaceship Earth, together with an inability to think in terms of prevention, that is today leading so many governments to invest in arms, instead of plowshares.

Despite the "softness" of political science, it is abundantly clear that human suffering on a massive scale is creating economic, social, political, and even military turmoil in many parts of the world. The choice for governments, and let's face it, for the taxpayers of this world, is either to find the means by which to pay now to stop the destruction of the natural resource base, or be prepared to pay later, possibly in blood, using tools that are already notoriously expensive, and whose very use would threaten to destabilize an already unstable world.

The ultimate choice is between conservation or conflict. Trees now, or tanks later.

This is an *international* Congress. But before considering action at the international level, let us be clear that the key to success lies at the *national* and *local* levels. There is a lot of loose talk about "international standards", both by those who fear all "standards", and by those who want more of them. But the only international environmental "standard" I know of is the one which protected every one of us who flew here on licensed commercial aircraft where it determines the quality of the drinking water on board. Governments can agree on treaties, such as the Antarctic Treaty, the Partial Test Ban Treaty, and others by which they accept mutual restraints that safeguard the environment, and perhaps—let us hope so—the Declaration of Bali may be a step in that direction. But the Declaration, and even a future Treaty based on it, will be only pieces of paper unless your workshops produce what are so aptly referred to as "Tools for the man on the ground." If you succeed in this I am confident that the financial and other support needed at the international level will be made available to help governments and people 'on the ground' to use these tools.

This year UNEP celebrated the end of its first decade. One of the many significant changes in the ten years since Stockholm—and since Yellowstone—has been the shift of emphasis from pollution and nature protection, to recognition of the need to integrate conservation and development, and to encourage the use of natural resources on a sustainable basis. Acceptance of the World Conservation Strategy, to which many of you have directly contributed, by governments in all parts of the world must now be translated into *national* strategies and action.

But in the intervening ten years since you last met, the world population has increased by 700 million and today farmers and ranchers in much of the developing world, especially Latin America, are being driven by their immediate needs and by short-term profit to dev-

astate huge areas in a one-time operation, at the cost of sustainable food production in their own countries. Looking at demographic projections, especially in Africa, where food *per capita* has been dropping for the past ten years, and where the population growth rate itself continues to grow, can anyone doubt these pressures will continue to mount?

I have sought to outline a division of labour between international and national organizations in the translation of the WCS into action on the ground, and have emphasized the key role at the international level in helping governments to *assess*, so as to manage their natural resources on a sustainable basis. With our partners in the UN System, we assist governments to achieve compatable and useful results through GEMS—the Global Environmental Monitoring System—in regard to:

- climate-related monitoring;
- the monitoring of long-range transboundary transport of atmospheric pollutants;
- health-related monitoring concerned with exposure to and effects of pollutants;
- ocean monitoring; and
- the monitoring of renewable natural resources.

The importance of natural resource monitoring as a basis for sound natural resource management is now clearly grasped, but one must bear in mind that all natural resources have an economic value to the countries in which they occur, and these countries must view them from a national point of view. Thus, the establishment of global natural resource monitoring networks is very different from establishing other kinds of monitoring programmes and is therefore being developed by encouraging the formation of appropriate *national* Ecological Monitoring Units through the provision of advice and by developing common methodologies.

The purpose of assessment and monitoring is to supply management agencies with the information needed for cost-effective action. GEMS helps fulfill this role at a number of levels. On the local level, various programmes develop new and efficient methodologies for collecting renewable resource data, so that national agencies or internationally-financed projects may work with the best tools available. Simultaneously, at the global scale, monitoring activities within GEMS become part of a network permitting exchange of ideas, data, expertise and methodologies, so that common problems are tackled in the same way.

UNEP's experience in coordinating and harmonizing assessment work in literally thousands of national institutions in all corners of the world demonstrates what can be done at the international level to lay a more rational basis for management decisions at the national level, even in the politically-difficult task of helping governments to assess natural resources within their sovereign territory. Documents are also available describing work currently underway with more than 100 governments in our Regional Seas Programme where problems of sovereignty are less harsh.

Considerations of sovereignty put real and proper constraints on the role of international organizations when it comes to decision-making at the national level. That is why the efforts of the UN System are devoted largely to the generation of 'guidelines' whose purpose is to encourage the national planner and decision-maker to ask the right questions at the right time so as to avoid a loss of investment or an environmental set-back. It is in this area that we look to this Congress with great hope.

I sincerely believe that if you can produce specific results which can serve as guidelines in the areas being addressed in your workshops, there will be no lack of support, including financial support at the international level, for those developing countries who need help in applying them. I say this despite the severe financial constraints under which all international as well as national institutions are now working.

The most difficult pressure to cope with on the natural resource base is the pressure exerted by poverty; by a *lack* of development. Development on an international scale is not the responsibility of any single organization. However, the initial phase of technical assistance, and all the pre-investment work needed to start the process throughout the developing world, and to develop the capacity of developing countries to attract large scale resources, is largely the responsibility of the U.N. System: Some thirty-five specialized and technical organizations take part in the U.N. Development Programme.

While flows of capital investment from the private sector play an important role, some would say as the "engine" of development, probably all would agree that foreign assistance can be useful in creating those conditions. But in the amounts available, this aid is today less and less able to start the engine.

In recent years the multilateral portion of Official Development Assistance (ODA) has increased less than half as much as the bilateral portion, and as to its purpose much of this is devoted to the expensive task of emergency food, disaster and refugee relief; treating the symptoms that result from earlier failure to take timely, preventive steps.

We are, I believe, facing a dangerous trend in which diminishing resources deprive the U.N. System of its ability to carry out the technical assistance and preinvestment work which lays the basis for loans and investments which are a critical ingredient of future growth in all parts of the planet.

From UNEP's experience in working directly with the private sector I am convinced that at top management levels, but all too often only at the top, there is good understanding and strong support for the World Conservation Strategy and for the concept of *sustainable* development. But there are many who lack foresight and proceed either in ignorance or in the belief that they cannot afford to take account of conservation. Since this phenomenon is particularly apparent at the local level, I strongly welcome the many constructive ideas in papers before this Congress on how to build co-operation between conservation and the private sector. This is an area which deserves more effort in the future, since we must avoid sterile confrontation in which all lose, and enlarge cooperation in which your insights and private sector management skills can set the future of this planet on a sustainable course.

The current annual report of the World Bank, "World Development Report 1982," presents an authoritative description of current and projected agricultural development that must go forward to meet the growing food demands of the planet. It seems to me that the Bank's statement contains real wisdom which States, particularly food-deficit developing countries, should follow in the years ahead. One of the implications is that increased inputs to boost productivity in good agricultural land, and the build-up of pressures on marginal lands, call for far better management practices, and this in turn requires better assessments and continual monitoring at all levels.

I want you to know that our many collaborators in the UN System, together with the World Bank, and all the multilateral, intergovernmental funding agencies with whom we work, are committed to a policy of incorporating environmental considerations in their funding activities. The same is increasingly true of the bilateral funding agencies and, as I said earlier, I am convinced that responsible private sector managers increasingly find it profitable to take the environment into account.

Those who are investing in the future—whether for national policy or for profit—are prepared to be responsive to the Strategy. But until you and we produce analytical tools to integrate conservation objectives into cold-blooded economic calculations in the development context, it will remain a concept that will not be translated into action.

I therefore hope you will be encouraged by the support which can be found if your efforts here in Bali lead to concrete results of the sort foreseen in the outstandingly thoughtful and constructive preparations for this Congress. It would be a fitting reflection of the shift from the narrow protectionism of the past, to the broadly-conceived conservation of today, and it would make your labors directly relevant and contributory to the goals you seek. I therefore salute those who have worked so hard to make this Congress the success we all want, and expect.

The Role of Protected Areas in the Implementation of the World Conservation Strategy

Lee M. Talbot
Director General
International Union for Conservation of Nature and Natural Resources
Gland, Switzerland

Human beings, in their quest for economic development and improvement of the quality of life, must come to terms with the reality of resource limitation and the carrying capacity of ecosystems, and must take account of the needs of future generations. This is the central message of modern conservation—as expressed in the World Conservation Strategy. As such, conservation is basic to human welfare, and indeed, to human survival. But it has not always been recognized as such.

Concern with conservation is not a new phenomena. Over two thousand years ago Plato eloquently recorded his concern about the hills of Attica in Greece, which had been denuded of their forest cover and had consequently lost their mantle of soil and their watercourses. They were, he wrote, "like the skeleton of a body wasted by disease." Further east, in the same period, protected forest areas were established in India, precursors to our modern national parks and reserves. Also in India, Emperor Ashoka established the first recorded "game laws," providing protection for certain species of mammlas, birds and fish. Both of these Indian developments represented conservation actions taken in response to the clear recognition of the need to control human activities to avoid harmful impact on wild living resources, which in turn adversely affected human welfare.

Throughout subsequent history there have been increasing examples of efforts, by governments, rulers, or individual landowners, to protect certain areas whose values were recognized. The efforts took modern form in 1872 with the initiation of the modern national park concept in America (with the establishment of Yellowstone National Park). And cohesion was provided to the scattered subsequent efforts through the First and Second World Conferences on National Parks.

However, the burgeoning human population, the increasing rate of development activities, and the even more rapidly increasing needs for effective development, combined with what was perceived as a preservationist approach to conservation, have created increasing conflicts between those concerned with conservation and those with development.

The irony of this conflict is twofold. First, the threats to the species and areas which the classical conservationists face and seek to overcome—habitat degradation and over-exploitation of resources—are exactly the same as the threats to human welfare which the developers face and seek to overcome. Second, development cannot succeed and be sustainable unless it is based on sound ecological conservation principles, and equally, conservation cannot succeed unless sound, sustainable development provides the human population with a better than subsistence existence.

Recognizing this situation, and with the invaluable assistance of UNEP, WWF, Unesco and FAO, IUCN produced the World Conservation Strategy in 1980. Since its appearance, the Strategy has received unparalleled endorsement by governments worldwide, the international development community, and the conservation community. The Strategy defines conservation as "the management of human use of the biosphere so that it may yield the greatest sustainable benefit to present generations while maintaining its potential to meet the needs and aspirations of future generations."

The three specific objectives of conservation as presented in the Strategy are: to maintain essential ecological processes and life support systems; to ensure that any utilization of species and ecosystems is sustainable; and to preserve genetic diversity.

The definition and objectives of the Strategy are

now widely accepted, as is its central thesis of the interdependence of conservation and sustainable development. The challenge, however, is to develop the tools—the policies and the methodologies to apply them—to implement the strategy. And this is where this Congress is expected to play a vital role.

Protected areas play an obvious and central role in implementation of the Strategy, in terms of the achievement of its three principal objectives. They play a key role in the maintenance of many ecological processes and life support systems; for example, the role of protected forests in the maintenance of water cycles is obvious and well known. Protected areas are essential for the maintenance of genetic diversity; nowhere is this better illustrated than in the tropical forests of our host country, Indonesia. And protected areas also contribute to assuring that utilization of species and habitats is sustainable, for example, by providing benchmark areas against which changes in the productivity of adjacent managed areas may be analyzed.

These are the clear physical contributions of parks and protected areas to the objectives of the Strategy. But we must remember that to be effective in terms of the strategy, the establishment and management of protected areas must be set within the social and economic development of the countries involved. A major problem of the past is that these areas were all too often seen to be in opposition to development, or at best, not to contribute to them.

We know they contribute, but how do we get the decision makers to recognize this fact? And perhaps a more basic question: do they really contribute effectively? Is our management of parks and protected areas responsive to the needs of development? I believe that all too often it is not.

Clearly there is a need for the traditional national parks, indeed, there is need for vastly more such strictly protected areas worldwide. But there is also a need for many additional kinds of protected areas, managed with different objectives for producing the necessary benefits to society.

One problem we have created for ourselves is that we have often sought a uniform approach to establishment of parks and protected areas; but here, as in other aspects of conservation, there is no single solution, no uniform approach that works in all places. True, a strict nature preserve must be strictly protected, but there may be as many types of approaches to that protection as there are nations which establish such reserves. And equally, the needs for different types of protected areas may be as diverse as the nations involved. Different countries have different needs, and different ways of determining and attaining their objectives.

The workshop sessions of this Congress will provide us with examples from around the world to illustrate how the various categories of protected areas and various types of management approaches are meeting the needs of countries of all economic, social, cultural, ecological and political backgrounds. Part of our challenge is to learn from this diversity and to develop the diversity of tools and methodologies needed to assure that parks and protected areas do indeed contribute to implementation of the World Conservation Strategy.

If we are to meet this challenge it will require some basic changes in philosophy, both on the part of some conservationists and of some developers. One such change involves a shift from the approach that a park is being protected *against* people, to the approach that it is being protected *for* people. By this I do not mean that we open the park to logging or hunting, but that we recognize that by protecting the area we are making a real contribution to human welfare. The physical management of the area may not change, but the political, financial and general public support will change, and the chances that the park will remain a park will be greatly improved.

In the same way there is need for a similar basic change in the development philosophy which sees a park or protected area as a waste of resources, rather than as a productive allocation of resources for other uses.

Only a few years back, most conservationists and developers would have said that these changes were not possible. Now, particularly since the emergence of the Strategy, there is growing recognition that they are not only possible but they are essential.

Indeed, earlier today we have heard from the representatives of the major international agencies represented here that they are willing and ready to help. That puts the responsibility back on us, the conservationists, to respond. I am convinced we will do it, and do it with real professionalism.

And this brings me to my final point. Protected area managers have developed from a variety of backgrounds, over the years, but have not yet evolved into an internationally recognized profession—in the way that wildlife management or range management are recognized. Yet effective management of protected areas requires a high degree of professional training and capability, and clearly deserves recognition as the professional endeavour it is. With protected area managers from some 80 nations, this Congress provides a unique opportunity for you to move toward true professional recognition, which would itself significantly advance the implementation of the Strategy.

I see this Congress as a major evolutionary step—indeed a revolutionary step—in the development of the management of parks and protected areas. It is now up to you, in the days ahead; you will determine whether we will emerge from this Congress having only held discussions which may represent a gentle evolution; or whether we will emerge having developed the tools for a true revolution which implements the World Conservation Strategy with tangible and lasting benefits to all mankind.

The Road to Bali:
An Audiovisual Presentation

Cottonwood Consultants
Alberta, Canada

The natural world. Diversity. Richness, and beauty transcending all political boundaries, the common heritage of all mankind. Images of ages long past reveal our eternal bond to the natural environment; not only the source of food and shelter, but also of inspiration.

But as our numbers multiply and our technology advances, the alteration of natural environments grows at an unprecedented pace. Urban-industrial growth, agricultural development, marine harvesting, water management projects—uncontrolled and poorly planned, they have destroyed extensive natural areas, and put the survival of many species in jeopardy; the remaining natural habitats are shrinking rapidly.

This must concern everyone: the quality of life depends on maintaining a healthy environment. When species and habitats are lost, we lose an important part of our past; as the productivity of forage, timber, fisheries, and wildlife declines, so does our standard of living. Ultimately, our very existence is at stake. Must our future be bleak? Not necessarily, for if we act now we can brighten the outlook for man and the natural world.

Over the last one hundred and ten years, a system of national parks and protected areas has evolved. This important conservation effort has provided many benefits, and is the foundation on which we must continue to build. Endangered species have been brought back from the edge of extinction, some to harvestable levels, but for many others, the future still looks uncertain.

Our understanding of the environment has greatly improved, but we need more research, more environmental education, and more trained people to actively manage protected areas.

Technical and financial support must be made available to help all countries. We now realize the complexity of the natural world, but only a mere fraction of the earth's surface lies in protected areas; serious gaps remain.

Some areas require strict protection; but the concept of protected areas must be expanded to allow a range of uses compatible with conservation. With this new approach, regional economies will benefit directly. If protected, wild species can be used to improve crops and livestock, and to develop new sources of food and medicine. With human use and conservation in balance, protected areas can ensure continued plant, animal, and water production, and they will benefit man in other ways. Protected areas are not a luxury—they are essential.

By the year 2000, at least a half million more species will vanish from the face of the earth; many ecosystems will be damaged or lost; and our vital soil, air, and water resources will be severely degraded.

With conservation and a stabilized population, we can maintain the fertile soil, fresh air, and clean water which support all life. It is *critical* that we act *now*. In conservation lies the future of Man.

Chapter 2
World Coverage of Protected Areas

The Natural Protected Areas of the World

Kenton R. Miller
Chairman, IUCN Commission on National Parks and Protected Areas
School of Natural Resources, University of Michigan
Ann Arbor, Michigan, USA

ABSTRACT. *Since the 1972 World National Parks Conference, there has been considerable progress in the establishment of protected areas; during this decade, the total number of areas rose from 1,823 to 2,671, and the area protected increased from 217 million ha to 396 million ha. While we celebrate this great progress in the establishment of protected areas, we remain humble in the face of the increasing demands of human populations. But science has been working during this decade to improve the technology of managing protected areas to attain social and economic objectives, as outlined in the World Conservation Strategy. Among the new management tools have been the establishment of management categories as determined by objectives, the classification of natural habitats for conservation purposes, and the creation of a monitoring and inventory system.*

1. INTRODUCTION

During the decade since the Second World Conference on National Parks, at Yellowstone and Grand Teton in the United States, a great deal of progress has been made in the parks and protected areas field. In these ten years the total number of units rose from 1,823 to 2,671; the area increased from 217,760,438 to 396,607,351 ha. This represents an increase of 47% in numbers of parks and protected areas, and an 82% expansion in territory. This is something about which we and all people can be proud: a cause for celebration, a reason to gather and share so great a human enterprise.

Yet, in the very process of working in the rural lands, the halls of government, the assemblies of international bodies, and the classrooms and research laboratories we have been sobered by the plight of people everywhere. North-South, East-West, rich and poor, ur-ban and rural, there are problems facing the welfare of people as never before in history.

Thus as we celebrate, we do so with caution and with reverence, for our accomplishments, even though they are the most dramatic of any decade in history, are severely tempered by what we have learned during this period.

The demands of people for the benefits of wild species and ecosystems expand at ever-increasing rates. The supply of our lands and waters still in a wild state is shrinking. We are conscious that in the next decade choices will be made to allocate the last of the wildlands in most parts of the world. Will they go to agriculture, forestry, fisheries, urban or industrial purposes? To permanent natural reserves? Or to desert, degradation and bush?

The 1970s and early 1980s have witnessed a crystalization of the science and the technology of conservation. While the bulk of work to be done lies ahead, we have an emerging field of *conservation biology* which is providing guidelines on the optimal characteristics of natural protected areas. And efforts are under way to step from the art of protected area management to the science and technology of managing reserves for various purposes.

The World Conservation Strategy, the preparation of which involved many of us here, has provided a focus to conservation. It has given a strategic framework for orienting choices regarding matters of importance to people and nature. And it has provided a practical way to relate conservation to development.

2. THE WORLD'S PROTECTED NATURAL AREAS (AUDIOVISUAL PRESENTATION)

Over the centuries, people everywhere have devised ways to regulate the protection and use of nature. With human settlements, industry, agriculture, forestry and fisheries replacing once-extensive wildlands, various ways to protect and employ key natural areas were evolved.

The advent of Yellowstone National park, quickly followed by Royal in Australia, Banff in Canada and Tongariro in New Zealand set the stage for modern management practices. Today, 110 years after Yellowstone, over 2500 protected areas have been established in 120 countries, containing some 400,000,000 ha. Let's examine some exemplary areas by major world biomes.

- In the humid tropics there are the Braulio Carillo National Park in Costa Rica, Selonga in Zaire, and Ole pupu Pue in Western Samoa.
- Parks in the high mountain lands include Sagarmatha, Nepal; Fjordland, New Zealand; Olympics, USA; Hauscaran, Peru; and Kilimanjaro, Tanzania.
- The grasslands and savanna biomes are typified by the Grasslands National Park, Canada; Serengeti, Tanzania in Africa, Kruger in Southern Africa; and the Emas of Brazil.
- The Lake District of the UK, Great Smoky Mountain National Park of the USA, and the mixed hardwood forest of Wolong Nature Reserve in China exemplify the temperate forest biome.
- The desert biome is represented by Paracas Nature Reserve in Peru, featuring the desert of Pacific coastal South America; the Repetek Ecological Reserve, Turkmen SSR, with a portion of the vast extension of Central Asia's Kara Kum; the Saguaro National Monument of Southwestern North America; and the recently established Asir Kingdom National Park in Saudi Arabia, a component of the deserts of the Arabian peninsula.
- The boreal forest of the Palaearctic is noted in the Terrasny-Priosny of the Soviet Union, and of the Nearctic in the Mt. McKinley National Park of Alaska.
- The tundra is featured in the many nature reserves in Sweden, and new parks in Northern Canada will include caribou, musk ox and other features of the Nearctic tundra.
- Twenty-nine research reserves have been set up on the Antarctic continent by the Treaty Powers.
- Canada's Auyuittuq on Baffin Island embraces both terrestrial and marine environments of the Arctic.
- The Great Barrier Reef of Australia features several reserves of aquatic environs; other aquatic reserves have or are being established in the coral reefs of the Bahamas and Caribbean, the marine mammals of coastal Argentina, the whales of Hawaii, and Alaska, the mangroves of Salamanca

Island National Park of Colombia, and the lagoon of Tonga.
- Islands are of special interest to conservation: world famous Galapagos Island National Park covers some 85% of the archipelago in Ecuador; the British Virgin Islands are establishing a system of protected areas embracing both terrestrial and marine habitats; and, here in Bali, many of us will visit and enjoy Bali Barat National Park.

The reasons for which these and hundreds of other protected areas have been established vary widely from country to country, reflecting differences in culture, economy and other features of human society. Some of the main reasons include the preservation of rare, unique and spectacular plants, animals and formations in nature, such as the Giant Sequoia of California, the Proteas of Cape Province in South Africa, China's panda, the rhino of Chitawan in Nepal, the caves of Guacharos in Colombia, and Victoria Falls in Zambia and Zimbabwe.

The maintenance of wild ecosystems is typified in Virunga National Park of Zaire with its outstanding diversity of habitats, and in the Manu National Park of Peru in the Upper Amazon basin.

Recreation and tourism are common in parks and protected areas throughout the world, where local people such as in Ybicui, Paraguay and Cibodas, Java can enjoy a restful day in the outdoors; where more physical skills can be tested, be it skiing in Tongariro National Park, New Zealand, or climbing Mt. Rainier in the USA; and where nature can be observed in a relatively undisturbed state in Lake Nakuru, Kenya, or San Salvador Island, Bahamas.

Closely related to recreational visits to natural areas are the opportunities for education about nature; such opportunities are available by the awesome crater of Poas volcano in Costa Rica, at the Loch of Lowes Nature Reserve in Scotland, and along the tracts of the Khao Yai National Park in Thailand with the well-trained staff.

Other reasons for national parks or different kinds of protected areas tie more closely with the material needs of people. Ensuring water supplies is a key factor in the mountain forests of Gomera National Park in Spain's Canary Islands; Guatopo National Park in Venezuela supplies potable water to the capital city of Caracas while it renders the other functions commonly associated with national parks. On the driest continent—Australia—the Kosiusko National Park in New South Wales contributes water for irrigation of agricultural lands outside the park, and the protection forests on the "mogotes" or haystack hills of the karst region of Cuba ensure the conservation of waters for agriculture in surrounding lands.

Quite different kinds of reserves involve the direct harvesting of plants and animals under technologies designed to ensure sustainable yields. The national forests of the USA, for example, provide for controlled timber harvesting, grazing and hunting, in addition to recreation and the protection of species and ecosystems of high value. In France, sheep grazing and mountain cheese production are elements in the management of the pre-park zone of the Pyrenees National Park.

In Botswana, and elsewhere in Africa, trophy and meat hunting for local residents and visitors are important to diet and economy. One of the greatest success stories of conservation in the past decade is found in the Pampa Galeras National Vicuna Reserve of Peru; rescuing the vicuna from near extinction, Peruvians, with considerable support from people worldwide, reestablished the population and instituted shearing and harvesting techniques to contribute once again to the well-being of the local people and the nation.

All protected areas, whether they are focused strictly on preservation, or controlled harvesting, or some combination, hold in common the need for research and monitoring to ensure their proper management. In Zimbabwe, the Shengwa Wildlife Research Station studies the movement of large animals among its other tasks. On the Galapagos, research on the giant tortoise is leading to programmes for survival of that endangered species. Scientists in the Virgin Islands of the Caribbean study chemical and physical pollution and the impact of various uses of marine parks and nearby lands and waters. In Los Glaciares National Park, Argentina, scientists study glaciation. In Virunga, recent efforts have focused on the hippo population problem.

Far less noticed is the contribution of research and monitoring in natural protected areas to society beyond reserve boundaries. In Hawaii Volcanoes National Park, seismographic instruments are linked to a global network designed to study earthquakes, volcanism and related phenomena. Similar efforts are under way in Brazilia National Park, Brazil.

And tying human welfare even more closely to nature, the effects of agriculture on soils and microclimate in comparison to wild steppe are being monitored in the Chernozem Biosphere Reserve in the USSR.

A growing concern for the survival of wild relatives of our crop cultivars and domestic animals, and of taxa valuable to pharmaceutical development and medical research, is leading to more specific efforts to conserve particular plants and animals and their habitats. Some examples are found in Iguazu National Park, Argentina, with the rosewood trees; in Ujung Kulon National Park in Western Java with the banteng; wild rice in Thailand and elsewhere in South East Asia; and the tomato in Lachay Reserve in coastal Peru.

Finally, perhaps no other site demonstrates quite so graphically the tie between protected areas, human welfare and ecosystems maintenance, as the Canaima in Venezuela. The great Guyana Shield which separates the Orinoco from the Amazon basin features high mesas or "tepuis" and clear rushing streams which flow through the Guri hydro-electric dam. This energy powers iron mines, steel mills, and Caracas. The national legislature augmented the size of the park from 1 million to 3

million ha in recognition of the value of this park to society.

In addition to these present needs, values are recognized in wild nature which relate to our ancient and historic past and our aspirations for the future. The earliest remains of one of man's most distant direct ancestors—*Homo habilis*—was found in Olduvai Gorge, on the shoulder of Ngorongoro Crater, Tanzania. More recent human history is found at the Cevenne in France, Machupichu, Peru, and Mesa Verde, USA.

The art and creativity of man is demonstrated in the Aboriginal cave paintings in Kakadu National Park, Australia, and the great Moi of Easter Island. The spiritual association between man and nature is shown in the Cagar Alam, Bali, and Mt. Fuji, Japan.

The ethical concerns for custodianship of all living things and for peace and harmony are reflected in the pride and enthusiasm by which people everywhere work to establish protected areas, and most recently, in the celebration of the 50th Anniversary of the International Peace Park by Canada and the USA at Glacier/Waterton.

These fundamental concerns and values were examined in the World Conservation Strategy. Developed by IUCN, WWF, and UNEP, with the strong support of FAO and Unesco, the WCS presents three objectives which tie conservation to development:

- to maintain essential ecological processes and life support systems;
- to preserve genetic diversity; and
- to ensure that any utilization of species and ecosystems is sustainable.

These three statements provide a target for what protected areas must cover.

The role of natural protected areas in achieving these objectives was recognized by the General Assembly of IUCN, meeting in Ashkhabad, USSR in 1978. Two policy papers explained the different types of protected areas already in use around the world and how they relate one to another and to the objectives of conservation and development.

The challenges for the coming decade are to:

a) evaluate present coverage of existing protected areas to examine their contents and integrity;
b) identify the gaps in the world system;
c) analyze present management to make sure that current policies, laws, and practices are appropriate for long-term goals; and
d) take action to establish new areas where coverage is lacking, and to enhance and revise existing areas, to provide security to species and ecosystems.

In order to ensure that the needs of people, both material and ethical, are met adequately, and that the biosphere is maintained, a worldwide network of effectively managed protected areas is a vital component of all conservation and development efforts. (End of audio-visual presentation)

3. CONCLUSION

Before we proceed to share our experience of this past decade and seek to derive principles to guide us in the coming years, it is basic that we examine the current status of protected areas:

How do protected areas look worldwide?
Why were they established?
How many are there?
What are their size and characteristics?

We have developed new concepts and tools to answer these and related questions. These include the concept of *management category*, a technology by which the management of protected areas can be focussed upon specified sets of objectives (IUCN, 1978a; IUCN, 1979).

The *classification of natural areas for conservation purposes* includes efforts to develop a biogeographic classification system for terrestrial environments (Udvardy, this volume), and a physical and biotic classification system for marine environments (Ray *et al.*, this volume).

The IUCN *Conservation Monitoring Centre*, and the *Protected Areas Data Unit*, at the Royal Botanic Gardens, Kew, UK, contain a data processing and storage capability which makes it possible to gather, store and analyze information on the vast network of protected areas. This ambitious effort, which you will all be able to inspect during the Congress, stems from the mandate given to IUCN by the United Nations Economic and Social Council (United Nations, 1959). Based on this request to inventory the national parks and related reserves of the world, IUCN established the Commission on National Parks and Protected Areas at Delphi, Greece. Thanks to the pioneering efforts of CNPPA members J.-P. Harroy, J. Henricot, Fred Packard and Sir H. Elliott, inventories were published in 1961, 1962, 1967, and 1971.

In this session of the Congress we will review the status of the protected areas of the world. From this overview and analysis of the status of protected areas several conclusions can be drawn:

- The amount of work thus far accomplished to establish a worldwide network of protected areas is impressive.
- The diversity in nature, culture and ways to manage protected areas to meet the goals of conservation and sustainable development is considerable.
- Given classification systems for terrestrial and marine environments, it is possible to evaluate the coverage of existing protected areas at a macro level of interest.
- The mechanisms now established by the IUCN Conservation Monitoring Centre make it possible to inventory and monitor the vast network of areas.
- Thus we can now begin to analyze and evaluate present coverage, identify gaps and focus financial and technical cooperation upon those areas of greatest priority.
- Finally, with these concepts and tools it will be possible to design action plans to assist countries to establish new areas where they are needed, to reorient existing areas as necessary, and to provide supporting institutions and governments with meaningful reports on progress, priorities and problems in achieving an effectively managed network of natural protected areas.

It is no accident that we are gathered in Indonesia, on this beautiful island of Bali, for this third gathering of those responsible for stewardship of the world's natural heritage. Recognizing the biological diversity of the tropics—that rainforests, tropical coastal zones and coral reefs hold the greatest wealth of living resources on the Planet—IUCN sought to celebrate this session in a tropical country. The people and the Government of Indonesia took the initiative to offer their lovely country as host to our deliberations, for which we are all most grateful.

The World Coverage of Protected Areas: Development Goals and Environmental Needs

Jeremy Harrison, Kenton Miller, and Jeffrey McNeely
IUCN Commission on National Parks and Protected Areas
Kew, UK; Ann Arbor, Michigan, USA; and Gland, Switzerland

ABSTRACT. *Modern civilization requires explicit means of conserving natural lands in order to bring benefits to mankind. One of the best means is through the establishment of protected areas, an effort that has matured over the past 110 years. This paper discusses how different parts of the world vary in their response to the need to establish and manage protected areas; provides a status report on the extent to which the international protected area network is covering natural ecosystems; suggests priorities for further action; describes a system which is monitoring the protected areas of the world; and outlines how protected areas can adapt to the even greater challenges that are sure to come.*

1. INTRODUCTION: THE INTERNATIONAL PROTECTED AREAS NETWORK

Since the first two national parks were established in the 1870s, 2,611 new areas have been created which are of sufficient status to be included on the *United Nations List of National Parks and Equivalent Reserves* (IUCN, 1982b); the total area protected as of June 1982 includes 3,397,316,382 ha. The rate of this growth is illustrated in Fig. 1, where both the number of sites protected and the area protected are plotted cumulatively from 1870 to 1982. Fig. 2 provides a histogram of number of sites and total new area protected for each 5 year period up to 1980. In Fig. 3 these data are broken up to illustrate the situation in each of the eight biogeographical realms.

Growth was slow in the early years, but began to pick up in the 1920s and 1930s, before being brought almost to a halt by World War II. By the early 1950s, momentum had begun to gather again and the decade from 1970 to 1980 saw about twice as many new areas created as had existed in 1969. This large increase in the rate of establishment of protected areas is also illustrated within a number of the individual realms.

To provide a bit more detail of the countries which are particularly well covered, Fig. 4 summarizes data from the 9 countries with over 10 percent of their land area protected (dealing only with countries larger than 20,000 square kilometers). There are also a few states which have remarkable figures hidden by the less impressive figures of the parent country; outstanding examples include India's Andhra Pradesh, with 10.4 percent, Australia's Tasmania with 12.8 percent, and the USA's Alaska, with 22.4 percent.

2. THE BIOGEOGRAPHIC BASIS FOR DETERMINING PROTECTED AREA COVERAGE

A major objective of the protected area system of the world is maintaining the diversity of species and ecosystems, but the listing of protected area coverage by country does not provide much information on how effectively the various natural ecosystems are being conserved. The problem of determining how well the ecosystem conservation objective is being met can be approached through biogeography, the science of distribution of species and ecosystems. Though a useful tool for the purpose, biogeography does have its limitations. Given the humbling indication that far less than half the world's species have even been scientifically described (Myers, 1979), it is unrealistic to expect mapping of individual species to be a workable tool in sufficient time to be useful; time is running out for major land-use decisions, so it is necessary to make the best use of the available information while a few options are still open. Further, botanists and zoologists each have their own ways of looking at the distribution of the organisms of their attention, rendering communication difficult and agreement on broad patterns of distribution next to impossible.

A compromise solution has been worked out for terrestrial ecosystems by Dasmann (1973) and Udvardy (1975; this volume). Both IUCN and Unesco are using the system to make a first estimate of the coverage of major living resources by protected areas. Each area is given a three-number code, which allows each protected area to be assigned a biogeographic context, and facilitates comparison of data on biomes, provinces, and realms.

The first approach to assessing coverage of the world's biota by protected areas is to examine coverage by biome, and biome within realm (Figs. 5, 6). It is important to appreciate that this does not mean habitat type; a protected area within a tropical humid forest biome may not necessarily contain tropical humid forest, and an area containing tropical humid forest could occur in another biome altogether (such as Mixed Island Systems).

It is also important to realize that the total area of each biome in each realm has not yet been determined with sufficient precision to assess percentage coverage. This can hide important differences in the figures. The list contains, for example, 67 areas covering 18,100,118 ha in the Tropical Humid Forest biome in the Neotropics, but only one area in the Lake System biome, of 36,180 ha. It would be misleading to assume that the Tropical Humid Forest Biome is therefore better protected than the Lake System biome in the Neotropical Realm, since roughly a quarter of the continent is in the Tropical Humid Forest biome but there is only one lake (Lake Titicaca) in the Lake Systems biome and the Reserva Nacional de Titicaca extends along at least 10 percent of the Peruvian shore.

In the same way, care should be taken when making comparisons within biomes. There are roughly 2.5 million ha of Subtropical and Temperate Rainforests or Woodlands protected in each the Antarctic and Neotropical Realms. This biome covers only New Zealand in the Antarctic Realm, but in the Neotropics the biome covers not only a large part of southern Brazil (large enough to hide several New Zealands), but also all of coastal Chile south of Temuco; therefore, the Subtropical and Temperate Rainforests or Woodlands biome is much better protected in percentage terms in the Antarctic Realm than in the Neotropical Realm, even though the total area protected is roughly the same.

3. USING PROTECTED AREA COVERAGE OF BIOGEOGRAPHIC PROVINCES TO ASSESS PRIORITIES

Comparison of the 193 biogeographic provinces suffers from many of the same limitations as biome comparisons; a 5,000 ha protected area in the relatively small

Malagasy Thorn Forest (3.10.04), for example, would protect a much larger section of that province than an equivalent-sized reserve would in the huge Somalian province (3.14.7). Coverage is patchy, but to determine exactly how patchy, more analysis of the figures is required, based on accurate estimations of the size of the provinces; this work is in progress.

For all of its limitations, the approach through biogeographic provinces does provide a useful tool for identifying major holes in the protected area network. While all of the biomes are more or less protected, 16 of the 193 biogeographic provinces have no protected areas at all, and some 33 provinces have fewer than 5 protected areas and an area of less than 100,000 ha protected. The rather crude tool of global biogeography suggests that these poorly protected provinces are where attention should be focussed to complete at least the most basic coverage of major ecosystems (Fig. 7).

It is clear that the global biogeographic approach provides useful information primarily at the global level. For national systems, the same biogeographic principles can be applied with considerably greater precision, yielding proportionally more useful results; outstanding examples of such applications include Costa Rica, Canada's Yukon (Environment Canada, 1981), the Amazonian region of Brazil (Jorge Padua, this volume), and the developing system of Biogenetic Reserves in Europe.

In addition, a number of other ecological principles beyond biogeography need to be considered when designing national systems of protected areas which aim at conserving a country's entire spectrum of plants and animals, and for determining action priorities for addressing weaknesses. Important among these are considerations of the size of the area required to maintain viable genetic diversity ("minimum critical size"), ways and means of ensuring that areas which are not protected still maintain value for conservation, local centres of diversity and endemism, and many others (Frankel and Soulé, 1981).

It is also apparent that the system has dealt only with terrestrial and freshwater biogeography to date; coastal and marine biogeography requires a rather different approach because of the "open" nature of the ecosystems involved and the long history of human use. A system based on marine biophysical provinces has also been presented at the World National Parks Congress in Indonesia in October 1982. This system has important applications in identifying the major gaps and weaknesses in the coverage of coastal and marine ecosystems, and should provide a biological basis to justify significant increases in the number and size of protected areas in these aquatic habitats (Ray, 1975).

4. A SYSTEM FOR MONITORING THE PROTECTED AREAS OF THE WORLD

The establishment of a protected area does not in itself ensure that the biota contained within the area will be saved. Theoretical advances in island biogeography and the design of protected areas suggest that any time the total area of an ecosystem is reduced, species diversity will decline until it reaches an equilibrium for the size of the ecosystem; further, few reserves will be large enough to protect viable populations of the larger, wide-ranging species such as tigers and elephants. Management must therefore have the capacity to deal with both "over-abundant species" which may be causing ecological damage in the lack of natural controls and with species whose populations are insufficient to maintain genetic viability.

Effective management is clearly the responsibility of the country involved, but international support can contribute to effective management in many ways. One important way is the 'monitoring of protected areas. IUCN's Commission on National Parks and Protected Areas (CNPPA) has been collecting information on protected areas for more than 20 years, ever since the 1959 United Nations resolution requested IUCN to form and maintain the *United Nations List of National Parks and Equivalent Reserves* (United Nations, 1959).

In 1979 CNPPA began to expand its information-gathering role by developing a more organized system of data collection. Coordinators for the various biogeographic provinces were appointed by CNPPA to compile detailed information about protected areas. At meetings in Costa Rica, Scotland, Cameroon, Peru, New Zealand and the USA and Canada, the coordinators presented data sheets on the protected areas in their parts of the world. Information on about three-quarters of the areas on the *UN List* has now been gathered, although the completeness of this information still varies widely.

CNPPA also collects other information such as management plans, published papers, maps, species lists, brochures and so on, and details of the conservation and protected area systems within each country. To ensure that the information held is kept up-to-date, CNPPA is developing a three-year review and publication cycle.

Such an increase in available information would be of limited use without an improved system for handling the data, so in May 1981 CNPPA (in cooperation with the United Nations Environment Programme and the US Nature Conservancy) inaugurated the Protected Areas Data Unit (PADU). This unit, which is part of IUCN's Conservation Monitoring Centre (CMC), is located at the Royal Botanic Gardens, Kew, England, where the CMC computer has been installed; the CMC operates within the auspices of the UNEP Global Environment Monitoring Centre (GEMS). PADU is responsible for the day-to-day collection of information on protected areas, and for filing that information both manually and on the computer in such a way that it can be retrieved on demand, in the most appropriate format.

By carefully assessing the coverage by protected areas of each biogeographical province on land or at sea (once the new system is operational), CNPPA will be able to identify gaps or weaknesses in the world-wide system of reserves; it will then be much easier to chart the development of new areas year by year, and to focus attention where it is most required. Also, comparison of protected area coverage with information on centres of diversity, endemism, or wild ancestors of domestic plants may bring to light previously hidden gaps in the system.

One of the main advantages of using computerised data files to hold the basic information is the ease with which these files can be manipulated. Data items can be sorted and selected using any character or group of characters within the file. For example, lists can be produced of protected areas of over 100,000 ha within Biome 1 in Latin America, all protected areas in Burma and Thailand in the Tropical Forest Biome, or all protected areas established between 1975 and 1980. Information in the files can also be quickly summarised for publication; volumes could be produced, for example, on protected areas containing tropical rain forest around the world, the protected areas of Brazil, or all the protected areas containing tigers. Examples which have already been published include the 1982 *United Nations List of Protected Areas* and the *IUCN Directory of Neotropical Protected Areas*.

4.1. Applications of the monitoring system

It is clear that each individual country has far more information on its own protected areas than could ever be handled by the CNPPA unit, and that most countries have the capacity to establish computer systems and to maintain their own information in ways that meet their own needs. There are, however, a number of good reasons for having an international 'macro-level' information system:

- Many international development agencies, if provided with quick and large-scale overviews of certain protected areas questions, would be able to design their projects to enhance sustainable development and to avoid adversely affecting particularly sensitive areas.
- IUCN, the World Wildlife Fund, and other international conservation agencies need a basis for determining high priority areas for allocation of scarce international conservation funds; such investments must be made on a rational basis, which is only possible when broad comparisons can be made.
- Unesco's Man and the Biosphere Programme and the World Heritage Convention require global information, the former in order to ensure that representative areas of all biogeographic provinces are established as biosphere reserves, the latter in order to ensure that sites nominated to the World

Heritage List are of truly "outstanding universal significance."

- The international effort to promote protected areas requires a centralized source of information for publications, requests from journalists, and other promotional and publicity uses.
- Scientists often need to make comparisons over the entire range of habitats or species ranges, requiring an international overview.
- Plant breeders need to know where wild ancestors of domestic agricultural crops can be found in protected areas, in order to locate sources of genetic diversity for improving crop breeds.
- Governments need to know what is being done in the field of protected areas management in other countries, in order to enhance their own efforts and to avoid repeating mistakes.

PADU will produce nothing that could not have been produced by governments or members of the CNPPA, given sufficient time and energy; the unit will provide only what is fed into it, but it will be able to produce the data very quickly and in many different configurations. It will not replace any of the human element in protected area management, but it will allow managers, development planners, conservationists, and scientists to be more efficient by providing the data needed, when it is needed, and in the form required.

Most important, collecting and presenting protected areas information in a professional and competent manner demonstrates to governments, development agencies, and individuals around the world that national parks and reserves are valuable land-use tools for managing areas which should, for various reasons, be kept in a natural or semi-natural state. Making protected areas data more accessible will help to ensure that the reserves can play their proper role in the process of socio-economic development.

5. ADAPTING TO THE CHALLENGES OF THE FUTURE

It might be felt that most of nature is either already within protected areas or will soon be so degraded by human pressure as to be worthless for conservation purposes. And indeed it may be difficult for many more major, fully-protected national parks to be created. But the gloomy perception that protected areas are doomed may be far off the mark, for there are several indications that protected natural areas are becoming more important, not less.

By defining the limits of conservation interest more broadly, as is being done by the *World Conservation Strategy*, the area of natural or semi-natural land which can attain useful human objectives can be greatly increased. One excellent example is Western Europe (Poore and Gryn-Ambrose, 1980). At the turn of the century, most forests were gone; France was merely 6 percent forested and Germany was little better. But today, much of Europe is covered in regrown dense forests which still contain a remarkable diversity of wildlife. These forests are generally under intensive management, but they still attain many of the objectives of conservation, providing water, timber, firewood, game animals, recreation, soil regeneration, clean air, and a host of other benefits.

A similar situation exists in the sea. The establishment and management of coastal and marine protected areas are in their infancy, but as the Law of the Sea begins to take effect and nations begin to realise that various forms of protection will increase the yield of fisheries rather than "close off the resource," a remarkable increase of areas under management protection can be expected.

The continuing expansion of protected areas is going to require much more effective management. It will no longer be a priority to put a fence around a nature sanctuary and leave it to its own ecological processes (though pure preservation may still be the best option in some areas). Clear and concise objectives will need to be established for each area, and management will need to focus activities in order to attain those objectives. This will require a greatly increased investment in human resources, in the development of enterprises for managing the natural estate, in education, and in research aimed at producing improved means of management. Such an investment would be well repaid by human societies living in a better balance with their environment.

Acknowledgements

This paper was prepared for IUCN's Commission on National Parks and Protected Areas in cooperation with the United Nations Environment Programme.

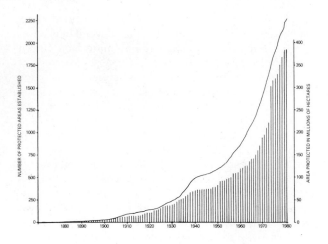

Figure 1. Number of sites protected and the area protected from 1870–1982. Source: McNeely, Harrison.

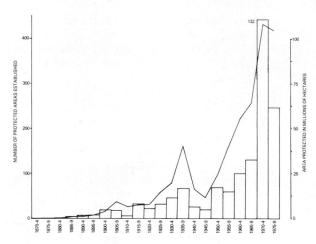

Figure 2. A histogram showing the number of sites and total new area protected for each 5-year period up to 1980. Source: McNeely, Harrison.

Figure 3 a–h. Number and size of protected areas established in each 10-year period within individual realms. The number of areas is represented by the graphs and the size of those areas by histogram. Source: Harrison, McNeely.

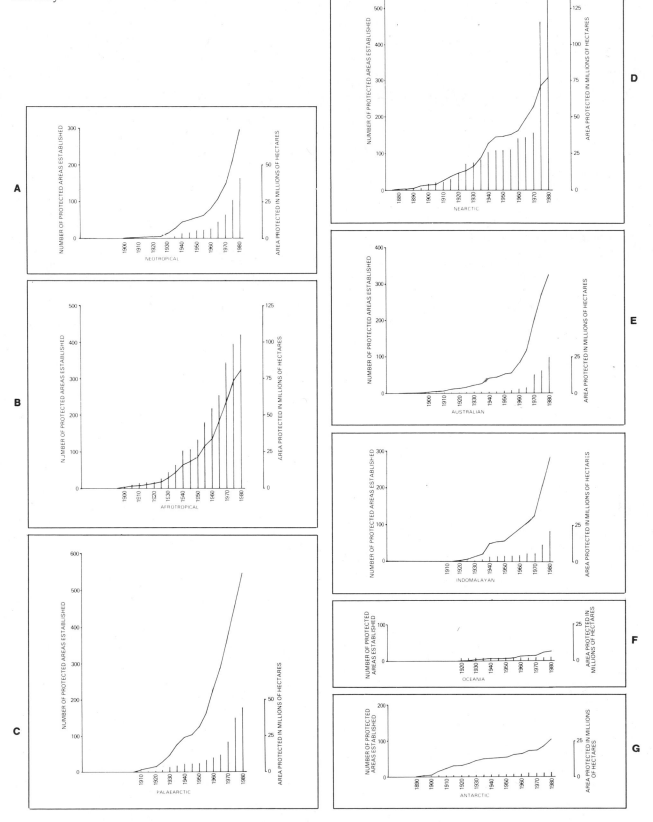

Figure 4. Countries of over 20,000 sq km with over 10% of the Land Area Protected

Country	Size of country	Population	No. of areas	Area protected	ha/sq km (ie %)	ha protected per 1,000 people
Botswana	574,978	726,000	9	10,439,300	18.16	14,379.20
Austria	83,848	7,509,000	5	1,111,898	13.26	148.08
Central African Rep.	622,996	2,610,000	12	7,499,800	12.04	2,873.49
Benin	115,763	3,377,000	5	1,377,550	11.90	407.92
Tanzania	939,762	16,553,000	15	10,830,700	11.52	654.30
Zimbabwe	389,361	6,930,000	25	4,394,400	11.29	634.11
Bhutan	46,620	1,232,000	1	525,000	11.26	426.14
Senegal	197,160	5,085,388	8	2,130,200	10.80	418.89
Rwanda	26,388	4,368,000	2	274,000	10.38	62.73

Figure 5. Protected Area Coverage of Biomes by Realm

Biome	Number of areas	Total area (ha)
1. Tropical humid forests		
Afrotropical	47	10,564,312
Indomalayan	150	13,315,263
Oceanian	10	3,031,863
Australian	81	2,506,065
Neotropical	67	18,100,118
	355	47,517,621
2. Subtropical/temperate rainforests/woodlands		
Nearctic	18	4,258,648
Palaearctic	34	1,296,584
Australian	28	875,494
Antarctic	100	2,627,415
Neotropical	21	2,273,643
	201	11,331,784
3. Temperate needle-leaf forests/woodlands		
Nearctic	49	22,947,056
Palaearctic	65	4,879,752
	114	27,826,808
4. Tropical dry forests/woodlands		
Afrotropical	204	59,920,323
Indomalayan	161	9,288,918
Australian	17	1,677,610
Neotropical	99	5,478,281
	481	76,365,132

Biome	Number of areas	Total area (ha)
5. Temperate broad-leaf forests		
Nearctic	79	2,082,297
Palaearctic	185	12,170,167
Neotropical	6	153,595
	270	14,406,059
6. Evergreen sclerophyllous forests		
Nearctic	8	553,645
Palaearctic	29	1,296,413
Afrotropical	18	75,157
Australian	368	6,314,739
Neotropical	3	34,054
	426	8,274,008
7. Warm deserts/semi-deserts		
Nearctic	21	3,469,878
Palaearctic	53	4,855,599
Afrotropical	46	33,995,712
Indomalayan	2	171,754
Australian	41	17,457,830
Neotropical	4	380,830
	167	60,331,320
8. Cold-winter deserts		
Nearctic	16	657,228
Palaearctic	28	6,850,030
Neotropical	4	99,793
	48	7,607,051

Figure 5 (contd). Protected Area Coverage of Biomes by Realm

Biome	Number of areas	Total area (ha)	Biome	Number of areas	Total area (ha)
9. Tundra communities			12. Mixed mountain systems		
Nearctic	15	96,298,958	Nearctic	80	8,033,335
Palaearctic	9	4,888,553	Palaearctic	145	7,012,256
Antarctic	7	49,741	Afrotropical	28	4,679,293
	31	101,237,252	Indomalayan	11	168,621
			Neotropical	54	8,478,358
				318	28,371,863
10. Tropical grasslands/savannas			13. Mixed island systems		
Australian	11	1,687,989	Palaearctic	6	34,814
Neotropical	20	7,078,067	Afrotropical	3	22,753
	31	8,766,056	Oceanian	27	381,279
			Neotropical	38	1,138,423
				74	1,577,269
11. Temperate grasslands			14. Lake systems		
Nearctic	23	365,623	Nearctic	3	157,184
Palaearctic	19	2,167,458	Palaearctic	1	18,300
Australian	36	514,753	Afrotropical	5	214,853
Neotropical	7	230,035	Neotropical	1	36,180
	85	3,277,869		10	426,517
				2,611	397,316,382

Figure 6. Coverage of the Biomes of the World by Protected Areas

Biome*	Nearctic	Palaearctic	Afrotropical	Indomalayan	Oceanian	Australian	Antarctic	Neotropical	TOTAL
1.	nr	nr	105,643	133,153	30,319	25,061	nr	181,001	475,177
2.	42,586	12,966	nr	nr	nr	8,755	26,274	22,736	113,317
3.	229,471	48,798	nr	nr	nr	nr	nr	nr	278,269
4.	nr	nr	599,203	92,889	nr	16,776	nr	54,783	763,651
5.	20,823	121,702	nr	nr	nr	nr	nr	1,536	144,061
6.	5,536	12,964	752	nr	nr	63,147	nr	341	82,740
7.	34,699	48,556	339,957	1,718	nr	174,578	nr	3,803	603,311
8.	6,572	68,500	nr	nr	nr	nr	nr	998	76,070
9.	962,990	48,886	nr	nr	nr	nr	497	nr	1,012,373
10.	nr	nr	nr	nr	nr	16,880	nr	70,781	87,661
11.	3,656	21,675	nr	nr	nr	5,148	nr	2,300	32,779
12.	80,333	70,123	46,793	1,686	nr	nr	nr	84,784	283,719
13.	nr	348	228	nr	3,813	nr	nr	11,384	15,773
14.	1,572	183	2,149	nr	nr	nr	nr	362	4,266
TOTAL (sq. km)	1,388,238	454,701	1,094,725	229,446	34,132	310,345	26,771	434,809	3,973,167

(* See Fig. 5 for names of Biomes)

Figure 7. Priority Areas for Establishment of Protected Areas

Provinces With No Protected Areas

Provinces With Less Than 5 Protected Areas or Less Than 100,000 ha Protected

Nearctic Realm

1.15.9	Arctic Archipelago
1.16.9	Greenland Tundra

Palaearctic Realm

2.18.7	Sahara
2.23.8	Tibetan
2.42.14	Lake Ladoga
2.44.14	Lake Baikal

Afrotropical Realm

3.12.17	Western Sahel
3.19.12	Guinean Highlands
3.23.13	Ascension/St. Helena Islands

Indomalayan Realm

4.16.12	Seychelles/Amirantes Is.
4.17.12	Laccadives Islands
4.18.12	Maldives & Chagos Is.
4.20.12	Andaman & Nicobar Is.

Oceanian Realm

Antarctic Realm

7.3.9	Marielandia

Neotropical Realm

8.42.13	Revilla Gigedo Is.
8.46.13	South Trinidade Is.

Nearctic Realm

1.10.7	Tamaulipan
1.13.9	Alaskan Tundra

Palaearctic Realm

2.28.11	Atlas Steppe
2.31.12	Scottish Highlands
2.39.12	Szechwan Highlands
2.40.13	Macronesian Islands
2.41.13	Ryukyu Islands

Afrotropical Realm

3.10.4	Malagasy Thorn Forest
3.24.13	Comores Islands/Aldabra
3.25.13	Mascarene Islands
3.27.14	Lake Ukerewe
3.28.14	Lake Tanganyika
3.29.14	Lake Malawi

Indomalayan Realm

4.4.1	Malabar Rainforest
4.14.4	Deccan Thorn Forest
4.12.4	Coromandel
4.19.12	Cocos-Keeling/Christmas Is.
4.27.12	Taiwan

Oceanian Realm

5.2.13	Micronesian
5.4.13	Southeastern Polynesian
5.6.13	New Caledonian
5.7.13	East Melanesian

Antarctic Realm

7.2.9	Maudlandia

Neotropical Realm

8.9.2	Brazilian Planalto
8.14.4	Guerreran
8.23.6	Chilean Sclerophyll
8.25.7	Monte
8.26.8	Patagonian
8.31.11	Argentinian Pampas
8.39.13	Cuban
8.43.13	Cocos Island
8.45.13	Fernando de Noronja Is.
8.47.14	Lake Titicaca

A Biogeographical Classification System for Terrestrial Environments

Miklos D.F. Udvardy
Department of Biological Sciences
California State University
Sacramento, California, USA

ABSTRACT. *This paper describes a biogeographical classification system for terrestrial environments. It represents a revision of a system that has been used by IUCN and Unesco since 1975. It accompanies a very large map which has been prepared in cooperation with UNEP and the University of Michigan; this map also includes the locations of all protected areas on the 1982 United Nations List, showing how the biogeographical classification system can be used to assess protected area coverage. The revised system will now be used widely for assessing protected area coverage at the global level. National and regional systems are now required to carry the system to the next level of detail.*

1. INTRODUCTION

In order to budget our economy, or to use our resources wisely, we have to know how much we have to start with. Following this simple reasoning, the World Conservation Strategy aims at cataloguing our resources to see what to protect. My task was to develop a system, already begun by Ray Dasmann (1973, 1974), which would classify the natural ecosystems of the world and their geographic distribution. The world's natural protected areas then can be charted on this basis, and we will know what we have and where it is.

The *biosphere* consists of the Earth's layer of living matter. A forest surrounds a meadow, is supplanted by scrub or barren rocks on a hilltop, ends abruptly at a lakeshore; these stands of various *ecosystems* have been classified into a system of biomes. *Biomes* are groups of ecosystems that are related, and which show similarity in both appearance and internal structure, for they are influenced by the same climate, soil conditions, and elevational conditions, etc. Biomes are characterized by their dominant plant and animal members, but since animals are elusive, biome classification is based on the vegetational component of their stands.

A stand of an ecosystem can be as small as that of the lichens crowding a single rock left uncovered by the arctic icefield of Greenland. It can be as large as the primeval forest that covered Bali from coast to coast, or even larger.

Where natural stands of ecosystems cover large areas in a uniform way, their mapping presents little difficulty at any scale. But we find these conditions only in a few areas of the world where the geology, the surface features of the land, and climatic conditions are rather uniform. Some parts of the pampas of South America, of the Sahara desert, and of the Congo rainforest come to mind.

Elsewhere the biological cartographer finds a mosaic of various ecosystem stands influenced by the landscape, by distance from the sea (continentality or oceanic influences), or by soil chemistry and the like. To chart this mosaic on a worldwide scale one has to compromise and simplify, ignoring the smaller units and emphasizing the most common or large ones. In this way the biosphere map, which is now usually based on satellite photographs, gets broken down into regional entities of land which we call *biogeographic provinces*. Theoretically, these smallest units in a hierarchial classification such as ours should be characterized by unique, local features. Each biogeographical province ought to possess a list of those of its plant and animal inhabitants which, if not unique, are at least blended in a unique proportion. But it is unrealistic to expect this to be done in a practical way for the biogeographical provinces of the world; it would be a mammoth task even for a team of biogeographers. But this task still must be done; attempts in this direction have already been initiated in certain parts of the world, e.g. the Australian Seabird Survey, the European Floral Atlas undertaking, etc.

Let me then state flatly that, though you might not expect it from a zoologist and avian zoogeographer, I have based the delimitation of my province units mostly on the vegetation, because it is the most logical indicator available. Most unique and endangered animals are restricted by their habitat selection mechanism to certain characteristic ecosystems. Where known to me, but in second place, I also considered unique faunal entities. Third, I used to a great extent the deliberations of floristic plant geographers.

Besides the two practical arguments that vegetation harbours animals and that vegetation is relatively easily mapped, the argument of uniformity of criteria also speaks for the vegetation: save for some tundra and rocky habitats, it is the *vascular plant* flora that makes up the visible and dominant vegetation. In plant geography, floristic and vegetational work can proceed side by side, complementing one another. In zoology we have as many geographies as there are major groups studied. What satisfies an arachnologist (about spiders) would not suit a chiropterologist (about bats) and vice versa.

The highest category of biogeographic entities is the "kingdom" of floristic botanists (in my 1975 report I called them "florists" but this expression prompted puzzled faces and some sarcastic remarks from colleagues whose native tongue is English), and "regions" of zoologists (faunists). Both are based on the uniqueness of occurrence of some higher taxa, families in most cases. This again is based on historic ties, or lack of such, between continents of the past. The eight *realms* of the system here presented deviates somewhat from the ones used by zoo- and phytogeographers. The Palaearctic, Nearctic, Neotropical, Afrotropical and Indomalayan realms have more or less traditional boundaries. The assigning of the Central American mountains to the Nearctic, those of Arabia Felix to the Afrotropical, Taiwan to the Indomalayan, the Thar Desert to the Palaearctic, though new arrangements in my approach, follow one or another earlier biogeographic system. I deviate most from the traditional approach in the realms of the southern hemisphere, in two respects. One is the establishing of an Oceanian Realm. All earlier biogeographic classifications considered the Pacific world an extension of the Oriental zoogeographic region or the Palaeotropical floristic kingdom; true, the biota spread hither mostly from neighbouring Asiatic coasts and islands, but the rapid evolution of island endemics in many of these archipelagoes makes this area unique.

The frozen world of Antarctica, least habitable and last explored continent, was mostly ignored by biogeographers of the past. Before the glacial epochs, though, it harboured a large fauna and flora, and in earlier geological periods it was the nucleus of the southern land mass, Gondwanaland, from which the other southern continents broke off one after the other. Thanks to the scientific explorations since the 1960s, survivors of this ancient biota have been detected, and Antarctica deserves to be put on the biogeographic map as a realm. Besides the continent itself and the surrounding island groups climatically allied with Antarctica, I consider New Zealand as part of the Antarctic realm. Its geographic position, surrounded by oceans on all sides, its small size compared to continental realms, and the modification and evolution of those species of Australian origin among its biota, militate against giving it a realm status or joining it to the Australian realm. Owing to an equable oceanic climate and great elevational variety, we find here preserved much of the ecosystems that seem to have covered Antarctica (or part of it) before glaciation. Though New Zealanders might not like being cut off from Australia in this system, it gives them a noble opportunity to scientifically and conservationally take charge of all Antarctic exploration

2. CRITERIA TO DELIMIT BIOMES

Since, as we have seen, biomes are manifest and observable by their vegetational component, the system of biomes used here is based on Unesco's (1973) vegetation classification, with great simplifications. On land eleven biomes are recognized as well as one lake biome. Two vegetationally complex units receive biome rank; islands and archipelagoes, highlands and mountain chains or massifs with complex zonation depending on altitude, slope exposure etc. deserve a special status on similar grounds.

A drawback of this broad ecological classification is that it is based on *zonal* ecosystems, i.e. those principally determined by the climatic zone and latitudinal position on the globe. The *azonal* communities (lakes, rivers, marshes and other wetlands, salt pans, caves, areas with mineral-deficient soil, etc.) are not considered, owing to the relatively small size of their stands and to a certain extent to the fact that they are geologically short-lived and thus do not usually evolve unique biota. Certain lakes are treated in this system, because they do have unique biota. Others, because they are residues of former sea intrusions and thus have relict organisms, are worth special attention by conservationists.

Each biogeographic province has a composite number consisting of three parts separated by point, as 2.4.3. or 8.35.10. The first number identifies the realm, from 1 to 8; the last number identifies the dominant biome of the province, from 1 to 14. The middle number is the serial number of the biogeographical province in question within its realm.

2.1. The revision of the 1975 system of biogeographical provinces

Scientific literature, both new since 1975 and older, has been considered. Especially helpful were recently published biogeographical maps. Foremost I had input, verbal or written, from colleagues all over the world, who often approached me with their suggestions and criticism or who helpfully answered my queries. IUCN and Unesco did everything from providing literature to mediating contact with local experts. Since the final text is yet to be written—and coordinated with the results of the twin projects concerning the oceans and their coasts— I am seeking, and hoping to get, further critical input from the members of this congress while we are in Bali and during subsequent weeks.

In the 1975 system we recognized 193 biogeographical provinces on land. At present we are listing 227 provinces, with three or four more pending for inclusion.

The NEARCTIC REALM is by and large unchanged thanks to its good foundation by Dasmann and subsequent ecogeographic mapping by R.G. Bailey (1976).

In the PALAEARCTIC, the Unesco map of Mediterranean vegetation and the new Council of Europe map (1979) helped with the western part of this realm, while colleagues V.V. Krinitsky and N.N. Drozdov mapped the biogeographic provinces of the Soviet Union and Wang Huen-pu supplied those of China. Their detailed work contributed to the increase of the number of Palaearctic provinces from 44 to 57.

In the AFROTROPICAL REALM Dr. White's vegetation map—not yet published but loaned to me by Unesco—is the main basis of revision. I also attached Arabia Felix (the mountainous areas of coastal southwest Arabia) to the Afrotropical, as many floral geographers and entomologists have done before me.

In the INDOMALAYAN REALM, we have now a better division of the Indian Peninsula owing to the vegetation mapping of Gadgil and Meher-Homji (1982), and of the archipelago of Indonesia.

Little revision was done concerning OCEANIA. Curry-Lindahl (1975; 1980) also considers Oceania as a separate entity, but his system is a little different from the one here employed. Final vegetational work is expected from the forthcoming monograph by Fosberg and Mueller-Dombois, who both kindly advised me regarding Oceania.

There was such upsurge of plant and animal geographic research in Australia during the last decade or so, that it was difficult for me, with only brief superficial experience on that continent, to make the revisions that the experts pointed out as highly necessary. Fortunately, Dr. Ovington assembled a group to adapt the vegetational knowledge of today to our system, and the result is the revised AUSTRALIAN REALM.

We have already mentioned the ANTARCTIC REALM, essentially unchanged. Following botanists, I assigned the outer-most coastal archipelago along the southern Chilean coast to this realm. It remains to the local experts to corroborate or correct this arrangement.

In South America itself, in the NEOTROPICAL REALM, the 1981 Unesco vegetation map enabled me to draw more accurate provincial boundaries and correct many details. More substantial changes were done, fol-

lowing correspondence with experts, in regard to Amazonia and neighbouring areas and to Chilean coastal biomes.

3. NEED FOR FURTHER IMPROVEMENTS

The map presented is a draft, subject to changes before it is printed. It needs additional input. Now, if those viewers in the practical and managerial conservation fields accept it uncritically because it was done by professionals, and the biogeographers present would leave it uncriticized since it does not serve fundamental science, this system will become something like the king's new robe: thin and translucent but accepted by ignorance. That is not what we want.

Our map also shows how much of the ecosystems are currently preserved in the form of national parks and other protected areas. Further ahead, I see the need to chart not only the potential natural ecosystem coverage of the earth, but what actually remains of it. A project mapping the economic, agrarian, industrial, recreational, and habitational uses of land would accomplish this.

BIOGEOGRAPHICAL PROVINCES

(1) THE NEARCTIC REALM
1.1.2.   *Sitkan*
1.2.2.   *Oregonian*
1.3.3.   *Yukon Taiga*
1.4.3.   *Canadian Taiga*
1.5.3.   *Lake Forest*
1.6.5.   *Eastern Forest*
1.7.5.   *Austroriparian*
1.8.6.   *Californian*
1.9.7.   *Sonoran*
1.10.7.   *Chihuahuan*
1.11.7.   *Tamaulipan*
1.12.8.   *Great Basin*
1.13.9.   *Aleutian Islands*
1.14.9.   *Alaskan Tundra*
1.15.9.   *Canadian Tundra*
1.16.9.   *Arctic Archipelago*
1.17.9.   *Greenland Tundra*
1.18.9.   *Arctic Desert and Icecap*
1.19.11. *Grasslands*
1.20.11. *Prairie Peninsula*
1.21.12. *Rocky Mountains*
1.22.12. *Sierra-Cascade*
1.23.12. *Madrean-Cordilleran*
1.24.14. *Great Lakes*

(2) THE PALAEARCTIC REALM
2.1.2.   *Chinese Subtropical Forest*
2.2.2.   *Japanese-Korean Evergreen Forest*
2.3.3.   *West Eurasian Taiga*
2.4.3.   *West Siberian Taiga*
2.5.3.   *East Siberian Taiga*

2.6.3.	Okhotsk Taiga		3.8.4.	East African Woodland/Savanna
2.7.3.	Boreonemoral		3.9.4.	Miombo Woodland/Savanna
2.8.3.	Manchu-Japanese Mixed Forest		3.10.4.	South African Woodland/Savanna
2.9.3.	Kamchatkan-Kurilean Mixed Forest		3.11.4.	Malagasy Woodland/Savanna
2.10.5.	Icelandic		3.12.4.	Malagasy Thorn Forest
2.11.5.	Atlantic		3.13.6.	Cape Sclerophyll Desert
2.12.5.	Northeast European Mixed Forest		3.14.7.	Western Sahel Desert
2.13.5.	Pannonian		3.15.7.	Eastern Sahel Desert
2.14.5.	Oriental Deciduous Forest		3.16.7.	Somalian Desert
2.15.5.	Oriental Forest-steppe		3.17.7.	Namib Desert
2.16.6.	Mediterranean Sclerophyll		3.18.7.	Kalahari Desert
2.17.7.	Sahara Desert		3.19.7.	Karroo Desert
2.18.7.	Arabian Desert		3.20.10.	Highveld
2.19.7.	Iranian Desert		3.21.12.	Arabian Highlands
2.20.7.	Thar Desert		3.22.12.	Ethiopian Highlands
2.21.8.	Kazakh Desert		3.23.12.	Cameroon Highlands
2.22.8.	Turanian Desert		3.24.12.	Central African Highlands
2.23.8.	Taklamakan-Gobi Desert		3.25.12.	East African Highlands
2.24.9.	Arctic Desert		3.26.12.	South African Highlands
2.25.9.	European Tundra		3.27.13.	Gulf of Guinea Islands
2.26.9.	W. Siberian Tundra		3.28.13.	Ascension and St. Helena Is.
2.27.9.	E. Siberian Tundra		3.29.13.	Seychelles and Mirante islands
2.28.11.	N. African Steppe		3.30.13.	Comores Islands and Aldabra
2.29.11.	Pontian Steppe		3.31.13.	Mascarere Islands
2.30.11.	W. Siberian Steppe		3.32.14.	African Lakes
2.31.11.	Mongolian-Manchurian Steppe		3.33.14.	Lake Victoria
2.32.11.	Anatolian Steppe		3.34.14.	Lake Tanganyika
2.33.11.	Fertile Crescent		3.35.14.	Lake Malawi (Nyasa)
2.34.11.	Iranian Steppe			
2.35.12.	South Scandes			
2.37.12.	Ural Highlands			
2.38.12.	Central European Highlands		(4) THE INDOMALAYAN REALM	
2.40.12.	Asia Minor Highlands		4.1.1.	Malabar Rainforest
2.41.12.	Krim Highlands		4.2.1.	Ceylonese Rainforest
2.42.12.	Kaukasus-Elburz Highlands		4.3.1.	Bengalian Rainforest
2.43.12.	Armeno-Iranian Highlands		4.4.1.	Assam-Burman Rainforest
2.44.12.	Afghan-Kirgiz Highlands		4.5.1.	Indochinese Rainforest
2.45.12.	Hindu Kush Highlands		4.6.1.	Tonkin-Chinese Tropical Forest
2.46.12.	Tien-Shan Highlands		4.7.1.	Malayan Rainforest
2.47.12.	South Siberian Highlands		4.8.1.	Sumatran Rainforest
2.48.12.	Tibetan Highlands		4.9.1.	Javan Rainforest
2.49.12.	Himalayan Highlands		4.10.1.	Borneo and Palawan
2.50.12.	Qilian-Shan Highlands		4.11.1.	East Malayan Islands
2.51.12.	Sichuan Highlands		4.12.1.	Filippine Islands
2.52.13.	Macaronesian islands		4.13.4.	Ganges Monsoon Forest
2.53.13.	Ryukyu Islands		4.14.4.	Rajastan
2.54.14.	Bonin islands		4.15.4.	Deccan Teak Forest
2.55.14.	Lake Ladoga		4.16.4.	Andhra Pradesh
2.56.14.	Lake Aral		4.17.4.	Coromandel
2.57.14.	Lake Baikal		4.18.4.	Ceylonese Monsoon Forest
			4.19.4.	Burmese Dry Forest
			4.20.4.	Thai Dry Forest
(3) THE AFROTROPICAL REALM			4.21.4.	Javan Monsoon Forest
3.1.1.	Guinean Rainforest Province		4.22.4.	Lesser Sunda Islands
3.2.1.	Congo Rainforest		4.23.12.	Transhimalayan Mountains
3.3.1.	Malagasy Rainforest		4.24.13.	Laccadives Islands
3.4.1.	Guinea-Congolian Forest		4.25.13.	Maldives and Chagos Islands
3.5.1.	Victorian Forest		4.26.13.	Cocos-Keeling/Christmas Is.
3.6.1.	South Congolian Forest		4.27.13.	Andaman and Nicobar Islands
3.7.4.	West African Woodland/Savanna		4.28.13.	Taiwan

(5) THE OCEANIAN REALM
5.1.1.   Papuan Rainforest
5.2.10. Papuan Savanna
5.3.13. Micronesian
5.4.13. Hawaiian
5.5.13. Southeastern Polynesian
5.6.13. Central Polynesian
5.7.13. New Caledonian
5.8.13. East Melanesian

(6) THE AUSTRALIAN REALM
6.1.1.   NE Queensland Rainforest
6.2.2.   Tasmanian
6.3.4.   Cape York
6.4.4.   Top End
6.5.6.   Western Sclerophyll
6.6.6.   Southern Sclerophyll
6.7.6.   Eastern Sclerophyll
6.8.6.   Murray Darling woodlands
6.9.6.   Brigalow
6.10.7. Western Arid
6.11.7. Northern Arid
6.12.7. Southern Arid
6.13.7. Eastern Arid
6.14.10. Northwestern Woodlands
6.15.10. Northeastern Woodlands
6.16.10. Northern Savanna/grasslands

(7) THE ANTARCTIC REALM
7.1.2.   Neozealandia
7.2.9.   Maudlandia
7.3.9.   Marielandia
7.4.9.   Insulantarctica

(8) THE NEOTROPICAL REALM
8.1.1.   Campechean Rainforest
8.2.1.   Central American Woodlands
8.3.1.   Northwest Coastal
8.4.1.   Atlantic Coastal
8.5.1.   Rio Negro
8.6.1.   Orinoco
8.7.1.   Manaus
8.8.1.   Guyanan Rainforest
8.9.1.   Solimoes
8.10.1. SW. Amazonas
8.11.1. Madeiran Rainforest
8.12.1. Serra do Mar Rainforest
8.13.2. Brazilian Rainforest

8.14.2. Brazilian Planalto Woodlands
8.15.2. Valdivian Forest
8.16.2. Chilean Nothofagus Forest
8.17.4. Everglades Woodland
8.18.4. Sinaloan Woodland
8.19.4. Guerreran Woodland
8.20.4. Yucatecan Woodland
8.21.4. Caribbean Dry forest
8.22.4. Caribbean Deciduous Forest
8.23.4. Ecuadorian Dry Forest
8.24.4. Caatinga Dry Forest
8.25.4. Gran Chaco Savanna
8.26.6. Chilean Sclerophyll
8.27.7. Pacific Desert
8.28.7. Monte Desert
8.29.8. Patagonian Desert
8.30.10. Llanos Savanna
8.31.10. Campos Limpos Savanna
8.32.10. Pantepui
8.33.10. Babacu Savanna
8.34.10. Campos Cerrados Savanna
8.35.10. Pantanal
8.36.11. Argentinian Pampas
8.37.12. Uruguayan Pampas
8.38.12. Volcanos
8.39.12. Parima
8.40.12. Northern Andean
8.41.12. Colombian Montane
8.42.12. Yungas Montane
8.43.12. Puna
8.44.12. Southern Andean
8.45.13. Bahamas-Bermudan
8.46.13. Cuban
8.47.13. Greater Antillean
8.48.13. Lesser Antillean
8.49.13. Revilla Gigedo Island
8.50.13. Cocos Island
8.51.13. Galpagos Islands
8.52.13. Chilean Pacific Islands
8.53.13. Fernando de Noronja Island
8.54.13. South Trinidade Island
8.55.14. Lake Titicaca

Acknowledgements

This paper was prepared for IUCN's Commission on National Parks and Protected Areas in cooperation with the United Nations Environment Programme.

Development of a Biophysical Coastal and Marine Classification System

G. Carleton Ray, Bruce P. Hayden, and Robert Dolan
Department of Environmental Sciences, University of Virginia
Charlottesville, Virginia, USA

ABSTRACT. *This paper describes the development of a marine biogeographical classification system to parallel the terrestrial system described in the preceding paper. This system was also included on a very large world map, with all coastal and marine protected areas indicated, showing how the system might be used to assess protected area coverage. It is recognized that a global classification system such as this one is useful primarily at the global level, and that it will need to be supplemented by national and regional systems at the appropriate scales. While it is impossible to devise a biogeographical classification system that pleases all specialists, this paper comes up with a rational and straightforward system which should be widely useful for conservation purposes.*

1. INTRODUCTION

The goal of developing an internally consistent world classification system is scientifically challenging. Terrestrial, coastal, and marine realms have been approached in quite different ways. Terrestrial biotic provinces have been classified by Udvardy (1975, this volume) largely on the basis of vegetation; this "world" classification draws boundaries of terrestrial realms though a presumably lifeless sea (Pielou, 1979). Coastal classification is largely by physical land forms and physical processes (Dolan, *et al.*, 1972); marine realms have been treated both physically (e.g., water masses) and biotically, and no one method dominates.

IUCN, as well as specialized agencies of the United Nations (particularly Unesco and FAO) have long recognized the need for a classification system. This Congress has recommended (No. 3, Marine and Coastal Protected Areas) that IUCN: "Develop as soon as possible an appropriate marine biogeographic classification scheme on global, regional, and national levels as a basis for ensuring adequate representation of different marine ecosystems in a wide range of protected areas". Ray (1975) suggested that the biogeography of the classic work of Ekman (1953) be adopted. Briggs (1974) now stands as the primary marine biogeography on a world level. However, none of these classifications entirely meets the practical needs of a system of protected areas. Therefore, IUCN has supported the efforts reported herein.

Unesco (1974) provides perhaps the best statement to date on objectives and criteria for protected areas, worldwide. Objectives are conservation, research and monitoring, and education and training. Criteria are representativeness, diversity, naturalness, effectiveness as a conservation unit, and uniqueness. Modified or perturbed areas are not excluded and difficult ecological concepts (e.g., "core" and "buffer" areas) are faced. Ray *et al.* (1981) have addressed these matters specifically with regard to coastal and marine areas. Nevertheless, to date, a suitable classification for application of those criteria and objectives has been lacking.

This paper describes an approach, with examples from the relatively well-studied Americas, in hopes that a useful classification will be made possible; Hayden, *et al.* (in prep.) are extending this approach worldwide. Problems will remain, particularly with regard to the consistency of land and sea approaches and coastal zone boundaries between their realms. Recognizing this, the practical necessity for a truly worldwide classification is immediate.

1.1 Special attributes of marine and coastal systems

Pielou (1979) has observed that profound differences in community structure and ecosystem function cause serious difficulties in designating terrestrial and marine biogeographic regions by similar methods. She further obderved, as have a number of scientists (e.g., Hesse, *et al.*, 1951), that: (1) vegetation does not form a structured environment in most marine systems; (2) the oceans are contiguous and marine species have greater ranges, generally, than terrestral ones; (3) the boundaries to dispersal are more subtle, but the closer to land, the clearer boundaries between regions become; (4) latitudinal zonation is more marked for marine species; and (5) the ocean is three-dimensional, meaning that biogeographical diffrences are ones of depth as well as of geographical location and that these are at right angles to one another. Further, all phyla of the animal kingdom and most classes are represented in the sea. Thus, life forms are much more varied, even though the total species are perhaps only a fifth of the land's. Taking such fundamentals into account, it should be apparent that a marine/coastal classification cannot be approached in the same way as for the land. In fact, Hesse *et al.*, (1951) stated that it is deceptive to divide the oceans into "domains". Pielou (1979) notes: "There is considerable doubt as to whether the waters of the open sea can and should be biogeographically classified".

An essential point concerns the "coastal zone". This is a broad ecotone that in many ways both divides and unites marine and terrestrial systems. Ray *et al.* (1981; after Ketchum, 1972) defined it as follows:

1) "The *terrestrial boundary* is defined by (a) the inland extent of astronomical tidal influence or (b) the inland limit of penetration of marine aerosols within the atmospheric boundary layer and including both salts and suspended liquids, whichever is greater.

2) "The *seaward limit* is defined by (a) the outer extent of the continental shelf (approximately 200 m depth) or (b) the limit of territorial waters, whichever is greater".

Within this broad band, ecological processes such as biological production, consumption, and exchange of materials occur at high rates. Definition (2b) is, of course, jurisdictional, not biophysical. It should be obvious that the coastal zone is very extensive indeed and that neither purely terrestrial nor purely oceanic approaches will suffice for its classification. Thus, it should not be assumed that a terrestrial classification extends to the water's edge. Where the boundary between land and sea lies is a difficult, unresolved question, the answer to which lies at the local process level. It is the coastal zone that has been most studied, to which marine "provinces" mostly apply, and for which the most urgent conservation problems exist, due to the fact that a majority of the world's population lives within it.

1.2 State-of-the-art

Briggs (1975) generally follows Ekman (1953) and has become the definitive reference of marine biogeography. He points out that most knowledge of the distribution of marine species is recent and fragmentary and over a century behind similar information for terrestrial species. He recognizes three "realms": (1) continental shelf—including marginal seas; (2) pelagic; and (3) deep benthic. He identifies provinces only for the former; provinces are not recognized "unless there appears to be good evidence, in the form of endemism, for doing so". His is a true geography, in that it includes maps depicting faunal assemblages.

However, there are other approaches. Hesse *et al.* (1951) took a basically ecological view in their classical treatment. They emphasized the fact that "the relations with the total environment are much more direct and obvious" among plants than animals. Terrestrial biotic provinces are defined mostly by rooted vegetation, but marine regions are basically zoogeographic. In this fact lies much of the difficulty in defining marine regions and provinces, especially in the open sea. Briggs noted general difficulties in correlating species distributions and water masses. He, therefore, separated the pelagic seas into epipelagic, mesopelagic, and bathypelagic divisions; the deep benthic areas are divided into continental slope, abyssal plains, and trenches. Similarly, Pielou separates the continental shelf and deep ocean as two basic "realms", noting that subdivision is less easy than for the land as the contrasts among units is less. Each of these realms provides two radically different habitats, the pelagic and the benthic. The ecological approach does not usually result in defining geographically distinct biotic maps. One reason is that geomorphological zones may or may not coincide with faunal ones, but some progress may, in time, be made in this regard. Notably, Menzies *et al.* (1973) have subdivided the abyssal environment into 5 regions and 13 provinces.

A third approach is historical and taxonomic. Darlington (1957) emphasized patterns and evolution of animal distribution and considered the vertebrate classes separately, MacArthur's (1972) treatment of geographical ecology is also concerned with such patterns. Unfortunately, this approach, as for the ecological, does not result in faunal assemblage maps.

2. APPROACHES

Two factors dominate our present efforts. First, the scope of this project permits us only a two-dimensional analysis. Second, we conclude, as have others before us, that the coastal zone deserves primary attention as the quality of the data base and distinctions among regions are best there. Further, we agree with Pielou (1979): "The evidence seems overwhelming that the boundaries of (coastal) biotic provinces are determined by modern abiotic (that is, physical) factors". Our approach, therefore, differs from that used by Udvardy (1975) for terrestrial areas in that we assume that the geophysical structure of coastal and marine environments "makes possible" a particular ecological response. Koppen (1936), Trewartha (1962), and Bryson (1966) have described the connections between climate and terrestrial biomes. The equivalent marine "biomes" or realms and their relationships to marine climates have been specified by Dietrich (1963). In general, little equivalent work has been done on the relationships between the attributes of the physical environment of coastal marine areas and biota at the global scale. Hayden and Dolan (1976) reported for North and South America a close association between coastal marine faunal distributions and along-the-coast units of the physical environment based on water masses, waves, tides, and currents.

To illustrate our approach, we will restrict ourselves in this paper to areas around these two continents. Space here does not permit a detailed discussion. This will be undertaken by Hayden *et al.* (in prep.). Suffice it for now to say that for the coastal margins, marginal seas, and archipelagos, we merge Bryson's and Dietrich's approaches in that we use the seasonal movements of both air and water masses by winds and currents to define coastal realms and to classify the marginal seas and archipelagos. The natural coupling of the atmosphere and the oceans ensures the integrity of the resulting organization.

The circulation of the atmosphere and the surface layer of the open ocean also define a system of natural regions and we applied Dietrich's classification to the ocean basin proper, outside the continental shelves. This serves well to delineate geographic areas occupied by ocean surface water masses of specific character. The results are consistent with our proposed classification of the coastal zone. This classification accounts for the circulation of the oceans, the temperature and salinity attributes of the ocean waters, and, indirectly, the presence of the major zones of upwelling.

2.1. Terminology

The literature reveals a wide diversity in the use of biogeographic terms. We use "biome" to signify an ecological formation in biotic terms. "Realm" is a major subdivision consisting of one or more "regions"; it is the same as the "domain" of Bailey (1980), but not equivalent to Udvardy's "realm", which is principally floristic. Hence, "biome" is an ecological conceptualization and "realm" implies a geographic division. "Region" refers to a specific, large area within a realm (Bailey's "division"), and "province" refers to an area within a region that can be justified either by endemism or by a characteristic biotic association. Obviously, there must be flexibility in use of all these terms.

3. RESULTS

Our approach results in defining a two-dimensional biophysical classification with the following fundamental biomes: open oceans, coastal margins, marginal seas, and marginal archipelagos. Figs. 1 and 2 illustrate this result, together with the biotic provinces; the latter align themselves well with the physical system. The limits of open oceans and marginal seas are based on the tabulations in: "International Hydrographic Bureau—Limits of Oceans and Seas" (Special Publication No. 23), Third Edition, 1953. We consider this listing preliminary for the particular purposes of this classification; nevertheless, it offers an internationally accepted standard. With regard to the archipelagos, there are three basic types: oceanic (contained within open oceans—e.g., Bahamas), those separating open oceans and marginal seas (e.g., Antilles), and those close to continental margins. The first two may be classified according to their positions within open ocean realms or their association with marginal seas. Marginal archipelagos, however, have distinct characteristics and merit special attention.

In addition, the scale of our efforts forbids consideration of smaller-sized coastal environments such as deltas, fjords, estuaries, etc. Nor do we consider the special case of oceanic islands. These merit a separate level of classification on their own and will be considered, in part, by Hayden *et al.* (in preparation).

3.1 The physical classification

3.1.1. Open ocean. The open ocean realms used here are adapted from Dietrich's (1963) classification of ocean surface waters. In Dietrich's work the circulation of the atmosphere and the surface layer of the ocean define a system of natural regions in a geographic sense. Dietrich sets aside several rather small geographic areas in a separate class due to the presence of "fast currents" such as the Gulf Stream in the Florida Straits. We do not apply this part of Dietrich's classification. The Dietrich classification delineates the geographic provinces occupied by water masses of specific character.

The nomenclature used by Dietrich is descriptive of the direction of advections of the surface waters. From equator to pole there are four broad zones: (1) the equatorial counter current (E); (2) the trade wind region (T); (3) the Horse latitudes (H); and (4) the west drift (W). There is a monsoon (m) type within the equatorial counter-current zone (Indian Ocean only). Within the tradewind zones there are west-bound (w), equator-bound (e) and poleward-bound (p) zones.

3.1.2. Coastal margins. For margins of ocean basins, ocean currents and atmospheric wind systems also define the delivery of air and water to both the terrestrial and marine parts of the coastal environment. While the geologic context of the ocean margins is complex, the distribution of collision and trailing-edge continental plates assures a measure of symmetry in the geology of the coastal environments. Cliffed coasts of the world are found most frequently along the west (collision) margins of continents and the great coastal plains along east (trailing) margins. The figures are coded so that similar areas can be quickly identified and the geographic symmetry of the classification can be easily seen from continent to continent. The following nomenclature is proposed:

REALMS OF THE WESTERN AND EASTERN CONTINENTAL MARGINS

Intertropical Realms—seasonally within the trade winds of both hemispheres.

Tropical Realms—persistently within the trade winds of one hemisphere.

Subtropical Realms—seasonally within the poleward extensions of the trade winds and within continental air streams.

Monsoon Realms—with seasonal and interhemispheric wind reversals (do not occur along North and South America).

Temperate Realms—within the westerly atmospheric and oceanic drifts of the mid-latitudes.

Subpolar Realms—within the circulation domains of the subpolar cyclones.

CIRCUMPOLAR REALMS

Arctic Realms—along the Arctic Ocean Coast.

Antarctic Realm—along the coast of the Antarctic Continent (does not occur along South America).

These realms are defined by such physical features as: presence of sea ice, storm tracks, currents, wind patterns, temperature and water density regimes, upwelling, weather patterns, and regional-scale landforms.

3.1.3. Marginal seas. Behind the ocean margin coasts one finds either the terrestrial environments of the continents, the marginal seas, or the marginal archipelagos. Where terrestrial continental environments occur, the coastal interface is simple in plan view. Where marginal seas and archipelagos occur, the coastal environment is complex. The marginal seas and archipelagos are classified according to the marginal ocean coast through which, and across which, ocean waters and winds flow. Each marginal sea and archipelago is related to the ocean realm adjacent to it. In several cases (*) there are seasonal reversals in the sources of waters entering the marginal seas, indicating that the marginal sea belongs to two different coastal realms. In such cases the marginal sea is listed under both realms.

The marginal seas shown in Figs. 1 and 2 are listed below (refer to marine charts for the seas' locations):

MARGINAL SEAS OF COASTAL REALMS

I.   *Arctic Coastal Realms*
 A.   *Beaufort Sea*
 B.   *Baffin Bay**
 C.   *Greenland Sea**
 D.   *Chukchi Sea*
II.   *Subpolar Coastal Realms*
 A.   *Davis Strait*
 B.   *Labrador Sea*
 C.   *Greenland Sea**
 D.   *Hudson Bay*
 E.   *Bering Sea*
III. *Western Temperate Coastal Realms*
   (none)
IV.   *Western Subtropical Coastal Realms*
 A.   *Gulf of California*
V.   *Western Tropical Coastal Realms*
   (none)
VI.   *Western Intertropical Coastal Realms*
   (none)
VII. *Eastern Temperate Coastal Realms*
 A.   *Gulf of St. Lawrence*
VIII. *Eastern Subtropical Coastal Realms*
   (none)
IX.   *Eastern Tropical Coastal Realms*
 A.   *Caribbean Sea*
 B.   *Gulf of Mexico*
X.   *Eastern Intertropical Coastal Realms*
   (none)

3.1.4. Marginal archipelagos. Archipelagos, as identified here, are restricted to those large island groups with direct ocean realm exposure; i.e. they border ocean realms and continents. They are analogous to marginal seas and are of the same size class. They contain different biotic associations than the adjacent continental coasts. In general, waterways between the islands are limited in extent. Archipelagos within marginal seas (e.g. Florida Keys) are not included, nor are those that separate marginal seas from ocean realms (e.g., Antilles—see above). Small island groups are also not included at present (e.g., Channel Islands of California). The marginal archipelagos included in our classification are (see atlases for locations):

1) The Canadian Arctic Archipelago—waters flow into this archipelago from the Arctic Coastal Realm and the Subpolar Coastal Realm through the Davis Straits.
2) The Alexander Archipelago—waters flow into this island group through the Subpolar Coastal Realm of Southeast Alaska.
3) The Archipelago Reina Adelaida—this archipelago is associated with the Subpolar Coastal Realm of the South Chile coast.
4) The Archipelago de Los Chonos—this archi-

pelago is equatorward of the Archipielago Reina Adelaida and is associated with the Temperate Coastal Realm of western Chile.

3.1.5. The biotic classification. Table 1 summarizes our classification of the Americas, slightly modified from Briggs (1974). Figs. 1 and 2 show how the provinces align with the physical regions identified above. The Americas include all five realms of the world, 10 of the 23 regions, and 17 of the 54 provinces (some regions have not yet been separated into provinces, so that the region and province are synonymous). There are fewer coastal/marine provinces than have been identified for the land. Further, our limited knowledge leaves certain oceanic islands in limbo (Briggs' "other islands"). However, these can be classified by our system by their positions within ocean realms (no ocean islands are shown on our figures).

4. CONCLUSION

The system we propose is only apparently complex. It is scientifically internally consistent and the figures reveal a good alignment between the physical and biotic classifications. This makes possible a *biophysical* description of coastal areas, which is the intent of Hayden *et al.* (in prep.). For example, one could describe Eastern Temperate-Virginian, Western Subtropical-Cortezian, Eastern Subtropical-Eastern South American, or Eastern Subpolar-Magellan coastal provinces; this makes possible a numerical computer entry system for easy data retrieval, as suggested by Ray (1975). The places where physical and biotic provinces overlap between areas are where "transitions" occur. As Pielou (1979) has pointed out, they are important in their own right and deserve special attention. Similarly, within ocean margin coasts and coasts of marginal seas and archipelagos, coastal landforms determine the specific character of the coastal environment. Those coastal landforms associated with the drainage of fresh waters into the oceans and seas are of special physical and biological significance. Accordingly, fjords, deltas and estuaries require attention as specific habitats or sub-provinces. Ray (1975) and Ray *et al.* (1981) recognized the importance of considering the habitat level within a classification. A matrix which cross-references provinces with habitats is necessary in order to assure that all habitat types within a province or region are included within representative protected areas. This is especially important when applying the classification suggested herein at the local or country level. Ecological processes should also be included within such a matrix; for example, the Bering Sea has been subdivided into three distinct sub-regions according to cross-shelf processes (Iverson, *et al.*, 1979), even though differences in species compositions may not be immediately apparent.

In the near future, it will become important further to develop this classification into the third, vertical, dimension. It will be equally important to align this system with that of Udvardy (this volume), as noted above. It must be emphasized that completely consistent land and sea classifications are probably not possible and probably not even desirable. Forcing marine classification into terrestrially-derived molds will have the inevitable result of inconsistency with the nature of marine/coastal systems. Even though theoretical and other difficulties will remain far into the future, we nevertheless feel that our system will serve the purpose of helping to establish a worldwide representative protected area system.

Acknowledgments

This paper was prepared for IUCN's Commission on National Parks and Protected Areas in cooperation with the United Nations Environment Programme.

Table 1: Biogeographic Classification of North and South America's Coasts (modified slightly from Briggs, 1974)

Realms	Regions	Provinces
1. Northern Hemisphere Cold Temperate and Arctic	1. Arctic 2. Western Atlantic Boreal 3. Eastern Pacific Boreal	1. Arctic 2. Virginian 3. Acadian 4. Aleutian 5. Oregonian
2. Northern Hemisphere Warm Temperate	4. Californian 5. Carolinian	6. San Diegan 7. Cortezian 8. Carolinian 9. Louisianan
3. Tropical	6. Eastern Pacific 7. Western Atlantic	10. Mexican 11. Panamanian 12. Caribbean 13. Brazilian 14. West Indian
4. Southern Hemisphere Warm Temperate	8. Western South American 9. Eastern South American	15. Peru-Chilean 16. Eastern South American
5. Southern Hemisphere Cold Temperate and Antarctic	10. Southern South American	17. Magellan

Notes for Figures 1 and 2

The insert box identifies coastal margins. Symbols and descriptions on the left are for western coasts, those on the right are for eastern coasts (see text). The marginal seas are associated with ocean margin coasts, as the symbols inserted within those seas indicate. Names of those seas and archipelagos are in the text; for exact locations, refer to maps and marine charts. Biogeographical province names are adjacent to the provinces and symbolized accordingly.

The ocean realms are identified by the following codes, after Dietrich (1963): E = Equatorial Counter Current; T = Tradewinds (w = west bound, e = equatorward bound, p = poleward bound); H = Horse Latitudes; and W = West Drift.

NATIONAL PARKS, CONSERVATION, AND DEVELOPMENT

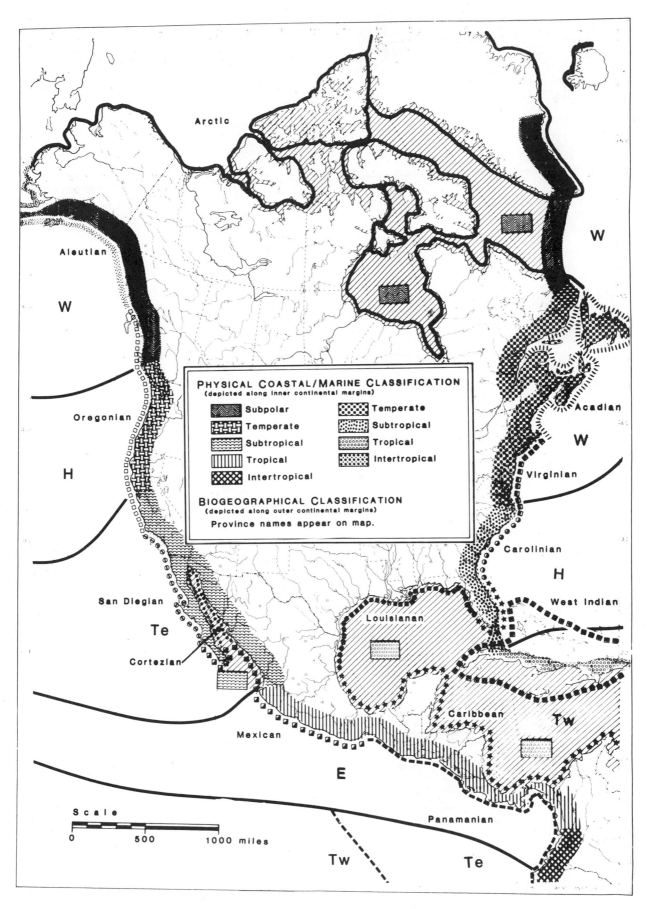

PHYSICAL COASTAL/MARINE CLASSIFICATION
(depicted along inner continental margins)

Subpolar

Temperate

Temperate

Subtropical

Subtropical

Tropical

Tropical

Intertropical

Intertropical

BIOGEOGRAPHICAL CLASSIFICATION
(depicted along outer continental margins)

Province names appear on map.

Arctic

Aleutian

W

Oregonian

H

San Dieglan

Te

Cortezlan

Mexican

E

Tw

Te

Panamanian

W

Acadian

W

Virginian

Carolinian

H

West Indian

Louisianan

Caribbean

Tw

Scale

0   500   1000 miles

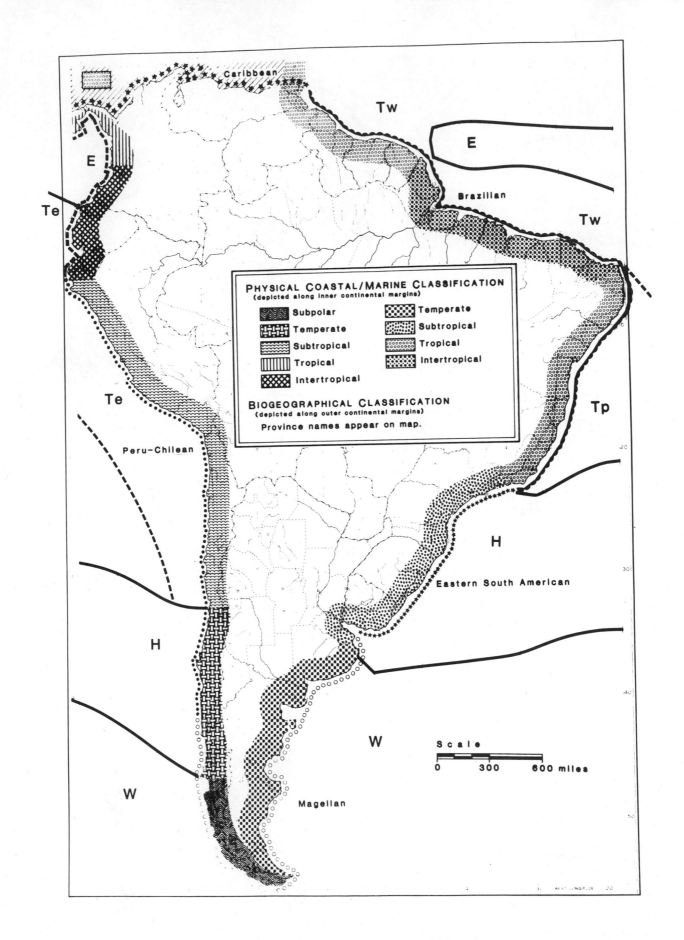

Caribbean

Tw

E

Brazilian

Tw

E

Te

Te

PHYSICAL COASTAL/MARINE CLASSIFICATION
(depicted along inner continental margins)

	Subpolar		Temperate
Temperate		Subtropical
Subtropical		Tropical
Tropical		Intertropical
Intertropical		

BIOGEOGRAPHICAL CLASSIFICATION
(depicted along outer continental margins)
Province names appear on map.

Tp

Te

Peru-Chilean

H

Eastern South American

H

W

W

Scale

0   300   600 miles

Magellan

Categories, Objectives and Criteria for Protected Areas

IUCN's Commission on National Parks and Protected Areas

ABSTRACT. *CNPPA's Committee on Protected Area Nomenclature worked for several years to produce in 1978 the first edition of this paper. Its major thesis is that the national park can be complemented by many other sorts of areas under conservation management; nomenclature of the different sorts of protected areas has obscured the important point that there are really relatively few basic objectives for which areas are established and managed. The nomenclatural confusion can be greatly eased by a system of categories based on objectives of management. Ten categories and their objectives are suggested in this paper, which is a revised edition of the 1978 paper, based on four years of discussion and the Bali Congress; this version applies.*

1. INTRODUCTION

The International Union for Conservation of Nature and Natural Resources is dedicated to the wise use of Earth's natural resources and to the maintenance of the Planet's natural diversity. Within the overall mandate and programme of IUCN, its Commission on National Parks and Protected Areas (CNPPA) is charged with the promotion and monitoring of national parks and other protected areas, as well as the provision of guidance for the management and maintenance of such areas.

During recent years, it has become apparent that many elements of the human habitat require special conservation attention if they are to bring benefits to mankind. For example, upstream river catchments require conservation management to ensure downstream food production; marine resources such as mangrove forests and coral reefs require careful management to ensure fisheries; and species such as elephants, vicunas, and sea turtles need to be protected in some parts of their range if they are to be productive in other parts.

How the conservation of nature can be interwoven with development is suggested by the principles of ecodevelopment outlined in the World Conservation Strategy. Natural resources can be managed in a variety of ways to support humans and maintain the human habitat; through the analysis of objectives for conservation, several categories of management for conservation areas can be defined.

The national park has been defined and criteria have been set forth (IUCN, 1969). Without altering these concepts, the national park can be complemented by other distinct categories, which when taken together can provide land managers and decision-makers with a broad set of legal and managerial options for conservation management on land and at sea.

The ideas of Hart (1966), Dasmann (1973), Forster (1973), Miller (1975), and Thelen and Miller (1975), have been interpreted into this paper, which also intends to include the conservation of cultural heritage where nature conservation is also involved, the potential of nations with older cultures and/or dense human populations, and the conservation of marine resources (Ray, 1975).

The recognition of a set of categories for conservation area management has several practical implications:

- At the national level, each nation can design a system of conservation areas which corresponds to its own resources and requirements. Such a system can assist the nation's responsibilities in the protection of finite resources while providing for human development on a sustainable basis.
- Based upon criteria for each category, regardless of nomenclature, each conservation area can be classified according to the objectives for which it

is being managed. Thus each nation can establish areas which fulfil the nation's particular needs yet receive world recognition for its contribution to world conservation.

- IUCN, the specialized UN agencies, and other institutions, can assemble and analyse information on national parks and other categories, allowing a more complete and realistic assessment of conservation areas to be made.
- Through access to IUCN's new Protected Areas Data Unit (PADU), this information can be stored and recalled, updated and printed quickly and easily; this will make the application of the data much more adaptable to real needs.
- The scientific community will have access to information regarding natural areas under all sorts of conservation management, not just within national parks.
- The tourism industry can have access to information on a wide range of natural and semi-natural areas suitable for recreation and tourism purposes. Expanded and diversified tourism has potential to both increase the support of natural areas and reduce pressure upon national parks.
- IUCN and CNPPA require a consistent framework within which to provide technical advice to international protected area programmes, including the Unesco Man and Biosphere Programme, the World Heritage Convention, the Global Environmental Monitoring System, and others.
- CNPPA can coordinate action with other IUCN Commissions on matters of high priority and strategic significance, such as: legal and policy structures for conservation categories; the planning of other-than-park categories; the development of educational programmes on conservation management in its several forms; the effectiveness of the various categories for species conservation; and the design of conservation management categories for marine resources.
- With a set of conservation categories among which a broad spectrum of conservation issues and objectives can be supported, IUCN can work more effectively with the development institutions. Conservation can be linked to water, protein, ecosystem productivity and diversity, pharmaceuticals, agriculture, livestock breeding, wood products, science education and the human environment in general. For example, projects to develop river resources should ideally include financial and technical support to establish some type of conservation management in the upstream catchment area; where a national park may be inappropriate, one of the other categories may address the local situation quite adequately. In any case, some recognized form of conservation can be provided.

Thus, this paper amplifies the scope of conservation management to be recognized by CNPPA, enabling IUCN to respond to the needs of the World Conservation Strategy. In a sense, more sophisticated tools are provided to perform a more complex task.

The categories should be considered as "members of the same family", free from dominance one by another. All categories are important, each with a different role, and only together can they adequately cover national and global resource management needs.

2. METHOD FOR THE DELINEATION OF CATEGORIES FOR CONSERVATION MANAGEMENT

The maintenance and development of the human habitat requires that some areas be retained in their wild state. The quality of water, the maintenance of genetic materials, the protection of scenic and aesthetic areas and the opportunity to enjoy and appreciate natural heritage, all depend upon the conservation of natural areas.

Other renewable natural resources include wood products, building materials, wild animal products (including fish), grazing from natural grasslands, and water for agriculture, industry, domestic use, and energy which can be produced on a sustained-yield basis.

Logically, some of these benefits can be received from natural areas or wildlands in perpetuity if management is properly designed and implemented. However, there are types of benefits which compete with one another; for example, it is physically and biologically difficult to remove wood products and study natural ecosystems on the same area. But the preservation of a sample ecosystem and research and monitoring can be readily done together if appropriately designed and controlled. Controlled tourism and species conservation can be compatible in both the terrestrial and marine environments.

Management categories can be designed and implemented so that each addresses a compatible set of benefits, without the pursuit of any one benefit ruling out the possibility of receiving other benefits. Commonly known categories which maintain the most options include the national park, wildlife sanctuary and forest reserve.

Even among generally compatible activities, conflicts may arise during particular seasons or on specific sites such as during nesting or calving periods or at critical habitats. These types of conflicts can be treated through a zoning system or a periodic restricted activity system.

Each benefit is related to specific objectives of management, such as the protection of rare or endangered species or habitats, the conservation of natural features of aesthetic value, and the conservation of areas where renewable resources can be utilized on a sustained-yield basis. Ideally all objectives and activities are related to environmental protection and to economic and social development.

Areas which are managed to meet specified compatible conservation objectives can be considered to be "protected areas"; they can be classified according to the objectives for which they are being managed. In contrast, however, the specific means required to meet the objectives of conservation will depend upon each particular situation and will vary with cultural, institutional, political and economic considerations.

Conservation categories provide the basis for clearly incorporating conservation into development (eco-development). Each category relates to one or several of the major goals of a nations's development plan: nutrition, education, housing, water, science, technology, defense and national identity. Viewed in this way, conservation categories become means for sustained development.

Taken together, these categories can be administered as a unified national system of conservation areas. In practice, the categories are generally divided among various divisions of central government; some of the categories may be administered by state, provincial or even private or corporate institutions. Multiple use areas or international categories such as the Biosphere Reserve and the World Heritage Site will often require cooperative administration among several institutions. What is important, however, is that a specified institution is made responsible and empowered to provide for the appropriate management of the resources.

3. CATEGORIES FOR CONSERVATION AREAS

CATEGORY I. Scientific Reserve/Strict Nature Reserve

Introduction. The rapid alteration of many natural environments has created a need for a category of management which will ensure areas free of human intervention and available exclusively for scientific research and environmental monitoring. These natural areas provide locations for research where a complete understanding of natural processes can be attained. In some situations scientific research may be limited to non-manipulative (observational) research in order to restrict the influence of human activity on the natural ecosystem.

Management Objectives. To protect nature (communities and species) and maintain natural processes in an undisturbed state in order to have ecologically representative examples of the natural environment available for scientific study, environmental monitoring, education, and for the maintenance of genetic resources in a dynamic and evolutionary state. Research activities need to be planned and undertaken carefully to minimize disturbance.

Criteria for Selection and Management. These areas possess some outstanding ecosystems, features and/or

species of flora and fauna of national scientific importance or are representative of particular natural areas; they often contain fragile ecosystems or life forms, areas of important biological or geological diversity or areas of particular importance to the conservation of genetic resources. Size is determined by the area required to ensure the integrity of the area to accomplish the scientific management objective and provide for the protection of the area.

Natural processes are allowed to take place in the absence of any direct human interference; tourism, recreation, and public access are generally proscribed. Ecological processes may include natural acts that alter the ecological system or physiographic features, such as naturally-occurring fires, natural succession, insect or disease outbreaks, storms, earthquakes and the like, but necessarily exclude man-made disturbances. The educational function of the site is to serve as resource for studying and obtaining scientific knowledge.

Use of the reserve should in most cases be controlled by central government. Exceptions may be made where adequate safeguards and controls for long-term protection are ensured and where the central government concurs.

CATEGORY II. National Park

Introduction. Governments have for some time recognized the desirability of establishing protective regimes over outstanding natural areas representative of the diversity of ecosystems of their countries and areas of jurisdiction so as to guarantee their protection and use for present and future generations. Rapid exploitation of natural resources has demonstrated that unless governments take decisive action to protect the most outstanding examples of the country's natural heritage, these resources may be lost. The continued trend of urbanization has increased the need to provide oppportunities for outdoor recreation and tourism in natural settings. Furthermore, the need for people to understand more fully the natural environment is of particular concern in an age of rapidly diminishing natural resources. Outstanding representative areas of a nation can serve to contribute to this understanding.

Management Objectives. To protect natural and scenic areas of national or international significance for scientific, educational, and recreational use. The area should perpetuate in a natural state representative samples of physiographic regions, biotic communities and genetic resources, and species in danger of extinction to provide ecological stability and diversity.

Criteria for Selection and Management. National parks are relatively large areas which contain representative samples of major natural regions, features or scenery where plant and animal species, geomorphological sites, and habitats are of special scientific, educational, and recreational interest. They contain one or several entire ecosystems that are not materially altered by human exploitation and occupation. The highest competent authority of the country having jurisdiction over the area has taken steps to prevent or eliminate as soon as possible exploitation or occupation in the area and to enforce effectively the respect of ecological, geomorphological, or aesthetic features which have led to its establishment.

The resource is managed and developed so as to sustain recreation and education activities on a controlled basis. The area is managed in a natural or near-natural state. Visitors enter under special conditions for inspirational, educational, cultural, and recreational purposes; sport hunting is not a compatible use, but culling for management purposes sometimes is required.

CATEGORY III. Natural Monument/Natural Landmark

Introduction. Most countries possess natural features of particular scientific and educational interest; however, they often receive no special national recognition. The features might include spectacular waterfalls, caves, craters, volcanoes, unique species of flora and fauna, sand dunes, etc., of such scenic, scientific, educational and inspirational importance that they merit special designation and protection; because of their uniqueness, these areas deserve greater protection for both scientific and public enjoyment.

Management Objectives. To protect and preserve nationally significant natural features because of their special interest or unique characteristics and to the extent consistent with this, provide opportunities for interpretation, education, research, and public appreciation.

Criteria for Selection and Management. This category normally contains one or more of several specific natural features of outstanding national significance which, because of uniqueness or rarity, should be protected. The specific feature to be protected ideally has little or no evidence of man's activities. These features are not of the size nor do they contain a diversity of features or representative ecosystems which would justify their inclusion as a national park. Size is not a significant factor; the area only needs to be large enough to protect the integrity of the site.

Although Category III areas may have recreational and touristic value, they should be managed to remain relatively free of human disturbance. These areas may be owned and managed by either central or other government agencies or non-profit trusts or corporations as long as there is assurance that they will be managed to protect their inherent features for the long term.

CATEGORY IV. Nature Conservation Reserve/ Managed Nature Reserve/Wildlife Sanctuary

Introduction. Although most of the other categories of management play important roles in protecting habitat for flora and fauna, it is essential that areas be established where manipulative management techniques can be applied to guarantee the stability or survival of certain species of plants and animals, through protection of breeding populations, feeding and breeding grounds, and critical habitat for protection of rare and endangered floral and faunal species.

Management Objectives. To assure the natural conditions necessary to protect nationally significant species, groups of species, biotic communities, or physical features of the environment where these require specific human manipulation for their perpetuation. Scientific research, environmental monitoring, and educational use are the primary activities associated with this category.

Criteria for Selection and Management. A Category IV area is desirable when protection of specific sites or habitats is essential to the continued well-being of resident or migratory fauna of national or global significance. Although a variety of areas fall within this category, each would have as its primary purpose the protection of nature; the production of harvestable, renewable resources may play a secondary role in the management of a particular area. The size of the area is dependent upon the habitat requirements of the species to be protected; these areas could be relatively small, consisting of nesting areas, marshes, or lakes, estuaries, forest, or grassland habitats, or fish spawning areas, or seagrass feeding beds for marine mammals.

The area may require habitat manipulation to provide optimum conditions for the species, vegetative community, or feature according to individual circumstances. For example, a particular grassland or heath community may be protected and perpetuated through a limited amount of livestock grazing; a marsh for wintering waterfowl may require continual removal of excess reeds and supplementary planting of waterfowl food; or a reserve for an endangered animal may need protection against predators. Limited areas may be developed for public education and appreciation of the work of wildlife management.

Ownership may be by the central government or, with adequate safeguards and controls, by lower levels of government, non-profit trusts or corporations or private individuals or groups.

CATEGORY V. Protected Landscape or Seascape

Introduction. In many areas of the world, distinctive landscape patterns are created by the integration of specific natural and cultural features that present aesthetically attractive land and water settings. These may result through traditional land use practices which have retained relatively large and scenic natural or semi-natural areas near urban centres.

At the same time, increasing population and leisure time and expanding urban areas are creating demand for additional recreation and tourism areas and facilities in aesthetic environments for citizens and visitors.

These natural and cultural areas are important because of their potential as reservoirs of genetic material and for their social customs and land use practices, which may be disappearing under the influence of modern technology.

Management Objectives. To maintain nationally significant natural landscapes which are characteristic of the harmonious interaction of man and land while providing opportunities for public enjoyment through recreation and tourism within the normal life style and economic activity of these areas. These areas also provide for ecological diversity, scientific, cultural and educational purposes.

Criteria for Selection and Management. The scope of areas that fall within this category is necessarily broad because of the wide variety of semi-natural and cultural landscapes that occur within various nations. This may be reflected in two types of areas: those whose landscapes possess special aesthetic qualities which are a result of the interaction of man and land; and those that are primarily natural areas managed intensively by man for recreational and tourism uses.

In the former case, these landscapes may demonstrate certain cultural manifestations such as: customs, beliefs, social organization, or material traits as reflected in land use patterns. These landscapes are characterized by either scenically attractive or aesthetically unique patterns of human settlement. Traditional land use practices associated with agriculture, grazing, and fishing are dominant. The area is large enough to ensure the integrity of the landscape pattern.

The latter case often includes natural or scenic areas found along coastlines and lake shores, in hilly or mountainous terrain, or along the shores of rivers, often adjacent to tourist highways or population centres; many will have the potential to be developed for a variety of outdoor recreational uses with national significance.

In some cases the area may be privately held and the use of either central or delegated planning control would be necessary to ensure the perpetuation of both the land use and life style. Means of government assistance might be required to improve the standard of living while maintaining the natural quality of the site through appropriate management practices. In other instances, the areas are established and managed under public ownership, or a combination of public and private ownership.

CATEGORY VI. Resource Reserve

Introduction. Despite the rapidly increasing utilization of the natural resources in the world, there still remain land and water areas for which the most appropriate utilization has yet to be determined. If these lands are not protected, occupation and use are likely to occur on an unplanned, single-use and short-term economic exploitation basis. This utilization without sufficient knowledge may result in resource deterioration and loss of longer-term economic and social benefits.

Management Objectives. To restrict use of these areas until adequate studies have been completed on how to best utilize these remaining resources; to protect the natural resources of the area for future use and prevent or contain development activities that could affect the resource pending the establishment of objectives which are based upon appropriate knowledge and planning.

Criteria for Selection and Management. Category VI areas will normally comprise an extensive and relatively isolated and uninhabited area having difficult access, or regions that are lightly populated yet may be under considerable pressure for colonization and greater utilization. In many cases, there has been little study or evaluation of these areas, so the consequences of converting these areas to agriculture, mineral or timber extraction, the construction of roads, or intensive fishing, dredging or mariculture is unclear. Similarly, use of the resources may not be appropriate because of the lack of technology, human or financial resource restrictions, or alternative national priorities. Consequently, natural, social, and economic values are not sufficiently identified to permit the area to be managed for specific objectives or to justify its conversion to other uses. On land, restricted access is implied so areas will normally require control, depending upon the pressures to enter and utilize the area. Areas may be owned or administered by government or public corporations.

Maintenance of existing conditions to allow for studies on the potential use for the designated areas is a prerequisite. No exploitation should occur with the exception of use of resources by indigenous inhabitants; ongoing ecologically sound activities are acceptable.

CATEGORY VII. Natural Biotic Area/Anthropological Reserve

Introduction. In some countries there may be a need for the protection of natural areas in which man is a component and obtains his livelihood by means that do not involve extensive cultivation or other major modifications of the vegetation and animal life. These individuals or societies may require special protection to maintain their existence.

Management Objectives. To allow the way of life of societies living in harmony with the environment to continue undisturbed by modern technology. Research into the evolution of man and his interaction with the land would be a secondary objective.

Criteria for Selection and Management. Category VII areas are characterized by natural areas where the influence or technology of modern man has not significantly interfered with or been absorbed by the traditional ways of life of the inhabitants. These areas may be remote and isolated and their inaccessibility may be maintained for a considerable period of time. The societies are of particular significance to the maintenance of cultural diversity; there is a strong dependence of man upon the natural environment for food, shelter, and other basic material to sustain life. Extensive cultivation or other major modifications of the vegetation and animal life is not permitted.

Management is oriented towards the maintenance of habitat for traditional societies so as to provide for their continuance within their own cultural mores.

CATEGORY VIII. Multiple Use Management Area/ Managed Resource Area

Introduction. Some terrestrial and marine areas can both provide protection to natural resource and ecological systems and yet contribute significantly to economic, social, and material needs of nations. The multiple function of these lands or waters can provide for a sustained yield of a series of natural products and services under proper management as well as for preservation of genetic diversity and protection of natural features and systems. Watershed protection, for example, may be of particular importance in addition to the timber, forage or wildlife aspect of the area. In the case of marine areas, protection of areas of great biological diversity may be of importance in sustaining the production of fish or other marine products.

Management Objectives. To provide for the sustained production of water, timber, wildlife (including fish), pasture or marine products, and outdoor recreation. The conservation of nature may be primarily oriented to the support of the economic activities (although specific zones may also be designated within these areas to achieve specific conservation objectives), or conservation may be a primary objective in its own right and given equal importance to economic and social objectives. Within the overall area, zones may be established in which either the conservation of nature or sustainable development is the primary objective.

Criteria for Selection and Management. A Category VIII area is large, containing considerable territory suitable for production of wood products, water, pasture, wildlife, marine products and outdoor recreation; parts of the area may be settled and may have been altered by man. The area may possess nationally unique or exceptional natural features, or may as a whole represent a feature or area of international or national significance.

Planning programmes to ensure the area is managed on a sustained yield basis is a prerequisite. Land ownership is under government control. Through proper zoning, significant areas can be given specific additional protection. For instance, the establishment of wilderness-type areas is consistent with the purpose of these areas as would be establishing nature reserves. Multiple use, in the context of Category VIII, is considered to be the management of all renewable resources, utilized in some combination to best meet the needs of the country. The major premise in the management of these areas is that they will be managed to maintain the overall productivity of the areas and their resources in perpetuity.

CATEGORY IX. Biosphere Reserve

Introduction. One focus of the Unesco Man and the Biosphere Programme, initiated in 1970, is to conserve representative natural areas throughout the world through the establishment of a network of biosphere reserves.

Management Objectives. To conserve for present and future use the diversity and integrity of biotic communities of plants and animals within natural ecosystems, and to safeguard the genetic diversity of species on which their continuing evolution depends. Biosphere reserves provide opportunities for ecological research, particularly baseline studies, both within natural and altered environments. These reserves have particular value as benchmarks or standards for measurement of long-term changes in the biosphere as a whole and are consequently important sites for environmental monitoring. Biosphere reserves provide facilities for education and training.

Criteria for Selection and Management. Each biosphere reserve will include one or more of the following: representative examples of natural biomes; unique communities or areas with unusual natural features or exceptional interest; examples of harmonious landscapes resulting from traditional patterns of land use; and examples of modified or degraded ecosystems capable of being restored to more natural conditions.

A biosphere reserve must have adequate long-term legal protection. Each biosphere reserve is large enough to be an effective conservation unit, and to accommodate different uses without conflict. Each reserve must be approved by the Man and the Biosphere International Co-ordinating Council before it can receive designation as a biosphere reserve.

Each biosphere reserve will be zoned to provide direction as to its management. Four zones may be delineated as follows: natural or core zone; manipulative or buffer zone; reclamation or restorative zone; and stable cultural zone.

CATEGORY X. World Heritage Site (Natural)

Introduction. The International Convention concerning the Protection of the World Cultural and Natural Heritage (Unesco, 1972) provides for the designation of areas of "outstanding universal value" as World Heritage Sites. These exceptional areas must be recommended by the signatory nation responsible for the site for declaration by the international World Heritage Committee. The sites include many previously designated protected areas.

Management Objectives. To protect the natural features for which the area was considered to be of world heritage quality; to provide information for world-wide public enlightenment; and to provide for research and environmental monitoring.

Criteria for Selection and Management. Areas to be considered under the Convention will be restricted to those which are truly of international significance. Natural sites must represent one or more of the following criteria:

(i) be outstanding examples representing the major stages of the earth's evolutionary history;

(ii) be outstanding examples representing significant ongoing geological processes, biological evolution and man's interaction with his natural environment;

(iii) contain unique, rare or superlative natural phenomena, formations or features or areas of exceptional natural beauty; and

(iv) be habitats where populations of rare or endangered species of plants and animals still survive.

Natural Heritage Sites must also fulfil conditions on the integrity of the site. Management of these sites stresses the maintenance of the heritage values, ensures the continuation of legal protection, and promotes the significance of each site to the country, its people and the world.

All sites have strict legal protection and are owned by government or non-profit corporation or trust for the long term. While recreation and on-site interpretation will generally be developed, some sites may be of such significance that public use will either be strictly controlled or prohibited.

Acknowledgements

This paper was prepared for IUCN's Commission on National Parks and Protected Areas in cooperation with the United Nations Environment Programme. The 1978 version of this paper was prepared in cooperation with Unesco and the Rockefeller Brothers Fund. The present paper has received significant additions by Dr. Graeme Kelleher which allow the categories to apply to both terrestrial and marine environments.

Chapter 3
Major Issues of the Future

The Survival of Species Genetic Diversity

Grenville L. Lucas
Chairman, IUCN Species Survival Commission
Royal Botanic Gardens
Kew, Richmond, UK

The Ark—being prepared for launching. Many here will remember the launching of another Ark, that of WWF some twenty years ago. And the concept then was to save the world's threatened species, as you recall from Recommendation No. 22 at the first World Parks Conference.

It is a great pleasure for me to see here today the co-founder and first chairman of SSC—the Survival Service as it was initially known—in the audience. Using the Ark analogy, Harold Jefferson Coolidge must have been the first Noah, starting SSC's work shortly after IUCN itself was founded in 1948. Sir Peter Scott carried on the tradition as a great helmsman—and I had the pleasure and honour of picking up the helm of this very large Commission in New Zealand a year ago.

Over a thousand active members of SSC are organized in some 65 specialist groups for animals, and are soon to be joined, I hope, by up to 25 plant groups. We are now called the Species Survival Commission. Our task may be said to be identifying the potential inmates of the ark and recommending the requirements for their long term survival.

The large network of our specialists—all volunteers—provides both a listening and intelligence network on the one hand, and a source of up-to-date data on the other, and this is focussed in many ways. One of the more visible developments is the creation of the IUCN Conservation Monitoring Centre (CMC), where a team of compilers has created the new Red Data Book series—probably one of SSC's more tangible products for IUCN. But this is only the tip of the new data base that CMC and the Wang computer is beginning to hold—one which will allow quick, accurate data to be available in many forms for the development of action plans where needed, highlighting problem areas and groups. This data management exercise is being carried out in association with the large SSC effort about to be launched to assess all threatened species and their needs in order to help the development of future programmes for IUCN. Together, these activities show the way the Commission is going.

Species are the flag-bearers—often for fund-raising—motivating peoples or governments to take action with regard to the habitat in which they live and of which they are an integral part. The original ecosystem is where the easiest and, one hopes, most successful maintenance of species should take place; where evolutionary pressures of a more natural kind can continue to take place, and where it is easiest to ensure species diversity.

Sadly, there are many species where numbers are so low or threats so great, that more drastic breeding or artificial propogation techniques have to be used to boost the population for reintroduction or bulking up in the habitat where appropriate.

One can hold the species in some *ex situ* situations, as in a seed bank for instance, but this is expensive; it can be dangerous (power cut); it is applying new "artificial" evolutionary pressures and certainly does not allow for genetic diversity except in a museum sense (the latter used to be something very important, let me say, in our agricultural and horticultural field—the need to have accurately reproduceable material for the mass market).

These techniques and botanic gardens, zoos, etc., have a vital part in species conservation now, and in the future. Bulking up for commerce may help generate a local trade; to support local activities, reserve support could be very lucrative, say, in orchid production or cactus growing for sale to tourists; so long as local controls are strong this could enhance the wild populations' chances of survival and expansion.

It is obviously more difficult with animal groups. We should not be afraid to have reserves that protect aesthetically pleasing species, species that are scientifically interesting, etc. This is a legitimate reason for their long-term survival.

Another consideration that the SSC and you have to face in the next 20 years is whether the parks and reserves that exist, or are proposed, are going to be enough for the maintenance of the majority of plant and animal species. What can be done for species by "fitting them" into and around urban, agricultural and forestry development? This is a very important way, I am sure, that we can enhance diversity both within the species and among species.

The Ark, the parks and reserves, can never be enough.

With all these considerations out of the way we come to the species/habitat/ reserve side of our work. There are some major problems. How do we choose the most representative areas for the maintenance of genetic diversity for this species or that?

If one looks at just the tree species in a tropical forest, you can never choose a sample big enough or representative enough to ensure *all* species are covered. However, by overlaying the information gained from different taxonomic groups and various disciplines one can see which configuration would obtain the largest number of species covered by a potential reserve. These data, with studies as to practical boundary and management problems, are familiar to you all, in the day-to-day compromise approach we all have to carry out.

The problem for SSC members increases with the decrease in the state of our knowledge, as one moves from temperate to tropical climes and from group to group.

The RDBs show that the data for the mammals and birds are most comprehensive, and those for plants and invertebrates least so. Magnitude of the taxonomic group also has a direct effect, though this does not have to be a crippling factor in conservation management advice. The threats are all too familiar; it is site selection which is the problem. But again there are often indicators to be had from the general species diversity in any one region. So selection of areas of importance is possible. Once this is done and the reserve or park is declared, then the work must really begin.

Appropriate scientific staff should be encouraged to look at the whole area in detail to establish the basic life support patterns of the mammals, birds, reptiles and amphibians, and fish. But please do not stop there— remember the plants. At the simplest level the inventory or checklist, for example, can be a problem to obtain, often because none exists. How many parks do we all know where you can obtain a glossy, coloured guide to the mammals and birds, but for a botanist like me, well. . . you might get a duplicated list of plant names if you are lucky.

And yet how many of those plants go to feed the animals and birds? The public would be interested to know and understand what the food chains or webs are. How many plants have a value to man—local or even more broadly as of potential pharmaceutical or chemical value? We should know. We must improve our knowledge and our awareness of these vital genetic resources. Man and all the animals we see in our parks and reserves depend on the plants one way or another, and yet they are the poor relations of our activities. How many times have the agriculturists had to return to the wild to find a nematode-resistant or fungal-resistant strain, to breed back into his crop, and where did it come from? The wild, and we have a responsibility to ensure that the "wild" within the reserve and park, and outside in the countryside as a whole, continues to maintain the greatest genetic diversity both within species, and the greatest range of species to keep all options open. Who knows what the future will require?

The SSC *can* help and stands ready *to* help wherever possible as it has done over the past 30 years.

The Permanence of Conservation Institutions

Wolfgang E. Burhenne
Chairman
IUCN Commission on Environmental Policy, Law and Administration
Bonn, Federal Republic of Germany

There are several members of CEPLA present at this Congress along with CEPLA's Vice Chairman, Michael McCloskey, and I am sure that they will take an active part in the discussions. I believe that this participation is very important, since it is my conviction that one of the major issues to be faced in the coming decade is the need for more interdisciplinary work.

We have, within IUCN, already proved this need in practice, and tried to reach across disciplines by setting up interdisciplinary groups, for example, the Programme Planning Advisory Group. A good deal, however, remains to be done, and meetings such as this provide a unique opportunity to identify areas of interdependence and intensify the dialogue.

The fact that this Congress is entitled "The World National Parks Congress" leads the provocative part of myself to remind you that you are dependent upon we lawyers for legal instruments to establish the protection for an area; only then can you start to fulfil your task. You may say that this is a typical attitude for a lawyer to take, and perhaps it is. But I will immediately admit that we depend upon you, to an even larger extent: indeed it is your knowledge and your experience which provides the substance to be included in our dry shell. Which area, why and how to protect it, are questions for which we need your answers in order to be able to devise an adequate choice of means.

One may consider that the past decade has witnessed considerable developments in the field of environmental law generally, and conservation law as a branch within it. This is valid for national legislation as well as for international conventions; of course, there is no reason yet to declare ourselves satisfied and we still—and will always—have a long way to go to achieve the objectives of conservation. In the particular field of natural area protection, I believe that there are three major tasks which we have to pursue in the next decade from a legal angle.

The first of these is the development of national rules for the protection of areas which, for given particular reasons are of special significance. Many countries now have such instruments.

They may not only include specific legislation on parks and reserves, other instruments may be available and equally useful for that particular purpose, for example, those on planning, zoning, forestry, etc. The task ahead of us here is to promote their systematic development on the one hand, and their adaptation to the state-of-the-art on the other. Again, your input is needed here as it is your experience and knowledge which determines this state-of-the-art.

A paper before you prepared by CEPLA member Barbara Lausche, has the very purpose of addressing the problems I have just mentioned. I shall hence not expand upon this, except to say that in spite of gaps and difficulties, the trend is encouraging and the direction clear.

The second task that I see ahead is the development of international instruments. Again, here one may consider the past decade encouraging, as more instruments have been developed during that period than ever before. On the other hand, we have to recognize that some are not fully adequate and others are marred by lack of implementation. This and the difficulties which are met in elaborating and negotiating international accords must lead us to a selective approach in promoting further binding regional and global conventions, in order to avoid unnecessary inflation. Thoughts for innovative future action in this field are submitted to you here in a paper prepared by another CEPLA member, Cyrille de Klemm, and I look forward to hearing your views on them.

The third task is somewhat related to your terms of reference and the whole concept of protected areas.

In 1972, there was an IUCN Commission on National Parks. Since then, not only has the Commission been renamed to include "protected areas" in its title, but the term has been generally accepted as reflecting a more modern approach to area conservation.

The concept leads me to think that your task is, in fact, much broader than that which you currently address.

Because, after all, what is a protected area? Not long ago I was reminded by a colleague from a neighbouring country of mine that all his country's open space "is more or less" protected. Is the fact that a private or public owner may not change the use of his land as he pleases not a protection? Is the prohibition to build in open spaces not a protection? Is a restriction on the use of natural resources of one's land not a protection? I would submit that such restrictions establish protected area status and that there is no difference in nature between this status and that of a park or reserve, but only a difference of degree.

I will, therefore, also submit that given CNPPA's name, these areas should be, and in fact, are your concern because they may be considered to be also "protected". This is a matter with which some of you may disagree. I am sure, however, that you will not disagree with me on the fact that if insufficient attention is given to these areas, most classical protected areas will become "isolated ecological islands surrounded by completely transformed habitats", as F. Bourlre said ten years ago.

It is essential to pay more attention to an arsenal of measures which would establish the principle of area protection *everywhere*. Understand me well—I am *not* suggesting that the goal of special or reinforced protection is futile, or would become redundant. Not at all; on the contrary, I think that it can only take its full significance in the context of a general protective status. What I am talking about may be compared to the system of reverse listing in species protection: the principle should be protection, while exceptions may be made—limited, regulated and controlled.

Am I controversial or unrealistic? If I am, maybe I am less so than one might think; after all, the idea that "sovereignty" at international level, or "property" at national level, obligates one is not new. After all, in how many countries of the world do we have legal controls, the aims of which are area oriented protection, which derive from this sense of social obligation? Their number is not negligible, and the form they take is varied. If land use planning legislation is certainly the most currently used means to implement this concept, many others are also used: laws on building, flood control, monuments and sites, avalanche protection, watershed protection, forestry, to cite a few at random.

There are, of course limits to this notion, and legal systems which recognize it provide for them: restrictions in the exercise of property rights for the public good must be counterbalanced by guarantees that these will not be imposed arbitrarily. I will also not deny that this concept of "social obligation" of property, or "property obligations" may fluctuate and vary according to the country concerned, its history, society and values. What matters in my opinion is on the one hand, the recognition of the principle and, on the other, its implementation in whatever legislative terms are appropriate in the country considered.

Giving attention to these general controls or, as I called it earlier, this principle of protection, is I believe, the most neglected and hence important task which we presently have ahead of us: clearly such controls are already far advanced in some countries, in an embryonic stage in others, and totally lacking in many.

My appeal to you today, is therefore, to obtain your support, assistance and counsel in promoting an "all-open-space protection concept", in which those areas which are now usually referred to as "protected areas" will be, and remain, the "jewels of the earth", fulfilling multiple functions, as they should and already aim at doing.

National conservation strategies should go a long way towards achieving such goals. It is essential that such strategies verify not only whether specific area-oriented controls are adequate, but also whether general area oriented controls are available.

I have spoken until now about what I feel is most lacking in my field. I see other problems, of a more limited nature, which we should address also, in order to better adapt legislation to management problems which you encounter. We should consider them together during and after this Congress. Our inter-Commission work is, after all, directed to finding solutions for each other's problems.

CAMROSE LUTHERAN COLLEGE
LIBRARY

Ecological Processes and National Park Management

J.D. Ovington
Chairman, IUCN Commission on Ecology

ABSTRACT. *The nature and inter-relationships of ecological processes are discussed. Examples are given of the effects on ecological processes of different management decisions and of their consequential impact on national park values. It is suggested that an understanding of ecological processes, as the functional elements of ecosystems, can assist park managers in the implementation of management plans and is especially relevant to research and educational activities.*

1. INTRODUCTION

As the ecosystem concept has evolved and as national park managers have gained greater practical experience, an early emphasis on a species-oriented approach to park management has been replaced by a more synecological, ecosystem approach. This change in emphasis is generally seen as having placed park management on a sounder ecological basis.

Perhaps the greatest challenge to sensitive park planning and management with this more holistic approach is the need to understand the complexity and dynamics of the ecosystems in national parks against a background of increasing use by people.

Difficulty in reaching an understanding originates in part from the diversity of species usually present in national park ecosystems. However, it is compounded by the multiplicity of interactions within species, between different species and between species and their environments. Natural changes in these interlocking inter-relationships greatly affect the stability of ecosystems and ultimately their capacity to accommodate different park uses.

As the number of visitors to national parks increases, the impacts of people on these inter-relationships also increases. In some cases visitor use has reached such proportions that the survival of some ecosystems is threatened and park values attractive to people are being lost.

Such considerations of ecosystem inter-relationships led Sir Frank Fraser Darling in 1980 to point out that "national parks, along with wildlife reserves and refuges throughout the world, are intimately concerned with the physiology of communities." The idea of ecosystem, or community, physiology with its implication of metabolic activity leads to consideration of what different operative processes are involved. Because park management involves the manipulation of ecosystems, park managers need to know the relative significance of these processes within specific ecosystems and their relevance to park management. As the life support mechanisms of ecosystems, ecological processes must be maintained by wise park management practises.

Three main kinds of ecological processes can be identified: first, species oriented processes such as natural succession, species competition and ecosystems evolution; second, transfer processes involving the movement of matter, minerals, water and energy; and third, environment oriented processes associated with changes in human impact, soil development and climate.

With natural succession the spatial distribution of ecosystems change. Furthermore, as ecosystems mature the rates and magnitudes of their ecological processes must be viewed against changing space and time dimensions.

Ecological processes are usually complex, each in itself consisting of an hierarchy of lesser processes. Taking transfer processes as an example, they involve the entire soil-plant-animal-micro-organism-atmosphere systems and are subject to various external influences (Figs. 1 and 2).

It is impossible here to discuss all ecological processes in relation to all ecosystem types. Therefore it seems best to examine two illustrative, controversial management activities practised in some national parks, namely prescribed burning and grazing by domestic stock, and to indicate their major consequences on five important ecological processes. These processes are: natural succession; organic production and decomposition; nutrient circulation; water circulation; and soil development.

2. PRESCRIBED BURNING

2.1. Reasons

Differences of opinion exist on the justification for prescribed burning as a management tool in national parks. Proponents of a deliberate burning regime under controlled conditions point out that in many areas fire, either natural or man-caused, occurs commonly. In these circumstances the existng natural systems may be regarded as fire tolerant and the survival of particular species or ecosystems depends on the incidence of fire. Prescribed burning may also be used as a park protective measure, preventing organic matter accumulation and the inevitable, destructive hot wildfires. Vegetation and dead litter may also be burned periodically as a protection measure around fire intolerant ecosystems such as rainforest, or around buildings.

2.2. Effects

Burning detracts from the scenic value of a national park but more important it can have dramatic effects, both short and long term, on ecological processes (Table l). Fire results in a rapid destruction of living things and dead organic matter, but in between burns recolonisation occurs and biomass accumulates. Thus a repetitive short-term cycle of natural succession is established which may give an appearance of long-term stability. However, in some areas repeated burning may result in a gradual progressive change in which ecosystem diversity and productivity are gradually but irreversibly reduced to the detriment of national park values.

3. GRAZING BY DOMESTIC STOCK

3.1. Reasons

Some conservationists are opposed to any grazing by domestic stock in national parks. Often they are concerned that once grazing is authorised there will be mounting pressure to manage the area to increase the grazing capacity and so place some park values in even greater jeopardy.

Other conservationists may accept some limited grazing for various reasons. Sometimes the area has been used traditionally for grazing by local people and the complete exclusion of domestic animals would create unacceptable hardships to poor people. Sometimes grazing may be permitted as a temporary measure in exceptional economic circumstances as when grazing flocks are threatened by some natural catastrophe, e.g., prolonged drought. Park managers may also use grazing animals as a management tool to maintain a particular stage of natural succession which they regard as a desirable park attribute.

The reality is that grazing by domestic stock does occur in some national parks for various reasons. Where this happens the responsible park managers need to understand the effects of this grazing on the ecology of the area.

3.2. Effects

The magnitudes of the various effects of grazing depend on climate and the initial conditions as well as the kind, number and distribution of grazing animals at particular times. While very different grazing regimes may be used, it is possible to identify certain general effects on ecological processes which park managers need to take into account (Table 2).

The two management examples direct attention largely toward localised effects of speciifc management practises. However, the management of a particular ecosystem may have side effects on ecological processes for other ecosystems and so have implications for the national park in total.

For example the Working Group on Mangrove Ecosystems of the Commission of Ecology has completed a report on the global status of mangrove ecosystems (Saenger, Hegerl and Davie, 1981). It is evident from this report that the management of a national park where mangroves are an important natural feature must be sensitive to the wealth of mangrove-inhabiting species present. It must also take into account both the internal ecological processes within the mangrove areas and the significance of these processes to other ecosystems and the regional economy.

Sometimes management activities elsewhere in a national park can be destructive of mangrove ecosystems and mangrove species. These activities are devastating where they adversely impact on ecological processes which maintain soil stability and provide for a natural inflow of freshwater and the input of plant nutrients into mangrove areas. The maintenance of these processes is critical if the mangrove ecosystems are to persist.

In turn, management, whether external or internal, which damages or destroys mangroves could have serious and widespread ecological consequences on other park values. For instance, the loss of mangroves can adversely affect waterfowl and marine species migration, the spawning and breeding of a variety of fish and shellfish important to local fishermen, the ecological balance of estuarine areas, particularly river mouths, and the stability of coastal areas by lessening their resistance to shore erosion and storm floods.

While the study of ecological processes is still in its infancy, a better understanding of ecological processes and the effects on them of different management practises could assist in improving park management now.

It can provide the scientific basis for safeguarding park values and in integrating park management with that of neighbouring areas. Such knowledge is especially relevant to research and educational activities in national parks. It is also important in enabling park managers to accommodate to the challenge of greater and more varied use of national parks as the world population increases and human aspirations grow.

Table 1: Some possible effects of prescribed burning on five ecological processes

Ecological Process	*Effects*
Natural succession	a. Curtailment of natural succession and ecosystem evolution b. Vegetation pattern reflects pattern of burns, the mosaic containing different successional stages c. Creation of bare areas which facilitates invasion of weed and exotic species d. Local breakdown of ecological balance between species e. Progressive reduction of species diversity depending on fire tolerance f. Progressive increase in uniformity with fewer ecosystems and specialised niches g. Migration and concentration of herbivores in areas with a flush of new, nutritious plant growth
Organic production and decomposition	a. Loss of biomass b. Reduced primary production and energy capture due to leaf loss c. Reduced secondary production at least until new flush of plant growth d. Diversion of photosynthate to plant shoots e. Reduction of organic turnover by decomposition
Nutrient circulation	a. Loss of elements by windblow of ash, smoke and volatization b. Diminution and simplification of nutrient cycle c. Reduced retention of nutrient capital in organic matter d. Reduced significance of litter layers in decomposition e. Enhanced loss of elements by surface run off and leaching f. Changed rate of nitrogen fixation
Water circulation	a. Reduction in interception of precipitation b. Increase in through fall c. Reduction in transpiration d. Increase in surface run off e. Reduction in moisture in upper soil layers due to greater evaporation f. Increase in soil moisture and higher water table g. Increase in water discharge
Soil development	a. Increase in soil erosion with loss of vegetation cover b. Reduction in soil breakdown by organic acids with loss of organic matter c. Formation of a base rich soil surface layer d. Increase in pH of soil surface layer affecting micro-organisms (e.g. nitrifiers) e. Darkening of soil with charcoal and loss of vegetation resulting in higher soil temperature f. Death and decomposition of plant roots g. Increase in nutrient loss by leaching h. Possible progressive long term decline in soil nutrient capital i. Increased salinity with loss of trees and raised water table

Table 2: Some effects of grazing by domestic stock on five ecological processes

Ecological process	*Effects*
Natural succession	a. Modification of natural succession by treading and selective grazing leading to dominance of unpalatable species b. Invasion of weed and exotic species c. Reduction of palatable tree, shrub and perennial species and expansion of grassland particularly of annual species d. Increased competition with native herbivores e. Excretion of dung and urine making vegetation unacceptable to native species f. Disturbance of native animal species by domestic grazing
Organic production and decomposition	a. Primary production diverted to ground level with loss of trees and shrubs b. Reduction in total biomass and possibly energy capture c. Decrease in biomass of native animals d. Natural decomposition process circumvented by grazing animal cycle e. More of primary production diverted to large herbivores f. Increased herbage intake leading to less litter and lower rates of decomposition
Nutrient circulation	a. Reduction in nutrient pool with fewer nutrients in vegetation b. Local and uneven re-allocation of nutrients according to distribution of faeces and urine c. Increased rate of nutrient circulation d. Replacement of slow cycling through soil organisms by more rapid, plant-animal cycling pools e. Initial stages of decomposition in rumen and gut of grazing animals f. Loss of nutrient capital with removal in animal products (meat, milk, hides)
Water circulation	a. increased surface run off b. Reduction in interception and transpiration c. Soil surface layers drier d. Increase in evaporation from soil surface with loss of vegetation cover
Soil development	a. Localised overgrazing resulting in soil erosion b. Increased exposure of soil especially where animals congregate c. Increased salinity with loss of trees and shrubs d. Increased soil compaction due to treading

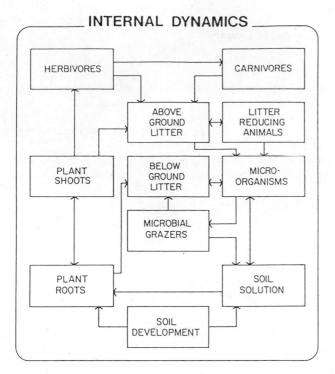

INTERNAL DYNAMICS

HERBIVORES

CARNIVORES

ABOVE GROUND LITTER

LITTER REDUCING ANIMALS

PLANT SHOOTS

BELOW GROUND LITTER

MICRO-ORGANISMS

MICROBIAL GRAZERS

PLANT ROOTS

SOIL SOLUTION

SOIL DEVELOPMENT

Figure 1. Flow chart to illustrate some internal ecosystem dynamics.

EXTERNAL DYNAMICS

INPUT
SOLAR ENERGY
ATMOSPHERIC (DUST)
PRECIPITATION
WATER FLOW (SURFACE and SUBSURFACE)
MIGRATION

OUTPUT
ENERGY RADIATION
ATMOSPHERIC (SEED and POLLEN DISPERSAL)
FIRE (VOLATIZATION)
LEACHING
WATER FLOW (SURFACE and SUBSURFACE)
MIGRATION
HARVEST

Figure 2. Some external processes affecting ecosystems.

The Relationship between Adjacent Lands and Protected Areas: Issues of Concern for the Protected Area Manager

Keith Garratt
IUCN Commission on Environmental Planning
Department of Lands and Survey
Wellington, New Zealand

ABSTRACT. *Protected areas are at one end of a spectrum of land uses ranging from strict protection to total development, and the protected area manager must take an interest in conservation on other lands. There are many physical and human linkages between protected areas and other land, and legal boundaries often have little effect on these linkages. Integrated regional planning provides a means of understanding these linkages and resolving conflicts in land use. Effective environmental planning requires adequate information and means of structuring and using this information in ways that can be understood by all interested parties. Successful integration of protected area management with management of other land requires adequate systems for involvement of local people and other organizations. These systems must be designed to suit local needs and to encourage involvement at all levels.*

1. INTRODUCTION

It is now an accepted fact that man is an integral part of the world's ecosystems and cannot consider himself independent of them. It has been realized that if man is to survive, he must understand the ways in which he is dependent on natural systems. He must learn to live in mutual harmony with the total environment, taking from it and contributing to it. In simple terms, man's total well-being can only be as good as that of the world in which he lives.

All cultures throughout history have developed traditions and practices which help them to live in harmony with the environment. There is no doubt that many of the so-called "primitive" cultures have much greater understanding of these needs than our 20th century industrialized societies. Often, these traditions and practices have been developed and carried on without any conscious thought about man/environment rela-

tionships. They developed out of experience and a growing instinct over many generations.

Rapid technological development and population growth in the last 100 years have in effect outstripped man's ability to adapt and evolve in this gradual fashion. Man's activities are causing a rapid degrading of the environment in which he lives. He has been forced to give urgent and concentrated attention to finding ways to ensure that a balance is restored between his demands on the environment and its capacity to restore itself. This concept of sustainable use of resources is a central theme of the World Conservation Strategy.

The establishment of protected areas is one of a number of strategies designed to restore a balance between man and his environment. However, it must be realized that it is only one facet of a much broader range of actions for environmental care. Protected areas alone will not cure the massive environmental problems that exist. This is recognized in the World Conservation Strategy which accepts the very broad scope of conservation, defining it as "the management of human use of the biosphere so that it may yield the greatest sustainable benefit to present generations while maintaining its potential to meet the needs and aspirations of future generations."

Protected areas must be seen as the most obvious and direct part of an integrated system of actions for environmental care in a region. They cannot be seen as islands which exist in isolation from their surroundings. They are important parts of the regions in which they are situated, and the mutual relationships and linkages between them and adjacent land must be understood and applied to management. These relationships are many and varied, but can be divided into two broad groups.

The first may be called physical relationships. These

are matters related to the actual physical environment. The second group can be called human relationships, and include all the various social, economic and cultural matters which are of importance to manangement or to the public.

2. PROTECTED AREAS—A HUMAN CONCEPT

A basic principle which is fundamental to this subject is that, although protected areas are primarily for the protection of *natural* species and systems, the whole process of defining differing types of land tenure, controlling land use by legislation and deciding the positions of boundaries is entirely a human *cultural* concept. These actions must be regarded as abstract tools which assist in wise physical management of the total landscape, with strictly protected areas being just part of the overall pattern of balanced land use.

Too often, the legal establishment of a protected area is seen as the sole target and its achievement is hailed as a total success for conservation. In some cases, this may be correct, particularly if the area has previously been under some real threat of destruction.

However, it must always be remembered that a signature on a legal document or the drawing of a boundary line on a map do not suddenly change the nature of an area or erect a barrier between it and the surrounding land or cut cultural or economic links with the land which local people already have.

Establishing of a protected area must be followed by wise management of the resources within it. Just as important, its whole physical, social and economic relationship with the surrounding regions must be carefully considered and necessary actions taken to ensure wise management of the total landscape.

To illustrate some of these concepts, let us assume that we know that an area of forest contains a population of a very rare bird species. It may seem logical to protect all or part of that forest. However, this attempt to protect the birds may be a complete failure if the protected area is not supported by other action. For example, the protection provided may mean nothing if the area contains only the bird's nesting area without necessary feeding areas; if it only protects their summer habitat and not their winter habitat; if the birds are killed for sport or food outside the protected area; or if the existence of the protected area itself is threatened by flooding or pollution caused by land clearance or land use in upstream catchments. In particular, the protected area is likely to fail if its produce is necessary for the livelihood of the local people, and no replacement for this produce is provided.

The message is clear that Nature does not recognize Man's laws and boundaries and that laws by themselves do not change human habits and traditions. Protected area management must therefore consider the physical and social environment of the broader region if it is to be effective.

3. SELECTING PROTECTED AREAS

The biogeographical principles used for selecting protected areas and planning a protected area system involve a thorough understanding of the total region. The planning of a protected area system should be part of an overall environmental planning exercise which also examines the needs for other means of integrating conservation and development.

It should also examine the impacts which the establishment of protected areas will have on the local population and find ways to soften or compensate for adverse impacts. Careful programmes of public participation and education may be required.

The more detailed discussion which follows on the various relationships between protected areas and adjacent land therefore applies just as much to selection of new protected areas as it does to management of existing protected areas.

4. INTEGRATED REGIONAL PLANNING

If the principles previously outlined are accepted, it is clear that planning for the protected area must consider issues beyond the protected area itself. Ideally, there should be an integrated planning system across the total geographical region. This then enables planning for the protected area to take place within the broader framework of regional objectives.

The precise ways in which such an integrated system would operate will vary according to the laws and customs of the particular country. If no formal planning system exists, it may be necessary for the protected area manager to act informally. In this case, his aim would be to establish continuing contact and discussions with other agencies with the aim of ensuring that all land management agencies understand each other's needs and problems. In particular, they need to understand the linkages and relationships which need to be taken into account in planning.

Descriptions of planning methodologies can be found in various texts (e.g., McHarg, 1969; Fabos, 1979). Basic features which are required in any effective system are definition of the extent and boundaries of the planning region in logical geographical, ecological or human terms; a system for collecting, storing and retrieving relevant and structured information; a system for analyzing and inter-relating the various categories of information, such as computerized land information systems or sieve mapping; an ability to define various planning options and to assess their consequences; systems for full cooperation and input from all relevant disciplines and organizations; systems for meaningful and effective public participation and consequent definition of realistic and acceptable regional planning objectives as a consistent framework for more detailed sectoral planning.

The following notes describe examples of regional issues and information related to protected area management. These are matters necessary to ensure adequate overall conservation management and should be taken into account in any regional planning process.

4.1. Physical factors

4.1.1. Flora and fauna. Adequate information on the distribution and types of flora and fauna in the regions is required. Specific matters which may be of particular importance are conservation significance of species or ecosystems in terms of rarity or threat; adequacy of representation of species or ecosystems in protected areas or under other forms of protection; existing or potential economic significance of species; daily or seasonal migration habits of wildlife species, either within or beyond the region; value of vegetation for erosion control and the significance of habitat types to wildlife survival.

4.1.2. Geology and soils. Information on geology and soils in terms relevant to land management is required. Some specific matters include presence of minerals of existing or potential economic significance; soil and rock stability; potential productivity of soils; representation of terrain types in protected areas and presence of significant geological features.

4.1.3. Hydrology. Matters related to water management which may need consideration include water quality and its significance for conservation in the region; needs for catchment vegetation protection to control water runoff and quality; water requirements for irrigation and human consumption; and the location, capacity and origin of underground water.

4.1.4. Scenic quality. If possible, the scenic qualities of the regional landscape should be assessed, some specific matters being identification of outstanding scenic features; representation of landscape types in protected areas and needs for scenic protection and enhancement outside protected areas.

4.2. Social and economic factors

4.2.1. Land tenure. Existing land tenures and traditional land rights are always a strong influence on land use planning. They are often the most difficult barrier to establishing effective protected area systems and conservation practices, and local people's rights must be respected whenever possible. Land tenure must therefore be carefully considered in the planning process. Some specific examples of matters to be considered are types and locations of land tenure; legal rights of owners; customary or traditional rights of owners; permanence of tenure; legal rights of the government; and expiry dates of leases.

4.2.2. Population distribution. Some aspects of population distribution can be important for conservation management, examples being impact of towns on the natural environment; recreational demands of urban populations; water supply needs of urban populations; outdoor education needs of urban populations; sewage disposal needs; air and water pollution from urban area; energy requirements and methods.

4.2.3. Social and economic factors. Conservation management and protected areas can have positive or negative economic effects for the local or regional population, and these should be assessed. Both short-term and long-term effects should be taken into account. The long-term potential economic benefits of conservation are seldom taken into account and particular care should be taken to ensure that they are adequately considered in regional planning.

Unfortunately, long-term economic benefits of conservation can seldom be stated in precise or definite terms, but the attempt should be made.

Examples of social and economic issues which might be considered are loss of access to productive land or forests in protected areas; loss of employment; need for access to firewood; employment potential in protected area management; shifting cultivation in areas of conservation value; potential for tourist use of protected areas; income and employment generated through tourism; long-term protection of sustained yield through conservation practices; prevention of flooding through catchment protection; and preservation of genetic diversity for long term economic use of species.

4.2.4. Cultural factors. There are often matters of cultural, historical or traditional significance which need to be seriously considered in regional planning. Some examples are presence of historic buildings; presence of burial sites; archaeological sites; geographical features of religious or traditional significance; traditional access or pilgrimage routes; traditional links with the land; and animals of religious significance.

4.3. Integration and planning

It can be seen from the above examples that, even looking only from the conservation viewpoint, there is a wide variety of matters which need to be taken into account in regional planning. Methods are required to analyze and handle the large amount of information collected, and various systems have been developed. Most involve some form of sieve analysis (McHarg, 1969; Fabos, 1979).

In its simplest form, sieve analysis involves the separate mapping of various factors and attributes relating to the land on transparent material. All categories are mapped at the same scale. This then enables the transparent maps to be overlaid in different combinations to examine the ways in which the various factors relate to each other. The effects of various planning proposals can be illustrated.

This type of process can be very effective as a basis for group consultation and discussion or for larger meetings. Often, this type of illustrated discussion among groups with conflicting or complementary aims can lead to mutually agreed solutions on such matters as land status and boundaries. By these methods, the issues involved can be quickly and easily understood by all concerned, and such a system is often much more effective than long written reports.

Computerized systems have also been developed for storage and analysis of resource information (Walker, 1982; Weber, 1979; Rogoff, 1978; Fabos, 1979; Walesh et al., 1977). Providing that the information is fed into the computer in a suitable fashion, it can provide very flexible and effective ways of handling and analyzing information. However, computerized systems may be less easily understood by people not expert in their use, and may therefore be less effective in developing cooperation and trust among local organizations and people.

4.4. The value of regional planning

Protected area managers often find themselves involved in disputes regarding the use of land or resources. Proposals for protected areas or other means of conservation often meet opposition. Conservation versus development conflicts are occurring in various parts of the world and often result in long and bitter argument. Often, the argument can run for years without any effective move to a solution to the problem.

The integrated planning approach described above can often assist and is very compatible with the principle of integration of conservation and development established in the World Conservation Strategy. It enables all parties to understand and discuss all the issues involved. Experience has shown that in most circumstances, when there is open and free consultation with all relevant information available in forms that everyone can understand, trust and cooperation increase and acceptable compromises are more easily reached.

An integrated planning approach therefore provides a framework and structure for resolving conservation/development conflicts and for pursuing the aims of the World Conservation Strategy. It also provides a means by which the role of protected areas in regions can be clearly established. This enables more effective protection of areas, and their more effective integration with balanced management of other land in the region.

The planning process can also be used to examine ways to compensate local people for losses in land or productivity through establishment of protected areas. This can be an extremely important issue for the local people. It can also be important for the protected area manager by lessening opposition to the protected area and by making it less liable to poaching or illegal removal of produce.

5. CONSULTATION AND PUBLIC PARTICIPATION

From what has already been said, it is clear that the protected area planner or manager cannot operate in isolation. Just as the protected areas themselves cannot be seen in isolation from other land, planners and managers must evolve close contact with managers of adjacent land, political authorities and local inhabitants.

A recurring theme in protected area literature from various parts of the world is fear, mistrust and opposition from local inhabitants and organizations (Sayer, 1981; Western, 1976; Molloy, 1982; Gardner & Nelson, 1981). They see economic resources being "locked up" in national parks and reserves. They often see no advantages to themselves.

Although these fears are sometimes misplaced, they are unfortunately often justified. Western notions of parks and reserves have often been transferred to developing countries without adjustment to suit local circumstances. In several countries, national parks have encompassed local villages. The villages themselves have been cut out from the park, but this means nothing if areas vital for their survival are then denied to the villagers without some alternative being provided (Croft, 1981; Garratt, 1981).

Protected area managers must therefore find techniques for developing a deep mutual trust and understanding with managers and occupiers of adjoining land and the public in general. The following notes discuss some available techniques.

5.1. Public participation procedures

Various techniques for public participation in management and planning have been developed around the world (Winge, 1978; Eidsvik, 1978; Shannon & Daubert, 1979; Reynolds, 1975). However, many are not suitable to meet the particular problems which occur when comparatively uneducated indigenous populations are involved. Even in highly developed countries, formal public participation procedures tend to favour those with education and wealth, and legal costs have in places become a real deterrent to participation.

Some participation techniques are largely ineffective because they only allow for reaction to plans put forward in a completed stage by park administration. Local people and organizations need to feel that they have made a real contribution to plans as they are being drawn up. It is only in this way that the necessary trust and interest can be built up.

Public participation procedures discussed here are therefore those which may be of use in getting direct involvement of local organizations and indigenous populations. The more formal, legalized procedures common in westernized countries are not discussed.

5.1.1. Informal consulation. There is no doubt that the most important technique in the short term is informal consultation. Although this sounds simple, it requires continuing effort, time and diplomacy by park managers and planners. Professionally trained staff must realize that local people may have specialized local knowledge of real validity for park management. They must make continual efforts to eliminate the automatic distrust that local poeple often have of highly educated "outsiders."

Park managers can gain trust and cooperation by showing landowners ways to improve the productivity of their own land by conservation practices, in return for their advice on park management (Halffter, 1981).

Similarly, park staff should establish close relations with organizations with land management or political responsibilities in the region. Regular informal discussions on matters of mutual interest can often forestall problems before they become serious. Proposals of the other agencies can be discussed and modifications suggested before they become entrenched in formal plans.

Experience has shown very clearly that friendly informal discussions at the right time, conducted in a spirit of trust and cooperation, are usually more effective in achieving conservation objectives than years of legal battles. It is often amazing just how little conflict really exists when all the facts are known to everyone, and each organization's objectives are clearly explained.

5.1.2. Advisory committees. Advisory committees selected or elected from the local population provide a way in which the local public can have a continuing knowledge of park management and contribute to it. They also provide a means by which management of the park can be integrated with management of adjoining land.

However, it is important that the advisory committees are given all the information required. If they are kept in ignorance and their advice appears not to be valued, this can do harm to good public relations.

5.1.3. Management committees. It is possible to give committees a direct management role, rather than just an advisory function. In theory, this is the ultimate method of involvement of the local population. However, experience has shown that this can sometimes cause problems. Committees can become overly involved in management trivia. For parks or reserves of national importance, a locally-based committee may give insufficient weight to the national or international values which the park or reserve is primarily intended to protect. Nevertheless, management committees should be considered as a serious option.

5.1.4. Education. In the long term, education is probably one of the most effective ways of integrating management of the protected area with that of the region. Education can of course occur at many age levels and in a variety of formal and informal ways. Park managers can give conservation classes in local schools; these should

deal with broad conservation issues beyond the park itself, but should demonstrate the interaction between the park and the region.

Schools and universities should be encouraged to use the park for education, either in the natural sciences, or for the development of character and self-reliance. Again, the park managers should participate. Where appropriate, camps or lodges for education purposes can be encouraged to establish in suitable locations within the park. Visitor interpretation facilities should be provided.

5.1.5. Employment. Often, the park can provide employment for local people, sometimes as a replacement for opportunities lost through creation of the park. In some cases, the park provides opportunities for easier or more lucrative employment than was available previously. For example, many Sherpas in Sagarmatha National Park in Nepal are providing guiding or portering services for tourist trekkers or mountaineers. Some say that they find this easier and more lucrative than their previous life of subsistence agriculture and trading (Garratt, 1981).

Use of local expertise for such projects as erection of bridges or buildings can result in an authentic architectural image for the park (Sayer, 1981).

5.1.6. Summary. The key to these various methods of public involvement is that they can result in the protected area becoming an integral and ingrained part of the social environment of the region. When this happens and local people automatically accept it as something which benefits them and their region, many difficulties can disappear and life can become much more pleasant and productive for the park manager.

6. OPTIONS FOR CONSERVATION MANAGEMENT

As stated previously, protected areas should be seen as only one technique for conservation, although perhaps the most extreme. Protected area managers and planners should do their part toward establishing a balanced pattern of integrated conservation and development across a region. The following notes discuss some possible techniques.

6.1. Controlled buffer zones

One possibility is to create a buffer zone adjoining or surrounding the protected area. This zone would permit limited levels of use while not imposing the strict limitations of the protected area or the more liberal land uses of the general region.

An example of this approach as applied to Kenya was provided by Lusigi (1981). He suggested, "that the ecosystem affecting national parks be designated a Wildlife Conservation Unit, with three land use categories—the national park, the protected area and the multiple use area."

In brief, he proposed that the national park area containing the wildlife populations and unique scenic areas would be strictly protected. It would be retained in a wilderness state with minimal development and roading. The protected area would surround the national park and contain the more intensive touristic facilities and maintenance and staff facilities. Restricted local grazing would be by permit only. Some managed harvesting of wildlife on a sustained yield basis would occur in this area.

In the multiple use areas, tourism facilities would be permitted, but the major purpose of the area would be wildlife management coordinated with resident livestock operations. Resident pastoral tribes would be permitted to establish or continue their traditional ways of life.

Of course, this particular system will not suit every situation, but the general concept of buffering the strictly protected area with partly controlled areas is important. The specific means of implementing such a system will also vary in different countries according to their customs and laws. Implementation is easiest when all the land involved is in public ownership, and the various uses can be established as leases or concessions, or undertaken by a government agency.

6.2. Conservation on private land

In order to achieve the necessary balanced pattern of conservation and development across a region, conservation principles must be applied to private land as well as to public land. This may be necessary to provide direct buffering for a protected area as previously described, or to protect resources which cannot be included in protected areas.

Means of achieving conservation on private land can be divided into three broad categories: control by regulation or laws; negotiated agreements with owners with monetary compensation; voluntary actions by owners.

Given the great variety of land laws and customs operating in various countries, it is difficult to discuss these techniques in detail, but the following notes discuss the principles involved.

6.2.1. Control by regulation. These techniques can range from direct restriction on land use by law to sophisticated zoning systems under a statutory planning process. In some countries, statutory planning systems have become complicated legal processes with wide provision for input or objections by owners and the general public, and provision for settling conflicts through the judicial system.

However, the basic principle of control by regulation or zoning is that, for the public good, private land-owners are restricted or controlled in the use of their own land.

Such controls can range over a great variety of activities. Matters which may be relevant to complementing or protecting a protected area system can include: controls on disturbance or clearance of native vegetation; controls on emission of pollutants to the water or the air; limits on grazing to prevent soil erosion; controls on drainage of wetlands; controls on subdivisions of properties; limits on building size and type; and limits on the type of land use.

6.2.2. Negotiated agreements. This type of technique can go under a variety of titles, examples being purchase of development rights, conservation covenants, purchase of easement rights, special leases and purchase of betterment rights. While they may differ in detail, the basic principle is that the owner enters into a legally binding agreement with the state or local government in return for payment. By the agreement, the owner undertakes to limit his use of the land in some way to achieve a desired conservation goal.

Again, the exact details of this technique will vary in different countries. Where a comprehensive land title system exists, the agreement is usually recorded on the title to the land involved.

6.2.3. Voluntary actions by owners. Landowners are sometimes prepared to protect areas or take conservation actions without requiring payment. They may become convinced that such actions are in their own best interests. Sometimes, an owner has a genuine wish to protect an area of forest or wetland because of his own traditional or sentimental attachment to it. In other cases, owners may simply act in the public good, but wish to retain ownership of the land concerned.

Protected area managers may be able to advise and encourage such owners in ways to protect natural systems. They may also be able to provide direct practical help. For example, they may offer help in fencing the area to be protected to prevent entry by livestock.

Some countries can provide legal support for voluntary protection of natural areas by land owners. For example, in New Zealand, the Reserves Act 1977 provides for Protected Private Land. Land in this category remains in private ownership, but the legal restrictions and offences provisions of the Act apply to the land concerned. In this way, the owner who wishes to protect an area has the legal support of the legislation but keeps the ownership and occupation of the land.

7. LEGISLATION

There is some difficulty involved in legislating for the type of integrated consultative approach to planning which has been suggested. One problem is that the presence of legislation imposed from central government level can itself provoke mistrust and opposition.

It may in fact hamper the development of the necessary informal consultation. Another problem is that when procedures are laid down in law, they become inflexible and can also become open to challenge through the legal system. Again, this conflicts with the basic objective of enabling effective and willing input from all sectors of the population.

It therefore appears preferable that in many circumstances, legislation should provide the means and opportunities to implement agreements on an integrated and balanced approach to land use, rather than providing a rigid legal process for the planning stages. The extent to which this can be achieved will vary in different countries, and some element of compulsion may be inevitable.

Apart from the normal provision for strictly protected areas, some examples of matters which may be provided for in law include: provision for negotiated agreements (covenants, leases, purchase of development rights, etc.); controls on air and water pollution; compensation rights for land owners; controls on water use; provision for multiple use or partly protected areas; flora and fauna protection; and protection of customary rights.

8. CONCLUSION

Protected area managers must recognize that strictly protected areas are not self-contained islands that can be managed in isolation from the surrounding region.

They are just one element of the total pattern of balanced land use. There are many physical linkages and relationships between protected areas and adjacent land. These must be understood and provided for in planning.

Just as important, there are human relationships between protected areas and adjacent land. Protected area managers must understand and provide for these. The physical and human linkages usually depend on each other. Physical protection may not be achieved without considering the human factors and developing systems of involvement by local inhabitants and outside organizations.

Most important of all, the protected area manager himself must not be isolated from the region. He must become an accepted and integral part of the regional community and be seen to be contributing to its total well-being through his expertise and knowledge.

Environmental planning at a regional scale provides the means by which conservation principles and the management of protected areas can be effectively integrated with development objectives in a region. It can thus contribute to integration of conservation and development, the basic objective of the World Conservation Strategy.

Acknowledgements

This paper was prepared for IUCN's Commission on National Parks and Protected Areas in cooperation with the United Nations Environment Programme.

How Protected Areas Can Help Meet Society's Evolving Needs

P.H.C. Lucas
Deputy Chairman
IUCN Commission on National Parks and Protected Areas
Department of Lands and Survey
Wellington, New Zealand

ABSTRACT. *This paper outlines the many ways that protected areas contribute to social and economic welfare, following the guidelines established by the World Conservation Strategy. Protected areas contribute to life-support systems, preservation of genetic diversity, sustainable utilization, conservation of natural heritage, recreation and tourism, and many others. The concept of protected areas is expected to evolve to meet society's changing needs primarily through devising ways and means of management to meet the real needs of people.*

1. INTRODUCTION

"To save ourselves—to enable us to live at our best and happiest, parks are necessary. Within national parks there is room—glorious room—room in which to find ourselves, in which to think and hope, to dream and plan, to rest and resolve." (Enos Mills, the "father" of Rocky Mountain National Park).

"There is nothing more practical than the preservation of beauty, than the preservation of anything that appeals to the higher emotions of mankind." (Theodore Roosevelt, conservationist and President of the USA).

"National parks are the conserving of resources that are not to be expressed in terms of money, but embrace the moral, spiritual, and educational welfare of the people and add to the joy of our living." (Freeman Tilden, author and philosopher).

"National parks are the cornerstone of the tourist industry." (a former chairman of the Tourist Hotel Corporation of New Zealand).

"National parks are a lock-up." (critics of recent national park extensions in New Zealand).

These are among the many and varied perceptions of national parks in countries which adopted the concept in the 19th century.

A perception of national parks from a country whose first park is still in the process of establishment illustrates the view of a citizen of a young nation on how national parks can help meet society's evolving needs:

"National Parks belong to the people. Every man, woman and child in the country has, as a heritage, these areas which are set aside forever to give pleasure to present and succeeding generations. Thus, those who use the parks have responsibility to themselves and to others to treat this great heritage with care and respect. Reserves are very important in the country. There are many important things in our life that could become rare. If we do not preserve or protect some of our lands and sea, these will be lost." (Kalati Poai, Department of Agriculture & Forests, Apia, Western Samoa).

This South Pacific assessment of the role of parks and reserves in the total environment recognizes their role as a resource for human enjoyment, inspiration and recreation; as a reservoir of genetic diversity; and as a heritage for the country and the world. This perception of the wide role of parks and reserves in meeting society's needs is not always appreciated in the wider world but the concept of protected areas is part of the South Pacific way of life, as illustrated in *tapu*, or sacred, forests, used as an integral part of the traditional mechanism for perpetuating natural resources.

As well, parks and reserves have been seen in many countries as a key mechanism in maintaining the life support systems necessary for human survival and to meet human aspirations. Increasingly, parks and reserves are recognized as basic elements in balanced resource management. In this context, as in their role in tourism, they have economic importance.

2. THE WORLD CONSERVATION STRATEGY

The World Conservation Strategy, suggests a comprehensive approach to what it describes as "living resource conservation for sustainable development." The goal of the Strategy is the integration of conservation and development to ensure that those modifications which occur to the world environment are such as will secure the survival and well-being of all people.

The Strategy says that conservation aims to ensure the continuing use of living resources for the benefit and enjoyment of mankind, keeping in mind the ethical imperative expressed in the belief that "we have not inherited the earth from our parents, we have borrowed it from our children."

The establishment and sound management of protected areas is a key element in achieving the goals of the World Conservation Strategy and is an integral component of sustainable development.

3. PROTECTED AREAS AND LIFE SUPPORT SYSTEMS

The maintenance of essential ecological processes and life-support systems is vital for all societies; archaeological evidence of ancient civilizations testifies to the fate of societies which ignored the need to maintain these systems and processes. Arthur Dahl, at the South Pacific Conference on National Parks and Reserves in Wellington in 1975, cited a South Pacific example. He referred to a small coral island originally surrounded by mangroves which had accumulated the sand, the material of which the island was built. However, the mangroves harboured mosquitoes so the island's residents cut all the mangroves to eliminate the mosquitoes. Said Dahl, "This was fine—it was a lovely improvement to their environment—until the next hurricane. The last time I visited the island all that was left was a pile of sand. There was nothing left of the buildings, the trees, the vegetation . . . . The mangrove had been an essential resource for the protection of that island, of the system on which the people depended. But it is only when we lose one of these natural benefits that we realise how valuable they are and that we must find enormous sums of money to re-establish that natural balance that we formerly had for free." This is a clear case where the establishment and management of those mangroves as a protected area would have been a key to maintaining the life-support system of that island.

The establishment of reserves to protect watershed forests is recognized as vital to the life-support systems in many countries. Some areas of New Zealand were devastated by floods in the 1930s, causing loss of life and the erosion of good agricultural land. The problem stemmed from the shrinking of watershed forests through unwise land clearance on steep erodible slopes and through the damage caused to those forests which remained by the introduction of alien browsing mammals into an ecological system which had developed in the

absence of browsing mammals. One step toward alleviating the problem was to establish the remaining watershed forests as protected areas, to plant additional protection forest and to introduce management practices designed to reduce the number of browsing animals. This emphasizes that functions of protected areas in meeting society's needs for watershed protection and soil conservation can be of even greater significance than their functions in scenery preservation, recreation and scientific value.

The government of Colombia has expanded its protected areas in watersheds to ensure the maintenance of water supplies on which major industrial and residential developement depends. The continuing supply of good quality water for human life and for industry is essential to the economic and physical well-being of many Colombians and the aim is to assure this supply through parks and reserves in the mountain hinterland.

In the Republic of South Africa, protected areas are being expanded to reduce sedimentation which is reducing the economic life of reservoirs in the massive Tuva scheme, designed to bring water to the Witwatersrand area of Transvaal. Deforestation in the catchments of new reservoirs caused some to be filled with sediment before the scheme was commissioned, leading to a programme of land acquisition, reservation and reforestation to improve the ecological health of the watersheds. How much better and more economic would protection of the catchments have been in the first place.

4. PROTECTED AREAS AND PRESERVATION OF GENETIC DIVERSITY

The World Conservation Strategy says that preservation of genetic diversity is both a matter of insurance and investment—necessary to sustain and improve agricultural, forestry and fisheries production, to keep open future options, as a buffer against harmful environmental change, as the raw material for much scientific and industrial innovation—and a matter of moral principle.

The establishment of parks and reserves has proved a key means of protecting genetic diversity, and of protecting species from extinction. It is in this area of species extinction that the issue of moral principle is particularly relevant. The involvement of human beings in evolution has brought many species to extinction and New Zealand is one country that does not have a good record in this field. However, major efforts are now being made in habitat protection through protected areas to preserve those species which are seen as endangered. These include plants such as a rare *Ranunculus* where a few plants remaining in an alpine environment were husbanded by a committed conservationist and, their habitat given reserve status; with careful field management the future of a threatened species seems assured. Efforts cover bird species such as the Takahe, rediscovered in the remote mountains of Fiordland National Park in 1949 and given even greater protection by legislation creating the takahe's habitat as a Specially Protected Area within the national park, with entry restricted to Wildlife officers and others who could contribute to the survival of the species. The work being done through management of parks and reserves to ensure the preservation of endangered species in many countries captures the imagination of people the world over, as the producers of natural history television films have found to their economic benefit.

The heavy dependence of modern medicine on the world's plants and animals is pointed out by the World Conservation Strategy, even though only a tiny proportion of plants and animals have been investigated for their medical and pharmaceutical values. By their major role as reservoirs of the world's genetic diversity, parks and reserves are playing a valuable part in meeting society's needs and have the potential for yet unknown contributions.

5. PROTECTED AREAS AND SUSTAINABLE UTILIZATION

Sustainable utilization is somewhat analogous to spending the interest and keeping the capital. The World Conservation Strategy points out that a society which insists that all use of living resources be sustainable ensures that it will benefit from those resources indefinitely.

The importance of sustainability of the world's fishing resources is highlighted by the shrinking numbers of the more dramatic species, such as whales, leading to international action for their protection, including controls on harvesting and proposals to establish sanctuaries and similar protected areas. The movement to create more marine reserves is seen in many parts of the world as an important means of ensuring that there are protected resources from which stocks may be replenished for harvesting outside the reserve.

Two examples from Peru illustrate how establishment of reserves is working toward sustainable utilization of wild species. The people of the region of Junin Lake historically had burned the reeds along on the shore of the lake to flush out the animals which were the people's major source of protein. Overburning reduced the habitat for the animals, leading to the inevitable reduction in the food supply. Now, a reserve has been established in the core area, to protect totally the breeding habitat for the animals. The surrounding area has been designated a hunting zone and, in this way, the Peruvians hope to ensure maintenance of the species and a sustained yield for the people.

The other example relates to the vicuna, a member of the camel family, whose extremely valuable, fine wool led to it being hunted almost to extinction. It was replaced largely by exotic sheep whose performance in the harsh environment of the montane valleys of the Andes was, to say the least, marginal. The Pampa Galeras National Reserve was set up to protect the habitat

of the few remaining vicuna in Peru. Habitat protection and protection from illegal hunters, achieved at the cost of injury and even death to park guards, has seen the vicuna flourish and expand in numbers to the point where breeding stock can now be made available to Andean farmers for meat and wool production.

Interestingly, the Peruvians describe their parks and reserves as "units of conservation" and they are proving the appropriateness of that title and demonstrating how protected areas can help meet society's evolving needs.

6. PROTECTED AREAS AND THEIR HERITAGE VALUE

The heritage role of parks and reserves is an intangible value of immense significance. Such is the diversity of plants and animals, that each region of the world finds itself the custodian of part of the world's heritage.

This has been recognized in the Unesco-sponsored Convention for the Conservation of the World Cultural and Natural Heritage, which seeks to marshal international resources in a cooperative effort to assist in the protection of the diversity of natural and cultural features that together represent the heritage of all mankind.

The World Heritage Convention encourages nations to identify features of their heritage that contribute significantly to the world's heritage in nature and culture. Many of the outstanding protected areas of the world have already been designated as World Heritage Sites, giving them an international stamp of quality and qualifying them to gain assistance from the World Heritage Fund where there is a need for the wider world community to cooperate in giving adequate protection. As an example, when Sagarmatha (Mount Everest) National Park in Nepal was made a World Heritage Site, it received support in personnel training, forest restoration and cultural preservation from the Fund.

But the heritage value of parks and reserves does not depend on international conventions. It belongs in the hearts and minds of the people of each nation. In this way protected areas contribute to society's needs for identity and pride. Kenya is one nation which has an immensely diverse wildlife resource and its pride in nationhood is based to a very large extent on its pride in wildlife. The proximity of Nairobi National Park to the Kenyan capital and the opportunity this brings for school children to visit the park and see the nation's wildlife for themselves contributes much to Kenyan national pride in its wildlife heritage.

The same pride in a country's natural heritage can be observed among school children whose opportunities of seeing wildlife in its natural habitat may be limited. Crowds of children visiting the natural history museum in Lima show obvious pride as they look at displays of Peru's heritage in wildlife, from the flamingo whose pink and white colouring gave Peru her national flag to the Andean condor known in Peru and the world in the song "El Condor Pasa." Papua New Guinea is another of the countries where pride in wildlife is honoured on the national flag.

What a tragedy, what a blow to national pride if all that future generations know of their unique heritage in nature is seen in museum displays and on the national flag.

7. PROTECTED AREAS AND THEIR RECREATIONAL VALUE

Inspiration, enjoyment and recreation are some of the benefits that people may gain from parks and reserves and the mountains, forests, seacoasts, lakes, rivers and other natural features they protect.

Much has been said in recent years in discussion on environmental issues about "quality of life" and, as the quest for material benefits has proceeded, there has been a growing realisation of the dangers of over-development and over-exploitation destroying the values and resources which give life a quality beyond that of mere survival.

Wise planning and protection of parks and reserves is an integral part of creating and maintaining an environment which provides for quality of life. The great weekend and holiday exodus of people from the huge cities of North America, Japan and Europe illustrates a desire to find recreation in a more pleasant environment than the cities provide, but the people concerned pay a high cost in both time and money in obtaining that recreation. How much better to seek to provide, as far as possible, for a range of recreational opportunities and experiences of nature near where people live. In this context a small natural area bringing "wilderness" into suburbia can be as significant to local people as a large remote national park.

In its system of national parks and reserves on the island of Upolu, Western Samoa has sought to protect resources of great recreational value and diversity. A marine reserve provides a safe viewing area of coral and small fish for swimmers equipped with mask or snorkel; a national park has educational displays in a visitor centre built in traditional style where craft-work can be seen and from which walking tracks give access to a natural features; a recreation reserve protects access to natural swimming pool with pleasant picnic spots; a scenic reserve has similar facilities as well as walking tracks and view points; a memorial reserve protects and interprets an historic feature; and a botanical garden being established will provide a display representative of the plants of the Pacific Basin.

Recreation is a key element in the constructive use of leisure time. The opportunities to enjoy leisure are tending to increase world-wide, whether from the benefits of affluence or the problems of unemployment. For whatever cause, parks and reserves provide an essential resource for the constructive use of leisure time in positive, healthy outdoor recreation. They provide, too, an essential resource for environmental education, giving the opportunity to observe natural processes at first hand and to appreciate, understand and assess the consequences of man-induced change in the environment. This leads hopefully to a more informed society capable of weighing up the implications of decisions which may affect the environment. These decisions become increasingly significant as the pressures on uncommitted natural resources grow.

8. PROTECTED AREAS AND THEIR VALUE FOR TOURISM

The importance of parks and reserves for tourism is nowhere more evident than in Kenya. Not only are the national parks and reserves a source of national pride, they are the cornerstone of the nation's tourism, an industry of great economic importance to the Kenyan people in both foreign-exchange earning and in employment opportunities.

The same applies in many countries but, without sound planning, there is the danger of tourism and the development it brings destroying the very resource on which it is based.

The mountains and rhododendron forests of Nepal are major attractions which help make tourism the Kingdom's major earner of foreign exchange. Most visitors enjoy the mountains and forests on foot, camping as they go in large parties of porters and other support staff who depend for cooking and heating on the forests which are relatively sparse and slow-growing at the high altitudes. The demand for fuel wood for these tourist parties was destroying much of the forest which is one of the Mt. Everest region's main attractions to tourists, an essential source of fuel wood and building material for the Sherpa people of the region and a stabilising influence in an erosion-prone region. So His Majesty's Government of Nepal has sought to solve the problem by establishing the area as a national park with provision of lodges, campsites with water supply and waste disposal facilities and tight constraints on the use of fuel-wood and encouragement for parties to be self-sufficient in fuel. At the same time, a programme of reforestation is under way with nurseries growing plants from seed drawn from the park itself. In this way, the Nepalese hope to see tourism in Sagarmatha National Park providing continuing economic benefit to the people of the region and to the nation as a whole, without adverse environmental effects.

The same potential for environmental damage exists with tourism in coastal areas, usually through development being undertaken in such close proximity to the coast or with architectural designs so dominant and out of scale with the landscape that the physical developments dominate the beauty of the coast which was the reason for the tourist facility in the first place. Another potential area of tension comes from tourist development, usually catering for overseas tourists, pre-empting prime beaches to the exclusion of the people of the region, with the inevitable and justifiable sense of injustice which results.

There is another very valid reason for not building too close to the coast, especially in an unstable coastal environment, and that is the obvious risk of damage to buildings from erosion. This seems obvious but it has not prevented the expenditure of millions of dollars on tourist development on the Gold Coast of Queensland, Australia, where buildings are so close to an eroding beach that costly and intrusive pipelines had to be built to pump sand from an estuary to an open beach where bulldozers endeavour to re-establish the beach that was the major reason for the development in the first place.

At the Second Pacific Conference on National Parks and Reserves in 1979, the Minister of State for Social Welfare of Fiji (The Hon. Ishwari Majpai) pointed out the impact in his country of the construction of tourist hotels and associated facilities. He quoted the loss of coral from sediment carried from construction of tourist hotels and associated facilities, from construction sites in Pacific Harbour, the construction of man-made islands and, groynes, and the blasting of boat channels or reefs resulting in the "drastic alteration of the equilibrium between sea and shore (rendering) the coastline more vulnerable to erosion in times of tsunamis and storms."

The provision of adequate coastal parks and reserves is a logical and effective means of alleviating many of these problems so that natural resources are protected and available to all and so that costly buildings and other facilities are safeguarded from possible damage.

There is growing interest in "nature tourism," tourism which is based on the enjoyment of natural areas and observation of nature rather than visiting cities. Organized groups from such conservation bodies as the Sierra Club in the United States travel widely, using cities and towns only as arrival and departure points in the countries they visit, and concentrate their time in national parks. Organizations such as the American-based Lindblad company specialize in nature tourism, visiting places which have experienced the minimum of adverse human impact; their schedules include visits to Pacific islands not normally frequented by tourists as well as to the Sub-Antarctic islands and to Antarctica itself.

As the world traveller becomes more and more blasé, so the wish to visit the unspoiled places will grow and the need to establish management which will ensure that the unspoiled places remain so. The parks and reserves concept is designed to provide the means of achieving adequate control. For example, the Lindblad company, like anyone else, must obtain the permission of the New Zealand government to land on Sub-Antarctic island such as the Auckland and Campbell Islands because of their importance as nature reserves. Landings are permitted only under strict conditions and under supervision, the same approach as has been adopted

by the government of Ecuador in preserving the Galapagos National Park, where guided visits protect nature and provide employment at the same time.

Some tourist companies are doing excellent work in nature tourism. One is the Tiger Tops organization operating a lodge and tent camp in the Royal Chitwan National Park in the lowlands of Nepal. This is nature tourism at its best, with the tourist company employing its own naturalists and guides and giving visitors a memorable experience involving travel by four-wheeled drive vehicle, elephant, raft and on foot. A director of this company has said that the confidence his company needs to continue to operate effectively is given by the assurance through national park status that the resource on which the enterprise is based will be protected in perpetuity. This type of operation has a low impact environmentally, is labour intensive and contributes socially and economically to the nation.

9. PROTECTED AREAS AS AN ELEMENT IN THE ENVIRONMENT

For many reasons—environmental, economic and emotional—there is a demonstrable need to identify key natural areas and to give them protection. The establishment of parks and reserves is the technique used most widely today to achieve this. But there is, of course, a cost. There may be direct productive benefit foregone in return for some intangible, potential, long-term benefit. It is impossible, for example, to measure in financial terms the difference between logging a stand of forest or preserving it if it happens to be the habitat of some rare bird. These are judgements that can be made only by the government of the countries concerned but, if the decision is made to forego some immediate economic benefit, and the cost is unreasonably high for the nation concerned, then there is clearly a case for regional or international support to in some way compensate the people who make the immediate sacrifice. On the other hand, there may well be long-term economic benefit in foregoing development, through maintaining other life-support systems by protection of water resources, ensuring a sustained yield from a fishery or from "reselling" the resource for tourism (an American national park superintendent has said of a stand of redwood trees in a national park that "the real dollars in those trees are tourist dollars").

Parks and reserves are not an optional extra but a vital part of the environmental scene. It is significant that in one part of the world where new land is being created—the Netherlands—an increasing proportion of the polders reclaimed from the sea is devoted to endeavouring to re-create nature, through forest and wild-life areas. How much better for those countries where the options are still open to establish protected areas now in advance of potential pressures so that the future is safeguarded.

"Ecodevelopment" is a word that has gained some

currency in recent years. It envisages economic development being undertaken in a manner which is ecologically sensitive, that is compatible with and takes advantage of natural systems. Protected areas need to be seen as a part of ecodevelopment as well as maintaining and enhancing the quality of human life, thus meeting society's needs in the wide variety of ways outlined.

10. PROTECTED AREAS IN A CHANGING WORLD

As protected areas are seen in the context of a changing world, there is a need to look at how the concept may evolve to meet society's changing needs.

The case study sessions illustrate the many and varied experiences, opportunities taken or lost, challenges met and yet to be met, in the work of managers and others involved with protected areas in a changing world, meeting situations very different from that in which the national park concept in the classic Yellowstone mould came into being.

Certainly, the ideal for a national park is still in the concept of a national park under public ownership and management and with only non-consumptive uses such as water, soil and forest conservation and public access for recreation, education and inspiration. This is the concept expressed by Freeman Tilden when he said, "When a tree falls down in a national park, it will lie where it fell. . . . The tree undisturbed will decay and become forest mould and supply the nourishment for future growths. It is nature's way."

But if this ideal is not capable of achievement, then it should not be an "ideal or nothing" situation and the most constructive compromise should seek the maximum preservation achievable in the context of social and economic realities. It is appropriate in this overview paper to comment on a few variations from the ideal which provide realistic approaches in the context in which they have evolved.

Nepal provides two examples of living with the realities of society's needs. In the lowland terai region just north of the border with India, rural dwellers strip the land of the resources they need for survival while, nearby, the grasslands of the Royal Chitwan National Park provide habitat for wildlife that is the basis for a tourist industry and which for 15 days a year is open to villagers in the region for the cutting of thatch for their homes. Today, the park's grasslands are the only local source remaining for this purpose, so their conservation is providing a renewable resource essential for human society. Up in the Himalayan mountain chain, the Sherpa people occupy alpine villages and graze their livestock in high alpine pastures while tourists trek to the Everest base camp. Sagarmatha National Park's management plan recognizes the need for continued development of Sherpa society and avoids any suggestion that the park region should be depopulated as has occurred in some cases; indeed, the park and its planning recognize that Sherpa society and culture are integral to the character and quality of the world's highest national park.

Where other societies continue to live in or use land that has become national park, there is growing recognition of the need to respect traditional activities of the people who for generations have lived, hunted and fished there. So, traditional rights are recognized in Kakadu National Park for the aboriginal people in Australia's Northern Territory and in the protected areas established and being established in the north of the North American continent, the home of Inuit peoples.

In other cases, it is traditional and customary land ownership rights that may be seen as barriers to the Yellowstone concept of public land ownership. Much of the land with potential for protected areas in Melanesia and Polynesia, for example, is held under some form of communal ownership. Here, a realistic approach respects the often-spiritual links of the people with the land and finds other means of achieving protection: by joint management arrangements or by long-term leasing with the owners' representatives having a voice in future management. This has happened with Maori land in New Zealand, part of Urewera National Park being managed under lease from the Tuhoe people while other Maori groups—the Ngati Tuwharetoa people and the Taranaki Maoris—have donated some of their land and retain a voice in management.

Countries with a long history of human occupation and modification have sought to meet the national park concept in other ways. The national parks of England and Wales do no meet the IUCN criteria for a number of reasons; most of the land remains in private ownership and, generally, in some form of pastoral production with whole villages incorporated in the parks. But the mechanism of control on the landscape and visual change, the strict protection of key natural areas, public ownership of the most significant scientific sites and most intensive public use areas all contribute to producing an environment which demonstrates man in harmony with nature. And it does this more successfully than in some other countries where there is strict management in the national parks and seemingly anything goes outside them.

It seems evident that increasingly, constructive compromise will need to be sought with mechanisms that will see protected areas established with the cooperation of local communities and landowners and with management arrangements which meet the needs of communities and owners but are compatible with an acceptable level of preservation of natural and landscape values.

May we take the exciting days which lie ahead in this Congress and convert them into exciting years as the challenges of the next decade are met in finding the most appropriate way in which national parks and other protected areas can better meet society's evolving needs.

Chapter 4
The Afrotropical Realm

Keynote Address: The Afrotropical Realm

Edward S. Ayensu
Smithsonian Institution
Washington, D.C., USA

ABSTRACT. *This paper summarizes the major needs and various responsibilities that lie ahead for both the decision makers and scientific communities who are concerned with protected areas in Africa. Such areas have a much more intensive role to play in the social and economic development of Africa, provided that conservation can be effectively integrated with economic development. There is room for both people and wildlife in this world, in spite of the tremendous pressures to exploit our living resources to the fullest.*

1. INTRODUCTION

Our concern for the well-being of Africa has now reached the stage where we must study the problems of conservation and development very critically, and not allow our emotions to sway us from looking at conservation in the total context of development. This type of an approach will bring us closer to the realities of life in Africa than we have hitherto allowed ourselves to be, and it will also lend more credibility to our efforts.

I say this because, for many years, conservation-oriented societies have pointed their fingers in accusation at development-oriented people who are trying to keep their local economy alive. Both factions should now start to work hand-in-glove to initiate programmes which will make our environmental resources more useful from the standpoints of both conservation and development.

In places where the concerns of wildlife and vegetation have been neglected, the governments and their decision-makers will have to be convinced, in no uncertain terms, that their national parks should be viewed as a major and vital portion of the productive sector of the economy. Financial considerations for conservation may depend on it.

It is not surprising that some of the less-developed countries become quite upset when they are told to preserve their environment in the face of their financial and economic crises. One African diplomat remarked to me a few years ago, when we met at the United Nations in New York, that most developing countries find it difficult to understand why affluent, over-developed countries are religiously preaching that poor countries should maintain large forest reserves. After all, he said, the developed countries have exploited their own environments to the full, and now they are rich. Why cannot the poor nations do the same thing to get rich and meet their balance of payment problems, before they start to talk about conservation? (Ayensu, 1976).

To elaborate on this prevalent, but correctable, viewpoint, I would like to mention a position statement made by the Government of Cameroon in 1971:

> "If it is recognized that the absorption capacity of the world environment has reached or soon will reach the saturation point and that it is important to the industrialized countries to diminish or completely stop unduly exploiting the free natural wealth (water, air and soil), it is not necessary for the developing countries to do the same thing; their imperative need for economic benefits interdict it. The industrialized countries should reduce their own onslaughts against nature to levels much below their historic share, and allow the other countries to utilize for their own benefit, in their turn, the natural availabilities of the air, sea, and land, not to mention the world population" (quoted in Johnson and Johnson, 1977).

To their credit, north temperate countries are, in fact, becoming more enlightened and are afforesting their environments and beginning to mend this situation.

Now, as I have said on several occasions (Ayensu, 1981), there is a certain sense of helplessness, frustration and even collective paranoia among many African specialists about the future of the continent. Such feelings are engendered because of the seeming inability of governments, particularly in the humid tropical regions, to handle the intricate and frustrating problems that confront their societies. I believe that the conservation and scientific communities, especially the biological sector, have a moral obligation to play an effective role in alleviating human suffering, by linking their research efforts to the socio-economic development of society. This pursuit is going to have to involve the manipulation of wildlife resources to some extent, often at a cooperative international level, if it is to be seriously effective and in harmony with the World Conservation Strategy.

One of the major issues confronting Africa is the lack of development of local expertise to assess and address with realism the problems confronting wildlife conservation. One assuredly could praise the persistence and ingenuity of the foreign experts who have, over the years, been persuading African governments to take heed of the concept of conservation, a concept which in itself is known to have been utterly alien to some of our traditional cultural concepts of free land use. However, the intention of these calls to conservation, and to link conservation with development, will become an effective reality only if the local scientific and conservation communities take a bolder initiative to confront their own goverments, appraise them of the situation, and present them with pragmatic and economic reasons why they should consider conservation objectives.

Before the times of national independence, a number of colonial countries in Africa had established some fairly decent forest reserves. These forest reserves were kept in very good repair because of the marshalling of resources by the colonial government. In fact, a number of them were actually designated as strict forest reserves. However, soon after independence, several of these reserves were plundered beyond recognition, so it seems obvious that the philosophy underlying the establishment of these reserves was misunderstood by many of the succeeding governments.

It has recently been asserted (Sabater Pi, 1981) that the Independence of Rio Muni in 1968, to become the Republic of Equatorial Guinea, totally frustrated the conservation measures which had been prepared by officials of the erstwhile Spanish colony. The wildlife, in particular the population of gorilla, is now so heavily exploited that it seems the only solution for their protection is the creation of national parks and reserves under strict control and a certain amount of international supervision. Although the gorilla is totally protected by legislation, it is inferred that actual protection does not exist. There are a number of comparable dilemmas in other African states, including Niger (Newby, pers.

comm.), and it is necessary that effective steps be taken to involve local supervision as well as visiting expertise to conserve these animals in well-maintained parks and reserves.

In order for national parks to have a more prominent role in responding to the challenging needs of society, the first thing to be ensured is that the local people are given due consideration. In this connection, Dr. David Kabala (Zaire) of the Unesco Regional Office in Dakar, Senegal, has made some pertinent observations. Groups of people such as the Pygmies, Masai and Bushmen, and others who exist as hunters and/or gatherers, have often had their culture and customs scoffed at and trampled on, to the extent that they often now "continue, at several places, to live, survive, in the margin of human society as elements of a second order".

The point being made here is that we need to study the ways to humanize the business of conservation, so that conservation will not be opposed to the legal claims of the local populations, especially when it comes to the creation of natural reserves and national parks where some of their rights are *de facto* ignored. If problems such as these can be solved in an equitable atmosphere, it will relieve a great deal of mental oppression and inferiority syndromes; and it will allow all people to respect their own dignity instead of being forced by circumstances beyond their control to reduce themselves to playing *tourist actor* or *curiosity* for the foreign visitors (emphasis Kabala's). Is any country immune to this?

Further to the issue of meeting the demands of people, I might mention that indeed, in for example Ghana, there have been some instances of difficulty in acquiring land for protected areas, and more particularly so when it is stool land where compensation is demanded by trustees (Johnson and Johnson, 1977). The stool system is heavily ingrained in the traditional culture of Ghana and in many other African countries.

2. IDEALS OF THE WORLD CONSERVATION STRATEGY

The World Conservation Strategy revolves around living resource conservation as a means to achieve sustainable development. If the object of development is to provide for social and economic welfare, the object of conservation is to ensure the Earth's capacity to sustain development and to support all life. As noted by Dr. Mostafa Tolba, Executive Director of UNEP, the starting point for the world community must be to meet basic human needs (Tolba, 1982).

A spectrum of deleterious effects is now facing Africa because the escalation of development has unwisely exploited natural resources. These problems essentially are soil erosion, desertification, loss of cropland, pollution, deforestation, destroyed and degraded ecosystems, and the extinction of species and varieties.

The 17 priority issues identified in the World Conservation Strategy all apply to one extent or another to the continent of Africa. Some of the issues, such as erosion, desertification, deforestation, and the lack of conservation-based rural development, are more acute in developing countries than in developed ones, and I therefore would like to concentrate for the most part on them, as they bear on the utilization of parks and reserves to meet society's needs. As much as we need to conserve species, habitats and ecosystems, we must not lose sight of the fact that it must be done in the context of the local human populations. This balanced approach will hopefully call for an end to the adversary atmosphere over the years between environmentalists and national and multinational development programmes.

3. MARGINAL LANDS UTILIZATION

During the past 100 years, mankind has helped to create a great deal of marginal land in Africa. As Dr. Tolba has said, the pressures of subsistence living may force farmers to cultivate marginal lands intensively, year after year. Such poverty-induced environmentally imprudent farming practices will in time turn once-productive soils into barren lands (Tolba, 1982). The people from these degraded lands have often moved to over-crowded cities in search of a livelihood, and they thus were called "ecological refugees" in the Global 2000 study (Ayensu, 1981). In fact, as of today, in North Africa as a whole there is an annual loss of at least 100,000 ha of land due to "desert-creep" (Galal, 1977). It has been recorded also that in the past 20 years, in the region south of Khartoum (Sudan), the acacia scrub zone has marched southward a distance of 90 km.

In July of this year, an immense cloud of hot dust from the Sahara travelled across the Atlantic Ocean and settled over most of Florida, in what scientists called the most significant outbreak of Saharan air to have reached that part of the United States since 1972. The cloud dramatically raised the air pollution level, but it was predicted that the dust would only cause some irritation to people who are not already in the best of health (Anon., 1982). The point here is that the dust cloud was 1,600 km long, from Florida extending eastward over the Atlantic, so it should remind us that, in the long run, as more land becomes converted into marginally productive soil, the more likely it is to contribute to these clouds which wander far from their genesis.

Before we even contemplate encroaching on the remaining forests, it would make for sound business sense to examine the marginal land we have created in various countries and try rapidly to restore a vegetative cover. Since we now do have a collective knowledge of the kinds of trees and shrubs to grow in order to bring the marginal lands into the productive sector of the economy, I am optimistic that we can restore marginal lands while studying and researching the potential of natural areas. I had the pleasure of chairing an international panel for the U.S. National Academy of Sciences which has produced a valuable report on *Firewood*

Crops: Shrub and Tree Species for Energy Production (U.S. National Academy of Sciences, 1980), and I would urge its amalgamation into local and national efforts to restore marginal lands to utility. Local plant species are always preferable to exotic species in replanting schemes, but in many cases the only choice available is the exotic species. A telling observation impinging on this has been made with reference to South Africa (Anon., 1980a): "Try to tell a man on the Cape Flats the evils of alien vegetation when he is using that vegetation for fuel and shelter and see what he thinks of conserving the *fynbos*." The *fynbos*, as we know, is the fastest disappearing land habitat in South Africa, yet it contains the richest flora of the world, with c. 6,000 species, most of which are endemic members of Proteaceae, Ericaceae and Restionceae (Huntley, 1978).

In regard to South Africa's marginal land, a report by the Wildlife Society of Southern Africa (Anon., 1980b) has attempted to explain that "the real cause is the lack of an appreciation of conservation principles by most of the Country's 77,000 white farmers who control 71 percent of the nation's land, while overgrazing in black homelands—where some 33 percent of the country's 25 million people occupy 12 percent of the land area—has reduced many areas to virtual deserts."

One hopes that, using all of the ingenuity and capabilities at the disposal of African governments, measures will continue to deal with the restoration of worthless and marginal land to some measure of productivity and equilibrium with the environment.

These poor lands are spreading up to the very boundaries of many parks and reserves, steadily encroaching as game animals and vegetation are plundered by poverty-stricken individuals for their daily needs. I can only conclude that such parks may in the future no longer be sanctuaries solely for the benefit of the affluent.

4. SOCIETY'S REQUIREMENTS FOR MEAT

Many people in Africa have a protein deficiency problem which even domestic livestock supplies cannot solve, and the people thus have applied more pressure on the bushmeat animals. In numerous countries, the meat of wild animals is actually preferred to that of domesticated species. It has been estimated that 50 percent of the people in Africa south of the Sahara depend on wildlife, including fish, insects and snails, as a source of protein in their diet (Afolayan, 1980). From my own observations based on extensive visits to African markets, this estimate is very conservative.

In Botswana, more than 50 species of wild animals, including elephant, ungulates, rodents, bats and birds, are eaten by rural people (Asibey, 1974). Even so, cattle remains as the backbone of the Botswana national economy and the cattle industry must be expanded due to political and economic pressures (Johnson and Johnson, 1977). It is believed that if huge tracts of land are to be protected for wildlife, then the wildlife will have to show an economic return which can bear some comparison with that of the cattle industry. Rural communities in the southern states of Nigeria derive 20 percent of their animal protein from bushmeat, especially in the coastal areas where cattle are susceptible to tsetse flies and other disease vectors.

It has been estimated that more than 80 percent of the fresh meat consumed in Ghana is bushmeat (Afolayan, 1980). Close to this figure is Asibey's (1974) observation that in some parts of Ghana, as much as 73 percent of locally-produced meat may come from wild animals, which is used as a supplement to domestic animal meat.

Even this selection of figures seems to indicate that if bushmeat could be rationally exploited on a sustained yield basis in Africa, it would lead to an economic justification for wildlife conservation. It also would give stiff competition to poachers and possibly make poaching uneconomical to the tribal villager, as well as the big businessmen and executives who are behind the scenes of illegal hunting in some countries.

5. STUDIES NEEDED IN TROPICAL AFRICA

During the Symposium on the State of Biology in Africa (Ayensu and Marton-Lefevre, 1981), which was held in April 1981 in Accra, Ghana under the auspices of ICSU and Unesco, I and others (Obeng, 1981 and Okali, 1981) called attention to the kinds of urgently required research results that can be obtained from field studies that would benefit the union of conservation and development for economic purposes. I would like to recall these to you for your consideration.

1) Development of a categorical system for including ecological data in epidemiological studies, which health researchers untrained in ecology can easily fill in.
2) The influence of phenology of leaf change on pest infestations.
3) Studies of the irregularity of flowering and fruiting periods in species of economic potential.
4) The life history, growth increments and regeneration capabilities of local tropical trees as related to their management potential for wood products and use in covering marginal land.
5) Ecology of fisheries in rivers and lakes, especially in waters slated for alteration by development; of great importance for human food values (cf. *Tilapia* and Nile perch).
6) Population biology studies of primates, with a view towards conservation and management of primates as a renewable resource.
7) Identification and selection of wild plant and animal species of new potential for medicine and food, coupled with propagation studies in botanical gardens and protected animal centres.
8) Studies of intact natural forests, for example in the Ivory Coast, could yield baseline information which can then be compared with yields in artificial industrial plantings of rubber, oil palm and other crops; in secondary forests resulting from cultivation; and in crops made by traditional agricultural methods.
9) Studies of aquatic systems to determine: whether nitrogen fixation occurs in African running waters; how pollution relates to the fertilization of aquatic ecosystems; and precisely what the vector snails of schistosomes really feed on.
10) The role of forests in rejuvenating soil fertility, especially by the nutrient "pumping" done by trees.
11) Agroforestry studies which can lead to a land production system that is more efficient than shifting cultivation, yet which will incorporate the valuable aspects of the practice of shifting cultivation, such as the use of a tree crop to rejuvenate soils during the fallow phase of the land use cycle. To achieve this objective we need to know much more about the kinds of tree species to be used, structural designs of the forest stands, the treatment for obtaining optimum canopy architecture, and the ideal tree/food crop mixtures.

The use of some zones within parks and other protected areas in which to conduct these studies will become important, because it is not going to be a realistic proposition for the institutions of the humid tropics to duplicate the kinds of highly sophisticated research operations that are taking place in the developed world, such as the building of biotrons which reproduce natural environmental parameters (Ayensu, 1981).

6. REGIONS REQUIRING PROTECTION

The World Conservation Strategy has indicated the priority biogeographical provinces for the establishment of protected areas in Africa at two levels. Priority is given to biogeographical provinces in which national parks and equivalent reserves protect a total area smaller than 1,000 sq km. These include mixed mountain and highland systems with areas spanning the borders of Ethiopia and Sudan, and South Africa and Lesotho, as well as evergreen sclerophyllous (Mediterranean-type) forests in southern Africa. Conservation of the southern African ecosystems has been extensively covered by Huntley (1978).

A higher priority is given to biogeographical provinces with no national parks or equivalent reserves. These high priority areas include warm deserts and semideserts in all, or parts, of Egypt, Libya, Algeria, Mauritania, Sudan, northern Chad, northern Niger and northern Mali. The other major high priority is the lake systems which occur in parts of Kenya, Tanzania, Zambia and

Malawi. For Madagascar, high priority is given to tropical humid forests in the east and the deciduous forests of the south, while the deciduous forests in the west have "ordinary" priority.

Tropical deforestation is a major world concern of today, and the present status of Africa's moist forests has been detailed by Myers (1980), and categorized according to the degree they are being converted to other uses. They have been divided as follows:

A. Areas undergoing broadscale conversion at rapid rates.
1) Much of *West Africa*'s mainly seasonal forests, due to timber exploitation and forest farming.
2) Much of *East Africa*'s relict montane forests, especially the mostly seasonal forests in northern Tanzania, due to timber exploitation, fuelwood cutting, and forest farming. Many endemics at the subspecies level occur here. The distribution of protected areas in relation to the needs of biotic community conservation in eastern Africa has been discussed in detail by Lamprey (1975).
3) Much of *Madagascar*'s lowland and upland rain forests, due to forest farming and timber exploitation.
B. Areas undergoing moderate conversion at intermediate rates.
1) Parts of the lowland and upland, seasonal and humid forests of *Cameroon*, due to timber exploitation and forest farming.
C. Areas apparently undergoing little change.
1) Much of the *Zaire Basin* comprising Gabon, Congo, and Zaire.

The southwestern lowland forests of Ivory Coast are part of a postulated Pleistocene refuge with exceptionally rich stocks of endemic mammals (Myers, 1980). Sadly, much forest in central and southern Ivory Coast has already been destroyed, and experts advise that with the current rate of deforestation we may see the total elimination of Ivory Coast's exploitable forests by 1985 (Ayensu, 1981).

Cameroon represents perhaps one of the richest floras in Africa and is an important centre of diversity and the so-called Pleistocene refugia. This is especially true along the border of Gabon. In Gabon, the extensive oil, manganese and uranium deposits present little incentive to forest exploitation, and there is not much population pressure due to the comparatively few people who reside there. In the People's Republic of Congo there are diverse and species-rich forests particularly in the northwest. Fortunately, in the Congo the population pressure on the forests is slight.

The valuable and high priority *lake system* resource has received some beneficial attention recently from the Government of Malawi. Malawi, with its population of 5 million, has one of the densest populations of any eastern African country. A special problem is the rising pressure on its freshwater fish resources (Anstey, pers. comm.), due to a higher intensity of fishing with im-

proved techniques and the impact of agricultural and industrial developments with their attendant pesticides, drainage, and pulp mill effluents.

We are thus doubly fortunate that, in December 1980, Malawi established the first deep water lake biotic reserve in Africa. This new Lake Malawi National Park is 6,868 ha in area. Africa is a land of superlatives, and Lake Malawi has its share; the lake has the highest rate of endemism among its fishes of any lake in the world, as well as the highest number of fish species, about 400 (mostly in the Family Cichlidae), of any lake in the world. We must congratulate Malawi for the creation of this first park in Africa declared primarily for inland aquatic flora and fauna.

7. INTERNATIONAL COOPERATION

As noted in the World Conservation Strategy, some living resources such as migratory species can be conserved only by international action. I believe that the African Convention for the Conservation of Nature and Natural Resources could become of great service to such action. The African Convention, which took effect as of July 1969, provides that "the Contracting States shall cooperate . . . whenever any national measure is likely to affect the natural resources of any other state" (Article 16). The Organization of African Unity (OAU) is the depository of the diplomatic instrument of this Convention, which was signed in 1968 by 38 African heads of state and government (Burhenne, 1970).

The African Convention is a regional agreement which covers many of the items we are concerned with in regard to the utilization of national parks and protected areas, such as floral and faunal resources, protected species, conservation areas, research, conservation education, and development plans.

Preceding the CITES Convention of 1973 by five years, the African Convention has an Annex List of Protected Species divided into Class A, species which shall be totally protected through the entire territory of the Contracting States, and Class B, species which shall be totally protected, but may be hunted, killed, captured or collected under special authorization granted by the competent authority. This Annex List is reminiscent of the Appendix I and II arrangement of CITES.

The conservation-oriented principles embodied in the African Convention could be of great utility in preserving species and habitats which cross international boundaries, and enhance ecosystem equilibrium in the process.

There are other glaring situations which call for the attention of international assistance, some of which I would now like to mention.

Cameroon. If international assistance could be given to finance material and personnel in the initial stages, it will encourage the Government to create marine parks where undisturbed mangrove and estuarine communities could thrive (Allo, pers. comm.).

Nile River. Kassas (1971) has urged that an international network of well-managed parks and reserves should be set up to save the tropical territories in the complex Nile River ecosystem. Work could proceed on the ecological relationships of pests to man, as well as upgrading the maintenance of the vegetation which is essential to the well being of the game reserves.

Tanzania. With regard to the international sharing of parks, Johnson and Johnson (1977) have reported an opinion that, in a sense, Tanzania is subsidizing Kenya's tourist industry by offering such prime attractions as Serengeti and Ngorongoro within striking distances, while bearing an unfair share of the costs of keeping such wilderness staffed with wardens and poaching patrols, as well as meeting the pressures for stringing the wildlands ranch fences.

Sahara and Sahel. Desertification often transcends national boundaries, and its arrest may well involve joint action by two or more countries (Tolba, 1982). In the harsh habitats of the desert and subdesert, antelopes such as the addax, oryx and gazelles are good resources for converting the coarse grasses into excellent meat without destroying the environment upon which they subsist, in contrast to destructive goats and cattle (Curry-Lindahl, 1974). It is difficult to establish efficient nature reserves for nomadic antelopes which wander great distances in irregular patterns following the paths of the erratic rainfall. The best way to save the wild desert herbivores would be inter-African cooperation, chiefly by Mauritania, Mali, Niger and Chad, with regard to strict hunting regulations, and education and information programmes.

Wildlife is the only natural resource that thrives in the arid lands of Sahara and most of the Sahel, since the land is mostly unsuitable for agriculture or permanent stock-rearing. But there is currently a lack of willingness to look at park and nature reserves wildlife as a useful, exploitable natural resource for meat, hides, hunting and tourism. Not least among the people who need to be convinced of the natural benefits of maintaining and eventually using the wildlife resources of dry, marginal lands are the major international funding and development agencies (e.g. World Bank, European Development Fund, U.S. AID), whose policies and money virtually dictate the way in which Sahelian development is going (Newby, pers. comm.).

There is a very urgent need for pilot projects to demonstrate once and for all that wildlife can be a valid alternative source of income, and may well be the best form of land use in the long run, considering the environmental factors of desertification and capricious climate. It has been noted that if we are to succeed in the Sahel, we must get away from the concept of traditional national parks and reserves, and into the realms of natural resource management units and multiple purpose land-use zoning (see also Myers, 1972).

As John Newby has expressed it, protected areas must become dynamic in nature, capable of changing their objectives with an evolving community of natural resources, and responding to the current requirements of the human population. From the beginning, it must be emphasized that the animals could be grown as a harvestable crop, rather than the practice of isolating these vanishing animals in open-air museums which are increasingly more threatened by poaching and habitat destruction.

To begin action, we need to create good protected areas in zones where wildlife still exists in viable quantities. Such key zones include (Newby, pers. comm.):

1) the Majabat of Mauritania and Mali;
2) the Air/Termit zone of Niger;
3) the Hoggar and surrounding Tassilis of Algeria;
4) the Ouadi Rime-Ouadi Achim area in Central Chad.

Norman Myers (1973, 1981a) has been an advocate of the concept that surplus (excess) wild animals in national parks should be sacrificed to provide food, hides, and beneficial revenue, and also of the concept of game ranching. In the Sahara and Sahel, this could certainly be explored from an international viewpoint in an attempt to solve the problems of this starving part of the African land.

8. FINAL STATEMENT

I have attempted to mention, in the foregoing discussions, some of the major needs and various responsibilities that lie ahead for both the decision makers and scientific communities who are concerned with national parks and other protected areas in Africa.

I believe that parks and reserves have a much more important role to play in the social and economic development of Africa. The protected habitats with their abundant species of wildlife and plants can be wisely utilized while at the same time protecting endangered species, if they are in ecosystems which are properly managed as a whole. The challenges are many to integrate conservation with economic development, and increased international cooperation is urgently required. More revenues from tourism, more abundant supplies of bushmeat, more adaptable management units, more protection from poachers, and more trained staff and financial assistance, are needs which press us from all angles. The rising tide of local human population threatens to engulf many parks, and must be given due respect while we try to correct the environmental imbalance caused by over-intensive local agriculture which causes land to change from viable to marginal in sight of the protected areas.

Regardless of what we contribute to the shaping of conservation policies and actions for Africa, let us remember that the welfare of the human populations should not be an isolated sector of our deliberations. There is room for both people and wildlife in this world, in spite of the tremendous pressures to exploit our living resources to the fullest.

9. Acknowledgements

I am grateful for the enthusiastic response which I received from my call for comments on the key issues facing African national parks and other protected areas. The information sent by many colleagues has allowed for a much broader picture of the commonality of problems and concerns in parks and reserves, and I wish to thank in particular the following for sharing their viewpoints with me: G. Achimbi (Mbalmayo, Cameroon), A.A. Allo (Garoua, Cameroon), J. Andriamampianina (Antananarivo, Madagascar), D.G. Anstey (Lilongwe, Malawi), V.S. Balinga (Yaounde, Cameroon), G.F.T. Child (Causeway, Zimbabwe), A. Doyen (Dakar, Senegal), A.R. Dupuy (Dakar, Senegal), J. Harrison (Kew, England), B.J. Huntley (Pretoria, South Africa), M. Kabala (Dakar, Senegal), W.J. Lusigi (Nairobi, Kenya), J.A. McNeely (Gland, Switzerland), N. Myers (Nairobi, Kenya), J. Newby (Niamey, Niger), B.A. Ola-Adams (Ibadan, Nigeria). I am also most grateful to my colleague Dr. Robert A. DeFillipps whose invaluable assistance helped me in the formulation of this presentation and to Mr. Marsha Cox for technical assistance.

The Impact of the Unexpected on the Uganda National Parks

F. Kayanja and I. Douglas-Hamilton

ABSTRACT. *Protected areas are subject to unexpected factors. Rinderpest and sleeping sickness epidemics, the compression of elephants in national parks, and internal security have all had major impacts. In Uganda, the National Parks were institutionalized under a Board of Trustees and were managed at a high standard, tourism—largely due to the national parks—was the country's second largest foreign-exchange earner. But the 1972 military coup brought catastrophy to the parks; tourism collapsed, the country's economy was ruined, and law and order broke down. Poaching by well-armed military personnel and government officials led to tragic reductions in wildlife populations, especially affecting elephants and rhinos. Following the war of liberation—which was itself another tragic episode for the parks—investigations by the Uganda Institute of Ecology found, rather miraculously, that the rangers were still at their posts and the National Parks organization remained intact with a tradition of dedication. For the future, the importance of training dedicated wildlife managers and educating a sympathetic public is stressed, if National Parks are to survive in Africa through the periods of turbulence that may lie ahead.*

1. INTRODUCTION

It is a truism to say that the best laid plans are often upset by unexpected events and, in the field of conservation, sudden changes may imperil species and ecosystems. Some unexpected events would be beyond the power of humanity to control, such as an asteroid colliding with the earth, which has recently been suggested as the cause of the Cretaceous extinction of the dinosaurs (Alvarez *et al.*, 1981). On a more imaginable scale, events like the progressive desiccation of the Sahelian zone, or sudden outbreaks of disease, such as the rinderpest pandemic which swept through Africa at the end of the nineteenth century (Simon, 1962), find no precedents or stereo-typed solutions. When, for example, sleeping sickness in the early years of the twentieth century, transmitted by the tsetse flies *Glossina* spp., desimated human populations, it was combated by colonial authorities in several areas by enforced migrations of people away from the tsetse zones, thus creating ideal conditions for recovery of wildlife populations.

With the foundation of National Parks, unexpected problems of island zoogeography arose. Often arbitrarily defined, the parks became surrounded by increasing human populations, preventing species from dispersing, and in some cases compressing them to high densities within the "safe" protected areas. Throughout the 1960s, one of the dominant national park problems in Africa was "the elephant problem". At that time, protected elephant populations had increased in density, both by natural increase and by compression to the point where they were destroying woodlands faster than they could regenerate, transforming landscapes and, in some instances, threatening other species, the diversity of the ecosystem, and even their own survival (Laws, 1970).

Among the most significant unexpected events of the last decade which have appeared on the continent are the severe economic problems, the breakdowns in political stability, the proliferation of automatic weapons and their use on wildlife. This paper, using events in the Uganda National Parks as an example, considers the need for flexibility in planning, including rapid decisive responses to crises and disaster, to enable protected areas to survive through turbulent times.

2. EARLY HISTORY OF UGANDA NATIONAL PARKS

The Colonial Governments, especially those in anglophone Africa, were appreciative of the value of wildlife and established, in effect, what was a conservation strategy (with little variation from state to state) (Kayanja, 1982). This strategy was exported from the developed world to the developing world. It was based on the establishment of national parks, an idealistic concept in which the protection of animals and plants was paramount, and game reserves, where the degree of protection varied and other forms of human use were tolerated. Outside of the parks, game laws restricted legal hunting to those who could pay for licenses.

The national parks in Uganda were established as a parastatal organization, run by an independent Board of Trustees with full legal and administrative control. The first two parks, the Murchison Falls National Park of 3860 sq km in the Western Boundary, and the Queen Elizabeth National Park of 1978 sq km in the south-west of the country, were gazetted by the Colonial Government in 1952. (They were later renamed Kabalega and Rwenzori, respectively, in the Amin era, but reverted to their original names in 1982). Both were areas of outstanding natural beauty. Murchison Falls National Park includes the swiftest flowing reaches of the Nile as it rushes 100 km past palm-studded islands before plunging over the Murchison Falls in three shattering cascades. Queen Elizabeth National Park is on the edge of Lakes Edward and George, linked by the Kazinga Channel, and includes over 100 overlapping craters, the result of a huge volcanic explosion in the past. Both areas possessed dense wildlife populations that included elephant, buffalo, hippo, waterbuck, bushbuck, reedbuck, hartebeeste, and kob. Murchison also had black rhino, giraffe and some of the most spectacular crocodile concentrations in Africa. White rhino were successfully introduced there from a threatened population west of the Nile, at Ajai.

Kidepo National Park, of 1442 sq km in the Karamoja District of the extreme north-east, was gazetted in 1962 after independence by Act of Parliament. It is considered by many to be the most beautiful of the three parks, containing two valleys of parkland savanna framed by jagged ranges of mountains. It contained most of the plains game normally associated with East Africa.

In the 1950s and 1960s, the viability of the national parks was reinforced by a rapidly expanding tourist industry. Katete (1968), the first African Director of Parks, stated, "Currently, the Murchison Falls Park attracts no less than 70% of the country's tourist business, valued at $9 million annually". The number of visitors entering the Murchison Falls Park rose from 7,500 in 1954 to 58,739 in 1970. Between 1960 and 1964, tourist revenues grew at a rate of 24.4% in Uganda, faster than either Kenya or Tanzania. On the basis of this trend, predictions were tentatively made that revenues from tourism could reach US $28 million by 1975 and US $85 million by 1980 (Laws, et al., 1975).

During the period immediately before and after independence, the Park's senior staff were mainly expatriates, who initiated a training programme for their African successors. The new African wardens learned their trade at first in the field on patrols. Later, the College of African Wildlife Management in Tanzania was used for further training. The National Parks developed as a strong institution, largely self-sufficient, with high standards of management and discipline (Willock, 1964). A strong emphasis was laid down that the parks should be of benefit to local people, and part of the gate revenues were paid to the local governments. The Uganda Parks also pioneered educational visits by Ugandan people of all ages, and in the 1950s were the first to encourage scientific research as a basis for managing the wildlife. Control of poaching was originally introduced with a sensibility for local feelings; persuasion was attempted and as few arrests as possible were made, especially in the Queen Elizabeth National Park, where fishing villages were long established within the park boundaries (Poppleton, pers. comm.).

A major problem in the Uganda Parks at that time was caused, in part, by the very effectiveness of the protection afforded to the animals. All three national parks suffered from an over-concentration of elephants. Laws, et. al., (1975), have traced the history of a distinct population of elephants in Murchison Falls National Park; i.e. those living on the South Bank of the Nile. This area, originally inhabited by people, was cleared in 1912 by government action to counter a severe sleeping sickness epidemic, thus creating an empty area, part of which was eventually to become a national park. By 1965, the elephants had increased until they had devastated the habitat to the point where their own reproductive success was lowered through malnutrition. In effect, recruitment and calf survival were so poor that the elephant population had actually entered a long, drawn-out population decline, which was masked by the fact that more elephants continued to immigrate to escape external harassment. The lowered reproductive rate which in former times may have acted as a natural regulating mechanism was unable to lower the density. Laws and his co-workers recommended culling and warned that in its absence the elephants could become virtually extinct (Laws, et al., 1970). Their work was based on an initial 300 elephants shot for scientific research, followed by 2000 cropped as part of a density-reducing experiment. They recommended that a further 4500 elephants should be cropped over a 4-year period (Laws, et al., 1975).

In summary, in the 1960s a well-ordered network of national parks existed, with firm political support, a sound economic basis, and an ecological problem of too many elephants. Planning was based on projections of long-term steady economic growth of the tourist trade.

3. THE ARRIVAL OF THE UNEXPECTED

Then, in 1971, with the military coup of Idi Amin, the parks suffered an unexpected impact of catastrophic proportions. Tourism collapsed and was banned in 1973, the country's economy was ruined, and law and order steadily deteriorated. With the dramatic world rise in the price of ivory, high government officials and security officers began to poach elephants in the national parks. Often senior officials would provide local hunters with automatic rifles so that they could bring in the ivory, rhino horn and meat. It was difficult or impossible for park wardens and rangers to cope with this situation, which had never been remotely anticipated.

From 1973 to 1976, the Uganda Institute of Ecology, in collaboration with expatriate scientists, made regular aerial surveys of the country; over the three year period, elephant estimates in the Murchison Falls Park dropped from 14,300 to 2,000, while in Rwenzori they declined from 2,700 to 700 (Eltringham and Malpas, 1980). The magnitude of these declines were confirmed in independent counts. Following this, no more surveys were allowed until the defeat of Amin's regime.

During the war itself, Amin's retreating troops occupied and passed through Paraa, the headquarters of Murchison Falls Park. When they left, they took at least 11 vehicles, boats, and many smaller articles of value. Two of the three hotels in the park were thoroughly looted and damaged; at the new hotel of Pakuba, soldiers systematically broke most of the windows and mirrors. The rangers fled into the bush. After the soldiers had gone, in a period of anarchy, local villagers looted whatever items the soldiers had left. By the end of 1979, Paraa was a gutted ruin. Record ivory had been stolen from the museum. Launches, riddled with bullets, lay half-sunk at their moorings, no vehicles were left, the workshops were emptied of tools, radios were smashed, the hotel and staff quarters had lost all furniture, blankets, linen, crockery, cutlery, the hotel had a gaping hole in the roof caused by the explosion of a rifle grenade, through which the rain poured.

Queen Elizabeth and Kidepo National Parks suffered less. Rangers had protected the buildings and neither of the hotels were looted, but the wildlife in Queen Elizabeth suffered heavy losses as the armies passed through (Van Orsdol, 1979).

Around all three parks there was an enormous proliferation of automatic rifles in the hands of poachers, ex-military personnel, villagers, and tribesmen, who were better armed than the rangers.

4. RESUMPTION OF MONITORING IN 1980

Faced with these conditions, the Uganda National Parks organization took its first steps towards rehabilitation. In 1980, the Uganda Institute of Ecology, in collaboration with scientists from WWF/IUCN, resumed monitoring by aerial survey. Both Queen Elizabeth and Murchison

Falls Parks were surveyed, using sampling techniques for all species, and total counting for elephants. Almost every species except Uganda kob showed a marked decline. Neither black nor white rhino were seen in Murchison, but ranger's reports indicated that a handful lingered on. The elephant populations had collapsed further. Only 150 were counted in the open areas of Queen Elizabeth, although 250 were seen just across the border in Zaire. In the north of Murchison, 1200 elephants remained out of a 1973 population of 5000, but in the isolated southern section the decline was even more catastrophic—only 160 remained out of a population that had numbered 9000 seven years previously (Anon., 1980c). It was from this group that five years earlier a cull of 4000 had been proposed (Laws, *et al.*, 1975). The prediction that the elephants would be reduced to virtual extinction (Laws, *et al.*, 1970) had come about, but for entirely different reasons.

Furthermore, there were clear signs that poaching was still in progress. Heavy gunfire could be heard almost every week from the park headquarters of Paraa, Chobe and Mweya, and fresh carcasses littered the elephant's range (Malpas, *et al.*, 1980).

5. POST-WAR CONDITIONS

The end of the liberation war had not led to any easing of the difficulties and hardship under which the National Park's staff laboured. Uniforms had not been replaced for years and were in rags. What little transport remained in the three parks was in poor running condition, spares were unobtainable locally, and there was a chronic lack of foreign exchange throughout the country. Fuel was often unavailable. Global inflation and recession added to the impact of the war, and helped to perpetuate economic dislocation. Food, which everyone could afford in the 1960s, became too expensive to buy, and in the Karamoja district in the north of the country, severe famine set in. Worst of all, the rangers were often unpaid; by May 1980 their pay was six months overdue, and it was impossible to feed them adequately.

In Kidepo, two rangers' children died of starvation, and yet the resident waterbuck and hartebeeste still lived in safety in and around the rangers' camp. In Murchison and Queen Elizabeth, in addition to the ivory poaching, commercial meat poachers were active, and found a ready market, since domestic stock meat was so expensive that the villagers could not afford to buy it. A few of the rangers supplemented their incomes by poaching, but by and large they remained at their stations and carried out their duties. Finally, the parks were cut off from headquarters in Kampala, with no radio communication and no aerial support for anti-poaching; travel outside the parks in the country at large was insecure, as the roads continued to be infested with bandits or armed factions.

6. FIRST STEPS TO REHABILITATION

It was clear at this stage that there was an immediate urgency to control the poaching and begin the rehabilitation of the parks. Unless steps were taken to reinforce the parks, the elephants and other wildlife would become virtually extinct.

At this point the Ministry of Wildlife and Tourism approached UNDP, but it took time for the project to be drafted, and still longer before it could be implemented. In the meantime the Board of Trustees accepted an offer from expatriate volunteers to provide an airplane and vehicle and to assist in anti-poaching. The national parks organization arranged the necessary clearances, and anti-poaching operations began on a shoe-string. A member of the EEC delegation on a visit to Murchison Falls witnessed the destruction of elephants and was impressed by the energetic efforts of the rangers to counter it. When the EEC were approached by government for vehicles for the parks they readily consented.

Conservation organizations were also approached and, although some concern existed in the minds of certain advisers that funds spent in Uganda would be wasted, the view prevailed that emergency assistance was justified. Frankfurt Zoological Society sent three land-rovers—the first new vehicles to arrive since the war—and they were put to immediate use.

For a year, the parks were run on a hand to mouth basis, and on the few donations coming in from outside. The WWF loaned a vehicle, bought and delivered the most vital spare parts, and ordered 500 uniforms and the first tactical VHF radios for anti-poaching. The Frankfurt Zoological Society provided further uniforms, paid for repairs to two aircraft, and ordered a 7-ton Bedford lorry. The African Wildlife Leadership Foundation provided offices in Nairobi to coordinate these activities, and a further Land-rover. The Mayor Foundation and a private benefactor, the late J.A. Mull, through the National Geographic Society, ordered a new Cessna 185 aircraft specially equipped for anti-poaching, to be loaned at running cost to the national parks. This was later replaced by a Rheim's Rocket donated by the People's Trust for Endangered Species. With the extra transport, it was again possible to provide food to the rangers, and with the gradual stabilization of government, the rangers were paid regularly. Fuel shortages were overcome through oodwill of Shell Petroleum Company, whose management made sure that parks did not go short. These improvements had a positive effect on the ranger force and wardens in the field, who felt that the outside world was supporting them. By the end of 1980, elephant poaching in Murchison Falls had greatly decreased.

7. UNDP AND EEC EMERGENCY AID

In this way, voluntary conservation aid from NGOs and individuals filled a vital gap from April 1980 to March 1981, while plans submitted to UNDP and EEC for more substantial aid were coming to fruition. These further proposals were justified in terms of economics: safeguarding an economic resource from destruction against the day when it could once more start making money. Under these programmes, UNDP helped to create an anti-poaching force and engaged the services of a Chief Technical Adviser who advised on Park's planning and administration and, together with an anti-poaching specialist, assisted in the formation, equipping, training and operations of the anti-poaching unit. The EEC complemented UNDP by providing 10 land-rovers, 3 lorries, 2 pick-ups, and spares. Once both programmes were underway and operating successfully, both agencies increased their support, UNDP by providing extra funds and food through the World Food Programme and EEC by recruiting the services of an engineer to rehabilitate the mechanical workshops, restore broken equipment and properly maintain the new vehicles.

It is interesting to note that in Uganda, both international aid agencies were geared to major disaster relief with respect to the famine in Karamoja. This meant that they were capable of responding swiftly and flexibly to government requests for an anti-poaching project, by drawing on emergency funds.

It may seem strange that in a country that was suffering from acute problems of security and famine, that tourism and wildife should receive a high priority in the government's recovery programme. But one of the most encouraging factors for conservationists in Uganda is the strong political support for national parks. This was due in part to the immense contribution that game-viewing tourism had formerly made to the foreign exchange earnings of the country, but also to a national pride in these unique and beautiful areas.

8. MAKING ANTI-POACHING WORK

In all three parks, the nature of poaching gangs had changed greatly since the first days of the parks. Formerly, poachers were almost entirely spearmen, and ranger patrols were equipped with one or two Greener shotguns at the most. Now, in Queen Elizabeth and Murchison, each poaching gang might number between five and thirty men and up to four would be armed with automatic rifles. In Kidepo, up to 35 armed uniformed men might be encountered from across the border in Sudan, with scores of porters.

The nature of anti-poaching tactics had to change. Rangers were now armed with automatic rifles. Some were supplied by the army, and the number of rifles steadily built up as more were captured from the poachers. Anti-poaching was organized on the principle of centrally controlled forces reacting to information from

NATIONAL PARKS, CONSERVATION, AND DEVELOPMENT

the peripheries. Mobile units were based at each park HQ, with patrols in the field operating under the direction of the Chief Park Warden and the anti-poaching specialist. The success of these operations depended on the quality and flow of information coming in, good communications, and mobility.

There were three main sources of information on poachers' whereabouts and activities. First, throughout each park were outposts. Some of these were not occupied all the time, but all were convenient for gathering information and as staging posts for patrols. Each post when manned contained three to four men who made reconnaissance patrols. Any gunshots heard, vultures seen, or tracks of poachers, were communicated to headquarter at the first opportunity. In the open country of Murchison, gunshots, under the right conditions, can be heard a distance of 15 km or more.

Second, once all the aircraft arrived, they too were stationed in each park, and made frequent patrols looking for vultures, dead animals, vehicle tracks, smoke and poachers' camps. An effective method at Murchison was to fly at night along the Nile when meat-drying fires were located. Frequently, aerial patrolling was combined with administrative visits to outposts.

Third, some of the most valuable information came from informers in the surrounding villages, who detailed the intentions of poachers and often commented on the success or failure of poaching expeditions. Information on exact dates, times, places and names of poachers, together with numbers, types and hiding places of illegal guns, proved invaluable.

Successful operations were improved by first class communications. VHF sets were installed to link ranger patrols, vehicles and airplanes, and proved highly effective. A long-range HF system was also installed, which linked all the parks with Kampala headquarters, greatly speeded up supplies and economized on unnecessary trips to town.

While all patrolling by rangers was done on foot, mobility was increased by delivering patrols by vehicle near to the area to be covered. A new series of airstrips was built, some in remote areas, and five rangers at a time could be carried by air and deposited with their equipment. Rangers were also supplied by air drops.

9. MONITORING THE EFFECTIVENESS OF THE RECOVERY PROGRAMME

By October 1982, the UNDP/EEC National Parks Project has been running for eighteen months. Although there are still many problems of supply and logistics, especially involving fuel, definite progress has been made. In all three parks there are hotels open for tourists. Launches have been repaired, and visitors can once again enjoy the river trips on the Kazinga Channel in Queen Elizabeth, or up the Nile to the Falls in Murchison. Ferries are operational across the Nile at Paraa, and the mechanical workshops have been overhauled

and restocked with most needed tools and spares. Limited road maintenance has been carried out. The parks still have a long way to go to regain their former status, but a start has been made. The trend in tourism has shown a slight upwards turn; Murchison Falls received virtually no visitors in 1979, but 2563 came from July 1980 to June 1981, and 7879 from July 1981 to June 1982, which corresponds to the 1954 level of 7500.

In Queen Elizabeth and Murchison the project has also succeeded in greatly decreasing poaching, especially of elephants. In Murchison, where efforts were first concentrated, success can be measured in terms of elephants found dead and numbers of guns recovered.

	Elephants found dead	Guns recovered
1980	120	14
1981	13	43
1982 (Jan.-Sept.)	1	23

In the first half of 1980, 112 elephants were reported killed, with the heaviest mortality occurring between April and June. It was also during this period that the first intensified anti-poaching operations were initiated. Poaching activity tailed off in the latter half of the year, with eight elephants reported killed. During this period, the number of army and militia road blocks on access roads to the parks also increased, making it more difficult to transport illegal ivory. In the first half of 1981, reported elephant mortality increased to 12, an increase associated with a new influx of loose guns available around the park (though the type recovered tended to be the Kalashnikov of the new army rather than the G3 of former times). By the end of June 1981, the situation was under control and only two more elephant carcasses have been reported since then. Queen Elizabeth has effected similar measures and no new elephant carcasses have been reported in the last 12 months. Loose rifles continue to be recovered in and around both parks, and in this way the park rangers assist the civil authority in restoring law and order to the country.

In the Kidepo National Park, a different situation existed. The elephant population was still relatively intact, with approximately 400 animals within the park, occasionally augmented by others from outside. An IUCN/WWF aerial survey took place in April 1981. The age structure of the population appeared much healthier than that of Kabalega, with a high proportion of young animals. However, a ratio of 27 dead to 73 live elephants was also recorded, which indicated a high recent mortality. This was supported by the record of elephant mortality reported by the Chief Park Wardens as follows:

	Dead elephants
1978	3
1979	10
1980	25
1981	38
1982 (Jan.-Sept.)	12

The main cause of mortality was increased poaching by armed men from across the border with Sudan. On numerous occasions, these were identified as elements of the Sudanese army stationed at a camp known as Bira, on the border of the park. The poaching was done both for meat and ivory. The poachers were aggressive and opened fire immediately on ranger patrols and any parks aircraft that came within range.

Despite protest from the Uganda government and the conservation bodies, the shooting still continued. Then, after a serious incident in October 1981 in which a ranger patrol was attacked by Sudanese soldiers in platoon strength and the National Geographic aircraft was hit by three bullets, stronger diplomatic protests were made. These led to an investigation on the Sudanese side and a termination of these incursions. Although this has considerably reduced the elephant poaching, other well-armed poachers continue to operate in Kidepo, and the ranger force is still stretched to its limits. This is particularly so in view of renewed shortages of food and fuel and continued logistical problems of supplying this remote park, which lies in an as yet insecure area.

A second series of aerial counts made in 1982 supports the view that the status of the elephants is much better than two years previously. In Kidepo, 420 elephants were counted, which showed no significant change from the previous year. In Murchison 980 elephants were recorded north of the Nile, which may represent a slight drop from the estimate of 1200 two years earlier; however, the elephants were mainly found in areas of dense vegetation, which obscured visibility. In the open areas of Queen Elizabeth, over 428 elephants were counted, a considerable increase on the 150 recorded in 1980. Evidently, they have emerged from the forest or have immigrated from Zaire. Furthermore, both Murchison and Queen Elizabeth are experiencing a massive regeneration of woody vegetation, triggered by the decreased elephant density. The recovery of habitat provides ideal conditions for the recovery of elephant populations, should their security continue to be guaranteed.

10. TRAINING

There is no doubt that the survival of the parks through the difficult years, and the beginning of their recovery, has been due to high standards of training in the past. The current UNDP project has trained 67 new rangers, who were selected for physical fitness by a competitive cross-country run.

There is, however, a shortage of wardens, and the present intention of the organization is to upgrade the calibre by recruiting from universities, while at the same time selecting men with an aptitude and liking for field work. Opportunities for training abroad are being sought. The vocational attitude of wardens and other officers will always be of crucial importance to the parks. Since their work is of international importance, recognition from the international conservation community can reinforce their motivation, and give an extra pride in their job.

11. CONCLUSION

The Uganda National Parks have survived a period of catastrophe, largely due to "islands of dedication" within the organization, and through the rapid and flexible aid which this has generated since the liberation war. It may be concluded more generally, in the continent of Africa, that political turbulence, civil strife, war, and failing economies, are ecological unpredictables of great impact, affecting the future survival of national parks and protected areas (cf. Lusigi, this volume). Unwavering international support for these institutions is vital in such times of adversity and instability.

What then will be the unexpected impacts of the future? We may hope and plan for rational economic development, for a self-sufficient tourist trade which earns foreign exchange for the benefit of the country, but if for any reason the economic scenario should fail, can we dare to hope that other unexpected factors can help to conserve Africa's natural resources, especially the national parks and the wildlife they contain?

Lusigi has suggested that many of the western-imported conservation ideas are alien to Africa, but human attitudes can change rapidly. Curiosity about other life forms is intrinsic to every child, and the success of wildlife clubs in Uganda, Kenya and elsewhere, shows the potential for presenting conservation in an "emotionally and intellectually satisfying" form, which could in time gain hold as a "conservation ethic".

Perhaps the new unexpected factor will be a growing enlightenment about the value of conservation, fostered through the universities, and through such movements as the wildlife clubs. Certainly, in Uganda, even now parties of students are visiting the parks in large numbers. Broad public and political support is essential if the wildlife is to survive the uncertain years that lie ahead for the continent of Africa.

Amboseli National Park: Human Values and the Conservation of a Savanna Ecosystem

David Western
Animal Research and Conservation Centre
Nairobi, Kenya

ABSTRACT. *The Amboseli ecosystem in Southern Kenya typifies the problems of conserving large migratory mammal communities in Africa. The changing pastoral herdsmen exerted increasing pressures on wildlife because the animals contributed nothing to the human economy, even though the value of wildlife nationally through tourism was considerable. A 15-year programme is described which has attempted to create an integrated use of the ecosystem by including the landowners in the benefits from the national park, thereby justifying continued animal migrations beyond its boundaries.*

1. INTRODUCTION

Amboseli National Park, which lies within an ecosystem typical of the open savanna habitats of eastern Africa, epitomizes the problems of conserving the spectacular large mammal communities found there. Like many other parks, Amboseli's wildlife migrates seasonally beyond the confines of its boundaries,—in this case onto land owned by Maasai pastoralists. Traditionally subsistence herders, the Maasai are fast changing in both their lifestyle and in their willingness to accept wildlife onto their lands, to which they have recently acquired legal title (Western, 1976). Within the park, which they used traditionally and communally until 1977, tourism has increased greatly over the past twenty years to the point of threatening both the welfare of certain wildlife and Amboseli's aesthetic appeal (Western and Henry, 1979). These factors raise a number of questions about the future of national parks in Africa. How can wildlife and wild places be conserved adequately when changing land usage, changing attitudes and dwindling open spaces compress large mammals into the confines of small parks, which are subject to use and harassment by increasing

numbers of visitors? To what extent will growing human numbers beyond park boundaries create demands for land within it? And how can the luxury of land devoted exclusively for wildlife be justified in the face of such pressures and claims?

Such problems are faced by nearly all African savanna parks and reserves (Myers, 1972). What is unique about Amboseli is that its policies directly address the conflict of man and wildlife within the ecosystem. The novelty of the approach lies in its efforts to reconcile conservation and alternative uses of land throughout the ecosystem by making landowners within it the recipients of economic and social benefits created by the national park. In this way the deficiencies in the ecological design of the park boundaries imposed by political constraints can potentially be made good by incentives (Western and Ssemakula, 1981). This principle has contributed directly to Kenya's national wildlife policies and to its development plans for wildlife conservation and tourism. The programme has been underway in Amboseli since 1977 and gives us some insight into the value of this approach to national parks development, the planning involved and the problems and shortcomings that arise. It is necessary to stress the need to view national parks within a broad ecological and human framework, rather than as biological islands— a view that arises from a purely preservationist approach to them.

2. THE AMBOSELI AREA

Amboseli (Fig. 1) is named after a dry lake basin of some 1000 sq km situated directly north of Kilimanjaro and along the Tanzania-Kenya border. The area has a rainfall of less than 400 mm annually and is dominated by open grasslands and lightly bushed savanna. The basin, fed by permanent springs from Kilimanjaro, is the only source of permanent water in the region. Wildlife migrants, including elephant, buffalo, zebra, wildebeest and gazelle, move over some 5000 sq km during the rains each year, then retreat to the permanent water sources of the Amboseli basin (Western, 1975). The ecosystem includes the entire seasonal range.

3. TRADITIONAL ECOLOGY

Man has long played a role in shaping the savanna landscapes and large mammal populations of eastern Africa. Over the last 3000 years or more, fire and the activities of domestic stock have contributed to the expansion of grasslands and of migratory plains animals (Bell, 1971). We cannot be entirely sure of the balance of domestic and wildlife numbers prior to the turn of the century, but based on the accounts of early explorers, we do know that both coexisted almost everywhere. Recent work suggests that pastoral livestock used the savannas in ways ecologically similar to wildlife migrants and that during droughts, the herdsmen relied on hunting to sustain themselves until their herds recovered (Western, in press).

The earliest conservation efforts did not seek to disrupt the prevailing human land practices. One of the first sanctuaries, the Southern Reserve, was intended first, to protect the wildlife herds from hunting, especially elephant, which were rapidly being depleted, and second, to guarantee the Maasai inalienable land rights in the face of encroachment by white farmers. The result was a hands-off policy which retained the traditional balance of pastoralist and wildlife in southern Maasailand long after changes were underway elsewhere.

But by the late 1930s efforts had been made throughout East Africa to establish national parks as a way of protecting wildlife. The reasons for conserving wildlife were thought by the colonial governments of the day to be justifiable—the preservation of "our" natural heritage, aesthetic appeal, scientific and educational values, the preservation of a diverse array of earth's creatures, and the economic potential of the parks—but the effect was to deprive nomads of the lands they had been guaranteed under earlier agreements. Instead, the land was devoted to wildlife under alien control. During this century, game laws have made wildlife all but redundant to pastoralists, and have increased the economic burden on them.

A few prime wildlife areas, Amboseli among them, had large pastoral populations whose traditional rights could not be ignored. Here national reserves were established, anticipating that they would soon become parks. The 3260 sq km Amboseli National Reserve, created in 1947 (the same year in which the first national park, Nairobi, was gazetted), was intended to protect its migratory wildlife from hunting. Though signaling

the intentions of the Kenya National Parks who administered it, the reserve acknowledged meanwhile the *status quo* between wildlife and pastoralists, who continued to use it. The boundaries, apart from circumscribing a known wildlife concentration centred around the Amboseli basin, were arbitrary.

Over the next two decades changes in the ecology of the Maasai gradually altered their traditional balance with wildlife. Previously both disease and lack of water had limited domestic stock, but veterinary improvements and water schemes subsequently allowed the rapid increase of cattle at the expense of wildlife (Western, in press; Prole, 1967). With independence approaching, the colonial government did not wish to alienate the Maasai by establishing a national park. Instead, in 1961 the administration of Amboseli was handed over to the Kajiado County Council, which represented a 20,000 sq km district of Maasailand, in the hope that local responsibility would create greater sympathy for the reserve, which was by then popular with tourists. Soon afterwards the Kajiado Council negotiated with the local Maasai of Amboseli to set aside a 78 sq km stock-free area which would protect the Council's wildlife assets.

During the 1960s a number of factors focussed national and international attention on Amboseli. Tourism grew rapidly following Kenya's independence in 1964 and by 1968 revenues from Amboseli amounted to some 75 percent of the Kajiado Council's annual income, giving them for the first time a tangible economic interest in the park. However, the Council had little expertise in managing the reserve, which suffered progressive deterioration. As livestock herds grew and increased their use of the basin swamps on which wildlife depended each dry season, and around which game viewing was centred, there were increasing demands from conservationists for full national park protection.

Partly to protect themselves from a new wave of agricultural encroachment into Maasailand after independence, and partly to stave off the gathering prospects of a national park, the local Maasai lobbied strongly for land tenure which would guarantee their rights to the entire region, including the Amboseli basin. They argued that revenues from tourism went only to the Council, over 150 km away, and contributed nothing to their own welfare, even though they alone suffered the costs of competition with wildlife. While wildlife had traditionally served as their "second cattle" during droughts, it no longer had any value to them. Why then should they lose their traditional dry season grazing grounds to benefit the Council, Government and the tourist? Their own answer was to seek exclusive land rights and to spear much of the wildlife, especially rhinos (Western and Sindiyo, 1972).

4. BACKGROUND STUDIES

By the late 1960s the conflicting claims on Amboseli and its highly publicized ecological deterioration created pressure on the Council and Government to resolve its future. However, little was known about the ecology of the ecosystem—the numbers of livestock and wildlife, their annual migrations, and their dependence on the Amboseli basin—or about the changes that were altering the traditional attitudes of the Maasai. To answer these questions I began a study of the Amboseli ecosystem in 1967.

It was learned that both wildlife and livestock migrated in essentially the same fashion between wet and dry season ranges (Fig. 2), and for essentially the same reasons. Permanent water, limited previously to the Amboseli swamps, restricted the dry season range of the migrants and therefore their carrying capacity. Water development schemes begun in the 1940s had increased the dry season range and carrying capacity of livestock, but some areas remained inaccessible.

The dispersal of wildlife over some 5000 sq km during the rainy season created insurmountable obstacles to conserving the entire ecosystem; some 6000 Maasai, 48,000 cattle and 18,000 sheep and goats depended on the same area and could not be relocated elsewhere. However, over 80 percent of the wildlife migrants did concentrate each dry season around the 600 sq km of the basin. Though this small area was the logical site to conserve, it would be inadequate as a self-sustaining national park; it was calculated that the large herbivore population would decline by 40 - 50 percent if confined permanently to the basin (Western, 1975). Similarly, if the Maasai were deprived of the basin's water and swamps, their livestock would decline by a similar level. Seasonal migrations were essential to maintain the present levels of both wildlife and livestock.

Tourism was also causing ecological changes. The growth of tourism (Fig. 3) had been largely fortuitous and the national parks were ill-prepared to cope with the management issues it created. The problem was perhaps more acute in Amboseli than elsewhere in Kenya—the combined result of heavy visitor traffic, fragile terrain and lax planning by the Council. Upwards of 30 vehicles (over one third of those in the park daily) might be located around a single predator; off-road driving was apparently destroying to the vegetation; only a small portion of the potential viewing areas was being used; rangers and drive-couriers were ill-trained in visitor interpretation and were willing to harass animals in order to obtain larger tips. The result was a severe stress on sensitive species such as the cheetah; unnecessary habitat destruction; deteriorating visitor satisfaction; and a complete lack of planning to remedy the situation, let alone to accommodate further tourism at that time increasing by about 25 percent annually (Henry, undated; Western, 1975; Mitchell, undated). At the same time, revenues from tourism are an important factor in the Kenyan economy, and particularly in earning foreign exchange; by the early 1970s Kenya was earning $60 million a year in hard currency from tourism (Republic of Kenya, 1976).

5. LAND USE OPTIONS

Table 1 summarizes a 1973 calculation of the economic potential of various options for land use in the Amboseli ecosystem. The arid region will support little apart from ranching and wildlife exploitation, and from the national point of view the most economically profitable of these was wildlife exploitation, which in 1972 grossed 166 times the cash income of livestock, or, more realistically, over twice the subsistence value to the pastoralist. Projecting tourism to full development, it was shown that wildlife would earn 18 times the annual income of a fully developed and commercialized beef economy (Western and Thresher, 1973).

However, the existing land claims by the Maasai and the lack of alternative areas for their relocation made it morally indefensible, legally difficult and practically impossible to deny their continued presence.

Moreover, the economic potential from exclusive wildlife use was only a little less within the 600 sq km basin area than over the entire ecosystem, quite simply because visitor capacity, no less than wildlife capacity, was limited by the dry season range (Western, 1975). To secure the future of wildlife in Amboseli and its economic potential in the face of changing Maasai land use and attitudes, it was necessary at least to guarantee the viability of the basin. The expansion of the park further afield would have been politically impossible and would have accomplished little.

Provided the lands beyond the basin remained accessible to wildlife, the total revenues from shared use of the ecosystem with livestock would in fact be greater than exclusive wildlife usage. Nonetheless, some fundamental questions were posed by this option: how stable would a basin park be if its wildlife depended on the whims of Maasai landowners beyond its boundaries? How would future changes among the Maasai affect the accessibility of the dispersal area? Who was to benefit from the tourist revenues—the Kenya Government, the County Council or the local Maasai? To what extent would the Maasai remain subsistence herders? Would they become more or less receptive to wildlife migrants on their land if they moved into the cash economy and could make use of the economic potential offered them?

The first plan for Amboseli placed before the Kajiado Council in 1968 proposed that 600 sq km of the basin should become a Maasai park—that is, with all the legal status of a national park, but vested in the Council. However, political pressures and vacillation within the Council denied that option and led to a stalemate. Meanwhile the attempts of the local Maasai to gain title to the entire region and to preempt a park were gaining momentum. To resolve the crisis, the central government stepped in and essentially forced the proposed plan on the Council, with the proviso that Amboseli would become a national park under government jurisdiction. Political pressures by the Amboseli Maasai forced the government to reduce the park to 488 sq km. Elements of revenue-sharing were retained: 160 ha of land surrounding the tourist lodge would remain Council land within the park and guarantee them its future income; the Council would also receive a portion of the gate receipts each year. The central government, for its part, would absorb both the developmental and recurrent costs of the park. The local Maasai would receive title to the remainder of the land in the ecosystem which would be cooperatively owned as group ranches. Once in possession of land title, they would be eligible for livestock development loans, although their real intent was more the security of land than its commercial development. The Presidential Decree that declared Amboseli a national park in 1974 recognized that the Maasai could not be displaced from the basin without alternative water and forage; it therefore guaranteed them new sources in exchange, and plans were made to deliver water from the swamps to the surrounding lands. Portions of the swamp were later detached from the park to give the Maasai adequate dry season pasture.

From the government's perspective the new park guaranteed the survival of a national wildlife asset, and one pivotal to the tourist trade. The revenue sharing arrangement with the Council earned their good will, ensured that other county councils would not be dissuaded from wildlife conservation and made money available for developments in Kajiado district as a whole.

But despite these progressive steps, the crux of the original plan lay ignored; those who bore the costs of supporting Amboseli's wildlife and who would determine its fate—the traditional Maasai occupants—were not included in its profits. Donor aid was essential to finance the pipeline which would give water to the Maasai in exchange for the national park, and the Kenyan Ministry of Tourism and Wildlife sought funds through a second phase of the World Bank's livestock loan, and from the New York Zoological Society. Both agencies financed the pipeline, making it a condition that the Maasai landowners in the dispersal zones benefit from the park.

The principle underlying the expanded plans was to show that in return for continued access to the entire ecosystem, Amboseli's wildlife could contribute economically to the landowers through a grazing compensation fee (to cover their livestock losses to wildlife migrants), through hunting and cropping on their land, and by accommodating tourist campsites, and possibly lodges. Non-monetary benefits could also be obtained through employment, and social amenities such as a school and a hospital, which would service park staff. Without access to the dispersal areas wildlife numbers would be halved and the projected net revenue would be reduced from $1.2 million to $0.8 million (Fig. 4). The net monetary gain of the park from continued use of the group ranches would thus be approximately $0.5 million, and the benefits from the park to the Maasai would ensure them an income 85 percent greater than they could obtain from livestock alone after full commercial development (Western and Thresher, 1973).

The Kenya Government's reformulation of wildlife policy in 1975, and the Wildlife Act of 1976, drew heavily on the Amboseli model as a way to justify wildlife on lands beyond national park boundaries. Articles were included in both documents which recognized and made possible such an approach. "Dispersal areas" were seen as a way to achieve this, and the legal basis for accomplishing it was set up. The National Parks and Game Department were amalgamated into the Wildlife Conservation and Management Department and charged with carrying out such an integrated approach.

If these new concepts required new legislation and administration to help justify wildlife in developing Kenya, they also called for planning and investment on an unprecedented scale. An interministerial planning committee (which among others included Tourism and Wildlife, Finance and Planning, Lands, Agriculture, Water, and outside consultants) drew up the detailed plans. Amboseli once again was the working model providing the foundation for a comprehensive proposal for wildlife and tourism development. Amboseli, and two national reserves, Mara and Samburu, would be developed as pivotal links on tourist circuits. Wildlife in each case would contribute to rural development in the dispersal zones. Tourism growth would be balanced with conservation objectives, and the economic benefits it brought locally. To achieve this would mean investment in improved viewing circuits within and beyond the parks, training programmes for guides, and the relocation of much of the park infrastructure, including the headquarters, outside the park boundaries where it would provide benefits to the rural community as well as to park staff. Amboseli would receive $6 million under the programme. The total national plan amounted to $37.5 million and is currently financed jointly by a World Bank loan and by the Kenya Government. It includes funding for a wildlife training institute, a wildlife planning unit, added anti-poaching funds, wildlife education and a number of studies to determine how wildlife and tourism can be better managed (Republic of Kenya, 1976).

6. SUCCESSES AND SHORTCOMINGS

Perhaps the single most successful aspect of the plan has been the demonstration to the Maasai ranchers that they can benefit from the park economically. Over the intervening years since the plan was drawn up, the Maasai have shifted increasingly to a cash economy as their per capita livestock holdings have fallen—the result of drought losses and a larger human population. In the process they have turned to the park as a source of employment, revenue, and social services. An annual compensation fee of $30,000 covers the losses they sustain in accommodating the park's wildlife; the first revenues they received have helped them build a local boarding school. In addition, the group ranchers have established a wildlife committee which meets monthly with the park warden, Bob Oguya, to discuss matters of mutual concern, interest and benefit. They have successfully negotiated a plan to relocate the tourist campsite on the group ranch where it adds to the ranchers' wildlife income, and helps reduce the pressure of visitors in the park. Firewood and road gravel, which are collected from the ranch, earn the owners additional income, and reduce the impact on the park. Recently the group ranch selected a full-time employee to work closely with the park in ensuring further benefits for the local Maasai.

The newly completed headquarters is located at the south-eastern corner of the park where it interferes minimally with wildlife and tourism, and where it provides a local community centre with a school and medical facilities. It should help reduce the congestion at the present headquarters of Ol Tukai, which is located in the central viewing area. The Wildlife Planning Unit, established to carry out national planning for parks, reserves and wildlife activities that require careful integration, has completed a detailed management plan which guides the implementation of the Amboseli programme. Finally, the network of visitor viewing tracts is partially complete, and where the standards have been maintained, has greatly improved the visitors' use of the area and reduced the impact caused by off-road driving.

A direct measure of the improved circumstances in Amboseli since 1977 can be gauged by the increased numbers of wildlife in the ecosystem and especially the park. Elephant had declined from over 600 in the 1960s to less than 480 by 1977, reflecting the poaching levels country-wide. Their numbers have since increased to over 620, with few animals poached. Rhino, which numbered over 150 in the 1950s, were virtually exterminated by 1977, with only 8 remaining, largely the result of spearing by the Maasai to show their political dissatisfaction with their prospects in Amboseli. Since then, the population has increased to 14 (Fig. 5) (Western, 1982). Not a single animal has been killed, despite the continuing losses elsewhere in Kenya. Other species, especially zebra and wildebeest, have increased substantially due to the exodus of domestic stock, which fomerly made up 60 percent of the liveweight of the basin's animals. Wildlife has also redistributed more uniformly throughout the park following the removal of Maasai settlements. The increased numbers and wider distribution should allow a higher visitor capacity for a given level of impact, as originally envisaged.

If hunting is also begun again shortly, following the temporary national ban imposed in 1977, the income of the ranchers from wildlife in the dispersal areas and from tourist revenues should increase substantially in the near future.

Despite the evident successes in Amboseli, there have been notable shortcomings in the implementation of plans. The water scheme that enabled the Maasai to relinquish their dependence on Amboseli was completed in 1977, but it has proved defective in design and deficient in cost-effectiveness. As a result the Maasai have frequently been forced to re-enter the park for water. Scheduled modifications should overcome the deficiencies. It is only then that the willingness of the Maasai to stay out during hard times will be demonstrated. Other aspects of the plan have yet to be implemented. For example, a project which would divert part of the deeper swamp outside the park and create new dry-season grazing for the Maasai has not yet begun, even though it was originally a contractual obligation of funding from the New York Zoological Society. Perhaps the gravest shortcomings arise in the implementation of plans for visitor management, and a continued reluctance by central government to include the Maasai as fully as they might in the benefits of Amboseli.

Standards of road design and building, visitor management and the management of the Maasai water scheme fall short of present needs. Ol Tukai has grown into an urban sprawl and there seems little hope of improvements in the near future. Part of the reason lies in the failure of the Ministry of Tourism and Wildlife to secure a management agreement with the Kajiado Council. The Council's only interest in Ol Tukai lies in its profits, and the national parks have no jurisdiction to manage and improve it. It takes time to build up the necessary foundation for so complex a plan as that called for in Amboseli; in the meantime it may be necessary to limit the number of visitors until those capabilities are developed.

7. OUTLOOK ON A LARGER WORLD

We can anticipate in the next century that no more than one or two percent of the earth's surface will be designated as national parks, an amount woefully inadequate to conserve more than a small portion of life's diversity. But it may not be necessary to rely on parks alone to serve as repositories of nature. Most parks could support but a fraction of their present biological diversity if their wildlife were barricaded from the lands surrounding them. Ecologists tend to argue for more park land and better ecological design of boundaries as a solution, ignoring the political constraints that denied more area at the outset. But there lies a greater and potentially more rewarding challenge barely addressed so far. Most of the earth's surface will remain rural, a checkerboard of farmland, ranchland, and forest, with between them interstices of roughland, wasteland, wilderness and the nondescript which shifts from one to another over time. We know that wildlife can survive in such areas. Indeed, despite its development, most wildlife does survive in the rural lands of North America, rather than within the diminutive parks.

The reason is that it benefits people to preserve wildlife in these areas, and there is a lesson here that may be widely applicable as much of the world elsewhere undergoes demographic and economic changes. The challenge that faces conservation is to ensure that wildlife does survive beyond the parks by demonstrating that its benefits there exceed its costs. Through time the balance between the two will change, as will our patterns of land use. We need to develop the principles that will justify wildlife in terms that match our changing values, for this alone will be the passport of wildlife across the confines of park boundaries.

Acknowledgements

The research and planning aspects of Amboseli's conservation owe much to numerous individuals and supporting institutions. Daniel Sindiyo, Warden of Amboseli in the late 1960s and currently Director of the Wildlife Conservation and Management Department (WCMD) contributed greatly to the formulation of the integrated principles outlined here, as did various Maasai in Amboseli, especially Parashino Ole Purdul and Kerenkol Ole Musa. Frank Mitchell contributed extensively to the economic justifications for Amboseli. Officers of the Ministry of Tourism and Wildlife, especialy the Permanent Secretaries and their staff, have been largely responsible for the acceptance of the plans. Staff of WCMD have contributed much to the successes in Amboseli, especially the Wardens Joe Kioko and Bob Oguya. Without their tactful handling of the human issues, little would have been accomplished. The New York Zoological Society has supported the programme both through the Kenya Government, and through support of my own studies.

Table 1. Gross revenues from existing and potential uses of Amboseli as calculated in 1973. Assumptions for the calculations are detailed in the development plans for Amboseli

| | $ Gross Return | |
	Park	Ecosystem
Total Wildlife 1972	1,200,000	+1,202,710
Total livestock 1972 (Cash Returns only)	3,000	4,200
Subsistence value livestock 1972	199,188	597,562
Wildlife potential (no livestock)	6,560,000	+8,030,000
Commercial livestock potential (no wildlife)	69,300	445,930
Combined wildlife and commercial livestock potential	6,560,000	8,285,580

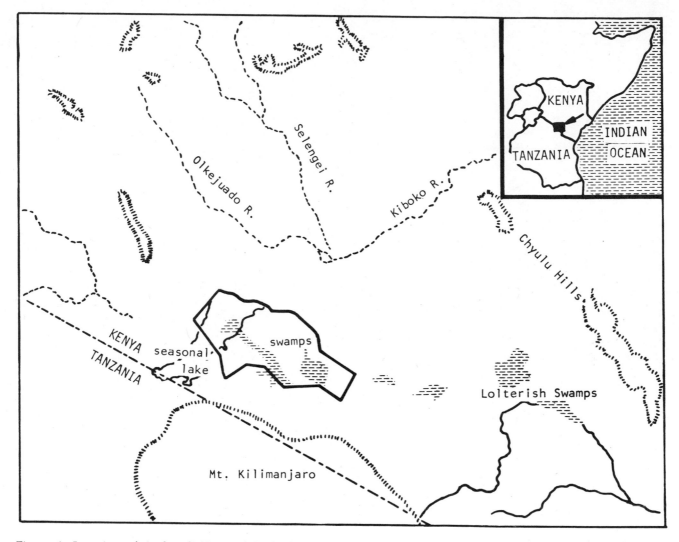

Figure 1. Location of Amboseli National Park (heavy line) and dispersal areas of the ecosystem.

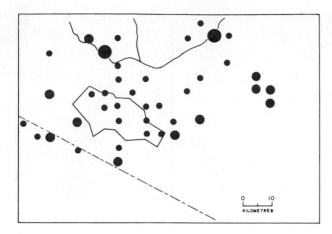

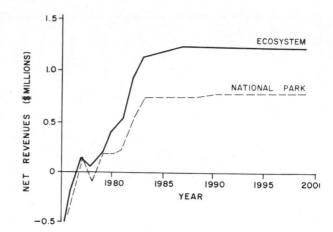

Figure 3. Growth of visitor numbers to Amboseli over the last thirty years.

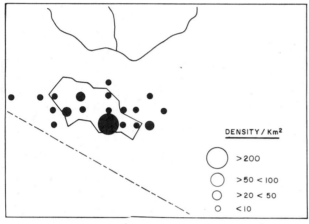

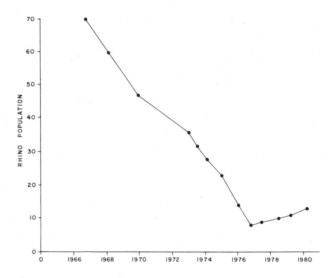

Figure 2. Seasonal movement patterns of wildebeeste, a characteristic migrant of the ecosystem. The dispersal phase occurs during the rains when water is widespread, the concentration phase in the dry season when water is restricted within the confines of the National Park.

Figure 5. Decline of the Amboseli rhino population reflects the trends throughout Eastern Africa but shows a marked turnaround in 1977 once the Park began to contribute to the welfare of the surrounding landowners (Western, 1982). ▽

Figure 4. Difference in projected net income depending on whether wildlife has access to the larger ecosystem or is confined to the National Park boundaries (see text for explanation).

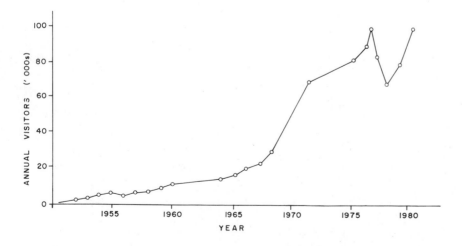

NATIONAL PARKS, CONSERVATION, AND DEVELOPMENT

Kenya's Experience in Establishing Coastal and Marine Protected Areas

Fred Pertet
Wildlife Conservation and Management Department
Nairobi, Kenya

ABSTRACT. *Kenya has long been a leader in nature conservation, and this holds true on the marine side as well as the terrestrial; the country has two marine national parks and two marine national reserves, with the first marine park in tropical Africa established at Malindi-Watamu in 1968. A series of other areas are also proposed for establishment in the future. These areas have a number of attractions and benefits to local people, including tourism and protection of breeding grounds of important species. In addition, the country has also instituted measures to control fishing, regulate shell collection and control pollution.*

1. INTRODUCTION

Kenya is one of the most active members in nature conservation in the world today. For instance, Kenya was among the first countries to launch the World Conservation Strategy in early 1980. In addition, Kenya was represented on UNEP's *ad hoc* Expert Group on the Draft World Charter for Nature convened by the UNEP Executive Director in August 1982 in Nairobi and hosted the United Nations University (UNU) Workshop in Mombasa. In practical terms, Kenya boasts 14 national parks and 24 national reserves totalling 43,615 sq km—including 25,396 sq km in parks and 18,075 sq km in reserves—or nearly 7.5% of the total area of Kenya.

The long catalogue of conservation areas includes two Marine National Parks and two Marine National Reserves which are the basis of the topic under discussion: the lessons learned by Kenya in establishing the coastal and marine protected areas.

UNEP (1980) defines "coastal zone" as "the maximum distance to which the influence of certain selected ecological factors extend landward and seaward from the seashore." In Kenya this zone may be said to extend for about 40 km inland.

The country has a shoreline of about 500 km, stretching from the Somalia border in the north to the Tanzania border in the south. The coastline is simple, without many indentations, a factor that hampers the establishment of harbours; in fact, only a few areas are suitable for harbours, that is, the Lamu archipelago and the Mombasa Island. However, the shoreline is endowed with magnificent beaches coupled with a chain of coral gardens which are the origin of Kenya's marine national parks and reserves (Fig. 1). The four marine national parks and reserves include Kiunga in the north and Kisite/Mpunguti in the south; between these two extremes are the Malindi and Watamu national parks and Malindi/Watamu national reserves complex.

1.1. Coastal vegetation

The coastal vegetation is influenced by a long history of human settlement and cultivation dating as far back as the fifteenth century, the Egyptians, Chinese, Greeks, and Portuguese all had trade links with the coast. However, the Arabs had the greatest influence, having settled for several hundred years before the British displaced them at the turn of the nineteenth century. The most characteristic vegetation is the coastal evergreen bushland, consisting of relatively dense stands of evergreen shrubs mixed with scattered trees. It is often interrupted by areas of cultivation. Characteristic woody plants are *Crossopterix febrifuga*, *Piliostigma thonningii*, *Lantana camara*, *Rhus natalensis* and *Grewia glandulosa*. It is not an important habitat for wildlife except for monkeys, birds and rodents.

The coastal palm woodlands are dominated by *Hyphaene* and *Borsassus* palms and occur on open grassland and on groundwater sites. Small but significant palm thickets are located northwest of the Lake Kenyatta Settlement Scheme and on the south coast around Ramisi.

The coastal rain forest is localized and restricted in distribution. It is characterized by such species as *Sterculia*, *Chlorophora* and *Memecylon*. Drier woodlands at the coast include stands of *Cynometra*, *Manilkara* and *Afzelia*, of *Brachlaena* and *Diospyros*, and of *Brachystegia* and *Julbernardia*. The *Brachystegia* woodland is the northernmost extension of the "miombo" woodlands that form a major biotic community of Tanzania and Zambia and is rapidly disappearing in Kenya.

The mangrove communities are dominated by *Rhizophora mucronata* and a few other species with similar ecology (Moomaw, 1960). The mangroves favour tidal creeks and lagoons and often require fresh water and water-logged mud. Major stands are to be found in the Lamu archipelago including the islands of Patte and Manda and also in the Vanga-Funze complex near the Tanzania border.

Finally, temporary pans of impeded drainage ("Ziwas") are common in the coast province and are characteristic of black cotton soils or where the water table is high. The common grass species here are *Echinochloa haploclada*, *Setaria sphacelata* and *Sorghum verticilliflorum*.

1.2. Drainage

The main drainage lines of the coast consist of the Tana, Sabaki and Ramisi rivers. There are however a few seasonal rivers and some which flow during the times of heavy flooding.

1.3. Climate

The coast has a humid tropical climate. The rainfall is largely associated with the monsoonal winds in combination with the orographic effects of the coastal hills and convection over the hot, dry hinterland immediately to the west. The south-east monsoon brings the long rains in April, May and June when more than half the annual precipitation usually falls. The long rains end in June in the north (Lamu) and in July in Mombasa (Moomaw, 1960). However, the intensity and reliability of rainfall decreases from the south northwards.

It is important to emphasize that this monsoonal climatic effect gives the coast of Kenya a unique character not repeated anywhere else on the Western Indian Ocean region. For instance, the west coast of Madagascar has a dry savanna climate which is different from that occuring on the Kenya coast due to lack of the monsoonal influence. Conversely, the east coast of Madagascar has a tropical marine climate because of the monsoonal influence. Because of the wider significance of the climatic influence on the Kenya coast, the pro-

tected areas should therefore be separated into coastal and marine zones (Fig. 1). Zone 1 includes, from the north, Boni and Dodori National Reserves and in the south the Shimba Hills National Park. Similarly the marine zone comprises of Kiunga, Malindi/Watamu and Kisite/Mpunguti. From the conservation point of view each park or reserve has its own interesting features.

2. THE NEED PERCEIVED IN KENYA FOR COASTAL AND MARINE PROTECTED AREAS

The objective of the Malindi/Watamu National Park was to conserve in the national interest, a representative feature of the coral reefs. Kiunga Marine National Reserve was the last one to be gazetted in 1973. The coastal areas include Boni and Dodori National Reserves and the Shimba Hills National Park.

2.1. Marine zone

Under this zone are three marine parks and reserves:

2.1.1. Malindi/Watamu Park/Reserve comprises a core park surrounded by a marine reserve which together occupy an area of about 240 sq km. The complex represents outstanding examples of coral beaches, tidal pools, coral gardens, fringing reefs and mangrove creeks protected within the boundaries of the park/reserve system (see Fig. 1).

2.1.2. Kisite and Mpunguti National Park. This system of parks is situated in the south coast and unlike Malindi and Watamu, functions to conserve marine life, including a group of waterless off-shore islands that are a home for an assemblage of pelagic birds.

2.1.3. Kiunga Marine National Reserve. Kiunga is situated on the northernmost point adjacent to the Dodori National Reserve close to the Somali border. Its function is to safeguard the important large nesting colonies of migratory seabirds on the off-shore islands and the superb and as yet unspoiled coral reefs. In addition, the mangrove thickets fringing the marine reserve harbour a wealth of birds, and the few creeks in the reserve are frequented by the rare dugong. Kiunga is the least developed of the marine parks/reserves.

2.2. Coastal zone

This zone is represented by one national park and two national reserves:

2.2.1. Dodori National Reserve. Dodori National Reserve is named after one of the major creek systems in north-eastern Lamu district. It extends to the Somali border on the northern side, whereas on the eastern seaward side it is contiguous with the Kiunga Marine Reserve. To the north it adjoins the Boni National Reserve.

Its main function is to conserve a major breeding ground for topi of the east Lamu population and to preserve an area of scenic beauty and important avian wildlife including pelicans and coastal waterfowl. Other than aerial surveys and boundary demarcation, little formal development has taken place but plans are in hand. The reserve has an area of about 850 sq km.

2.2.2. Boni National Reserve. The Boni National Reserve covers 1240 sq km in the north-eastern area of Garissa District adjacent to the Somali border. It is centred on the extensive Boni Forest which is the only ground water forest in Kenya. Boni provides a major sanctuary habitat for the east Lamu and southern Garissa elephant herds. Ecologically it it virtually unexplored; it was possible that *Apalis chariessa*, thought to be extinct, may still survive in this area.

3. PROPOSALS FOR NEW COASTAL AND MARINE RESERVES

In addition to the existing coastal and marine parks, the Wildlife Conservation and Management Department (WCMD) is keen on the protection of some critical areas on the coast before they are completely destroyed. These include:

3.1. The proposed Ras Tenewi Coastal Zone National Park

The present marine parks in Kenya do not protect the terrestrial features adjacent to them. The proposed Ras Tenewi Park (Fig. 1) is therefore intended to bridge this gap by combining a marine component with a terrestrial one. It is situated north of the Tana River delta on a headland south of the Lamu archipelago. The new reserve has an area of about 350 sq km divided into 105 sq km of land and 245 sq km of water. Apart from the extensive coral reefs, the reserve encompasses several rocky islands which are important nesting sites for migratory seabirds primarily terns and gulls. The sooty gull, *larus hemprichii*, breeds here as well as various terns - the noddy *Anous stolidus*, roseatte *Sternus dougallii* and white-checked, *S. repnessa* (Von Someren, 1981). In addition the area is an important breeding ground for the marine turtles which have become threatened throughout their range in the world, including Kenya. Three species are known to occur, the olive ridley *Lepidochelys olivacea*, the green *Chelonia mydas* and the hawksbill, *Eretmochelys imbricata*. In fact, at the World Conference on Sea Turtles Conservation in 1979, in the only recommendation that referred to the East African coast, the Ras Tenewi area was selected for establishment of a coastal zone marine sanctuary for sea turtles (IUCN,

1979). Dugong, whose presumed distribution along the Kenya coast ranges between Malindi and Kiunga, is supposed to occur in the Tana River estuary close by. Other tourist attractions of the Ras Tenewi area include historic ruins and tomb at Mwana as well as concentrations of elephant and topi *Damaliscus korrigum*.

3.2. The proposed Diani Marine National Park Complex

Comprising of Similani and Kaya Pungu in the north and Chale Island in the south, these are the only areas which would conserve marine caves with their large colonies of bats. The caves are of great cultural and religous significance to the fishermen, as evidenced by sites selected for practising witchcraft.

Similani is particularly famous for its caves, which harbour several thousand bats; the two most important species in terms of biomas and size are the large fruit bat, *Rousettus aegypticus* and the insect eating bat, *Hipposideros commersoni*. All in all, there are about 8-9 species of resident and migrant bats whose periodicity is closely linked with the movement and concentration of insects. For instance, large numbers of bats arrive at the Similani Caves around March/April and September/October which is the peak breeding season for insects. However, as soon as the insects start to die off or to move out at the onset of the long rains in the intervening months, the bats follow suit.

At the moment the bat populations are free from contamination with toxins because there are no insecticides being used on the Kenya coast. However, their main threat comes from the loss of critical habitat which is being destroyed by the enterpreneurs who buy land from the local people to build beach houses. The Chale islands are well protected and, like Kiunga, are an important nesting site for several species of birds.

4. NATIONAL MONUMENTS AND THREATENED HABITATS

These fall under different types of management, including the Trustees of the National Museums of Kenya, the Forest Department and those areas under the protection of the local people for cultural or religious purposes, but without proper legal status. The Tana River Delta has no protection and is seriously threatened.

4.1. Areas under the Trustees of the National Museum

These are represented by three important museums. The Fort Jesus, Gedi Ruins and Lamu museums are situated at Mombasa, Malindi and Lamu respectively. The three museums are of immense archaelogical interest as they contain valuable fossils and other scientific materials of past civilizations.

Other significant historical sites under the National Museum along the coast are located at Kipungani, Matondoni, Mpeketoni, Ndau, Kiwaiyu, Shanga, Tokosa, Siyu, Jumbaba, Mtwana and Muarani. All these monuments are of great tourist attraction.

4.2. Areas under the protection of the Forest Department

Two important nature reserves are located at Sokoke and Witu and require stricter control.

4.3. Areas under the protection of the local people

These comprise of the areas normally known as the "Kayas." The Kayas consist of coral or limestone caves within groups of trees, some of which are considered "sacred groves" and others as refuges from raiders in the long past. As such, the flora has been preserved and recently found to contain several new or little-known species with very limited distribution.

For instance, at Chasimba Kaya are found important tree genera, e.g., *Cola octolobioides*, *Savia fadeni*, and *Caesalpina dalei*. Kaya northeast of Mwara contain the genus *Holmskioldia* and is the type locality of the African Violet *Saintpaula rupicola*. Pangani Kaya represents *Micrococca scariosa* and *Oxystigma msoo* (National Museums, 1982). In addition, the caves harbour great concentrations of different species of bats. However, the invertebrates have not yet been studied.

4.4. Tana River Delta

Virtually unexplored in recent years and endangered due to proposals for agricultural development, the Tana River Delta is the only known locality for the native bird, *Cisticola restricta*. *Apalis chariessa*, preserved at the National Museum and thought to be now extinct, came from Mitoli on the Tana, near Garsen. Two important waterfowl lakes or swamps, Belissa and Shakabobo, are wildfowl sanctuaries and wetlands and require protection under the Ramsar Convention. There are also important heronries in the area, with some 15 species of breeding birds. Small mammals include the local Red duiker *Cephalophus natalensis*, and the Tana squirrel *Paraxerus palliatus tanae*, an important species in this type locality. The snake *Aparallactus guentheri* is only known from this area and Mt. Mbololo. The frog *Hylarana bravana* was first recorded from the Tana River Delta. Important flora include *Rhus quartiniana*, *Maerua triphilla*, *Commiphora riparia*, *Combretum tanaensis* and *Terminalia brevipes*, all of which are limited or rare in distribution along the coast.

5. PROBLEMS ENCOUNTERED IN COASTAL AND MARINE CONSERVATION

5.1. Fishing

Controlled fishing has little adverse effect on Kenya's marine parks. However, socio-economic pressure has led to the down-grading of certain portions of national parks to reserve status in order to allow fishing, e.g. the Malindi/Watamu Reserve surrounding the Malindi/ Watamu National Park area. Similarly, Kiunga, although located on government waters, is accorded reserve status to accommodate fishing. On the other hand, uncontrolled commercial fishing, particularly for prawns, is causing problems to the marine reserves. For instance, trawlers now enter shallow estuaries and lagoons where prawns concentrate and probably damage fish eggs and larvae of the ocean bottom. As a result, breeding may be interferred with because fish larvae spend their first stages of life in these shallow creeks, feeding and developing; in turn the recruitment of coral fishes would be affected.

Fishing for only commercially important fishes may also lead to an ecological imbalance due to unfavourable selection. Similarly, the collection of lobsters creates problems because they are not protected under the Wildlife Act. The majority of lobsters occur outside the marine parks but they need protection because they are slow breeders. Many lobsters that are trapped have been observed to be gravid and it is possible that the reproduction within the population is being interferred with through restriction of genetic diversity. Clearly, a separation must be made between traditional and commercial fishing if the marine parks/reserves are to be safeguarded in the future.

5.3. Shell collection

A recent study has revealed that shell collection within the protected areas is causing concern; the main collectors are probably visitors and their guides. The study revealed that collection took place at Kiunga, Malindi and Shimoni with the favourite shells being those of *Cypaea tigris*, *C. mauritania*, *C. rufa*, *Ovula ovum* and *Lambis lambis*.

5.4. Conflict of uses

Coastal hotels want to adapt the Malindi and Shimoni marine areas for water sports for their visitors. Apart from being aesthetically unacceptable, water skiing would pose danger to gogglers, especially if the numbers of skiers increases. The mooring of boats in the corals is damaging the corals, as is snorklers standing on the coral.

5.5. Problem of entrance gates

Coupled with the problem of water skiing is the problem of illegal entry into marine parks and reserves. The major problem to planning is the location of tourist facilities on the shore. The land base of the park and reserve is invariably restricted because the land is owned by the urban and municipal councils. Besides, the visitors have access to the marine parks and reserves at several points and many avoid the entrance gates through ignorance. This may mean that a certain amount of revenue is not collected.

5.6. Lack of skilled manpower and proper training

Wardens and rangers manning the marine parks have either wrong training or no training at all. For instance, the wardens have all trained at the Wildlife College Mweka, Tanzania, where emphasis is on terrestrial parks and reserves with only casual reference to the coastal and marine parks in theoretical work. The lack of interest in these areas is further supported by lack of appropriate titles for the wardens assigned to the marine reserves. This is a serious ommission in such an important training institution.

5.7. The problem of irrigation schemes and the hydro-electric dams

Kenya has constructed a series of dams along the Tana River for producing electricity, aimed at making the country self-sufficient in energy requirements. The method used is called "cascade development of the river", based on a system of power stations. Large dams along the Tana River are located at Masinga, Kamburu and Kitaru. Unfortunately, poor land husbandry on the slopes of Mt. Kenya is causing serious soil erosion, leading to siltation of the dams which may reduce their lifespan. The silt load is estimated by the Tana River Development Authority (TRDA) as between 9.2 and 14.3 million ton/year, which is affecting the proposed Ras Tenewi Reserve. Similarly, siltation emanating from the Sabaki River in the south is affecting Malindi National Park. In addition, no study made to assess the impact of the dams on fauna and flora, and particularly the fish. A case in point are two species of eels, *Anguilla* spp., which travel from the ocean upstream to spawn in the cold streams on Mt. Kenya. In the absence of fish-ladders to facilitate eel migration, it is not yet known what the long-term effect will be. Similarly, fish, *Labeo* spp., go in the reverse direction to the ocean along the Tana and Sabaki Rivers.

5.8. The problem of endangered species

Two marine animals, turtles and dugong, are endangered in Kenya. The marine turtles are unfortunate in that they do not enjoy adequate protection outside the present sanctuaries. Thus, the fishermen and the other people at the coast are at liberty to catch the turtles unhindered. At the moment, the Wildlife Conservation and Management Department does not have enough marine scouts to patrol the shores beyond the marine parks and reserves.

Dugong only enjoys token protection around Kiunga and Malindi/Watamu areas. However, its critical range, like that for the marine turtles, is outside the protected areas, being situated around the mouth of the Tana River.

5.9. Exploitation of timber and charcoal burning

In the Shimba Hills, cutting of timber by the Forest Department and the burning of charcoal, intensive cultivation and uncontrolled bush-fires are destroying the national reserve. The problem of the Shimba Hills is further complicated by the forest and game management, which do not seem to be in harmony with each other. For instance, whereas the game department advocates strict conservation and non-interference of the natural resources, the forest department allows timber exploitation and massive re-afforestation. This type of dual management of a common resource can only be harmful to the resource's future.

The mangrove forests are cut to supply poles to an existing market in the Middle East a factor that may have adverse effects in the future.

6. SOLUTIONS PRESCRIBED

6.1. Control of fishing

As a deliberate way of safeguarding marine parks and reserves, the Fisheries Department has supported the Wildlife Department, which is the custodian of marine parks, by introducing regulations to control subsistence fishing within the marine parks. First, a buffer zone/reserve was established around the parks for subsistence fishing. In addition, only certain methods are allowed, such as setting correct size of nets and outlawing of spear-fishing and harpooning. The use of explosives or water-rifles are prohibited.

6.2. Limitation on shell collection

Shell collection is regulated through a licensing system which establishes quotas; collection is allowed on designated areas only. Occasionally, a ban on shell-collection may be imposed as a conservation measure.

6.3. Safe-guarding of rare or endangered species

With regard to the endangered marine species the Government has given them complete protection and, by ratifying CITES, has ensured their protection on an international scale. The list at the moment includes all the marine turtles and the dugong. The status of other marine species is reviewed regularly with a view to extending this protection.

The ban on hunting and the sale of wildlife trophies was aimed at further safe-guarding these species.

6.4. Role of research

The Government encourages research with the view to enhancing the understanding of marine ecosystems for better conservation. For instance, the protection and care of nesting sites for marine turtles at Malindi by the Warden is aimed at ensuring better success of the hatchlings.

6.5. Control of pollution

The municipal councils governing the coastal cities are being encouraged to properly plan their sewage systems as a way of minimizing the discharge of effluents into the ocean to reduce the pollution of the parks and reserves. Further afield, the Ministry of Agriculture is involved in education campaigns for better soil conservation through proper methods of land husbandry, in line with the World Conservation Strategy. This would have a beneficial effect on the parks. It is further hoped that the Law of the Sea will have a beneficial effect once it becomes functional.

6.6. Discipline of settlement schemes

An effort is being made to encourage new settlement schemes to use other forms of fuel such as cow dung and gas to safeguard trees. If this effort is successful, it should be possible to safeguard the mangrove forest and the Tana River Delta including the coastal rain forests.

7. MANAGEMENT PLANNING

The Wildlife Department established a Wildlife Planning Unit in 1978 with the objective of preparing management plans for all of Kenya's parks and reserves. The management plans will help the Department in allocating funds and manpower to each park. In addition, the

Research Division is providing scientific information relevant to planning, such as numbers and distribution of various animal species. In addition, sociological studies are being encouraged to ascertain the visitor perception of the marine parks for better planning to enhance visitor enjoyment. The introduction of tourist facilities, e.g. underwater trails and visitor centres, are subjected to research before arriving at decisions. Thus, research is complementary to planning.

8. ROLE OF MARINE PARKS WITHIN THE PARK SYSTEM

The coastal and marine protected areas of Kenya fulfill an important role of protecting unique and delicate habitats, such as coastal rain forests, saline grasslands, sand dunes, coral reefs and some of the off-shore islands. A system plan under preparation has identified gaps in the protection of Kenya's natural regions, particularly in the coastal region, e.g. the Ras Tenewi and Diani areas.

9. ECONOMIC IMPORTANCE OF MARINE PARKS

Of about 500,000 visitors coming to Kenya each year, only 5% visit the marine parks. Thus the marine parks are not a prime attraction. They also employ few people. Despite this weak base, coastal hotels are primarily based on tourism, and the tourist industry employs many people directly involved in hotels and transportation. Indirectly, it adds to the economy through interlocking activities involving tourist spending.

10. RELATING KENYA'S EXPERIENCE TO UNEP'S EAST AFRICAN SEAS PROGRAMME

Kenya's conservation programme for the coastal and marine protected areas is primarily concerned with the protection of marine ecosystems. Priority is given to fragile habitats such as the mangrove thickets and coral reefs and to the rare and endangered fauna, e.g. turtles and dugong.

Protection is also extended to representative biotic communities such as the palm woodlands, alkaline grasslands, beaches and dunes.

Kenya's guidelines for establishing parks and reserves, safeguarding of marine ecosystems and preservation of rare species are identical to the UNEP's Action Plan for the East African Regional Seas Programme. The country recognizes major threats to marine resources as being associated with urban developments taking place in Mombasa, Lamu and Malindi.

11. CONCLUSIONS AND RECOMMENDATIONS

Coastal and marine protected areas have positive and negative aspects. On the positive side, they conserve rare or fragile ecosystems including habitats of threatened fauna and flora. These areas may also serve as a baseline for observing ecological changes in other unprotected areas. Economically, these areas are important as they support tourism which is second to agriculture in contributing to the Gross National Product of Kenya.

But these areas can also have a negative impact. For instance, the coastal reserves of Boni, Dodori and Shimba Hills harbour the deadly tsetse fly that transmit a fatal disease to domestic livestock. This is a major stumbling block to agricultural development. In addition, control of fires within the parks has interferred with the natural course of events necessary for the elimination of the vegetation that harbours the fly.

Conflict also exists between park and traditional rights of fishing and shell collection.

On another scale, there is a growing land problem associated with the development of tourist hotels. Because the beach plots for erecting lodges and other tourist facilities such as night spots and casinos are scarce, the local people are enticed by entrepeneurs to sell land for purposes of tourist development. Further inland, the local people are laying more emphasis on cash crops rather than subsistence crops in order to supply to the expanding tourist industry. This shift away from subsistence cultivation may in time contribute to food shortage and famine, particularly during severe drought.

However, the advantages of having the coastal and marine protected areas far outweigh their disadvantages. The land under parks is more secure than that under other forms of use, such as agriculture which is exploitative in nature. Today, the marine parks and reserves face several challenges. For example, lack of qualified manpower is a major drawback. Realising this shortcoming Kenya is establishing a Wildlife and Fisheries Training Institute with help from the World Bank which will train wardens in techniques of managing both the terrestrial and marine reserves.

All these problems underscore the need for scientific research and planning. UNEP, IUCN, WWF, Unesco, UNDP and FAO can assist the East African countries by providing the necessary technical assistance to solve some of the problems outlined above.

Acknowledgements

This paper was prepared for IUCN's Commission of National Parks and Protected Areas in cooperation with the United Nations Environment Programme.

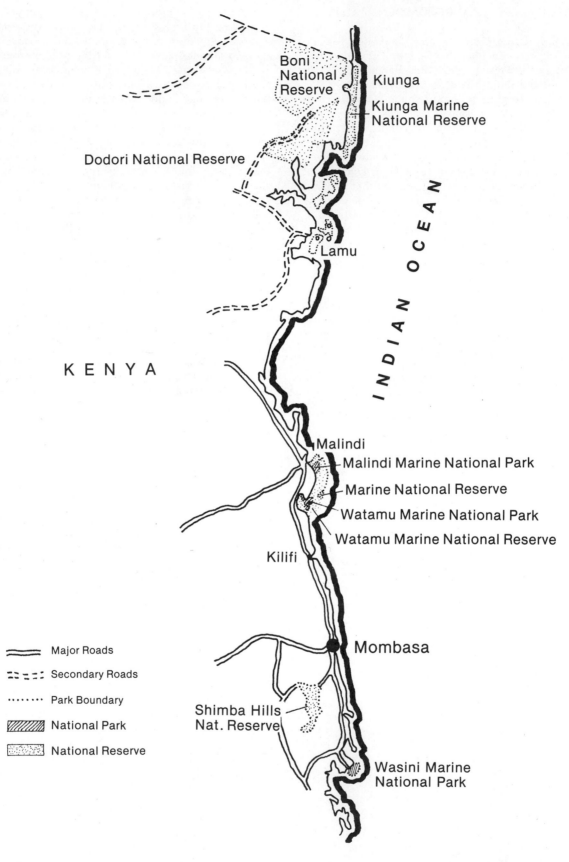

Figure 1. Coastal and marine parks of Kenya.

108

Training Protected Area Personnel: Lessons from the College of African Wildlife Management

G.T. Mosha and J.W. Thorsell
College of African Wildlife Management
Moshi, Tanzania

ABSTRACT. *The College of African Wildlife Management trains middle-level managers for the anglophone countries of Africa. Nearly 1,000 graduates from 16 countries are now in important positions in virtually all of the protected areas in eastern Africa. Lessons which have been learned over the 19-year history of the school are summarized, and future problems are fully discussed. Primary among these are the need to secure appropriate funding, and the importance of modifying the curriculum to reflect the expanding importance of resource management in east Africa.*

1. INTRODUCTION

Located at 1400 m elevation on the slopes of Mt. Kilimanjaro in Northern Tanzania is the campus of the College of African Wildlife Management. Established in 1963, the College is the pioneer training institution serving anglophone Africa. In these first 19 years, the College has produced 924 Certificate and Diploma graduates from 16 countries; graduates are now responsible for management duties in virtually all of the protected areas in eastern Africa.

This paper presents a summary of the College's facilities and programmes, reviews its outputs, suggests some lessons we have learned and discusses some of the issues which we face in the future.

This paper is based on material compiled by the then-Principal, Dr. Felix Nyahoza in his monograph on the College, published by the African Wildlife Leadership Foundation in 1981. Our interpretations and opinions, however, are our own and do not necessarily represent official views of the Governing Body of the host government.

2. DESCRIPTION OF THE COLLEGE

The 21 ha site of the campus was chosen for the advantages of its location near various types of parks, reserves and game controlled areas. These include the savanna grasslands of the Serengeti, the plateau area of the Ngorongoro highlands, the montane forests and alpine moorlands of Kilimanjaro and Meru, the alkaline lakes of the Rift Valley, and the marine resources of the Indian Ocean. There is no other protected area training institution that operates in such a variety of life zones, ranging from glaciers at 5900 m through to coral reef and coastal zone habitats.

College facilities are equally extensive. We maintain a fleet of some 20 vehicles including buses and Unimogs for student transport, four-wheel drive pick-ups, and smaller vehicles. A workshop compound and stores area support our transport section. We also maintain field equipment that can accommodate up to 125 people under canvas. Specialized equipment such as field glasses, microscopes, and audio-visual equipment, although limited, is also part of our inventory.

Residential buildings include five student dormitories, 18 senior staff houses and six support staff housing complexes. For teaching purposes there are an administration building, 12 faculty offices, two lecture halls, one auditorium, one laboratory, a museum display and one study room. There is also a large library, a taxidermy room, an armoury and a weapons training area. Recreational facilities are provided in the form of a social hall, a soccer field and courts for basketball, tennis and squash.

Our physical plant is thus a substantial one. It follows that our maintenance budget is also substantial and our replacement value almost inestimable.

Teaching faculty however, are the real foundation of any educational institution. Their competence, experience and enthusiasm are the main contributors to the the effectiveness of training. The teaching staff at Mweka is composed of a Principal, a Deputy Principal and 14 Instructors of various ranks. An additional 60 support staff (cooks, drivers, secretarial, grounds crew) are also employed.

For the 1981/82 fiscal year the total budget for recurrent costs of the College was just under $500,000. Approximately 50% of this went towards teaching expenses (salaries, library, camp supplies), 25% towards student accommodation costs, 16% towards vehicle and building maintenance and 8% towards office administration. In addition to this, a total of three Instructors are sponsored by outside sources.

During the same year our capital budget expenditure was US $333,000. This was primarily provided under a Denmark-sponsored development project which is making $1.75 million available for new facilities and staff training. Additional counterpart money provided by the Tanzania Government for development amounts to $260,000.

Over the past ten years the average total number of students in attendance was 80. In 1981/82 we had 77 students from 11 different African countries registered. The student tuition fees, which have recently been raised to $6,000 per annum, do not cover operating costs. Over the past four years the Government of Tanzania has provided an average subvention of 27% of total operating costs in order to cover this deficit. This is the direct subsidy cost of the operation of Mweka by the host country.

3. PROGRAMME DESCRIPTION

The thrust of the training programme at Mweka is directed to middle-level managers. The College continues to have this focus, which leads to the majority of graduates being employed in assistant and senior field officer posts.

Three levels of courses are offered. The Certificate course requires an ordinary secondary level education and is intended for posts at the Assistant Warden level. The Diploma course requires a Certificate in Wildlife Management or an advanced secondary level of education for entry and and is designed to produce senior field officers. Both courses require two years to complete. Students must also have previous field experience and are admitted only through a sponsoring organization.

The Post-Graduate Diploma course is intended for University graduates who wish to take up senior posts in park and wildlife management. This one-year course is custom-designed to fit the career requirement of the individual student and requires the conduct of a research project leading to a Dissertation. To date, 25 Postgraduate Diplomas have been awarded.

There is also provision for the College to organize special courses on various topics. These are usually done on a specific request by the organization employing the particular student; such courses have been mounted in herbarium techniques, zoo management, taxidermy, ballistics and tourism.

The College curriculum has evolved over the years and is continuously being updated to keep it relevant. The most recent revision was completed in 1981 and is contained in a detailed 64-page syllabus.

The content of the training programme tries to strike a balance between a general background in ecology and conservation and practice training in the various skills involved in wildlife and protected area management. One third of the training is done on field practicals.

Courses are grouped in three main subject areas:

1) Natural Sciences, including mammalogy, ornithology, herpetology, geography, earth science, invertebrates, and botany.
2) Wildlife Management, including wildlife management techniques, range management, surveying statistics, vehicle mechanics, diseases, photography and ballistics.
3) Estate Management and Conservation Education including park management, planning, administration, law enforcement, conservation education, construction techniques and outdoor survival techniques. (Diploma course students are given more in-depth material, particularly in general management, planning, administration and public relations).

The Mweka graduate is therefore prepared to step into a field management position with a good general knowledgement of the environment he is dealing with as well as the practical skills involved in managing it. The capabilities of Mweka graduates and their subsequent performance has been commended on numerous occasions by the various organizations employing them.

4. PERFORMANCE INDICATORS

The question of how to evaluate the success of an educational institution is a difficult one as there are few empirical measures to do so and a long-term perspective is required. Five criteria are discussed here and collectively should provide the reader with an impression of our relative success in meeting our objective of training effective protected area managers.

4.1. Student output

From the initial 25 students who entered the College in 1963 an additional 899 have followed them for a total graduating class to date of 924. Geographically these students were from Tanzania (333), Kenya (247), Ghana

(55), Zambia (50), Uganda (43), Nigeria (42), Ethiopia (32), Sudan (22), Botsawana (18), Malawi (13), Sierra Leone (10), Liberia (9), Cameroon (7), Somalia (6), Egypt (4) and UK (1).

The production of this quantity of qualified protected area and wildlife managers is matched by few other schools of our nature. This output is further reinforced by knowledge that the great majority of Mweka graduates have continued careers in this field. The waste or drop-out rate that the various sponsoring organizations have suffered is known to be below 20%.

4.2. Student placement

Another measure of our success in providing qualified protected area managers is the current positions that many College alumni now hold. Virtually every protected area in East Africa has personnel who have been trained at Mweka, including the majority of wardens and semi-wardens. Several have distinguished themselves beyond this level. For instance, the Directors of Wildlife in Tanzania, Zambia and Malawi and the Deputy Director in Ghana are Mweka graduates. Two others are Assistant Directors with the Kenya Wildlife Department.

Former students are also heading other wildlife training institutions. These include the Wildlife School at Garoua, Cameroon, the Bussa school in Nigeria, the Ghana Game Scout school, the Mazambique Game Ranger School and the Pasiansi Institute in Tanzania. The Deputy Principal of this College is also a former student.

Another one of our graduates, now Warden incharge of Tsavo National Park, recently was awarded the IUCN International Parks Valor Award.

4.3. Programme leadership

The College has served as a model for the development of the wildlife training schools mentioned in the above section as well as the new Naivasha Institute in Kenya. Not only former Mweka graduates but Instructors as well have dispersed to provide conservation leadership in many different parts of the world. Many of our former Instructors are now in various related posts with IUCN, Unesco, FAO and UNDP. Two others are currently training wildlife personnel in the Central African Republic and Sierra Leone.

4.4. Recognition of Mweka qualifications

Many of our diploma course graduates have gone on to further their education. Recognition of their Diploma for University entry has now been given by many institutions in Australia, Canada, the United Kingdom, USA and Africa. Many of these have also been accepted for post-graduate degrees. A Diploma or Certificate from Mweka is thus not only recognized regionally but is widely known and accepted as a qualification for entry to programmes of higher education.

4.5. Conservation dividends

It is estimated that over 12,000,000 ha of land in various eastern African countries have been established as some form of conservation area since 1965. It may be safely concluded that Mweka's programmes have directly and indirectly had a positive role and influence on the conservation attitudes and achievements of participating countries. As many of these areas are developed for economic purposes (e.g. tourism and trophy hunting) it can also be concluded that the Collee has contributed substantially to the development of these countries resulting from wildlife-based tourism and sustained use of natural resources. The recognition of the College's contribution to conservation in Africa resulted to our being selected as a WWF recipient for 1981 of the International Award for Conservation Merit.

5. SOME LESSONS

Looking back over our nearly two decades of operation it is possible to identify some of the lessons we have learned that may offer guidelines to other training institutions. These are discussed below.

5.1. Timing

The establishment of the College coincided closely with the attainment of independence in eastern Africa in the early 1960s. It was increasingly recognized that "localization" of many of the posts in the national parks and wildlife departments would require a major regional effort in formal taining of local staff. As one of the founders of the College noted at an IUCN Symposium which led to the launching of the College:

> "Training . . . must be formalized, standardized, properly organized, largely centralized and soundly administered with adequate equipment and facilities. It is clear that that what is needed to meet these requirements is the organization of "Wildlife Management Training Schools" on a regional basis . . . to train up the largely missing middle ranks" (Kinloch, 1963).

The appropriateness of the timing of the establishment of the College was also given a strong endorsement in the following statement of the then Prime Minister J. Nyerere made at the same symposium and known as the Arusha Manifesto:

"The conservation of wildlife and wildspaces calls for specialist knowledge, trained manpower and money and we look to other nations to cooperate in this important task—the success or the failure of which not only affects the continent of Africa but the rest of the world as well."

Mweka, then, was an idea whose time had come, the right type of institution at the right time.

5.2. Political support

One of the key strengths of the College has been the continuing support from the highest political levels. The Arusha Manifesto has been followed up by a continued subvention from the Tanzanian Government for operating expenditures. This has increased steadily from US $15,000 in 1963 to $134,000 in 1980/81. Despite political differences that occur from time to time between neighbouring states, the College has largely stayed above these and regional attendance has continued.

5.3. Multi-institutional funding sources

The Mweka programme has been given support from an exceptionally wide variety of agencies. The governments of USA, Germany, Canada, UK and Denmark have all provided equipment and instructors to the College. UNDP/FAO have also contributed here. The Government of Kenya has provided an Instructor for the past three years. Both UNEP and Unesco have provided scholarship funds for students and instructors.

Various non-government agencies have added substantial inputs as well. These include the African Wildlife Leadership Foundation, Rockefeller Brothers Fund, IUCN/World Wildlife Fund, Frankfurt Zoological Society and the Ford Foundation.

This diversified range of input from six governments, three UN Agencies and five NGOs has made the College widely known to potential donors and in turn has reinforced the international view of Mweka.

5.4. International flavour

As an institution serving regional needs, the College has brought together students from 15 African countries. As indicated above, Mweka Instructors, too, bring knowledge and viewpoints from many different countries. One of the strengths of Mweka, the fostering of international understanding and the global role of wildlife and protected areas, is further enhanced by the presence of instructors of many nationalities over the years and the representation on the Governing Body of 10 members from seven countries.

5.5. Emphasis on field practicals

During the 1981/82 academic year at Mweka, students in both the Diploma and Certificate courses spent a total of 67 days on field safaris. Comparing this to the 156 days spent in classrooms, field time is thus 30% of total learning time.

While the desirability of field training is notable it must also be recognized that this requires a substantial input in terms of equipment and safari vehicles. The equipment requirements for safari has been itemized in a previous section. Under the Unesco World Heritage Fund $60,000 is being made available to purchase new tentage for instructors and students which is one reflection of the high cost of undertaking field safaris.

5.6. Cooperative links with related agencies

As indicated above, field exercises in the various protected areas of Tanzania are an integral part of the syllabus. In turn, these safaris require cooperative relationships with the various land agencies involved. On the one hand, these agencies provide free use of facilities in their areas as well as contributing resource personnel to meet with the students during the exercises. The Departments of Game, Fisheries and Forestry, as well as the Tanzania Wildlife Corporation, National Parks and Ngorongoro Conservation Area Authority all have provided substantial field input to the College programme.

On the other hand, the College has provided these agencies with various services as well including conduct of game control and live animal trapping exercises, maintenance of facilities and data collection. Various reports by instructional staff and post graduate dissertations have been submitted to and acted on by these agencies. The cooperation between the College and the various related Government agencies is thus a symbiotic one, with important practical benefits accruing to each partner.

5.7. Staff training programme

Provision for strengthening the teaching capabilities of the academic staff has been included in the development plans for the College. The majority of teaching staff have Bachelor degrees from regional universities where training programmes in environmental subjects are not well developed. Accordingly, 8 staff have received support for graduate study at North American universities (in particular the University of New Mexico). Currently, through the DANIDA sponsored programme, 12 scholarship-years are being provided. It is the aim of the College to have the majority of instructors trained to the Masters degree level.

Another method of staff training has been through the International Seminar on National Parks. Four of our Instructors have been sponsored on this valuable course by the United States and through the World Heritage Fund. Add-on study tours were usually also included. It is anticipated that at some future time the College could play a role in sponsoring a similar international seminar in the East African region.

A third technique for reinforcing teaching resources was the provision of short term (two months) specialist attachments to Mweka by 11 members of the US Park Service. The team-teaching attachments focussed on providing feedback with park specialists and resource materials for teaching and reference. Both College staff and students gained from this exposure, but the disadvantages of minimal orientation time for the advisors suggested that two months was not an adequate period for adaptation.

Training of support staff (secretarial, finance, library) has not been neglected and is done at the regional level. Further efforts here need to be developed.

6. PROBLEM AREAS: FACING THE FUTURE

Looking forward we anticipate some modifications and new directions in our programmes if our one over-riding problem, that of funding, can be solved. These will now be discussed.

6.1. Funding

Like most institutions worldwide, we continue to face serious limitations on aspects dealing with our financial requirements. As outlined above, we have received generous support to date in our infrastructural development from many sources. The fact is, however, that there is no assured source of funding for the future. This is of great concern in light of the increasing difficulty of the United Republic of Tanzania to continue its subsidies in the face of other pressing social and economic commitments.

The root of our funding problem is the growth in recurrent costs which have increased threefold in the past six years. During this period we have had to raise the annual student fee from $2,200 to $6,000. Few countries in anglophone Africa will be able to afford this fee and enrolments are expected to decrease, causing a serious set-back to the progress of conservation on this continent.

We must emphasize that the only solution to this problem is the continuation of external support based on the regional role of the College. *How to obtain this support and assure it on a long term basis is the key issue facing the College in the future.*

6.2. Regional role

What will be the impact on Mweka of the possible development of other regional training institutions? Proposals for similar Colleges have been made for Malawi, Zambia, Nigeria and Ghana and a World Bank-financed wildlife school is due to open in Kenya this year. Will international funding be even further dispersed with a proliferation of similar institutions? It is suggested that to foster cooperation among these and other training centres that a regional coordinating body be established, possibly through IUCN. The duplication of programme offerings in an era of scarce funds could be reviewed and curriculum integration fostered by such a body.

6.3. Faculty research and consulting activities

College Instructors have in the past been encouraged to undertake various investigational projects in local wildlife areas. Some funds for these projects have been available and most have contributed effectively to teaching activities as well.

To further encourage this involvement the College will take a more active role in soliciting research and project funds as well modifying the teaching time-table to allow more time to be devoted to these activities. By extending our staff capabilities beyond teaching, it is anticipated that academic staff will demonstrate the capacity of the College to be of practical use to various development agencies which in turn, may allow funds to be channelled to associated College functions as well as contributing to professional development.

6.4. Curriculum modifications

Flexibility to modify the curriculum to adapt the College to changing needs has long occupied a great deal of effort. The most recent revision of our syllabus was made in 1981 to include, among other things, greater emphasis on conservation education and new approaches to protected area management planning.

In tune with the *World Conservation Strategy*, our curriculum has been expanding beyond basic wildlife biology to give increased attention to environmental issues in general, land-use planning, and the sociology of conservation. To reinforce our capabilities in these areas, we currently have a staff member undertaking graduate studies in natural resources planning in Canada.

Curriculum changes can most efficiently be reviewed by consulting former students as to their impressions on the adequacy of their training and relevance to current responsibilities. A study of this nature was completed by FAO in 1974 and another is needed to provide more current feedback and monitoring.

6.5. Expansion of offering

In concert with a higher profile through expanded research and contract opportunities, the College is also considering becoming more active in extension activities. These would include refresher courses, seminars and workshops on specialized topics within the scope of our competence.

With a strengthened faculty and improved seminar facilities, such programmes will be initiated when funds are available. At this time the College is proposing to co-sponsor a planning workshop on marine parks and coastal zone management. This would be carried out in cooperation with Tanzania National Parks, CNPPA and UNEP's Regional Seas Programme.

Other workshops being planned for a wide range of target groups include the subjects of wildlife clubs, conservation education and capture methods.

6.6. Course handbooks and teaching aids

Considerable experience has been accumulated at Mweka from both the classroom and field operations on the many aspects of protected area management in East Africa. The compilation of this material into loose-leaf manuals for use by both students and instructors is a project we have launched with assistance from the US National Park Service.

A first draft of the parks course manual is currently being revised. Further illustrative materials are being collected from the region and from information gathered at the World National Parks Congress. Our manual in fact will be an East African version of the book on *Managing Protected Areas in the Tropics* being prepared at the Congress.

Along with the production of course handbooks we are currently assessing the reinforcement of the teaching aids that are available. Both our audio-visual capabilities and library are in need of strengthening. The availability of foreign exchange is a major limitation here and we have gratefully benefited from our liaison with the US National Park Service in this regard. Another project to refurbish our wildlife museum is also being pursued with the African Wildlife Leadership Foundation.

6.7. Field demonstration area

Finally, the College is currently finalizing the acquisition of an off-campus environmental study site. Discussions with the Game Department have indicated that a 20,000 ha site adjacent to Arusha National Park will be made available to the College for teaching, research and wildlife utilization functions. The actual management of the area will be the responsibility of the College and has potential to produce significant revenue as well as providing a close-in site for permament teaching and research facilities.

In conclusion, we believe that the College of African Wildlife Management has gone a long way towards meeting the principles of the Arusha Manifesto. With the continued cooperation of those who have assisted us in the past and in the spirit of the *World Conservation Strategy* and the Bali Congress we would hope to do even more in future.

Acknowledgements

We would like to thank our Colleagues at Mweka for their assistance in developing this paper as well as the Danish International Development Agency for sponsoring attendance of two lecturers to this Congress.

The Role of Protected Areas in Catchment Conservation in Malawi

A. D. C. Kombe
Chief Game Warden
Department of National Parks and Wildlife
Lilongwe 3, Malawi

ABSTRACT. *Malawi is a small country with a dense and increasing population. At the same time, a relatively high proportion of the land area is designated as protected area. The primary objectives of conservation in Malawi are preservation of ecological communities and catchment conservation; this paper emphasizes the latter objective. Catchment conservation is a basic tenet of land husbandry, and for this reason most protected areas are located on land classified as unsuitable for development, particularly the highlands and escarpments. The value of this protection is demonstrated through its effect on streamflow and through its role as the basis of the extensive system of gravity fed rural water supplies. Conservation areas in Malawi are currently experiencing heavy pressures from the expanding population. The key to overcoming these pressures is raising production in agricultural land, not opening up protected areas, which play an integral role in the National Land Use Plan in maintaining productivity in the developed areas, and ensuring a satisfactory environment.*

1. INTRODUCTION

Malawi is a small country with an area of 95,000 sq km, roughly equal to that of the state of Indiana, or 3/4 of the size of the island of Java. However, with a population of 6 million people, its average population density is over 60 per sq km. While not high by the standards of southeast Asia this puts Malawi into the top five countries in Africa in terms of population density.

At the same time, the percentage of protected land in Malawi is high: 12% is allocated to National Parks and Game Reserves, 5% is allocated to National Parks and Game Reserves, and a further 5% to Forest Reserves, giving a total of 17% of the land area devoted primarily to conservation.

In this situation of high and increasing population density, we must ask, first, why the area devoted to conservation is so large, and second, why the Government of Malawi feels it necessary to maintain the conservation areas in the face of increasing pressure on land.

The object of this paper is to answer these questions.

2. THE OBJECTIVES OF CONSERVATION IN MALAWI

The primary objective of conservation in Malawi is to preserve representative examples of wildlife communities of the country for aesthetic and scientific reasons. The second objective of conservation is to assist in maintaining the productivity and water supplies of the agricultural areas of the country through catchment conservation. Some of the forest reserves have the additional objectives of conserving and developing forest products for direct use, for example, fuelwood, timber and pulp.

This paper will concentrate particularly on the second objective, the role of protected areas in catchment conservation.

3. LAND HUSBANDRY PRINCIPLES

Catchment conservation is a basic tenet of land husbandry. It is based on the principle that certain areas are unsuitable for cultivation or other forms of exploitation because these uses damage not only the areas themselves but also land beyond their boundaries, through erosion, siltation, loss of vegetation and cur-

115

tailment of surface water supplies. Such areas are usually those with steep slopes and erodible soils.

For many years, the Malawi Government has been strongly committed to the principles of land husbandry, and the relevant technical services have surveyed and classified all land in the country according to its capability. About 20% of the land has been classified as unsuitable for cultivation, and it is primarily here that protected areas have been designated. The distribution of protected areas can be understood in terms of a brief outline of the geography of the country.

4. AN OUTLINE OF THE GEOGRAPHY OF MALAWI

Malawi is a long, narrow country situated astride the lip of part of the African Rift Valley system. As such, the country consists of a series of plateau areas separated by a series of escarpments. There are three major plateau levels, with two major escarpment series separating them. The high plateaus, standing at above 2000 m a.s.l., are the Nyika, Vipya, Zomba and Mulanje plateaus. These are separated from the middle plateaus by high escarpments.

The middle plateaus, which are part of the great Central African Plateau, at about 800 m a.s.l., make up the Mzimba, Kasungu and Lilongwe plains to the west of the Rift, and the Phalombe and Namwera plains to the east. These are separated from the low plateaus by low escarpments.

The low valleys, making up the floor of the Rift Valley, include the Lakeshore plain, the Middle Shire Valley and the lower Shire Valley.

One may summarize the ecology of these land regions as follows: fertility and hence agricultural potential is lowest on the high plateaus and increases as one goes down to the very fertile Rift Valley floor; rainfall and water availability are greatest in the highlands and escarpments and decrease as one goes down to the relatively arid Rift Valley floor; and erosion tends to be highest in the upland and escarpment areas, and lowest on the middle and lower plateaus.

Therefore, in terms of land capability, the middle and lower plateaus are most suitable for intensive exploitation, the highlands and escarpments best suited to conservation.

5. THE DISTRIBUTION OF PROTECTED AREAS

Because the different land regions differ in climate and soils, they support different ecological communities. For this reason, sections of each have been designated as conservation areas for the primary purpose of conserving representative examples of the major biotopes. Examples are Kasungu National Park, Liwonde National Park, the old part of Lengwe National Park, and Vwaza Marsh Game Reserve, which are located on the middle

and lower plateaus in areas where catchment conservation is not usually considered to be of critical importance.

The areas designated as conservation areas for reasons of catchment conservation include most of the Forest Reserves, Nyika National Park and its extensions, Nkhotakota Game Reserves, and the extensions to Lengwe National Park and Majete and Mwabvi Game Reserves.

The result of this approach is that most of the high plateau areas are protected, as well as a high proportion of the escarpments. A progressively lower proportion of the middle plateaus and valleys is protected except in areas of very high biological interest (Lengwe and Liwonde National Parks) or in areas with other physical obstacles to development.

6. THE VALUE OF CATCHMENT CONSERVATION

It is not always easy to demonstrate directly the value of catchment conservation, usually because of lack of sufficiently long data series of comparable controls. However, a good example is provided by comparing stream flow on the Bua and Dwangwa rivers, which drain adjacent catchments in the Central Region of Malawi. The upper Bua catchment is largely open to cultivation and has experienced a massive expansion of agriculture over the last 10 years, particularly in the form of tobacco estates, at the expense of the indigenous *Brachystegia* woodland. The upper Dwangwa catchment, by contrast, is largely protected by the Kasungu National Park.

It has recently been demonstrated by the Department of Lands, Evaluation and Water that run-off from the upper Bua catchment, as measured by stream flow, was 50% higher during 1970-1980 than during 1954-1964, a decade of comparable rainfall in quantity and pattern. The adjacent catchment of the upper Dwangwa, by contrast, showed no change in the amount of run-off between the two decades.

The problems associated with such an increase in run-off are of course well known, involving loss of topsoil, siltation of the lower catchment, and reduction of dry season flow. The stream flow data indicate that these problems may be anticipated in the Bua catchment, but not in the Dwangwa catchment, whose headwaters are protected.

7. GRAVITY-FED RURAL WATER SUPPLIES

The Bua-Dwangwa example is the more impressive since both catchments are very flat and not considered as high erosion risk areas. The problems are of course potentially much greater in the upland areas and escarpments. These areas are the sources of much of the available surface water in the country, but at the same time are the most susceptible to damage by improper land use.

Their importance as water supplies is demonstrated by the gravity-fed rural water supply system, initiated in 1969 and still under development. In this system, water is piped from inlets on streams in highland areas with protected catchments, and distributed by gravity pressure to settlements in the relatively waterless plains below. At present 43 such projects have been completed or are under construction, which will supply water to 960,000 people, or about 16% of the national population. The system is relatively cheap and simple to install and maintain, involving no machinery or fuel costs, while the water is clean and hygienic without the use of filters of treatment. In the words of the system's originator, Mr. Lindsay Robertson, "Instead of fighting against nature, we are allowing nature to do our work for us." The essential feature of the system is, of course, protection of the catchments concerned.

8. CONCLUSION

The present conservation situation in Malawi is relatively favourable. However, the protected areas are currently being subjected to increasing pressures, both in terms of illegal exploitation of resources (i.e. timber, meat, ivory, etc.), and in terms of pressures to open them to cultivation.

The basic problem is, of course, the increase in the population, currently estimated at 2.7% per annum, bringing with it an increasing need for production of food and other resources. The question of population control is currently under discussion. In the meantime the key to a successful land use plan is increased production on land already under cultivation, not the opening up of protected land. Development in this direction must be backed up by education and public relations, conveying the significance of conservation as an integral component of the national land use plan.

The message, briefly, is this:

The people of Malawi are the owners of a capital asset in the land. We cannot expect to reap dividends from the entire capital. We must use part of it in maintaining the state of the productive capital. Just as owners of mechanical plants spend money and effort in maintaining their plants, so we as owners of the land must continue to manage the conservation areas as a maintenance service to the rest of the country, so that its inhabitants can continue to produce resources on a sustainable basis, and can enjoy the products in a satisfactory environment.

Acknowledgements

This paper was prepared for IUCN's Commission on National Parks and Protected Areas in cooperation with the United Nations Environment Programme.

Managing Wildlife for People in Zimbabwe

Graham Child
Director
National Parks and Wildlife Management
Harare, Zimbabwe

ABSTRACT. *Large mammal populations have increased in the Chirisa Safari Area (170,000 sq km) since it was set aside some 20 years ago as an area for research into tsetse-vertebrate host relationships. Surplus elephant are now being culled to protect the habitats. Benefits from this culling and recreational hunting accrue to the local communities living around the area, through the provisions of a pragmatic policy that views wildlife as a natural renewable resource that can and should be used correctly for the benefit of people. Success over the past three years has encouraged the expansion of this concept in this part of Zimbabwe and its application elsewhere in the country.*

1. INTRODUCTION

Beginning in the late 1950s Zimbabwe has evolved a pragmatic policy toward nature conservation which recognizes wildlife as a renewable resource with special attributes which can and should be used to enhance rural productivity for the benefit of the landholders, their communities and the State. This paper outlines the history of the Chirisa Safari Area, which came into being as a result of the excellence and appropriateness of the research being done in the area, but which has also benefitted from the philosophy of managing wildlife with the interests of people in mind.

2. HISTORY OF CHIRISA SAFARI AREA

The Chirisa Safari Area lies in the Sebungwe region of northwest Zimbabwe, in an area infested with tsetse and of a generally poor agricultural potential. Tsetse precludes pastoralism, and between 1919 and 1959/60

some 805,000 head of 36 species of large mammals were shot on tsetse control operations. By this time, Weitz (1963) had perfected a technique for analyzing tsetse blood meals and surveys in the Sebungwe had shown that four species were the preferred hosts—warthog, bushpig, kudu, and bushbuck—and these and elephant and buffalo were the main species shot. The last two species were destroyed chiefly because they damaged the fences which by this time flanked the hunting corridors and because they transported the fly mechanically across them.

A temporary research base to study tsetse-vertebrate relationships was set up in December, 1964. The research programme evolved in line with a policy that was pertinent to the improved welfare of remote tribal communities as well as to wildlife conservation and tsetse control problems. At that time the land was an unoccupied tribal area and it was decided to make it a game reserve from which benefits, including revenue, would go to the neighbouring rural communities so as to generate an appreciation of the value of wildlife. This was a farsighted administrative decision in the mid-1960s; it was enshrined in legislation and the Chirisa became a Safari Area in 1975. In the meantime the research programme was put on a permanent basis and the Sengwa Institute of Wildlife Research was established in 1970.

The decision to establish this institute was most appropriate as the northern Sebungwe Region, which now has six major protected areas (Fig. 1), is well endowed with wildlife but, as noted, is infested with tsetse and is generally marginal or submarginal for conventional agriculture (Martin and Taylor, 1982).

The original programme, which included measuring the changing numerical trends in resident large mammal populations (now in its 17th year) and an in-depth study of the biology of warthog (Cumming, 1975), (which incidentally pioneered the large-scale use of radio telemetry in the study of large African mammals), has gradually been expanded. Studies have included work on various aspects of the vegetation, its relationships to soils and its use by animals, as well as research on specific large mammals, such as elephant.

Besides the obvious value to management decisions of the research at Sengwa, this work was instrumental in delaying tsetse control hunting and in securing the Chirisa Safari Area as a protected area in the first place. This was largely a question of convincing administrators whose first concern was the welfare of people in an area with a rapidly expanding population. Even at that early stage it was appreciated that it would also be necessary to persuade the local rural communities in the neighbourhood of the benefits to themselves of retaining the protected area in the face of intensifying land shortages and far-reaching policy decisions were taken which have benefitted the area through the controlled use of the wildlife resources.

3. OPERATION WINDFALL

Due to population growth and influx from other areas, the elephant population of Sebungwe had increased from about 1500 in 1924 to about 9000 at present, this in spite of the shooting of 5400 head in tsetse control operations since 1960 (Cumming, 1981). The decision to reduce elephant numbers in Chirisa in order to conserve the full spectrum of plant communities in the Sengwa Wildlife Research Area provided a vehicle for "Operation Windfall".

The Natural Resources Board, the national conscience on environmental issues, with considerable persuasive and legal power to correct environmentally damaging practices, became critical of the Department of National Parks and Wild Life Management as a conservation agency of the Government, for permitting so many trees to be killed before taking effective remedial action. Allowing elephants to destroy forest conflicted with the Board's national campaign against the wholesale destruction of woodland by people and there was a risk that Government could be held responsible for favouring animals over people, at the expense of trees. As a result, 380 elephant were culled in 1980 and 375 in 1981, all from within the 370 sq km research area; this decision to reduce elephant populations in Chirisa was based purely on the need to conserve vegetation and habitat diversity.

Having made this decision, based on the best evidence available, there were several consequential decisions that had to be taken. These included a requirement that the best possible use be made of any products of the management action. Products could be sold to best advantage or be made available to local people at a nominal charge. Here the decision was relatively simple because of an earlier Government commitment toward Chirisa which allowed all revenues earned in the area to accrue to local communities. This fact, and the local absence of the skills and machinery needed to process raw ivory and elephant hide, determined that the hide and ivory should be sold to best advantage while the bulk of the meat should be sold locally. The local people also benefitted from the employment opportunities provided at a time when they were not busy with agricultural crops.

In anticipation of the 1978 population reduction exercise, officials of the Department in the field met with their counterparts in the District Administration to plan the programme. Culling elephant and processing the carcasses presented considerable logistical and technical problems if the operation was to be humane, yield quality products and mesh with research. The idea of Operation Windfall (a mnemonic for "Wildlife Industries For All") emerged during these meetings (Martin, Conway and Dix, 1977). Bridging finance was made available so that the exercise would be undertaken on a profit-making basis. It was agreed that certain charges, including the salaries and incidental expenses of Departmental staff, should not be debited against the operation as they were a fair charge to research and management (See Tables 1 and 2).

Previous research suggested the removal of three major population units, or clans, and it was decided to use the 1980 cull to test the effects of removing one of these, consisting of about 400 animals. A comprehensive radio collar marking programme was carried out with a view to answering questions relating to the short-term disturbance effects of this shooting and long-term monitoring of the reoccupation of the culling area.

In the short term there was some minor disturbance limited mainly to groups of elephant within the clan concerned. In the second year it was decided to retain a predetermined number of animals to provide a known population in which to observe post-culling behaviour. These groups were radio marked and all others were removed.

3.1. Culling and processing products

During culling, a suitably-sized group of elephant is located from the air, and the ground party, of two or three hunters and their assistants, are then guided to the group by radio. In such a tightly coordinated operation the pilot, who is also an experienced hunter, is informed of the wind direction by the men on the ground who he then guides to the group to be shot. Killing is quick and effective and the shooting is usually over within one minute.

The killing is done so rapidly that the group does not disperse and the carcasses remain conveniently close to each other. Each carcass is numbered and the cuts to remove panels of hide are marked out. While the skinning and butchering proceeds, useful scientific data on reproductive status, stomach contents, physical condition and age are collected.

During Operation Windfall, 110 labourers were employed to skin and cut up the carcasses which were then transported to a processing yard, where the hide was flensed, washed and salted and the meat was cut into thin strips, brined and sun-dried on wire mesh racks. A further 110 workers were employed on these activities and on preparing the products for market.

3.2. Safari hunting

Although the Chirisa is viewed as a potential National Park and the ecosystems are protected accordingly, its present status as a Safari Area allows more freedom of use. In particular, recreational trophy hunting is permitted. This is strictly controlled and has minimal effect on wild populations of birds and mammals, but provides a significant economic return.

Hunting in Safari Areas in Zimbabwe is either sold as individual hunts with a predetermined quota for each hunt, or an annual quota is offered on tender to a registered safari operator. Chirisa falls into the latter category and in 1980 realized US$74,200. 1981 was the first of a 5-year agreement with a different operator and yielded US$86,720 for the rights and quotas noted in Table 3.

3.3. Results

There are already signs that the vegetation in parts of Chirisa is responding positively to the reduced elephant pressure. The closely monitored cull confirmed the Department's earlier experience which suggested that the removal of whole family groups of elephant results in minimal disturbance to the behaviour of resident elephant populations. The reduction exercise yielded additional useful scientific data and US$416,969 in cash from products sold. Recreational hunting added US$158,300 over the two years to yield US$1.68 per ha/year. While this high return was dependent on a superabundance of elephant, it meant that US$556,230 in profits was paid to the local District Council at a critical stage in the history of the area.

The people have benefitted from the availability of a good supply of high quality protein and already they have requested an increase in the price of this meat so as to prevent a few customers from cornering the market, and to ensure its wider distribution. The hides and ivory, either in a raw or manufactured state, have earned useful foreign currency and have generated economic activity at various levels from the Sebungwe to the cities.

One old man, who witnessed the payment of royalties to his District Council, was heard to say that he would not again complain and demand the destruction of elephant that entered his crops, instead he would take home any sick animal he found so that he could nurse it back to health.

Against these positive responses there are several negative factors. Despite propaganda and the relatively high levels of productivity that can be sustained from the safari operations, there is a danger that the local people will be disappointed as the return in meat and cash declines once excessive populations are curbed. There are also signs of growing disagreement in regard to where the revenue derived from wildlife should be spent, between the people living in parts of the district where wildlife is plentiful and those from more populous and politically more influential areas where it is scarce. This may explain why some District Councils elsewhere in Zimbabwe have shown a reluctance to inform their grass roots constitutents of the direct benefits to the area of the proper use of its wildlife.

4. DISCUSSION

An acceptance that wildlife in Zimbabwe is a renewable resource was encouraged through legislation and administrative action over a period of 17 years. This culminated in the promulgation of the Parks and Wild Life Act in 1975. This act allows a landowner to use his wildlife at will and to benefit from such use. Abuses are curbed by his local conservation committee and are subject to unilateral action by central Government, if necessary. In the seven years since the Act came into force, these provisions have not been invoked.

This philosophy has favoured wildlife on privately-owned land, but the principle was not applied to communally-occupied tribal land by the pre-independence Government. Operation Windfall is the first major move toward rectifying this situation. Already there is less antagonism against wildlife as instead of being viewed as state property, it is appreciated as a resource to be used by the local community. A number of Councils already, after only one year, are examining the allocation of some of their land for wildlife management programmes.

There are many examples in Zimbabwe of well-stocked National Parks or Safari Areas adjoining underdeveloped communal lands. It is hoped this practice will be extended to other areas in the interests of breaking down the "hard edge" effect of these two forms of land use, and plans are being developed for these principles to be applied to the entire Sebungwe region (Martin and Taylor 1982). Consideration is also being given to the creation of more buffer zones around protected areas where, technically, the interests of wildlife would diminish outwards and those of agriculture in the reverse direction, but where the local people and the protected area administration would have a mutual interest in the proper use of the wildlife. This does, however, require careful biological research, into the implications, and broad public consultation, before it can be implemented.

Large mammals like elephant, buffalo and lion represent a uniquely African and highly marketable cash crop that is less sensitive to world commodity price fluctuations than most conventional primary products. Areas of low agricultural productivity like Chirisa have an opportunity to provide a valuable harvest that can rival any from conventional agriculture while requiring less intensive inputs and placing less strain on the ecosystems of the area. The controlled harvesting of wildlife is of long-term advantage to the protection of the animal resource both by maintaining a healthy habitat and by increasing its material value both locally and nationally.

Without the demonstration provided by the use of wildlife in Chirisa, development in the Sebungwe, outside of its six protected areas, would have continued to be toward intensified agriculture. Already this has led to serious ecological deterioration and this would have accelerated in the face of the political demands of a rapidly expanding human population expecting enhanced living standards from a precarious ecological base. Wildlife would have been eliminated, either intentionally to make way for agriculture or through the destruction of its habitat.

Acknowledgements

I am grateful to Dr. David Cumming and Mr. Rowan Martin of the Department of National Parks and Wild Life Management and Professor Kenton R. Miller, Chairman, Commission on National Parks and Protected Areas, who read and offered valuable comments on the draft of this paper. Mrs. Isabel West kindly typed the Ms while Mr. Claud Dzotizeyi prepared the figure.

Table 1. Costs of Elephant Population Reduction in Chirisa Safari Area in Zimbabwe dollars

Year	Number cropped	Costs					
		Labour $	Supplies(1) $	Transport $	Flying $	Drugs/Ammo $	Total $
1980	380	20,344	3,880	13,153	6,500	700	44,577
1981	375	23,096	6,561	11,427	7,979	700	49,763
Total	755	43,440	10,441	24,580	14,479	1,400	94,340
Av./Carcass		57.53	13.83	32.55	19.16	1.85	

(1) Estimated—ivory not yet sold.

Table 2. Income from Elephants Removed from Chirisa Safari Area in Zimbabwe dollars

Year	Number cropped	Earnings				
		Meat $	Ivory $	Hide $	Other $	Total $
1980	380	9,599	70,676	70,511	487	151,273
1981	375	9,750	75,000 (1)	64,926	7,917	157,593
Total	755	19,349	145,676	135,437	8,404	308,866
Av./Animal		25.6	193	179	11,1	409,09

(1) Estimated—ivory not yet sold.

Table 3. Hunting Quota Offered in the Chirisa Safari Area in 1981 including gross earnings for 1980/1981

Species	No.	Royalty per Animal Z($)	Species	No.	Royalty per Animal Z($)
Elephant, male	5	2,000	Warthog 4	25	
Elephant, female	10	700	Baboon 30	10	
Lion 3	1,000		Porcupine	1	15
Leopard 8	600		Civet 2	25	
Buffalo, male	15	350	Total value of Trophies		40,995
Buffalo, female	5	150	75% refund on untaken		
Sable 2	600		Trophy Animals		2,735.50
Eland 2	350			$38,259.50	
Kudu	200		Concession hunting rights fee 1981		24,000.00
Reedbuck 5	100		Trophy fees paid 1981		38,259.50
Waterbuck	2	300	Population reduction revenue 1980/81		308,866.00
Zebra 10	250		Concession/hunting fees paid 1980		55,000.00
Impala 24	30		2 year total =		$426,125.50
Bushbuck 6	100		Therefore, Gross product per ha. =		
Duiker 6	15				
Grysbok 6	20		$\dfrac{426,125.50}{171,200} =$		$2.49
Klipspringer	4	75			

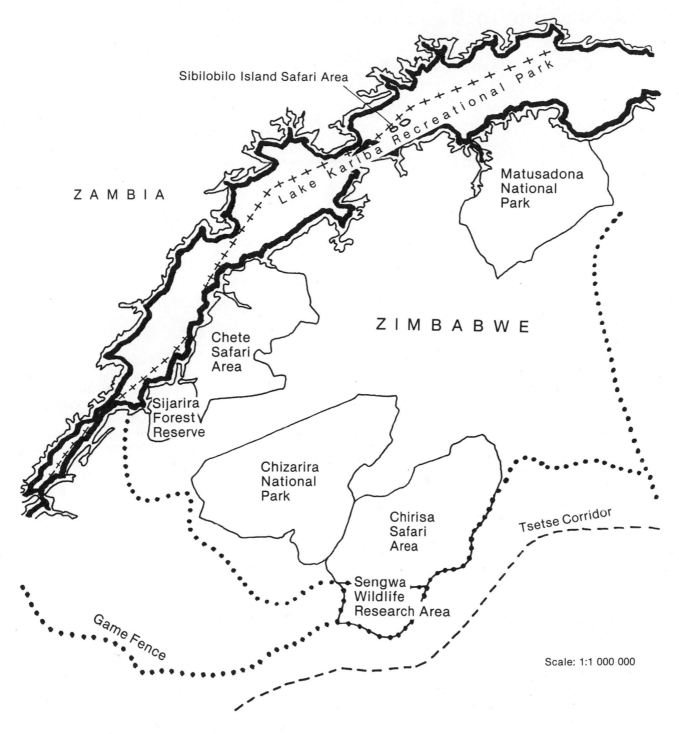

Figure 1. The Sebungwe region of Zimbabwe showing the Chirisa and other protected areas and the tsetse control hunting corridor of which the Sengwa Wildlife Research Area was originally a part.

Anti-Poaching in Botswana

Decreanor Dwililan Mangubo
Department of Wildlife and National Parks
Maun, Botswana

ABSTRACT. *Botswana's approach to anti-poaching is to institute active management of all wildlife resources in the country. The Department of Wildlife and National Parks has full powers of arrest of those who violate the regulations, but is also carrying out an active public relations campaign involving public conservation education, public meetings, and seminars for local decision makers; this campaign aims at increasing the awareness of the value of the wildlife resource so that the people themselves help to control poaching. Difficulties include the lack of sufficient manpower, funds, equipment, and infrastructure.*

1. INTRODUCTION

The Republic of Botswana is landlocked, bounded by Zimbabwe in the east, South Africa in the south, Namibia (South West Africa) in the west and northwest and Zambia in the north. Botswana has an area of 570,000 sq km and has an estimated population of just under 1 million. About 2/3 of the country is covered by the sandy Kalahari desert.

1.1. Wildlife

Botswana is endowed with a fascinating variety of African game. Herds of desert species, e.g. gemsbok *Oryx gazella*, cape hartebeest *Alcelaphus buselaphus*, and springboks *Antidorcas marsupialis* may be seen roaming the grasslands of the Kalahari from north to south. Going along in the same movement are thousands of wildebeest *Connochaetes taurinus* migrating from south to north utilizing water holes or pans before they dry.

In the north are the only two rivers of perennial water, the Okavango and the Chobe. Both these rivers have their source in Angola and bring in flood from April to August. The Okavango spills into the northwestern corner of Botswana and forms the internationally famous swamps of the 16,000 sq km Okavango Delta. The Chobe river which forms the north international boundaries between Botswana and the Caprivi Strip of Namibia and also between Botswana and Zambia, runs for over 300 km before it pours its waters into the Zambezi river. There is a distributary of the Chobe called Savuti which pours its water into the Mababe depression. These systems of rivers support enormous herds of elephants *Loxondanta africana*, zebras *Equus burchelli*, buffaloes *Syncerus caffer*, hippopotami *Hippopotamus amphibius* and giraffes *Giraffa camelopardalis* just to mention a few. Found side by side with these game herds are predators such as lions *Panthera leo*, spotted hyaena *Crocuta crocuta*, leopards *Panthera pardus*, etc.

In an effort to preserve and protect wildlife in Botswana the Government has declared all vertebrates game animals so that no person is allowed to utilize these animals without a licence or permit, and perhaps the most important measure, areas abounding in game animals were proclaimed or declared national parks, game reserves, or sanctauries. A new addition to these are the wildlife management areas (WMAs) where wildlife utilization will be carried out.

1.2. Conflicting land uses

National parks, game reserves and game sanctuaries occupy 17% of the total area of Botswana. This percentage is indeed very high at this stage of the world human population explosion, which stimulates a scramble for land. Although Botswana is sparsely populated, signs of growing land demand are evident. In 1971 the population was just above 650,000; by 1981, preliminary results of the census showed a rise to over 990,000. New technologies, new developments, and more people all need space in order to survive. For example, a farmer who had 50 head of cattle in 1971 may have 300 head of cattle today and the area he occupies is by far greater than before, say 4,900 ha. New towns spring from the desert as more mines are being discovered. Wildlife migration routes are being blocked by new towns or migrations are being deflected into areas where human interests are high, thus necessitating killing of animals in defence of property. In Botswana, however, plans for any land use form have been developed to take stock of all interests including wildlife. If farms are being proposed or established, corridors are provided so that animals have access to areas where they can find food. But the biggest problem is veterinary cordon fences which are erected in the middle of migration routes to stop animals from coming into contact with cattle, as foot and mouth disease is contracted by animals (the spread or outbreak of foot and mouth affects 75% of the people as cattle herding is the mainstay of Botswana). Ugly scenes of entangled game are seen every day along fences. This situation is unacceptable to all concerned but nothing has been done as it has the sanction of government. As the disease is controlled through improved vaccination programmes, these fences should be removed.

2. NATIONAL PARKS, GAME RESERVES AND SANCTUARIES

Botswana being a developing nation has problems of developing, managing and policing its national parks, game reserves and sanctuaries. Funds for establishing infrastructure such as game viewing roads, demarcated boundaries, tourist facilities and information signs are inadequate. Lack of trained personnel and, equipment make the task of maintaining national parks and protected areas more difficult. In Botswana the situation is further aggravated by the very nature of these areas; they are either too sandy or too swampy to penetrate by ordinary means.

2.1. Controlled hunting areas

The country has been divided into several blocks called "controlled hunting areas"; where hunting quotas are determined, thus controlling the number of persons hunting in each area. Licences are then sold for each animal against the number determined. It is easy to see and gauge if any species is in abundance or scarce by returns given after the hunt or by reports as given by hunters. No person is allowed to hunt in any area other than the one endorsed by license. While hunters are in the field, wildlife officers check on the conduct of hunters and to ascertain that they only shoot the allowed numbers. Constant or regular patrols have a deterrent effect on poaching activities.

2.2. Controlling poaching in general

The Department of Wildlife and National Parks is charged with the responsibility of controlling or stopping illegal hunting (the Botswana Police are, however, also empowered and entrusted with that responsibility). The Department staff of slightly above two hundred is thinly distributed throughout the country. Each game reserve, national park, sanctuary or controlled hunting area has a statutory instrument establishing it or declaring and defining its boundary. Whenever possible boundaries follow known physical features to avoid confusing people with imaginary lines. Where this is not possible, outlines or sign posts are made and placed where they can be of help.

2.3. Field camps

Field camps are built at strategic locations, for example at District Headquarters or at the entrance of each game reserve or national park. Three or more officers are stationed at each camp. Vehicles are provided to vitally strategic places; foot patrols or boat patrols are also embarked upon. Due to financial constraints, not as many field camps are constructed or as many people employed as are necessary to do the job. Because illegal activities pertaining to hunting and trading in trophies become more intense year after year and the shortage of resources is a problem, government has sought assistance from interested persons who provide information and are also empowered to arrest wrongdoers. These people are designated Honorary Game Officers.

2.4. Wildlife conservation education

There is an Education Unit in the Department of Wildlife and National Parks which is charged with the responsibility of promoting public awareness, disseminating information, and interpreting wildlife legislation to the people. In order to succeed in formulating and implementing policy on wildlife conservation, people have to accept the policy; to achieve this, people must be educated to understand the value of wildlife to all mankind. The unit addresses public meetings in villages and schools, and thereafter show slides or films. Departmental staff stationed in field camps go around as well in their respective districts, holding public meetings at village meeting places. Here villagers and wildlife officers converge in a free atmosphere to discuss problems facing one another and share ideas about the best methods or principles to be followed in fostering conservation of wildlife. Information obtained from villagers is amalgamated into the plan of strategies for the development of the wildlife resource in their area; information obtained is also incorporated in the drafting of wildlife legislation. This is a very crucial event in a democratic set-up. If there is no consultation between government and the people, an area of confrontation is born and an anti-wildlife feeling gained so that poaching can go on unabated.

2.5. Involvement of local institutions

The involvement of local institutions in the affairs of the Department pertaining to the management of the wildlife resource has enhanced public awareness. In our case, each district has a District Council and a Land Board. The District Council provides inputs into management plans, and revenue collected from the sale of game licenses is shared between government and district councils; in this way the district council can generate revenue to provide services to the people in the form of clinics, schools and improved roads, etc. The Land Board is the custodian of all tribal land; it is charged with the responsibility of allocating land and settling land disputes. If Safari Companies want to lease areas for hunting or for photographic safaris, applications are made to the Land Board, which consults with the Department and the District Council in deciding on the applications. Money realized from leased lands goes directly into the coffers of the Land Boards. This money is used to maintain the Board and also to expand the activities of the Board in meeting the demands of the people. As these institutions deal with people every day, they are able to inform the public of the benefits of preserving and protecting wildlife. Having the support of the above institutions, the Department activities are better understood and appreciated and hence less confrontation is experienced and successful anti-poaching operations are made possible.

3. TRAINING INSTITUTIONS

The object of having public support and cooperation cannot be achieved without quality staff, so Government has established a wildlife Training Centre in Maun, a village on the outskirts of the Okavango, to train wildlife managers. It is an in-service training institution; all officers recruited in the Department go through an induction course, including a seven months certificate course. All officers are put through the course at intervals, so they become better qualified and prepared to discharge their duties through such courses.

Every year at the end of the seven months course, a seminar on wildlife conservation is organized. Participants are drawn from Safari operators, District Councils, Land Boards, Government Officers and villagers. By educating people in the role that wildlife plays in nature, and in the development of the country, abuse of the resource through poaching and other illegal activities is decreased.

4. MEMBERSHIP OF INTERNATIONAL ORGANIZATIONS

Botswana is a Party to the Convention on International Trade in Endangered Species of Wild Fauna and Flora (CITES) and as such endeavours to enforce the dictates of this Convention inasfar as trade in fauna and faunal products is concerned. It should be understood that poaching, as in the case of elephant, increases with the monetary value of the animal concerned. Since in Botswana all dealers in wildlife and wildlife products are known in that they require permits or licenses, all of which are issued by the Department of Wildlife and National Parks, it would not help any poacher to approach these dealers with his illegally obtained trophies. This therefore argues for the existence of an underground organization through which illegally obtained trophies are channelled to buyers outside Botswana. Should such poached products escape the country somehow then other parties of CITES will be on the lookout for them. Indeed several European countries as well as the USA have come back to us on exported wildlife products purporting to have been legally obtained from Botswana but whose expert permits were either missing or different from the known Botswana permits.

5. CONCLUSION

Botswana could do more and is actively endeavouring to do more but the lack of sufficient manpower, funds and equipment such as vehicles, radios, arms and ammunition, as well as the lack of sufficient, adequate or in some cases of any accommodation at all makes the task somewhat difficult. With a little bit of help from our friends, however, we think we can manage to reduce, since it is impossible to actually eradicate, poaching.

Acknowledgements

This paper was prepared for IUCN's Commission on National Parks and Protected Areas in cooperation with the United Nations Environment Programme.

We All Want the Trees: Resource Conflict in the Tai National Park, Ivory Coast

Harald H. Roth
National Parks and Wildlife Adviser to the Government of Ivory Coast
Abidjan, Ivory Coast

1. INTRODUCTION

We all want trees? I would rather say: We all *need* trees. The Global 2000 Report to the President of the United States concludes that "of all the environmental impacts, deforestation probably poses the most serious problems for the world, particularly in the developing countries". An estimated 40% of the tropical moist forests that had historically covered this planet, have already been permanently lost. The remaining tropical forest cover is disappearing so rapidly, that without stringent conservation measures this unique resource will be exhausted and transformed into man-made landscapes within the next 30 years. The case history of the Tai National Park is the story of an effort to conserve the last large primary rainforest in West Africa.

2. VEGETATION ZONES OF AFRICA

In Africa one has to distinguish between the large Congolese-Biafran rainforest block and the Guinean rainforest belt, separated from each other by the Dahomean V. This distinction is important because the Guinean forest belt contains a large number of plant and animal species endemic in that region only. At the same time West Africa is the region in which forest destruction and transformation is advancing more rapidly than in any other region of the world: by 1976 the moist forest cover had regressed already by 76% and projection by FAO indicates that by 2000, 47% of the remaining closed forest area will be lost.

2.1. Vegetation zones of the Guinean region

Within the Guinean forest zone one has to distinguish between the semi-deciduous moist forest and the evergreen lowland rainforest. The distribution of the forest elephant in West Africa indicates best the degree of fragmentation of the lowland rainforest left. Remaining patches are rarely larger than 150,000 ha; the only large rainforest left untouched is the Tai complex in the southwest region of Ivory Coast. With its buffer zone and adjoining game reserves, it comprises today an area of no less than 750,000 ha.

3. CONSERVATION AREAS IN WEST AFRICA

The Tai National Park is the only well-established conservation area in the Guinean forest zone, large enough to preserve the flora and fauna endemic to that zone. In Liberia, which has next to Ivory Coast the most important rainforest area, efforts are under way to establish some 130,000 ha of primary forest as the Sappo National Park, but this has still no legal status. In Sierra Leone, the last rainforest, the Gola complex, representing 4% of the original forest area, is currently being scheduled for timbering. In Ghana, once so rich in forest resources, the only developed forest conservation area comprises the Bia National Park of only 8,000 ha surrounded by some 60,000 ha of game and forest reserves.

Of the total of areas zoned for conservation in West Africa, 92% are savanna lands and only 8% moist forest. This highlights the particular problem and urgency of conservation action in the West African forest zone.

4. TIMBER EXPLOITATION IN THE IVORY COAST

The south-west region of Ivory Coast bordering Liberia was almost uninhabited until the 1950s, when large scale timber exploitation started. By 1968 timbering had reached the Tai forest, which had already in 1926 been declared a Forest and Wildlife Refuge by the French administration. Upon representation by the IUCN in 1971 the President of the Ivory Coast himself had partly declared this Forest Reserve as a National Park. Timber exploitation was halted at its periphery in the last minute. In 1977, a buffer zone was created in which no settlement is allowed and in which timber exploitation is being phased out. Timber exploitation, however, remains to be a potential threat to the Tai National Park as the forest resource of the country becomes totally exhausted.

5. REGIONAL DEVELOPMENT OF THE SOUTHWEST OF IVORY COAST

Development of the south-western region of Ivory Coast within the past 15 years has been one of the fastest in all of West Africa. Immigration of people from the north has boosted the population of this region from 2 persons/sq km in 1968 to about 7 persons/sq km in 1978, and is projected to reach 27 persons/sq km by the end of the century. Two major hydro-electrical plants are being developed on the Sassandra river, inundating some 50,000 ha of forest. South of the park 350,000 ha of forest are being transformed into paper pulp plantations.

Approximately 40,000 ha of forest are being cleared every year for shifting cultivation. The total surface of agro-industrial plantations around the park has developed from 1,700 ha in 1967 to 36,000 ha in 1980; the total surface of coffee and cocoa plantations has increased from 4,500 ha in 1975 to more than 10,000 ha in 1980.

Due to the rapid development of the south-western region the Tai National Park has become the last island of primary forest in a more or less man-made landscape. Settlement along with agricultural development has not yet penetrated into the park, but its pressure on the boundaries of the park is building up. Illegal timbering at one time or another has modified about one third of the park. Poaching is heavy everywhere in the park and very difficult to control. A summary of the conservation actions taken to date is shown in Table 1.

What is this heritage we are trying to conserve? The Tai forest contains some 1,300 different species of higher plants, of which 54% occur only in the Guinea zone; 16%, i.e. about 150 species, are endemic in the Tai region. The total of animal species occurring in the Tai forest has been estimated at some 2,000. Of the 54 larger mammal species known to occur in the Guinea rainforest belt, 47 are found in the Tai National Park. Several of these, like the Pigmy Hippo, Jentink's and Zebra duiker, the Green colobus monkey and some of the viverrids have a very restricted range within the Guinea region only. Five of the mammalian species of the Tai National Park are included in the Red Data Book. These figures highlight the uniqueness of the Tai National Park and the reason why we all should be concerned with its conservation.

Table 1: History of the Conservation of the Tai Rain Forest Complex in Ivory Coast

Year	National Action	Size of area	International Action
1926	Creation of a "Wildlife and Forest Refuge" between the rivers Cavally and Sassandra	1,000,000 ha	
1933			Inclusion of the "Sassandra Reserve" in the London Convention on the Protection of African Fauna;
1956	Consolidation of status into Game Reserve	425,000 ha	
1971			IUCN Mission and proposal for National Park;
1972	Declaration of Tai National Park	350,000 ha	
1973	Reduction of size of Tai National Park in favour of timber conservation	10,000 ha	
1973			German National Parks fact-finding mission;
1974	Creation of independent National Parks Organization		
1975			French study on Tourist potential of Tai National Park;
1976			Commencement of UNESCO/MAB Project Tai;
1976–78			German inventory survey of Tai National Park and management proposals;
1977	Redelimitation of Tai National Park and creation of buffer zone	350,000 ha 66,000 ha	
1978			Unesco declaration of Tai National Park as Biosphere Reserve;
1978–81			WWF project on delimitation of Tai National Park;
1981	Phasing out of timber exploitation in the National Park buffer zone		
1981–1982	Reorganization and reenforcement of National Park administration		Inclusion of the Tai National Park in the IUCN conservation programme "Primates and Rainforest";
1982	Extension of National Park buffer zone	70,000 ha	Inclusion of the Tai National Park in the Unesco List of World Heritage.

The Role of Protected Areas in Saving the Sahel

John Newby
Direction des Eaux et Forêts
Niamey, Niger

ABSTRACT. *Using the Aïr and Ténéré National Nature Reserve, a proposed area of some 8 million ha, the study shows the immensely important role that protected areas and wildlife can play in the wise use of Africa's arid lands. Potentially valuable wildlife resources in the Sahel are rapidly dwindling because of over-hunting, but lack of funds forbids anything but cursory action to stop the decline and this is likely to continue until the wildlife totally disappears or its real potential is recognized and exploited. Throughout the Sahel the aim should be a mix of traditional forms of resource conservation and more modern land-use approaches such as wildlife culling within zoned conservation units; such zoning needs to be flexible and allow for changes in management as resource abundance and local imperatives change. Eventually it should be possible to transfer much of the decision-making and land management to the local populations, who can be expected to act rationally to their own advantage.*

1. INTRODUCTION

The Republic of Niger is on the verge of establishing its first nature reserve since Independence in 1960. The Aïr and Ténéré National Nature Reserve will, when created, not only be the largest protected area in Africa (8,015,000 ha) but also the first wildlife reserve in the Sahara. The following case study outlines the reserve's history and the rationale behind the decision to create it. In doing so, the study endeavours to emphasize the immensely important role that protected areas and wildlife can play in the wise use of Africa's aridlands and ultimately, in the rational, long-term development of their natural, cultural and historical resources.

Niger (1,267,000 sq km) is one of the vast Sahelian states that lie within and to the south of the Sahara.

Two-thirds of the country is made up of arid and hyper-arid habitats that receive less than 400 mm of rainfall annually. The vegetation of this Sahelo-Saharan zone ranges from sparsely wooded steppe in the south to the barren and waterless sand-seas of the Sahara in the north. Where there are mountains, enclaves of Sahelian vegetation grow in the valleys and drainage pans. In spite of its waterless nature, the Sahelo-Saharan zone was until recently the home of large numbers of highly adapted aridland ungulates such as the addax *Addax naso maculatus*, the scimitar-horned oryx *Oryx dammah* and several species of gazelle (*Gazella* spp.).

In 1979, IUCN, WWF and the Zoological Society of London, mounted a joint expedition to Niger. The expedition had two aims; to assess Niger's desert and sub-desert fauna; and to make concrete proposals to the Government of Niger (GON) on how its aridland fauna might be effectively protected. The expedition rapidly discovered two important facts:

- that Niger's aridland fauna was not only highly threatened but had largely disappeared from most of its recent range;
- that the mountainous areas of the Aïr and Termit were perhaps the last strongholds of Sahelo-Saharan wildlife in the country.

Considering the urgency of the situation, work was immediately started on studying the ecology of part of the Aïr and neighbouring Ténéré desert. Although the major aim of the survey was to inventory the natural resources of these areas, a great deal of time was spent quantifying habitat degradation, especially among the area's trees. The Tuareg nomads of the Aïr are comparatively sedentary and in an area devoid of large expanses of grassland, the pastoralism they practise depends a great deal on the existence of healthy stands of browse species like *Acacia* trees; during drought years, trees may be the nomads' sole source of fodder. In 1979, the effects of the major drought that afflicted the Sahel during the late 1960s and 70s was most evident; many trees had died and others were in poor shape following over-utilization. However, even a cursory glance at the area under study revealed that unlike many other parts of Niger, wildlife was still varied and relatively abundant. Dorcas gazelles *Gazella dorcas*, Barbary sheep *Capra lervia* and ostrich *Struthio camelus* seemed particularly well represented and apart from the plains-living oryx, the other Sahelo-Saharan species could all be found.

Following its work, the expedition published a synthesis of its findings (Newby and Jones, 1980) to form the basis of a project proposal that would permit the GON to request funds for the establishment of a protected area in the Aïr. The expedition's report was greeted enthusiastically by the GON and prompted IUCN/WWF to initiate a specific project for the country (IUCN/WWF Project 1624).

In 1980, IUCN/WWF sent Newby back to Niger to assist the authorities in the preparation of an in-depth study of the Aïr and to outline concrete proposals for the establishment of a protected area.

While the fieldwork was being carried out, WWF began raising funds for the project. In 1981, the project's financial success was guaranteed when WWF International received an ear-marked donation US$450,000 from an anonymous donor. In the same year in the United Kingdom, WWF secured a further US$80,000 and the Fauna and Flora Preservation Society, Marwell Preservation Trust Ltd., the People's Trust for Endangered Species and the Zoological Society of London joined forces to launch a fund-raising appeal called "Operation Scimitar Oryx". When the reserve is officially gazetted, the funds raised will permit the GON to undertake a comprehensive programme to conserve its aridland wildlife, flora and habitats.

2. THE ENDANGERED SAHELO-SAHARAN FAUNA

Concerned by reports from all over the northern arid zone of Africa that wildlife was severely threatened, IUCN, WWF and UNEP initiated a wildlife survey in 1975. The reports submitted (Lamprey, 1975; Newby, 1975a, Trotignon, 1975) showed that each of the principal large mammal species of the Sahel and Sahara had undergone serious reductions in their distribution. Many of the species could be classed as vulnerable, and the addax and scimitar-horned oryx were highly endangered and risked extinction unless prompt remedial action was taken. As a result of the project, a group of consultants met in Morges in 1976 and drew up a framework for the conservation of the Sahelo-Saharan fauna. The establishment of a comprehensive and well-run net-

work of protected areas was deemed necessary. At that time only one reserve existed, Chad's Ouadi Rimé-Ouadi Achim Faunal Reserve, and it was unanimously decided that the Chadian government be aided in maintaining its long-standing commitment to preserving aridland wildlife. Up until the escalation of civil unrest in 1978, the Ouadi Rimé reserve benefited from financial and technical assistance from IUCN/WWF (Project 1327). When the reserve finally had to be abandoned, the world lost its only Sahelo-Saharan wildlife reserve; with it went a sizeable proportion of the world's addax and, staggeringly, up to 80% of the total scimitar-horned oryx population. Among the areas recommended for action at the Morges consultation was the Aïr Mountains.

Six years after the Morges meeting, Africa is still without a valid Sahelo- Saharan wildlife reserve and the status of the region's mammals has considerably worsened. Addax exist in small remnant herds across the Sahara but the oryx is now restricted to two small areas in Niger and Chad. It is as yet too soon to know exactly how the Chadian wildlife has fared during the civil war but reports are far from encouraging. As the larger antelopes disappear, the smaller gazelles and the ostrich become prime targets for hunters. A status review of the Sahelo-Saharan fauna prepared for IUCN (Newby, 1981), shows that the current situation is precarious with the scimitar-horned oryx down to as few as 1500 in the wild.

3. THE FAUNA'S DECLINE

The decline of the Sahelo-Saharan fauna has been a spectacularly rapid one. During the 19th century, the first European travellers marvelled at the wealth of wildlife they found in the arid zone of West Africa (Barth 1958-60, Nachtigal 1881). As late as the 1950s, wildlife populations were still considered abundant throughout much of the Sahel. A decade later, very little remained. Populations of oryx, addax, dama gazelle *Gazella dama*, slender-horned gazelle *G. leptoceros* and ostrich had been radically reduced by ruthless overhunting. Although the increase in the number of automatic weapons has had a drastic effect on wildlife numbers, the advent of desert-going vehicles makes hunting in the wide-open spaces of the Sahel child's play. Petrochemical and mineral prospectors, military and armed administrators were and still are the major culprits of the worsening wildlife situation. In spite of the fact that most Sahelian states have banned hunting, outlawed the possession of firearms and have specific laws to protect their aridland fauna, the carnage goes on and for the most part it is the legal possessors of arms who are responsible.

While over-hunting is by far the principal and most direct cause for the decline of the fauna, other factors are also important. Although adequately adapted to cope with arid conditions, wildlife suffers from prolonged drought through the disappearance of pasture. The desert ungulates have evolved migration to solve the problems posed on vegetation by a capricious climate. Within the zone, rainfall is totally unpredictable in time, space and quantity, and precipitation usually varies by more than 30% from one year to the next. Unfortunately, the expansion of rain-fed or irrigated agriculture is restricting migration patterns, often resulting in closer contact between man and wildlife and, invariably, increased hunting. The scimitar-horned oryx has particularly suffered, having been deprived of vital hot season grazing by domestic stock now that water for them is available. The possibilities to poach have also increased and because of poaching's sporadic nature, it is virtually impossible to control on a widespread front.

4. WILDLIFE FOR DEVELOPMENT

As has been indicated by increasing desertification and habitat degradation, economic development of the Sahel is a difficult task. The provision of permanent water, although allowing nomads regular access to hitherto difficult-to-exploit pastures, has led to overgrazing and the removal of the plant cover that prevents erosion and arrests desert creep. Under natural conditions, nomadism is kept in check by the availability of water and pasture and habitat overuse is rarely possible. Deep-well permanent water leads to sedentarism and sedentarism leads to overgrazing. Swift (1975) succinctly points out the pitfalls of the recent and widespread policy to develop nomadism along non-traditional lines. In addition, nomadic movement patterns are becoming cramped by agricultural development to the south, so the inherent capacity of nomadism to cope with fluctuating resource abundance is being destroyed.

In many ways, but to a lesser degree of perfection, nomadic pastoralism mimics the way in which the wildlife exploits its environment. Advanced physiological, morphological and behavioural adaptations permit wildlife not only to exploit marginal arid habitats but, considering the environmental constraints, to be highly productive. Unlike domestic livestock, Sahelo-Saharan wildlife needs no permanent water supply, most of the species being able to satisfy their water requirements by feeding on moisture-rich plants. Furthermore, through its diversity and selective feeding habits, the wildlife can exploit the various habitat strata without the risk of over-exploiting any one of them. Considering the waterless environment, the patchy distribution of pasture, the unpredictable rainfall and ecologically-sound productivity of the Sahelian fauna, every effort should be made to exploit wildlife as an economic resource valuable to humans. Unfortunately, wildlife in the Sahel is being treated as a last option when nothing else will work. At the risk of irking the protectionists that staunchly resist the logic behind the rational utilization of wildlife resources, it is probably fair to say that unless the practice can be initiated in the Sahel, the wildlife will go and go very rapidly indeed.

Apart from the production of meat and valuable hides, tourism is another valid way of conserving wildlife under the auspices of economic development. Given a basic infra-structure of protected areas, tourism could become a lucrative prospect for localized communities and while, as Swift (1975) says, protected areas may be undesirable ". . . for the benefit of well-fed foreign tourists, scattered through an ecological wasteland inhabited by undernourished people," they could, if well designed, serve as useful test grounds for developing and demonstriong the economic viability and ecological supremacy of the Sahelian wildlife resource.

Realistic development of wildlife is being hampered both in and outside the Third World by the notion that protected areas must be inviolate. While there is a very definite need for the traditional type of park or reserve, conservation would be greatly encouraged if more emphasis were put on multi-purpose conservation zones and other management units. To survive, wildlife must be considered a harvestable crop rather than the anachronism it is becoming in ever-dwindling and encroached-upon preserves. New parks and reserves ought to be conceived and established with a view to a change in their function as and when the situation warrants. At the moment, it is imperative to protect the fauna as effectively as possible or it will soon become extinct, but we can be realistically optimistic that once protected, the wildlife will quickly increase to exploitable levels.

5. CONSTRAINTS ON PROGRESS: HUNTERS AND HUNTING

Unlike many ecological problems, the root cause for the disappearance of the Sahelo-Saharan wildlife is readily identified—over-hunting—and, theoretically, once identified is possible to combat. Secondary causes such as direct competition for land and loss of habitat through desertification or overuse are of minor importance for most species. Mining, for example, should pose virtually no threats to wildlife but as it is, the areas around mines are invariably totally hunted out. When the mines and minerals have gone nothing exploitable will be left at all.

Because of good wildlife laws, all hunting in Niger has been banned and is therefore illegal; yet it is widely practised in the absence of law enforcement. To understand something of the difficulties involved in controlling hunting it is necessary to look briefly at hunting itself. Most rural Africans are hunters at heart and probably will always be so as long as game exists. It is dangerous to be dogmatic about the effects of traditional forms of hunting on wildlife. In a context devoid of modifying factors such as modern weapons, vehicles and changing land-use patterns, traditional hunting, in spite ot its widespread and often intensive nature, did not have a significant effect on wildlife numbers. Lack of water and great distances are serious constraints on hunting on foot, horse or camel. Observations made by this author on traditional hunting in central Chad revealed that while the smaller and more numerous herbivores were hunted all the year round, the larger addax and oryx could only be hunted systematically during certain times. Oryx were most vulnerable during the hot season, and at the beginning of the wet season, when at the southern end of their migratory range. During the cold and later wet seasons, they could usually maintain sufficient distance between themselves and potential hunters. Observations on the hot season distribution of wildlife, when it is physically most vulnerable to attack, are of the utmost importance to the planners and managers of Sahelo-Saharan reserves. Exploiting this sort of information permitted park rangers in Chad to control oryx to such an extent that numbers rose by some 60% over a four-year period (Newby, 1980).

At the risk of being dogmatic, it is probably fair to say that, with the exception of particularly rare species, traditional hunting is still largely insignificant to wildlife numbers. What is perhaps more to the point, considering its widespread nature, is that it is virtually impossible to control.

Commercial hunting is another matter and in many parts of the Sahel has reached alarming proportions. Whole areas are being systematically hunted out and while the oryx, dama gazelle and ostrich have long-since disappeared, the dorcas gazelle populations are rapidly dwindling. Hunting is carried out by professional hunters armed with artisanal firearms and wheel-type foot-traps and snares. The meat and hides obtained are prepared in the bush for clandestine sale in the larger rural centres. Considering the scale of operations in some areas, it is difficult to say whether the trade goes on because of the complicity or complacency of the local authorities. It is hard to believe that they are totally ignorant of it.

In spite of numerous private and more publicised warning from the highest authorities, the armed forces persist in hunting wildlife. They are often the only legal possessors of firearms and while they should theoretically uphold the laws of the land, are invariably the prime perpetrators of wildlife massacres.

In most Sahelian countries, wildlife and protected areas are the responsibility of the *Eaux et Forêts*. As in most francophone states, *Eaux et Forêts* action in the field of wildlife conservation centres on the repression of offences. In the vast Sahelian nations, total repression of hunting is an impossibility and even partial action in specific areas would require means beyond those currently available. By and large, there are adequate numbers of non-specialized field personnel but higher, well-trained cadres and equipment are sadly lacking. Even where there are vehicles for wildlife protection, funds for fuel, spares and repairs are totally inadequate for the task at hand. Considering the low priority that wildlife conservation enjoys, motives to do anything at the bush level is understandably poor. Rather than being a complaint, these statements are nothing but a realistic appraisal of the actual situation. Vast sums of money,

even if available to the governments, would rightly be used to better the more immediate needs of their people.

6. SOUND LIMITED ACTION AND THE WILDLIFE POTENTIAL

At its most terse, the wildlife problem in the Sahel can be stated thus: potentiallly valuable wildlife resources are rapidly dwindling because of over-hunting; lack of funds forbids anything but cursory action to stop the decline and this is likely to continue until either the wildlife totally disappears or its real potential is recognized and exploited.

The socio-economic constraints influencing the demise ofthe Sahelo-Saharan hardly leave room for optimism but without it, most wildlife conservationists would be long-since redundant. "Never say die" is most certainly the catchphrase of the professional! It would appear that two prime requirements are prerequisites for the recovery and long-term health of the Sahel's fauna.

6.1. Critical evaluation of the potential of wildlife resources

Until now, the aridland wildlife has at best been treated as something that exists but that has no forseeable long-term value. Like the minerals of the earth, it is for lack of insight being treated as an expendable non-renewable resource. Governments must ask themselves what wildlife can do for them in the Sahel. Considering the environmental and economic constraints on the Sahel and especially the thousands of square kilometres of marginal aridland, wildlife is ecologically an undeniable trump card. It is unfortunately often treated as an 'either/or' subject instead of being considered a valuable complement to other socio-economic activities. In the face of 21st century state-of-the-art technology and development, it is not considered 'sexy' enough to warrant serious consideration. While it would be totally unrealistic to suggest that, wildlife could replace livestock as the number one source of protein or provide an economic livelihood for rural populations, it may be feasible locally and once again, one must stress the complementary role that wildlife could play. In the past, a healthy wildlife resource has played an important role for nomadic and semi-nomadic peoples during periods of drought and famine—and drought is an old friend of the Sahel's. Just as it is wise to store grain for times of famine, it should be desirable to encourage the growth of healthy wildlife stocks.

Not least among the people to be convinced of the potential value of wildlife are the international funding and development agencies like the World Bank, the European Development Fund and the United States Agency for International Development. The policies, influence and money of organizations like these are virtually dictating the way in which Sahelian development is going. There is urgent need for pilot-projects (Duncan and Esser, 1982) to prove once and for all that wildlife can not only be a valid alternative source of income and form of land-use but in some areas may well be the best form of land-use. It must be emphasized that aridland wildlife requires little or no management, no expensive wells to water it, no herders to ensure its access to grazing, little or no veterinary care to keep it in good health and, last but not least, no fears that it will degrade its habitat.

6.2. Sound limited action

Considering the social priorities and the economic restraints facing the Sahelian governments, nationwide action to conserve wildlife is impossible. Action must be selective and based on a careful assessment of potentials and priorities. There is no hope of success if the available funds are spread too thinly and properly conceived, specific projects not only stand a better chance of success but also of finding funds. The same comments also apply to the funding agencies. Instead of saying "we have 100 projects in 100 countries which may or may not succeed," would it not be better to say "we have 3 projects in 3 countries that are succeeding"? Evidently not and until funds for wildlife conservation can be truly internationally-secured, this is unlikely to happen. Funds need to be obtained and used objectively and not solely on the whims of charitable organizations and their albeit generous patrons, otherwise species are going to disappear before the general public has even realized they existed. Tough decisions are needed and need to be firmly adhered to. But who makes the decision to cut off the rhino and save the oryx because it could feed people? And besides, the sale of rhino horn and ivory could also feed people if taken out of the hands of wildlife's mafia of profit-hungry entrepreneurs. This may well sound like heresy to orthodox conservationists but it might just be the only way to keep animals like the rhino and elephant alive in the decades to come. Would this be acceptable? Or will we just sit around blithely discussing the ethics of such an action while the species disappear inexorably into oblivion?

7. ACTION IN NIGER

The creation of a protected area in the Aïr Mountains and Ténéré Desert (Fig. 1) of Niger is a good example of realistic planning and use of valuable natural and cultural resources. The decision to establish the protected area was motivated by five main factors:

- the disappearance of the aridland fauna;
- the increase in habitat degradation;
- the destruction of rich archaeological sites;
- the desire to conserve a part of Niger's natural

heritage for aesthetic, cultural, educational and scientific reasons; and
- the desire to broaden the country's tourist infrastructure.

The protected area was conceived with the aim of maintaining, as far as possible, the traditional forms of land-use, not to evict or compromise the lives of the people who live within and off the area's resources.

The actual zone chosen was selected on the strength of 10 other criteria:

- wealth of fauna;
- great floral variety;
- wealth of geographic, topographic and geological features;
- outstanding cultural, historical and pre-historical value;
- highly important tourist potential;
- possibilities of managing and protecting the zone efficiently;
- low population density;
- presence of a road network making it accessible;
- presence of an existing administrative infrastructure; and
- overall outstanding beauty among Niger's and the Sahara's aridlands.

More important, it will provide the GON with a prestigious focal point on which to concentrate its various commitments to conservation, rural development and tourism.

Unlike many protected areas that are created on the strength of one or two outstanding features, it was decided to inventory as large an area as possible, study its demographic and socio-economic characters and then delimit boundaries that would best attain the project's aims, the chances of success and the hopes focussed on the region. Between 1980 and 1982, seven lengthy field-trips were carried out by the WWF consultant and technicians from the *Eaux et Forêts*. While new areas were visited on each trip, a regular programme of ecological monitoring and wildlife census was initiated. Although an inventory of all the area's natural resources might take years to finish, a useful framework has been established within which new data can be inserted and updated. Apart from the people directly involved in the fieldwork, the regional *Eaux et Forêts* personnel have benefitted from the wealth of information on areas that they rarely visit through lack of means. The establishment and subsequent running of the reserve will greatly enhance the regional infrastructure and its efficiency. The fieldtrips and subsequent analysis of data have provided the Nigerien technicians with valuable training in ecological survey, practical conservation and game management. It has initiated many to the techniques of fieldwork, data collection and analysis. Furthermore, it has been valuable at all levels in bringing out the potential importance of wildlife. To many people it came as a pleasant surprise that wildlife still existed in the area at all.

The boundaries eventually selected for the reserve were chosen after much critical scrutiny and in accordance with a number of factors predetermined as being highly important. These were:

- Validity in terms of the biological requirements of the wildlife;
- lease of recognition;
- the possibility of controlling the delimited area; and
- the inclusion of potentially valuable tourist assets

The work of delimiting the reserve was greatly aided by the previous experience gained in managing Chad's Ouadi Rimé reserve. Although predominantly sub-desert in character, the reserve is similar in size (7,795,000 ha), harbours a similar fauna and is influenced by comparable socio-economic and environmental factors.

8. STEPS TO COME

In way of a conclusion it will be useful to briefly outline the various steps and procedures required before the proposed national nature reserve is officially designated and legally gazetted. Although the scientific aspects of the proposal have already met the approval of the administration's technical services, the documentation requires study by both the higher national and regional government and by the traditional authorities in the region where the reserve will be situated. Comments and criticisms made at these levels will be evaluated and amendments or modifications made as and where necessary. After approval by the Council of Ministers, a decree will be prepared for signature by the Head of State.

While all this is going on, *Eaux et Forêts* will have initiated the recruitment of personnel for the reserve. Plans will be made as to equipping the reserve, managing it and budgeting for its running. In the early stages planning must be open-ended to allow for changes as and when these become necessary or obvious in the light of experience and the tasks at hand. Once the nuances of everyday work become apparent it will be easier to deal with longer-term objectives such as habitat and vegetation rehabilitation. It will also be easier to recognize and exploit the possibilities to include the local population not only in the management of the area but also in planning the policies that will govern land-use and natural resource utilization.

Not only in Niger but throughout the Sahel, we should ideally be aiming at a mix of both traditional forms of resource conservation and more radical (to traditionalists) land-use possibilities such as wildlife culling within zoned conservation units. Zoning needs to be flexible and to allow for changes in management as factors such as resource abundance and local imperatives change. Eventually it should be possible to transfer much of the decision making and land-management to the local populations for their benefit, the region's and that of the nation.

By comparison with what is happening in most of the world's protected areas at the moment, these ideas may sound like futuristic pipe-dreams but the time is rapidly approaching when nothing but radical concepts will satisfy the needs of mankind and wildlife alike. The sooner these concepts are tried, the sooner we can be satisfied that all our efforts have not been in vain.

Acknowledgments

This paper was prepared for IUCN's Commission on National Parks and Protected Areas in cooperation with the World Wildlife Fund.

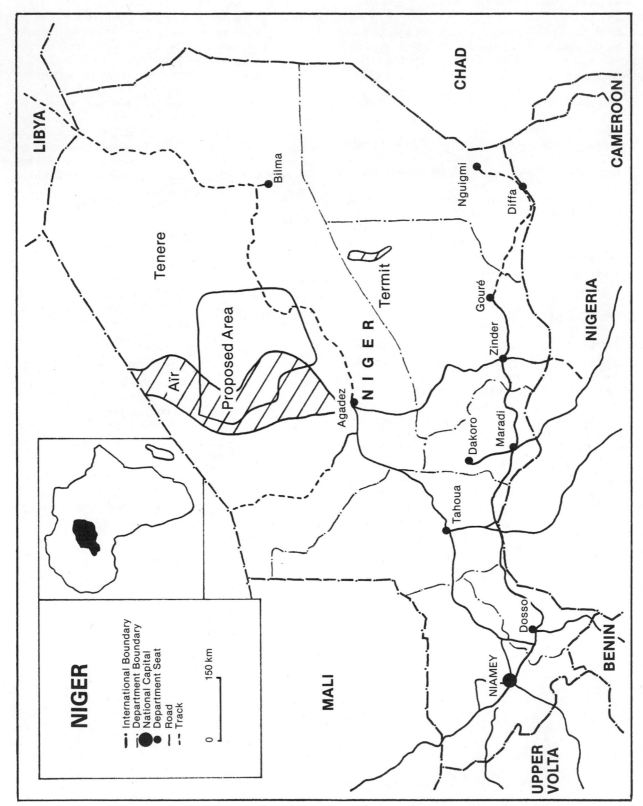

Figure 1. Proposed protected areas in Niger.

NATIONAL PARKS, CONSERVATION, AND DEVELOPMENT

Future Directions for the Afrotropical Realm

Walter J. Lusigi
Project Coordinator
Unesco Integrated Project on Arid Lands
Nairobi, Kenya

ABSTRACT. *The crisis confronting the present system of protected areas in Africa is largely due to the fact that the system is a continuation of conservation policies that fail to recognise the needs, fears and values of the local people, and which are ill-suited to today's development problems. This paper analyzes the trends leading to the present situation and suggests a possible new approach recognizing three basic choices to be made. First, where it can be shown that the conservation of a certain unique ecosystem should have priority, the state has an obligation to secure the land for conservation as by the creation of national parks and reserves (in consulatation with surrounding populations). Second, and at the other extreme, there will be areas where there will be intensive use to the exclusion of any protection activity. Third, between these two extremes, land use plans for the remaining land should assume a degree of compatibility between various competing uses such as wildlife, animal husbandry and agriculture.*

1. INTRODUCTION

The problems of political and socio-economic development which have faced the continent of Africa in recent decades have had profound effects on the conservation movement and the conservation of natural resources in general. Amid competing priorities, such as education, health, food, infrastructure, economic development, agriculture and cooperatives, conservation has unfortunately not received appropriate emphasis. Despite considerable change on the international scene in conservation policies, principles and practices, accompanied by experimentation with new ideas, tropical Africa seems not to be keeping pace. Most conservation systems are still protective of natural resources in the face of demands for increased use from the people.

Although the list of protected areas is very impressive, and has indeed increased in the last decade, largely due to international support and pressure, the question still looms large whether these reserves are viable in the long run within the present institutional framework.

There is first the question of acceptance. Conservation plans implemented in tropical Africa, which have been largely outgrowths of Western conservation needs, fears and values, rather than those of the people whose livelihood is most affected, have not been accepted by the people in the form in which they are currently being presented. In many cases there has simply been no assessment of human needs, and planning still assumes that these countries will develop in the same way as Western countries and that these ideas can be transplanted without modification. Despite claims to the contrary, conservation as presented now remains an alien idea, and the transformation necessary to make it emotionally and intellectually satisfying in its new environment in Africa has not taken place.

Effective conservation reflects a state of mind. In my judgement, the purely economic benefits now popularly advanced as a justification for nature conservation will not in themselves save the African natural heritage. A common failing in the implementation of conservation programmes in the past has been the scant regard that has been given to the so-called "human factor". The existence of a human population in a place presupposes a complex of ethnic, social and biological influences and interactions. If these are not understood and adequately incorporated into conservation plans, the consequences can be serious, and even disastrous.

The publication of the World Conservation Strategy in 1980 was a major landmark in the history of conservation and will undoubtedly serve to unify some of the differing approaches adopted by biologists working in Africa. These differences in approach have crippled the development of realistic conservation policies in the past. Conservation plans acceptable to the people under the prevailing conditions of socio-economic development will have to be based on an appraisal of cultural, political, ecological and socio-economic factors that can balance resources policy with local human needs in both the short- and the long-term.

Another major development that has had a significant impact on conservation activities in tropical Africa in the last few decades has been the high rate of population growth in what are largely agricultural economies. The resulting population pressure on protected areas demands that the conservation system be developed to fulfil a set of realistic objectives and multiple functions, if the protected areas are to survive.

Finally, in addressing ourselves to the future of protected areas there are a number of sensitive questions that must be faced realistically. Can there be effective conservation in the middle of the political turmoil that has characterized Africa in the last two decades? Can there be effective conservation in the absence of realistic land-use policies? Can there be effective conservation within political systems where people often unscrupulously exploit specific scarce resources? Can there be effective conservation in the absence of a realistic conservation education system? Can there be effective conservation in the middle of over-populated, poverty-stricken and largely hungry agricultural communities?

Can there be effective conservation while governments are impoverished by inflation and increasing economic pressures? Can there be effective conservation amid a generally degrading environment suffering from various forms of land-use malpractice? Lastly, can there be effective conservation without the support of the local populations?

I submit that these questions, some of which are hardly ever considered in discussing protected areas, will have to be taken seriously if the future of protected areas in tropical Africa is to be secure. It is not, of course, possible to make any single observation that will apply equally to all African countries. I am, for instance, aware of a number of positive efforts being made in conservation policy in certain countries. If what I say here may not have relevance to every particular case, yet my comments in general are based on a majority of the cases. In a paper of this scope, it will not be possible to go into specifics, so that I have chosen to talk in rather general terms, but I believe the main points are clear and generally applicable. My references to protected areas include national parks and forest reserves, whose protection criteria I consider largely the same. If I appear over-critical, that does not mean that I am pointing an accusing finger—I am myself an African and I fully share and accept part of the blame.

I propose now to look at past and present major trends affecting the conservation of protected areas in Africa. I will then discuss what implications these have for future trends and how in my opinion conservationists could be involved in meeting the new challenges.

2. A HISTORICAL PERSPECTIVE

The wind of change which blew through Africa in the 1960s converted the most universally colonized continent into the world's greatest assembly of newly independent states, receiving their independence at almost the same time. Their existence was in most cases due neither to the exigencies of geography nor to ethnic divisions. As they stand now, they represent the ultimate results of the disastrous rivalry for colonial aggrandisement of the "great powers" at the end of the nineteenth century. They are also the inheritors of the imperial institutions, especially in administrative structure and education, which with the end of colonialism suddenly lost much of whatever socio-economic relevance they had ever possessed. Of these institutions, conservation was probably the least understood by the new rulers and the one which they were, perhaps, least prepared to take over. Whereas in education there was already a Western-educated elite, and in administration already some locally trained officials, in conservation there was a near vacuum. Indeed, one of the rallying cries in the fight for independence was to "recover the lost land", some of which of course lay in protected areas, such as parks and forest reserves. With independence, African states inherited a system of protected areas which consisted mainly of national parks for the protection of wildlife, and of forest reserves for the protection of important water catchments. The system had been set up largely in response to outside pressures and interests, and there had been little consultation with local populations during its formation. Moreover, many areas had been set aside at the cost of displacing traditional cultural practices.

Game laws which restricted local traditional hunting had already hardened local attitudes towards conservation efforts. Protected areas had therefore neither the full sympathy nor the support of the former nationalists who were now the rulers, nor was there support from the local populations.

Despite their seeming indifference toward conservation, many African states emerging into independence during the 1960s were quick to adopt the preservation of indigenous fauna and flora as a matter of prestige. This was, of course, inspired by the "new consciousness" towards nature conservation developing in the 1960s outside Africa. It was also a reaction to fears expressed by Europeans that the new African states would not pay sufficient attention to such matters in the inevitable atmosphere of "accelerated development." Let there be no mistaken notion that when several African states signed the OAU "African Convention on Natural Resources and Protected Areas", and even with the statements of support which followed, that rarely meant total commitment to the cause of conservation. The political import of such statements and of all the grand resource-management plans should not be overlooked, for although many sound national conservation objectives have been declared, subsequent practice has shown that there was often enough no real sincerity behind them.

It is against that background that the following sketch of the main factors operating in the present situation should be read. Many of them, of course, also derive from the historical situation.

3. MAJOR TRENDS AFFECTING PROTECTED AREAS

3.1. Exploitation and management of protected areas

Having declared a commitment to the conservation of protected areas, the new states now face the question of their management. As we have seen, there was a general lack of qualified protected area management personnel who had both professional commitment and emotional understanding of what they were expected to do. Although sympathetic international organizations immediately set up training programmes both locally and abroad to meet this need, it was going to take some time to produce the people needed, and this meant that for a time, the management of protected areas was left completely in the hands of petty administrators and former army privates to whom conservation meant anti-poaching or poaching. The lack of qualified and sympathetic protected area managers and of general integrity and seriousness about conservation led to a wave of exploitation of wildlife, forests and protected areas in the period immediately following independence. Poaching and illegal trading in game trophies and plant products became epidemic across the continent. The sad thing about this exploitation was that it was not done by the local populations, for whom there would at least have been some excuse, but by the very people who were supposed to be the custodians of the resources they were managing. It was not until several game and plant species were in danger of extinction that general international pressure was again brought to bear to save these protected areas. This pressure was coupled with the signing of a treaty on trade in endangered wild species. But despite all these pressures and international incentives, there seem not to have developed local bases for strong conservation action. Although the rate of illegal over-exploitation has slowed down now, the question is, for how long? It is my view that while international pressure has been very successful in maintaining a grid of protected areas across the continent, the success has been mainly a matter of buying time. There must now be realistic conservation policies that can be implemented before that time runs out.

3.2. Protected areas and changes in governments and political systems

Following the wave of independence in Africa came the bewildering wave of violence, manifested in coups d'etat, secessions, and tribal clashes, which swept across the continent from East to West Africa. The past two decades have been characterized by ever-changing policies and political systems, and this trend is still going on today; at the time of writing this paper there are still reports of fighting in various corners of the continent and the wave of refugees moving from country to country continues. These political upheavals are taking their own toll of the protected areas and of efforts to enforce a realistic conservation policy. Amid warring factions, wildlife has of necessity often been the only source of food for hungry soldiers. And wildlife and other valuable resources from protected areas have often been made to supply the quick gains needed by the opportunists who emerge as temporary winners in these struggles. It is not possible to say when the situation will stabilize, but conservationists should not only hope for the best but also prepare for the worst. They must therefore try to develop policies that can maintain the wholeness of protected areas against this background. I will be discussing this in more detail later, but it seems to me that the only hope is for the conservationists to turn their attention to the rural populations that live around protected areas. If such populations can be brought to realize the benefit of these protected areas, they will be able to hold them against any army.

3.3. Land reform

In many African countries the question of land and its ownership is perhaps one of the most sensitive today. It was indeed the ownership of so much land by so few expatriates, while the local populations were pushed into reserves, that was a main issue in the struggle for independence in many countries. Land ownership is fundamentally important in African tribal organization, as people are entirely dependent upon land for all the material needs of life, through which spiritual and mental contentment is achieved. It was therefore to be expected that land reform and an organized land-use system would have been the priorities of these new nations from the beginning. Unfortunately, this has not been the case in many countries in the last two decades. The use of land has been left to opportunism and expediency, and with increasing populations the situation is now so critical that fears have been expressed about the continued viability of protected areas if present trends continue.

Without denying that there may in some cases be total commitment by governments to the concept of protected areas serving as wildlife sanctuaries, it is felt that there may not be sufficient awareness of the dangers likely to undermine the effective continuation of sound conservation policies. Should populations continue to expand at present rates, and unless alternative proposals for human employment and endeavour can be found and implemented, there will arise an insistent clamour for portions of parks to be excised to permit subsistence farming. Eventually, parks could be completely engulfed. Conservationists must in the future push for a development of realistic land-use policies and systems in which parks will have their own place.

3.4. Local views of the present network of protected areas

We have already seen that conservation, as it is currently presented, has not been accepted by the people most immediately affected, and remains an alien idea. I should like to enlarge here on a few of the factors that have contributed to this state of affairs.

Apart from a few isolated examples like county council reserves, by and large the needs of local populations have received little consideration. First, the European settlements pushed many of them out of their homelands; then game laws which allowed hunting by permit only made their normal subsistence hunting illegal; and finally, the land taken for national parks dislodged still more people from their homes.

To the local rural populations around parks and reserves, therefore, protected areas have been seen as the mechanism that forced them from their homes, while confrontation with the game laws has sent many of the men to prison; these are experiences that have reinforced the negative attitude toward protected areas.

The continuation by independent governments of the old conservation policies of absolute protection has further aggravated the attitudes of local populations. In Kenya, for example, there is now a total ban on hunting, a move which is supposed to curb the legal and illegal practices of the more influential, but which drastically penalizes the subsistence hunter. The present protected areas are therefore surrounded by populations that have little sympathy for the park system or for conservation efforts in general. In my opinion, to gain any degree of acceptance throughout the population, the conservation effort simply must be aimed at cultural mores and the restoration of the long-standing ties between man and his natural environment.

3.5. Cultural considerations

Living in balance with the environment was an integral component of African cultures. For example, the concentrations of plains herbivores that we now seek to conserve exist only because of a tolerance for wildlife in some African cultures, in which the individual was taught to co-exist with the natural world around him and to see himself as part and parcel of the system.

Many traditional African religions referred specifically to the preservation of natural things and made it taboo to kill more than was needed for survival. Wildlife, which supported life and gave spiritual satisfaction, was hunted for food and clothing but was also used in tribal ceremonies and rituals. The communal land-ownership system was also designed to enhance living in balance with nature. In pastoral societies, wildlife was regarded as "second cattle", and was especially used during droughts, when domestic cattle were scarce. Through the years, African communities evolved a form of co-existence with the wildlife around them which permitted both to survive. The neglect of these survival strategies is a tragic loss which should be redressed in the future.

In contrast to the African way, most Western efforts at conservation have been resource-oriented—an outgrowth of Western history and heritage and of the focus of the institutions within which most biologists work. The African outlook toward natural things is largely commodity-oriented, and this view must undoubtedly be incorporated in the future planning of protected areas. It certainly cannot be assumed that nature will be regarded in the same way in all cultures—an assumption that has in fact coloured the approach to national parks in Africa in the past. For example, the practice of allocating a single purpose to land—as in the case of parks—is foreign to African culture. To ensure the survival of the national parks in the long run the system must be adjusted to recognize this fact, and to include "perpetuation and use".

3.6. Population trends

Of the many factors that are having an impact on protected areas in Africa, perhaps the most important is human population growth. Many African countries have recorded population growth rates ranging from 2 to 4 percent; some countries in Africa have the highest rates in the world. Despite a growing tendency of urbanization, 90 percent of African populations are still rural, deriving their livelihood from agriculture and livestock. While population increases, the amount of productive land is strictly limited, and most areas have already reached their human carrying capacity. It is estimated that by the year 2000, a great part of this rural population will be forced to find other occupations and to settle elsewhere, simply to avoid starvation. A great deal of Africa's land receives only erratic rainfall, and this is destined to remain rangeland, suitable only for grazing and capable of supporting only sparse nomadic populations. But even in these harsh areas, there has been a population explosion, and many people in the region have now been surviving on famine relief for a number of years.

Increases in human population put pressure on national parks in the same way that they put pressure on other rangelands, and many national parks in East Africa are in fact already being threatened by surrounding populations.

3.7. Economic trends

Except for a few giants like the Sudan, Nigeria and Zaire, most African countries have few exploitable minerals or oil, which means that they will have to support themselves entirely from the land. This is a major constraint on their development, since it is unlikely that countries compelled to base their development on agriculture will ever be able to achieve the same standards of living as the industrialized nations. Despite this, national targets call for a rapid rate of development; coupled with the rapid growth in population, there is growing pressure to develop every piece of land to the maximum, and some of that pressure is directed at national parks. Conservationists must accept the fact that, in order to survive, national parks must be made to serve purposes other than those for which admission fees are charged—photography and game viewing.

3.8. Tourism and protected areas

Tourism, which is largely based on the wildlife resources of the national parks, is today one of the most important foreign-exchange earners for many African countries. Unfortunately, this has been seen by many governments as the sole justification necessary for maintaining protected areas within their boundaries. Given the common lack of mineral resources, the concern of governments with deriving some capital out of tourism for other development projects is understandable. But little of that money directly benefits the local populations surrounding the parks, who, with their land appropriated to create these parks, now see wildlife wandering freely across the boundaries to use and often to damage the land that remains to them. It all adds fuel to their resentment of the parks.

There are at least two other factors which strain the people's relationship with the park system. The less important is the fact that entry to the parks is beyond the reach of most local people, few of whom own cars, which are necessary before one can enter most parks. It is an ironical situation; these people have moved for generations on foot among the animals in what are now called parks, but they must now have a permit and a car to do the same thing. More fundamental is the fact that the structure of African societies is such that few would use the parks for recreation even if the gate fees did not exist. Because of the extended-family system, spare time and extra money are usually spent with relatives and friends; the type of recreation represented by the parks is a low priority for most people, even for those who can afford it. Land and wildlife are seen as commodities, not as a resource base for recreation. To gain some degree of acceptance, conservationists will have to restore the traditional interaction between the people and wildlife and also systems of direct benefits to the people.

3.9. Wildlife populations

The wildlife herds in Africa today are only the remnants of the far larger herds of previous times. But even with their reduced numbers, they cannot be completely accommodated within the existing parks. When the parks were established, little attention was paid to the needs of migratory herds or to the conservation of complete ecological units. This is why animals so often wander across park boundaries and on to private land. One solution would be to increase the size of the national parks to cover the year-round needs of the migratory animals, but the pressure of human population on the borders of the parks makes this solution politically impossible. In addition, some of the migratory populations range over several thousand square kilometres, and many countries could scarcely contain parks large enough to satisfy all the year-round needs of such herds. It follows that the management of national parks must not be concentrated entirely within the park boundaries, but must be extended to include the surrounding areas, and this emphasizes yet again the need for good will and tolerance for wildlife from the people living near the parks. To foster that good will, they must be compensated directly and promptly for the damage done by wildlife to their land, and they must also benefit directly from the tourist income by being involved in the trade at the local level.

Another consequence of the national park system is that the concentration of game in limited areas is damaging the restricted habitats. The solution may involve some form of controlled cropping to strike a new balance between the size of herds and the land available to support them. Because of the 'preservation' attitude on which the national parks were founded, habitats are changing and becoming increasingly unsuitable for some species. There may be need for habitat manipulation to maintain suitable habitats for all the species of game.

3.10. Forest reserves

Forest reserves generally occur in areas where the land is suitable for a number of other alternatives like intensive farming. Forest reserves also generally occur in high population density areas where they are under considerable pressure. The last few decades have seen the increased exploitation of forests which are being largely used for fuelwood and the land put under intensive cultivation. Many indigenous forests are also now experiencing high commercial pressure for valuable timber in order to generate adequate capital to support various development activities. As population trends will continue to increase in the foreseeable future, and the needs of government for more capital to support these populations will still increase, conservationists will have to join governments in finding suitable alternative energy sources so that pressure on the remaining forest reserves can be contained. Forest destruction in the past decade has been accompanied by the worst cases of soil erosion, which has endangered very important water catchments. Conservationists will have to join other agencies in soil conservation efforts and in designing the appropriate uses for high potential land.

4. THE FUTURE OF PROTECTED AREAS

From this brief review of the developments and factors affecting conservation areas in the past few decades, it is pretty clear that the future of national parks and protected areas is going to be dim unless urgent measures are taken to implement a realistic policy that will be acceptable to the local people. Everything points to the need for a new approach that can withstand the present violent political, social and economic development activities. Past conservation efforts have at least been successful in demarcating a system of protected areas whose perpetuation must now be ensured by realistic policies and plans. I am convinced that amid economic and political turbulence, realistic conservation can only be achieved by the local people, and indeed mainly by the rural populations. It is only the people themselves who can defend the protected areas against any pressures. Future conservation efforts, therefore, should take as their starting point the restoration of the balance between nature and the people.

I would like now to sketch out some broad propositions for what I see as the future direction of our national parks and protected areas policy in Africa. I would like to emphasize that these are broad propositions rather than specific ones, and although they are made with reference to national parks, they should apply equally to other categories of protected areas, like forest reserves. It is the general overriding principle of bringing conservation to man that is important. This approach is not new; it is in fact the principle of the biosphere reserve system which is also being promoted by Unesco, and already the idea is being experimented with in the Ngorongoro area of Tanzania. In what follows, I have used the term "conservation unit", merely for lack of a better expression. I am open to suggestions for a better term, should this one not be acceptable to other views.

5. THE CONSERVATION UNIT APPROACH

5.1. Major factors for consideration

Only rarely can a wildlife park be established so as to include an entire ecosystem, especially in regard to the year-round needs of migratory species. To establish and develop a park without management control of the surrounding land will therefore lead to great problems in managing both the animals and the area. Unless these seasonal habitats of migratory species in the park are also controlled—protected from fencing, overgrazing and unplanned cultivation—the herds are likely to be decimated and the migrations hindered or stopped. When this happens the park wildlife will no longer be a viable part of a large, dynamic ecosystem, but will consist only of remnant resident groups. This "outdoor zoo" may remain attractive to tourists, but part of the world's heritage of migratory herds, made up of a variety of species, will be lost.

Park management must therefore be coordinated with management of the surrounding lands. But a wildlife park must also be culturally and economically valuable to the local people if it is to be a permanent institution, capable of surviving changes in political regime and periods of financial stress; few developing nations can afford the luxury of a park for purely aesthetic or philosophical reasons. It is essential to consider local economies and local traditions in addition to ecological factors when parks are being planned.

5.2. Proposed concept

I have argued that a broader concept of wildlife-park development is necessary, and it is suggested here that a coordinated management system be developed, consisting of various categories of land use in addition to the national park itself. This would include one or more ecosystems, but would also consider ethnic and political boundaries, thus making the ecological management of the area coincide with the political administration. My suggestion is that the ecosystem influencing national parks be designated as a "conservation unit", consisting of three land-use categories: the national park, the game reserve, and a multiple-use area.

5.3. The national park

This would include primary wildlife populations or areas of special interest, or unique scenic features. Managed as an IUCN Category II area, there would be minimal development; only those roads necessary for management and minimum tourist use would be established, and a wilderness atmosphere with little or no human interference would be encouraged. Under special circumstances, prescribed burning and water development would be used to maintain the wildlife range carrying capacity. The objective would be the preservation of a wildlife ecosystem and/or a unique scenic area; tourism, game viewing and occasional use for important tribal wildife ceremonies would be of secondary importance.

5.4. The game reserve

These areas, surrounding the park, would include locations for intensely developed tourist lodges and their associated facilities. Restricted local grazing would be allowed by permit only. Roads would be of a higher standard, and airstrips would be permitted near the lodges. The protected areas would permit both controlled grazing and controlled tribal hunting for the local people, and lodges and game viewing for tourists. This type of area would coincide with IUCN Category IV or Category V.

Wildlife management would involve harvesting animals on a sustained-yield basis, both for the sale of meat and hides and to control the herds migrating in and out of the park. Cropping methods would be designed to avoid interference with tourist activities, through selected harvest and night shooting; animals could be approached again for photography the day following cropping, since they would not associate vehicles with shooting; this method has been used most effectively in South African parks. Live capture of animals for sale could also be used to control the population, and prescribed burning and water-development programmes would be introduced to maintain or increase the carrying capacity of the range.

5.5. The multiple-use area

These large zones would surround the game reserves. Tourism would be permitted, but the major purpose of the area would be wildlife management coordinated with resident livestock operations. Wildlife management would be given priority, but resident pastoral tribes would be permitted to establish or continue their traditional ways of life. Safari hunting concessions might be permitted within these areas, and game-cropping programmes, as established in the game reserve, would also be operated. The use of fire and water developments would form part of the management plan. The multiple-use areas would thus accommodate grazing, residence, and tribal hunting by the local people, and tourism, organized mainly by local residents, as well as wildlife management coordinated with livestock. This corresponds to IUCN Category VIII.

As Fig. 1 shows, the entire wildlife conservation unit should be managed as a single entity, with marked and patrolled boundaries and entry only through manned gates on access roads.

There would be a number of advantages in such an approach:

- Unique wildlife populations, habitats or scenic features would be preserved;
- The portions designated as parks would retain a wilderness atmosphere without being isolated;
- Migratory wildlife populations would be maintained, by controlling their ranges inside and outside the parks;
- Wildlife populations would be harvested as necessary outside the park, to protect the habitat and to prevent one species from dominating the park or the ecosystem;
- Harmony between the local people and wildlife would be restored, by involving the people directly in wildlife management and by removing unnecessary restrictions on their way of life. Livestock numbers would be controlled—but so would the wildlife population;
- The local people would reap some of the economic benefits of the parks: from tourism, through wages and the sale of souvenirs; and from game cropping through wages for skinners and meat processors and the income from sale of meat and of live animals;
- Safari hunting would be controlled by the community, and the income—concession fees, trophy fees, meat sales, wages—would accrue to the community, thus reducing unemployment.

6. HOW CAN THESE NEW STRATEGIES IN CONSERVATION BE REALIZED?

Attempting to answer this question is perhaps the most difficult part of my present task. It is not possible to suggest a single approach that will apply uniformly to all States, in view of differing political approaches and systems, differing levels of development, and difference in the available natural resources and wealth in general. It is therefore a matter of necessity that the suggestions made in this part be general and broad. However, as land resources are finite and there is a limit to the ecological abuse that they can support, there are a few fundamentals that must be observed by any nation. It is basically this that gives me the courage to make the following suggestions.

6.1. Land-use policies and plans

It is not possible to realize any effective conservation without specific and realistic coordinated policies and programmes for the use of a nation's land resources. As land-use policies are lacking in many African countries, priority will have to be given to the development of such policies and plans. Conservationists should therefore join in government efforts and encourage the development of a framework which will recognize protected areas as viable land-use systems. Conservationists must go out of their way to assist in the design of land-use systems that are not specifically dominated by the idea of protected areas but which will have a big effect on how conservation areas are viewed. An intensive irrigation scheme, for example, may be planned for an area that may not itself be a protected area; its implementation can, however, have great effects in reducing the pressure that would otherwise have been brought to bear on a protected area. Conservationists should be involved in the development of any such scheme.

6.2. Education and training

The crisis in which protected areas find themselves at present requires an urgent conservation education effort that should reach the whole population almost immediately and probably all at the same time. This means that the conservation education effort will have to be intensified at all levels of society.

6.2.1. The local rural level. There will have to be a mass conservation education campaign aimed at reaching all the rural populations, but concentrating on populations surrounding strategic protected areas. This will have to be simple and able to accommodate both literate and illiterate populations. The main thrust of this mass education campaign will have to be traditional in its approach, drawing on already-existing conservation practices and building on them any new approaches.

6.2.2. Formal education. Schools and colleges alike will need some special form of conservation education. It is sad that despite many years of independence, satisfactory curricula have not yet been developed in conservation. In Kenya, for example, wildlife conservation is reaching the students in high schools not through the normal education curricula but through the wildlife clubs, which consist of some 20 or 30 students in each school. Conservation education should be made mandatory for all students as part of their formal education and not be treated just as a hobby. It is equally sad to observe that despite two decades of independence many institutions of higher learning do not have specific departments of conservation. To take my own country of Kenya again as an example, the Biology of Conservation course offered in the Department of Zoology at the University of Nairobi has not been able to produce more than ten graduates in the last two decades. This is not what I mean by conservation education. I am proposing specific Colleges of Natural Resources at universities, able to produce 500 qualified graduates in conservation every year.

As it will take time to train such well-qualified teachers, I propose that for the suggested campaign a crash course for local teachers be introduced, which need not be at a high level. Thousands of unemployed high-school leavers could be absorbed for this purpose.

6.2.3. Conservation education for administration and policy makers. This is one of the most difficult groups, since many of the individuals that make it up believe that they already know everything there is to know about conservation, which is far from being the case.

With very few exceptions, administrations are staffed by people who have never been exposed to conservation education. This is too often a group that looks upon conservation as backwardness and for whom development means cities, intensively farmed landscapes and mass agricultural production systems.

There must be a concerted effort to reach this group, since in it are found the decision makers and even the policy makers in parliaments. In recent debates on conflicts between wildlife and people, it has not been unusual to hear from seemingly very knowledgeable parliamentarians that wildlife should be eliminated. Seminars will have to be designed for these groups and somehow they will have to be made to listen.

7. PROTECTED AREA MANAGERS

Past effort in protected area management has largely gone into the training of park wardens. This may have been reasonable in terms of the policies and thinking of the time when wardens were considered as park protectors and trained mainly in keeping away poachers. Managers of the protected areas proposed in this paper will have to be very different. They will have to be people trained in general conservation and basic ecology. They will be exposed to all natural resource disciplines: forestry, hydrology, watershed management, wildlife conservation, range management and outdoor recreation. The new generation of protected area managers will also be exposed to basic sociology, economics and public relations. The most important requirement is that they should not be 'protectionists' but rather sound land-use managers with a deep appreciation of the importance of conservation in the trade-offs between various competing land uses.

To be successful, the protected area manager will have to identify himself with the community in which he is working—it is the local community who will in fact be the strength behind him. He will have to join in the community's development activities related to land management and help and participate in the organization of its socio-economic development and cultural activities. He should assist the local people in the distribution of the benefits accruing from conservation activities like tourism, hunting and population control of wild animals. The protected area manager should form the link between conservation goals and the administration, and that means that he will have to work hand-in-hand with the local chiefs and the political administrative authority in the district. It will be his duty to make sure that the conservation education campaign proposed above continues even after the formal programmes are completed. This will have to be done through his participation in the various community gatherings and meetings. Finally, the protected area manager will need to be somebody with a very broad outlook and mature judgement and with both a professional and an emotional commitment to the cause of conservation.

8. INTERNATIONAL COOPERATION

The approach to international cooperation in the field of conservation should be based on the principle that the unique resources we are seeking to conserve, although they are contained within the national boundaries, are of significance to mankind as a whole.

A great many of the positive developments in conservation in Africa have been largely due to international assistance and to either direct or indirect pressure on nations to protect certain unique resources. In Kenya, for example, under the new Wildlife Conservation and Management Act, the Government has established a wildlife fund, managed by trustees to solicit and receive donations for approved projects. The degree of Kenya's dependence on such assistance in wildlife matters can be judged from the following admission in the 1974-78 Development Plan: "Should the targets for private donations not be met, it will be necessary to reduce levels of some wildlife activities below those planned."

Through the WWF, FAO, IUCN, the African Wildlife Leadership Foundation and many other donors, financial assistance and the provision of experts for various wildlife projects have been obtained. As already noted, the increased number of parks and protected areas is mainly due to the work of a few dedicated foreigners who, with international financial backing, have continued to work behind the scenes.

At the time of writing this paper, worldwide inflation has hit African countries perhaps harder than any others, and nations on the continent are struggling for the bare maintenance of even their essential services in health, education and agriculture. It is doubtful whether such approaches as those suggested here could be undertaken without generous donations from abroad. Africa will therefore continue to count on international assistance, and it is even to be hoped that this will be stepped up in the spirit of preserving our unique resources for posterity.

9. THE ROLE OF INTERNATIONAL AGENCIES

The new strategies suggested here demand extensive inputs in both finance and expertise. In many African countries the present administrative machinery for protected areas is still weak and there is a general lack of high-level expertise to develop the new materials needed for the suggested campaign. It is here that international agencies should be called upon to assist.

In the first place, international agencies should be looked to for assistance with the crash programme to prepare conservation teachers at all levels. They should also provide the technical backing to develop the educational materials that will be needed in the short term, while we are laying the foundation for the long-term development of these materials nationally. International agencies can also be expected to assist governments in the identification and organization of possible funding sources to support the new conservation ventures.

In making these suggestions, it is recognized that most of these approaches are already being exploited to some extent. What is being suggested here is that they must be stepped up, if the needed awareness is to be achieved.

Of importance in this regard will be the coordination of these efforts at the international level, to avoid duplication and to make really efficient use of the available financial and manpower resources. IUCN should be able to fulfil this role very well.

10. CONCLUSION

The crisis confronting the present system of protected areas in Africa is largely due to the fact that this system is a continuation of old conservation policies that failed to recognize the needs, fears and values of the local people, and which are ill-suited to today's development problems. I have tried briefly to analyse the trends leading to the present situation and have suggested a possible new approach. There is every reason to believe that even at this seemingly late hour, the implementation of imaginative policies as suggested here would go far to remedy the present critical position.

Since many African countries have limited alternative sources of wealth, the land must be developed by every means. But development must take the form most suited to the prevailing circumstances and the purposes to which an area is best adapted. The natural surplus can be legitimately used and tourism can be fostered without detriment to the continued existence of the resources.

Whatever the future of protected areas in Africa may be, it is conditional upon the degree of support derived from the people locally. This underlines the necessity for enlisting popular support from the people primarily concerned by letting conservation fulfil, in part, their expectations, needs and traditions.

The conservation approach suggested here recognizes three basic choices to be made. First, where it can be shown that the conservation of a certain unique ecosystem should have priority, the state has an obligation to secure the land for conservation, as by the creation of national parks and reserves. This should be done in consultation with surrounding populations. Second, and at the other extreme, there will be areas where there will be intensive use to the exclusion of any protection activity. Third, it is suggested that elsewhere land-use plans should assume a degree of compatibility between various competing uses, such as wildlife, animal husbandry and agriculture. In my opinion, all approaches adopted with regard to conservation (and this I have observed all over the world) must be based on compromise.

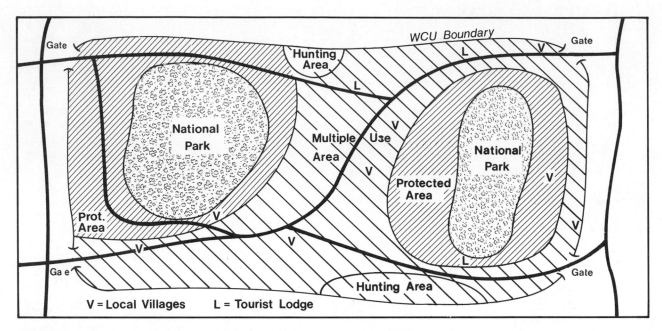

Figure 1. A diagrammatic model of a wildlife conservation unit. The entire unit would be managed as a single entity, with distinctive land uses for the national parks, the protected areas, and the multiple use areas.

Chapter 5
The Indomalayan Realm

Keynote Address:
The Indomalayan Realm

M.K. Ranjitsinh
Secretary, Forests and Tourism
Government of Madhya Pradesh
Bhopal, India

ABSTRACT. *The Indomalayan Realm contains some of the world's most ancient civilizations, but it also harbours some of the wealthiest natural habitats in the world in terms of species diversity and endemism. Despite very dense populations in most countries, there still remains a surprising amount of nature. Many problems still remain, including inappropriate placement and design of protected areas, lack of personnel and finance, threats from inappropriate development projects, insurgency, and shifting cultivation. However, governments are becoming much more aware of the need for effective management of protected areas; many have established ministries of the environment, research on wildlife management and other protected area matters is increasing, and training institutions have been established.*

1. INTRODUCTION

The illiterate but ingenious Indian ruler, Maharaja Ranjitsingh of the Punjab, when shown a map of India depicting the territories of the incipient British Indian empire in red, remarked that soon all would turn red. History proved him right, for the whole subcontinent came under British hegemony. Perhaps the most interesting maps of modern times are satellite photos showing the environmental status of planet earth and the variations in forest cover, where the deforested and inhabited areas show up in various shades of red. At the rate at which the forests of the Indomalayan Realm are vanishing, it requires no pundit to predict that the whole landmass will soon show red on those photographs!

2. THE ONLY CLIMAX FOREST IN THE FUTURE?

The population of Asia, excluding the USSR, increased from approximately 1887 million in 1950 to about 3182 million in 1975, and is expected to rise to 5312 million by A.D. 2000 (Ranjitsinh, 1979). In Nepal, one ha of land must now support 9 people. The present standing wood volume in cubic metres per person in Asia is 15, as against the world average of 75. According to FAO, approximately five million ha of forests are "lost" annually in Asia (Tiger Paper, 1978). Some 8 million ha are burned and temporarily cultivated every year, by approximately 200 million shifting cultivators affecting about 300 million ha of forest. It is estimated that almost 30 percent of the officially-designated forest areas of some of the south and southeast Asian countries are put to such usage (Ranjitsinh, 1979). According to the National Economic and Social Development Board (NESDB) of Thailand, the total area of forests in that country has been reduced from 58.3 percent in 1952 to 39 percent in 1973 and a mere 33 percent in 1978. Some experts predict that at the current rate of reduction all forests would have gone by 1987, while optimists might grant the Thai forests a few more years. The National Environment Protection Council (NEPC) of the Philippines reports that one third of the total land area of that country is now susceptible to erosion. In Indonesia 12 million people are engaged in shifting cultivation, affecting a total forest area of 37 million ha. The Malaysian National Forestry Council warns that at the present rate of logging, Malaysia, which is losing forests at the rate of 275,000 ha a year, would have lost its forests by 1990. At the current rate of destruction, Nepal is expected to lose its forests by the end of the century. Pakistan has today only 3.5 percent of its territory under forest cover

(Ranjitsinh, 1979). In India, though the official figures record about 23 percent of the land area as forest land, barely 2 percent is under forest cover approaching its natural richness (Gadgil, 1982). In countries like Sri Lanka, Malaysia and India, large forests areas have been given to Forest Corporations for conversion into man-made forests.

Yet among all the gathering gloom and grave prognostications, a most heartening phenomenon emerges. Aerial photographs of the Petchabun Range in Thailand show the national parks and the protected areas—Nam Nao, Phu Kradeung and the rest—still intact, while dessication is fast overtaking the rest of the forests. Southward, a dark patch emerges in sharp contrast with the clear-felled areas all around; that dark patch is the Khao Yai National Park. The pristine forests of the Periyar Sanctuary in Kerala still survive, surrounded though they are by some of the most densely inhabited areas in the world. Yet a little northwards, the magnificent forests of the Cardamom Hills, a reserved forest but not a part of the protected areas system of the country, have all but gone. The transformation that greets one upon entry into isolated "pocket paradises", like Ranthambhor in India and Ujung Kulon in Indonesia, is almost unbelievable. The scenario and the richness inside the precincts bear no resemblance to the stark world of despoilation immediately outside.

It is in this context that the significance of the protected areas systems of the Indomalayan Realm have to be assessed. The holocaust which has engulfed the forests and other wildlife habitats has not, by and large, seriously affected these areas—not as yet. It is only in these tracts that not only the magnificent fauna and flora of this region, but nature as such, has hope for long-term survival. In many countries, these protected areas may well be the only places where natural climax forests will survive in the twenty-first century. The implications and ramifications of such a surmise are only too obvious.

The matter assumes even greater significance when one considers two aspects pertinent to this realm. First, the incredible richness and diversity of the faunal and floral wealth of the region and the niche it therefore occupies in the world heritage; and second, the endemism and the threat of extinction that faces so many life forms.

3. BOUNTY OF NATURE

The tropical moist forests of south-east Asia are among the oldest forest types in the world, being at least 30 million years old (Richards, 1964). Unit for unit, they are also the richest biotic region in the world. Java has 4500 plant species, Sumatra 6000, Sulawesi 5000 to 6000, Philippines 7000, Peninsular Malaysia 8000 and Borneo 9000 to 10,000. The State of Brunei with an area of 5000 sq km has 2000 tree species while Holland with an area 7 times larger in size possesses only 30 (Myers, 1979). Indonesia's forests are estimated to contain about 25,000

species of plants, 500 species of mammals, 1500 species of birds and perhaps a million species of vertebrates and invertebrates (Sumardja, 1980a).

The Sunda Shelf alone boasts of 732 species of birds, as against a tally of 398 for the whole of Europe west of the USSR, an area 4 times as large (Medway, 1978). The Oriental Zoogeographical region, though the smallest in the world, has the largest number of the non-aquatic large mammalian families of the world. Twenty-one out of the 36 species of wild cats of the world, 5 out of the 8 bear species, one of the two elephant species, 3 of the 5 rhinoceros species, 18 of the 41 deer species and 7 of the sub-family Bovinae comprising of wild buffaloes and wild oxen, are found in this faunal region.

4. ENDEMISM AND THE THREAT OF EXTINCTION

Next to the oceanic islands, south Asia has one of the greatest degreesof endemism in the world. Almost half of the bird species of the Malay Peninsula and more than half the mammalian species of the Philippines are endemic (Myers, 1979). To quote a few examples, the Abbott's booby *Sula abbotti* is now found only on Christmas Island south of Java and the Narcondam hornbill *Aceros narcondami* only on the Narcondam Island of the Andamans. The unique island of Palawan is the only home of the Palawan peacock pheasant *Polyplectron emphanum*, and the white-eyed river martin *Pseudochelidon sirintarae*, has so far been recorded only on Thailand's largest freshwater lake, Bueng Buraphet, which is also one of the last habitats of the Siamese crocodile *Crocodilus siamensis*. The red-faced malkoha *Phaenicophaeus pyrrhocephalus* endemic to Sri Lanka, is now perhaps confined only to the Singharajah forest. The Rochschild's starling *Leucopsar rothschildi* in recent times at least was localized only in what is now the Bali Barat Reserve on the island of Bali, Indonesia.

The Mentawai islands west of Sumatra hold four endemic species of primates, two of which have split into separate subspecies; an endemic species of squirrel *Callosciurus mentawi* and 10 other endemic subspecies of mammals (McNeely, 1980). The endangered Indus dolphin or susu *Platanista indi*, is confined only to the lower Indus water system.

The Kuhl's deer *Cervus kuhli* occurs only on the small Indonesian island of Bawean and the Calamian deer *Cervus calamianensis* on the small Calamian group of islands in the Philippines. The dwarf anoa buffalo *Bubalus depressicornis* is found only on Sulawesi and the tamaraw *Bubalus mindorensis* on Mindoro alone. The unique babirusa pig *Babyrousa babyrussa* with tushes that subscribe a circle over its head to earn it the local name of pig-deer (babi-rusa), occurs only on Sulawesi and the adjacent Togian islands. The Nilgiri thar *Hemitragus hylocrius* is found only in the southern parts of the Western

Ghats and the Indian wild ass *Equus hemionus khur* only in the Little Rann of Kutch, both in India.

The plant *Hubbardia heptaneuron*, now believed to be extinct, was recorded only from the spray zone of the Jog Falls of the Sharavati River in Karnataka, India. The unique orchid *Dendrobium pauciflorum* has been recorded in only two sites in Sikkim and West Bengal in India. The only known population of the lenteri palm *Areca concinna*, numbering about 1000 specimens, occurs only in a swamp 2 to 4 ha in extent in the Kalutara district in Sri Lanka and is threatened with a change in the drainage pattern.

The only known wild population of the rattan *Ceratolobus glaucescens*, numbering not more than 30 plants, is now confined to a locality near Pelabuanratu on the south coast of west Java, and the only wild population of the palm *Maxburretia rupicola* is confined to the tops of 3 limestone hills—Batu caves hill, Bukit Takun and Bukit Anark Takun, all within 40 kms of Kuala Lumpur in Malaysia (IUCN, 1978b).

The problem is further compounded by the fact that faunal species are not always adaptive to change. Harrison (1968) found 76 species of mammals in lowland forests in west Malaysia, as compared with only 11 indigenous species in areas converted to rubber and oil palm cultivation in the neighbouring tracts. Only 5 percent of the tropical birds could adjust to a change from a forest to a non-forest habitat (McClure and Osman, 1968).

Add to all this localization the tremendous demographic pressure which has been increasingly exerted for centuries and it is not surprising to find a long list of candidates for extinction. Of the thousand species and subspecies of vertebrates in the world that are deemed to be endangered, more than a quarter exist in Asia. The Red Data Book of the IUCN lists 61 species and subspecies of mammals alone that are threatened in South Asia; eighteen out of the 29 forms of threatened deer listed by the IUCN occur here.

The world population of the Javan rhinoceros *Rhinoceros sondaicus* numbering altogether about 50, seek refuge in the Udjung Kulon National Park in Indonesia, and the world population of the Asiatic lion *Panthera leo persica* numbering less than 200, in the Gir National Park in western India. The only safe haven for the Kashmir stag or hangul *Cervus elaphus hanglu*, numbering not more than 400, is the Dachigam Sanctuary in Kashmir. But the pride of place amongst the mammalian subspecies threatened with extinction in the wild in the world, must surely go to the Manipur brow-antlered deer *Cervus eldi eldi*, confined to less than a 20 sq km habitat in the Keibul Lamjao National Park in Manipur, India. Down to 14 animals in 1975, a population of 30 specimens was reported in 1979.

The purpose of this lengthy prelude is to stress the one factor which I feel should be the central theme for the national parks of the Indomalayan Realm: that the assured long-term future safety of this wondrous floral and faunal wealth, much of it so localized and endangered, lies only in the protected areas of the nations of south and southeast Asia. From this standpoint, therefore, the parks of this region are perhaps the most important in the world. To safeguard this world heritage, the parks need to be established to protect diverse and unique habitats, biomes and ecosystems, relict and threatened populations of living organisms both terrestrial and aquatic; to achieve this the protected areas must be of adequate size, inter-linked as far as possible and, above all, appropriately protected and managed. At the same time, there is an urgent need to involve the people, for even national parks and sanctuaries can remain safe in the long run only with popular support.

5. FACTORS WHICH IMPEDE THE ESTABLISHMENT AND EFFECTIVE MANAGEMENT OF PROTECTED AREAS

Predictably, the main problems stem from demographic pressures and the need to develop the economies of the nations of the region. The world "conservation" is still synonymous in some minds with the word "protection". Even in the minds of the educated and of the decision-makers, protected areas are still identified as an elitist concept, as non-utilized tracts, and hence a waste of resources. The peoples whose practices and privileges of exploitation, legal or otherwise, have been curtailed or stopped due to the establishment of protected areas have, understandably, found it the most difficult to acquiesce. Grazing of livestock and collection of firewood and other forest produce with the concommitant disturbance and incidence of fire, have been the greatest banes of the protected areas on the Indian subcontinent. This exploitation, linked to the existence of human populations and cultivation that is permitted in most wildlife sanctuaries, is the main reason, together with the revenue from legal timber extraction, that has prevented the state Governments of the Indian Union from converting more sanctuaries into national parks than they have done so far.

Many of the protected areas, particularly in the Indian subcontinent, have been a legacy from the colonial past. They were originally hunting reserves and had been established mainly for the number of sporting animals and birds they held. The early approach to management, therefore, was species-protection oriented, which is now gradually changing to habitat conservation methods. However, the ecosystem approach which takes into account representative and unique ecosystems with a view to include them in the protected araes system, has not quite been launched. Many ecosystems, particularly grasslands, coastal and marine areas, remain very inadequately represented in the national protected areas systems.

Threatened species like the Siberian cranes *Bugeranus leucogeranus* and the hangul are not safe once their seasonal movements take them outside the precincts of their winter haunts—the Bharatpur National Park and the Dachigam Sanctuary, respectively. In many instances the major portions of relict populations of threatened species like the lion-tailed macaque *Macaca silenus*, the pygmy hog *Sus salvanius*, the Javan wart hog *Sus verrucosus*, the false gavial *Tomistoma schlegeli*, the white-winged wood duck *Cairina scutulata*, and Cabot's tragopan pheasant *Tragopan caboti*, to name just a few, still live outside existing protected areas.

Many of the protected areas are too small and too isolated with the destruction of suitable habitats around. Forty-one sanctuaries of Sri Lanka have areas less than 50 sq km each, many of them being less than 250 ha and that too not clearly demarcated. The breakdown of corridors and the resultant isolation of populations has had the most adverse impact on large mammals like the elephant *Elephas maximus*, causing destruction of the habitat in the confined areas by the pachyderms themselves, irascibility among the animals, and depredations and damage to human property outside the protected area precincts. Where the forest canopy has been removed, as in the parks of India, Malaysia, Sri Lanka and Thailand, exotic weeds like *Lantana camara*, *Eupatorium odoratum* and *Strobilanthus collusus* are taking over to the detriment of the grasslands and forest understorey. In the Manas Tiger Reserve and the Jaldapara Sanctuary in eastern India, both important for the populations of the Indian rhinoceras *Rhinoceros unicornis* that they hold, the exotic *Mikania scandens* is choking the trees and the grasslands in the open patches. Biological control of these weeds has not begun, and it is too dangerous to experiment with herbicides.

Applied research which could be utilized for practical managerial purposes in protected areas is still in a nascent stage in the region. An impetus to this, including establishment of a few field research stations, is of primary importance.

Lack of finances and the consequent lack of protective personnel, is an almost universal major drawback. There is approximately one person to man 90 sq km in a Thai National Park, and one persson to patrol about 340 sq km in a wildlife sanctuary in that country. Lack of personnel is also acutely felt in Sri Lanka, Burma and Indonesia, and those that are in the field are inadequately paid.

Inadequate enforcement of legislation, inadequacy of the laws to assist appropriate management and protection, and the leniency of the law courts in dealing with offenders, is noted in varying degrees in Thailand, Indonesia, Philippines and Bangladesh.

The threat of hydroelectric and irrigation projects affects the Silent Valley and the Indravati National Park in India and Taman Negara in Malaysia, to name a few. It has already inundated prime habitat in the Corbett National Park in India.

Feral buffaloes in Yala and Wilpattu National Parks of Sri Lanka, particularly in the former where they number about 15,000, are a cause of serious overuse of the areas they concentrate upon, especially around the *villus* or ponds.

The lack of trained personnel is universal, and is the single most important factor impeding data collection and scientific management. This is also a major reason why comprehensive surveys to determine status and distribution of endangered species have not been adequate.

Tourism is still in its infancy in the parks and sanctuaries of the region. However, in parts of Yala and Wilpattu National Parks of Sri Lanka, Periyar in south India and Khao Yai in Thailand, excessive concentration and overuse in some restricted areas is being felt.

In Vietnam, Kampuchea and Laos, an area justly famous for its wildlife and holding rare and localized life forms like the Kouprey *Bos sauveli*, the Imperial and Edward's pheasants, *Lophura imperialis* and *Lophura edwardsi*, the ravages of a fierce and long-drawn war resulting in both hunting and habitat destruction, including defoliation through chemical warfare, has meant a very severe set-back to all conservation efforts in the region. The impact of 50 million kg of pesticides sprayed over 2.4 million ha in South Vietnam (McNeely, 1975) cannot but be lethal to wildlife. The unsettled conditions in this whole region precludes setting up of effectively protected areas, at least in the near future.

The activities of the shifting cultivators—*kaingineros*—and the fires that convert woodlands into *Imperata* grasslands, is the biggest law enforcement problem in the Philippines national parks (Grimwood, 1974). The field officers in the charge of these parks are further handicapped by the fact that they are not the masters of these areas under their jurisdiction, being subordinate to the local forest staff. And logging still poses a threat to the protected areas of Southeast Asia. Both Taman Negara and Endau Rompin in west Malaysia are so threatened, and the 73,000 ha Mt. Apo National Park on Mindanao Island in the Philippines, containing several endemic species and a population of the extremely endangered Philippines eagle *Pithecophaga jefferyi*, may be reduced to less than 14,000 ha to accommodate settlers and logging interests (Myers, 1979). A sawmill has been established close to Gunung Leuser, the most important of Sumatra's protected areas and one of the last strongholds of the Sumatran rhinoceros *Dicerorhinus sumatrensis*. 30,000 ha of prime lowland dipterocarp forest in the Sikunder area, a part of Gunung Leuser, has been ceded for logging. Kerumutan Reserve (120,000 ha) and Way Kambas (130,000 ha) also in Sumatra, have both been logged and largely destroyed, even though the latter was specially set up to protect the Sumatran rhino. Commercial plantations have been established in the Baluran Reserve (FAO, 1976a), and large chunks of the natural forests of the Bali Barat Reserve in Bali have been converted into teak.

6. FACTORS WHICH HAVE ENCOURAGED THE ESTABLISHMENT AND EFFECTIVE MANAGEMENT OF PROTECTED AREAS

This grim tale of dessication and lost ground would seem to suggest that the cause is lost. On the contrary, both the intelligentsia and the decision-makers are rapidly coming to accept the fact that protected areas are the future hope of natural forests and fauna, and that these areas have many other important uses.

One of the best and easiest ways to save an important watershed is to establish a protected area there. It is an interesting phenomenon that while the people come to accept the complete stoppage of exploitation, as is with most national parks, it is far more difficult to enforce controlled usage which the wildlife sanctuaries mostly strive to achieve. Once the principle of non-use comes to be accepted, as it does surprisingly soon, the clamour dies down. On the other hand, controlled exploitation and rotational grazing, for instance, are a constant source of friction and defiance in wildlife sanctuaries. Thailand has overcome this problem by making their wildlife sanctuaries free from exploitation and thus on a par with the national parks in this regard.

In China, the purpose for the establishment of protected areas is fourfold—for the protection of the whole natural landscape; for the protection of special types of ecosystems; for the protection of rare species of animals and plants; and for tourism and recreation (Wang, 1980).

According to the UN List of National Parks and Protected Areas, the protected areas system of the Indomalayan Realm which began with the establishment of the first area in 1918, covering 32,633 ha, had increased to 10 areas in 1928 extending over 229,636 ha. By 1938 the number had increased to 43 with an area of 3,312,854 ha; by 1958 to 85 areas encompassing 4,742,055 ha, and by 1968 to 116 areas covering 6,486,791 ha. Thereafter, the increase has been even more dramatic. By 1972 there were 150 protected areas and by 1978 there were 257, covering an area of 16,389,417 ha. By the latest count there were 292 areas protecting 22,275,030 ha (IUCN, 1982b).

Most countries of the region have also sizeably enhanced their budgetary allocations for nature conservation. In the Bangladesh First Five Year Plan (1973-1979), a financial allocation of TK. 20.06 million was sanctioned exclusively for the preservation of tiger habitat in the Sunderbans. Indonesia's Third Five Year Plan, in which conservation is being given high priority, there is a budget of approximately 2 million dollars for 1978/79 and a projected three-fold increases in the total area of reserves to 10 million ha. The WWF has also pledged a support of $1.2 million to Indonesia.

In India, US$10.01 million have been spent over a seven year period under Project Tiger, and a total of US$15.16 million has been earmarked for it in the current Five Year Plan. The WWF is assisting with an additional US$1 million. The Federal Government also gives financial assistance to state Governments in conservation projects like the conservation of the three crocodile species and the conservation of important protected areas. The state of Jammu and Kashmir is earmarking US$600,000 for the conservation of the Dal Lake watershed which will benefit the Dachigam Sanctuary, the only safe haven for the gravely endangered hangul or Kashmir stag.

West Malaysia will be spending the equivalent of US$8 millions on nature parks, reserves and on the conservation-cum-management of wildlife. Special attention will be given to the conservation of endangered species like the Sumatran rhinoceros, seladang, elephant, tiger and tapir.

There is another factor which augurs well for both establishment and improved management of protected areas. Most nations have established separate departments and ministries for the environment, and though the management of wildlife and national parks still remains under the aegis of the forest departments in most countries, separate agencies within the administrative set-up are coming about. No more are the wildlife sections the dumping grounds of unwanted personnel of the forest department; though the youthful lot that is now coming into the field and at managerial levels is not widely trained in wildlife management, they have travelled and have been exposed to the conservation philosophy. What were a handful of conservation enthusiasts scattered about in some of the countries ten years ago, have now become a nucleus in each country, a band of determined and dedicated managers.

7. CURRENT STATUS OF THE PROTECTED AREAS IN THE REALM

An examination of the coverage of the protected areas of the world's various biogeographical realms reveals interesting facts. 152 of the 355 protected areas in the tropical humid forest biomes, and 161 of the 482 areas in the tropical dry forest and woodland biome, are in the Indomalayan realm. There are, however, only 2 protected areas in warm deserts and semi-deserts out of a world total of 171, and 11 in the mixed mountain systems out of a total of 344, in the Indomalayan realm. This is partly understandable as it is due to topography and vegetation; but what is not encouraging is the fact that there are no tropical grasslands nor lake system nor mixed island system biomes represented in the protected areas system of our realm (IUCN, 1982b).

7.1. Protected areas by biogeographic province

The above-mentioned preponderance of the coverage of forests and the relative and even total negligence of arid and semi-arid areas, grasslands and of island ecosystems, is reflected in the distribution of the protected areas in the various biogeographical provinces of the Indomalayan realm. There are 20 protected areas in the

Malabar, 24 in Indochinese, 8 in south Chinese, 14 in the Sumatran, 19 in the Javan, 11 in the Celebesian, and 30 in the Bornean and 11 in the Malayan rainforests. There are 80 areas in the Indus-Ganges, 27 in the Thailandian and 30 in the Ceylonese monsoon forests. The Burman rainforest and monsoon forests, with 1 and 6 areas respectively, are poorly represented, as is the Ceylonese rainforest with only one area protected. But the drier forests, thorn forests, grasslands and island ecosystems are in a worse predicament. The Coromandel biogeographical province has only one protected area (Point Calimere), the Deccan thorn forest 2, and the Thar desert another 2. The Philippines has 8 areas listed, but the Seychelles and Amirantes Islands, Laccadive Islands, Maldives and Chagos Islands and the Andaman and Nicobar Islands have no protected areas listed at all. Yet these islands contain highly endemic and rare fauna, particularly avifauna, such as the Seychelles magpie robin *Copsychus sechellarum*, the Seychelles owl *Otus insularis*, the Seychelles warbler *Nesillas sechellensis*, the Nicobar megapode *Megapodius freycinet nicobarensis*, and the Andaman teal *Anas gibberifrons albogularis* (IUCN, 1982b).

7.2. Strengths, weaknesses and gaps

The main aspects have already been discussed above and are not repeated here. There are some features, however, which need to be elaborated upon and others discussed.

Marine areas are very poorly represented in the protected areas system, and those that have come about like the outstanding Tarutao National Park on the borders of Thailand and Peninsular Malaysia, are still heavily fished and corals destroyed by explosives to kill the fish. Lagoons like Lake Chilka on the Orissa coast in India, the largest lagoon in the region; coral areas like those off Rameshwaram in the gulf of Manaar, south India; and large inland drainage lakes like Tonle Sap in Kampuchea and Lake Toba in Sumatra, are outside the pale of the protected areas system. Though both Bangladesh and India have established tiger reserves in the Sunderbans, the largest single mangrove area in the world, mangrove areas by and large are poorly represented in the protected areas system, particularly in Thailand, Burma, Malaysia, Philippines and Indonesia (Christenson, 1979). More protected areas are also needed on the Trengganu coast of West Malaysia to protect the rookeries of the leathery turtle *Dermochelys coriacea*.

Belatedly, wildlife research is gaining momentum in some countries. In Malaysia research has been undertaken, among others, on the great argus pheasant *Argusianus argus*, the Sumatran rhino, tiger, elephant, Seladang *Bos gaurus*, and tapir *Tapirus indicus*.

In Indonesia, with the collaboration of foreign scholars, research has been carried out in a number of areas, notably in Ujung Kulon, and Gunung Leuser. The Anoa in Sulawesi, the Javan tiger in Meru Betiri and some of the apes are also subjects of study. In India, research has been carried in the Gir National Park, particularly on the lion, in Kanha, particularly on the tiger and the central Indian barasingha, *Cervus duvauceli branderi*; and in Bandipur, particularly on the Chital *Axis axis*, and the wild dog *Cuon alpinus*. Research has also been carried out on the behaviour and ecology of the lion-tailed macaque, the common langur *Presbytus entellus*, the great Indian bustard *Choriotis nicriceps*, and the blackbuck *Antilope cervicapra*. In Thailand, the Kasetsart University and the Department of Agriculture are carrying out useful applied research. Elsewhere, research in wildlife aspects needs a very great impetus. Furthermore, the research topics that have been undertaken are largely the more spectacular mammalian and bird species. Very little work has been done as yet on the ecosystems of the region and the effects of demographic and biotic factors that are brought to bear upon these ecosystems.

The urgent need for trained personnel to man the protected areas has been already mentioned. With the number of protected areas that are available, it is not a very viable preposition to start an elaborate training school in wildlife management at the national level, with the exception of India and Indonesia; India started a training programme at Dehra Dun over a decade ago, and a school of Environmental Conservation Management has been established at Ciawi near Bogor, in Indonesia. But what really is required is a regional school for wildlife management which would benefit the trainees from countries who do not or cannot start their own training programme. The teaching staff, the equipment and the scope of teaching could be expanded to fulfil the needs of a regional school, to the benefit of all trainees, the rapport that would be established among the individuals from the different nations of the region would stand in very good stead, and the resulting cooperation would be very helpful in the formulation and implementation of international conservation policies and conventions. In fact, such a training school at present would perhaps be the single greatest need at the regional level in the field of nature conservation in the Indomalayan Realm.

Acknowledgements

This paper was prepared for IUCN's Commission on National Parks and Protected Areas in cooperation with the World Wildlife Fund.

Protected Areas and Turtle Eggs in Sabah, East Malaysia

G.S. de Silva
East Coast National Parks Regional Office
Sandakan, Sabah, East Malaysia

ABSTRACT. *This case study describes the circumstances which caused the near disappearance of two species of marine turtles from three island rookeries in the Sulu Sea of East Malaysia. It describes how establishing protective measures was able to bring the species back to a productive level. The economic importance of turtle products is discussed, along with the threats such values have caused. Continuing problems lead to the suggestion that international marine sanctuaries need to be established for sea turtles between Sabah and the Philippines.*

1. INTRODUCTION

This case study describes the circumstances which nearly caused the extinction of 2 species of marine turtles nesting on 3 island rookeries in the Sulu Sea and describes how the situation was brought under control by the timely intervention of the Sabah State Government. It also indicates circumstances leading to the compulsory acquisition of 3 privately-owned island rookeries. These rookeries were constituted Bird and Game Sanctuaries and approximately 5 years later were converted into the Turtle Islands National Park. After the main problem was eliminated, others arose. Some were solved; a few continue to exist. Events are narrated chronologically as the writer has been with the project since he proposed it in 1965.

All turtle rookeries in protected areas administered under the National Park Ordinance and the Fauna Conservation Ordinance have been visited by the writer. Pulau Sipadan, a remotely situated Bird and Game Sanctuary, has been very infrequently visited and the reason for this is mentioned elsehere. Comments are based on the writer's personal observations and experiences, and authentic reports from fishermen, seafarers, islanders and official records which were rummaged for pertinent material.

The economic importance of turtle eggs, meat, shell, etc. is discussed and some re-export figures are provided together with an account of the suppression of the trade in turtle products. To draw attention to an urgent need, occurrences near the Sabah/Philippine territorial boundary in the Sulu Sea are narrated. Finally, it is suggested that an international marine sanctuary be established.

As very little was known about marine turtles in Sabah waters, investigations were undertaken during the period 1964-1965 to establish the status of the Green Turtle *Chelonia mydas* and the Hawksbill Turtle *Eretmochelys imbricata*. For this purpose all known rookeries were visited; to facilitate evaluation, attempts were made to coincide visits with the local turtle nesting period. This was no easy task as travel by sea became hazardous due to rough seas and the threat of piracy. Travel by road was sometimes impossible during the rains.

During the course of the investigation, it became clear that the Green Turtle and the Hawksbill Turtle were vulnerable while at sea and on the beaches. Both species were in danger of extinction due to the complete removal of the fruits of their reproductive efforts, incessantly and methodically from every nesting beach for over 50 years. Furthermore, the situation was aggravated by the illegal slaughter of turtles in Sabah waters by fishing vessels. As a result of these two devastating factors, it was envisaged that the turtle populations which existed had little chance of survival. The repealed Turtle Preservation Ordinance of 1914 and the Turtle Preservation Ordinance No. 5 had afforded the turtles meagre protection.

The principal protected area discussed in this paper is the Turtle Islands National Park, (1,740.21 ha), encompassing the islands of Pulau Selingaan (8.09 ha), Pulau Bakkungan Kechil (8.49 ha), and Pulau Gulisaan (1.61 ha) and the surrounding coral reefs. The islands lie approximately 40 km northeast of Sandakan in the Sulu Sea. Other nesting areas of lesser importance are also found in the area, and data on the period of nesting and nesting intensity are available.

For some time it has not been possible to freely visit the various rookeries in the Sulu Sea and elsewhere because of the threat of piracy. On one occasion, the vessel in which the writer was travelling was fired at by pirates. On another occasion, the writer witnessed the gunning down of a small fishing boat near Pulau Bakkungan Kechil, within the Turtle Islands National Park. Departmental staff while working on P. Bakkungan Kechil have been fired at with small calibre automatic weapons by the crew of a Filipino trawler. In 1977, an attempt was made by Filippino "refugees" to establish a colony on P. Bakkungan Kechil. They were soon removed by the police. On 9 July 1977, the island was the scene of a bloody battle between pirates and the Sabah police. Although naval and marine police patrols have greatly increased, caution must be exercised when travelling the seas in this area.

2. STATE CONSERVATION POLICIES

To obtain an idea of the existing state of affairs it is expedient to review past and present turtle conservation policies of the state which was formerly known as British North Borneo.

Beginning in 1927, colonial administrators made attempts to conserve the Hawksbill which was hunted for its shell; conservation proposals began when the Board of Directors of the Chartered Company sent their officers in the colony a report by James Hornell on the Turtle Fisheries of the Seychelles. This report and subsequent action resulted in Gazette Notifications 227 and 228 of 1928. The latter prohibited the capture of turtles for 12 months from 1 January 1929. Later, Morrell studied the situation and submitted a report on the turtle industry of North Borneo and *inter alia* recommended a closed season every alternate year for 6 years. According to records, the 1929 closed season was imposed and partially successful. The other seasons were not enforced as the trade in sea produce was driven from Kudat to the Philippines, unrestricted fishing (for turtles) was carried out in Philippine territory; and there were difficulties of control.

In 1933, exclusive licences to collect Green Turtle eggs for 3-year periods were issued by the Resident, Sandakan; a licence was subject to cancellation at one year's notice and it prohibited the collection of Hawksbill eggs, though it is extremely doubtful whether the successful tenderer abided by the stipulated conditions.

On 26 June 1948 the Government of the Crown Colony of North Boreno handed over to the Philippine government the richest of the turtle islands situated in the Sulu Sea. Prior to 1964, Turtle Preservation Ordinance No. 5 of 1952 was laxly administered by the authorities concerned; presumably, their main difficulty was to enforce the law on remote islands and beaches. Perhaps, except for an occasional visit to a rookery, nothing else could be done.

When the Fauna Conservation Ordinance 1963 came into force in July 1964, the undisputed control of turtle farms and all matters connected with turtle conservation passed into the hands of the Conservator of Forests and Chief Game Warden and a conservation policy was recommended by the writer who was then Assistant Chief Game Warden. After the recommendations were accepted by government, the issue of Turtle Licenses for the purpose of killing turtles ceased immediately and the closed season in March for turtle egg collection on turtle farms and any area reserved for the collection of turtle eggs was to be strictly enforced. The former policy was carried out, but owing to the paucity of staff, inadequate transport and the threat of piracy in the Sulu Sea, the later directive could not be enforced (incidentally, Batasara, an egg collector, was killed in 1964 by pirates while collecting turtle eggs).

Native rights were safe-guarded under the ordinance and natives still collect without a license all turtle eggs laid in Native Reserves. After a conservation policy was formulated in 1964, the Resident, West Coast, indicated that an invidious situation had arisen in the Kota Belud District owing to the fact that natives in the district had to pay licence fees for collecting turtle eggs from traditional harvesting areas, whereas their coastal brethren in other parts of the state were granted "native rights". After the situation was investigated, it was found that only small numbers of turtles nested seasonally in the remote areas involved, and that traditional native egg collecting areas were involved; due to difficulties of control in extremely remote areas, it was recommended to Government that the Kota Belud District and the islands involved be declared native turtle egg collecting areas. After the establishment of these native reserves no other concessions have been granted up to date. It appears that all ethnic groups claiming "native turtle rights", under the law have been placated.

Eight turtle farms were constituted under the Fauna Conservation (Turtle Farms) Regulations of 1964. Turtle farms under the Regulations are not marine culture facilities but island rookeries where licencees could harvest turtle eggs under supervision and control of the Chief Game Warden.

Out of the 8 islands—Pulau Selingaan, Pulau Bakkungan Kechil, Pulau Gulisaan, Pulau Tegapil, Pulau Laukayan, Pulau Bilean, Pulau Koyan Koyan and Pulau Nunu Nunukan—only the first 3 were privately owned under title. However, as almost all the turtle eggs were laid within the government reserve on each island, the State permitted the collection of eggs under licence and exercised control. The government reserve on P. Selkingaan was 15.08 m from high water mark; on P. Gulisaan there was a foreshore reserve of 15.24 m. Although the title in respect of P. Bakkungan Kechil was said to have been lost or destroyed during the Japanese occupation, government collected royalty and exercised control on the harvesting of eggs on the island beaches. As the other farms were remotely situated in the Sulu Sea and the haunts of pirates, little control was exercised. Nevertheless, an occasional licence was issued.

Although Pulau Tegapil, Pulau Lang-Kangan, Pulau Bikan, Pulau Koyan Koyan and Pulau Nunu Nunukan were constituted as Turtle Farms in 1964, they are remotely situated in the Sulu Sea and yield few eggs. As the seas surrounding these islands were the haunt of pirates, the writer, except for an occasional visit, was unable to enforce the law and regulate the harvesting of turtle eggs. It was virtually impossible to get any staff to live on the islands as they were not desirous of having their pensions or gratuities paid posthumously. Visiting fishermen and others collected the eggs for domestic use and for sale on the mainland.

Incidentally, the seas around P. Bilean are heavily exploited by fishermen with explosives. Fish bombing in this area has gone on sufficiently long to exterminate marine fauna and at the same time adversely affect breeding turtles found there. Explosives are purchased from the gypsies of the sea. On one occasion, the writer surprised a small boat near Pulau Bilean manned by a crew of 3. They were energetically engaged in collecting fish killed by explosives. When investigations commenced, the boat was deliberately capsized so that whatever was in it was sunk. Although the crew of the sunken boat claimed to hail from Banggi Island near Kudat, none of them could produce proof of identity which every Malaysian is equipped with. However, their speech indicated that they were undoubtedly from a neighbouring country. As attempts were made to recover what was sunk (explosives?), and right the capsized boat, a large fishing vessel was sighted steaming towards P. Bilean. As her size and shape indicated that it was an alien vessel, further investigations were terminated according to the dictates of prudence.

Egg collecting records from the Turtle Farms (P. Selingaan, P. Gulisaan and P. Bakkungan Kechil) for the period 1947-1964 are scanty and were haphazardly maintained. However, from the data extracted and summarised from the files made available by the District Officer, Sandakan, it can be established that most of the eggs harvested from the 3 islands were those of the Green Turtle. It can also be established that in 1947, the 3 islands yielded a harvest of 706,960 eggs.

From 1950 to 1964, the exclusive rights to collect turtle eggs were given out by competitive tender, and the price steadily increased from US$250 in 1950 to $10,000 in 1964.

It has to be appreciated that the demand in Sandakan for turtle eggs is insatiable, which is the main reason for the steady rise in the tender price for turtle eggs; this speaks for itself with regard to the consumer demand for turtle eggs. When the effect of the tender system was examined, it was realised that the system

(i) increased the price of eggs to the public, (ii) caused tremendous dissatisfaction to the owners of the islands and (iii) encouraged the entry of a number of Chinese middlemen into the business whose principal function was to appropriate the profits.

In 1965, the tender system was suspended and it was decided to assist the owners of the 3 islands by giving them the exclusive rights to collect turtle eggs without going through the customary tender procedure.

Turtle egg collecting licence fees for the period 1965-1971 averaged about US$6,000 per year; 290,000 to 680,000 eggs were collected annually. The islands ceased to be turtle farms under Gazette Notification No. 882 on 13 November 1971 but licencees were permitted to harvest turtle eggs until the licences expired in December 1971, as they had already paid the full year's fees. Furthermore, the licencees had to be given some time to remove their property and livestock from the islands.

Prior to 1972, Sandakan was supplied with eggs from the 3 turtle farms conveniently located in the Sulu Sea. At times, however, the supply was augmented with harvests from the islands towards Kudat. The price, of course, was subject to fluctuation. During the optimium laying months, a glut of eggs made the price fall and suppliers quickly ceased flooding the market. When the 3 islands became game sanctuaries, egg harvesting ceased on 31 December 1971 but Sandakan continued to be supplied by Filipino barter traders with harvests from Bakkungan Besar and Taganak. The price of turtle eggs in Sandakan rose from US$0.05 in 1971 to $0.20 in 1972 and $0.25 in 1982.

From the information on harvest level and prices, it is speculated that the 1971 harvest from the 3 islands could have been sold in Sandakan at US$25,000.

Prior to 1972, Saburi, the egg collector on P. Selingaan, profitably marketed turtle eggs in Kota Belud and Kota Kinabalu during the off season in those places. He also purchased eggs from the Philippine island of Bakkungan Besar to increase his stock and evade customs duty. These eggs were also marketed in Sandakan. Even though the licencees were to some extent deprived of their harvests by their employees, who were also their relatives, no one complained as everyone involved presumably profited.

This state of affairs went on happily for the purveyors of turtle eggs, but disastrously for the animals. Due to the demand for the commodity and the prevailing price of eggs it was impossible to get the islanders to co- operate. In 1970, the writer was reliably informed that there was a demand for turtle eggs in Hong Kong's red light district, but the potency of turtle eggs as an aphrodisiac is as yet unproven. Various ethnic groups consume turtle eggs but members of one group in particular relish it for the "stamina" it provides. Occasionally, small quantities of turtle eggs are taken from Sandakan by Chinese travelling to Hong Kong. These gifts are said to be highly appreciated by the recipients.

Turtle eggs are sold in Kota Belud during the season and cost about US$0.15 each. During the off season, eggs are sold at $0.25 each. The sale of eggs harvested from nearby beaches contributes to the welfare of the natives in those places as they have very little or nothing to sell from their remote and unproductive lands. Turtles are also slaughtered by the local inhabitants and the flesh is sold locally but the carapace, plastron and flippers are sold to Filipino barter traders as there is no local demand. It is now known that the egg harvest during the season has dwindled and fewer turtles come ashore to nest.

At present large quantities of turtle eggs are brought to Sandakan from the Philippine islands of Taganak and Bakkungan Besar by traders who report that the collection of eggs in their respective islands is not subject to control. Their imported consignments are quickly distributed to retailers; in this regard, it is noted that competition was brisk even in colonial times and it is interesting to observe that in 1954 the late Hj. Sanukong complained to government that his sale of turtle eggs in Sandakan was affected by imports from Taganak. Customs duty then charged for eggs from Taganak was 5%, i.e. the duty on sea produce. Repeated complaints compelled the Resident at Sandakan to recommend to the competent authority that the duty on turtle eggs be raised to 10%. What happened subsequently is unknown as the old files and records are missing.

The massive harvests of 1967 (677,275), 1969 (650,330), 1970 (539,593), and 1973 (510,272) have not occurred since. From 1974 to 1980, the yearly harvest in the National Park has been in the region of 300,000+ eggs; the harvest for 1981 was 285,853. Ten years of intensive conservation work have rolled by, and with some reservations it can be said, if given time, the populations may recover from the battering they received for over half a century. But the success of our efforts depends largely on the co operation of a friendly neighbouring country—the Republic of the Philippines.

3. CONSERVATION

3.1. Need for conservation

Even 20 years after the cessation of hostilities in the Pacific, the Japanese were blamed for the decrease of turtles in Sabah waters. Presumably, a convenient scapegoat was available as large numbers of turtles were indiscriminately slaughtered in the various rookeries when food was scarce during the occupation (de Silva, 1968). Who can blame the Japanese for this? However, the real reasons for the decline appear to have eluded notice:

- for 50 years or more, i.e. up to 1970, the reproductive efforts of every turtle were methodically removed from practically every nesting beach, predominantly for material gain;

- illegal hunting in Sabah waters by local fishing vessels to surreptitiously supply the ever-increasing demand for turtle meat on the mainland;
- the slaughter of turtles outside the territorial waters of Sabah by Filipino fishing vessels;
- frightening away of gravid females approaching the nesting beaches by brightly illuminated fishing vessels;
- killing of fish with explosives near islands frequented by nesting turtles; and
- slaughtering of nesting turtles by local inhabitants in coastal areas without any inhibition whatsoever.

When it was realised that it was impossible for any species of turtle to survive under these critical conditions, conservation measures were adopted.

3.2. Conservation measures

When conservation policy was formulated, it was realised that although drastic measures were immediately necessary to safeguard the Green Turtle and Hawksbill Turtle, it was impolitic to antagonise ignorant islanders and coastal dwellers as the concept of totally exploiting an easily procurable resource was ingrained and conservation of any sort was alien to them. In view of the fact that it was humanly impossible to control every rookery in the State, it was decided to concentrate on the most important turtle rookeries (P. Selingaan, P. Bakkungan Kechil, P. Gulisaan) in the Sulu Sea. Initially, a closed season in March was imposed but it was very difficult to travel to the islands at this time because of the prevailing northeast monsoon. When this problem arose, it was envisaged that if the islanders became actively involved in turtle conservation and observed what conservation measures were implemented elsewhere, they would, in due course, cooperate with the authorities; labour problems on the islands would also be eased or solved.

On 1 August 1966, in spite of opposition from the owners of P. Selingaan, a hatchery for experimental purposes was established on the island. Eggs were purchased from several licencees with great difficulty and there was a time when government tendered the collection rights to collectors and purchased the eggs for conservation purposes.

This situation went on for several years, with protests from licencees to persons of eminence and authority. Although government paid the prevailing market price for eggs in Sandakan for those purchased on the islands, the reluctance of the licencees to part with even a portion of their harvests was due to the fact that the whole year's harvest had been sold by them to Chinese middlemen, for a profit, at the beginning of the year when the licences were issued. It was therefore obligatory for the original licencees to hand over the entire year's harvest to middlemen in Sandakan.

As the 1966 experiment on P. Selingaan yielded the necessary information and provided newly recruited staff with the basic training in hatchery techniques, hatcheries were established on P. Gulisaan and P. Bakkung Kechil in March 1968. During 1968, it was possible to utilise most of the eggs laid on P. Selingaan and P. Gulisaan for hatchery purposes as turtle egg collecting licences were not issued for administrative reasons. The islanders resented this and tampered with several hundred clutches on P. Selingaan which were eventually spoiled; some clutches were stolen on P. Gulisaan (de Silva, 1969a).

The presence of rangers was also hotly resented as other illicit activities were observed and curbed. Apart from raping the nesting beaches, the collection of sand and coral for mainland construction projects was actively encouraged by the islanders for material gain. Sand was taken at all times of the year and the few feral nests which escaped the collectors were inadvertently dug up. The reefs surrounding the islands were heavily exploited and the coral sold in Sandakan to construction agencies. However, conservation policy was implemented without fear or favour and the law vigorously enforced.

As a result of the antagonistic attitude of the licencees during the period 1966/1971 only 14.2% (431,615) of 2,991,125 eggs were used to produce hatchlings. During this period it was observed that egg collectors on the 3 turtle farms energetically harvested practically every egg laid on the beaches. They refused to even consider that their energies were directed toward the extinction of the turtles and disregarded the fact that the survival of turtles depended on mass egg production and conservation.

Since 1966, trawler fishing close to the islands had considerably increased and a random check revealed that hatchlings and adult turtles were sometimes caught in the nets. As uncontrolled operations posed a threat to the turtles, the State Fisheries Department in 1973 co-operated by prohibiting trawling operations within one mile of the islands; the trawler fishermen have honoured the ban.

4. GAME SANCTUARIES AND NATIONAL PARKS

4.1. Acquisition of private property

Oviparous turtles must concentrate on rookeries at the same time of the year to ensure that a good portion of the hatchlings reach the sea. If only a small number of hatchlings are produced, avian and marine predators can exterminate them. As only a fraction of the eggs laid on turtle farms close to Sandakan were available for hatchery purposes, fewer hatchlings reached the sea. Numerical date indicate that only 286,803 hatchlings reached the sea in the 6 years from 1966 to 1971. This was considered quite insufficient if the species was to

be rescued from imminent danger and permitted to survive. Furthermore, there was the alarming and undisputable fact that over-exploitation of eggs for over half a century, without permitting any opportunity for recruitment by allowing eggs to hatch, had resulted in a population of aged animals. A stage would certainly have been reached when the old turtles started to die without replacement and the numbers would drastically drop. Clearly, it was impossible for any population to recover from such an onslaught. As it was not practicable to eliminate the other factors which also contributed to the decline of the turtle population and at the same time protect their habitat from commercial exploitation, the State Government agreed to acquire the islands for conservation purposes.

In 1972, by Gazette Notification No. 504 of 27 June 1972 the 3 islands were constituted Game and Bird Sanctuaries by the Governor, and remained so until 30 September 1977. During the period 1972 to 1977, the islands were under the absolute control of the Chief Game Warden and all eggs laid on the rookeries were utilised for hatchery purposes. However, occasionally, thefts of eggs occurred on all 3 islands. The culprits were from Pulau Libaran whose main traditional source of protein was restricted with the acquisition of the islands; the thefts usually took place at night when the staff were asleep.

By Gazette Notification No. 490 of 18 August 1977, the State Government constituted the 1740.21 ha Turtle Islands National Park on 1 October 1977. The National Park not only encompassed the 3 islands but also the coral reefs between them. The move was imperative to protect the coral reefs from commercial exploitation for construction work and the surrounding sea from fish bombing. Apart from this, small but brightly illuminated fishing vessels anchored off the islands to clean and pack fish for marketing. The brightly illuminated fishing vessels frightened away turtles approaching the nesting beaches, and the discarded fish, offal and edible refuse dumped into the sea attracted large numbers of sharks and predatory fish to the vicinity of the islands; these scavengers of the sea attacked hatchlings when they entered the water after release on the natal beaches. In addition, survivors of the initial attack became disorientated and swam toward the brightly illuminated fishing vessels and were preyed upon by predators in the vicinity of the trawlers, and the foul discharge of bilges and toilets and the jettisoned cans, bottles and plastic containers contaminated to some extent the coral reefs and island beaches.

5. INTERNATIONAL TURTLE SANCTUARY

Very close to the Sabah territorial boundary and the Turtle Islands National Park are the Philippine Islands of Boaan, Bagnan, Taganak, Liliman, Langaan and Bakkungan Besar. Together they form a well-defined group of turtle rookeries. As far as the writer is aware, egg harvests obtained from Taganak and Bakkungan Besar are marketed in Sandakan at all times of the year; the harvesting and marketing of the eggs is probably the only source of income to the impoverished islanders. G. de Silva (1969b) reported that Filipino fishing trawlers hunted turtles in the Sulu Sea and the Celebes Sea. Hunting in the former area has not ceased; it still occurs near P. Bakkungan Kechil and P.Bakkungan Besar and catches are disposed of within 72 hours in Zamboanga. Polunin (1975) quotes an estimate of 5,000 large Green Turtles captured annually in the Sulu Sea. Trawlers operating between P. Bakkungan Besar and P. Bakkungan Kechil are armed, and crews use swimming or copulating turtles as targets; putrid carcases with neatly punctured carapaces are occasionally found floating near Bakkungan Kechil. Fish bombing by islanders from across the border is common on both sides of the border near the islands of Bakkungan Besar and Bakkungan Kechil; when attempts are made to apprehend them, they conveniently sail across the international border which we do not cross for obvious reasons. Under these conditions, the conservation work undertaken on the Sabah islands is negated within a distance of about 2-16 km.

It is therefore imperative that preventative action be taken in the areas involved. Without being presumptious, it is suggested that Philippine conservation authorities take cognisance of what is happening in the Philippine islands near the Sabah Turtle Islands National Park and consider the protection of the islands involved and the surrounding seas near the territorial boundary. It is also suggested that the Philippine islands be converted into Turtle Sanctuaries. After this is done, an international sanctuary should be constituted. This proposal was mooted at the Washington Sea Turtle Conference in 1979 by the writer, but unfortunately no progress has been made as yet. A fervent appeal is again made to the agencies concerned to give this matter their serious consideration.

Acknowledgements

The writer is deeply indebted to Tan Sri Datuk T.J. Jayasuriya, Chairman, National Parks Board of Trustees, Sabah, for the help, facilities, and envouragement given to undertak turtle research on the islands; to Mr A.J. Hepburn, Natural Resources, Chief Minister's Department, for critically reading and editing the manuscript and to Dr George Balazs, University of Hawaii, USA, for sending reference material from time to time. Finally, the writer wishes to express his appreciation to Miss N.L. Chan and Miss Veronica S.Y. Chok for patiently deciphering his heavy, illegible hand and typing the drafts and manuscript and checking statistics from numerous files.

This paper was prepared for IUCN's Commission on National Parks and Protected Areas in cooperation with the World Wildlife Fund.

How to Protect Coastal and Marine Ecosystems: Lessons from the Philippines

Amado S. Tolentino, Jr.
National Environmental Protection Council
Ministry of Human Settlements
Quezon City, Philippines

ABSTRACT. *Using Philippine examples, this paper analyzes the legal and institutional approaches to the effective management of coastal and marine protected areas. It presents the Philippine coastal and marine zone situation, outlines the master plan for managing these areas and discusses the use of law as an environmental management tool. It offers legal and institutional approaches to the effective management of coastal and marine protected areas, including: a well-defined coastal zone policy; serious implementation and strict enforcement of coastal zone legislation; and a coastal zone management programme including a master plan, a coordinating mechanism to ensure implementation of policy with development, use of interagency and multi-disciplinary approach, and a management systems framework.*

1. INTRODUCTION

This case study aims to help define a new and expanded role for coastal and marine ecosystems in the process of socio-economic development. Using Philippine examples, it will analyze the legal and institutional approaches to the effective management of coastal and marine protected areas, based on the goal of achieving and maintaining a balance between economic development and environmental quality.

The study also presents the Philippine coastal and marine zone situation, its management problems, the Master Plan for Coastal Zone Management, and the management systems framework, emphasizing the use of law as an environmental management tool.

2. SETTING

The Philippines lies just off the southeastern portion of the Asian continent and on the eastern rim of the Pacific Ocean. Due to its physical location and configuration, the country is rich in valuable coastal ecosystems, such as reef flats, sandy beaches, embayments, coastal wetlands, estuaries, mangrove swamps, coral reefs and sheltered coves, which serve important biological and economic functions.

Considering the archipelagic nature of the country, the Philippine coastal and marine areas are significant elements of the nation's environment, there are 18,417 km of shoreline and 82% of the country's provinces are coastal. Clearly, coastal and marine resources are critical to the livelihood of the Filipino people. In addition, the coastal zone is the locale of a number of significant infrastructure projects, the focus of urban and industrial development, the site of many historical landmarks and the setting of numerous prime recreation areas (NEPC, 1979).

But the Philippine coastal and marine zones are beset with problems. These can be attributed to a series of conflicts among coastal utilization, coastal resources and natural coastal features. Problems associated with the non-extractive utilization of the coastal and marine zones are in the form of natural hazards; pollution due to domestic, industrial and solid wastes; and environmental problems due to dredging, oil spills, shore structure and reclamation (Juliano, 1979).

3. CONSTRAINTS

Some 50 existing government institutions are directly or indirectly involved with coastal zone research or management in the Philippines, but none has a direct responsibility for management as a whole. Naturally, in their operations, there are overlaps in effort and conflicts in jurisdiction, often arising from poor communication or coordination between agencies. A few examples may be cited: until the issuance of Presidential Decree 1968, corals were being thrown back and forth between the Bureau of Fisheries and Aquatic Resources and the Bureau of Mines; mangroves have been disputed by the Bureau of Forest Development, the Bureau of Fisheries and Aquatic Resources and to a certain extent by the Bureau of Lands; and marine parks and reserves are in no man's land with the Philippine Tourism Authority coming onto the territory previously claimed by the Bureau of Forest Development, the Bureau of Fisheries and Aquatic Resources and the Natural Resources Management Centre, not to mention the National Environmental Protection Council. It is not always clear where the jurisdictions of the Maritime Industry Authority, the Philippine Ports Authority and the Philippine Fish Marketing Authority begin and end. How well do the Bureau of Flood Control and the Bureau of Port Harbours and Reclamation coordinate their dredging activities, be they for different reasons?

Aside from the overlapping and conflicting jurisdictions, other limitations and restrictions on the orderly development of coastal and marine zone programmes are: lack of necessary political support; absence of a clear-cut policy and specific legislation on coastal zone management; lack of adequate funds, manpower and technical equipment; and lack of highly trained personnel not only to enforce regulations but also to teach, demonstrate and carry out badly needed research.

4. ADDRESSING THE PROBLEMS

In 1977, three landmark pieces of legislation were enacted in the Philippines: the Philippine Environmental Policy; the Environment Code; and the law creating the National Environmental Protection Council (NEPC). The Philippine Environment Policy sets forth the broad environmental policies for the country, recognizes the right of the people to a healthy environment and renders compulsory the submission of environmental impact statements for environmentally critical projects or projects located in environmentally critical areas. The Environment Code, on the other hand, deals with the Philippine environment in its totality and not on a fragmented basis; its primary concern is the establishment of management policies and quality standards for the environment, pollution control being merely one of its many aspects (NEPC, 1981).

4.1. The Coastal Zone Management Programme (CZMP)

The NEPC was created as the central authority that will rationalize the functions of government agencies charged with environmental protection and to oversee, unify and integrate the planning, management and implementation of the government's environment programme. In 1977, it embarked on CZMP, a programme to protect and manage the country's coastal and marine zones. An Inter-Agency Task Force (IATF) composed of 22 environment-oriented and coastal zone-related agencies was organized through a Memorandum of Agreement, defining the agencies' participation in the CZMP and their respective tasks and responsibilities.

Among the significant works done by the IATF during the first 3 years have been: definition of the Philippine coastal zone; inventory of coastal zone resources; a study of coastal zone utilization and activities; inventory of coastal zone-related legislation; and identification and assessment of manpower and institutions with coastal zone research and management capabilities.

In the inventory of coastal zone-related legislation, it was discovered that a coastal zone policy has yet to be formulated and given a definite official and legal direction. Furthermore, the legislation simply provided for full exploitation and utilization of coastal zone resources for purely economic gains with less consideration to sustained-yield management or environmental protection.

In the study of existing institutions, it was found that the research effort directed to the coastal zone has never been given the emphasis it deserves; funding, facilities and manpower are very limited. In regard to management, a fresh look at the list of interested institutions revealed that only a third are primarily involved in coastal zone affairs. In fact, this should be enough to take care of coastal zone management in the country, if there were a single coordinating authority. There is little doubt that such a mechanism would remove many of the present difficulties including policy and decision-making problems, and will lead to more efficient functioning of the various agencies.

After these studies, the IATF formulated a Master Plan for Coastal Zone Management. The plan contains the terms of reference of the CZMP and concepts of potential programmes and projects, including goals, objectives and strategies to attain the desired ends. Activities and projects were categorized in the Master Plan as follows: information and data generation; research; education and public information; development and restoration; and policy and institutional studies. It also defines the Philippine Coastal Zone:

"The coastal zone is the strip of land and adjacent lake or ocean space (water and submerged land) in which the land ecology and land use directly affect lake and ocean space ecology and vice versa. Functionally, it is a broad interface between land and water where production, consumption and exchange processes occur at high rates of intensity. Ecologically, it is an area of dynamic biochemical activity but with limited capacity of supporting various forms of human use. Geographically, the outermost boundary is defined as the extent to which land-based activities have a measurable influence on the chemistry of the water or on the ecology of biota.

"In determining the boundaries of the Philippines coastal zone, the point of reference used is the zero mark or mean sea level in the 1:50,000 topographic maps and governed by the following limits: (1) The outermost limit is the 200 m (100 fathom) isobath except at embayments in which case the 200 m isobath at the mouth of the bay, gulf or cover is extended across. In cases where the 200 m isobath is less than three kilometres from the shorelines the three-kilometre distance will be adopted. The internal waters are likewise considered part of the coastal zone. (2) The innermost boundary is one kilometre from the shorelines except at places where recognizable indicators for maritime influences exist like mangroves, nipa swamps, beach vegetation, sand dune, salt beds, marshlands, bayous, recent marine deposits, beach sand deposits and deltaic deposits in which cases the one-kilometre distance shall be reckoned from edges of such features."

4.2. The coastal zone management systems framework

The Master Plan was followed by the development of a management systems framework for the implementation of the CZMP. The framework identifies the different components of the coastal zone management system, notably: programme planning and development system; project management system; programme evaluation system; and information and coordination network.

4.2.1. Programme planning and development system (PPDS).
Programme planning and development is concerned with the processes of strategic planning, target setting, prioritization and goal formulation. The output of the PPDS is strategic, based on the master plan and approved priority projects.

4.2.2. Project Management System (PMS).
The PMS is concerned with project operations planning, implementation, monitoring, evaluation and re-planning. The output of the PMS consists of project plans, monitoring reports, and evaluation, all of which are fed as inputs to programme evaluation.

4.2.3. Programme Evaluation System (PES).
Based on the outputs of the PPDS and PMS, the process of pro-

gramme evaluation consists of comparing planned against accomplished project outputs. The PES results serve as a basis for management action decision, policy formulation and the succeeding process of programme planning and development.

4.2.4. Information and coordination network.
The network serves as the mechanism to institutionalize the linkages and coordination among participating agencies/entities for information exchange and monitoring of activities and, most important, in the implementation of plans and projects.

4.3. The coastal zone management programme structure

The main focus of the structure of the CZMP, which supports the designed CZMP systems framework, is the setting up of a strong secretariat to oversee the CZMP implementation and the inclusion of the regional provincial, municipal and *barangay* (village) structure. The support components of the CZMP structure are:

- The Ministry of Human Settlements (MHS). Serves as the umbrella ministry of the CZMP and provides top-level institutional support to the NEPC.
- The National Environmental Protection Council (NEPC). Serves as the lead agency in the implementation of the CZMP and coordinates all the programmes/plans/projects/activities of all member agencies.

4.4. Strategy for implementation

The scope and areas covered by the CZMP necessitates continuing and workable inter-agency collaboration, requiring the institutionalization of an Information and Coordination Network. A Memorandum of Agreement (MA) among agencies/entities vital to coastal zone management serves to identify the project's lead agency as well as specific agency involvement; it may also facilitate budgetary releases for inter-agency projects. The MA also defines in detail the points for coordination and specific duties, responsibilities and accountabilities of the various agencies.

A number of implementing structures is tapped for the CZMP at the national, regional, provincial, municipal and village levels; in generating CZMP programmes and projects at each level, the lead agency provides technical and/or funding assistance (including assistance at the various levels). The coordinating bodies are assigned the functions of programme management (programme planning, development, and evaluation) while the implementing structures are concerned with project implementation and management.

5. COASTAL ZONE LEGISLATION REVIEW

In the Philippines, the promulgation of conservation laws are usually in response to sectoral needs or emergencies, and are generally characterized by gaps, duplications and even conflicts. In many instances where the laws are unified and holistic, the implementation is the problem; there may be no provision for enforcement. In cases where responsibilities in the implementation of sectoral components fall on the shoulders of different agencies, the lack of coordination is often the cause of failure.

To complement the CZMP, the NEPC embarked on a coastal zone legislation review to determine the adequacy of existing legislations on the coastal zone; to identify gaps and overlaps in existing legislation; and to recommend amendments/new legislation on coastal zone management.

In 1980, the NEPC Inter-Agency Legal Committee recommended a coastal zone policy as follows:

"It is hereby declared a policy of the State to pursue a continuing programme of effective management of coastal zones to meet the socio-economic development needs of our country for the benefit of present and future generations. In pursuing this policy, it shall be the responsibility of all government bureaus, agencies or instrumentalities, including political subdivisions involved in coastal management, to instill awareness to the public about the dangers of the degradation of environmental conditions in the country's coastal zones and encourage active participation of the people in all undertakings to conserve and enhance the country's coastal zones."

The Legal Committee also argued strongly for more serious implementation and enforcement of coastal zone-related legislation, like the environmental impact assessment law which assures integration of environmental consideration on the development programme of projects. Indeed, law which is not implemented in any form or which is not enforced for any reason is not materially binding; its existence may satisfy political and administrative conscience but it has no effective impact on the problems with which it is supposed to deal. It may have some initial deterring effect but this will disappear as soon as it becomes evident that the law will not be enforced. Even a law that has been implemented through regulations can remain ineffective because of lack of funds, personnel and equipment (Zamora, 1981).

Above all, successful implementation and enforcement of laws presupposes a conservation-oriented education of the people. To achieve this end, a programme of environmental education should be adopted in all schools. It should begin from the lowest grade and continue up to the college level, complemented by the same concentration in informal or adult education.

6. RESULTS

In the last few years, two notable coastal zone projects made use of the legal and institutional approaches as described above. Those are: a Study of the Effects of Silt Load on the Coastal Ecosystem of San Fabian, Pangasinan, and the Coastal Zone Management Studies for Hundred Islands.

6.1. The effects of silt load on the Coastal Ecosystem of San Fabian.

Siltation, one of the critical problems of the Philippine coastal zone, is well illustrated in the coastal area of San Fabian, Pangasinan. A study on the effects of silt load in the town's ecosystem was thought to give valuable information that could be applied to other similar areas in the future.

The project utilized an inter-agency and inter-disciplinary approach, with the scope of investigation covering the biological parametres (vegetation, aquatic plants, fish and shellfish etc.), physico-chemical parametres (construction materials, heavy metals, surface and ocean water quality etc.), and socio- economic parameters (coastal zone utilization; fishing, residential, agricultural, recreation; and culture status; health and safety, population density, etc.).

Agency responsibilities were delineated in a Memorandum of Agreement among the Fishery Industry Development Council, National Environmental Protection Council, Philippines Atomic Energy Commission, National Pollution Control Commission, the Bureau of Lands and the Environmental Centre of the Philippines.

At the conclusion of the project's implementation period, it was able to determine the degree of silt load, the components of the ecosystem, the effects of silt load to the various components of the ecosystem in the study area, and develop a system of monitoring the silt load and other sources of pollutants in the Bued-Cayanga River.

6.2. Coastal Zone Management Studies for Hundred Islands

The Hundred Islands, located in the northern portion of the municipality of Alaminos, Pangasinan, constitute one of the unique coastal formations in the Philippines. Its resources, however, are at the mercy of various environmental stresses resulting from unregulated human activities. A study was therefore geared toward the formulation of policies and guidelines for the rational management of the coastal features of Hundred Islands.

The NEPC was the coordinating agency, assisted by the following as cooperating agencies: Bureau of Forest Development; Bureau of Fisheries and Aquatic Resources; Bureau of Mines; Ministry of Tourism; and the University of the Philippines Marine Science Centre. A

Memorandum of Agreement was drawn among them and following the coastal zone management programme systems framework, the study was able to determine existing environmental attributes of the project site and came out with a conceptual management plan for Hundred Islands.

7. CONCLUSION

There are two levels upon which the above study may be of value. The first is the broad level of awareness, or understanding of the existential context in which we humans are part of nature and interact with the elements in it. This is the reason the World National Parks Congress aims to define a new and expanded role for protected areas in the process of socio-economic development, particularly in developing countries.

At a more practical level, the study suggests legal and institutional approaches to the effective management of coastal and marine protected areas to countries which are similarly situated. These approaches include: a well-defined coastal zone policy; serious implementation and strict enforcement of coastal zone-related legislation; a coastal zone management programme including a master plan; a coordinating mechanism to insure implementation of policy; use of inter-agency and multidisciplinary approaches coordinated by a Memorandum of Agreement; and a management systems framework for the implementation of Coastal Zone Management Programmes. Out of these approaches, it is hoped, would come more effective working concepts for coastal and marine zone management. As changes are made, the legal and educational systems can help define the path toward increasing preservation of the dignity of nature and the dignity of humanity within it.

Acknowledgements

This paper was prepared for IUCN's Commission on National Parks and Protected Areas in cooperation with the United Nations Environment Programme.

Aquaculture, Forestry and Conservation in Malaysian Mangroves

Ong Jin-Eong
School of Biological Sciences
Universiti Sains Malaysia
Penang, Malaysia

ABSTRACT. *Malaysia's 650,000 ha of mangroves are under the jurisdiction of the various State Forest Departments. Some 20% of mangroves have been lost through "reclamation" by the woodchip industry in the past twenty years. Another 20% has been earmarked for possible aquaculture development in Peninsular Malaysia. A comparison between sustained-yield management for forestry and conversion to aquaculture shows that aquaculture development is economically precarious. A conservation plan involving sustained-yield management and the establishment of mangrove protected areas is suggested. Seed materials from the protected areas will ensure genetic vigour for sustained-yield management.*

1. INTRODUCTION

Mangroves comprise some 650,000 ha (about 2%) of the total land area of Malaysia; about 110,000 ha occur in Peninsular Malaysia, while the rest are in Sabah and Sarawak. In Peninsular Malaysia, some 20% of the mangroves have been reclaimed in the last 20 years (Ong, 1978). The major mangrove forests in Peninsular Malaysia are under some form of sustained yield management by the different State Forest Departments. In recent years the loss of mangrove areas is due mainly to excision for port and airport facilities, industrial estates and, to a lesser extent, agriculture. In Sabah and Sarawak, another 20% has been licensed for woodchip production (estimated from figures of annual coupes given by Chai, 1977 and Liew, 1977). It appears that no new licenses are being issued in Sabah and Sarawak for the production of woodchips (the socio-economic returns being poor and the degradation to the mangrove being a problem—Nair, 1977, and Ong, 1978).

The Ministry of Agriculture has estimated that about 27,000 ha of land in Peninsular Malaysia is suitable for brackish water fish culture (in Gedney, *et al.*, 1982). This presumably is mostly mangrove land, which means some 20 to 25% of the mangroves in Peninsular Malaysia has been earmarked for aquaculture use. Indeed, the Fisheries Development Authority (Lembaga Kemajuan Ikan Malaysia or Majuikan), has started the initial phase of a giant aquaculture scheme by acquiring some 300 ha of forest in the Sungai Merbok Mangrove Forest Reserve, Kedah. It would thus appear that aquaculture presents the greatest threat to Malaysian mangroves in the near future.

The aim of this study is to examine the various implications of developing aquaculture schemes in mangrove forests as compared with sustained yield management for timber production and suggest the most rational use of this so often misunderstood ecosystem.

2. TWO MANGROVE SYSTEMS

This will be done by examining two mangrove areas in Peninsular Malaysia:

i) The Matang Mangrove Forest Reserve, which is under sustained yield management for charcoal, poles and firewood by the Perak Forest Department; and

ii) The Sungai Merbok Mangrove Forest Reserve, which is being developed into a major aquaculture scheme by Majuikan.

165

2.1. The Matang Mangrove

Sustained yield use of mangrove forest is seen at its best in the Matang Mangrove Forest Reserve, which contains about 40,000 ha of forests dominated by almost pure stands of *Rhizophora apiculata*. It is situated in the state of Perak and is under the jurisdiction and management of the Perak Forest Department. The forest has been under sustained yield management since the early part of this century.

2.1.1. Management plan.
The forest has been worked under a 30- to 40- year rotation plan is now in its third rotation; the annual coupe for clear-felling is about 1,000 ha, with trees clear-felled in patches of a few hectares in an area. Clear-felled timber is used mainly for the manufacture of charcoal, the rest being for firewood. After clear-felling, the slash (i.e. small branches, twigs, leaves, fruits and stumps) is left to decompose naturally. This slash usually becomes neglible after about two years. In certain areas natural regeneration of young plants is good so no planting is necessary but in areas where regeneration is poor, the area is planted with *Rhizophora apiculata* propagules, at about 1.2 m intervals. In some areas it is necessary to manually remove weeds like the mangrove fern *Acrostichum* before replanting can be carried out. It is estimated that some 50% of the clear-felled areas need artificial replanting.

The seedlings are allowed to grow unattended for 15 years, at which time the first thinning is carried out. A 1.2 m stick is used during this process. Any tree within a radius of 1.2 m (the stick) of the central tree is removed. The aim of this thinning is to obtain poles which have a diameter at breast height of about 15 cm. Poles are used for scaffolding by the local building industry, pilings and fishing stakes. Apparently this is not intended as a silvicultural treatment although an unpublished (Gong, Ong & Wong) study indicated "natural thinnings" occur to a very significant extent between 10 and 15 years. A second thinning is carried out between 20 and 25 years with a 1.9 m stick and the trees are finally clear-felled at about 30 years, ending the rotation. This rule-of-thumb system (Watson, 1928) appears to have worked remarkably well although there has been a drop in yield between the second and third rotations (the first rotation figures cannot be used for comparison because the first fellings were of larger trees more than 30-40 years old); the reason for the decrease in yield is not known (Tang *et al.*, 1980).

2.1.2. Socio-economic factors.
A number of villages are located within mangrove forests. The population is either involved with forestry or the fishing industry. It has been estimated that the forest industry provides employment for a direct work force of about 1,400 and an indirect work force of another 1,000 (Ong, 1978). The estimated annual total value of mangrove forest products in the area is about US$ 9 million (Haron, 1980).

The fishing industry in the same area provides employment for an estimated direct work force of about 2,500 and an estimated indirect work force of another 7,500 (Ong, 1978). Based on the value of prawns and cockles landed in 1979 of US$ 32 million for the whole State of Perak (Tang *et al.*, 1980), it is estimated the total annual value of the Matang mangrove fisheries to be at least on the order of US$ 30 million.

Thus, it can be seen that the fishing industry in Matang provides employment (directly or indirectly) for 4 times as many people as the forest industry and the value from fishing is at least 3 times that derived from forestry. Matang is the best mangrove forest in Malaysia (and possibly in the world). The returns from the forest industry will probably be less in lesser managed forests. This vividly illustrates the value of the fishing industry in the mangrove environment.

2.1.3. Ecological implications.
Since the pioneering works of Heald (1971) and W.E. Odum (1971) there is now ample circumstantial evidence to demonstrate the dependance of coastal fisheries on mangroves. Certain species of penaeid prawns, including *Penaeus indicus*, *P. merguiensis*, *P. monodon* and most species of *Metapenaeus*, are dependant on mangrove forests for shelter during their juvenile stages (Macnae, 1974). While in some areas the correlation between prawn landings and mangrove area is good the relationship does not hold in other areas; it is not possible to generalize and say "no mangroves: no prawns." In Peninsular Malaysia there is also a good correlation between prawn landings and mangroves (Gedney *et al.*, 1982) and a number of studies (T.L. Ong, 1978); Sasekumar and Thong, 1980; Thong and Sasekumar, 1980; Leh and Sasekumar, 1980) have shown the presence of significant amounts of mangrove detritus in the guts of many important commercial fishes in coastal waters.

Unfortunately, direct or quantitative evidence to link mangroves and coastal fisheries appear lacking. The vital question, "How much mangroves can be removed in any particular area without adversely affecting the adjacent coastal fisheries?" as yet cannot be answered. There is an urgent need for concerted research efforts in this area.

In the Matang Mangroves some 10 tonof mangrove litter is produced per hectare per year (Gong *et al.*, 1980; Ong *et al.*, 1980a). Slash produced by thinnings and clear-felling adds significantly to this amount (Wong *et al.*, 1982). Thus the practice of sustained yield production of timber in Matang can coexist in harmony with coastal capture fisheries. Efforts should be made to have fisheries input to the present management plan since any alternate use or change in management plan may have an adverse effect on the fisheries.

Until more information becomes available it appears that the system of management as practiced in Matang should be maintained and encouraged, though this management results in almost a monoculture of *Rhizophora apiculata*. Conservation is essentially rational use, and I have previously suggested a pragmatic approach

NATIONAL PARKS, CONSERVATION, AND DEVELOPMENT

(for Peninsular Malaysia) of preserving about 1% of mangroves for posterity and maintaining most of the rest as practiced at Matang until such time as we have a better understanding of the ecosystem (Ong, 1982). The close association between man and mangroves has made it such that there is no truly virgin stand of mangroves in Peninsular Malaysia.

2.2. The Sungai Merbok Mangrove

The Sungai Merbok Mangrove Forest Reserve is used here to illustrate the use of mangroves for aquaculture. The reserve is made up of 18 forest compartments with a total area of 4176 ha. The vegetation is dominated by *Rhizophora apiculata* and *Bruguiera parviflora*. Some 1,500 ha on the north bank of the Sungai Merbok (known as the Ban Merbok area) had been previously reclaimed for rice cultivation but the development of acid sulphate conditions has resulted in the land lying idle. Compartment 15, comprising 307 ha, has recently been excised for aquaculture by Majuikan. The reserve is under the jurisdiction of the Kedah Forest Department.

2.2.1. Forest Management Plan.
The forests are thinned and clear-felled under a plan similar to that at Matang but there is no silvicultural treatment like weed extermination and planting. Regeneration is completely left to nature, yet the forests are surprisingly good (Ong *et al.*, 1980a). The lack of selective planting has resulted in a forest of mixed species, some of the Compartments in this forest are specifically set aside for the use of fishermen in the area.

2.2.2. Aquaculture Development Plan.
Majuikan and the State Government of Kedah are developing an aquaculture scheme here. Already some 50 ha have been converted into ponds and its associated infrastructure. The rest of the mangrove is being studied for further conversion. A master plan for the development of the whole mangrove estuary into a major aquaculture scheme is being undertaken. The objectives of the scheme are to provide gainful employment to the farmers and fishermen in the area and to raise their living standards. The overall development plan will "include aquaculture installations and regional and local settlement centres with communication systems, infrastructure, and utilities (water supply, electricity, sewage, roads, etc.) and amenities (schools, hospitals, recreational centres, etc.), conducive to creating an attractive living and working environment" (Majuikan, 1979). The plan includes a socio-economic evaluation as well as an environmental impact assessment. A baseline ecological survey has already been completed (Ong, *et al.*, 1980b). It is expected that the scheme will involve the economically depressed population of about 15,000 in the area.

2.2.3. Economics of pond aquaculture.
A recent assessment (Gedney *et al.*, 1982), showed that, in the Malaysian context, culture of the tiger prawn, *Penaeus monodon* in ponds provides the best returns. A net income of between US$-4,200 (i.e. net loss) to US$16,800 per ha of pond per annum was estimated, depending on the survival rate of the prawns. Majuikan has started culturing tiger prawns in their new ponds. Input/output calculations have shown that, unless seed and feed costs can be reduced, the project will face serious economic problems unless a remarkably high survival rate of 60% can be achieved. With better technology, it is possible to reduce the cost of seeds but it is unlikely that the cost of trash fish for feeding will go down since with more ponds, demand will become greater. Already Malaysia is a net importer of trash fish (Gedney *et al.*, 1982). Only under ideal conditions will it be possible to approach the net income of over US$12,000 estimated by Gedney *et al*. It is evident that the risks are great as an economic venture, which may account for the paucity of private enterprise in brackish water pond aquaculture.

2.2.4. Ecological implications.
The high organic content in mangrove soils, iron in the soil and the ever-present sulphate from tidal seawater makes practically all mangrove soils susceptible to acid sulphate conditions should oxidation of the soil occur. This often happens during pond construction, when the soil is exposed to air and oxidized. When this happens the pH of the ponds often drops to 3 or less—a condition not conducive to pond culture. It is sometimes possible to control this condition with the use of lime and careful control of water levels, but this can prove uneconomical. It is not known if mangroves will recolonize ponds abandoned as a result of acid sulphate conditions. If recolonization can take place, it may be possible to restore the mangroves.

The aquaculture system used by Majuikan involves feeding the prawns with trash fish (with plans for the use of pellitized food at a later stage); it is not known if this is more efficient than the natural system in the mangrove waterways.

Since the aquaculture ponds rely on a supply of water from the adjacent mangrove waterways, it is vital that the water is of good quality and unpolluted. It is thus important that steps are taken to ensure that pollution upstream from the mangroves is well controlled; any laxity could result in catastrophe for the ponds. Pond operators will automatically put great pressure on the relevant authorities to enforce strict control, and the surrounding mangrove areas will benefit from this control.

The main problem now for Majuikan is to decide how much of the mangroves can be converted to aquaculture ponds and the associated infrastructure without adversely affecting the adjacent coastal fisheries. There is no ready answer to this; it will take some years of concerted research effort to solve the problem. Unless the aquaculture scheme within the mangrove ecosystem can improve on the productivity (in terms of either quality or quantity), then such use of the mangrove ecosystem is a wasteful one. This is a vital consideration for resource managers. The mangrove is nature's own aquaculture system with a number of advantages. An artificial system has the advantage of relatively easier harvest and selection of particular species but nature's system is vastly more stable and less susceptible to diseases and epidemics. Unless the artificial ponds can very significantly surpass the natural system, the establishment of aquaculture ponds may be a case of robbing Peter to pay Paul with the possible added cost of having to compensate Peter after.

3. CONSERVATION

One concept of conservation is that of total preservation for the sake of posterity. While such a concept may have its proponents in the developed nations (where conflict between prosperity and posterity is sometimes thought to be minimal), a more pragmatic concept may have to be applied in the less developed countries (where rapid growth in prosperity is often a primary target of national development). The concept that would be generally acceptable is one that regards conservation as the rational use and mangement of resources. Indeed, this concept does not necessarily exclude the narrower concept of total preservation for posterity.

Since most of the world's mangroves occur in the less developed countries, conservation plans are more likely to succeed if based on the concept of rational use and development rather than one based on preservation for posterity (if a certain amount of prosperity is not achieved, there may be no posterity left to preserve for).

Conservation of mangroves in Malaysia would thus involve a plan or strategy for its rational use and management. As a background to this, it would be necessary to demonstrate the usefulness of mangroves. This can then be followed by a national strategy for rational use and management.

3.1. The value of mangroves

The mangrove ecosystem is in all likelihood the most productive (in terms of net productivity) of all natural ecosystems; its timber yield alone is greater than those of land forests (Tang *et al.*, 1980) and its very considerable contribution to adjacent coastal fisheries (especially the prawn fishery) makes this ecosystem too valuable to be neglected or callously ravaged (as has sometimes been the case in the past).

Ecologically these forests appear to be involved in stabilizing soil and checking erosion in the riparian and littoral zones as well as providing nourishment (from mangrove litter) to aquatic organisms in the mangrove and adjacent coastal ecosystems.

3.2. Major uses of mangroves

At present there are three major uses of mangroves: sustained yield management for the production of charcoal, poles and fuelwood (as seen at its best at Matang); harvesting of woodchips with little serious attempt at regeneration (as seen in Sabah and Sarawak) and the conversion of mangroves into aquaculture ponds (as at Sungai Merbok).

The use of mangroves as now practiced by the woodchip industry can do irreparable damage to the mangrove ecosystem as well as affect the adjacent coastal fisheries. It is possible, however, with proper planning and good management, for the woodchip industry to use the mangrove ecosystem on a sustained yield basis similar to that seen at Matang.

The conversion of mangroves for aquaculture ponds is not a use of mangrove but a replacement of the ecosystem with ponds. As practiced now, it is extremely wasteful—especially when less productive coastal land can be used for the same purpose. Add to this the acid sulphate potential of mangrove land and the precarious economic returns and the balance tilts against this wasteful use. However, a breakthrough in the state of art of prawn culture in the foreseeable future is a good possibility (e.g., the drastic reduction in the production cost of seeds). If this happens, prawn culture becomes economically very attractive, and mangroves, because of their coastal location will no doubt be the main targets for conversion to ponds.

One advantage of having aquaculture ponds (as well as other aquaculture activities like cockle and floating cage culture) is that deterioration of water quality caused by pollution will have a dramatic effect in terms of fish kills, ensuring that the relevant authorities keep a close check on pollution of the ecosystem.

3.3. Mangrove National Parks

The first National Park in Malaysia that includes the mangrove ecosystem is the Bako National Park in Sarawak. The Klias National Park in Sabah consists of mainly mangroves. There is, however, no mangrove national park in Peninsular Malaysia, only two almost insignificant areas of Virgin Jungle Reserve (VJR). It is suggested that a mangrove national park be established in Peninsular Malaysia, preferably in the state of Johore, where more natural mangroves can still be found. The number of mangrove Virgin Jungle Reserves should be appreciably increased.

Apart from the usual arguments for the establishment of national parks (and VJRs) there is an additional strong argument here. The management system in Matang (in its third rotation) has seen a drop in yield. Although the actual reason for this reduction in yield is not known, the use of selected (e.g. high yield) seeds could have prevented this. Also, the current practice may have resulted in the reduction of genetic vigour.

NATIONAL PARKS, CONSERVATION, AND DEVELOPMENT

Availability of seeds (propagules) has also been a problem. Mangrove national parks and VJRs would certainly be excellent sources for seeds and genetic material. The proposed mangrove national park for Peninsular Malaysia should include a complete ecosystem (from the freshwater to seawater) and it is not unreasonable to suggest that the area should be not less than 1 percent of the total mangrove area on the Peninsula. The area of Mangrove VJRs should also be increased to at least 1 or 2 percent of the total mangrove forest reserves.

4. CONCLUSION: A STRATEGY FOR RATIONAL USE AND MANAGEMENT

It is evident that at present the most rational use of mangroves in Malaysia is the sustained yield system as practised in Matang. It is also possible to manage mangroves on a sustained yield basis for the woodchip industry (although this is not done at the present). Certain mangrove areas may be suitable for conversion to aquaculture ponds.

The strategy for rational use and management of Malaysia's mangroves should follow a national mangrove management plan based on the following guidelines:

- for the time being mangroves should be used on a sustained yield basis and managed along the lines used in Matang;
- the management plan used in Matang should be improved with greater research input. There should also be a significant input from fisheries research;

- the use of mangroves for aquaculture should be further researched and explored before major efforts at implementation;
- the conversion of mangroves to aquaculture ponds should proceed with extreme caution and carefully evaluated both ecologically and socio-economically;
- the use of *hutan darat* or land forests of the mangroves for conversion to aquaculture ponds should be thoroughly investigated before productive mangrove forests are used for this purpose;
- a number of mangrove national parks and Virgin Jungle Reserves (each covering at least 1 percent of the mangrove area in Peninsular Malaysia, Sabah and Sarawak) should be established; and
- funding should be obtained for much-needed scientific and socio-economic research on the mangrove ecosystem; the establishment of a National Mangrove Research Institute is opportune.

A National Mangrove Committee has already been established in Malaysia. It is hoped that this Committee will show its effectiveness by drawing up a national mangrove management strategy for the Government's consideration. This is a matter of ugency. Unless such a strategy is adopted soon, Malaysia's unique and rich mangroves will disappear, leaving the country poorer for the loss.

Acknowledgements

This paper was prepared for IUCN's Commission on National Parks and Protected Areas in cooperation with the United Nations Environment Programme.

Vulnerable Marine Resources, Coastal Reserves, and Pollution: A Southeast Asian Perspective

Alan White
Environment and Policy Institute
East-West Center
Honolulu, Hawaii, USA

ABSTRACT. *The distribution of vulnerable marine resources, coastal reserves and pollution sites in southeast Asia as compiled for the* Marine Policy Atlas of Southeast Asian Seas *(Morgan and Valencia, eds. in press) are presented by brief description to accompany the display of maps of scale 1:16,000,000. The vulnerable marine resource distributions include estuaries, beaches, mangroves, coral reefs, sea turtles, crocodiles, seabird colonies, dugong, whales and dolphins. Coastal reserves include all the various designations of marine reserves in the region which border on the coast or have jurisdiction over marine areas. Priority sites for management of marine resources are determined by particularly strong aggregations of vulnerable marine resources, productive fisheries and the presence of marine reserves. This paper focuses on geographical distribution and aggregations which have implications for national and regional marine reserve selection and management programmes.*

1. INTRODUCTION

A Draft Action Plan for the Conservation of Nature in the ASEAN Region has recently been formulated by IUCN. The first two priorities set by this plan are establishment of a network of ASEAN reserves, and institution of measures to protect endangered species (IUCN, 1981). The need to maintain essential ecological processes and life-support systems, to preserve genetic diversity, and to ensure the sustainable utilization of species and ecosystems are emphasized as uniting criteria of potential projects. A network of protected areas is regarded in the plan as one of the most effective ways to conserve ecosystems and their constituent wildlife. Stress is placed on finding common criteria for establishing an adequate reserve system of regional and national importance and of benefit to the local population (ASEAN Report, 1980).

The collection of data for the compilation of a series of environmental maps of the Southeast Asian region was prompted by these priorities. The general distribution of the various marine resources must be known before more site-specific studies can be made. Those areas with viable populations of vulnerable marine animals and intact coastal ecosystems can be identified by combining the respective maps. Those areas often associated with productive fisheries and proposed or implemented reserves can be isolated as priority areas for conservation. Descriptions of areas where pollution is significant and is conflicting with the priority conservation areas are needed information for constructing a feasible regional conservation plan and for the ultimate location and formation of marine resources.

Information on the distribution of marine resources and pollution that could affect them comprises the part of this paper. These data have been compiled by library research utilizing the most current national and regional field reports, symposium and workshop proceedings, interviews with persons from major southeast Asian countries, and personal observation in the Philippines. References for the distribution of each resource and pollution source are identified in the *Marine Policy Atlas of Southeast Asian Seas* (Morgan and Valencia, in press).

2. VULNERABLE MARINE RESOURCES

2.1. Estuaries

Estuaries occur at the mouths of most Southeast Asian rivers and are thus common features in the region. A few large estuarine systems are found in the deltas of major rivers, such as the Mekong, Chao Phaya, Irrawady, and Kapuas river systems. Intermediate and small estuaries are numerous and occur along all the continental and larger island coasts. Only small islands completely lack estuarine systems. Coasts of particular estuarine dominance include the Irrawady region of Burma, parts of the eastern gulf of Thailand and southern Vietnamese and Chinese coasts, the western Malay Peninsula, and the low, northeastern coast of Sumatra, south and eastern Borneo, scattered areas in Java and Sulawesi with a dominance along southern Irian Jaya and the gulf of Papua New Guinea. The Philippines and most small islands have few major estuaries.

2.2. Beaches

The primary large sand beaches of the region occur on coasts exposed to wave energy, such as the south-facing coasts of the Sunda Archipelago, the eastern coast of the Malay Peninsula, the Gulf of Thailand, exposed coasts on the eastern and western shores of the Philippines, northern Borneo, and the northern New Guinea coast. Secondary beaches of smaller size and more localized characteristics are distributed widely throughout the region. These beaches are associated with coral reef formation, small islands, and particular circumstances of coastal formations combined with alongshore currents and sediment availability from rivers. Beaches associated with rivers occur throughout the region on one or both sides of a river mouth, depending on the predominant currents. The beach length and width varies with the river sediment contribution and the shoreline contour.

2.3. Mangroves

The largest concentration of mangrove forest remaining in Southeast Asia is in Indonesia, with an estimated 3.6 million ha; three quarters occurs in Irian Jaya and Sumatra. The second largest concentration is on the southern coast of Papua New Guinea and is considered to be one of the least disturbed mangrove areas in the world. Other major mangrove forests are found along the southwest coast of the Malay Peninsula and at various places along the coast of Borneo.

2.4. Coral reefs

Fringing coral reefs occur throughout the region and are usually associated with small- to medium-sized coastal islands. Larger island and continental coasts support reefs to a lesser extent due to high sedimentation rates, turbidity, and low salinity associated with river outlets.

The Andaman, Nicobar, Mergui, and western Thai coastal islands all support coral reef growth, some in good condition. The Gulf of Thailand has limited reef areas. Coastal islands of the Malay Peninsula support coral reefs, but the peninsular coast in general has none.

The most extensive coral reef area for one country occurs in Indonesia, reflecting its 81,000 km coastline and 13,000 islands. Coral reefs are well represented in the Mentawai Archipelago, along many coasts in the Sunda Archipelago, and islands in the Java and Banda seas and north central Indonesia. Southern Papua New Guinea has limited reefs because of terrestrial runoff, but the north coast and islands are fringed with reefs in some areas. The Philippines also has extensive reef growth with its 18,000 km coastline and 7,000 islands. Once again, the more remote, smaller islands support the better quality and more extensive reefs. The Sulu Archipelago and Sulu Sea islands, Palawan Island, Cuyo Islands, some smaller Visayan islands, and some eastern, Pacific-facing coasts support much coral reef area. Most islands in the South China Sea have fringing reefs, but the southern Chinese and Vietnamese coasts noticeably lack reef growth.

2.5. Sea turtles

Five species of sea turtles occur in the region. Sea turtles nest on sandy beaches and normally breed in protected estuarine or reef waters; they feed and bask in similar locations, generally over reef flats. They are often observed swimming in deeper water near the reef edge or farther offshore. The single largest concentration of sea turtle nesting occurs along the east coast of the Malay Peninsula, where more than one million eggs are deposited annually. Other important confirmed sites include the Turtle Islands in the Sulu Archipelago, selected beaches and islands in the Gulf of Thailand, along the southern coasts of Sumatra and Java, selected islands in eastern Indonesia, and northern Irian Jaya.

2.6. Crocodiles

Crocodiles frequent estuarine, swampy areas near large river mouths and mangrove areas. They are also seen infrequently in open water over shallow reef flats. Known breeding sites are few; those remaining are located in remote areas away from human population centres. Four species are known in the region. *Crocodylus porosus* (saltwater crocodile) numbers have been drastically reduced; the largest concentrations occur in Papua New Guinea, but it is also reported in Flores and Timor, the Moluccas, and the Kai and Aru Islands of Indonesia and a few areas in the southern Philippines. *Crocodylus novaeguinea* (New Guinea crocodile) is reported in eastern Indonesia and Papua New Guinea. *Crocodylus mindorensis* (Philippine crocodile) is Endangered in most of its range; probable sites may include Mindinao, Jolo, Busuanga, Palawan, Negros, Samar, and Mindoro in the Philippines. *Crocodylus siamensis* is Endangered in Thailand, Laos, and Kampuchea (where it is a purely freshwater form); it is reported to occur in Indonesia, but no further information exists on its range or frequency.

2.7. Seabird colonies

Marine birds include shore birds, vagrant waders, and oceanic seabirds. Seabirds often have dense breeding concentrations near the shore in undisturbed areas. These colonies of oceanic seabirds are scattered thoughout the region, primarily on smaller islands away from the presence of humans. Seabirds are more common near productive waters and seem to be correlated with established or probable areas of upwelling and associated fisheries.

2.8. Dugong

The only inshore mammal occurring in the region is the sea cow or Dugong. It is strictly a marine species, inhabiting sheltered, shallow tropical and subtropical coastal waters. Dugong feed in intertidal and subtidal areas on sea grasses, although they will feed on algae if sea grasses are scarce. Dugong generally rest in deep water during the day, coming inshore at night to feed in sea grass communities. Dugong migrate, although they may also occur as local residents; during calm weather they will move from protected into exposed waters. There is little information on their present population numbers, although known healthy populations still occur in Indonesia, particularly in the Aru Archipelago where there is a fishery producing about 1,000 dugong annually, and New Guinean waters, where groups of 20 to 50 individuals are still common. Sporadic sightings indicate some presence in the western Java Sea, along the coasts of southern Borneo, Java, Sunda Islands, the western Malay Peninsula, and in the Sulu Sea.

2.9. Whales and dolphins

There is a high diversity of whales (11 species) and dolphins (24 species) in the region. Little is known about migration routes except that which can be inferred from sightings. A few species are still relatively abundant, while most are seen only rarely and are thought to be remnants of once larger populations, or outside their normal range. Most sightings are in southern Indonesia and localized near channels between major islands where the animals are concentrated after emerging from larger bodies of water.

3. COASTAL RESERVES

The location of marine tourist sites and research stations is correlated strongly with the larger population centres or areas with good transportation links. In contrast, marine reserves are distributed more evenly and are associated with environmental features that require protection and management. There is also a correlation between the better quality, acccessible marine reserves and tourist sites. In Thailand there is a strong grouping of such sites along the sandy shores of the upper Gulf and centred near or on Phuket Island in the south. Peninsular Malaysia has numerous sites near and north of Penang and along the Trengganu coast; Sabah and Sarawak have only a few sites. A concentration is evident around Jakarta in western Java and along the south Java coast extending to Bali. Other such areas in Indonesia are sparse except for those sites around Ambon, Seram. The Philippines has many reserves or tourist sites, with a proliferation near and south of Manila on Luzon and in the central Visayan region.

Marine reserves in the upper gulf of Thailand reflect an effort by the Thai government to protect beaches for tourism and several small islands with coral reefs and sea turtle nesting. Western Thai reserves also reflect an interest in tourism and the protection of wetlands, with their associated fauna. Eastern Peninsular Malaysia has extensive sea turtle nesting beaches and small offshore islands, which have prompted reserve formation. Western Peninsular Malaysia offers some recreational sites and extensive wetlands with shorebirds and mangrove forest. Sumatra has a few reserves although sites in the pristine western islands of Mentawai are proposed. The concentration on western Java is composed of small island sites with coral reefs attractive for tourists, a national park at Ujung Kulon, and extensive beaches with nesting sea turtles. Local tourists frequent sites on the south coast. Sites on and near Bali serve to protect some sea turtle nesting and coral reef areas while serving international tourism. Central Indonesia is well represented by legislated reserves for particular environmental and faunal features, while Seram has several sites for the management of coastal or small island coral reef and fishery resources.

Irian Jaya and Papua New Guinea have a few reserves that are primarily terrestrial but include some mangrove, dugong, and crocodile habitat areas and beaches which host sea turtles. A concentration of marine reserves near Manila in the Philippines serves local and international tourism and normally includes beaches and some coral reef sites. The many legislated reserves in the central and northern Visayas are predominantly efforts to protect mangrove forest, associated wildlife, fishery resources and some small island-reef areas. A dearth of information and presumed non-existence shows the coasts of China, Vietnam, and Kampuchea to have no marine reserves; there may be only one in Burma.

The marine reserves with existing management are very few; the legislated areas without management are much more numerous, with Indonesia and the Philippines having the most. Proposed sites, although not clearly defined, are also numerous. The total of all existing, legislated, and proposed sites comprises only the coastal-marine interface of the region or in any single country, and the managed and protected areas comprise only a fraction of these areas.

4. POLLUTION

4.1. Sewage

Sewage includes wastes from both human and industrial sources and since many areas of Southeast Asia have dense coastal populations, the pollution resulting from untreated or inadequately treated sewage can be great. Most Southeast Asian cities lack sewage systems, and the wastes from their large populations enter the sea either directly or via rivers. The highest population densities include the entire island of Java, the west coast of the island of Taiwan, the Hanoi-Haiphong urbanized region of Vietnam, the mainland coast of China (particularly the Hong Kong-Guangzhou region), the metropolitan areas of Manila, Thanh Pho-Ho Chi Minh City, Bangkok, and Kuala Lumpur, and some other areas in the Philippines and Indonesia. The most extensive pollution regions are in the Strait of Malacca, the upper Gulf of Thailand, the Hong Kong region, on the north and west coasts of Taiwan, and in the Manila and Jakarta metropolitan areas.

4.2. Hydrocarbons

Hydrocarbon pollution is widespread. Tarballs have been reported in various areas in the South China Sea, along both coasts of peninsular Malaysia, south of Sumatra and Java, and particularly in the southern Sunda Archipelago. High hydrocarbon content is often evident near oil ports, some shipping routes, and at various locations along the coasts of peninsular Malaysia, Sumatra, and Java. The most important crude oil tanker routes originate outside Southeast Asia, in the Persian Gulf, and transit the region via the Malacca Strait, the South China Sea, and the Luzon Strait. The route for tankers too large to navigate the Malacca Strait is via the Lombok and Makassar Straits and the Philippines Sea to Japan. Indonesia is the largest oil producer in Southeast Asia and therefore has the largest number of oil terminals. Many of them are single or multi-buoy moorings that can handle very large tankers. The ports of Dumai, Pangkalan Susu, Port Dickson, Pulau Bukum, and Singapore, all on the Malacca-Singapore Straits route, make this passage extremely pollution-prone. Other large oil ports are in Brunei (Serai), Malaysia (Miri, Labuan, and Pulai terminal), Hong Kong, and on the island of Taiwan. Smaller ports are located in Thailand, Burma, and Kampuchea.

4.3. Industrial estates

The high concentrations of industrial activities in the inner Gulf of Thailand, in Peninsular Malaysia, on Java, and in the Manila bay area are evident. In the Northern part of the region the west coast of the island of Taiwan is a notable source of industrial-based pollution and existing industrial estates. There is little industrial activity in eastern Indonesia, and information is unobtainable for Burma and not complete for the coasts of China, Vietnam, and Kampuchea.

4.4. Agriculture and forestry

Agricultural activities are the source of a number of water pollutants. Among these are animal wastes, pesticides, and compounds containing nitrogen and phosphorus that are prime constituents of commercial fertilizers. The primary pollutant resulting from forestry activities is sediment from the eroded topsoil, which is a consequence of excessive and careless logging. Accelerated deposition of sediments in Indonesian coastal waters is evident along the densely populated areas of Java and Madura. In the coastal waters of Sumatra and Kalimantan, sedimentation has increased recently due to commercial timber operations. High sediment loads characterize most rivers in Malaysia and are particularly high in peninsular Malaysia. In the Philippines, nearly 30% of the total land area is subject to major soil erosion problems. The deposition of silt from runoff into the Gulf of Thailand has resulted in the formation of a delta of some 3,695 sq km and now extends considerable turbidity into the inner Gulf waters.

4.5. Mining

Mining pollution has become a significant source of coastal water pollution in Southeast Asia. In Thailand about 70% of the tin is mined from coastal waters off the west coast, near Phuket. Dredging and suction boat operations have made these waters turbid. Similarly affected areas include the west coast of peninsular Malaysia, Bangka and Belitung Islands. Philippine waters, particularly those off Luzon, Negros, Cebu, Samar, Balabac, and the Calamian group, suffer from considerable pollution due to terrestrial mining activities. Less extensive patches of polluted waters are located off the coast of Sarawak, north and east of Jakarta, and in Kepulauan Lingga.

5. CRITICAL AND PRIORITY AREAS

5.1. Pollution and vulnerable resources

The obvious zones of direct conflict between pollution and vulnerable marine resources are near densely populated coasts, cities, where industry is established or developing, where medium to large rivers carry increasing sediment loads or other pollutants, and where mine tailings enter the marine environment. Areas of unpredictable pollution are near major sea lanes and ports.

To a certain extent the more important aggregations of vulnerable resources do not now occur near or in the most pollution-prone areas because they have been disturbed or often destroyed. Reefs and mangroves, for example, are affected directly by quantitative increases in pollution and have receded from these areas. Vulnerable marine animals, although adversely affected by pollution, are normally heavily exploited in populated areas and now survive mostly in the less-disturbed, more pristine environments.

Pollution and marine resource conflicts are most evident in the upper Gulf of Thailand, along the west coast of Thailand near Phuket and Peninsular Malaysia, around Belitung and Bangka Islands, the north coast of Java, parts of southern Sulawesi, along the developed areas of Sarawak, Brunei, particular sites in the central and southern Philippines, (especially near the regional urban capitals, where vulnerable resources still survive). These areas in general are not likely to support large populations of vulnerable marine animals and healthy ecosystems now, and are less likely to in the future. They should thus receive a lower priority status for location of parks and reserves with goals of long-term preservation and management.

5.2. Priority sites for management

Strong aggregations where several vulnerable species and ecosystems occur in combination with rich fisheries and marine reserves, or where very large populations of one particular resource survives in a healthy state, occur in the Andaman and Nicobar Islands, Kepulauan Mentawai, parts of the eastern Sunda Archipelago, Kepulauan Aru, parts of southern Irian Jaya and Papua New Guinea, along northwestern Irian Jaya and offshore islands, parts of Seram, Halmahera and northern Sulawesi, selected islands in the Sulu Sea, and Palawan. The subjective choices of what resources should be emphasized cannot be addressed here. Relative size of populations, ecosystem extent and diversity, distance from infringing pollution sources, and current management attempts might all be important criteria for choosing priority reserve sites. A few possible examples are:

- the Aru Archipelago in eastern Indonesia where four species of turtles nest and dugong and crocodile populations survive in an environment of relatively pristine mangrove forests and some coral reefs;
- sites on the northern Great Barrier Reef and islands in the Torres Strait where extensive coral reef areas are intact and are accompanied by sea turtle nesting beaches;
- several recently-formed Indonesian national parks which include coastal areas with reef and mangrove habitat, some populations of sea turtles, dugong, a few crocodiles, seabirds, and indigenous beach vegetation; these include Ujung Kulon in West Java, Baluran in east Java, Bali Barat in Bali, Komodo in Nusu Tenggara Province and Manusela in central Seram;
- parts of the east coast of the Malay Peninsula where dense sea turtle nesting occurs;
- Apo Reef and Tubatahha Reefs in the Philippines where extensive, mostly intact, coral reef ecosystems occur;
- selected smaller islands north of Papua New Guinea were dugong and sea turtle populations survive supported by seagrass;
- sites in the Nicobar Islands where four species of sea turtles reside along with some crocodiles, seabirds, and dugong with supporting mangrove, coral reef and beach habitat.

Many more sites could be choosen by using the information provided here. It is intended that the included broad perspective highlights the important areas and the methodology used may help guide decision makers where site-specific choices should be made now and in the future.

Better Than Machines: Elephants in Burma

Saw Han
Nature Conservation and National Parks Project
Working Peoples' Settlement Board
Rangoon, Burma

ABSTRACT. *There are about 6500 wild elephants in Burma, mainly confined to the five mountain ranges; this represents some 40% of Southeast Asia's elephant population. Other than by timber extraction the habitats of the elephants are undisturbed; there is little conflict between man and elephants but it is not unknown. There are also some 5400 domestic elephants, ninety percent of which are engaged in the timber industry. The timber industry replenishes its stock of elephants from the wild, controlled by the Forest Department. Capture methods are keddah, mela-shikar, and immobilization. In Burma elephants are totally protected by the Wildlife Protection Act, and the Public Property Protection Act. The latter is a severe law to protect the public property. New legislation is being written to protect the habitat as well as the species; the Nature Conservation and National Parks Project has recently been launched, and one of its tasks is to establish elephant sanctuaries and ranges in addition to a series of National Parks and Nature Reserves.*

1. INTRODUCTION

Burma is situated between 10° and 28°N latitudes and 92° and 101°E longitudes. The country is generally hilly in the east, in the north and the west. The central region, with the exception of the Pegu Yomas is rather flattish. The total land area is 676,577 sq km of which 57% is forest covered. The 387,280 sq km of forests can be divided roughly into 8 floristic zones. These floristic zones are again sub-divided into 47 forest types which include climax, sub-climax and seral communities.

In addition, there are extensive areas of bamboo brakes which together with the bamboo component of the evergreen and deciduous forests constitute some 18,000 sq km of almost pure bamboo. With abundant bamboo resources, there is enough food for the elephants and their habitats are still well preserved and undisturbed.

Timber is second to rice as an export commodity. Some 102 million log tons of timber were extracted in 1980, and timber extraction will be increased yearly. The forests are managed under the Selection System, with a felling cycle of 30 years; this system has been in use for well over a hundred years.

2. BURMESE ELEPHANTS

With a good percentage of the land still clad in forests and few development works encroaching on elephant territories, the future of the wild elephants holds good promise; the elephant habitats are still well preserved in the forest reserves (99,378 sq km) and in the wildlife sanctuaries, numbering 14 and 13, established and proposed respectively (Figure 1).

Estimates of the wild elephant population vary with the sources. The number in 1942 was 5500, Smith's estimate in 1949 was 5000, Williams' in 1950 gave 6000. Tun Yin came with a figure of 6500 in 1959 and Wint in 1962 gave 9057. Hundley's figure for 1980 was 6008. Thet Hun's estimate of 6560 is the most recent estimate and the figure is said to be a very conservative one. His estimate will be regarded as a good working estimate for the moment.

The number of domestic elephants in 1982 is 5398. These elephants belong to the Forest Department (baggage only), the Timber Corporation (baggage and timber elephants) and private individuals (baggage and timber elephants).

After young elephants undergo training, they are

put to work as baggage elephants. They become expert timber elephants at around 18 years of age. They work as such for up to 55 years, after which they are retired. They usually do not live long after retirement.

Elephants are better than machines for forestry and on many counts. They are used in all situations such as slippery, soft and boggy soils, and in fairly steep topography; a gradient of 30% is quite easy for them. They can work under conditions unfavourable for tractors. Depending on the size of the animal, a timber load of 1-3 tons can be easily skidded over a distance of 1 km. On rugged terrain, larger loads are skidded by elephants working in tandem of 2 or 3 animals. Elephants belonging to the Timber Organization extract 150 log tons per season of about 7 months; privately owned elephants extract up to 300 tons.

They are not only useful but also virtually indispensable in the operation known locally as *Ye-lite*. Frequently, after the streams have been in spate, the logs are scattered and left high on sand banks; elephants collect the logs and put them back into the streams. This is work which no heavy machines can do. Sometimes logs are piled-up in huge log jams, which are broken up by elephants; again this is no work for machines. The elephants do the work at high risk to themselves and the riders.

Machines are limited by the configuration of the terrain and ground conditions, weather, system of management, high initial costs, and scarcity of spare parts. Elephants are superior to machines in all these respects.

The conservation of the environment is one of the most important factors in forestry, and in particular when management is based on the selection system which is totally dependent on the natural regeneration of teak and other important tree species. The use of elephants in logging causes little environmental disturbance. This is not so with the heavy machines, which not only destroy the natural regeneration but also disturb the soil and cause erosion.

Besides, the elephants work for about 35 years before they are retired. This is roughly equivalent to 3 generations of machine life.

Thus elephants are amphibious, weather-proof, multi-purpose four-legged timber tractors that require little maintenance and energy input. The whole forest is the source of their energy.

3. CAPTURE OF ELEPHANTS IN BURMA

Wild elephants are captured to replenish the timber elephants of the Timber Corporation. The method most widely used is the keddah, where a herd of elephants is driven into a large and sturdy corral; lesser-used methods are mela-shikar (roping individuals) and immobilization.

The Forest Department controls the capture of the elephants and there are 60 keddah blocks over the whole country. The capture limit for the current year is 150 and during the 7-year period ending 1980-81, only 716 elephants were captured against the permitted limit of 1400. Each year a certain number of blocks is opened according to the stipulated number of catch. A block may be opened for 3 successive years, depending upon the number of elephants.

Once an area is closed to capture, it is placed under recuperation. Areas where the population of the wild elephants are intrinsically small, are also placed under recuperation so that the population will eventually increase through self-regeneration.

4. PROTECTION OF ELEPHANTS

Wild elephants have been protected ever since the Elephant Preservation Act of 1879, which was later amended in 1883. The Act was superceded by the Wildlife Protection Act of 1936 and its amended version of 1956.

Elephants are declared as totally protected animals under the Wildlife Protection Act. Lately, in addition to the laws mentioned, they are given added protection under the Public Property Protection Act of 1963, a more severe law.

The future programme for the protection of the wild elephants will be much more effective with the implementation of the Nature Conservation and National Parks Project. The project will cover such activities as the establishment of a series of natural parks and nature reserves, writing of the new legislation for the protection of the wildlife, and the drafting of legislation on the national parks. Strict control on the illegal trade in wildlife and the products thereof shall also be included in the new legislation.

5. CONCLUSION

To sum up, there are about 11,000 elephants wild and domestic, of which 46% of the domestic elephants are State-owned. With a yearly increase in the volume of timber extraction and owing to the specific advantages of elephants over machines, more timber elephants will be needed. In the light of the extraction power of each elephant the timber industry would need about 4800 elephants as of today and more will be needed in the future.

Therefore in keeping with the perpetuation and use principles of elephant management, wild elephant stock will have to be conserved and increased so that the offtake can be sustained. Measures are also being taken to protect the habitats, establish sanctuaries and ranges where possible under the aegis of the Nature Conservation and National Parks Project.

Figure 1: Wildlife Sanctuaries (Existing and Proposed)

Existing	Area in sq km	Proposed	Area in sq km
1. Pidaung	703.93	Kyaukpandaung	132.61
2. Chatthin	268.18	Rhi Lake	10.36
3. Shwe-U-danang	119.14⎱	Zamual	38.85
	206.82⎰		
4. Mayunjo	126.88	Lemro	44.50
5. Wethtikan	4.53	Thitsone	90.65
7. Shwesettaw	551.67	Byingye	39.19
7. Taunggyi	16.06	Yegauk	910.22
8. Kahilu	160.58	Ngwedaung	5.18
9. Kelatha	24.48	Htu Lake	14.58
10. Mulayit	138.56	Hlawga	30.56
11. Moscos Islands	49.21	Peikthanoe	2.59
12. Thamihla Islands	0.88	Mayingyi	103.60
13. Minwuntaung	205.88	Inle Lake	642.32
14. Htamanthi	2150.73		
Total	4727.54	Total	2065.21

River Basin Development and Protected Areas in Sri Lanka

Lyn de Alwis
Director
Department of Wildlife Conservation
Colombo, Sri Lanka

ABSTRACT. *This paper describes the Accelerated Mahewali Project, which represents the first opportunity in Sri Lanka for the integrated and mutually supportive development of a system of protected areas with different management categories in order to bring benefits to both wildlife and people. This favourable situation has been brought about by a realization of the benefits that protected areas can bring, including control of sedimentation rates, mitigation of crop damage, and buffer zone development, as well as flood control, bank stabilization, fisheries conservation, opportunities for tourism, provision of local employment, conservation of genetic resources, and provision of educational and recreational opportunities.*

1. INTRODUCTION: HISTORICAL BACKGROUND

The tradition of an agricultural way of life was brought to Sri Lanka by the farming forefathers of the Sinhalese people, who first settled in the northwestern and southeastern arid zones of the island. These people were obliged to adapt their existing agricultural skills to the climatic regime of those areas, which divided the year into distinct growing (wet) and harvesting (dry) seasons. When necessary, these people found it easy to colonise the sparse arid zone forest by making use of the dry season to resort to a labour-saving method of clearing land for agriculture. This was to slash and burn patches of forest, a system known locally as *chena* agriculture. For some time, a single crop fed by the northeast monsoonal rains was sufficient to meet their needs. As the population increased, however, people were gradually forced further inland into areas where they found rainfed agriculture was insufficient to produce enough food, especially rice (their staple grain), to meet their annual requirements.

This situation created an incentive to devise ways and means for growing a second crop. Thus the 3rd century BC saw the emergence of the rudiments of river basin development. Seeing the irony of rivers flowing idly through the parched land, the ancient Sinhalese kings and their engineers determined to harness them to irrigate their fields. Initially, they built only an anicut across a river to impound sufficient water which could be led by a canal to a series of large tanks (or reservoirs), the overflow from one feeding the next. These reservoirs were built by constructing massive earth bunds to required heights. The water was released from the tanks through sophisticated sluices and other hyrdro-engineering devices designed to control the rate of flow, and dispersed to the fields in the river basin via a system of irrigation channels. The second crop made possible in this way led to a surplus above subsistence grain requirements, which was used to support a growing governmental structure. Later on, the technique of building dams directly across rivers or their major tributaries was developed, thereby greatly increasing the irrigable area.

During the 11th century A.D., the administrative and cultural centre of the Island moved to Polonnaruwa. It was here in the 12th century that King Parakramabahu the Great built the vast 3,110 ha tank which until recent times remained the country's largest irrigation reservoir. This "Sea of Parakrama" brought under cultivation 12,000 ha of land in the Mahaweli River basin.

It is important to mention at this point that a great religious and cultural tradition was also establishing itself in the country. Based on Buddhism, which had been brought to Sri Lanka around the year 300 B.C., this included protection to all living creatures. Successive Sinhalese kings considered it their duty to declare Sanctuaries, as is evidenced by the chronicles, e.g. the edict of King Nissanka Malla in the 12th century A.D. who, "ordering by beat of drum that no animal should be killed within a radius of seven gav (1 gava = 5 km) from the city of Anuradhapura, gave security to animals. He gave security to the fish in the twelve great (irrigation?) tanks. He gave security to birds."

Culturally, we see the emergence of the elephant as the only noble and majestic animal worthy of participating in religious festivals, including the one where the Lord Buddha's relic casket is carried in procession.

These two traditions were to play a vital part in wildlife protection, valid even to the present day.

2. MAJOR CHANGES COME TO SRI LANKA

By the 14th century however, the scenario changed again. The Polonnaruwa era was over, and there was a steady movement of people into the south-west and the hills. The great irrigation works fell into disuse and disrepair. It was only as these areas came under rapid development that conflict between man and wild animal emerged in any very significant way. In fact, one of the earlier references to crop damage by elephants is given by Robert Knox writing of the Kandy area in the 17th century, the beginning of three simultaneous processes that continued for 3 centuries: wildlife was forced out of the hills and wet zones into the less-populated lowland dry zones; the human population increased greatly; and colonial aims and values had far-reaching influence on national life.

As soon as the people had started moving into the southwest, which has so much rain that there is no proper dry or harvesting season, they began losing their agricultural and hydro-engineering skills, and turned to trade in spices which grow wild, and cash crops like coffee and later, coconut, tea and rubber. These trends were encouraged by the colonial powers who, with regrettably few exceptions, did not attempt to revive old skills or rehabilitate the old tanks and irrigation systems.

However, in 1940, with the human population numbering 5.9 million, it was estimated that a staggering 800,000 ha needed to be brought under cultivation to achieve self-sufficiency in rice. Where was this land to come from? The Government turned to the dry zone, the last stronghold of wildlife. Indeed, as early as the 1930's the then Minister for Lands (later Ceylon's first Prime Minister), the Hon. D.S. Senanayake, had set several colonization schemes in motion.

It must be stated, however, that it was during Mr. Senanayake's stewardship as Minister for Lands that far-reaching changes in wildlife protection were also instituted. For instance, he abolished the Resident Sportsmen's Reserves and Game Sanctuaries, where shooting was allowed, and created in their place, in 1938, Sri Lanka's first national parks at Yala and Wilpattu. In 1937 he removed laws pertaining to wildlife from the Forest Ordinance and enacted a separate Fauna

& Flora Protection Ordinance. He was a visionary, for these reforms coupled with existing traditions ensured protection to wildlife as in pre-colonial Sri Lanka.

Simultaneously with the vast settlements made under the new irrigation schemes, other landless people were settling in the dry zone on an *ad hoc* basis as squatters, and the ancient legacy of *chena* cultivation underwent a revival. Together these processes led to an upheaval in the dry zone, and by 1950 Sri Lanka's natural forest cover had dwindled to 45%. As a result, the remaining wildlife populations were exposed to a new and severe set of problems and pressures.

The dubious future of wildlife took a grip on public attention. On the one hand there was an outcry on religious grounds, on the other the conservation community created an awareness that wildlife, particularly the elephant, was heading rapidly towards extinction. One consequence of this attention was the creation of an autonomous Department of Wildlife in 1950. Unfortunately, the new Department ran into teething troubles due largely to paucity of both personnel and funds. It did not really mature until after 1965 when it began evolving in four important directions: the abolition of shooting on licence; the introduction of a scientific attitude to conservation; an educational programme in schools; and the creation of a series of new protected areas as recommended by a Committee appointed for the purpose. There also emerged new thinking on linking protected areas by jungle corridors and the first corridor was declared in early 1970.

During this period, the Minister in charge of wildlife conservation was none other than the present President, who remains a great protagonist of the cause.

3. CONSERVATION FOR DEVELOPMENT: WATER AND ELEPHANTS

There was by that time an awareness of the tremendous seriousness of the situation among people of all walks of life. By 1969 the Government, too, had realized that the Department of Wildlife Conservation should be represented on various development bodies if haphazard alienation of land was to be controlled. However, these encouraging trends received a setback during the period of severe economic recession and food shortage that spanned the years 1970 to 1977. During those years the people were encouraged to clear and cultivate every inch of land by any means. Widespread *chena* greatly aggravated the problems of wildlife conservation by creating discontinuous forests in which animals were virtually trapped. The numerous "pocketed" elephant herds we have today are largely a legacy of those days of haphazard and uncontrolled land development.

Happily, we learned our lessons from those mistakes. In 1977, on my re-appointment to the Department after a lapse of seven years, my staff and I carried out several surveys in an attempt to redeem lost land. We appraised Government of three serious situations that could be arrested only if proper conservation measures were employed even at that late stage. These were:

- the removal of forest cover from hills and river banks had virtually eliminated the dry weather flow in rivers, used for agriculture and the generation of hydro-power;
- the destruction of the water catchment areas of the larger irrigation reservoirs had accelerated their siltation which in turn was jeopardizing agriculture in the respective river basins; and
- crop damage by marauding elephants from "pocketed" herds was crippling the settlers economically.

As expected, the Government responded positively and I was asked to make suitable recommendations for rectifying the situation. In the meantime, the Department was again put back on relevant decision-making Institutes. Special mention must be made of the Mahaweli Development Board, which at the time was in charge of the largest-ever and most ambitious river basin development scheme the country has ever known (the Mahaweli Authority has superseded the Board). In 1978, Cabinet issued an administrative directive that there should be no new clearing of land without reference to the Department. Even at district level, any new scheme is now subject to comments from the Department. We are now in a position to help integrate conservation concerns with modern river basin development.

We made three important recommendations to Government. They were:

- that all catchments of reservoirs be made National Reserves (either National Parks or Nature Reserves);
- that wherever possible these catchments be interconnected by Jungle corridors, preferably along river banks; and
- that all National Reserves have a one-mile wide Buffer Zone.

Based on these recommendations, which were strongly supported by non-governmental organizations and the general public and, of course, wholly accepted by the Cabinet, we first set about redeeming three important protected areas.

First, the 31,000 ha Uda Walawe National Park, which includes the Uda Walawe Reservoir, its surrounds and about 16 km of both banks of the Walawe Ganga (River), was taken in hand. This park, although mooted in 1969 and hastily declared in 1973, had some 800 squatter families engaged in slash and burn agriculture. The erosion from the slopes was taking massive loads of silt into the Reservoir, thereby threatening the irrigation of some 20,000 ha of land. These families were offered land under the same scheme and in two years the catchment was cleared of them and the park reha-

bilitated. Today, four years later, Uda Walawe is rich in elephants, spotted deer and bird life.

We next tackled the problems of the Somawathiya Sanctuary. The problem here lay in the annual clearing of the banks of the Mahaweli Ganga for cash crops, predominantly tobacco. The 22,000 ha reserve is an ecological masterpiece, watered by Sri Lanka's largest and longest river, the soils replenished by alluvium. The flood plain is studded with *villus*, shallow basins of water rich in aquatic life and which grow lush succulent grasses including two varieties of *Brachiaria*. Between the villus too, is grass excellent for grazing. Until the tobacco cultivators resorted to annual clearing, the river banks had good evergreen forest cover. As is to be expected, it was a paradise for elephants. Indeed it is believed that the 600-800 elephants which live in this flood plain are a subspecies or at least a distinct race, popularly known here as the marsh elephant.

Somawathiya well illustrates the rigours of population expansion, for over a period of about 15 years, the number of itinerant tobacco cultivators swelled from a few dozen to over a thousand. Not only that, they brought thousands of cattle for grazing and, more recently, began growing food crops for profit. Their activities ruined the environment and I was afraid that the "Marsh" elephant would disappear altogether from this sylvan plain. Not only was there serious competition for grazing but the elephants were also being prevented from coming to the river by the cultivators in defence of crops.

For four long years we waged battle and in the end succeeded in getting the cultivators out of the sanctuary area. Our current thinking, backed by the Technical Consultants to the Mahaweli Authority, is that the sanctuary should be up-graded to a National Park, for the area cries out for pasture management and other improvements to habitat, e.g. due to overgrazing by cattle, *Brachiaria* has been choked by weed species (cocklebur and abutilon) greatly reducing elephant activity on the western side.

The third example of the close link we have established between river basin development and a protected area is the Wasgomuwa Strict Natural Reserve (SNR) which by its IUCN Category I status should be a "holy of holies". Alas, in the early seventies it had been taken up for colonization and in fact when we went in there in 1977 a flourishing settlement greeted us. The 27,500 ha reserve was pockmarked with *chenas* and literally hundreds of squatters were living happily. Back in Colombo to protest about it, we received our next shock, when we were told that Wasgomuwa would form part of the downstream development under the Mahaweli scheme. Indeed there it was on the map, as "System E."

There was no time to lose. We prepared a memorandum showing that Wasgomuwa had been declared a SNR back in 1940 because it was a unique landscape with a range of hills (Sudukanda) down its centre, covered with cloud forest. The dry weather flow into the

Mahaweli in the east and the Amban Gange in the west was brought by the streams trickling from its peaks. In fact today we realise that not only is it just a beautiful landscape, but with our advanced knowledge, that it is a unique ecosystem.

A decision could be taken only by the highest in the land, I was told. So thither we went and, before long, Wasgomuwa received a Presidential reprieve. The irony of it was that the 2000-odd squatters were resettled under the very scheme which threatened to destroy it. Within one year the large elephant herds returned and now Wasgomuwa is back as a wildlife refuge.

There is a different lesson to be learned here. An isolated SNR, with all its severe restrictions on movement within it, is very vulnerable. It is easier for the intrepid squattter to carve it out, than for the Department to protect it. The general public are not allowed in and thus have no emotional attachment to it. It is doomed. I therefore recommended that Wasgomuwa be made into a National Park and that recommendation has been accepted. It will then have a far better chance of survival with support from the public, who will be captivated by its unique scenery.

4. THE MAHAWELI SCHEME: DEVELOPMENT WITHOUT DESTRUCTION

I have repeatedly referred to the Mahaweli Scheme. Let me make it the final chapter of this paper.

The Mahaweli Diversion Project, popularly known as the Mahaweli Scheme, entails the harnessing of our largest river by not simply one dam, but by an elaborate system of diversions through tunnels to feed a network of existing as well as new reservoirs. It will irrigate land not only in its own basins but in the basins of several other rivers which have insufficient water in the dry season. The scheme aims at providing water for two seasons in the year thereby aiming at self-sufficiency in food. It also aims at providing land for thousands of landless families.

To discuss the whole scheme here would be quite impossible and I shall only touch on what is known now as the Accelerated Mahaweli Programme (AMP) which concerns development in the lower river basin. It is termed "Accelerated" because in 1977 a decision was taken to make a 30-year scheme possible in 5.

There are an estimated 800 elephants in the AMP area, and these are representatives of but one of 7 endangered and 2 vulnerable animal species found there. In all, some 95 species of endemic animals and plants have been identified in the Mahaweli region. Construction of water works and other man-made modifications of the natural ecosystem in the AMP area is expected to reduce this prime wildlife habitat by about 27,000 ha. This will displace animals from their home ranges and will crowd others into what is remaining. Excessive crowding will lead to an overuse of habits, resulting in a decrease in the quantity and quality of wildlife pop-ulations and more displacement and concentration of remaining populations in limited areas. As a consequence, agricultural development and human settlements that are planned for the AMP will be increasingly vulnerable to animals (particularly wild elephants) living in overcrowded conditions. Crop losses and homestead destruction will be inevitable.

It is in this context that the conservation process and the establishment of protected areas comes into its own, and their additional role in mitigating the likely wildlife impacts of the AMP has been recognised also, for two reasons. First, unless something is done to compensate for the loss of high quality wildlife habitat as the AMP resettlement scheme gets underway, wildlife, especially elephants, in these areas will inevitably come into conflict with farmers as they compete for space. This will result in substantial crop damage as well as damage to dams, bunds, and irrigation channels. Second, there is great appreciation of the important contribution that the elephant and other wildlife make to national pride, a respect for tradition, the quality of life, and the promotion of tourism.

In consequence of all the above, the Government of Sri Lanka has placed a very high priority on the upgrading and establishment of protected areas in the prime wildlife habitats, in the catchments to reservoirs, and along the major river banks of the AMP area. The existing Somawathiya Sanctuary is to be expanded to an area of 52,000 ha and upgraded to National Park status. The Wasgamuwa Strict Natural Reserve (27,972 ha) is also to be made into a National park. Two other major new protected areas, the Maduru Oya National Park (40,000 ha) and the Floodplain National Park (15,000 ha) are to be created. These parks will be inter-linked by additional forest reserves and jungle corridors both to confer maximal ecological and genetic resilience on the system, as well as to safeguard the routes taken by elephants between their wet season feeding and dry season watering areas. Furthermore, each park will be bordered by a 1.6 km-thick buffer zone, which will both help reduce conflict between animals and agriculture, and be managed to bring direct benefits to people living in the surrounding areas. While annual crops or permanent dwellings would not be permitted, we envisage that the buffer zone might include areas of perennial tree crops, fuelwood or exotic timber plantations; and the harvest of indigenous timber for non-commercial use, grazing, collection of dead firewood, fruit, rattan, *beedi* leaves, honey, ayurvedic medicinal plants, and, perhaps where appropriate, the utilization of some species of wildlife like water buffalo for agriculture could all be allowed.

The AMP represents the first opportunity in Sri Lanka for the integrated and mutually supportive development of a system of protected areas with differing management categories such as National Parks (IUCN Category II), Forest Reserves (Category VI), Jungle Corridors (Category III or IV), and Buffer Zones (Category VIII), for the benefit of both wildlife and people.

The total area to be managed in this way (134,972 ha as national parks alone) far exceeds the total of new and improved agricultural land to be developed under the AMP (107,150 ha). This is one of the few, perhaps only, examples where the protected areas within a development scheme exceed the agricultural and settlement areas in extent.

This favourable situation has been brought about by a realization of the benefits that nature conservation, can bring to the people through the establishment of protected areas. Some of these, such as control of sedimentation rates, mitigation of crop damage, and buffer zone management, have been touched on already, but the list could be expanded to include flood control, bank stabilization, conserving fisheries, providing opportunities for tourism, providing local employment, conserving genetic resources, providing educational and recreation opportunities and so on.

5. CONCLUSION

Our proposal for a system of protected areas within and adjacent to the areas to be developed under the Accelerated Mahaweli Programme is a textbook example of the World Conservation Strategy in action, "conservation for development". In Sri Lanka today environmental factors are being given full consideration and attention for the supportive role they can play in the processes of social and economic development. Accordingly, the AMP will not be the first and last example. The ways and means of integrating conservation and development are currently under active consideration in relation to other schemes elsewhere in the country. In closing, it is probably fair to claim that the evolution of this awareness of the need for sound environmental management, both among the people and the decision-makers of Sri Lanka, is due in no small part to the traditional interest and value they have attached to wild life. And the fact that the elephant has long been a symbol of conservation in our country has been reaffirmed convincingly by the overwhelming public response to a fund-raising campaign centred on the elephant which was launched, under the title "Let Them Live", by HRH Prince Philip during his visit to Sri Lanka in March 1982, in his capacity as President of World Wildlife Fund.

It is a happy outcome, therefore, that while it is the elephant that potentially would suffer most from the proposed river basin development programmes, it is the elephant that will also perhaps benefit the most from the integration of environmental factors into the AMP and other schemes as described in this paper.

What to Do When You've Succeeded:
Project Tiger, Ten Years Later

H.S. Panwar
Project Tiger
Ministry of Agriculture
New Delhi, India

ABSTRACT. *This paper reviews the progress and future of India's Project Tiger. The action imperatives include strengthening the protected area network to make it functionally efficient and biogeographically representative; ensuring that the management of such areas is compatible with local communities; and providing a strong conservation orientation to community development in the forested regions of India. Project Tiger has stimulated the evolution of a coordinated development strategy for the forested regions of India, based on the realization that the people, the forests, and the wildlife either thrive together in a balanced environment, or stagnate together in a wretched one.*

1. INTRODUCTION

Although sparked off by an urge to save the unique and the gravely endangered striped feline, the Indian Project Tiger was essentially formulated on an ecosystem concept. The special Task Force of the Indian Board for Wildlife (IBWL) that prepared the project proposal in November 1972 gave the following as its basic objective: "To ensure maintenance of a viable population of tiger in India and to preserve, for all times, areas of biological importance as a national heritage for the benefit, education and enjoyment of the people".

This was re-emphasized in Prime Minister Shrimati Indira Gandhi's launching address for the project in April 1973: "But the tiger cannot be preserved in isolation. It is at the apex of a large and complex biotope. Its habitat threatened by human intrusion, commercial forestry and cattle grazing must first be made inviolate."

With every stride of the project, the validity of its ecosystem approach has been vindicated and this con-

currently has led the strategies to be strengthened along these lines.

The project has been in action now for a decade. It has been hailed for its successes not only in putting the endangered tiger on a course of assured recovery but also with equal, if not greater, appreciation for saving some of the unique specimens of the wild ecosystems of India. While justifiably happy with the achievements to date, those involved in the project are operating under no illusions. They are aware of, and are indeed preparing to meet, the complex and challenging task that lies ahead in order to consolidate the gains and to sustain the tempo of progress. This case study traces the background leading to the formation of the project, summarizes its progress and achievements, and goes on to highlight the strategies for the coming years.

2. THE PROBLEM

While fossil evidence suggests that it evolved in Siberia, the tiger has found its best home on the Indian subcontinent. This versatile supreme predator thrived all over the expansive wilderness of the sub-continent, adapting itself admirably to a wide variety of environmental situations, from the high altitude cold coniferous Himalayan forests to the steaming Sunderbans mangrove forests, from the flat swampy reed beds of the Himalayan terai to the rugged scorched hills of the Indian peninsula and from the scrub-thorn semi-deserts to the lush wet evergreen rainforest. An estimate placed the population of tigers in India at the turn of the century at 40,000. Even if this was an exaggeration, the picture was dismal when an all-India tiger census in 1972 revealed that only 1827 survived.

183

Intensive human demographic pressures gathering momentum toward the latter part of the 19th Century accounted for a progressive diversion of more and more wilderness areas to agriculture. Direct pressures against wildlife also increased from the early part of this century and particularly major species like the tiger came under heavy persecution at the hands of the colonial-feudal hunters. The totalitarian controls inherent in the admimistrative structure of the pre-independence era were responsible for the protection of still sizeable belts of forests. With the crumbling of these controls in the post-independence era, the scene changed rapidly; extensive privately owned forests, lying in between remote reserved forest blocks, soon became liquidated to meet the land hunger. Paucity of resources for inputs to enhance productivity from existing holdings, and the rapid increase in population, and the urge of the popular state governments to give relief to the people all combined to generate a permissive atmosphere that allowed the land use to drift afloat on expediency. Marginal lands unfit for sustained agriculture were brought under the plough without soil conservation safeguards. Village pastures likewise were reclaimed for cultivation, pushing the cattle inevitably into the hitherto sparingly-grazed reserved forests.

The forests, besides industrial removals of timber and firewood through operations under the forestry working plans, also had to bear the brunt of villagers' increasing domestic demands; this overuse and abuse undermined the productivity of the reserved forests. The expanding development activity took a heavy toll of areas under forests for irrigation and power projects, industrial use, roads and the like. In the guise of crop protection and tribal hunts, villagers decimated the prey base of the tiger. The adversity was heightened by the legal and illegal hunting by the urban hunters, pillaging the forests on nocturnal forays by jeep. With cattle penetrating deep into interior forests and the major carnivores faced with the paucity of wild prey, the incidence of cattle lifting by wild predators went up. This led to poisoning of tigers and leopards by the graziers, assisted and encouraged by the unscrupulous traders of skins, who multiplied to channel the boom to the big-money metropolitan markets. The legal deterrants and their enforcement levels both failed utterly to keep pace with this onslaught.

3. BACKGROUND

It was only in the late 1960s that the gravity of this devastation and its correlation with environmental ravage began to be felt, but by then much of the damage had been done. A number of national parks and sanctuaries were constituted in the sixties, but only a few enjoyed a reasonable measure of protection and management for reasons of low priority in resource allocation to nature conservation. Habitat destruction along with the hunting pressures had brought the status of

wildlife in India to its lowest ebb ever, as the sixties yielded to the seventies. The rural people felt a mounting scarcity of fodder for their cattle and timber and firewood for their domestic use. While on the one hand, the green revolution and advanced industrialization prepared the country to turn the corner, the drag of irrational land use on the other hand held out hazardous environmental portents. It was in this setting that serious pleas for urgent conservation action began to be made.

The precariously depleted status of tiger throughout its range of distribution in Asia came in sharp focus at the 10th General Assembly of IUCN, held in New Delhi in November 1969. The IBWL took it up strongly and the concern generated both among the conservationists and the Government caused a series of actions to be taken in quick succession. A countrywide ban on hunting of tiger was declared in July 1970. Although wildlife and forestry were state responsibilities under the Constitution, the Federal Parliament, with prior authorization from state legislatures, enacted the Wildlife (Protection) Act in September 1972, substantially enhancing legal protection levels for wildlife and its habitat in general and for the endangered species and special conservation areas in particular. After considerable training and trials, an all-India tiger census was conducted in May 1972 and this indicated the tiger population of the country to be a mere 1827. This left little doubt that unless positive field conservation action was taken urgently the chance for the tiger's survival was thin. In the meantime, in April 1972 the Government of India appointed a special Task Force under the auspices of the IBWL in order to advise it on a programme for sustained preservation of tiger in the wild. Mr. Guy Mountfort, a Trustee of the World Wildlife Fund-International (WWF), met the Prime Minister in April 1972 and offered WWF assistance for such a programme.

4. CONSTRAINTS

4.1 Adverse land use

The Task Force was convinced that this programme, which soon came to be designated as "Project Tiger," should take to an environmental approach. But almost all the prospective areas that could have been brought under the project were under commercial forestry operations besides being subject to the pressures of rural demand for stock grazing areas, and for firewood, small timber and other forest products. Even remote small valleys carried human settlements with peasants toiling on marginal lands without any soil conservation safeguards, and consequently obtaining very poor crop yields; because of remote locations in compact forest blocks, cattle and crops were ceaselessly threatened by wild animals. Lacking adequate field enforcement, poaching of wild animals and wood was widespread. The wildlife habitat itself was depleted from overgrazing, rampant fires, an impoverished water regime and soil erosion. Unregulated and excessive stock grazing not only contributed to the habitat degradation but also undermined fodder productivity and proliferated weed growth. The low productivity of the depleted pastures did not allow the health and productivity of cattle to improve, even as their population kept increasing in step with the growing human population. Obviously this form of unsound land use and the interior location of villages in the otherwise large and unbroken forest blocks was highly unsatisfactory to the people and nature conservation alike. Yet there was little doubt that any conservation action entailing restrictions on the current land-use practices and relocation of interior settlements would meet with resistance, not so much from the people—if suitable alternatives were provided—but from politicization of the issue at local levels.

4.2 Scarce financial resources

It was imperative that at least parts of the areas to be brought under the programme would have to be rendered free from forestry operations, sacrificing sizeable forest revenues. Besides this, money would have to be found for protection and development activity in order to rehabilitate the areas. With the scarce resources of a developing economy charged with meeting the basic needs of a huge and burgeoning population, this two-way financial squeeze could certainly not be conducive to very large allocations becoming available for the project. Further, from practical considerations it was not possible for the project to cover all the tiger bearing areas of the country. The Task Force therefore concluded that the project would initially have to address itself to a few selected prime areas only.

4.3 Other constraints

Except for a few small limitations preventing ecologically ideal conservation units, enough areas potentially suitable for development of tiger habitat were available. Legal protection levels had already been substantially reinforced with the promulgation of the Wildlife (Protection) Act (1972), although much would depend upon the extent of staff and infrastructure support permitted by the funds that became available. Personnel could also be found within the State Forest Departments who could make a beginning by shouldering the primary responsiblity for protection and habitat development. Further, with their technical forestry background, such people could easily acquire the necessary proficiency in wildlife management, if helped by short orientation and training courses.

5. ACTION

5.1 Choice of areas

The Task Force developed a strategy based on the formation of tiger reserves with a sizeable core area, free from all human use, surrounded by a buffer zone where wildlife-oriented forestry operations and conservation-oriented land use is permitted. Proposals were invited from the states for tiger reserves and the Task Force finally selected areas to represent as many biogeographic types as possible in the range of distribution of tiger habitat in the country, and to be amenable to concerted conservation action.

5.2 Management plans

This was soon followed up by preparation of management plans for each reserve, to describe the attributes and the limiting factors of the habitat and prescribe ameliorative measures.

The guiding principles on which the management plans were prepared were:

- To seek to eliminate all forms of human exploitation and disturbance from the core areas and rationalize these in the buffer zones;
- To limit habitat management to the repair of damage done by man and to seek to restore the ecosystem to as close to its natural functioning as possible;
- To build up the habitat by mitigating limiting factors arising out of abuse and over-use and thus to build up the wildlife populations to the intrinsic carrying capacity of the habitat, scrupulously avoiding management assistance capable of pushing the growth of populations beyond this stage; and
- To carry out research on the habitat and wild animals and carefully monitor the ongoing changes in flora and fauna.

The management plans identified the core and buffer areas along with tourism zones. They carried various management maps and a large pool of information on climate, terrain, geology, soils, vegetation and fauna. The legal status of forests and the burden of rights and concessions were also documented, along with information on location of villages and their human and cattle populations.

A number of management measures were aimed at mitigating the limiting factors. Thus under anti-poaching a network of outstation patrol camps, entry check posts and support in the form of vehicles, boats, elephants, even camels, wireless sets and firearms were envisaged. "Reamelioratory management" included measures like stopping grazing in core areas and regulating grazing in buffer zones, relocating villages from core areas, fire protection, soil and water conservation works in denuded areas, and eradication of weeds in over-grazed parts. Measures under "compensatory development" included creation of waterholes to replace those within the same eco-complex but denied to wild animals because of human habitation, or in compensation of those lost on account of lowering of water tables due to forest destruction. The intent was to rejuvenate the habitat to its natural intrinsic carrying capacity; manipulatory management aimed at any general or specific hike in the carrying capacity was totally excluded.

5.3 Launching of Project Tiger

Project Tiger was launched in the 1973. The Central Government offered additional budgets for staff, equipment and works in the nine tiger reserves that were created, while the states were required to continue staff and financial inputs at the same level as obtained at the inception of the project. The project was essentially to supplement the then-current levels of nature conservation activity in the area concerned. The states were also called upon to give up forestry operations, stock grazing and other forms of human use, including human habitation, in the core areas. The Prime Minister's observation, in her launching address for the project, hastened the pace of these actions:

> "Forestry practices, designed to squeeze the last rupees out of our jungles, must be radically reoriented at least within our national parks and sanctuaries, and pre-eminently in the tiger reserves. The narrow outlook of the accountant must give way to a wider vision of the recreational, educational and ecological value of totally undisturbed areas of wilderness. Is it beyond our political will and administrative ingenuity to set aside about one or two percent of our forests in their pristine glory for this purpose?"

Eight tiger reserves came into existence within the fiscal year ending 31 March 1974; the ninth followed early the following year. An executive cell headed by Director Project Tiger also became functional in the Union Ministry of Agriculture to coordinate and administer the implementation of the Project. The largest-ever nature conservation effort in Asia thus got off the mark. Soon the field operations for protection and habitat development started and, fueled by progressive successes, quickly gathered momentum. There were exchanges of fire with poachers, raids and legal proceedings; the poachers' gangs were effectively busted. In the course of these operations a few of the staff laid down their lives while many suffered assaults. On the other hand, expanding the long-term advantages of conservation-oriented land use predominated the approach toward communities living in or near the reserves. With the offer of viable alternatives this approach started paying off and even the seemingly impossible task of village relocation got off to a start. Similarly, halting of stock grazing in the core areas was effected in quick phases and forestry operations in the core areas were immediately abandoned, quickly bringing tranquility to the core areas. Field works for soil and water conservation and habitat restoration commenced simultaneously. This effort got a boost with vehicles, boats, wireless sets and other equipment received through World Wildlife Fund assistance.

5.4 Strengthening of the project

In the years that followed, some tiger reserves were strengthened by increasing their core and buffer areas. Two more reserves were added in 1978-79, taking the tally to 11 and the total area to 15,800 sq km of which the extent of core areas was 5,142 sq km (Annex I). The project itself, initially contemplated for only 5 years, was decided to be continued with increased allocations. The Prime Minister herself agreed to head the Steering Committee of the project. The enhanced programme for the early 1980s was approved. This included further enlargement of some reserves, intensification of protection and habitat development activity in the buffer zones, strengthening of protection and research staff, widening of the scope of wildlife research and the taking up of some more new reserves. In its latest meeting on 1 July 1982, the Steering Committee decided to add four new reserves with the objective of including some unrepresented tiger habitat types and improving the geographic distribution of conservation areas in the country (Annex I).

5.5 Financial aspect

From inception in 1973 up to 1979-80 a total of US$5.6 million was spent on the project. The States in addition spent US$4.5 million, taking the total to US$10.01 million. In the 5-year period from 1980-81 to 1984-85 the sanctioned outlay for the project stood at US$11.11 million. The States during this period would provide an additional US$5.05 million, raising the total outlay to US$15.16 million. As for the WWF contribution, a total amount of US$763,000 had been utilized from the inception of the project up to October 1981, against the pledged assistance of US$1 million. This was used for buying equipment, organizing study tours and visits of experts for special courses and advice on monitoring research.

5.6 Research and training

Once implementation began it became necessay to obtain more information and to monitor the changes and trends in vegetation and animal populations in order to keep an eye on the habitat conditions and to evaluate the efficacy of management practices. Three IUCN experts were invited to advise on floral and faunal monitoring programmes. A research committee of Project Tiger personnel and the Director of Wildlife Research and Training was formed to devise a comprehensive package of wildlife research in tiger reserves. In addition to general monitoring, several studies on individual problems and animals were undertaken. Attempts were made to evolve census techniques for animals and these ranged from total enumeration to sample counts. A dependable and practical technique for tiger censuses based on pug marks was evolved. More elaborate studies on tiger sociology, land tenure and aberrant behaviour (including man-eating) were undertaken. Detailed study of habitat based on aerial photo-interpretation and ground checks was initiated. A number of wildlife research fellowships were awarded by the Government, enabling university scholars to take up studies on animals and habitats; some of them have already presented their theses.

An International Symposium on the Tiger was organized in Delhi in February 1979. A number of scientists from IUCN, Smithsonian Institution, and other Asian countries, besides Indian participants, attended the 3-day Symposium. A large number of papers on habitat, prey species and the tiger were presented at the Symposium, which culminated in the adoption of resolutions emphasizing tiger conservation as a vital aspect of total environmental preservation in the countries harbouring it. With WWF assistance, some Project Tiger personnel went on a study tour to East African national parks and research centres. Two courses on the techniques of immobilization and radio-telemetry of animals were organized. The Directorate of Wildlife Research and Training has trained a large number of personnel, many of whom have joined tiger reserves. Recently a 3-week workshop on techniques in wildlife research and management was conducted in Kanha Tiger Reserve in collaboration with the US Fish and Wildlife Service; five of the nearly 60 participants were from other Asian countries. The US and Indian instructors at the workshop are now interacting to produce a manual of techniques suitable for Indian conditions.

5.7 Interaction with the communities

All the areas formed into tiger reserves carried human habitation and varying degrees of human use. Environmental reamelioration of these areas on a core-buffer pattern inevitably required such uses to be curtailed and disciplined. This was a delicate humanitarian problem, particularly because most of the people involved were toiling on marginal lands, supplementing their livelihood with stock grazing, collection of edible and commercial forest products, employment in forestry operations, etc. There was no question that for all the uses,

alternatives would have to be provided by readjustments in the areas outside the reserves. However, the already-advanced abuse and overuse had undermined the productivity of the areas around the reserves. A beginning was made in explaining to the local communities the advantages of conservation-oriented practices that could restore and sustain the productivity of the multiple use areas. While it was possible to convince the people of the advantages of practices like contour bunding of fields, improvement in cattle breeds, gradual reduction in cattle population and rotational grazing, the field translation of these ideas is still in a formative stage. This requires involvement of the various community development agencies and reorienting their programmes so as to be in harmony with basic conservation dictates essential for marginal lands and hilly forested tracts.

6. RESULTS

In the tiger reserves, the intensive protection and habitat development effort registered striking successes. Core areas extending over 5,142 sq km were rendered free from forestry operations, which at current prices would mean an annual revenue loss of some US$11 million. Forty villages, with a total population of nearly 6,000 people, were relocated from the core areas with full rehabilitation facilities and adequate agricultural land. Grazing control measures resulted in a reduction in stock grazing pressure of over 100,000 head, rendering the core areas free from grazing. Strict anti-poaching in the reserves and nearby areas brought the poaching incidence to levels next to negligible. Restorative management and compensatory development resulted in rapid rejuvenation of habitat conditions in the reserves. The recovery of ground and field level vegetation was quick and phenomenal and if one entered a reserve from other adjacent forests, the difference would be too obvious to be missed. Water regimes improved, with streams retaining their flow longer and some once-seasonal watercourses becoming perennial. Strikingly low monsoon silt load in the streams of the reserves as compared to that in streams of adjacent areas, signified the success of soil conservation measures. Fire protection not only led to increased fodder availability during the lean period in summer but also to formation of humus on the forest floor, resulting in increased organic activity, efficacious nutrient cycling and revitalization of the water regime.

With fodder, water, tranquility and protection extending over a much bigger area, there was a steady rise in the animal populations and a wide ranging dispersal of animals, assuring more efficacious use of habitat. The population of tigers went up from 268 in 1972 in nine reserves to 757 in 1981 in eleven reserves. The population of tigers in the country rose from 1,827 in 1972 to 3,015 in 1979, based on the two all-India censuses conducted in these years. Besides the tiger, a number of other endangered species like swamp deer, elephant, rhino and wild buffalo benefitted substantially in the reserves. Not the least accomplishment has been the significant improvement in the preservation of overall floral and faunal diversity in the reserves, particularly the core areas enjoying total environmental protection.

7. CONCLUSIONS

The success in the implementation of Project Tiger in its first decade has abundantly vindicated its ecosystem approach. Further, the experience gained in exploratory beginnings made to involve communities leaves no doubt that the ecosystem approach should now logically expand to encompass the communities that live around the tiger reserves, in order to ensure and sustain wide-based conservation advantages. Indeed, this has led to the identification of action imperatives that should constitute the main thrust of the conservation effort in the coming years, particularly for an intensive programme like Project Tiger. These are:

- To strengthen the network of conservation units so as to make it functionally efficient and biogeographically representative;
- To ensure that the constitution and management of such units is compatible with the communities; and
- To provide a strong conservation orientation to community development/welfare programmes in the forested regions.

7.1 Network of conservation units

Protection, however effective, and management, however scientific, of small units cannot be of much long-term conservation advantage. Such successes are bound to be short-lived and limited for three reasons: first, if the land surrounding such effort-sustained "oases" continue to deteriorate in productivity and available resources for the communities, the oases are bound to succumb one day to the "have not" syndrome; second, for ecological, particularly genetic, considerations, such isolated islands may not after all discharge the "gene bank" function so idealistically expected of them; and third, the overall environmental function of such infinitesimal units is also likely to be of little national, much less global, significance. It cannot therefore be disputed that the future success of any field conservation effort is going to be shaped in the multiple-use areas that surround the main conservation units. Logically, therefore, the effort should be to evolve a network of "core conservation units" occupying the least molested pockets in the still surviving extensive forest tracts, even if the latter are currently fragmented by human habitation and denuded interruptions. Representation of as many biogeographic types as possible and improvement in the

geographic distribution should further guide the selection.

7.2 Constitution and management of conservation units

In order that the conservation units have a secure position and also serve the communities, it is necessary that the core units are surrounded by buffer belts, in turn surrounded by the much vaster multiple-use areas. Needless to say, it may be difficult to find areas conforming to such idyllic concepts of concentric circles, but a pragmatic configuration capable of discharging the varied functions is all that is required. The inevitable curtailment of community uses in the core areas has to be compensated by alternatives; however, the real breakthrough from enhanced productivity can only come when a conservation-oriented development programme reameliorates the multiple-use areas.

7.3 Conservation-oriented community development

There are two strong reasons why the multiple-use areas in the forested regions need priority conservation action: first, they are deteriorating further from their already-depleted and regressive condition, under the pressure of demands of the communities; and second, there is no other way of providing relief to the villagers who ironically are reeling under the aftermath of an ecological boomerang so unwittingly set off by themselves through a rapid and now advanced environmental ravage. It must be remembered that for the people living in the forested regions, there just do not exist any other employment alternatives; agriculture and cattle raising on marginal lands will continue to be their mainstay for livelihood.

The community development activity has so far not produced the desired improvement in the economic conditions of the people living in such tracts and the environmental ravage is continuing largely unabated. This is mainly because the current land use practices and the development programmes are not in tune with basic conservation dictates. The very nature of terrain and soil preclude any highly intensive agricultural or animal husbandry practices, which, assisted by irrigation, have brought about the magic of 'green' and 'white' revolutions in the plains. The enormity of the problem calls for drastic changes in sectoral allocations and priorities. Since the basic cause of the malady is impoverished productivity of the fundamental resource, the land (whether under agriculture, pasture or forests), relief cannot be brought about without addressing the current faulty land use practices. It need hardly be emphasized that the productivity of agricultural lands and cattle in this tract cannot go up without bringing back the forest cover, because both water regime and cattle fodder depend upon it.

The programme of Project Tiger in the coming years envisages, besides taking up some new tiger reserves, interacting with other community development agencies in the buffer zones of tiger reserves and around them, with a view to reorienting in accordance with conservation imperatives their programmes involving or influencing land use.

Project Tiger thus hopes to catalyze the evolution of a coordinated development strategy for the forested regions based on the realization that the people in these regions, the forests and the wildlife either thrive together in a balanced environment or will all suffer together in a wretched one. It is hoped that just as the successes in ecosystem conservation in tiger reserves, particularly in the core areas, have provided a rationale for the management of conservation units, the results of these actions may lead to coordinated programmes for the management of nature conservation areas on the one hand and the development of communities in the forested regions on the other. On this will depend the sustainable success of Project Tiger.

ANNEX I: TIGER RESERVES UNDER PROJECT TIGER

Existing Tiger Reserves	Total area	Core area
	Sq km	
1. Melghat (Maharashtra). The deciduous forests dominated by teak and bamboo	1571	311
2. Palamau (Bihar). The eastern peninsular forest with an interesting association of sal and bamboo	930	200
3. Simlipal (Orissa). Moist miscellaneous forests of the East (Champ and Sal)	2750	300
4. Kanha (Madhya Pradesh). The Central highlands of peninsular India (Sal and miscellaneous forests)	1945	940
5. Bandipur (Karnataka). The miscellaneous forests of the Western Ghats	690	335
6. Corbett Park (Uttar Pradesh). The Central foothills of the Himalayas with sal as the dominant species	520	320
7. Manas (Assam). Eastern foothills of heavy rainfall with *terai* riverain, reeds and swamps, semi-evergreen and ever-green forests	2840	391
8. Ranthambhor (Rajasthan). The dry deciduous open forests of the Aravalis and Vindhyas in the West	392	167
9. Sunderbans (West Bengal). Tropical estuarine mangrove forests and other littoral vegetation	2585	1330
10. Periyar (Kerala). Moist deciduous, tropical wet-evergreen and semi-evergreen forests	777	350
11. Sariska (Rajasthan). Dry deciduous forest in the heart of Aravalis range, with sandy valleys carrying scrubthorn and grasslands.	800	498
Total:	15,800	5,142

Tiger Reserves to be Created		
12. Nagarjuna Sagar (Andhra Pradesh). Rugged hills in the middle reaches of Krishna with dry mixed deciduous forest	3000	1200
13. Namdapha (Arunachal Pradesh). Low level (200 m above MSL) riverain to alpine (6000 m above MSL) through moist deciduous and tropical wet evergreen forests	1808	695
14. Indravati (Madhya Pradesh). Tropical mixed moist deciduous forest with rich grasslands along Indravati river	2084	1258
15. Buxa (West Bengal). Riverain, *terai*-bhabhar, reed-swamps and semi-evergreen forest of the eastern foothills.	745	313
Grand total:	23,437	8,608

Human Dimensions in Wildlife Management: The Indian Experience

V.B. Saharia
Director
Wildlife Institute of India
Dehra Dun, India

ABSTRACT. *This paper outlines a number of basic issues in wildlife conservation and protected area management programmes. Using three different cases in India, (Gir, Palamau and Dudhwa), the paper stresses the importance of linking local people with the conservation programme through identifying wildlife as part of a resource system in the socio-economic sense. It is also important to have an institutional framework where analysis of environmental impacts of development projects become mandatory processes in project planning.*

1. INTRODUCTION

1.1. Human dimensions: a resource paradigm

A conceptual framework for relating the cultural, socio-economic and political aspects of wildlife resources into management and development programmes is provided by Firey's (1980) resource paradigm; ideas of development, self-sufficiency and cultural dimensions provide linkages to the resource system at the local, regional and national levels.

Firey considers natural resources, including biological resources, as types of landed capital which are different from other types of capital primarily in the degree to which non-human factors have affected their evolution and development. In this view, biological resources are not just tangible entities like trees and timber or tigers and elephants. Such resources are as much social concepts as biological entities, for resources are the product of social processes that define them initally as potentially useful things and then provide the means by which to convert them for social purposes. A resource system is thus looked upon as a hierarchy of interactions, comprising a set of resource processes, structured toward achieving a particular objective. Tourism in a national park is an example of what Firey calls a "resource system". "Resource processes" include information gathered by biologists and others relating to the environment and the survival needs of its plants and animals; the processes involved in advertising the nature of the area and marketing its image; the activities of individuals and organizations to protect the integrity of the park against competing interests and claims; building of roads, visitors' camps and hotels; and interpretation services.

On the other hand, a set of resource processes consisting of gathering of fuelwood; collection of fruits, tubers and roots as food; hunting of wild animals; and grazing of livestock, constitute a resource system of a tribal village situated in or in close proximity of such a national park.

Different social groups may have a perception of the resource system within their own frame of reference which is not necessarily connected to the assumptions of others. Firey suggests four broad frames of reference to describe the resource phenomena:

- *The ecological approach* relates to the entities and interactions of the physical habitat and its living organisms;
- *The economic approach* relates to the various resource processes connected with the utilization of the resource system and also the development processes through which the existing resource system is sought to be incorporated into larger socio-economic units at the state or national level through the development planning process.
- *The cultural approach* relates to society's social or-

ganizations and their value judgements derived from their social, traditional and cultural constraints; and

• *The normative approach* relates to the society's institutions and its rules and regulations.

1.2. Outline of the case study

The present case study derives from the theoretical model outlined above. It is divided into three sections: the first section outlines resource processes characterising the wildlife resource system in India within its ecological, socio-economic, political and normative frames of reference; the second section presents three cases which highlight the various human dimensions of wildlife management in India; and the third section analyzes the human dimensions of the wildlife conservation problem in the background of the Indian experience.

The case study has been conducted by the author as a part of the study-tours conducted by him with the trainees of the Diploma Course in Wildlife Management (a post-graduate programme conducted by the Directorate of Wildlife Environmental Research & Education, Forest Research Institute & Colleges, Dehra Dun, for in-service professional foresters in India). The Dudhwa and Palamau cases formed part of a special study, to prepare a model for relating resource processes with wildlife habitats in managed forests, for Orientation Courses for Divisional Forest Officers in India.

2. WILDLIFE AS A RESOURCE SYSTEM AND AREAS OF CONFLICT

Though the preservation of species of wild fauna and flora is a well-defined objective, the concept of wildlife as a resource-system in the socio-economic sense is rather amorphous. Trophy hunting has been historically considered a leisurely pastime of the princes in old princely States who maintained their own shooting preserves in pre-independence India, and a few privileged elites under the British Colonial rule. Wildlife-oriented tourism has also focussed more attention to the rich and affluent foreign tourist. Game management for organized hunting, as practised in Europe or America, has not been practised in India, and the common man by and large does not associate wildlife as a resource system of any consequence in an economic sense. On the other hand, in a primarily agricultural society the nuisance value of wildlife, for crop-depredations, damage to poultry and cattle-lifting is more pronounced in people's minds. Trade in wildlife and wildlife products is confined only to a few items, mainly consisting of skins and furs and handicrafts based on imported African ivory. Among plants the major trade is in orchids of nursery origin. Some clandestine trade in rhino horn and musk takes place, though strict legal measures are adopted to control it. The export value of wildlife and wildlife products was US\$8,046,480 in 1978, \$4,592,640 in 1980 and \$4,276,480 up to December 1981 (Prasad, 1982). The declining trend is indicative of the government's efforts to reduce wildlife trade at all levels. Hunting of most of the species in major parts of the country is prohibited and stringent laws have been framed to control domestic as well as international trade.

2.1. Wildlife habitats and resource processes

Preservation of wildlife habitats is a major area of conflict with different resource processes. Most rural societies which live in or on the fringes of forest areas live on subsistence levels; tribal peoples constitute a major section of such societies. Their resource processes are intimately linked with forest resource systems which form the main wildlife habitat in India. These resource processes can be identified as follows:

• Keeping large stocks of unproductive cattle. These cattle are not looked upon as milch cattle, but as a type of wealth in times of need and providing dung for fuel and some organic manure for their fields. They exert heavy grazing pressure on the forest vegetation (particulary in drier parts), converting these layers into bare ground or producing growth of weeds unpalatable to both cattle and wildlife as well as retarding regeneration of the tree species;
• Practising subsistence cultivaton on marginal lands or shifting cultivaion in certain parts;
• In times of scarcity or famine, subsistence on tubers, flowers and fruits of some forest plants;
• Fuelwood removals and removal of minor forest produce for personal use as well as for sale in small quantities for subsistence living;
• Working as unskilled labour in forestry operations;
• Removing small timber, bamboos and thatch grass for construction of houses; and
• Occasional tribal hunts as parts of rituals or ceremonies.

Most of the development activities, like vast irrigation and hydro-electric projects, resettlement programmes, mining, and road building, tend to overlook wildlife values altogether or consider them trivial and dispensable compared with benefits of these projects which entail their destruction or degradation.

Forestry practices have also become more commercialised in view of rising demands of industrial wood, pulpwood and construction timber. Large scale plantation programmes of fast-growing exotics have been undertaken in grassland savannas, scrub and deciduous mixed forests as they were low timber- producing areas though rich in wildlife.

In this setting, conservation of wildlife habitats has come to be looked upon as a negation of all human activities. More areas are being taken out of regular forest working and constituted as national parks and sanctuaries for protection of wildlife. There were only six national parks in India in 1970; by 1980 there were 19 and the area had increased from 1270 sq km in 1970 to 7186.28 sq km. Similarly, the number of sanctuaries increased from 128 in 1970 to 204 in 1980 and the corresponding area increase was from 25,611 sq km to 80,446 sq km. In terms of percentages the area under national parks and sanctuaries rose from 3.38 of the total forest area in 1970 to 11.69 in 1980.

Since most of these protected areas have been constituted from managed forests, with their own sets of resource processes, wildlife programmes lead to a number of conflicts which are related to the social economic and political frames in which these measures are adopted. The cases which follow in the subsequent sections will highlight the various issues involved.

3. THE GIR CASE

The Gir forest in the Saurashtra peninsula of Gujarat is a 1,500 sq km tract of semi-arid woodland supporting a dry, open-canopy deciduous forest with stunted teak as the principal species; less than a century ago, the forests of Gir covered 3 times the area they have today. The most recent figures available indicate that more than 63% of the land adjacent to the sanctuary is now under cultivation. Within this tract live nearly 200 lions which constitute the only free living population of the Asiatic lion *Panthera leo persica* in the world.

In addition to the lion, the Gir ecosystem is dotted by small pastoral settlements of cattle graziers, called the Maldharis. The settlements in which the Maldharis live are called "*nesses*." In 1972, there were 129 Maldhari *nesses* in the Gir having 845 families and a population of 4,802. The cattle population, mostly buffaloes, was estimated at 16,852. Until about 20 years ago, the Maldhari and his buffalo formed a part of the Gir ecosystem and were fully integrated with the ecology of the lion.

With the disappearance of the forest all around the Gir and most of the lands adjacent to the Gir sanctuary coming under cultivation, a heavy influx of nearly 48,000 non-resident cattle came into the Gir during the monsoon every year. During drought years, all too common in Saurashtra, cattle from all over Saurashtra and Kutch came to graze in Gir and the whole forest area became a vast cattle camp. The situation resulted in extreme over-grazing leading to the invasion of weeds and loss of all natural regeneration, heavy soil erosion, and degradation of forests. All types of wildlife inhabiting the region were naturally affected by this abuse of the land, leading to the heavy reduction of the wild ungulate prey base of the lion. Studies by the Gir Ecological Research Project revealed that 80% of the diet of the Gir lion was buffalo or cattle.

Milk yield of stock fell down. The loss of cattle by predation, falling milk yields, and degradation of the ecosystem effected the Maldhari economy very badly. The conflict resulted in frequent cases of poisoning of lions on cattle kills.

3.1. The Gir Lion Sanctuary Project

In 1972, Government of Gujarat started the Gir Lion Sanctuary Project to save the Gir ecosystem. The objectives were: the protecting the lion; and improving the socio-economic conditions of the Gir Maldhari.

An area of 1412.12 sq km was declared a Sanctuary; a core area of 258.71 sq km was declared a National Park in 1974. The project enviaged the following:

- Stopping grazing by all non-resident cattle. To achieve this, a 1-m high rubble wall extending over a length of roughly 400 km has been erected all along the periphery, with live hedges on either side. Barricades have been erected on water courses.
- A programme of resettlement of the Maldharis outside the sanctuary on its periphery was designed, which provided for 3.2 ha of cultivable land thoroughly ploughed at government cost provided free to each family; a plot of 610 sq m given as a house site free of charge; a subsidy equivalent to US$271 with a loan equivalent to another US$271 given to each family for house construction; free transport of household effects and dismantled material from old sites to the resettlement site was provided; since the Maldhari was not traditionally a cultivator, small agricultural implements were also provided for initiating the Maldhari into agriculture; and community facilities created included drinking water supply, primary school, approach road and community centres.

In addition, health care and medical services were provided and the Maldhari were linked to other community development programmes, particularly for dairy development and veterinary aid. The total cost of resettlement worked out to US$623.80 per family, exclusive of the US$271 given as loan. By March 1980, 517 out of a total of 845 Maldhari families had been resettled in 14 resettlement sites; the remaining families are still being resettled.

3.2. Results of the Gir Project

The results of these actions on the Gir ecosystem have been spectacular. The prey base, the wild ungulate biomass, more than doubled betweem 1970 and 1977, with the population of wild pig increasing from 110 to 2400, spotted deer from 4500 to 8500, and four-horned antelope from 250 to 1000.

The lion population increased from 180 in 1974 to

205 in 1979. The resettlement of the Maldharis and their socio-economic development as a part of the conservation project is not only an attempt to improve the resource processes of a subsistence society but also to expose them to the modern processes of development.

4. THE PALAMAU CASE

Situated in the State of Bihar, Palamau is one of the 11 Tiger Reserves constituted in the country under Project Tiger. Palamau has long been one of the best tiger areas in Bhihar. The reserve has an area of 928 sq km. There are 35 revenue and 9 forest villages in the reserve inhabited by about 8,400 people; the villagers are mostly tribal.

4.1. The Resource Practices

The various resource practices include: practising marginal rainfed agriculture. The area being drought prone, crop failures are common and the villagers have to depend on fruits, flowers, roots and tubers collected from the forest to supplement their dietary requirements. Mahua *Madhuca latifolia* flowers and fruits constitute an important item of diet which all the villagers collect and store to meet their year-round requirements. Crop depredation by wild animals is a common feature.

Mehtos are professional graziers who keep large stocks of buffaloes, cows and oxen and graze their cattle in the forest. The cattle are of very poor breed and produce hardly any milk. They are primarily looked upon as a sort of wealth for special needs like marriages or for periods of scarcity when they can be sold to get some ready cash. The total resident cattle in the reserve is estimated to be about 24,000. In addition, quite a few cattle camps were established in these forests and all the forests were open to grazing throughout the year.

Hunting is not practised by the tribals but they certainly try to grab an opportunity to snare the animals especially wild boar and spotted deer. They even try to steal away the carcass of sambar, barking deer or wild boar if freshly killed by tigers, leopards and wild dogs.

The villagers have claim over forest produce from the "right holders coupes" for construction of their houses, agricultural implements and fuelwood. They also depend partly on the work provided through various forestry operations in the area (this has been stopped since the creation of the tiger reserve).

4.2. Habitat conditions

The forests of Palamau are tropical dry deciduous with sal; some portions in the south constitute moist deciduous sal forests. Bamboos form an important understorey. Prior to the establishment of the project, fires used to sweep through the whole area annually, making the forest floor bare. Grazing intensity was heavy in areas, particularly close to habitation. Sahaya (1979) has estimated that the total ungulate biomass in the Palamau Tiger Reserve is 7712 kg per sq km, of which 1894 kg is the wild ungulate biomass and 5818 kg is comprised of cattle; cattle thus constituted 3 times the biomass of the wild ungulate population in the reserve. There was evidently heavy competition for grazing especially in the scarce period of summer. Commercial exploitation of bamboos was combined with heavy browsing pressure by elephants and gaur; fires and heavy grazing added to the depletion of the rich bamboo forests of the area. Palatable grasses and shrubby vegetation was replaced by weeds like *Cassia tora* and *Xanthium* and regeneration of tree species was poor. Most of the water holes dried up during summer and there was competition for water between man, cattle and the wild ungulates.

4.3. The action

The various management actions undertaken in the park include: 20l sq km area of the park has been declared as a core area where all grazing and human activity has been stopped; cattle coming from outside the park and cattle camps have been stopped; strict fire protection measures have been adopted; and all forestry work in the reserve has been suspended.

However, the most interesting aspect of the management of the reserve is the attempt at socio-economic integration of the villagers inside the park instead of removing the villagers from the park and resettling them outside. I visited many villages in the Palamau Tiger Reserve with the Park Director to study the approach that he has adopted and had talks with a number of villagers to assess the impact of these practices. R.P. Singh's approach can be summarized as follows:

4.3.1. Water development. Singh has located aquifers in various stream beds and tapped them progressively throughout the summer to provide water holes; 400 such water holes have been developed all over the reserve. An interesting feature is that separate water holes have been developed for the village cattle so that the village cattle do not have to go into the forest and compete for water with the wild ungulates.

4.3.2. Stall feeding. Though grazing has been stopped in core areas, grazing in the rest of the area is still allowed. The villagers are, however, being gradually introduced to the concept of stall feeding and rotational grazing. With strict fire protection, water improvement works and closure to grazing, some of the areas now have high growth of grass even during summer. These grasses become too coarse for the wild ungulates, and are a fire hazard. The villagers are engaged in cutting these grasses as a fire protection measure for which they get paid. The cut grass is then allowed to be taken away free by the villagers for stall feeding the cattle (fresh sprouts coming after grass-cutting are being used again by ungulates). Singh is persuading the villagers to adopt methods of hay-making and silage together with a programme of improving the breed of the cattle and developing milk yields, with veterinary help.

All the cattle of the villagers are also being vaccinated against foot and mouth disease as part of a programme of veterinary care being provided to the villagers. This has the twin benefit of controlling spread of disease among wild ungulates as well as protecting the cattle themselves. After some initial resistance, the villagers are now appreciating this programme and coming forward for vaccination in greater numbers.

I met some of the villagers. They are getting used to the idea of taking the cut grass for stall feeding and appreciating the benefits of closures which provide more grass to their cattle. The suggestion that stall feeding will also increase the availability of cattle dung for manuring their fields also appeared appealing to the villagers.

The villagers' conflict with the park appears to be based on the damage to their crops by wild pigs, elephants and deer, in that order. They feel aggrieved that they cannot protect their crops and kill any of the animals. The project management is allowing them facilities to engage their own unemployed village people for keeping a watch on the fields against the wild animals at the cost of the project. The project is also supplying fuel to make torches to scare away elephants and other wild animals. Battery cells are also provided for torches for people to move in the dark. Fire-crackers are also provided. Though these steps have reduced damage, the villagers are still not totally free from crop depredation. They particularly want to be allowed to capture or kill wild pigs partly as a measure of protection and partly as compensation for crop depredations to provide them with protein food.

4.4. Results of the Palamau project

Socio-economic development in Palamau is linked with the conservation programme *in situ*; the villagers are gradually made aware that their development, in a sense, is linked to the conservation of wildlife and is treated as a part of the total improvement of the habitat in which they live.

Villagers in the Project area now appear to have a better appreciation of the conservation programme. The habitat has shown significant improvement; bamboo forests have revived; the water regime has improved; villagers no longer complain of water scarcity; and development of water holes, well dispersed in the park, have helped in the dispersal of wildlife.

The villagers were asked if they would like to be rehabilitated outside the forests with more modern amenities. The majority response was a clear "No," because of their prime dependence on forest resource systems. Forests provided a measure of security during periods of drought when crops failed; the sustenance

came from roots, tubers and fruits from the forests. Fuel and fodder was also free in the forest. Cattle manure was available to fertilise their fields. Outside the forest and its resource system, the tribals felt insecure and helpless.

5. THE DUDHWA CASE

Situated on the Indo-Nepal border in Kheri District of Uttar Pradesh, Dudhwa is one of the last remnants of an unique habitat, called the *tarai*. Lying just below the Himalayan foothills, *tarai* is a narrow belt of marshy flood plains which sprawl across the states of Uttar Pradesh, Bengal and Assam in India and the adjoining countries of Nepal and Bhutan—a length of more than 1000 km. The original *tarai* landscape consisted of vast alluvial meadows of tall grasses and reeds (locally called *phantas*, *chaurs* or *tappars*), dotted with shallow ponds and marshes, with stretches of raised alluvial plateaus (called *damars*) containing the finest sal forest of the country. The *tarai* was one of the richest wildlife habitats of India before most of it was colonized and put under agriculture.

In the Kheri District between the Sharda river in the south and Suheli river in the north, was a strip of *tarai* grassland about 10 km wide and 70-80 km long. All this area was reclaimed during the 1950s, as a result of influx of refugees from Panjab, after partition.

Rich farms of sugarcane, rice and wheat have replaced most of the grasslands. Although most of the marshes too have been drained and colonized, it is estimated that about 80 patches, 2-8 ha in extent, still remain unclaimed. This rich habitat harboured species of flora and fauna which are now classified as rare and endangered. Among these are the swamp deer *Cervus duvacelli*, the Gangetic gharial and the tiger. The great Indian Rhinoceros, the wild buffalo and the pygmy hog, though no longer found in the area, are believed to have existed here in the past. The area also contains populations of hog deer, chital, sambar, barking deer, and wild boar. A herd of 31 elephants has also migrated into this tract from Nepal.

In 1977, a 490 sq km area north of river Suheli was declared as Dudhwa National Park. In the north, an additional area of 123 sq km has been declared as a buffer area, and extends up to the international boundary of Nepal. The southern portion of the Park (about 100 sq km in area) is the flood plain of Suheli river, comprising the typical *tarai* grassland and marsh. Cultivated fields of sugarcane and rice adjoin the park boundary south of Suheli. Sixty villages, with a population of about 60,000 and nearly an equal number of cattle, lie within a distance of 5 km from the park boundary. Three sugar mills are also located in this tract.

The buffer area in the north consists of raised *damar* plateau land containing rich sal forest. Some 41 tribal villages of the Tharu tribe, with a population of about 16,000, are located in the buffer area. The cattle population of the Tharus is about 15,000.

After the formation of the park, all grazing within the park was stopped. Tharus in the buffer area were given special concessions, to graze their cattle, to get free timber and fuel and to fish. Villagers in the south are rich farmers and have no concessions except removal of thatching material from 15 November to 10 December on free passes, and a cartload of fuel per family.

5.1. Man-eating tigers

The unique ecosystem of Dudhwa National Park is one of immense scientific and ecological value to scientists, ecologists and wildlife managers; but the rich sugarcane belt south of Dudhwa has become the centre of one of the biggest controversies between man and wildlife.

In the last 4 years, 93 people have fallen victims to man-eating tigers. Most of these man-eating cases have taken place in sugarcane fields outside the park boundary, though stray cases of man-eating have also occurred within the park.

The resentment which these man-eaters have evoked in the people has posed a challenge to the very concept of wildlife conservation in the country. In a recent article, Shahi (1982) has taken a survey of people's views in the area. Some of the views are produced below:

- Hari Singh, farmer of Bhira village who has a farm near the park: "Sugarcane crop grows best in the Sharda valley. This is a favourite spot for sugarcane growers. Sugarcane in a sense is also an extension of the grasslands—home of the tigers. The conflict is natural. Government figures of 90 human kills of past 4 years are wrong. In Bhira village alone, 20-25 people have been killed. Tigers have lost fear of man and his gun as we cannot shoot them."
- Harjot Singh, farmer of Sampurna Nagar: "Law is a cruel joke on man. If man kills a tiger, he has to pay a fine of Rs.50,000 (US$5,986) and undergo 10 years imprisonment. If tiger kills a man, compensation is Rs.5,000 (US$598). If Government wants to protect tigers why should it be done on our heads? Could the Government not find a more remote and hilly terrain than this inhabited human tract? We do not want any right to go into the forest for shooting tigers, but if the tiger creates havoc in our fields, we should have the right to kill it. If Government does not give us any means of self-protection, it should keep its tigers in bounds."
- Kewal Krishan, Advocate, Patpura Village: "If Government cannot keep tigers in bounds, at least the Wildlife Protection Act can be applied more reasonably. It is a travesty of law that a man trying to drive away a tiger creating havoc in his own field should be subject to fine."

In 1979, a team consisting of Choudhury and Sinha (1980) was appointed by the Government of India to investigate the problem of Dudhwa man-eaters. The team brought out the following aspects of the man-eating problem:

- The alluvial grasslands of Kheri and Pilibhit districts in U.P have been historically great tiger lands and the annual take from these protected tigers has been constantly high until the ban of tiger shooting was imposed more than a decade ago.
- During the last 2 decades much of the tall grass and the vast spread of the valleys has been replaced by equally tall and dense sugarcane. The tiger continues to stay here, adapting itself to the seasonally fluctuating heights in the stands of cane, the denser population of farm people and livestock and the mechanised sophistication in cultivation.
- In those dynamic tiger areas of *tarai* grassland forests, cases of accidental man killings have been very rare and deliberate man-eating virtually unknown. Local enquiries confirm that prior to March 1978, there had been no instance of a man-eater in Kheri District, except in 1952 and 1962 during the large scale reclamation of the *tarai* grassland forest.
- Human kills by tigers started again in March 1978 in three different areas, one inside the Dudhwa National Park and two outside the park.
- Though some of the tigers living in sugarcane fields and reed-beds outside the park can be considered resident, there is also a seasonal influx into crop fields of the normal tiger prey followed by its predator from Dudhwa Park. One of the reasons for this periodic influx from Dudhwa to the adjoining fields is the absence of the proper grazing succession between coarse, medium and tender feeders among the herbivores. During the monsoon, the grasses of Dudhwa become too tall and coarse for the swamp deer as well as the chital and hog deer. Bovines, particularly the gaur and buffalo, are coarse feeders which are absent in Dudhwa. In Kaziranga, the buffaloes and the rhinoceros occupy this niche. The Asiatic elephant also can share the tall grass niche, but their population is very low in the park.

5.2. Actions

A number of actions have been taken to handle this sensitive situation: the Government is keeping a close watch on all cases of man eating. A man-eater, once it is established, is promptly destroyed; a compensation of US$598 by the Government is paid for each human kill; a trench-fence is being dug along the southern boundary of the Park to prevent emigration of the ungulates from the Park to the cultivated fields; a programme of introduction of rhinoceros, as a coarse feeder, is being worked out; and a suggestion has been made to link the Kishanpur Sanctuary, situated in the south, with the Park by acquiring the cultivated fields between the two areas.

5.3. Some key issues

Some of the key issues which need answering in the above study are:

Why were there no cases of man-eating between 1952/1962 (when large scale reclamation of *tarai* grasslands took place) and 1978? Is there any connection between formation of Dudhwa National Park in 1977 and start of man-eating cases from 1978? Has there been a flaw in management? If man has intruded into the tiger's habitat, should tiger conservation be given up? Is man prepared to retreat and give up the area he has rehabilitated to wildlife? Is it really a conservation vs. development conflict? Should the laws formed by man, be weighed against man himself to favour wildlife? Will people whose lives are threatened allow wildlife conservation to be practised, whatever the scientific and ecological values of the area and the species?

6. CONCLUSIONS

The theoretical model outlined and the three cases presented in the study highlight the following basic issues in any programme of wildlife conservation and management of protected areas:

- The human dimension issues are more particularly relevant to the developing societies where most of the development action comes from government initiatives, and the perception and value judgements of different groups of people, both in regard to development and to the value of wildlife resources, may be widely different.
- In India, and the same may be true for other developing countries, wildlife conservation has come as an ecological programme concerned mainly with species conservation based primarily on western concepts. Most of the protected areas have been carved out from existing forest areas where forestry and other resource exploitation were already being practised. Stopping these resource practices normally results in a number of conflicts.
- In light of the Indian experience, wildlife conservation programmes in developing countries will have to be viewed in the context of the various resource processes which are linked with these areas. Socio-economic development of the people, particularly the subsistence societies linked with these areas, will have to form a part of the conservation programme. The success of both the Gir and the Palamau cases have amply demonstrated this. However, the approach of integrating the resource process of the people with conservation *in situ* will be more suitable (as demonstrated in the Palamau case) as opposed to removing the people away from the protected areas and practising conservation in isolation.

- A more positive approach in identifying wildlife as a resource system in the socio-economic sense will have to be adopted if wildlife conservation programmes are to be fully appreciated by the people, the politicians, the planners and the decision makers. Wildlife values tend to be overlooked by planners and decision makers, only because these values are not quantified and do not form a part of the resource system in the economic planning process. These aspects can be developed by taking up projects of game farming for furs, skins and meat, all of which can be highly profitable activities which can be developed at the village-level society. These can be integrated in the forestry management programmes where most of the wildlife habitats lie, and people associated with these programmes at local and community levels. In addition, the non-consumptive uses of wildlife, particularly wildlife-oriented tourism, has to be organised on a much larger scale, particularly keeping the middle and the lower-middle income group in mind. It is this group which determines the various economic processes which constitute a resource system.
- Wildlife-man conflicts as in the Dudhwa case have to be studied in depth. The cause of conservation cannot be served if wild animals are looked upon as a scourge on society. The maxim that most wildlife species which are harmful to man are really "ecological dislocates" should be kept in mind. The man-eating tigers of Dudhwa are not in any sense aberrant tigers but a product of some management decisions whose impact has to be properly evaluated without losing any time.
- The normative processes which guide various professional groups, development planners and politicians have a great bearing on conservation programmes. Quite often, wildlife and conservation considerations do not enter planning process and cost-benefit analysis because of the lack of mandatory provisions. These need an institutional framework where analysis of environmental impacts of various development projects become mandatory processes in project planning. In this connection, India has initiated a suitable machinery by establishing a separate Department of Environment whose job it is to over-see various development projects at the national level. A corresponding legal framework has to be developed in this context.
- Conservation education at all levels is necessary. The most important target group in India is recognised as that consisting of professionals whose activities have a bearing on the natural ecosystems, primarily planners and administrators. Quite often decisions are taken by this group because the conservation issues involved appear too trivial to them, compared to the immediate benefits which they see from a particular development programme. An appreciation of long-term environmental issues, and development of skills to evaluate them, can be built up only through well-designed education programmes, case studies and orientation camps.

NATIONAL PARKS, CONSERVATION, AND DEVELOPMENT

A Delicate Balance: Tigers, Rhinoceros, Tourists and Park Management *vs.* The Needs of the Local People in Royal Chitwan National Park, Nepal

Hemanta R. Mishra
Tiger Ecology Project Nepal
Kathmandu, Nepal

ABSTRACT. *This paper describes the conflicts inherent in trying to establish an effective national park in an area of important agricultural use. It points out the costs in human lives due to attacks by tigers and rhinos, the destruction of crops by wild animals, and the cost to villagers of doing without the resources of the park. On the other hand, the area surrounding Chitwan has been virtually denuded of firewood and thatch for housing purposes, proving the value of strict protection. In order to bring benefits to the local people, the most reasonable option has been shown to be the removal on a planned basis of grasses for thatch and reeds; these have provided, in the 5-year period from 1978 to 1982, some 334,000 kg of grass worth an estimated US $2.9 million.*

1. INTRODUCTION

Aldo Leopold, an outstanding naturalist of great vision, stressed the need to understand the relationship between the human environment and wilderness areas within the context of ecosystem inter-dependencies. Though Leopold's ideas were concerned with game management in the United States, his wise words have universal application to national parks and reserves in any country irrespective of geographical location or socio-economic background.

More recently Kellert (1979) emphasized the needs for understanding the human dimensions of conservation programmes, particularly the human and non-human dichotomy which requires recognition of the interaction between the natural resources and those who use or abuse them.

The 1970s witnessed an upsurge in the conservation movement, and this led to the realization that national parks and reserves are not only a whim of the affluent but a basic necessity for human survival. In the small Himalayan Kingdom of Nepal the national parks and reserves are not only of aesthetic value but are vital to conserve soil, water and resources for the future (Blower, 1971; Eckholm, 1976).

His Majesty King Birendra Bir Bikram Shah Deva proclaimed the country's first National Park and Wildlife Conservation Act in 1973 to ensure that nature conservation formed a vital part of the government's socio-economic development plans. Several international organizations such, as FAO, IUCN, the Smithsonian Institution, WWF, Frankfurt Zoological Society, New Zealand Government and many others have provided financial and technical assistance to the Kingdom.

By 1978 four national parks and three wildlife reserves (Fig. 1) were established both in the Terai and the high Himalayas to represent different ecosystems throughout the country (Mishra, 1974).

Legal, administrative and financial provisions by His Majesty's Government secured the Chitwan National Park from the axe, plough and grazing encroachment. Thanks to the personal involvement of influential and dedicated persons like His Royal Highness Prince Gyanendra Bir Bikram Shah, this national park proved to be a classic example of a success story where governmental determination backed by local and international expertise changed a depleted area into one of the most outstanding national parks in the world.

The ungulate crude biomass is estimated to have increased from about 2,000 kg/sq km in 1974 (Seidensticker, 1976) to about 5,000 in 1980 (Mishra, unpublished). The population of the rhino alone is reported to have increased from about 100 in 1968 (Caughley, 1968) to at least 300 in the next ten years (Laurie, 1978), as poaching was completely controlled. The population

197

of the tiger was estimated to be less than 25 in 1974 (Poppleton and Mishra, 1974) and the present estimate is over 60 (Smith and Mishra, 1980). However, these increases have been associated with heavy damage to agricultural crops, loss of livestock and even casualties of human life in Chitwan, bringing park management in direct conflict with the local people.

The objective of this case study is to outline the sources of conflict between park management and local people, and to describe real incidents and the perspectives of the local people.

2. THE SETTING

The national park (Fig. 2) lies in the Chitwan district of the Nepal terai, near the Indian border. The River Rapti demarcates the northern boundary of the park from densely cultivated areas. The Reu river separates the park from farm land on the south while the Naryani River forms its western boundaries. It is only on its eastern side that the national park is bounded by forests. During most of the year the Rapti and Reu rivers are crossable by humans and their cattle. The Churia mountain range bisects the park into catchments draining into these rivers. The area of the park when first gazetted was 544 sq km, but was increased to 894 sq km in 1978.

3. THE REGION'S NATURAL SYSTEMS

The climate in Chitwan is sub-tropical and is dominated by the southeast monsoon. The average annual rainfall is about 250 cm, with most occurring between June and September. Two other seasons are pronounced. The post-monsoon season between November and January is cool with the daily average temperature reaching 24°C during the day and dropping to about 7°C at night. The months of March to May are hot and dry with the temperature reaching as high as 40°C and rarely dropping below 20°C.

The geology of the area and soil type are described by HMG (1968), Hagen (1969) and Berry et al. (1974). The Churia range of the Siwalik hills is characterized by sandstones, conglomerate quartzes, shales and micaceous sandstones; the valley floors are formed by rich alluvials of high fine sand content and silt from seasonal flooding.

The vegetation is dominated by almost monotypic stands of Sal Shorea robusta which occupy 70% of the park area. This straight-boled deciduous tree occupies all of the Churia ridges and most of the well-drained parts of the national park. In places it is associated with other trees such as Terminalia bellirica, Dalbergia latifolia, and Anogneissus latifolia. The shrub and herb undergrowth is poor in species but the grass Themeda caudata grows prolifically on the forest floor.

Riverine forest and grasslands form a mosaic along the banks of the rivers and islands, and are maintained by seasonal flooding and frequent changes in the courses of the rivers. Riverine forest occupies about 7% of the park, the most common species being Bombax cebia, Trewia nudiflora, Acacia catechu and Dalbergia sisso. Grasslands occupy about 20% of the area; some are derived from past agricultural settlements, while others are in the initial stages in the succession from newly deposited alluvium to forests. The lower banks of the rivers are dominated by Saccharum spontaneum, which is the first species to colonise dry river beds. Old village sites which were cleared in 1964 are occupied by Imperata cylinderica, a species much in demand as thatch grass. Saccharum narenga grows as mixed stands with other tall and dense species such as Arundo spp, Typha elephantina and Cyperus spp (collectively referred to as "elephant grass"). About 3% of the area is occupied by rivers, streams and other permanent water bodies.

The national park contains Nepal's only surviving population of the great one-horned Asiatic rhinoceros. The park also has a population of tigers and is one of the major "Operation Tiger" areas. Other large mammals include leopard, wild dog, sloth bear, gaur, sambar, chital, hog deer, the barking deer, and the wild swine. The swamp deer, formerly a common species of the area, was extirpated from Chitwan in the mid-sixties. Smaller mammals such as monkey, otter, porcupine, yellow-throated marten and civet are also common throughout the park. Aquatic species include the Gangetic dolphin, the mugger crocodile, and the Endangered gharial. Over 350 species of birds have been reported from Chitwan and there are at least 60 species of fish in the rivers and oxbow lakes inside the park.

4. HUMAN ECOLOGY, AGRICULTURE AND LAND USE PATTERNS

The Tharus are the only indigenous people of the area, and little is known about their origin in Chitwan. Though people of all castes and from all parts of Nepal have recently colonised the Chitwan area, the Tamangs form the majority.

In 1980 there were 320 villages around the national park comprising approximately 52,250 households and 261,300 persons; immigration and a high rate of population increase have almost doubled the human population since 1970. There is no current estimate of the domestic cattle population, though Seidensticker (1976) estimated the cattle density to be 27,895 kg per sq km in 1974 along the fringes of the national park.

The pattern of land use in the Chitwan valley is similar to that of most of the inner Terai. Berry et al., (1974) described traditional systems of farming in the adjacent Nawalpur district, and recently Milton and Binney (1980) described the seasonal cycles of planting and harvesting in areas near the park. Rice, the main crop, is planted between June and July and it is harvested between November and December; where there is permanent water, it is planted and harvested earlier. In such land, dal (pulses) is planted after the rice harvest. Maize is planted before the monsoon rains on dry and sloping land and it is harvested in August/September.

Major winter crops of wheat and mustard are planted in November/December, and are harvested four to five months after planting. Domestic cattle are often allowed to graze on recently harvested land and their dung provides fertilizer for the next crop. Barley and millet are cultivated in some wetter areas, and chiles and tobacco are planted in small patches of land surrounding houses. Fruits such as banana and mango are also grown.

Farming techniques are primitive compared with those used in developed countries. Ploughing is done manually or by use of bullocks. Irrigation is by small canals excavated annually between fields and major water sources. Domestic cattle, mainly cows and water buffalo, provide both milk and bullocks for ploughing and pulling carts. Villagers also keep goats and sheep; the male offspring of the former are often castrated and reared for meat. Human ecology and socio-political features were described by Milton and Binney (1980) and descriptions of the people and their culture were given by Bista (1967).

5. FACTORS AFFECTING THE ECOSYSTEM OF THE NATIONAL PARK

Fire, grass cutting and tourism are the main human factors that directly affect the ecosystem of the park. In addition there are over 400 park staff who live scattered throughout the park area and about 40 domestic elephants are regularly grazed in the park.

Annual burning of grassland in Chitwan valley is an ancient human practice (Laurie, 1978; Bolton, 1975). The grasslands and the surface litter of the sal forests burn between January and April. Early fires are made by villagers after the thatch grass harvest. Villagers follow the fire which burns the leaves and young dry shoots of the dense grasses, leaving the stems and reeds clear which are then cut; this practice eases the collection of thatch for the villagers. Late fires during the dry, windy period from March to May are also induced by man but can also be caused by lightning (Wharton, 1968). Annual fires seem to maintain the grasslands and a few species of shrubs; *Bombax* is the only fire resistant tree that is encroaching the grasslands (Troth, 1976). Regrowth of grasses after burning is rapid and they often reach 2-3 metres before the first monsoon shower. Every year villagers are permitted to collect thatch grass in the park and over 100,000 people are engaged in this activity for a two-week period (Section 8.2).

The Royal Chitwan National Park is a popular destination for overseas tourists visiting Nepal, with the Tiger Tops sector and the Saurah sector the major points of destination. Governmental control on tourist concessionnaires and the number of domestic elephants used by tourists have restricted the effects of tourism to a low level. Furthermore, high costs and the general limitations of infrastructure have also helped to keep the number of visitors to a manageable level. Tourism has also been the main source of revenue, though the total revenue obtained is still far less than Government inputs.

There is little other human disturbance in the park, and this is restricted to the edges. Poaching has been controlled, but thatch grass, bamboo, and fuel wood are occasionally stolen. A little grazing encroachment occurs but is again also restricted to the fringes of the park. The rivers are heavily fished, mainly by a little-known group of people, the Botes, who depend upon fish for their livelihood as they own no land.

6. THE HUMAN DILEMMA

In Chitwan, there are four basic areas of conflict between park management and the local people. Each case will be described by narrating real incidents as they have occurred in the last five years.

6.1 Loss of life

One misty morning in December 1978, Trilochan, a school teacher from a village on the border of the park, was walking toward the river to perform his morning ablution. At the same time a young male tiger was padding up a gully near the river to seek refuge in the adjacent forest. The schoolmaster entered the top of the gully just as the tiger was approaching the rim from the other side. Both man and beast panicked at this extremely rare and surprising encounter, and the schoolmaster was attacked and killed instantaneously. This incident was enough to cause a small riot by local villagers against the national park. Fortunately, the tiger carried a radio collar, and with the aid of Smithsonian Tiger Ecology Project personnel the animal was captured and translocated within 24 hours to Kathmandu Zoo (Mishra, 1981). This operation was necessary to calm the anger of the local population.

From then until 1982, four other humans have been killed by tigers and one tigress alone was responsible for killing three persons. The latter incidents were responsible for a rumour spread by unscrupulous politicians that park authorities had deliberately released a man-killer to keep people out of the national park. The national park authorities made a wise decision by destroying the tiger, an act which was witnessed by several hundred villagers. This act demonstrated that despite the full legal protection afforded tigers, the park authorities care about human lives.

Lato, a simple teenaged lad, was taking his cattle to graze in a patch of forest adjacent to the national park when he was attacked and killed by a rhinoceros that was returning to the park after a night spent raiding crops. Damai, a tailor, was walking through the public right of way to go to the bazaar when he encountered a rhino with a calf. She chased him and gored him to death. Every year 3 to 5 people are killed or badly mauled by rhinoceros as both humans and animals move constantly along the fringes of the national park. While these killings are rare compared with deaths by natural or other causes, statistics to this effect mean little to the bereaved families. Furthermore, there is little effective control as long as people and animals use common areas. While the national park is not legally liable for such accidents, any death by park wildlife produces resentment against the park and polarizes public opinion.

6.2 Loss of livestock

Ram Prashad was proud of a buffalo he bought with savings from nearly four years of hard labour. Unfortunately the animal could not resist the lush green grass across the river inside the park and one morning he wandered about a kilometer inside the boundary, where he was killed and devoured by a big male tiger. Since it is illegal to let domestic cattle into the park, Ram could have been fined. He has no legal recourse but he will hold a grudge against the park for as long as he lives.

The loss of domestic cattle to large carnivores has diminished since grazing inside the park was effectively controlled. However, since there is little grazing land outside the park, cattle of the bordering villages often wander into the park and are killed by tigers and leopards. It has been estimated that domestic cattle constitute 30% of the tiger kills in an area adjacent to villages (Tamang, 1979).

6.3 Problems arising from park regulations

Every morning Kumar used to take his cattle for grazing inside the forests. While he grazed the cattle, his cousin Siva collected fuel wood, honey and other forest produce. Since the national park was established, Kumar has to graze the cattle along the open banks of the Rapti river where there is little grazing and ensure that any of his cattle do not cross the river into the national park to avoid paying a fine of five Rupees (US $0.40) for any animal found grazing in park land. Now his cousin has to travel up to 16 km miles every day to collect fuel wood. Little does Kumar realize that the national park cannot sustain grazing pressures nor will there be any trees left if fuel wood collection is not stopped. He regularly sees strange-looking foreigners going through the jungle on elephant back and fails to understand why an area is set aside at the expense of his liberty to do whatever he was doing before in the jungle.

His maternal uncle who has come for a visit has to rush back soon since movement through the park is restricted after sunset nor can his friends take a few shots at birds and ducks with their catapults. His father complains that there are so many guards he cannot sneak into the forests and quietly shoot a wild boar for a feast for his elder son's wedding. He fails to understand why these animals are protected if no one can eat them. This is just an example given and is based on a conversation I had with some of the young boys around Saurah. Like many Nepalese, they tell their story with humour and sarcasm. They accept the national park regulations as one of the many nuisances they have to face as a part of their struggle for survival and avoiding capture is the only reasonable alternative.

6.4 Problems arising from crop destruction

Crop destruction is the main source of conflict with the local communities and is probably the most important factor to be overcome in successful management of the park. Despite this there has been to date only one preliminary ten-month study of this problem (Milton and Binney, 1980).

In particular, this study revealed that rhinoceros and people cannot co-exist without increasing public resentment against the national park. The rhinoceros is a unique endangered ungulate but it is also a local nuisance to many of the villagers that have to tolerate its constant intrusion in the farmlands. Crop damages by wildlife in some of the villages ranged from 10% to 100% of the crop planted (Milton and Binney 1980) and the monetary value of crop loss was high (Table 1).

Following Milton and Binney's study and before the frustration of the local community erupted, the government decided to undertake the gigantic task of resettling over 7,000 people from the wildlife nuisance area to an alternative site with better soil fertility and no rhinoceros or other wild herbivores. This was in accordance with the demands of the local people. The national park also had an interest in resettling villagers from this area since it would ensure revival of the grassland ecosystem over an area of about 40 sq km. This action was possible only because the interests of the local community and park authorities were in agreement and the government had alternate areas. However, this was a solution for only about 10 of the 320 villages that surround the park, and there are not many areas left where other similarly-affected villages can be shifted. Nor is further relocation of villages politically or economically feasible. No matter how large or small a park may be, there will be farmlands across the park boundary and crop raiding by wild ungulates will be a constant source of conflict.

Efforts to fence Chitwan's park boundaries have failed. Fences were not effective against rhinoceros or seasonal torrents of the monsoon. In fact, a fence that is effective against the mighty rhinoceros as well as lesser creatures and can still sustain the high floods of the monsoon is simply beyond the means of the country. This clearly indicates the need for research and studies to minimize agricultural damage without having to destroy wild ungulates.

7. BENEFITS FROM THE PARK: VIEWPOINTS OF THE VILLAGERS

No project is viable in the long run unless the local people are involved in the processes and derive benefits from the programme. This section is a brief attempt to appraise how local people view the benefits and is based on interviews and discussions with some of the leaders of the local communities.

7.1 Benefits from tourism

Unlike in the Sagarmatha National Park (see Jefferies, this volume), the people of Chitwan are not directly involved in tourism. In the last eight years the annual number of visitors to Chitwan has increased from less than 1,000 to over 8,000, with an average stay of three nights for tourists. However, the park revenue from tourism constitutes less than 25% of the government financial inputs. It is also unlikely that the budget of the national park can be subsidized wholly from tourism.

Most visitors to Chitwan are non-Nepalese since few nationals can afford the prices and facilities that generally cater to western tourists. Thus the national park "consumers" are outsiders who have little interest in local problems.

Tourism is also a service-oriented industry; but because of the local shortage of educational opportunities, the chance of a local villager being employed is very slim, and only a few locals are employed in menial jobs. It is obvious that tourism has not generated local jobs as the tourist industry forecasted. Most of the well-paying jobs are taken by qualified and experienced people from outside Chitwan, or even from outside Nepal, with the possible exception of staff of the Tharu Village Camp, a resort located outside the national park boundary. Tourist facilities might increase opportunities for local employment, but further increases in tourism will be detrimental to the national park. Furthermore, the objective of the national park is not entirely to promote tourism.

One of the detrimental effects of tourism has been the rapid rate of inflation in Chitwan. Tourism is a "consumer" industry and unless its influx can be matched with a parallel increase in production of goods and materials, a tourist tends to consume more than the area produces and the law of supply and demand pushes the prices up. For example, the price of an egg was US$0.04 in 1978 and US$0.10 in 1981. Similarly, the price of a chicken rose from US$1.5 in 1978 to US$5 in 1981. In Saurah, one of the centres of tourism, the prices of rice, vegetables, cooking oil, kerosene and other products have increased more rapidly than in other parts of Chitwan. Thus, except for a few traders and merchants of the nearby towns, most people in the vicinity of the national park are losing instead of benefiting from tourism.

There is little doubt that the country as a whole is being enriched by the tourist industry and some of the benefits filter down to the community around the national park through the Government's development programme. With the increase in the government's education and training programme the people of Chitwan will someday be actively involved in tourism in a manner parallel to the Sherpas of Solo Khumbu. But at present the concept of selling the idea of a national park from the benefits to the local people from wilderness-oriented tourism has not been successful and is unlikely to have any positive effect within the next decade.

7.2 Employment by the national park

The national park is the biggest employer of the local people but as with the tourism sector, it can only provide seasonal jobs and only a small segment of the local population derives direct benefit from it. Other than in the form of limited employment from tourism and the national park, the local people derive no direct monetary benefits by the existence of a national park in their area.

7.3 Conservation of soil and water

The biggest benefit of the national park to the district is its role in the conservation of soil and water. With the control of grazing, the southern banks of the Rapti river have stabilized. Over the last decade it has been clearly demonstrated that vegetation along the banks of the river stabilize the monsoon torrents. But these benefits are neither realized nor appreciated in local communities. Floods and landslides are believed to be acts of God rather than the results of mismanagement of land. The lack of an effective conservation education and publicity programme is responsible for the local communities' failure to realize the importance of the park in conserving soil and water. Furthermore, most villagers are preoccupied with the day-to-day struggle for existence. When the source of their next meal is a major worry, principles of soil and water conservation have little relevance.

8. EFFORTS TO MINIMIZE CONFLICTS WITH LOCAL PEOPLE: THE CHITWAN EXPERIENCE

The villagers' perspective of the park had been negative and the park authorities were faced with pressure to compromise the park principles. During the last five years two experimental approaches to change the negative view of the villagers have been undertaken to minimize such conflicts. One is a public relations campaign where an effort is made to diffuse local hard feelings by direct communication. The other is to provide the local villager with renewable park resources as a form of compensation for the losses or difficulties posed by the existence of the national park.

8.1 The "Panch Vhella" (a forum of community leaders)

In most countries of Asia, national park planners and managers are foresters or biologists who are more at home in forests than in local villages. Experience and training in public relations programmes at a community level is lacking because such programmes are difficult to devise and there are important differences from area to area even within the same country. The result is a general lack of communication with the local people. To most local people the park staff are viewed as watch dogs to ensure that they do not have access to the resources they had been using or abusing in the past. Thus, they are generally cautious in dealing with the park staff, and conversely, experience has taught the park staff to regard most villagers with some suspicion.

Since 1977 the park authorities have assembled a group of villagers, school teachers and leaders of the local communities once every year to discuss the problems of the local people and the needs of the national park. The people meet for 2 days at park headquarters where they are housed and fed by the park staff. They are also given a tour of the park. During the 2 days a series of meetings are also held where the park hears the complaints, grievances and views of the local villagers. Attempts are made to solve or provide answers to each and every issue raised. The park staff also explain why some of the demands, such as grazing or timber exploitation, cannot be permitted.

The biggest impact of these meetings has been psychological, since the local people are beginning to feel that they are being involved in park processes that affect them. Though these gatherings were envisaged to allow park staff to learn of the real problems faced by local people, they have also allowed us to demonstrate the complexities of various problems to the local people. These gatherings have also given the local people a chance to "blow off steam" against the park or against other government programmes.

8.2 The annual grass harvest

Since 1978 local villagers have been permitted to enter the park to collect grass for building materials. Most houses in Chitwan are roofed with thatch grass, and the canes of tall elephant grass have been used traditionally to construct walls and partitions both outside and inside the house. These materials are now available only in the national park.

A nominal fee of US $0.02 is charged for each permit per household. The fee's purpose is to keep a record of people entering the park rather than generate revenue. One permit allows each household to harvest and remove as much grass as its members are able. The entire season lasts for 15 days in the month of January. The villagers spend the first week harvesting thatch grass, after which they set fire to the grasslands. The tall grass canes are removed after the fire burns most of the leaves and other dry parts. Motorized vehicles and bullock carts are not permitted, so both rich and poor have equal opportunity to take as much as they require. Many of the latter also make a living out of harvested grasses by selling crafted products in nearby towns and villages.

Villagers come to the park from as far away as 50 km. Between 30,000 and 50,000 permits have been issued per annum and over 66,830 tons of grass in average is removed annually. The value of the produce based on a minimum price during the grass cutting season has ranged from US $444,431 to as high as US $891,985 per annum. From 1978 to 1982, over 334,154 tons of grass valued at nearly US $3 million have been harvested from the national park. The regrowth of grass after the harvest and burn is rapid.

The national park authorities view this programme in three ways. First, any park system in the midst of a densely populated area must consider the local community as a part of reserve management.

Second, by allowing the local people limited access to a resource central to their livelihood, the programme illustrates one principle of conservation in terms that villagers can understand. Most villagers who farm a few hectares do not understand the aesthetic or intellectual arguments for preserving natural ecosystems since they are too busy trying to feed themselves. However, they recognize that most tall grasses outside the park have disappeared, and that the reserve is protecting those that are left in the district. Furthermore, the tall grasses never matured to their full height before the national park was established because they were constantly cropped by domestic cattle. Thus, grass cutting has been one of the most powerful educational and public relations tools for the national park.

Third, the grasslands are a successional stage that has been maintained for hundreds of years by human activities (Wharton, 1968) and the annual grass cutting programme may be the most effective and economical ways of maintaining this ecosystem. Over 100,000 people are mobilized without financial burden to the government treasury, and even with its meagre fees the park has already collected over US $15,385 during the last five years.

Obviously the situation in the Terai is somewhat unusual since we are dealing with a rapidly renewable resource. The application of the same principles for fuel wood or timber collection would be self-defeating. The short- and long-term effects of this massive periodic influx of people on the fauna is not known. However, it is an effective means of compensation to the local population for the restriction imposed by the park legislation and the consequent damage of their crops or property. In short, it is a practical trade-off.

9. DISCUSSION AND CONCLUSIONS

Talbot (1979) pointed out that as conservation efforts become successful they automatically conflict with other human interests. Problems once perceived as of a biological nature become political, economic, social and cultural ones. The people-park conflict in Chitwan and other reserves in Nepal verify this prediction. The efforts to diffuse human antagonism against the national park Chitwan have only "bought some time" because the conflict will increase with the disappearance of the few remaining patches of the forests outside the national park that have fulfilled the need for fuel wood and grazing land. Once these are lost, the pressures of the growing population will be directed to the national park. Thus the future of the park depends upon how quickly alternate resources vital to the local people can be generated and how fast effective measures against animal damage can be executed.

Most parks and reserves in the Indian sub-continent are islands in a sea of human population. Biologists have elaborated on the relationship between shape, size and other parameters of the park to maximize species diversity, but the hard reality is that existing park systems have been brought about by a compromise between a variety of interest groups. There is very little doubt, for example, that the reserves in the Terai of Nepal would not have been in existence without the sport hunting interests of the country's past rulers.

Some land-use planners have suggested that parks and reserves should be established in "marginal" land where they will be more secure from human pressures. Adherence to this belief alone would wipe out most reserves from southern Asia, since most lands where parks and reserves can be effectively established are also good for agriculture or other human usage. Furthermore, in Nepal we find the term "marginal land" too vague, since our experiences even in the remote Himalayas reveal that no land is marginal, including the high slopes of Mt. Sagarmatha where human usage is indeed competitive and has been largely responsible for the deterioration of the environment.

Human usage of national parks has been a subject of intensive studies and IUCN has documented guidelines for planning national parks for human use. This has also been a subject of discussion since the first World Conference on National Parks 20 years ago and it has been the focus of many technical meetings of the IUCN. The emphasis, however, has always been on visitation by humans, their recreational and aesthetic needs and tourist interests. There has been far too little discussion of the use of national parks by the local people whose primary interest is simply survival. The emphasis on tourism in the national parks has been used and abused by various interest groups. In Chitwan, economic returns from tourism have clearly failed to motivate the local populace in favour of the national park as anticipated. In contrast, our preoccupation with hopes that tourism will catalyze local support or change public attitudes seem to be self-defeating since the benefits from tourism were overplayed both by government authorities and tourist organizations. Furthermore, how does one explain to the villager that a tourist can use the national park for recreation because he is wealthy whereas the resident of the area must be subject to restriction and cannot use the resources for his daily existence?

The tug-of-war between wildlife and park management versus the local people of Chitwan is not restricted to Nepal, but is going on in parks and reserves throughout most of the developing world. The relationship between wildlife, tourists, national parks and the local people must be symbiotic rather than antagonistic; the benefits must be mutual in the form of jobs, markets, prestige, sentiment, or even thatch grasses.

The timely task for park planners is to explore and foster means of co-existence beyond the park boundary and into local communities. If this is not achieved, national park and reserve systems in the developing world will perish as sand castles on the beach, and the insights of naturalists like Aldo Leopold will have been for nothing.

Acknowledgements

My research work in Nepal was supported by the Smithsonian Institution. Dr. Christen Wemmer provided the technical advice particularly in the preparation of the final draft of this report. I am grateful to him for also correcting the English language of this paper. Tirtha M. Maskey collaborated in all the processes in gathering the information in Chitwan and his help in the final compilation of the data on grass cutting was very valuable.

Jeffrey A. McNeely provided the basic guidelines and above all the encouragement that were needed to view the complexities of the people-parks problem. Drs. J. Siedensticker, I.R. Taylor, and G. Binney also made some valuable comments. Last but not least, many of the local people provided much of the information frankly and honestly, if not bluntly, as to how they view the national park and I am grateful to them. The staff of the HMG/Elephant Camp, guards of the national park and other staff, and the staff of the Tiger Project were always cooperative and provided much of the local support.

This paper was prepared for IUCN's Commission on National Parks and Protected Areas in cooperation with the World Wildlife Fund.

Table 1. Estimated Percentages of Crop Loss in Some Villages Adjacent to Chitwan National Park 1977–1978

Name of village	Rice	Wheat	Mustard	Maize	Vegetable	Average	Economic value of combined crop loss US $	Estimated loss from 1975–1978 (%)
Padampur	60	60	40	60	60	50	615	60
Bhimpur	60	50	50	60	20	48	92	60
Piperiya	50	50	30	30	20	36	285	50
Khekheryia	30	20	30	20	15	23	258	35
Jitpur	10	15	15	10	10	12	38	10–20
Dhidouli	50	50	40	60	40	48	92	50
Bhawanipur	80	90	85	100	60	83	500	80–90
Marchouli	50	40	75	6	40	53	N/A	75
Jaimangala	85	80	70	90	60	77	N/A	80

Source: Milton and Binney, 1980

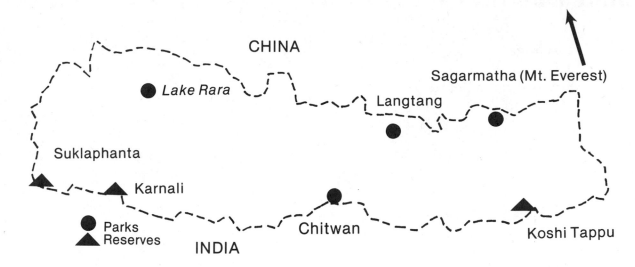

Figure 1. Nepal's national parks and wildlife reserves.

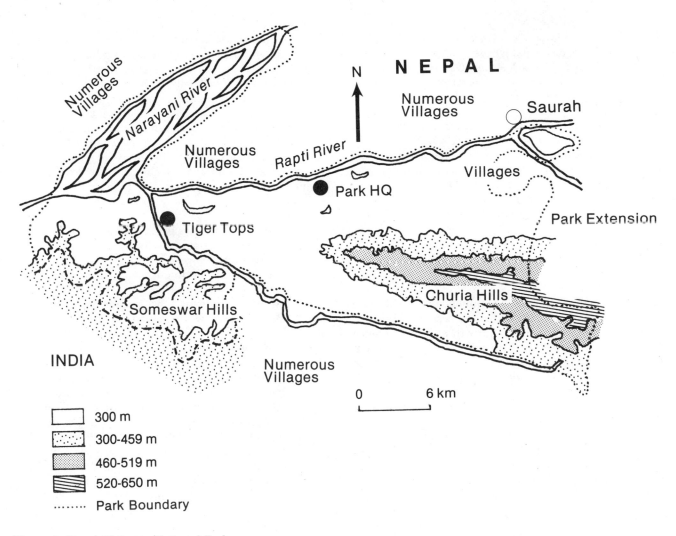

Figure 2. Royal Chitwan National Park.

Future Directions for the Indomalayan Realm

Kasem Snidvongs
Secretary General
National Environment Board
Bangkok, Thailand

ABSTRACT. *It appears that we are close to the limit of the area which can be established for preservation of natural conditions in the Indo-Malayan Realm. Our primary concerns must be on how the increasing population and development pressures will affect the status of protected areas, how to effectively manage the existing areas, and how to convince the decision-makers that the areas are truly worth saving. Each of the countries in the realm differs significantly in socio-economic and political structures; since many of the problems in protected area management are non-technical problems, the varying social, political and economic settings are likely to result in significantly different problems in managing similar environments in different countries. Future directions must continue to adapt to these variable conditions.*

1. INTRODUCTION

Most of the countries in the Indomalayan Realm are developing countries rich in natural resources but suffering from rapid population growth and questionable economic development which has involved inefficient and wasteful utilization of natural resources. The population growth and economic development activities have generated concern about our natural areas and consequently over the last twenty years the number of protected natural areas has tripled and their area quadrupled. In 1962 there were 96 protected areas covering about 5 million ha in the Indomalayan Realm; today nearly protected areas cover over 22 million ha. That is significant and impressive growth. It is also a huge amount of land and water surface area to manage and protect.

Obviously, this growth was influenced by the increasing pressure of people and nations to use natural areas in such a way that they are no longer valuable in their natural state. The need for land and water and the resources and uses they can yield to support agricultural and industrial growth for our burgeoning populations will increase phenomenally in the future; thus the costs of protecting these natural resources and processes will paradoxically be questioned more and more, while their value to society continues to increase. There is a limit to the area which can be established for protection of natural conditions and I would say that, in most countries of the Indomalayan Realm, we are close to that limit.

Our primary concerns must be:

- How will increasing population and development effect the status of protected areas, both in quality and quantity?
- What must we do to effectively manage and protect the natural areas?
- How can we convince the "competition" that these areas are truly worth saving?

The purpose of this discussion is to look at these issues, which will determine the future directions required to successfully establish and manage protected areas. In order to provide a look into the future which is at least relatively comprehensive for the Indomalayan Realm, I decided that it was important to obtain a diversity of outlooks of experts throughout the Realm. To accomplish this a list of "point-counterpoint" type issues was distributed and comments solicited and received from experts in Thailand, Malaysia, Burma, India and Indonesia. The point-counterpoint issues follow:

1a. The present general directions of establishment and management of national parks are appropriate for the Indomalayan region.

1b. Present efforts towards establishment and protection have been failing and new directions and efforts must be found.

2a. The basic problems in protection are due to government policies including inadequate budgeting and conflicts in development goals.

2b. The basic problems in protection are due to lack of technical management capabilities in line agencies. Protection would be adequate, provided there is provision of sufficient resources including budget.

3a. Conservation of protected areas cannot be achieved without improved administration and management ability.

3b. Administration and management ability are not important limiting factors and their improvement, even with sufficient resources, would not achieve optimal protection.

4a. Conservation of protected areas could be achieved if governments in the Indomalayan Realm realized and recognized the value of conservation.

4b. Recognition of the value of conservation by governments is not a major limiting factor to conservation of protected areas except in a few countries.

5a. In order for conservation to be achieved, local people must be educated about the benefits of conservation.

5b. Education about the benefits of conservation is not a major limiting factor and in many areas this would not eliminate the problem of protection.

6a. Local people must be made to sacrifice their short-term needs in order to achieve the long-term benefits of conservation.

6b. Local people should not be made to sacrifice short-term needs for the sake of long-term benefits from conservation.

7a. Conservation does not now conflict with short-term developmental goals of developing countries.

7b. It is a fact that conservation now conflicts with the immediate developmental goals of developing countries.

8a. The conservation of protected areas must be achieved with more armed power and will power in this realm.

8b. The conservation of protected areas will not be achieved simply with more manpower and will power and some innovative approaches are required.

9a. Tourism could benefit conservation of protected areas if its volume were increased.

9b. Tourism as now conceived mainly benefits the wealthy and will not help conservation in this realm significantly.

9c. Tourism would not contribute much to conservation of protected areas because the tropical rain forest does not attract tourists.

2. OUTLINING DIRECTIONS

In July 1981, the Foreign Correspondents Club of Thailand sponsored a panel discussion on wildlife conservation. The panel comprised several government, academic, and international experts responsible for the management of protected areas. At the end of the panel discussion a concensus was reached that, despite the valiant efforts of dedicated conservationists to date, our approach in Thailand is failing and it is time to recognize this and to seek a new approach or formula which has a fair chance to succeed.

On a realm-wide basis it appears that most countries are headed in an appropriate general direction of establishing protected areas, but the level of successful protection varies considerably. Some areas are well protected, others not protected at all and the majority are protected at some level in between. Thus there seems to be a need to redirect management efforts to achieve more effective protection. Revisions of current management practices or development of new directions will be determined by: (i) government policies; (ii) administrative needs; (iii) financial requirements; (iv) manpower and expertise requirements and; (v) local social and economic conditions and needs. It is obvious from the responses to the "point-counterpoint" issues that each government will need to assess the relative importance of each factor to determine the most important or controlling factors inhibiting successful establishment and protection of national parks and other protected areas.

3. GOVERNMENT POLICY AND PLANNING: FIGURING OUT WHERE WE STAND

Most governments in the Indomalayan Realm have gone on record as setting high priority on protection of national parks. All too often it seems that such high priority actually exists only in the government agencies charged with the responsibility to plan and manage national parks. When a potential conflict in a proposed use of such areas comes up, we find that the priority for protection was never firmly incorporated in the overall priorities of the government development policies and plans. Thus it is difficult to rank a development policy priority relative to protection of a given area and decisions on the use of the area tend to be geared toward utilization for quick-return economic development unless conservationsts can strongly support the value of the area in its protected state. Because of the rather disjointed priority ranking, each time a situation arises where there is a conflict in the use of a protected area, this convincing action must be repeated.

Thus there is a need for the governments to effectively incorporate the policies on protected area establishment and management as an integral component of social and economic development policies, strategies and plans. This means that the policies should reflect the status of all potential land/water uses in terms of priorities so that there is a clear understanding of what uses will and will not be allowed. If the priority status of maintaining protection of national parks is low on the list as compared to, for example, mineral resources or water resource development, then we will know that efforts should be focussed on re-orienting government policy to favour protection of national parks. Also, if this is the case, it should indicate to the agencies charged with establishment and management of national parks that they may need to adjust their policies to manage parks better so that their track record is favourable for convincing a government of the high priority requirement for protecting national parks.

I often have the feeling that one of the reasons that protected area management is not integrated with overall development planning is because the programmes are too dispersed and too vague in terms of how effective they can be expected to be. We push for establishment of more and larger protected areas without showing a concrete need and without a track record showing that the areas can be effectively protected and managed. To really gain some stature in development priorities, agencies responsible for protected area management must be able to submit development-type plans to the decision-makers in the government which impress the decision-makers as being well thought out and planned over a five-or ten-year planning period, including necessary manpower and budget requirements. Such plans should present a comprehensive programme, to show the decision-maker the estimated costs of the entire programme, as well as the benefits to be expected. An analysis should show the land/water areas to be included, the operating management procedures and controls to be applied, and projections of what the wildlife and natural area conditions will be like in 20 or 50 years both with and without project conditions. In other words, the programmes should be planned and processed in the same manner as other public development projects and by doing so will be better planned and get the appropriate level of attention from decision-makers.

4. ADMINISTRATION AND MANAGEMENT: LET'S GET INNOVATIVE

The importance of sound and effective administration and management of protected areas was weighted as "very important" and "not very important" in the responses I received. As an administrator, I feel that this diversity of opinion reflects reality: the concept of the purpose of administration and management seems to vary from place to place. I believe that any redirection in establishing and protecting natural areas must take into account the effectiveness of current administration and management practices and the administrators and managers are going to have to come up with some innovative schemes to be able to receive the budgets and trained manpower which they require. I don't think

this will happen unless administrators and managers attempt to pin down the causes of failures and then risk some new approaches to management. The ideas of enhancing development, mainly of rural local populations and local regional, national and international tourism do not necessarily reflect management policies and thus will fail if management and administration are not adjusted to maximize the potential for success.

Once appropriate administrative and management schemes are devised it will be necessary to re-educate the professional staff of protected areas so that the new schemes can be put into effect. Finally, the schemes must be flexible (follow a research and development approach) and revised with practice and experience. In taking this approach we can solicit the help of: academics and students who will contribute to the development and at the same time gain expertise in the application of new management schemes; concerned government agencies which will influence and be influenced (be in tune with and support) new schemes, and; international assistance agencies interested in assisting and learning from such research and development.

5. CONCLUSIONS: LET'S GET COORDINATED AND INTEGRATED WITH DEVELOPMENT

As a policy-maker and administrator, it is my opinion that any approaches to establishment and protection of natural areas, whether utilizing contemporary or innovative technologies, will have limited success because of the demand for such areas for development and everyday human-use, *unless* such approaches are integrated into the overall development scheme. Agencies charged with protection areas can no longer sit back and say, "These resources are protected for future generations so they can not be used." Those future generations are going to exert more pressure on utilizing protected areas for development than we have faced to date because they will need to use them. We are running out of resources. Therefore our approach must be to maximize the use of protected areas to obtain the most benefits for most people and still maintain a level of suitable protection. To accomplish this will not require "opening protected areas" to developers but will require management schemes which area managers and administrators can implement and bring maximum sustained benefits to the people. I would like to suggest for your consideration a few future directions that might be appropriate for protected areas in the Indomalayan Realm:

- Given that most of the countries of the Realm are based on ancient civilizations which grew up in the major river basins where rice could be grown, it is apparent that most of the people have little cultural link with the tropical forest where most protected areas are found; indeed, most governments look on the forest- and hill-dwelling peoples as potential security threats which must be drawn into the mainstream culture as quickly as possible. It is therefore necessary to develop innovative education programmes at several levels: at the rural "aborigine" or "hill-tribe" level, to show the people that the central government does have their best interests at heart when it tries to encourage them to change some of their destructive land-use practises and when it establishes protected areas in lands they once considered theirs; at the urban level, to inform the decision-makers and the educated populace about the importance of the forested areas and the role that national parks and other categories of reserves are playing in ensuring a productive environment; and at the individual protected area level, to develop interesting and informative intepretive programmes so that visitors who may know virtually nothing about the forest will leave with a positive impression in their minds. A new corps of interpreters in protected areas is needed, and should be considered a high priority in any protected area management plan.

- Given that most countries in the realm are already implementing protected area systems, it is important to improve the flow of information between the different countries. While this already occurs to some extent on an *ad hoc* basis, I feel that information exchange should be better institutionalized. This may be something that IUCN could help with, in cooperation with FAO, Unesco, and UNEP. Information flow is too sluggish and needs to be speeded up considerably if it is to help the situation.

- The existing areas need to be managed more effectively. While there has been notable progress in management planning in such places as Indonesia, most of the Realm still lacks management plans for even the key protected areas. I would like to see a crash programme to develop a capacity in each protected area department to prepare and implement management plans for each protected area. This might require some external help at the beginning, perhaps in the form of workshops for training protected area planners. It would also stimulate governments to decide on the objectives for each of the protected areas. It seems clear that if we wait for policy direction from some amorphous leadership in a remote capital, we will need a lot of patience; better by far to get moving ourselves and inform the central government planners what protected areas can do to help implement national development plans, and what steps are required to ensure that protected areas make their maximum contribution. This is surely the way to stimulate an increased flow of budgetary support.

- It is also important to realistically assess the source of our land-abuse problems. When I look at why forests have been destroyed in Thailand, I quickly learn that the rate of forest destruction has been paralleled by a remarkable increase in the export of crops grown on once-forested land: maize, sugar cane, cassava, rubber. People are not clearing forest to grow their own food, they are clearing the forest to make money which contributes to the national economy and, by supplying the industrial countries in North America, Europe, and Eastern Asia, contributes to the productivity of the world. This process cannot stop, if we wish to maintain even the present level of political and social stability in the Realm. Rather, we must make the process work better. We must encourage the various steps being taken to rationalize land use and to make the best agricultural land more productive; we must stress the role of protected areas in ensuring the flow of vital irrigation water; we must ensure that protected areas are seen as a source of genetic material for the crop improvement programmes involving local fruits and vegetables. Almost as important as helping ourselves, we must ensure that the industrialized countries, who are making a fair profit when they sell us manufactured goods, pay us a fair price for producing the agricultural commodities which they require and which are destroying our forests; we might also reasonably expect them to assist our efforts to establish and maintain our protected areas which help ensure the environmental conditions which will permit us to continue supplying them with the needed agricultural commodities.

- Another measure which should be implemented immediately is the establishment of some demonstration "pilot projects" where integrated rural development is really leading to an improvement in human welfare. Such areas, to quote from our colleague from India, Dr. Samar Singh, would encompass forms of land use such as contour bunding of agricultural fields to prevent soil erosion, simple irrigation systems, breed improvement, pasture improvement, scientific grazing practices, fire-wood plantations, and energy alternatives; the pilot project should be carried out in each country in areas surrounding a national park or reserve, which would form the "core zone" for the rural development scheme. This would require the innovative administration and management I referred to earlier, in order to formulate an overall rural development policy in which protected areas form a crucial part. Such a pilot project would demonstrate that local people need not sacrifice anything to ensure the integrity of a national park; quite the opposite, for postive action in the buffer zone would bring real benefits to the people.

None of the future directions outlined above is particularly new or innovative, nor difficult to implement.

All that is required is the will of governments, the professionalism of protected area managers and planners, and a modicum of cooperation among ourselves so that lessons once learned need not be unnecessarily repeated.

Finally, I think it is important to note that each of the countries in the Indomalayan Realm differs significantly in their socio-economic and political structures. Since many of the problems in protected area management are non-technical problems, the varying social, political and economic settings may result in significantly different problems in protecting and managing similar environments in different countries or regions. The responses to my point-counterpoint issues definitely indicate that solutions must be developed and tested and implemented, utilizing future directions that conform to the local regional and national setting.

Acknowledgements

When Jeffrey A. McNeely, Executive Officer, CNNPA, requested me to prepare a paper for this Congress when we met at the 15th Session of the General Assembly of IUCN, Christchurch, New Zealand, in October 1981, I was rather reluctant to accept this difficult responsibility. After consultations with Warren Evans and Warren Brockelman both of whom I have the priviledge of having been closely associated with in the field of environmental management in Thailand, I decided to accept this task. Warren Evans especially has encouraged and inspired me throughout the preparation period. My deepest gratitude goes to them. Many people whose interests and dedication in conservation have made significant contributions to this paper. Without their straightforward views, valuable suggestions and experience in protected areas, it would have been very difficult to discuss future directions on a "realm-wide" basis. I received comments on the "point-counterpoint" issues listed in this paper from experts in India, Burma, Indonesia, Malaysia and Thailand. My sincere gratitude is extended to the following for their contributions: Hans Banziger, Warren Brockelman, Robert Dobias, J. Futardo, Mohd. Khan bin Momin Khan, W. J. van Liere, John MacKinnon, Clive Marsh, H.E. Emil Salim, Samar Singh, Jeffrey Sayer, and Gary Wiles.

Chapter 6
Indonesian Protected Areas

Keynote Address: The Balinese View of Nature

Ida Bagus Mantra
Governor of Bali

1. INTRODUCTION

The perception of an individual or society towards "something"—like nature or art—cannot be separated from the overall system of values and the perceptions of life adopted by society as a whole. In their daily life and living, the Balinese—95% of whom are Hindus—cling to and behave according to their beliefs in Hinduism. To a very large degree activities of Balinese people are a reflection of their religious spirit.

If we study this matter further, through the traditional lontar palm leaf scrolls, and the "Purwa Dresta" (Book of Traditions), it is evident that almost every aspect of life, including utilizing potential resources, is related to religion. In social life generally, Hindu believers in Bali adopt attitudes based on formulae which are in accordance with their beliefs and which are in harmony with their environment. One of these accepted formulae is the Panca Crada (five beliefs) which are:

- Belief in the existence of Brahman (only one God);
- belief in the existence of Atman (a soul in every living thing);
- belief in the existence of Kharmapala (reward to every deed);
- belief in the existence of Purnabawa (reincarnation of every soul); and
- belief in the existence of Moksa (eternal freedom).

Assured of these basic beliefs, the Balinese make them a starting point to face the challenges of life in this world.

A Balinese Hindu attempts to maintain a proper balance between harmony and conflict in every stage of life, so he expects that there will always be movement from one balance point to another one which is better and more in line with existing conditions and potentials. Eventually he will reach a strategic goal of his religion: *Moksa*. Simply speaking, Moksa is eternal freedom from suffering, which one can then enjoy at the end of one's life; it is attained through: unity between the soul (*Atman*) and the Spirit of the universe (*Paramatma*); and unification of the *Sarira* (physical body) of the human creature with the physical part of the universe. Therefore, it can be concluded that unity between human and universe is the final destination to be reached.

In line with that, all activities in Balinese life have become phases of effort in reaching the final destination. The Unity (afterward) can only be accomplished if, from the very beginning, there have been harmonious relationships between man as the "contents" on one side, and the universe as the "container" on the other. This relationship is considered the ideal to be maintained.

The religious mystical doctrines of the harmony between man and the universe, including *Tatwa* (Philosophy), *Susila* (Ethics), *Widya* (Awareness, Conscience), and *Rituil* (rituals) are all combined in a relationship which is harmonious and demonstrates an appropriate balance between man, nature and culture. Since harmony and balance are required, the doctrine is flexible and dynamic.

The implication of all this basic philosophy of Balinese Hinduism is a realization that man as a creature with tastes and senses will never be satisfied with his own self. Man is always searching, investigating, and trying to deeply understand the true meaning of life; and he keeps changing his environment, physically as well as socially, aiming at new cultural adaptations to his needs.

2. BALINESE PERCEPTION OF NATURE

Within the Balinese attitude toward life, there is an inseparable unity among men, between man and God, and between man and other living creatures. Therefore it is simply impossible to be able to describe one aspect without possessing a full understanding of the whole matter. If this unity is not taken into account there will be a greater chance to fail than to succeed in any endeavour; and even if it should succeed, it must still be admitted that such an effort would have not reached the depth of the real essence. This requirement for unity and harmony must be kept in mind as we discuss "Balinese Perceptions of Nature", which will require the ability to reduce something of an abstract character into something of a concrete one.

For example, the harmony between macro-cosmos (the universe) and micro-cosmos (human affairs) which is most desired and is to be passed on to the next generation, is similar to the harmony shown in the relationship between the embryo (*manik*) as "contents" and the womb (*cecupu*) as "container".

The embryo as the contents plays an active role, moving and developing itself, but within natural confinements of the space available, without damaging it or transgressing the restrictions of the womb as its container. On the other hand, the womb as the container willingly widens itself, always providing vital substances for nurturing the embryo as the contents; it takes good care of it, not too tightly holding it or acting like a prison. This, then, is analogous with humankind (micro-cosmos) as the contents, which plays an active role, changing and developing itself (in accordance with the teaching of Satwam, Rajas and Tamas), but which still has the responsibility to preserve the continuity of nature (macro-cosmos) as the container and the source of vital substances and good care.

To successfully provide continuity according to what is most desirable in the teachings of Hinduism, some principles are also outlined which can be used as basic guidance in the interior design of human buildings and settlements. Those mystical techniques are described in the old literatures of *Purwa Asta Bumi* (for design of construction) and *Asta Kosala Kosali Begawan Wisman Karma* (for architecture).

In the modern-day Bali Regional Plan, it is clearly emphasized that we should apply these traditional approaches in managing the living environment today—using humans as a starting point. Implementation is expected to be based on the philosophy *Tri Hita Karana* (three causes of righteousness) which should create the impression of true harmony—a harmony which comes from the integration of form, construction and design, maintenance, utilization, and ritual use.

This Balinese attitude and behaviour towards natural design and the living environment can still be seen in the present time in many parts of the island. It is seen, for example, in regional designs, or in village layout, in individual homes and other lving environments. There, at least in the Balinese view, it demonstrates harmony and integration of society's physical, sociocultural and socio-economic relationships, and shows a proper combination between man, nature and culture which gives balanced moves and yields. All this is but a reflection of the views of life Balinese have adopted, which come from the teachings of Hinduism.

3. CONCLUSION

Knowing and admiring nature is also one of the starting points to understand, to be aware of and to know oneself; and to realize that all happenings in the universe are simply creations of and controlled by God Almighty.

Belief in the teachings of Hinduism, which teaches that nature is the source of all beauties, wonders, and inspirations, are basic views of the Balinese. So too is their belief in "Oneness" between man and nature, resulting in their sense of responsibility as human beings (micro-cosmos) to maintain harmony between themselves and nature (macro-cosmos).

Indonesia's Network of Protected Areas

Effendy A. Sumardja, Harsono, and John MacKinnon
Directorate of Nature Conservation
Bogor, Indonesia

ABSTRACT. *This paper describes the criteria for different categories of Indonesian protected areas, including national parks, nature reserves, game reserves, recreation parks, hunting reserves, and protected forests. It defines the sorts of human activities which are permitted in each of the categories, and provides a list of areas that are suitable as national parks or equivalent status, both in the short term, the medium term and the long term. A total of 40 such areas are suggested for Indonesia. The threats to protected areas are also covered.*

1. INTRODUCTION

Indonesia lies in the Indomalayan and Oceanian Realms (Udvardy, 1975) and faces the same problems as most other tropical countries—unchecked population growth but continually decreasing biological productivity. As forest is cleared and converted to agriculture, the proportion of productivity which can be consumed by humans may increase but the total energy productivity certainly decreases and soils become degraded as they are stripped of their cover.

The Government has recognized the urgent need for conservation, based on the desire to promote the cultural and economic development of the Indonesian people in harmony with their natural environment. Government policy states that all forms of natural life and examples of all ecosystems within Indonesia must be preserved for the benefit of future generations. In particular, the air, water, soil, plants, fish and animals upon which people depend must be protected.

Conservation in Indonesia has been achieved through the maintenance of a system of protection forests to protect water sources and soils on steep or high land, the maintenance of a system of strict nature reserves

(*Cagar Alam*) and game reserves (*Suaka Margasatwa*) and the adoption of a number of laws and regulations controlling the exploitation of living resources including logging regulations, game laws, protected species laws and others.

Four types of reserves are currently defined under the Basic Forestry Law No. 5, 1967 of Indonesia:

1. *Nature Reserves* or 'Cagar Alam' (IUCN Category I) in which no management or human interference with the environment is permitted.
2. *Game Reserves* or 'Suaka Margasatwa' (IUCN Category IV: Managed Nature Reserves) in which the natural balance of the environment must not be disturbed but low levels of management, visitor use and utilization are permitted.
3. *Hunting Reserves* or 'Taman Buru' (IUCN Category VIII: Multiple Use Managed Area) are managed specifically for hunting and fishing.
4. *Recreation Parks* or 'Taman Wisata' (IUCN Category V: Protected Landscape) which are maintained for outdoor recreational purposes.

As of March 1982 the protected areas of Indonesia totalled 299 locations with an area of 11,267,540.06 ha. This reflects the wish of government to promote conservation in the country with the rapid increase of Protected Areas from 4 million ha in the first Five Year Development Plan (Repelita I) to 11.2 million ha in the third year of the Third Five Year Development Plan (Repelita III).

Fig. 1 shows the general criteria for different status of protected areas in Indonesia, and Fig. 2 indicates what types of activity are permitted or prohibited in

214

each type of reserve. Fig. 3 shows the distribution of reserves throughout Indonesia.

New legislation is currently in draft to cater for the establishment of National Parks and conservation buffer zones.

In the following sections of this paper we briefly outline how the protected areas are designed and the methods and criteria for selecting reserves; major weaknesses in the system of reserves and their management; and steps being taken to overcome the weaknesses.

2. NATIONAL PARK DEVELOPMENT

2.1 Criteria for national parks

The Indonesian Government has embarked on a programme to develop a system of National Parks in addition to the other categories of reserves. This programme is receiving budgetary priority for development. The first five National Parks in Indonesia—Gunung Leuser, Ujung Kulon, Gunung Gede-Pangrango, Baluran and Komodo—were declared in March 1980 (Sumardja, 1981).

While being managed for the enjoyment and benefit of the nation, national parks are also intended to protect and preserve the natural heritage of the nation. These Parks should conform to the international criteria outlined for national parks by IUCN, but: in the case of Indonesia, which is so richly endowed with extensive wild areas, it is possible to place further criteria to ensure that only the best areas are selected as national parks and to ensure that these will be of benefit to the local people.

a) *Size*: In Indonesia it is possible to raise the size criteria for National Parks to 100,000 ha for National Parks on the large islands: Sumatra, Kalimantan (Indonesian Borneo), Sulawesi and Irian Jaya; and 10,000 ha for the smaller islands: Maluku, Nusa Tenggara and Java.

b) *Conservation*: To ensure that National Parks serve an important conservation function, only areas scored as priority 1 in the National Conservation Plan should be considered.

c) *Recreation*: To achieve desired levels of recreational and educational use, National Parks should all be reasonably accessible from major population centres or tourist areas.

d) *Regional benefits*: National Parks must be clearly seen to be in the regional interest so that their establishment will constitute a benefit, rather than an added hardship, to the rural people living around them. Such benefits can include: preservation of high quality living environment; protection of water sources; establishment, where necessary, of buffer zones; job opportunities (working in the park or created by local tourism industry); special developments around parks, e.g. schools, road improvements, irrigation improvements; and in rare cases where it is necessary to translocate people further away from parks they must be given compensatory land holdings of at least the same value as their original lands.

2.2 National strategy for national park development

To afford even coverage of major biotypes and adequate access to the public, the area of National Parks on each island or island group should be roughly proportional to the area of wild habitat available while the number of national parks should be roughly proportional to the size of the population. Thus Java requires several smaller national parks while Irian requires few but very large Parks. It is hoped that at least part of a national park can be located within each province and this would pave the way for the possibility of establishing a separate Directorate for National Parks.

At present, however, the national parks will be administered by a special Sub-Directorate under the Directorate of Nature Conservation (PPA). Each Park will be managed by a "Kepala Sub-Balai" and eventually these may be upgraded to the level of "Balai".

National Parks are generally large and complex areas which are managed by dividing the parks into zones which define specific objectives for portions of the parks. The zones within those parks covered include various combinations of the following: strict nature reserves; managed nature reserves; recreation areas; and cultural areas. To the extent possible, facilities for visitors—especially overnight accommodation—will be kept on the park's periphery. In our case, a surrounding buffer zone which is devoted to agro-forestry activities has been added for the benefit of the local population and to lessen their dependence on the park or reserve itself (Sumardja, 1980b).

2.3 Provincial parks and other special categories

Several reserves which do not quite reach national park standards could be developed by local government because of their regional importance. Choice of criteria would be similar to those for national parks but size limits could be smaller, levels of conservation priority and human disturbance less strict and management controlled by local government rather than by PPA.

Especially important reserves may be recognized by international conventions, e.g. World Heritage Sites or ASEAN Heritage Reserves where development could be assisted by funds from the relevant convention secretariats. These categories could include important gene resource reserves which are too remote to warrant development as parks.

Another important category of reserves is the Biosphere Reserve identified under Unesco's Man and the Biosphere Programme. These are selected by the National MAB Committee, organized under the Natural Biological Institute (LBN) and chosen because of their importance for scientific research, education, monitoring and conservation. Such special status is useful for upgrading areas of high scientific or conservation importance even though they may be too affected by human influences to qualify as national parks. Several biosphere reserves already exist in Indonesia, e.g. Tanjung Puting, Siberut, Lore Lindu, Komodo and Gunung Gede-Pangrango, but others are planned, e.g. Apo Kayan.

2.4 Marine reserves

The enormous dependence of the Indonesian people on the sea and its resources explains why some 80% of the total population are found living in coastal regions. The inshore habitats are at the same time the most productive but also the most vulnerable marine habitats. Within Indonesia there is mounting evidence of resource decline due to over-exploitation or uncontrolled destructive influences, so it is now vital for Indonesia to establish a strategy for conservation of marine resources to be included in the Indonesia Protected Areas Network.

The strategy for conservation of marine resources should have three main components:

- Selection and establishment of a system of marine reserves to protect examples of all major ecotypes;
- Development of marine national parks and recreation areas to promote non-destructive uses of the sea and increase revenue from marine conservation; and
- Establishment and enforcement of an adequate system of laws and regulations controlling the use of marine resources.

The needs for establishment of marine reserves are determined by mapping of marine resources; this is currently in progress, e.g. mapping distributions of different coral reef types, sea grass beds, mangrove forests, turtle nesting areas, bird nesting islands, main vertebrate and crustacean fisheries and sea current patterns. On the basis of this data, conservation needs for habitat and species resources can be identified.

The coastal and marine parts of already-declared terrestrial reserves should be evaluated for their usefulness and where appropriate incorporated into the marine reserve system. The same guard force and infrastructure would serve both and it is good policy to have the landward side of marine reserves protected to prevent inland pollution and silting problems.

In order to fit conservation into the overall land-use policy for the province, to assess national conservation needs, to provide a basic conservation reference document to government planners, and to ensure that all major ecosystems are included in conservation areas, UNDP/FAO have assisted the government in the preparation of a National Conservation Plan for Indonesia (eight volumes) (MacKinnon, 1981 & 1982).

3. DESIGN OF THE RESERVE SYSTEM

Before selecting any areas for reserves it is necessary to have an overall design for planning a whole system of reserves. In recent years a great deal of scientific effort has gone into the theory and practice of reserve design (MacKinnon, 1982). Two main lines of research have been most helpful in designating reserves.

3.1 The theory of minimum size

Since making reserves larger than necessary would be a wasteful use of land resources, attempts have been made to identify the minimum size required to include viable populations of all essential component species in each ecotype. The theory depends on determining what is the minimum viable size for plant and animal populations, then measuring the densities of the rarest resident species and multiply up the area until sufficient land is included. There are two ways of estimating the minimum viable size of populations:

a) genetic and mathematical estimates of the numbers of breeding individuals needed to maintain natural levels of genetic heterozygosity for a given species' sex ratio and levels of outbreeding. Estimates for this vary widely but are usually numbered in thousands, with 5000 as a medium figure;

b) the second approach involves looking at populations on small islands to see what are numerically the smallest stable surviving isolated populations. Again figures in the order of 5000 are suggested.

If we use this figure of 5000 individuals as a rule of thumb, we would estimate that for rich lowland rainforest, where most tree species are present at densities of less than one tree per hectare, and many species at densities as low as 1 tree per 10 ha, to include viable populations of most tree species a reserve would need to be at least 50,000 ha for the richest habitat. Slightly smaller areas would suffice for less species-rich habitats because densities are higher. In a country the size of Indonesia, such large reserves could still in practice be established but it is not so easy to include all the native animals.

The rarest animals in the forest occur at densities even lower than 1 per 10 ha. Tigers, for instance, may be as rare as 1 per 20 sq km, i.e. a reserve of 10 million ha would be required to contain a viable tiger population. Clearly it is impractical and impossible to acquire such large areas as reserves, suggesting that active intervention by management authorities may be required to save these species.

3.2 Island biogeographic theory

This theory predicts that as land outside reserves is converted to other uses the isolated reserves will be cut off from similar habitat and will function in the same way as oceanic islands whose population dynamics have been well studied. We can therefore conclude that no reduced area of reserve can ultimately retain all its original species when it becomes isolated from similar habitat but that species numbers will fall due to increased levels of local extinctions. However, it is clear that the larger the reserve, the less severe these species losses will be and the slower the rate at which they will be lost.

It is evident, therefore, that substantially large areas must be declared reserves if they are to be expected to preserve the bulk of species in Indonesia. The Directorate General of Forestry have approved PPA's plans to expand the reserve system to reach a target of about 10% of the forest areas of the country.

Given this go-ahead and the knowledge that for successful conservation we need large reserves, we must still decide how best to apportion this allotted area. Should there be one huge reserve in the richest part of the richest island? Or should all islands be adequately covered? If all islands are to be covered, should there be one large reserve per island, or several smaller ones?

Government policy, states that all habitat types and all species must be protected. It is impossible to do this with just a few large reserves, so to implement Government policy there should be reserves in each distinct biogeographic zone and within each zone every major habitat type should be represented in a reserve.

In view of these facts the following model for the reserve system design has been selected for adoption as part of the Conservation Strategy.

- The major biogeographic divisions of Indonesia must be identified and a comprehensive system adopted as part of the Conservation Strategy.
- Within each biogeographical division, the main priority should be the establishment of large major ecosystem reserves selected to include a continuum of many habitat types including, if possible, the richest examples of those habitats.
- Smaller reserves should augment these major reserves by protecting habitat types not yet represented in the system or covering region variants of habitats already included.
- Small reserves are included in the system to provide necessary recreational, educational or research facilities or to protect unique sites of special interest or beauty.

- Some small reserves may be included to protect specific localized species or sites, e.g. *Rafflesia* reserves, nest areas of important species etc.

Even with an extensive system of reserves some extinction of species is probable within each biogeographic division. Species protected in several divisions have a better chance of overall survival, so preference should be given to protecting endemic species.

4. NATIONAL CONSERVATION PLAN

To guide the selection of new reserves the Government of Indonesia has produced, with FAO assistance, an eight-volume National Conservation Plan, including an introductory volume, six regional volumes, and a concluding volume on legislation, research, education, development, management plants, species conservation, etc.

Each regional volume has general introductory chapters for each island followed by specific chapters for each province. For use at the regional level planning it is sufficient to have Volume I, Volume VIII and the relevant regional Volume only.

The aims of regional volumes are to: aid in the selection and justification of new nature reserves and revision of existing reserves; identify conservation priorities among existing and proposed reserves; give direction to the future development of reserves; and provide a clear plan against which the conservation consequences of future developments can be assessed. (For instance if a hydroelectric dam is planned in area A, it can be seen from the Plans maps which areas of conservation interest and which natural habitats will be affected and from the text and tables what the conservation importance of such areas and habitats may be).

Priority Ratings are accorded to different areas of conservation interest. *Priority 1* is accorded to areas of major conservation importance whose omission from the reserve system would constitute major gaps in the habitat coverage. *Priority 2* is given to areas that would make useful additions to the reserve system by filling in minor gaps and duplicating habitats so that local extinctions of species in one reserve are not irreversible. *Priority 3* is accorded to areas of low conservation value. They generally should not be retained as national reserves, though some may still justify protection as provincial recreation areas or environmental protection forests.

Recommendations are included to guide future development. For instance, urgency for protection may depend more on current threats than on overall conservation priority. Similarly, suitability for tourist development is quite distinct from conservation importance.

Priority ratings and recommendations are based on three different types of evaluation:

1. *Genetic gain/loss values* are rough estimates of the probability that omission of a given area from the reserve system will result in extinction of a given number of genes. This index is for assessing the genetic value of ecosystem reserves, and is based on the combination of several factors:
   - The size of different habitat types contained in the area (habitat types are defined on physical, climatic and vegetation parameters);
   - The rarity of those habitat types (measured from maps of their original distribution);
   - The rate at which such habitat types are being lost (measured from maps of remaining climax vegetation made from satellite photos, aerial photos and land use maps);
   - The degree to which such habitat types are under-represented in the present reserve system;
   - The species richness of such habitats (measured in the field or taken from an island/habitat matrix of accumulated data); and
   - The degree of distinctiveness of the area concerned (based on known levels of island and local endemism).
2. *Socio-economic Justification.* This score lists the social and economic benefits—including beauty and aesthetics, research or recreational potential, protection of particular species of interest or value, unique examples of flora or geology, etc.—of protecting the area measured against its alternative land uses. As a general rule any area scoring half or more of the maximum possible points on this index can be strongly justified. Areas much below half should be regarded as unrealistic. All reserves, irrespective of their objectives must score adequately on this index.
3. *Management viability scores* determine whether a given area is viable as an isolated ecological unit and whether it can indeed be successfully managed. Again half of the maximum possible score is a rough guideline of reasonable viability, but ecological viability is not necessary for some small sites of interest such as recreation areas or artificially managed populations of particular species.

To summarize these three types of evaluation: Score 1 determines the genetic resources importance or desirability of acquiring an area as a reserve; Score 2 reflects whether the reserve is justifiable; and Score 3 reflects whether it will work. All three scores are considered in according priority ratings and recommendations.

5. CURRENT MANAGEMENT PROBLEMS

The major problems in the protected areas network can be divided into two categories: areas and ecosystems,

and management (Sumardja and McNeely, 1980). Areas which are still relatively poorly represented include Irian Jaya, Kalimantan, the Lesser Sundas, and Maluku. Ecosystems which are still under-represented include most notably tropical lowland rainforest, including the lowland dipterocarp forests which are so economically important to Indonesia. Although the islands of Indonesia are surrounded by sea, marine ecosystem conservation is only beginning been enacted.

5.1 Boundaries not clearly marked in the field

Boundaries should either follow clear natural boundaries such as rivers and shorelines or be marked by a clear path and regular concrete numbered marker posts. Occasional notice boards should announce what the boundary is.

5.2 Inadequate directives are given to guards as to their duties

This is caused by various factors such as lack of management plans; Regional Heads and even District Heads living too far away from and rarely visiting reserves; lack of directives from the Directorate or Balai office. Each officer should be issued with clear terms of reference and a written job description, which includes his routine duties.

5.3 Lack of discipline and responsibility

No one is going to perform assigned tasks unless they are: a) requested; b) checked upon; c) appreciated when performed; and d) reprimanded or penalized when not performed. There must be a clear line of penalty responsibility, from the Director to the lowest guard; any officer giving directives should be held responsible for ensuring that the instructions are carried out. Regular reporting and checking is the key to establishing such a line of responsibility.

5.4 Lack of reward and motivation

Guards receive low salaries. As they receive these salaries whether they perform their duties or not, there are no incentives for good performance so many occupy their time in other interests. It is recommended that project honoraria are allocated on a piece-rate basis for additional performance beyond the basic routine duties. Motivation can be further improved by the introduction of merit awards, travel (extra pay) and courses (upgrading).

5.5 Inadequate equipment

Guards must be provided with the minimum basic equipment if they are to operate effectively, e.g. uniforms (field and town), belts, hats, boots, capes, bush knife, pack, notebooks, malaria pills, etc., and if they are expected to live in remote locations away from their own villages they need adequate quarters. They must have access to field stores such as plastic roofing, paraffin stoves, cooking sets, binoculars, compasses and maps if they are to perform field work.

5.6 Inadequate training and briefing

All staff must attend suitable training programmes to ensure that they are competent to perform their duties. Senior staff training courses are run at Ciawi and Gunung Batu, but local courses should also be organized to teach lowest level guards: knowledge of the law and regulations relating to their reserve; knowledge of the main plants and animals in the reserve, their status and relevant game laws; familiarity with their area of duty particularly all paths and boundaries; map reading competence; trail and boundary maintenance; mode of patrolling; procedures of arrest and reporting abuses; guidance of visitors; and basic survey and inventory methods.

It is recommended that regional training courses (basic training and regular refresher courses) for guards should be run in all major reserves with guards attending from elsewhere in the region.

5.7 Lack of institutional back-up

Many guards are afraid to take action against, or report abuses by, village heads, police or military officials, senior family relatives, etc. for fear of reprisals. This can only be solved if the supervisors are firmly supportive in pressing prosecutions and generally backing their field staff. Why should a guard take physical risk (e.g., apprehending armed poachers) or make himself unpopular with local officials if there is no follow-up to his report? It is important that the supervisors seek strong support for the game laws from Governors and District Officers and cooperation from local police and military heads.

5.8 Lack of respect and sympathy for conservation goals by people around reserves

This can be partially improved by education and extension projects but however much people may agree with the need for reserves they will still abuse them if the benefits for so doing are large and the risks slight. The only solution is a firm protective force so that the risks of regular reserve abusers evading detection are small and the penalties serious.

6. THE FUTURE

A much-expanded system of National Parks and equivalent areas is planned. These areas fall into three categories:

a) Parks already declared and currently being developed;
b) those for which management plans are completed and which are suitable for middle term development; and
c) those areas identified as suitable as National Parks or equivalent status but for which management plans are not yet complete or whose priority for development is low. These areas are listed for long-term development, dependent on the availability of funds, completion of management plans and the success of the first Parks.

Fig. 4 lists the various reserves in each category and indicates which areas need the most development—the protective infrascture, buffer zones, recreational facilities or research facilities. The table also indicates if processing of legal boundaries is still needed before these areas can be declared.

Indonesia also aims to keep open the widest range of man's future development options by maintaining high genetic diversity. To achieve conservation, several programmes are needed which hopefully will relieve pressure on the protected areas network in Indonesia (MacKinnon, 1981).

a) *Protection of priority conservation areas must be stronger* than that for other forest categories, e.g. production and protection forests, so that if forest land is lost to irresistible land hunger the most valuable reserves are the last forests to go.
b) *Reaching population stability* is a great challenge; the sooner this is reached, the higher are the standards of living and quality of life that can be attained in Indonesia.
c) *Crops must be diversified* to give agriculture greater ecological and economic stability. Agricultural practice and technology must be improved, and better crop varieties must be found and propagated. Better use may be made of the unused sunlight falling on the sea, e.g. by draining areas of the Java Sea or devising floating agricultural rafts. Current wasteland must be brought back into agricultural production. Wasteful and destructive forms of agriculture must be brought under control; over-mechanization of agriculture is not ecologically effective and, in a country with a huge unemployed workforce, not economically necessary.
d) *Alternative energy sources must be found*, to take pressure off demands for firewood. Wind, tidal, thermal, solar and nuclear energy uses should be developed.

e) *Increased industrialization should be promoted*. Indonesia must earn more foreign capital by selling *manufactured goods* rather than rely on its dwindling natural resources, particularly in urban areas.

f) *Conservation ethics must be developed*. The Indonesian people have a long tradition of belief in the balance of nature, a love of beautiful forest, plants, scenic views, animals, and clean water. The importance of the "quality of life" must be stressed through formal education and introduced into the national philosophy, "Pancasila", with which it is very compatible.

g) *Well enforced environmental laws* are needed to control pollution of seas and waterways, air pollution, land toxification and radioactive leakage, protection of coral reefs and fringing mangroves, food quality controls, etc. Legal practice must be tightened up.

h) *Production forests must be seen as more than timber*. They must continue to produce all those products traditionally harvested from forests which are part of the Indonesian way of life, including: house poles, firewood, palm wood and hardwood for tool handles, etc., bamboos, rattans, barks, fibres, thatch leaves, wild honey and fruits, resins, fish and game meat, orchids, medicinal plants, etc.

To obtain maximal benefit over the longest timespan, harvesting must be done on a *sustained yield* basis. Most of this harvesting has traditionally been done for domestic use but there are several areas where potential for commercial and export harvesting is possible under suitable management. Examples include: game meat (deer, processed wild pig), skins (reptiles and some ungulates), pet birds (e.g. some parrots that are agricultural pests), primates for scientific research (macaques are agricultural pests in many areas), rattans, resins, some wild fruits, honey, etc.

Much research has already been carried out, particularly on maximizing timber yield from managed production forest, but little attention has been given to these minor forest products whose value through continuous harvest is often greater than that gained by a "once off" logging operation. Morover, such harvesting is ecologically sounder, environmentally less destructive and much better attuned to the socio-economic situation in Indonesia, providing year-round employment and benefitting a wider range of the rural population.

Hopefully, plantations in the future will be more like natural forests, i.e. will combine different types of timber trees, hardwoods and softwoods (upper canopy), and also have fruit trees (middle canopy), rattans, vines and wild animals in them to provide a much greater yield. Such forests should never be 'logged over' but single trees would be cut and removed when they fall naturally or are judged to be past prime reproductive age. A great deal of research and experimentation needs to be done in this field.

7. CONCLUSION

As land and forest resources become rarer, the reserve system will come under increasing need of socio-economic justification and also the individual reserves will become more like islands in their species composition, i.e. species diversity will drop toward new lowered equilibria. PPA will therefore 1) have to have much better information on species/area needs to justify its land holdings, and 2) have to employ increased levels of management to artificially maintain high levels of gene exchange between isolated reserves and undertake species specific management projects whenever reserves are found to be too small to support viable populations of important species.

The current reserve system is being planned on the pessimistic assumption that survival of wild species outside reserves cannot be relied upon, and that habitats outside reserves will largely be converted or destroyed. If management of permanent production and protection forests outside reserves is radically improved, it is quite possible that such pessimism is unwarranted and smaller reserves as core areas surrounded by wide production forest buffer zones would be adequate to achieve conservation goals. PPA currently holds larger areas of montane forests in reserves than are probably needed. So long as the only alternative use for these areas is protection forest, this is justifiable but the need for protection forests could be seriously challenged if production forestry could be done in a way which did not lead to erosion and reduced water absorption. It is also possible that other alternative ground cover may be found for important catchment areas that is as efficient as natural forest.

The long term view for conservation in Indonesia, however, is much more promising than in many other tropical countries. The country is large, the natural resources of tremendous value, the climate favourable, the seas rich, the soils, especially in volcanic areas, fertile, and the population is active, intelligent, inventive, law-abiding and keen to maintain high living standards.

Figure 1: General Criteria for Different Protected Areas

Taman Nasional (National Park) — Large relatively undisturbed areas of outstanding natural value with high conservation importance, high recreation potential, of easy access to visitors and clearly of benefit to the region.

Cagar Alam (Nature Reserve) — Generally small undisturbed fragile habitats of high conservation importance, unique natural sites, homes of particular rare species, etc. Areas requiring strict protection.

Suaka Margasatwa (Game Reserve) — Generally medium or large areas of relatively undisturbed stable habitats of moderate to high conservation importance.

Taman Wisata (Recreation Park) — Small natural or landscaped area or site of attractive or interesting aspect of easy access for visitors where conservation value is low or not threatened by visitor activities and recreation oriented management.

Taman Buru (Hunting Reserve) — Medium or large-sized natural or semi-natural habitats with game hunting potential, i.e. large enough populations of permitted game species (pigs, deer, wild cattle, fish, etc.) where demand for hunting facilities exists and of easy access to would-be hunters. Such reserves should be of low conservation importance or have conservation values that are not threatened by the hunting/fishing activities.

Hutan Lindung (Protection Forest) — Medium to large areas of natural or planted forested land on steep, high, erodable, rainwashed lands where forest cover is essential to protect important catchment areas and prevent landslips and erosion but where conservation priorities are not so high as to justify reserve status.

Figure 2. Activities Permitted Prohibited (X) in Different Categories of Protected Area

	Taman Nasional (according to zones)	Cagar Alam	Suaka Margasatwa	Taman Wisata	Taman Buru	Extralimital Buffer Zones	Protection Forests
Growing Food Crops	X	X	X	X	X	X	X
Growing Tree Crops	X	X	X				
Human Settlement	X	X	X	X	X	X	X
Commercial Logging	X	X	X	X	X	X	X
Collecting herbs and firewood	X	X		X	X		
Hunting	X	X	X	X		X	
Fishing		X	X	X			
Camping		X					
Scientific Collecting with permit		X					
Active Habitat Management		X					
Non-exotic Introduction		X					
Collecting rattan + poles with permit	X	X	X	X			
Mineral Exploration		X		X			
Wildlife Control		X					
Visitor use		X					
Exotic Introductions	X	X	X		X		

Figure 3. Development of Natural Reserves in Indonesia as of December 1981

Location	Area (million ha)	% Forest	% Reserves	Planned additions
Sumatra	47.4	57	5.6	modest
Java and Bali	13.8	9	3.0	modest
Kalimantan	53.9	60	4.7	modest
Sulawesi	18.9	62	6.0	modest
Nusa Tenggara	6.8	24	2.8	extensive
Maluku	7.5	76	0.9	extensive
Irian Jaya	42.2	94	9.7	extensive
TOTAL	190.5	62	5.9	c 4.6

Figure 4.

A. AREAS ALREADY DECLARED AS NATIONAL PARKS AND CURRENTLY UNDER DEVELOPMENT

No. Name	Area/ha	Province(s)	Protection	Recreation	Research	Buffer Zone	Protection status processed
1. Gn. Leuser NP	964,000	Aceh/N. Sumatra	high	moderate	high	high	yes
2. Ujung Kulon NP×	60,000	West Java	moderate	high	moderate	moderate	yes
3. Gn. Gede-Pangrango NP	15,000	West Java	moderate	high	moderate	moderate	yes
4. Baluran NP×	25,500	East Java	moderate	high	low	low	yes
5. Komodo NP×	59,000	E. Nusa Tenggara	low	high	low	low	yes

B. AREAS IDENTIFIED AS SUITABLE FOR MIDDLE TERM DEVELOPMENT AS NATIONAL PARKS (NP) OR EQUIVALENT

No. Name	Area/ha	Province(s)	Protection	Recreation	Research	Buffer Zone	Legal status processed
1. Bromo-Tengger NP	67,600	East Java	moderate	high	low	moderate	part
2. Lore Lindu NP	200,000	C. Sulawesi	moderate	moderate	moderate	low	most
3. Kutai KPA×	200,000	E. Kalimantan	high	low	high	low	yes
4. Bali Barat NP×	90,000	Bali	high	high	low	moderate	part
5. Sumatera Selatan I (Barisan Selatan NP)	356,800	Lampung/Bengkulu	high	low	high	high	yes
6. Meru Betiri NP×	50,000	E. Kalimantan	moderate	moderate	low	moderate	yes
7. Dumoga-Bone NP	300,000	N. Sulawesi	high	moderate	moderate	high	yes
8. Manusela NP×	180,000	Maluku	low	low	moderate	low	part
9. Tg. Puting NP×	305,000	C. Kalimantan	moderate	low	high	high	yes
10. G. Kerinci-Seblat NP	1,600,000	Bengkulu/S. Sumatra	high	moderate	high	high	part
11. Pulau Seribu NP	P.M.	West Java	moderate	high	moderate	high	no

Figure 4 (cont).

C. AREAS IDENTIFIED AS SUITABLE FOR LONG TERM DEVELOPMENT AS NATIONAL PARKS (NP) OR EQUIVALENT STATUS (KPA) (1989–94)

No.	Name	Area/ha	Province(s)	Development needs				Protection status processed
				Protection	Recreation	Research	Buffer Zone	
1.	P. Siberut NP˟	150,000	W. Sumatra	low	moderate	high	low	part
2.	Berbak NP˟	190,000	Jambi	high	low	moderate	low	yes
3.	Way Kambas KPA˟	123,500	Lampung	high	moderate	low	low	yes
4.	Ijen NP	100,000	East Java	moderate	moderate	low	high	yes
5.	Yang NP	400,000	East Java	moderate	moderate	low	low	part
6.	Karimun Jawa KPA (Marine)	P.M.	Central Java	moderate	moderate	low	low	no
7.	Merapi-Merbabu NP	200,000	Central Java	moderate	low	low	low	part
8.	Gn. Palung NP˟	100,000	W. Kalimantan	moderate	moderate	moderate	moderate	part
9.	S. Kayan-Mentarang (Ulu Malinau portion) KPA	400,000	E. Kalimantan	low	low	low	low	part
10.	Gn. Rinjani NP	125,000	W. Nusa Tenggara	low	moderate	low	low	part
11.	Tangkoko-Dua Saudara KPA˟	8,867	N. Sulawesi	low	moderate	low	low	yes
12.	Morawali NP˟	160,000	C. Sulawesi	low	low	moderate	low	yes
13.	Lolobata NP	191,000	Maluku	moderate	low	moderate	moderate	no
14.	Aru MP˟	130,000	Maluku	low	low	moderate	low	part
15.	P. Dolok KPA˟	600,000	Irian Jaya	moderate	low	low	moderate	yes
16.	Wasur KPA˟	120,000	Irian Jaya	high	moderate	low	moderate	yes
17.	Gn. Lorentz NP˟	1,675,000	Irian Jaya	low	moderate	high	low	yes
18.	Foja-Mamberamo NP˟	1,442,500	Irian Jaya	low	moderate	high	low	no
19.	Teluk Cenderawasih NP (Marine)	P.M.	Irian Jaya	low	moderate	low	low	no
20.	Sangkulirang NP	100,000	E. Kalimantan	low	moderate	high	low	no
21.	Siak Kecil-Duri KPA	100,000	Riau	high	moderate	high	high	no
22.	Bukit Raya NP	400,000	C/W. Kalimantan	moderate	low	moderate	low	part
23.	Rawa Opa KPA˟	200,000	SE Sulawesi	high	low	high	moderate	part
24.	Batimurung-Leang-leang KPA	1,000	S. Sulawesi	moderate	high	low	low	yes

Note: Reserves marked with x have additional marine habitats.

Nature Conservation and Rice Production in the Dumoga Area, North Sulawesi, Indonesia

Effendy A. Sumardja, Tarmudji, and Jan Wind
Directorate of Nature Conservation
Bogor, Indonesia

ABSTRACT. *This paper describes the proposed Dumoga-Bone National Park, located in the middle of the northern arm of Sulawesi. Shaped like a large U, the reserve surrounds the Dumoga Valley irrigation scheme, funded by the World Bank. Concern about possible deforestation of the Dumoga watershed resulted in an agreement between the Government of Indonesia and the World Bank to provide appropriate financial support to develop and protect the water catchment area proposed as the Dumoga-Bone National Park, one of the first instances in Indonesia where a major development funding agency fully recognized protected area conservation as an integral part of development. The paper discusses the problems encountered, the strategy adopted to solve the problems, and the results obtained to date.*

1. INTRODUCTION

The proposed Dumoga-Bone National Park is located in the middle of the northern arm of the island of Sulawesi (Celebes) and consists of some 3,000 sq km of primary tropical rainforest with an altitude range of 100-2000 m. The conservation history is of very recent date (Rodenburg and Palete, 1981); the first identification survey was made in 1977 by Dr John MacKinnon (WWF) and PPA North Sulawesi, with the area becoming established as a reserve in 1979-80.

The reserve stretches in an east-west direction along the arm and extends almost from north coast to south coast at some places. At the eastern end, the Dumoga Valley is bounded on three sides by the reserve and at the western end the Bone valley opens onto the Gorontalo plains. This case study will restrict discussion to the Dumoga Valley area and the surrounding Dumoga water catchment section of the reserve.

The development of the area is very closely related to the World Bank funding of the Dumoga Valley Irrigation Schemes. Concern about the deforestation of the watershed area in the Dumoga basin culminated in an agreement between the government of Indonesia and the World Bank to give considerable financial support toward the development and protection of the water catchment area proposed as the Dumoga-Bone National Park. This is one of the first instances where a major development funding agency has fully recognized conservation as an integral part of development.

The following sections discuss the problems encountered, the values of concern and the strategy put forward to solve the problems while safeguarding the natural values of the reserve, and finally the results obtained so far.

2. PROBLEM STATEMENT

Problems encountered to date include:

- Initial deterioration of Dumoga forest environment through ecologically unsound land-use;
- Negative impacts of present land-use on the fertile Dumoga Valley and its productive capacity for rice and other agricultural produce, and the welfare of the different social groups including transmigrants from Bali and Java (both spontaneous and organized), migrants from neighbouring areas and the original inhabitants of the valley; and
- Threats to the wildlife of Sulawesi and its unique forms occurring in the northern part of the island.

3. BACKGROUND

The Dumoga Valley and its surroundings were largely forest-covered until some 20 years ago, apart from a few settlements along the main rivers Ongkak, Dumoga and Pusian. Between 1940 and 1945 some small scale migration occurred with rice-field farmers moving in from the Tondano area, Minahasa region, because of heavy pressure on the few existing rice-field areas in that region.

The population in 1961 amounted to 8,000 people (i.e. more than 1500 families), the local inhabitants of the Mongondow tribe being dependent on shifting agriculture and coconut plantations. Population growth was gradual until 1963/1964 when the first transmigrants (594 families) were moved from Bali because of the eruption of the Gunung Agung volcano. Their impact on population growth was substantial as a number of relatives and neighbours followed them. As a result the population more than doubled in the decade 1961-1971.

With a valley area of some 30,000 ha and a population of only 17,827 people there is, as yet, no concern about over-population. The government has plans to transmigrate more people and to develop large irrigation schemes for rice cultivation in the valley, including the Kosinggolan Scheme (already started in 1967) and the Toraut Scheme and several small-scale (so-called *Sederhana*) Schemes.

From 1971 to 1974 some 4500 people from Java and Bali were transmigrated and again many others followed them spontaneously (exact data about numbers not available). Other large scale developments in the last ten years (1971-1981) include:

- Construction of the Dumoga Valley highway (in the period 1974-1976);
- Further construction of the Kosinggolan Irrigation Scheme; official opening of the weir by the President of Indonesia at the end of 1975;
- World Bank involvement to upgrade the scheme, starting in 1980. This project should be completed in 1983, and at present the primary and secondary canals are almost ready. The tertiaries are under construction and many roads have been developed.
- Construction, with World Bank funding, of the large Toraut Irrigation Scheme, starting in 1981; the irrigation system needed to develop some 7000 ha of rice-fields should be completed by 1985.

The effects of these developments on land-use include the following:

- The valley, almost forest-covered up to 20 years ago, is now totally opened up, as are parts of the steep hillsides at the border of the valley.
- The watershed area (approximately 20,500 ha) of the Kosinggolan Scheme has been heavily opened up for agriculture with more than 10% of the for-

est-cover gone, including 4% in the park area. Because of this there is insufficient water to irrigate 3000 ha of rice-fields, let alone the 5000 ha planned for the area. Siltation of the waterstorage lake above the weir is increasing (without proper monitoring, the data is inexact).

- The watershed area of the Toraut Scheme (approximately 25,000 ha) has suffered only slight damage with 0.8% of the forest opened up above the weir.
- The watershed forest in the valleys of the feeder rivers has been damaged at many places in both the Kosinggolan and the Toraut area. The potential to use these river systems for additional water has now been greatly lowered and siltation of the canals is more likely to occur due to the ongoing process of encroachment onto the hillsides.

Two groups of people are mainly responsible for the problems: the original inhabitants, and the spontaneous migrants from neighbouring areas. The original inhabitants sold their valley land to the transmigrants and moved into the forest areas to practise their traditional land use of shifting agriculture including the opening of forest and extensive forms of planting of annual crops such as upland rice, corn, and cassava. Some of their recent settlements occur several kilometres inside the forest at strategic fertile locations.

The encroachment of the spontaneous migrants from the Minahasa and Mongondow area is, on the other hand, of a much higher magnitude, as their numbers are much higher. Their share of the present valley population is estimated to be more than 55%, compared with only 11% ten years ago. Many of the spontaneous migrants are by tradition shifting cultivators, though some are cashcrop farmers, both looking for 'dry' land, often to be found at the forest (i.e., the Park) borders.

The construction of the Dumoga Valley Highway clearly initiated this spontaneous migration (the rapid population increase since 1974-1976 coincides with the completion of the main road). Maintenance roads built along the canals bordering the valley during the last five years greatly facilitated access to the forest/Park borders and accelerated encroachment of the catchment area.

Forest protection programmes for the area began in June 1980 when the Directorate of Nature Conservation, funded by the World Bank "Dumoga Watershed Protection Project", began to recruit forest guards and build guardposts. In July 1980 a WWF Consultant was recruited with the responsibility for producing a management plan for the Dumoga Reserve (Rodenburg and Palete, 1981).

Forest boundaries at the valley borders were established as late as 1979/1980 by the Forestry Service and Forestry Planning. A large stretch of the 100 km valley border/park boundary was put too far uphill under pressure from the local village people and village chiefs. With few forest guards and an unsuitable boundary, the movement of some 300-400 families into the Park could not be prevented.

4. CONSTRAINTS

The following are the main constraints at present:

- Apart from generally outlined rice-field areas and detailed plans for the construction of irrigation systems and road infrastructures, a land use plan for the valley and surrounding does not yet exist.
- All valley land is under ownership, including a substantial number of absentee landlords. Resettlement of people within the valley is assumed impossible.
- Some of the people legally occupying the foothill areas outside the park are reluctant to move out. They cannot be blamed for a wrong boundary alignment.
- A small area inside the park has been planted with cashcrops such as cloves and coconut. Removal by force will probably encounter heavy resistance. Note: Cashcrops outside the park in areas that should be included under watershed protection as a buffer zone to the park will be left and destruction or replanting will not be needed.
- Intensification of land use in the valley is only partly successful. Transmigrants are most advanced and have received much attention from the government. Local people used to traditional extensive forms of land use are, however, in need of guidance to make more intensive use of their lands. Transmigrants live in separate villages and thus have little influence upon the land use practises of other inhabitants of the valley.
- The population is almost 100% agriculture-oriented and other jobs are hardly available. People with higher education in general leave the area.

5. INTERVENTION

As mentioned above, the World Bank concluded there was a need for an integrated approach of planning and development and extended the loan agreement with the government to the funding of the Dumoga Watershed Protection Project under WWF Consultancy and under the responsibility of PPA. This loan includes US$ 700,000 for a three year development period.

A management plan prepared under this project gives direction to the development process. Funds were used to recruit guards, to build guardposts, etc., and to patrol boundaries as well as to prevent further encroachment.

The government has decided to revise the boundary to establish a buffer zone at the border of the valley at the base of the foothills. The government has also taken steps to rehabilitate the watershed forest through the replanting of denuded hillsides and is planning to resettle the people who encroached the Park area at locations outside of the valley. A land use plan by the government is to be executed by the local university; this plan includes the whole valley area outside of the Park.

The government gives high priority to the protection of the Dumoga-Bone area and agreed to develop it into a National Park. This will guarantee that substantial funds will become available for further development under the Fourth Five Year Development Plan.

The total area of the National Park will be approximately 300,000 ha, large enough to guarantee the survival of many endemic species of Sulawesi island and some specific forms endemic to this northern part of the island.

6. RESULTS TO DATE

The Indonesian Government, PPA, and the local government have initiated an integrated approach to tackle the encountered problems of environmental deterioration, watershed forest cutting, and threatened wildlife.

This has led to a large investment under World Bank Loan to fund the protection of the Dumoga watershed, initially to guarantee sufficient and regular water supply for the irrigation development schemes and, in a second stage, to extend the efforts to develop a National Park of some 300,000 ha including the Dumoga and Bone areas. Additional projects anticipated to be funded by the government include the establishment of a Regional Nature Conservation Training School, a Field Research Station and facilities for recreation and tourism.

Some 35 guards have been recruited in the two-year-old project, and a headquarters complex is being built which includes an office, education centre, staff house and a guesthouse. Five guardposts are being built. The budget includes an allocation to revise the major part of the Dumoga Valley park boundary. This work is being implemented.

The government is finalising plans for the resettlement of the people who encroached the Park. It is anticipated that funds will be more than sufficient to resettle all the people. Law-enforcement action by the local government and patrolling by PPA has halted further encroachment in a number of areas.

7. CONCLUSIONS

One effect of improving accessibility through building of the Dumoga valley highway and the maintenance roads along irrigation canals is accelerated population influx. Such impact should have been anticipated before construction started and necessary actions planned beforehand. One of the actions should be an advance programme of forest protection before people start to encroach upon forest areas. Encroachment is hard to stop and damage of watershed forest may take several decades to recover. A programme for replanting, resettlement and law-enforcement is very costly and also very frustrating for the local people involved.

Gradual growth and small scale development is preferable to rapid development under large scale investment projects if a policy of development based on ecological principles is to be followed. In this context it may also be concluded that the small scale, *Sederhana* Irrigation Development Schemes, set up in close cooperation with local farmers, has shown a high success rate, and a relatively low cost with only minor forms of negative impact upon the environment.

Extension work to speed up to land use intensification especially among the original inhabitants and traditional shifting cultivators is much needed.

Land registration may well be a major instrument in regulating land use, spontaneous migration, and absentee land-ownership. The programme should especially be applied to land areas on the border of reserves/parks, buffer zones and enclaves in the reserves.

Population density projections should be based upon potential and existing cultivable areas and not include protected forest areas, reserves, and parks. An area may in fact already be under heavy population pressure while population density figures do not show this, as a large area of forest is included as "living" space. This may lead to wrong government decisions.

Indonesia's Experience in Training Protected Areas Personnel

H.M. Duryat and L.P. van Lavieren
School of Environmental Conservation Management (Ciawi)
Bogor, Indonesia

ABSTRACT. *This paper describes the methods being used to train personnel to manage the greatly expanded protected area system of Indonesia, describing the training course for field level managers at the School of Environmental Conservation Management located at Ciawi in West Java. It describes the personnel structure of the Directorate of Nature Conservation and shows how the curriculum of the school is related to the personnel needs of the Directorate. It discusses some of the problems that have been faced, including financing, the value of the diploma, participation from other institutions, marine conservation and regionalization. It is hoped that the school will become increasingly regional in the future, provided that a number of basic issues can be successfully addressed before proceeding with such an expansion.*

1. INTRODUCTION

A start was made on establishing a system of nature reserves in Indonesia prior to independence, under the protection and management of the Botanical Gardens at Bogor. Since 1957 nature conservation has come under the umbrella of the Forestry Department and in 1971 a separate Directorate of Nature Conservation was created within this department. As a result, the majority of the staff in charge of the management of nature reserves have been recruited from officers with a forestry education.

Although these foresters have contributed substantially to the establishment and maintenance of nature reserves in Indonesia, in many ways forestry training does not cover the multifarious aspects of nature conservation and wildlife management. Apart from further training, most Indonesian foresters need to re-orient their approach toward a non-consumptive use of tropical primeval forests.

In Indonesia today a total of 11.2 million ha of land and sea have been established for nature reserves, a four-fold increase over the past eight years. The planning, development and management of such a huge area (about 3.5 times the size of the Netherlands) requires large numbers of properly trained personnel at various levels of responsibility.

Recently, a number of biologists and ecologists have been trained at Indonesian universities but, as with most university courses, their training has been theoretical rather than aimed at solving practical problems encountered in managing nature reserves. The day-to-day management of protected areas is in fact the task of a highly-trained professional. This paper reports on a training course for protected area managers begun in 1978 at the School of Environmental Conservation Management, Ciawi, West Java. It discusses our experiences so far, outlines the constraints encountered and suggests future steps toward regional training cooperation in South-East Asia.

2. MANPOWER PLANNING

In general three categories of personnel for management of protected areas can be identified. At the highest level are directors and subdirectors and university-trained biologists, ecologists and other specialists. Park planning, wildlife and habitat management, outdoor recreation and visitor management have attained the status of separate disciplines at many universities in both temperate and tropical regions of the world; the main tasks of these specialists are to conduct in-depth ecological and biological studies, to inventory and survey the protected ecosystems, to study the behaviour, needs and impact of visitors, to develop methods and techniques for the management of wildlife and habitat, to evolve a programme of conservation education and interpretation, to design and supervise the construction of the area's infrastructure, and to establish laws and regulations. In most countries the planning, establishment and management of reserves has now become such a complex issue that only a team of specialists can do the job properly. Most conservation departments in developing countries cannot afford to employ many specialists on a full-time basis and instead enlist the cooperation of universities and other research institutions.

The second category of personnel includes intermediate level staff, such as park superintendents and wildlife wardens. Their principal task is the supervision and implementation of management programmes and the day-to-day running of the areas as a recreational site for visitors. Proper training of intermediate level staff is crucial for the success of conservation programmes; not only are they the first to be aware of undesireable biological and ecological changes, encroachments and infringements, they must also be able to analyze the causes and to implement measures for solving problems as they arise.

The third category of personnel is the subordinate staff, including guards, scouts and guides. Their tasks are many and various and may include law enforcement activities and visitor control but also such duties as making inventories or routine observations of wildlife and habitat, assisting research scientists and the control of problem animals. Their training is usually organized in brief (1 to 3 months) in-service courses in the field.

Manpower planning has become a matter of urgent concern in the Directorate of Nature Conservation (PPA) in Indonesia. The area of reserves and parks is to be expanded further during the forthcoming Five Year Plan, starting in April 1983, to around 20 million ha. Many of the existing and newly-established reserves include important catchment areas and play a vital role in the well-being of the low-income rural population of Indonesia; the management of these reserves must be improved and intensified as many are under mounting pressure from human encroachment (Indonesia's 1981 population of 154 million is expected to increase to 200-230 million by 2000).

In view of the expected expansion of its responsibilities, PPA will require an increasing number of staff at all levels. An assessment of required manpower was made in 1981 for both PPA-headquarters in Bogor and for staffing the regional units (Daryadi, 1981). A summary of PPA's future staff requirements is given in Table 1.

3. SCHOOL OF ENVIRONMENTAL CONSERVATION MANAGEMENT

The School of Environmental Conservation Management was established in 1978 as a joint endeavour between the governments of Indonesia (Ministry of Agriculture, Agency for Agricultural Education, Training and Extension) and the Netherlands (Ministry of Foreign Affairs, Directorate General of International Cooperation). The School is located in Ciawi, West Java. The principal objectives of the School are to train the intermediate level personnel—"Kepala Balai" and "Kepala Sub-Balai" for the Directorate of Nature Conservation for Indonesia. Since its creation, the school has enjoyed general financial, technical and moral support from both the Indonesian and the Netherlands governments. The Indonesian contribution includes all running costs, buildings and facilities, catering and lodging of the participants, teaching materials, uniforms and salaries and allowances for a number of local instructors, and adequate supporting and administrative staff. The Netherlands contribution includes four qualified consultant-instructors, vehicles, large amounts of field and office equipment, and a number of fellowships.

The initial target as projected in the Schedule of Operations was to train a total of 240 intermediate level staff by 1983, but this has now been revised in view of the manpower planning document outlined above (see Table 1).

4. CURRICULUM

Intermediate level personnel involved in the management of nature reserves should be able to understand the complexity and functioning of ecosystems and to monitor and evaluate conditions and trends in components of the system. They should be able to evaluate the impact of human activities on the ecosystem and to take measures to curb undesireable changes. This requires a basic knowledge of biology, ecology, soil and water conservation and habitat and wildlife management techniques.

Valuable supplementary courses such as a routine repair and maintenance of equipment (vehicles, water-pumps, generators, outboard engines etc.), personnel management and office routine are included in the curriculum. Finally, a number of complementary courses such as First Aid, Photography and Survival Techniques are deemed important. The training course at Ciawi identified background sciences, management techniques and supporting subjects; coefficients of importance are given below.

1) Highest coefficient: Management techniques
   Habitat management
   Wildlife management
   Management of Conservation Areas

2) Medium coefficient: Scientific background
   Biology and Natural History
   Ecology
   Conservation Education and Intepretation
3) Lowest coefficient: Supporting subjects
   Introduction to environment conservation
   Conservation Law
   Economic aspects of environmental
     conservation
   Taxidermy
   Map reading
   Control of firearms
   Mechanics (simple)
   Office routine
   Personnel management
4) Extra-curricular subjects
   First aid
   Survival techniques
   Photography
   Zoo management
   Snorkeling, diving
   Sports
   English

The course is of 9 to 10 months duration, comprising 20 weeks of classroom instruction (544 hours lectures and 102 hours demonstrations and laboratory work) and 15 weeks of fieldwork in various parks and reserves in Java, Bali and southern Sumatra. Usually, fieldwork alternates with brief periods at the School preparing reports, analyzing data and getting ready for the next field trip. Emphasis is put on the practical application of class and field instruction.

During the first semester (October-March), a number of one- or two-day excursions to relevant institutes, museums, botanical gardens and zoos are organized. Extra-curricular activites include lectures by guest speakers and specialists in the field of environmental conservation and other subjects, slide programmes and films and also students' participation in the preparation and planning of intepretive programmes, guide-books, etc.

4.1 Ciawi's achievements

Although no attempt has been made to evaluate the effects of the training courses so far given at Ciawi, without doubt the School has contributed to the improvement of the management of protected areas in Indonesia. More important, the School has boosted the image of PPA and the status of its personnel. Already the management of most important parks and reserves throughout Indonesia is now planned, implemented and supervised by Ciawi graduates.

Four training courses has been completed since October 1978; total of 124 Indonesian and 3 foreign participants have attended the courses to date.

From experience we have learned that there are considerable problems of organization in dealing with groups of over 30 students in one class; moreover, the transfer of knowledge and skills, particularly during field exercises, becomes less satisfactory when the group size exceeds 30. At present, dormitory and catering facilities at the Ciawi School are limited to 40 participants, but we feel that the ideal number of participants for each course is 30.

4.2 Constraints

4.2.1. Timing and organization. Initially, the Ciawi School aimed at upgrading the skill of personnel of PPA already in service. This has caused certain constraints in the timing and organization of the course. The participants had to be released from PPA duties for the duration of the course. In many cases they were also separated from their families for a long period of time which tended to undermine morale.

4.2.2. Heterogeneity. A problem encountered in most in-service training is the range of experience of the participants. Participants in the first four courses at Ciawi varied from freshly-trained university graduates with little or no field experience to very experienced officers a few years away from retirement. Lack of homogeneity in previous education and experience of the candidates is one of the greatest handicaps to the effectiveness of training courses. However, it is almost impossible to have all participants with the same level of education and experience when the course is given to personnel already in service. Similar problems have been encountered at both African colleges, and a partial solution is to introduce an age limit, e.g. in Garoua, since 1978, participants must be between 17 and 30 years of age. Another solution would be to recruit candidates directly from among high school or university graduates.

For these direct-recruits, the diploma of the Ciawi School could then become a prerequisite for entering PPA's service. It is expected that this will happen in the near future.

4.2.3. Financing. It is a fortunate situation that until now the Ciawi School has known little or no financial constraints. However, a nine to ten months training course involving five to six field trips of 7 to 14 days duration is a costly enterprise. Very few countries can afford to maintain special training institutions for protected area personnel. In fact, both African Schools would not have operated successfully without generous financial and technical support from both international and national public and private organizations. Indonesia is investing an amount of US $ 7,000 for each Ciawi graduate, not including the salaries of participants and staff. If the standard of the course is to be maintained, particularly the realization of the targeted number of fieldwork days, it may be necessary to apply for external financial assistance or to call for international or regional cooperation.

4.2.4. Language of instruction. In view of the expected future regional role of the School, English was chosen as the language of instructions. Most hand-outs, documents and library books are in English, but the command of the English language of most participants proved inadequate. For this reason, a five-week refresher course in English is organized at the beginning of the school year, i.e. during September and early October. The results of these courses are rather disappointing. Many participants do not fully realize the necessity of having a good command of English and miss part of the instruction. Most Indonesian instructors teach in Bahasa Indonesia. So far this has not caused major problems among the foreign participants as these were all from Malaysia. However, when countries other than Indonesia and Malaysia are going to use the Ciawi School, *all* instruction and teaching materials will have to be in English. This may present problems for a number of local staff members.

5. FUTURE DEVELOPMENTS

5.1 New recruits

When direct recruitment from school leavers is implemented, the minimum requirements for admission should be clearly defined; applicants should have passed sixth level education or hold an equivalent qualification, be physically fit, show a keen interest in nature conservation, have a good work incentive and show initiative. They should also be prepared to fulfil their future duties by living in remote areas, often having to work away from their families under arduous conditions.

5.2 Value of the diploma

The diploma of the School should be a qualification for admission or promotion in the ranks of the Civil Service, i.e. its "civil effect" should be clearly stated and accepted by the participating governments. Newly recruited staff should already be put on the pay-roll on a probationary basis during their training. Definite employment in the service should depend on whether they complete their training successfully.

5.3 Participation from other institutions

Apart from the expected continuous demand for training for PPA staff, other institutions in related fields may wish to use the Ciawi School for training of their intermediate level personnel. These could include the Forestry Department (now responsible for visitor management in protection forests and buffer zones adjacent to parks and reserves on Java), the Office of Tourism, University faculties of Nature Conservation and Wildlife Management, etc.

5.4 Marine conservation

In view of the vast area of seas and oceans in the South east Asian region, it would be sensible to pay special attention to marine conservation and island ecology. The current curriculum of the Ciawi School does include some marine ecology and management of marine parks, but these courses should be expanded.

5.5 After service

There will be a continuous need for "after service" training, i.e. refresher courses, seminars and workshops on specific subjects, new techniques and new developments for Ciawi's alumni. These short courses should be arranged either once a year or once every second year. The spirit of the alumni could best be maintained by issuing a School newsletter or journal (four issues a year), which should be sent free of charge to all Ciawi graduates.

5.6 Regionalization

The possibility of promoting the Ciawi School into a regional school for South east Asia has been considered from the beginning. Project proposals have been forwarded to ASEAN countries and many countries seem to be interested. It is hoped that further steps toward regional cooperation will soon be taken in order to lessen the financial burden to Indonesia, and to guarantee continuation of the School on a permanent basis.

If the School did become a regional centre, it is likely that internationl organizations such as UNDP (FAO), World Bank, EEC and bilateral agencies for technical cooperation would also take a keen interest and support it financially and technically.

At present we have no reliable estimate of the numbers of staff who might come to Ciawi from interested countries in South east Asia. A questionnaire on this matter is currently being processed through the Ministry of Development supervision and Environment of Indonesia. It is expected that training needs in the region fully justify further investment in the Ciawi School.

One of the conditions for success would be to simplify and standardize the Indonesian government's procedures for invitation and admittance of prospective students. Furthermore, some of the School's facilities should be extended and improved. Teaching staff would need to be of high standard and fluent in English. It is recommended that before developing the Ciawi School as a regional Southeast Asian training school, the problems and advantages of regional participation be studied carefully at both regional African Colleges.

Table 1. Nature Conservation Staff Requirements

Staff level	Demand		Currently Employed		Vacancies	
	Central Office	Regional Units	Central Office	Regional Units	Central Office	Regional Units
Directors, Sub-direct.	7	8	5	—	2	8
Chief Wardens	110	519	32	114	78	405
Rangers	156	2418	40	674	116	1744
Guards	77	1498	30	891	47	597

National Parks and Land Use Policy

I Made Sandy
Directorate of Land Use Planning
Jakarta, Indonesia

I Gusti Made Tantra
Forest Research Institute
Bogor, Indonesia

Kuswarta Kartawinata
Herbarium Bogoriense
Bogor, Indonesia

ABSTRACT. *This paper describes land use patterns as the net result of conflicts between individual, sectoral and public interests, suggesting that population increase and rising demands will result in fierce competition for the use of land in the future. It is seen as essential to involve local communities to share full responsibility for protected areas with the officially appointed managers from the protected area agency. At the highest level of government, priorities must be given to the various alternatives of land use.*

1. INTRODUCTION

Few of us would deny the importance of conserving nature, whether for reaons of scenic beauty, rare species or even out of religious considerations. In spite of this recognition, however, it must be admitted that it is becoming more and more difficult to keep preserved areas intact. Reports of poaching of supposedly protected species keep coming in. Most recently, the mysterious deaths of several rhinos in the Ujung Kulon National Park have been reported. Another disturbing report also came recently from the Province of Riau, where local people raised complaints of being chased out of their traditional fishing ground by the Forest Police, since that part of forest land, including several lakes located within the area, had recently been declared a nature reserve. Apparently the conversion of the area into a nature reserve was not known to the local people.

The Kutai Nature Reserve in East Kalimantan is located next to a rapidly developing industrial community, the Bontang LNG (Liquefied Natural Gas) project and related urban activities. It appears that the nature reserve and the industrial community will not be able to coexist peacefully for much longer.

Discouraging though the outlook might be in maintaining nature reserves in the future, there is still hope, provided of course that the right steps are taken when opportunities arise.

"Primitive" tribes have a deep understanding of maintaining an equilibrium of some sort with nature; many such tribes don't take more from nature than their real needs, so they actually never create waste. They seem to be aware of the fact that if their natural habitats go, they too will perish. In all their "primitiveness", they seem to be very much aware of the stake they have in keeping their natural environment intact.

If we look at the development programme in PELITA III (3rd Five Year Development Plan), we find that every branch of the Department of Agriculture plans to expand the area of land under their crops. New plantation areas of sugarcane, rubber and oil palm will be opened, in addition to cattle ranches and reforestation programmes.

Agriculture is not the only programme with plans for areal expansion. The same is true for industry, mining, and, not the least, settlement or transmigration programmes. No less than 500,000 families are planned to be migrated toward the end of PELITA III and another 1,000,000 families for PELITA IV. One can imagine the magnitude of land clearing activities that will be required to support these people in the future, and the conflicts that might ensue if all of the areal expansions of the agricultural programmes of PELITA III are implemented to the full.

It is among the noise of the sound of bulldozers, tractors and chainsaws on the one hand and the crackle of forest fires of the local shifting cultivators on the other that we must try to find a piece of land to conserve various types of natural ecosystems, including the habitats of rare species, for the benefit of science, society and future generations.

2. LAND USE

Land use and land rights, especially in developed areas, are two different but inseparable things. Access to land is not only determined by physical factors but even more so by legal factors. Administering the use of land, therefore, is in essence administering conflicts. There are conflicts between the interests of individuals and the more noble interest of the public, as well as conflicts of the interest of one sector versus the interest of another sector. These conflicts are further aggravated when greed and ignorance come to play their parts.

To determine the best use of land on the basis of its physical capability alone is not difficult but, in most cases, it is the legal factor that stands in the way of proper land use. It is with a view to overcoming this legal obstacle that some kind of procedure must be established.

Land use policy is, in essence, development policy, in that the latter must be there first. Land use policy then must accommodate whatever and wherever space is required for the implementation of that development policy mentioned.

If the government believes that for the well-being of society, the establishment of national parks is urgent, then in the first place it must be so stated in its development programme. After that policy has been adopted, the department managing the affairs of land must accommodate that policy by setting aside a piece of real estate as required, and free from legal handicaps.

The first step in the procedure is a policy decision by the highest authoritative body, which in the case of Indonesia is the President, to designate a piece of land for a certain purpose, such as a national park. This decision must be supported by necessary facts, so that when challenged, the urgency of it is reasonably defensible. A policy decision short of a presidential one will be very difficult to enforce, should conflict arise with other equally urgent projects such as mining, which usually leaves no option for choosing different sites. A presidential policy decision setting priorities also combats the possibility of land being expropriated by eminent domain.

Sangkaropi in Central Sulawesi was declared a nature reserve by the Minister of Agriculture. The Department of Mining, however, has found a large deposit of high grade copper and nickel. Which one has to be sacrificed?

Sangkaropi is of course not the only case of such conflict. More popular is the case of Meru Betiri, where a whole community has to be evacuated particularly for the sake of one pair of tigers, whose existence is even doubted by the populace. Recent investigations, however, reported that the tigers are still inhabiting the area.

A more detailed account of this case and similar other cases elsewhere is presented in the Appendix.

Although the majority of Indonesia's population eke a living from small subsistence agriculture, the most serious threat to protected areas might not come from this sector of society. But, when it does happen, the main reason is either because the farmers have not been informed that the areas have been declared protected areas, or because the boundaries are not clearly demarcated.

More serious threats come from those who knowingly enter nature reserve boundaries, because they are lured by lucrative profits. The profit may be derived from the sale of logs, rare species or animal parts like ivory, rhino horns, or crocodile hides. Profit hunting of this latter type is unfortunately not carried out in the primitive way, but rather with full sophistication; sadly, it is not a rare occasion when government officials are involved in these illegal activities. It is therefore quite necessary that government officials concerned, especially conservation managers, are trained in such a way that they are not easily caught by the lure of easy profits.

As a rule it can be stated that local people honour the existence of parks and other protected areas, once they are established. The threats upon them usually come from non-indigenous migrants or settlers. The Sangeh Nature Reserve in Bali, for example, has never been disturbed in spite of political and social upheavals that occurred in the areas surrounding it. This may be due to the local people respecting the existence of the forest and the temple within it so that squatting by outsiders anywhere near the site is not possible. As a result, the reserve and the temple have been left to the care of the local people.

Quite different is the case of the Batuangus Reserve in North Sulawesi. Not trespassing over the reserve boundary, the Sangir people started a small settlement near the border of the Batuangus Reserve north of Airperang, known by the name of Makawide. But now Makawide has expanded in such a way that it is located well within the original boundaries of the reserve. The increasing urban activities of the harbour of Bitung, of course, has given this small hamlet a boost to its present growth.

In similar fashion, the Berbak reserve is threatened not by the indigenous people of Jambi, but rather by Buginese settlers who came to establish tidal irrigation ricefields around the reserve. These once-small settlements are now thriving towns, whose people occasionally slip across the reserve boundaries to get some ducks and deer or destroy whole areas for new fields before they are caught.

The examples mentioned above imply that in order to secure the existence of protected areas, we must involve as many local communities as possible right from the beginning and charge them with responsibilities for the management of the reserves. The involvement of local communities is in fact in line with the concept of Biosphere Reserves, which has a great advantage of being more flexible than the concept of national parks. Many aspects related to human populations (density, distribution, settlements, way of life, etc.) that cannot be accommodated in the concept of national parks and other protected areas are an integral part of biosphere reserve perspectives.

Not only should human populations not be kept out of certain areas of reserves, but their future needs for land expansion and improvement of their well-being should be taken into consideration (Maldague, 1981). The application of the biosphere reserve concept in the establishment and management of national parks and other protected areas can mitigate land use and social problems resulting therefrom. It has been shown to work successfully in Mexico (Halffter, 1981a), and in Indonesia it has been partially exercised in some national parks. It should be emphasized that the biosphere reserve system is not intended to replace other conservation efforts, but rather to support and complement them (IUCN, 1979).

3. CONCLUSION

The land use pattern of an area as we find it today is the net result of conflicts between individual, sectoral and public interests. Land use policy must accommodate development policy.

Planned use of land can only proceed when a certain procedure is followed. If protected areas are considered urgent, then Presidential policy decisions must rate their priority over other uses. In this way conflicts with other interests can be avoided.

It might be more fruitful if local communities are invited to share full responsibilities and care of protected areas instead of trusting the management solely to officially appointed managers.

The application of the biosphere reserve concept can mitigate land use and social problems and should be encouraged further in future establishment and management of parks and other protected areas.

APPENDIX

It has been suggested above that to avoid conflicts of interest among government agencies, individuals and public sectors, Presidential Policy Decisions are required for the designation of national parks and other protected areas. The following are cases on conflicts in one proposed national park and two other protected areas, presented as examples.

1. MERU BETIRI GAME RESERVE

The Meru Betiri Game Reserve in East Java has a total area of 50,000 ha. It was designated as a game reserve by the Minister of Agriculture in 1972, to conserve the habitat of Javan tiger *Panthera tigris sondaica*, banteng *Bos javanicus*, barking deer *Muntiacus muntjak*, leathery turtle *Dermochelys coriacea* and other wildlife. The vegetation of the area includes beach forest, mangrove, swamp forest and mountain forest.

In view of the fact that it has been reported to be the last resort of the Javan tiger, an endangered species according to the IUCN *Red Data Book*, the Government of Indonesia, in this case the Directorate of Nature Conservation and Wildlife Management proposed to convert the game reserve into a National Park and extend the area to include also the Bandealit and Sukamade tree crop plantations with the total area of 2,154 ha.

The problem is, however, that the plantations are situated as an enclave within the proposed park and have provided employment to many families who also settled within the estates. The establishment of plantations (rubber, coffee, cocoa, and coconut) was based on a long-term contract between the government and the proprietor of the estate. The contract, however, terminated on 23 September 1980, in accordance with the Presidential Decree No. 32, 1979.

To follow closely the IUCN criteria for national parks, people living within the area have to be moved out. Disputes cannot be avoided. People living in the area and public at large raised their complaints and questioned such an action and priority-setting: why is a pair of tigers more important than the established plantation and the people living within it?

Conflicts and disputes may not arise should the concept of biosphere reserves be exercised in establishing this park. People can live in the area and the plantation can continue to operate, but they should be involved in protecting and maintaining the reserve; these are not impossible things for them to do, and in fact various reports show that they have been instrumental in protecting the reserve and the wildlife it contains.

2. KERUMUTAN GAME RESERVE

The Kerumutan Game Reserve with the total area of 120,000 ha in the Province of Riau, was designated as a game reserve by the Minister of Agriculture in 1928.

In 1973, however, aerial photographs showed that most of the game reserve area had changed a great deal. Settlements, shifting cultivation areas and small but scattered rubber plantations owned by local people had developed. From the point of view of conservation, the conditions of the reserve were so bad that it could not possibly function as a reserve.

In 1979 the Minister of Agriculture issued another Decree (No 350/Kpts/6/1979) stipulating a replacement of the much-damaged game reserve with another neighbouring and much better forest of the same size. At the same time the Minister of Agriculture also ordered the Directorate-General of Forestry to establish a definite boundary of this new game reserve.

This case shows the existence of conflicts among various sectors in a society that needs the same land for different purposes. Such conflicts should not be left unsolved, but rather an action should be taken immediately which reflects a development and land use policy that has been adjusted to local conditions and needs.

3. KUTAI RESERVE

The Kutai Nature Reserve was proposed in 1932; it covered about 2,000,000 ha surrounded by natural boundaries. The Sultan of Kutai issued a Decree, and on 25 July 1936 the Governor of Kalimantan in Banjarmasin approved it, but the area was reduced to 306,000 ha.

After the World War II the Minister of Agriculture confirmed the legal status of the reserve and designated it as a Game Reserve by Decree (No. 110/Un/1957, dated 14 June 1957). During the last fifteen years the existence of the reserve has been threatened by a number of human activities, in particular poaching, logging operations, and industrial development.

In 1968 100,000 ha of the area located along the coast was excised and within this area oil drilling and logging activities were allowed to operate. Another 60,000 ha in the southern part of the reserve were later conceded to a logging concession, P.T. Kayu Mas. Meanwhile the 100,000 ha logged-over forest, now occupied by farmers, oil wells, log-loading bays, and roads, was then returned to the reserve in 1971 to compensate the loss of the 60,000 ha virgin forest in the southern part (Minister of Agriculture Decree No, 280). The nominal size of the reserve as stated in the decree is 200,000 ha, but according to the "Proposed Management Plan, Kutai Reserve, East Kalimantan, Indonesia" produced by the "WWF Indonesia Programme", November 1979, the area of forest remaining within the reserve was less than 140,000 ha, and was expected to decrease further as logging operations were continuing. The reserve is now surrounded by logging concession areas and a damaged coastal strip on the eastern side. The Directorate of Nature Conservation is very concerned about the situation and has to save the valuable, intact and remaining forest. As the result of a consultative meeting on nature conservation in East Kalimantan held in Samarinda on 8-9 February 1980, it was agreed that the conversion of Kutai game reserve into a National Park was acceptable.

The above accounts indicate that decisions at a ministerial level are not powerful enough to guarantee the integrity and continuity of any reserves.

NATIONAL PARKS, CONSERVATION, AND DEVELOPMENT

National Parks and Rural Communities

Soekiman Atmosoedarjo
Professor of the Mulawarman University
Samarinda, Indonesia

Lukito Daryadi
Directorate General of Forestry
Jakarta, Indonesia

John MacKinnon
UNDP/FAO National Parks Development
Project, Bogor, Indonesia

Paul Hillegers
School of Environmental Conservation Management
Ciawi, Indonesia

ABSTRACT. *National park development in Indonesia is still at an early stage; none of the first parks are yet fully developed and in no case have the buffer zones and other community projects yet been implemented. But existing government programmes of extension and agro-forestry can be adapted to conservation needs. Indonesia already has much experience in all of the components of the proposed methods for minimizing friction between local people and national parks and in maximizing benefits from these areas. This paper describes a number of these social programmes for protected areas which are being implemented in Indonesia, with hopes that such information will prove useful to other countries facing similar problems.*

1. INTRODUCTION

Land use planning by designation of areas for specific uses produces a pattern of areas with different management objectives. It results in boundaries which did not exist before and restricts the expansion of each form of land use. Adjacent land uses will inevitably have mutual influences, and the degree and extent of these influences depends on the respective land use objectives and the communities living in these areas. This paper is devoted to the interactions and relationships that exist between national parks/protected areas and neighbouring rural communities, especially in Indonesia.

About 60% of the 2 million sq km of Indonesian land is forested (unexploited and logged-over forests), 8% is under permanent agriculture (7% smallholders and 1% estates) and the remaining 32% is occupied by other land uses including considerable areas of denuded and bare critical land. The country includes a full spectrum from some of the least disturbed and least populated areas in the humid tropics, e.g. Irian Jaya with an area of 42 million ha but a population of only 1.1 million (2.6 persons per sq km) and 98% of its natural vegetation left, to some of the most densely populated areas, e.g. Java with an area of 13.5 million ha and a population of 91 million (674 persons per sq km) and only (8% of its natural vegetation left.

The Indonesian population is the fifth largest in the world (150 million) containing many different ethnic groups. The majority depend on subsistence agriculture (i.e. most of their stable food, protein, fuel and other coommodities are either directly collected from nature or grown for their own consumption and do not enter the cash economy). The rural population is a very heterogeneous, ranging from isolated groups who live completely on the gathering of forest products and shifting cultivation to sophisticated farmers who are well integrated into the market economy.

The country as a whole can be characterised as humid tropics but in fact there is a broad range of climate from ever-wet to seasonal monsoon. In addition, because of the country's fortuitous position straddling the gap between two major biogeographic regions and the high levels of island endemism in the transition zone, the country boasts longer species lists and greater diversity of biological communities (including very extensive marine habitats) than almost any other country in the world.

With respect to this great natural wealth of species, Indonesia has embarked on an ambitious conservation programme. Apart from an extensive system of environmental protection forests to preserve water sources and prevent soil erosion in steep and erosion-prone areas, the government has ordered a major expansion of its system of Strict Nature Reserves, Game Reserves, Recreation Forests and, more recently, National Parks. In every case, the success of such reserves depends upon the relationship that develops between the reserve management and the neighbouring rural community.

2. GOVERNMENT OBJECTIVES AND POLICY

One of the general objectives of the Indonesian Government is "the protection of nature and wildlife specifically for scientific, cultural, national defence, recreational and tourist purposes; . . . providing various means of living for the people in and around the forest; . . . Nature conservation and protection are directed to the conservation of ecosystems instead of merely protecting species, through the designation of suitable forest areas as nature reserves." Further, Indonesia has adopted the generally-accepted IUCN criteria for internationally recognized National Parks, but has added some specific criteria of its own. Among these is the stipulation that Indonesian National Parks must also be clearly seen to be in the regional interest so that their establishment will constitute a benefit, rather than an added hardship, to the rural people living around them.

These general objective, policy and management directives place active commitments on the Government to ensure positive benefits to the rural communities when a reserve or national park is established. Indeed, the Government has already developed a strategy for rural community development with objectives which include all the prerequisites to observe these commitments. The general objectives for rural community development not only correspond with the Forestry Policy but they provide a more solid base for rural planning. The objectives read:

"1. to conserve the forest, land and water resources;
2. to increase the income and prosperity of the local community and farmers in critical land areas;
3. to improve the attitude and responsibility of the local community members as preservers of natural resources."

Perum Perhutani—a semi-Government Forestry Cooperation—already has ample experience in drawing up and implementing rural community development programmes. Figure 1 portrays an outline of the rural development objectives in Indonesia and the programmes that have been developed by the Foresty Department and Perum Perhutani.

3. MAXIMIZING BENEFITS FROM NATIONAL PARKS

The onus is on Government to show that the rural community is better off with, rather than without, such parks. This stipulation can be easily met in cases where direct benefits evidently exceed the negative effects of the establishment of a reserve/national park. Direct benefits for the local community which accrue from a national park/reserve may include:

- Conservation or safeguarding of resources, i.e. landforms, rocks, water, soil, microclimates, plantlife, wildlife, fish.
- The balance of the regional environment. This may be the regulation of runoff and the reduction of flood peaks. Decreased rapid surface flow reduces erosion hazard and prevents flooding and sedimentation of valuable agricultural land and irrigation systems.
- Ensuring sustainable supplies of water, wildlife, fish, plants and plant products. Undisturbed catchment areas regulate and filter water runoff so that a steady flow of unpolluted water will be available for domestic and agricultural use. Wildlife and fish will find a refuge where they can breed, restore a healthy population size and from where they can disperse to areas where people are allowed to hunt or fish.
- Employment created by the establishment, development and management of the park. Dependent on the objectives, the habitats and the size of the park, many kinds of labour have to be called in, i.e. to construct and to maintain the infrastructure, accommodations, visitor commodities etc., to manage the habitats and wildlife, to guard and to patrol the park, to man visitor centres and offices, to guide visitors, etc.
- General stimulation of the local economy. Non-local visitors require lodging, food and beverages during their stay in and around the park. Souvenir sales, local craft shops and home and small scale industries to make these articles will get a boost. Often new markets for local agricultural products originate due to better roads and will increase cash crop production. The stimulation of the local economy results in more job opportunities.
- Provision of recreation and tourism possibilities for local, domestic and international visitors. The park will give those living close to it ample time for a regular breather; it will be a healthful resort with creative and aesthetic relaxation opportunities for the region.
- Educational use of the park for visiting classes of school children, student parties, nature lovers groups, scout movements, etc.
- Research uses of the park will not only be of interest for a limited number of national and foreign scientists but it will again bring more money

into the region and provide more jobs as research assistants, guides etc.

The existence or establishment of a national park will always result in some frictions and problems with local communities or individual families living close to the park area. These problems are inherent in the restrictions that must be placed on use of and access to the park (in some cases people have to be actually encouraged to move out of the park areas) and to the negative mutual influences of two different forms of land use. In Indonesia the main disadvantage of a reserve or national parks is that it restricts the land use and consequently takes away subsistence possibilities of the rural community or part thereof. Inevitably local people will try to take advantage of the reserves/parks resources through:

- Encroachment by shifting cultivation or even by permanent agriculture. Fertile, continuous water-fed sites are especially susceptible to encroachment and are difficult to regain once occupied.
- Exploitation of: timber for building materials, for agricultural uses or for sale; fuelwood; fodder; food such as seeds, nuts, fruits, edible palm shoots, fungi, and roots; forest products which can provide cash income, i.e. bamboo, rattan, resins, gums, seeds, tannin, medicinal plants, etc.; honey; and animal protein from hunting and fishing.
- Destruction of dangerous and pest species.

The negative effects which accrue when a reserve or national park directly adjoins agricultural land include the following:

- Foraging in the park of domestic animals such as cattle, water buffalo, goats, sheep etc.
- Intrusion and invasion of the park by exotic plant and animal species, pests, and diseases, wildfires.
- Intrusion and invasion of the agricultural lands by destructive and pest animals, weeds, other pests and diseases, fires.
- Pollution of the park by domestic and agricultural detergents and pesticides, soil products from water and wind erosion, litter from visitors, etc.

Maximizing the benefits and at the same time eliminating or minimizing the mutual negative effects is the easiest way for park management to assure the welfare and cooperation of the rural community. Government can maximize these benefits to the rural community by developing as many different activities and uses of the national parks as are mutually compatible and consistent with the objectives of the parks and involving local people wherever possible. In addition Government could:

- Develop suitable barriers or boundary fences to limit damage done by wildlife to community property. In the case of pest species (e.g. pigs, mon-

keys and rats) this may involve suitable control operations.
- Develop compensation systems for damage done by protected animals.
- Select national parks so as to minimize land-use competition and, where possible, to coincide with other protection needs where environmental benefits are clearest (i.e. include important water catchment areas and critical areas provided these areas meet national parks criteria), and in accessible areas where tourism benefits will be appreciable.

4. RURAL COMMUNITY DEVELOPMENT

In cases where Government wants to establish a park in the national interest, but which appears to be disadvantageous to those close to the park—in spite of the direct benefits from the establishment—then some positive investments and assistance to the local community must be included in the overall land-use package. This policy of Government has to be applied so that conservation is seen as part of the development process rather than a handicap to development—in line with IUCN's World Conservation Strategy—and out of general fairness to the community concerned. This policy is in practice essential to the success of national parks as it is clear that they will fail until they receive the respect and the support of the local rural communities. There are many ways in which Government could compensate local communities to loss of access to or rights within nature reserves and national parks.

4.1. Optimization of land use according to a sound capability classification

This could include a change in cultivation system, i.e., irrigation of dry land; altering the rotation period by planting perennial crops instead of annuals or vice versa; switching from arable farming to shrub, tree or grassland cultivation or vice versa; reforestation; combinations of forestry with agriculture and/or animal husbandry. Soils and water conservation management, different soil tillage and planting techniques could improve existing farmlands. Government could introduce and stimulate these changes through setting examples on Government land, extension, grants, credits, assistance in cooperatives etc. In the last few decades, especially in areas outside Java, slash and burn practices have stripped large forests and have converted huge areas into alang alang *Imperata cylindrica* fields. Government is implementing different programmes aiming at the settlement of shifting cultivation communities in order to protect remaining forests and to prevent further devastation of areas under fallow. For instance, in the Population Resettlement Programme started in 1972, families are provided with parcels of cleared arable land, building materials for housing, social amenities and food, seed and fertilizers for an initial period. The Nucleus Estate and Smallholders Programme is a cooperation between small plantation farmers and large plantation enterprises established by forest concessionaires.

The allocation of extensive forms of land use between areas with conflicting land use objectives (agriculture and parks) can help to minimize the mutual negative effects. On state land Government could establish buffer zones, around parks consisting of areas of state land falling under the overall management of the park authorities, but generally outside the park boundaries proper, where certain levels of utilisation are permitted for the local community. Through the concept of buffer zones it is intended, where possible, to interpose an intermediate land-use zone managed to benefit the local community while at the same time offering an extra layer of protection to the reserve. Various forms of agriculture would be permitted within the buffer zone. The actual form of land use that is most suitable will vary from situation to situation but within the limitations placed by the actual buffering needs of the reserve/park, management can generally be aimed at maximizing the benefits to local people.

Buffer zone development around Indonesian reserves and parks is still a new concept. Guidelines for buffer zone development have been recommended by FAO and PPA and are still the subject of Government review, but no legislation for the establishment of such buffer zones yet exists. Nevertheless there do exist ample examples of new land uses that are suitable for buffer zones. For a long time, agroforestry has been commonly practised and today various different systems of mixed, strip-and inter-cropping are used successfully. The humid tropics are suitable for the plantation of perennial bush and tree crops such as tea, coffee, pepper, cinnamon, cloves, nutmeg, cocoa, oilpalm, coconut, rubber, fruits, etc. Firewood shortage forced the Forest Department a long time ago to establish tree and shrub plantations for energy production.

4.2. Provision of social amenities

These include training centres, housing, water supply, electricity etc. Government has already provided many of these facilities for local communities through different programmes. The Magersaren Programme creates small villages for forest labourers, including houses, water supply and a community centre for religious and educational purposes. Another programme consists of the building of central bath and wash facilities in villages with clean water drawn from undisturbed forest watersheds.

4.3. Improvement of education, extension and information systems

A typical example of transfer of knowledge through community personalities is the MALU programmes. MALU stands for the close cooperation between the responsible forest officer, the mantri, and the head of a village, the Lurak. The residence of the mantri in the village functions as information and extension centre. Here, seedlings of fruit trees and other perennials are raised in small model nurseries and distributed to the villagers to be planted in home gardens and on village lands vordering forest areas. Through the mantri, people are advised on and assisted in apiculture, sericulture, growing fodder, medical plants, fuelwood etc.

5. HOW TO EARN COMMUNITY SUPPORT

To gain community support it is necessary to indeed ensure that development will be a benefit to the community. It is then necessary to undertake extension programmes so that local people understand the objectives of the national park and their own direct and indirect benefits. Extension can be achieved through direct approaches by specialised extension teams or mobile units, by inviting village representatives to meetings, by introducing conservation education into school courses, by the activity of nature lover groups and through general media such as television, magazines, newspapers, education centres, etc. In practice, the direct approach is best and mobile education units in North Sumatra and Aceh received very good response to their slide programmes and film shows in villages. A number of suitable programmes have been made and such units are being established in other areas.

PPA will never have enough guards to physically patrol and protect all parts of all reserves so if reserves, are to be respected, local communities will have to help protect them. To achieve this, each community adjacent to a park will have to be made responsible for the actions of their own individual members. Luckily there usually exist in most parts of Indonesia traditional rules or *adat* to control individual behaviour, particularly with respect to exploitation of communal resources. The idea of community taboo is also still strong in most rural areas. It is important to harness and build on these existing traditions to get villages to respect park regulations. These same *adat* principles are also extremely useful in helping devise the framework for developing harvest and utilisation rights and control within buffer zones.

Government can declare buffer zones, devise regulations, give advice and even assistance in establishing plantations etc. but the labour and main expense of marking, planting and working of the buffer zones must come from the communities that are to benefit from them. Elaborate recommendations have been devised that try to find a formula that will give fairness to all concerned and avoid acting as a magnet that attracts ever more people into the privileged zone around the park. Again, there is quite a lot of local tradition in organizing community cooperatives in Indonesia; fishing cooperatives, agricultural and agroforestry cooperatives and marketing cooperatives can all be used as a basis for organizing buffer zones.

Ultimately the guard force must be available to arrest and to prosecute the park abusers where necessary. So long as there is no penalty for reserve abuse no amount of extension and goodwill can achieve protection.

6. EXAMPLES

While no park in Indonesia can be said to be fully developed nor any buffer zone fully established, it is worth describing some of the practical examples and case studies that exist in Indonesia of the successful operations of some of the suggested ideas.

6.1. Recreation development at Ujung Kulon, Gunung Gede-Pangrango and Pangandaran

The contrast of the situation in three parks in West Java is instructive.

Ujong Kulon, Indonesia's showpiece reserve, is a rare piece of coastal lowland forest of high conservation value with rare Javan rhinoceros and an abundance of easily-viewed wildlife; but it has never attracted large numbers of visitors despite large financial investment in the reserve, including several excellent guest houses. The problem is the difficulty and expense of access. The overland access route is over terrible roads with no proper bridges while the alternative access involves prohibitive charter of uncomfortable fishing boats and a rough seven-hour sea passage. The local communities adjacent to the reserve are completely bypassed by what visitors there are so that there are no rub-off benefits from the park. Little extension work has been done, the local people do not respect the reserve and abuses in the eastern part of the park remain very serious.

Gunung Gede-Pangrango is of less conservation value and has few animals to be seen by visitors, but has an attractive botanical garden and the park itself has a challenging climb, good views, beautiful forest scenery and waterfalls, a good trail system and an information centre. As a result, several thousand visitors enter the park each year and although they do a great deal of damage in littering and graffiti, they bring a considerable income to the local people, who run weekend refreshment stands and several of whom are employed in the reserve. The reserve is thus fairly well respected and apart from a bit of illicit firewood collection is reasonably unabused.

Pangandaran, a tiny coastal isthmus with a nature reserve and small recreation forest, offers visitors well-laid-out walks through a forest covering interesting

limestone blocks with curious caves. There is an abundance of almost-tame wildlife—deer, banteng, monkeys—and some attractive sea beaches for bathing. The entrance fee is kept at a very modest 100 Rp (US$0.15). There is almost no accommodation in the park so that the village benefits from all the visitor accommodation, refreshments, sale of souvenirs and running of boat trips over the coral reefs. As a result, the whole area is now in a tourist boom with half a million visitors each year and no serious threat to the forest.

6.2. Recreation forests by Perum Perhutani

Apart from PPA, the State Forest Cooperation for Java, Perum Perhutani, has had considerable experience in developing Recreation Forests. Perum Perhutani is responsible for the management of about 3 million ha of forest area consisting of a wide variety of man-made and natural forest types, e.g. teak and pine plantations and beach, mangrove, lowland, mountain and deciduous monsoon forests, located all over Java in varying and beautiful landscapes. Since 1976, as part of the multiple use policy of the forest resources in Indonesia, the management started to develop the recreation function of their forests. For this purpose an increasing number of forest areas are scattered over Java to serve as Recreation Forests; substantial investments are made in visitors' facilities such as camping grounds, parking lots, nature trails, day and night shelters, etc. Apart from these selected forest areas, many well-visited forest sites are equipped with picnic areas and rest stops. The number of people who are using these facilities is overwhelming and Perum Perhutani is unable to cope with the demand.

6.3. The encouragement of private organizations

Much can be achieved through the activities of private and non-governmental organizations to foster appreciation of wilderness and protected areas. In Java, for instance, there are already 300 Nature Lover Groups and in addition the *Pramuka* or Scouting Movement is of widespread popularity. The Minister of Development Supervision and the Environment has drawn together many of these groups into a representation body called *Wahana*, whose secretariat is housed in his offices. A good example of such a non-government organization is the Green Indonesia Foundation, which publishes a regular illustrated nature magazine aimed at students and interested nature lovers, produces slide programmes with commentaries about reserves and other conservation issues, publishes posters, stickers, educational booklets etc. and also lays on exhibitions at public fairs, conducts extension services and runs a mobile educational unit showing wildlife and environmental films.

6.4. Forest, land and water conservation

The Forest, Land and Water Conservation Programme in the current Five Year Development Plan is a major effort to conserve forests, to battle further degradation of critical lands and to develop rural communities in forest areas. The programme consists of reforestation and greening of State lands as well as private lands, terracing of agricultural lands and the construction of checkdams for regulating run-off, sedimentation of eroded soil materials and irrigation purposes. *Penghijauan*, the nationwide greening programme, is financed by the Ministry of Home Affairs. It combines the facilities and goodwill of the local authorities, the labour forces of the local communities and the managerial skills of the Ministry of Agriculture (the Directorate of Reforestation and Land Rehabilitation), to implement tree planting projects in critical areas. The type and size of the plantations and the tree species to be planted depend on the local needs and the site requirements and may consist of fruit tree orchards, fuelwood plantations or timber and pulp plantations.

6.5. Buffer zones

While detailed guidelines now exist for the establishment of buffer zones no official buffer zones around reserves have yet been established. However, there exist some plantations adjacent to reserves that already act as buffers. Baluran National Park, for instance, is bounded by an extensive teak plantation which is carefully managed and does clearly help to protect the reserve from agricultural encroachment and invasion by livestock and fire. Moreover, since this monoculture is rather sterile for wildlife, it deters deer and pigs from wandering out of the reserve. As a buffer zone, the plantation provides benefit only to the plantation employees. It could certainly do more to assist local communities if the profits were shared with villages. Other experiences, such as tea plantations around Gn. Gede-Pangrango National Park and the durian and coffee groves adjacent to Gn. Leuser National Park and Kirinci Reserve, confirm the effectiveness of plantations as conservation buffers. In addition, it is clear from experience that fruit or berry plantations survive better than firewood plantations which tend to be cut as fast as they can be planted.

6.6. The involvement of *adat*

Introduction of *adat* principles into the exploitation of buffers is again still to be tried out. However, in some cases the existence of strong traditional regulations and taboos are clearly being harnessed directly to reserve needs. In Siberut Island, for instance, the new management plan for a major reserve includes a large 'Traditional Use Zone' where local people who maintain very strong rules about disturbing the balance of nature and have lived in a stable balance with the forest for hundreds of years will be permitted to continue most of their traditional harvesting of wood, medical plants, fruits, thatch, fish and game that is hunted with bows and arrows. By getting the local people to jealously protect these rights in the Traditional Use zone, the inner sanctuary zone becomes completely protected from other outside pressures.

Figure 1: Outline of the rural community development objectives and programmes in Indonesia

General Objectives		Specific Objectives			Programmed
Rural Community Development	1. Conserve forest land & water resources	Outside Java		Forest, Land & Water Conservation	Reforestation
					Terracing
					Checkdams
				Shifting Cultivation Management	Resettlements
					Nucleus estate smallholders
					Isolated community development
					Transmigration
					Development estates of export crops
				Information and Extension	Radio & TV
					National Campaigns
					Emphasis on farmers on critical lands
	2. Increase income & prosperity of local community & farmers in critical land-areas		1. Increasing efficacy of forest lands	Agroforestry — Tumpangsari	Mixed-cropping (rice, corn) during first years of tree plantation establishment.
				Agroforestry — Mama	Strip-cropping of fast growing trees and annual agriculture (rice, corn).
				Agroforestry — Tanaman Sela	Inter-cropping under older tree plantations (grass, medicinal plants, firewood).
	3. Improve attitude & responsibility of local community members as preservers of natural resources	On Java & densely populated areas	2. Increasing carrying capacity of land around forest lands	Reforestation	
				Malu — Agriculture	bee keeping
				Malu — Sericulture	silk caterpillar culture
				Malu — Fodder	elephant grass
				Malu — Fruit trees	mango, jack-fruit, citrus
				Malu — Medicinal plants	Curouma xanthorrhiza, C. domestica, Zingiber officinale / Dioscorea spp., Kaempferia galanga, etc.

General Objectives	Specific Objectives	Programmed		
		Fuelwood		Gliricidia sepium, Calliandra calothyrsus, Leucaena laucocephala, etc.
		Checkdams	Erosion Control	
			Irrigation	
		Terracing		
		Reforestation		
	3. Development of local community	Magersaren	Housing	
			Facilities	mosque, community hall, etc.
		Cooperative		
		Water Supply		
		Information & Extension		

Involvement of Politicians in the Development of Parks and Protected Areas

Prijono Hardjosentono
Directorate-General of Forestry
Jakarta, Indonesia

F. Hehuwat
Chairman
Green Indonesia Foundation
Jakarta, Indonesia

B. Soemarmo
Director
Ragunan Zoological Garden
Jakarta, Indonesia

ABSTRACT. *This paper provides some basic approaches to convincing politicians about the need for nature conservation. It covers approaches both from the top and from the bottom (the grass roots approach) and describes a number of political issues in nature conservation; these include suggestions that problems should be presented with their solutions, the importance of timing, and the importance of non-governmental conservation organizations in achieving political aims in conservation. The paper then describes a series of steps through which conservationists may discover how best to involve politicians in their conservation movement.*

1. INTRODUCTION

It would be rather unrealistic to assume that a blanket answer could be formulated to the question of how to involve politicians in conservation, as political conditions and customs differ from one nation to another, and quite different approaches are determined by local rules of political play. Nevertheless, some basic approaches can be defined.

2. THE NATURE CONSERVATION SYSTEM

The issue of Nature Conservation has been dealt with *in extenso* and it is not the intention to discuss this matter in detail here. Suffice it to say that, for a National Nature Conservation System to function properly, a number of basic requirements must be met, most important among which are:

- A "national vision" (or "outlook upon life") which favours nature conservation. This would express itself in a general public awareness of the plight of nature conservation, or the political will to include nature conservation as a fundamental building block in the development process, or both of these.
- An adequate and appropriate amount of scientific knowledge and technical know-how to plan, execute and evaluate a nature conservation policy.
- An institutional framework of organizations to implement this conservation policy.

The body of this paper will concern itself with the first item, in which the political issue of Nature Conservation is embedded and we will consider how to earn the involvement of politicans in the implementation of the conservation policy.

3. THE POLITICAL ISSUE

In the origins of nature conservation as a political issue, it is sometimes possible to distinguish two different types of development:

Development from the top. In this situation, politicans or political parties "pick up" the issue of nature conservation as a political issue. This can arise either from an awakening of Nature Conservation awareness or genuine concern about the deterioriation of the environmental quality, *or* for pure political gains to be used against political opponents. If the party carrying the

245

nature conservation banner happens to gain a victory or come to power, then it might be expected that the national development policy will be characterized by a concern for environmental quality (assuming that the conservation lobby sticks to its platform policy). Raising the issue of nature conservation in political spheres usually has a spin-off effect of increasing the general public's awareness of nature conservation.

Development from the bottom or "grass roots". In this situation a growing awareness of the issue of nature conservation develops within the society, and is expressed by the spontaneous coming into being of numerous groups and organizations concerned about nature conservation. This public awareness (and the subsequent activities of the groups and organizations) can then exert pressure upon the political establishment which may react by taking up the conservation issue as a political issue.

In many countries both developments have taken place simultaneously, and as they reinforce each other it is often difficult to distinguish between "the chicken and the egg". Any distinction between the two is therefore only relevant if conservationists want to raise the issue of nature conservation in the political sphere, because they may call for different approaches. It should also be realized that each development has its pros and cons. The broad-based "grass roots" approach is usually slower in achieving tangible results, but as its driving force is genuine and idealistic it creates its own informal monitoring and evaluation system whereby citizens critically watch and oversee the politicians in action and judge the ecological soundness of development programmes. The approach from the top can achieve quicker results, but it might not be based on personal conviction but political opportunism and the intensity of commitment might be determined by other factors such as the state of the national economy, influence of local interest groups, etc. Furthermore, the results in terms of nature conservation will only be as good as the quality of the executing bureaucracy. For these reasons it might be concluded that both approaches should be pursued together to obtain optimal results.

4. APPROACHES TO INVOLVE POLITICIANS

The essence of the matter is to involve the politician(s) in furthering the cause of nature conservation, without questioning whether this is done out of conviction or to achieve political gains. The politicians' involvement is necessary for obvious reasons: to raise the question of nature conservation to a national and public level; to introduce nature conservation into national development plans, including education, laws and regulations, budget and personnel allocation; to establish an executing organization; and to achieve these objectives within as short a time as possible, as in many cases not much time is left for nature conservation efforts.

Depending on whether action comes from above or below, there will be a slight difference in the order in which various steps are taken. Bearing in mind the broad spectrum of political structures and cultures of different countries, each of which needs its own appropriate strategy, a number of pointers are listed below, which seem to work under various political conditions. The issues have not been classified systematically but broadly we can distinguish between politically exploitable issues and "pitfalls".

5. POLITICAL ISSUES OF NATURE CONSERVATION

a) *Incubation period of the problem*. Short-term problems are more saleable politically than long-term problems, solutions are more saleable than problems; and short-term solutions are more saleable than long-term solutions.

b) *Rate and magnitude of problems*. Catastrophic short-lived phenomena are more obvious and understandable than are slow but continuous processes, e.g. a flash-flood caused by deforestation is more attention-catching than slow, ongoing soil erosion.

c) *Problems should be presented with their solutions*. The conservationists' practice of being content with a role as doomsday prophets should be discarded. It is unfair to let conservation amateurs grapple with problems, while the professionals stand aside as sceptical onlookers.

d) *Although difficult, problems should be presented as quantitatively as possible*. The same holds true for any solutions offered. In this respect, a great deal more has to be done on the cost of abusing the environment.

e) *Questions regarding arable land and jobs are "powder-kegs"*. Strong feelings are likely to be awakened when conservation measures require actions affecting these two subjects, so the solutions and arguments should be prepared in an especially careful and detailed manner.

f) *Timing is of paramount importance*. This also means that opportunites have to be exploited to the fullest ("riding the tide").

g) *Industrial pollution is usually a safe topic*. Industry affects the lives of a great number of people, and is usually a good topic with which to start or rally support for a conservation lobby in politics.

h) *In an effort to acquire areas to be zoned for nature conservation, it is a wise policy to try to acquire an area as large as possible covering a wide spread of habitats*. In view of our incomplete knowledge of the natural mechanisms operating in different ecosystems, especially the tropical forest ecosystem, it is sound practice to set aside as large an area as possible to accommodate unforeseen future requirements.

i) *Non-governmental conservation organisations and nature lover groups represent a potential and actual asset to achieve political aims in conservation.* To enhance and optimise the usefulness of these organizations, some sort of formal or informal nation-wide network should be established encompassing them. This would also prevent or minimise conflicts on environmental issues between those organizations, which would only create unnecessary confusion among both public and politicians.

j) *As early as possible the press and other kinds of mass-media have to be enlisted in the conservation movement.* The mass-media represents a powerful and effective tool for informal (public) education to raise the nature conservation awareness of both the general public (society) and the politicians.

6. ACTIVE INVOLVEMENT OF POLITICIANS IN THE DEVELOPMENT OF PARKS AND PROTECTED AREAS

All countries have different political conditions and customs, but by following a line of reasoning as outlined below, conservationists may find guidance on how best to involve politicians in their conservation movement.

a) Politicians are a group of people who act as architects or designers of the social structure of the human community and the set-up of government in a country.

b) Although politicians may belong to different parties or political alliances, in fact they all share the same political goal: a human community enjoying sustained prosperity, peace and justice, generation to generation throughout the ages. No less than the politicians, the international conservationists with their World Conservation movements are also aiming at sustained prosperity for all mankind. Their slogan is: "Conservation is not for the sake of conservation alone, but for the benefit and enjoyment of the people".

c) A "grass roots" conservation movement is free from any political persuasion and does not depend on any one government system, so it need not be affected either by prevailing political struggles between parties within a country or by struggles between different countries. In fact the reverse may be true; a conservation movement, by stressing common goals, can lessen political tensions between parties and even between nations. Therefore, in any country and at any time, conservation movements can be so organized as to get support from any existing political grouping or ideology.

d) To attain this prosperity for mankind it is vital that we husband the world's natural resources, including the diversity of species maintained in a proper balance with their ecosystems. The extinction of any species or wasteful destruction of resources and the consequent disturbance and imbalance in nature reduce the quality of life for man himself.

e) Because the politicians and the conservationists hold parallel attitudes regarding the role of natural resources in the future destiny of all mankind, it should not be very difficult to earn the involvement of politicians in the development of the conservation movement. Conversely, to act against the conservation movements and their activities when these are properly executed and organized, is to act against the main goal of any political grouping; it would also make the party concerned very unpopular, especially in the eyes of the conservation-minded members of the populace.

f) To increase the participation of the politicians in development of parks and protected areas, it is necessary to increase and deepen conservation awareness both among the politicans themselves and the voting/general public. To achieve this, conservationists should try to meet regularly with members of such political institutions as parliament, the provincial councils, etc., to discuss conservation matters and problems in language which the politicians understand. Such meetings should be followed by on-the-spot visits by politicians to conservation projects in the country, accompanied by competent conservationists; such tours provide a favourable opportunity for proper discussions with the main aim of broadening the conservation experience of the politicians and increasing their conservation awareness.

g) It is wise to involve influential politicians in the development of important conservation programmes, such as establishing outstanding national parks etc. Politicians may also be involved in formulating new laws and regulations dealing with conservation before these are submitted to the government and the parliament. Outstanding influential politicians should be regularly supplied with written conservation materials (books, periodicals, reports etc.) to keep them continuously in touch with the conservation movements in their own country and the rest of the world.

h) If there are good conservation films available, it is very worthwhile to show them to the interested politicians and their families. It is also worthwhile to encourage politicians and their families to holiday in the national parks. They will personally experience the role of national parks in unifying members of a family into a whole, so necessary in this very unstable world. The whole family will also enjoy a holiday amid the delights of nature and see what the national parks have to offer the public.

i) Politicians who have given outstanding service in the development of conservation movements should be recognized both nationally and internationally, with awards and honours such as the IUCN awards.

j) It seems also beneficial to establish organizations which can develop close cooperation and understanding between conservationists and politicians and allow a continuous exchange of ideas. The eventual goal is to turn politicians into enthusiastic conservationists and teach conservationists to become skilful and intelligent politicians.

7. CONCLUSIONS

In the foregoing discussion we have proposed a number of approaches to influence politicians in favour of nature conservation and to acquire their support for conservation aims. Nevertheless, it should be realized that for a national nature conservation policy to be successful the ideals and the motivation of the cause should be firmly entrenched in the society. This can be achieved both through the formal education system in schools and by informal education aimed at increasing public awareness. The cause of nature conservation should never be left to the politcians alone but should be based on broad public support.

Development of Marine Conservation in Indonesia

Aprilani Soegiarto
National Institute of Oceanology
Jakarta, Indonesia

Soewito
Directorate of the Management of Aquatic Resources
Jakarta, Indonesia

Rodney V. Salm
UNDP
National Park Development Project
Jakarta, Indonesia

ABSTRACT. *Two-thirds of Indonesian territory is covered by seas so there is an urgent need to develop a marine protected area system in order to conserve representative examples of Indonesia's valuable and rich marine ecosystems. This paper discusses the concept of marine conservation in Indonesia, describes progress to present, and outlines a plan for further development of marine conservation. Thirteen areas have been declared as marine protected areas, although there is as yet no fully established management for any of them. In addition, 42 proposed marine protected areas are listed, along with 24 existing terrestrial protected areas which include a marine component. There are four broad activities of Indonesia's marine conservation programme, including strategy formulation, establishment of a team of marine conservation specialists, establishment of protected areas, and establishment of a Sub-Directorate of Marine Conservation within the Directorate of Nature Conservation.*

1. INTRODUCTION

The Indonesian archipelago consists of thousands of islands surrounded by a complex system of waterways. Two-thirds of the Indonesian territory is covered by seas. Lately, as a side effect of our drive for economic growth and development, these waters have come under increased stress, particularly those that are adjacent to population and industrial centres. Therefore, it has become apparent that there is an urgent need to develop a marine park system in Indonesia in order to conserve representative samples of our valuable and rich, but vulnerable, marine ecosystems.

2. THE PHYSICAL ENVIRONMENT OF INDONESIA

Geographically, the Indonesian archipelago is situated between the Pacific and the Indian Oceans, between 94E and 141E and 6N and 11S. The archipelago consists of more than 13,000 islands and has more than 81,800 km of coastline, possibly the longest in the world. The Indonesian territorial seas can be divided into several parts: the shallow Sunda shelf in the west, the Sahul shelf in the east, deep ocean to the south and deep seas, straits and channels in the middle.

Because of its geographic location, the Indonesian archipelago is strongly governed by a monsoon-type climate. The northwest monsoon generally lasts from about December to February and the southeast monsoon from June to August; during the northwest monsoon the wind blows eastward and brings heavy rainfall to most of the western parts of the Indonesian archipelago. Rainfall combined with the heavy runoff of many rivers from the Greater Sunda Islands (Sumatra, Java and Kalimantan) result in turbidity and conditions favouring establishment of mangroves. At the same time, surface currents from the South China Sea bring low salinity water into the western part of the Java Sea and push the higher salinity eastward. With the onset of the southeast monsoon, these low salinity waters are transported back westward and into the Java Sea and South China Sea. They are replaced by waters of higher salinity from the Macassar Strait and the Flores Sea, east of the Sunda Shelf.

The maximal westward penetration of the high salinity water masses generally occurs in or around September. The deep seas of central Indonesia (e.g. Flores, Banda, Ceram, Moluccan and Sulawesi Seas) generally remain extremely clear and favour development of extensive coral reefs. For further review of the oceanographic features of the Indonesian waters refer to Soegiarto (1979a) and Soegiarto and Birowo (1975), and for their relationship to marine parks see Soegiarto (1979b).

The Indonesian coastline consists of three different bottom types: rock, sand or mud. Their distribution is partly governed by the degree of water energy (current patterns and wave actions). Along the coastline one can find various types of habitats, such as coral reefs, mangroves, sago, nipa and other swampy forests.

3. MARINE CONSERVATION

3.1 The concept

On land the principal conservation issues are the saving of unique species (e.g. the Javan rhinoceros) from extinction and the safeguarding of last examples of vanishing habitats. These activities often seem in direct conflict with basic human needs for land, particularly on crowded Java.

In the sea the principal conservation issues include controlling the destruction of productive habitats, the heavy exploitation of species which has resulted in depletion of stocks and in some cases, even endangered their survival. These control measures are not in conflict with human land or resource needs; on the contrary, marine conservation aims are to safeguard resources for sustainable harvest by fishermen and coastal residents.

The strategic objective of marine conservation in Indonesia is to yield food and security to its burgeoning population through preventing the disappearance of species and the degradation of critical habitats (i.e. those important to species or of high productivity). Establishment of a system of reserves for the natural replenishment of communities and species stocks in nearby exploited or damaged areas is the major tactical objective. In addition, these protected areas will help to maintain genetic resources, and provide for tourism development, for fisheries, for research and education and for contribution to the national prosperity through the generation of foreign exchange from exports.

The conservation issues in the sea are so different from those on land that marine conservation has suffered from the direct transfer of criteria and definitions which have evolved to meet terrestrial needs. For example, long-established traditions do not permit commercial harvest of resources in terrestrial conservation areas, but there are many types of fishing which do not conflict with conservation objectives. In the proposed Pulau Seribu Marine National Park, commercial fishing by island residents will be permitted in the buffer zone, and open water fisheries are recommended for consideration in the intensive use zone of the park after its establishment (Salm et al., 1982a, 1982b).

It is not easy, and indeed not even necessary, to exclude people from reserves in the densely-populated coastal zone of countries like Indonesia. People can be integrated into the protected areas by establishment of multiple use reserves (IUCN Category VIII). In the proposed Pulau Togian Multiple Use Reserve, for example, island residents will be able to continue subsistence and commercial fishing throughout most of the reserve (Salm et al., 1982c). However, certain areas, designated "Replenishment Reserves," will receive total protection. Fishing by non-residents will be prohibited throughout the vast reserve area. Hence, while the residents will lose some traditional areas to total protection, they will gain by the safeguarding of breeding stocks of overfished valuable species in the replenishment areas and by elimination of competition for resources by non-residents. Residents, who have dugout canoes or small boats, cannot compete with non-residents who come well-equipped in large and faster boats and who remove boatloads of trochus shells, pearl oysters and coconut crabs. To assist PPA management of the reserve, it is proposed that village chiefs be given responsibility for protection of replenishment areas and fishing grounds in their neighbourhood.

Multiple use reserves enable fulfilment of both resource conservation and utilization objectives. It is clear that in Indonesia there is need for a new category of conservation areas in which there is primary emphasis on managed resource exploitation, but in which all activities and developments are restricted which might jeopardise continued exploitation. Such reserves would perhaps be classified best as a category of Resource Reserve (IUCN Category VI). They could be large or small areas in which resource use is strictly managed within sustainable limits and where protection extends not to the resource but to its habitat.

For example, in many parts of Indonesia, sections of beach have traditionally been leased for the collection of all turtle eggs. It will be impractical to consider total protection of all of these beaches, which would meet formidable opposition by local residents. However, their cooperation might well be obtained if conservation efforts were geared more directly to their needs. Active habitat protection could be implemented to avoid damage to nesting beaches by sand mining or developments. Breeding turtles could be protected by the banning of turtle hunting and fishing with nets off the nesting beaches during the nesting season. Harvest of eggs could be kept within sustainable limits by leaving a percentage of the eggs to hatch in situ or in a hatchery located on the same beach.

Such exploitable resource reserves, although atypical protected area, would make a valuable contribution to conservation, especially of such species as the green and hawksbill turtles. They would perhaps best be placed under the jurisdiction of the Directorate General of Fisheries. PPA would retain responsibility for managing other types of protected areas.

3.2 The practice

The development of marine conservation in Indonesia is still in its formative stage. At the moment only 0.2%

of the staff of the Directorate of Nature Conservation (PPA) work exclusively on marine conservation. Only 1.1% of all the established parks and reserves are exclusively marine (i.e. marine parks at Pulau Banda, Pulau Pombo and Pulau Kasa in the Moluccas), and they lack management plans. However, some terrestrial protected areas which border the sea also make a useful contribution to marine conservation.

Previous projects working with PPA, such as the UNDP/FAO National Parks Development Projects or IUCN/WWF Indonesia Programme, have had minor marine components. At first glance this disparity between land and sea may seem incredible in an island nation whose territory is 70% ocean (excluding the 200 mile Exclusive Economic Zone). But it is understandable. Endemism, which is far more prevalent on the islands than in the sea, has endowed the land with many unique species now threatened with extinction. The survival of these species and of vanishing habitats has been of paramount concern, especially since it may seem in direct conflict with the increasing needs for land by Indonesia's expanding population. Such conflicts are far more visible on land than underwater and, from the conservation point of view, they have been far more urgent. The loss of such species and forests from Indonesia is a total loss from the world. The loss of marine species (e.g. turtles or dugongs) or habitats (e.g. coral reefs or mangroves) would be Indonesia's loss alone; these would survive elsewhere in the world, albeit in a world poorer for the loss. While the struggle continued on land to prevent extinctions, marine issues were relegated to lower priority. Species such as giant clams *Tridacna gigas* were eliminated from much of their former range; whole families of certain commercially valuable fishes (e.g. carangids, lutjanids, lethrinids, serranids) became rare or actually disappeared from many reefs; and naturally productive habitats, such as coral reefs and mangroves, were degraded by damaging fishing practices, pollution, siltation or clear-cutting. Now attention has turned to the sea.

PPA has found itself with the mandate to protect, conserve and manage coastal and marine habitats valuable to fisheries and tourism in addition to strict conservation of all endangered, vulnerable or depleted species. That 0.2% of the PPA staff has a task too large for even the remaining 98%. Fortunately, expansion of the marine conservation programme is planned during the upcoming 5 year development cycle which begins in 1984.

During 1981 a Marine Conservation Section was formed within PPA. The section has a staff of four, of which only one so far has training in marine science (actually fisheries management), experience in snorkelling, diving and survey. The section falls under the Sub-Directorate of Nature Reserves and Protection Forests. Although not ideal, this arrangement is a starting point. Consolidation of marine activities can only occur with further development of expertise. The establishment of a Sub-Directorate of Marine Conservation will be a goal of the next development phase in PPA.

The progress in establishment of protected marine areas is summarized in Table 1 (see also Robinson *et al.,* 1981). Their locations are depicted in Figs. 1 and 2. There are 3 marine parks, 2 recreation parks and 7 marine reserves declared but awaiting management plans and development. A further 3 marine parks (including 1 marine national park) and 28 marine reserves have been proposed. Seaward extension of the boundaries of one reserve has been effected and is proposed for 3 national parks and a further 7 reserves, one of which (Bali Barat - Pulau Manjangan) would be upgraded to a national park. A total of 24 terrestrial parks and reserves which border the sea have a coastal component (e.g. turtle nesting beach or mangrove). These areas contain a variety of elements, some more important than others.

There are three small coral reef reserves in Indonesia, all in the Moluccas, at Pulau Banda, Pulau Pombo and Pulau Kasa. Their total area is 4,600 ha, or less than 0.05% of the total protected area in Indonesia. The process of establishment has progressed as far as legal declaration and some limited management. Formulation of management plans and their implementation is the next step. The boundary of Tangkoko-Batuangus Strict Nature Reserve has been extended 500 m seaward to include offshore reefs; additional reef areas will be protected by extension of national park boundaries at Komodo, Ujung Kulon, Krakatau, Baluran and Bali Barat. Of these Bali Barat probably makes the greatest contribution to reef conservation, but the total value in the national perspective of their areas is small.

Indonesia has a great variety of reef types (patch, ocean atoll, shelf atoll, barrier and fringing reefs, faroes, knolls and shoals) of large size, high species diversity and considerable value. These important reefs are being surveyed and suitable locations are being proposed as reserves. The goal will be to retain the value of these reefs to fisheries, research and recreation by establishing a network of coral reef reserves and national parks linked by current corridors whose function will be to safeguard breeding stocks of valuable commercial species, samples of different reef environments and communities, and areas of value to tourism, research and education.

There are 130 reserves which have the protection of mangroves as a principal aim. Mangroves are also found bordering 14 other protected areas where they are of secondary interest. A further 9 proposals for mangrove reserves have been approved by provincial Governors and a great number of proposals are being processed. Proposals will be solicited from the Department of Fisheries and research institutions to help establish protection and management of those mangrove areas most valuable to fisheries production, research, education and conservation of genetic resources. There remains the need to classify mangroves by type, diversity, biological production, contribution to fisheries and value to endemic or particular species, and to include examples of each into the reserve system.

Turtle nesting beaches are well protected in 2 reserves, Meru Betiri and Cikepuh, and 1 national park, Ujung Kulon, all on the southern coast of Java. Turtles receive varying amounts of protection in 6 other reserves. However, relative to other nesting beaches in Indonesia, these are of lesser importance. Pulau Semama, East Kalimantan, has recently been declared a turtle reserve by local government; once approved and declared a reserve by central government, enforcement can begin and Indonesia will have an important green turtle reserve. It is not known to what extent Indonesia shares its turtle populations with neighbouring countries. There is evidence that the green turtles *Chelonia mydas* of East Kalimantan are part of a larger population shared by Indonesia, Sabah and the Philippines; that the turtles of northwest Kalimantan are shared with Sarawak; that the leatherbacks *Dermochelys coriacea* of Irian Jaya are part of a population shared with northern Papua New Guinea and that the leatherbacks of south Sumatra are shared with the Andaman and Nicobar Islands. Clearly the conservation of turtle stocks in Indonesia will require multi-national cooperation.

Of the 5 turtle species regularly occurring in Indonesia, only 3 are protected by law (Leatherback, Olive Ridleys and Loggerhead); the other 2 species (Green and Hawksbill) suffer heavy and unregulated exploitation. There are plans to achieve sustainable harvest of these 2 species, but not protection.

Dugong habitats as yet are not protected anywhere in Indonesia. Although dugongs themselves are protected, this law is not generally known or adhered to by coastal residents who continue to hunt them. There is still very little known of their distribution and movement, location and size of populations and conservation needs.

A dugong sanctuary has been proposed off southeast Aru. When established, this site will help safeguard what is probably Indonesia's largest dugong population. The proposed Teluk Cenderawasih Reserve in Irian Jaya also has the protection of dugongs and their habitats as one of the principal aims. Extension of the boundaries of existing protected areas in Kalimantan to include offshore dugong habitats will further safeguard dugong stocks. There are 4 other proposed reserves in which dugongs repeatedly occur. Like turtles, dugong populations are almost certainly shared with Papua New Guinea and Indonesia and their management would benefit from collaborative efforts. Here Indonesia can benefit greatly from the experience of dugong census and conservation in Papua New Guinea.

All whales and dolphins are protected in Indonesia. Other than the small scale traditional whale fishery off Lembata Island, there is no whaling in Indonesian seas. Indonesia has a vital role to play in the Indian Ocean Sanctuary, as the major migration route for great whales between the Indian and Pacific Oceans is through the Banda Sea and straits between Timor and Flores. Indonesia has not ratified the Indian Ocean Sanctuary or acceded to the International Convention for the Regulation of Whaling to become a voting member of the International Whaling Commission, but these are currently under consideration.

Still under-represented in protected areas are samples of beach forests, seabird nesting sites and rookeries, mudflats important as feeding areas for migrating waders and the habitats of marine invertebrates (such as giant clams, commercial trochus, pearl oysters, and coconut crabs) which are seriously depleted in some areas and urgently in need of management. No marine invertebrates are protected in Indonesia. Reserves are proposed for seabirds and some marine invertebrates, but important mudflats and beach forests have still to be identified.

4. THE PLAN FOR FURTHER DEVELOPMENT OF MARINE CONSERVATION

The principal problem facing marine conservation in Indonesia is how to control the continued destruction of productive habitats that are important to the livelihood of local residents and to the national economy; total value of recorded fisheries production in 1979 was $ 537,548,800 (Anon., 1980c) and of exports was US$ 236,827,000 (Anon., 1981)).

Another major problem is control of the current heavy exploitation of endangered and vulnerable species, such as turtles, dugongs, giant clams and coconut crabs, so that these can continue to contribute to the communities which currently exploit them. Certain of these species and habitats may well be critically endangered in Indonesia. However, we know little about them, they are of less socio-economic importance than turtles and dugongs or are not globally endangered, and we are limited in scope by inevitable financial constraints, so we concentrate initial efforts on the conservation and management of reefs, mangroves, turtles and dugongs.

Consistent with the objectives of the *World Conservation Strategy*, the overall objective of Marine Resource Conservation and Management in Indonesia is to achieve controlled development of the marine environment, sustainable utilization of Indonesia's diverse marine resources and protection of habitats critical to the survival of commercially valuable, endangered, vulnerable and other selected marine species. Toward this end, PPA will establish a system of marine multiple-use, resource and strict nature reserves and marine national parks; build within the organization a cadre of suitably trained personnel to manage these areas and to continue development of marine conservation; help develop public education programmes, essential legislation and appropriate enforcement tactics; and cooperate with other relevant research and management agencies.

There are 4 broad activities of this programme. Strategy formulation and establishment of a marine conservation specialist team are the beginning and lead to the longer term objectives: establishment of protected areas and establishment of a Sub-Directorate of Marine Conservation. There has been progress in all 4 activities.

Table 1. Existing and Proposed Marine Protected Areas and Terrestrial Protected Areas with Marine Components in Indonesia

Category	No.	Name of Area*	Province	Total	Area (Ha) Coral Reef	Mangrove	Marine Conservation Element
Declared Marine Park/Reserve							
1. Management/Protection Established	—	—	—	—	—	—	—
2. No Fully Established Management/Protection	1.	Mas-Popaya-Raja SNR	N. Sulawesi	160	—	—	seabirds
	2.	P. Kasa MP	Maluku	1,100	1,000	—	coral reef
	3.	P. Pombo MP	Maluku	1,000	500	—	coral reef
	4.	P. Banda MP	Maluku	2,500	?	—	coral reef
	5.	Gunung Api SNR	Maluku	80	—	—	seabirds
	6.	P. Manuk WR	Maluku	100	—	—	seabirds
	7.	Sabuda-Tataruga WR	Irian Jaya	450	50	—	nesting turtles, coral reef
	8.	Teluk Yotefa RP	Irian Jaya	1,650	—	—	recreation
	9.	Muara Angke SNR	Jakarta	15.4	—	15.4	mangrove
	10.	P. Kembang RP	S. Kalimantan	60	—	?	mangrove, recreation
	11.	P. Kaget WR	S. Kalimantan	85	—	85	mangrove
	12.	Teluk Kelumpang SNR	S. Kalimantan	66,500	—	13,750	mangrove
	13.	Hutan Bakau Pantai Timur Jambi SNR	Jambi, Sumatra	6,500	—	6,500	mangrove
Proposed Marine Park/Reserve	14.	P. Web-P. Beras SNR	Aceh, Sumatra	3,000	—	—	coral reef
	15.	Siberut (Teluk Sarabuda, P. Kecil, P. Panjang, P. Saibi, P. Kaininggit, P. Laba Buinan) SNR	West Sumatra	15,227	?	?	coral reef, mangrove
	16.	P. Tikus SNR	Bengkulu, Sumatra	—	?	?	coral reef
	17.†	P. Seribu MNP	Jakarta	108,000	?	?	coral reef, fringing mangrove, nesting green and hawksbill turtles, research & education, tourism
	18.	Segara Anakan-Nusakambangan SNR	Central Java	22,077	?	?	coral reef, mangrove, nesting green turtle
	19.	Karimunjawa WR	Central Java	111,625	?	—	coral reef, tourism
	20.	P. Pemenang MP	Nusa Tenggara	2,000	?	—	coral reef, tourism
	21.	P. Karimata SNR	W. Kalimantan	77,000	10,000	—	coral reef
	22.	Semana-Sangalaki SNR	E. Kalimantan	?	1,000	—	nesting green & hawksbill turtles, coral reef
	23.	P. Maratua-Karang Muaras SNR	E. Kalimantan	?	10,000	—	coral reef
	24.	P. Birah-Birahan SNR	E. Kalimantan	?	?	?	coral reef, beach vegetation, nesting turtles
	25.	Pamukan SNR	E. Kalimantan	10,000	—	10,000	mangrove
	26.	Muara Sebuku SNR	E. Kalimantan	110,000	?	55,000	mangrove
	27.	Kepulauan Bunaken MP	N. Sulawesi	49,375	?	—	coral reef, mangroves, tourism
	28.	P. Pasoso WR	Central Sulawesi	?	?	—	coral reef, nesting green turtles
	29.	P. Togian MMUR	Central Sulawesi	?	?	?	coral reef, coconut crab, nesting green & hawksbill turtles, dugong, mangrove
	30.	P. Peleng SNR	Central Sulawesi	?	?	?	dugongs, coral reefs, nesting green turtles
	31.	P. Samalona SNR	S. Sulawesi	5,000	?	—	coral reef, nesting green turtles
	32.	Kawi-Kawia (= Kahabia) SNR	SE Sulawesi	?	—	—	seabirds
	33.	Teluk Dalam-Teluk Lasolo SNR	SE Sulawesi	?	?	—	coral reef, dugong

Table 1 (cont). Existing and Proposed Marine Protected Areas and Terrestrial Protected Areas with Marine Components in Indonesia

Category	No.	Name of Area*	Province	Total	Coral Reef	Mangrove	Marine Conservation Element
	34.	Selawat Wawonoi SNR	SE. Sulawesi	?	?	—	coral reef, dugong
	35.	Selat Muna SNR	SE. Sulawesi	?	?	—	no information
	36.	P. Penyu SNR	Maluku	?	?	—	coral reef, nesting green turtle
	37.	Aru Tenggara SNR	Maluku	200,000	?	?	dugongs, nesting green & hawksbill turtles, mangrove, saltwater crocodile, coral reef
	38.	Raja Ampat SNR	Irian Jaya	2,976	?	—	coral reef
	39.	Kepulauan Ayu-Asia WR	Irian Jaya	904	?	—	coral reef, green turtles
	40.	N. Coast Vogelkop (5 beaches) WRs	Irian Jaya	?	—	—	nesting green & leatherneck turtles
	41.	Teluk Bintuni SNR	Irian Jaya	450,000 +	—	450,000	mangrove
	42.	Teluk Cenderawasih MR	Irian Jaya	?	80,000	?	nesting green & hawksbill turtles, dugong, saltwater crocodile, *Tridacna gigas* & other giant clam species, coral reef, mangrove
	43.	P. Mapia WR	Irian Jaya	1,557	?	—	coral reef, nesting hawksbill turtles
	44.	P. Sayang WR	Irian Jaya	?	—	—	nesting hawksbill turtles
Declared Terrestrial Reserves Bordering the Sea							
1. Seaward Extensions Exists	45.	Tangkoko-Batuangus SNR	N. Sulawesi	1,250	?	—	coral reef
2. Seaward Extension Proposed	46.	Krakatau Islands WR	W. Java	?	?	—	coral reef, nesting green & hawksbill turtles, research & education
	47.	Ujung Kulon NP	W. Java	72,000	?	?	coral reef, mangrove, nesting green and rare leatherback turtles
	48.	Sancang Cipatijah WR	W. Java	2,500	—	?	mangrove, nesting turtles
	49.	Pananjung-Pangandaran SNR + RP	W. Java	2,500	?	—	coral reef, recreation
	50.	Baluran NP	E. Java	4,000	?	?	coral reef, mangrove, milkfish fry nursery
	51.	Bali Barat-P. Menjangan WR	Bali	6,220	810	310	coral reef, mangrove, tourism
	52.	P. Moyo WR	Nusa Tenggara	?	?	—	coral reef
	53.	Komodo-Padar-Rinca NP	Nusa Tenggara	34,271	?	?	coral reef, mangrove, turtles, plankton rich seas, whale sharks, manta rays, whales
	54.	Tanjung Api SNR	Central Sulawesi	?	?	—	coral reef
	55.	Anggremeos WR	Irian Jaya	2,500	?	?	coral reef, mangrove, dugong
3. No Seaward Extension, but includes Marine Component	56.	P. Berteh WR	E. Sumatra	500	—	?	mangrove
	57.	Berbak WR	Jambu, Sumatra	190,000	—	?	mangrove
	58.	Way Kambas WR	Lampung, Sumatra	130,000	—	?	mangrove
	59.	Sumatra Selatan WR	Lampung, Sumatra	356,800		—	nesting green turtles
	60.	P. Dua SNR	W. Java	8	—	?	mangrove, waders**
	61.	P. Bokor SNR	Jakarta	15	—	—	waders**
	62.	P. Rambut SNR	Jakarta	18	—	?	mangrove, waders**
	63.	Cikepuh WR	W. Java	8,127.5	—	—	nesting green turtles
	64.	Teluk Baron SNR	Yogyakarta, Java	2.4	—	—	? recreation
	65.	Nusa Barung SNR	S. Java	6,100	—	—	nesting green turtles
	66.	Meru Betiri WR	E. Java	50,000	—	—	nesting green, hawksbill, leatherback & Ridley turtles
	67.	Banyuwangi Selatan WR	E. Java	62,000	—	—	nesting green turtles, seabirds
	68.	P. Manipo WR	Nusa Tenggara	2,000	—	—	seabirds
	69.	Tanjung Puting WR	Central Kalimantan	335,000	—	11,000	mangrove**

Table 1 (cont). Existing and Proposed Marine Protected Areas and Terrestrial Protected Areas with Marine Components in Indonesia

Category	No.	Name of Area*	Province	Total	Area (Ha) Coral Reef	Mangrove	Marine Conservation Element
	70.	Kutai WR	E. Kalimantan	200,000	—	?	mangrove**
	71.	Pleihari Tanah Laut WR	S. Kalimantan	35,000	—	4,000	mangrove**, nesting green turtle
	72.	Panua SNR	N. Sulawesi	1,500	—	?	mangrove
	73.	Morowali SNR	Central Sulawesi	200,000	—	?	mangrove**
	74.	Lampoko-Mapie WR	S. Sulawesi	2,000	—	?	mangrove
	75.	Tanjung Peropa WR	SE. Sulawesi	38,000	—	?	mangrove
	76.	Watumohai HP	SE. Sulawesi	50,000	—	?	mangrove
	77.	Gunung Lorentz SNR	Irian Jaya	1,675,000	—	301,500	mangrove**
	78.	P. Dolok WR	Irian Jaya	600,000	—	99,000	mangrove**
	79.	Wasur WR	Irian Jaya	225,000	—	6,180	mangrove**

† recently declared a SNR, due to be classified a MNP.
* P = Pulau (= island), MP = Marine Park, MNP/NP = Marine National Park/National Park, RP = Recreation Park, HP = Hunting Park, SNR = Strict Nature Reserve, MR/WR = Marine Reserve/Wildlife Reserve, MMUR = Marine Multiple Use Reserve.
** Element of major interest

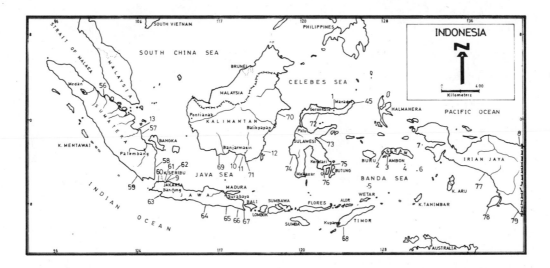

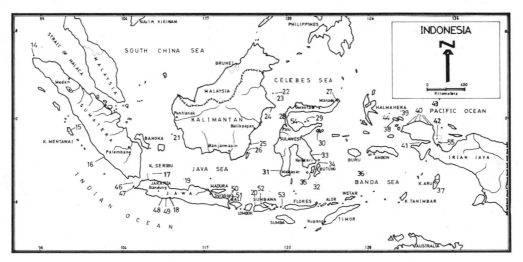

Figures 1 and 2. Indonesia, with existing and proposed protected areas shown.

Chapter 7
The Australian Realm

Keynote Address: The Australian Realm

D.F. McMichael
Department of Home Affairs and Environment
Canberra, Australia

N.C. Gare
Australian National Parks and Wildlife Service
Canberra, Australia

ABSTRACT. *Australia has a long history of national parks, beginning with Royal National Park in 1879. Since that time, Australia has developed an extensive system of protected areas which reflects the federal structure of the Australian Government, with each state having its own system. As a result, there is considerable diversity in approach, manpower, and budget between the various states. Australia has also suffered what may be a unique problem in the world: the sheer abundance of land in an essentially natural state. However, this is balanced by a number of particularly critical areas, such as the rainforests of New South Wales and Queensland and the wilderness of Southwest Tasmania.*

1. HISTORICAL BACKGROUND

When Europeans first came to settle on the east coast of Australia almost 200 years ago, they found a land in which the indigenous aboriginal people lived in almost perfect harmony with nature. The Australian Aborigines were hunter-gatherers, to whom the cultivation of crops, the building of permanent dwellings, the formation of permanent settlements, and the extraction and use of minerals were all unknown and unnecessary.

That is not to say that the Aborigines had no significant impact on the natural environment. On the contrary, it seems certain that since the arrival of the Aborigines over 40,000 years ago, the Australian environment has been markedly altered through their manipulation of the natural ecosystems. Their principal management tool appears to have been fire. As well as using fire for comfort and cooking, the Aborigines used it as a hunting tool. There can be little doubt that the incidence of fire in Australian ecosystems was markedly higher as a result of Aboriginal activity than it would have been in their absence. Nevertheless it seems likely that over many millenia a new balance was reached, in which the numbers of human beings and their lifestyles were finely adapted to the environments in which they found themselves.

The European occupation of Australia changed all that. They brought with them values and a technology which had evolved in a different environment, and imposed them, without ever questioning their right to do so, on the ancient people and ecosystems which confronted them. Within one hundred years, the greater part of Australia's non-arid land had been transformed into an agricultural/pastoral landscape, with alien animals predominating and exotic plant species widespread. As the natural areas shrank before the axe and the plough, most of the animals retreated to the remnant habitat, or slipped quietly into extinction. The Aboriginal people too were generally unable to cope with this onslaught, and either declined in numbers or retreated to the more remote areas of their former tribal lands.

There were some areas of Australia to which European culture did not penetrate, or where it failed to become established. In particular the arid central and western parts, much of the tropical north, and the wet and rugged south-west of Tasmania, remain to this day largely unsettled, though not necessarily uninfluenced by the new Australians. Not surprisingly, these more-or-less natural areas are regarded today as having high nature conservation value. Regrettably they are also seen by some as areas still available for exploitation, by applying the scientific knowledge and technology of the 20th and 21st centuries.

Despite the rapidity with which Europeans occupied and transformed the land, a few were acutely aware of the beauty and interest of Australia's natural environment, and concerned about its wildlife. Hear the words of John Gould in 1863:

"Short-sighted indeed are the Anglo-Australians, or they would long ere this have made laws for the preservation of their highly singular, and in many cases noble, indigenous animals . . . . . without some such protection the remnant that is left will soon disappear, to be followed by unavailing regret for the apathy with which they had been previously regarded."

So it was that, as long ago as 1879, Australia's first National Park was established in rugged coastal bush and heathland immediately to the south of the growing city of Sydney. This was the world's second National Park, and for more than a century now, it has provided successive generations of Sydney residents with their most accessible area of natural bushland, rich in plant and animal life, and containing some spectacular coastal scenery. Many of Australia's leading natural scientists and conservationists owe their interest in nature to their early experience in this priceless piece of Australia's heritage.

Royal National Park (as it is now known) was soon followed by other National Parks or equivalent Reserves in the other colonies (as the states were then called). By the turn of the century, there were a variety of areas in most states reserved under one designation or another, and variously described as being for the preservation of fauna and flora, for public recreation, or for the preservation of scenery. These areas provided the federation of states, known as the Commonwealth of Australia when formed in 1901, with a network of protected areas serving a variety of social purposes. They were not "national" parks and reserves in the normal sense of the word—that is, they did not become the responsibility of the new Government. But in every other sense they constituted a "national" system, since they were generally protected in similar ways, and were used by the Australian people, inveterate travellers all, as recreation destinations and were perceived as conservation areas for the distinctive Australia fauna and flora.

Nevertheless it was not until the middle of this century that any significant attention was paid to the overall conservation status of Australia's flora and fauna and the ecosystems which they constitute. The rising tide of public interest in nature conservation coincided with the great economic boom which followed the Second World War. There had always been a far-sighted few who had pressed the need for a more comprehensive system of parks and reserves, and while they had some successes, there was little sense of urgency until the great flood of developments associated with the boom began to make inroads into the remaining pockets of natural bushland with which Australians had long been familiar.

During the 1960s and early 1970s nature conservation in Australia turned professional. Up to that time, the business of identifying and setting aside areas of land with nature conservation value had been a part-time interest of a few Government officials, as often as not in response to protracted lobbying from local enthusiasts and the various community conservation and recreation organizations. The parks and reserves which had been established were, by and large, managed by one or a few untrained rangers, if they were managed at all. None had any published management plan, and few if any had been the subject of any resources survey. The various pieces of legislation under which they were established varied widely from state to state, and not all the parks and reserves were secure against inappropriate use or even exploitation of the timber, water and mineral resources which they contained. Further- more, the range of ecosystems contained within the parks and reserves then established was very limited. Almost all of them had been selected because they contained attractive forest coupled with high scenic value. Many were located in rugged mountainous regions, others were coastal, but few were on the inland plains or in the arid interior. There were exceptions such as Ayers Rock-Mt. Olga National Park and the Tanami Desert Wildlife Sanctuary in the Northern Territory and the Simpson Desert National Park in Queensland (Mosley, 1967).

Movement toward better legislation commenced in 1956 with passage of the Victorian National Parks Act, while the Queensland Forestry Act 1959 enunciated separate management principles for state Forests and National Parks. In 1967, under a strong and vigorous Minister, the state of New South Wales adopted a new National Parks and Wildlife Act, for the first time bringing nature conservation under the umbrella of one organization—a National Parks and Wildlife Service. Other states, territories and the Commonwealth followed this trend, so that by 1982 comprehensive nature conservation legislation existed in some form or other in each part of the Federation.

As a result of this increased activity, the amount of land reserved primarily for nature conservation has risen to over 30 million ha, equivalent to about 4% of Australia's land area.

So far we have dealt only with land reserved specifically for nature conservation, or purposes closely related thereto such as the preservation of scenery, and for public recreation. However, land was reserved for many purposes in the Australian Colonies/states, some of which resulted in the preservation of extensive areas in an essentially natural condition, thus contributing to the overall area of land in its natural state, and hence to nature conservation. The most significant of these purposes was forestry.

When Europeans first settled in Australia, the timber producing trees with which they were familiar were, of course, missing. The search for timber was an important factor in the opening up of the lands of eastern Australia to settlement by Europeans. Some species of Australian trees were found to produce particularly good timbers for a variety of purposes, and they were eagerly sought out and harvested, with little regard for the future. The classic example is the species known as Australian Red Cedar *Cedrela toona*, which was once abundant in the coastal rainforests of northern New South Wales. These rainforests were known as "The Big Scrub" and they were cut down mercilessly as the cedar was harvested during the latter part of the 19th century. By the turn of the century, all 75,000 ha of the Big Scrub had vanished, save only a few remnants which are so small as to make doubtful their capacity to survive in the long term.

Early in the 20th century, the need to reserve areas of land containing high quality timber, and areas suitable for the establishment of plantations, especially of introduced softwood species such as the Monterey Pine *Pinus radiata* became apparent. In each state, large areas of land have been reserved for forestry purposes, and much of this remains either in a near natural state (11.5 million ha at 30 June 1978) or as regenerated native forest following earlier timber harvesting. As such it contributes significantly to the habitat available to native Australian plants and animals, though it cannot be said to be "secure" habitat, because most of it is subject to management practices designed to maximize timber production, and to exploitation in one way or another. Some areas are destined to be selectively logged on a sustained yield basis, and here the nature conservation value is high. Others will be subject to clear-felling for wood-chips, and subsequently allowed to regenerate as native forests over rotations varying between 40 and 120 years. These too can have considerable nature conservation importance, as it has been shown that virtually all the species originally present in an area are re-established within 10-15 years of clear-felling providing sufficient reservoirs of undisturbed habitat are left in close proximity to the clear-felled areas (Loyn *et al.*, 1980). Some areas of the forest estate are, however, destined for clearing and planting of introduced *Pinus* species, and these will have little residual nature conservation value.

Other areas which can have high nature conservation significance are those reserved to protect water catchments, especially those providing the water supply of the larger cities.

In recent years, there has been considerable pressure from the nature conservation movement in Australia to have some of the lands at present reserved for forestry and water catchment protection purposes transferred to the National Park and Nature Reserve system. In some cases, this has been suggested because the value of the area for recreation is high; in other cases it is because of the ecosystems contained in them, or because they provide extensive habitat for native plants and animals in areas otherwise lacking it. Where there are no powerful reasons for retaining such lands for their original purpose, or where that purpose is compatible with national park/nature reserve status, these pressures have often been responded to by the transfer of the land in question. In other cases, however, the lands have been seen as still required for the original purposes and the pressure for transfer has been resisted. This has led to some bitter controversies, a number of which are still continuing.

In summary, we can say that the Australian Realm has, in less than 200 years, been transformed from a continent largely in its natural state, to one which is dominated by European man and the species he brought with him. There are, however, still substantial areas in a natural or near-natural state, and a significant area of land has been reserved for nature conservation, or purposes closely aligned with it. The area specifically reserved for this purpose is growing daily, and it can be expected to continue to do so for some time to come. The extent to which the existing reserve system preserves an adequate sample of Australian ecosystems and species will be examined next.

2. CURRENT STATUS OF PROTECTED AREAS IN THE REALM

The biogeographic provinces proposed by Udvardy (1975) for the Australian Realm were based primarily on vegetation, and have been recently reviewed by Australian scientists who have suggested amended boundaries currently under consideration by Australian nature conservation authorities.

Specht (1981) has separately examined the relationship between secure reserves and vegetational association and has concluded that many Australian plant communities (formations and alliances) are now reasonably well conserved in the network of reserves proclaimed throughout Australia. Nevertheless he commented that "undoubtedly efforts need to be made in all regions of Australia to overcome deficiencies in the National System of Ecological Reserves" and identified seven major plant formations as being virtually absent from, or poorly conserved in the network:

1) Tropical/sub-tropical tussock grasslands in the coastal and semi-arid zones, and in south-eastern Queensland.
2) Mulga *Acacia aneura* and related *Acacia* tall shrubland communities of the semi-arid zone of Queensland, New South Wales, Northern Territory and South Australia.
3) Low shrubland (shrub steppe) communities dominated by *Atriplex* spp. and *Maireana* (*Kochia*) spp. in semi-arid southern Australia.
4) Temperate tussock grasslands (*Themeda*, *Danthonia*, and *Lomandra*) of western Victoria and South Australia.
5) Brigalow *Acacia harpophylla* open forests in central and south-eastern Queensland.
6) Savannah woodland communities (dominated by many *Eucalyptus* spp) in the wheat belt of south-eastern Queensland, New South Wales,

Victoria, Tasmania, South Australian and Western Australia.

7) The Mallee open-scrub (*Eucalyptus socialis* alliance) in the wheat belt of north-western Victoria and the adjacent Murray lands of South Australia.

Specht pointed out that "the first three formations listed . . . form a vital part of the pastoral industry in the semi-arid zone of Australia" but noted that "large, but degraded conservation reserves could still be acquired". He went on to say that "the last four formations lie within the wheat belt/improved pasture zone of Australia", and that "only small 'islands', plus roadside corridors, still remain".

While every effort should be made now to correct these deficiencies in the system, it is worth remembering Specht's earlier assertion that "undoubtedly efforts need to be made in all regions of Australia to overcome deficiencies". There is still a lot of "in-filling" to be done before there will be an adequate sample of the ecosystems and species of Australian fauna and flora contained within the Australian nature conservation reserve system.

Although the Australian Realm consists of a single country, it does not have a single system of protected areas. In fact it is a federation of six sovereign states, one large self-governing territory (the Northern Territory), one small internal "Federal" territory (the Australian Capital Territory), and the small number of "external" territories, mostly oceanic islands, many of which are uninhabited. It is therefore appropriate to consider the nature conservation systems operating in the various states and the internal territories. While there are differences in the precise details by which lands are reserved and managed for nature conservation purposes, the differences now are relatively insignificant. A recent publication entitled "*Nature Conservation Reserves in Australia* (1980)" (Hinchey, 1981) briefly described the systems operating in each state and territory at that time. Since then a new law has come into operation in the Australian Capital Territory which aligns it more closely with the other states.

The reasons why this degree of uniformity now exists will be dealt with later. The important point to be made is that it was not always so. Because the states have sovereignty over land within their borders, and in the absence of any specific mention in the Australian Constitution of Federal Government power relating to nature conservation, it follows that this function is almost wholly the responsibility of the state Governments (and for all practical purposes, of the Territory Governments).

Generally speaking it can be said that areas reserved for nature conservation have a very high degree of protection in Australia. For the most part they are securely reserved against any form of direct exploitation, be it for timber, flora and fauna, or minerals. Some contain areas which are available for tourist development, but generally under strict control and usually with the objective of providing accommodation for visitors to the parks and reserves, and facilities to enable them to enjoy the natural features. While developments of this kind sometimes create controversy (for example, the resort development in Kosciusko National Park to provide for skiers) most are considered to be conforming uses.

There have been a few cases where the boundaries of national parks or nature reserves have been altered in order to allow valuable resources lying within them to be exploited, but in such cases there has often been a compensating addition of adjacent land. More often the boundaries of the protected areas have been drawn in the first place to exclude specific areas subject to exploitation. In some cases this has resulted in enclaves of exploitation, especially mining, within national parks, but usually such areas have been at the margins. Whether enclave or marginal, the exclusion of areas from a park or reserve to permit active exploitation to continue is always viewed with hostility by the nature conservation movement, and some of the most prolonged and vehement disputes which have occurred in Australia over nature conservation issues in recent years have been about such matters—for example, the exclusion of known Uranium-containing ore bodies from Kakadu National Park in the Northern Territory. But it remains true that these situations are the exceptions. Most protected areas have satisfactory boundaries, are permanently reserved for nature conservation, cannot be subjected to uses which are incompatible with the primary objective, and can only have their boundaries altered with the consent of the appropriate legislature.

3. FACTORS AFFECTING THE ESTABLISHMENT AND MANAGEMENT OF PROTECTED AREAS

3.1 Impeding factors

The single factor which most impeded the establishment of protected areas in Australia was the sheer abundance of land in an essentially natural state. It seems a truism that when people are surrounded by naturalness, there is little incentive to reserve and protect it. Although the transformation of the landscape took place very quickly following European settlement, the small population generally did not feel any sense of loss because there still seemed to be a sufficiency of naturalness available in the areas left unaltered.

Since the beginning of this century, however, there has developed an increasing awareness of the fact that the bush was disappearing, that the fauna and flora were diminishing in number and range. Despite this, it was not until the 1960s that any significant increase occurred in the area of land reserved and protected. Why was this? Because the new Australians, derived for the most part from the British Isles and to a small extent from other European countries, had brought with them an essentially Judeo-Christian view of the world which places man in the ascendency over nature. The widely held view was, and still is, that land that is not "productive" of some usable output is wasted and to be feared.

The distinguished Australian poet, author, and conservationist, Judith Wright, has eloquently told the story in an essay entitled "Wilderness, Waste and History" (Australian Conservation Foundation, 1980). She writes about present-day attitudes as follows:

"Our own dreams have shrunk to more realistic proportions, and our politicians now merely want to sell as much iron, coal and uranium as possible from the still untamed north and west of the continent, regardless of the wastelands which will follow. The concept behind this ambition is of course still the same—the Wilderness must be turned to account, even if in the process it becomes an even more unproductive waste—and the psychology behind it is I think also the same: a continuing and deeply instinctive fear and dislike of the unknown, of country of which man is not in control and which pays no tribute to his economy and his technological powers".

These attitudes have generally operated to produce powerful resistance to almost every proposal for a national park or nature reserve. The arguments which are advanced against the establishment of a new protected area are varied, but they all stem from two basic propositions:

a) that some valuable commodity, be it timber, minerals, grazing opportunity, or tourist development opportunity, will be "lost" or "sterilized" or "locked up"; and

b) that a threat to adjacent productive or occupied land will arise from the protected area—either from wild animals (predators, competing herbivores) or plants (weeds) or from uncontrolled wildfire.

Another factor which has operated to impede the establishment of protected areas is lack of money to buy land. This has been particularly important in those regions which have been extensively subdivided and settled, but where the land has remained largely in its natural condition, for example in the Southern Mulga/Saltbush Biogeographic Province. Here the opportunity exists to obtain comparatively large areas of land for nature conservation purposes through purchase of grazing properties, but they cost a great deal of money and governments have not been willing to provide sufficient funds to enable all desirable purchases to be made. In other regions, money is required, not so much to purchase very large areas, but for smaller areas which are needed to increase the size of existing reserves or to remove enclaves of non-conforming use. Again sufficient funds are seldom available to permit all areas of

value to be acquired. However, in recent years Governments have significantly increased the funds made available to nature conservation agencies for this purpose.

A further factor which has affected the development of a coordinated national approach to the establishment and effective management of protected areas is the division of powers between the states and the Commonwealth in the Australian Federation.

The Australian Constitution left power over land and land use generally with the states, the Commonwealth Government's jurisdiction being for the most part confined to those territories over which it retains full power. The Commonwealth does, however, have sovereign power over the sea bed, and it is because of this that the Great Barrier Reef Marine Park is being progressively established under Commonwealth legislation, with participation in management by the state of Queensland.

One result of the division of powers in Australia was that each state adopted a different approach to protected areas establishment. This led to differences in the terminology used, the regulations adopted, and the kinds of places included in the protected area system. To a large extent these reflect differences in the cultural and historical origins and development of each of the colonies which became states, accentuated by the vastness and climatic diversity of Australia. Yet in recent years there has been a tendency towards greater uniformity of approach, to which we shall return later.

The main factors impeding effective management of protected areas in Australia have been the lack of knowledge of management principles for natural areas, and the lack of trained manpower. It is only in very recent times that scientific study has been applied to Australian ecosystems—to find out how they work and what needs to be done to them to attain specific management goals—and to date, only a very little knowledge has accumulated. Despite the commendable efforts of organizations like the Commonwealth Scientific and Industrial Research Organisation (CSIRO), the state and Federal nature conservation agencies, various state government research organizations, the universities, and funding bodies such as World Wildlife Fund (Australia), there is still a great knowledge vacuum as far as most ecosystems and most species are concerned.

Even where knowledge is available, it cannot always be applied. To do so requires skilled manpower, able to understand the principles and apply the techniques to give effect to them, and this is not always available. It is not just a matter of training. Even the best-trained natural area manager cannot apply his knowledge and skills if he does not have the time and the resources to allow him to do it properly. Time is always the great enemy, and of course its absence is no more than another measure of inadequate resources. However, the situation is improving. During the last two decades there has been a substantial increase in the number of protected area managers, many of whom have had university level training in relevant disciplines.

3.2 Encouraging factors

Despite all this, we must remember that it is not yet 200 years since European settlement began in Australia. With the approach of the Bicentenary in 1988, it is important also to consider those factors which have encouraged and continue encouraging the establishment and effective management of protected areas.

An important factor has been that the dominant cultural force has been, until recently, very unified. That is to say, until after World War II the great majority of non-Aboriginal Australians were of British stock and spoke a common language. They had a common legal tradition deriving in large measure from British forms and practice, and perhaps most important, there was a relatively high level of equality among people—that is, there were few large land-owners, many small holdings, and larger amounts of land remained under control of the Government. In addition, the Australian people have been very mobile, moving frequently between different parts of the country in pursuit of jobs or economic opportunity. Thus despite the "tyranny of distance" there has always been a rapid exchange of information and ideas throughout the country, and what was found successful in one state was quickly tested in another.

In recent decades the fact that Australia is a federation with a central Government has ensured that any reluctance by a state to act vigorously has resulted in requests for Commonwealth intervention (even though the Constitutional power of the Commonwealth to take the action proposed may be the subject to debate). This in turn has spurred the states to make greater efforts, because the last thing they want is the central Government encroaching upon their traditional areas of responsibility.

Another important factor has been the biological interest, indeed uniqueness, of the Australian fauna and flora. This has stimulated scientists and others interested in nature, to move vigorously to preserve and protect the fauna and flora, and of course the responsibility is much easier to demonstrate if your country is wholly responsible for a fauna and flora, than it is if the responsibility is shared with other countries. Further, the rapid change in the distribution and abundance of species has been obvious to anyone who cared to notice, and this too has promoted public interest in protected areas.

The emergence of strong advocates from time to time over the past 100 years has given impetus to the protected area movement. Individual public figures and community organizations have exerted a steady pressure for better legislation, a more comprehensive reserve system, and a more professional approach to management.

An important result of this swell of public concern and Government activity has been the development of cooperative arrangements among the states and the Commonwealth to promote fauna and flora conservation and protected area establishment and management.

The annual Ministerial conferences begun in 1967 were formalized in 1974 as the Council of Nature Conservation Ministers, known as CONCOM. It consists of the Ministers responsible for nature conservation matters from each of the six states, the two mainland territories (the Northern Territory and the Australian Capital Territory) and the Commonwealth Government. It is supported by a Standing Committee of senior officials, the Directors of the various state and Commonwealth National Park and Wildlife Services (Ministers and officials from Papua New Guinea and New Zealand also attend by invitation).

A major role of CONCOM has been to address the problem of achieving effective cooperation on a national basis on important nature conservation issues. Working groups of officers from each state and the Commonwealth have been appointed to consider and report on a variety of nationally important problems such as endangered fauna and flora, the use of remote sensing, law enforcement, sub-professional training, and the classification and nomenclature of protected areas.

CONCOM considered and approved appropriate roles in the Federal system for the Australian National Parks and Wildlife Service (ANPWS), established by the Commonwealth in 1973. As well as framing national nature conservation principles for Commonwealth Government endorsement and recommending national policies, the Commonwealth Service has a number of roles aimed at cooperation with and among the states, as well as the development of research, survey, inventory, monitoring, training, and education programmes of national importance. It also has responsibility for establishing and managing marine parks outside areas controlled by the states, i.e., outside the three-mile limit from the coast.

Under the umbrella of CONCOM much progress is being made towards increased cooperation and the best use of resources and expertise in the national interest among the states and the Commonwealth. For example in the past few weeks the first Regional Seminar, sponsored by CONCOM and organized on its behalf by the ANPWS, has brought together senior management personnel from the states, the Commonwealth, New Zealand, and Papua New Guinea to examine and learn from field management situations in three states and the Australian Capital Territory.

CONCOM has been a powerful factor in the development of a common attitude at Government level within Australia towards legislative provisions, the nomeclature used, and the management practices which apply to protected areas.

4. SPECIAL TOPICS RELEVANT TO THE REALM

4.1 The Aboriginal people and national parks

As emphasized at the beginning of this paper, the Australian Aborigines had a special relationship with the land, and lived in harmony with nature. There are still numbers of Aborigines living in parts of Australia in close association with their ancentral lands. In recent years, there has been a movement to restore to the Aborigines title to these lands, some of which have high nature conservation value. One such area is the Alligator Rivers Region in the Northern Territory, where the Aboriginal owners have entered into formal arrangements with the Australian National Parks and Wildlife Service, for their lands to be leased and reserved as the Kakadu National Park, subject to their having the right to live in traditional ways on it. This has proved to be a very effective working relationship, satisfactory to the Aborigines and to the National Park managers, and is regarded with considerable interest as a model for similar arrangements elsewhere. Of special interest is a programme under which Aboriginal men and women are being trained to become rangers and eventually managers in the Park established on their land.

4.2 The Great Barrier Reef

This extraordinary system of coral reefs and related ecosystems is protected by a unique legislative arrangement which provides a protective framework within which reasonable use of the reef system may continue. The Great Barrier Reef Marine Park Act defines the Great Barrier Reef Region, within which areas may be declared as part of the Marine Park. Once declared, the areas are fully protected against mining and related activities including oil drilling, but other forms of exploitation, including commercial fishing and tourism, are permitted where appropriate. To date two major areas of the Region have been declared as part of the Marine Park, amounting to 48,000 square kilometres. The Region covers 348,000 square kilometres, though it does not follow that all of it will eventually be declared since it is arbitrarily defined simply to enclose the whole of the Great Barrier Reef. The Great Barrier Reef Marine Park Authority is required by law to prepare a zoning plan for each area declared; this plan is placed on exhibition for several months, during which time the public have an opportunity to comment on it, and the Authority is required to take the public comments into account before the plan is finalized and comes into operation. Day-to-day management of the Park is carried out with involvement of agencies of the state of Queensland, under a formal agreement between that state and the Commonwealth.

4.3 International agreements and their significance

A number of international conventions and agreements have important relationships to Australia's protected areas. Perhaps the most important of these is the Convention Concerning the Protection of the World Cultural and Natural Heritage (the World Heritage Convention).

Under this Convention, the Great Barrier Reef, the Willanda Lakes Region, and Kakadu National Park have already been included on the World Heritage list. Two other natural areas have been nominated for addition to the list and will be considered at the World Heritage Committee's meeting later this year, Lord Howe Island off the coast of New South Wales and a series of Wilderness Parks in south-western Tasmania.

Great controversy surrounds the latter area, because it is the central part of one of the last great temperate wilderness areas of the Southern Hemisphere. It is also an area with considerable hydro-electric potential and the Tasmanian Government has decided to build a major dam in the area for power development which it regards as essential for Tasmania's economic growth. The nomination of the area for inclusion on the World Heritage List has brought great pressure to bear on the Tasmanian and Commonwealth Governments to find ways to protect the area; the outcome remains uncertain at this time. (Editor's note: In December 1982, the World Heritage Committee added Western Tasmania Wilderness National Park to the World Heritage List and the Australian Cabinet approved the building of the dam. The controversy continues).

Other conventions and agreements to which Australia is a party and which give international standing to protected areas are the Ramsar Convention on Wetlands of International Importance and the UNESCO Man and the Biosphere Programme. Twelve Australian Parks and Reserves have been designated as Biosphere Reserves, and two areas have been identified for protection under the Ramsar Convention. Another Agreement having significance for the establishment and management of protected areas is that between Japan and Australia in relation to Migratory Birds and Birds in Danger of Extinction. Recent discussions have taken place between the two countries following consultation among the states and Commonwealth. It seems likely that international conventions such as these will increasingly be used to give status, and therefore additional protection, to important protected areas in Australia.

4.4 Staff training

A major step forward in improving capacity to establish and manage successfully the protected areas in the Australian Realm is the attention being given to training and development of staff. Twenty years ago the number of graduates in protected area management could virtually be counted on the fingers of one hand. Today most park services have a variety of professional skills represented in their ranks, and much attention is being given to staff training and recruitment programmes designed to furnish skilled professionals for the investigation, planning, and management of parks and reserves. Not only are full degree and post-graduate courses available at a range of universities and colleges, but subprofessional courses of an applied nature are available to produce more people at the technician level for day-to-day management.

To some extent competition among states and the Commonwealth has produced this range of improved training opportunities. At the same time there have been excellent examples of seminars and workshops involving interstate and international participation and co-operation. In a new development, the Australian National Parks and Wildlife Service has provided a training officer to help the South Australian Service develop a comprehensive training programme for its field staff, and the two Services are about to cooperate in an Aboriginal ranger training programme in the Flinders Ranges of South Australia.

4.5 New technology

The tightening of the purse-strings in public administration all over the world has not been escaped in Australia. One effect in protected area management is an accelerated effort to adopt new technology in such management, and the training of staff to understand the new tools and put them to best use. Remote sensing and the use of computer modelling are but two examples of this new trend, which will greatly assist capacity to assess and manage natural areas in the eighties and onwards towards the year 2000.

4.6 Public participation

In the past decade there has been more formal involvement of private citizens in the process of selection and management of protected areas in Australia. There is now a widespread statutory requirement for members of the public to have an opportunity to make representations concerning plans of management. Similarly the practice of having advisory or consultative committees is developing as a major factor in achieving positive community involvement.

Shortage of public finance and related resources has also contributed to further efforts being made in two fields: the making of arrangements between Governments and private landholders for the protection of natural areas on the latter's land (thereby avoiding costly land acquisition); and the involvement of volunteer groups to assist Government agencies in some aspects of park and reserve management.

4.7 Commonwealth-state cooperation

As will be evident from what has been mentioned previously, a key factor in protected area establishment and management in Australia is the fact that the country is a federation of sovereign states and one large, self-governing territory. This has, on the one hand, prevented the establishment of a centrally controlled National Park system such as found in the United States or Canada. It has, on the other hand, led to a good deal of healthy competition among the states, in striving to establish "the best" system of protected areas, and to cooperation among the states and the Commonwealth in the development of policies relating to such matters as ranger trainig, fire management, wildlife management, control of scientific research, control of exotic and pest species, the siting and design of visitor facilities, and the regulation of park users.

During the three year period (1973-1975) of the Australian Labor Party Government, the Commonwealth National Parks and Wildlife Conservation Act was passed by Parliament. This Act provided for the establishment of the Australian National Parks and Wildlife Service, and also provided authority for the Commonwealth to establish protected areas on land owned by the Commonwealth. The passing of this Act caused great consternation among the states and the Northern Territory, who regarded nature conservation, and particularly the establishment of protected areas, as matters of state concern and beyond the Commonwealth's accepted role.

Yet in retrospect, this and other Commonwealth legislation, including the Great Barrier Reef Marine Park Act, have played a role in stimulating further interest in and development of protected area establishment and management in Australia. Controversial as was the creation of the Australian National Parks and Wildlife Service (ANPWS) in 1975, it is now being accepted as a positive force in Australian nature conservation, providing an opportunity to foster cooperation and encourage a national approach to major issues.

Previous mention has been made of the role of the Council of Nature Conservation Ministers (CONCOM). As a result of its consideration of the issue of cooperation among the states and the Commonwealth a clear and positive role has emerged for the ANPWS. It is the Commonwealth's principal adviser on nature conservation matters and controls three national parks, one on Christmas Island in the Indian Ocean, and two in the Northern Territory. Of the latter, Kakadu, involving agreement with Aboriginal landowners, is a landmark in protected area management which has already given rise to interest both in Australia and internationally. Both of these Northern Territory parks feature cooperation between the Commonwealth and the Northern Territory in day-to-day management operations. Cooperative programmes among the Commonwealth and State and Territory Services have been initiated in fields such as resource surveys, management planning, and staff training, as well as the examination of possible areas for marine reserves along the Australian coast.

There are therefore very encouraging signs that from the controversy and even conflict, of 1975, a new era has emerged featuring very positive cooperation among the Governments and agencies of the Australian federal systems. Friendly rivalry and competition add a new dimension, in the Australian tradition, to produce fresh ideas and make best use of the resources and individual skills of each agency and its staff toward solving the nation's nature conservation problems. At the First World Conference on National Parks twenty years ago, the total Australian delegation consisted of five people and only two states were represented by officers from small parks branches within much larger Departments. Today the Australian States, Territories, and the Commonwealth are represented by directors or senior officers from well-established protected area agencies, and there are numerous persons from Australia involved. Over 2500 persons are directly employed by Government nature conservation agencies in Australia at the present time.

The papers being presented at this session will graphically illustrate the stage which we have reached in protected area management in the Australian Realm, and perhaps give some indicators of the way ahead as we approach the 21st century.

Australia's Great Barrier Reef Marine Park: Making Development Compatible with Conservation

Graeme Kelleher and Richard Kenchington
Great Barrier Reef Marine Park Authority
Queensland, Australia

ABSTRACT. *The Great Barrier Reef is the largest system of coral reefs and associated life forms in the world, covering an area of some 300,000 sq km off Australia's northeast coast. The Australian Government has established a management regime over the area which provides for multiple use of this great system while ensuring that its natural qualities are protected. The paper describes the management regime, which is based on scientific research, public involvement and zoning of areas to separate incompatible activities and to reserve areas for the uses to which they are best suited.*

1. INTRODUCTION

As the 1970s drew to a close, there was growing international acceptance of two related concepts affecting national parks. One was the end of the doctrinaire disputes between those who sought to protect and conserve the natural environment and those who argued for unrestricted large-scale exploitation of natural resources. Those disputes have largely been replaced by the realization that both conservation and development are necessary, and must be made compatible each with the other. The second concept was the notion of "buffer areas" around protected sites. While IUCN defines national parks as large areas free of exploitation, where one or more ecosystems are not materially altered by human activities (IUCN, 1977), in fact such parks have tended to be relatively small areas of territory in a nearly natural state, surrounded by much larger areas where economic activities proceed more or less unimpeded. The sudden transition from highly protected areas to areas of relatively little protection causes a number of problems, and there is increasing awareness of the benefits of "buffer zones"—areas which permit some forms

of economic activity, but which still afford some measure of protection. Such a concept implies land use planning over a much larger area, and of much more sophistication.

Both those ideas have been widely applied to terrestrial parks. But they also have applications for marine parks. Australia's Great Barrier Reef Marine Park, legally established in 1975, embodies both of these concepts.

The Park is divided into sections, each of which usually encompasses some thousands or tens of thousands of square kilometres. Each section is divided into a series of zones, with highly protected zones being generally adjacent to, or surrounded by, zones which provide for moderate protection. Adjacent to or surrounding these are zones with very few restrictions indeed. The zoning plan allows for any reasonable activity, the concept being to separate incompatible activities, to ensure that reasonable uses are permitted to occur in areas for which they are suited, that activities do not cause unacceptable damage to the Reef and, most importantly, that the natural qualities of the Reef are conserved for present and future generations. In many ways the concept and the way it is applied are similar to town and country planning in the terrestrial environment.

2. DESCRIPTION

The Great Barrier Reef can be described in biophysical terms as the largest system of corals and associated life forms anywhere in the world, covering an area of some 300,000 sq km on Australia's continental shelf. It stretches for almost 2000 km along the north-eastern coast of Australia in a complex maze of approximately 2,500 individual reefs, ranging in size from less than 1 ha to more than 100 sq km. In the north the Reef is narrow and its eastern edge is marked by a series of narrow 'ribbon' reefs but in southern areas it broadens out and presents a vast wilderness of 'patch' reefs separated by open water or narrow winding channels.

The Reef Region (Fig. 1) is known for its faunal diversity and number of endemic species. The 71 coral cays are the breeding and nesting places for some of the 242 species of birds recorded for the region. Six species of turtle are recorded in the region, making it one of the world's most significant turtle breeding areas. Whales, dolphins and dugong occur in the area, although the number of species is unknown. An estimated 1500 species of fish and over 300 species of hard corals have been recognized. Many species of echinoderms, crustaceans, and other invertebrates are important in the kinetic processes of the Reef and over 4000 mollusc species have so far been collected from the Region.

2.1 Socio-economic description

The Great Barrier Reef or parts of it have been explored and used by man since prehistoric times. Australian Aboriginal fishermen used the area more than 15,000 years ago. Since the coming of Europeans, the Reef has supported commercial enterprises based on harvesting its natural resources: beche de mer, turtles, scallops, prawns and pelagic and demersal fishes. It has also been a centre of scientific research and of commercial and non-commercial recreational activities.

Utilization of the Reef for a variety of activities is increasing rapidly. Fishing for prawns and demersal and pelagic fishes is carried out commercially and for recreation, and the total landed value for commercial fisheries production in the Reef region has been estimated at approximately $20 million annually. Tourism also is a major regional industry, much of it focussed on the Reef. From April 1979 to March 1980, approximately 2 million visitor trips were made to the Reef, the islands and adjacent mainland, and in 1979 visitors to the Reef region spent approximately $100 million in direct travel-related expenditure.

On the adjacent mainland, development of agriculture (mainly sugar-cane production) and industry is rapid. There are also major mineral recovery projects in operation or proposed which are relevant to the management of the Reef, particularly in relation to the quality of freshwater flows into the marine environment, and to the volume of shipping.

3. LEGISLATION

In the late 1960s and early 1970s the development of industry coincided with increasing public concern, in Australia and overseas, for the future of the Reef. The passage by the Australian Parliament of the Great Bar-

rier Reef Marine Park Act in 1975 was an indication of the urgency of this widely expressed concern. The Act established the Great Barrier Reef Marine Park Authority, and gave it the following functions (Great Barrier Reef Marine Park Act, 1975):

"a) To make recommendations . . . in relation to the care and development of the Marine Park including recommendations from time to time, as to:

    (i) the areas that should be declared to be parts of the Marine Park; and

    (ii) the regulations that should be made under this Act;

b) to carry out, by itself or in cooperation with other institutions or persons, and to arrange for any other institutions or persons to carry out, research and investigations relevant to the Marine Park;

c) to prepare zoning plans for the Marine Park . . .;

d) such functions relating to the Marine Park as are provided for by the regulations; and

e) to do anything incidental or conducive to the performance of any of the foregoing functions".

Australia has a federal system of government, and administrative arrangements tend therefore to be complex. The Great Barrier Reef Marine Park Act is federal legislation, but because it has profound implications for the state of Queensland, various arrangements for coordination have been made. The Authority is a 3-man statutory body, with one of its members nominated by the Queensland Government.

The Authority reports to a federal Minister who is the convenor of a 4-man Ministerial Council, comprising two Ministers from each of the 2 governments (federal and state), which coordinates the policies of the two governments on Great Barrier Reef matters. Day-to-day management of the Park is carried out by officers of the Queensland Government.

4. MANAGEMENT PHILOSOPHY

Important and expanding uses of the Great Barrier Reef Region must be carefully managed if its essential natural qualities are to survive the increasing pressures being imposed upon it. An understanding of the Reef and the processes which maintain it is necessary before sensible decisions can be made about competing uses, and before limitations can be placed on potentially destructive uses. The aim is to ensure a level of usage which is consistent with maintenance of the ecological system and which will be accepted as reasonable by society. Put briefly, the Authority believes that opportunities for human enjoyment and use of the Reef should be maximised, consistent with the conservation of the natural qualities of the system which give it its unique value. In practice regulation is deliberately held at the minimum considered necessary to achieve conservation objectives.

This philosophy is expressed by declaring sections of the Reef as parts of the Great Barrier Reef Marine Park and by developing zoning plans, which specify what uses may occur within each zone and the conditions under which those uses may proceed. Initially the Authority has concentated on incorporating the most heavily-used areas in the Marine Park, so that protective management regimes can be established. Since this facilitates public usage of the area, this policy contributes to public enjoyment of, and benefit from, the Reef.

Once the general area proposed for a Park Section is identified, the Authority develops inventories of physical and biological resources and their use to help establish the precise boundaries of the Section. Some understanding of the likely effects of different uses, or combinations of uses, on the ecological characteristics of the Reef is required. In addition to our own research programmes, and those of universities and research institutions, much information is gained from the public, particularly those who use the area.

This type of information—but in more detail—is also required for developing zoning plans. The emphasis is on determining the comparative properties and qualities of different areas (usually individual reefs) in a Park Section, so that decisions can be made on what uses each area is best fitted to sustain.

Market forces will have already taken into account many of the factors which would be considered in establishing a zoning plan. Our experience has been that these mechanisms have frequently resulted in developments which are compatible with the natural qualities of the immediate environment. It would be a rare event for a zoning plan to prohibit an activity if substantial investment had been made in that activity prior to creation of the Park Section. Very careful attention is therefore given to determining the kinds and intensities of use which have already developed in an area, and the process of creating a new section of the park and zoning it to restrict some activities involves a great deal of consultation with interested parties and the public.

5. ESTABLISHING A PLAN

The Capricornia Section of the Park (Fig. 1) illustrates the method used to develop a zoning plan (see Appendix I for the 12 steps involved in establishing a zoning plan). The plan had to encompass 22 reefs, six shoals, and the surrounding waters; a number of planning constraints emerged for each.

Nine reefs—Tryon, Masthead, Fairfax, North West, Irving, Lady Musgrave, Erskine, Polmaise, Lady Elliott—were so accessible and so heavily used that any form of restriction which could not be demonstrated to be essential would be unacceptable.

Three reefs - Heron, (tourist resort, research station, Queensland Marine Park), Wistari (Queensland Marine Park) and One Tree (research station)—had use predetermined by prior development.

The island of Wreck Reef, a prime Loggerhead Turtle nesting site—was clearly a site of such conservational significance that it merited a high level of protection.

One reef—Llewellyn Reef—was a very good example of a raised lagoonal platform characteristic of the Capricorn/Bunker Group of Reefs. It merited preservation as a reference area.

Another reef—Fitzroy Reef—was of such importance as an all-weather anchorage that restrictions could cause difficulties under national and international conventions on navigational safety.

These constraints effectively limited the zoning options for 14 of the 22 reefs. The remaining 8 reefs were generally more than 90 km from the nearest mainland harbour or boat ramp. The constraints in turn evoked a number of planning factors. Despite suggestions from the public, there was little likelihood that commercial and recreational fishing could be treated separately. Any controls intended to protect demersal fish stocks would have to apply to all methods of fishing. Some activities were seen to be incompatible with others—for example spearfishing was incompatible with fishwatching, and unrestricted fishing was incompatible with scientific research.

There was a demand for areas open to the public where only minimal exploitation would be permitted. However, an important public use of such areas would be light recreational fishing.

The need to set aside some areas—but not a majority of the Section—for research and preservation was widely accepted.

The continued use of the shipping lanes between Lady Musgrave and Lady Elliott Island and along the eastern and western edges of the Section was essential.

The draft zoning plan established five zones (Table 1), and included provision for 3 types of protected areas (Table 2). As required by the Act public comment was sought on this draft zoning plan. Again a policy was adopted of actively encouraging public representations, and this resulted in a number of modifications to the plan. One was the creation of a new zone—Marine National Park 'B' for Llewellyn Reef—in response to widespread demand for a reef open to the public but entirely free from fishing and collecting. Another involved changing the distance from the reef crest affected by such legal provisions as Seasonal Closure Areas in order not to reduce the availability of some protected anchoring areas.

One major modification to the zoning plan involved changing the zoning of one area in order not to close an important scallop fishing area, a change made at the request of local fishermen.

The Zoning Plan (Fig. 3) and regulations came into effect on 1 July 1981. Management and monitoring arrangements are still developing. Only by monitoring the effectiveness of the Zoning Plan over a period of years will it be possible to determine the extent to which the objectives of the Marine Park are being satisfied. The Authority's policy is to achieve management goals largely by education and by obtaining the cooperation of the public, rather than by direct enforcement, and the intent is to achieve the minimum level of regulation compatible with the conservation and the well-being of the Great Barrier Reef.

6. RESEARCH AND MONITORING

Adequate knowledge of the baseline (or reference) ecological characteristics of the Reef is essential in order to monitor the changes wrought by man's activities. It is also necessary to be able to predict roughly the type and scale of effect likely to be produced by individual activities and combinations of them, so that the intensity and distribution of usages can be controlled—but not overcontrolled—in a manner compatible with the conservation of the Reef's natural qualities.

At the same time, management decisions will always have to be taken on the basis of incomplete knowledge and understanding. The realistic aim of management-oriented research must be to progressively reduce the areas and degrees of uncertainty. The information required by the Authority falls into three principal areas:

Resource Analysis, which comprises understanding and measuring the systems which make up the Great Barrier Reef Region. The aims are the compilation of an inventory of physical, chemical, biological, human and human-built resources, as well as the identification of processes and the development of models which will enable the state of the area to be monitored and the processes occurring within it to be described.

Analysis of Use, which defines the uses of the area, their physical, chemical and biological effects, their value and economic importance and which measures their intensity and distribution. The aim is to predict future levels of use and their potential effects.

Information Management, which aims to ensure that adequate information is available for analysis and interpretation, and to develop methods of presenting information for research, management and education.

The three categories of research have been developed into research programmes as shown in Table 3.

The titles of the research programmes given in Table 3 are probably adequate to indicate their scope. Each programme has precisely-designated goals designed to meet a particular management information requirement, and each research project has a specified time limit to allow the Authority to discharge its major statutory responsibilities—recommending areas to be part of the Marine Park, the development of zoning plans, and management tasks. Most of the research is contracted out.

7. PRESENT STATUS OF THE PARK

The Capricornia Section of the Park has been zoned and managed since July 1981. It covers an area of about 12,000 sq km of the most southerly extent of the Reef, an area that is heavily used. Our experience there has been encouraging. People who love and depend on the Reef evidently are assured that a management regime has been established which is at once both practical and effective. The only complaints we have received have been that the level of policing is inadequate. We know that this is true but it takes a long time to obtain approval to employ people and to recruit and train them. The situation will improve rapidly.

Late in 1981 two further sections of the Park were created in the latitudinal centre of the Reef, and extending in part to the mainland coast. Called the Cairns and Cormorant Pass Sections, they cover an area of 35,000 sq km. It will be a good indication of the general applicability of the Marine Park concept if we are able, as we did for the Capricornia Section, to develop zoning plans which are accepted by the public as reasonable and competent. We are now in the process of developing those zoning plans with active public participation.

8. PROSPECTS

Some 14 percent of the Great Barrier Reef Region has been incorporated into the Marine Park, which now covers an area of 47,000 sq km. It is by far the world's largest marine park, and the only one of its kind.

In some ways the Great Barrier Reef Marine Park is an experiment on a grand scale. Nevertheless principles are being followed in its development which have often been successfully applied in terrestrial parks. Provided the Park Authority and other government agencies continue to be democratic, moderate and judicious in the exercise of their responsibilities, public support in Australia for the Great Barrier Reef Marine Park will continue to grow from its present high level. This new Marine Park concept might well serve as a model for management of marine and terrestrial areas in other parts of the world, particularly since the declaration of 200-mile economic zones in territorial waters has led many nations to seek ways of managing their marine resources. In the process it may help to achieve one aim of the World Conservation Strategy: long-term harmony between man's activities and his environment.

APPENDIX I: STEPS INVOLVED IN ESTABLISHING A ZONING PLAN

(a) The Great Barrier Reef Marine Park Authority collects and evaluates baseline information for a specific sub-region of the Reef Region.
(b) Information is sought from the public about past,

present and possible future uses of the sub-region.

(c) A report is prepared and presented by the Authority proposing that an area of the sub-region be declared a Section of the Marine Park, and proposing a name for the Section.

(d) This report is submitted to the Great Barrier Reef Ministerial Council and, if endorsed, to the Federal Executive Council for consideration.

(e) If approved, the Section of the Marine Park is declared, by Proclamation, by the Governor General.

(f) After the proclamation of the new Section, notices of the intention to prepare a zoning plan are placed in local, state and national press, soliciting representations from the public.

(g) A draft zoning plan and outline of the effects of probable regulations are prepared by the Authority, and submitted to Ministerial Council for consideration.

(h) Public displays of the draft zoning plan and a document outlining the effects of probable regulations are made at various centres throughout Queensland and the other States, seeking further representations.

(i) The draft zoning plan is revised, if necessary, in the light of public submissions. A report is prepared for the Minister conveying the recommended zoning plan, the representations made to the Authority and comments by the Authority on how those representations were taken into account.

(j) The report together with the zoning plan and appropriate draft regulations are submitted to the Ministerial Council for consideration for endorsement.

(k) If the Minister does not refer the zoning plan back to the Authority for further consideration, he lays it before both Houses of the Federal Parliament.

(l) If within 20 sitting days there are no motions passed by either House disallowing the plan, the Minister by public notice specifies the date on which the zoning plan will come into effect. The regulations which implement and support the zoning plan usually come into effect on the same date as the zoning plan, and are laid before both Houses of the Federal Parliament for 15 days, during which period they too are subject to disallowance.

Table 1. Zoning Areas in the Great Barrier Reef Region

General Use 'A' Zone—includes all the shoals on the Section as well as Lady Elliott Island; covers more than 80% of the area of the Section. No restriction on use other than:
a) that provided by Section 38 which prohibits operations for the recovery of minerals except for the purposes of research,

b) commercial spearfishing and spearfishing with SCUBA.

General Use 'B' Zone—includes about 18% of the area of the Section. Provisions are the same as for General Use 'A' Zone with additional prohibition on trawling and the navigation of vessels greater than 500 tonnes.

Marine National Park Zone—Heron Island and Wistari Reefs. Conservational management primarily for tourist purposes with fishing allowed subject to gear restriction (one hand held line or rod and no more than two hooks).

Scientific Research Zone—One Tree Island Reef. Specific provision for scientific research in an area as far as possible unaffected by other uses.

Preservation Zone—Wreck Island and Llewellyn Reefs. Specific provision for management of an island reef and a lagoon reef as far as possible unaffected by human use.

Table 2. Protected Areas in the Great Barrier Reef Region

Reef Appreciation Area—An area of a reef, in a zone which normally permits fishing and collecting, in which fishing and collecting are excluded in order to enable the public to observe reef life relatively undisturbed by human activity.

Seasonal Closure Area—An area, known to be of importance to the breeding of particular animals, which may be closed during the breeding season.

Replenishment Areas—Seven areas, two of which may be closed at any time for a period of up to 3 years. The concept is at present experimental and is designed to test whether, as has been suggested, periodic closure will increase the productivity of demersal reef fisheries.

Table 3. Research Programmes in the Great Barrier Reef Region

Category	Programme
Resource Analysis	1. Bathymetry and Survey
	2. Oceanography
	3. Marine Geology
	4. Marine Chemistry
	5. Marine Ecology
Analysis of Use	6. Inventory of Uses
	7. Impacts of Uses
	8. Management Strategies
	9. Socio-economic Studies
Information Management	10. Great Barrier Reef Data Bank
	11. Mechanics of Information Transfer

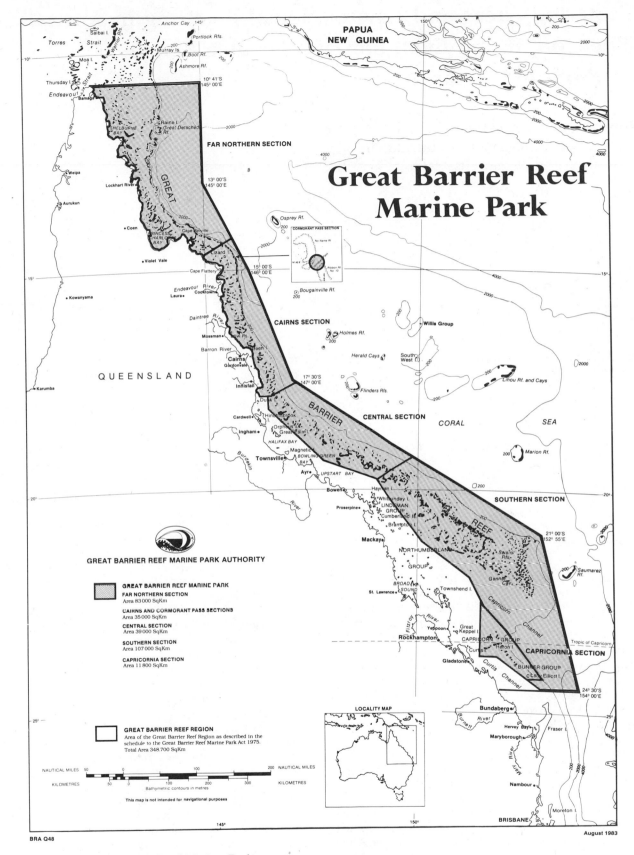

Great Barrier Reef Marine Park

PAPUA NEW GUINEA

FAR NORTHERN SECTION

CORMORANT PASS SECTION

CAIRNS SECTION

QUEENSLAND

CENTRAL SECTION

CORAL SEA

SOUTHERN SECTION

GREAT BARRIER REEF MARINE PARK AUTHORITY

GREAT BARRIER REEF MARINE PARK
FAR NORTHERN SECTION
Area 83 000 SqKm

CAIRNS AND CORMORANT PASS SECTIONS
Area 35 000 SqKm

CENTRAL SECTION
Area 39 000 SqKm

SOUTHERN SECTION
Area 107 000 SqKm

CAPRICORNIA SECTION
Area 11 800 SqKm

GREAT BARRIER REEF REGION
Area of the Great Barrier Reef Region as described in the schedule to the Great Barrier Reef Marine Park Act 1975.
Total Area 348,700 SqKm

CAPRICORNIA SECTION

LOCALITY MAP

NAUTICAL MILES   50   0   100   200 NAUTICAL MILES
KILOMETRES   50   0   100   200   300 KILOMETRES
Bathymetric contours in metres

This map is not intended for navigational purposes

BRA Q48

August 1983

Figure 1. Great Barrier Reef Marine Park.

Protected Areas and Environmental Planning in Australia: The Continuing Evolution of a Diverse Range of Protected Areas

John Geoffrey Mosley
Australian Conservation Foundation
Hawthorn, Victoria, Australia

ABSTRACT. *This paper discusses the range of categories of protected areas which can be used to achieve a variety of conservation objectives. It discusses the moves in Australia to diversify the range of protected areas, including conservation in state forests, conservation in private lands, and conservation of Aboriginal lands. The application in Australia of "other protected areas", including landscape protection areas, resource reserves, anthropological reserves, and multiple use management areas, is discussed. Each of these areas is making an important contribution to conservation in Australia, and can be even more important in the future.*

1. INTRODUCTION

The value of national parks and nature reserves in conserving natural environment and wildlife is well understood and widely supported both by conservationists and the general public in most countries. In contrast, the use of other categories of protected areas to achieve a variety of conservation objectives is not so well developed, and awareness of the potential of these measures is limited even among conservationists.

The hesitancy which exists about developing other protected area categories also extends to proposals for the introduction of functionally defined systems of protected area classification. Few countries can point to the existence of an operational classification introduced for the purpose of achieving better definition and coordination of a variety of protected area categories.

Notwithstanding these facts, in most countries a variety of other protected areas are being used and comprehensive classification systems have been proposed. Important stimulus for these efforts has come from study of approaches being used in other countries and from the classification system developed by IUCN's Commission on National Parks and Protected Areas (CNPPA) (IUCN, 1978a).

Making further progress with these measures is a major challenge for the conservationist. National park and nature reserve administrators have many skills, including a capacity for advocacy, which could be applied to this task, but no-one should be blind to the fact that the field of other protected areas is more complex, less certain, and less comfortable than most of the current endeavours of national parks practitioners.

Progress in Australia with other protected areas is probably typical of that in most of the so-called "developed nations". Australia cannot offer impeccable lessons or perfect models. Nevertheless, an analysis of the state of the art of conservation of "other protected areas" in Australia does provide some valuable pointers for further progress in this field as well as illustrating the immensity of the task awaiting those who have the courage to venture into this field.

2. BACKGROUND

Of the settled continents, Australia is the most uniform in terms of its physical and cultural environment. After Antarctica, it is also the continent which receives the least precipitation—70 percent of Australia is classified as arid or semi-arid. Australian soils are relatively infertile so that the production capacity of the country is comparatively low. Again after Antarctica, Australia has the smallest human population—15 million (1982)—even though its mainland area is greater than that of mainland United States (less Alaska).

More important still for this discussion is the fact that Australia was the last of the settled continents to be invaded by Europeans. The Aboriginal people practised little or no cultivation and with the likely exception of the dingo *Canis familiaris dingo* appear not to have introduced any alien plants and animals. Their main environmental impact (caused by their practice of burning the vegetation for easier movement and attraction of kangaroos for hunting) was to extend the grasslands at the expense of the forest. It is still less than 200 years since the first European settlement was established (the bi-centenary will occur in 1988), so modern impact on the environment is of very recent origin. In some of the more remote parts of the continent the impact of European man dates back to less than hundred years. As a result, the pre-European elements of the landscape are still important over much of Australia and it is not surprising that, like their New World counterparts, Australian conservationists have been largely concerned with promoting the understanding and protection of the natural environment and its wildlife.

In spite of the relatively small size of the population, the aridity and the limited fertility of the soils, this has been an uphill battle. The domestic sheep and cattle and introduced feral animals such as the rabbit and the cat have spread rapidly over the vast plains. Only the hardiness of the native vegetation prevented the landscape from losing most of its indigenous character in the face of the onslaught of domestic stock and feral animals. As it was, the combination of introduced predators and grazing and trampling on habitat had a highly destructive effect on much of the native fauna, particularly the smaller ground-living mammals. Although a quarter of Australia is officially classified as "other land not commercially used", no part of the continent has been unaffected by the plant and animal introductions of the European colonists (Table 1).

The Unused Land is largely sandy desert in the centre, mallee woodland on the southern fringe and rugged mountainous areas in the north. About a third of this is Aboriginal land. The greater proportion of the continent—65 percent—is agricultural land, most of it used for grazing on a relatively extensive basis.

The lands which have retained their pre-European character to the greatest extent are the forested areas in the rugged mountain areas of the peripheral humid zone. The humid zone is the home of 75 percent of the population, the majority of whom live in urban settlements (over 80 percent of Australians live in towns with a population of over 2,500). The humid zone also has the best growing conditions for grass and other crops and, not surprisingly, the humid zone is the area in which the fiercest land-use conflicts occur.

The conservation movement developed in the cities in the late nineteenth century and was soon engrossed in efforts to protect wildlife and set aside conveniently located and scenically attractive areas as national parks. Other strands in the movement which developed included a response at the turn of the century to the wasteful use of forested areas in order to protect their timber values (leading to the establishment of permanent forest reserves), and a move in the 1930s and 1940s to counter soil erosion caused largely by over-grazing.

Australian society is a paradox. Much of its ethos, and the image it presents to the outside world, is closely related to the peculiarities of the Australian environment and to the encounter with the bush and the interior ("the outback") of the European invaders, and yet the majority of Autralians live in a few large coastal cities in which life is not greatly different from that in the cities of Western Europe and North America. It could be argued that Australians have demonstrated by the nature and location of their settlements their dislike for the rural areas and the interior, but the popularity of such activities as bushwalking, motor touring and hobby farming and the continued preoccupation of Australian arts and letters with the rural environment, are evidence that Australians are not altogether satisfied with their urban existence and indicate the strong reservoir of support which exists for conservation programmes.

There is one other important factor which needs to be explained before turning to the discussion of conservation through other protected areas. In 1901, when the self-governing British colonies in Australia formed the federation known as the Commonwealth of Australia, the responsibility for the control of land and resources and the protection of the air and water was left with the constituent governments of what now became the six states. This control extended to very large areas of Crown land, much of which still remains in state ownership to this day. The current tenure situation is set out in Table 2 (Commonwealth of Australia, 1981).

An important feature of land ownership in Australia not stated in Table 2 is land with which Aboriginal groups are closely associated; some 73 million ha of land are held by Aboriginals in one form or another. The Aboriginal population still retains a close affinity with the land in much of northern and central Australia and there are many Aboriginal reserves in the states of Western Australia and Queensland. These reserves and former reserves in the Northern Territory and South Australia are generally areas which are commercially useless for activities such as grazing and timber production. In the Northern Territory and South Australia the recognition of Aboriginal claims by traditional owners has resulted in the granting of freehold title to many of the reserve areas. To date the Governments of Western Australia and Queensland have strongly resisted the granting of similar rights to Aboriginals in their states.

3. MOVES TO DIVERSIFY THE RANGE OF PROTECTED AREAS

As a result of state and Commonwealth responses to the dedicated efforts of several generations of conservationists, Australia today has eight still-expanding systems of national parks and nature reserves which occupy 4 percent of the country. In Tasmania, national parks and other nature conservation areas occupy 14 percent of the state. Western Australia has 5.6 percent of its territory in parks and nature reserves, and two other states, Victoria (4.9 percent) and South Australia (4.4 percent) are close to the 5.0 percent suggested by some earlier commentators as a minimum provision. While the aim of conserving the natural environment by means of state-owned reserves has been the major pre-occupation of the conservation movement, other factors have stimulated an interest in the development of other types of protected area. The interest stems from the difficult challenge of achieving conservation on private land and in combination with productive land uses.

3.1 The landscape protection movement

Perhaps the most interesting movement for the diversification of the protected area system has been that which has sought to provide special protection through town and country planning measures for areas of coastline or countryside. In most cases the lands which were the focus of attention were scenically attractive farming areas close to large cities. The private National Trusts provided some of the leadership for the efforts to obtain special status for these areas, particularly in New South Wales where a category of "scenic preserve" was suggested, but generally progress was a result of the efforts of local conservation groups, such as those which worked for the protection of the Adelaide Hills in South Australia and the Mornington Peninsula in Victoria. The pleas of these groups were sympathetically received by town and country planners versed in English traditions of amenity preservation, but the problems of translating these proposals into plans and regulations acceptable to Australian landowners and politicians was often found to be insurmountable. The political climate has generally been so hostile that the few successes in this field should be of considerable interest to other park professionals who have to work in a country with strong traditions of protecting the rights of private landowners.

3.2 Conservation in state forests

Another field which has offered obvious scope for environmental protection outside the national parks has been in the state-owned forests. The native forests are of considerable value to the community not only as a source of timber but also for watershed protection, the retention of habitat for wildlife, and the provision of an interesting and stimulating locale for inspiration and a variety of forms of recreation. In most states, the government forestry agencies were established before the national park authorities. Notwithstanding, except in Queensland for 60 years, the management of national parks was seen as being an inappropriate role for the forestry body and the major task of protecting wildlife

and areas of outstanding national scenery was left to the national parks and wildlife authorities. Where the forestry authorities wanted to maintain control over a large forest but saw the case for reserving some small parts, some special statutory or administrative provision for systems of forestry-controlled reserves was made. In consequence, the forestry authorities were predisposed towards feeling that conservation objectives were being met largely by national parks or these special forest reserves.

From the late 1960s onwards, public criticism of the forestry services for the priority given to short-term wood production against other uses became very strong. This caused the forest services to claim that they did in fact practise multiple-use, but there is little evidence of it and none of the state acts relating to forestry provide a definition of multiple-use or make its practice mandatory (French, 1980). Of the 32.7 million hectares of forest land in Australia, forestry legislation gives the forestry authorities the power to allow logging on all but the 3.6 million hectares which are national parks or closed water supply catchments.

The clearing of native forest for the planting of rapid-growing softwoods (mainly exotic) and the growing influence of practices associated with pulpwood harvesting, such as clearfelling and shorter rotations, constitutes a major threat to the non-wood values of the forests. Even if multiple-use regimes were achieved, many Australians would worry that too great a flexibility for change would lead to a gradual lowering of protection goals and standards.

Until protection of non-wood values is presented in legislation and a strategy is drawn up which would relieve the native forests from carrying the main burden of wood production by transferring this role to plantations established on former farmland, it is likely that Australians will continue to seek the conservation of nature largely through national parks and nature reserves.

3.3 Wildlife and habitat protection on farmlands

Another major group of "other protected areas" is that resulting from the efforts of landholders to obtain assistance in their efforts to protect wildlife and wildlife habitat. Most states have offered wildlife "sanctuary" or "refuge" status to private landholders.

Over the last five years there has been growing interest in the protection of trees for their amenity, hydrological and shade value. The rapid decline of trees in the rural environment due to old age and insect attacks has helped to create an awareness of the need for a concerted approach to this problem. To date this has not resulted in the invention of any new category of protected area, but the South Australian Government has passed heritage agreement legislation under which the state helps landowners with the retention of significant areas of native vegetation and Victoria has introduced a grant system to subsidize tree planting and other tree regeneration work on farms.

3.4 Conservation on Aboriginal lands

Since the lands which were made available to the Aborigines in northern and central Australia were regarded as areas which were virtually useless for pastoralism, they are areas which have retained much of their nature conservation value. Consequently, there was concern among Australian conservationists that these areas may be damaged by future economic development by the Aborigines. Solutions were sought in two directions: persuading government to make suitable additional areas available on which the Aborigines could develop economically viable pastoral ventures; and obtaining agreement from the Aborigines that conservation would be an objective of the management of their lands.

The first arrangements for conservation on Aboriginal Reserves in the Northern Territory were made under the Wildlife Conservation and Control Ordinance of 1962 which declared five areas to be sanctuaries. One of these, the Tanami Desert Wildlife Sanctuary, covered 3,752,900 ha. While this arrangement protected the wildlife, it restricted Aboriginal movement; the Aboriginal tribal owners wanted complete ownership so that they could determine their own use of the land and way of life. When the Woodward Commission made its report to the Federal Government recommending comprehensive legislation for Aboriginal land rights, it made specific reference to the conservation question. The Australian Conservation Foundation (ACF) had meetings which established the mutual conservation interests of the Aboriginal and conservation groups and supported the Aborigines in their land claims for areas such as that now included in stage I of Kakadu National Park (Australian Conservation Foundation, 1978).

3.5 Register of the national estate

Another facet of the conservation movement which has been developed to an advanced stage in Australia has been the establishment under federal legislation of a Register of the National Estate. While not strictly a protected area measure, it has the aim of strengthening protection. This approach, which began with the passage of the Australian Heritage Commission Act in 1975, had its origin with the classification and listing work begun by the various state-based National Trusts in Australia. These still continue their work but the Register of the National Estate, which covers both natural and cultural sites, is fully national in scope. The so-called "first generation list" completed in 1980 lists 6,600 places (Macmillan Company of Australia, 1981). It is expected that the second generation register will take a decade or more to complete and will involve a systematic review of all categories.

The Register includes items which are otherwise protected by State or Territory laws as well as those which are not. The general effect sought is to increase public and official awareness of the importance of the sites. The Commission describes it as a "protective inventory" (Australian Heritage Commission, 1982) but the strength of protection afforded by the Act has yet to be tested. The Register does indicate the possibilities for superimposing a relatively uniform national classification category on sites and areas which vary widely in terms of degree of protection and form of administration. Clearly there is considerable scope for the use of this approach for the functional classification of protected areas across the nation.

4. OTHER PROTECTED AREAS: THE PRESENT POSITION IN AUSTRALIA

Turning now to look at the Australian "other protected areas" in more detail and with particular reference to individual innovations which might be of interest to overseas practitioners, it is useful to use the IUCN classification. Only the last four categories (V-VIII) are relevant to this discussion.

4.1 Protected Landscape (IUCN Category V)

The IUCN category of "Protected Landscape" appears to embrace two generally quite different sub-types of protected area in Australia: 1) large stretches of protected countryside; and 2) smaller publicly owned reserves important for recreation. It is difficult to classify some areas, but in general, in the case of the areas in the first sub-type which I will call "Landscape Protection Areas", most of the land is likely to have been modified by agriculture and settlement and to be in private ownership (although it is common for such regions also to include patches of publicly-owned bushland). Most of the areas which fall into the second sub-type, which I will call "Landscape Recreation Areas", still have their natural cover, but in any case they are publicly owned. They are usually not greatly different in character from national parks except that most are smaller and recreation ranks relatively high in the objectives of management. The intensity of recreational use varies greatly from area to area.

4.1.1. Landscape Protection Areas (V.1). The conservation of the amenity value of large stretches of rural or coastal country (sub-type 1) is largely approached by means of town and country planning legislation. While a number of Australian authorities have called for serious attention to be paid to the potential for this type of protected area (National Estate Committee of Enquiry, 1974 and Australian Conservation Foundation, 1975), no comprehensive legislative provision for a system of such areas has been made in any state. What has been achieved has arisen from efforts to protect individual areas because of their outstanding and often threatened character. The piecemeal progress which has been made is summarized in Table 3. The four states of southeastern Australia all have a number of conservation or landscape protection zones which are applied in local authority planning schemes. The Department of Environment and Planning in New South Wales has devoted considerable attention to the development of a comprehensive system of "Environmental Protection Zones" integrating the different private and public protected area categories. The conservation effort has been used very effectively along the coast (Coastal Lands Protection Scheme) and along escarpments. Implementation of the environmental protection zones is by local government authorities but the central department is trying to encourage the use of the system and its terminology.

4.1.2. Landscape Recreation Areas (V.2). A category of protected area in which recreation is a major objective of preservation and management does not fit readily into the IUCN classification. Some commentators for instance have felt that reserves for recreation should be classified as Multiple-Use Management Areas (Category VIII) because recreation is an economic activity. In Australia, the systems of protected areas established under this category contain a wide spectrum of areas varying from natural area reserves little different from most national parks, except in terms of size, to areas which are largely altered in state.

Unlike the landscape protection areas, they are all on public land. Some landscape recreation areas are located on a major physical feature such as a river or lake, or near a cave or waterfall, and it could be argued that some of these fit more appropriately into IUCN Category III (Natural Landmark). In some of the man-modified areas such as the regional parks of Tasmania, activities such as grazing are permitted.

As will be seen from Table 4, several states have developed state-wide systems of areas in this category. Areas which have been added to this category since its introduction include new reserves of relatively small extent which in earlier years would have been dedicated as national parks. Thus the development of the category is gradually resulting in Australian national parks becoming closer to the IUCN concept of national parks as spacious areas. Future classification of national parks is likely to build up the landscape recreation areas category still further.

4.2 Resource Reserve (Category VI)

Vacant Crown lands in Australia are no longer regarded as land awaiting alienation into private hands but until they are earmarked for some specific public purpose, it could be argued that they fall loosely into the Resource Reserve category. Only Victoria has taken steps to formalize this situation by identifying "uncommitted Crown lands" as a land bank category. It has done this as part of a comprehensive evaluation of all public lands (including national parks and reserved forests). A special organization called the Land Conservation Council was set up under the Land Conservation Act in 1970 to carry out this task. The process involves the making of recommendations to the State Government for each of the "study areas" into which the State has been divided. Each study area is reviewed at approximately five-year intervals. Areas which the Government believes should not be immediately allocated are placed in the uncommitted Crown land category.

Such a category cannot serve its purpose fully unless all its values (and hence its options for various forms of resource or land use) are maintained. In the case of uncommitted Crown land in Victoria as well as elsewhere, there is inadequate protection of natural area values against damage by forestry operations. An attempt to overcome this problem was made for a period in the Victorian Alpine region where a special committee advised the Premier on the approval of roading and logging proposals in an attempt to maintain the value of land for future national park dedication.

While there is no similar category of formal resource reserve elsewhere in Australia, the situation is somewhat similar in Western and Central Tasmania, where "Conservation Areas" (National Parks and Wildlife Act) and "Protected Areas" (Lands Department) both have been established. In both cases the whole area was proposed by conservationists for national park dedication. The category is seen as allowing flexibility of future land use decision-making as well as allowing some current multiple-use.

4.3 Anthropological Reserve (Category VII)

By 1982 considerable progress had been made in establishing protected areas in this category. The traditional owners had leased the Stage I Kakadu National Park (645,000 ha) to the Director of the Commonwealth National Parks and Wildlife Service and an agreement and management plan (Australian National Parks and Wildlife Service, 1980) provided for the joint use of the area as a national park and for traditional uses by the Aboriginal owners. In 1981 the Cobourg Peninsula Aboriginal Land and Sanctuary Act vested the land on the Peninsula in a trust for Aboriginals and declared the land to be a national park. A Board comprising 4 Aboriginal members and 4 members from the Conservation Commmission of the Northern Territory has been established. The Northern Territory Government has also proposed a joint management arrangement for Uluru (Ayers Rock) National Park and for other national parks under claim in the Territory. However, no agreement has been reached yet between the Northern Territory

Government and the Aboriginals over the future protection of the Tanami Desert Wildlife Sanctuary, Australia's largest wildlife reserve; the sanctuary status of this area lapsed in August 1982.

Elsewhere in Australia, the Aboriginals are too involved with their struggle to obtain repossession of their ancient lands to give first priority to proposals for conservation arrangements while most of Australia's urban-based conservatonists are too preoccupied with their own battles in more southern lands to become involved with this movement.

4.4 Multiple-Use Management Areas (Category VIII)

Reference has already been made to the problem of whether to regard state forests as true multiple-use areas (Table 5). Forest agencies generally have the authority under legislation to practise multiple-use management but the provision is discretionary and is not universally applied.

The other major type of multiple-use arrangement in Australia is one aimed at protecting wildlife or wildlife habitat on farmland. The New South Wales Wildlife Refuge System is probably the best-known example of this kind. It is a completely voluntary scheme. The Refuge is dedicated at the request of the owner over the whole or part of an agricultural property. There is provision for technical advice to be given, management plans to be drawn up, and financial assistance provided for the wildlife objective.

5. CLASSIFICATION SYSTEMS

The advantages of an overall classification system for resource allocation, evaluation of adequacy, public understanding, and management have been described in an earlier paper (Mosley, 1978). With so much innovation in the other protected area fields and with the national parks and wildlife bodies being made responsible for the administration of some of the categories, it is not surprising that some thought has been given to the introduction of comprehensive classification systems. At some time or other most States have reviewed their systems and some adjustments in terminology and control such as those relating to state recreation areas in New South Wales have occurred. For instance in all States and territories except Western Australia and Victoria, the control of national parks and wildlife has been placed under a single authority. Currently the Tasmanian Government is considering the transfer of regional parks, state recreation areas and protected areas from the Lands Department to the National Parks and Wildlife Service.

The centralization of responsibility for the various categories should hasten the development of compre-

hensive classification systems at the state level, but at the national level it is the strong state rights attitude which is the main obstacle to progress. The Australian Council of Nature Conservation Ministers (CONCOM) in 1973 appointed a Working Group to review the categories and nomenclature for protected areas in Australia against IUCN guidelines. The Standing Committee of CONCOM endorsed the desirability in the long term of a nationally uniform system and referred the matter back to the Working Group to further develop the needed concepts.

A new Working Group was convened in 1979 to examine the application of the new IUCN terminology. In its report (Working Group on Selection and Classification of Protected Areas, 1980), the new Working Group noted that the IUCN system could be introduced and applied by mutual agreement independent of any change to local legislation or administration. The Working Group gave an indication of the changes which would be needed if the areas were reclassified, noting that some fairly drastic changes would take place creating some short term political criticism or public confusion. It said that in the period since 1974 the position in Australia had deteriorated, and recommended legal standardization of nomenclature as rapidly as possible. With some minor adjustments, the Working Group found the IUCN system suitable for Australia and recommended action be taken within five years to incorporate the finally acceptable terminology into appropriate State and Commonwealth legislation.

After sending the report to the individual Governments for comment, CONCOM in 1981 concluded that implementation of the recommendations on a national basis would be difficult at the present time but agreed the work should continue. Although reports on progress in this field are to be on the agenda of the annual meetings of CONCOM, effectively the matter has been shelved.

6. CONCLUSION

A considerable amount of progress has been made in the development of other protected areas in Australia and there have been considerable benefits. Several of the new categories perform a valuable complementary role to National Parks and in some situations are being used as buffer areas. Other protected areas also have intrinsic values so that they are greatly widening the overall conservation effort. Certainly there are some disadvantages in them in that governments sometimes use the new categories as a means of avoiding the justified allocation of lands into national parks.

It is worth noting that there is a considerable degree of convergence in the developments in the various Australian states in terms of both new categories and arrangements for administration. Thus it is reasonable to hope that further progress can be made. One of the main needs is for more information to be provided on management objectives and benefits of each of the other protected area categories. To some extent this goal can also be sought by the promotion of overall classification systems. Even if this system is applied informally to the existing areas without resort to change of legislation or jurisdiction, it can do much to educate the public to the value of having a wide range of protected areas. It is now up to the conservation bodies, such as the Australian Committee of IUCN and the ACF, to undertake a public education campaign in this field.

Table 1: Land use in Australia

Land Use	Approx. area in thousands of hectares	%
Urban	1,000	0.7
Forestry (State-owned and private)	29,000	3.8
National Parks and equivalent reserves	31,000	4.0
Unused for any commercial purpose	200,000	26.0
Farming and grazing (includes cropped area of about 15,000)	500,000	65.1
Miscellaneous	7,000	0.9
TOTAL	768,000	100.5

Source: Division of National Mapping, 1980.

Table 2: Land tenure in Australia (1979/80)

Private Land	Area in thousands of hectares	%
Alienated	90,200	11.8
In process of alienation	24,000	3.1
Crown Lands		
Leased or licenses	404,200	52.6
Reserve or uncommitted	250,000	32.5
TOTAL	768,300	100.0

Table 3: List of Landscape Protection Areas (Category V sub-type 1)

State	Area	Measure	Comments
New South Wales		*Environmental Protection Zones* Includes Wetlands (7(a) and (b))	These zones are established under guidelines drawn up by the Department of Environment and Planning and administered by local authorities.
		Scenic (7d)	Applied chiefly to areas with "high visual quality—outstanding, unusual, distinctive or diverse character".
	Illawarra Escarpment	Escarpment (7e)	(Mainly hill areas forming a backdrop to towns.) Control over vegetation important.
		Foreshore Protection (7(f))	Designed to give statutory effect to Coastal Lands Protection Scheme. Two sub-categories: 7f(1)—to preserve important elements of coastal scenery by restricting development, 7f(2)—lands due to be acquired by the Government.
	Hillend	Historic Site 7(h)	
Victoria	Upper Yarra Valley and Dandenong Ranges 3,000 square kilometers	Regional Strategy Plan (Upper Yarra Valley and Dandenong Ranges Authority Act)	Act gives increased protection for special features and the character of the Region. Sets up Authority for Region and gives special protection to areas of regional significance. Strategy Plan provides for 'Rural Landscape' and 'Landscape Living' Zones.
	Southern Mornington Peninsula	Conservation Plan and Statement of Planning Policy	Controlled by local Shires. Minister assisted by Westernport Advisory Committee. Plan provides for development control in relation to 'land units', 'natural systems' and 'cultural elements'.
	Metropolitan Parks in Melbourne Region	Statements of Planning Policy	Large parks contain private and public land. Administered by Board of Works assisted by advisory committees.
	Mount Macedon	Statement of Planning Policy	
South Australia	Adelaide Hills Face Zone	Planning and Development Act	Applications for major developments are referred to State Planning Authority for decision.
	Flinders Ranges (Area of Development Plan)		
Western Australia	Parks and Recreation Reserves in Perth Metropolitan Region (32,000 hectares)	Perth Metropolitan Regional Plan	Out of 32,000 hectares, 5,000 are in private ownership. Development control administered mainly by local authority but regional matters referred to regional authority for decision.

Table 4: List of Landscape Recreation Areas (Category V sub-type 2)

State	Name of Protected Area	Comments
Queensland	Environmental Parks (Land Act)	Same security of tenure as National Parks. System controlled by National Parks and Wildlife Service, individual area managed by local government trustees.
New South Wales	State Recreation Areas (SRA) (National Parks and Wildlife Act).	Overall administration passed from lands Department to National Parks and Wildlife Service in 1980. Each area is managed by a private trust.
		The 4 categories of SRA include coastline areas, water storage areas, river valley areas, and special interest areas. Stronger emphasis on recreation than most State systems in this category.
Victoria	Other Parks (National Parks Act)	Same security of tenure as national parks. Includes 'State Parks' and 'Coastal Parks'. Controlled and managed by National Parks Service.
Tasmania	Regional Parks (Crown Lands Act)	'Regional Parks' and 'State Recreation Areas'—mainly near urban areas or on coastline. Controlled by Department of Lands. Low security of tenure. Not seen as being permanent reserves. Cater to forms of recreation not allowed in national parks. Multi-use arrangements in some areas.
South Australia	Recreation Parks (National Parks and Wildlife Act)	Mainly small areas near Adelaide. Some are former national parks. Controlled by National Parks and Wildlife Service.

Table 5: List of Multiple Use Areas (Category VIII)

Protected Area Category

Queensland	1. State Forest	Tasmania	1. State Forest
	2. Brisbane Forest Park (Brisbane Forest Park Authority)		2. Conservation Area (National Parks and Wildlife Act)
	3. Departmental and Other Purpose Reserve		3. Protected Areas (Lands Department)
New South Wales	1. State and National Forest		4. Game Reserve
	2. Wildlife Refuge	South Australia	1. State Forest
	3. Water Catchment Areas		2. Sanctuary
	4. Game Reserve	Western Australia	1. State Forest
Victoria	1. Reserve Forest		2. Game Reserve
	2. Wildlife Management Cooperative Area	Northern Territory	1. Protected Area
	3. Wildlife Sanctuary		2. Sanctuary

Increasing Pressures for Resources Exploitation in an Area of High Nature Conservation Value, Southwest Tasmania

P.K. Bosworth
Tasmanian National Parks and Wildlife Service
Tasmania, Australia

ABSTRACT. *Southwest Tasmania occupies 25 percent of the smallest state of Australia and is one of the last three major temperate wilderness areas in the world. It has many features which warrant its conservation, but the area also has potential for the production of water power, minerals and timber as well as for tourism and recreational development. Developing these resources would greatly reduce its conservation value. Efforts have been made to conserve the area and to minimize the detrimental effects of development but these efforts have not solved the basic conflict between conservation and resource development.*

1. INTRODUCTION

Southwest Tasmania is increasingly being looked at by some as a resource to be exploited and by others as a significant large temperate wilderness area warranting very careful protection. This case study examines the possibilities of reconciling these views and means of minimizing adverse effects and maximizing protection.

The paper first states the basic problem at present being experienced, provides a brief summary of the conservation values of Southwest Tasmania, and describes the development of the area's resources, present resource development proposals and the effects of these proposals on the conservation values of the area. Means which have been developed to minimize adverse affects from these proposals in Tasmania are then described and their effectiveness evaluated.

2. PROBLEM STATEMENT

The conflict between resource development and nature conservation within southwest Tasmania has reached a decisive stage in Australia. On the one hand the region has potential for water power, forestry and recreational development and perhaps for mineral exploitation; as a result, resource development interests want to explore and exploit the region. On the other hand, the area includes the major part of the last large temperate wilderness area in Australia, and one of the last three large temperate wilderness areas remaining in the southern hemisphere. As a result, conservationists believe that it should be preserved intact.

3. BACKGROUND

Tasmania, the smallest state of Australia, is an island of 68,000 sq km situated in the Southern Ocean just off the southeast corner of Australia. It is part of a Federal system of government, where the state government has responsibility for most decision making and is wholly responsible for the state's national parks. The population is concentrated in the north and east; the southwest is largely uninhabited because of its harsh climate and inaccessibility.

All of the area (14,350 sq km) known as Southwest Tasmania is proclaimed as a Conservation Area (IUCN Category VIII Multiple Use Management Area). Basically, Conservation Areas only protect wildlife, so economic development may be permitted in them. However, the legislation does require the preparation of management plans, and these can provide for the protection of other values. Within the Conservation Area some 644,000 ha have been declared as State Reserves and have the highest legal protection. exploitation is not permitted in these areas unless the specific development activity is approved by both Houses of Parliament. These

State Reserves include National Parks, Nature Reserves and Historic Sites (IUCN Categories II & IV).

3.1 Physical features

The Southwest wilderness has been recognized by IUCN as one of the world's largest temperate wilderness areas, and an area of world scientific and conservation significance. It has also been recognized by Unesco's International Biological Programme (Project Aqua) as a unique wilderness of incomparable significance and value. (Editor's Note: Western Tasmania Wilderness National Park was added to the World Heritage List in December, 1982).

Landforms include a diversity of glacial, fluvial, karst and coastal features; during the Pleistocene the area was the most glaciated in Australia. The core of the region comprises a broad belt of folded Pre-Cambrian metamorphic rocks striking generally north-south. These form the spectacular quartzite ranges of the Southwest and are separated by flat valleys of limestone, conglomerates and tertiary sediments. Large belts of cavernous limestone exist, particularly along the lower Franklin and Gordon Rivers and these contain numerous karst features. A huge crater left by a meteorite (one of only two known in Australia) occurs in the heart of the area.

With the second-highest rainfall in Australia (up to 3600 mm annual average), the Southwest has some impressive river systems. The larger rivers have cut across mountain ranges to create awesome gorges, particularly in the Franklin-Lower Gordon Wild Rivers region. Countless waterfalls, ravines, rapids, placid reaches and river terraces occur on these rivers. Only two of Tasmania's large rivers, the Franklin and the Davey, now remain in their natural or wild state, the Franklin being the last major wild river left in Australia.

The coastline in the Southwest is particularly rugged, with sandy beaches alternating with rocky headlands, lagoons and cliffs.

3.2 Biological features

The vegetation is a mosaic of temperate rainforest, heathland, sedgeland and eucalypt forest (Fig. 1). The temperate rainforest extends from sea level to over 1000 m altitude but occurs principally along river valleys and fire-protected slopes. These forests are the Australian stronghold of the Gwondwanaland elements of the flora. They constitute a primaeval vegetation type which is gradually being replaced by the "Australian" element of flora because of climatic change, increased fire frequency and decreasing soil fertility. Human activities have hastened this trend.

The sedgeland consists predominantly of buttongrass, a tussock sedge with distinct globular "buttons" of seeds on the end of long stalks. The buttongrass plains cover a large area of poorly drained peaty soils

and have replaced the forest in some areas which have a history of recurrent fires. The alpine heath or montane moorland consists mainly of dwarf shrubbery comprising many plants unique to Tasmania. Patches of coniferous forest occur sporadically throughout the higher altitude areas.

Approximately 165 plant species endemic to Tasmania have been recorded in the Southwest; twenty-nine of these are only to be found in the Southwest and some are rare and endangered.

Only one systematic faunal survey has been conducted, and only in a part of the region. Nevertheless, knowledge of the vertebrate fauna at least is reasonably complete and is sufficient to stamp the area as of great importance for the conservation of Australian fauna. Twenty-one species of native mammals have so far been recorded, representing two-thirds of the 32 species known in Tasmania. Two of these are considered to be rare and endangered; in addition, the Southwest may be the last habitat of the Tasmanian tiger *Thylacinus cynocephalus*. Endemic species occurring in the area include the Tasmanian devil, *Sarcophilus harrisii*.

Two of the 159 bird species recorded in the area are considered to be rare and endangered. The orange-bellied parrot *Neophema chrysogaster*, breeds only in the Southwest and is one of the rarest parrots in the world, with a known population of only 200 birds. The ground parrot *Pezoporus wallicus*, is also internationally recognized as being endangered.

The Southwest has major scientific value both because it is undisturbed, and because it contains a diverse terrestrial and freshwater invertebrate fauna of great importance to world biogeography. Of the 4,500 terrestrial invertebrate species recently found in a small part of the area, over 25 percent are new to science.

3.3 Cultural features

The early Tasmanian Aborigines arrived in Tasmania over 20,000 years ago and were cut off from mainland Australia by the rising waters of Bass Strait after the last great Ice Age, to become one of the longest-surviving isolated populations the world has known. They successfully adapted to the sub-Antarctic environment of those times, and as the climate changed learned to exploit most habitats in the rapidly-evolving landscape.

This island population of 5,000 people evolved a complex society, and survived for 900 generations before being obliterated in one generation by the most rapid genocide in history, following the occupation of Tasmania by Europeans. There is no full account of their society; only one ethnographer made any major observations of their lifestyle, and this at the time when the Aborigines were undergoing the stress of extinction. All that can be known of these vanished people is held precariously in the rapidly-disappearing material archives dotted on the landscape: the remains of their occupation sites, quarries, rock engravings and stone arrangements.

Little archaeological investigation has been carried out in the Southwest although many sites have been recorded in coastal areas. However, in January 1981 an archaeological team from the Tasmanian National Parks and Wildlife Service and the Australian National University discovered a prehistoric occupation site in a limestone cave on the Gordon River and prehistoric stone tools at open sites on the banks of the Denison River. Another expedition in March 1981 led to the discovery of one of Australia's richest archaeological sites, in a large limestone cave on the Franklin River. Already minor excavation work in Fraser Cave has confirmed it as a unique site. In March 1982 a further expedition discovered eight more archaeological sites in the heart of the Southwest, including a spectacular cave, much larger than Fraser Cave, containing massive archaeological deposits. Eleven prehistoric sites are now known from the wild rivers area of the Southwest, confirming it as one of the most important archaeological regions in Australia. While still only partially explored, the number, age and richness of the sites now makes the area as significant as the great cave sites of southern France. The Ice Age hunters of Southwest Tasmania have been likened to the reindeer hunters of Ice Age Europe. This, the southernmost extent of man during the last glaciation, is now known to be far older (20,000 years) than any known occupation in the Americas.

Documented European history of the Southwest began with Tasman's sighting of the west coast in 1642. Recorded history shows that the west coast was a landfall for the French expedition under Marion du Fresne in 1772, and other French and English expeditions up to the establishment of the first European settlement of Tasmania in 1803. A timber industry based on the extraction of Huon pine, *Dacrydium franklinii*, a particularly durable timber found only in Tasmania, started at Macquarie Harbour in 1816 and continued with the establishment of a penal institution at Sarah Island in 1822. Communications, supply and the shipment of Huon pine back to the main settlement of Hobart on the southeast coast (now the capital of Tasmania) were hazardous operations, and the settlement closed in 1834. Timbering, whaling, sealing, fishing, mining and trade, mostly along the coast, continued from 1834 to 1883; however habitation was limited to isolated timber camps on the upper reaches of rivers, and whaling and timber operations in Port Davey.

The first main phase of development and inhabitation of the Southwest came with a mineral exploration boom at the turn of the century, but this quickly faded. The second main, and more permanent, phase of development and habitation began in the 1960s and 1970s with the development of the Upper Gordon hydro-electric scheme, which included the building of roads, impoundments, villages and associated works in the middle of the Southwest.

4. RESOURCE DEVELOPMENT PRESSURES AND CONSEQUENT PROBLEMS

Water power, forestry, mineral exploration and extraction, communications, beekeeping, fishing, recreation and nature conservation are the principal potential land uses in the Southwest. Nature conservation and recreation are the most extensive land uses at present, followed by forestry activities, water power developments, and mineral exploration and extraction.

The issue of fundamental importance for the Southwest is now the conflict between increasing pressures to exploit its resources—water power, minerals, forests and recreational facilities—and the need for continued conservation of nature. These increasing pressures include proposals for intensive mineral exploration, the exploitation of most of the accessible forest, the development of the remaining water power potential and improved and extensive recreational facilities, access and shelter.

4.1 Mining

Minerals have attracted people to Southwest Tasmania since 1816. At the present time 46 percent of the Southwest is Conservation Area which has not been proclaimed as State Reserve, and which is therefore available for mineral exploration and mining. Approximately half of this, 25 percent of the Southwest as a whole, is already covered by mineral exploration licences, but only a small part (8 percent) is covered by actual mining leases.

Past mining has frequently left longstanding scars on the landscape. The dual effects of smelter fumes and the cutting of firewood to fuel the smelters have created a "lunar landscape" in one area on the outskirts of the Southwest. While it is often claimed that mining and mineral exploration only affect a small part of the land surface, these claims ignore the problems caused by improved access, roads, erosion, altered fire frequency and the introduction of exotic animals, plants and diseases in areas of high nature conservation value.

4.2 Forestry

The unique rainforest trees were used by the early convict settlers for shipbuilding, and this use still continues today, but these species now also form the basis for a valuable craftwood industry. However, the greatest pressures on the forests of the Southwest occur on its eastern margin where the eucalypt forests are being clear-felled for woodchips and sawlogs.

While only about 18 percent of the Southwest is subject to forestry rights, this actually includes over half the forest in the area. Direct problems as a result of forestry activities are the clearing and alteration of native vegetation and habitats and the destruction of archaeological sites. Of particular concern is the intentional replacement of rainforest with more commercial eucalypt forest. As with mining, there are indirect problems associated with forestry, such as the improved access, altered fire regimes, erosion, and the introduction of exotic pests, animals and diseases.

4.3 Recreation

Because of its unique scenery, Southwest Tasmania is a prime tourist and recreational resource. Bushwalking, mountain climbing, rafting and canoeing in the area are regarded by recreationists as the ultimate experiences of their type. At least 12,300 Tasmanians and 26,000 other visitors used the Tasmanian wilderness directly in 1978. The demand for wilderness is increasing rapidly and conservative estimates show that it will increase by over 100 percent in the next 10 years. Rafting and canoeing the wild and scenic rivers has become a major and rapidly-increasing recreational use of the Southwest; the number of expeditions has grown from 5 in 1978/79 to over 1000 in 1981/82. This last year has also seen an influx of commercial operators, with six licenced operators on the Franklin River in 1981/82 charging approximately $500 per person for a 10-day trip. Many more visitors come to view the Southwest wilderness from the outskirts, the most popular access areas being the Gordon River (60,000 visitors annually), Strathgordon (50,000 visitors annually), Lyell Highway and Cockle Creek.

4.4 Water power

The debate over the development of hydro-electric projects in Southwest Tasmania is a classic example of the conflict between the desire to exploit natural resources and the desire to conserve natural sites. The potential of water power in the Southwest was first demonstrated in 1911, when wood used to fire mine boilers became too expensive and a small hydro-electric scheme was built on the western edge of the area. The pressure for ever-larger schemes has increased since then.

In 1955 the proclamation of what was then Lake Pedder National Park was regarded as an important step in the process of conserving Southwest Tasmania. But only eight years later the Tasmanian Government applied for and received a grant to build a road 90 km into the heart of the area to investigate the potential for hydro-electric development. Subsequently, despite the secrecy that surrounded the proposals, it became clear that the Gordon River Power Development involved the inundation of environmentally- unique areas around Lake Pedder. The proposal considered no alternatives and did not include an adequate environmental assessment; despite this, it was hastily introduced into the Tasmanian Parliament and approved.

In the meantime, a limited biological study of the area found a scientifically-important ecosystem with some 20 species endemic to the area. Increasing public concern then induced the Australian Parliament to appoint a Committee of Inquiry in 1973. The Committee recommended that the proposal be delayed while alternatives were considered, and the Australian Federal government offered funds to the Tasmanian Government. The offer was refused and the project went ahead as planned. The development involved the creation of two large impoundments and associated dams, power stations, roads, transmission lines, quarries and villages. Together these total four percent of the area of the Southwest. The Hydro-Electric Commission also has a second large project known as the Derwent Scheme which involves roads and canals at the northern end of the Southwest, as well as numerous roads, tracks, gauging and rainfall stations, camps, helipads and minor works associated with potential projects in the wild rivers area of the Southwest.

But it is the recent proposals for hydro-electric development in the Southwest that most effectively demonstrate the effects of increasing development pressures on areas of high nature conservation value. In 1979 the Hydro-Electric Commission submitted to the Tasmanian Government a "Report on the Gordon River Power Development Stage 2". It recommended the integrated hydro-electric development of the Gordon and Franklin Rivers within the heart of the Southwest. The proposed scheme is shown in Fig. 2.

At the same time the National Parks and Wildlife Service submitted a detailed proposal for a Wild Rivers National Park. In essence this proposal presented a conservation alternative to the land use proposed by the Hydro-Electric Commission for the Franklin-Lower Gordon River region. In addition, the National Parks and Wildlife Service reviewed the Hydro-Electric Commission's Environmental Statement for the proposal and found that it did not provide an adequate consideration of environmental matters. The proposed scheme would destroy over 16 percent of the Southwest wilderness, as illustrated in Fig. 3, and would also split the Southwest into two very much reduced wilderness areas. It would destroy some of the last wild rivers in Tasmania and the last major wild river in eastern Australia, as well as almost all of the important cave and karst features of the Southwest. It would flood one of only two meteorite craters in Australia, and alter the landscape with large scale impoundments, villages, roads, transmission lines, quarries and associated works.

In addition, there are 24 rare species of plants whose main populations are known to be in the catchments to be flooded; 18 of these rare species would be threatened if the scheme proceeded and the remaining world habitat of Huon pine occurs only in Tasmania; 35 percent of its remaining habitat would be flooded by the proposed scheme.

Two endangered bird species, the orange-bellied parrot and the ground parrot, would suffer loss of substantial areas of habitat if the scheme proceeded. The azure kingfisher *Alcyone azurea*, a threatened species in Tasmania, would be affected because the dam would eliminate native freshwater fish from all upstream catchments. These native fish are the major constituents of the azure kingfisher's diet. In addition, the broad-toothed rat *Mastacomys fuscus*, which is also endangered, would lose substantial areas of habitat.

The provision of access deep into the very heart of the Southwest is one of the major environmental drawbacks of the proposed water power scheme. Tasmanian history shows that the provision of road or water-borne access greatly accelerates the loss of conservation values through the alteration of fire regimes and the introduction of exotic plants, animals and diseases. In addition, the archaeological sites of world significance which have recently been discovered in the limestone caves of the Southwest would be destroyed by the artificial lake. Their value to science would be lost forever.

5. ATTEMPTS TO SOLVE THE PROBLEMS

These are obviously major drawbacks to this scheme, and Tasmania has developed several means of attempting to overcome or ameliorate some of them. In 1975 the Tasmanian Government established a Southwest Advisory Committee to study the use, development and management of the region. After 3 years of investigation, the Committee recommended that there be a moratorium on further developments in Southwest Tasmania; that the whole Southwest region be declared a conservation area; that management plans be prepared; that legislation be enacted to establish a system of land-use determination, and to appoint a permanent independent authority to advise on all future decisions concerning Southwest Tasmania; that an inquiry be held into forestry in Southwest Tasmania; and that the Federal Government of Australia be asked for special funding for Southwest Tasmania to finance conservation in the region.

In 1979 the Tasmanian Government substantially accepted the Committee's recommendations, but not those dealing with the establishment of an independent commission on the Southwest. Instead, an independent "Southwest Tasmania Committee", was set up to consider matters referred to it by the Premier. No inquiry into forestry was initiated.

Although it is hampered by lack of staff, the Southwest Tasmania Committee has taken a positive and in-

dependent role in broad land use planning and policy formulation.

In 1976, as a first stage in planning and managing the region, the Australian Government was asked to finance a detailed survey of the resources of Southwest Tasmania. The survey, begun in 1977, has just been completed, producing a total of 25 Discussion Papers, 20 Occasional Papers and 22 Working Papers, plus an intensive final report and appendices. The Survey provides much of the detailed basis for the planning and management of the conservation values of the Southwest.

Unfortunately, the Tasmanian National Parks and Wildlife Service has not been able to secure funding to enable it to undertake the planning and management required to cope with the increased pressures on the Southwest. Some steps have been taken, however. The Tasmanian National Parks and Wildlife Service, in association with the Mines Department, has prepared guidelines for mineral exploration within the Southwest Conservation Area. Exploration licences will not be issued or will be terminated unless the guidelines are followed. The Forestry Commission is now required to prepare Forest Management Plans for areas within the Southwest Conservation Area, in consultation with the National Parks and Wildlife Service. The plans must allow for public involvement, and preliminary work on management plans has been initiated, although no staff are specifically assigned to that task.

6. CONCLUSION

The means which have been developed to overcome or ameliorate some of the environmental problems caused by increasing pressures for resource exploitation in Southwest Tasmania are reasonably effective, despite a lack of supervision of agreed controls. However, this wilderness area is now at a turning point. Further resource development and compromise land use decisions will completely destroy its nature conservation value.

Planning and management cannot provide a solution to the basic problem of conflict between pressures for the exploitation of resources and conservation of the wilderness, which is the essence of the present situation in Tasmania. They cannot because these two uses are incompatible. Tasmania needs to decide if it wants to maintain such remaining wilderness areas or develop them. If it decides to maintain them, then resource exploitation cannot proceed in these areas.

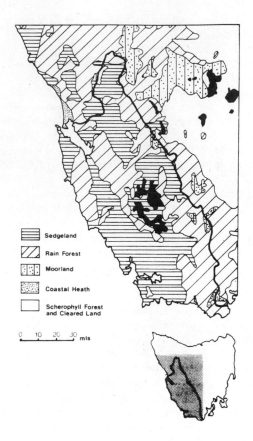

Figure 1. Vegetation map of South West Tasmania.
Source: Tasmanian Atlas, Davies, 1965.

Figure 2. Man's historical impact on South West Tasmania over time, 1780–1980.

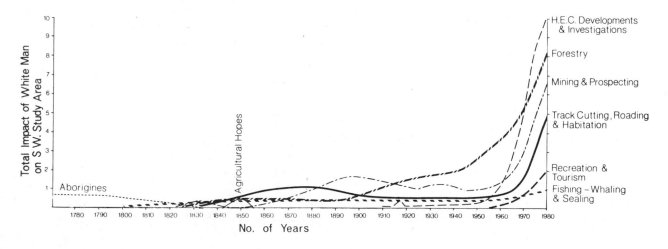

NATIONAL PARKS, CONSERVATION, AND DEVELOPMENT

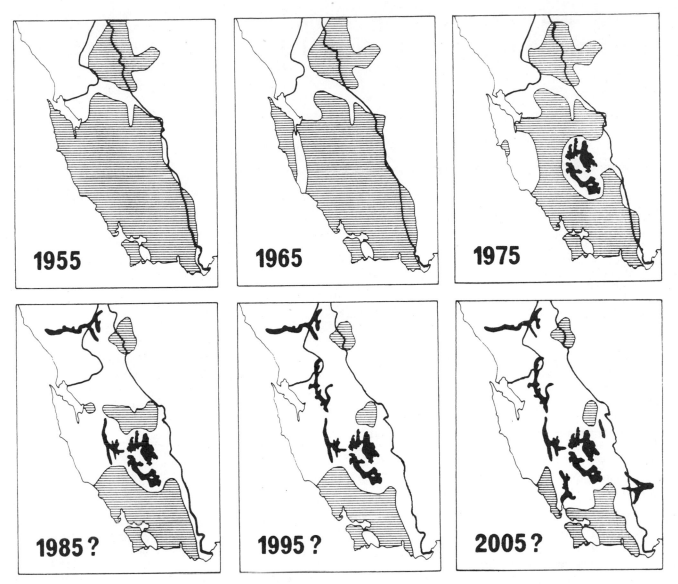

Figure 3. If development of the South West continues at its present unencumbered rate, by the year 2005 the wilderness areas may shrink to a fraction of their present levels. Black areas are lakes formed by hydroelectric schemes. Source: South West Tasmania Resources Survey.

People and Their Park: An Example of Free Running Socio-Ecological Succession

Allan M. Fox
Queanbeyan, Australia

ABSTRACT. *This paper describes the impact of people on a small unnamed park which has significant ecological attractions, cultural deposits and archeological values. Through the years the impact of humans has changed dramatically, and protected area management has evolved to respond to this different human pressure. Protected areas will receive appropriate attention from public and government only when staff are well motivated and well trained, the purposes and objectives for protected areas are clearly spelled out and accepted, and there are programmes of management which involve the public.*

1. INTRODUCTION

This paper describes the impact of people on a small park which has significant ecological attractions, cultural deposits and archaeological values including Aboriginal art galleries. The period of park development cuts across the development period of the Park Service itself. The example is typical of the problems I see widely existing in Australia today, where severe financial and staff constraints have set services back a decade or more. Many of the problems arise from pre-park days and the political system, but Aboriginal attitudes to the land provide understandings and beliefs which may help us attain more successful management programmes.

There has been a tendency when looking at systems problems to initiate narrow specialist lines of research. The opportunity to observe the impact of human pressures on a particular area is rare, probably because of time-span constraints on individual observation. Just as succession and zonation of life has been a useful tool in developing management programmes in other land use areas, the biological and physical successions caused by changing user impacts on the park systems can be useful in providing a basis for understanding the management problems and planning for their solution. Concepts such as the Recreation Opportunity Spectrum seem to arise from such observations, as do land use spectrums from land systems studies (Clark & Stankey, 1979; Clark, 1982).

2. THE PROBLEM

I am currently preparing plans for two very different parks, one a large piece of beautiful arid South Australian wilderness the other a highly significant 25,000 ha wedge of land which starts in the city of Brisbane and has been established as a recreation area for the city. In the first case some parts on the perimeter are sustaining heavy use and there are conflicting demands for use of the interior—4-wheel drive vehicles, trail bikes, wildlife conservation, wilderness walking, nature study, painting and photography, mining, grazing. In the second, there are a million potential users on the doorstep of the steep eucalyptus-covered and rainforested ridges. Both areas have already a history of pre-park use. The question of the relevance of this historical use continually appears in terms of problems with neighbours, political problems, "traditional" use, provision and maintenance of improvements and public expectations.

At the same time, this historical use provides guidelines or directions for future management programmes, for training the manager and for educating the visitor.

This paper looks at the history of one small area which provides lessons for developing an understanding and from this an appreciation of the complexity of problems surrounding the management of a park and its public.

3. THE SETTING OF THE CASE

3.1 A land of wild honey and kangaroo steaks

For perhaps 50,000 years or more the Aboriginal people have lived in a part of Australia which we will call "Our Valley". Sometime in the Aboriginal dreamtime the great ancestors had wandered the interior of our land and had traced the rivers and had discovered the mountains and valleys. They found the insects, the fish, the reptiles, and the marsupials—all of the animals and the plants as well. For all intents and purposes, in these discoveries they had "created" the world for man.

They learned where the plants and animals lived, how the fires were followed by the succulent *Solanum*, how fire could be used to drive animals into a trap, how the fresh green feed after a fire would attract the wallaroo, wallaby and kangaroo. Seasons were named after the way they affected life. The landscape about the Aboriginals, the hills, waterholes, rocks, trees, valleys, headlands and rivers reminded them constantly of their great ancestor spirits' epic journey of creation. These journeys were told in story, song and dance. They were a constant reminder of the rules of living; there were stories, for instance, of camps set on dry deltaic fans being washed out by violent flash floods in the season of storms.

One group of most fortunate Aboriginals found "Our Valley" set in a sedimentary range deep in the arid zone, perhaps in a not-so-arid time. "Most fortunate" because rising in the red sandstone range, the creek which eroded out the valley at times carried heavy volumes of water; in pouring over the bars of conglomerate rock, the water swept loose pebbles about like a hammer drill and cut deep rockholes in shaded clefts which stored cool life-giving waters even in the harshest drought. Narrow floodplains of rich silt formed from the sand and dust residue of the summer dust storms and on these grew lush grass and many old red gum trees, their hollow limbs providing homes for cockatoos, parrots and native bees. The valley and its rockholes were the key to life in the area, for surrounding this island of rocky hills were desert sand ridges covered with acacia, spinifex and cypress pine. Not that the ridges did not have a life of their own, but the biomass there was strictly limited by lack of water; when it rained there was plenty . . .in drought very little.

Over some thousands of generations of occupation by Aboriginals a kind of wisdom of nature had evolved to the extent that the clan using the resources of the valley as a base never grew much beyond 40 persons. Even then occupation was not full term—in certain seasons when the hopping mice populations boomed on the nearby sandhills, the people would wander far for a month or so. At other times they would walk far to the east to attend ceremonies by the river. When they returned, their accumulated biodegradable garbage of the previous occupation had become part of the soil. At each campsite, stones long used for grinding food were cached away; chips, broken stone tools, bones and ashes built up around the campsites telling this story of long ago.

Meanwhile the walls of overhangs and caverns under the dipping sandstones carried a record of the passing generations in white, yellow and red ochres—emu, kangaroo, people, weapons handprints and images of things sacred to the Aboriginal. On the wall of a huge cavern was a great king brown snake, a representation of a most important ancestor being which created much of the landscape. In other places where the surfaces were smooth and flat, people perhaps a thousand years before, had pecked out intricate designs of animals and people who shared "Our Valley". One great gallery, tilted to a 30 degree dip and fractured into huge blocks, covered a hectare or more and was suffering the ravages of time.

Our Valley and its inhabitants had ebbed and flowed together as one landscape over perhaps 3,000 human generations.

3.2 Our Valley becomes a piece of real estate

Living conditions in Our Valley has always had it ups and downs but these were usually the result of natural phenomena—fire, droughts, floods, storms and occasional disease. Then sometime before 1845 a shadow of the changes to come passed across the land. New diseases swept the land whenever people met people—measles, smallpox and later syphillus. Port Jackson (Sydney) was the focus. Horses and sheep came with explorer Charles Stuart and passed to the west of the valley on their way to discover the Channel Country for white men. Giles came by and those ill-prepared explorers Burke and Wills made camp there, all lured by the permanent water. But they even then found the Aboriginals weakened by disease in their desert paradise drifting in to the sheep and cattle stations being developed along the great river to the east. Giles left behind a horse yard made of stones near the great dipping gallery of peckings while Burke and Wills left a low stone dam used to raise the water level of a rock hole. The richness and diversity of the human heritage within Our Valley was growing with each visitor.

Sheep and cattle came hard on the heels of the explorers and again the waterholes drew them in like magnets. Just out from the rough rocky hills, permanent homesteads were built and the landscape between was blocked in with fences of wire. Tracks and coach roads formed links between the homesteads and the distant towns; Cobb and Co. brought in their yankee coaches and one of the horse-changing stations was built at the mouth of the valley. The water attracted the stock but when the stock had eaten the scrub off the hills the holes became silted, despite the walls which were built across the rockholes in an attempt to delay the inevitable erosion.

Goats, donkeys and camels came and ran wild. The hill kangaroos were evicted from their rocky shelters by the goats and the beautiful little rock wallabies were pushed further and further back into the rocky fastnesses of red gorges and cuesta tablelands. The landscape was dying.

Kidman, the "cattle king", bought the surrounding pastoral leases and in an attempt to beat the droughts began vast movements of stock over lands he controlled larger in area than Great Britain, but in the end drought was winning. Some sheep stations lost 100,000 sheep and more in a year. But after each drought the land never reached its previous condition. The plants and animals of the interior are very resilient indeed and in small islands of nearly undisturbed lands amid the rocky hills relicts survived. Goats were on the rampage, however, and even these rare wild places were threatened. The pastoral leases were dying. Lands surrounding Our Valley were becoming true deserts. Person after person was fired as more economic machinery took over the labour and by the mid-twentieth century pastoral companies, banks and insurance companies with their far off shareholders, most of whom had never seen the arid lands, held most of the leases. The absentee landlords demanded greater and greater returns for their investments, forcing managers to economize further and to thrash the land.

By the mid-nineteenth century the last Aboriginals who had been able to live on the land for 3,000 generations drifted as dispirited people to the stations and the towns. In just 4 generations most of the Europeans were on the same drift, leaving the land fit for little more than feral goats. As people fit to husband this land, the European Australian had been a disaster, not intentionally or out of malice, but by a sheer lack of an understanding of the processes of the natural systems.

In the 1930s and 1940s, however, some Europeans working in a large provincial city and with an interest in observing nature began to be aware of the cultural and natural riches of Our Valley. A use for land of such value was being tried elsewhere: land for inspiration, education, recreation and science. The concept of national parks and reserves was on the move, albeit slowly, and rumours of this fascinating land in the interior reached some ears in government.

3.3 The third wave, or Let us have another try

The motivations of the third wave of interest was markedly different from that of the second. Most of its protagonists talked conservation but meant protection. "How can we protect the great red cave of the king brown snake?" "How can we stop people from removing the carvings and artefacts?" "How can we save the last of the rock wallabies?" . . . and so on.

There were fifteen conservationists in the first busload I took to the valley in 1953 and road conditions were so rough that by the time we got there, only 3 days remained to explore the place. We camped by a rockhole surrounded by red flaking sandstone walls which looked immense because the plants struggling to survive looked like a bonzai garden. Around our camp were masses of chert, quartz and fine-grained volcanic flakes indicating where the original inhabitants squatted making tools.

Even though this was a peak holiday period, there were no other visitors, so we wandered through the intricate maze of hills, gorges, crevices and cliffs without interruption and with the feeling that at any time we could be the first to discover a new cavern of art. There was a primitiveness about the place that stirred our imagination. At night we built our fires and the ruddy light danced off the walls as it had for fifty thousand years of campfires. Above, in the velvety blackness of the desert night, the constellations blazed.

Ten years later I returned with two busloads—46 people—some of whom were conservationists but there were many there because it was a cheap trip. Where there had been a few tents hidden among the rocks there were now 22 pitched on a dusty worn space—a township of tents. The firewood forage now took half an hour and by the look of the eucalyptus and acacias many had been disappearing into campfires for some time. The valley filled with smoke and campground noise. No animals dare drink from the soapy waterholes until the valley of humans was asleep. Next day our line alone stretched a hundred metres and ahead around the corner one could always hear others. The air of mystery had gone for good! Already, over the past ten years thousands of pairs of feet had etched the track to the Snake Cave deeply into the soil by the creek. Leaning trees had fallen into the creek and "Kodak" gleamed golden from a stagnant waterhole. Chalk lines outlined the paintings and the red desert varnish on the sandstone pavements was giving away to crunching hobnails. Clearly these trends spelled disaster.

At about this time the State political parties, and particularly one young and vigorous politician, were beginning to take note of the growing list of nature conservation controversies. With a change of government the vigorous politician became Minister and proceeded to draft a National Parks and Wildlife Bill. With the passage of this Act, "Our Valley" became a Historic Site for the better management of its cultural and natural resources. Here surely would be a place to demonstrate the impact of new management. Cash was available, the staff new and enthusiastic and sometime in the near future moves would be made by government to expand this small area into a truly great national park by taking in adjacent grazing leases. To achieve this end, the skeptical people of the arid zone would need a demonstration of the technical skill of the new administration. Just as significantly, the Minister needed public goodwill and the respect of his colleagues so as to produce the political support to boost "his" national park project. Such was the political environment.

First, some form of residential staff was needed and

preferably a person from the dry country. . .no good having a city guy, there'd be too many perceived barriers of understanding. Two of the dying race of stockmen were showing a keen interest in the idea. These were local men who knew cattle or sheep and who "knew" the land. So old Bob was appointed as first ranger. He arrived with his horse and camp gear and a more popular character with visitors would have been hard to find. The visitor was Bob's whole world. In the daytime he would guide them and spin stories of Aboriginal wars (that never were) and provide a sample of the artefacts for those interested enough to fill their pockets. When I suggested that these were part of the Reserve he simply replied, "I know where there's a lake full of these things in Queensland, I'll get a Toyota load when they run out here". Then at night he would light a roaring campfire, squat on his elastic-sided boots, give his issue hat rim a couple of rolls and proceed to spin fascinating yarns about the droving days. To top the evening off he would bake a damper in the coals and brew a pot of hot black tea. Absolutely superb interpretive methods. . .but the message? "The blacks were disappearing anyway, poor people; there are stacks of artefacts for all to sample and this was sure God's country when sheep was King!"

Bob had two other strong attributes; he was a builder of fences over the roughest terrain and he was a super tidy character once clear of his camp. The first led to the construction of a track for his Toyota and gear through very fragile sandstone formations and a powerful barbed wire fence which kept goats out, hung the hill kangaroos and impaired the movement of people. Chainsaw, jack hammer and crowbar left a deep impression on the trees and sandstone. His attribute of tidiness had far-reaching effects still dictating to the manager. He carried a rake everywhere to "straighten up" the country. Aboriginal factory sites distributed according to the resources and needs of the people were raked and the "untidy" flakes hidden from view. In another location a tumulus of unknown meaning was rebuilt. But the greatest memorial to his clean habits was the long 30 degree slope of the petroglyph gallery. Some of the glyphs were so old that the slabs had subsequently split and had begun their slow slide downhill. Between each great slab and holding the slope more or less together were ton of rubble. Careful not to damage the surface, Bob with rubbertyred barrow patiently cleaned out the slots and crevices, taking the rubble off site and hiding it . . . ton and ton of it. The process of slope movement accelerated. Bob's time was just about through and the local people were most impressed with his diligence and industry.

Phase two of "industrial management" swung into action with the appointment of a highly qualified engineer. Roads, camping areas, water supply, an airfield (the Minister was a pilot), toilets, showers and a visitor centre/staff accommodation block were on the drawing boards. The contract architect too was of the highest academic standing and had numerous prize-winning designs to his credit in the eastern cities. Both men had no previous experience in an arid environment.

As throughout all time, the water supply problem had to be solved first because already the Minister's public relations programme was convincing many people to visit "Our Valley"; by 1969 hundreds were camped there during school holidays.

An inspection of the site and aerial photos showed an ideal place for a concrete wall where the creek cut through a narrow cleft in the sandstone. No matter that a silt-filled rockhole lay just upstream. Environmental messages were everywhere. Each of the rockholes had had several layers of sandstone slabs concreted across the bars to raise the water and silt levels. Trees 30-40 years old were growing in the backed-up silt. On the shadowed walls upstream from the dam site, vague lines of peckings told stories of the Aboriginals: emus now gone, wallabies now gone, euros much rarer. It was reasoned that the country above was all rock so "silting shouldn't be a problem". Forget the indelible story on site. Anyway an impatient Minister wanted the job done.

A finely curved wall in white concrete, the new Service's first "major engineering project" was completed. But where once there were rugged red walls and deep in the shadows down under the rocks the gleam of water, now there was the antithesis of it all—smooth white lines, an intrusion as violent as a rifle shot. Word went to a very proud engineer, "camouflage it!" A ready supply of sandstone slabs lay innocently in a line down below. These were fixed to the wall and it now looked somewhat in character. Smiles were short lived. It is likely that one of the few extant reminders of the ill-fated Burke and Wills expedition, their dam, was now stuck to the concrete wall. As the waters rose someone noted the drowning of ancient artwork.

In the meantime the great blocks of petroglyphs were sliding downslope.

About that time a major mining company of the region had broken new ground in corporate responsibility by making a large financial contribution towards the construction of a Visitor Centre. The Minister understandably demanded quick action. There was no plan of management yet for this area. The Minister's Advisory Committee of Architects met and the task of designing the Centre was let.

The location of the site for main visitor contact seemed obvious. In the lower valley conveniently close to the entrance gate a tributary valley joined our main creek by way of a broad floodplain. It was in fact a deep deltaic fan built during massive downpours. In the short term the least costly place to build; easy for excavations and a level building site. Oh where were the Service geomorphologists? The time will surely come when that fan will be covered by rushing, turbid waters. However, one is loathe to dwell too long on the site problem as the development of effecitve drainage embankments and channels to protect the "developments" may well do greater damage to the site. Better to leave the building to that future flood and the termites and let it provide its best value—for the education of all managers who would treat the processes of Nature with disrespect.

The plans showed a lack of understanding of the environment. For example, the western and northern walls were of glass. Apart from the difficulties imposed on display designers, the building would have become a super hot house. Hot air drainage was designed by way of a fixed wooden louvred clearlight for the length of the roof ridge. Immediately below lay a full ceiling. Sand storms are a common summer phenomenon and are particularly heavy on this lower valley floor fed by the wide sandy creek bed. One could envisage the ceiling collapsing under the load of trapped sand and dust.

Building materials too were only a slight challenge to the voracious termites of the desert. Termites in Our Valley were perhaps the most important organism in the nutrient recycling system, being specially adapted to cutting up and breaking down the toughest woody tissue. Natural selection, however, has produced a genus of a fine lumber-producing tree growing on the nearby drylands which is termite resistant. For some reason best known to the architect this tree was specified in only parts of the construction. Non-resistant timbers were brought in at considerable additional cost. Within a year much of this timber was little more than a paint or lacquer shell.

For a brief moment the solution seemed to rest in replacement and heavy regular treatments of Dieldrin. Then someone reminded the operations people that the water storage tanks had been built as foundations for this building. So second time around resistant timbers were used and pesticides applied sparingly.

With such short-sighted enthusiasm by the young National Parks and Wildlife Service (and I was part of it), Nature was set to deal out a lesson of the style of the biblical plagues of Egypt. Soon after the building was completed and the inspection hatches covered with vinyl flooring and at least one partition wall, a rare wet season took place and frog populations swelled to plague proportions. One way or another some thousands made for the security of our great concrete tanks and died there. The problem was considerable!

As for the Minister's airfield, the visitor centre lay about 500 metres from the end of the east-west runway and the approach was right across the visitor camping area and the major art site—heavy competition for an interpreter weaving his tales of the ancient painters of the great gallery. One of the finest stands of old beefwood trees Grevillea striata stood too close to the eastern end so in the cause of safety the chain saw quickly removed 500 years of rare old trees, some of the few remaining after the second wave of exploitation.

In the meantime, rain was finding silt to wash into the dam and the great slabs of sandstone carrying the petroglyphs were continuing their accelerated slide down hill. Oh for that geomorphologist.

Silting was becoming a critical problem and the solution was seen in the constructon of silt traps (small dams) in each of the tributaries leading directly into the main dam. These were built and for a year or so little silt reached the dam but inevitably the traps filled. What do we do now? Build a higher set of dams on the silt terraces? Clearly there was ample sand and dust carried by the wind to ultimately fill any and all dams just as all previous dams had been filled since sheep and goats had arrived. Two solutions seemed available—a cock in the base of the dam walls to unload the silt downstream in times of flood, or the regular cleaning of the silt traps. The second alternative was followed. Access was consequently built across the rugged terrain of the tops so that trucks or trailers could get in. So now where once the wind sighed through the pines and acacias and the red sandstone showed no human interference—a wild place where the human spirit could briefly forget the torment of development—crushed white rock, wheel tracks, and barbed wire fences laced this miniature wilderness and killed its wildness. An essential quality had been lost forever.

Perhaps the main reason for the reserved status of Our Valley was the richness of its Aboriginal art. It wasn't long therefore before the petroglyph gallery was closed to the public so that "provision could be made for the reduction of vandalism and damage". Remember the problem of the sliding slabs initiated by the simple process of Ranger Bob clearing rubble from between the blocks? Opportunity seemed to knock for the Service—the new ranger appointed came with a very successful experience in rock drilling and his experience was immediately called upon. The simple solution was obvious—drill the slabs and peg them down. Still no geomorphic advice was called, as the solution seemed simple.

Holes were drilled and stainless steel pegs were driven through the slabs and into the basement. Almost unbelievably, the process of downhill movement continued with the massive pegs bending and the blocks veering about. Further holes were drilled in the gaps between the slabs and more pegs inserted but now with massive wooden wedges inserted over the pegs to act as the rubble had so adequately done for thousands of years. The sliding subsided but soon the wood was cracking. . .nylon replacement wedges solved the immediate problem.

And so the story goes on through all of the period of major development. Six and a half years after its establishment as a Historic Site, a plan of management was adopted—a situation which because of lack of finance and manpower is the rule rather than the exception in Australia today.

4. CONCLUSIONS

In almost all instances the construction, maintenance and public interface programmes had followed a reactive model. Primary criteria for the development decisions had been basically politically oriented and the developments had been established with haste and without adequate consideration of the special environmental problems existing in the arid zone. The whole Service experience had been in the temperate eastern lands.

The case raises many relevant questions:

Should managers let enthusiastic politicians have their head?

How can managers lead the politician?

Does a rich budget necessarily lead to good management?

Does enthusiasm necessarily lead to sound management?

Is rapid growth necessarily effective growth?

Does the staff realize that they are developing public perception as to what park management is about?

Does the staff really represent the Service?

Does the staff know what the organization is about?

Do high qualifications of staff and consultants necessarily mean that we can expect the most effective and appropriate work?

Do we ever know enough about the places we manage?

Do we seek answers to our problems where the problems are, or do we as a matter of course get them somewhere else?

How responsible are advisory committees?

Will a plan of management necessarily lead us along a trouble-free path?

Do we know what specialist information we might need and who those specialists might be?

Why do we decide to embark on construction programmes?

Are visitor centres there primarily as foundations for some political statement?

There are many human forces working to take over the direction of park management programmes—political, industrial, concession/commercial, influential public elements and so on. No one these days seriously questions the value of museums, libraries and other traditional institutions; protected areas require a similar stature with the public. Such halcyon days for the park manager will not arrive until staff are well motivated and well trained, the purposes and objectives are clearly spelled out and accepted and there are programmes of management, preferably constructed using processes of which the public are aware and in which the public have been involved.

One of the problems which few of us face is related to the diversity of humans in the population. As the opportunities offered by a particular park change, the visiting public changes along with it. Most of these changes are generated by the management authorities and their perceptions of public needs. A sense of history and a knowledge of the original purposes for the dediction of the area will help to modify these perceptions and to pin them down so that they don't engender continuous change. Each new public will reinforce the benefit of change, but back in the community there will always be a public in retreat from these changes. More than a sense of history is needed if we are going to maintain a stable system of reserves. In the beginning we must look at our resources and ask, what are the highest opportunities these resources offer? Then and only then should the works people design the aids for the effective utilization of these opportunities.

In the end, however, what happens will depend largely upon the way the Director and his staff can verbalize a common and agreed philosophy.

Fire and Pest Species:
A Case Study of Kosciusko National Park

G. Medhurst and R. Good
National Parks and Wildlife Service of New South Wales
Sydney, Australia

ABSTRACT. *As with almost all the Australian biota, the native flora and fauna in Kosciusko National Park have evolved under a natural fire regime. However, the fire regime of prescribed burning does not duplicate natural fire occurrence and gross changes in plant communities may eventually result. The frequent removal of ground litter similarly can provide a potential for recolonization by alien species, catchment instability and erosion. The structural changes in the plant communities also provide potential habitat for feral animals such as the rabbit, pig, cat and horse. The increase in numbers of these species has contributed to the problems associated with wild dog and dingo management.*

1. INTRODUCTION

Prescribed burning has long been used as a protection management technique over the majority of forest and woodlands in Kosciusko National Park, by the the Hume-Snowy Bush Fire Prevention Scheme which has responsibility for fire control and suppression within the park and surrounding forested lands. All burning proposals are based on the removal of accumulated litter (fuel) which is deemed to present a potential fire hazard. Park management is now examining the need for such extensive burning based only on a single criterion, particularly where inadequate consideration is taken of other management objectives, such as habitat improvement or species management, and where the long-term effects of prescribed burning are not known.

Conversely, the Service accepts that it has a statutory obligation (under the Bush Fire Act, 1949) to prevent as far as possible the spread of fire from the park to neighbouring lands. There is also an obvious need to take measures to protect visitors, park assets, recreational facilities and lessee developments from fire.

Park managers must therefore strive increasingly to achieve a more satisfactory balance between essential protection activities and nature conservation principles. To date, this balance has been clearly weighted in favour of the former.

A lack of data on fire effects will always exist and some fire management objectives are needed; fire is accepted as a natural environmental factor. The approach taken in Kosciusko National Park by park management personnel has been to critically analyse prescribed burning proposals. The influence of litter removal is considered to reduce catchment stability and increase erosion potential. During the past years when grazing and associated burning was common, widespread erosion did occur within the park and in some construction sites during the construction of the Snowy Mountains Hydro-electric Scheme; catchment stability is essential to the operation of the latter scheme as well as for the maintenance of a stable vegetation cover to exclude exotic plant species.

Unfortunately, the many years of grazing and construction provided an opportunity for the invasion of these lands by exotic species and these sites now serve as propagule sources for further invasion. Agricultural lands acquired as part of the park also serve as distribution areas for weed dispersal, particularly for species such as Blackberry *Rubus fruticosus*, St. Johns Wort *Hypericum perforatum* and many thistle species. These species are now widespread and due to the difficulty of control are considered pest species.

Most construction sites have had various reclamation techniques applied to them and many exotic trees and grasses were used as stabilising species, such as

Willow (*Salix* spp.), Birch (*Betula* spp.), Clover (*Trifolium* spp.), and grasses (*Loluim, Poa, Agrostis* spp.). Other exotic species were inadvertently introduced with stabilizing agents and many of these have become widespread in the park, e.g., Sorrell *Rumex acetosella*. While these plant species do not themselves occur in 'pest' populations or present major management problems, their occurrence has led to other problems, particularly the significant increase in animal populations utilizing roadside habitat or visitor use areas, with the resulting road deaths and nuisance animals requiring specific management and control.

Some exotic and feral animal species have reached pest proportions. These animals are feral pigs and cats, rabbits and wild dogs. Brumbies (wild horses) may be considered in the pest category although their population exists at a relatively low level and the damage to natural ecosystems is not dramatic. For many pest plant and animal species, control and eradication programmes are in operation within Kosciusko and provide an interesting case study.

2. MANAGEMENT PROBLEMS

2.1 Fire and pest plants

The management of planned and unplanned fire is becoming an increasing source of conflict between fire control authorities, park personnel and managers of private and public lands adjoining the park. Park neighbours have long viewed it as an area of non-management where wildfire ignition potential exists, due to park visitor use and where hazard-level fuels (greater than 8 ton/ha) occur, providing the potential for devastating wildfires which may pose a threat to their lands. Many of these fears may date from experience in 1939 when vast areas of vacant Crown land and forest became sources of ignition for devastating fires. The concern of the private landholders has influenced the Hume Snowy Bush Fire Prevention Scheme to orient its fire control planning within the park towards protection of private lands adjacent to the park, with little consideration of park conservation objectives. This orientation has occurred despite the fact that the Hume Snowy Bush Fire Prevention Scheme (involving representation from the National Parks and Wildlife Service, Forestry Commission, Soil Conservation Service, Snowy Mountains Hydro-Electric Authority and local government/neighbours) was set up on a cooperative basis to ensure the protection of the water catchments on which the Hume-Snowy hydro-electric and irrigation schemes are based. Fire management has been based almost solely on the reduction of hazard-level fuels below an arbitrary level of 6-8 tons/ha. Fuel levels of this order are deemed to be sufficiently low to provide a heat energy level which can be readily suppressed. The concept of prescribed burning to reduce fuels is not questioned but fuel and vegetative cover removal and its influence on catchment instability was not recognized and this led to a questioning of the role of prescribed burning in catchment management.

Research has found that in sclerophyll forests up to 25t/ha of litter (fuel) is required to prevent potential erosion from run-off on slopes up to 10 degrees; the level of cover must increase proportionally with slope; as slope doubles the rate of run-off increases four-fold. Similarly, the rate of spread of a fire increases in the same order for increases in slope, with the slope vector enhancing the damaging effect of a fire front upon vegetation.

In a park where the majority of the land has slopes in excess of 10 degrees and the mean slope is approximately 20 degrees it is obvious that there is a high potential for fires to have a significant effect on vegetation and ground surface cover.

Infrequent high intensity wildfires (10-20 year intervals) will always be a major perturbation and cause catchment instability but the period of instability is usually short as the summer fire season is followed by mild weather conditions conducive to a rapid regeneration of ground cover. With the very frequent prescribed burning (3-7 years), instability is often continuous, with ground cover being maintained at a low level. Erosion is an end result of much prescribed burning; these eroded areas have in many places been recolonized by aggressive and very competitive exotic weeds.

Improved fire control techniques (particularly the use of helicopters for transport of fire fighters and for application of incendiaries in backburning) may have reduced the need for such large areas of the park to be subjected to fuel management burning.

2.2 Pest animals

As with fire and weeds, introduced animals are often of more concern to neighbours of the park than they are to park management. This is particularly so with respect to dogs and pigs, which have the capacity to cause substantial damage to sheep flocks and in the case of pigs to crops as well.

The dogs of concern can be either feral dogs (wild domestic dogs) or dingo (native dog). Neither appear to have an adverse effect on the park environment, and dingo is protected within the park confines.

Pigs can have a significant impact within the park because of their foraging habits; when foraging for plant food they turn the soil over so that the area looks as if it has been ploughed, devastating certain delicate plant communities in the park.

Rabbits are a general nuisance to both the park managers and neighbouring landowners because of their well-documented life style. Within the park they only occupy disturbed areas (previously cleared and grazed) which have since been incorporated into the park, retarding a return of native vegetation.

Wild horses appear to have only a negligible impact on the park and are of no concern to neighbours. Numbers are kept low by natural mortality, occasional licensed trapping and poaching.

The pig is without doubt the worst pest as far as the park is concerned because of the disturbance it causes to the environment. On the other hand most management efforts are directed towards dog control particularly in the park/private property interface where neighbours are affected.

3. MANAGEMENT STRATEGIES

3.1 An example of planned burning: Burn Block 143

This burn block of 11,980 ha is located within the rugged Bogong Mountains to the east of Jounama Pondage. Bogong Mountain (1380 m), Numbananga Peak (1500 m), Pillared Rock Ridge (about 1600 m) and Jounama Peak (1718 m) form some of the higher terrain within this rugged and diverse landscape. The slopes from Jounama Pondage at 400 m to Malabar Mountain (1139 m) are extremely steep, including many slopes of 26 degrees.

A number of fire trails, including the Pethers Hut, Cotterills and Wargong fire trails, form along with the Pethers Hut ruins, the only type of modification to the area.

The altitudinal range found within this block is reflected by the eucalypts present. The associations include:-

E. dives - E. macrorhynca	(500 m)
E. rubida - E. radiata	(600 m)
E. rubida - E. radiata - E. bridgesiana	(800 m)
E. pauciflora - E. delegatensis - E. dalyrympleana	(1200 m)

The burning block is located partly within the Blowering management unit and partly within the Bogong Peaks management unit. The emphasis is towards nature conservation management, with concentration on its special scientific values and opportunities for solitude.

Relative to the criteria established in section 2.1, the following areas would be excluded from burning: all of the steep lands of the western fall, Malabar Mountain area; all of the steep eastern facing lands that descend to the Peak River; and the higher areas (above 1360 m) of the Bogong Mountain Range including Pillared Rock Ridge and Big Plain Peak.

The greater portion of the burn block area is excluded on this basis, leaving only the higher (average altitude 1200 m) core of the block that may be prescribed burned. This central area is also considered to be significant for park management objectives in terms of nature conservation values and as a reference area. The objective for burning the central core area of the block would only be to protect the catchment areas of Rings Creek, McGregors Creek and a number of tributaries to the Peak River.

The Bogong Peaks management unit has been recognized as an important reference area, from which the use of broad area fuel reduction on a park-wide basis may be monitored. This concept is consistent with:-

- the park's status as a Biosphere Reserve, and the requirements for reference areas in relation to man's land use patterns.
- the planning concept for a special scientific area for the Bogong Peaks.
- an ability to reduce fuel on lands surrounding the Bogong Peaks as a basis for fire protection.
- the very rugged nature of the Bogong Peaks and the difficulty of fire suppression within the majority of the management unit.

It is recommended that for this block the practicalities of implementing a no prescription burn policy for Bogong Peaks be explored in terms of property responsibilities, simulated wildfire events for various fuel loads, and an ability to control wildfire events given the fuel-reduced perimeter strips. This approach would be documented in detail as a basis for Management Council consideration and procedures would be developed for dealing with a wildfire event.

Further, areas of steep slope and sub-alpine areas within the burn block should be excluded from prescription burning, and the remaining area of the burn block should be excluded from burning for the 1982 season because of the "lower than optimum" fuel load required for catchment protection. Finally, the management objective for maintaining the Bogong Peaks Management Unit as a reference area (relatively to man's use of fire) under the terms of managing the park as a Biosphere Reserve, should be examined in detail, as a basis for permanently excluding the management unit from prescription burning. This will require a full assessment of the implications of not reducing fuel in terms of property protection, control of wildfires, and benefit in terms of monitoring and research.

Given that the area was last burned during 1975/76, the average fuel loads (from Preplan) were determined, for 1200 m, to be 15 ton/ha. This figure is below the recommended catchment protection fuel load of 17.5 ton/ha for this altitude. A Preplan wildfire simulation for this area found that for present fuel loads a crown fire, (for a 14 degree slope) with a most likely flame length of 23 m and an approximate spotting distance of 6 km would develop. With fuel reduction, the wildfire would still be a crown fire. Therefore, the prescription burning would not lower the wildfire intensity to a controllable level for simulated Mt. Youngal blow-up conditions.

This vastly improved planning procedure is still undergoing trial by the Service and evaluation by the Hume Snowy Bush Fire Prevention Scheme but appears likely to provide the answer to the vexing question of matching nature conservation needs to perceived fire management responsibilities.

3.2 Pest plants

Many exotic plant species now exist within the park, some in pest populations. Many other exotic species have been introduced for use in roadside stabilization programmes, e.g., Willows (*Salix* spp,), but these pose no threat to natural communities as they have no potential to spread and are readily removed.

The exotic species in pest populations are those which are competing directly with the native vegetation and which have the capacity to utilize habitats unsuitable to native species. These habitats are generally isolated and inaccessible, providing the ideal conditions for the exotic species to become established but making physical control and eradication almost impossible. Blackberry and St. Johns Wort have become well established in this way, their distribution throughout the park being assisted by animal movements through the park and by visitor activities. Blackberries occur commonly along streams and rivers and further spread along watercourses is assisted by the carriage of propagules in the stream flow.

Management strategies in the past have endeavoured to reduce the area of occurrence of Blackberry by the application of chemical sprays to live plants and the burning of dead canes. Using this approach, only weed communities of easy access near roads and tracks can be eradicated. Eradication of a widespread, aggressive weed such as Blackberry is not feasible, particularly when only accessible areas are treated; it is largely a waste of resources in time and costs (except when it is effective in preventing spread to new areas) so control rather than eradication must be the basis for treatment. The strategy now is initially to determine the full distribution of the weed species and identify the source points of importance at the headwaters of each stream or river. Initial attack with control measures is then centred on these areas where feasible, and eradication is undertaken progressively downstream of the source points. Further downstream, minimal control of spread of the weeds from the riparian communities into other natural vegetation is undertaken. The overall strategy is thus to eradicate the weeds at the source points and restrict other areas of occurrence to the riparian communities or existing infestations. Similar strategies and approaches are taken to control other pest species which are distributed along roads, fire trails and service tracks. This approach based on control makes more cost-effective use of funds available for weed control.

The strategy to be adopted for weed infestations associated with prescribed burning and wildfire is very difficult to generalize, being site specific. Weed infestations in burned and eroded lands are very dispersed and disjunct so that a systematic eradication and control programme as developed for weeds of stream and road-side communities cannot be adopted. The control strategy is that adopted to ensure catchment stability as outlined in fire management. If effectively implemented, this provides little potential for further weed invasion and spread. Only large areas of existing weed populations where eradication can be ensured are treated with herbicides or other mechanical eradication programmes. An important time factor has to be considered in the treatment of these large areas as recolonization by native species is slow and the potential for re-invasion by weed species is high. Continual monitoring is essential so that early eradication of re-invading weed species can be undertaken. The time factor places limitations on the number of areas which can be treated at any one time so eradication/control will be a very slow and ongoing process.

Mechanical eradication programmes for species such as thistles and St. Johns Wort need also to be integrated with rabbit and other pest animal control programmes.

3.3 Pest animals

Most of the park management's control efforts relate to introduced animals which have an impact on neighbouring landowners. The dog control programme is the largest, followed by rabbit and pig control. All these animals are controlled using "1080" poison baiting techniques. Dingo is only baited in the peripheral areas of the park. Wild horse control is limited to licensing commercial operators to remove them.

The feral dog/dingo problem will be a continuing one despite the baiting programmes unless sheep grazing is discontinued in areas adjacent to the park. The rabbit programme on the park will diminish as the previously degraded areas revegetate and become unsuitable habitat. Considerable success has been achieved with pig control; only a maintenance programme is necessary now.

4. CONCLUSIONS

Unfortunately, experience to date has been that the programmes on which effort has been concentrated are those for which the economic/sociological or political pressure has been greatest. As a professional resource management agency, the National Parks and Wildlife Service aims to shift the balance towards programmes which are designed to protect or enhance the park environment. The following quote is very relevant:

"In spite of recent advances, aids and comprehensive plans, controlled burning programmes will not be totally successful unless the manager is fully aware of the basic properties of the resources under consideration and the ways that these resources react with fire. These basic principles cannot be ignored, compromised or breached without serious backlashes . . . . Part of the art of controlled burning is being able to extrapolate, synthesize and generalize in a holistic manner so that basic principles of the resources and the fire can be clearly identified. Management guidelines are dictated by the inherent biological-environmental composition of the resources and not by any economic, sociological, technological or political expediencies" (Vogl, 1979).

Of course, in the real world of park management the economic, sociological and political pressures will always bear heavily. Management can best minimize these pressures through a process of resource assessment/management planning and a commitment to adhere to planning directions.

In the case of Kosciusko National Park a breakdown of traditional attitudes will not be easy, but will be aided by improved liaison with neighbours, other government authorities, the Hume Snowy Bush Fire Prevention Scheme, the Wild Dog Destruction Board, the Kosciusko National Park Advisory Committee (set up under the National Parks and Wildlife Act, 1974 to advise the Service on the management and protection of the park), and through various public involvement strategies.

Future Directions for the Australian Realm

D.A. Johnstone
Director
National Parks and Wildlife Service of New South Wales
Sydney, Australia

ABSTRACT. *In order to adequately respond to the challenges presented by growth in population and the economy, the protected area manager in Australia should be aware of the need to be dynamic, to adjust to socio-economic changes over time and, when necessary, to do things differently. A diversity of approaches may be most appropriate for the different states of Australia, in order to take account of their different sizes, populations, stages of development and ecological factors. Traditional concepts of "national parks" may need to be modified, and greater emphasis placed on planning control rather than ownership by the Crown. In order to decide among the many alternatives available, protected area managers will need to have a clear set of objectives in mind; establishing these objectives should be their first task for the future.*

1. INTRODUCTION

One of the most simple but important tasks facing protected area managers in Australia in the next decade will be to maintain a practical optimism regarding the future in the face of increasing world political and economic problems. Without this optimism they may fail to adequately, or perhaps advantageously, respond to the changes that may occur.

In Australia, changes requiring new initiatives are expected as a result of continued population and economic growth and increased individual propensity for recreation. These factors have the potential to significantly affect both the expansion and the management of the protected areas estate. Continued growth will place increasing pressure on the nation's land resources and thereby make it more difficult than in the past to establish additional protected areas of the national park or reserve variety. Similarly, this growth, along with increased levels of recreational activity, will place additional pressures on existing and new protected areas once established.

The capacity of protected area managers to respond to change requires the appreciation of a dynamic or flexible approach to administration and management. They should be aware of the likely need to do things differently in the future. Although lessons may be learned from other countries, Australian protected area managers will need to formulate an approach that recognizes Australia's specific historical, cultural or social factors. I would place first on the list of these factors the traditional and constitutional role of the subnational governments (state governments) in land management.

In the last decade the protected areas estate in each state and the Northern Territory of Australia was expanded considerably. There are indications that some further expansion is likely, although it is not possible to predict its magnitude. However, one thing is clear— the extent and direction of expansion will, in part, depend on the protected area managers' ability to take advantage of the prevailing socio-economic conditions. In addition, they will need to re-examine former approaches to management, to examine all the alternatives available to achieve nature conservation objectives, and to apply those which give the best results in the prevailing circumstances.

This paper identifies some of the possible socio-economic trends which could affect protected area establishment and management in Australia, and describes possible strategies for dealing with them.

2. A PHILOSOPHICAL PERSPECTIVE

Efforts by any individual in any field to predict the future are fraught with uncertainty. Although the future may be predictable, it is by definition uncertain. I am reminded of the words of Ray Dasmann at the Second South Pacific Conference on National Parks and Reserves held in Sydney, Australia, in 1979:

"I have examined crystal balls and watched the flight of birds, the behaviour of schools of fish, but I can't forecast the future with any confidence. The best I can do is perhaps like the Polynesian navigators of centuries past, say that I believe there are safe shores ahead, but I do not know if we will reach them."

I too believe that there are safe shores ahead and will attempt in this paper to identify some of these safe shores for Australia. Unfortunately as a *Homo sapiens* I am not equipped with the navigational expertise of the great sea turtles and must rely on estimations as to what these safe shores might be.

I am by nature a person not inclined to dwell on the pessimistic side of events, past, present or future. In part my propensity for optimism is a direct result of my ideas (philosophies if you like) regarding nature and people's relation to it. I am concerned that pessimism about the future could be the ultimate justification for the careless and wanton destruction of our natural heritage. At one extreme there might be the view that there is no point in preserving such heritage for future generations if there are not going to be any, or similarly that there is no point in attempting to preserve this heritage now because growing social, cultural or economic pressures will eventually make preservation impossible. Therefore, as a person who believes in the idea that human survival and welfare depends on the conservative use of natural resources, I feel an obligation to be optimistic about the future and naturally that includes the future of protected areas in the Australian realm.

There is another philosophical stance which I suggest may be important in this discussion. It is summed up by the following quotation from J.P. Hartley's "The Go-between":

"The past is like a foreign country; they do things differently there."

There are important messages inherent in this quotation. First, if this statement holds true for the past it may also hold true for the future. That is, the future is like going to a foreign country; things can be done differently there. Of course, the validity of this statement depends on the proposition that things are in fact done differently in "foreign" countries, and that is the second message in the quotation. That is to say, the ideas and perceptions about protected area administration and management in one country may not be valid for other countries. A simple way of combining these two messages is to say that cultural differences exist in both space and time and such differences may demand a completely different set of criteria on which to base the administration and management of protected areas.

There has been a tendency to apply criteria developed in one or more countries to other countries, or similarly to apply criteria developed in the past to the problems of today. It is my contention that this approach is unecological. It is accepted that physical and ecological differences should be taken into account when formulating plans of management for different protected areas around the world; similarly, cultural variations also should be taken into account if ecologically sustainable results are to be achieved. It would be fair to say that the World Conservation Strategy objective of promoting the development of a National Conservation Strategy for each country is a recognition of the importance of cultural variances between countries. Similarly the 1st and 2nd South Pacific Conferences on National Parks and Reserves were, in part, a recognition of the fact that this region has certain specific cultural characteristics that require an approach to the administration and management of national parks different from that of other regions. In fact, at the 2nd South Pacific Conference held in Sydney, Australia, in June, 1979, it was revealed that, despite the availability of other forms of protective status, some countries in this region are concerned that, under existing criteria, none of their protected areas apparently qualify for inclusion in the *United Nations List of National Parks and Equivalent Reserves* because of the continued occupancy by man exercising traditional rights. As a result the Conference recommended:

"That IUCN review the definitions of protected areas for nature conservation purposes with the view of respecting customary land ownership and of determining acceptable traditional use rights that can be accommodated without prejudicing the high principles and management standards espoused by the present definitions."

This recommendation exemplifies the problems which can arise from attempts to apply uniform standards, methods or criteria across a broad spectrum of cultural or ecological units, or for that matter through time. Although I would support the value of standards such as the IUCN classification system for protected areas (IUCN, 1978a), particularly as a model for action, I also suggest that in the future it may be beneficial to think again about the desirability of applying anthropocentric uniformity to what would otherwise be a beautifully complex and diverse natural world.

It is with these ideas in mind that I propose to discuss future directions for the Australian realm.

3. THE AUSTRALIAN ADMINISTRATIVE FRAMEWORK

There seems little doubt that the world has changed and will continue to change. Just over 200 years ago Australia was populated by a relatively small number of Aborginal people who lived in relative harmony with their environment and as a race had done so for at least 40,000 years. Although Aboriginal people may have participated in ecological changes to the environment, this participation was interactive rather than dominant—that is, ecocentric rather than anthropocentric. The Aboriginals had no need for national parks. They only had to step a few feet in any direction, away from their camp-fires or sheltered rocks, to enjoy the national park experience. However, with the invasion (and I use this word in its ecological sense) of the Australian realm by other races, certain changes occurred. One of the most significant was the introduction of the concept of land ownership and the vesting of all lands in the Crown.

The concept of land ownership is of course a fundamental part of industrialized economies but has been also a necessary pre-requisite to the establishment of national parks and reserves. As a result, and perhaps ironically, most modern day Australians, unlike early Aboriginals, must not only travel some distance for, but must pay for, a national park experience, both in terms of direct payments such as entry fees and through the support of the government authorities to acquire and manage the parks. As wages and land values increase, so then must these costs also increase.

In this respect, there are similarities between Australia and the USA where the currently popular concept of a national park began. But there are also major differences. For example, in Australia the great majority of the land vested in the Crown (public land) was in the right of the constituent states; that is, it was and still is "owned" by the government of the state. As a result the states are the major land managers, and hence are the traditional administrators of national parks and other protected areas. For example, in 1863 Tasmania passed laws protecting some scenic areas, in 1879 the Royal National Park was established in New South Wales and Victoria's first national park at Tower Hill in the western district was declared in 1892. Therefore, in Australia, state governments have the traditional responsibility for the establishment and management of national parks and other protected areas. This responsibility was reinforced when statewide legislation to protect flora and fauna and to establish protected areas was enacted in all states by the mid-1950s. All states and the Northern Territory now have specialist authorities for the administration of protected areas. Alternatively, in the USA a large proportion of land was vested in the Federal Government. As a result, the way was clear for the establishment of a federal park system. This difference in governmental responsibility for land management between Australia and the USA is one example only of differences between a variety of governmental systems worldwide. Many have unitary systems of government with land management being the responsibility of central government, others have a variety of national and sub-national governmental systems. Because of these differences in the nature of governmental responsibility for protected area management throughout the world, and the consequent differences in approach as a result of different political, social and economic policies, what may be an appropriate course of action in the USA or other countries may not be a viable proposition for Australia. Similarly, what may be the best course of action for a particular state of Australia may not be the best course of action for another state.

Over many years the governments of the states have gained considerable experience and expertise in management. I believe that protected areas will be best served if this firm foundation of experience and expertise is built upon and consolidated by strengthening cooperation and collaboration between state and Federal government administrations responsible for their management, particularly through the Council of Nature Conservation Ministers (CONCOM) (McMichael & Gare, this volume).

Cooperation between protected area authorities and non-government organizations is also important. In Australia this is now achieved through the Australian Committee for IUCN. I feel that further cooperation between these groups and other sectors of the community, including industry, will be achieved in the next decade through the National Conservation Strategy for Australia. The achievement of this cooperation will be one positive reason for an optimistic view of the future of protected areas in Australia; all interested sectors of the Australian community will have to work together to encourage governments at all levels to adopt appropriate nature conservation policies.

4. THE FUTURE OF PROTECTED AREAS

The recognition of important variables when applying or comparing ideas and practices from country to country hold equally when looking into the future. Relationships and ideas that hold today may have little validity tomorrow. The Royal National Park was established in 1879 for what was called "the public," but today, with increased population, urbanization and industrialization of the Sydney region, protected area managers must address themselves to servicing "the masses" who arrive in their motor vehicles who have expectations and behaviour patterns conditioned by today's social environment. The advent of the computer chip, and other advances in technology, may create user expectations which will be entirely different from those of today.

In addition, in the last ten years international cooperation and treaties have created the new concept of an "international" park or protected area, such as Biosphere Reserve or World Heritage Site. The expectations this creates in the user may be quite different from those of current users of "national" parks.

Perhaps problems inherent in predicting the future occur in the field of protected area administration and management to a much greater extent than they occur in the more established, better funded, and technically supported fields of business management in the private sector or transport in the public sector. In the case of protected areas, there are many more intangibles to add into the predictive equation such as human perceptions and behaviour. Although most of the intangibles relate to the recreation side of the park use spectrum, they also have the potential to affect the ecological integrity of protected areas.

Changes in perceptions and behaviour of the masses will not only directly affect protected areas through recreation pressures, but will also affect future acquisition of lands as well as the ability of the protected area managers to manage them. Some specific examples are discussed below.

4.1. Expanding the protected areas estate in the Australian Realm

The area of Australia's total 768,242,785 ha that is reserved for nature conservation is steadily increasing. On 30 June 1981, 4.1% of Australia (excluding external territories) was reserved for nature conservation, distributed as in Table 1.

Table 1 shows that there have been significant increases in the areas set aside for nature conservation in most states since 1968. All states have pursued a programme of land acquisition and the 1981 figures quoted above no doubt have increased in most cases. In New South Wales, for example, the total area reserved for conservation has increased to 2,993,876 ha or 3.74% of its total land area (as at 31 December 1981).

However, because the rate of increase in the protected areas estate fluctuates considerably from year to year, it is impossible to propose a trend for the future. The important point is that acquisition of additional land is being carried out and is likely to continue while there is a perceived need for these additions. The perception of need is both resource-based and user-based. At present, Australians appear to have accepted the ideology that additional lands for nature conservation are required for ecological reasons. In part this ideology has been the result of a series of Commonwealth reports such as the Report from the 1972 House of Representatives Select Committee on Wildlife Conservation and the 1974 Report of the Committee of Inquiry into the National Estate. At the state level, individual environment and conservation administrations have produced studies designed to identify nature conservation needs of particular regions, habitats or species. The series of reports produced by the Western Australian Department of Conservation and Environment on Conservation Reserves for Western Australia is an example of

that state's continuing concern for expanding the protected area estate. In particular, the report on the Darling System (Western Australia Department of Conservation and Environment, 1981) makes recommendations which if implemented could result in a further 5.5% of the region being dedicated in some way as "parks and reserves."

The identification of the need for further acquisitions is also assisted by scientific reports. A recent study (Leigh, et al., 1981) has listed 2,206 species of Australian plants as rare or threatened; of the species listed, only 842 are believed to occur in parks or reserves. Similarly, a draft report on the conservation status of Australian animals suggests that there are 26 mammal, 22 bird, 7 reptile and 6 amphibian species which are rare, vulnerable or endangered. The ecological need for the establishment of further protected areas is clear.

However, more detailed information would be a major advantage, particularly in regard to the setting of priorities for preservation. Such priorities could be incorporated into a set of nature conservation objectives at national and sub-national levels. A set of conservation objectives has been proposed for the National Conservation Strategy (Commonwealth Department of Home Affairs and Environment, 1982). Some of the objectives relevant to this paper are to:

- further develop knowledge of species' habitat and land use capabilities through ecological surveys;
- identify and protect habitats for economically, culturally or ecologically important or threatened species of wildlife;
- further develop and enlarge the conservation reserve system to ensure comprehensive representation of species and plant and animal communities, both terrestrial and aquatic;
- retain representative samples of natural landscape and habitats in developed areas;
- ensure that parks and reserves are large enough to conserve species even under adverse conditions such as drought;
- promote alternative regional tourism and recreation facilities which will ease pressure on more fragile conservation areas.

As a strategy for the next decade, protected area managers will need to encourage the formulation and adoption of a set of objectives for their individual administrations.

Ecological justification for parks, however, may turn out to be less important than demographic justification—that is, demand for recreation. Such factors as increasing population, increasing income, more leisure time and the growth of personal transport may accelerate demand to use natural areas for recreational purposes. In the Australian context, recreational considerations would be a major factor in the justification of the establishment of protected areas in close proximity to major or growing urban areas.

Whatever the objective of acquiring additional areas, the success of a proposal for additions to the protected areas estate may also depend on the nature of the proposals themselves. In Australia there are two basic means of achieving the objective of expanding the protected areas estate:

A. Reserving public lands or purchasing private lands for inclusion in the protected areas estate, for management as category I to IV areas of the IUCN classification system.

B. Controlling the use of public lands or private lands so that they have a major or subordinate nature conservation purpose, thereby creating protected areas of the IUCN Category V, VI and VIII variety.

The capacity to carry out either of these means of expanding the protected areas estate will require the resolution of competing land uses. Increasingly, areas of land are being set aside for agriculture, industry, mining, to accommodate urban sprawl and to meet numerous other demands of Australia's high consumption and rising population. For example, public land suitable for nature conservation may also be required for forestry, active recreation, water catchments or reservoirs, mining, or urban subdivision. On the other hand, most private lands of interest to nature conservation would be currently used or set aside for agriculture, although some will be required for other uses such as mining, forestry, water storage or urban development. In all cases, the rate at which these lands can be changed to protected area use depends largely on the development of the Australian economy and the pressure this places on natural resources.

Since the 1950s, Australia has had an expanding economy. Recent growth in the gross domestic product ranges from 9.6% in 1968-9 to 5.1% in 1973-4 and to 2.9% in 1981. Although there have been fluctuations, there has been a general trend towards a reduction in the rate of growth during the 1970s. I do not have access to reliable predictions regarding the future growth of the Australian economy, but I feel it would be safe to say that growth will continue, however moderate this may be. However, it is clear that a steady, modest growth in the economy of around 3% along with sustained levels of welfare and increases in population will create increased demands upon the nation's land resources. The 1992 forecast for Australia's population is approximately 17.5 million, which represents an increase of approximately 2.4 million over the predicted population of 15.1 million for 1982 (Australian Bureau of Statistics, 1981). As a result of these trends, it seems likely that protected area administrators will be less and less able to establish additional protected areas using means "A" described above.

On the other hand, the achievement of protected area objectives using means "B" above, although subject to the same socio-economic trends, will not be as re-

stricted by them. The main reason for this is that the protection or conservation of lands in private ownership does not prevent alternative land uses as do IUCN Category I and II protected areas, but only restricts those uses to the extent necessary to meet the secondary nature conservation needs.

In Australia, as in many other countries, restrictions over land use are applied through town and country planning legislation and land-use zoning. In New South Wales, for example, the relevant legislation is the Environmental Planning and Assessment Act, 1979. This Act contains a wide variety of provisions relating to planning matters and environmental assessment of development proposals, which are highly desirable from a general environmental point of view. Of particular interest are the provisions relating to rural zoning. Under the Act, local planning authorities are required to use a set of planning zones in their planning instruments which include a number of environmental protection zones aimed at protecting the following types of land units: escarpments; archeological sites; historical sites; scientific sites; wildlife refuges; wetlands; estuarine wetlands; foreshores; scenic areas; and water catchments.

Land uses that would be inconsistent with the purposes of the above zones are either controlled, restricted or prohibited by local planning instruments. The degree of control exercised by a local planning authority over the uses permitted is largely at the discretion of the authority, although intervention by the Minister administering the Act or his department is possible under the provisions of the Act.

The New South Wales National Parks and Wildlife Service takes a cooperative and consultative approach, and liaises with local authorities during the preparation of plans in order to promote nature conservation objectives as much as possible. Although possible, stronger controls aimed at nature conservation over development on private lands have not been attempted, possibly because of the equity and compensation issues that this would raise. However, in the long term it may be found that it is more effective to utilize planning controls to achieve nature conservation objectives, even where this may require compensation, rather than attempting to reserve public lands and/or to purchase private lands. Indeed as the pressure on the nations's land resources grows, this approach may become a significant alternative to land purchase programmes.

Few states of Australia have comprehensive legislation that would enable the application of controls over private lands aimed at preserving their conservation status. The development of such legislation will be an important task for the future. This legislation could be aimed at applying planning controls as in New South Wales; developing special heritage agreements as in South Australia; applying special covenants over the title of the land; or a combination of these approaches.

Aside from this, there is the more general need of incorporating ecological criteria into the planning process so that important or threatened ecological units are identified prior to approval of developments that may destroy them. In this regard, the draft National Conservation Strategy for Australia suggests that there is a need to incorporate ecosystem evaluation and land suitability studies in the planning process (Department of Home Affairs and Environment, 1982).

4.2. Managing the protected areas estate

4.2.1. The problems identified. Providing that Australia maintains a steady state of growth in its economy, however modest, there should always be public funds available to manage protected areas. Although the degree of funding may vary according to the political situation, and this is not predictable, it is not likely that such variations will be significant. That is, established programmes and authorities based on recognized government policy commitments require on-going financial resources and are generally funded accordingly. Although variations in the economy may result in some tightening of government spending, there is no reason to think that nature conservation administrations in Australia will be severely affected by this. Unfortunately, there is also no reason to think that such administrations will be granted an increased proportion of the total public finance cake. What may be more important is the demands that will be placed on the funds available for management from increasing visitor pressures, development pressures around protected areas, and additions to the protected area estate that may require an increased level of management activity per unit of protected area in order to sustain its present level of ecological integrity.

4.2.2. Implications for management of increasing the protected areas estate. Although normally considered an entirely desirable course of action, increasing the protected areas estate may place immediate demands on management resources which may not be necessarily met by increased supply. There is every indication that the allocation of public funds to protected area management administration will be the subject of government restraint in the early years of the next decade. Real increases in funding may be possible, but are likely to be minimal.

Clearly, if increases in recurrent expenditure are less than required to cover increases in the size of protected areas to be managed, then the intensity of management must inevitably decrease. Protected area managers will need to ensure that management does not fall below levels necessary to sustain the ecological integrity of established protected areas. In some instances this might mean foregoing the establishment of new low priority areas so that existing high priority areas may be managed adequately. This task, although easy to define, may not be as easy to carry out. This is because certain decisions on priorities for managment or establishment are often taken in a political context and are outside the protected area managers' sphere of control; and decisions on priorities for management or establishment require a clear set of criteria or corporate objectives on which to base these decisions.

Protected area managers are not always able to formulate these objectives because of inadequate research into the existing state of the environment, both within and outside protected areas. Encouraging such research will be a major task for the next decade. Without this information and the objectives they may lead to, tradeoffs between establishment of new areas and management priorities of existing areas cannot be made.

4.2.3. Visitor pressure. There seems little doubt that in Australia, increased population and increased leisure time resulting from decreased hours of work will increase the demand for recreation in protected areas. Increased mobility, longer holidays and leisure periods and a larger percentage of disposable income have been indentified as the major determinants of visitation growth in the United States (Clawson, 1972).

In the United States these determinants resulted in substantial increase in national park visits from 8% to 10% annually in the 3 to 4 decades prior to 1972 (Clawson, 1972). Similarly, in Japan the number of visitors jumped from 140 million in 1960 to 300 million in 1970 (Senger, 1974). Australia also seems to be following a pattern of increased visitation; increases in the order of 12% have been recorded for many Australian national parks in a number of different states (Fox, 1974). In New South Wales it has been estimated that visitors to national parks have increased at a rate of 15% to 17% since 1976. However, unlike the USA, demand for outdoor recreation in Australia cannot be reliably predicted on the basis of distance costs associated with travel to the park. Variations to models of projected demand based on travel costs occur because many park resources are located near cities. For example, access to park resources from Sydney is such that travel time and visitation costs are minimal and therefore not significant factors underlying visitor decision-making.

On the whole, park visitors tend to visit the national park nearest to where they live, as the majority of visitors do not discriminate between the resources of one park and those of another. A recent study (Macquarie University, 1976) of visitors to three national parks near Sydney found that approximately 90% of visitors had travelled less than 30 km. For the majority of visitors to a near-city national park, their visit to the park is an opportunity for a family picnic or barbecue in a natural setting, lasting on average from three to four hours (Inness-Brown, 1977)

There seems little doubt, therefore, that visitor pressure on the category II protected areas (national parks) will continue to increase. Protected areas near the capital cities will be prime recreational targets, with a rule-of-thumb increase in the order of 12% per year. Protected area managers may respond to this increasing recreational pressure by:

a) acquiring additional lands;
b) directing recreational use away from protected areas; and
c) increasing developments within protected areas.

The acquisition of additional lands has already been discussed. Predicted heavy demands for recreation may provide additional justification for acquisition of further lands. The alternative responses are considered below.

4.2.4. Directing recreation away from protected areas. There are two methods of achieving this objective. One method is to take the direct and somewhat negative approach of restricting use by methods such as quotas or 'house-full' park closures. The second method is to encourage the development of alternative recreational centres.

As far as I can ascertain, restricting use has been used rarely in Australia to date. In New South Wales it has been occasionally necessary to restrict vehicle access to parts of the Royal National Park near Sydney on heavy use days, namely Sundays in the summer. Similarly, there is a bed quota in the ski-resort areas of Kosciusko National Park. However, with increased recreational pressure this method may become a more important alternative in the future. Unfortunately, quotas tend to be a politically sensitive issue. The alternative of pricing controls should not be considered because of the inequitable access to protected areas that this may create.

In most cases, it may be possible for protected areas managers to provide alternative recreational facilities. In New South Wales, for example, State Recreation Areas which are essentially regional parks providing high-intensity visitor opportunities, fall within the administrative responsibility of the Director of National Parks and Wildlife. Similarly, other state administrations have responsibility for protected areas which have a prime recreational function. Such areas are complementary to the national park system in that they are established close to centres of population to direct recreation pressure away from national parks. For example, State Recreation Areas within 100 km of Sydney receive a similar number of visitors per year to national parks.

Increasing developments within protected areas, of course, may be unacceptable in protected areas which have a prime nature conservation function and where the recreational facilities to be provided will significantly interfere with the ecological integrity of those protected areas. Because the legislation which governs the administration of protected areas in the various states of Australia implicitly includes nature conservation as a prime objective of management, it is not likely that managers will be forced by political or other reasons to compromise protected areas of the category I to IV variety, to the point where nature conservation interests are overruled by recreational interest. This is my optimistic view. However, there are at least three means of avoiding the situation should it become a potential problem:

• gain public support for the nature conservation purpose of protected areas using interpretative and educational materials; and/or
• encourage the development of mandatory environmental assessment legislation that binds public authorities and necessitates the development of environmental impact statements for developments, including those in protected areas, whether by the protected area managers or others; and/or
• promote the amendment of the relevant state legislation governing the administration and management of protected areas so that nature conservation is explictly defined as a prime objective of that legislation.

4.3. Development pressures

As the Australian economy expands this is also likely to place greater pressures on existing and future protected areas, both directly such as in the case of mining within the protected areas and indirectly such as pollution from developments surrounding protected areas.

Development activities within protected areas such as mining are not a common feature within Australian national parks or similar protected areas. As an optimist, I have no reason to believe that this situation will change significantly in the next ten years. In the very long term, as energy resources become depleted, it may be inevitable that some compromises are made.

Development activities surrounding protected areas may also be a problem. Mining or urban development adjacent to a protected area may result in significant environmental degradation or loss of public amenity within protected areas. Predictions Australia-wide in this regard are not possible as local and regional factors are the most important. I suggest that Australia could sustain considerably more urban growth, industrialization and mining without affecting existing protected areas, providing these activities are directed away from these areas. This presumes that buffer zones around protected areas are recognized as essential to the protected areas system. Again these buffer zones would fall within the ambit of town and country planning legislation and appropriate land-use zoning.

Where the development of buffer zones is not possible, protected area managers would need to ensure that development activities surrounding these areas are carried out in a manner that results in the lowest impact. One way of doing this is to take an active interest in the environmental impact assessment process normally associated with major developments in Australia. In practical terms this would mean making submissions on exhibited environmental impact statements, participation in environmental inquiries, constant liaison with environmental protection authorities and, where possible, direct liaison with development proponents, with a view to achieving modification of proposals and the incorporation of conditions of development and operation designed to minimize adverse environmental effects.

5. CONCLUSIONS

Pressures on protected areas in Australia will continue to increase as a result of growth in population and the economy. These factors are likely to increase demands on the nation's land resources for such purposes as water supply, timber production, agriculture and mining. Competition from these land uses will make it more difficult to establish additional protected areas, particularly of the IUCN Category I and II variety. Increasing demand for recreation along with the developments associated with urban expansion are likely to add pressure on established protected areas.

In order to respond adequately to these challenges, the protected area manager in Australia should be aware of the need to be dynamic, to adjust to socio-economic changes over time, and, when necessary, to do things differently. In some cases this may mean following a course of action different from that followed in other countries, to take account of Australia's particular historical social and cultural conditions. Indeed, it may be desirable for the different states of Australia to maintain different approaches to take account of their individual size, population, stage of development and ecological factors.

In other cases, changes in socio-economic factors may require an approach different from that taken in the past. Traditional concepts of "national parks" may need to be modified, and greater emphasis may need to be placed on planning controls rather than ownership by the Crown. There are many possibilities and only a few have been discussed here. Protected area managers will not be able to decide between these alternatives unless they have a clear set of objectives in mind. Establishing these objectives should be their first task for the future.

Table 1

	Total Area (sq km)	Area proclaimed as national park etc. (sq km) (June 1981)	% of Total Area Reserved 1968	1977	1981
New South Wales	801,600	29,760	1.1	2.3	3.7
Victoria	227,600	8,840	0.9	1.0	3.9
Queensland	1,727,200	28,980	0.6	0.7	1.7
South Australia	984,000	43,720	1.2	3.2	4.4
Western Australia	2,525,500	142,400	0.5	1.5	5.6
Tasmania	67,800	9,150	4.2	9.9	13.5
Northern Territory	1,346,200	50,060	3.5	3.7	3.7
Australian Capital Territory	2,400	610	1.9	4.1	25.4
Australia	7,682,300	313,520	1.2	2.1	4.1

Source: Department of Home Affairs and Environment (in press)

NATIONAL PARKS, CONSERVATION, AND DEVELOPMENT

Chapter 8
The Oceanian Realm

Keynote Address: The Oceanian Realm

Birandra Singh
Conservation Officer
National Trust for Fiji
Suva, Fiji

ABSTRACT. *Conservation has always been a crucial issue for the survival of the peoples in the various islands of the Oceanian Realm. The introduction of new methods of transportation and communication brought the indigenous inhabitants in contact with new ideas, styles of living and technologies for resource use, greatly affecting the traditional conservation concepts. New methods of conservation have had to be introduced, which include adaptations of the traditional protected area system to the specific situation in the Pacific islands. One major difficulty is the traditional land tenure system, which has led to a number of specific adaptations.*

1. INTRODUCTION: HISTORICAL BACKGROUND

1.1 Pre-industrial resource use

As was common to most societies in the pre-industrial era, the inhabitants of the many islands in the Oceanian Realm had a pattern of living dependent very much on the coastal or terrestrial resources that were available to them at the time. The coastal inhabitants were natural swimmers and seamen, which aided them to reap harvests from the seas and reefs. Micronesians were the only Oceanian people who did deep sea fishing.

The inhabitants living along waterways towards the middle of islands developed methods of obtaining game from the forests which included pigs (probably originally introduced by the early arrivals on the islands), birds and large lizards. Both coastal and inland peoples also practised slash and burn agriculture—primarily growing rootcrops and leaving the land fallow after harvest—and collected fruits and root crops growing wild near the settlements.

Enough examples can be given to illustrate that there was a great tradition of conservation practice in the Pacific, especially through the use of "taboo" areas or practices; these taboo systems had extraordinary socio-religious power. No doubt there were exceptions but these probably depended on the availability of plentiful supplies in relation to the size of human population. Where population pressures were high, resource utilization destroyed the natural environment, e.g. grasslands of Marquesas, Papua New Guinea and western Viti Leva (Fiji). In Fiji we also know that some bird species including a pigeon were hunted to extinction in the 18th century. The prehistoric inhabitants of the Pacific islands practised intelligent conservation, and used technologies adequate for those times; but they also depended on the sanctions of social customs to be successful. Conservation seems to have been almost entirely "economically" oriented, producing crop surpluses which were needed for ceremonies, military campaigns (also to withstand seige) and storm-induced famine.

1.2 Trends in resource utilization over the past century

During the past century, as visits to this region increased with arrivals from Europe and Asia, a commercial value was established for almost all resources. The trade established with the visitors initially meant obtaining firearms and the know-how to use them, leading to fierce clashes and aligning of settlements closer to coastal areas for easier contact with the traders.

The introduction of new methods of transportation and communication also brought the indigenous inhabitants of this region in contact with new ideas, styles of living and technologies for resource use. This has affected and will undoubtedly continue to affect the traditional conservation concepts in the future. Even if the intentions of the new arrivals were good, their end result has been the slow eradication of traditional practices that maintained the delicate balances between humanity and nature. Tourism, industralization and the introduction of intensive agricultural systems based on exotic species of plants and animals are bringing about far-reaching changes.

The rapid deforestation of the higher islands that has taken place over the past century is a major concern to scientists, conservationists and other inhabitants of this realm. The forests on quite a number of islands are being extracted for export earnings; mines on different islands are fast removing the mineral wealth of the islands. Records show an increase in fish catch every year with the introduction of modern fisheries technologies. The rapid increase in tourism in the region has also led to modifications and alterations in the landscape and seascape of the coastal areas. The increase in population has created a demand for more lands for settlements and therefore removal of forests or reclamation of swamps (mangroves), involving quite large earthworks. Some of the changes may be necessary to respond to people's needs and aspirations, but present exploitation tends to be on a "grab what I can now" basis with little or no concern for the future. The point is not to stop utilization of resources, but to ensure there is a wise use so that the balance of nature is maintained.

1.3 Trends in resource protection, especially through protected areas, over the past century

Some of the earliest formal conservation action recorded from this realm has been the establishment of forest reserves in Fiji (the earliest dating back to 1914); some control of grass and forest fires in the Society Islands and Mangareva; closed seasons for pearling in the Gambier Archipelago and in the Tuamotus; and the creation of Hawaii National Park.

During the 1930s, the first real attempts were made for protected areas and their management in the region. Examples include the establishment of a seabird breeding colony on the island of Gunuerg Api (1937) and the declaration by the Chilean Government of Juan Fernandez and Rapa Nui (Easter) islands as national parks (1935). These and other initiatives were brought to a halt with the outbreak of war. During the war, the extent of damage done to the ecosystems in the Oceanian region probably reached its all-time peak. After the war, very little significant contribution was made towards conservation until the mid-sixties.

Almost all the present protected areas and the legislation related to protected area systems in the realm have been enacted within the last twenty years.

2. CURRENT STATUS OF PROTECTED AREAS IN THE OCEANIAN REALM

2.1 Protected areas by country

American Samoa has had a territorial park system for some time, financed in part by the US Government under a grant-in-aid programme initiated in the mid-1980s.

In the *Cook Islands*, the island of Manuae has been dedicated a "World Island for Science" and two reef areas totalling 250 ha were established as national parks in 1972.

In *French Polynesia* there are no National Parks, but two areas on Tahiti Island (Mount Marau and Pari Coast) are at present under consideration. French Polynesia has a number of reserves:

Leeward Islands: Scilly Lagoon (1971)
Tuamotu: Robinson Reserve (atoll de Tararo) (1978)
Marquesas: Eiao (1971), Monotane (1971), and Hatutu (1974).

All these, except Scilly atoll, are uninhabited.

In *Fiji Islands*, eight nature reserves and an animal sanctuary have been established:

Reserve	Feature
Tomaniivi (Mt. Victoria) 1,350 ha	rainforest, sub-montane cloud forest
Nadarivatu, 93 ha	tropical rainforest
Naqaranibuluti (Mt. Lomalagi) 280 ha	rainforest
Draunibota Island, 2 ha	small island
Labiko Island, 0.3 ha	small island
Vuo Island, 1.2 ha	small island
Vunimoli, 20 ha	tropical rainforest
Ravilevu, 4,000 ha	tropical rainforest
Yadua Taba Island, 60 ha	crested iguana sanctuary

Fiji has produced a plan for a system of protected areas which is yet to be implemented.

The *Hawaiian Islands* have two major protected areas. The Hawaii Volcanoes National Park contains two active volcanoes; Kilauea supports a magnificent tropical rainforest, while Mauna Loa supports more open forests with a unique flora. It is also a habitat of many endemic species of birds. Haleakala National Park is a volcano which has been dormant for over 200 years, in the crater of which the extraordinary silversword plant is found.

In *Kiribati* (formerly the Gilbert Islands) there are no national parks but there exist bird sanctuaries on Christmas, McKean, Birnie and some of the Phoenix Islands.

In *New Caledonia*, conservation action was started in the 1950s and has resulted in the following types of protected areas:

A. *Reserves:*
    (i)   *Two integral reserves*: where the ecological system is protected absolutely and nature is left to its own devices.
    (ii) *Three botanical reserves*: where the flora alone is protected.
    (iii) *Six forestry reserves*: where the forest as a living community is protected but where man may exercise a controlled interference.
    (iv) *Three game reserves*: where terrestrial fauna is protected.
    (v)   *One fishing and game reserve*: where terrestrial and aquatic faunas are protected.
B. *Eight integral protection perimeters*: where mining activities are forbidden.
C. *One marine reserve*: where the lagoon-coast-islets ecological system is integrally protected.
D. *A botanical and zoological park in Noumea and the Thy Forest near Noumea*: where the public is educated in the nature of the country and the biology of the local fauna is studied.
E. *Four large zones of partial protection perimeters*: where prospecting and exploitation are controlled.

Papua New Guinea is a leader in protected area systems among the developing countries of the Oceanian Realm, with the following status at present:

Varirata National Park: situated in the Astrolabe Range about 40 km from Port Moresby, the park covers an area of about 1000 ha. It comprises both rainforest areas and open savannas typical of the Port Moresby area.

McAdam National Park: situated in the Bulolo River Gorge between the towns of Bulolo and Wau, the park covers an area of approximately 200 ha. It contains one of the last virgin stands of *Araucaria*.

Talele Islands Provincial Park: situated off the north coast of East New Britain, the park consists of a group of eight islands varying in size from approximately 2 to 4 ha.

Nanuk Island Provincial Park: situated on the direct canoe route from Kikopo in East New Britain to the Duke of York Islands, this 4 ha island is used as a staging point for those travelling by canoe.

Cape Wom Memorial Park: situated about 13 km from the town of Wewak, this Historic Site is the point at which the Japanese surrendered in 1945. It covers an area of approximately 55 ha.

In addition to these areas, negotiations are at an advanced stage for the establishment of a national park at Mt. Wilhelm, Mt. Kemeagi, Mt. Mosavi (a district park behind Central Government Buildings), Waigani, Vaigana Swamp, Paga Hill and the declaration of Kokoda Train and Bulldog Train as a national walking track. In addition 2 marine reserves Matupore Island near Port Moresby and Fly Islands in Morobe Province.

Apart from the areas committed to the management of the National Parks Board, the Wildlife Section of the Department of Lands, National Mapping and Environment control some reserves. These comprise mainly Game Management Areas where the wildlife resource is harvested in accordance with conservaton practices agreed to by local people.

The *Solomon Islands* has one national park, the Queen Elizabeth Park (6,080 ha) which is under public ownership but subjected to traditional rights by inhabitants of four enclaves enclosed within the park boundaries. There are seven bird sanctuaries on small islands.

On *Tonga*, almost 40 years ago, in 1940, 'Ata, the Minister of Lands, gazetted a park reserve at Haveluloto along the shores of Fanga'uta lagoon. In 1972, King Taufa'ahau Tupou IV declared 2 reserves: at Mui Hopohoponga and at the Ha'amonga Trilithon. Mui Hopohoponga is a 2 km stretch of beach on the extreme eastern end of Tongatapu. The Ha'amonga Trilithon, the Stonehenge of the South Pacific, is a 23 ha reserve.

Under the Parks and Reserves Act of 1976, Tonga has gazetted two national parks, which comprise the entire islands of Monuafe and Molinoa, and five marine reserves. Two reserves are the reefs which surround the islands of Malinoa and Monuafe and the other three are reefs at Pangaimotu, Hakaumama'o and Ha'atafu.

Tonga will soon have a major terrestrial park on the island of 'Eua, which lies 19 km south south-east of Nuku'alofa. Being the geologically oldest island in Tonga, having considerable altitudinal variation and being lightly settled and developed, 'Eua possesses the most extensive undisturbed habitats in the Kingdom. The proposed national park on the east side of the island encompasses 1,400 ha and four major habitats: the ringing reef; the coastal region; the eastern ridge; and the ridge summit.

In 1974 *Western Samoa* passed legislation to provide for a National Parks and Reserves system. A year later a comprehensive approach was undertaken through a study by IUCN and UNDAT, one of which recommended the reservation of 6 percent of Western Samoa's land area (38,220 ha in national parks). The following is the present situation in Western Samoa:

Tusitala Historic and Nature Reserve: A 1968 ordinance set aside approximately 128 ha on Mt. Vaea, which is subsequently being incorporated into the 1974 National Parks and Reserves Act. This area includes much of a small hill located in a commanding position immediately behind Apia. Robert Louis Stevenson (Tusitala) was buried on Mt. Vaea near the summit. Additional land has recently been added at the base and this area is to be developed as a botanical garden together with picnic, and walking areas.

O Le Pupu - Pu'e National Park: This area of 3,000 ha

was set aside by the Government as the country's first National Park in March 1978, although it has not yet been formally gazetted. This latter matter awaits the survey of the boundaries. The land was previously government land and stretches from the southern coast to the dividing ridge at Mt. Fito on Upolu Island, thus providing a range of ecotypes found on the island. It is hoped that O Le Pupu-Pu'e will serve as a demonstration area and thereby foster wider public and political support for the concept of National Parks and Reserves.

Togitogiga Recreation Reserve: This reserve was set aside by Government in 1978. It is a small riverside area containing 2 waterfalls and a very popular swimming hole. It has recently been surveyed to enable it to be formally gazetted as a Reserve. The area lies adjacent to the O Le Pupu - Pu'e National Park and the proposed park Headquarters area.

There are a number of areas currently under consideration for reservation in Western Samoa, including Palolo Deep, a small area of coral reef close to Apia. Work is currently underway to improve public access to the area and develop an underwater nature trail. Lake Lanuto'o is also on Upolu Island and is situated on the main divide to the West of O Le Pupu - Pu'e National Park; the proposal is centred around Government land but includes Customary land, Freehold, and Government Corporation Land. The area has significant recreation, and soil and water catchment protection values.

3. FACTORS WHICH HAVE IMPEDED THE ESTABLISHMENT AND EFFECTIVE MANAGEMENT OF PROTECTED AREAS

The purpose and the need for protected areas was traditionally recognized but due to the rapid industrialization and agricultural expansion in the Pacific nations, most of this traditional knowledge has fallen by the wayside. Only on remote islands where the inhabitants depend on nature's resources for their survival has such knowledge been passed from one generation to another.

In the Oceanian Realm one of the most important features in planning for protected areas is the question of land tenure and traditional rights. On most of the island nations a large percentage of the land is owned by the communal owners. The ownership of this land passes from one generation to the next and it cannot be alienated. A majority of the existing protected areas are on land already alienated to the government in the past. Today almost all areas that are in dire need of protection lie within customary ownership. It is a very slow process to convince the customary owners of the importance of conservation areas and the long term benefits (if any) associated with such designations.

The other problem faced by a lot of the island nations is finance to establish and manage protected areas. The economies of the nations are such that protected area systems are not recognised as being of high priority because the returns from these areas cannot be counted in dollars.

In Fiji we have realised that if forest areas are to be protected then the communal owners must be compensated with the same amount of money that they would receive if their timber had been logged. To raise this amount of money within a country is a very massive task when today's societies do not reap their harvests from nature, but are dependent far too much on finished products found in supermarkets and shops for which they have to pay from their earnings.

The smaller nations in this realm are faced with further problems of employing personnel to manage areas. The management costs involved if the islands are widely scattered are fairly high and almost all nations other than Papua New Guinea lack trained personnel or funds to train their manpower needs.

4. FACTORS WHICH HAVE ENCOURAGED THE ESTABLISHMENT AND EFFECTIVE MANAGEMENT OF PROTECTED AREAS

One of the major factors that has encouraged the creation of protected areas in the Oceanian Realm is conservation education, which has been included in almost all school curricula. Also the attendance at seminars, workshops and conferences has enlightened many decision makers towards protected area concepts.

At national levels the renewed interest in traditional cultures and lifestyles has given rise to rethinking about the traditional conservation practices and methods of resource utilization.

The existence of legislation dating back to the days when these countries were colonies, protectorates, or territories associated with European and Asian powers has also been a significant factor promoting the creation of protected areas. But this legislation desperately needs modification and revision.

The interest of industrialized countries in keeping island nations in this region as "island in sun with white sandy beaches fringed by coconut palms and with a backdrop of tropical forests" has meant that some funds are available from tourist ventures for protected area systems.

Also the pressures from the scientific community in relating the extinction of species to man's impact on island ecosystems has contributed towards an increased awareness of protected area systems.

The help of IUCN and WWF, together with aid from developed countries, has helped many an island nation prepare plans for protected area systems, train personnel and successfully establish national parks and reserves.

Finally, the rapidly depleting resources of the island nations should give rise to thoughts of the use of national parks and reserves as key mechanisms in maintaining the life support systems necessary for human survival. The governments in the region should recognize that parks and reserves are basic elements in balanced resource management.

5. SPECIAL CONSIDERATIONS

5.1 Marine protected areas

Traditionally, marine protected areas were created by closing an area to total resource use by imposing socio-religious *tapus* (taboos). These restrictions were imposed by members or inhabitants of villages (settlements) holding traditional fishing rights. The traditional fishing rights were rights enjoyed by owners over areas from mangrove swamps to the outer reef slopes.

With the commercial exploitation of resources many colonial powers viewed these traditional rights as "problems". These later gave rise to legislation in some countries which gave birth to the conception "freedom of seas" as evidenced by the disappearance of such rights from Hawaii, the Mariannas, Ponape and American Samoa. In countries like Fiji and Papua New Guinea, such rights are in existence and protected by legislation.

The present-day method of establishing and managing a marine protected area must always encourage participation or benefits for the traditional fishing rights owners or nearby coastal settlements or villages. Such participation is of utmost importance, especially in smaller nations with a severe limitation of funds. This type of proposal is viewed by the inhabitants of coastal areas as their development so there is general surveillance of a protected area with little or no cost outlay. In Fiji, thought has been given to allow certain traditional subsistence fishing to continue in legally proclaimed protected areas to prevent conflicts. Consideration has also been given to the involvement of coastal inhabitants and traditional fishing right owners in tourism-related business opportunities that will open from establishment of marine parks.

Most of the nations in the Oceanian Realm face the problem of lack of funds for proper management of protected areas. It is very easy to forget the vastness of this realm and the non-availability of proper communications and transport network systems in the island nations. Tonga, for example, has five marine parks and the staff have one small boat and a bicycle for management purposes. Fiji, having a reef system second to that of Australia and four hundred islands, has not been able to carry out very effective and appropriate surveys to determine the locations of marine protected areas because of lack of transportation.

5.2 International conventions

Unesco's Man and the Biosphere Programme is of particular interest to the island nations but unfortunately most of the island nations do not belong to Unesco, and it is difficult for them to join in other inter-governmental endeavours because of restricted available funds and a shortage of trained personnel to attend international meetings.

The South Pacific Convention for the Conservation of Nature still has to be ratified by some countries. The South Pacific Regional Environmental Programme has been accepted by governments as a part of UNEP's Regional Seas Programme and I hope will support protected area systems.

The convention that was proposed by the International Biological Programme concerning conservation of Islands for Science, has some willing contenders but has yet to be presented to a forum of the island nations.

Much more can be said about other special considerations, including the need for training, the special role of indigenous people, and the importance of systems planning. All of this is significant, and indicates that the Oceanian Realm is taking seriously the need to establish protected areas for the continued social, cultural, and economic well-being of its people.

Wildlife Management by the People

Navu Kwapena
First Assistant Director
Division of Wildlife, Office of Environment and Conservation
Konedobu, Papua New Guinea

ABSTRACT. *Papua New Guinea is a country rich in cultural and natural resources, where 98 percent of the land is held by customary landowners. This presents problems in establishing national parks and other sorts of protected areas, but a method has been evolved to use tradition to conserve nature. This involves the establishment of Wildlife Management Areas, parcels of land of any size, reserved at the request of landowners for the conservation and controlled utilization of the wildlife and its habitat. Sixteen such areas have already been declared, and 80 more are proposed, including both marine and terrestrial areas. An example of one such area is provided.*

1. INTRODUCTION

Papua New Guinea is rich in traditional culture with a tremendous amount of wildlife supported by its diverse habitats. The rugged, steep slopes of the country are covered with an abundant growth of natural vegetation ranging from sea level to the mountain tops, making it extremely difficult to travel from one place to another; because of the generally difficult access of the country, much of the wildlife is unspoiled.

All of the wildlife habitat in Papua New Guinea is owned by either individual clans or under a complex form of village ownership, so the traditional use of wildlife and its habitats will continue and be encouraged. However, care must be taken to manage these resources wisely.

The Division of Wildlife within the Ministry of Environment and Conservation has been charged by an Act of Parliament to protect, manage and control wildlife and utilization of its habitat. The National Parks Division ensures that parks, nature reserves and other scenic sites are completely protected and well maintained. The Environment Division monitors large-scale developments and controls noise, water, air and total environmental pollution problems.

The Papua New Guinea Constitution also guides the protection and proper use of our natural resources and environment: "We declare our fourth Goal to be for Papua New Guinea's Natural Resources to be conserved and used for the collective benefit of us all, and be replenished for the benefit of future generations".

We accordingly call for:

a) wise use to be made of our natural resources and the environment in and on the land or seabed in the sea, under the land, and in the air, in the interests of our development and in trust for future generations;

b) the conservation and replenishment, for the benefit of ourselves and posterity, of the environment and its sacred, scenic and historical qualities; and

c) all necessary steps to be taken to give adequate protection to all our valued birds, animals, fish, insects, plants and trees.

There are six relevant pieces of legislations which are protecting the natural resources of Papua New Guinea: Fauna Protection and Control Act (1966); Crocodile Trade Protection and Control Act (1974); Conservation Areas Act (1978); Environment Planning Act (1978); International Trade Act on the Endangered Species of Wild Flora and Fauna (1979); and National Park Act (1982).

This paper explains how the people in Papua New Guinea manage wildlife and how the present legislation tries to enforce these traditional wildlife management practices. Today many of the rural people in Papua New

Guinea still follow their traditional Melanesian way of doing things which include hunting, fishing, gathering, subsistence farming using the bush fallow rotation method, dancing, singing, chanting, and still practicing magical powers as well as believing in dreams. Traditional wildlife management has been reorganized and has been incorporated in the Fauna Protection and Control Act 1966. Throughout Papua New Guinea, local people are encouraged to protect, control and declare their traditional wildlife habitat areas as Wildlife Management Areas.

2. LAND TENURE: A PROBLEM AND AN OPPORTUNITY

The land mass of the island of Papua New Guinea is so rugged and diversified that most of its natural resources are either unexplored or unexploited. Nearly 75 percent of the country's population (3 million) is still living in the rural areas and some tribes are still in remote areas where they are isolated by steep mountain slopes and rugged drainage systems.

About 98 percent of the total land is still under customary land ownership; the remaining 2 percent is alienated land. Because the wildlife habitat areas are under local land ownership, it is almost impossible to acquire land for public use; at present there are many demands from landowners asking the Goverment either to pay the adequate value of land occupied by the Government before Independence (16 September, 1975) or to return the lands.

Even though the National Land Registration Act (1977) is trying to help settle disputes and land compensation claim payments, it has some disadvantages in that it does not provide for acquisition of any new land and does not allow for declaration of land which the State has not already acquired or held title over; because of these land registration and legal land compensation problems it is difficult to acquire any new land for conservation use.

Because of these land problems it may take some time for the Government to divert customary lands into sound use. While the Government is facing land acquisition and compensation problems, large-scale application of modern technology for exploiting the resources is rapidly increasing at an alarming rate. The question is, what shall we do now? Shall we allow the large-scale development projects to go ahead without any proper environmental assessment and scientifically sound conservation measures? Are there any alternative ways of implementing forestry ecosystem conservation and proper management of wildlife and its habitats on land which is held under traditional tenure?

3. USING TRADITION TO CONSERVE NATURE

With 700 different dialects spoken by the people there is a great language communication barrier as well as numerous traditions and customs. The communication difficulties and the complicated customary practices in regards to land ownership, natural resource use and so forth make it almost impossible for Papua New Guinea to adopt modern technology in implementing scientifically sound conservation projects. However, some of the traditional practices are complex and sophisticated and make sense in conserving and maintaining natural resources on a sustainable yield basis in the PNG Melanesian life style.

3.1 Traditional conservation practices

3.1.1. Traditional practices that deliberately set out to conserve wildlife resources. There are a number of traditional practices that deliberately set out to conserve wildlife resources. For example, among the Maopa people of the Marshall Lagoon area, there is a type of hunt with the use of fire which is permitted only once a year and is rotated between different locations each year. This traditional hunting season is called "Iwatha-kala" and lasts for a week ("Iwatha" means a digging stick for cultivating the land and "kala" means food). When the people finish their cultivation work with digging sticks and start to harvest their crops, a special hunt is held, along with fishing and exchange of food among relatives and between neighbouring villages.

The advantage of this traditional mode of hunting is that people select, from three available areas of bushland which are used by the whole community, the area with the most animals and thickest vegetation. Once an area has been selected and hunted in, it will be left alone for another two to three years to allow the bush to regenerate and the animals to return. (At present, with the introduction of modern weapons, population pressure and destruction of habitat, it is doubtful whether the animal population can long withstand the changes that are taking place).

3.1.2. Unintended conservation measures. There are certain traditional beliefs or practices that were not necessarily deliberately designed to conserve wildlife but had unintended conservation effects. For example, the Kewabi-speaking people of the Southern Highlands completely protect the bowerbirds *Amblyornis macgregoriae* (Kwapena, 1980), because this bird is used as an augur to discover who future wives or husbands will be.

The Kumbeme people also believe that the long, black plumes of the Long-tailed Bird-of-Paradise *Astrapia stephaniae* represent the long, black-dyed grass skirts worn by women in the area. It is believed that if a young man dreams about this bird, a yound bride will be coming his way. Because of this and other beliefs associated with the bird, it is not killed for its plumes in the Lalibu area.

Another example of possibly unintended conservation consequence comes from the Morehead District of the Western Province, where there is a belief that only men are allowed to enter a sacred forest area called Mirikiri. Before the men can enter the area for traditional use, they have to be decorated and to perform a ritual which the landowner initiates with a dance and a song. Women are not allowed to come to this sacred area while the ceremony is proceeding, and other men are not allowed to enter the area without the landowner performing the rituals. Because of these traditional restrictions, Mirikiri is kept sacred and not disturbed by any development. This area is now under investigation by National Parks and Wildlife Officers.

In many parts of Papua New Guinea only those people who can demonstrate ownership of an area and who have hunting ability are allowed to take or hunt wildlife in those areas. People who do not have land or any ability to hunt are not allowed to kill wildlife there. Traditional land ownership is one way of protecting wildlife and its habitat, prohibiting access to those who are not landowners (Kwapena, 1982).

3.1.3. Traditional wildlife depletion.
In Papua New Guinea there are also a number of traditional customs and practices that did not or do not help to conserve wildlife resources, but tend to deplete them. In several parts of the country large ceremonies require the killing of wildlife such as cassowaries, a practice clearly detrimental to wildlife populations. The PNG wildlife film "Thunder Woman" illustrates the massive killing of pigs and cassowaries in the Highlands.

Bird plumes play an important part in ceremonies in Papua New Guinea. In nearly every traditional song-fest in the country, plumes of birds of paradise are worn. For example, thousands of plumes were used in the South Pacific Festival of Arts in Port Moresby in 1980. Plumes are also used in cultural exchange, compensation for payback killing, bride price and gifts among friends and relatives.

In certain places, people only use one species of bird of paradise; in others, they may use more than one species. For example, the people on the north coast of Papua New Guinea only utilize Lesser Bird-of-Paradise plumes *Paradisaea minor*; on the southern coast of Papua, people use Red Bird-of-Paradise *Paradisaea raggiana*. In the central highlands, especially in Mount Hagen and Mendi areas, the people use more than one species of bird of paradise; for example the upper Mendi people favour the use of King of Saxony *Pteridophora albert* and the Blue Bird-of-Paradise *Paradisaea rudolphi* plumes (Kwapena 1980).

Large numbers of plumes are needed for ceremonial purposes. If demand for plumes continues, the wild population of birds of paradise may not be able to withstand the pressure. Spring (1977) illustrated some vivid photographs of birds-of-paradise plumes utilized by thousands of people at the 1977 Goroka Show. Various authors (Healey, 1973; Liem, 1975; Megitt, 1958; Rappaport, 1976; Waithaman, 1974; Dwyer, 1974; Blumer and Menzies, 1972; and Blumer, 1968) also indicated the social, cultural, economic and nutritional values of wildlife which people use for their living.

In the East and West New Britain Provinces, a large number of megapode eggs are harvested each year. This protein resource has been used for generations. The people of Garu village of Talasea, West New Britain Province, and the Matupit people near Rabaul in East New Britian Province eat the eggs on many different occasions. Lavege Village and other surrounding villages of Cape Hoskins use these eggs with other protein foods in celebrating or saying farewell to the dead; because thousands of eggs are collected regularly, this over-collection may soon result in a reduction of the Megapode population.

3.2 New problems in relation to wildlife resources

Because of population pressure at present, rapid growth of roads, modern hunting and collecting technology, forestry and agriculture, mining, fishing and resettlement schemes in various parts of Papua New Guinea, wildlife and its natural habitats are threatened. Some of the major factors which contribute directly or indirectly to a decline in wildlife populations and the destruction of the habitats or ecosystems in which wildlife exists are:

- clearing and selective logging of forests;
- large-scale agricultural development for oil palm, rubber, cocoa, coffee and other projects which replace large tracts of wildlife habitats;
- easier access for hunters to remote habitats because of improved road transport;
- trade in wildlife for modern goods and other items including money (Heaney, 1982 and Kwapena, 1980). Plumes of birds of paradise are particularly heavily utilized in the highlands, and crocodiles in lowland areas;
- hunting with shot-guns, replacing the old form of hunting wildlife using bows and arrows. In my research I found in 1967 that there was only one shot-gun in the Mendi area, but in 1978 there were 150; Downes (1977) also reported the increase in the use of shot-guns and ammunition in Papua New Guinea;
- large-scale mining, which reduces the natural habitats of wildlife populations;
- human population increase, resulting in heavier demands for food, and resettlement schemes which also affect natural wildlife habitats, as the population clears more forest for gardens or for other purposes.

Some of these traditional practices continue, while others have ceased. Beliefs about particular species and sacred areas and restricted access to hunting land still help to conserve wildlife, but in some areas increased harvesting has occurred because of larger human populations or increased demand for wildlife for ceremonial purposes (see Healey, 1982 and Kula, 1982). Other practices have died out or sacred areas have been destroyed.

4. LIMITATIONS IN DECLARING CONSERVATION OR WILDLIFE MANAGEMENT AREAS

The major constraints which hinder development of conservation areas (Fig. 1) are as follows:

a) Both Conservation and Fauna acts do not adequately protect the areas; the local people, as the owners of the land, still have access to these areas and may collect or harvest wildlife whether dead or alive.

b) Most people are well aware of the value of land so they are very reluctant to sell to the Government. Traditionally and culturally, forest and wildlife are part of their ecosystem and people value their land more than anything else.

c) There are always financial and manpower problems due to the poor national economy, and there are no training and research facilities for wildlife and habitat conservation.

d) Politically and financially, the Papua New Guinea Government at present gives low priority to non-profit making projects such as wildlife conservation and environment protection, national parks and so forth. Even though people are willing to declare their areas as Wildlife Management Areas, the Government is reluctant to provide money to develop these.

5. WILDLIFE MANAGEMENT AREAS TO ENCOURAGE TRADITIONAL CONSERVATION PRACTICES

One of the major actions taken is the encouragement of traditional conservation practices using existing legislation to create Wildlife Management Areas. Under the Fauna Protection and Control Act, the Minister for Environment and Conservation can declare a Wildlife Management Area (WMA), a parcel of land of any size, reserved at the request of the landowners for the conservation and controlled utilization of the wildlife and habitat.

Many of these areas have already been declared in the country. They are run by committees of people with traditional land rights in them. Each committee is chosen by the people and decides on rules for looking after the area. These rules are made law only when they have the support of all the people. When these rules are published in the Government Gazette they become laws like any other laws in Papua New Guinea. The rules can be changed if new problems arise or if the reason for making the rules has disappeared. Hunting and the use of plants and trees is not stopped in a WMA unless there is a special reason to do so; when rules are made to correct a problem with a specific species, this does not affect the use of other animals eaten or used by the people. Appendices 1 and 2 give an example of a WMA and its rules.

Landowners can take as long as they wish to decide on the size, committee, rules and other matters related to a WMA. Some areas have taken five years or more before complete agreement was made and before the WMA was gazetted; three years is the usual minimum.

When a final field report on a proposed WMA is received at headquarterss, a brief report is presented to the Minister for Environment and Conservation, to inform him and obtain his approval to take other steps. The chief draftsman of Lands Division then prepares a legal boundary description, and the Office of Legislative Counsel prepares a declaration which includes boundaries, committee members and name of area. The declaration is then signed by the Minister, and often a press release is made at the same time.

There are 16 declared Wildlife Management Areas, 5 awaiting gazettal notice and 75 proposed, including both Marine and Terrestrial Reserves (Fig. 2). The 16 existing WMAs cover approximately 480,000 ha. By declaring more WMAs, it is hoped that Papua New Guinea will be able to manage and protect most of the endangered species of Wildife and their habitats for the people and the nation.

Apart from Wildlife Management Areas there are 7 National Parks and Nature Reserves declared, 17 approved areas waiting to be gazetted, 16 proposed and another 44 potential areas under investigation. The declaration of National Parks Areas is covered under the National Parks Act (1982). The Conservation Areas Act (1978) can also be used to declare other categories of protected areas, including Sanctuaries, Nature Reserves and others.

Apart from the above areas there are six major areas to be investigated and declared if possible to preserve the representative population of the 33 species of birds-of-paradise found in Papua New Guinea.

As a result of having the three pieces of legislation protecting Wildlife Management Areas, National Parks, Conservation Areas and the total environment, we are able to protect some of our nationally unique species of wildlife.

6. CONCLUSION

The long-term future of wildlife and its habitat in Papua New Guinea is in doubt due to the effects of development. Material and social changes in the country, particularly economic growth, are increasing the dangers of over-exploitation of the animals and the deterioration of their habitat.

Conservation of wildlife in Papua New Guinea has two objectives: preservation of the existing wildlife populations for use in traditional and cultural ways; and the saving of any relict populations of species endangered by exploitation or any other causes.

The slowing or halting of development is not an effective nor satisfactory wildlife management tool in present-day Papua New Guinea. Rather, both in policy and practice, the preservation and wise use of wildlife should be one of the benefits sought from national development planned on an ecological basis. Unless the village people are fully involved and support wildlife and its habitat conservation it is most unlikely to save a significant number of animals or areas of habitat.

Government policy is that protected wildlife may not be commercially exploited, but preserved for use by the people in traditional and cultural ways. This policy can be greatly strengthened by the establishment of wildlife management projects in the village hunting areas, aimed at controlling shot-guns, the commercial plume trade, trespass and adverse changes in the habitat.

Therefore, in view of the national importance of wildlife and the urgent need for practical action to maintain the existing populations, it is recommended that the Government establish and maintain a special programme in the Wildlife Division. This programme should direct a national effort by the village people themselves, to preserve a resource which they own and the future of which they control. This programme would include the following steps:

- A thorough survey of existing traditional conservation practices, which may be useful to wildlife resource management planning and conservation;
- Wise use of available traditional practices in conserving our wildlife and its habitats;
- A system to preserve sufficient representative areas to contain the most endangered species of flora and fauna and their habitats; and
- International, national, provincial and community governments, and local leaders to work together in solving, developing and conserving the forests and the wildlife resources of each community.

APPENDIX 1: RULES FOR TONDA WILDLIFE MANAGEMENT AREA

The rules of the area gazetted in March 1976 include:

- Only customary landowners may hunt freely in the area.
- A tourist may hunt deer, duck and fish only and must have a separate licence for each.
- Each hunter must be accompanied by an official guide.

- All hunting by tourists must be west of the Bensback River.
- Licences are to cost K2 each.
- A limit of five is set on the number of deer or duck killed.
- Tourists may pay K1 to enter the area.
- Royalties payable are:
  K15 for each deer killed
  K2 for each duck killed
  K0.30 per kilo of fish caught.
- The carcasses of the dead animals are to remain the property of the licence-holder.
- The agents may issue licences and hold fees and the royalty payments in trust for the management committee.

The committee requested that the rules be amended to further reduce the killing of the wildlife. In the Gazette of December 1976 the rules were amended to include:

- A person wishing to hunt in the area with a gun must have a firearm permit from the Police Department before applying for a licence to hunt in the area.
- Hunters may not shoot or fish on the land between the Bensbach and Morehead Rivers.
- Hunters may not hunt from a vehhicle or boat whether moving or stopped.
- Royalties payable are:

First deer	K5
Second deer	K20
Third deer	K30
Fourth deer	K50
Fifth deer	K60

Duck and fish remain the same.

APPENDIX 2: AN EXAMPLE OF A WILDLIFE MANAGEMENT AREA: TONDA WESTERN PROVINCE

The people in the Tonda area of the Western Province wanted development and to participate in the cash economy. Most of their land was used only for hunting, with limited subsistence agriculture in the coastal area. The main source of cash income was the sale of crocodile skins, but many years of overhunting had reduced the numbers of crocodiles and the cash income.

Tonda is an area of outstanding importance of wildlife conservation, as it carries heavy populations of deer, wallaby, wild pig, duck, cassowary and many other forms of wildlife. These were previously used for subsistence purposes only - food, ornamentation and for exchange ceremonies. However, the people were aware that their wildlife held additional values.

With careful management and control measures the wildlife could be utilized in the following ways:

- farming of crocodiles for export of skins
- trade in wild pigs, cassowary, wallaby and cuscus
- farming and harvesting of deer for meat and other by-products
- a controlling committee of landowners, councillors and departmental advisers to draft rules and issue hunting and fishing permits for the area
- increased extension work on village industries
- local equity in all commercial ventures in the area

It was therefore proposed that the landowers have the area declared a management area with provision for continued traditional ownership of the land, continua-

tion of customary hunting and royalty payments by outside or commercial hunters. The main rules gazetted in 1976 are listed in Apendix 1 of this paper.

The Tonda WMA has potential for further developmentof its rich wildlife resources: through large-scale deer farming and associated industries, village farming of crocodiles (for export), cassowaries (for Papua New Guinean markets) and deer (for local consumption). There are also opportunities for tourist development, manufacture of artefacts and some employment related to these activites. Tourist services would centre on observaton and photography of wildlife, as well as hunting, fishing and camping.

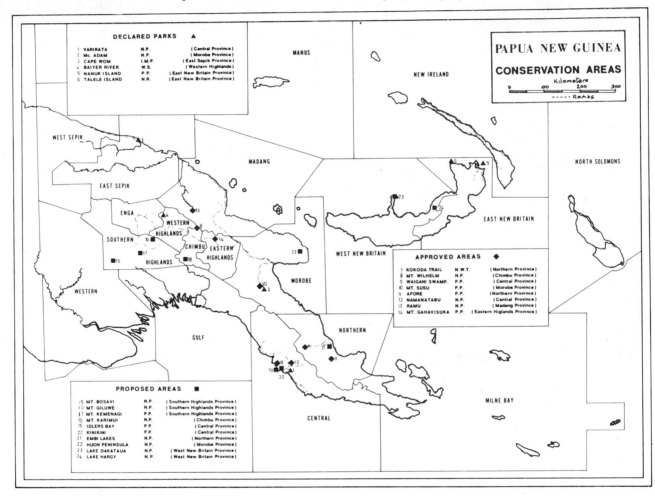

Figure 1. Conservation areas of Papua New Guinea.

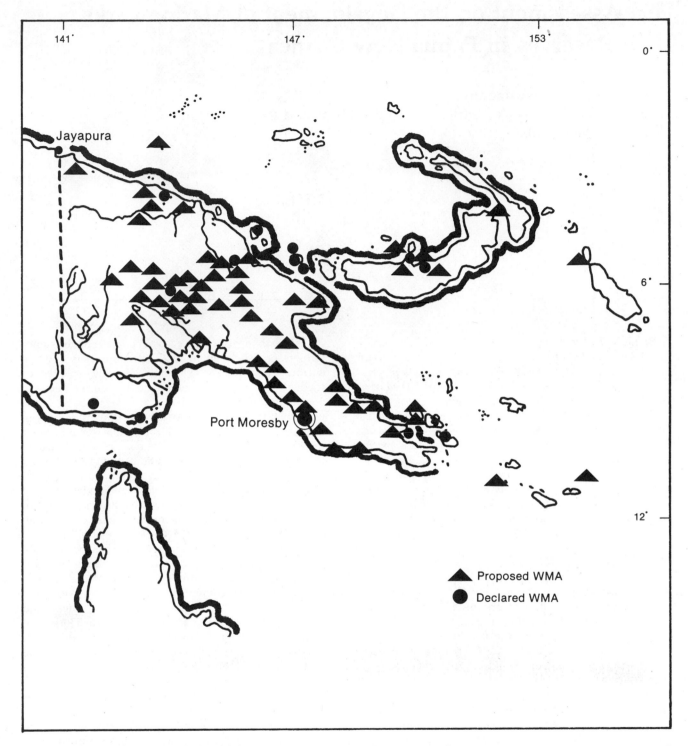

Figure 2. Proposed and declared wildlife management areas in Papua New Guinea.

An Assessment on the Development of Marine Parks and Reserves in Papua New Guinea

John Mark G. Genolagani
National Parks Service, Office of Environment and Conservation
Papua New Guinea

ABSTRACT. *The Papua New Guinea National Parks Service has tried since the early 1970s to establish marine protected areas. This development, however, has made very little progress in establishing additional reserves due to the traditional ownership systems, limited manpower and finance, and lack of enforcement and training. This account is an assessment of the problems in establishing marine parks and reserves, while discussing preliminary needs, actions and future developments and support that is needed. Within this framework, a case study on the proposed Horseshoe Reef-Tahira Marine Park is presented. The experience of the Horseshoe Reef Marine Park is then discussed to identify appropriate actions and support that is needed for marine conservation on a national scale.*

1. INTRODUCTION

The marine waters of Papua New Guinea (PNG) comprise some 65% of her territory and cover some 7,300 km of coastlines, excluding a declared 200-mile economic zone which covers 308,800 sq km of ocean (Perry, 1982; PNG Foreign Affairs 1982). There are several major river systems which run over 1000 km before reaching the sea, a number of large lakes, and extensive marine and fresh water wetlands. Most of the coastal population still employ traditional fishing methods but these are being superseded by outboard motors and monofilament nets. The marine resources contribute to the national economy; the average total value of marine resource exports (tuna, crayfish and prawns, shells, and crocodile skins) in 1980 was K33 million.

Although PNG has been fortunate in not experiencing large scale marine environmental problems such as over-exploittion of fisheries and widespread oil pollution, there is a rising concern for protection and management measures for marine resources.

More than 90% of the coastal people are subsistence farmers or fishermen in PNG, and the reefs and the surrounding waters have been traditionally exploited for food, shells, corals and other marine life for personal adornment, artifacts for daily use and currency. However, this strong dependence is being undermined along the Papuan coast, as the realization that some of these marine resources may have economic potential has led to an increasing commercialization of many traditional resources (Pernetta and Hill, in press). To protect traditional uses for the future while accommodating social changes and economic development, it is necessary for conservation and management measures to be implemented now.

The need for protected reserves has been established and proposed by different Government departments (e.g., Primary Industry; Lands, Surveys and Environment), Government institutions (e.g. Motupore Island by the University of Papua New Guinea), and even by non-governmental agencies (e.g. the Horseshoe Reef Marine Park by Tropical Diving Adventures, Ltd.). However, it is the Division of Wildlife and the National Parks Service (NPS) of the Office of Environment and Conservation (OEC) which have been entrusted specifically to establish and develop marine nature reserves (Andrews, 1980).

The Wildlife Division has made a significant contribution in marine conservation by developing a working model suited to PNG under its Wildlife Management Area programme (Spring, 1980; Kwapena, 1980; Hudson, 1980). The NPS has in the meantime established protection of a representative biological area (Talele Islands Nature Reserve) and nature or historic parks for visitor and recreational uses (Nanuk Island Provincial Park, Cape Wom International Memorial Park), but has experienced considerable problems, similar to those of the terrestrial reserves (Eaton, 1980; Gorio, 1980); these programmes have now been discontinued due to lack of finance. It appears that only if enough revenue can be generated from conservation areas will they warrant recognition by decision makers, a requirement which the established marine reserves have failed to meet.

It is obvious, however, that there is already interest in establishing 'marine nature reserves' based on money-making ventures by some provincial governments (e.g., Manus, Madang, Morobe and Milne Bay Provinces) and also private organizations (e.g., Tropical Diving Adventures, Port Moresby Sub-Aqua Club).

The purpose of this account is to describe the problems and constraints in establishing an envisaged pioneer marine park, the Horseshoe Reef-Tahira Marine Park in the Bootless Inlet, near Port Moresby, Central Province, and potential conflicts that may arise. It is hoped that the experience of the reserve may suggest appropriate approaches in realizing a more practical marine conservation strategy for PNG.

2. HORSESHOE REEF-TAHIRA MARINE PARK

2.1. Background to the area

The Central Province, in the south-eastern portion of PNG, has received considerable attention due to the primacy of Port Moresby, the seat of the National Government as well as the Central Provincial Government; it also serves a dual function as an administrative and commercial centre, providing opportunities of employment which encourages urban drift, while its 'youthful demography' is giving rise to a high natural population growth.

The Papuan coastal lagoon covers a surface area of some 200 sq km and borders the open ocean (Coral Sea) by a discontinuous coralline barrier reef, referred to as the "Papuan Barrier Reef" on the narrow continental shelf. The configuration of the coastline and the barrier reef at the north-west of the Papuan coastal lagoon show a funnel-shaped opening (Caution Bay) into the lagoon while toward the southeast the lagoon is narrowed where the fringing reefs and the barrier reef meet. The barrier reef is discontinuous with four major and many small channels. There are two major embayments, Port Moresby harbour and Bootless Inlet. Within and outside the embayments in the lagoon, are some coral fringed islands. The embayments and the adjacent coastlines are sheltered by low hills at a maximum height of 300m while the Owen Stanley Range towers to over 1,000m above sea level behind a narrow coastal plain.

The Bootless Inlet and its surrounding coastal environments have been under occupation for some 2000 years by the Motuans (Swadling, 1981) and fishing activities have formed part of their livelihood due to the frequent poor seasons of garden yields (Groves, 1977). This area has a relatively low rainfall and marked dry seasons and subsistence farming has led to a savanna vegetation (Paijmans, 1982). Fishing was not even sufficient to cater for different populations of the area, perhaps due to economic warfare (Oram, 1980), or the depletion of marine resources (Groves, 1977; Oram, 1981). This has been very significant even under European occupation; as Groves (1977) reports, "A major function of *hiri* (trade), Motu themselves insist, was economic. Without it they would not have subsisted, for in the frequent poor seasons neither their gardens nor their inland exchanges of fish for banana and tuber yielded sufficient staple food to tide them over the months immediately preceeding the annual harvest." The items of this traditional trade with the Gulf of Papua and their eastern neighbours included clay pots, sago, logs and shells (Lacey, 1982); it was the shells in the form of armshells and other ornaments that was the major item for ceremonial currency and, even at present, for bride prices.

The marine resources of the area are limited; from existing accounts it appears that fishing activities have been restricted by and large to the fringing reefs while very little attention has been focussed on activities on the barrier reef.

The urban development of Port Moresby is directly imposing social and economic changes, particularly in the use of marine resources, for instance the depletion of shells at the Pari Village (Swadling, 1980) and holothurians for pech-der-mer (Shelley, 1981). In addition, the extraction and transport of minerals from the area has had some impact, such as the discarded copper ore slug in the mangrove stands in Bootless Inlet (Johnstone, 1977), and the transport of the copper ore from the OK Tedi development in the Western Province into the Port Moresby harbour for eventual export (Moore, 1982).

The Horseshoe Reef Marine Park was first proposed in 1978 by the Tropical Diving Adventures Pty. Ltd. (TDA) based in Port Moresby, who specialize in water-based recreational activities, particularly SCUBA diving and underwater photography. The proponents themselves have recently changed the area's name to Tahira Marine Park (Coleman, 1982). As a portion of the barrier reef off the Bootless Inlet next to the Nateara Reef, the reserve is exclusively marine in that it includes no islands or coastal areas; this includes the coral reefs as well as the surrounding seas to an area of 295.9 ha. The reserve was proposed primarily to make aware to the coastal villages the effects of reef fishing on coral reefs in the area by protecting the Horseshoe Reef; however, terms regarding local participation in the establishment and management of the reserve have not been defined.

An official declaration to establish the area is still in process. Few surveys have been, so physical descriptions (physical profile, diversity and distribution of different species) are scanty and there are no assessments of its conservation and management needs; the objectives of the reserve have not been defined and there is no management plan.

The reserve is primarily a portion of the barrier reef in the shape of a horseshoe; the southern portion of the reef is exposed during the low-water spring tidal levels while the northern side is submerged. The submerged south-eastern end of the reef is connected to the adjacent submerged reefs while the north-west end immediately borders the Padana Nahua channel, one of the four major channels of the western sector of the Papuan Barrier reef. The most comprehensive data to date of its marine life is given by Coleman (1982).

2.2. Coral reefs

Coleman (1982) in his faunal survey of 1980 over a period of about 60 hours, recorded 70 coral species, including 37 species of hard corals in the genera *Acropora, Seriatopora, Stylophora, Pocillopora, Montipora, Fungis, Herpolitha, Parahalomitra, Coniopora, Porites, Echinopora, Favia, Hydnophora, Leptoria, Oulophyllia, Galaxea, Lobophyllia, Lithophyllis, Pectinia, Physogyra, Euphyllia, Dendrophyllia, Tubastrea* and *Turbinaria.*

2.3. Large animals and special sites

Large animals recorded in the same survey include wobbegongs *Orectolobus dasypogon,* catsharks *Hemiscyllium ocellatum,* and sharks *Sphyrna lewini, Carcharchinus spallanzani, Charcharchinus* sp, *Triaenodon obesus.* No turtles or dugongs were recorded.

A special site within the reserve is the 'Parama', a wreck that was sunk as an artificial reef and houses the major attractions of the reserve, a big grouper named Nessie, a moray eel *Gymnothorax flavomarginatus* and Fred Parker, a sea snake *Laticauda colubrina.*

2.4. Present human uses

Although the major traditional coastal villages of Pari, Tubusereia and Barakua are fishing villages, their activities on the reef are not known in detail though fishermen are occasionally seen on the reef. In addition, people from new settlements in the Tahira and the Mirigeda areas of the Bootless Inlet fish within or on adjacent reefs. The fishermen use either spear guns and mono filament gill nets for fish, but other marine resources such as shells may be collected. Some city dwellers have ventured into night spear fishing and occasionally intrude into the reserve area. Clearly, the area is vulnerable to pressure from other coastal populations as well as from its traditional users.

2.5. Problems in establishing the reserve

The initial problem in establishing the reserve was its boundary description, a function of the Lands Division

(which is independent of the National Parks Service although they are both within the same Lands, Surveys and Environment Department); the proposal was submitted in December 1978 and the boundary descriptions were not completed until August 1980, after a period of more than two and a half years. This boundary description had to be submitted to the Department of Justice for approval and forwarded to the Lands Department for gazettement under its legislation; this step was completed on 9 July 1981.

This gazettal was for the public to show, within a three month period, causes why the area could not be used for conservation purposes. There were no complaints or enquiries as such and the reserve would have been declared Government land and finally the National Park Act of 1982 would have declared the NPS to be responsible for its management. None of this, however, has been done since the area was found to be within a traditional fishing zone and therefore the area must be subjected to valuation for compensation payment to the traditional owners before it can be managed by the government. A further problem has been realized in that this is the Lands Division's first experience with marine areas, and hence there is a lack of personnel who can do the valuation of marine resources underwater. Furthermore the traditional owners still have to be identified, since the survey by NPS in 1979 and the reports that followed have failed to mention the traditional owners of the area.

Meanwhile, due to the sensitive nature of land compensation for areas under customary ownership, the establishment procedure for the reserve has been suspended. In conclusion, reserve establishment at present is a very lengthy process and it is apparent that followup visits have been non-existent, both to the reserve and to the coastal villagers; lack of training in conducting field surveys, reporting and drawing up management plans has made the problem worse.

A major constraint has been a failure to consider how and to what extent will the traditional owners and non-traditional owners will participate in the reserve's establishment, although this was one of the terms that was agreed with Tubusereia and Barakua villages in 1979. The NPS in the meantime has limited manpower and lacks the resources to commit itself to enforcement measures. Perhaps the ultimate test for the NPS is in making a set of compromises between the traditional owners and the Tropical Diving Adventures.

The TDA use the reserve as their base of operations and can be regarded as a significant component for its revenue. The traditional owners, on the other hand, pose a potential concern in that plans or compromises proposed between the three parties (NPS, TDA, and traditional owners) may not be acceptable, and a demand for a higher percentage of the revenues of the marine park by the traditional owners is not impossible. The primary concern here would be over shares for the traditional owners, fees to be imposed by the NPS, and profits the TDA need to earn for its operations.

From the above, it is obvious that the NPS has given the reserve in practical terms a very low priority. And one may ask, why? Most of the senior technical officers attribute the lack of attention to the marine parks and reserves concept being new. The rural populations have very little understanding of the concept of marine nature reserves, and even to those acquainted with 'marine parks' the term implies 'tourists and money' with very little consideration for conservation of the environment.

The current situation is that the only NPS Officer involved with marine matters (writer of this account) has only a basic marine sciences background and very limited experience in field surveys and in preparing management plans. Further, the NPS has very limited general resources, particularly on equipment, with only two sets of SCUBA diving gear available. It may, therefore, be premature at this stage to embark on such a programme due to constraints of finance and staff.

Thus it is only when the availability of finance can be assured that the Horseshoe Reef Marine Park or other marine reserves can be established.

2.6. Needs for the future

Due to the sensitiveness of the customary ownership of the area and potential conflicts that may develop, the reserve's immediate establishment has been put off for an indefinite period to identify appropriate actions. The basic needs recognized include: 1) more biological data such as for coral species number/diversity and distribution, dominant coral assemblages, concentrations of adults, juveniles, and breeding sites of lobsters, commercial fish distribution, known concentrations of endangered, threatened, or highly sought after species, and the presence of marine turtles and dolphins; 2) socio-economic data including identification and location of fishing villages, fishing grounds, location of industry, agricultural areas and proposed developments, and sites of specific interest; 3) determination of the conservation potential of the area through assessments of conservation values, threats and socio-economic considerations involved; and 4) a management plan.

3. EXPERIENCE FROM THE HORSESHOE REEF MARINE PARK

The experience of the Horseshoe Reef Marine Park shows that establishment of marine reserves in PNG is a very lengthy process which reflects the situation for the terrestrial reserves as well (Eaton, 1980; Gorio, 1980). Coupled with this is the lack of data on environmental, biological and socio-economic aspects of the coastal populations and their traditional uses of the environment; such data is necessary to prepare management strategies or propose necessary changes as new problems are encountered. This shows the need for a marine conservation unit which will include a cadre of trained personnel who can ensure wider public awareness and the development of marine conservation.

Note that within this account there is no mention of the Central Provincial Government (CPG) being involved, simply because it has not been involved. The NPS have failed to cooperate with the CPG, but the CPG has also ignored the possibility of the NPS to assist its own conservation efforts. This is at least partly due to the availability of finance within its own budget for initiating its own projects, such as the Idlers Bay Reserve near Port Moresby. Since the NPS lacked financial resources to purchase and develop the area from its traditional owners, the CPG purchased the area to be a provincial project without NPS assistance. However, due to lack of consultation and cooperation, there has been no development, and the CPG is envisaging returning the land to the traditional owners.

The development of the Horseshoe Reef MP to ensure direct benefits (e.g., payment of fees, local employment, protection of marine species and habitats) will meet some of the Provincial Government's priorities on protecting the welfare of the Central Province people, so this could be an initial point for the NPS to discuss with the CPG, particularly regarding finance.

With regard to traditional ownership, the Division of Wildlife has pioneered a model suited to PNG in the form of Wildlife Management Areas (WMA) (Kwapena, 1980), where a reserve's rules and regulations for its management and enforcement are created and implemented by the traditional owners of the reserve while the Wildlife Division assists in technical and resource management aspects. Major concerns with the WMA model include providing alternative means to generate local revenue to the villagers and the degree of authority that traditional owners or the NPS shall exercise over each other.

Where the people may be inconvenienced by conservation measures to the extent that they lose money, the model needs to provide alternative marine resources; an example of this is where the Kiwai people of the Western Province have been suggested to look to barramundi and crayfish—which have virtually unlimited and lucrative market and wildstocks for more intensive fishing—as alternative commodities from dugongs. However, the people need new techniques, such as catching crayfish alive so they can be marketed; the Dept. of Primary Industry could be requested to assist in such training.

With regard to the second concern, the traditional owners may neglect important conservation values of a reserve for economic exploitation and the Government can have very little control over such activities.

In view of this, local people and the NPS may need to reach a compromise between the WMA model and a more conventional marine parks system.

The viability of establishing Marine National Parks in PNG is greatly affected by recreational tourism, but PNG lacks a tourism base. As Ranck (1982) points out, there is considerable potential but costs of services and accommodation are very high when compared to similar facilities in neighbouring countries. This is due partly to the national economy depending on extraction of minerals, plantation products, timber and fisheries, which seem less risky than tourism but contribute to PNG's expensive accommodation industry. As long as PNG's national currency stays very strong in comparison to other currencies, recreational tourism may remain a minor development in the national economy.

4. ACTION AND ENVISAGED DEVELOPMENTS

To establish and develop a system of marine reserves, critical habitats, ranges of endangered species, and sites for tourism need to be identified. This is a constraint since the environment of PNG has been very little studied and so true interests as to conservation may not be known for some time yet (Dahl, 1980). However, preliminary sites have been compiled for field surveys, and Table 1 shows the areas of priority as proposed by different bodies and individuals.

Since there is no national strategy and thus a lack of guidelines for a marine conservation strategy, there is still considerable groundwork to be done. This includes developing a marine conservation strategy and establishing a marine conservation specialists team at the initial stages to enable the longer term goals of establishment of marine protected areas and a marine conservation unit.

The development of a marine conservation strategy would follow the national conservation strategy when it is prepared. Forming and developing a marine conservation specialist team is already in process due to the amalgamation of NPS into the OEC.

As for in-service training on marine conservation, PNG is inconvenienced by the discontinuation of the marine turtle and dugong projects where the national staff were being trained under the Wildlife Division. Under NPS there have been no training programmes, so an appropriate training programme will have to be developed.

4.1. Staff and resources available within the OEC

With the constraints of finance, manpower and training, the establishment of a small unit is envisaged which would be oriented mostly to efforts to assist local people in managing the way they use their environment in the light of recent alterations of life style. The unit would have a nucleus of officers of varying degrees of experience in village-based management work, drawing on all the organizations involved and on their active support to develop the skills and experience needed to improve the environmental conditions of the country.

Acknowledgements

I am grateful to the IUCN for enabling me to realize this manuscript, with special mention to Mr. Jeffrey McNeely for his comments and personal assistance. I am also indebted to Dr. Rodney Salm for his encouragement, and to Dr. Nicholas C.V. Polunin for additional comments.

A word of appreciation extends to all those who directly or indirectly contributed, particularly Dr. Lance Hill, Dr. Peter Eaton, Mr. Bob Halstead, and the staff of the Wildlife Division and the National Park Service. Finally, thanks and appreciation to Mr. Neville Coleman for making available his 1980 survey data, Mase Asigau and Wendy U. Lewa for typing the manuscript.

Table 1. Existing and Proposed Marine Protected Areas and Terrestrial Protected Areas with Marine Components in Papua New Guinea

Category	No.	Name of Area*	Province	Total	Area (Ha) Coral Reef	Mangrove	Marine Conservation Elements
Declared Marine Park/Reserve							
1. Management/Protection Established	1.	Talele Island NR[1] (1973)	E. New Britain	—	—	—	seabirds, coral reef, mangrove
	2.	Nanuk Island pp[1] (1973)	E. New Britain	12	—	—	seabirds, coral reef, recreation
	3.	Maza WMA[2]	Western	184,230	—	—	dugong, coral reef
	4.	Swataeteae WMA[2] (1977)	Milne Bay	—	—	—	turtles, coral reef
	5.	Baniara Islands PA (1975)	Milne Bay	—	—	—	no information
	6.	Long Island WMA[2]	Madang	—	—	—	marine turtle breeding areas (hawksbill, green turtles) seabirds, coral reef
	7.	Crown Island WS[2] (1977)	Madang	—	—	—	marine turtle nesting areas
	8.	Bagiai WMA[2]		—	—	—	Marine turtles, coral reefs
2. No Fully Established Management/Protection	9.	Garu WMA[2]	W. New Britain	—	—	—	no information
	10.	Horseshoe Reef MP[1]	Central	395,9	—	—	coral reef recreation, tourism, research and education
	11.	Unei Island VR[1]	East Sepik	—	—	—	coral reef, fish, seabirds
	12.	Fly Island MP[1]	Morobe	—	—	—	coral reef
Proposed Marine Park/ Reserve (by N.P.S. and Wild-life Division)	13.	Vuvulu Islands	Manus	—	—	—	coral reef
	14.	Ninigo Groupo	Manus	—	—	—	coral reef, turtle
	15.	Hermit Islands	Manus	—	—	—	coral reef, turtle, wildlife
	16.	Western Islands	Manus	—	—	—	seabirds, coral reef
	17.	Sabben Islands	Manus	—	—	—	no information
	18.	Alim Islands	Manus	—	—	—	no information
	19.	Baluan Islands	Manus	—	—	—	dugong
	20.	Lou Islands	Manus	—	—	—	dugong
	21.	Los Negrosls	Manus	—	—	—	dugong
	22.	Rambutyo Islands	Manus	—	—	—	dugong
	23.	St. Mathias Group	New Ireland	—	—	—	turtles, wildlife, coral reef
	24.	Islands between New Hanover & Kavieng	New Ireland	—	—	—	no information, could be coral reef
	25.	Djaul Islands	New Ireland	—	—	—	no information
	26.	Tabar Islands	New Ireland	—	—	—	coral reef
	27.	Lihir Group	New Ireland	—	—	—	coral reef
	28.	Tanga Islands	New Ireland	—	—	—	coral reef
	29.	Feni Islands	New Ireland	—	—	—	coral reef
	30.	Pinipel-Nassau Group	N. Solomons	—	—	—	coral reef
	31.	Kulu, Manus, Passu	N. Solomons	—	—	—	coral reef, seabirds
	32.	Duke of York	E. New Britain	—	—	—	wildlife
	33.	Hoskins Bay	W. New Britain	—	—	—	no information
	34.	Cape Gloucester	W. New Britain	—	—	—	dugong
	35.	Arawe Islands	W. New Britain	—	—	—	dugong**
	36.	Cape Anukur	W. New Britain	—	—	—	coral reef
	37.	Tumelo Ali, Seleo & Angel Island	West Sepik	—	—	—	coral reef
	38.	Shouten Islands	East Sepik	—	—	—	no information
	39.	Murik Lakes	East Sepik	—	—	—	no information
	40.	Chambri Lake	East Sepik	—	—	—	no information
	41.	Kuvenimas Lake	East Sepik	—	—	—	no information
	42.	Yimas Lake	East Sepik	—	—	—	no information
	43.	Manam Island	Madang	—	—	—	coral reef** research & education**
	44.	Hansa Bay	Morbe	—	—	—	coral reef**
	45.	Astralobe Bay	Madang	—	—	—	coral reef**
	46.	Umboi Islands	Morbe	—	—	—	mangrove
	47.	Tami Islands	Morbe	—	—	—	coral reef
	48.	Labu Lakes	Morobe	—	—	—	coral reef
	49.	Salamaua Peninsular	Morbe	—	—	—	coral reef
	50.	Mangrove Island	Northern	—	—	—	wildlife, coral reef
	51.	Cape Nelson	Northern	—	—	—	no information
	52.	Trobriand Islands	Milne Bay	—	—	—	coral reef, turtles, seabirds
	53.	Woodlark Islands	Milne Bay	—	—	—	coral reef, seabirds
	54.	Goodenough Islands	Milne Bay	—	—	—	coral reef, seabirds, turtles
	55.	Fergusson Islands	Milne Bay	—	—	—	coral reef, seabirds, turtles
	56.	Normanby Islands	Milne Bay	—	—	—	coral reef, seabirds, turtles
	57.	Pocklington reef	Milne Bay	—	—	—	coral reef, seabirds, turtles

Table 1 (cont). Existing and Proposed Marine Protected Areas and Terrestrial Protected Areas with Marine Components in Papua New Guinea

Category	No.	Name of Area*	Province	Total	Area (Ha) Coral Reef	Mangrove	Marine Conservation Elements
	58.	Misima Islands	Milne Bay	—	—	—	dugong, coral reef
	59.	Yela Islands	Milne Bay	—	—	—	coral reef, turtles
	60.	Calvados Chain	Milne Bay	—	—	—	coral reef
	61.	Conflict Group	Milne Bay	—	—	—	coral reef, seabirds
	62.	Engineer Group	Milne Bay	—	—	—	seabirds**, coral reef
	63.	Ware Islands	Milne Bay	—	—	—	seabirds, coral reef
	64.	Killerton Islands	Milne Bay	—	—	—	mangrove
	65.	Milne Bay Islands	Milne Bay	—	—	—	dugong, coral reef
	66.	Abau	Central	—	—	—	mangrove, recreation, dugong**
	67.	White Beach RF	Central	—	—	—	mangrove, recreation
	68.	Coutance Islands	Central	—	—	—	coral reef**, turtles
	69.	Papuan Barrier Reef	Central/Nat. Capt. Milne Bay	—	—	—	coral reef, tourism, research & education, turtles, recreation
	70.	Motupore Island MR	Central	—	—	—	research & education** coral reef, mangrove**, seagrass
	71.	Lealea Salt Flats	Central	—	—	—	mangroves**
	72.	Taurama Beach RP	Nat. Capital	—	—	—	tourism, recreation, coral reef, seagrass**
	73.	Idlers Bay P.P.	Central	—	—	—	tourism, recreation, coral reef, mangrove
	74.	Kerema	Gulf	—	—	—	mangrove**
	75.	Kikori	Gulf	—	—	—	mangrove
Declared Terresterial Reserves Bordering the Sea							
1. Seaward Extension Exists	76.	Cape Wom IMP[1]	E. Sepik	55	—	—	recreation, stoll, beach forest
2. Seaward Extension Proposed	—		—	—	—	—	—
3. No Seaward Extension, But Includes Marine Component	—		—	—	—	—	—

* MP = Marine Park, MNP/NP = Marine National Park/National Park, HP = Hunting Park, SNR = Strict Nature Reserve, MR/WR = Marine Reserve/Wildlife Reserve, PP = Provincial Park, PA = Protected Area, WS = Wildlife Sanctuary, WMA = Wildlife Management Area
** Element of major interest
[1] National Parks Service (Division)
[2] Wildlife Division
***Papua Barrier Reef—extends along the south-east of Papua New Guinea (across the National Capital District, Central and Milne Bayu Provinces)

Envisaged Design; Achievements; and Principal Goals of the Marine Conservation Programme, Papua New Guinea (based on Fig. 3 Salm et al., 1982)

Data Review and Collation—Preliminary Identification of Conservation Needs (Development Stages)

Strategy Formulation	Establishment of Protected Areas	Establishment of Marine Conservation Specialists Team	Establishment of a Marine Conservation Unit
Definition of Data Elements (nonexistent)			
Data gathering + mapping	Preliminary survey	Legalisation by ministerial decree	Recruitment of suitable project manager and counterpart staff (nonexistent)
Data analysis	Assessment of conservation value and needs at different sites (nonexistent)	Identification and invitation of members	Assignments to experts seconded from national institutions or abroad (needs developing)
Data Synthesis			
Identification of: • Potential Conflicts • Themes for Action • Priority Sites for Action	Identification of sites for protection (7 (WMA) completed, none under NPS) Detailed survey (none) Production of management plan (none)	Working meetings Development of government policy and legislation for use of productive habitats and selected species	In-service training (none) Regional study tours (none) Misc. level training abroad
Five (?) Year Plan for Development of Marine Conservation	Declaration (3 in existence, continuing) Establishment of Parks/ Reserves	Monitoring, review, revision, advising on Marine Conservation Programme	Marine Conservation Unit in NPS. Assistant Chief of Operation (A/C00) Marine Conservation Section Chiefs: • Marine Parks & Reserves • Habitat Management • Species Management • Planning • Survey and Research 4 National Park Managers

Biological Principles Relevant to Protected Area Design in the New Guinea Region

Jared M. Diamond
University of California Medical Center
Los Angeles, California

ABSTRACT. *This paper uses the New Guinea region to illustrate biological principles relevant to the design of terrestrial reserves. Biological input into the initial selection of protected areas must include answers to three sets of questions: What are the major types of habitats that support biologically distinctive communities? What are the major biogeographic districts that constitute separate centres of endemism? How much area is required for effective conservation? Each of these questions is considered for the New Guinea region.*

1. INTRODUCTION

This paper uses the New Guinea region to illustrate biological principles relevant to the design of terrestrial reserves. The scope of discussion is restricted to biological considerations and does not review socio-economic and political considerations (but see Kwapena, this volume, and Genolagani, this volume). The geographic scope is restricted to the "New Guinea region" of biogeographers: i.e., New Guinea itself, other islands of the Sahul Shelf north of Torres Strait, the southeast Papuan islands, and nearby north coast islands off the Sahul Shelf (mainly those of Geelvink Bay = Teluk Cenderawasih, but not the Bismarcks, Solomons, or Moluccas = Maluku). Scope is further restricted to terrestrial biota. Space restrictions preclude discussing the equally important problems of marine conservation.

The New Guinea region is divided between two nations: Papua New Guinea in the east, and Indonesia (Irian Jaya province) in the west. In its species diversity and endemism, New Guinea is one of the world's biological treasures and is really a small continent. Famous and distinctive species include birds of paradise, bowerbirds, cassowaries, mound-builders, tree kangaroos, and bird-wing butterflies. Compared to other areas of the world, New Guinea is fortunate in still possessing large areas of natural habitat, and it has yet to suffer any documented extinctions. However, threats to its biota are accumulating from logging, forest clearance by an expanding population, the illegal bird trade, and overhunting.

Proposals for national parks were prepared when Papua New Guinea was still an Australian mandate and Irian Jaya still a Dutch colony. Discussion of these proposals has continued since independence and transfer to Indonesia, respectively. Papua New Guinea now has a National Parks Board, Office of Environment and Conservation, and Wildlife Division, while Irian Jaya province has a Directorate of Nature Conservation office and a resident representative of IUCN/WWF. Numerous conservation areas are under discussion, but at present the only effective and actively managed one is Varirata National Park near Port Moresby, the capital of Papua New Guinea.

Biological input into the initial selection of protected areas must include answers to three sets of questions:

- What are the major types of habitats that support biologically distinctive communities?
- What are the major biogeographic districts that constitute separate centres of endemism?
- How much area is required for effective conservation?

2. HABITATS

New Guinea's mountains rise to over 5,000 m. From lowland rainforest one ascends through hill forest, oak forest (*Castanopsis*), southern beech forest (*Nothofagus*), subalpine forest, and alpine grassland to glaciers on the highest peaks. Almost all species occupy only a fraction of this altitudinal gradient. For instance, 90% of New Guinea bird species have altitudinal ranges spanning less than 1700 m and many span less than 300 m. Even species with broad spans, such as certain birds of paradise and bowerbirds, may require the whole span and be unable to survive in a fraction of it; they breed at high altitudes but live as immatures at low altitudes. Species diversity decreases with altitude, but the proportion of endemics increases. Hence the foremost habitat consideration in reserve design is that reserves must be selected to represent all altitudinal bands.

In addition to this vertical sequence of communities, there is also a horizontal sequence at the same altitude. While most of New Guinea is covered by forest of various types, extensive dry areas of south New Guinea are covered by savanna woodlands of *Eucalyptus* and *Melaleuca*, with a biota more similar to that of Australia than to the rest of New Guinea. Other non-forest communities include grassland (in the mountains largely anthropogenic), strand vegetation, extensive marshes, several major rivers (Fly, Sepik, Mamberamo with its tributaries the Rouffaerˆariku and Idenburgˆaritatu, and Digul), and several lakes of modest size (Rombebai, Chambri, and Murray in the lowlands, Wissel and Anggi in the mountains). Among specialized forest types New Guinea's mangrove forests are the most extensive in the world, and its swamp forests (especially those dominated by sago *Metroxylon sagu*) are also extensive. Substrates associated with distinctive forest types include limestone, ultrabasic rocks, and alluvium. On a given substrate, forest species can differ between high-rainfall and low-rainfall areas (e.g. the fruit doves *Ptilinopus pulchellus* vs. *P. coronulatus*).

3. BIOGEOGRAPHIC DISTRICTS

I mentioned that New Guinea is really a miniature continent, i.e., it is large enough to have produced radiations of birds and mammals by speciation completely within its own boundaries, not just by invasion from the outside. The reason is that New Guinea is large enough, and tropical populations sufficiently sedentary, that initially conspecific populations in different parts of New Guinea can become genetically isolated. New Guinea contains many centres of endemism, each with its own set of endemic species. For instance, among the ribbon-tailed birds of paradise (genus *Astrapia*), the species *A. nigra* is confined to the Arfak Mountains, *A. rothschildi* to the mountains of the Huon Peninsula, and *A. spendissima*, *A. mayeri*, and *A. stephaniae* to the western, central, and eastern portions respectively of the Central Dividing Range. Thus, it is not enough to have one reserve for each habitat type: there must be multiple reserves in different parts of the New Guinea "continent."

Clearly, information about species distributions and centres of endemism is critical in deciding where reserves are needed to protect local species. The Central Dividing Range runs east-west for 1500 km with no passes under 1500 m. Hence, for those hill-forest species confined to elevations under 1500 m the populations of the northern and southern watersheds are isolated, and each watershed has endemic taxa. For species living over 1500 m endemic taxa replace each other east-to-west, as in the examples of *Astrapia* species given in the preceding paragraph. The four main divisions are the southeast peninsula of Papua New Guinea west to about Menyamya, the central highlands of Papua New Guinea west to Strickland Gorge, the Star Mountains and Jayawijaya Mountains, and the Snow Mountains and Weyland Mountains.

Isolated from the Central Dividing Range by a "sea" of lowlands inhospitable to montane species are eight mountain ranges along the north coast (Huon, Adelbert, Bewani/Torricelli, Cyclops, Foja, van Rees, Wandammen, Arfak/Tamrau) and two on the south coast (Fakfak and Kumawa). All have endemic montane species, such as the previously mentioned *Astrapia* species of the Arfak and Huon Mountains. Of these isolated ranges, Arfak/Tamrau and Huon have the highest mountains and are richest in endemics.

Just as New Guinea's mountains are carved into island-like centers of endemism for montane species by its lowlands, so too its lowlands are carved into districts with endemic lowland species by its mountains. The three main lowland biotas are that south of the Central Dividing Range, that north of the Central Dividing Range, and that of the Vogelkop Peninsula at the west end of New Guinea. For instance, each of these three districts has a different species of crowned pigeon (genus *Goura*), large mound-builder (*Talegalla*), and streaked lory (*Chalcopsitta*).

The offshore islands similarly fall into three categories. First come those islands off the north and southeast coasts that lie off the Sahul Shelf, that lacked recent land connections to New Guinea, and that were colonized overwater from New Guinea. Of these, Biak is the largest and has the most endemic species, followed by Kofiau, Tagula, the d'Entrecasteaux group, and Numfor. The islands of the Sahul shelf (Aru, Japen, Salawati, Batanta, Waigeu, Misol) had intermittent land connections to New Guinea during the Pleistocene and received overland some colonists that subsequently differentiated, especially on Waigeu and Batanta. Finally, New Guinea's numerous scattered small islands share some species ("supertramps") absent from the New Guinea mainland and also serve as important breeding sites for marine turtles and certain pigeons.

4. AREA

Besides specifying in what parts of New Guinea and in what habitats reserves should be located, biologists can also offer guidelines about how large a reserve needs to be. Reserve area affects whether particular species can maintain self-sustaining populations within the reserve, and how many species the reserve can maintain.

Suppose one studies how a species is distributed over habitat patches (e.g., woodlots in open country) or over islands of different areas. One finds for most species that there is some minimum area below which the species is certain to be absent as a resident, and some larger area above which it is almost certain to be present, while its probability of occurrence increases from 0 to 1 with increasing area. The minimum area requirement varies greatly with species. Common forest flycatchers and rats may be able to persist for decades in a woodlot a fraction of 1 sq km in area, while eagles and tigers would require thousands and possibly tens of thousands of sq km. The reasons are several-fold. First, territory size determines the area required for even a single pair of a sedentary species to survive briefly. Second, the larger the area and hence number of breeding pairs, the less likely is a population to go extinct within a given time. Finally, a species that occupies different habitats at different seasons needs a reserve containing all these habitats for its population to be self-sustaining.

The larger a reserve, the more species will it contain. As a rough rule of thumb, a 10-fold increase in area doubles the number of species. Part of the reason is that, as a reserve gets larger, it can sustain populations of species with larger area requirements. Another reason is that larger reserves contain a greater variety of habitats and hence more species confined to specialized habitats absent from smaller reserves.

The New Guinea biota includes many species requiring very large areas for self-sustaining populations. Even the largest land-bridge island of the Sahul Shelf, Aru (7800 sq km in area), has lost more than half of its sedentary bird species since rising sea-level cut Aru off from the New Guinea mainland at the end of the Pleistocene. Among these species requiring very large areas are ones with huge territories such as the New Guinea Harpy Eagle *Harpyopsis novaeguineae*; ones confined to specialized habitats, such as the bird of paradise *Seleucides melanoleuca*, a denizen of sago swamps; and flocking species that wander widely in search of food, such as the parrot *Pseudeos fuscata*. If such species, which include many of New Guinea's most distinctive endemics, are to survive in the wild, it will be necessary to maintain somewhere in New Guinea an ecologically diverse block of land tens of thousands of sq km in area. None of the reserves currently under consideration in Papua New Guinea remotely approaches this size. However, such a reserve could be created in Irian Jaya if plans are implemented to connect the proposed Mamberamo, Foja, Jayawijaya, and Lorentz reserves.

Indigenous Island Peoples, Living Resources and Protected Areas

Bernard Nietschmann
Department of Geography
University of California

ABSTRACT. *This paper describes how indigenous island peoples use and manage living marine resources, the significance of those resources to islander society and culture, and the importance of this information in the design of protected areas. It considers cultural ecology and its application to island study and management, ecological characteristics of tropical islands, reefs and coastal waters significant to management strategies, Torres Strait environments and resource history, living marine resources and indigenous conservation, and the implications of these considerations for protected area specialists and indigenous island peoples. It provides a series of nine guidelines for protected areas and indigenous island peoples, concluding that legislated protected areas can meet the needs of indigenous peoples only if those peoples are involved in the design and establishment of new protected area programmes.*

1. INTRODUCTION

1.1 Indigenous conservation

This is a study of how indigenous island peoples use and manage living marine resources, the significance of those resources to islander society and culture, and the importance of this information in the design of protected areas.

Because of the limited resource base of islands and the ecological fragility of tropical reefs and coastal waters, indigenous peoples using these areas have adopted many strategies for controlling exploitation and encouraging protection. Another way of thinking about this is to consider that programmes of resource management and environmental protection are already in operation wherever indigenous peoples live in traditional settings. Re-

source conservation programmes may be more successful if they are adapted to and include indigenous conservation techniques. Many island peoples have very sophisticated ways of regulating the use of living resources. In that most of these environmental management strategies are carried out through cultural and social means that link people to their environment and to each other, new programmes introduced to protect an area could endanger an indigenous culture, create resource conflicts, and fail to achieve the goals of protection (Barker, 1980; Telander, 1981). It is argued here that indigenous peoples, such as the Torres Strait Islanders, have much to teach the outside specialist. They also have much to lose if they lose their traditional adaptation to their environment.

1.2 Background of the study

Research supported by the National Geographic Society and the Australian National University was done during 1976-77 and 1980 in the Torres Strait Islands, Queensland. The 150 km wide strait separates Papua New Guinea from the Australian mainland, and joins the Coral and Arafura seas. With my wife and son I lived for more than 16 months on Mabuiag, one of the mid-Western Islands, located near 10°S latitude and 142°E longitude. This area is listed as part of the Papuan biogeographic province (Udvardy, 1975).

1.3 Objective of this study

Discussion will be directed to consideration of 1) cultural ecology and its application to island study and management; 2) ecological characteristics of tropical islands, reefs and coastal waters significant to management strategies; 3) Torres Strait environments and resource history; 4) living marine resources and indigenous conservation; and 5) the implications of this study's findings for protected area specialists and indigenous island peoples. Research from Torres Strait will be augmented by findings obtained by other investigators who have worked on topics concerning tropical island people and resources.

2. THE ECOLOGY OF CULTURE AND RESOURCES

2.1 Interactions of culture and environment

Investigators in geography, anthropology and other fields have accumulated considerable research demonstrating that culture (a society's shared beliefs, knowledge and technology) provides the common means by which people adapt to and modify environments (Bennett, 1976; Hardesty, 1977; Jochim, 1981; Moran, 1979; Netting, 1977). The cultural relationships that link people in a society to a specific biotic and abiotic environment are as important to understand as those "things" being linked (i.e., the individual, the household, the village, an island, a coastal environment, and so on).

2.2 Cultural ecology

An approach used by geographers and anthropologists to study and understand these human-environmental relationships is called cultural ecology (other terms with slightly different meanings are human ecology, ecological anthropology, resource ecology). This approach focuses on the relations between individuals, society, culture, and environment, including biota and physical elements and processes. Cultural ecologists are interested in how culture shapes a society's conception of the natural world and how it provides the means to solve problems of resource management. The emphasis is on how people adapt to and modify their environments, how they organize, structure and give meaning to the natural world, and how they regulate and manage resources, both living and non-living. The environment, society and culture are studied as parts of continuous human-ecological systems that are maintained and changed by internal and external factors.

2.3 Resources as cultural appraisals

The natural world is an interacting, inter-connected complex of biotic and abiotic elements and processes. To study and use the natural world each society relies on systematic methods of categorization (language, science, folk science) to differentiate particular things from the complex whole. The natural world contains many potential resources, only some of which are recognized and relevant to a particular cultural group. Thus resources are cultural appraisals and as such cannot be disengaged from their cultural context. The natural world becomes a specific type of environment with specific resources (living and non-living, renewable and non-renewable) because of cultural selection.

In that resources are a cultural concept as much as they may be a biological fact, those things that are differentiated as "resources" by one group of people may not be recognized by another group of people—even in the same environment, whether that environment is terrestrial or marine, the resources living or non-living, the area protected or unprotected.

Indigenous peoples also use logically consistent taxonomic systems for identifying and classifying their natural world (Berlin, Breedlove and Raven, 1974; Conklin, 1972). Some indigenous societies may recognize more things or "resources" in an environment than would a scientist from the outside (Lvi- Strauss, 1966. Thus, an unrecognized problem might occur when protected area specialists and national or international conservation agencies introduce a resource protection-conservation programme that includes *fewer* resources than are recognized and used by the indigenous inhabitants. A type of resource "impoverishment" occurs because the environment would be seen to contain fewer resources. The status of a living resource (abundant, rare, threatened, endangered) is a reflection of environmental change, its exploitation history, and its cultural recognition (i.e., the *Anopheles* mosquito is not considered a resource, nor does its low population in some areas constitute it being classified as "locally endangered").

2.4 Culture as a resource

Because culture is in part a means to identify resources for a human group and to organize and pass on problem-solving knowledge about how to use and manage them, it constitutes an integral part of the human environment. This is why cultural ecologists speak of "bio-cultural environments".

For a specific society and place, culture is a resource in itself because through culture, environments are conceptually constituted, the means and controls of exploitation are organized, and cumulative resource knowledge stored, taught and used. The cultural resources of indigenous peoples are based on hundreds, often thousands, of years of empirical experience with the ecology of living resources in specific environments. Conservation of the cultural resources may be critical in promoting and achieving conservation of the biological resources.

3. TROPICAL ISLANDS, REEFS AND SHALLOW WATERS

3.1 Ecological characteristics

Tropical islands, reefs and shallow coastal waters have many specific ecological characteristics that facilitate resource exploitation but hinder resource conservation (Byrne, 1979; IUCN, 1976a; McEachern and Towle, 1974; Odum, 1976; South Pacific Commission, 1973). Presented briefly here are some of the important ecological aspects that might influence resource management strategies of indigenous peoples.

3.2 Islands

The most significant ecological characteristics of islands result from their isolation. Isolation favours the development and survival of unique biotas that may be considered part of "evolutionary museums". As such, islands have been attractive in the study of evolution (Darwin, Wallace), the development of island biogeography models of extinction-immigration rates and equilibrium (MacArthur and Wilson, 1967; May, 1978; Simberloff, 1982), to preserve as parks and reserves (Dorst, 1974; McEachern and Towle, 1974), and as "islands for science" (Elliott, 1973a, 1973b). Because many "island-like" ecological situations exist on mainlands (a national park is often considered to be like an island), the study of islands and island peoples has relevance beyond sea islands (IUCN, 1980b; Orians, 1974; May, 1978; MacArthur and Wilson, 1967; Fosberg, 1965).

3.2.1. Types of islands.
Islands may be distinguished by type (continental, atoll, volcanic, raised reef), and by relative locations (isolated, island cluster, island chain). Type and relative location influence resource occurrence; for example, Niue, an isolated, raised reef island, will have fewer terrestrial and marine resources than will the largely volcanic island cluster of Western and American Samoa just to the north.

3.2.2. Island characteristics that affect living resources.
Islands have a narrower range of living resources than do mainland areas of comparable size. This is largely due to the capriciousness of accidental overseas dispersal (Wiens, 1962) and the limiting conditions imposed by insular environments. Prior to human migrations, the establishment of a plant or animal on an island was largely a chance event, influenced in part by the island's age, size, elevation, distance from a colonizing source on a mainland or another island, and existing habitat quality (relative abundance of soils, fresh water, vegetation). In general, younger, smaller, lower, more distant islands will have a smaller and more disjunct range of living resources than will older, larger, higher, closer islands (MacArthur and Wilson, 1967).

3.2.3. Island life.
Because of relative conditions of insularity (a limited land area surrounded by water) and remoteness (distance and frequency of biotic contact), island biota are in many ways different from mainland biota. Islands are characterized by a limited number of species, the absence of important animal and plant species, a high degree of endemism, and modified ecological behaviour (i.e. ground-dwelling birds) of many species (Holdgate and Wace, 1961; Wiens, 1962). Whereas isolation creates and protects these biological characteristics, the living resources are extremely vulnerable and susceptible to change when isolation is broken down ("ecological boiling" from further accidental introductions, colonization by humans and their domesticates and "fellow travellers"—weeds and rats, and temporary visits by scientists or tourists). Because of high endemism and biotic fragility, more historical extinctions and endangered species occur on islands than on mainlands.

The living resources and environments of islands are dynamic and ever-changing. Disturbances are a natural part of island ecosystems (cyclones, droughts, accidental colonizations). The distinctive character of island biota often results from the nature and frequency of disturbances, not just from isolation itself.

3.2.4. Islands and boundaries.
Islands are limited land areas bounded by water. The land-water distinction is only one of several boundaries (political, economic, cultural, ecological) that may affect delimitation of islands. From an ecological perspective, islands are part of a land-water system that overlaps the shoreline boundary. Exchange of terrestrial and marine materials is frequent and ecologically significant. For example, sandy beach soils are enriched by additions of wind-, wave- and tide-carried fragments of marine plants and animals; and fringing reefs, lagoons and inshore waters receive island-derived sediments and freshwater outflow.

An island does not stop or start at the water's edge. This is of significance in understanding how island peoples have adapted to the overlapping and edge effects of adjacent land-reef-shallow-sea systems. Ecological and cultural boundaries are important considerations for specialists who may be called on to establish and justify boundaries for protected areas.

3.3 Coral reefs

Coral reefs (platform, fringing, barrier, atoll) are among the world's most biologically productive and diverse ecosystems (Goreau, Goreau and Goreau, 1979). Limited to shallow, clear, warm, well oxygenated, and unpolluted salt water, coral reefs are biological islands surrounded by the ocean sea. Large amounts of nutrients are concentrated in the high standing crops of fish and invertebrates. Many materials and nutrients are recycled and loss from the reef reduces the amount available for future recycling (Grigg, 1979).

Coral reefs are vulnerable to disruption because of their shallow water accessibility and concentration of habitat. They are easily depleted by intensive fishing and they can be affected by near and distant changes in the marine environment caused by dredging, silting, pollution, and changes in water temperature, salinity and clarity.

Reefs adjacent to islands are important because they may provide the major source of protein to island people, they protect the island from storm waves, they bound and protect inshore lagoons, and they supply biotic materials for shoreline enrichment.

3.4 The shallow water marine tropics

Tropical coastal waters contain four of the world's most productive yet fragile ecosystems: coral reefs; seagrass communities; lagoons and estuaries, and sea-edge mangrove forests. Because of their productivity, species diversity, spatial concentration and accessibility, these environments are attractive areas for human exploitation (Kapetsky, 1981; West, 1976). Indigenous use of resources from these fragile environments has to be exceptionally sophisticated to permit sustainable exploitation.

4. PERSPECTIVES ON ABORIGINAL TORRES STRAIT

Torres Strait (Fig. 1) contains a diverse yet fragile spectrum of island and marine environments and resources. Consideration of the general characteristics of the area's maritime geography and previous patterns of indigenous resource use will provide useful perspectives on the contemporary situation.

4.1 Torres Strait islands and waters

No two islands are alike. Each is different in its own environmental history and environmental setting. As elsewhere this is true in Torres Strait with its wide range of island types: continental in the west; alluvial in the north; volcanic in the east; and coral cay in the centre. Reef types include fringing, platform and barrier (the northern end of the Great Barrier Reef marks the eastern edge of Torres Strait). Coral reefs are extensive and well developed in the shallow waters that mark the western limits of the Strait. Here too exist vast shoals of sand and mud, in some places anchored by beds of seagrasses; elsewhere the shoals migrate in sand waves across the bottom, driven by strong currents. Seagrasses (*Thalassia hemprichii, Enhalus acoroides, Halophila* sp. *Thallasodendron ciliatum, Halodule pirifolia, Cymodocea* sp., *Zostera* sp. and others) occur on reefs, shoals of unconsolidated materials, and along island sand and mangrove alluvium margins. Seagrasses are more prevalent in the

shallow waters of western Torres Strait (10-15m) with its varied and extensive complex of island, reef and shoal, than in the eastern Strait with its greater depth (30-50m) and fewer reefs.

With its diversified, productive and compact marine environments, Torres Strait is the most ecologically complex part of one of the largest continental shelves in the world, stretching some 2000 km long and 1000 km across (Jennings, 1972). Torres Strait lies within the Indo-Pacific marine faunal province, the world's richest in species diversity. Whereas the sea is species-rich, the islands are species-poor. Torres Strait is a floristic and faunistic boundary between the Australian and Oceanian biogeographic realms, between the wet, tropical environments of New Guinea and the dry, sub-tropical environments of Australia (Wace, 1972). Different ecological conditions on the island and the intervening water barriers have limited the north-south spread of many plants and animals and their establishment on the islands.

Fluctuations in weather, tides and currents, and the movement of marine fauna add further ecological complexity. The tropical wet-dry climate creates significant shifts in precipitation and wind direction. During the monsoon season (December through April), the wind and rain are from the northwest; about 85 percent of the annual average of 1628mm (Thursday Island) falls during the monsoon wet. In the tradewind season (May through September), southeast winds are brisk and frequent but rainfall is slight and scattered. Occupying the narrow constriction between two large seas, and situated astride the convergence of two out-of-phase tidal regimes—those of the Indian and Pacific Oceans—Torres Strait has a complex pattern of tides and tidal currents. Tides are mixed with two highs and two lows occurring daily; during the twice-monthly spring tide, a range of 3.5 metres is common. This is significant because in such shallow waters, vast areas of reef, island margin, and seagrasses are alternatively opened and closed to fish, turtles, dugongs and people. Strong tidal currents accompany the massive up-down shifts of the tides. In constricted reef passages the tidal currents can reach 6 knots (Endeavour Strait has the fastest tidal currents of any commercial sea passage in the world). Tidal currents, rather than sea swells, transport nutrients, move and oxygenate the water that promote coral growth and that produce the dominant east-west elongated platform reefs. With a high tidal range and strong tidal currents, the rhythmic up and down and in and out movement of sea water strongly influence the temporal and spatial occurrence and accessibility of marine biota.

Molluscs, crustaceans, and many species of fish are more or less sedentary in various reef and nearshore zones, while other fish range more widely with the tides and changes in seasons. Dugongs *Dugong dugon* and green turtles *Chelonia mydas* are herbivorous and move frequently with the tides to and from the shallow reef and island-edge seagrass pastures. Green turtles make periodic, 2- to 4-year interval migrations to island nesting beaches at Bramble Cay (eastern edge of Torres

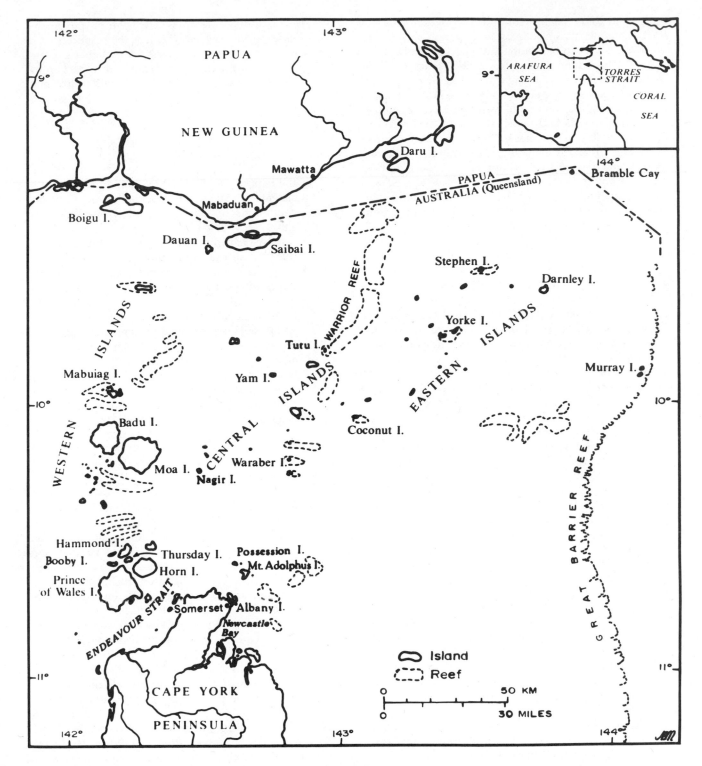

Figure 1. Map of Torres Strait area, showing islands and reefs.

Strait) and Raine Island (south along the Great Barrier Reef). Dugongs may also make long-distance migrations but this has yet to be demonstrated scientifically.

It is important to note from the discussion so far that the populations of living marine resource important to Islander subsistence are periodically concentrated and then dispersed through regular and predictable changes in weather (winds and rains), tides and tidal currents, and during life cycle phases (fish and spiny crayfish spawning, green turtle mating and nesting, and dugong mating and birthing on distant reefs). The island-sea resource environments are varied, closely spaced and ever oscillating. These common insular-maritime characteristics present significant problems for indigenous and non-indigenous resource managers.

4.2 Past Torres Strait Islander subsistence

This brief reconstruction of previous Islander use of living resources is based on the handful of accounts available from the early period of prolonged European contact starting in the mid-19th Century (Haddon, 1901-1935; Moore, 1979).

The people referred to as Torres Strait Islanders are part of the Melanesian culture area but they also have some cultural influences from aboriginal Australia. Subsistence strategies varied greatly from island to island but in rough outline two main patterns were evident: in the eastern volcanic and northern alluvial islands the emphasis was on horticulture and fishing; while on the coral central and igneous western islands with their poor soils and scarce freshwater but good reefs and seagrass pastures, the emphasis was on fishing, marine hunting, and reef foraging, with some horticulture on some islands.

The individual island patterns were much more complex. For example, on the mid-Western Islands of Badu, Moa and Mabuiag, Islanders used a wide range of subsistence adaptations to ensure a bountiful return. On the islands, bananas, yams, and taro were grown in small raised fields, and wongai plums *Mimusops browniana* and native almonds *Terminalia catappa* were collected. Bivalves, gastropods, and crabs were foraged from the reefs exposed at low tide. Mangrove forests along protected island margins provided crabs, oysters, and a wet season food made from beaten and cooked viviparous seedlings of the mangrove *Bruguiera gymnorrhiza*. Fishing was important and done by the use of hook and line, diverse spears from single to multi-prong, large stone fish traps, and underwater spearfishing. Marine hunting of dugongs and green turtles tapped the productivity of the extensive seagrass pastures and provided large amounts of meat and fat.

Dugongs and turtles were harpooned from canoes, turtles were also caught by using line-carrying remoras, and dugongs were harpooned from portable hunting platforms erected over seagrass feeding grounds.

Few island people anywhere were or are capable of supporting themselves with just the resources from their island and adjacent waters. A sustainable island adaptation usually meant minimizing the impact on the easily depleted local island-reef base—with its low populations of many species concen- trated in limited geographical areas, and by acquiring resources from other areas.

In Torres Strait, resource availability was maintained by these cultural adaptations:

- the temporal and spatial rotation of different subsistence activities that provided efficient but discontinuous subsistence from any one species or site;
- resource expeditions to distant islands and reefs that also spread exploitation pressure;
- frequent ceremonies, rituals, and prohibitions which diffused and accentuated subsistence pressure;
- trade for goods with other Islanders, and Papuans and Aborigines, extended the limited resource base of any one island and integrated many locales into a single regional trading network; and
- frequent inter- and intra-island feasting and gift giving served to spread out resource accumulations during times of plenty and to accumulate obligations for reciprocal treatment for future times of scarcity.

4.3 European intrusion

European seafarers entered Torres Strait by the early 17th Century, perhaps earlier. After the establishment of the Australian colony in 1788, movement through the Strait and sporadic contact with Islanders became more frequent. In the 1860s, the European discovery of abundant beds of pearl shell, and later, trochus and *bche-de-mer* (trepang), attracted divers and crews from many places including England, the Pacific Islands and Japan. In 1871 the London Missionary Society began to Christianize the Islanders, a process turned over to the Anglicans in 1914. Queensland annexed the islands in 1872 and Thursday Island was made the administrative and commercial centre. Initially to protect the Islanders against the ravages of the pearl shellers, but later to continue a policy of containment of non-whites, the islands were established as reserves to be locally governed by elected representatives but administered by Queensland's Department of Aboriginal and Islander Advancement (DAIA) which controls most forms of transportation and communication, and runs and supplies the stores that are on each island. Many men joined the all- Islander Torres Strait Light Infantry Battalion during World War II and they or their families still receive pensions today. State and Commonwealth social benefits contribute in part to Islander incomes. In 1948 they became Australian citizens; in 1961 they gained the franchise; and changes in state and Commonwealth legislation in 1965 and 1966 gave them some of the rights enjoyed by most other Australians. Pearl shell was over-exploited by Europeans and only four or five pearl luggers work the grounds today, down from the more than 200 in the area at the turn of the century. The major marine economic activity in the area today for the Islanders is diving for spiny crayfish ($8.00/kg for tails). "Europeans" (white Australians) trawl for prawns.

As a result of missionary directives, political hegemony, public health policy, and lack of adequate boats for extra-regional transport, the old trade networks are gone. The inter- and intra-regional dependency that augmented local subsistence has been partially replaced by centralized state and federal control of the Island economy. Queensland ships goods to the islands and the Commonwealth provides Islanders with the money to buy the goods. Household incomes are based on social benefits, remittances from relatives working on the mainland, earnings from crayfishing, and from government jobs held on the reserve islands and private jobs on Thursday Island.

Some 4500 Islanders live in Torres Strait, with 2000 on Thursday Island, and 2500 living on the 13 outer islands which are reserves. Outsiders cannot visit the reserve islands without special permission from specific island and regional committees. Another 5000 Islanders live on the mainland, mostly at Bamaga (nothern Cape York), Cairns, Townsville and Brisbane.

Two things stand out about islands and islanders that are important when considering issues of resource conservation and protecting insular and marine areas. First, for resident islanders, continued access to local resources provides culturally and nutritionally important materials and promotes cultural continuity. Each island has its own local living resource base which yields sustenance and cultural and social identity. Second, for islander emigrants and residents, continued contact with their home island is of utmost significance. One's identity comes in large measure from one's home island. If you are an islander, your island place of birth may be more important than your current place of residence. A return visit, correspondence, or a visit from an island relative are sufficient to maintain ties with the island home. People who were born on mainlands often cannot appreciate the significance of place that islands evoke of their peoples. Forced relocation of islanders usually leads to tragic consequences, as happened with the resettlement of people from Bikini and Eniwetok Atolls in the Marshall Islands (Kiste, 1974; Mason, 1954).

In Torres Strait, island place and resource are central to Islander identity and self-image. Many of the former traditional resource adaptations remain in the midst of modern influences and many modern influences have been adapted to fit Islander traditions. Islanders are culturally ambidextrous, they can participate in both modern and traditional worlds. But it is access to the traditional that permits participation in the modern. To do otherwise would be to become nobody.

5. CULTURE AND RESOURCES IN THE ISLANDS

The critical importance of living resources to indigenous island peoples and the methods they use to control resource harvest can be better understood by closer examination of a single island. The following material pertains to Mabuiag, one of the mid-Western Islands (see also Nietschmann, 1977; Nietschmann and Nietschmann, 1981).

5.1 Living marine resources

Living resources from the sea are overwhelmingly more important in diet, labour and prestige than those from the land. Exploitation of the sea for subsistence focuses on dugongs, green turtles and fishes. Securing these resources is the major activity of most men, and many women fish. Crayfish are taken by free divers and the tails frozen and sold to buyers on Thursday Island.

Fish are caught throughout the year during several recognized seasons using a range of gear (seine nets, hooks with various baits, different spears, and spearfishing). Using hand lines and seine nets, women bring in the most fish and are the most consistent fishers. Men spear fish on reef flats and under- water. At any one time people seek specific species, but during the course of a year they commonly exploit some 30 of the 130 species they name and I was able to identify. Most of the species of fish caught regularly have large stocks on nearby and distant reefs and waters (jacks, tuskfishes, perches, rock-cods, snappers, mackerel, mullet, garfish, coral trout, and various stingrays).

Dugongs and green turtles are similar in that they are the world's only large animals that graze on the pastures of the sea and convert the primary production of the extensive seagrasses into abundant and flavourful meat. Big and good tasting, confined to shallow waters, and air breathing, dugongs and green turtles have been important sources of high quality protein for indigenous island and coastal peoples. Increased exploitation during European colonial expansion, coastal habitat modification, and the spread of market economies led to the demise of dugongs over much of their East Africa-Western Pacific range and of green turtles throughout their pan-tropical range. In many places, populations of these species are locally extinct, threatened or endangered. Reasonably large populations are still to be found in coastal waters of northern Australia, including Torres Strait, and New Guinea (Elliott, 1981; Heinsohn, 1981; Hudson, 1981; Spring in press).

In Torres Strait, dugongs and green turtles are hunted for subsistence only, not for commerce. Queensland legislation enacted in 1968 and 1969 allows the state's Aborigine and Islander peoples to take these animals for their own needs but prohibits exploitation for market or by others. Thus, hunting pressure is determined by the subsistence needs of the resident indigenous populations.

Dugongs are large (250-300 kg) marine mammals. They have low reproductive rates and grow slowly to maturity. Therefore, they are very susceptible to over-exploitation. Green turtles (90-150 kg) are marine reptiles that have greater reproductive rates but because they are mass social nesters, females are vulnerable to human exploitation on the beaches. Hatchling loss is high from predation by birds, crabs and fishes. Thus, the turtle population is vulnerable because loss from overharvesting of adults may not be compensated because of natural nest and hatchling losses. Nesting beaches used by Torres Strait green turtles (Bramble Cay, Raine Island) are protected by isolation and legislation. Adult dugongs and green turtles are generally too big and too well protected to be preyed upon by anything in the sea except very large sharks and that is probably rare. The size and status of dugong and green turtle populations is strongly influenced by the carrying capacity of sea-grasses, loss from diseases and old age, recruitment from other populations, and exploitation by humans.

5.2 Hunting dugongs and green turtles

Hunting is not simply a means to get meat to eat. To be sure, the hunting of marine animals in Torres Strait provides the major source of protein and is the major activity for many Islander males. But it is more. Hunting is the means by which an adult male may fulfil some obligations as a husband, father, uncle, son-in-law, brother-in-law and Islander. It is one of the ways a person is taught about the sea and society.

Hunters have the ability to obtain elusive animals from an often rough sea and to train others to do so. Through the education of a hunter, knowledge about natural history and culture history is passed on and maintained, obligations for sharing and conservation are taught, and the skill, training and experience to live from the sea are accumulated.

Hunters don't hunt because they have to. They hunt despite the fact that they have ready access to market products and to sources of money that could buy imported tinned meat and fish. Animal protein itself is not the issue; the maintenance of a lifestyle is. Money obtained from several sources in a household will be used to purchase an aluminium dinghy ($1200), outboard motor ($1200-1800) and petrol ($18.00 for 20 litres) that will be used to hunt dugongs and turtles for meat that will be given away (Fig. 2). More than 100 years ago missionaries stopped the New Guinea trade that supplied Islanders with canoe hulls for outriggers. Today the Islanders rely on dinghies and outboards for hunting, fishing and travel between islands. Because hunting is limited to subsistence, outboard-powered dinghies do not increase the catch, they reduce the effort to acquire the catch (see Johannes, 1978 for similar comments on this point concerning Pacific Islanders).

There is nothing in traditional Torres Strait Islander society to push the economy to transcend subsistence. Once sufficient fish, turtles and dugongs are taken to meet the food needs and social obligations of the villagers, exploitation ceases. In population-dependent resource exploitation there is no point in taking more than can be eaten. Furthermore, fish, turtle and dugong are not just out there for the taking—the "environment as super- market" view. Successful hunting and fishing require highly skilled efforts in small boats in frequently stormy seas.

Marine hunting, fishing and foraging on reefs and beaches provide dependable, efficient and culturally relevant sources of animal foods. During one year on Mabuiag Island, the average daily yield from these activities was about .45 kg per person (Fig. 2).

Figure 2. Amounts of cleaned meat obtained from marine sources for subsistence, September 1976 through August 1977, Mabuiag Island.

	Number taken	Butchered, clean meat weight
dugong	109	12,493 kg
green turtle	131	5,984 kg
fish		1,770 kg
squid, crayfish, crabs hawksbill eggs, molluscs		535 kg
		20,782 kg

5.3 Environmental knowledge

Many individuals who write books and articles about the sea and people who subsist from it assume that marine resources are "unpredictable", "uncertain" and "problematic", and that "the sea is a dangerous and alien environment" (see the review of the anthropological literature on fishing by Acheson, 1981). Torres Strait Islanders do not approach the sea or its resources from this point of view. To them the marine environment is part of their home. Much is knowable and predictable. The sea is continually studied and the knowledge gained from generations of seafarers is taught and learned.

Environmental knowledge is extremely complex, wide-ranging and logically ordered. For example, more than 80 terms are used to distinguish different tidal and associated sea conditions. Rather than simply recognizing differences in high and low tide levels, Islanders have developed an elegant system that keeps track of the four daily tides and their changes in height and current speed as these increase and decrease between spring and neap tides twice monthly. This knowledge helps them predict the appropriate time and location to go hunting and fishing. Similar information is taught about winds, and the behaviour and natural history of fauna and flora and other aspects of the island-sea environment that makes it predictable, useable and understandable. This knowledge is probably the most valuable resource in Torres Strait. Other island and coastal peoples have similar sophisticated descriptions and understanding of their environments (Cordell, 1974, 1978; Forman, 1970; Johannes, 1977, 1978, 1981; Klee, 1976, 1980).

As with many other indigenous peoples, environmental knowledge of this calibre is an intellectual achievement of considerable magnitude. If subsistence alone were the object of this knowledge, then the Islanders are solving a problem with a solution more complicated than the problem itself. Environmental knowledge is extensive and extends well beyond mere subsistence. Based on local environments, this knowledge satisfies subsistence and intellectual requirements. Lévi-Strauss (1966) observed that animals and plants are not known as a result of their usefulness; they are deemed to be useful or interesting because first of all they are known.

5.4 Indigenous management

The use of living resources is managed. As with many other islanders, the Torres Strait people traditionally conserve island and sea resources, safeguarding vulnerable biota from depletion due to overharvesting. Westernization has eroded some of the traditional conservation methods, but many still remain and are regularly used. These include:

- "fallow" rotation of hunting and fishing areas to permit faunal recovery;
- preference for large, adult dugongs and turtles that are especially hard to catch, which serves to validate skill, provide an esteemed return and bypass most of the younger, smaller animals;
- hunting emphasis on the quality of the catch rather than the quantity;
- hunting and fishing done in phase with appropriate tides, winds, seasons, and sea conditions, which increases exploitation efficiency but makes it sporadic over time;
- taking more than enough to share within kin networks is considered greedy and unsatisfactory behaviour and not socially condoned;
- because they have absolute confidence in their environmental knowledge and hunting abilities, Islanders do not over-exploit animals when they may be especially abundant at any one time, preferring instead to let the sea "store" the animals until they are needed;
- using traditional gear for most hunting and fishing (out- boards are used only to get people *to* a prospective hunting or fishing area); and
- maintenance of traditional rights to specific is-

lands, reefs and waters (sea tenure) works as a type of "limited entry" regulation that works to reduce exploitation pressure.

Village and island ownership of sea and reef space establishes limited entry fishing rights and serves to control exploitative intrusion by people from other villages or islands. Sea tenure was once prevalent among indigenous island and coastal peoples and is still important in some places (Johannes, 1977, 1981; Cordell, 1974, 1978). McCay (1981) pointed out that "most known cases of indigenous fisheries management hinge upon the movement of access to fishing *space* rather than levels of fishing effort." Many marine species are highly mobile or migratory and are difficult to manage because some aspects of their life cycle may be carried out on the other side of political boundaries or are too distant to be encompassed by a local management programme—be it indigenous or non-indigenous (Carr, 1967; Marsh, 1981; McCay, 1981).

Indigenous forms of sea tenure differ greatly from European-derived forms. Torres Strait Islanders, as many island peoples elsewhere, do not consider the sea and its resources to be a "commons" open to anyone who has the ability to enter the water. Instead, each island community has the rights over resources that occur in specific reef and water areas.

Torres Strait Islander management of living resources is based on two general approaches: 1) local cultural regulation of selective exploitation of marine fauna to provide food for small communities of people; and 2) local control over sea and reef space for each "home" island.

In addition to these, pressure on stocks of fishes, green turtles and dugongs is further reduced because of migration (permanent and circular) of Islanders to the mainland, frequent rough sea conditions, sporadic supplies of petrol on the outer islands, and frequent breakdown of outboard motors.

5.5 Islands and islanders

Islanders view their islands not merely as a place of residence and a supply of resources. In Torres Strait, the island where one was born establishes home, history and specific social relationships with other Islanders near and distant. As one Islander explained to a visiting mainlander: "The island is the people."

Islands and associated reefs and waters are intimately known and myriad features are named. These names establish identify, territory, and history. Many indigenous peoples emphasize *where* a past event happened rather than *when* it happened (Harwood, 1976). History occurs at places; seasons change at times.

For Torres Strait Islanders their history and their myths and legends are indivisibly tied to specific island and reef and water places. There is a geography to history. For example, part of Mabuiag Island history is the story of two brothers, Deibu and Tekui, who quarrelled over sharing fish they caught. As a result, their spirits went up to the sky leaving their human forms behind, turned to rocks located on a frequently travelled trail to a favourite fishing spot. Often told, this story is reified because the history is *there*. Each island has scores of legends such as this one which provide moral and cultural guidelines that are relevant to these people and these places.

The environment is visible history for Torres Strait Islanders. It is a storehouse of their past, a sort of huge library. Place-anchored history provides a stabilizing effect and is an important aspect in the persistence of Islander culture.

To understand a place or a resource one should endeavour to understand the viewpoint of the inhabitants. For indigenous peoples environment and biota may represent mythological and cultural significance that may not at first be appreciated by an outsider. Each place has many environments.

Islands for islanders are important resources to conserve. Many of the small, distant, outer islands are losing population through emigration to larger islands and mainlands. However, this movement is but a point in a very old pattern of population shifts. In the near future many islander emigrants may very well return to their home islands because of growing support for self-determination, cultural revitalization movements, and the declining capacity of metropolitan places to offer jobs and services.

6. PROTECTED AREAS AND INDIGENOUS ISLAND PEOPLES

Acknowledging that every situation may be unique and must be evaluated on its own terms, certain general guidelines are presented here that concern small tropical islands, living resources and indigenous peoples.

- Although islands are clearly bounded by water, ecologically and economically they and their indigenous inhabitants are part of larger, sometimes distant, systems. It might therefore be relevant to consider the nature (degree of permeability), not just the location, of proposed boundaries for protected areas.
- Island ecologies are particularly vulnerable to the introduction of exotic species and the exportation of biotic materials that reduce the amounts available for recycling. Exotic living resources should not be introduced and local living resources should not be "mined" for export.
- Even though coral reefs are part of more open, continuous marine ecosystems, in many respects they are underwater islands because of ecological boundaries. Protection of coral reef habitat is a critical but difficult task because the three-dimensional water environment can transport pollutants

and biocides across ecological and administrative boundaries to be dispersed throughout the reef environment. Reefs can be protected in part by education and cooperation of non-indigenous and indigenous peoples.

- Environments are created by people through use and classification. "Home island", "my people's place", "evolutionary museum", "island for science", "protected areas", are all types of classification of environment for what may be the same island. Environments and resources are cultural appraisals. There cannot be only one sanctified, official, sacred interpretation of what is an environment any more than a single interpretation can be advocated for what is a traditional culture (Wendt, 1978). Definitions and delimitations of protected areas should be multicultural.
- Culture is an integral part of environment. Neither exists without the other. Island peoples are intimately tied to islands through family, history, sense of place, and environmental knowledge. Culture is a resource and should be so treated.
- The use of living resources by indigenous peoples may be only one aspect of their overall significance in a larger context of complex knowledge, beliefs and attitudes which relate the resource to a wider system of people, important cultural sites, and the mythological past (Chase, 1981). Resource exploitation by indigenous peoples represents more than securing just the resource. It is part of socialization, moral education, the teaching of social and economic responsibilities, an expression of skill and ability. As a result, limitations on resource use imposed by outsiders may be strongly contested. Adversary positions on resource conservation and area protection should be avoided. It is to the mutual advantage of indigenous peoples and protected area specialists to wisely control the use of biota and environments.
- Indigenous island peoples manage living marine resources. Some of the ways they do this is to regulate access to the resources and to restrict access (sea tenure) to the place where the resources are found. That they are effective is evidenced by the co-survival of people and living resources over often hundreds or thousands of years on islands and reefs. Indigenous conservation methods have stood the test of time and are relevant to local ecological situations, while protected area and conservation programmes are often highly theoretical and extrapolated from western cultural and environmental situations. These programmes should recognize, support and utilize indigenous resource management methods and indigenous people.
- Islands, reefs, and inshore waters are very diverse habitats. Resource management plans that integrate and involve indigenous peoples should also be diversified. Multiple use plans may be the most

attractive (different times and places for subsistence and protection; different islands for different purposes, core areas and buffer areas).

• So that legislated protected areas meet the needs of indigenous peoples those peoples must be involved in the design and establishment of new programmes. Islanders must be heard from. The remarks on conservation problems made by Mr. B.F. Weilbacher from Saipan at the IUCN-SPC "Regional Symposium on Conservation of Nature—Reefs and Lagoons" in Noumea in 1971 are as appropriate now as they were then:

"Who determines what is best for whom? After all, it is we islanders who are the endangered species and will eventually be the victims or hopefully beneficiaries of the various answers to these problems. Perhaps in seeking these answers instead of relying on their advanced technological status the scientists, experts or foreign administrators concerned should take more notice of the knowledge possessed by the islanders themselves. It has often been stated that many of the scientific wonders achieved in highly developed countries have in fact been experienced or made use of by islanders through their empirical association with nature and their environment, so that proper consultation with them could well help to solve some of our dilemmas. I do not like to see the islanders and their islands simply being made into human zoos, where scientists and other research personnel conduct their experiments without due regard for the traditions as well as the general welfare of the inhabitants" (Weilbacher, 1973).

Traditional Conservation Methods and Protected Marine Areas in Oceania

R.E. Johannes
CSIRO Marine Laboratories
North Beach, Western Australia

ABSTRACT. *Local fishermen in Polynesia, Micronesia and eastern Melanesia have an understanding of shallow tropical fisheries which can be invaluable to marine resource use planners. Their knowledge is often superior to that obtained from conventional resource surveys. They have also developed traditional methods of conservation that provide a variety of opportunities for those concerned with establishing and managing protected areas. Recognition of traditional fishing rights can be an important factor in protecting fisheries from over-exploitation. An understanding of local traditions is essential for marine resource use planners.*

1. INTRODUCTION

In areas where recorded knowledge of local environments and biota is inadequate, the knowledge possessed by amateur naturalists can play a vital role in siting protected areas (Margules and Usher, 1958). For the marine environments of the tropical Pacific islands, it is the local fishermen who possess this knowledge. Further, an understanding their customary patterns of marine resource use is essential in designing management programmes compatible with local customs and sentiments.

The warm, clear waters around the islands of Polynesia, Micronesia and eastern Melanesia have provided these fishermen with exceptional conditions for studying their prey at close range. They have made the most of this opportunity, developing their profession over many generations to levels of sublety and complexity unexcelled in other preindustrial cultures. Several centuries of contact with continental colonizers has eroded their traditional knowledge and skills. But what

remains still constitutes an encyclopaedic reservoir of practical sea lore—knowledge which has been described by one team of marine biologists as being "of a stupefying richness, and at times of such precision that the corresponding poverty of our own conceptions makes enquiry very difficult" (Ottino and Plessis, 1972).

Studying their knowledge during the past few years has provided a host of valuable insights into the nature of shallow tropical marine resources. Information obtained in this way is often superior in important respects to information gained by means of conventional resource surveys performed by imported consultants constrained by insufficient time and money. For example, what may look like an insignificant and relatively barren islet to a reserve planner during a site inventory made in one season, may be thronged with breeding sea birds, or in rarer cases, breeding sea snakes, in another.

Certain otherwise unremarkable beaches may come alive with spawning land crabs during certain lunar periods and seasons (Johannes, 1981) or serve as rookeries for nesting sea turtles.

Many island fishermen also know that year after year a wide range of reef food fish aggregate at specific locations to breed at particular seasons and at particular phases of the moon (Johannes, 1981). The number of marine fish species known by biologists to breed at particular locations on a fixed lunar cycle has more than doubled in the past decade as a direct result of information provided by Pacific island fishermen; in fact, such breeding grounds will rarely be discovered *without* assistance from fishermen. These areas may not always coincide with areas judged to be important on the basis of aesthetic qualities, species diversity, and the other common criteria for choosing protected areas, but they often deserve protection from the standpoint of fisheries conservation. Islanders themselves sometimes protect such areas with traditional taboos.

In fact, Pacific island fishermen possess a wide range of traditional methods for protecting their marine resources (Johannes, 1978). Long before continental peoples, they became aware that marine fish stocks have finite limits. This is because their islands have no continental shelves; their seafood stocks are confined largely to nearshore reefs and lagoons and are thus particularly vulnerable to overharvesting. In consequence, they devised and practiced almost every basic form of modern marine fisheries conservation measure centuries ago, long before the need for marine conservation was even recognized in western countries. (It was only about 90 years ago that western biologists first began to realize the marine fish stocks were vulnerable to over-fishing).

2. TRADITIONAL LIMITED ENTRY

Restriction of fishing effort has been achieved by the use of closed seasons, closed areas, size restrictions, gear restrictions and—the most important of all fisheries management strategies—restricted entry (Johannes, 1978, 1981, and in press). These customs present a variety of potential opportunities (and headaches) for those concerned with establishing and managing protected marine areas.

Throughout most of Oceania the right to fish in a particular area was controlled by a clan, chief or family. Generally this control extended from mangrove swamps and shoreline across reef flats and lagoon to the outer reef slope. It would be difficult to over-emphasize the importance of some form of limited entry such as this to sound fisheries management. Without some control over fishing rights, fishermen have little incentive not to overfish since they cannot prevent others from catching what they leave behind. This is a central tenet of modern fisheries management. Under modern conditions the government must assume the sole responsibility for placing and enforcing fisheries conservation measures. This is a difficult and expensive responsibility under the best of circumstances; it is close to impossible in most tropical artisanal fisheries. Typically there are far more boats, more species in the catch, and more distribution channels (both subsistence and market) to monitor and regulate than in high latitude fisheries of similar sizes. And there is usually much less money and expertise available with which to do it.

Before these problems became obvious, colonial powers in the Pacific sometimes destroyed traditional fishing rights in the name of the now discredited concept of "freedom of the seas"—or simply because such customs prevented colonists from expropriating the islanders' fish, pearl oysters, trepang, or whatever else in the sea offered a profit. Traditional fishing rights have largely disappeared from island groups such as Hawaii, the Mariannas, Ponape, and American Samoa. But in other island countries, such as Fiji, Palau, Yap and much

of Papua New Guinea, these rights are not only still practiced but also protected through explicit or implicit legal recognition.

Studies of traditional fishing rights have begun only in the past few years in Oceania. But it is already clear that the phenomenon is nearly as complicated in some Pacific islands as its terrestrial counterpart—that very complex and contentious subject, traditional land tenure. Some of the implications of traditional fishing rights are outlined below for those concerned with protected marine areas.

Traditional fishing rights are not just a means of conserving fish stocks. They evolved in part as a means of minimizing conflicts and distributing resources effectively, and are woven into the social fabric of the cultures that possess them. Efforts to protect coastal waters by means of various sorts of protected areas are not likely to succeed if they are carried out in the absence of an understanding of such customs and a willingness to consider them as an integral part of any proposed new system of management.

This is not to suggest that such customs should be thought of as irrevocably fixed. They evolve as conditions change. Thus legislation that freezes these customs may create problems by preventing fishermen from responding effectively to the introduction of fishing technology that facilitates the exploitation of previously inaccessible fishing areas, or to changing demographic patterns or economic conditions. In Palau, for example, where taxation by Japanese colonists in the 1930s placed a new burden on fishing villages, one village with fishing rights above its needs voluntarily ceded some of these rights to other less well-provided villages who needed additional income from fishing to pay their taxes (Johannes, 1981).

As resources are discovered or made accessible by improved fishing technology, villagers will naturally wish to extend their traditional fishing boundaries to encompass previously untenured waters. If legislation prevents them from doing so by rendering their fishing boundaries unalterable, the government imposes upon itself, unnecessarily, the sole responsibility for placing and maintaining effective restraints on exploitation.

Although traditional fishing rights facilitate the conservation of fish stocks, they cannot, without additional constraints, prevent depletion if the perceived needs of the owners exceed the maximum sustainable yield. Today in many Pacific island areas where the subsistence needs of fishing rights owners do not by themselves place undue pressure on stocks, the demand for fish for export to markets in larger population centres may combine with local needs to overtax the stocks. However, owners may opt to reject external demands.

For example, several years ago the aggressive fishermen of one Palau municipality borrowed money to buy a fishing boat that would enable them to catch enough fish to export to Guam. They quickly fished their stocks down to a level at which it no longer paid to keep the boat in operation. As the fish stocks dwin-

The Oceanian Realm

345

dled they began to eye the reefs belonging to nearby villages whose waters were not so heavily fished. But the people of these villages had seen their ambitious neighbours deplete their own fishing grounds and refused them entry, thereby preventing the depletion from spreading (Johannes, 1981).

A similar situation pertains today in Loniu, a village on the island of Manus, Papua New Guinea, that is ideally situated for exporting fish to the nearby fish-poor district centre of Lorengau. Loniu villagers say that catching fish for sale outside their village would overtax their fishing grounds. They have restricted their own fishing activities accordingly. Such examples demonstrate the fact that third world villagers often recognize and try to stay within the productive limits of their natural resources.

It may be useful, where such enlightened self-interest is found, to recognize villagers as official wardens of protected marine areas, thereby enhancing their effectiveness as resource managers. But the absence of legally sanctioned village fishing rights will tend to undermine this strategy. For example, dynamiting of reef fish, although illegal, is widespread in Western Samoa. But although village leaders have recently been given enhanced legal responsibilities for enforcing environmental laws in their villages, they cannot control dynamite fishing because traditional fishing rights are no longer recognized in most areas. Thus they cannot prevent people from elsewhere from using dynamite in their waters, nor can they prevent their own fishermen from using dynamite elsewhere. Returning the traditional control over who fishes on nearby fishing grounds to villagers could alleviate this problem.

Where traditional fishing rights are legally recognized some of the legal problems associated with establishing new protected marine areas may be circumvented. The situation in Hawaii is illustrative. Here the right to harvest seafood in local coastal waters was controlled by the chiefs prior to western contact. In their desire to open coastal waters to the public and to business interests, American colonists set out to destroy this system about 80 years ago. In 1900 an act was passed which stipulated that the government should condemn and buy up private fishing rights. But although condemnations and purchases have been made sporadically since then, about 40 small parcels of coastal waters (referred to incorrectly but commonly as "konohikis") remain under nominal private control today.

Although the total area of unalienated konohikis is small, they appear to present coastal planners in Hawaii with a novel set of opportunities for establishing protected marine areas with a minimum of procedural difficulty. Unfortunately no one has tested their legal and practical implications for contemporary resource management. In Hawaii, a tangle of complex, sometimes conflicting, federal, state and county regulations make an alteration in the usage of state-controlled coastal waters difficult. However, the owners of konohikis have the legal right, tested before the U.S. Supreme Court, to lease

their fishing grounds, and to restrict fishing activities therein (Kosaki, 1954). Thus, using appropriate konohikis, marine parks might be established in Hawaii with considerably less procedural wrangling and fewer management problems than would be encountered in public waters.

3. NEGOTIATING WITH FISHERMEN

Where protected status is being sought for waters over which villagers exert either legally recognized or de facto control, they cannot be expected to cooperate with reserve or park planners in the absence of some consequent benefits. Planners should thus have some incentive in mind; lease payments, greater legal recognition of local village authority, better protection from outside encroachment, enhanced income from tourism, and others.

The degree to which fishing rights are elaborated and enforced depends upon their perceived value. Populations are burgeoning in the Pacific islands and the demand for fish outstrips the local catch in most island countries. The value of traditional fishing rights is thus increasing. This is not an unmixed blessing for marine resource managers. It would be a mistake to romanticize traditional island fishermen, to view them as ideal conservationists living in perfect harmony with nature and one another. Greed and opportunism are endemic here as elsewhere, and the introduction of export markets and cash economies has tended to exacerbate these traits. Written records of traditional fishing boundariess often do not exist, and it is not surprising under the circumstances to find that villagers will invent "traditional" fishing rights if there are advantages to be gained by doing so.

Information obtained from villagers on their fishing rights and customs is thus liable to be more reliable if it is elicited prior to discussing the establishment of a protected area in their waters. Ideally such investigations should be pursued as a general policy in all coastal areas prior to their being considered for any new uses, thus reducing the need later for circumspection on the part of the planners. Unfortunately, it seems too late for this more forthright approach in many island areas.

In areas where fishing rights are secure, their possessors may choose to reject the establishment of protected areas. What can be done in such circumstances? An alternative rarely available on land is often available in coastal waters—the establishment of protected areas in untenured waters adjacent to major population centres. Fishing rights in waters in the vicinity of major population centres in Oceania have rarely persisted because the pressure of the large numbers of migrants from other districts and countries has overwhelmed the traditional rights of the original inhabitants. Here the government can establish a protected area without fear of violating existing custom. For example, a marine park is maintained in untenured waters adjacent to Suva, the capital of Fiji. Enforcement of management regulations is simplified by the proximity of such reserves to population centres, where they are readily subject to surveillance.

Of course, marine waters exposed to substantial pollution cannot serve well as protected areas. But areas remain near many population centres in the Pacific islands where pollution or construction has not overwhelmed marine ecosystems. The Palolo Deep Reserve in Western Samoa, for example, is very close to an area heavily affected by sediment and sewage pollution from the capital, Apia, but prevailing currents carry this pollution away from the reserve.

Overfishing is usually a problem near district centres. But once reef areas are protected, they will repopulate with fish in a few years. Marine animals and plants are more mobile than terrestrial biota and, providing that the essential framework of living corals remains, reef fish communities can rebuild relatively quickly (Brock, Lewis, and Wass, 1979).

4. PRESERVATION OF TRADITIONAL FISHING PRACTICES

Protected marine areas provide opportunities to help preserve valuable traditional fishing practices. Such practices were part of a complex of activities that once enabled Pacific islanders to be totally independent of the outside world. Today no Pacific island group is self-sufficient. Island fishermen rely heavily on outboard motors from the U.S., fish-hooks from Norway, fishing nets from Japan, and a wide range of other imported consumer goods. Because islanders do not have the resources to balance their imports with exports, high and rapidly growing trade deficits plague the region. The past few decades have seen massive foreign aid (by the standards of island economies) to make up the difference. In Micronesia, for example, roughly 90 percent of all economic activity depends on U.S. financial assistance (Carter, 1982). But as economies falter in developed countries, foreign aid programmes are among the first targets of budget-conscious governments. As with other Pacific islanders, Micronesians currently face a substantial decrease in foreign aid and an involuntary return to greater self-sufficiency. The success of this retrenchment will depend upon how effectively islanders' traditional skills can be resurrected. Yet traditional sailing vessels have completely disappeared from some Micronesian cultures, along with the knowledge of how to build them and sail them. Woven palm fronds rather than imported nets were once used throughout much of the area to entrap large numbers of reef fish (Johannes, 1981). This practice has ceased in most island groups and only a few old men remember how it was done.

These and many other traditional activities are of interest to tourists, and income from tourism could thus provide incentive to reactivate or maintain them. In this way tourism in protected areas might be employed to help maintain valuable traditions for a time when economic considerations may dictate their wider adoption.

Another avenue for exploration in connection with the establishment of protected marine areas is provided by the existence of traditionally sacred marine sites. The protection of sacred sites on land has received considerable attention in some parts of the world, but very little effort has been made to identify and protect similar marine sites. Although their existence around some Pacific islands is clear, there appear to be no published records.

Many of the customs discussed here are not restricted to Oceania. The last few years have witnessed expanding interest in methods by which fishermen regulate their catches in other parts of the world. Customary fishing rights and other practices that function to protect marine resources in Indonesia have been reviewed by Polunin (1982). Similar customs can be found among native fishermen in Africa (Kapetsky, 1981), Sri Lanka (Alexander, 1977), Brazil (Cordell, in press) and elsewhere. Similar *de facto* arrangements, sometimes in conflict with government regulations, also exist in modern technologically advanced fisheries (Cordell, in press). The growing interest among social and biological scientists and marine resource managers in such customs ensures that many more will come to light. And a growing recognition that ignoring such customs in the past has contributed to innumerable failures in tropical marine resource management provides hope that future management efforts will be more successful.

These comments provide only brief sketches of some of the general problems and opportunities presented to marine resource managers by Pacific island fishing lore and customs. Even within a relatively homogenous cultural and biogeographical area such as, say, Polynesia, unique circumstances will face the resource manager or developer of protected areas on virtually every island, and often even at different locations on single islands. There is thus no substitute for detailed, locale-specific research into local fishing lore and customs in order to take advantage of the opportunities and minimize the problems they present.

People Pressure and Management of Limited Resources on Yap

Marjorie V.C. Falanruw
Yap Institute of Natural Science
Yap, Western Caroline Islands

ABSTRACT. *The Pacific island of Yap once had a very dense human population, some eight times higher than at present; the pre-contact culture was adapted to sustaining many people on limited island resources, and many of these sustained utilization methods could be adapted to current problems. The study of such mechanisms could also be of wider application in densely populated countries. Crucial to the sustained production of natural ecosystems is to regulate human use of natural resources, and social organization has provided for such regulation as a result of social stratification and specialization, territoriality, resource apportionment, limitations on harvest, effective sanctions, and group spirit. What is required for the future is the evolution of a suitable "neo-tradition" of resource use, which fully involves conservation considerations.*

1. INTRODUCTION

Insular situations excite scientists. From time of Darwin, there has been interest in the unique species living in such isolation and concern for the vulnerability of island ecosystems to change. In the world of today, most islands are the home and ultimate source of support for human populations. Some of these island people have a long cultural history of surviving with their limited insular resources, sometimes reaching fairly dense populations. As the world's population increases, and proportional per capita resources decrease, we can learn from the adaptive features of the cultures of island people who have, in effect, already experienced living under such conditions.

Yap once had a very dense population and evolved a culture adapted to sustaining many people on limited island resources. With contact, the population decreased, but it is now rising rapidly again, with money,

energy, goods and technology provided from outside contributing to a lifestyle out of balance with resources. When external aid is withdrawn, attempts to support a rising population with a consumptive lifestyle could lead to exploitation of local resources on an unsustainable basis. It will take conscious recognition and effort to avoid resource depletion and environmental degradation which could place Yap among the obligatory dependent states of the world. The means of resource management in the past and the dilemma of resource protected areas in the future is the subject of this paper.

2. BACKGROUND

2.1. Geography

Yap state lies in the Western and Central Caroline Islands, and is one of the 4 Federated States of Micronesia, a political entity emerging out of the Trust Territory of the Pacific. The state center consists of a group of high islands of basaltic origin totalling about 100 sq km and known collectively as "Yap." Outer islands total 19 sq km and include 11 inhabited and 4 uninhabited atolls or low islands and extensive banks and shoal areas. The State covers about 1 million sq km of ocean.

2.2. Population

The population of Yap alone is thought to have been as high as 40,000 in pre-contact times (Underwood, 1969). Yapese dance chants lament a time when young betelnut fell from the tree, a poetic allusion to the fact that not only the old died, as expected, but also the young and vigorous. People blamed the misfortune on their own misbehaviour. Most historians attribute such population declines to post-contact epidemics. Early German reports (Thilenius, 1917) give the population of Yap as 7,464 in 1902. The population continued to decline through the Japanese occupation and by 1946 there were only 2,478 people on Yap (Useem, 1946). During the American administration of the island, however, the population has increased rapidly and the 1973 census of 5,139 people showed that the population of Yap had more than doubled. The population increase in the outer islands of Yap has also been great, going from 4,760 in 1946 to 7,870 in 1973.

3. MANAGEMENT OF LIMITED RESOURCES IN THE PAST

The precontact population of 40,000 people postulated by archaelogists and anthropologists for mainland Yap give a population density of some 400 people per sq km. It is remarkable how a population anywhere near this great could have been maintained and even have energy to voyage afar for cultural tokens such as the famous stone money.

The achievement was not easy and Yap and her people bear the signs of hard times and harsh discipline in the past. While there remain many unknowns, four factors appear to have been important in the management of resources; adaptive methods; appropriate timing of activities; energy conservation; and management of people using resources.

3.1. Adaptive methods

Most of Yap island and lagoon have been modified into an anthropocentric food production system. Most villages of Yap are situated in the narrow coastal area between mangroves and hills. The natural vegetation of these areas was probably swamp forest similar to but less extensive and species-rich than those to be seen in Palau, Ponape, and Kosrae (Stemmermand and Proby, 1978). Hardly any such vegetation is present on Yap today. Low areas were deepened and connected with channels and raised paths and drained planting areas created with the hand-excavated fill. Useful trees were planted in the drained areas and with time these tree gardens became relatively self-perpetuating via the recycling of nturients of fallen leaves as in natural forests. The forest canopy protected the soil from erosion by the often torrential downpour, and the ditches, often stone lined, directed an aerated flow of water through the system of channels and low areas. Silt and nutrients were trapped in the low areas managed as taro patches. Human energies involved largely the pruning of the forest to select for useful trees, transfer of excessive organic material from low area to raised areas, and the

simultaneous harvesting and replanting of the taro patches.

Areas more inland of villages were utilized for gardens of *Dioscorea* yams mixed with other crops. The making of such gardens required the opening of a "skylight" in the forest canopy. This was done during the dry part of the year when a limited area was burned and a variety of crops planted. With the resultant ash fertilizer and beginning rains, crops generally grow fast and form a multi-layer vegetative cover over the soil by the time the heavy rains come. After several harvests, these gardens are allowed to go fallow so that the canopy reforms and soil nutrients and structure are regenerated.

The seaside of most Yapese villages is lined with mangroves. These have been modified via selective logging for termite resistant wood, landfills, paths created along the inner margins, and the development of fish ponds in some areas. Landfill activities of the past involved the building of a rock seawall and then filling of the area with coral debris and sections of turf cut from seagrass beds. This activity was at least partially responsible for the development of coastal mangrove depressions functioning as silt traps. Most villages also built a peninsula through the mangrove fringe. This peninsula was paved with rocks and became the site of a house for fishermen and their gear, providing access to the sea and an outpost to watch for the approach of enemies. While most ecologists talk of the land-building effects of mangroves, many Yapese today complain about the erosive effects of mangroves and their associated fauna, especially crabs, on the paths and land built by their ancestors.

Mangroves are valued by both ecologists and Yapese as a nursery area for fish and other sea life. The rich muck also provides habitat for clams and crabs, important as a source of protein during times when conditions are inclement for fishing, or when fishermen are not available. The coastal mangrove depression was kept clear of corals by men who utilized the area for catching mangrove crabs in traps, fishing with handnets, and as a nearshore water route.

Beyond the coastal mangrove depression are generally extensive seagrass meadows. These areas, known to be highly productive by biologists, provided feeding areas for fish retreating to deeper areas toward the mangrove or reef. These areas also were generally kept clear of corals to select for a habitat for favoured fish, including rabbitfish. Fishing in these areas involved the use of hand nets, the driving of fish into gill nets, or surround nets set to utilize tidal extremes. During low tide, the area provided a foraging ground for women and children. The seeds of the seagrass *Enhalus* were eaten by children to assuage hunger pangs and prolong their stay in the area. The strong fibres of *Enhalus* were utilized to make a fine-mesh net said to have lasted for generations, and areas were protected so that this seagrass could grow especially long and thus provide long strands for nets.

The mangroves, fishponds, coastal mangrove depressions and seagrass meadows were most important in day-to-day fishing and as such served an "icebox" function. Fishing for bigger fish in deeper holes and channels within the lagoon involved line fishing and group net fishing, which was generally reserved for special occasions when large amounts of fish were needed. Fishing beyond the reef involved sailing canoes and the use of hand lines and nets for catching flying fish.

One of the most notable features of Yap's reef flats are stone fishweirs. These structures are generally in the form of huge arrows pointing towards the reef, or zigzag patterns of stone along the reef edge. They are situated in relation to current patterns so that fish are directed toward the apex and diagonals of the stone walls where traps are placed. When traps are not in place fish are directed and concentrated but can swim away with the high tide. Thus the weirs, while permanent, do not harvest continuously.

In the past, fishing involved considerable ritual and taboos, including abstincence from activities of the land and women. Fishing efforts farthest from land required the longest isolation and men had to remain in men's houses along the shore where they and their gear would not be contaminated. The assistance of a magician was employed for special fishing expeditions and this man had to isolate himself for an even longer period.

3.2. Appropriate timing

The timing of food production and correlated social activities was quite structured and involved the services of specialists called *tamerong* who proclaimed the best time for different activities. The work of this shaman was difficult. Yap lies near the intertropical convergence zone and the initiation of the tradewind season is irregular and the island is sometimes subjected to a monsoon pattern of torrential rainfall and a dry period. It was important to orchestrate the activities of each year to harmonize with that year's weather conditions. Predictability being limited, the activities of the shaman also involved magic and Yap has been known for possessing powerful magic. The agricultural shaman moved from one established sacred place to another with passing seasons and performed magic associated with food producing activities and a series of social celebrations associated with the seasons.

The coordination of efforts resulted in a focus of group concentration. To a great extent, the Yapese food production system might be classified as "nature intensive," as opposed to modern energy-intensive agriculture and traditional Asian labour-intensive agriculture. Rather than rearrange the environment and expend great amounts of energy and chemicals, people's activities are directed to the most effective use of microhabitat and natural phenomena. This requires a good deal of knowledge of nature in order to predict, for example, where

to plant a yam so that its roots can gain nutrients or where to place a net to take advantage of the movements of schools of fish often associated with currents of rising and falling tides.

The isolation of fishermen in men's houses provided an ideal setting for the preparation of gear, a more exacting process during the days of natural fibres and materials. It also provided a mix of fishing activity and discussion of experience that contributed to the growth of individual and group ability. Though couched in terms of avoiding contamination, this isolation probably also served to free women to become immersed in their own specialty of gardening. The tripartite tree, taro patch and dryland garden agricultural system served to assure food throughout the year despite variable weather phenomena. The time of greatest production of breadfruit was counterpoint to the period of the yam harvest, and the production of taro patches provided a back-up system.

3.3. Energy conservation

The "nature intensive" food production systems of Yap of the past appear to have minimized the expenditure of energy per calorie of harvest. Fire was used for clearing and energy for weeding was minimized by the closure of the canopy. Cooking the main bulk of food was done generally once a day with carefully-tended fires; fuels commonly utilized include the husks of coconuts and of *Inocarpus* nuts and whatever wood might be available as by-products of harvested food and the food production system.

Fishing methods were largely passive. Marine transport involved the use of lightweight poled bamboo rafts and lightweight sailing canoes for fishing and near-shore travel, with specialized canoes utilized for carrying large loads and making ocean voyages.

People lived close to the most frequently utilized resources so that even energy for movement was minimized. In addition, a system of social stratification and territoriality further proscribed individual activity. The social and territorial system of Yap seems to have managed cooperation and competition in a way which allowed for vitality but minimized the expenditure of energy. Wars were carefully managed by paramount chiefs to conclude with the killing of certain parties or achievement of pre-set objectives. The real currency of Yapese culture was the calorie, and the most lavish cultural displays involved the gathering and redistribution of food, and the showing of manpower and the achievements of manpower. Tokens of such achievement, such as golden tumeric powder and stone money, were largely used, not for purchases *per se*, but for social interaction and keeping the peace.

3.4. The management of people using resources

Resources can only be managed if there is a way to regulate people's use of these resources. The social organization of Yap provided for such regulation as a result of social stratification and specialization, territoriality, resource apportionment, limitations on harvest, effective sanctions, and group spirit.

3.4.1. Social stratification.
It is said on Yap that people come and go, but the land remains forever. Lands have names associated with them and these names are conferred on appropriate people. These lands and their associated people and marine areas are ranked. There are 3 paramount groups of equal rank, each with a series of lesser ranks subject to their request, having specialized functions. The highest ranks are chiefs called *pilung*, or "voice of the people." This group organizes the activities of their people for the good of the community and applies sanctions when necessary. The commands of a chief is reinforced by his shaman. The group as a whole was protected by a warrior class which is somewhat privileged by virtue of the danger of their function. Other groups served as artisans; the least influential group had no land of their own and provided services in return for the privilege of living on land and receiving protection. By 1966, however, Underwood (1969) reports that the population distribution on Yap was more related to favourable environmental conditions than to class membership. Thus the population and living situation of the lowest group probably fluctuated with the population density of Yap, living conditions being least favourable when proportional resources were most limited. As such, it probably provided a valve for population overflow by defining who would survive during times of extreme hardship.

3.4.2. Territoriality.
All land in mainland Yap is owned and subject to a complex land tenure system. In general, lands were inherited through the male line but tended by women and inherited by their children, thus giving some rights to the matrilineal line. Fathers could expect service from sons in return for eventual land, and women were assured the use of their husband's land subject to their production of children and good behaviour. Land ownership involved multiple rights of use and one piece of land might belong to one person but be subject to the consent of another, be lived on by a third, and harvested by a fourth party. This complex system of land control resulted in considerable diversity in management while preventing widespread changes to large pieces of land.

Limited areas were designated for collective use by specific groups such as chief's houses, men's houses, and women's menstrual houses. Main paths were used collectively but even here there was often a separation of women's and men's paths. Areas between villages were designated as playgrounds and here children could play and make noise. Otherwise the peace of the village was not to be disturbed.

3.4.3. Resource apportionment.
The harvests of group fishing efforts are distributed according to appropriate patterns. The most striking examples of resource apportionment are the reservation of certain species to certain groups. Throughout Yap State, turtles are chiefly food. Anyone catching a turtle presented it to a chief who would divide it in an appropriate manner. Even the specific parts of the turtle were destined to go to particular people. Fruitbats and eels were other resources limited to a particular group, though because this group is not so socially influential, the ban takes the form of the items being distasteful to other groups. In other areas of the Pacific, such as Tonga, fruitbats are reserved for chiefs, so it seems that certain species are culturally recognized as being a limited resource.

3.4.4. Limiting harvests.
Harvests are sometimes limited by the placing of a restriction on an area. This might be done for a number of reasons, such as prohibiting harvesting from the lands of a person who died for a period after their death. On other occasions, a fishing area might be put off limits until fish were again large and plentiful.

Other restrictions were more subtle. An individual making an especially large catch generally did not go fishing again right away as it was considered bad to harvest too much at once. Luck in fishing should be shared rather than used for one's own benefit.

Fishing areas were owned by relatively few estates so that permission was required from the overseer in order to fish there. Many fishing methods were the prerogative of certain individuals. Fishing was a male activity and men involved in group fishing were assembled according to cultural relationships.

Yapese of the past did not trespass on the property or resources of others. The seriousness of trespassing varied with distance of relationship and individuals entering the equivalent of another municipality without a good reason might well have been killed. Even today, the boats of people fishing in other's territory are confiscated. These territorial restrictions placed considerable limitations on the loci of individual activity.

3.4.5. Effective sanctions against misbehaviour.
Chiefs and the community of Yap in the past had powerful sanctions against misbehaviour. An individual's right to land could be alienated as punishment for misbehaviour. This was a very serious thing, for it involved one's own name and social standing. For the young who had not yet inherited land, there was the prospect of not inheriting land or some secret knowledge from a parent.

Supernatural sanctions were also present in the past. Chiefs had an associated shaman who could apply spells and bring bad fortune. At more individual levels, there was a strong sense of need to do things in order to be pleasing to spirits past and present.

3.4.6. Group spirit and individual satisfaction. The social system of Yap provided a superstructure with specialized functions so that everyone was part of the whole. In being named, one obtained a role in Yapese society and responsibility to live one's life appropriately. Regardless of rank, there was pride in fulfilling one's role well. Today this interconnectedness is most strikingly demonstrated in Yapese dance, where groups of up to a hundred or more move together as if connected by the same nerve system. Each strives to be in harmony with the other dancers in the line, but also to dance the best. Thus though there is curtailment of the range of individual movement, there is no curtailment of individual excellence. The result is group excellence.

Thus in the past, there was a rhythm to life, a division of labour, and everyone knew their relationship to each other and to their resources. No individual other than a chief could exploit more than his share of resources and no good chief would request more from his people than they could reasonably produce, as the sustainability and balance of the system had to be maintained. It was rather like a rhythmic dance between people and their resources.

4. PROBLEMS OF THE PRESENT

While Yapese culture of the past appears to have been relatively well adapted to the Yap ecosystem, the impact of the huge population had its effect. Today there are extensive areas of degraded soil which bear the signs of too frequent burning and too intensive use. There are few wild places on Yap, and few unique form of life compared to relatively nearby islands such as Palau, Ponape and even Guam. Some species such as *Tridachna gigas* have been wiped out completely. The harsh discipline and curtailment of individual freedom were other costs of such a dense population.

Today the population of Yap state is growing very fast and consuming a great deal more. Import of goods, energy and technology have made it possible to forestall the consequences of trespassing the basic rules of caloric self-sufficiency and sustainability of lifestyle so that anthropocentric indicators of the island's limitations are now lacking.

Since the time that traditional human ecosystem on Yap functioned to the fullest, there have been epidemics, World War II, and the successive influence or administration of the islands by Spanish, Germans, an American Irishman, Japanese and Americans. Throughout these presences, Yapese carried on their affairs as if the outsiders were just passing through. Interaction with one another remained the most important thing in life. The visitors, however, had their impact. O'Keefe's big-ship technology brought an end to the spirit and adventure of voyaging afar for stone money. Population declines and World War II brought great hardships to a people whose social, energy and food production systems were so highly organized and finely tuned.

The U.S. administration has been more benevolent, especially in the last 17 years when large sums of money have been spent on the islands. While the Administering Authority had its ideas about the use of these funds for "development", local concentration has largely been on making use of the new resources to make life easier and to carry out social obligations. The ways of getting the new resources differs and especially the activities of men have switched from concentration on food production to use of the new inflow of resources. The timing of the workday and fiscal year differs from that of natural phenomena and correlated social activities. The consumption of energy has increased very greatly as people commute from village to town and an electrical system is extended to the outermost villages.

Concurrent with the rise in population is an increase in the proportion of young people. With a very large percentage of the male population working at government jobs in town, there are less opportunities for young men to learn traditional technologies. Patterns of land tenure are changing and there is a lack of effective sanctions against misbehaviour and declininng control over people's use of resources. Life is no longer a harmonious dance between people and their resources and satisfying roles and recognition of excellence is fading. The disharmony is having its impact on the high proportion of youth exposed to an American TV lifestyle and being relatively undirected in their own heritage and its prospects for the future. The incidence of crime and suicide has risen.

Scientists' recognition of the value of many traditional practices is coming at a time when there is a rush for development based on the Western formula of applying lots of money, energy, strong chemicals, and powerful technology. The changes which are possible via the application of these resources are fast, spectacular and so attractive that they lead people to disparage their own resources, technologies and traditions of production. The unpredictability and lack of control over appropriations and programmes initiated outside the state enforces an instinct to get what one can when it's available and people do not always pause to evaluate what they are losing in the parocess. Thus, for example, the availability of money, machines or SeaBee construction teams dictates the bulldozing of roads during periods of heavy rain, turning carefully drained and landscaped paths into quagmires, disrupting the pattern of nutrient flow and aeration through taro patches, and eroding the soil into the lagoon where its impact is not noticed as most of the men are in school or in town.

5. PROSPECTS FOR THE FUTURE

Prospects for sustainable development seem dismal. Yap, however, is entering the world's "development stage" at a pivotal point in human history, when goals of short-term affluence are being replaced by goals of long-term sustainability and survival. There will be compelling inertia to play the development game by the old rules of exploitation, but there are signs, however, of growing recognition that all is not going well, and that the resource consciousness of the past is still present.

5.1. Fruitbats—A minicase

Yap's only indigenous mammal is the fruitbat *Pteropus yapensis*. These flying animals were used in the past by a portion of Yap's population. On the nearby island of Guam, however, where they are a delicacy of the Chamorro cuisine, they have been hunted to near extinction and are now protected as endangered species. About 1974, a few individuals on Yap began shipping frozen bats to Guam where they could be sold for a high price. With recognition of the money to be earned, exports increased and as the practice became commercialized traditional apportionment of the resource to certain groups were ignored. The rate of harvest became unsustainable, populations of fruitbats declined rapidly, and it seemed Yap would emulate Guam. This was noticed by Yap's leaders, many of whom still live close to natural reality, and reinforced by an ongoing U.S. Forest Service study of fruitbats (Falanruw, 1982). As a result, the First Yap State legislature placed a ban on the killing and export of fruitbats until such time as populations increase and a sustainable rate of harvest is determined. Work is continuing to determine the best "neo-traditional" ways to manage the resource. It is notable that the legislation was passed by some of the very people earning most from the trade, thus demonstrating their concern for long-term sustainability over short-term profit.

5.2. Plans

There are other indicators of concern for the sustainable use of local resources. The Preamble of the Constitution of the State of Yap begins: "We the people of the State of Yap: Desire to live in peace and harmony with one another, our neighbours, and our environment; Recognize our traditional heritage and villages as the foundation of our society and economy. . . " There are provisions in this Constitution for the recognition of traditional resource rights as well as for other conservation functions.

The draft of Yap's Five Year Development Plan includes a provision for an Office of the Environment which would develop comprehensive environmental management programme for Yap, contribute to environmental education and do research in environmental management. There are plans for an agroforestry study which would document and evaluate many traditional land management practices. There are also plans to develop opportunities for youth to learn traditional as well as modern skills.

The first steps of recognition have been taken. The next problem, of course, is how to do things right. On such small islands, mistakes can have far-reaching environmental consequences and there is generally only one chance to do things right. There are no precedents to follow, and somehow problems have to be foreseen before they are experienced. The management of Yap's resources on a sustainable basis is a great challenge.

The Compact of Free Association being negotiated to end the Trusteeship provides for the local development of standards and procedures to protect the environment similar to a number of U.S. environmental acts, such as the National Environmental Policy Act and the Clean Water Act. How this is done is critical. If the body of U.S. legislation is merely transferred as is, it will have little more effect on conserving resources than at present (Falanruw, 1981), and will mainly provide jobs for outsiders and outside groups, and for local people who learn to go through the proper motions. Then when U.S. funds are used up, the function will be dropped.

5.4. Recommendations

More lasting would be the evolution of suitable "neo-traditions" of resource use. A version of environmentalist existed in the shamen of old Yap. Because many of the practices of the profession were enforced by no longer credible religious and social sanctions, however, their function has been overlooked and the profession has almost disappeared. Perhaps the time has come to develop Neoshamen, whose profession would be based on the fullest knowledge possible of Yapese culture, the laws of the natural world, and the same reverence for life inherent in the discipline and religion of their forefathers.

The work involved in the evolution of such a strategy of environmental management would involve at least the professions of ethnobiologists, traditional elders and their younger counterparts-in-training, a lawyer, and appropriate scientists and administrators. Traditional practices relating to resource use should be recorded by the ethnobiologist, elders and younger counterparts. A lawyer would compile the standards and objectives of environmental legislation required under the Compact. An ecologist, an ethnobiologist, and neotraditional environmentalists would evaluate the standards and objectives and traditional practices to determine their functional aspects and what measures are needed to fill gaps for effective resource management. Finally, the whole team would work together to determine where a synthesis can be made between Yapese practices and U.S. environmental legislation. The result would be a suggested body of legislation including traditional practices having conservation value and satisfying the human spirit; neotraditional syntheses of traditional and western practices; and other environmental regulations needed to deal with present-day problems which are not covered by traditional or neotraditional practices.

The work will not be easy but it will be meaningful as a model for people living in the most limited of ecosystems. In many respects, the issues addressed in the microcosm of Yap are those of the larger world. The difference is that on Yap they are at a more human scale, and therefore are more immediately possible. Thus Yap and other inhabited islands could provide models for the world of the future when the most modern thing will be the sustainable use of resources.

The outside world can help by educating devel-opment advisors to the limitations of island ecosystems and the need for appropriate methods, timing, and evaluation of inputs required for results, their impact, and whether these are sustainable. Opportunities are needed for practical training in applied ecology for sustainable development to assist with the development of a corps of local scientists, and support is needed for sustained efforts of local scientists committed to solving local problems so that neotraditional strategies of sustainable resource use may evolve.

The Nature Conservancy of Hawaii's Endangered Forest and Bird Project

Henry P. Little
The Nature Conservancy of Hawaii
Honolulu, Hawaii, USA

ABSTRACT. *This case study describes the effort of a private conservation organization to help conserve the endangered bird fauna of the Hawaiian islands. A third of the bird species known at the time of European contact are now extinct, and another third are currently endangered. The protected area system of Hawaii was not established with species conservation in mind, so many areas of concentration of endemic species are not covered by protected areas. The Nature Conservancy identified 14 potential reserves to help fill the gaps in the system and is now working to purchase these areas or otherwise gain control over their use. As a result of this effort, a number of lessons have been learned for wider application.*

1. INTRODUCTION

In recent years individuals and institutions concerned with the alarming loss of species world-wide have become increasingly interested in the preservation of both tropical forests and island ecosystems. The Hawaiian archipelago is one area where the destruction of tropical forests and the disruptions of fragile island ecosystems are occurring at an alarming rate, putting in doubt the future survival of many endemic Hawaian species of plants and animals.

This paper recounts briefly what one organization, The Nature Conservancy (TNC), has done and plans to do to preserve Hawaii's full array of natural biological diversity. Of course, the Conservancy's Hawaii effort is but one of many in the state. The programme has consisted principally of translating scientifically-based recommendations for selection, acquisition and management natural areas into effective action in both the private and governmental sectors. Therefore, this paper will focus on the "how to get the job done" aspects of species conservation in Hawaii, leaving to others explanations of the programme's scientific underpinnings.

2. HAWAII'S NATURAL BIOLOGICAL DIVERSITY

Volcanic in origin, the Hawaiian archipelago was colonized inadvertently by plant and animal species borne by the wind and sea and by birds. Here, on the earth's most isolated land mass, evolved a unique array of plant and animal species, some 96% of which are found nowhere else in the world. For example, from a colonizing population of a single passerine bird species, some 47 different species and subspecies of Hawaiian honeycreepers (Drepanididae) evolved.

With the arrival of Polynesian man in 400-500 A.D. and of Western man in 1778, a biological dismemberment began which continues unabated today. Twenty-three of some 70 endemic bird species extant in 1778 are extinct, and another 29 currently are endangered. An estimated 66% of Hawaii's vascular plants too are threatened with extinction, as are many species of land snails and insects. And despite federal, state and private efforts to reverse these trends, the ratio of words to actions has weighed heavily with the former, and few truly effective biological conservation programmes have been initiated.

3. THE NATURE CONSERVANCY IN HAWAII

The first decade of the Conservancy's conservation efforts in hawaii, from 1968 to 1979, was distinguished more by the organization's failures that by its achievements. The Conservancy established the Kipahulu Valley Preserve in 1968, but since then, under joint Conservancy-U.S. National Park Service management, the 5,500 ha preserve has suffered substantial degradation, principally due to feral pig-induced invasion of exotic plants. The failure to plan for the proper management of this preserve has been a costly lesson for the Conservancy, in terms of both biological losses and loss of Conservancy credibility.

Similar planning shortcomings undermined Conservancy efforts to open and sustain a professionally-staffed office in Hawaii in the mid-1970's. Moreover, the absence of a local professional staff and of a network of supportive local community and business leaders rendered ineffective a well-funded Conservancey effort to acquire in 1975 the 1,500 ha Kilauea Forest Preserve, which most local naturalists consider to be Hawaii's best remnant native forest ecosystem.

3.1. The launching of the Endangered Hawaiian Forest Bird Project (EHFBP)

It was from this rather chequered history that the Conservancy in 1979 endeavoured to build a viable, comprehensive biological conservation programme in Hawaii. It was largely from the findings of the U.S. Fish and Wildlife Service's Hawaiian Forest Bird Survey. that the Conservancy launched the EHFBP. The availability of extensive information on the populations and distributions of endemic forest bird species, the threats to and the essential habitats of these populations, and the requisite management of these habitats, enabled the Conservancy to chart a carefully planned programme aimed at preserving Hawaii's beleaguered forest bird species.

Rather than discuss exhaustively the steps taken by the Conservancy to initiate the EHFBP, I will outline briefly only the important events in the project's evolution. Perhaps more important, I will highlight what I believe were the principal "lessons learned" from both early and recent Conservancy efforts in Hawaii. I should add that all along the Conservancy's goal has been to preserve the full extent of Hawaii's natural diversity and that the decision to focus initially on forest birds was dictated both by the availability of information and by the marketability of a bird conservation effort.

3.2. Sequence of events

1979

1. Formulated EHFBP (5 year) Plan: 14 potential preserves identified; 7 targeted for TNC action.
2. National TNC gave San Francisco staff permission to deficit finance the project until major EHFBP campaign could be launched.

1980

1. Established volunteer EHFBP Steering Committee, consisting of 5 local leaders from Hawaii business, government and community sectors.
2. Established volunteer EHFBP Scientific Advisory Committee, consisting of 8 highly respected local scientists.
3. Hired local professional staff, consisting of project director, project field representative and secretary.
4. Identified 3-4 priority preserves on which to focus all staff efforts until one notable "success" (i.e., an option to acquire one priority' preserve) had been achieved.

1981

1. Narrowed focus to acquiring the 1225 ha Molokai Ranch parcel of the proposed Kamakou Preserve (Molokai), and the 2375 ha Haleakala Ranch parcel of the proposed Waikamoi Preserve (Maui).
2. Developed preliminary long-range (5 year) preserve management plans for the Kamakou and Waikamoi preserves.
3. Secured an option to purchase for $150,000 a perpetual conservation easement over 1225 ha Molokai Ranch parcel, Kamakou Preserve, Molokai. Ranch retained limited water development and transport rights.
4. Converted Steering Committee into 18-member Board of Trustees of newly created Nature Conservancy of Hawaii (TNCH). Board given full authority for all EHFBP decisions.
5. $3 million EHFBP fundraising campaign launched to cover for the next 2 1/2 years all projected land acquisitions ($800,000), preserve management ($1,800,000) and staff operating ($400,000) expenses.
6. $1 million challenge grant secured for project by national Nature Conservancy.
7. Two additions (120 ha) added to Kipahulu Valley Preserve to fill out the preserve's redefined boundaries.

1982

1. $1,400,000 raised to date for $3 million EHFBP campaign (includes $1 million challenge grant).
2. Option secured for $300,000 purchase of perpetual conservation easement over 2375 ha Haleakala Ranch parcel, Waikamoi Preserve, Maui. Ranch retains limited water development transport rights.
3. Management lease secured for 20 ha Newell's Shearwater nesting site on Kauai.
4. Project scientist hired and detailed 1985 Kamakou Preserve Management Plan prepared by

project scientist and Scientific Advisory Committee.

5. Purchase of Molokai Ranch parcel, Kamakou Preserve completed.
6. Grassroots/public education programme launched to foster widespread awareness of and support for EHFBP.
7. Discussions held with State of Hawaii and quasi-public Bishop Estate regarding cooperative management of state and Bishop Estate lands within the proposed Kamakou Preserve.
8. TNCH Board Chairman elected to TNC national Board of Governors.

1983 Goals:

1. Complete EHFBP to the extent that:
   a) $3 million raised;
   b) a total of 7-8 EHFBP preserves established by year end 1983;
   c) adequate management programmes, adequately staffed and funded, planned and initiated on all preserves including Kipahulu Valley (Maui), Waikamoi (Maui), Kamakou (Molokai), Hakalau (Hawaii) and Kaluahonu (Kauai);
2. Broaden scope of TNCH's activities in an effort to protect Hawaii's full array of national biological diversity.
   a) initiate modest, in-house inventory (based on TNC's "natural heritage programme" methodology) of Hawaii's flora and fauna;
   b) prepare a "natural diversity scorecard" for Hawaii, specifically identifying the "gaps" in the array of protected diversity in the state;
   c) select and design 5 preserves which will protect the highest priority "gaps";
   d) secure $3-5 million in "high risk" capital to finance the protection of both EHFBP preserves and the new preserves identified in c) above;
   e) turn day-to-day operations of TNCH over to local staff director;
   f) develop 5,000-person local membership to TNCH;
   g) develop sources of funding for on-going annual TNCH operating budget ($200,00/yr).

4. LESSONS LEARNED

Recognizing that experiences of one individual or one organization in one place at one time may have little relevance to others working elsewhere in the future, I will simply outline what lessons I have learned during my brief work in Hawaii.

4.1. Steps to building a successful programme

1. Secure funding for 2-3 years of "start-up" operations.
2. Develop or tap into a good data base which identifies the "gaps" in protected diversity.
3. Prepare business-like 3-5 year operating plan, which includes:
   a) targeted elements of natural diversity;
   b) preserve selection;
   c) preserve design;
   d) level of protection (e.g. legal rights) desired;
   e) preserve management planning and implementation;
   f) development of "local" volunteer leadership;
   g) hiring and training of local staff;
   h) programme budget; and
   i) fundraising.
4. Organize local leadership.
5. Hire and train staff.
6. Focus on achieving 1-2 very important marketable, tangible results within 2 years.
7. Once initial project success is achieved:
   a) solidify local leadership;
   b) launch large scale fundraising campaign; and
   c) prepare to expand scope of programme.
8. Evaluate results annually, update long range plans every two ears, and prepare annual operating plans each fall.

4.2. Important determinants of success

1. Good planning, long range and annual, for all aspects of programme.
2. Substantial "front end" funding.
3. Incentives from national organization to local leadership, such as:
   a) "front end" operating funding;
   b) challenge grant;
   c) loan of experienced personnel to train local staffs and to initiate programme; and
   d) local Board—national Board link.
4. Excellent local leadership.
5. Excellent local staff, who first and foremost are salesmen.
6. Objective, comprehensive data on status of biological diversity.
7. Close ties with land-owning entities and institutions, private and public.
8. Conservation proposals presented within the context of economic development, as it is from this viewpoint that decision-makers will be evaluating your programme.
9. Incredible persistence; ability to bounce back from failures, of which there will be many; flexibility to adjust initial expectations to reality.
10. Public acceptance of programme.
11. Cost-effective management of preserves.

5. CONCLUSION

As is evident to those who have read this paper, the Conservancy's EHFBP can hardly be considered a success at this time. Rather, some signs of success are beginning to appear on the distant horizon. The future fate of the EHFBP and of other Conservancy initiatives in Hawaii, however, will depend largely on the Conservancy's ability to solidify its relationships with large public land-owning entities, to develop effective, low-cost preserve management programmes, and to marshall adequate public support for biological conservation in Hawaii.

It is hoped that others engaged in species conservation activities elsewhere will find in the Conservancy's Hawaii experience a useful idea or two which will enhance the likelihood of their success, upon which so much depends.

Future Directions for the Oceanian Realm

Arthur Lyon Dahl
South Pacific Commission
Noumea, New Caledonia

ABSTRACT. *Islands are biologically distinctive, due to their isolation and resulting independent biological histories. Therefore, each island must be conserved in its own right. The peoples of the Pacific islands have developed cultures and traditions with an important conservation element. However, present trends, based on external sources of food, capital, and labour, are placing much of the natural and cultural heritage of the Pacific region at risk. It is apparent that protected area conservation must deal both with the natural biota, and the cultural context in which it has existed for hundreds of years. Protected area approaches imported from the mainland are not appropriate, but the IUCN Category VIII Multiple-use area, Category V Cultural landscape, and Category VII Anthropological reserve are all highly relevant for the Pacific. Conservation must build on the existing strong community spirit and traditional cultural means of conservation to evolve a new approach to benefit both people and nature.*

1. INTRODUCTION

The Oceanian Realm is characterized by the occurrence of small island systems in a vast expanse of ocean. It is the specificity of the island situation that gives this region its importance for conservation, and that constrains the kinds of conservation action that can be contemplated. This paper focusses on future directions for conservation in the area served by the South Pacific Commission and the South Pacific Regional Environment Programme (Micronesia, Melanesia and Polynesia excluding Hawaii and New Zealand), since this region shares many common features.

The Pacific Islands tend to be small, scattered and isolated. The region has a population of about 5 million inhabiting a total land area of only 550,000 sq km in a sea area of over 29 million sq km, giving a population density of 9 persons per sq km. Excluding Papua New Guinea, the population is under 2 million on a land area of 88,800 sq km in a sea area of over 26 million sq km (population density 21 persons per sq km). While the population is decreasing on some smaller islands because of outmigration, the general trend is for rapid population growth placing increasing pressure on very limited resources.

It is in the nature of islands to be biologically distinctive, and principles of island biogeography have been developed to explain this. In general, the immigration and extinction rates of organisms are related to the size of the island and its distance from centres of colonization. In Oceania, the great isolation of many islands has led to high rates of endemism. The region has been estimated to have about 2,000 ecosystem types in 20 biogeographic provinces (Dahl, 1980). This rich natural heritage is the responsibility of very small and scattered populations with limited human, scientific and financial resources. It is unreasonable to expect that the burden of conserving this heritage should be borne by the people of the region alone.

The peoples of the Pacific Islands have developed cultures and traditions with an important conservation element. The people are strongly attached to their land, and in general learned to live in harmony with their limited island resources. The frequent taboo areas were the equivalent of parks and reserves. Intensive management practices and controls were developed for each species where required to maintian their abundance. There was in general a strong sense of local responsibility for the natural resources necessary for survival.

Given the benign climate and natural productivity of many islands, material development was limited to essentials and most efforts went into human relationships and social interactions. It is this strong cultural foundation for conservation that gives hope for the future.

Unfortunately, present trends are placing much of the natural and cultural heritage at risk. With development and population growth, the conflicts between resource uses have been accentuated, and some countries are rapidly approaching the absolute limits of some essential resources such as soil and water. The centrifugal forces resulting from immersion in the outside world are destroying the autonomy and self-sufficiency of island societies. There is an increasing dependence on imports and aid, associated with a loss of a sense of responsibility. The joint trends of urbanization and the marginalization of rural areas are transforming the structure of island communities and the peoples' relationship with their natural resources. However, the strong pressures for westernization are being increasingly countered by a search for new lifestyles and approaches to development more appropriate to the island condition. As people experience the increasing stress on their resources as a result of short-sighted exploitation, they raise more questions about their future. In the recent review of the State of the Environment in the South Pacific (Dahl and Baumgart, 1982), a large majority of countries in the region reported problems of soil erosion, water and lagoon pollution, forest loss, and endangered species. Efforts are now under way through the South Pacific Regional Environment Programme to assist countries in resolving these problems.

2. PRESENT STATE OF CONSERVATION ACTION

A good start has been made on the protection of natural areas in the region with the creation over 100 parks and reserves in some 15 countries. However, these protected areas still include only a small proportion of the fauna, flora, unique sites and ecosystems of the South Pacific region. Progress has been slow, and with the very limited resources available for conservation in island countries, the foundation is still insecure. In general, the legal measures providing for the creation of protected areas are well in advance of the political commitment to conservation. Few parks and reserves have been created in most countries, and where they do exist, governments lack the finance and manpower to develop and manage them. Some parks have had to be abandoned, and others are under pressure. In the present situation in most island countries, we cannot expect much improvement with the conservation approaches tried to date.

The status of the Convention on Conservation of Nature in the South Pacific is indicative. The Convention was drafted in 1976, and signed that year at a plenipotentiary meeting in Apia, Western Samoa. However, no country has yet ratified it, and the political support seems inadequate to make any rapid progress.

Meanwhile, there is a steady reduction in the remaining natural areas as more land is cleared, pollution increases, and resource exploitation is intensified. The number of endangered species and ecosystems is uncomfortably large, and would certainly be larger if better information were available.

3. FUTURE DIRECTIONS FOR CONSERVATION

It is clear that, in island societies, where the people much more than the governments control the land and its resources, conservation actions must be based on popular understanding and support and must be adapted to the limited small island situation where single-purpose reserves are seldom possible. The following are some requirements for the future progress of conservation in the Oceanian Realm.

3.1. Information

A prerequisite to effective conservation is better information on natural areas and species. There are few scientists in the region, and the understanding of many island ecosystems is still very rudimentary. What information exists is generally in foreign experts and overseas research institutions and thus largely unavailable locally where it is most needed. Many conservation tragedies are the result of simple ignorance of the value of an organism or site. Areas and resources of conservation interest must be identified and mapped, sometimes even down to individual trees where these are very rare. This information should be produced in forms useful both for planning and for education. Regular monitoring is then required to identify trends, such as loss of forest cover or degradation of coral reefs, that may threaten conservation objectives.

Both of the above can be done with outside assistance if necessary, but it may be even more important to restore the local knowledge of species and areas. Traditional island societies had their fishing masters, hunters, healers and sorcerers who passed on their deep knowledge of the natural world and its uses from generation to generation. These people controlled the use of resources based on their intimate knowledge and their powers of observation. Their information was locally available and frequently consulted. However, the impact of missionaries and modern educational systems has undercut and all but eliminated this traditional environmental management. It is important to try to salvage what little traditional knowledge remains as a basis for renewed resource management approaches.

3.2. Protected areas

Much more flexibility is needed in the approaches to the protection of species, ecosystems and habitats. Most legislation in the region was copied from often inappropriate examples elsewhere, but already some experiments in new approaches have been tried and others could be considered. There is a trend towards permitting the limited traditional use of organisms rather than establishing a total prohibition which is unenforceable.

Two examples are the wildlife management areas in Papua New Guinea and the farming of species under pressure to meet the commercial demand. New Caledonia has established a rotating marine reserve, in which three sections of the barrier reef are closed successively for three-year intervals. There has been discussion of the possibility of family reserves on land held in communal family ownership. A modification of the principle of the traditional fallow system could require a certain percentage of the land be held in forest, allowing some land clearing and use as other areas of forest regenerate. Reserved areas will frequently need to cater to multiple uses where these are compatible, such as watershed protection, medicinal plant collection, the cutting of trees for canoes or house posts, and other appropriate uses. Reserves may be more successful if they follow the pattern of traditional taboo areas. It may in some instances be necessary to include local inhabitants and their activities within a conservation area, or even to manage a whole island so that essential natural features are preserved alongside human activities.

3.3. Local support and responsibility

Central authority still tends to be weak and limited in its scope in most island countries, particularly in the many areas and islands that are remote from the seat of the government. Conservation in such areas will only be effective if supported by public opinion and particularly by the customary land owners. Where traditional authority is still respected, it should be used to enforce conservation actions, reinforced as necessary with laws and educational programmes.

Customary land tenure has been seen as a major barrier to park and reserve creation, but it could be turned into an asset through approaches in which the customary owners themselves help to define the conservation actions required, and make and enforce the necessary regulations with the support and encouragement of national authorities. This approach has showed promise in the wildlife management areas of Papua New Guinea (Kwapena, this volume). Such approaches do not involve taking away family land (which would be politically unacceptable even where it is possible), but apply controls protecting the resources on the land while leaving the peoples' ties to the land undisturbed. Local protection should be recognized by and enforceable under national law, and where development or management of the site as a conservation area is required, some financial and technical support could be made available.

It will still be necessary to find ways of sharing the burden on those land owners who are denied development opportunities because their land happens to have conservation interest. In many islands, it is not possible to provide other land in compensation, and spiritual and ancestral ties with the land cannot be replaced.

The conservation of marine and coastal areas presents a particular problem. Many parts of Oceania had traditional marine tenure systems which allowed for limited access and local responsibility for the management of fisheries resources.

However, European legal systems have made such areas public, creating a new "tragedy of the commons". It may be necessary to restore traditional systems of marine resources ownership to achieve the effective management and conservation of these resources.

A basic principle for conservation in the Pacific islands should be to decentralize authority and responsibility to a level where enforcement is possible and where the greatest knowledge of the resources exists. In most instances, this will be the village, family or island level.

The essential support for this decentralized conservation will be strong and continuing public education campaigns and the provision of extension services. This may indeed be the most appropriate type of conservation activity on a national and regional basis. Since the populations involved are small, a moderate commitment of resources should make it possible to reach a large percentage of the population.

3.4. Integration with planning and development

The small land area of islands makes for greater conflicts in resource use. Conservation must therefore be closely integrated into the planning process, and not just set aside as the responsibility of a national parks unit. The reservation of natural areas should be seen as a kind of development which contributes to resource management and tourism as well as to nature conservation. In the many countries of Oceania where tourism is a major economic activity, there is a great need for more park development to improve the tourist experience and to prevent the industry from destroying the very resources on which it depends.

Most countries with islands of any size should aim for a few major national parks for tourism, public education and the protection of significant ecosystems, plus many small sites under local responsibility for areas of ecological, scenic, historic or recreation interest.

Rural communities should be encouraged to return to their pre-missionary state where they saw their activities as part of nature rather than working against nature. Their development should respect the continuity of the natural systems on which they depend.

3.5. Local resource managers

A pilot project is now being developed in the region to implement the future direction for conservation and resource management described above through the training of local resource managers. These people will be trained to bring modern scientific experience together with the traditional approaches and knowledge which have proven their effectiveness over generations, so that they can take on an advisory and management role in their own local community. The trainees will research the past use of local resources, and learn basic scientific methods so that they can design and carry out their own experimental trials and resource monitoring.

They will have continuing access to scientific advice, and contribute to national planning and data collection, while carrying out their primary role of guiding the development and uses of the resources of their community. They must have the agreement and support of the traditional authorities and the community for their new role, which will be comparable to the wise men of pre-European communities or local scientists in a western country. The presence in each village of a local resource manager who is aware of the need for conservation and knows what requires protection should catalyse more effective conservation action than could ever be imposed from the national level.

4. CONCLUSION

These future directions for conservation in Oceania may not seem practical when viewed from a European, African or American perspective, but they reflect the realities of the small isolated island communities in the region.

The Oceanian Realm probably has more unique natural areas and endemic species per capita than any other region. There are probably also more governments and government ministers per capita, but with much less at the base of the governmental pyramid to actually execute programmes. Government officers need to be generalists rather than specialists, and it will never be possible for island governments to carry out the same range of functions or responsibilities as in larger countries. Much more responsibility must therefore be left with the people themselves.

There is in the Pacific a strong community spirit and a sense of regionalism that is expressed through effective regional institutions, but there is also a strong resistance to the imposition of approaches from the outside. Past attempts at conservation have too often come from outside and been supported largely by expatriates. A new approach is needed, building on the foundation of the traditional island ways. The rapid erosion of those traditions that achieved effective conservation must be reversed. It is fortunately not too late to turn the tide with education and creative solutions to conservation problems, and thus to save a significant part of the rich natural heritage of the Oceanian Realm.

Chapter 9
The Antarctic Realm

Keynote Address: The Antarctic Realm

Hon. Jonathan Elworthy
Minister of Lands and Forests
Wellington, New Zealand

ABSTRACT. *The Antarctic Realm epitomizes many of the problems and challenges involved in applying the principles of the World Conservation Strategy, especially in relation to the fragile ecosystems that are typical of the island environments of New Zealand and other isolated islands in the sub-Antarctic. The issues are highlighted in the future of the largest land mass in the Antarctic Realm, the Antarctic Continent, with its surrounding seas. A wide variety of conservation mechanisms will be required, including means other than public ownership. The case studies presented for the Antarctic Realm will illustrate lessons on how conservation and development are being integrated in a variety of settings.*

1. INTRODUCTION

As elsewhere in the world, there is change in the Antarctic Realm in the social, economic and political environment in which protected areas are established and managed. The realm epitomizes many of the problems and challenges involved in applying the principles of the World Conservation Strategy (WCS), especially in relation to the fragile ecosystems that are typical of the island environments of New Zealand and other isolated islands in the sub-antarctic. The issues are highlighted in the future of the largest land mass in the Antarctic Realm, the Antarctic Continent, with its surrounding seas.

Increasingly, the demands human society is placing on natural resources are closing off the easy options that existed in the past when the first national parks were established in remote or mountainous areas with little or no apparent social or economic potential foregone.

The WCS recognizes today's realities by emphasizing the need for "living resources for sustainable development" and my Government has endorsed this approach by adopting the principles of the WCS. It has taken the principles further by encouraging the development of a proposal for a New Zealand Conservation Strategy. The drafters of the NZ Strategy have identified issues of the day clearly by the title they have given to the proposal: "Integrating Conservation with Development".

Looking back to the proceedings of the first two world conferences on national parks, it seems to me that the first in Seattle in 1962 looked primarily at parks as entities in themselves; the second conference in 1972 at Yellowstone/Grand Teton saw parks more in the context of the physical environment in which they existed; and this congress is looking at protected areas in the context of the whole fabric of society. In this respect, it clearly reflects the WCS recognition of national parks and other protected areas as an integral part of the conservation of Earth's living resources essential for human well-being and sustainable development.

With world social and economic problems ever-pressing, there are costs and benefits involved in the establishment and maintenance of protected areas which society must assess. One of the problems for protected areas is that it is easier to measure the potential of resources available for directly productive uses than to measure the more intangible benefits of protected areas. Certainly, the value of protected areas for tourism is measurable but the values of water, soil and forest conservation are less readily identifiable and it is certainly not possible to measure in money terms the considerable but intangible benefits of what the New Zealand National Parks Act calls "inspiration, enjoyment, recreation and other benefits" that may be gained from national parks.

There is also the literally immeasurable value of knowing that protected areas exist, in knowing that there are some parts of the world which still retain minimum evidence of human impact. That, of course, is one of the great arguments for the protection in a largely unmodified state of Antarctica itself. Of those who argue for preservation of the Antarctic environment, only a small minority can ever hope to visit there but many more can share vicariously in the experience, particularly through television.

2. ANTARCTICA

Antarctica epitomizes the dilemma of the times. Depending on point of view, it is a wilderness at risk to be protected at all costs, it is a continent up for grabs, or it represents an opportunity to apply the principles of the WCS, which sees some productive potential from the resources of the continent and the surrounding seas but only after careful consideration of the environmental impact. This approach was endorsed by the Fifteenth General Assembly of IUCN, held a year ago in Christchurch. The comprehensive IUCN resolution on Antarctica urged the maintenance for all time of "the intrinsic values of the Antarctica environment for mankind and the global ecosystem" and stressed the need to ensure that "all human activities are compatible with the maintenance of these values."

The IUCN approach was arrived at after much careful consideration and constructive debate. It represents, I believe, a carefully considered and realistic view. A full evening's presentation on Antarctic issues and devoted to exploring options for Antarctica led to the establishment of a working group whose efforts in turn led to the adoption by the General Assembly of the comprehensive resolution which is quoted in the case study paper on Antarctica.

It is interesting to compare the extent to which Antarctica was seen as an issue at Christchurch and given such in-depth study with the extent it was debated at the First and Second World Conferences on National Parks. In 1962, the record shows no presentation on Antarctica, while in 1972, the proceedings record only one substantive comment on the region. In spite of that—or perhaps because there had been no in-depth consideration of the issues—the 1972 conference adopted a recommendation that aimed for the establishment of Antarctica as the first World Park, under the auspices of the United Nations.

The IUCN General Assembly last year, after much more careful study, did not opt for such an idealistic—or some might say unrealistic—approach. Instead, it urged that there be ascribed to the Antarctic environment as a whole "a designation which connotes worldwide its unique character and values and the special measures accorded to its planning, management and conservation."

IUCN recognized the benefits of international co-operation in relation to Antarctica in its resolution at Christchurch last year. The General Assembly acknowledged "the achievements of the Consultative parties in their stewardship under the Antarctic Treaty in protecting the Antarctic environment from harmful interference."

Since territorial claims to Antarctica were frozen with the coming into force of the Antarctic Treaty in 1961, the consultative parties under the Treaty have worked with a high degree of constructive cooperation in recognition of the Treaty's fundamental principle that "it is in the interest of all mankind that Antarctica shall continue forever to be used exclusively for peaceful purposes and shall not become the scene or object of international discord."

New Zealand, as one of the original parties to the Treaty, continues to endorse that principle while recognizing that the demands of world society cannot be ignored in terms of gaining benefit from those resources which may prove capable of economic use on a basis which is compatible with the principles of the WCS.

The IUCN resolution on Antarctica gives the Antarctic Treaty parties a clear message from those whose primary concern is with conservation of nature and natural resources. It is a message that New Zealand certainly endorses.

3. THE SUB-ANTARCTIC

The same pressures which have brought Antarctica into increasing prominence apply to the isolated environments in the sub-Antarctic region of the Antarctic Realm. The Campbell Island case study typifies the conservation issues involved: the scientific value of small island ecosystems; their fragility and vulnerability to change; and the growing world interest in them for tourism and other economic purposes.

Islands, once seen as of value only as bases for whaling or sealing, as depots for shipwrecked mariners or as the setting for unsuccessful attempts at human settlement, are today under an increasing focus of attention. Some of the smaller islands must be among the most pristine ecosystems in the world; others are much modified by grazing from domestic animals which have become feral and are variously seen today as environment modifiers deserving to be destroyed or as evolutionary species having an historic and scientific interest which justifies their retention in conflict with the concept of strict nature protection.

And over all this, the new impact of human interest: on the one hand, the desire of people, many with a deep concern for nature, to visit the world's remote places; and, on the other hand, the application of new technology which is making the extraction of petroleum and other minerals a possibility with its likely demands for shore facilities.

The rationalizing and harmonizing of these considerations with the status of islands such as Campbell as nature reserves is dealt with through the management planning technique but there are two problems here. One is that remote, little-known island groups do not have a body of informed public opinion able to contribute significantly to the public participation opportunities that exist under the planning process. The other problem is that, while resource exploration in the surrounding seas may have little or no impact on nearby island reserves, the discovery of resources of economic potential can dramatically change the situation and bring understandable pressure to reassess management priorities from those who have invested substantially in exploration and those who, from a distance, see the benefits to mankind of tapping a newly-found resource to far outweigh the value of a remote island in the southern ocean.

4. THE PRESERVATION/USE CONFLICT

The same sorts of value judgements which are inherent in the integration of conservation with development in Antarctica and in the sub-Antarctic are even more evident when the issue is one of committing potentially productive resources to protected area status in areas where people live. This dilemma of preservation for wider national good versus production to maintain the viability of resident communities is highlighted in the case study of the reservation of commercially important lowland forests in the west coast of the South Island of New Zealand.

As I said earlier, it is a dilemma which did not face our predecessors to the same extent when establishment of national parks tended to happen in areas of little or no resident population or little or no known economic value. Some cynics have suggested that some past decisions have been made on the basis that "It's no good for anything else; let's make it a national park." If that were ever even partly true, it is certainly not true today.

As another of the case studies in this realm points out, there is a new emphasis on moving towards a representative system of protected areas in New Zealand. This is a practical application on a country basis of the broad goal of international conservation to see the widest possible range of ecosystems protected. It is a most desirable goal totally in harmony with the WCS. It is a goal which is recognized in New Zealand legislation and to which our National Parks and Reserves Authority is committed. Like all worthwhile goals, it is one which will not be easy to achieve.

Some of the problems in achieving it are covered in a number of the case studies: the need to identify gaps in the existing system of protected areas; the extent to which human impact and introduced species have modified the New Zealand environment; the social and economic impact of taking decisions for preservation where there is a problem posed for community viability; and I would add a growing reluctance among many in society to seeing more land moving from private hands into state ownership.

5. THE REPRESENTATIVE SYSTEM CONCEPT

The establishment of protected areas has, in many cases, relied on individual or group enthusiasm and/or emotive argument. These are and will continue to be important. But when it comes to making value judgements about the commitment of a natural resource to protected area status, enthusiasm and emotion are no longer enough in the face of often-competing demands for that resource.

It is in this context that I believe the concept of a national biogeographic scheme is important in identifying ecological regions and districts, enabling existing protected areas to be fitted into the framework of these regions and districts to assess their representativeness and providing a guide for the selection of new protected areas needed to achieve representativeness.

When the present framework is fleshed out and information is in place, it will be much easier for those in government at all levels to make informed judgements on the commitment of natural resources to production or protection. This will benefit the credibility of the conservation movement as our often-limited knowledge in the past has led to concerns to protect a particular area as the last remaining habitat of some endangered species being repeated in later years in relation to some other area. This can easily lead to politicians and public alike becoming cynical at what they may see as exaggerated claims made as a case for protected area status.

6. THE INTRODUCED ANIMAL PROBLEM

Better knowledge and its presentation on a systematic basis will help greatly in identifying priorities for protection. At the same time, the extent to which animals and plants—as well as humans—have successfully colonized New Zealand with consequent modification to its natural environment poses problems. Options for protection of some ecosystems have been closed off by their modification and a conflict of philosophies has developed towards the extermination of introduced animals in protected areas and their acceptance as a positive and desirable addition to public interest and recreation in the form of hunting.

Plants and animals have been introduced to New Zealand for many reasons, from a desire of settlers both Polynesian and *pakeha* (European) to be surrounded by the familiar and the useful and to provide a hunting resource. As the case study on this topic shows, great problems have been created where introductions have flourished in the wild, nowhere more than in the impact of rodents on native birds and of introduced browsing mammals on native vegetation.

NATIONAL PARKS, CONSERVATION, AND DEVELOPMENT

The result has been not only the modification of many ecosystems, but the establishment of a hunting resource which has great attractions to many. Conflict between those who see deer and the North American elk or wapiti as introduced animals to be exterminated in the interests of nature preservation and those who see them as a recreationally valuable hunting resource has been further complicated by the extent to which these introductions have become valuable commercially.

The advent of helicopter-based hunting for the meat industry and, more recently, for live capture to stock domestic deer farms, has generally reduced introduced animal numbers to levels where there is significant recovery of native vegetation. This, in turn, has heightened pressure from recreational hunting interests to accept the continued presence of these animals as a desirable part of national parks and other protected areas and not, as other groups see them, as a continuing barrier to the preservation of nature.

The problem of the decision-maker in this situation is one of seeking a course of action that is justified, justifiable and meets with broad public acceptance. This tends to become increasingly difficult in an era where issues tend to be debated through the media and in uncompromising terms rather than through balanced discussion designed to seek middle ground.

7. BALANCED DECISION-MAKING

This need for constructive dialogue between different interest groups with differing objectives is graphically illustrated in the case study on the reservation of lowland forests of commercial importance, particularly to small locally resident communities. This case study highlights a range of issues: the national interest in relation to regional and local interests; the responsibility of the wider community to find a means of compensating in some form or other for economic potential foregone; the unfortunate adversary situation which may develop between small communities which feel beleaguered by what they see as well-organized pressure groups financed by affluent city dwellers; and the image of national parks seen by some as areas "locked up" for the benefit of an elite minority.

I am sure there are means by which society can move away from open confrontation towards constructive dialogue and balanced resource decisions which take into account the varying interests of people of the locality, the region, the nation and the world.

This surely is the challenge of the World Conservation Strategy which we are endeavouring to pick up in the New Zealand Strategy—the challenge of integrating conservation with development and achieving sustainable use of resources. This sustainable use has as an integral part of it the identification of those areas where preservation should be paramount. At the same time, wherever possible and compatible with preservation, there is a need for us to remember that protected areas are established to meet society's evolving needs: parks are for people.

We need to communicate to people more effectively the values of national parks and other protected areas and the recreational opportunities they offer in a way that gives the lie to the "lock-up" allegation. We also need to improve our processes of public participation and decision-making to take better account of conflicting viewpoints, interests and aspirations so that proposals are developed as part of a total package rather than in a unilateral way without apparent regard for their economic, social or environmental implications.

It has been with these points in mind that I have initiated the merger of the two major land-administering organs of government in New Zealand—the Department of Lands and Survey and the New Zealand Forest Service. The merged department will have land management responsibilities for 54 percent of New Zealand's land resource and its aims in the management of public lands are to conserve soil, water biota and historical and cultural values; to contribute to economic and social development by productive use of resources; to provide for public enjoyment of recreation, scenic and social values generally; and to arrive at an appropriate balance of uses by synthesis rather than conflict.

The Departments' proposals for implementing the merger recommend integration of conservation and development in each major operating sector of the merged department—in plantation forestry, in farming, and in indigenous forest/open country management. In this latter area, where the new organization will be responsible for national parks and a wide range of other protected areas, there will also be a responsibility in relation to other indigenous forest land to balance demands for production with the claims of preservation.

With a policy and overview role, it is proposed to have an Indigenous Forests and Open Country Commission, independent of officials. This Commission would absorb the present responsibilities of the National Parks and Reserves Authority and add to them responsibility for policy in relation to all publicly-owned indigenous forest and open country. That Commission would have the task of working with the department in seeking to achieve balanced land use proposals which the public would have the opportunity of reacting to before decisions were made.

Another factor to which I have referred is the extent to which nature preservation is being achieved in New Zealand by mechanisms other than public ownership. Various techniques by which land-owners voluntarily accept constraints over the use of their land exist today and are being used increasingly. They depend on the landowner being aware of the particular values which may exist on his or her land and on landowner confidence in the administrative mechanism to achieve appropriate protection. This technique and others like it offer valuable means of achieving nature conservation goals while leaving land in private ownership.

In conclusion, like the rest of the world, the Antarctic Realm has a need for a representative system of protected areas in the context of living resource conservation for sustainable development. I believe the case studies will illustrate some lessons—negative and positive—from which we can all learn as we endeavour to best serve the world community and the societies we represent. I believe the steps being taken under the Antarctic Treaty and in New Zealand are positive steps towards achieving the goal of integrating conservation with development.

Finding Ways and Means to Conserve Antarctica

P.H.C. Lucas
Director General
Department of Lands and Survey
Wellington, New Zealand

ABSTRACT. *Until the late 1950s human impact on the Antarctica continent stemmed from the challenge of exploration. Then, the International Geophysical Year (1957-58) saw the beginning of a continuing programme of scientific research, while territorial claims were frozen with the adoption by interested nations of the Antarctica Treaty which entered into force in 1961. The Treaty provides for Antarctica to be used only for peaceful purposes with concentration on scientific research and safeguards for conservation of its flora and fauna. Mineral resource exploration and possible extraction has become a recurring issue since evidences of hydrocarbons were found. The effectiveness of the Treaty in preserving the Antarctic environment is assessed.*

1. INTRODUCTION

The qualities and the natural resources of Antarctica have been the subject of many publications, both popular and scientific. A recent one sums up in its title both the qualities and concerns about the southern polar regions: "Antarctica: Wilderness at Risk" (Brewster, 1982). The purpose of this case study is to discuss the existing mechanisms for conservation of Antarctica and to assess the best means of ensuring effective protection of the region for the future.

The 15th General Assembly of IUCN, meeting in Christchurch, New Zealand, in October 1981, was in no doubt about the significance and values of the region. Participants prefaced a resolution on the subject by "recognizing the importance of Antarctica and its Continental shelf and the Southern Ocean for the world as a whole, particularly in maintaining the stability of the global marine environment and atmosphere, and the paramount importance to mankind of its great wilderness qualities for science, education and inspiration."

Interest and concern for Antarctica has grown in recent years. It is noteworthy that at the First World Conference on National Parks in Seattle, USA, in 1962, there was no presentation on polar regions although a recommendation was adopted in support of the Antarctic Treaty. Ten years later, at the Second World Conference at Grand Teton National Park, USA, the only speaker reported in the Conference Proceedings as discussing Antarctica was Dr. Ricardo Luti of Argentina, who said that "The Antarctic ecosystems are very unstable. Their rather simple structure, due to their relatively recent origin, makes them very susceptible to any impact, even that of the very presence and movements of man, the alterations caused being sometimes irreversible. Much of the region is in a quasi-pristine state, but its recent history offers examples of total or partial devastation of appreciable fractions of its ecosystems, basically comprising some of its rich fauna: there has been "a no man's land" destructive approach to exploitation of seals, whales, penguins, and other species for their skin, meat, oil, use as fertiliser, and even, in the case of penguins, their eggs, although the exploitation of the latter can easily be organized on conservation lines . . ."

Luti stressed the need for integrated ecological studies and full protection of representative areas and of endangered species. He stressed the need for an international approach and stressed the need to accept "the challenge of mutual cooperation, possibly involving the establishment of a coordinated chain of natural areas by countries claiming rights in Antarctica." The meeting noted that the fragility of the ecosystems of polar regions were such that "industrial developments and resource exploitation may be fatal unless properly controlled." It also noted adverse influences in Antarctica "now being caused by the establishment of scientific bases and tourist facilities" and commented that the extension of these developments must be carefully watched. The conference proceedings record that the "meeting was in favour of the idea of an international Antarctic park, although the intensive research required for such a project was emphasized."

Three days later, the Second World Conference on National Parks at its concluding session adopted a recommendation "that the nations party to the Antarctic Treaty should negotiate to establish the Antarctic Continent and the surrounding seas as the first world park, under auspices of the United Nations." Soon after this, the New Zealand Government proposed giving Antarctica world park status, but the other Antarctic Treaty Parties failed to respond to the initiative and New Zealand's subsequent policy approach to Antarctica conservation has not included the world park option.

So in 1982 at the World Parks Congress in Bali, Indonesia the search continues for ways and means to conserve Antarctica.

2. ANTARCTICA

The *World Conservation Strategy* defines Antarctica and the Southern Ocean "as all the land and sea south of the Antarctica Convergence (the well-defined but fluctuating line where the cold surface waters of the Southern Ocean sink beneath the warmer waters of the cold-temperature Atlantic, Indian and Pacific Oceans). Much of this area—that is the entire area south of 60 degrees latitude except for the 'high seas'—is covered by the Antarctic Treaty" (Fig. 1).

The Antarctic continent has a total area of some 14 million sq km, or about one-tenth of the globe's land surface, an area larger than Europe, and half again as big as the USA. Ninety-eight percent of the continent is covered by ice, and the Antarctic ice cap contains some 70 percent of the globe's freshwater. Permanent ice shelves 100 to 250 m thick have formed at various places along the coast. These ice shelves are themselves vast and spawn equally huge icebergs; the Ross Sea ice shelf is the size of France, and some years ago a single iceberg the size of Luxembourg was discovered in the Weddell Sea. Each year some 1.4 thousand million metric tons of ice break off and melt in the Southern Ocean. In addition, Antarctica more than doubles in size each winter, with the formation of pack ice which stretches more than 1100 km from the shore.

Precipitation inland is very light. Annual snowfall at the south pole is the equivalent of less than 2.5 cm of water, far drier than most deserts. On the coast, snowfall is 500 mm annually; in the interior it is about 50 mm. While the interior is virtually lifeless, the Antarctic oceans and coastal regions are among the most biologically productive in the world. For more than 50 years, Antarctic waters were the world's major whaling grounds, until over-exploitation reduced whale stocks to the point that the primary commercial species—suc-

cessively blue, fin, sei and sperm whales—have become too rare to hunt commercially, and only the smaller minke whale is now taken in Antarctic waters. Instead, commercial exploitation is beginning to turn to the substantial reserves of fin fish and krill *Euphasia superba*, a type of oceanic shrimp) found in Antarctic waters.

Antarctica has been described as "the coldest, driest, windiest, least accessible, worst known and generally the most unpleasant of all the seven continents," (Mitchell and Tinker, 1980) and Capt. Robert Scott, who died with all the members of his expedition shortly after reaching the south pole on 17 January 1912 noted in his diary: "Great God This is an awful place." But from another point of view is is also a demilitarized, unpolluted wildlife sanctuary dedicated to free scientific enquiry and international cooperation, thanks mainly to a unique treaty which has governed human activities in Antarctica since 1959. The treaty, now signed by 14 "consultative parties" and acceded to by 12 other states, has been largely successful in protecting the Antarctic environment, and in promoting international cooperation in Antarctic exploration and research. But it is facing new tests, arising primarily from the growing pressure for commercial development of Antarctica's resources: fish, krill, and, possibly, oil.

Antarctica has a relatively brief human history. After the early voyages of discovery and the first landing in 1895 by the Belgian explorer Adrien de Gerlache, the frozen continent has seen two clearly definable eras of human contact. First was the "heroic age" of Antarctic exploration which reached its peak early this century. The explorers of a number of countries mounted expeditions to Antarctica, some with and some without the authority of their governments; many of these early explorers claimed to have taken possession of the areas they had discovered on behalf of their countries and by 1930 seven states laid claim to parts of Antarctica: Argentina, Australia, Chile, France, New Zealand, Norway and United Kingdom.

The second era of man's involvement in the continent began with the International Geophysical Year (IGY) in 1957/58 when numerous scientific stations were set up in Antarctica, marking the beginning of the scientific era. Scientific endeavours under the IGY programme led to an understanding of the fragile nature of the Antarctic environment and its significance as a regulator of the climate of a large segment of the southern hemisphere.

The IGY brought a new spirit of cooperation to Antarctic affairs. The previous era had been marked by increasing competition, with conflicting claims giving rise to international tensions and attempts to consolidate sovereignty being matched by equally vigorous attempts to rebut and deny those claims on the part of non-claimants. However, the IGY programme brought a breathing space through an understanding that activities during this period would be purely scientific, without implications for claims of sovereignty. Increasingly, it became clear that a long-term solution was required, one which should include among its principal aims the continuation of scientific cooperation among states and the protection of the environment by some formal arrangement which would regulate the activities of states in Antarctica and prevent activities which might jeopardise the environment. Such a framework was achieved on 1 December 1959, with the signing of the Antarctic Treaty.

3. THE ANTARCTIC TREATY

Briefly, the Antarctic Treaty provides for Antarctica to be used only for peaceful purposes, principally scientific research. Conservation of the living reources of the land is provided for under the Treaty by "Agreed measures for the Conservation of Antarctic Fauna and Flora." Monitoring of the state of conservation and scientific advice on conservation are provided by the Scientific Committee of Antarctic Research (SCAR) of the International Council of Scientific Unions; the Committee was established in 1958 to coordinate research in Antarctica.

Twelve nations participated in the conference which produced the treaty—which entered into force on 23 June 1961—and all of them had established a close interest in Antarctica either through exploration, the conduct of scientific research, or their proximity to the continent. The 12 countries—the seven claimants plus Belgium, Japan, South Africa, the USA and the USSR—are the signatory powers. Poland (in 1977) and the Federal Republic of Germany (in 1981) have since been added to the list of Consultative Parties with full voting rights to amend the treaty. All states may accede to the Treaty; acceding parties cannot vote but agree to abide by the Treaty's provisions and such agreed measures as the Consultative Parties develop for protection of the environment. Brazil, Bulgaria, Czechoslovakia, Denmark, the German Democratic Republic, Italy, the Netherlands, Papua New Guinea, Peru, Romania, Spain and Uruguay have acceded to the Treaty.

The Treaty provides for the use of Antarctica for peaceful purposes only: freedom of scientific investigation and exchanges of scientific information and personnel. It has no expiration date and remains in force indefinitely, but provision was made for a review of its operation 30 years after it entered into force, at the request of any of the Consultative Parties. The Consultative Parties also meet every two years to review scientific research, discuss matters of common interest and formulate measures and recommendations to further the principles and objectives of the Treaty.

The Treaty provides for specific measures to regulate the impact of human intervention on Antarctica and for the preservation and conservation of its living resources. For example, it prohibits military bases, nuclear explosions or the disposal of radioactive wastes in Antarctic, making it the most comprehensive disarmament programme in the world, and the only one which specifically provides for on-site inspection.

The treaty also seeks to promote scientific research through international cooperation. Research data is exchanged after tabulation, analysis and publication, and research projects in the fields of biology, earth sciences, glaciology, atmospheric sciences, ocean studies and biomedicine have been conducted or are under way.

4. CONSERVATION UNDER THE ANTARCTIC TREATY

In 1964, some of the Consultative Parties concluded an agreement for the conservation of Antarctic flora and fauna through "interim measures," pending approval by all the Consultative Parties. The measures provide that:

a) the killing, wounding, capturing and molesting of any native mammal or bird is prohibited, except with a permit;
b) the parties agree to minimize harmful interference to habitat, and alleviate the pollution of coastal waters;
c) Specially Protected Areas may be designated for sites of outstanding scientific interest; and
d) the introduction of non-indigenous species is prohibited, except by permit.

The interim measures have since been supplemented by the designation of Specially Protected Areas, Sites of Special Scientific Interest and Marine Sites of Special Scientific Interest. Over twenty sites have been so designated by mutual agreement and information on them is held in the IUCN Protected Areas Data Unit (PADU).

The Consultative Parties have also made recommendations which are of major importance for general environmental protection. Among them:

• In 1970 it was recommended that SCAR be invited to identify the extent of human interference in the area and propose measures to minimize harmful effects of man's activities. Guidelines produced by SCAR have been adopted by the Consultative Parties;
• The Consultative Parties have adopted a number of recommendations directed at ensuring that tourism does not prejudice the conduct of scientific research, the conservation of fauna and flora and the operation of Antarctic Stations;
• In 1977, the Consultative Parties adopted a special resolution which recognized their prime responsibility for the protection of the Antarctic environment from all forms of harmful human interference, agreed to give due consideration to environmental impacts in planning future activities, agreed to refrain from activities that have an inherent tendency to modify the Antarctic envi-

ronment (unless appropriate steps are taken to foresee the probable modifications and to exercise appropriate controls on harmful effects), and agreed to continue monitoring the Antarctic environment and to inform the world community of any significant changes caused by man's activities.

In addition, the Consultative Parties negotiated a Convention on the Conservation of Antarctic Seals, which came into force in 1978. It prohibits the taking of Ross, Southern Elephant and Southern Fur seals, sets quotas for Crabeater, Leopard and Weddell seals, and provides for the establishment of an inspection system should commercial sealing begin.

According to an IUCN information package prepared in 1981, these "impressive achievements have been recognized by the international conservation community," and it has generally been acknowledged that the Treaty has "served well to maintain the relatively undisturbed nature of the Antarctic and Southern Ocean ecosystems," which it covers. The Consultative Parties have been praised for their conservation initiatives under the Treaty and related actions.

But the IUCN package went on to say that in recent years several concerns for the future of the conservation of the area had arisen. These were classified into three groups:

- the issue of resources exploitation in the area;
- the issue of the confidential nature of the decision-making process for the area;
- and the issue of the involvement of the international community in the decision-making process and in the benefits which might be derived from resources exploitation in the area.

5. RESOURCES EXPLOITATION

The IUCN document recognizes a number of flaws in the existing treaty arrangements. From the outset, the 14 Consultative Parties met in private and made decisions in private. One consequence is a proposal from Third World nations, to have administration of Antarctica taken over by some more representative body, like the UN. Suggestions include provisions for wider sharing of the economic benefits expected to flow from the commercial exploitation of Antarctic's resources.

Those resources are believed to have considerable potential; there is impressive circumstantial evidence for the presence of oil fields in the region, as well as evidence of mineral deposits. However, fish stocks, and particularly krill, are probably the most readily-exploited resources. The 1977 catch of Antarctic fin fish was 279,239 metric tons, and the catch of krill was about 123,000 metric tons. Since krill are an important link in the Antarctic food chain—they provide the principal food for five species of whales, three species of seals, three species of squid, about 20 species of fish, and numerous

species of birds—and since this is a new fishery which is only beginning to be exploited, conservationists are concerned. Krill are found only south of the Antarctic convergence, and their habit of swarming—one expedition reported netting krill at the rate of 40 metric tons per hour—makes them particularly vulnerable to overfishing. At the same time a number of countries have been excluded from traditional fishing grounds by the spread of 200 mile Exclusive Economic Zones (EEZs). Krill has a sizeable potential—the sustainable catch is variously estimated at 1 to 150 million metric tons per year (even the lower figure would make krill one of the 10 largest fisheries in the world)—and is increasingly seen as an attractive alternative to traditional fisheries.

As early as 1977, the development of commercial fishing interests in the waters surrounding Antarctica prompted measures for the establishment of a sound conservation system to prevent over-fishing and protect the integrity of the Antarctic ecosystem. After several years of effort, the Consultative Parties, the Federal Republic of Germany, and the German Democratic Republic adopted a Convention on the Conservation of Antarctic Marine Living Resources in May 1980.

The Convention is considered a landmark in international conservation law in taking an ecosystem approach. It covers all species of living organisms of the treaty area, and requires that harvesting or related activities prevent the population of harvested species from falling below the levels necessary for recruitment, maintain the ecological relationship between harvested, dependent and related populations; restore depleted populations; and prevent or minimize the risk of non-reversible changes in the marine ecosystems.

5.1. Mineral resources

In 1972, drilling in the Ross Sea Continental Shelf provided the first evidence of hydrocarbons in Antarctica, thus opening up the possibility of large-scale exploration leading to extraction of minerals not only from the continent but also from the ocean floor. In response to these developments, in 1975 the Consultative Parties to the Antarctic Treaty recommended that their Governments study the environmental implications of mineral resources activities in the Antarctic Treaty Area, and that SCAR be invited to make an assessment of possible environmental effects if exploration and exploitation were to occur.

At the same time, the Consultative Parties decided to refrain from any activities of exploration and exploitation. This voluntary restraint has been confirmed at subsequent meetings of the Consultative Parties, while the possibility of developing guidelines for mineral exploration was being discussed; it has been agreed that these guidelines should include methods of assessing the possible impact of mineral resource activities on the Antarctic environment; of determining whether mineral resources activities will be acceptable; and of establishing rules relating to the protection of the Antarctic environment. A meeting to negotiate such guidelines was convened by the New Zealand Government in Wellington in June 1982.

6. OTHER ISSUES

The Consultative Parties' practice of making decisions in private has given rise to criticism, and the IUCN and other groups, have requested greater opportunities to participate in meetings under the Treaty and its conventions. Some participation does exist. For example, IUCN was invited to participate in a meeting under the Convention on the Conservation of Antarctic Marine Living Resources, following a resolution on the Antarctic Environment and the Southern Oceans adopted by the IUCN 15th General Assembly in 1981. Subsequent to that, IUCN was invited to participate in a meeting under the Convention on the Conservation of Antarctic Marine Living Resources.

7. WAYS AND MEANS

In the search for ways and means of conserving Antarctica, a predominant factor must be the realities of international politics for, by agreement, those nations with claims in Antarctica and others which have declined to make or recognize claims have since 1961 accepted the freezing of their interests under a regime with a strong conservation emphasis.

Whatever may be said in criticism of the manner in which the Consultative Parties have taken decisions, there is no doubt that the Treaty has been effective in conserving the Antarctic environment to date, and has proved sensitive and responsive to potentially harmful developments. This is evident in measures to safeguard the environment from disturbance caused by scientific study itself, by the impact of tourism, and by the potentially adverse effects of commerial use of Antarctic seals and other marine living resources. Initiatives have also been taken to begin protecting the environment from the possible impacts of mineral exploration and extraction.

The existence of controls on the natural resources of Antarctica, with the agreement of the states active in scientific research there, probably provides as sound a base for conservation as can be realistically expected. Twenty-six states have acceded to the Treaty and are thus committed to its measures, and this reinforces the value of the Treaty as a conservation mechanism.

The world park concept for Antarctica, raised at the Second World Conference on National Parks without any in-depth discussion or investigation and not taken up by the Consultative Parties, was discussed at meetings associated with the 15th General Assembly of IUCN in 1981. As a concept it did not survive the careful consideration of options which led to the resolution

adopted by the General Assembly. However, the resolution did recommend that the Antarctic Treaty Consultative Parties should "ascribe to the Antarctica environment as a whole a designation which connotes worldwide its unique character and values. . ." An appropriate designation would certainly help focus public interest and concern, but more important than any designation is a sensitive and responsive set of agreed measures to ensure the Antarctic environment is safeguarded from the adverse effects of change. The consultative mechanism provides for arrangements to be reviewed each 2 years and for consequential adjustments to be made as the need arises.

With increasing financial constraints, it is evident that international conservation bodies lack the resources—as well as the powers—to operate other than through such mechanisms as the Antarctic Treaty. What the conservation movement has as its most potent weapons are the commitment and knowledge of scientists, and the growing public concern for environmental conservation. Educational programmes can be prepared to inform and influence public opinion which, in turn, is capable of influencing those governments with direct involvement in Antarctica, and encouraging others to accede to the Treaty. Such a growth in public consultation can only lead to a more open approach by the Consultative Parties, while public pressure could lead to further scientific studies and the identification of a representative range of Antarctic ecosystems and rare and endangered species.

The need in Antarctica is for a dynamic system of management capable of adjusting and adapting to new technology and new pressures. The present Specially Protected Areas are generally very small and essentially designed to protect habitats against disturbance and modification by scientific studies. This may be adequate while Antarctica remains predominantly unmodified but would be quite inadequate to cope with such developments as the extraction of minerals, for example. In such a situation, it would be essential that a fully representative system of protected areas be identified and given appropriate status. Such an approach would be in the interests of conserving the Antarctic environment and in preserving the continent's wilderness quality, not only for the few who may be able to experience it but also for those who enjoy it vicariously through books and films, or who are satisfied simply by knowing that the Antarctic wilderness exists.

A basic need would be to ensure that, after the identification of a broad spectrum of representative protected areas, there would still be adequate controls for conservation of the balance of Antarctica. Given this, a greatly expanded representative system of protected areas—both terrestrial and marine—could be the subject of new measures under the Treaty or even of a new convention giving them recognition analogous to that of World Heritage Sites.

8. CONCLUSION

Antarctica is the most remote and inhospitable of the earth's continents, and the history of human habitation there is a very short one. Man's main activities in Antarctica to date have been those of exploration and scientific research. The Antarctic Treaty of 1959, which was founded on the principle of conservation of the fragile Antarctic environment, has laid a firm basis for the regulation of human activity on the continent. The Treaty has proved to be an outstanding success. Its disarmament provisions are the world's most comprehensive, and the only ones specifically providing for on-site inspection. A remarkable degree of international cooperation in scientific research has been achieved for over 20 years, and the Treaty has also provided an umbrella for wide-ranging measures to protect and conserve the unique ecology of Antarctica. Virtually every form of impact by man on Antarctica, including tourism, has been regulated by the Treaty Parties, who meet regularly to renew existing measures and to ensure through new measures that the aims of the Treaty are maintained.

The Antarctic Treaty states are currently elaborating a programme to govern any eventual exploration and exploitation of the mineral resources of Antarctica, and in particular to protect the environment from man's potentially damaging activities. Clearly, the Antarctic Treaty offers the most practical mechanism for effective conservation of Antarctica and the Southern Ocean. Nevertheless, there is a need for more scientific research and all states must be urged to enhance the effectiveness of the Treaty.

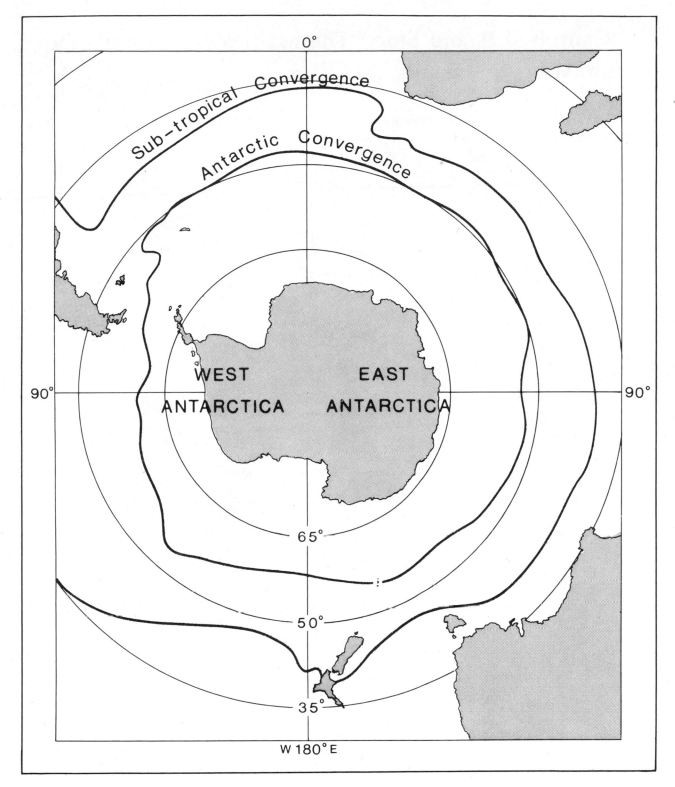

Figure 1. The Antarctic continent.

The Campbell Island Story: The Management Challenge of Sub-Antarctic Islands

N.D.R. McKerchar and W.T. Devine
National Parks and Reserves Directorate
Wellington, New Zealand .

ABSTRACT. *Campbell Island illustrates that distance, climate and isolation have not been sufficient barriers to man and his accompanying animal and plant invaders and that island flora and fauna are vulnerable, although sometimes quite resilient after human settlement ceases. The Nature Reserve has a national administrative structure which guarantees the best scientific advice and management coordination. While resources for surveillance are generally limited for related New Zealand reserves in the Sub-Antarctic, there is a permanently manned Meteorological Station on Campbell. This is critically important for management, as activity in fishing and oil exploration increases in the surrounding seas.*

1. INTRODUCTION

1.1 The sub-Antarctic Islands

There are 16 island groups in the sub-Antarctic Zone of the Southern Ocean (see Fig. 1) and 6 of these form part of New Zealand (NZ). The latter are all on a submerged plateau connecting them geologically with the mainland. The NZ sub-Antarctic islands lie to the east and south of the mainland, from the Chatham Islands on the boundary of the sub-tropical convergence at 44°30'S to Campbell Island at 52°33'S. The Chathams are the only group which are at present settled and farmed. The remaining five groups are nature reserves administered by the New Zealand Department of Lands and Survey (L & S).

Of the remaining 10 island groups in this zone administered by other countries, 4 are listed in the 1980 United Nations List of National Parks and Equivalent Reserves: Macquarie (Australia), Iles Kerguelen and Iles Crozet (France) and Prince Edward (S. Africa).

1.2 Campbell Island

While the Campbell Island group is classed as sub-Antarctic, the group has certain features which appear to be due to the influence of the East Australian Current (notonectian). Lying at longitude 169°08'E, due south of the NZ mainland, it is made up of one large island (Campbell) and several offshore islets and stacks. Campbell Island has an area of 11,268 ha and its largest offshore island is Jacquemart at about 40 ha.

Seen in outline from the sea, Campbell Island is generally rugged with a number of scattered peaks of over 450 m. The highest, Mt. Honey (569m), and three others on the south coast are already eroded back by sea and weather to the vertical plains of the peaks themselves. This high block is almost separated from the more uniformly elevated northern block by Perseverance Harbour, penetrating the east coast to a distance of 8 km. The resistant southwest block is almost unique in sub-Antarctic island structure. The coasts on the south and west now strike across what must have been the heart of the island (Fig. 2).

The islands are the remnant of a dissected volcanic dome and nearly two-thirds of the main island is covered by volcanic flows. The island was subjected to the action of ice during the Pleistocene but there are different opinions on the origins of the glacial landforms. There is a pronounced topographic influence on soil development; deep peat occupies flat and gently sloping areas, but on steeper surfaces is generally less than 2m thick. Erosion is widespread and conspicuous as a result of the mass movement of peat, especially over impervious bedding planes in the sedimentary rocks. Wind erosion is also very significant at higher altitudes and appears to be accelerated by sheep grazing.

The anticyclonic weather of the Campbells is characterised by overcast skies and drizzle. The annual rainfall is about 1450mm, but the occasional passage of a deep depression over the islands produces heavy rain, and falls of more than 250mm in a day have been recorded. Westerly wind is the dominant climatic element. The mean annual temperature is approximately 6°C.

The plant life and terrestrial animals are in the main similar to those of apparently newer islands and are in fact less rich in variety and degree of endemism than are those of the Auckland Islands, to which most of them are closely related. Both the higher latitude and position further east place the Campbells in a colder belt and impose restriction on the development of a flora and fauna that appear to have been derived mainly from the north through the Auckland Islands. There is no tree forest, but in scattered localities a dense scrub of grass trees (*Dracophyllum scoparium* and *D. longifolia* with *Coprosma ciliata*, *C. cunceata*, *C. pumila* and *Myrsine divaricata*). The greater part of the island is covered with tussock and a variety of herbaceous plants. Apart from fine taxonomic distinctions that can be made in some groups, there is nothing strikingly distinctive about the terrestrial fauna. There is however a considerable annual breeding influx mammals and marine birds; the group is the main breeding ground of Southern Royal Albatross.

2. HISTORICAL BACKGROUND

2.1 Human occupation

The human history of the Campbell Island began with the whalers and sealers when it was discovered in 1810 by F. Hassleborough in the brig *Perseverance* owned by Campbell and Co., of Sydney. His initial haul of 15,000 fur seal skins brought many more sealers, until, eventually, the yield fell away to an unprofitable level.

At about the time of the final decline of the animal oil industry, the NZ Government offered pastoral leases over both Auckland and Campbell Island, and the latter became a sheep station in 1896 until it was abandoned in 1931. Limited licences for fur seals were also offered and whaling was revived in 1910 from shore stations. A coast-watching station was set up and occupied in July 1941 and a manned meterological station has since been maintained. The research programme has covered meterology, ionospheric recording and biology.

2.2 Scientific expeditions

In 1840 the Ross Expedition from England carried out the first surveys and scientific work on the Islands. A second expedition was sponsored by the government of France in 1873 to observe the transit of Venus. Many place names derive from this visit (Fig. 2). In the postwar years three scientific expeditions were made by

physicists and biologists, including a visit by the Danish research vessel *Galathea* in 1951. There have been numerous scientific visitors to the Islands from NZ more recently, with the last major expedition in 1975/76.

2.3 Declaration as protected area

After the pastoral leases expired, Campbell Island was held as unoccupied Crown land (IUCN Category VI) by L & S and not put to any use until the coast-watching station was established. However, in 1954, in recognition of its natural values (see section 3) the Campbell Island group was made a reserve for the preservation of flora and fauna.

Under current NZ legislation the group falls into the Nature Reserve classification and meets the criterion of IUCN Category I (Scientific Reserves/Strict Nature Reserves). The purpose of the reservation, specifically, is defined in the Reserves Act 1977 as ". . . protecting and preserving in perpetuity indigenous flora and fauna or natural features that are of such rarity, scientific interest of importance or so unique that their protection and preservation are in the public interest".

2.4 Introduction of animals

Sheep, goats and pigs had been liberated at various times prior to attempted settlement of the main island. They were intended to provide sustenance to the shipwrecked but none of these animals survived for very long. Norway rats *Rattus norvegicus* were reported as well established on the main islands as early as 1874 and are still abundant. Feral cats are also present but scarce.

Large-scale modification of the vegetation was precipitated by the introduction of sheep (Merino breeds for the most part) and cattle in 1895. Sheep numbers peaked in 1910 at a population of about 8,500. When farming was abandoned, 4,000 sheep and 20-30 cattle were left behind and their offspring became feral (see section 3.1 for current situation).

3. RESOURCE EVALUATION

3.1 Ecological importance

Atkinson and Bell (1974) had this to say of New Zealand's sub-Antarctic islands: "Each of these islands is unique in terms of the plant-and-animal system it supports. Together they are an integral part of the sub-Antarctic ecosystem; for these specks of land in a vast stretch of highly productive ocean are the only possible breeding grounds for huge numbers of sea birds and many seals." These sea birds and seals are mostly top carnivores in food relationships and thus play a key role in the ecology of the southern oceans.

The Campbell Island group has many endemic species and subspecies with invertebrates and especially arthropods figuring significantly. Many of the other organisms are found only on one or more of the other five New Zealand sub-Antarctic island groups. The merits of preserving all remaining species, forms and rare genetic material cannot be questioned. That some of these species, including the Campbell Island teal, the probable subspecies of pipit and some invertebrates, have either been wiped out on the main island or are threatened is a matter of great concern.

There are several interesting plant communities, both natural and induced. These include the contrasting vegetation patterns on either side of the stock fence (see section 4); the tussock/cushion "lane" which Meurk (1980) attributed to persistent high water tables; and several biotic plant associations at seabird nesting colonies and sea mammal resting and breeding grounds.

No alien plant species which have established in the Reserve have become noxious (in the sense of threatening the niche of an indigenous one). Meurk (1977) suggested that if grazing animals are totally removed, artifically disturbed communities would slowly develop into new climax associations in which a group of less than 24 proven alien species will become integrated while the remaining 60 or so introduced species will form transient or persistent populations around human habitation.

"Certainly Campbell Island could be considered one of the finest of all albatross islands, for five species occur there during the breeding season, and few, if any, other islands of the world have so many" (Bailey and Sorenson, 1962). It is also notable as the stronghold of the rockhopper penguin.

3.2 Offshore islets

The inaccessible and almost completely unmodified offshore islets have special importance as habitat of wildlife formerly common on the main island but now absent there or present only in reduced numbers. These wildlife refuges will serve as pools for recolonization of the main island in the future. One near-shore islet has a Norway rat population, however, illustrating the continuing risk of rodent spread.

3.3 Scientific values

The reserve, especially the offshore islets, affords an opportunity to study areas which are relatively unmodified and which have high intrinsic values because of the endemic species and the unique communities which occur. The biota of these islands is a statement of the history of dispersal, climatic events and community interactions that have occurred to date. As such, they are of great interest to ecologists and biogeographers.

An understanding of island ecosystems such as those of Campbell may greatly assist general environmental management in the future. Natural biological systems on mainland areas are becoming more and more insular in character as they are fragmented by land development. As the vegetation patterns of the main island have been modified over the last few decades by burning and grazing, an opportunity now exists to study their recovery after release from grazing pressures.

3.4 Meteorological values

Because of its location in the Southern Ocean, the meteorological station on Campbell Island is an invaluable component of the New Zealand and the global weather reporting network.

3.5 Educational values

The existence of comparatively unmodified ecological systems is a valuable teaching tool for imparting an understanding of the natural constraints within which mankind must live. The use of popular science publications, movies and TV can take the otherwise largely inaccessible Campbell Islands to the people of New Zealand and overseas.

3.6 Scenic and recreational values

The coastal cliffs, peninsulas, islets and offshore stacks are the most spectacular scenic aspect of Campbell Island and these can best be viewed from the sea. The main attractions are the wildlife and plants of the islands which are of special interest to the naturalist. The cost and limited availability of transport to the islands is a deterrent to most would-be tourists (but see section 4.5).

3.7 Historic values

The Campbell historic sites reflect a range of human activities over a time span of at least 150 years, on a compact land area. Such a site assemblage, in a generally unmodified state, is rare on the New Zealand mainland and is considered to be of national importance (Palmer and Judd, 1981).

3.8 Economic values

Although the Campbell island group has little commercial value, that of the nearby seas and seabed is considerable. Unfortunately, the exploitation of some of these resources could greatly affect the islands' wildlife and ecological systems if there are not sufficient restraints. Competition with man for fish, squid and krill could seriously diminish bird and seal populations. On the other hand, the continuing decrease of commercially-exploited whale populations may cause a decreased natural competition for food with some bird populations.

Intensified use of the surrounding area would magnify the risks associated with entry to the Reserve. The danger of oil spills from ship refuelling operations and shipwrecks would also be greater. Oil exploration and exploitation, should oil be found, would be an even greater threat because of the extremely rigorous climate.

4. CURRENT SITUATION

4.1 Feral sheep and cattle management

The noted botanist and plant geographer Dr. (later Sir) Leonard Cockayne (1855-1934) visited Campbell Island about seven years after the establishment of domestic sheep flocks at a time when their numbers stood at about 4,500. It was his opinion that there had been in the history of botanical science no better opportunity for investigating the effect of man with his introduced animals, fire and plants, upon a described purely virgin vegetation. Studies of these induced changes have continued since then and other botanists have improved knowledge of the composition and general condition of the flora.

By 1941 the sheep numbers had declined to 2,000 and fell again by half during the intervening period to 1962, with no sign of any change to the general trend. In the same period, the feral cattle herd generally remained static at about 15-20 beasts.

In 1969, when counted again, the sheep population was found to have increased to 3,000. This again raised concern over their presence in a reserve dedicated to the preservation of indigenous flora and fauna, although at that time there was no law requiring that they be removed. The strategy of taking sheep off half the island at a time was decided on to help determine how best to manage the reserve's vegetation and wildlife and to lessen the risk of creating new and unexpected conservation problems (for example, it was thought that the grazed vegetation might favour albatross nesting). A post and wire fence was erected across the "waist" of the island in 1970 and the sheep on the northern half were shot. (The range of the cattle is naturally restricted to the southern end of the island.)

A monitoring programme was set up and research into the biology, population ecology and agricultural value of the sheep and cattle was intensified. However, because of a number of factors but mainly the isolation of the reserve, it has not been possible to coordinate research tightly, and study objectives have not therefore been fully satisfied (see section 5.3). Apart from containment, and the taking of an occasional animal by meteorological staff for food and by scientists for necropsy, the sheep and cattle left on the Island have not been managed.

4.2 Management of flora

The known vascular flora of Campbell Island now stands at 218 species, subspecies and hybrids. Of these 81 are adventives. Mosses comprise 119 species, 3 varieties and 1 form. Over half were only reported as recently as 1974. There are several interesting plant communities, both natural and induced. These include the contrasting vegetation patterns on either side of the fence (section 4.1), the tussock/cushion "lane" associations, and several biotic plant associatons at seabird nesting colonies and sea mammal resting and breeding grounds.

Many indigenous plants on Campbell Island are "rare" by IUCN definition (on an international scale) but only two species have a restricted distribution on the island. The most localized plants are those which are at the limits of their geographic range or are relatively recent arrivals. There are no endemic vascular plants.

Many indigenous plant species are depleted on the main island because of past human occupation. One goal of erecting the fence was immediately to remove any possible threat by sheep which might lead to local plant extinctons. There has been remarkable regeneration of the unique megaherbfield associations in some parts of the reserve north of the fence since sheep were removed, indicating the effect sheep in particular have had on the vegetation in the past.

Apart from exclusion of the sheep from the northern side of the main island no management or manipulation of the vegetation is undertaken. Potentially aggressive species such as broom *Sarothamnus scoparius* and gorse *Ulex europaeus* are monitored. As many past changes are considered irreversible, the emphasis of management is on exclusion of fire and on preventing new plant introductions.

4.3 Management of introduced predators

Cats are only one of the factors involved in the depletion of bird and insect populations on the main island but their removal might allow the rehabilitation of some bird species. These feral predators are scarce in number and their extermination is the long-term aim. Meteorological station staff are allowed to kill them on sight.

The Meteorological Station staff lay rodenticides around buildings but there is no wider attempt at control of Norway rats for conservation reasons. It is recognized that these rodents pose the greatest existing threat to the island ecosystem and that extermination would be desirable. However, this is impracticable, in the state of present knowledge, using acceptable techniques. The Norway rat is not significantly controlled by the cats.

The prevention of other rodent introductions of their transfer to offshore islands is emphasized. The ship rat *Rattus rattus* is considered the greatest potential threat. Should such an introduction be detected an intensive localized extermination campaign would be undertaken in the hope of preventing this species becoming naturalized.

4.4 Management of indigenous birds and marine mammals

There are no endangered vertebrate species in the reserve and the threatened subspecies are still represented in the offshore island fauna. The emphasis of management is therefore on protection of natural life support systems in the expectation that the animals will then be quite capable of maintaining their own populations (conflicts with other interests are dealt with in sections 4.5 and 5). At the same time, with the restoration programme underway changes in the environment of the main island and its effect on wildlife must be anticipated.

The protection of some indigenous species (including large invertebrates) is not possible in the main island bcause of feral predators. However, the offshore islands afford sanctuaries for them, albeit in lower numbers. With this limitation, the aim is to seek natural distributions, numbers and interactions of indigenous species.

While sea birds and mammal species found on the islands are also protected under New Zealand law in the territorial sea, the marine habitat is not managed in their interests and, beyond the reserve's foreshore, they are outside the jurisdiction of L & S.

4.5 Management of visitors

The aim is to see the least possible degradation of the qualities of the reserve and to ensure that wildlife behaviour is altered as little as possible by human influences. In achieving this aim the presence of a meteorological station has both advantages and disadvantages. It provides a means of law enforcement, a base for scientific studies and some assistance with monitoring programmes. There are, however, problems associated even with such limited human habitation in a nature reserve. These are not only from the direct impact of station staff (about 10 persons) and their servicing, but the indirect effects of the base attracting other visitors (especially ships on the way to and from the Antarctic). Unauthorized landings, however, are probably deterred, reducing the risk of *Rattus rattus* introduction. On balance, the station is accepted as being compatible with the preservation of the island's flora and fauna. In any case, meteorological use pre-dated reservation.

The station is administered and manned by a different government agency from L & S but mechanisms for coordination and consultation have been set up and there is a great degree of cooperation. Staff maintain the station to a high standard and in general sympathize with nature conservation.

Apart from invitees to the station, entry to the reserve is by permit granted by L & S. Strict rules govern scientific research and access is mainly limited to scientists and reserve managers. The offshore islets are visited only in special circumstances. General tourism is not permitted. Day visits on a limited basis are allowed to the main island by especially supervised international cruising expeditions. Lindblad Travel Ltd. has been the principal recipient of permits to date. No commercial tourist interest has arisen from New Zealand. The degree of latent demand has not, however, been tested.

5. CURRENT ISSUES AND FUTURE INTENTIONS

5.1 Planning

A management plan for the reserve is being finalized by L & S. Preparation follows a statutory process involving public participation. The main interest, however, has been institutional. Apart from public notification nationally in newspapers, no special arrangements were made for general public consultation.

5.2 Economic resources

Early in the nineteenth century, seals were slaughtered for their fur and oil but these animals are now fully protected by law. There is no current conflict of interest.

The islands were leased for pastoral farming from 1895-1937 but their isolation from markets and inhospitable nature led to the abandonment of farming in 1931. A renewed interest is unlikely.

The surrounding sea has a number of economic resources and conservation conflicts will arise:

(a) Wet Fish. At present few New Zealand fishing boats venture this far out, but the area is frequented by Russian, Korean and Japanese fishermen. An increase in fishing activity in the area can be expected since the introduction of New Zealand's 200 mile exclusive economic zone (EEZ).
(b) Whales. Between June and October southern right whales congregate around the Campbell Islands.
(c) Krill. There is a growing interest in harvesting this resource.
(d) Squid. Already being harvested by foreign and joint venture boats.
(e) Petroleum. Prospecting licences are held over approximately 557,000 sq km of marine shelf

and islands south of New Zealand. Should prospecting begin, there is likely to be strong pressure for the provision of shore facilities for these operations.

There are no known mineral resources of interest around Campbell Island. Manganese nodules are restricted in distribution and grade and are not of commercial interest.

The grant of fishing licences within the EEZ by the New Zealand Ministry of Agriculture and Fisheries (MAF) is subject to Government environmental protection and enhancement policies. Because of deficient knowledge and scant public interest (perhaps through the information gap) the welfare of island wildlife is not a paramount consideration and L & S has no direct jurisdiction.

The New Zealand region has the greatest diversity of seabirds on earth, with over one-third of all varieties occurring there as breeders or visitors. The sub-Antarctic islands form the major remaining reservoirs of many of these species. L & S and the New Zealand Wildlife Service recognize that these seabirds are vulnerable to any threat which affects their food supply because of their extreme specialization.

While not of direct concern to Campbell Island management as a nature reserve, the sheltered waters of its bays, inlets and harbours are important to right whales which habitually bear their calves and suckle them there. Concern over their food supply and disturbance is also therefore adopted by reserve managers. A strategy for dealing with these food resource issues is currently being considered as part of a wider New Zealand Conservation Strategy. IUCN has urged the Government of New Zealand to make available the funds needed for research and management to conserve the endemic animal and plant communities of its offshore and outlying islands (Resolution 15/28 of the 15th Session of the IUCN General Assembly, Christchurch).

Procedures for dealing with shore-based communication facilities for oil exploration are set out in the draft policy statement attached as Appendix 1. New Zealand lacks experience in dealing with the wider conservation implications of marine oil exploration but overseas experience is being studied.

5.3 Research

Permanent photo-points have been established on both sides of the fence to compare long-term changes in the vegetation with and without sheep. There is a photographic record of several thousand exposures. It was started in 1970 and has been repeated and expanded in 1971/72, 1975/76, 1976/77, 1977/78 and 1979/80. This record, along with botanical descriptions and maps of vegetation quadrats, has documented dramatic changes in the vegetation where the grazing pressure has been removed to the north of the fence. However, it is still

too early to anticipate with confidence the final repercussions of complete sheep removal.

The plant communities of Campbell Island have been mapped and studied, and a project on the primary production of the vegetation is underway. Some geological and soil investigations have been carried out and there has been a reconnaissance survey of soil erosion on the island.

Several studies on the birdlife have been completed or are underway, with particular emphasis on numbers and distribution. The breeding royal albatross population has been mapped and counted on seven occasions since 1968. It has remained much the same on both sides of the fence and is increasing.

Invertebrates have been collected and more detailed studies made on several groups. The food habits of Norway rats and feral cats have been the subjects of preliminary investigation. The sheep population has been counted and its distribution mapped on eight occasions since 1960, and a study has been made of the feral cattle and what limits their range. Substantial progress was made during the 1975/76 expedition with studies of the biology, ecology and agricultural value of the feral sheep and cattle. A small flock of sheep was collected from Campbell Island for the Ruakura Agricultural Research Centre by the 1975/76 expedition and these animals are now proving useful for genetic and other scientific studies away from the island. However, there still appears to be a need for more agriculturally orientated research on the island in such fields as sheep behaviour.

The research needs of management will be reviewed in the near future. Implementation is severely constrained by the highly competitive situation with funding and by other man-power priorities.

5.4 The future of the feral sheep and cattle

Publication of the draft management plan revealed a dichotomy of scientific-conservation opinion on this matter. By statue now applying to nature reserves ". . . the indigenous flora and fauna, ecological associations and natural environment shall as far as possible be preserved and the exotic flora and fauna as far as possible be exterminated." However, as well as ministerial discretion, there is an obligation for scientific features to be ". . . managed and protected to the extent compatible with the principal or primary purpose of the reserve." Opinion is at present being evaluated against these legal principles and possible policy options. A course of action is expected to be decided on before the end of 1982.

5.5 Administration and public involvement

L & S convenes an advisory and coordinating committee of 11 state employees representing a range of disciplines and Government agencies with an interest in the planning and management of the sub-Antarctic islands. To ensure a free exchange of official information and frank expression of views the Committee meets in private and its constitution is limited to state employees. The Committee is responsible to the Director-General of Lands (permanent head of L & S) and was formed in 1967. Its terms of reference have been reviewed from time to time, mostly recently in 1981.

While the Committee advises the department on day-to-day management and policy, the National Parks and Reserve Authority, a public body set up under the National Parks Act 1980, has general oversight of administration and management of outlying island nature reserves among its responsibilities.

While the public is excluded from the direct decision making of the Committee (other than through the Authority), the Committee and L & S are legally bound to comply with the management plans for each of the outlying island reserves in the exercise of their functions. These plans have to be kept under continuous review and the Minister of Lands may from time to time require L&S, with the advice of the Committee, to revise any policy. The public therefore has an opportunity to ensure social values are reflected in administration and management.

6. CONCLUSION

The Campbell Island Nature Reserve has been used as a case study to illustrate state-of-the-art techniques for the management of New Zealand's protected natural areas in the Antarctic Realm. These techniques have been developed over a 30-year period. They reflect growing appreciation of the values of the reserve. At the same time, resource exploitation is closing in around these reserves and their vulnerability is a matter of increasing concern.

The paramount importance of Campbell Island and related Nature Reserves is that they include the best of the few remaining island groups in the world which have avoided the most destructive activities of man. Feral populations of sheep and cattle on the main island are being managed to determine their final disposition in the best interest of the Nature Reserve and (as a genetic resource) mankind generally. Norway rats and feral cats have eliminated breeding colonies of some bird species on the main island of the group but populations exist on the offshore islets. The indigenous flora also remains intact and dominant over exotic plant communities.

The role of reserves like Campbell Island is evolving at present to satisfy a growing public need for both vicarious and actual experience of wild and remote places with their unusual and often unique plants and animals. This must be kept within bounds and preservation must remain their major function or the world stands to lose the very attractions which people are seeking to enjoy. Apart from overseas cruising expeditions (Lindblad), there are at present few opportunities for people to visit the Nature Reserve other than for scientific studies which

have been promoted for management purposes. As a result, however, there is a lack of a supportive, knowledgeable lobby in New Zealand for proper conservation of Campbell Island and its related reserves.

Current threats to the protection of these reserves illustrate what has become a truism that no "island of nature" can survive untouched in a "sea of unrestricted development". The global society needs to evaluate whether it can afford not to have controls on the use of the ocean which are as comprehensive as those on land and as rigorously applied and policed. The future of the sub-Antarctic islands is bound up with marine conservation and with decisions to be made on exploitation of resources of the Southern Ocean and the Antarctic Continent.

The New Zealand Government accepts its international responsibility to preserve these islands containing as they do the breeding grounds of such large numbers of migratory birds and endemic plant and animal communities. While a fragile balance exists, New Zealand has so far succeeded in preserving it. However, a comparision with other current national efforts in the sub-Antarctic zone would be of value.

APPENDIX 1: CONTINGENCY POLICY: COMMUNICATION STATIONS IN OUTLYING ISLAND NATURE RESERVES

Background

The Ministry of Energy in June 1981 advertised internationally inviting applications for marine petroleum exploration areas on the continental shelf south and east of the South Island. The whole area is still in an early phase of exploration and there has been comparatively little activity to date and few wells have been drilled. (Hunt Petroleum, and Phillips and Petrocorp hold earlier exploration licences). Increased activity round the sub-Antarctic Islands is expected. Past experience has been as follows:

a) Hunt International Petroleum Company of NZ applied for permission to install a transmitter in the Snares in 1974 but did not proceed. In 1976 the Company renewed the application but then withdrew it.

b) In 1977 the Company proposed putting accommodation for drilling rig crews with helicopter or aircraft landing facilities on Campbell Island and a refuelling facility at the Auckland Islands (barge with helicopter pad) but later withdrew the application.

c) In May 1981 Phillips Petroleum Company Far East (Oklahoma, USA) acting on behalf of Hunt/Petrocorp/Phillips applied for approval to erect a telemetric station in the Auckland Islands to facilitate a highly accurate navigation system required for seismic surveys (HO file RES 1/5/4/4). As there was no authority, under the provisions of the Reserves Act 1977, to grant the permission sought (and to cover the broader matter of communication stations in reserves generally) Section 48A was written into the Act by an amendment in 1981 and provided for the grant of permits for such facilities. The application did not proceed as the Company decided the station was not essential until possibly when drilling started.

General Policy

Use of sub-Antarctic and Kermadec Islands Nature Reserves for Communication Stations.

1. To prohibit the use of the reserves as sites for radio, electric, or electronic communication stations unless it meets all the following criteria:
   a) The station cannot be readily provided in an environmentally less sensitive site on the mainland or (as a last resort) another Island, or installed on a moored vessel, (or if another alternative such as a seafloor transponder navigation system cannot be substituted);
   b) The station does not prevent the proper and beneficial management, administration and control of the reserve;
   c) The station does not threaten the survival of any species of indigenous flora or fauna;
   d) The station would not materially alter or permanently damage other features of the reserves.

2. To grant a permit under Section 48A of the Act allowing the use of a site/sites, if the above criteria are met, provided:
   a) No building, dwelling, mast, structure is to be erected, and no track or other work is to be constructed or undertaken and no plant or machinery is to be brought into the reserve which is not essential for the construction and operation of the station.
   b) No landing is to be made or entry to the reserve outside the station area allowed except in accordance with an authorization under Section 57 of the Act.
   c) The facility is to be removed and the site left in a clean and tidy condition on expiry of any associated right granted under any other Act (e.g. Petroleum Act 1974).
   d) The design, materials and siting of buildings and structures are to be in accordance with the specifications of the permit.

Implementation

A. Each application for a permit under Section 48A of the Act is to be accompanied by a written statement dealing with an assessment of the environmental impact (EIA) of the proposal by the applicant. This is to include:
   (i) Function of the station and importance to the applicant's operations;
   (ii) Parameters used in site selection with explanations where necessary;
   (iii) Other sites or alternatives considered and reasons rejected;
   (iv) Schedule of buildings and structure required and justification (function, size, materials, foundations etc.);
   (v) Schedule of other works including tracks and landing and mooring facilities and justification;
   (vi) Schedule of plant and machinery to be used during construction;
   (vii) Schedule of plant and machinery to be permanently installed/operated at the station and justification;
   (viii) Details of precautions to be taken against:
   • introduction of exotic flora and fauna
   • marine pollution
   • fire
   • litter
   (ix) Description of methods of intended waste and sewage disposal and assessment of environmental impacts;
   (x) Arrangements for manning during and after construction (numbers, frequency of changeover, type of vessel, use of helicopter etc.);
   (xi) Arrangement for servicing (type of vessel, frequency of landings, use of helicopter, nature of fuel supplies and any other dangerous goods);
   (xii) Other measures to be taken to minimize or avoid damage to the environment in the course construction or operation of the station.

B. On receipt of the EIA the Director-General will seek advice on the application from the Outlying Islands Reserves Committee (OIRC) and comment from the Commissioner for the Environment.

C. If the OIRC recommends the grant of a permit and the Commissioner for the Environment does not require an environmental impact report (EIR) the Director-General will publicly notify the proposal unless provision for the station has already been made in an approved management plan for the reserve.

D. The decision on the application will take into account the public interest as revealed by objections and submissions. If approved, the permit will be subject to stringent conditions ensuring the protection of reserve values and such other terms and conditions as the Minister of Lands determines.

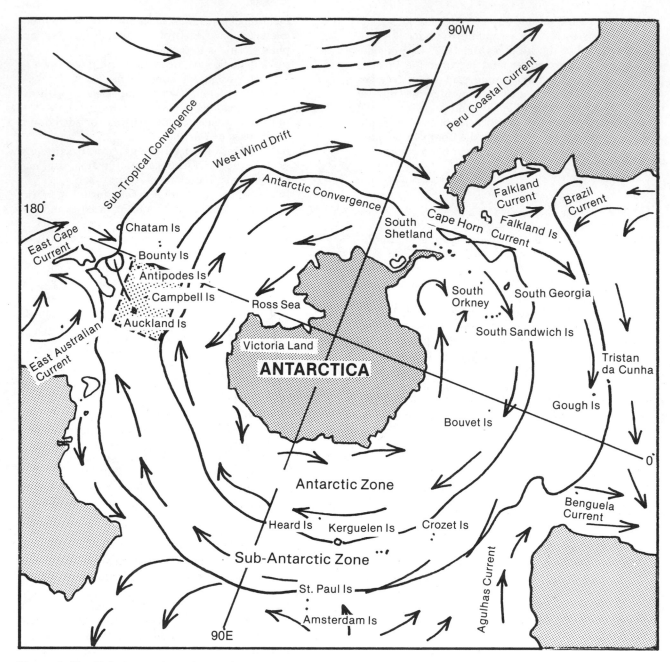

Figure 1. The Sub-Antarctic region and associated physical features of the Southern Ocean.

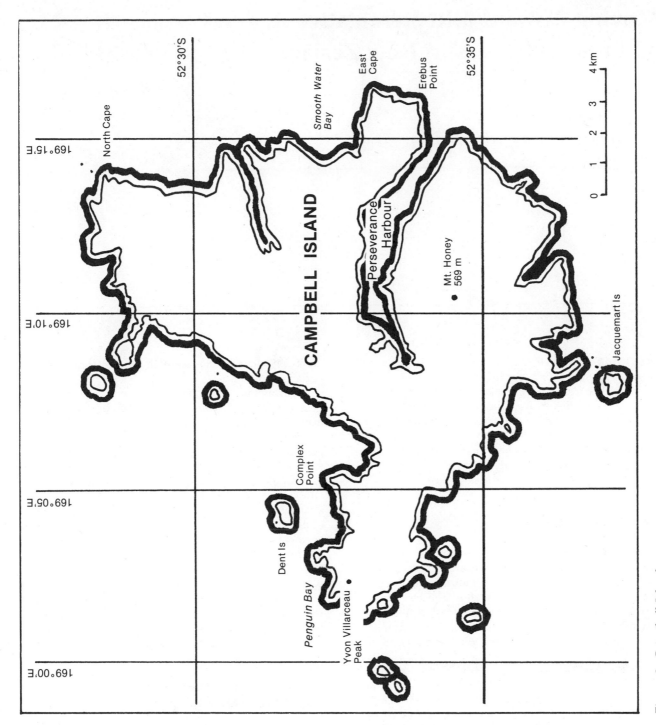

Figure 2. Campbell Island.

Moving Toward a Representative System of Protected Areas in New Zealand

P.R. Dingwall
Senior Scientist
Department of Lands and Survey
New Zealand

ABSTRACT. *Although New Zealand has more than 1500 protected areas, extending over 16% of the total land area and encompassing a wide range of management objectives, the system is biased ecologically toward upland forested terrain. Recent developments in legislation, policy making, administration and information gathering reveal a new commitment to extend the protected area network to lowland and non-forested environments, thereby protecting a fully representative range of the country's natural biota and landscapes.*

1. INTRODUCTION

New Zealand has a long record in the establishment and management of protected natural areas, dating from the earliest period of European colonization in the latter half of the 19th Century. The well-established practice of land protection has produced today a comprehensive network of parks and reserves extending over some 16% of the country's land area, both on the mainland and on surrounding islands.

This protected area system, replete with elaborate administrative, legislative and management structures, is an extremely diverse one which affords wide-ranging management opportunities and varying levels of protection and use of natural resources. Critical examination of the coverage of the protected area system, however, reveals a strong bias toward higher altitude and forested landscapes which inadequately reflects the true ecological diversity of New Zealand's natural environment. Thus, lowland native forests, for example, are seriously under-represented in reserved areas, despite the fact that they have been depleted to the greatest extent in the conversion of some 70% of the country's original forest cover to farmland and exotic forest (Ni-

cholls, 1980), and they contain most of our rare and endangered biota.

During the past decade, however, we have witnessed a remarkable shift in the philosophical basis for extending the protected area network, toward a greater emphasis on securing a truly ecologically representative system. This change in attitude reflects in part a response to initiatives occurring in the international nature conservation movement, and a revitalization of early efforts to establish widely representative reserves in New Zealand. But above all it signifies the growing influence of a scientific rationale for the establishment and management of protected areas. This case study describes the purposes for which protected areas are established in New Zealand and examines the legislative and institutional arrangement for their management. It traces the origins and development of the concept of ecological representation and reveals some of the practical steps being taken to redress the ecological imbalance in the present system of protected areas.

2. MANAGEMENT OBJECTIVES OF NEW ZEALAND PROTECTED AREAS

There are thirteen classes of protected area (those terrestrial areas in which the preservation and protection of the natural environment is either the principal or a major objective of management) in New Zealand, ranked in Table 1 according to the relative extent of land covered. The whole network comprises 1,505 individual areas, extending over a total of 4,480,707 ha.

2.1 National Parks and allied reserves

New Zealand's *National Parks* generally satisfy internationally accepted principles for national park management established at the 10th General Assembly of IUCN in New Delhi in 1969. They contain scenery of such distinctive quality and ecological systems or natural features so beautiful, unique or scientifically important, that their preservation is in the national interest. There is a legal requirement that native plants and animals be preserved and those that are introduced be eliminated, as far as possible. Subject to conditions necessary for the protection of natural features, members of the public have freedom of entry. Land can be excluded from a national park only by Act of Parliament, so the security of status is extremely high.

Where in a national park there is an area of special ecological or cultural significance in which the resources protected are particularly rare, endangered or vulnerable to disturbance and must be strictly guarded from visitors, then a *National Park Specially Protected Area* may be established. Such areas are created or revoked only by the Government-General, and public access is by ministerial consent and permit only.

Nature, Scientific and *Scenic Reserves* all have as their principal purpose the protection and preservation of natural ecosystems in perpetuity. They also all have the same degree of security, with revocation of reserve status being by Gazette Notice following public notification and the hearing of objections. In detail, however, they differ according to the permissable uses and degree of protection afforded. Thus, emphasis in nature reserves is given to unique habitats normally containing rare and endangered species of biota, where control of public access is essential to maintain the natural state and access is by permit only. Scientific reserves stress research and education values rather than strict nature preservation. Public entry is restricted only in special cases, while research and monitoring by scientists is encouraged and limited manipulation of the natural environment is permitted for approved experimental purposes. Scenic reserves are managed essentially according to the principles for national parks. Members of the public have freedom of entry and facilities may be provided for recreational activities compatible with ecological protection.

2.2 State Forest Parks and Reserves

Forest Parks are multiple-use management areas aimed at facilitating public recreation in accordance with other purposes for which a forest is managed, including timber production and the protection of natural areas. Approaches to landscape protection are more liberal than in national parks, and there is a lesser degree of permanency as forest park status can be revoked by an Order-in-Council.

Forest Sanctuaries are intended especially to provide absolute protection for rare forest associations or faunas. Public access, while not prohibited, is strictly controlled and the highest possible security is afforded sanctuaries, since revocation of their status requires an Act of Parliament.

State Forest Ecological Areas are essentially multi-purpose scientific reserves set aside to protect rare habitats of forest floras or faunas, or representative forest ecosystems which maintain genetic diversity and are natural reference areas for ecological research and monitoring. Public access is normally unrestricted, and revocation is by Gazette Notice so their legal security parallels that of nature, scientific and scenic reserves.

2.3 Wildlife Reserves

Three types of reserves are directed specifically at wildlife protection. The *Wildlife Sanctuary* gives absolute protection to fragile wildlife habitats or rare and important wildlife species, which are highly susceptible to disturbance and must be protected from uncontrolled public entry. They can be revoked either by Proclamation or Gazette Notice, so are accorded a relatively insecure status which many consider incompatible with their important protective role.

A *Wildlife Refuge* is a multi-purpose reserve protecting both native and introduced wildlife. It secures important habitat for protected native wildlife but also serves as a refuge for waterfowl during the game bird shooting season. At other times public access is usually unrestricted. Refuges can be revoked by Proclamation so require an additional reserve status to ensure their security.

Wildlife Management Reserves are aimed at facilitating hunting and fishing and the public appreciation of wildlife. Public access is, therefore, unrestricted and habitat manipulation is permitted. Revocation provisions parallel those for wildlife sanctuaries, so security of status is low.

2.4 Reserves on private land

There are three classes of reserve enabling nature protection to be extended to freehold and leasehold land in New Zealand.

Protected Private Land is essentially a private scenic reserve wherein the Crown, by agreement with the landowner, provides protection either in perpetuity or for a specified term. Public access provisions are also by agreement. Security of status is low as, unless the agreement is in perpetuity, it is not binding on successive owners.

Conservation Covenants, administered by the Crown, and *Open Space covenants*, administered by an independent Trust, are not reserves *per se*. Rather, they are legal contracts whereby the landowner voluntarily agrees that the land be managed to retain its essentially natural character. Provisions for public access, the degree of nature protection, and the duration of protective measures vary according to conditions in the convenant. While open space covenants are binding on both existing and subsequent landowners, in neither case is covenant status a guarantee of permanent protection.

2.5 Comparisons of management objectives

Table 2 is a guide to the comparative management objectives of the various types of protected area, as individual classes are ranked according to the degree of protection of natural features. Conversely, this ranking also reveals the degree of flexibility in management and multiplicity of uses permitted. It also establishes the relative position of New Zealand's protected areas in a hierarchical classification system of conservation management established by IUCN (1978a). This is helpful in grouping separate statutory classes of parks and reserves having essentially the same management objectives and protective status.

3. LEGISLATIVE AND ADMINISTRATIVE FRAMEWORK

The management of New Zealand's protected areas falls primarily into three government ministerial portfolios—Lands, Forests and Internal Affairs—and involves the administration of six principal statutes (Fig. 1).

In administering national parks under the National Parks Act 1980, the Department of Lands and Survey works cooperatively with an independent National Parks and Reserve Authority and twelve Boards with district responsibilities. The department is responsible for day-to-day administration of parks and provides professional and ranger staff for park management. The responsibilities of the Authority and Boards include, among others, policy formulation, management plan approval and new park planning.

Under the Reserves Act 1977, the department is responsible for the identification, purchase and management of reserves. Maritime Parks are also administered under this Act or under separate legislation. A maritime park, rather than a separate protected area class, is simply an administrative grouping of existing terrestrial reserves which facilitates coordinated management of geographically separate reserves in coastal environments.

The department also services the Queen Elizabeth II National Trust, an independent body financed from private donations and subscriptions and from government grants, whose primary responsibility is the negotiation of Open Space Covenants on private land.

The New Zealand Forest Service has a responsibility for establishing and managing protected areas in State Forests under the Forests Act 1949. It is assisted in all

aspects of park management by State Forest Park Advisory Committees, and in the design and management of protected areas by a multi-disciplinary Scientific Coordinating Committee.

Under the Wildlife Act 1953, control and management of wildlife sanctuaries, refuges and management reserves are the responsibility of the Wildlife Service of the Department of Internal Affairs. Some management responsibilities are delegated to private organizations such as Acclimatization Societies.

4. EVOLUTION OF THE CONCEPT OF REPRESENTATIVE RESERVES

The value of securing an ecologically diverse and representative reserve system was appreciated almost from the beginning of the nature conservation movement in New Zealand, and was soon recognized within the political realm. The remarkable politician and conservationist H.G. Ell, during an active parliamentary career in the first two decades of this century, continually urged the government to establish inalienable reserves over the typical plant life found in all districts of the country (Roche, 1981; Dingwall, 1981). He was also the architect of the Scenery Preservation Act 1903, the first statute in New Zealand devoted to reserving land for nature conservation, which laid the foundations for our present system of Scenic Reserves.

During the investigations of a Royal Commission on Forestry in 1913, Ell's arguments were strengthened by support from natural scientists. The eminent government botanist Leonard Cockayne and, particularly, Charles Chilton, Professor of Biology at Canterbury University College, advocated the establishment of a wide range of reserves especially over non-forested areas such as alpine meadow, swamp and sand dune environments.

The promise of these early initiatives for a widely representative reserve system was never fulfilled, however, and the steadily expanding reserve network soon exhibited a strong bias toward forested areas, especially on uplands, and secondarily to areas containing natural "curiosities".

Several factors contributed to this evolving pattern of forest reserves. The prevailing socio-economic climate in the young and vigorous agricultural colony gave prior attention to the replacement of native plant cover by introduced grassland and the settlement of land for farming. Land of easy contour and at lower altitudes, suitable for settlement, was excluded from reservation, thus effectively limiting reserves to higher and steeper terrain where farming was impractical and the timber was not commercially exploitable.

The retention of forests at higher altitudes was also vital for preventing accelerated runoff and soil erosion. The marked increase in flooding, soil erosion and sedimentation was ample evidence of the consequences of indiscriminate clearing of catchment forests. The government responded by approving the reservation of forests at the sources of rivers, along stream margins and on steep slopes for "climatic" and other catchment protection purposes (Wynn, 1979).

The early conservation movement was strongly motivated by aesthetic considerations and a concern for the preservation of scenery. Landscape artists and nature writers nurtured a fascination for mountains and forests, or "bush", which were the dominant landscape images (Shepard, 1969; Johnston, 1981). This resulted in the overwhelming attention accorded to mountainous and forested environments in selecting reserves to protect the country's scenic heritage.

Efforts in scenery preservation also encouraged a growing interest in reserving natural "curiosities" such as geothermal phenomena, glaciers, and other geological formations. Hot springs, in particular, were regarded as beneficial health resorts and as tourist attractions and they became the site of some of our earliest reserves.

Renewed interest in ecological representativeness occurred only after the major phase of reserve acquisition had concluded and the essential character of the reserve system had been decided. It came principally from within the scientific community; Kealy (1951) noted the desirability of extending protection to a wide range of remnant forest types, and Grimmett (1956) sought protection for adequate and representative areas of all major plant and animal associations and examples of unmodified soils. This theme was taken up again by Atkinson (1961) who stressed the benchmark value of representative examples of soil reserves and made suggestions for their systematic selection.

Following completion of the first regional biological surveys of reserves, the ecological imbalance in the habitat types protected was dramatically revealed. For example, Kelly (1972) showed that in Canterbury, whereas forests occupied only approximately 15% of the landscape prior to the arrival of Europeans, they comprise some 80% of the area protected in reserves, and there are serious deficiencies in the reservation of natural grassland, shrubland, swamps and coastal dunes. He expressed the hope that at least one good example of every vegetation type, natural community and habitat in the country would be properly protected.

During the 1970s the value of ecological representativeness as a guiding philosophy in the establishment of protected areas was recognized by the land administering authorities (Thomson and Nicholls, 1973; Dingwall, 1977), and the concept eventually won expression in legislation and official government policy for protected area management.

In 1976 an amendment to the Forests Act gave the Minister extended powers to undertake surveys for ecological purposes and to acquire and use land for, among others, the protection of the natural environment and wildlife, and for a wide range of scientific purposes. The Forest Service policy on the reservation of indigenous forests (N.Z. Forest Service, 1977) specifies that repre-

sentative examples of each forest ecosystem should be preserved and that State forests should continue to be reserved as sanctuaries or dedicated scientific areas. The rapidly expanding network of Ecological Areas, guided by the advisory State Forest Scientific Coordinating Committee, testifies to the practical effectiveness of this policy.

Perhaps the clearest expression of the representative area concept in legislation occurred with the passing of the Reserves Act 1977. This comprehensive statute expresses as one of its principal purposes to ensure, as far as possible, the survival of all indigenous species of flora and fauna, both rare and common, in their natural communities and habitats, and the preservation of representative samples of all classes of natural ecosystems and landscape which in the aggregate originally gave New Zealand its own recognizable character.

The National Parks Act 1980, a major revision of the original Act that had guided national park management for almost 30 years, contained as one of its most innovative features specific reference to the preservation in parks of ecological systems and natural features of scientific importance. This represents a significant endorsement of the scientific rationale for national parks. Draft national park policy notes that criteria for selecting new park areas will give consideration to including ecological systems and sequences, landscapes or landform types not adequately represented in the park system at present.

4.1 International Influences

The stimulus for acceptance of the concept of representative areas in New Zealand came also, in great measure, from international sources. Project 8 of Unesco's Man and the Biosphere (MAB) Programme is directed toward the establishment of a global series of Biosphere Reserves encompassing representative areas of the world's major ecosystems (di Castri and Loope, 1977). This programme complements the work of the IUCN Commission on National Parks and Protected Areas, aimed at elaborating the conceptual and procedural framework for establishing and managing an ecologically representative network of protected areas. This, in turn, is a key element in the *World Conservation Strategy*. The proposals for a New Zealand Conservation Strategy (N.Z. Nature Conservation Council, 1981) reveal acceptance of these principles, and the movement toward a representative protected area system in New Zealand is a logical expression of attempts at adopting these guidelines in the national context.

5. GIVING EFFECT TO THE REPRESENTATIVE AREA CONCEPT

The statutory and administrative commitment to a nationally representative system of protected areas carries with it the challenge of establishing mechanisms and resources which give effect to this programme on the ground. Here, there are two fundamental requirements. The first is an inventory of all natural communities and landscapes found in the country which should be protected. The second is a critical analysis of communities and landscapes in existing parks and reserves with a view to assessing the adequacy of ecological representation and identifying gaps. Recent developments reveal that positive progress is being made in meeting these needs.

5.1 Improving the information base for nature conservation

A national assessment of New Zealand biota and landscapes is hindered by the absence of a coordinated biological survey and mapping scheme. Thus, there is no checklist of vegetation types, wildlife habitats or landscapes which characterize New Zealand and should be represented in protected areas. Although we have a register of threatened and endangered plants and vertebrate animals (N.Z. Nature Conservation Council, 1981) there is no equivalent listing of communities and landscapes under threat and no recognized procedure for ranking and evaluating their conservation status.

A recent inventory of remnant lowland forest stands (Park and Walls, 1978), while limited in scope geographically, is an enlightened initiative in the identification and conservation ranking of threatened and diminishing habitats. It has already produced an encouraging surge of interest in Open Space Convenants from private landowners.

A similar inventory approach is now incorporated in a regional land inventory scheme conducted by the Department of Lands and Survey. This scheme, which produces single-factor maps and interpretive overlays to rank resources for various uses, including nature conservation, is a promising planning tool for identifying potential park and reserve areas. However, the map scale of 1:100,000 presents limitations for site selection and design.

Another major advance in improving the data base for natural resource protection is the recent establishment of a national Biological Resources Centre. The Centre has began the task of developing procedures for a national inventory of biological resources and evaluation of sites meriting protection. It is also promoting a programme of regional resource surveys using as an information framework a recently developed national biogeographic scheme.

This biogeographic scheme is modelled on a system devised for identifying representative reserves in State forests (Nicholls, 1979). It divides the country into 82 ecological regions and 235 ecologicl districts and is a refinement on a national scale of the global system of biogeographic realms and provinces developed for IUCN by Udvardy (1975). Ecological regions are distinguished essentially by gross differences in rock type, landforms, climate and vegetation type. They are subdivided into districts where there is a significant homogeneous element, such as a local climate, or a topographic discontinuity. This biogeographic scheme, the first of its kind in New Zealand, will be invaluable not only as a framework for assembling data for nature conservation purposes, but also as a reference against which to examine the ecological representativeness of existing parks and reserves and a guide for their further selection.

5.2 Assessing resources in existing protected areas

Notwithstanding the considerable effort at survey and research, our knowledge of the character and scope of resources already protected in parks and reserves remains markedly deficient. The burgeoning system of reserves in State forests has a relatively substantial information base, and the selection process involves application of a rigorously scientific set of ground rules emphasizing biological integrity, representativeness, and diversity, which requires a good understanding of the natural resources.

Similar attention to scientific principles has accompanied the establishment of many nature and scientific reserves, and their information base is always improving through their continuing research function.

The situation is worse, however, for the longer-established scenic reserves, most of which were selected in the absence of ecological considerations or resource assessment. It was not until the late 1960s that a national biological survey of scenic reserves was begun and it remains incomplete.

What has also been lacking is a comprehensive uniformly-designed checklist of resources in all types of protected area. In an attempt to satisfy this need, a Register of Protected Natural Areas in New Zealand has been compiled, as a joint project of the Department of Lands and Survey, Forest Service and Wildlife Service; the Register is now in its final stages of preparation.

The Register is a milestone in improving our understanding of the protected area system in New Zealand. While it adds little new information, it provides for the first time in one document a comprehensive summary of administrative details for the more than 1500 protected areas, and systematically lists physical and biological features, including rare plants and animals, plus archaelogical and historical information and evidence of human modification.

The information contained in the register is highly variable in quality and there are gaps in the available information, but exposure of these deficiencies should stimulate increased research effort. It is intended that the register be computerized for better storage and retrieval of information and to enable its manipulation for analysis. The register will be an invaluable aid in an objective assessment of the full complement of resources under protection and in revealing the gaps.

6. CONCLUSION

New Zealand has developed a comprehensive and extensive system of protected areas accommodating a wide range of conservation management objectives, and supported by an elaborate legislative framework. However, on closer examination from an ecological perspective this apparently favourable situation is revealed as somewhat illusory. The protected area network is overwhelmingly confined to higher altitude forested terrain and fails to fully represent the diversity of New Zealand's biota and landscapes.

This ecological imbalance is the product of a land allocation process that has favoured the conversion of lowlands to farmland, and generally accorded protective status to areas lacking demonstrable economic potential. Moreover, the protected area programme has been strongly motivated by aesthetic concerns and protected areas have generally lacked a systematic or scientific basis for their establishment.

In recent years this situation has changed dramatically and the movement toward a fully representative system of protected areas is gaining momentum, stimulated by an increased attention to scientific principles in the design of protected area systems, in both the global and New Zealand's own national context.

There is now a clearly expressed commitment by government, and adequate legal provision, to protect what remains of lowland natural environments. Encouraging progress has also been made in developing the necessary procedural and information requirements for this. There is no room for complacency, however. Extension of protection to lowland ecosystems will be difficult, for the reservation process will inevitably produce conflict with other competing and incompatible uses of land. Meanwhile, the depletion of natural areas is continuing apace and there is an urgent need to secure examples of lowland environments and ensure the protection of a sample of our whole natural heritage. Recent developments suggest that this challenge has been accepted.

Table 1: Number and extent of New Zealand's protected areas, as of 1 January 1981

Protected Area Class	No.	Total Area	% New Zealand land area
National Park*	10	1,968,600	7.35
State Forest Park**	18	1,424,465	5.32
Scenic Reserve***	1,162	401,398	1.50
Nature Reserve	49	197,311	0.74
National Park Specially Protected Areas	5	190,234	0.71
State Forest Ecological Area	36	59,915	0.22
State Forest Sanctuary	14	16,287	0.06
Wildlife Refuge	53	15,271	0.06
Wildlife Management Reserve	79	11,106	0.04
Scientific Reserve	27	2,723	0.01
Open Space Covenant	31	1,615	0.006
Wildlife Sanctuary	12	197	0.001
Conservation Covenant	9	159	0.001
	1,505	4,480,707	16.02

*Excludes national park specially protected areas; ** Excludes sanctuaries and ecological areas; *** Includes protected private land*

Table 2: Classification of protected areas according to management objectives for protection and use

NZ Protected Area Class	IUCN Conservation Management Class
National Park Specially Protected Area State Forest Sanctuary Nature Reserve Wildlife Sanctuary	Scientific Reserve/Strict Nature Reserve
National Park	National Park
Scenic Reserve Scientific Reserve State Forest Ecological Area Open Space Covenant Conservation Covenant Wildlife Management Reserve Wildlife Refuge	Nature Conservation Reserve/Managed Nature Reserve/Wildlife Sanct'y
State Forest Park	Multiple Use Management Area/ Managed Resource Reserve

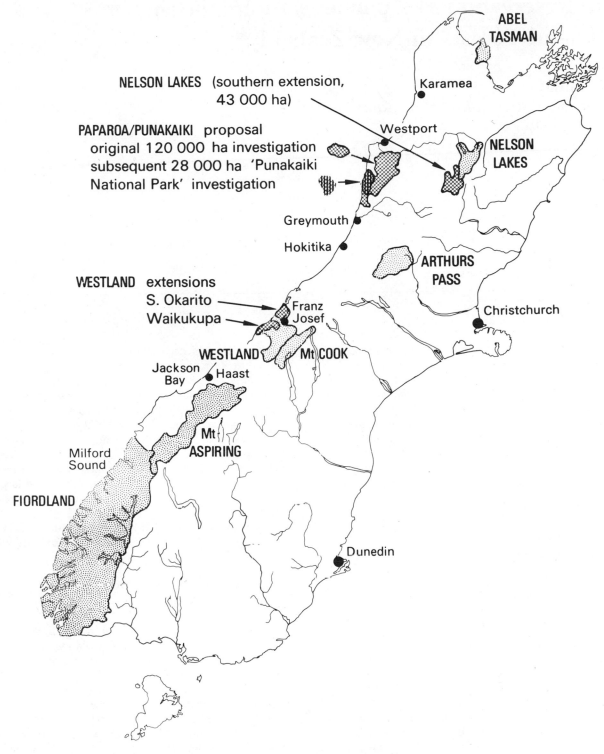

Figure 1. Existing national parks, South Island, New Zealand, showing three proposed additions (or new park) in the West Coast region.

The Reservation of Commercially Important Lowland Forests in New Zealand

L.F. Molloy
Department of Scientific and Industrial Research
New Zealand

ABSTRACT. *The lowland indigenous forests of New Zealand are of international importance, for the long isolation of the islands has preserved a flora which retains many of the elements of the ancient supercontinent of Gondwanaland. Whereas 1200 years ago indigenous forests covered nearly 80 percent of New Zealand, today just 23 percent remains. The case study charts the changes in public attitudes and government policy during the past decade, particularly with reference to the indigenous forest of the West Coast of the South Island, a resource sought by the timber industry in the face of public concern about the need to preserve as much as possible of the nation's lowland forest remnants. A number of conclusions are drawn which should be applicable to developing countries attempting to balance forest production with the need to preserve a representative range of protected areas.*

1. INTRODUCTION

When the early Polynesian voyagers reached New Zealand 1200 years ago they were confronted by a heavily forested landscape. About 78 percent of the land was forested; the rest consisted of mountaintops, wetlands and areas of grasslands around the volcanoes of the Central North Island and in the semi-arid intermontane basins of the South Island. Much of this new land, Te-ika-a-Maui, was extremely rugged and mountainous. Half of New Zealand's area of 270,000 sq km consists of land with slopes steeper than 28 and nearly 60 percent of the land lies above 300m altitude. However, in the coastal regions and the limited area of lowlands, there were dense tracts of tall forest. For 1,000 years, until the beginning of European colonization early in the 19th century, the Maori people used these forests by hunting and gathering or extracting specific trees for canoes,

construction and decorative carving; some areas were cleared for agriculture, particularly for the kumara tuber.

In the eastern "rain-shadow" regions, particularly in the South Island, large areas of drier forest were destroyed, probably by fires associated with the hunting of the 27 species of now-extinct flightless birds generally known as moas. By the time planned European settlement began in 1840 the forest estate had dwindled to just over 50 percent of the land; today only 26 percent of New Zealand is forested, 23 percent as the largely montane remnants of the primeval indigenous forests, and 3 percent as plantations of exotic softwoods (primarily *Pinus radiata*) which have now virtually replaced the indigenous forest as the nation's source of timber.

2. IMPORTANCE OF REMAINING INDIGENOUS FOREST

Inevitably, most of the forest clearance by both Polynesians and Europeans was in the lowlands, particularly those luxuriant forests on the deeper, more fertile soils suited to pastoral agriculture. The extent of this loss of lowland forest below 300m altitude since European settlement is shown in Fig.1. On the more populated North Island, about 80 percent of this lowland forest has now been cleared and most of the urban population have to travel considerable distances to glimpse any remnants of their once-magnificent forest heritage.

The lowland forests of New Zealand are not only of national importance; many consider them to be of international importance for the forests of the New Zealand biological region (approximately the Neozealandia Biogeographical Province of Udvardy, 1975) may be the best surviving examples of the forests of the ancient southern supercontinent of Gondwanaland. More tropical Gondwanaland fragments, such as Queensland, New Guinea and New Caledonia, still share much of this ancient flora but, in contrast, New Zealand has been more isolated—a cluster of islands separated from the Australia-Antarctica remnant of Gondwanaland for 60 to 80 million years. Many distinctive elements of the New Zealand "bush" today—the podocarps (the genera *Podocarpus*, *Dacrydium* and *Dacrycarpus*), kauri *Agathis australis*, southern beeches *Nothofagus* and the 'celery pines' *Phyllocladus*—have coexisted for as long as 130 million years during their evolutionary development on the ancestral New Zealand landmass.

In terms of their botanical composition and location these indigenous forests can be conveniently grouped into 4 broad classes:

- *kauri*-dominated forests in the warmer parts of the North Island lying north of latitude 38°S;
- *podocarp* forests of the lowlands (with large trees such as rimu, miro, matai, totara and kahikatea);
- mixed *podocarp/beech/hardwood* forests of the lowlands; and
- *beech* forests of the montane and subalpine regions (largely unmerchantable).

The first two forest classes have borne the brunt of timber exploitation. The kauri forests of Northland still contain some of the largest trees in the world, once prized as a source of spars for sailing ships. Kauri timber was used in all manner of building construction in colonial New Zealand, and subsequently, these magnificent forests were further plundered for an exudate, kauri gum, found in the soil beneath the tree. Today there are only about 1200 ha of virgin dense kauri forest left in a small number of forest sanctuaries, although the commercial value of kauri is so high that it is being replanted in cutover indigenous forest in the Auckland and Northland regions.

The lowland podocarp/hardwood forests have suffered a similar fate to the kauri, for throughout the North Island and the eastern parts of the South Island the pioneer imperative was to clear the forest so that the land could be farmed. This huge resource of potential commercial timber was largely squandered and burned. As a result, the New Zealand Forest Service was formed in 1919 to try and bring about the conservation of these merchantable forests and, at the same time, establish faster-growing exotic trees as a timber substitute.

The only commercially important indigenous production forests that remain today are confined to three regions:

- the podocarp/hardwood forests of the volcanic plateau of the central North Island (Pureora and Whirinaki forests);
- the podocarp/hardwood and podocarp/beech forests of the West Coast of the South Island; and

- the silver beech and podocarp forests of western Southland.

While the continued milling of the remaining indigenous forests of the volcanic plateau and western Southland has generated national conservation controversies, such industries are only of local socio-economic importance. The situation in the West Coast is entirely different, however, for indigenous milling is of considerable economic significance in this region with a long history of resource exploitation. Long before the indigenous timber of the West Coast began to run out, there had been the gold rushes and the widespread mining of coal; both appear to have followed a "boom and bust" cycle and this traditional mining philosophy also seemed to apply to the forests. Because the West Coast forest controversy illustrates so precisely the different opinions that individuals, communities and governments can hold about any natural resource, it has been chosen as a case study from the many other examples of public concern over the continued milling of indigenous forests in New Zealand. As a case study it highlights many differences in values that sectors of our society place upon natural landscapes:

- differences between central and regional government in development priorities;
- the different aspirations and lifestyles of isolated rural communities compared with more affluent urban populations;
- how traditional resource exploitation is at variance with modern conservation attitudes;
- how people whose livelihood comes from milling or mining a natural resource find it difficult to relate to those who want to recreate in, or study, such a natural landscape which may now be rare in other parts of the country.

3. THE WEST COAST ENVIRONMENT

The forests of the West Coast are the outstanding remnant of the lowland forests of primeval New Zealand. They are a product of the interplay of many environmental factors in a land continually drenched by rain from the prevailing westerly winds that strike the wall of the Southern Alps (average height of 2000m, up to 3500m in Westland National Park). This mountain chain (including the two northern outliers, the Paparoa Range and Tasman Mountains) extends 600 km from the Heaphy River in the north to Milford Sound in Fiordland. In places, the mountains reach the coastline, but generally there is a narrow strip of coastal lowland, 5-10 km wide, between the Tasman Sea and the great Alpine Fault which cuts across the western foot of the Southern Alps. It is no exaggeration to describe the climate of the West Coast as unique in the world. No other temperate region has such a combination of regular distribution of intense rainfall (as much as 13,000 mm per year), relatively high sunshine hours, and a mild climate with comparatively little variation between summer and winter temperatures.

Small wonder then that the dense temperate rain forests of the West Coast have been likened in structure and luxuriance to those of the tropics.

Although the West Coast is only 9 percent of the area of New Zealand it contains about 45 percent of the remaining merchantable indigenous forest. Most of the forests on floodplains and the better soils of the alluvial terraces have been converted into productive dairy farms; the remaining forests now predominate on two landforms, the hill country slopes (predominantly old glacial moraines) and the flat-surfaced fluvio-glacial outwash and glacial terraces.

Historically the forests on these landforms were "mined" for their timber, clearfelled with no attempt at retaining a forest structure and ultimately degraded to "pakihi" wastelands, through a rising water table and very low soil fertility (because of the high rates of leaching). The New Zealand Forest Service attempted to institute improved methods of logging ("strip-felling", "selection-logging") and silviculture in an attempt to regenerate the forests and perpetuate a sustained-yield. It is a complex story of trial and error but, with hindsight today, we have to accept that too little was done, too late, in a socio-economic climate that still placed a higher value on pioneer development than forest conservation.

Today, the West Coast regional economy is remarkable for its dependence upon primary industry. Twenty-eight percent of the region's workforce is directly engaged in primary industries (agriculture, forestry, mining and fishing) compared with 12 percent so engaged for all of New Zealand. In 1976 an estimated 19 percent (workers plus dependants) of the region's population were dependent on forestry, indicating the importance of forestry to the economic and social fabric of this very isolated region which has somewhat vulnerable rail and shipping links with the rest of New Zealand.

4. NATIONAL PARKS AND PROTECTED AREAS ON THE WEST COAST

New Zealand has an enviable reputation for the high proportion of the country that has been established as protected areas. National Parks and Reserves (under the Reserves Act, 1977) cover over 27,000 sq km, or 10 percent of the area of New Zealand. Most of this land is mountainous, huge tracts of the Southern Alps, volcanoes, glaciers, fiords and subalpine beech forest, but the lowland forests of New Zealand were cleared or milled to such an extent that they only occur as relatively small remnants within the national parks and reserves system. Although 10 percent of the land may be protected it has been estimated that only 0.5 percent of the land has been reserved where it also had a productive potential for agriculture or forestry.

Consequently, there has been very little sacrifice for the traditional pastoral and forestry industries in the evolution of the New Zealand parks and reserves system. However, the 1970s ushered in a decade of sharply increasing forest conservation consciousness in a public galvanised by the folly of government and industry attempts, in the late 1960s, to raise the levels of Lakes Manapouri and Te Anau in Fiordland National Park. Inevitably, it was to the West Coast, with its shining alps, tall podocarp forests, glaciers, lakes and dramatic coastline, that New Zealand's increasing urbanised public looked for the opportunity to preserve the best of the remaining indigenous landscapes of the lowlands.

5. THE WEST COAST FOREST CONTROVERSY EMERGES

This national concern for the preservation of remaining lowland forest came into focus with the government announcement in 1971 that the NZ Forest Service intended to call for proposals to use large areas of previously unmerchantable beech and beech/podocarp forest in the North Westland/Buller subregion. This "beech scheme" initially envisaged the conversion of 100,000 ha of these forests to exotic plantations and the management of another 150,000 ha for long term production of beech and podocarp timber. A fundamental rationale of the scheme was the establishment of a major industry, such as a pulp or paper mill, to use the large amount of defect wood in the beech forests. Ultimately the exotics established in the ashes of the cleared forests would sustain the bulk of such an industry.

The Forest Service attempted to zone the forests for multiple uses—scientific reservations, recreational areas, riparian strips along waterways, and even the conversion of small areas with suitable soils to farmland. In addition, the Forest Service sought the advice of technical experts and subjected the proposals to analysis by a wide range of government and quasi-governmental agencies, many of them with an environmental brief. Gradually, a comprehensive set of research programmes was established to assist in the delineation of protected areas, refine silviculture, and improve the logging and regeneration of the forests—in all, a commendable effort unparalleled in the investigation of any of New Zealand's major natural resources up to that time.

Inevitably, however, the proposals ran into a storm of public protest as well as a degree of opposition from other government agencies such as the Commission for the Environment and the Wildlife Service. Understandably, the proposals for the conversion of indigenous forest to exotics were vehemently rejected by a wide body of conservation opinion. It was not that this conversion was anything new but it was on an unprecedented, coordinated scale. Along with similar, but smaller, conversion proposals in the North Island and eastern Southland, it flew directly in the face of changing public attitudes, particularly those of a younger, more articulate, urban section of the population.

The whole complex chain of investigation and decision-making for the West Coast forests since 1971 was fairly simple until 1975 but became increasingly complicated as government attempted to bring the different factors together in the formulation of a West Coast Forest Policy in 1978. The implementation of that 1978 policy has since become extremely complicated, with many interacting investigations, public initiatives and administrative decisions up until the time this paper was written in July 1982.

Major forestry conferences in 1974 and 1975 had faced up to revising the management policy for indigenous forests. Bowing to public concern, the Forest Service (and ultimately government) accepted that henceforth logged indigenous forests would be perpetuated *as indigenous forests* and only converted to exotic forests where there were over-riding local socio-economic reasons. It was a major victory for the conservationists both within and outside government. It set in train a series of major consequential changes for the West Coast forest industry and the future of the lowland forests and their fauna.

In 1975, the New Zealand Government rejected the large-scale proposals of industry for the pulping of the West Coast beech forests, largely because of the likely environmental impact. To implement the policy revisions, the Forests Act 1949 was significantly amended in 1976 to require the Forest Service to manage State forests for "balanced use" (not just the production of timber) and allow more public involvement in decision-making about the use of indigenous forests. "Balanced use" could only be achieved with good resource information, so the scientific and inventory investigations into the West Coast forests increased.

By 1977 the fundamental philosophical differences between the protagonists were painfully clear and attitudes were very polarised. On the one hand a range of conservation, preservation and recreation organizations had made the protection of adequate forest reserves on the West Coast into a major political issue. The West Coast population, on the other hand, had been rather slow to realize the magnitude of the policy changes but from 1977 on they rallied behind the local forestry industry and assailed the conservationists, the National Parks Authority, the political party in government, and even the Forest Service with demands to stop "locking-up" the resources of the region.

5.1 Forest Service attempts to balance the use of West Coast forests

By this time the Forest Service had made commendable attempts to delineate on a sound scientific basis representative reserves ('ecological areas') within the State forests. When the North Westland/Buller subregion was evaluated in terms of its geology, landforms, soils, climate and biota, 12 'ecological districts' were recognized

and the Forest Service attempted to reserve at least one major 'ecological area' representative of each district. This role of assessing ecological representativeness fell to a Scientific Coordinating Committee which brought together the scientific expertise of the Forest Service and that of a number of other agencies with research responsibilities for native freshwater fish, birdlife, soils and indigenous plants.

The ecological area exercise is probably one of the most successful outgrowths of the controversy, for this approach has since been developed by the NZ Biological Resources Centre into a provisional system of 82 'ecological regions' (subdivided into 235 'ecological districts') for all of New Zealand (Simpson, 1982). However, the scientifically important 'ecological areas' were only one part of the Forest Service's attempts to zone the forests for multiple uses; in addition to production zones, there were recreation zones (natural environment, amenity and wilderness) which offered a gradation in recreation development and opportunity.

5.2 National park proposals for West Coast forests

While the Forest Service was widely praised for its thorough work in delineating representative ecological areas, these reserves were still too narrow in their scientific concept to capture the imagination of the conservation movement. To many members of the public they seemed akin to sanctuaries solely for the satisfaction of a scientific elite. Popular concern for the preservation of indigenous landscapes of outstanding interest or beauty was still expressed, as it always has been in New Zealand, in demands for new or extended national parks. A number of proposals emanated from sections of the public but only 3 of them gained significant support:

(a) a 43,000 ha addition to Nelson Lakes National Park, consisting of montane and subalpine beech forests in the upper Buller River catchment on the western slopes of the Spenser Mountains at the southern boundary of the existing park;

(b) an extension of Westland National Park across the densely forested piedmont west of the Alpine Fault to the Tasman Sea. This would include approximately 26,000 ha of the great lowland terrace podocarp forests of Waikukupa and southern Okarito State Forests near the famous Franz Josef and Fox Glaciers, an outstanding example of a "mountain-crest to the sea" park; and

(c) a new Paparoa/Punakaiki National Park of about 120,000 ha based on the Paparoa Range and the Punakaiki coast with its dramatic limestone scenery. The proposal contained a significant area of lowland podocarp/hardwood forest lying in a basin containing an outstanding complex of limestone caves on the western side of the Paparoa Range.

The addition to Nelson Lakes National Park doubled the size of the existing park but generated very little opposition locally because valley-floor grazing was not affected and most of the forests were unmerchantable and peripheral to the West Coast indigenous timber industry. It conformed to the traditional view of New Zealand national parks—mountainous and remote with no real productive value.

The Okarito/Waikukupa and Paparoa proposals were just the opposite. They contained significant volumes of podocarp timber (1,600,000 cu m and approximately 160,000 cu m, respectively), and both resources were deemed essential to the continuance of the indigenous timber industries in the South Westland and Buller regions, respectively.

Both proposals were exhaustively evaluated over many years and a bitter and acrimonious conflict ensued. Feelings ran high in the extreme wings of both camps. On the one hand, conservationists were ridiculed and ostracised in the small communities and threats were made to shoot the colony of rare white herons which had been adopted as the symbol of the forest preservation groups; on the other hand, mill saws were sabotaged by nails driven into trees scheduled for logging.

5.3 Okarito and Waikukupa additions to Westland National Park

The small South Westland farming and timber communities of Harihari and Whataroa were united in their opposition to the national park extension for they feared that their isolated settlements would become economic and social backwaters (tourism notwithstanding) like so many West Coast communities before then. Others, however, believed that a lowland forest extension to Westland National Park would recapture something of the pioneering spirit of the historic coastal hamlet of Okarito, the site where:

- the Dutch navigator, Abel Janzoon Tasman, made the first European discovery of New Zealand in 1642;
- where James MacKay purchased the West Coast for the Crown from the Maori people for a mere 300 in 1860; and
- a gold-rush boom town sprang up in the mid-1860s to become briefly a thriving port which even had survey plans for a "Colonial University of Okarito".

The proposal for the Okarito/Waikukupa forest extension to Westland National Park has undergone many vicissitudes since the National Parks Authority (NPA) recommended its inclusion to government in August 1977. The eventual addition, in July 1982, of southern Okarito and Waikukupa forests to Westland National Park was the culmination of possibly the longest and most bitter forest conservation issue in New Zealand. But the price was high, for the *quid pro quo* was the promise to establish up to 10,000 ha of exotic plantations in South Westland, the only significant region of the country which still had no exotic forest and substantially retained an indigenous character. To establish these plantations it would be necessary to clearfell large areas of cutover indigenous forest north of Okarito.

The decision was clearly a political attempt to find some sort of compromise acceptable to all parties. However, in its stark simplicity it was a reversion on a massive scale to earlier philosophies, a rejection of the multiple-use concept so cherished by the Forest Service and the demise of the professional forester's dream of a large indigenous forest working circle within which the terrace podocarp forests would be selectively logged on a 50-year cycle to sustain a yield of high-quality timber sufficient for a modest local processing industry. Interspersed with this timber production, Forest Service had still hoped to retain recreational opportunities and wildlife corridors in the large area of cutover forest. Instead, the decision on the one hand preserves an outstanding pristine lowland forest but, on the other, may sacrifice up to 10,000 ha of existing indigenous forest which, although modified, still retains significant wildlife and scenic values.

The Government decision to forego the production forestry option and add the forests to the national park does not spell the end of indigenous forestry in South Westland but it does hasten the inevitable reduction to a low yield which can be sustained in perpetuity—enough for one sawmill. One estimate (Salmon, 1981) puts the timber supply from immediately logging the entire sustainable yield for the first 50 year cycle within the forests of southern Okarito and Waikukupa at an amount which would maintain the 4 existing major mills for a period of no more than 8 years. However, it is widely recognized that the agricultural and forestry communities of Harihari and Whataroa should not be seriously disadvantaged. Changes in employment will be necessary but there is a determination to maintain these communities by developing viable rural economies, even though they may be based on different natural resources. Just how this change in the direction of regional development can be achieved with as little social disruption as possible is highly debatable. One matter, however, is clear: it is going to be difficult to find 10,000 ha of suitable land for exotic trees in this landscape of highly-leached soils. The physical and nutritional limitations of the soil are coupled with remoteness from markets to such an extent that South Westland would be the least likely area (after Fiordland) where any forest entrepeneur would want to invest his capital. The trees will grow but there may be problems of windthrow on these old moraines, a problem which has bedevilled the Forest Service's attempts to establish an acceptable method of selectively logging the indigenous podocarp forest.

An increase in tourism associated with the development of recreational facilities and a family holiday complex at Okarito should be one positive regional development to come from the park extensions. In 1980, about 110 jobs, or three-quarters of all employement, in Franz Josef and Fox Glacier townships were tourist-related. Furthermore, an "economic impact study" (Pearce, 1982) has indicated that annual expenditure by visitors to the existing Westland National Park is around $4.2 million, with another $1.7million being spent elsewhere in Westland County by these park visitors.

The tourist-oriented communities of Franz Josef and Fox townships adjoining the existing Westland National Park generally support the national park addition for they can see how the forests and coastline, lagoons and historic relics complement the existing largely alpine park with its austere grandeur and recreational attractions which are necessarily the preserve of the skilled mountaineer.

Yet the average length of stay for all visitors to the glaciers is currently only 1.5 days; the wider spectrum of recreational opportunity in an extended park should induce visitors to spend longer in the park, thereby gaining a better understanding of the ecology of the park and, at the same time, making an even more significant contribution to the local economy.

But it is difficult for communities like Harihari and Whataroa that have pioneer roots and families that have produced generations of bushmen (timber millers), to make the transition to service industries such as tourism. They take pride in their bush skills in a region where people value rugged independence and reliance upon primary industry. There are perhaps other limited employment opportunities—a resurgence in historical gold-mining of the "black-sands" along the coast or State-assisted development or flood-protection of the limited area of alluvial soils with agricultural potential. But there is really no easy way of adjusting to change.

5.4 The Paparoa/Punakaiki National Park proposal

The Paparoa/Punakaiki national park proposal was the Buller sub-region "mountain-crest to the sea" equivalent of the Okarito/Waikukupa forest additions. In contrast, however, this proposal was much larger (120,000 ha), and of very diverse geology and topography. Here the conflict with the forest industry was not as large although the relatively small podocarp resource is deemed by Forest Service to be critical to "bridging the timber gap" for sawmills in the Buller sub-region where there is no prospect of a sustained yield and the forests are still subject to the traditional "cut down and get out" approach. However, the geographical diversity of the Paparoa region has meant that it is considered highly promising for mineral exploitation, particularly limestone (for cement making) and coal.

The national park qualities of this very rugged stretch of mountain land, coastal cliffs, canyons and karst landscape have been a matter of public debate since the

National Parks Authority began to investigate the area in February 1977. Two impressive reports (Native Forests Action Council, 1979; Dennis, 1981) on the national park qualities of the area have been produced by one of the more prominent conservation organizations, the Native Forests Action Council, and the area has been subjected to very detailed scientific and recreation evaluation. Despite all this effort the National Parks Authority in May 1979 was unable to agree that the whole area under investigation was of national park quality. Most of the proposed park would have been a rugged mountainous wilderness with a reputation for severe weather and a low potential for public use. The ecological values of much of the proposed area were obvious but the Authority probably accepted that the Forest Service comprehensive zoning of the area made adequate provision for representative reserves of areas of ecological importance.

But the "Paparoa National Park" proposal sprang to life again with the release of the Forest Service's Buller Forest Management Plan in January 1982. By this time the former NPA had been replaced by a new National Parks and Reserves Authority (NPRA) as a consequence of the passing of the National Parks Act 1980. Under this new Act the Authority has a broader mandate in the assessment of potential national parks, including more emphasis upon ecological representation, as distinct from scenic quality and recreational opportunity. In May 1982 the NPRA decided that there was a *prima facie* case for a smaller area of 28,000 ha in the Punakaiki and Fox River area being of appropriate quality for national park recognition. An investigation of such a "Punakaiki National Park" is now being carried out by the Department of Lands and Survey and a fundamental part of this planning process is inviting submissions from the public and close consultation with regional government (the West Coast United Council).

The Punakaiki National Park proposal could materialize into New Zealand's 11th national park—the first new park for 20 years—and one that would add an exciting new element to the system with its very dramatic coastline, limestone canyons and caves and luxuriant lowland forest, much of it bearing a superficial resemblance to the tropical forests of SE Asia because of this unique combination of mild, superhumid climate, and higher-fertility soils derived from limestone. Interestingly, local communities do not appear to harbour the degree of opposition to such a park as that shown towards Okarito and Waikukupa. The indigenous timber industry in the Buller region is in an even worse supply position but it is not so important to the regional economy as in South Westland. Coal, cement and agriculture also contribute to a more diversified economy. There are also social differences; for instance, the Buller region contains a significant number of rural smallholdings, many occupied by "urban refugees" who have shifted to this region to seek an alternative lifestyle. In the main, these immigrants tend to reflect a positive attitude towards protecting the remaining lowland forests in the region, attitudes shared by a large section of New Zealand's urban community.

6. CONCLUSIONS

There are many lessons to be learned from these tortuous indigenous forest controversies of the past decade. I suspect that few of them are unique to New Zealand; most of them probably apply to other countries which are also trying to make the painful adjustments involved in sustaining resource use and reserving protected areas. The conclusions to be drawn from our experience include:

6.1 Demise of sustained-yield indigenous forestry

The opportunity for the sustained yield (on a 200-250 year rotation) from the formerly widespread podocarp forests has now largely passed—a monumental conservation failure in New Zealand's history. The death knell of the indigenous timber industry in New Zealand is now being sounded as the industry finds itself severely pressured by the demands of a largely urban population which wants the forest remnants preserved. Despite the earnest if somewhat belated conservation efforts of the Forest Service, the indigenous timber industry is fundamentally responsible for its own predicament by failing long ago to reduce its cutting rate to a level which the diminishing forest estate could sustain in perpetuity. For too long these timbers were undervalued and not enough was done to promote their specialist use in high value products.

6.2 Need for dialogue

Governments need to be aware of, or anticipate, changing public attitudes in a parliamentary democracy like New Zealand. With hindsight, so much of the conflict could have been avoided if the Forest Service had developed in the 1950s and '60s the effective methods of public consultation (through conferences and draft management plans) that they had to adopt in the mid-1970s. But the National Parks Authority also lacked ways in which it could involve the public in the formulation of national park proposals and, at a regional government level, the Town and Country Planning Act had not been revised to allow for the establishment of regional planning with its provisions for input from the interested public and other government agencies.

6.3 Resource information

Often insufficient information on the extent and nature of our lowland forests was available at the time that events forced political decisions to be made. Again, the need for such information—timber volumes; silvicultural trials; logging/regeneration techniques; soil, botanical, wildlife, hydrological and recreational data—would have been a high priority if managers and politicians had anticipated the changing situation and the critical importance of this information in planning for future balanced use of the forests.

6.4 Compensation

Central Governments need to face up squarely to how isolated communities, such as those on New Zealand's West Coast, can be compensated for foregoing the use of some of their natural resources in the national interest. Clearly, in the forestry situations outlined in this case study there is a wide gulf between national and regional aspirations. Monetary payments have been used to compensate logging companies for cancelled timber cutting rights at Pureora in the central North Island but this approach was not used by central government for the much more serious West Coast situation. The *quid pro quo* of exotic plantations (which will take up to 40 years to mature) is no real substitute for a comprehensive plan of regional development to assist such economically disadvantaged communities.

6.5 Image of national parks

The public image of national parks and reserves needs to be significantly improved in areas with a long-standing pioneer tradition. The "lock-up" myth must be dispelled and the whole philosophy of "conservation with development" enshrined in the World Conservation Strategy needs to be promoted at all community levels. Parks must be seen to be for people and not just the preserve of scientists and conservationists. At the same time, though, local communities must be encouraged to be involved with the park, to take pride in it as an area which is so important a part of their national heritage that it has been preserved regardless of the wealth and employment foregone.

6.6 Key role of environmental conservation organizations

The indigenous forest controversies over the past decade have spawned several new, aggressive and highly organized groups dedicated to preserving most of the remaining virgin, lowland indigenous forest. The more extreme preservationist groups generated considerable resentment at their "ends justify the means" tactics. Nevertheless, their contribution, as well as that of the more traditional nature conservation and outdoor recreation organizations, has been a major one in achieving balanced forest use and extensions to the national park system.

6.7 National-Regional rivalry

The whole indigenous forestry issue has done more than any other issue to heighten regional consciousness and set in train the difficult, but important, exercise of regional planning. For despite the isolation of the West Coast from the rest of New Zealand, the isolation of the different communities *within* the region has sometimes been an even stronger factor, often leading to parochialism. The local government administrations in the West Coast are now trying to take a more regional approach to planning through the West Coast United Council (WCUC). Unfortunately, the WCUC initially tried to hinder the establishment of national parks, reserves and wilderness areas through the provisions of its planning scheme. In this action the United Council ran headlong into the legitimate concerns of the Forest Service and the Department of Lands and Survey who are charged with administering the various public lands of the region—93 percent of the land on the West Coast. Although an approved regional planning scheme binds central government, these departments of State were clearly unhappy at being dictated to by regional government in the use of the lands they administer under Acts of Parliament. Consequently, the relationship between central and regional government on the West Coast is going to be a very sensitive one for some time as both parties attempt to strike a balance in the use of the region's resources.

Finally, all protagonists in the lowland forests debate have learned a great deal about each others' points of view and I believe that we are painfully evolving ways of planning for the many different commodities and experiences that these forests can provide. Our record of forest conservation has not been a good one, but it is probably no worse than that of civilizations and cultures in other biogeographic provinces of the world. As a people we could learn much from the forests themselves, for in their gradual evolution they have survived many environmental crises since the ancestral New Zealand landmass was launched into the Southern Ocean 60 to 80 millions years ago. The forests developed ways of adapting to changing environmental conditions; they managed to conserve their energy and nutrients, with each plant and animal playing an important part in the ordered structure of a community which attempted to maintain its stability through its diversity and resilience in the face of environmental hazards. This web of forest life has been lost in so many parts of the globe that many New Zealanders are determined that the small areas of lowland forests remaining in this land must be protected, not only for their international significance, but because we as a nation will be so much poorer for losing something of our ancient inheritance that contributes in many small ways to the fabric of our everyday life.

Yet, I am sure that many will be aware of regions in their own nations that face similar problems to those of the West Coast of the South Island of New Zealand, that are isolated, with depressed economies based on the traditional exploitation of non-renewable resources. Their antipathy to 'experts' and outsiders is an expression of their inevitable frustration and issues such as the use or preservation of indigenous forests act as a focus for their concern. Perhaps the West Coast is a microcosm of a global problem facing us all: conservation and protected areas are still seen as a luxury only afforded by the wealthy, rather than a necessity for survival and economic well-being in the long term.

Acknowledgements

This paper was prepared for IUCN's Commission on National Parks and Protected Areas in cooperation with the United Nations Environment Programme.

Figure 1. Indigenous forest of New Zealand below 300 m.

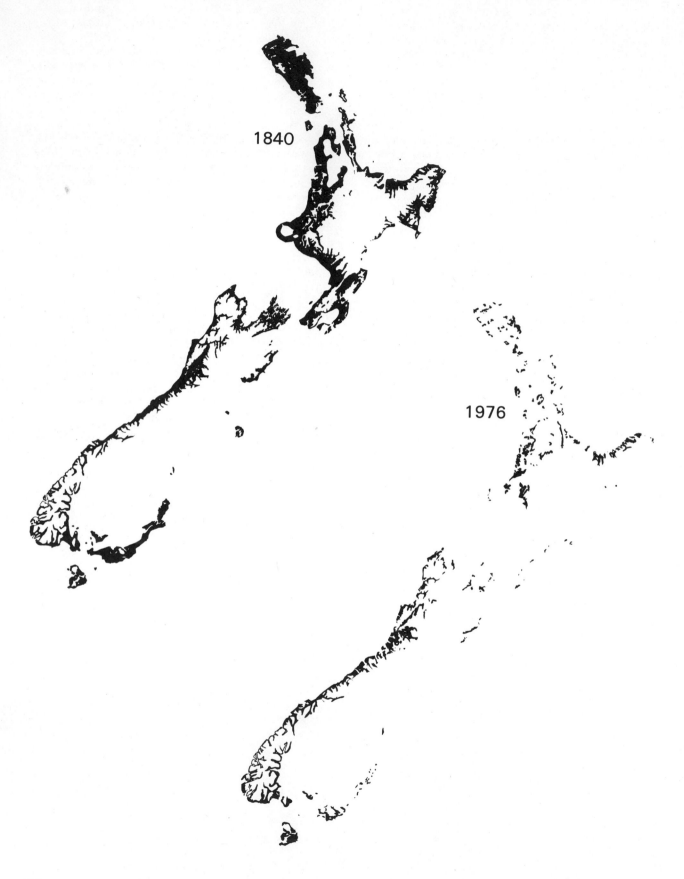

Protected Areas and Introduced Species in New Zealand

Carolyn W. Burns
Department Zoology
University of Otago
Dunedin, New Zealand

ABSTRACT. *New Zealand's native flora and fauna have evolved in the absence of browsing and grazing mammals and contain many species found nowhere else in the world. During the 1800's many species of animals and plants were introduced, some of which have spread widely, flourished, and now threaten the preservation of native species in protected areas. Problems include competition with native plants, predation of native birds and invertebrates by introduced rodents, and damage to vegetation by introduced ungulates and possums. For this reason, extermination of introduced plants and animals in national parks and several kinds of reserve is a stated policy in legislation, although control is often the only feasible management goal. A framework for the management of exotic species in national parks and reserves is provided by general policy and individual management plans for each protected area. The public play an essential role in the preparation of both policy and management plans.*

1. INTRODUCTION: SCIENTIFIC SIGNIFICANCE OF NEW ZEALAND'S NATIVE SPECIES

Several factors contribute to the scientific interest internationally of New Zealand's native flora and fauna. First, species are present whose ancestors date back to the Mesozoic when New Zealand was part of Gondwanaland. The native conifers, for example rimu *Dacrydium cupressinum*, kahikatea *Podocarpus dacrydioides*, totara *Podocarpus totara* and kauri *Agathis australis*, extend back some 250 million years; some native frogs, the reptile tuatara *Sphenodon punctatus* and perhaps some carnivorous snails existed in the New Zealand part of Gondwanaland as far back as 150 million years ago. The flightless moa *Dinornis* spp. and kiwis *Apteryx* spp., and the ancestors of the southern beeches *Nothofagus* spp.

were present also about 80 million years ago when New Zealand first began to drift away from Australia and Antarctica.

Second, the long period of New Zealand's isolation has produced a high degree of biological endemism; that is, of plants and animals found nowhere else in the world. The distinctive character of New Zealand's flora and fauna extends to almost all the major classes where more than half the species are unique to New Zealand (Fig. 1). Many of these species have distinctive morphological and physiological adaptations which add to their scientific interest.

And third, there is a low species diversity among several groups and many groups are absent or represented by only one species. This is expressed most dramatically in the terrestrial mammals, of which New Zealand possessed only 2 species of bats before the arrival of Polynesians about 1200 years ago; these stalwart voyagers brought with them a dog, which has since died out, and a rat *Rattus exulans*. Thus, New Zealand's native vegetation evolved in the absence of grazing and browsing mammals (although the effects of browsing by moa must not be overlooked), its invertebrates evolved in the absence of rodents and hedgehogs, and its birds in the absence of mammalian predators. Ecological niches characteristically occupied elsewhere in the world by small mammals are, in New Zealand, occupied by birds or invertebrates—a point brought out in popular articles when the ground-dwelling parrot, kakapo *Strigops habroptilus*, now one of New Zealand's rarest birds, is referred to as an "avian rabbit" and the giant wetas *Deinacrida* spp., which are among the largest insects in the world, are called "invertebrate mice".

2. INTRODUCED SPECIES

Into this scene, deliberately and accidentally over the past 200 years, Europeans have introduced thousands of species of plants and animals, to the extent that the present number of introduced plant species equals that of the native species at about 2000 species each (Molloy *et al*; 1980) and approximately 20 species of introduced mammals occur now in the wild. Following the deliberate introductions of mammals for meat by the early explorers, others were introduced in the late 1800s for sport, fur and the control of introduced rodents and rabbits. Patterns of spread and establishment varied. A few animals failed to establish; some, such as the hare *Lepus europaeus* and mouse *Mus musculus*, spread quickly until all suitable habitats were occupied; others such as the rabbit *Oryctolagus cuniculus* and possum *Trichosurus vulpecula* were assisted by repeated secondary liberations (Gibb and Flux, 1973). No one knows the number of native invertebrates that existed before Europeans arrived in New Zealand because the taxonomy of several invertebrate groups, notably insects, is still incomplete and some have been lost as a consequence of the introduction of exotic species without ever having been recorded (Ramsay, 1978).

A feature of introduced species in New Zealand is their remarkable vigour compared with that in their country of origin. In the United Kingdom, gorse *Ulex europaeus* is cultivated; in New Zealand, it has flourished and spread to such an extent that it is a noxious weed. Red deer *Cervus elaphus* thrive in New Zealand, reaching population densities unheard of in Europe.

2.2 Effects on native species

This influx of new species has caused new stresses from competition, predation and disease, some of which are illustrated later in this paper. Others, related to introduced plant pathogens and invertebrates, are not discussed owing largely to lack of information. It is a sobering commentary on the repercussions of introduced species in New Zealand that of the 41 species of rare and endangered species of endemic terrestrial vertebrates listed in The Red Data Book of New Zealand (1981), 17 of 21 species of birds, 7 of 14 species of lizards and amphibians and a species of bat are known or suspected of having reached this status through predation by rats, cats or mustelids; competition with introduced trout is thought to have caused the decline of 2 of 5 species of fish; and the decline of more than half of 61 species of vascular plants listed in the Red Data Book has been brought about by competition with introduced plants or by the grazing, browsing and associated trampling of introduced mammals.

3. PROTECTED AREAS

About 10% of New Zealand's land surface (2.7 million ha) is reserved in a manner which reasonably guarantees the preservation of flora and fauna (Nature Conservation Council, 1981). The major pieces of legislation related to the conservation of natural ecosystems within protected areas are the National Parks Act 1980, Reserves Act 1977 and Forests Act 1949. Other means of protection are included in the Wildlife Act 1953, Marine Reserves Act 1971 and Land Act 1948; there are several ways in which areas on private, leasehold, endowment and Maori lands may be protected under the Reserves Act 1977, the Queen Elizabeth II National Trust Act 1977 and Historic Places Act 1980. The largest areas of state-owned land for nature conservation are national parks, indigenous state forests and state forest parks. However, the priority given to preservation differs; whereas national parks (and some reserves) are managed primarily for preservation and recreation, state forest parks and state forests allow for extractive use. The management and contol of exotic species in New Zealand come under several acts, the two major ones relevant to protected areas being the Wild Animals Control Act 1977 and the Noxious Plants Act 1978.

4. POLICY CONCERNING INTRODUCED SPECIES IN PROTECTED AREAS

The topic of exotic species in protected areas in New Zealand is an immense one. To provide a framework within which to examine the current problems and issues raised by introduced species, I begin by considering relevant sections in the National Parks Act and Reserves Act and then consider some policies prepared by the National Parks and Reserves Authority (NPRA) relevant to these sections which are being circulated for public comment. These policies, evolved over many years, have been honed by ecological imperatives, scientific responsibilities, recreational demands, economic realities, and a respect for people's traditions; they reflect past, present and potential problems and solutions. Each draft policy is stated (underlined) after which examples selected from national parks and reserves are used to illustrate the background to the policy. The location of protected areas referred to is shown in Fig. 2.

The National Parks Act 1980 requires that "except where the Authority (NPRA) otherwise determines, the native plants and animals of the parks shall as far as possible be preserved and the introduced plants and animals shall as far as possible be exterminated". A comparable legislative requirement exists in respect of introduced plants and animals in scientific, nature and scenic reserves under the Reserves Act 1977, although not in respect of other categories of reserve (recreation, historic, government purpose) under this Act.

4.1 NPRA Draft Policy, July 1982—Plants

"Use of introduced tree species to control erosion or for other purposes will be subject to prior approval of the Authority and will only be permitted where the nature and extent of erosion or potential erosion is considered to pose a significant threat to maintaining other park values.

Existing non-spreading introduced trees of proven historic significance may remain at the discretion of the Authority, and vegetables and non-spreading shrubs and flowers may be planted for domestic purposes by occupiers of park land in areas authorized in accordance with the management plan".

4.1.1. Lodgepole pine *Pinus contorta.* Many areas of New Zealand are naturally erosion-prone and this tendency has been accentuated by the activities of deer and other introduced ungulates in several parks and reserves. Attempts to control erosion by planting trees have often made use of the rapid-spreading introduced *Pinus contorta*, dense infestations of which now occur in the tussock grassland and scrubland adjoining Tongariro National Park. The encroachment of *P. contorta* into the park would result eventually in a major vegetational modification from an association of natural native tussock and scrub unique to this part of New Zealand into one of exotic pine forest and would be completely contrary to the objectives for which the park was created. In Tongariro National Park, trees are removed by hand-cutting; however, in dense infestations outside the Park, a variety of techniques involving roller crushing, rotary slashing and burning is being used with hand-cutting for trees on steep eroding land. Although the use of *P. contorta* in erosion control has lessened recently, the species is well-established in both North and South Island where expensive control programmes are likely to continue to be required.

4.1.2. Marram grass *Ammophila arenaria.* Introduced to stabilize coastal sand dunes, this species has become so well established that few marram-free dune communities remain. On Codfish Island, a nature reserve off the coast of Stewart Island, and coastal Fiordland National Park, marram grass is being removed by hand digging and poisons.

4.1.3. Heather *Calluna, Erica.* Some of the early botanists to visit New Zealand expressed doubts about the survival of the indigenous flora in the face of aggressive introduced species. Later botanists, however, accede to the view that most introduced plants do not invade and displace native species in primitive communities until the communities are disturbed by man and animals (Healy, 1973). In Tongariro National Park, two species of heather, introduced to provide cover for game birds, have spread to such an extent that control by chemical, biological or physical means is not possible. Nor may control be necessary since scientific advice indicates that without damage by fires, heather will eventually be sup-

pressed by native plants (Tongariro National Park Board, 1979).

4.1.4. *Clematis vitalba.* This wind-dispersed soft woody vine which climbs over and smothers shrubs and trees, leading to eventual death, is causing increasing concern in protected areas on both main islands of New Zealand. Since the problem is worsening, a seminar will be held later this year to review present knowledge, explore avenues for future research and control, and publicize the problem more widely.

4.1.5. Gorse *Ulex europaeus.* Owing to its aggressive tendency to invade land cleared for agricultural and other purposes, gorse has long been classed as a noxious weed in New Zealand. This classification now poses problems for the management of some protected areas because research has revealed that gorse can form an excellent "nursery" cover for regenerating native tree species. Since gorse has high demands for light, it dies back when the emerging tree canopy develops.

4.1.6. Common weeds, long-established herbs and grasses. Many exotic weeds of developed land—blackberry, gorse, broom, lupin, thistles, briar rose—succeed in parks and reserves only along tracks, roads, fence lines, and around buildings where the native vegetation has been disturbed, the tree canopy opened or the area visited frequently by vehicles and man. Often these plants can be removed by hand, cut, or sprayed in the most frequently used areas and in places where native ecosystems are in jeopardy. While endeavours are made to keep these introduced weeds to a minimum by such methods, the NPRA acknowledges that for some long-established introduced herbs and grasses, eradication, or even control, would not be practical.

4.2 NPRA Draft Policy, July 1982—Animals

"Although ultimate extermination of introduced animals will be aimed at, the immediate objective shall be the reducation by all available means, of their numbers to a level the native flora and fauna can tolerate. Where necessary the extermination of introduced animals in particular areas will be undertaken if this is possible".

This policy underlines several problems which I illustrate by recent case studies related to red deer, stoats, possums, goats and feral cats in protected areas.

4.2.1. Control of introduced mammals. The Wild Animals Control Act 1977 provides the legislative framework for the control of many of the introduced mammals which now cause problems in new Zealand. In national parks and reserves, control operations for wild animals, as defined in this Act, which include deer, goats, chamois, tahr, pigs and possums, are carried out in accordance with Wild Animal Control Plans. These plans are prepared by the New Zealand Forest Service in consultation with the Department of Lands and Survey and local National Parks and Reserves Boards. Permits for commercial and recreational hunting and recovery are required; permits for ground operations are issued by the Commissioners of Crown Lands.

4.2.2. Red deer *Cervus elaphus*.

New Zealand's equable climate and predominantly evergreen native vegetation combines a long growing season with a year-round food supply for herbivores. This feature, aided perhaps by an absence of large predators, allows deer populations to increase rapidly and keep permanently close to the food limit with no marked seasonal relief from browsing or die-off in winter for the vegetation. Botanically, there is a loss of preferred species and, in severe cases, removal of the ground and shrub layer, thereby preventing the regeneration of canopy species. In mountain lands, areas of high rainfall, steep gradients and soil instability, the animals by their grazing, browsing and trampling upset the stability of the habitat and accelerate erosion.

4.2.3. Extermination policy.

In the 1960s a policy to exterminate wild ungulates in New Zealand was modified to one of controlling their numbers "at a level indicated as sufficiently low by the condition of the vegetation" (Gibb and Flux, 1973). However, for national parks and three classes of reserve, the extermination clause has remained in legislation (see 4.1 above) despite some criticism and suggestions for its amendment (Williams, 1979). The clause has been retained in the belief that extermination should be the *principle* on which administration of our national parks and reserves is based even if a more flexible policy is required to allow for the realities of the situation in some circumstances.

4.2.4. Role of introduced species in Takahe decline.

"*A . . . reduction . . . of their numbers to a level the native flora and fauna can tolerate*" is sufficiently flexible to allow for a spectrum of control from damage prevention to complete eradication. In the Murchison Mountains of Fiordland National Park, in the specially protected Takahe Area, lives the sole surviving wild population of the endemic and formerly widespread takahe *Notornis mantelli*, now one of the world's rarest species. Between 1967 and 1972 the number of birds declined 40%. This dramatic decrease coincided with a period when red deer began to compete with takahe for their staple diet of certain *Chionochloa* spp. tussocks after the deer had eliminated their own favoured species. Predation by stoats *Mustela erminea* was responsible for the death of some adult birds. A programme of deer control is being carried out effectively in the Murchison Mountains and palatable native species are regenerating. However, King (1978) was forced to conclude from her research on stoats in the park that control of the overall number of stoats in the Takahe Area is, in the foreseeable future, completely impracticable. Fluctuations in stoat numbers are associated with spectacular changes in mouse *Mus musculus* numbers which are related to, among other things, the periodic seeding of the native beech *Nothofagus* spp. Beech mast normally occurs a year after a hot summer (Lavers and Mills, 1978). If these apparent relationships are confirmed by further research, effective protection of takahe by "saturation trapping" in specific areas during peak stoat years may be possible.

4.2.5. Possum *Trichosurus vulpecula*.

Introduced from Australia repeatedly in the 1800s, this brush-tailed marsupial has spread slowly throughout New Zealand, reaching the northern North Island only recently. Their mainly vegetarian diet (buds, flowers, fruits, seeds and fresh shoots) has caused extensive death of the dominant canopy trees, rata *Metrosideros* spp. and kamahi *Weinmannia racemosa* in parts of Westland. Besides these species, they exploit several other native trees and shrubs frequently killing them, thereby exposing the forest to windthrow and erosion. Although the extent of damage directly attributable to possums is not always readily separated from salt spray, insect damage and the effects of other introduced animals, their role in the decline of some species in protected areas is well-documented. On Kapiti Island, a 2000 ha nature reserve off the coast of Wellington, farming was abandoned in 1897 and a luxuriant native forest became re-established despite moderate numbers of possums but without ungulates after goats were removed in 1928. Possum trapping had occurred, but in 1968 it ceased for several reasons: the need for regular trapping had never been clearly demonstrated; there were rumours that many native birds were being killed by traps; prices for possum pelts were low; and it was difficult to find people to do the trapping (Orsman, 1982). It was hoped that in the absence of trapping a balance might develop where natural regeneration would replace the few trees killed by possum browse as appeared to be the case on Codfish Island, a nature reserve off the coast of Stewart Island. However, after 12 years, possum numbers showed no signs of stabilizing and the vegetation continued to suffer. The possums were feeding on northern rata *Metrosideros robusta*—a slow-growing tree and an important source of food for nectar-eating birds in summer—more than before, and were thought to be disturbing the breeding of the little spotted kiwi *Apteryx owenii*, of which the only known population lives on Kapiti Island. On advice from the Department of Scientific and Industrial Research, commercial trapping was reinstated in February 1980; since then, 12,000 possums have been removed. There are now too few possums to make commercial trapping worthwhile and studies are underway to determine ways of eradicating possums from the island.

4.2.6. Feral cats *Felis catus*.

On Little Barrier Island (3055 ha), an important nature reserve off the east coast north of Auckland, feral cats have, for many years, posed a threat to ground-nesting petrels and other birds. Recently, intensive poisoning and trapping has rid the island of cats on what is probably New Zealand's only example of predator extermination.

4.2.7. Feral goats *Capra hircus.* Introduced by Captain Cook and liberated on off-shore islands as food for castaways, goats have been responsible for much vegetational damage on islands as well as the mainland. On Arapawa Island in Cook Strait there is a scenic reserve containing one of the few remnants of the former coastal vegetation characteristic of this region. Also present on the island are feral goats alleged by a local inhabitant to be descended from the original strain released by Captain Cook in 1777. The native vegetation has suffered severe damage from browsing by these goats and rooting by feral pigs. So, in an attempt to meet the requirements of the Reserves Act and to ensure that any special genetic qualities represented by these goats are not lost to mankind, goats have been made available to goat farmers and game parks and a breeding herd has been removed to a Crown-owned farm on the mainland; the numbers of goats remaining are being strictly controlled.

4.3 NPRA Draft Policy, July 1982

"Both commercial and recreational hunting will be encouraged by methods most appropriate to the individual park. No charge will be made for hunting permits issued by the Commissioner to commercial or recreational hunters".

4.3.1. Recreational hunting, conflicts and compromises. Exotic animals contribute to the appeal of, and use of, parks by recreational hunters. The NPRA policy encourages these users. However, intensive programmes to eradicate or control animal numbers to preserve ecological values arouse anger among recreational hunters over loss of recreational benefits. There is added resentment when the areas were protected through the initiatives of recreational hunters. The New Zealand Deerstalkers' Association (NZDA) represents a well-organized and powerful lobby which protects the interests of recreational hunters, including pressing for the retention of the localized herds of rusa, fallow and Virginia deer which have been established in New Zealand and for a herd of wapiti *Cervus canadensis nelsoni* in Fiordland National Park. The latter is the only wild herd of wapiti in New Zealand and is much prized by hunters, although the animals have hybridized with red deer to varying degrees. Pressures to remove the wapiti from the park to safeguard ecological values are being strongly opposed by the recreational hunters. After considering the arguments, the Government has decided to relocate a wapiti herd outside the park and a 3-phase programme began in January 1982. The aims of the programme are to remove 500 animals from the park, 300 of which are destined for upgrading of their wapiti characteristics by breeding in captivity before relocation in a suitable area in the wild outside the park; the other 200 are destined

for farming. The relocation area has yet to be decided and proposed sites will be the subject of an environmental impact report and public submissions, although the widespread and continuing problems created by deer in New Zealand would seem to beg the ecological wisdom of introducing a herd of these animals into any part of New Zealand where they do not occur already.

4.3.2. Economics of commercial hunting. Difficulties arise in parks when the numbers of animals removed by recreational hunters are insufficient to lessen the damage to ecologically tolerable levels and commercial hunters are allowed in. The advent of commercial venison removal by helicopters in the 1970's and, more recently, of live deer recovery for deer farms, has reduced the numbers of readily accessible animals for recreational hunters. However, commercial deer hunting, like possum trapping, is strongly influenced by the market for meat, skins and live animals and quickly becomes ineffective as a method of wild animal control at low population densities or when prices are low. Escalating costs of helicopter fuel now threaten the economic viability of commercial hunting, as do deer and possum farming.

4.3.3. Park income from exotic species. The present policy allows for concessions to be granted to commercial operators and for licence fees to be imposed for the use of park resources, generally on a royalty basis. In Fiordland National Park, and more recently, Urewera National Park, commercial hunting is used as a method of controlling deer populations to the financial benefit of the park. Before the revision of the National Parks Act 1980 which requires all revenue accrued to a park to be paid into a consolidated fund, this source of revenue to Fiordland National Park sometimes aroused ethical scruples, perhaps tinged with jealousy, among members of other park boards working under financial stringencies.

4.4 NPRA Draft Policy, July 1982

"The ecological impact of control techniques and their effectiveness on target populations should be monitored, with the aim being to replace techniques with adverse ecological impacts or little effectiveness with more acceptable methods. Public safety must always remain an important factor when considering and implementing techniques for the control of introduced animals".

4.4.1. Monitoring, poisons and non-target species. The wild animal control plans which are prepared include provision for monitoring the effectiveness of control on the target populations and of the techniques being used. The Wildlife Service, which has responsibilities for protecting native fauna under the Wildlife Act, is called in frequently to monitor the effects of the control programme and of the techniques being used—trapping, poisons etc.—on non-target, native fauna. As a result of some deaths of native birds during control programmes with '1080'-poisoned carrot baits for deer and possums, the carrot-cutters have been redesigned to reduce the proportion of chaff, or fines, which are picked up by birds and a more target-specific method of poisoning deer in native forests has been developed. It involves painting 1080-gel on the leaves of a broad-leaved preferred food shrub. The poisoned branch is tied down with string to browse level where it is out of reach of ground-feeding birds and invertebrates. Improvements to the adhesiveness of the gel in high rainfall climates are still needed but the method has been used successfully on Stewart Island and on Secretary Island, Fiordland National Park.

4.4.2. Policing commercial control operations. Wild animal control plans define the areas and times of year when commercial hunters can operate for reasons of public safety and to allow public access to parks and reserves during peak holiday periods. In both Fiordland National Park and Urewera National Park the policing of commercial operations has proven difficult and even dangerous at times, but limiting the number of operators, meeting with them regularly and insisting on better identification markings on helicopters appears to be reducing the number of infringements of the control plans.

4.5 NPRA Draft Policy, July 1982

"Emphasis will be placed on the prevention of new introduction of undesirable plants and animals".

4.5.1. Islands. Nowhere is this emphasis more important than on New Zealand's 634 offshore and 30 outlying islands, which range in latitude from subtropical (the Kermadecs 30°S) to subantarctic (Campbell Island 52°30'S) and in size from about 0.4 ha to 900 sq km (Chatham Island) (Williams, 1973). Parts of the larger offshore islands can be farmed or afforested economically without endangering unique plants or wildllife, but the wisest use of most islands is as reserves for scientific, educational and recreational purposes (Atkinson and Bell, 1973) and many of them have been so reserved. Most of the islands are free of deer, possums and even of some exotic weeds. Although goats were liberated on several offshore islands and cattle and sheep were released on some of the larger outlying islands, most have never been exposed to browsing and grazing mammals and at least 83 of 147 biologically significant islands are still rodent-free and, on another 40, only one species of rodent is present (Dingwall *et al*; 1978). At present, rats or mice, once established on an island, cannot be removed and the changes in the indigenous fauna which follow often become irreversible within a year or so of the rodents' arrival.

A recent example is given by the Big South Cape Islands, off Stewart Island, the largest of which is approximately 400 ha. Solomon Island (*c.* 25 ha) in the group was the only remaining habitat for the South Island saddleback *Philesturnus carunculatus*, Stead's bush wren *Xenicus longipes variabilis*, Stewart Island snipe *Coenocorypha aucklandica iredalei* and probably also the Stewart Island short-tailed bat *Mystacina tuberculata robusta* until an irruption of ship rats *Rattus rattus* in 1962-4. Other birds such as parakeets *Cyanoramphus* spp., bellbirds *Anthornis melanura melanura*, fernbirds *Bowdleria punctata stewartiana*, robins *Petroica australis rakiura* etc. were very common before the irruption as were many insects, including wetas. The irruptions caused robins and fernbirds to disappear from the island and the extinction of the saddleback, wren and snipe. The rats gained access to the island from the mooring lines of fishing boats (Bell, 1978).

There are three main problems to be faced in attempts to keep new introduced species from reaching New Zealand's offshore islands: the conservation value of maintaining rodent-free islands is not widely recognized by the public nor specifically in legislation; policing is inadequate on remote islands; and pressures are increasing to use the islands for communications installations and shelter for fishing boats during storms.

Recently, the NPRA concurred in a permit being issued to a fisherman for landing and mooring on Snares Islands, which are biologically significant and rodent-free sub-Antarctic island nature reserves. The permit, with strict conditions of use attached, was agreed to on the grounds that to refuse the permit could engender ill will among local fishermen to the extent that, under the present inadequate policing of the islands, illegal moorings and landings, which are known to occur, might increase and place the islands at greater risk than a few strictly controlled landings.

4.5.2. Proposed new introductions. Despite a legacy of problems throughout New Zealand related to introduced species, proposals to introduce new species are still considered seriously. At present, grass carp *Ctenopharyngodon idella* are undergoing trials for possible release in waterways to combat problems related to the excessive growth of introduced water weeds. Last year, the introduction of mink *Mustela vison* to establish a fur-farming industry was being contemplated.

4.6 NPRA Draft Policy, July 1982

"The use of herbicides, pesticides and poisons will be permitted only under stringent controls and where no other effective alternatives are available".

The use of poisons for controlling introduced plants and animals is discussed in the management plants for national parks and reserves. Separate proposals for large scale management programmes involving the use of poisons are drawn up prior to their implementation. In a programme aimed at eradicating mysore thorn *Caesalpinia decapetala*, purple guava *Psidium littorale* and African olive *Olea africana* which are threatening the indigenous subtropical flora of Raoul Island, a nature reserve northeast of New Zealand, spraying with the herbicide was not initiated until it had been established that indigenous flora which might also be affected was represented elsewhere on Raoul Island and that adverse effects on birds were unlikely (Devine 1977). Hand pulling and ringbarking have proven effective alternatives for Mauritius hemp *Furcraea foetida* and shore hibiscus *Hibiscus tiliaceus*, two other pernicious adventives on the island.

4.7 NPRA Draft Policy, July 1982

"Cooperation with local and regional authorities, district noxious plants authorities, adjacent landowners and other agencies in the implementation of these policies will be encouraged".

Discussion and cooperation locally are essential, especially where the source of introduced species is an adjacent landowner. Where park and reserve boundaries abut on pastoral land, stock are apt to wander into the forest for food and shelter, with consequent damage to the vegetation. Illegal wintering of cattle in adjacent reserves occasionally still occurs but has largely been overcome through boundary fencing with the cooperation of the farmer, although frequently financed by the Crown.

4.8 Domestic Animals

Since dogs and cats disturb and prey on native birds, and since the risk of pets escaping is too great, domestic animals and pets (exception: seeing eye dogs) are prohibited from national parks unless they have been specifically authorized by the Commissioner of Crown Lands. Specially trained dogs for management or security purposes may be permitted.

In parks and reserves where there is a traditional use of horses, for example Urewera National Park, this use is accepted but the ecological impact of the horses is assessed from time to time and control measures introduced if necessary.

4.9 Fish and Fishing

Many of New Zealand's waterways, including those in parks and reserves, now contain exotic species, mainly trout *Salmo* spp., which were introduced last century and are now a widely-valued recreational resource. For this reason, NPRA policy allows not only recreational fishing for these species but also, if introduced species are already present, for the release of fry or fingerlings of the same species where it can be shown that there has been a signifcant reduction in stock. Releases of this nature occur in Fiordland National Park, for example. The policy stipulates, however, that no introduced species of fish will be released into park waters where native fish only are present or where fish have not been reported. Like the deerstalkers, the fishermen's lobby is powerful and pressures to release trout into new areas can be strong.

4.10 Grazing

Sheep and cattle grazing is not considered to be in keeping with the primary purposes of the National Parks Act. However, since there are areas within parks which have been grazed for many years, generally predating the establishment of the park concerned, the policy makes provision for grazing to be continued under specified conditions, provided the land already exists in predominantly exotic pasture species, there is no risk of erosion, the animals are effectively controlled and the public's use of the park is not affected detrimentally. The policy allows also for grazing by introduced species as a management tool where scientific study has shown this to be necessary, or to protect particular park values, native species or important habitats.

5. CONCLUSION

The lessons learned from introduced species in the management of protected areas in New Zealand are encapsulated in the NPRA policies outlined above. They relate to the dangers to native flora and fauna of introducing exotic species, the problems of eradication or control, and the difficulties of achieving a balance between protecting the native flora and fauna and providing for the recreational use of the parks for hunting and fishing the now-established exotic species.

Stated succinctly, some of these lessons are:

- Give top priority to preventing new introductions into protected areas where they do not occur.
- Minimize the extent to which buffer zones can act as a source of exotic invasions.
- Precede any large scale eradication or control programme with research to assess the management goals, feasibility and best approach. Control programmes may just perpetuate a problem when it can be shown that native vegetation will eventually suppress introduced plants, or exotic animal densities will fluctuate between stable limits without intolerable damage to native flora and fauna. "Successful" control programmes may actually stimulate increased growth rates, migration and reproductive performance.
- In all large-scale control programmes for introduced species, include provisions for monitoring the effects on non-target species.
- Eradication of some introduced species is possible in particular areas on the mainland and on islands, but such exercises are time-consuming and expensive.

- Eradication, or even population control, is not possible at present for mustelids and rodents in New Zealand.
- Deer are a recreational asset in parks and reserves, but recreational hunting is ineffective as a means of wild animal control.
- Recreational hunters who benefit from exotic species in protected areas quickly become pressure groups opposed to extermination whenever extermination becomes possible.
- Commercial hunting is effective as a means of wild animal control only at high population densities and when the economics are favourable.
- Deer-farming and possum-farming outside protected areas now threaten the economics of exotic animal control in national parks and reserves based on the commercial recovery of meat, fur and live animals.

- The presence of deer has greatly increased the difficulties of balancing preservation and recreational values of national parks and reserves in the light of economic realities.
- Policies concerning introduced plants and animals, domestic animals, grazing, fish and fishing in parks and reserves in New Zealand provide a valuable framework for management.
- Public involvement in the preparation of policy and management plans for protected areas is essential.
- A wider recognition by the public of the international significance of New Zealand's flora and fauna and of the problems caused by introduced species in protected areas is needed to promote understanding of, and support for, restrictions and conditions related to the use of national parks and reserves.

Figure 1. New Zealand native flora and fauna.

Group	No. of living species native to New Zealand	% species endemic
Mosses and ferns	1,170	35
Conifers	20	100
Flowering plants	1,813	81
Invertebrates—worms, snails, spiders, insects	c 12,658	94
Freshwater fish	25–26	85
Amphibians	3	100
Reptiles	c 38	100
Terrestrial birds	65	57
Terrestrial mammals	2	100

Sources: Nature Conservation Council Technical Subcommittee 1981. Molloy, L.F. (ed.) 1980.

Figure 2. Location of national parks of New Zealand and reserves referred to in the text.

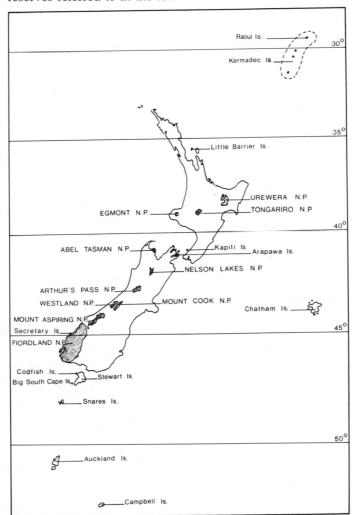

Future Directions for the Antarctic Realm

David A. Thom
Chairman
National Parks and Reserves Authority of New Zealand

ABSTRACT. *Owing to its unusual features, the Antarctic Realm must be discussed under separate headings for Antarctica, the Southern Ocean and New Zealand. Future directions for the Antarctic Continent require strong leadership from IUCN, increased investigative effort focussed on areas of development interest, the application of open information policies by the Treaty Nations, and increased responsibility by NGOs. It is paramount that the hitherto successful conservation policy remains effective. Similar conditions apply in relation to securing a sufficient understanding of the ecosystem of the Southern Ocean. Future directions for New Zealand include institutional development, widening the conservation responsibility, communication effort, representative and marine reservation, anticipatory policies, the cultural integration of the representative system and its referencing in global frameworks.*

1. INTRODUCTION

The Antarctic Realm lies within the context of a vast ocean area. It has thus much in common with Oceania, but differs greatly in respect of an extreme climatic range, and in its inclusion of a continental land mass. The realm contains a very low human population, fewer than 3.4 million people, of which 3.2 million reside in the islands of New Zealand. The control of human activity in Antarctica is exercised through a treaty of nations.

Apart from the Antarctic Continent, the Antarctic Realm is comprised of island groups within and adjacent to the vast marine wilderness of the Southern Ocean. Perhaps more than in any other region of the earth, consideration of a realm and its future leads to speculation on the ecosystem relationships within the realm; of the continent, the islands, and the Southern Ocean. A characteristic feature of the Antarctic Realm is the fundamental significance of marine ecosystems. All marine mammals and sea birds on sub-Antarctic island reserves are dependant on the oceans for their food—protection of terrestrial areas and resources cannot be considered separately from conservation of marine environments and resources.

For these reasons it is not practicable to make general statements about the future directions of the Realm as a whole. I have therefore approached future directions for the Antarctic Realm from three standpoints:

- In relation to the Antarctic continent which is under the direction of international treaty;
- In relation to an understanding of the ecosystem of the Southern Ocean; and
- In relation to the populated area with conventional government—the islands of New Zealand.

2. THE ANTARCTIC CONTINENT

The 1980 Convention on the Conservation of Antarctic Marine Living Resources came into force this year. The latest round of talks on the Antarctic Minerals Regime emphasized the urgency of elaborating a Regime in the face of increased pressure to permit exploration/exploitation. Delegations reaffirmed the principle that protection of the Antarctic environment should be a basic consideration and that work should proceed on establishing mechanisms to ensure appropriate environmental safeguards. This parallels, in essence, the IUCN reolution on Antarctic minerals.

The Antarctic experience is unusual in that development issues are now being raised within an agreed conservation policy. This is the inverse of the more normal situation in which conservation finds itself frantically endeavouring to reserve residuals and remnants in the face of established industries and related social attitudes. The success of the Antarctic Treaty draws attention to the fundamental issue of political will. It draws attention also to the value of cooperation, and to the case in which the shaping of policy appears to be paced by, and in step with, the growth of the information base.

In all these aspects the Antarctic experience is unusual. Success may be due on the one hand to the general belief that conditions were so harsh that exploitation was severely constrained, and on the other to lack of confirmed information as to the nature and extent of useful resources. There has, accordingly, been an absence of strong political pressures in favour of resource development, a situation further promoted by the absence of an electorate.

However, notice has been given in recent discussions of the Treaty nations, in the pressures mounting from nations outside the Treaty, in the increasing public knowledge of Antarctica, and in the accumulation of information itself, that the Antarctic situation may now become increasingly political. This is in the sense that the laudable long-term objectives of the Treaty will increasingly be subject to short-term pressures, and it is on the political arms of governments that these pressures will be felt. The effect of such pressures is, generally, to unbalance the relationship between the soundness of the information base, and short- and long-term policy. The Antarctic provides an opportunity to maintain the balance, seldom maintained elsewhere; indeed, an imbalance is often deeply embedded in national political and institutional structures.

The Antarctic also illustrates a general trend to increasing competition for resources. This may be allied to stringent economic circumstances, and the whole may be allied to general decline of resource availability. The effect again is to increase the pressure towards decisions which favour the short term at the expense of the long. Again the pressures fall on the political arms of governments.

But can the Antarctic situation be maintained under growing pressure? Powerful lobbies will develop. Politicians will need convincing and well founded advice, in which they can have confidence and conviction. Anticipatory policy requires acceptance that the pace of events is accelerating, and the allocation and steady escalation of investigative resources. Priorities for the programming of investigation need to take full account of the nature, location, and timing of possible development pressures. Unless the required investigation is then carried out in time to develop the necessary framework of conservation policy, conservation may lose control.

In this situation, the primary need for future directions in the Antarctic is conservation leadership and influence at both international and national levels. We must look to IUCN to provide this, and to exercise the greatest possible range of influence by formal means as well as by informal means such as direct contact with Foreign Ministers by elder statesmen of IUCN.

Such leadership would also seek to impress non-government organizations and national IUCN committees with the need to take responsibility within their individual national situations for strong representations to their own governments.

A condition for the success of such activity is full and free availability of information about the deliberations of the Treaty Nations, and the work of the scientific programmes carried out by their scientific organizations.

At the scientific level, further direct linkage between scientific committees of IUCN and the scientific coordinating committee of the Treat Nations is necessary.

In addition to the foregoing policy steps, aimed at strengthening the conservation framework in the face of mounting development measures, action programmes can be proposed. The following illustrate the type of field action which would strengthen the conservation framework:

- A critical review of protected areas in Antarctica, with the objective of obtaining a documented inventory of protected resources, extensions of existing protected areas, and identification of new areas representing the full diversity of Antarctic terrestrial and freshwater ecosystems.
- Instigation of a management planning exercise for protected areas of Antarctica and the southern islands of Insulantarctica.
- Design of a biogeographic system for coastal and marine environments of the Antarctic Realm, as a basis for the selection of widely representative marine protected areas.
- Preparation of an Atlas of Protected Areas of the Antarctic Realm as a major reference source for management and for use in educational and interpretative programmes.
- Preparation of attractive, informative and authoritative documents on protected areas specifically for fostering and assisting tourist activities, especially in Antarctica and the southern islands.

3. THE SOUTHERN OCEAN

Most productive of the oceans of the world, the Southern Ocean has been well characterized by Professor E.C. Young in his paper for the workshop on Managing Coastal and Marine Protected Areas (Young, 1982): "Physically this is an enormously robust system, with the swirling water mass driven by the westerly winds. It is well able to withstand the puny impact of man. But biologically it is vulnerable, with much of its organic production channelled through a single harvestable species of crustacea—the ubiquitous krill *Euphausia superba*.

"The impact of the deep permanent ice-cover on Antarctic biology and climate cannot be overstressed.

There is little ice-free shore-line, and none not scoured clean of larger life forms, and few places anywhere where soils and freshwater can provide habitats for more than a tenuous existence for a cold- adapted fauna and flora. There are few suitable breeding places on land for birds and mammals, so that breeding concentrations are limited and as no food is available, these animals depend directly or ultimately on the fertility of the seas. On the continent there are no territorial animals apart from mites and insects''.

Against the background of that evocative description, one can sense the importance, and the fragility of islands like the Campbells (McKerchar and Devine, this volume). They are few, and the margins for mistakes in management are slim and unforgiving. Some of the islands are still rat-free, and the introduction of rats on these would amount to a major conservation disaster for the bird life which is part of the Southern Ocean ecosystem.

Conservation of the botany of the islands is not any less important. Remote and in severe latitudes, there is a high degree of endemism in the plants. But these islands, like the Antarctic itself, are the subject of increasing development pressure from tourism. The prospect of demands for bases for oil exploration is not remote. Without much more knowledge of the place of these islands within the Southern Ocean ecosystem, managers lack vital information.

Future directions for the Southern Ocean are similar to those for Antarctica. The same sort of leadership is required, together with the same sorts of linkages and connections between IUCN and the scientific agencies working in the Southern Ocean as have been proposed for the Antarctic. The objective should be the piecing together, openly, and through international cooperation, of an immensely superior account of the ecosystem of the Southern Ocean.

4. NEW ZEALAND

4.1 Institutional development

New Zealand National Parks administration passed into a phase of institutional change and development with the coming into force of the National Parks Act 1980. This established a citizen policy-making body (the National Parks and Reserves Authority) and 12 regional boards covering New Zealand. Executive administration of the policies set by these bodies within the legislation is carried out by the Department of Lands and Survey.

Elworthy (this volume) has described the prospect of further institutional change in the form of a Commission which would add responsibility for policy in relation to all publicly owned indigenous forest and open country to those at present directed to National Parks and Reserves. In concept such an institutional change would establish a body able to implement the

intentions of the World (and New Zealand) Conservation Strategies, to provide more real choices within the lands under its policy overview, and to guide the process of highly public information and policy formulation which is necessary in today's world.

4.2 Widening the conservation responsibility

The institutional proposal described by Elworthy also widens the conservation responsibility. This is a matter of fundamental importance once the general objective of management is seen to be conservation rather than exploitation. Within such an objective, conservation must extend and demonstrate its managerial capacity in the field of sustainable production. It is necessary, in other words, to show how sustainable production, within the concept of conservation, can be made to work.

Widened responsibility extends to solving (in a real and viable sense) the social and economic difficulties of applied conservation policy, like those described by Molloy (this volume). Widened responsibility includes also the perception and development of anticipatory policy, a matter discussed below.

4.3 Communication

There are a number of examples from New Zealand, of situations which arose or became unnecessarily polarized because the arts of communication were not utilized. In the background can often lie a pervasive half-understanding of the values and cultural importance of protected areas.

The National Parks Act of New Zealand promotes communication and openness, incorporating specified public notice and response procedures in relation to management planning and proposals to extend national parks. It is now clearly evident that major communicating effort from national park administration with all sectors of use has become an essential vehicle for policy formulation. It is also an essential aspect of public support, confidence, and understanding. Among future directions for New Zealand therefore lies major effort to communicate by every means available, informally as well as by procedure, about protected area values.

In the increasing role of conservation in relation to political decision-making, it is vital to establish communication, credibility, and confidence. As to communication, there is no substitute for personal contact. Credibility and reason are inseparably related. Confidence is the product of good advice, firmness, and consistency.

4.4 Completing the representative system

Dingwall (this volume) has described New Zealand efforts to move toward a representative system of protected areas which have resulted in a provisional statement of ecological regions and districts. The adequacy of existing reservation will be tested against the provisional subdivision. The implications of such testing are confirmation of existing reservation, and its modification, extension and replacement.

Already, its potential practical usefulness in conservation management can be glimpsed. For example, Burns (this volume) discusses the particular problem of the wapiti *Cervus canadensis* in Fiordland National Park, and government proposals to remove this much prized hunting herd. Recreational hunters are strongly opposed to removal. It is not inconceivable that well-founded definition of the ecological region in which the herd is at present located, and knowledge of the range of the animals in relation to the region, would permit consideration of their retention. The requirements of any such sector of an ecological region or district for this purpose would be clearly that boundaries would permit control of the herd's range, and that comparative monitoring of the state of vegetation was feasible. It goes without saying that the sector would be of sufficient area to support the herd, and that the balance of the ecological district was sustainable.

Future directions in completing the system lie not only in fieldwork, the identification of deficiencies and threatened areas, and the inventories which accompany a major effort to achieve a representative system, but also in carrying through the investigations into national park extension and new national park areas which have been proceeding for more than a decade. The results of these investigations have now to receive the final assessments and exposure to public procedures which are requirements of the 1980 National Parks Act.

The completion of these two streams of work (national park extension and representative reservation) will largely complete the framework of nature reservation in New Zealand. Regrettably, and this is very clear from the focus of attention on marine reservation at this Congress, New Zealand is very much behind many other countries in its attention to marine reservation.

Future directions for New Zealand must include energetic efforts to evolve nationally appropriate concepts, and institutional and managerial arrangements for marine reservation.

4.5 Formulating anticipatory policies

Molloy (this volume) clearly demonstates a situation which resulted from a lack of anticipatory policy. In the situation he describes, indigenous forests had declined beyond the point at which a transition into sustainable yield production was feasible. In consequence, political controversy and pressures led to reservation, which forced decline and change on local communities leading in turn to further political reaction, limited options, and difficult national/regional compensation issues.

In late stages of the controversies, conservation interests in New Zealand had glimpsed the significance of anticipatory policy, and were posing options for the continued economic and local support of affected communities. By this time, attitudes had polarized, and conservation did not enjoy the credibility needed for the objective consideration of proposals. The lessons of the experience are to do with the forecasting of resource decline, public involvement in the making of public policy, and in the value of anticipatory policy.

An excellent example of a situation in need of anticipatory policy is given by Burns, who refers to the general decline of commercial deer hunting by helicopter in national parks. The operation is losing its commercial attractiveness due to rising fuel costs, low animal numbers due to heavy pressure in the immediate past, and the establishment of farmed deer herds.

Anticipatory policy must now be developed for a situation in which animal numbers will rise due to release of commercial deer hunting pressure. National parks administration will then have available a forecast situation, will know how, when and where to act, and the extent of funding required.

4.6 Attending to the survival of the system

It is clear from the many case studies presented at the World National Parks Congress that some New Zealand experiences are shared widely. Molloy has described conflicts generated by proposals which appeared to affect the life styles of communities adjacent to the parks. Burns has referred to conflicts over recreational deer hunting with bodies which are essentially supporters of conservation.

It is apparent that policies of reservation must be sensitive and responsive to the social and economic circumstances of the people and lands surrounding the reservations. It is essential for the survival of protected areas systems that they must become supported and accepted within the regions and culture of their countries. One would expect, with time, to find successful national, even regional, variations emerging, with a detectable cultural and regional variation of policy guiding the affairs of the natural areas, themselves so highly representative of a distinctive situation.

Rigid models of protection will tend to generate conflicts which may erode the public support which is the ultimate protection. Survival depends on the sensitivity with which protected areas can be integrated into the culture and land use of their countries. Future directions include the study and development of the mechanisms needed.

4.7 Locating the system in context

As described by Dingwall, New Zealand has a provisional definition of ecological regions and districts as a basis for the selection of representative reservation. A future direction which has already been identified in this paper is the development of marine reservation.

Global biogeographic frameworks for terrestrial and ocean systems have been discussed at this Congress. The monitoring of the developing New Zealand systems to ensure their location and referencing within the global frameworks will be a future direction for New Zealand.

Chapter 10
The Palaearctic Realm

Keynote Address: The Palaearctic Realm

Francois Ramade
Laboratoire de Zoologie et d'Ecologie
Université de Paris Sud
Paris, France

ABSTRACT. *The Palaearctic Realm is the largest in the world, stretching from Iceland to Japan. It has had an ancient and profound impact by man on its various ecosystems from the very beginnings of the agricultural revolution, yet there are still many areas where nature has adapted to humans and where conservation values are still respected. Over 41 million hectares are contained within the protected areas of the Palaearctic, but lake and river ecosystems are still poorly protected, as are temperate broadleaf forests and highland orophyllous habitats. The need to develop scientific research, especially in the ecological field, in the various protected areas is emphasized.*

1. INTRODUCTION

The Palaearctic Realm is, by its area and the diversity of the ecosystems it contains, the main biogeographical area of the world. Traditionally, ecologists divide the Palearctic Realm into four areas: the Euro-Siberian; the Mediterranean; the Aral and Caspian; and the Chinese.

Some specialists also include an Arctic area consisting of the Tundra and the Niveal zones of the Northern Euro-Siberian area. The Southern boundaries of the Mediterranean and the Aral and Caspian areas are still highly controversial, but are generally established at Latitude 30 degrees South.

2. HISTORICAL BACKGROUND OF THE USE OF NATURAL RESOURCES IN THE PALAEARCTIC REALM

The Palaearctic Realm was affected by demographic pressures at a very early stage; the oldest civilizations appeared independently and at about the same period of time in the Eastern Mediterranean Basin and in the valleys of temperate China. Thus it is no coincidence if the resources of the Chinese and Mediterranean Areas are among those which have been over-exploited and degraded.

At the beginning, the Mediterranean area was covered with forests dominated either by sclerophyllous (several species of oaks) or needleleaf species. For thousands of years, the joint action of the axe, fire and overgrazing led to the extinction of the climatic woodlands which today remain as relicts in remote areas. On extensive areas of low quality and fragile soils, forest ecosystems were replaced by degraded vegetation dominated by shrub (Corsican maquis, for example). Over-exploitation of Mediterranean forest ecosystems led to the dramatic erosion of soils which was aggravated by the special climatic conditions of the area.

Temperate China is also an example of an area in the world where natural resources have been especially degraded through human action. Deforestation and the resulting erosion have been enhanced by the very nature of the montainous biotopes: 85% of the whole area is above 1000 m. Whereas 70% of temperate China was covered by forests at the end of the Paleolithic Era, today the forest covers only 8%. On the other hand, 39% of the total area is eroded and/or desertified due to man's action.

The history of nature and natural resource use in Atlantic and Central Europe is somewhat different; although it may seem strange, the "natural" environment there is less degraded than in the areas described earlier, in spite of a very high population density (sometimes more than 200 per square kilometre).

In Western and Central Europe, there is virtually no primitive habitat left, but the productivity of the vegetation and the soils is not highly altered, although these were deeply modified by man's activities. The ecosystems to be found from the North-Western Iberic Peninsula to Central Russia result from the deforestation of the deciduous temperate forests—the great Hercynian Forest—which covered the area for the last ten thousand years. The brown forest soils of these biotopes are very stable and this is the reason why it was possible to develop in Europe a high quality rural area with remarkable agricultural productivity. As a result, deciduous climatic forests were progressively restricted to poor soils.

Thus, most of the so-called "natural" ecosystems of middle Europe have in fact been modified or even created by man. The grasslands of Atlantic Europe and the genista or heather moors are good examples of such ecosystems.

Furthermore, it took so long to modify the different habitats during historical times that nearly all European fauna (with the exception of the bigger species) were able to adapt to the alterations of their biotope.

As a consequence, nature conservation in Europe does not generally aim at the survival of primitive ecosystems—except for some primitive forest relicts—but at the protection of secondary habitats and communities resulting from man's continuous action during historical times.

3. NATURAL RESOURCE USE AND PROTECTION TENDENCIES

As everywhere else, use of living resources has increased considerably during the last century. With regards to forest resources, exploitation of the primitive needleleaf forest—Taga—covering a wide area of the Euro-Siberian region has progressed rapidly. In vast areas of the Mediterranean region and China, degradation of the secondary vegetation canopy was accelerated under the joint impact of traditional practices and marginal lands development due to demographic factors and, in turn, aggravated soil degradation.

The temperate steppe of Eurasia is another ecosystem which was profoundly disturbed by man in the past century. Once development of Eastern European steppes was completed, nearly the whole of the unaltered steppes of central Asia was given over to agricultural development wherever rainfall was sufficient. The last vast unaltered steppe of the world—in Kazakhstan—was developed in the 1950s.

Where there was not enough rainfall, traditional use for extensive pastoral purposes was increased and overgrazing resulted in grassland degradation in most of the Aral and Caspian area (from Syria to Pakistan) as well as in Northern Africa.

With regards to wild fauna exploitation, hunting pressure increased considerably in the last century. In France, for example, where the hunting pressure is unfortunately the highest in the world, the number of hunters increased from 300,000 in 1880 to more than 2,000,000 at the end of the past decade.

Aquatic ecosystems, whether freshwater or coastal, have also suffered from intensive use and alteration during this period. The destruction of wetlands through draining in order to reclaim land for agriculture was particularly strong in the western part of the Palaearctic Realm—Europe and the Mediterranean Basin. In the whole of the Palaearctic, the development of dams and other water projects construction on rivers has had a negative impact on fish populations important for the continental fisheries.

Tourist development on the coast and in the mountains has been very important in the Western Palaearctic area during the last decades and is a new source of disturbance for environments which until then had been relatively protected from intensive use.

This is a matter of great concern for the whole of the Mediterranean coastal fringe where anarchic urban development together with exaggerated tourist pressure have often hindered the establishment of land or marine natural reserves aimed at the protection of exceptional ecosystems.

Finally, industrialization causing air as well as continental and coastal water pollution has resulted in the degradation of many habitats. Acid rain is an example reminding one of the extent to which an industrial pollutant can degrade natural resources far away from its emission site.

In the area under consideration and even in any given country of the realm, resources protection measures and particularly the establishment of protected areas varies from one place to another. However, there has been a considerable increase in the number of areas under protection. In 1909, there were only two National Parks in the whole of the Palaearctic Realm: the Swedish National Parks of Sarek and Sonfjallet, covering an area of 200,000 ha. Today, some 40,000,000 ha are protected throughout the Palaearctic Realm.

All developed countries implement strict measures to protect the air, water, soils and all living resources. At the same time, most of the developing countries of the Palaearctic realm have taken in the past three decades legal measures to protect nature and natural resources and the National Parks and Protected Areas network has expanded. However, considerable differences exist in the density and the quality of the network, from one country to another, as is shown in Tables 1 and 2.

Table 1 indicates that each of the main land and freshwater biomes is under some sort of protection.

Table 2 concerns the distribution of Protected Areas in each biogeographical province of the Palaearctic Realm. Considering the rather high number of provinces—some of which cover a limited area—as defined by IUCN (Udvardy, 1975) and used by the Protected Areas Data unit, we have amalgamated some of the data.

4. PROTECTION STATUS IN THE WHOLE OF THE PALAEARCTIC

We included in the tables the main data on the protected areas of the Palaearctic Realm collected by IUCN's Protected Area Data Unit (PADU); however we have had to modify some of them when we were told of errors concerning the figures on one protected area or another.

Table 3 has been prepared from computerized data collected by PADU. It shows the areas of the National Parks and Equivalent Reserves for each country of the Palaearctic Realm, the proportion of the Protected Areas compared to the total area and the protected area compared to the population.

Data followed by a question mark concerns countries not to be found on IUCN's list or countries where the real status of conservation in the so-called protected areas is doubtful. We have used the 1981 World Population Data Sheet of Washington's Population Reference Bureau as a source for each country's population.

Table 4 shows the increase in the protected areas of the Palaearctic Realm since the beginning of the century.

The study of Tables 1–4 summarizing the statistical data on protected areas of the Palaearctic Realm allows one to draw a certain number of conclusions on nature conservation tendencies and the present status in the Realm:

- There has been a considerable increase in the area of National Parks and Equivalent Reserves in the 20th century, from 230,000 ha in 1909 to 41,391,000 ha in 1982.
- Most of the protected areas are located in the Euro-Siberian biogeographical area where they cover the widest range of ecosystems and biotopes compared to the total number of natural systems in this area.
- Legal measures—and especially nature protection laws implemented in Protected Areas—are best implemented in the Euro-Siberian area. This neither means that protected areas of the Euro-Siberian area guarantee the survival of all the types of natural environments to be found, nor that the park and reserve management is always perfect.
- Although the 410 Protected Areas of the Euro-Siberian area make up a rather complete network, there are still some gaps in the protection of this wide biogeographical zone.
- Looking at map 3 of the World Conservation Strategy, "Priority biogeographical provinces of the land for the establishment of protected areas", one notices that protection measures are quite inadequate for three types of ecosystems. The first one is the lake and river ecosystems: in Europe and Siberia, only a few lakes, ponds or river sections are under protection. In France, for example, there are plans to develop the last "wild" 100 km of the Rhne to produce hydro-electricity; this will

totally disturb the aquatic and coastal species. Similarly, temperate broadleaf forests as well as several mountain or highlands orophyllous habitats are, even in Western Europe, inadequately protected.

- When comparing the proportion of Protected Areas relative to the total area of the national territory in every country of the realm, one cannot but notice the considerable differences.
- With the exception of Austria and Czechoslovakia, no state has more than 10% of its territory under protection.
- However paradoxal this may seem, there is no negative relationship between population density and the extent of the protected areas. In the U.K., which has one of the highest population densities in Western Europe, more than 6.1% of the territory is covered by Natural Reserves and other Protected Areas. On the other hand, in France or Spain, where the population density is the lowest, less than 0.8% of the territory is protected.
- In the *Chinese biogeographical area*, the number of National Parks and Equivalent Reserves varies widely. Their total number is over 100 for the four countries concerned (China, Mongolia, The Republic of Korea, Japan). Japan, with national parks and other protected areas covering 9.14% of its territory, is well ahead of the other countries. In China, the different natural reserves only cover 0.18 percent of the total area. There is not yet a park in the Tibetan region and priority actions should be taken to protect the Chinese-Himalayan mountains and highlands.
- The World Conservation Strategy underlines the urgent need to reinforce Protected Areas and to extend the areas under protection of subtropical forest and temperate rain forest in Southern China, Mongolian and Manchu steppes, semi-deserts and the cold deserts of Eastern China and the Himalayan area.
- The *Aral and Caspian area* has about 100 protected areas but great differences exist in the numbers and in the strict management of National Parks and thus in the efficiency of the protection.
- In the Soviet Union, there is at least one park or equivalent reserve in every biogeographical zone and nearly all types of ecosystems are protected.
- At the other end, neither Syria nor Iraq are on the UN List. The political situation in Iran and Afghanistan makes it impossible to know whether the extensive area covered by National Parks in both countries is really under adequate protection.
- The Western Anatolian province forests are listed in the World Conservation Strategy among the priority areas for the establishment of Reserves.
- The *Mediterranean biogeographical area* is the one with the most severe conservation problems in the whole of the Palaearctic Realm. There are about 50 protected areas covering less than 600,000 hec-

tares in 15 countries. Several Eastern Mediterranean nations are not on the UN List and for the whole of Northern Africa, Tunisia only with 2 percent of its territory under protection, is in a good position among the whole of the Palaearctic Realm countries. Moreover, the World Conservation Strategy lists the Southern part of the Mediterranean region as a high priority area for the establishment of steppe and desert reserves.

Urgent conservation measures need to be taken for the coastal and island systems as well as for the marine zones where, in many countries, inter-coastal and circumcoastal zones are highly threatened by development and pollution. It is therefore urgent to establish a sufficient number of well distributed National Marine Parks. Let us underline that had such protected areas been created at the begining of the 1960s, some populations of threatened species could have been saved, such as the western Mediterranean monk-seal, which still visited the area of Scandola in Corsica at the end of the decade.

5. FACTORS IN THE ESTABLISHMENT AND MANAGEMENT OF PROTECTED AREAS

5.1 Positive factors

During the last two decades, a number of universal or specific factors enhanced the establishment and expansion of protected areas in the whole of the Palaearctic Realm. A series of conferences and other international meetings, such as Unesco's 1968 Conference on use and conservation of the Biosphere, the 1970 European Year for Nature Protection, and the 1972 Stockholm Conference on Human Environment, have played an essential role in the development of the network of national parks and other protected areas network by making politicians aware of the seriousness and urgency of nature conservation problems.

Several International Organizations have also played an important part in the field: UNEP, Unesco and its Biosphere Reserves, and IUCN and its constant influence on the different governmental agencies concerned.

Finally, the very active non-governmental organizations of Europe and Japan have influenced decision-makers to establish more protected areas or to extend the existing ones. In many cases, the first Nature Reserves of Western Europe were created by such non-profit NGOs. It is not necessary to recall the role of U.K's National Trust in this field. Similarly, the first French Strict Nature Reserve—the Camargue—was created in 1928 by an NGO, the Socit nationale de protection de la nature, some 32 years before the first French legislation on National Parks was passed.

Whereas in the countries concerned, public awareness is still too often based on aesthetic criteria, the major advantage for a country's economy of the sound conservation and management of natural resources or of the protection, for example, of genetic resources or watershed forests plays a decisive role in the decision making of governments concerning the establishment of National Parks. The World Conservation Strategy clearly underlines the urgent need to integrate ecosystem protection to development programmes.

5.2 Negative factors

Several negative factors interfere with the establishment of protected areas or with the implementation of efficient conservation measures inside Protected areas.

Among them we shall note the high urbanization pressures in connection with tourism which are being exerted upon the natural environment in many Western European countries and in the Mediterranean Basin. This results in a pernicious degradation of and a permanent encroachment on the last undisturbed natural areas left in these biogeographical provinces.

Nowadays, it has become more and more difficult to find on the Northern Mediterranean coast—from Gibraltar to Albania—a large enough natural zone to create an ecologically viable reserve.

Development for tourism also goes against the establishment of National Parks in mountain areas. Thus, in France, the Mercantour National Park created in 1979 saw its area reduced and its boundaries modified compared to the original project (early 1960s) for in the meantime, two important ski resorts had been built on the area proposed as National Park.

The implementation of effective protection is hampered by the opening of ski runs inside protected areas. IUCN's 16th General Assembly (Christchurch, New Zealand, October 1981) took a resolution on the matter in relation to Cairngorm Reserve in Scotland. The problem of ski run development inside National Parks is to be found from Pallas-Ounastunturi National Park, Finland, to several protected areas of the Southern Alps. Finally, in many Western European countries, protected areas attract a lot of tourists and this brings about a problem of "human erosion". Trampling visitors destroy the herbaceous vegetation and may even hamper forest regeneration in the most popular reserves.

Some groups of hunters lobby to influence governments and are an obstacle to the establishment of parks in many nations of the Palaearctic Realm. This is especially strong in latin European countries. In France, for example, local hunters have often been opposed to the establishment of new protected areas. Through their action, hunting is allowed or has been re-opened for certain species in several National Parks. They successfully opposed banning of hunting in most of the National Reserves created since the mid-1970s.

Poaching, which exists in many areas of the Palaearctic Realm without being as dramatic as in other biogeographical areas, is locally a serious obstacle to the efficient protection of the fauna.

Agricultural or forestry development projects concerning some threatened ecosystems are also elements against the establishment of National Parks and other protected areas. Today, one of the most serious problems in several countries of the Palaearctic Realm is the drying up of vast wetlands for agriculture. Many projects relating to the establishment of new reserves are countered by the pastoral use of the concerned areas and by projects to convert some of them for wheat crops as well as by forest exploitation of some woodlands which need urgent and strict protection.

Deficiencies are noted in the whole of the Palaearctic Realm where several countries are not yet part of certain Conventions or International Agreements. This hampers the efficiency of conservation measures taken in the so-called protected areas. In Western Europe, several countries do not apply rules edicted in the EEC framework or at a wider level. Many nations of the Palaearctic Realm have not yet accepted the Ramsar or Washington Conventions, and only a limited number of IUCN's member States have set up a National Conservation Strategy.

6. CONCLUSION

To conclude this overview of the problems of protected areas establishment and management in the Palaearctic Realm, we shall emphasize the need to develop scientific research, especially in the ecological field, inside National Parks and protected areas. As well as a good understanding of basic biocenotic phenomenons, it is highly desirable to be able to monitor the potential evolution of these areas, whether it is spontaneous or man-induced. The predominant role of National Parks and other protected areas in the conservation of genetic diversity demands the precise monitoring of the species composing the living communities protected.

Table 1: Protected areas in each large continental biomes of the Palaearctic Realm

Biome	Total area protected (hectares)
Temperate rain forest	1,419,821
Temperate deciduous forest	7,144,259
Southern sclerophyllous forest	1,383,213
Boreal needleleaf forest	4,877,282
Temperate steppe	2,167,458
Hot desert	4,855,599
Cold desert	6,856,280
Arctic tundra	4,888,553
Mountain biomes	7,780,872
Freshwater ecosystems	18,300
	41,391,630

Table 2: Distribution of the Palaearctic Realm protected areas according to biogeographical provinces

Province	Biographic code	Total area protected (hectares)
Arctic region		
Iceland, Spitzbergen	2.05.05, 2.25.09	
Wrangel Island	2.26.09	4,588,826
Euro-Siberian tundra	2.27.11	2,961,254
Sub-Arctic birchwoods	2.06.05	600,260
		8,150,340
Euro-Siberian region		
Atlantic Europe (includes British Isles.)	2.08.05, 2.09.05	1,908,936
Iberian Highlands	2.16.06	215,782
Central European Highlands	2.32.12	2,311,235
Balkan Highlands	2.33.12	416,703
Altai Highlands	2.35.12	935,093
Middle European Forest	2.11.05	790,720
Boreonemoral	2.10.05	685,051
Pannonian	2.12.05	127,755
Pontian Steppe	2.29.11	532,033
Mongolian-Manchurian Steppe	2.30.11	79,080
West Eurasian Taiga	2.03.03	
East Siberian Taiga	2.04.03	4,877,282
Kamchatkan	2.07.05	964,000
		13,843,670
Mediterranean region		
Mediterranean Sclerophyll	2.17.07	546,584
Steppes and deserts	2.13.05, 2.19.07, 2.28.11	75,255
		621,839
Aral and Caspian region		
Arabian Desert and Anatolian-Iranian Desert	2.19.07, 2.20.08, 2.24.09	1,678,016
Turanian	2.21.08	1,165,804
Takla-Makan-Gobi Desert	2.22.08	4,507,850
Aral Sea	2.43.14	18,300
Caucaso-Iranian Highlands	2.34.12	2,234,303
Altai and Pamir-Tian-Shan Highlands	2.35.12, 2.36.12	654,000
		10,258,273
Chinese region		
Chinese Subtropical Forest	2.01.02	287,205
Japanese Evergreen Forest	2.02.02	1,132,616
Himalayan and Szechwan Highlands	2.38.12, 2.39.12	1,020,200
		2,440,021

Table 3: Data on national parks and other protected areas for each country of the Palaearctic Realm

Country	Total area (000 Km²)	NP and other Protected Areas (000 ha)	Ratio protected area/area total	Population (000)	Protected area per capita (m²)
Afghanistan	648	131	2	16	79.9
Albania	29	13	4.4	3	45.2
Alberia	2,382	2	0.01	19	1.03
Austria	84	1,265	150.8	8	1,686.5
Belgium	31	4	1.3	10	3.9
Bhutan	52	525 (?)	—	NA	—
Bulgaria	111	84	7.5	9	94.7
China	9,561	1,690	1.8	985	17.1
Czechoslovakia	128	1,324	103.4	15	859.7
Denmark	43	29	6.8	5	56.9
Egypt	1,100	1	0.009	44	0.2
Finland	337	961	28.5	5	2,002.9
France	551	387	7.0	54	71.6
German Dem. Rep.	108	3 (?)	—	17	—
German Fed. Rep.	249	415	16.7	61	67.7
Great Britain	244	1,490	61.1	56	266.5
Greece	132	97	7.4	10	101.4
Hungary	93	262	28.3	11	245.1
Iceland	103	829	80.5	.2	248.5
Iran	1,648	3,174 (?)	—	40	—
Ireland	70	21	2.9	3	60.9
Israel	21	34	16.4	4	87.2
Italy	301	336	11.2	57	58.7
Japan	370	3,380	91.4	118	287.0
Jordan	98	37	3.7	3	110.6
Korea, Rep. of	99	237	24.1	39	60.9
Libya	1,760	140	0.96	3	451.6
Mongolia	2,500	4,579	18.4	2	27,058.8
Morocco	445	38	0.85	22	17.43
Nepal	141	295	21.0	14	205.0
Netherlands	34	74	23.47	14	15.5
Norway	324	3,580	92.0	4	8,730.0
Oman	213	1,021	48.0	1	11,340.0
Pakistan	804	343	4.3	89	38.6
Poland	313	136	4.3	36	37.9
Portugal	92	136	14.8	10	136.0
Rumania	238	94	39.7	22	42.0
Saudia Arabia	2,150	450	20.9	10	432.7
Spain	505	285	5.6	38	75.3
Sweden	450	1,175	26.1	8	1,415.6
Switzerland	41	34	8.2	6	53.6
Tunisia	164	32	19.8	7	49.1
Turkey	781	272	34.7	46	58.7
USSR	22,402	12,964	5.8	268	483.7
Yugoslavia	256	687	26.8	22	305.1

Table 4: Increase in the protected areas of the Palaearctic Realm since the beginning of this century

Year	Area protected (1000 ha)	Year	Area protected (1000 ha)
1910	230	1950	6,181
1920	665	1960	8,962
1930	2,660	1970	21,500
1940	4,961	1980	41,391

Protected Areas in the United Kingdom: An Approach to the Selection, Establishment, and Management of Natural and Scenic Protected Areas in a Densely Populated Country with Limited Choices

John Foster
Director
Countryside Commission for Scotland
Battleby, UK

Adrian Phillips
Director
The Countryside Commission
Cheltenham, UK

Richard Steele
Director General
The Nature Conservancy Council
London, UK

ABSTRACT. *This paper describes the approach developed in the United Kingdom for selection, establishment and management of protected areas, identifying the important features of this approach, explaining these in terms of the circumstances prevailing in the UK and drawing attention to the achievements of the system and the outstanding problems. The challenge in the UK has been to develop conservation policies, including those for protected areas, in a relatively small and very densely populated country with very little unaltered natural environment, but where there is a strong public demand for conservation action. Since the total protection of extensive areas of unaltered natural environment is not an option in the UK, it has been necessary to find ways of integrating conservation with other land uses.*

1. INTRODUCTION

This case study describes the approach developed in the United Kingdom (UK) in the selection, establishment and management of protected areas, stressing the role played by government. It identifies important features of this approach, explains these in terms of the circumstances prevailing in the UK, and draws attention to the achievements of the system and outstanding problems.

The challenge in the UK has been to develop conservation policies, including those for protected areas, in a relatively small and very densely populated country (the total population of 55,883,000 gives an overall density of 229 persons per sq km) with very little unaltered natural environment, but where there is a strong public demand for conservation action. Since the total protection of extensive areas of unaltered natural environment is not an option in the UK, it has been necessary to find ways of integrating conservation with other land uses. It has also been necessary to coordinate as far as possible conservation action between the public and voluntary sectors.

2. BACKGROUND

2.1 Physical character

At its nearest point the UK lies only 32 km off the mainland of north-west Europe. It consists of the three countries of Great Britain (England, Wales and Scotland) and Northern Ireland (the UK does not include the Channel Islands and the Isle of Man, which are direct dependencies of the Crown). By European standards it is a medium sized country, but a small one in world terms, covering just over 244,000 sq km. Largely because of its island character, it has, however, a remarkably long coastline of 15,000 km.

The northernmost islands of Scotland are on the same latitude as southern Greenland and no part of the UK is as far south as any part of Japan or the USA, except Alaska. In spite of its northerly position, the UK enjoys an oceanic climate with relatively mild temperatures, a long growing season and ample rainfall, due to the proximity of the Northern Atlantic current. However, prevailing conditions deteriorate rapidly to the north and the tree line in the north and west is only a few hundred metres above sea level.

The UK has a very varied geology. Recent sedimentary rocks in southern and eastern parts have been gently folded during the Alpine mountain-building process. To the north and west progressively older rocks, some of them rich in coal, occur until ancient igneous and metamorphic rocks outcrop, especially in Scotland. Northern Ireland is complex geologically, but much affected by tertiary volcanic activity. Quaternary glaciation has left its mark. Ice extended over all but the southern part of England and greatly modified the mountain scenery of Scotland, north-west England, north Wales and Northern Ireland.

This varied geology gives rise to a varied scenery, and associated vegetative cover. Gentle hills, barely rising above 200 m, and broad vales characterize much of southern and eastern England, but the scenery of northern and western England—and still more that of Wales, Scotland and Northern Ireland—is marked by extensive moorland and mountains, reaching 1,000 m. The Scottish Highlands contain mountainous areas with sub-arctic characteristics, rising to over 1,300 m. The coastal scenery is correspondingly diverse, with practically all temperate coastal types in evidence; the west coast of Scotland is characterized by fjords. Offshore islands are numerous, especially to the west and north of the mainland of Scotland.

Little unmodified landscape remains—excepting, of course, much of the sea coast. Most of the original forest cover, and large carnivores, have disappeared from the countryside. However, both the farmed landscape and the uplands still contain relict areas of native vegetation providing some wildlife habitat and scenic attractiveness.

Of the total population in the UK, 75 percent are urban dwellers. Rural population densities are relatively high in the lowlands, but are as low as 4 persons per sq km in remoter districts of north-west Scotland. The proportion of the population which is directly dependent on agriculture for a living (3.5 percent) is among the lowest in the world.

2.2 Constitution

Each of the 4 distinct components of the UK has its own institutions and traditions of government.

Although constitutionally one State since 1707, Great Britain has adopted flexible methods of government adapted to the needs of its constituent elements. England and Wales on the one hand, and Scotland on the other, have different systems of law, land tenure, education, local government and, for domestic matters, different government departments and different legislation. Welsh and Scottish issues are dealt with by Government departments based in Cardiff and Edinburgh respectively and grouped under Secretaries of State for Wales and Scotland, who are members of the Cabinet. Long-standing and well-developed systems of local government exist. These operate at two levels: in England and Wales at county and district; and in Scotland at region and district (except for the three island groups—Shetlands, Orkneys and Western Isles—which have single tier, all-purpose authorities).

Northern Ireland has substantial delegation of powers for matters concerning the administration of the province, presently overseen by the Secretary of State for Northern Ireland. The system of local government with currently limited powers comprises district councils and area boards.

The UK joined the European Economic Community in 1973 when it adhered to the Treaty of Rome.

2.3 Legislation

Conservation legislation in the UK has developed alongside a comprehensive system of town and country planning legislation built up over more than half a century. In England and Wales, the county councils are responsible for preparing 'structure plans' dealing with major policy subjects, including communications, population, employment and environment. These plans require the formal approval of central government. Thereafter, district councils prepare and themselves adopt 'local plans' for various purposes for whole or parts of their areas. Control of most forms of new development rests with the district councils (or national park authorities where they exist), with a right of appeal to central government by aggrieved parties. Planning control covers all but very minor new developments and includes changes of use of land, but excludes most agricultural and forestry operations.

In Scotland, the arrangements are broadly similar within the two tiers of local government, i.e., region and district. In Northern Ireland, land use planning is a function of central government. There are no national park authorities in Scotland or Northern Ireland.

3. CONSTRAINTS

3.1 Physical environment

There is very little undisturbed natural environment in the UK. Apart from the higher mountaintops and the cliffs and foreshores of the sea coast, the land surface has been modified by man in the course of use over many centuries. Conservation in the UK cannot, therefore, mean only the protection of natural habitats or undisturbed landscapes.

3.2 Land ownership

Land in the UK is mainly owned privately, the units of individual ownership varying greatly in size from region to region; they are interspersed with land held by central and local agencies of government for specific purposes, such as defence, forestry and water-gathering. The establishment of protected areas—whether by public bodies, private individuals or voluntary bodies—has had, therefore, to take account of the presence of numerous long-established interests.

3.3 Primary land uses

The primary land uses of farming and forestry have long been regarded as a key to the protection of the character of the countryside and its resources. However, with increasing economic pressures and the greater opportunities for intensification afforded by modern technology, farmers and foresters are now coming under criticism on the grounds that their activities can damage the environment, especially wildlife. With farming, this is particularly so in the fertile lowlands of eastern and southern England and with forestry in the uplands of the north of England and parts of Wales. However, as farming and forestry are largely excluded from the system of planning control (although strongly influenced by grant-aid and fiscal measures) only limited constraints can be imposed on them; considerable reliance must therefore be placed on a voluntary approach. Nevertheless, there are administrative procedures for seeking compromise or adjudicating between productive and environmental interests, and in some circumstances sensitively designed farming and forestry can make a valuable contribution to environmental values.

3.4 Cultural background

Regional differences, developed over the centuries, abound in the UK. Sometimes these find expression as suspicion of authority—particularly any new form of centralized authority. Not surprisingly, conservation, as a comparatively new and unfamiliar idea (at least in the form of a conscious public policy) has encountered some resistance, for example in the remoter upland areas where conservation values are often particularly high. On the other hand, there has been a marked growth in support for conservation among the general public in recent years, as evidenced, for example, by the large audience for conservation programmes on television and radio, by the membership of voluntary conservation bodies, and by the numbers visiting sites of conservation importance.

3.5 Socio-economic considerations

In the more heavily populated parts of the UK there are strong outward pressures from a number of conurbations and major cities for development and recreational use. These create a competition for land use, place a strain on normal farming activities, threaten habitats and cause landscape damage.

In the more remote upland areas, there is frequently pressure for development to maintain an acceptable socio-economic infrastructure for the communities involved. In many areas, both in the uplands and in the lowlands, a degree of prosperity is essential if the acceptable man-made elements of the landscape are to be maintained. All of this calls for a careful balance between conservation and socio-economic policies which is not always easy to achieve. Such policies must also take account of the UK's position within the European Economic Community: extensive parts of the UK, mainly in Scotland, have been defined as Less Favoured Areas in which special community programmes for socio-economic development apply.

3.6 Institutions of government

The various institutions of government in each of the four countries of the UK both reflect and reinforce social, cultural and economic differences. This adds a further complication to what is, for a variety of other reasons, already a complicated situation and makes a UK-wide response to conservation requirements difficult. Even within the individual countries of the UK, regional and local differences deriving from the structure of local government, again based on long-standing traditions and practices, render uniformity of response difficult at local government level.

NATIONAL PARKS, CONSERVATION, AND DEVELOPMENT

3.7 Finance

In the UK, as in most countries, there is intense competition for public funds, with economic and social demands frequently taking precedence over environmental considerations. The costs of conservation, in terms of the direct management costs of protection and opportunity costs arising from restriction on the economic uses of land, have to be thoroughly justified by reasoned argument before they can be met out of public funds. There is also the added problem of determining the most appropriate balance between central and local government sources of funding conservation costs.

4. ACTION

The history of the conservation movement in the UK can be traced well back into the 19th century, when farsighted individuals first began to express concern about the loss of cherished features of the countryside. Four distinct, but related, movements can be identified which explain much about attitudes to conservation in the UK today; i.e. nature conservation; landscape conservation; historic buildings conservation; and public enjoyment of the countryside. While this study concentrates on the first two of these, without the other two strands the story of conservation in the UK would be incomplete. Historic buildings and settlements are integral parts of the rural scene and much of the pressure for safeguarding places of natural and scenic interest in the countryside has been coupled with demands for greater public rights of access to them.

4.1 Development of powers for conservation

The National Trust has been active in the preservation of places of historic interest and natural beauty since 1895 and secured Parliamentary support for this in 1907. Moreover, some local authorities have also long been active in protecting areas of countryside for public enjoyment. However, government took little part in conservation until 1945. By then, public pressure for nature and landscape conservation had led to the commissioning of several important studies on the subject. As a result, the Nature Conservancy was established by Royal Charter in 1949 and powers to establish nature reserves and other areas for nature conservation in England, Wales and Scotland were provided in the National Parks and Access to the Countryside Act of 1949. That Act also established the National Parks Commission, with responsibilities in England and Wales for designating National Parks and Areas of Outstanding Natural Beauty. In 1968, the landscape protection responsibilities of the National Parks Commission were extended to the countryside of England and Wales as a whole and its title changed accordingly to that of the Countryside Commission; at the same time the Commission's Committee for Wales was established. In 1973, the Nature Conservancy Council (NCC) replaced the Nature Conservancy as the statutory body responsible, among other things, for advising Government on nature conservation matters.

In Scotland, to which the national parks provisions of the Act of 1949 had not applied, the Countryside (Scotland) Act of 1967 established the Countryside Commission of Scotland, with landscape protection responsibilitis over the whole of the Scottish countryside.

Responsibility for policies for nature and landscape conservation in Northern Ireland rests with the Department of the Environment for Northern Ireland under legislation of 1965, amended in 1972. In exercising this responsibility, the Department is advised by the Nature Reserves Committee and the Ulster Countryside Committee.

In addition, the Forestry Commission manages seven forest parks in England, Wales and Scotland, the first of which was established in 1935. While timber production is the main purpose, within these parks the Forestry Commission pays regard to nature conservation and landscape interests and particularly to provision for informal recreation. They correspond most closely to the Category VIII Multiple-Use Management Areas of the IUCN classification. The Forest Service of the Department of Agriculture for Northern Ireland manages nine forest parks, the first of which was opened in 1955.

In parallel with the establishment of national agencies responsible for nature and landscape conservation and the designation of the protected areas themselves, various powers have been introduced which enable areas to be conserved and managed by public bodies in ways appropriate to their character. The most important of these powers are:

- to control new development and uses of land under the established system of town and country planning legislation (by local authorities);
- to acquire or lease land and manage it for nature or landscape conservation (by the Nature Conservancy Council and local authorities);
- to undertake conservation measures e.g. to improve derelict land, plant trees, provide countryside ranger services (principally by local authorities);
- to make management agreements with private landowners to conserve wildlife or landscape features of value (by the Nature Conservancy Council, Countryside Commission for Scotland and local authorities);
- to give exemption from capital transfer tax to owners of land of outstanding scientific or scenic interest in return for undertakings to manage the land so as to retain its conservation value (by the Treasury, on the advice of the Nature Conservancy Council and/or the Countryside Commissions);

- to acquire, by private treaty sale, land of outstanding scientific or scenic interest at lower prices which take account of the vendor's tax liabilities (by the Nature Conservancy Council, local authorities, the National Trusts and others);
- to receive land (normally of outstanding scientific or scenic interest) accepted by the Treasury in lieu of tax (the National Trusts, local authorities and charitable organizations such as local conservation trusts);
- to delay land use changes potentially harmful to nature conservation in Sites of Special Scientific Interest so as to provide time to conclude a management agreement; or, as a last resort, compulsory purchase orders (by the Nature Conservancy Council). Similar, but less comprehensive, powers exist to delay certain agricultural changes which might affect the landscape of national parks (by national parks authorities).

Where undertaken by local authorities, including national park authorities, some of these conservation activities can be supported by grants from the Nature Conservancy Council and the Countryside Commissions. In addition, the Nature Conservancy Council and Countryside Commissions have powers to grant-aid voluntary bodies to acquire and manage land for nature and landscape conservation purposes. The National Heritage Memorial Fund is empowered to make financial contributions towards the acquisition of land of outstanding wildlife or landscape conservation value.

4.2 Selection, establishment and management of nature conservation

Arrangements in Great Britain (i.e. England, Wales and Scotland) are considered before those for Northern Ireland, which differ in a number of respects.

4.2.1. England, Wales and Scotland. A national strategy for nature conservation in Great Britain was formally prescribed in 1947 in two government White Papers. These declared that a number of representative key areas should be protected, covering all major natural and semi-natural habitats and with geological and physiographic features represented for their own intrinsic interest. This key area concept found its main expression in the designation of National Nature Reserves (NNRs) and the notification of Sites of Special Scientific Interest (SSSIs). In addition certain woodland SSSIs, owned and managed by a government department or public body, are given the non-statutory designation of Forest Nature Reserves (FNRs).

Following a more detailed survey, a review was published in 1977 of the areas in England, Wales and Scotland of national or international importance for nature, but excluding marine areas which are to be the subject of a separate review, and geological sites for which a review is currently in progress. Based on the criteria of size, richness and diversity, naturalness, rarity, fragility and the extent to which they represented characteristic habitats and communities, the review identified 735 key sites. The conservation of these key areas is regarded as essential for nature conservation in Great Britain.

Sites of high international significance were identified separately, especially those habitats, communities and species which are rare on the global scene. Sites thus designated are mostly high-quality examples of ecosystems and communities and contain species with a very restricted European distribution.

The Nature Conservancy Council, and its predecessor the Nature Conservancy, has to date established 182 NNRs in England, Wales and Scotland, covering a total area of over 139,000 ha and ranging in size from 2 ha to 25,950 ha. National Nature Reserves are established and managed for the conservation of flora, fauna and geological or physiographic features, and to provide special opportunities for research and study. They are owned, leased or managed by agreement by the NCC, and many meet the criteria for IUCN protected area Category I. There are also 9 FNRs covering 900 ha. Legislation has recently been enacted to allow the establishment of marine nature reserves.

In addition, 3,877 SSSIs, covering 1,361,404 ha, have been notified by the Nature Conservancy Council to local planning authorities and land-owning interests concerned. These are subject to consultation and control over alterations to management practices which would adversely affect their nature conservation interests.

Unesco has certified 13 areas in the UK as Biospheres Reserves under its Man and the Biosphere Programme. Although no Biogenetic Reserves have been designated for the Council of Europe's network, the Nature Conservancy Council is currently preparing recommendations. The Council has also identified 130 sites for possible designation under the Ramsar Convention on Wetlands of International Importance, especially as Waterfowl Habitat; 19 such Ramsar sites have so far been designated. The Nature Conservancy Council is currently discussing with the government sites which might be identified in accordance with the requirements of the EEC Directive on the Conservation of Wild Birds.

In addition to the work of the Nature Conservancy Council, local authorities have established 84 local nature reserves. The role of the *voluntary bodies* is especially significant, however, with a number of important wildlife reserves owned or managed by voluntary conservation bodies. Many of these reserves are designated as Sites of Special Scientific Interest and several form part of National Nature Reserves. The main bodies concerned are: The Royal Society for the Protection of Birds (RSPB), with over a third of a million members, which has 86 reserves in the UK (the RSPB covers Northern Ireland as well as Great Britain) with a total of 42,270 ha; the county conservation trusts, the Scottish Wildlife Trust and their national association, the Royal Society for Nature Conservation, which own or manage 1,300 reserves in Great Britain covering 44,530 ha; the National Trust, within whose property there are 350 Sites of Special Scientific Interest covering more than 82,000 ha; and the National Trust for Scotland.

4.2.2. Northern Ireland. Following the passing of the Amenity Lands Act (Northern Ireland) 1965, it was agreed to follow a broadly similar policy to that in operation in Great Britain for the establishment of National Nature Reserves (NNRs) and the notification of Areas of Scientific Interest (ASIs). At a very early stage a general survey of all identified habitats was undertaken, following which a selection of suitable sites for NNRs and ASIs was made. The criteria used in selection were generally similar to those used by the Nature Conservancy Council.

There are currently 36 NNRs, covering a total of approximately 3,052 ha and ranging in size from 1 to 789 ha; the Department of the Environment for Northern Ireland owns, leases or manages by agreement all reserves. In addition, 47 ASIs covering approximately 74,000 ha have been notified.

No Biosphere or Biogenetic Reserves have yet been designated; one site has been designated under the Ramsar Convention with two other sites identified for possible designation. A list of sites has been drawn up which may be identified in accordance with the requirements of the EEC Directive on the Conservation of Wild Birds.

4.3 Selection, establishment and management of Scenic Areas

Because arrangements differ so much between England and Wales, Scotland, and Northern Ireland, the areas are described separately.

4.3.1. England and Wales. Under the National Parks and Access to the Countryside Act, 1949, the Countryside Commission (until 1968 the National Parks Commission) designates National Parks and Areas of Outstanding Natural Beauty, subject to confirmation by the appropriate Secretary of State. The Countryside Commission also defines a third category of protected scenic area, Heritage Coasts, in consultation with the local planning authorities.

The ten existing National Parks are extensive areas designated between 1950 and 1955 for their scenic beauty and their potential for open air recreation. They do not correspond to national parks in the sense of IUCN Category II, but rather to Category V (Protected Landscape) and to Category C of the Council of Europe classification (one of the national parks, the Peak District, has been awarded the European Diploma of the Council of Europe). They cover 13,600 sq km—9 percent of the area of England and Wales—and have a combined resident population of 237,000. All but one of the parks are mainly in upland areas, covering the finest moor and mountain scenery; the exception is predominantly an area of fine coastline in Wales. While further areas may be designated, there are no firm plans to this end at present.

The parks are administered by national park authorities, i.e. special boards or committees of local government, one-third of whose members are appointed by government after consultation with the Commission. Since 1974, each park has had its own national park officer (appointed in consultation with the Countryside Commission) and administrative, technical and field staff, the total number of staff employed in all the parks being just under 500. Each park authority is responsible for day-to-day control of development and follows stringent policies to protect the quality of the landscape; each also provides management services (e.g. rangers and interpretive staff) along lines set out in its national park plan, which must be reviewed by the Commission before it is adopted. Total annual expenditure by all the park authorities is nearly US $16.2 million, three quarters of which comes from central government in the form of an annual grant against an approved programme, based on the advice of the Commission.

The parks contain small towns, villages, small industries, working farms and many other economic activities. Indeed the appeal of much of the landscape of the parks lies in the harmonious way in which villages, farms and woodlands fit into the scene.

While designation of the parks does not affect land ownership, some areas which are particularly beautiful and popular with visitors, may be acquired by the national park authority; more often, however, it is voluntary bodies, such as the National Trust, which acquire land in the parks for conservation and public enjoyment, often with grants from the Countryside Commission. The role of the Commission is otherwise advisory and on occasion it may assist a park authority in resisting damaging development proposals.

The 33 designated *Areas of Outstanding Natural Beauty* (AONBs) also fall within Category V of the IUCN classification. Further AONBs may shortly be designated. Most are relatively extensive and all are selected for their scenic beauty. Together they cover nearly 14,500 sq km— 9.6 per cent of the area of England and Wales—and include a variety of landscapes such as hills, moorlands, river valleys, lowland heaths, chalk downlands, coastal scenery, islands and forests. As with National Parks, designation does not affect ownership; unlike National Parks, however, designation of AONBs does not imply a specific programme for recreation. However, some AONBs contain extensive areas of land in public or voluntary protective ownership.

AONBs are designated by the Countryside Commission, which has similar advisory responsibilities towards them as towards National Parks. However, in other respects arrangements to secure the national interests in their planning and management are much more limited, and responsibility for AONBs rests largely with the local authorities concerned. The emphasis in

AONBs is on protection from damaging forms of development, but increasing attention is being given by some local authorities to their positive management.

The 35 *Heritage Coasts* have been defined by the Countryside Commission and the local authorities along 1,161 km of the finest coasts of England and Wales—26.3 per cent of the whole coastline. Some Heritage Coasts coincide with established National Parks and AONBs. Besides reinforcing protection, heritage coast definition implies intensive management for conservation (and recreation), for example through ranger and interpretive services. The landward depth of heritage coasts rarely exceeds one kilometre. Definition does not affect ownership. This type of protected area may be considered Category III National Monuments in the IUCN classification. Further heritage coasts may shortly be defined.

In addition to the foregoing three categories of protected areas, there are two further unique areas. The New Forest, in southern England, contains extensive tracts of largely undisturbed forest, heath and bog ecosystems. The Broads, in eastern England, which is a complex of slow-moving rivers and shallow man-made lakes, is another area where special measures have been taken to protect the scenery, which the Countryside Commission recognizes as of national park quality; a special Broads Authority has been established with funds from the Commission and local government.

Finally, there are a number of smaller areas in England and Wales both within and outside the official category of protected area, where scenic protection is provided through ownership by local authorities, voluntary bodies and private individuals, often with financial assistance provided by the Countryside Commission. For many years, a number of local authorities have been active in acquiring land for conservation purposes often to secure also rights of public access. Collectively local government ownership now makes a significant contribution to the conservation of the landscape heritage of England and Wales.

The role of *voluntary bodies* is equally important, and the rapid expansion of public support for their work has been a conspicuous feature in recent years. Thus, the National Trust, which was established in 1895, now owns 182,000 ha of fine countryside and coast in England and Wales (and Northern Ireland), which is managed for the protection of its natural beauty and for public enjoyment; its ownership includes more than 5 percent of the area of the National Parks. The Trust, which is supported by over a million members, enjoys a privileged taxation status and may uniquely declare its properties inalienable (i.e. they cannot be sold, mortgaged or compulsorily acquired without the express will of Parliament). The Woodland Trust was set up more recently to acquire and protect woodlands and now holds over 700 ha. Some voluntary bodies undertake practical conservation tasks, such as tree planting, much of it within protected areas; many thousands of individuals are involved in such work. In addition, the national and local nature conservation voluntary bodies described earlier protect sites which are important in terms of scenic quality as well as nature conservation.

4.3.2. Scotland. For reasons now only of historic interest, the powers contained in the National Parks and Access to the Countryside Act 1949 to establish National Parks did not extend to Scotland, even though Scotland contains more substantial areas of relatively remote country and coastline than elsewhere in the UK.

However, National Scenic Areas, of which there are 40, covering 10,105 sq km—12.8 per cent of the area of Scotland—have been defined by the Countryside Commission for Scotland. These have been selected on different and—in scenic terms—a more selective basis than applies to national parks and AONBs in England and Wales. They fall within IUCN Category V, although a few of the more remote areas come close to meeting the requirements for Category II. Since 1981 planning authorities have had to refer planning applications for certain classes of development within these areas to the Commission to secure the national element of interest. No other arrangements for the national interest exist within them, but local authorities are expected to reflect the scenic importance of the areas in their planning and management strategies. Definition does not affect ownership nor imply any specific programme for recreational provision.

As well as National Scenic Areas, there is also a similar pattern to that of England and Wales of protected areas within the ownership of local authorities, voluntary bodies and private individuals. The National Trust for Scotland, established in 1931, owns 44,445 ha of scenically important countryside and coast protected for its quality and for public enjoyment.

4.3.3. Northern Ireland. There are no national parks in Northern Ireland, although the Amenity Lands Act (Northern Ireland) 1965 contains powers for designation of such areas.

Eight Areas of Outstanding Natural Beauty have been designated and two others recommended. These cover a range of mountain, valley, lake, moorland and coastal landscapes and, as in England and Wales, designation is intended to afford a higher degree of planning control to limit or prevent development detrimental to scenic quality. Their sizes range from 2,000 to 101,000 ha and together they account for approximately 18 percent of the total area of Northern Ireland. The National Trust owns 2,633 ha of open countryside in Northern Ireland.

5. RESULTS

5.1 Achievements

The conservation achievements in the UK since the foundations were laid with the National Parks and Access to the Countryside Act of 1949 have been considerable. While the creation of protected areas is only one reason for this, it has without doubt been the key to the protection, indeed sometimes survival, of endangered species and habitats, and to safeguarding the finest scenery of the UK for public enjoyment. All this has been achieved in a period of rapid economic and industrial change.

Seven particular achievements deserve special mention.

5.1.1. Establishment of a network of nature and landscape conservation areas.
The first, and most outstanding, achievement is that there exists in the UK, within the mosaic of many different public and private ownerships and long established land uses, a recognizable network of key areas and sites protected for conservation and identified at a national level by government agencies. In summary the network comprises:

a) in England, Wales and Scotland, nature conservation areas established as National Nature Reserves (182) and Sites of Special Scientific Interest (3877);

b) in England and Wales, scenic areas designated as National Parks (10) and Areas of Outstanding Natural Beauty (33) and defined as Heritage Coasts (35);

c) in Scotland, scenic areas defined as National Scenic Areas (40); and

d) in Northern Ireland, nature conservation areas designated as National Nature Reserves (36) and Areas of Scientific Interest (47), and scenic areas designated as Areas of Outstanding Natural Beauty (8).

Complementing and supplementing this national network, local government and voluntary bodies have secured extensive areas of land for conservation through ownership and management agreements. The Nature Conservancy Council and the Countryside Commissions have stimulated this trend, especially through grant aid. The chief national voluntary bodies are the National Trusts, the Royal Society for the Protection of Birds, and the Royal Society for Nature Conservation with its associated trusts in England and Wales, the Scottish Wildlife Trust and the Ulster Trust for Nature Conservation.

5.1.2. Integration of conservation with land-use planning.
The well-established and generally comprehensive land-use planning system in the UK helps ensure that protected areas are indeed conserved against many of the pressures that are placed upon them and helps secure at least a partial integration of such areas into the planning of the environment as a whole. Integration might be still more effective but for the independence of local levels of government, the separation of the nature and landscape conservation systems and the limited coordination so far achieved in national policies as they affect rural land use.

5.1.3. Collaboration between national conservation agencies and local government.
Though national conservation agencies identify the national priorities by designating protected areas, local government is usually involved in their subsequent conservation. In the case of nature conservation areas, this is secured indirectly through land use planning and, less often, directly when local authorities own and manage nature reserves. In the case of landscape conservation, the role of local government is critical, since the protection of AONBs and National Scenic Areas is principally their responsibility; and in the National Parks, where special arrangements exist to secure the national interest, local government plays the key role in ensuring that the parks are conserved. Though the priorities of the national conservation agencies and local authorities do, on occasion, diverge, local government as a whole has shown itself increasingly responsive to conservation requirements, both within the nationally-designated areas and outside.

5.1.4. The contribution made by voluntary conservation bodies.
The voluntary conservation bodies command very extensive public support in the UK and a number of them have developed considerable expertise and competence in the management of land for nature and landscape conservation. While national conservation agencies have set the framework by designating protected areas and defining the policies, voluntary bodies have played a vital role in securing the ongoing management of many such areas; for example, they manage a number of National Nature Reserves by agreement with the Nature Conservancy Council and extensive parts of the national parks within the broad guidance given by the national park plans. Bodies such as the National Trusts can guarantee continuity of management policy over many years. This partnership between voluntary and official bodies is particularly important in the UK, where it is more highly developed than in most countries outside the USA. Voluntary bodies also play a special role as catalysts and pressure groups in support of the objectives of the national conservation bodies; the sheer size of their membership now gives them considerable political influence.

5.1.5. Collaboration between public agencies and private individuals.
The machinery now exists for protection by formal agreements between public agencies and private owners of land to maintain particular aspects of natural or scenic interests, with lump sum or annual payments made in consideration for the special type of

management or restriction of use involved. Protection of conservation values on private land can also be secured through agreements which provide fiscal exemption or relief to landowners in return for certain management undertakings.

5.1.6. Development of conservation expertise.

A body of expertise has grown up over the past thirty years in the selection, establishment and management of protected areas. This is evident in the professionalism shown by staff in the public sector at a variety of levels, from field staff (rangers etc.), through middle management to those holding senior policy roles. There is also a large body of voluntary expertise, for example, voluntary rangers deployed both by public bodies and voluntary bodies. Through systems of communication and training, the individuals concerned constitute an informal network of professionals engaged in conservation. The presence of this network helps to overcome some of the coordination problems which would otherwise arise from the complex structure of conservation responsibilities in the UK. The fact-finding and monitoring work of the national conservation agencies is also relevant by providing a basis for advice which can be used in resolving conservation problems on the ground.

5.1.7. Development of skills in conservation education.

In recent years, the skills and techniques for managing recreational use of the countryside have been developed and applied widely. One important purpose has been to help people enjoy protected areas without damaging their essential qualities. Particular emphasis has been placed on high quality of design, control of visitor numbers in sensitive areas and reinforcement of the conservation message through interpretive facilities, including over two hundred centres ranging in their degree of sophistication from major interpretive centres to mobile information caravans, several hundred nature trails and a wealth of interpretive literature. Together, these enable people to enjoy and understand the importance of protected areas and thereby reinforce the public commitment to their conservation.

5.2 Problems

Though progress in conservation in general, and in protected areas in particular, has been considerable, problems remain. These are broadly of three kinds: those within the protected areas themselves, those in official policies towards conservation; and those in public and political attitudes towards conservation.

5.2.1. Within protected areas.

People live and work in many of the nature conservation protected areas and in all the scenic protected areas of the UK. Indeed, conservation of such man-modified environments may depend upon maintaining a level of human intervention; for example, traditional forms of farming help to protect the wildlife and scenic quality of the uplands. Problems arise when:

a) the traditional economy declines. For example, increasing economic pressures lead to a declining agricultural work force; woodlands and hedgerows cannot then be so easily managed in ways which favour wildlife conservation and traditional landscape features, such as stone walls, become neglected and fall into disrepair. Doing nothing, therefore, is rarely a conservation option in the UK;

b) traditional low-intensity land use practices give way to more intensive practices. For example, the drainage of wetlands or the ploughing up of rough grazing can mean the destruction of valued habitats or changes in the landscape features in protected areas;

c) protected areas have within them, at the time of establishment, land uses which are incompatible with the purposes of protection. Examples have included land for military establishments and mineral development, many of which have proved very difficult to remove;

d) new developments take place in protected areas, either to improve the local economy or to serve the requirements of the national economy; these may have a damaging impact on wildlife and scenery. Examples in the past have included the provision of new roads or reservoirs in or affecting national parks or National Nature Reserves; and

e) recreation and conservation objectives come into conflict with one another, as where sensitive wildlife or scenic interests suffer from damage by large numbers of visitors.

Policies and techniques have been devised to help deal with some of these problems. For example, although agriculture and forestry operations are outside planning control, recent legislation provides for the making of management agreements between public agencies and landowners or farmers, with the object of managing land in accordance with conservation requirements in return for payment in compensation for income foregone.

5.2.2. In official policies.

Problems arise:

a) when conservation is accorded a generally lesser status than economic and social factors, on occasion being taken into account only at an advanced stage in the decision-making process. As the World Conservation Strategy argues, conservation requires to be incorporated fully within the process at all levels from the outset. If this is not done, the policies followed by government tments may differ as they affect conservation interests;

b) when the demands created by the need to conserve protected areas exceed the available funds. For example, the demands placed on the budgets of the Nature Conservancy Council and the two Countryside Commissions exceed the resources which they believe they require for effective conservation on a national basis;

c) because there are inherent dangers in the separation of the nature and landscape conservation systems. While this provides the useful opportunity for two conservation voices where only one would otherwise be heard, it can also lead to duplication of effort and it makes public understanding of, and support for, conservation objectives that much more difficult. To capitalize on the positive aspects of there being two systems, the various national conservation agencies must collaborate closely in all their activities. In Northern Ireland the two aspects are dealt with by one government department.

5.2.3. In public and political support. In the last analysis, the conservation of protected areas will only be secured on a lasting basis if there is sufficient public and political support, especially within the protected areas themselves. The UK public has shown itself increasingly aware of the need to conserve protected areas in recent years—an interest that has been reflected in the level of public debate over recent Parliamentary legislation, in the large audience ratings for television and radio programmes on conservation topics, in the rapid rise in membership of voluntary bodies concerned with conservation and in the willingness of people to give their own time to voluntary conservation effort. However, many politicians and policy-makers probably still see conservation as marginal when compared to economic and social considerations, although there are indications that some of them are now responding to the increasing level of public interest. This trend may be given new impetus by the publication of a series of reports, sponsored by the national conservation agencies and a consortium of voluntary bodies, designed to focus the attention of the public and decision-makers on the relevance to the UK of the recommendations in the World Conservation Strategy.

6. CONCLUSIONS

In the UK, the selection and establishment of areas for nature conservation and landscape protection have had to be integrated with a long-established pattern of urban and rural settlements and land ownerships and uses. Management of the areas has had to have regard to the kinds of pressures which arise within a small country where population concentrations are heavy, distances are short, people enjoy a high degree of individual mobility and there is a strong public desire to use the countryside as a place of leisure.

Throughout the period of selection and establishment of protected areas there has existed a comprehensive system of statutory land-use planning at national and local levels, into which the areas have been fitted. In addition, account has had to be taken of a system of local government which enjoys a significant degree of autonomy and of a number of powerful voluntary bodies with strong views on how conservation should be achieved, whose political standing has grown as their membership has increased.

What then are the principal lessons to be learned from the UK experience which are likely to be of interest to other countries? The following would seem to be the most relevant.

6.1 The need for a range of types of protected areas

The very small amount of unmodified natural environment in a country is no reason for not establishing a system of protected areas and the range of types within the IUCN categories is such that countries can adopt those most suited to their particular character and needs. In the UK, a variety of kinds of protected area with different levels of protection has been established; in some places, indeed, two or even more types of protected area overlap one another. While this may appear confusing at first sight, experience has shown that it works in practice and fits into the complicated and intensive land use and ownership patterns of the UK.

6.2 The need to update legislation

As well as establishing basic conservation legislation with adequate powers for the range of types of protected area required, it is important to monitor the operation of the legislation. In the UK since 1945 there have been several major pieces of legislation relating to protected areas. These have sought, *inter alia*, to make good shortcomings in earlier legislation and to respond to changing attitudes and circumstances, e.g. to public concern over the need to protect fine coastline (which led to the adoption in England and Wales of the Heritage Coast concept) or over the effect of the intensification of agriculture on conservation values (which led to legislation for management agreements).

6.3 The need for local support within protected areas

Support from those most directly affected by the existence of protected areas is essential. With areas established exclusively for conservation purposes, i.e. within IUCN Categories I and II, this is often easier to achieve than in the multiple-use protected areas most often found in the UK where private landowning and local community interests may see the existence of a protected area as a constraint on the reasonable pursuit of their economic interests. Considerable effort has been needed to establish and maintain policies which secure the essential values of such areas and at the same time support the social and economic aspirations of local communities in a manner compatible with conservation objectives. In any particular area, a variety of ways of integrating conservation and economic development may need to be tested, with a willingness on occasion to modify certain conservation policies to secure local support.

6.4 The need to involve the voluntary sector

The importance of the voluntary sector in the UK has been demonstrated. It brings valuable additional manpower, competence and finance to the conservation of protected areas. Indeed its combined conservation 'estate' considerably exceeds that held by public bodies. Moreover, it constitutes a strong political pressure on government in support of conservation interests. It is a force to be encouraged, supported and helped to achieve practical ends. As the voluntary sector increases in influence, its activities are becoming complementary to those of the public sector with which it needs to work closely.

6.5 The need for wide support for conservation

Although the voluntary sector is strong in the UK, conservation nevertheless continues to be seen by some politicians and senior officials of government as a minority interest. The effort, now well established through communication and interpretation provision, to help people enjoy and better understand the importance of protected areas is essential if the public is to give its support for protected areas, and for the measures necessary to secure their consideration. The interest created by the publication of the World Conservation Strategy in the UK, as in other countries, provides a timely opportunity to foster this vital growth in public support for conservation.

6.6 The need to be involved in international activities

Many conservation problems must be tackled internationally, e.g. conservation of migratory species or control of transfrontier pollution. Countries can also usefully learn from one another's experience, however different their physical, social and economic character. The UK has played a full part in international conservation through membership of various organizations, adherence to a number of international conventions, and research and monitoring activities of relevance and value to countries outside the UK. Those people directly involved with conservation within the UK recognize the value of these links and the importance of expanding them.

The UK system of nature and landscape conservation can be summarized as operating under three main heads: specific elements of designation; land use planning control; and influence by a wide range of interests. Strictly protected areas, as understood by the terms of IUCN criteria, are few and of these many do not have the protection of ownership by a public conservation agency.

Possibly the most relevant message from the UK experience for other countries—especially those which have been long settled and are heavily populated—concerns the mixture of designation, planning control and influence which has developed over the years. Although it is complicated and sophisticated, it is a logical package for the circumstances which prevail in a country of the character of the UK. It has done a great deal for nature and landscape protection in the wider countryside, but seen from outside the UK it may appear that its effectiveness would be reinforced by a policy which increased the extent of ownership of key areas of national importance by public and voluntary conservation bodies.

7. THE WAY AHEAD

This case study has sought to describe and critically analyze the status of protected areas in the UK today. Looking ahead, it seems likely that public interest in conservation will grow further, that the influence of the voluntary sector will expand and that politicians will respond to these trends by strengthening the effectiveness of conservation policies generally and protected area policies in particular. This may lead to sharpened conflict between conservation and economic considerations, especially between conservationists and many who own or manage farms and forests. It will therefore be all the more important to reinforce the means of cooperation between these two interest groups, and to find and exploit ways in which economic and conservation aims can complement each other in the terms sought in the World Conservation Strategy.

Another consequence of an increase in public interest in the UK could be a major debate on the role of the national conservation agencies, vis-a-vis each other and in relation to central and local government and the voluntary sector. A third development could be a call for a critical review of the various systems for protected area conservation which have grown up, with a view to their rationalization. While this must all be conjecture at present, it seems likely that public interest in protected areas in the UK will be sufficiently strong in the years ahead to bring about significant innovations in how such areas are selected, established and managed.

Acknowledgements

The assistance of many individuals involved in protected areas in the UK is gratefully acknowledged, particularly contributions from the Department of the Environment, Welsh Office, Scottish Development Department, Department of the Environment for Northern Ireland, Forestry Commission and National Trusts; as well as former and present colleagues from the Countryside Commission for Scotland, the Countryside Commission (for England and Wales), and the Nature Conservancy Council.

ANNEX 1: THE NATIONAL TRUST AND THE NATIONAL TRUST FOR SCOTLAND

The National Trust, which operates throughout England, Wales and Northern Ireland, and the National Trust for Scotland, despite the impression given by their names, are private charities with membership open to everyone. This note explains their character, functions and legal status and demonstrates the important part which the Trusts play in the conservation of land and buildings and in the pattern of protected areas throughout the United Kingdom.

The *National Trust* was founded in 1895 by three people with the vision to see that the heritage of natural and man-made beauty required organized protection if it were to survive. Their aim was to establish a responsible body '. . . to act as a Corporation for the holding of lands of natural beauty and sites and houses of historic interest, to be preserved intact for the nation's use and enjoyment'.

Through the National Trust Act of 1907, the Trust acquired the unique privilege of being able to declare its land inalienable (land so declared cannot be sold, mortgaged or compulsorily acquired without the express will of Parliament). Although the Trust receives no direct subsidy from the government it enjoys certain important taxation advantages. It may receive and dispose of gifts without either the donor or the Trust being liable to Capital Gains Tax and legacies made to it are exempt from Capital Transfer Tax.

The Trust is assisted in some of its land purchases within England and Wales by the Countryside Commission, which also helps the Trust to meet the cost of providing a ranger service on much of its open coast and countryside. The Trust is, however, sufficiently free of governmental funding to pursue its aims without the disruption often produced by political change.

From modest beginnings the Trust has now developed into the largest private landowner in England, Wales and Northern Ireland, owning 184,633 ha of the most beautiful countryside, protecting by ownership nearly 750 kilometres of coastline (half the coast worthy of permanent preservation) and opening to the public over 200 historic houses and gardens.

In recent years the membership of the National Trust has grown rapidly, from about 200,000 in 1970 to well over one million in 1981. It continues to receive or acquire fine properties and can justly claim to be one of the largest and most successful conservation bodies in the world.

Among the Trust's duties is the protection of plant and animal life and it is notable that about one-third of the Sites of Special Scientific Interest of Grade 1 quality, that is of international importance, belong to the Trust. In all, it owns some 350 SSSIs totaling over 48,000 ha.

The *National Trust for Scotland* was founded in 1931. Its membership now exceeds 110,000 and its landownership, mainly of mountainous country, extends to 44,445 ha.

The aims, interests and legal and taxation position of the National Trust for Scotland are for the most part similar to those of its sister Trust. The National Trust for Scotland has been a leader in the field of interpretation and information for visitors; for example, many of the famous Scottish battlefields are so equipped. It has also taken a lead in developing a ranger service whose staff, in addition to protecting countryside in their charge, are trained to inform visitors about its natural history and the problems of conservation.

International interest in the National Trusts is growing and there are now similar bodies in many European countries and in the United States, Australia and New Zealand. As a result of a recent visit to Britain a National Trust may also be established shortly in Japan.

A Regional Approach to Marine and Coastal Protected Areas: The Mediterranean Sea

Hedia Baccar
Ministry of Agriculture
Tunis, Tunisia

ABSTRACT. *This case study demonstates the importance of the regional approach to protected areas in the Mediterranean region. In the field of marine protection, the United Nations Environment Programme has adopted the regional approach to environmental issues, believing that in this way, efforts could be concentrated on the special problems of each area and all concerned governments would gradually become involved in the safeguarding of their marine environment. Problems of balanced management in the Mediterranean imply that development and implementation of measures to control pollution and monitor protected ecosystems require coordination and intervention at the regional level. The different measures and interventions would cover a series of activities concerning protection of the Mediterranean environment, particularly along the coastal fringe. Among these measures, management of protected areas can only be considered in the context of coordinated action.*

1. INTRODUCTION

1.1 Purpose of the study

This case study demonstrates the importance of having a regional approach to the problems of protected areas in the Mediterranean eco-region. In the field of marine protection, the United Nations Environmental Programme has adopted a regional approach to environmental issues, believing that in this way, efforts can be concentrated on the special problems of each area and that UNEP would thus serve as a true catalyst while helping all concerned governments to gradually become more effective in the safeguarding of their marine environment.

UNEP and the concerned governments have decided to develop action and survival plans for ten regions, among which the Mediterranean Sea is the first where UNEP has launched, with the help of the UN System, coastal States and specialised institutions, an Action Plan approved in Barcelona in 1975 and aimed at the protection of the common sea. The plan has four sections:

- juridical (Barcelona Convention and related Protocols);
- scientific (research and marine environment monitoring project);
- integrated planification (Blue Plan and priority actions programme); and
- institutional and financial.

The latter section follows a regional approach through the creation of a Coordination Unit and of Regional Activity Centres (CAR/RAC), including CAR/Fight against Pollution (Malta), CAR/Blue Plan (France), CAR/Priority Actions Programme (Yugoslavia), and CAR/Protected Areas (Tunisia).

1.2 Mediterranean Action Plan (MAP) background

The Action Plan, developed in 1975 to implement measures to protect and develop the marine environment and coastal areas of the Mediterranean, was followed up by a Conference of Plenipotentiaries (Barcelona, 1976) where the Coastal States and the European Economic Community approved a Convention and two Protocols which came into force on l2 February 1978:

- Convention for the Protection of the Mediterranean Sea Against Pollution and related Protocols (Barcelona Convention).
- Protocol for the Prevention of Pollution in the Mediterranean Sea by Dumping from Ships or Aircraft.
- Protocol concerning Cooperation in Combating Pollution of the Mediterranean Sea by Oil and other Harmful Substances in Cases of Emergency.

A third Protocol, for the Protection of the Mediterranean Sea against Pollution from Land-Based Sources, was adopted in Athens in May 1980. The fourth Protocol, concerning Mediterranean Specially Protected Areas, has just been adopted in Geneva (March 1982).

Activities undertaken in relation to Specially Protected Areas come under the Management and Environmental Legislation section of the Mediterranean Action Plan and are covered more precisely by the fourth Protocol.

2. PRESENTATION OF THE PROBLEM: THE MEDITERRANEAN SEA

From the point of view of its natural resources, the variety of its landscapes, cultures and civilisations, the Mediterranean Sea is one of the richest areas of the world. It is the only region where three continents meet and it is where human activities have had the stongest impact; these include industrialization, intensive urban and tourist development, and uncontrolled expansion of coastal populations.

The Mediterranean Sea also has a considerable economic potential, some of the most important activity areas being fishing (commerciallly valuable species), mineral resources and tourism (55 million tourists on the western coast only).

Mediterranean countries share the same will to protect their common sea which has always been a narrow link between the North and the South, the rich and the poor countries. The Mediterranean is a semi-closed sea whose waters are renewed very slowly (it takes about 80 years); it has an ecological unity although it consists of four seas (the Alboran Sea, the Western Mediterranean Sea, the Adriatic Sea and the Eastern Mediterranean Sea). All of them are distinct ecosystems which are each important for the ecoregion as a whole.

The salinity of the Mediterranean Sea is one of the highest of the oceans (37 g/litre), and the sea is one of the richest in species (7000 species) but also one of the most polluted. Its low productivity might be threatened as much by the massive pollution coming from the coasts and the back country as by overexploitation of its biological resources (760,000 tons of fish cropped in 1976, according to FAO).

These resources, common heritage to all coastal countries, can only be managed on a regional basis; protection, although it is the responsibility of the National authorities, depends on cooperation between all States. It has been noticed that the scarce measures taken at the national level could only have positive results for protection of the Mediterranean ecoregion if they were to be coordinated, followed up and specially planned on a regional basis. Therefore, it has become obvious that there was an advantage for the Mediterranean States to develop a mechanism which would allow national decisions and actions to be considered in the context of a regional approach.

A study by IUCN (Baccar, 1977) on Marine Parks and Reserves has established that there were only about 20 parks around the Mediterranean Basin. This gives only a fragmentary idea of a problem which should be considered as a whole, through an integrated approach.

3. THE NEED FOR A REGIONAL APPROACH

As previously mentioned, the Mediterranean region is unique from the point of view of its fauna and flora but also of the ecosystems which comprise it. This explains why the regional approach has become necessary in the field of Protected Areas.

Some animal species are endemic to the region, while others breed, feed, nest and survive in different areas. The best example of the latter is migratory species whose protection calls for cooperation between several States, again emphasizing the idea of regional cooperation.

Although the many socio-economic activities and the use of natural resources vary from one country to another according to the level of development, there is no doubt that interdependance can be found between the main activity centres: exploitation of marine resources; development of transportation and communication; tourism; and so on. All these activities must be considered from a regional point of view in order to avoid one country's activities interfering with another's. A regional approach will also facilitate exchange of information and experience, comparisons of data, and setting up of a Mediterranean network which will take into account national as well as regional needs for conservation.

The will to cooperate at the regional level was stressed in March 1982 when the Protocol on Protected Areas was signed. Aimed at enhancing cooperation between coastal States, its preamble underlines "that it is imperative to protect and, whenever necessary, to improve the status of natural resources and sites of the Mediterranean as well as the situation of the region's cultural heritage by creating specially protected areas including marine areas and their environment and, to achieve this objective, expresses the will to set up tight cooperation between the areas."

The Contracting Parties have agreed to cooperate and to coordinate their actions in this field, adopting the Protocol of which article 12 stipulates:

"The Parties establish, as far as possible, a cooperation programme for the creation, planification, management and conservation of Protected Areas throughout the Mediterranean region, taking fully into account all existing networks, including Unesco's Biosphere Reserves Network. Characteristics of the Protected Areas, acquired experience and identified problems will be shared through regular exchanges of information."

Cooperation will be channeled through the Regional Activity Centre for Protected Areas created in Tunis by decision of the Contracting Parties to the Barcelona Convention at their 2nd meeting (Cannes, 1981). On the basis of the regional approach, the Centre's activities will include:

- Identification of conservation needs acording to regional necessities;
- Exchange of experience, methods and international cooperation for conducting surveys and selecting criteria of identification of critical areas to be protected. More than anything else, establishment of protected areas acquires all its meaning at the regional level; protection of migratory birds, for example, can only be considered in this perspective;
- promotion of regional and sub-regional classification systems of habitats;
- development of measures to protect migratory species;
- development of possibilities to exchange ideas and personnel;
- promotion of training activities at the regional level;
- technical advice on the implementation of relevant aspects of protected areas of the Convention on Protection of the Mediterranean Protected Areas against Pollution and of the Protocols concerning Protected Areas;
- keeping up regular contacts with regional or international organizations active in the field of protected areas conservation;
- support to regional studies on identification of critical coastal and marine habitats, carried out from an ecological, biological and socio-economic point of view; and
- establishment of a regional classification system of habitats from which a representative network of protected Areas could be selected, established and managed. The network would allow protection of rare and commercially important species, promote conservation of the diversity of habitats and species and make it possible to monitor ecological processes in the whole area.

With protected areas established on the basis of a representative classification system, each State would have the opportunity to contribute to regional cooperation and benefit from it. Each country would be responsible for the protection of riches shared with its neighbours and the whole region.

4. CONSTRAINTS AND INTERVENTIONS

Created by the Mediterranean Coastal States, in order to protect endangered species of fauna (including the monk seal and marine turtles) and flora, marine parks will be reserves of genetic material and reference zones for scientific research on ecological problems, especially in areas threatened by pollution or other socio-economic activities.

Since the most ancient times, Mediterranean man has tended to dump his wastes in the sea, and the recent high rate of population growth has made the situation worse because pollution is proportional to population growth. Thus, to industrial pollution is added pollution from urban wastes and from agricultural development. Today, the natural purification mechanisms of the Mediterranean are largely overwhelmed and pollutants can no longer be completely biologically decomposed.

The Mediterranean Sea, potentially very rich in biological resources, is also overexploited by man; degradation of the marine environment is accompanied by extinction of the coastal fauna and flora vital to Mediterranean man.

Resources are therefore twice threatened by the consequences of human activities; pollution and overexploitation are leading to the extinction of marine resources, uncontrolled coastal development, and transformation and drying up of wetlands.

In order to protect critical habitats (fish breeding zones, wetlands, etc.) on which depend productivity and conservation of species, it is urgent to establish a zonation of activities, to be used for protection of certain natural habitats, for guiding development, and for reference. Zonation will follow common principles and guidelines in order to ensure integrated development of the entire ecoregion.

5. CONCLUSION

Problems of promoting balanced management in the Mediterranean environment imply not only the development and implementation of measures to control pollution and monitor protected ecosystems but also to identify and coordinate means of intervention at the regional level. The different measures and interventions will cover a series of activities concerning protection of the Mediterranean environment, particularly the coastal fringe. Among such measures, management of protected areas can only be considered in the context of coordinated action.

Only in this perspective can a protected areas network in the Mediterranean Basin be set up and organised in order to compensate the imbalance between the different "settlement plans" of the coast and to avoid further degradation by protecting certain fragile parts of the coast. Only by following such an approach will the Mediterranean States reach equilibrium between socio-economic development and protection of their environment.

Mediterranean countries have agreed on the principles and guidelines to create and manage protected areas. They also have come to a basic agreement in this field where, more than anywhere else, disorderly action and lack of coordination would lead to irrational management of protected areas, the equilibrium of which is a necessary condition for the conservation of Mediterranean ecosystems. The regional approach is therefore essential. It is the only way to harmonise interventions so as to protect the Mediterranean for present and future generations.

Acknowledgements

This paper was prepared for IUCN's Commission on National Parks and Protected Areas in cooperation with the United Nations Environment Programme.

National Park Development and Its Economics: Experience from Plitvice National Park, Yugoslavia

Josip Movcan
Plitvice National Park
Yugoslavia

ABSTRACT. *A large number of national parks seem to be located in economically under-developed areas. Consequently, they frequently face the problem of inadequate financing. Using the Plitvice National Park in Yugoslavia as an example, this paper points to some ways of improving park revenues. Efficient park management, good organization and control of park attendance, together with suitable package tours, may not only improve park financing, but may also contribute to the welfare of the region where the park is located.*

1. INTRODUCTION

The world today is divided into economically developed regions and those which make great efforts to become developed. The world of national parks, too, follows a similar path. Some parks are wealthy and well developed while the others hardly survive. National economies of their respective countries are not willing to withdraw claims on the exploitation of natural resources and are also reluctant to provide financial means for their conservation as it merely burdens their meagre budgets. We have to find ways and means of improving the economic welfare of those who need help and give hope to the others who deserve that status but cannot reach it for economic reasons.

Using the Plitvice National Park as an example, the aim of this paper is to give consideration to some possibilities that in given circumstances may have an influence on the improvement of the economic status of national parks. My wish is, also, to point out the problems that characterize such development. It would be also wise to exert an influence on governments to view nature conservation in national parks as a possible source of economic growth of the regions where they are lo-

cated. I wish to develop and elaborate the following thesis:

* in well-developed parks, attendance and sight-seeing at their beauty spots can be efficiently organized and thus bring in part of the income vital for self-preservation and survival;
* visitors to a national park seem to be very good customers and consumers of various services (e.g. tourism and recreation, catering and hotel services, shopping trade, transport, cottage industry, and the like), which should be activated and evaluated; and
* the services offered to visitors initiate the production and processing of consumer goods and other activities (agriculture, building trade, crafts, park maintenance and upkeep, manufacture of souvenirs, etc.) within the park boundaries.

All the activities stated above play an important part in the employment of the local population. In other words, this is of great effect—either indirect or direct—for the economic stability of a given region without needing to exploit the natural resources in a national park.

The Plitvice National Park was granted the legal status of a national park in 1949. The park lies in a mountainous region of Yugoslavia and is from 417 to 1280 m above sea level. It is 80 km from the Adriatic Sea and about 140 km from Zagreb, the capital of SR Croatia. The park covers an area of 19,200ha of which 14,500 ha are forests, 200 ha lakes and streams, and the rest are meadows and arable land in the vicinity of villages and hamlets. At the time when the area was declared a national park, the village population amounted to 1,100.

The basic natural phenomenon here is the process of travertine (tufa) making: rain waters which disappear into the ground in the karst area beyond the lakes emerge here again enriched with dissolved carbonates of lime. In the clear streams and transparent waters, in ideal ecological conditions, the carbonates of lime are deposited, encrusting on vegetation which transforms them into a porous rock tufa or travertine. Travertine forms walls across streams and rivers and these walls sometimes grow into big barriers which accumulate lakes behind them, the lakes being interlinked with cascades and waterfalls. This miraculous biodynamic system has been continuously operating for thousands of years, suffering considerable destruction only in the glacial periods of the Pleistocene Epoch.

This beautiful system of lakes and waterfalls with their tributaries is surrounded by well-preserved forests of beech, fir, spruce, and pine. On lower slopes near the lakes, where the climate is warmer, elements of sub-Mediterranean vegetation are found. Meadows and the other areas are a result of the traditional way of life here, when inhabitants used to raise cattle. The meadows with many species of flowers and an occasional small village amid them are very picturesque against the mountainous landscape of thick, wild forests.

The magnificent beauty of the Plitvice Lakes was discovered relatively late and it was only at the end of the 19th Century that the first hotel was built on the slope above the biggest of the Plitvice Lakes. Very soon a small group of catering establishments appeared by the side of it. With two other localities, the pre-war catering trade had about 750 beds. Further urbanization tendencies of the time were stopped by the outbreak and destruction of World War II.

A new hotel, the Plitvice, was built on the site of the first hotel which had been destroyed. However, the cost of its infrastructure was much higher than its economic potential. Then two more hotels were built, making a complex whole along with their infrastructure. Their total accommodation capacity approximately equals that of all the pre-war tourist establishments in the area. Further expansion of the hotel building within the national park has been deliberately put to a stop. Until 1970, the hotel industry in the area had its own management. The management of the national park, on the other hand, had to face a very complex problem of financing its activities, including protection and conservation of its forests and waters. Very difficult economic conditions after the war forced the park management to provide financial means by felling of trees. As the felling was not extensive for safety reasons, the financial means supplied in this way could hardly cover the needs of the personnel. There were no financial resources whatsoever for park development. The first gleam of hope came when the modernization of the roads started; all of a sudden there was a surge of public interest in the Plitvice Lakes, and this led to the idea of organized visits and sightseeing to the park and the introduction of an admission charge. Money started to flow in and park development could proceed.

However, some new problems appeared. European motoring started to infiltrate into the delicate texture of the Plitvice Lakes. Roads were winding around the lakes with the cars coming and going in search of beauty spots at Plitvice and further away at the sunny Adriatic. It was certainly a great challenge for the national park.

On the other hand, the hotel trade, anxious to expand and improve the standard of living of its employees, sensed the importance of ever-growing tourism. These two sides could not possibly solve their problems on their own. This led to the merger of the two sides, and one large working organization, the Plitvice National Park, also develops tourism and other supporting activities in a broader region. Such policy opened the doors of banks which were now willing to finance the park development.

In the last ten years, the merged management has succeeded in solving the problems of protective infrastructure and the standard of living of the park's employees; cars and other motor vehicles have been banned in a large part of the park and the park has organized its own transport of visitors by electric buses; and a powerful scientific and research presence has been developed. New tourist facilities are being erected on building sites in the north and south access routes to the national park trying to preserve elements of autochthonous architecture. Within its region, the park also develops agriculture and food processing, shops and the building trade. There are 1,600 employees in the park and in this way the material basis for widening of the protected area is being created.

Rapid development of any kind results in a number of new problems, which are also present in our park. Young people and experts have been educated and trained to work in production. They want to produce wood in forests, wheat in the fields, they want to build big and comfortable houses and settlements; in a word, they want to use and exploit the existing natural resources. Here they often encounter tasks which are sometimes opposite to those prevailing in the general psychosis of commercializing everyday life. Evaluation of aesthetics requires a very refined sense of action in nature. Therefore, we feel it is highly necessary for new employees of the park to exchange ideas with those who have already achieved considerable successes in "the park education".

There are also problems with the village population, since they, too, crave for rapid growth and development, which eventually leads to gradual urbanization. Great efforts have been made to stop such tendencies within the boundaries of the national park. The mistakes made at this stage will certainly show in the field of financing.

2. THE NATIONAL PARK DEVELOPMENT

If we wish to have well-organized visitation to the national park, it is necessary to give special consideration to its development; we have to bear in mind that nature is highly susceptible to damage in its beauty spots. Therefore the park development has to comprise both the protective measures and efforts to make the given area accessible to the public. In evaluating the park capacity for the reception of visitors and in selecting the means of their transport, it is very important to think of the weather conditions, the configuration and suitability of landscape for its development, and to evaluate the duration of such visits. In Plitvice, the highest number of visitors is usually recorded in July and August, though nature here is at its most beautiful in spring and autumn. Most visitors (two-thirds) spend only a few hours in the park, while the others stay for the night in our hotels, motels, camp sites and in private rooms in the nearby villages.

A well-developed national park must have modern access routes, one or more reception areas, a well-studied network of internal park roads, a satisfactory system of information services, health services and resting places and shelters in case of bad weather. All the above facilities should be provided with adequate infrastructure which meets the nature conservation requirements.

The park access routes are public thoroughfares. The best thing is if they only touch the national park boundaries but do not pass through it. In the Plitvice National Park there is also a transit road which separates one-third of the park area in the north from the rest of the park. That road is today used for all heavy traffic. The number of vehicles using the road in the busy season amounts to more than 10,000; they make noise, cause bustle and bring pollution and thus hinder appropriate park development. When that road too is replaced by a planned ring road to the north of the park, this area will become a national park in its real sense.

The entrance reception area on the access road is where admission tickets are sold; visitors can also park their cars there and get information, use sanitation and catering services, etc. If possible, it is the most economic to have just one entrance reception area, but the Plitvice Lakes today have two of them situated deep inside the park territory; when the northern ring road has been built, these reception areas will be moved to the north and south access routes to the park.

The Plitvice internal road and transport network consists of former public roads, the system of pathways and waters of bigger lakes. Sets of electric buses (panoramic buses) run along the roads, electrically-powered passenger boats transport visitors across the waters of the lakes, and the pathways built as causeways of rough-hewn wood in some susceptible spots provide access to the lakes for hikers. The entire system of pathways has been conceived in such a manner that it offers visitors a choice of circular movement, depending on the time available (the minimum duration of a visit being three hours). The car park capacity and the carrying capacity of pathways and causeways are the best regulators of the number of park visitors.

General and instructive information is given orally in many foreign languages, audiovisually by means of brochures and informative signs and sign-posts which are marked at the back of the admission ticket. The entrance reception areas are provided with restaurants and souvenir shops, and bigger stop-overs and resting places have small refreshment stands.

The three hotels in the national park fit in with the landscape surrounding them; they are well-established, offer high standards of equipment and services and are provided with the protective infrastructure. The same infrastructure is also used for all the other facilities available to the national park visitors.

3. THE PARK ECONOMICS

The Plitvice Lakes is one of the few national parks that provides financial means from its own sources, i.e., its income is the result of its own trade and activities. The exceptional beauty of the area, its favourable transport and geographical position, steadfast management and long-term bank loans have led to the development that was neither easy nor simple. The specific quality of this institution is that apart from its primary activity of nature conservation it has also developed its economics, based on the services offered to the park visitors. The main economic factors are:

- The admission ticket to the national park, the price of which is from two to four US dollars depending on the age and social group of visitors, is in fact a compensation for the package of services which comprises car parking and attending, transport by panoramic bus and electric boat within the park, upkeep of pathways, causeways and other park facilities, sanitation and information services. The ticket itself is a kind of a souvenir, giving information and being used for publicity purposes. Very few visitors so far have complained about this kind of admission charge.
- In the park one can hire boats, bicycles, and horse carriages; there are also special guided tours and trips and also day fishing permits which have a charge. The park also takes care of the world-famous River Gacka, known for its trout; it organizes various gatherings and conferences of scientific and cultural significance.
- The catering trade here consists of classical, rustic and self-service types of restaurants, picnic areas and small park facilities such as barbecue stalls, log cabin cafes and refreshment stands. These small places are very economic since they cost little to build and can cater for a large number of visitors.
- Camping sites seem to be growing in demand and are increasingly popular year by year. This fact

called for a detailed and expert analysis which resulted in building a new and more adequate camping site at the access route to the national park (it is now under construction). The old camping site located within the park will be rebuilt and converted into the Promenade of the brides and bridegrooms who have their wedding ceremony under the Plitvice waterfall; there will be also showrooms for young sculptors.

- The hotel trade, which could hardly cover its annual expenses in earlier years, has become a profitable business branch. It has been spreading south and north of the park access routes where there already exist motel facilities. Work has also started on building infrastructure of a large hotel and catering complex near the north access route to the park. It will boast a new camping site and youth hostel facilities.
- The market trade had a very modest beginning with the sale of souvenirs and necessities for the local population. Today there is a well-developed system of shops in the region. New wholesale and warehouse facilities are being built in a small neighbouring town, which will make supply more efficient and lower transport cost.
- Forestry is an activity that gives relatively modest results due to the primary protective role of the national park forests—those of the highest quality have been declared reserves. Corrective and sanitary felling of the trees generally cover the expenses of this trade.
- The building trade has been developing in two directions. First, it relates to the upkeep and maintenance of the buildings and other facilities within and outside of the park. The other activity concentrates on the industrial production of chalets and log cabins intended for tourist purposes. This trade has its own transport means and machinery needed for the preparation of building sites.
- Food production has become a very important part of the economy; the national park has started cooperation with many individual producers of meat, dairy products and vegetables in the region.

It has taken over considerable agricultural areas in the vicinity, tilled the land and started sheep and cattle breeding for the production of milk and calves. The agricultural products obtained in this way are sold to the park's own hotel and catering establishments. Also, large hunting-grounds for game are being established in the nearby mountain regions in order to attract hunters, off-season.

Finally, I would like to point out that the national park and its economics has never suffered any losses since the merger, which shows that it is always possible to solve problems if we join forces. The economic policy of the park contributes to the employment of new labour and to the education and training of young workers.

4. CONCLUSION

Natural characteristics of national parks around the world are different in many ways although their major goals are similar; the possibilities for their development are specific to their local situation. It is rather difficult to suggest to others which road of development to take using *one* national park as an example. It is, however, possible to present the experience gained, both in the positive and the negative sense.

In this paper, an effort has been made to consider some possibilities in the organization of supporting activities in parks using the Plitvice National Park in Yugoslavia as an example. It can be concluded that efficient park management, good organization and control of the park attendance, along with suitable package tours, can certainly contribute to the economic welfare of the area where the park is located; it is necessary to study the possibilities of financing programmes to support the development of national parks at international and national levels. The activities stated in the paper must never come into collision with nature conservation and they may exert a positive influence on the park economics and, more broadly, on the region where the parks are located.

Abruzzo's Bears: Reconciling the Interests of Wildlife and People in Abruzzo National Park, Italy

Franco Tassi
Chairman
Italian Committee for National Parks and Equivalent Reserves
Rome, Italy

ABSTRACT. *Italy's Abruzzo National Park has been the site of an innovative approach to management of a severely threatened ecosystem. This involved bringing real benefits to local people, educating them in the importance of the national park for their own benefit, and establishing visitor centres in each of the villages of the park to spread the benefits of park visitors evenly among the local people. It also led to considerable local employment, as well as educational benefits. A system of zoning was established to guide human activities. Many Italians now feel that saving Abruzzo's bears will also help save people.*

1. INTRODUCTION

About 15 years ago, when the World Conservation Strategy was not yet conceived, a simple but significant experience of reconciliation between conservation and development was started in Italy, among quite a bit of difficulties. The country itself, though extremely well-provided with natural features, had no remarkable traditions in the field of nature conservation, and the people had no deep commitment to such goals; as a result, the efforts of a small group of individuals trying to affirm nature's rights faced particular difficulties. This is the story of the efforts of these individuals to save Abruzzo National Park.

2. HISTORY OF ABRUZZO NATIONAL PARK

One of Italy's oldest and most popular National Parks, Abruzzo protects about 40,000 ha of mountains, forests and prairies hosting precious wildlife—including the last Abruzzo brown bears, Abruzzo chamois and Apennine wolves—in the Central Apennine Range, just in the middle of Italy, a two-hour drive from Rome or Naples.

Created in 1922, the park has had a long and very complex history of conservation problems, successes and defeats. By the 1960s, Abruzzo National Park was under heavy pressure of exploitation and speculation, but Italian conservationists did not accept the idea of a park abandoned and lost. In a very unfavourable climate for conservation principles, there began a growing awareness of the necessity to change completely the Italian attitude toward nature.

So in 1968 a new campaign was started, mainly on behalf of the Association Italia Nostra, with the cooperation of the young World Wildlife Fund Italian Appeal and with increasing help from part of the press and public opinion. This campaign was inspired to embark on a new and original cultural approach: our major effort was devoted to demonstrate the utility of the park for human society. Instead of emphasizing only its well-known natural, ecological and scenic values to a well-inclined and sensitive minority, we tried to show to the indifferent and selfish majority that the park was there for their advantage too. Instead of representing only a limitative entity, it could produce real benefits for all.

At that time, the utility of a modern national park, conceived in a broader vision of its cultural, social and economic values, was hardly understood at the level of local people and politicians (the park has 5 villages inside of its boundaries, and 13 more inhabited centres are near by). For them, the national park was a symbol of limitations and prohibitions, and their main objective seemed to be simply to eliminate it as soon as possible. To some of them, the national park was acceptable only as a publicity label for their commercial enterprises in the field of tourism and connected matters.

The situation evolved only when we could demonstrate—not only theoretically, but in practice—that the park, properly managed, was capable of bringing real advantages to the local people. But this approach required a great change in the national parks policy in Italy, an idea which received little support and was poorly understood by both central and local powers.

We had to manage the park as a creative and very active agency, promoting new kinds of intervention. Management included not only conservation itself, obviously and forever our first priority, and scientific research, especially devoted to matters related with nature conservation; but we also gave high priority to education and its specific applications to the park's reality. We considered visitors a special category of guests, who should not be confused with tourists in the common, broader sense; visitors need to be oriented to be reasonable users of the park, in the sense of World Conservation Strategy, treating the park's resources with restraint and respect.

The promotion of tourism in the park had resulted in extremely heavy impact, and we had to fight against this traditional and consumptive idea of tourism in natural areas—new roads, ski resorts, real estate developments and so on—which was leading to consumption and collapse of a very precious and unique resource.

On the contrary, we proposed and created new alternative structures—visitor centres, museums, information points, trails, picnic grounds and wildlife areas—which proved to be most successful in attracting, selecting and controlling visitors. Some of these structures, such as the Pescasseroli Visitor Centre inaugurated in 1969, were introduced for the first time in Italy and were later imitated in other parks.

Furthermore, we encouraged local people to become the first actors on the screen, hosting guests in their homes (instead of pressing for new second houses for city folk, or for luxurious hotels connected with external promoters and interests). We stimulated school visits during the low season, encouraged the creation of simple hostels, and permitted limited camping facilities very close to the villages.

Most of the local people soon began to understand that well-managed visitors to the national park could very well satisfy their economic needs; actually, all their traditional productive activities (such as grazing, timber harvesting, and hunting) resulted in great decline not only owing to park limitations, but due to the general trends of the economy in all the Apennines. So the people began to see that one old tree or a wild animal could give more benefit to the local community if preserved as a permanent attraction, instead of being destroyed and consumed for one day's individual need or amusement. Defending better conservation and use of the park would mean larger and surer incomes and lead to a better future for the park as well.

Eventually the local people became interested in preserving habitats and species not only for scientific, aesthetic and ethical considerations, but also for their own better living. According to a conservationist's rough but effective image, local people (as predators) should exploit a certain number of visitors (as prey) in order to survive; but just for this aim, as well as for nature's wealth, all the environment should be preserved.

Some figures might explain the situation better than many words. During the past few years we have had more than 1 million visitors per year, including 300,000-400,000 in the system of visitors centres, five of which were in operation in 1980, and where all visitors buy tickets and are individually counted. Economists estimate an average stay in Abruzzo of 1-3 days, with an average expenditure of at least $28 per individual, yielding a total amount of about US$28,000,000 (40 billion lire) to the local economy, on the basis of the most conservative evaluations.

Moreover, the park helped develop jobs; no less than 50 permanent and 50 temporary staff are directly working in the park organization, but it was estimated that each job in this field produces 5-6 indirect employments in connected services such as lodging, catering, and so on. It is also generally recognized that this way of non-destructive and non-consumptive use of the environment gives up to 100 times more benefits (from the existing resources, and without spoiling them) than previous private interventions.

Local people are quite ready to accept and maximize benefits from the park, but do not always look with the same attitude at all the connected limitations. Conflicts of interest still exist, of course, and often prove to be difficult and slow to clear up. But the substance of the park's reality is being accepted more and more—what seemed to be absolutely impossible only ten years ago—and problems arise now especially at a different level, concerning the management of the park.

The park dilemma today is that it is under many points of view a local entity, but it has to be managed as part of the national heritage. So we try to follow the well-known principle, *"Think globally, act locally"*.

3. CONSERVING TOP VALUES

It has been very often emphasized that involvement of local people is essential: this is certainly true, but our experience says that you ought to involve not only local people—which might mean sometimes only a slow trend toward a better conservation-development balance—but also, and especially, the whole society in the country. In fact, you very often need strong support for the most urgent park needs, and you should not risk waiting for a greater awareness of the local reality; otherwise you might lose some of the park's best values, especially the ones I call the "top-values".

I mean by this term the most important, perennial and high values, which are at the same time the ones that local people often find useless and difficult to appreciate. Virgin forests, ancient big trees, decaying wood, wilderness areas, predators and superpredators, endemic plants and insects are some of the most typical "top values". Top values include peculiar features—unique scenery, aesthetic quality, rare and curious objects—which were particularly appreciated by romantic early naturalists; but from a modern perspective they also include such abstract matters as biological complexity and diversity, sophisticated inter-relations in ecosystems, and genetic resources. Their conservation involves a major long-term investment.

We are aware that such top-values cannot survive, unfortunately, intact and totally unspoiled everywhere in the world; we are conscious that a reasonable level of exploitation—or better, a sustainable yield—of natural resources is necessary for the survival of humanity. But we have made the parks our last frontier, where we try to let natural values survive. And we hope possibly to use the national parks to extend nature conservation values even further through the countryside.

In other words, the parks with their top values (inspiring supreme landscapes, extraordinary natural elements, precious genetic resources) represent the environmental hope of rescue, both spiritual and material, of the whole of human society.

4. THE STRUGGLE FOR ABRUZZO NATIONAL PARK

The symbols of the struggle for nature in Italy have been, for many years, the animals of the Abruzzo National Park and especially the Abruzzo brown bear. In order to let the people sympathize with this animal, we used all modern methods, including mass-media and publicity (and even car-stickers with a small, appealing bear and the motto "your friend the bear"). Furthermore, we developed a system of compensation and incentives (such as paying indemnities for damage to cattle, providing food in critical seasons and offering prizes to agriculturalists for maize cultivation in marginal lands), without forgetting the enforcement of the laws against hunting and poaching. The interest of this restricted Apennine bear population has substantially increased, after scientific research proved its clear distinction from any other European brown bear.

Considering the conservation of the ecosystems as a whole as the most significant task of Abruzzo National Park, we devoted ourselves also to the restoration of parts of such ecosystems that had been previously damaged and spoiled by man. In this spirit, we reintroduced with success two species which were formerly represented in the park's fauna, the Roe deer and the Red deer. And we had a very interesting experience creating for the first time in Italy and in Europe, in 1969, what we called "wildlife areas": fenced large natural areas boasting individuals or families of the rare animals of the park—there were always some wounded, imprinted or abandoned specimens—for many different objectives, ranging from acclimatization and scientific research to visitor attraction and educational purposes.

Very happily, such areas have worked very well, especially for local people; for instance, in the case of the Apennine wolf, we were able to persuade the villagers that those animals were to be preserved and were really substantially harmless to man.

It would have been impossible to manage a national park which included villages and productive lands without a system of zones. It is clearly unrealistic to consider wilderness areas and inhabited areas the same way, so a very simple zoning system, related to the main land uses, was gradually established in the park:

• Zone A Strict nature reserve (deserving absolute protection) (IUCN Category I);
Zone B Natural environment (supporting only very limited traditional activities) (Category II);
Zone C Countryside (protecting cultural landscapes) (Category V); and
Zone D Villages and other inhabited areas (promoting kinds of development reconcilable with park aims) (Category VIII).

Furthermore, a buffer zone of about 60,000 ha has been established around the park. It is generally assumed that the future big and modern Abruzzo National Park should include this buffer zone, integrating all the environment having common features and priority resources, totalling more than 100,000 ha in the Central Apennines, covering parts of the territory of 3 regions—Abruzzo, Latium and Molise—in a master plan of conservation and management.

In our feeling, sound management of a modern park in a densely populated country such as Italy is a serious and very difficult task which involves interdisciplinary activities, including not only biology, ecology, law, planning, architecture and public organization sciences, but also economy, sociology, public relation techniques and many others.

Our major efforts are being now devoted to transform Abruzzo National Park in a self-supporting agency, meeting its costs with its own income. Our situation seems to be a little bit more difficult than the well-known—and admirably managed—case of Plitvice National Park (Movcan, this volume), since our national park authority is not the owner of the land and depends on the existence of the villages inside of the park and must share powers with many other public authorities. For instance, many of the productive activities, especially in the field of the services related to tourism, are being exploited by the local young people (a system of cooperative associations having been developed) on the basis of agreements with the park's authority (whose services are usually compensated with a contribution of 20% of the net income to the park's budget, as a symbolic payment for the general services assured by the park itself).

5. CONCLUSION

To say that all the problems have been solved would be certainly over-optimistic. In a living national park, as in any other living creature, new problems always arise and to state that everything is static, could only mean that it has died.

Nevertheless, a workable approach has been developed, and today nobody in Italy dares to claim that nature conservation and national parks are not beneficial to human needs. While it was formerly common to hear "before protecting the bears, think of the people", now people are beginning to understand that to preserve the bears may mean to save the people too.

Threshold Approach to the Definition of Environmental Capacity in Poland's Tatry National Park

Jerzy M. Kozlowski
University of Queensland
Brisbane, Australia

ABSTRACT. *This case study presents a planning method for defining the environmental carrying capacity of a protected area through the identification of boundary constraints, "Ultimate Environmental Thresholds" (UETs). It shows how it can be practically applied, using the Tatry in Poland. The method is aimed at allocating rational use and evaluating ecosystem carrying capacity, drawing on a broad intra-disciplinary approach and integrating a number of diverse elements.*

1. INTRODUCTION

This case study presents a planning method for defining environmental carrying capacity through the identification of boundary constraints, called Ultimate Environmental Thresholds (UETs), and its practical application in the Tatry—a Polish mountain ecosystem which has been a National Park since 1955. The method is oriented at rational use allocation and ecosystem evaluation, one of the major fields upon which implementation of the World Conservation Strategy depends. The concept of UETs originated some years ago and successively developed in research programmes and practical planning.

2. PROBLEM SETTING

To designate an area as a national park, nature reserve or wilderness may protect it from certain kinds of exploitation but it does not guarantee that the environment will not still be endangered. Indeed, the problem of misuse or overuse of protected areas is worldwide and it often happens that the very natural resources to which those areas owe their attractiveness or value are threatened. Therefore, it is always important that human activities in protected areas be kept within the environmental capacity of such areas. The proper assessment of the environmental capacity is most significant in protecting valuable ecosystems from various forms of degradation by human activities. This poses a twofold problem: first, to assess the capacity; and second, to establish the right system of environmental management. One of the activities which directly and commonly affects protected areas is tourism. It takes many forms, some of which can adversely affect the quality of the natural environment and even impair the ability of the ecosystem to maintain itself. Tourist activities with their accompanying infrastructure of tourist-related services tend naturally to concentrate in areas with the most attractive natural qualities. Frequently these activities have destructive impacts on places where the resistance of the natural environment to damage is lowest. Therefore, certain touristic developments should be excluded or at least restricted in some areas or parts of areas where the natural qualities or living resources are threatened. This statement points to the significance of providing appropriate working tools for planners and managers, allowing them to define environmental capacity as expressed by: areas, development levels, and time periods to which various forms of tourism should be confined.

3. BACKGROUND

Existing methods of evaluating the capacity of the natural environment for various activities fall into two main categories: those aimed at measuring attractiveness to visitors; and those aimed at identifying quantitative lim-

450

itations. The second category is less developed than the first. Most commonly the definition of capacity is limited to overnight tourists and to holiday-makers while the indicators are primarily specified in relation to the capacity of tourist facilities (e.g. number of beds, seats in restaurants, etc.). Moreover, in Western Europe and in the United States this capacity is almost solely determined by the sociological aspects (i.e. satisfaction and security of tourists).

In contrast, methods which are environmentally oriented usually regard vegetation as the key element determining capacity and other, often more significant, elements are ranked lower in to importance. The tendency to use mathematical models (or equations) as tools for defining capacity can also be noted. To suggest that these could satisfactorily account for all interrelations among the environmental elements, as well as for their links with touristic activities, seems questionable. In fact, there are no fully reliable planning methods or techniques oriented at the definition of such environmental capacities. Hence no environmentally sound basis can be provided for decisions on whether or not to exclude certain activities from certain areas or for decisions on what level of activities should be permitted. This is an obvious gap in the environmental planning methodology.

An attempt to close this particular gap in knowledge was started in 1968 as the continuation and extension of theoretical ideas characterising so-called Threshold Analysis, applied in urban planning (Kozlowski and Hugues, 1972). Since one of the targets of environmental planning is the identification of opportunities and constraints posed by natural ecosystems to different forms of human activities, it was considered appropriate to introduce the threshold concept into this planning. An "amenity threshold" was first introduced in a subregional plan for the Central Borders in Scotland (Scottish Development Department, 1968).

Later, in the plan for the Podtatrze region in Poland, a method was developed for determining if any recreation and tourist activities could be permitted without exceeding "ultimate thresholds" (Kozlowski, 1975). Development of the major concept of "ultimate environmental thresholds" (UET-s) followed and their four dimensions—territorial, quantitative, qualitative and temporal—were identified in 1976 (Kozlowski, 1977). At the same time, as a result of a special research project, a method for identifying UET-s in the development of tourism was formulated (Baranowska-Janota, 1977) and applied in the Physical Plan for the Tatry National Park (TNP) in Poland (Kozlowski, et al., 1979) where continually increasing pressure from various forms of tourism and sport indicated a firm need to define and impose territorial, quantitative, qualitative and temporal restrictions on these activities. This practical application led to further refinement and the final formulation of the UET Method (Baranowska-Janota and Kozlowski, 1981).

4. RESEARCH ACTION

The research programme based on the UET concept and designed to address the problem of environmental capacity was aimed at the formulation of a planning method founded on a reliable theoretical basis but simple enough to become a real, *practical* help to planners and managers in the field. The main aspects of this method are outlined below.

4.1. Major definitions

UETs have been defined as the stress limits beyond which a given ecosystem becomes incapable of returning to its original condition and balance. Where these limits are exceeded as a result of the functioning or development of particular tourist or other activities, a chain reaction is generated leading towards irreversible environmental damage of the whole ecosystem or of its essential parts. Identification of such limits is certainly essential both for planners and managers. Three types of UETs were distinguished:

- *territorial UETs* which are location-oriented and indicate areas from which given activities should be excluded; these thresholds can be presented cartographically as lines on a base map;
- *quantitative UETs* which are capacity-oriented and indicate levels of development that must not be overstepped by particular forms of tourist activities; these thresholds can be presented numerically as a maximum number of users (or services for tourists) which may be accommodated in a given area; and
- *temporal UETs* which are time oriented and indicate periods of time during which access may be permitted and to which different forms of touristic activities must be confined; these thresholds can be presented in time units (hours, days, months, etc.).

It has been assumed that the "quality" of tourism depends on the type and amount of accompanying services (such as hotels, trails, chairlifts, parking sites, etc.). Therefore, instead of introducing separate qualitative UETs it was recommended that the tourist-related services be treated as an integral part of tourist activities and be dealt with accordingly in the proposed approach.

4.2. Approach to the definition of environmental capacity

The three types of UETs jointly define ultimate environmental carrying capacity for different forms of tourist and recreational activities (such as hiking, potholing, downhill skiing, mountaineering etc.) that exist or are expected in a given area. Therefore a basic prerequisite to the definition of UETs is the formulation of a list of these forms subdivided into "activities" and "services" which then must be characterized by standards, intensity, frequency, etc. It is assumed that the main factor determining development possibilities from the viewpoint of environmental protection requirements is the quality of the natural environment. There are considerable difficulties in measuring this quality; it can, however, be expressed by means of selected characteristic features which can be measured, or at least objectively defined in relation to various elements of this environment. In this approach the quality of natural environmental elements is defined by degrees of "uniqueness", "transformation" and "resistance" which can together indicate the extent of protection required from the effects of a particular tourist activity.

Uniqueness can be determined by the frequency of occurrence of a given environmental element or, more often, of its particular components within the whole country or, at least, its regions. The spatial differentiation of this occurrence can be characterized in three classes: "unique", "rare" and "common." To give an example, the occurrence of relict stone pine forest is a unique phenomenon within Poland, while the occurrence of pine forests is a common phenomenon. Taking another example: bison are unique, as they live only in the Bialowieza National Park, while black grouse should be classified as rare and wild boar as common. Degree of uniqueness dictates the necessity to protect rare or particularly threatened environmental elements from the adverse effects of tourism.

Transformation indicates how far any given environmental elements or their components have changed as compared with the original state (that is the state in which self-regulating natural mechanisms were working and the balance between biotic and abiotic factors was maintained). Three distinct degrees of transformation can be distinguished: "minimal," "partial" and "total." The last can be further subdivided into "reversible" and "irreversible." To give an example: a single instance of water pollution in a stream is minimal transformation, while cutting down a section of a forest can be classified as partial. Extermination, within a local area, of a species endemic to a region is a total though reversible transformation, but extermination of a species endemic to this area is not only total, but irreversible.

Such information is of great importance in determining the extent of protection necessary from the effects of different types of tourist activities, particularly if these effects are superimposed on existing transformations due to previous human activities or ecological factors. The process of the environment's return to the original state may then be impeded and the transformations may become more serious.

Resistance of a given environmental element to damage from specific forms of tourist activities can be evident in its ability both to withstand negative effects and to self-regenerate, with the help of natural forces, allowing the element to return to its previous state. It is essential to note first, that each component may have a different degree of resistance to damage at a different time (of the year, month or day), and from different causes, and second, that the very location of this component affects the degree of its resistance. For example, in the case of wildlife, this may be during the mating and breeding seasons; for vegetation, during the early stages of establishment; for soils, at the time of high saturation levels, etc. Vulnerable locations for specific elements of the environment may be, for instance, backwoods in the case of some wildlife species, areas of initial soil development, the upper-forest layer, etc. The three following classes of resistance can be distinguished: "full resistance," meaning that a given element has such capacity for self-regeneration that a particular use or activity does not bring about lasting damage; "minor resistance," meaning that some capacity for self-regeneration exists but its process is too slow to fully counteract the adverse impacts involved; and "very low resistance," meaning that owing to lack of self-regenerating capacity, the effects of particular use or activity will lead to irreversible damage of the element concerned.

4.3. The process

The suggested process leading to the definition of the environmental capacity is subdivided into the following major phases:

Phase 1: *Preliminaries*, which begin with the selection of the best means for data gathering, followed by decisions on which forms of touristic activities and which elements of the natural environment should be taken into account. These decisions would be derived from analysis of "potential environmental threats," by considering the relations between various activities and various elements. The character, intensity and duration of an activity could be of particular significance in identifying these threats.

Phase 2: *Evaluation of environmental quality and definition of partial territorial UETs*, which first leads toward the identification, for each environmental element, of its various degrees of uniqueness, transformation and resistance and of their geographical location. Next, from synthesis, partial territorial UETs are defined for each activity considered.

Phase 3: *Definition of combined territorial UETs*, where by overlapping partial territorial UETs as imposed on any form of activity by all the environmental elements involved, the combined UETs are defined. The principle of combining each partial threshold is shown in Fig. 1. The resulting UETs for each activity can be shown together on one map or separately. They indicate areas from which particular activities must be excluded.

Phase 4: *Definition of quantitative and temporal UETs*, in which the first task is to identify specific localities within the areas, for which both the above thresholds need to be defined. These should be localities of distinct identity such as a section of trail, a place of rest or a stopping point. Next, from results obtained in Phase 2 and from supplementary evidence for each locality and for each activity, quantitative and temporal UETs are defined. Quantitative UETs indicate environmental capacity expressed as the maximum number of tourists which can be allowed at any one time to be in a given locality without the stress limit of the environment being transgressed. Quantitative UETs are thus defined for each activity as determined by all environmental elements involved. The most severe partial thresholds determine the final UETs as shown in Fig. 2. Finally, the temporal UETs for particular activities are defined, indicating the acceptable duration for particular activities or the sensitive periods (e.g. mating season) during which some activities may need to be totally excluded.

4.4. Management implications

The method not only defines a total environmental capacity for the whole area but may assist in indicating optimal (in given circumstances) distribution of tourists by revealing the capacities of the various localities considered. A major problem is then, of course, how to attain such a distribution in reality. It may not be practicable trying to close the access to a given area when the number of visitors in this area reached threshold magnitude; the desired distribution might better be attained by appropriate management (steering) of tourist flows, that is, by making access more difficult to particular entry points or to specific overloaded areas while increasing the attractiveness of those having spare capacity. To make this possible the resource manager needs to know the reasons for the existing distribution of tourist flows and the means by which they can best be altered. A properly programmed simulation model should be of major assistance as it will reveal the changes in the distribution of tourists resulting from such factors as closure of some trails, opening of new trails, increasing or decreasing the attractiveness of some localities, changes in quality and profile of visitors, closure of some entry points, opening of new entry points, etc. A simulation model fed with appropriate input data, including UETs, will assist the planner or the manager to determine appropriate actions or means to keep tourist activities within the identified environmental capacity of the area. Such a model would be a very important supplementary tool for the practical application of results emerging from the UET Methods.

5. PRACTICAL RESULTS

5.1. The case study area

The reason for using the Tatry National Park (TNP) for the case study is obvious since the method was first tested in the process of preparing the plan for this park. In addition, however, this particular mountain ecosystem offers such a rare combination of widely differing threats and pressures that the validity of the approach and the constraints in its application can be better exposed. The TNP, with its alpine character and accumulation of natural values, is a unique "monument of nature" in Poland. At the same time, general interest in this area encourages multiple use of the park through different types of tourism, sport and recreation. This brings a number of conflicts (man vs. environment and man vs. man). The park exhibits several areas of considerable and severe damage caused by natural calamities, to which the mountains are very susceptible; the area is small and damage resulting from such calamities alone is a major problem in attempting to maintain its existing range of ecosystems. These transformations from the natural state are further aggravated by inappropriate use.

The park covers 21,000 ha, of which 57 percent is zoned as strict reserve (total exclusion) and 43 percent as partial reserve (partial exclusion). Forest occupies 70 percent of the area, followed by 20 percent wasteland and rock, 9 percent alpine meadows and clearings, and 1 percent water. The park attracts over 3 million visitors per year. They use, among other things, 12 tourist hostels, 27 km of roads, 8 parking lots and 254 km of marked trail.

The basic structure of visitor activities during the 1973 summer season was as follows:

Hiking	700,000 people -	31.8%
Group excursions	800,000 people -	36.4%
Qualified hiking (experienced skiers only)	636,000 people -	30.7%
Climbing	22,000 people -	1.0%
Cave exploration	2,000 people -	0.1%

The volume of ski activities reached approximately 250,000 people in the period December 1972 - April 1973.

5.2. The scope of approach

The approach presented below outlines the process of analysis and evaluation of the natural environmental elements, as well as the definition of boundary limitations on the use of the TNP environment. The major input was provided by initial decisions on the type of activities thought permissible in the park and on the general conditions which should be imposed upon them. Thirteen forms of use (e.g. scientific field research, hiking, qualified hiking, conducted tours, downhill skiing) and nine forms of services (e.g. overnight accommodation and mountain rescue service) were finally listed.

To more clearly illustrate the UET Method, the case study was restricted to the four most characteristic and potentially damaging touristic activities in the park together with the four forms of accompanying services. These were: general hiking, qualified hiking, conducted tours, and downhill skiing; and overnight accommodation, restaurants, mountain trails and ski lifts correspondingly. The analysis of stresses and transformation of the natural environment in the TNP has demonstrated that existing types of visitor activity endanger primarily vegetation, water, topography (relief) and fauna. Therefore, the process of determining uniqueness, transformation and resistance centred on these four environmental elements.

5.3. The process

The analytical part of the approach started by identifying potential threats to the natural elements from the four selected forms of activities and services. This was followed by defining criteria and classifying the degrees of the elements' uniqueness, transformation and resistance. For the sake of brevity, the classification will be described in some detail only for vegetation and the definition of UETs for the services will not be further discussed.

5.3.1. Defining uniqueness.
The Tatry vegetation is very special in the context of Poland. To evaluate uniqueness, rare species were identified and the various plant associations found in the area were defined. Data were gathered to determine factors responsible for spatial patterning of individual species and communities. Frequency of occurrence was considered in the context of the whole country and of the region i.e. the Tatry mountains. According to the former, plant communities were subdivided into three groups: unique, rare and common. "Unique" communities were those which were exclusive in a given area; they were primarily endemic. Typical examples in this category were the following plant communities: relict stone pine forests *Cembro piceetum*, dwarf mountain pine brushwood *Pinetum mughi carpaticum*, sycamore maple weeds *Phyllitido aceretum* or Norway spruce hedges above the upper timberline. "Rare" communities were those which appeared also in several regions; however their occurrence was not widespread. Beechwood *Fagetum carpaticum*, fir forest *Piceetum abietotosum*, high mountain spruce *Piceetum tarticum* and meadow associations *Gladiolo agrostidetum tipicum* were put into this category. "Common" communities included exogenous Norway spruce stands and mat grass meadow associations (e.g. *Nardojuncetum squarrosi*). These occur throughout the country and in a range of different environments.

5.3.2. Transformation.
To analyze transformations, comparison was made between known areas of natural vegetation and areas currently occupied by vegetation know to be either introduced or successional. Preserved fragments of primeval vegetation often served as a model, and results from paleobotanic studies together with historic information were also used. Changes of species composition, expulsion of native forms and ecotypes,

changes in plant communities and removal of the plant cover on steep slopes were recognized as major transformations from the natural state. Three grades of transformations were distinguished: none (or minimal), partial and total. "Partial" transformation included: decrease in the number of indicator species (e.g. fir in the fir/spruce forest association); mechanical injuries to vegetation that did not produce complete degradation; possible succession of ecologically diverse meadow communities composed of native species to forest associations, etc. "Total" transformations were: total destruction of vegetational communities; destruction of native species, varieties and ecotypes of trees; and the occurrence of meadow communities of low value in place of forest associations. Some of these were then classified as "irreversible."

5.3.3. Resistance.
Evaluation of resistance was preceded by definition of "potential threats" that may result from the analyzed touristic activities. For example: trampling of plants and ground cover, injuring roots or breaking of branches may result from hiking, qualified hiking and conducting tours; downhill skiing may more likely be associated with tearing away of turf. The two following factors were identified as those which determined the degree of resistance: "sensitivity" to disturbance and damage, and "capacity" for natural regeneration. The following elements were indicated as having major influence on these factors in the Tatry environment:

- the biological properties of the vegetation such as anatomical and morphological structure which influence natural resistance to mechanical injuries;
- relief, since in steep terrain any removal of or disturbance to the protective vegetational layer leads to increased risk of erosion. This in turn limits the capacity of vegetation to regenerate;
- type of bedrock, which influences soil type, the rate and intensity of erosion and thus the possibilities for regeneration (the most critical are localities with loose, stony, scree or easily sliding bedrock);
- elevation above sea level, as specific vegetation types have differing altitudinal tolerances, hence vegetation growing near the upper reaches of its habitat is of low vitality.

Resistance to intrusion of foreign species was also considered important as it was found that changes in habitat conditions due to disturbance led to the creation of secondary habitats, more vulnerable to invasion by foreign species. As a result of the evaluation, three classes of resistance were defined: "least resistant," including all plant communities growing on bedrock, scree-like or shallow soils where slopes are over 30%, the upper timber line zone, relict Scots pine associations etc; "more resistant," including dwarf mountain pine brushwood, areas where a slope is over 30% but with compact bedrock, the meadow associations, etc.; and the "most resistant," like mat grass meadow communities and fragments of *Firmentum* and *Trifido distichetum* associations which occur on gently sloping areas.

5.3.4. Territorial and temporal UETs.

The integrated results of the evaluations allowed the definition of those properties (or their combinations) which impose a territorial UET to tourist activities under consideration and imply the total exclusion of tourists from the areas contained within this threshold. These properties were as follows:

- very low resistance and unique (including relict Scot pine associations, high mountain scree, herb brush associations etc.);
- very low resistance (including all plant communities on areas where the slope is greater than 30% on scree, stony or sliding bedrock);
- undergoing transformations with minor regeneration capability (including partially damaged dwarf mountain pine brushwood and fragments of a devastated upper timberline).

Analyses of varying resistance of plant communities to destruction and of the time necessary for their regeneration also allowed the determination of temporal UETs. They were, among others, proposed for the spring season in relation to the beech forest association, which has a large regeneration capacity provided that seedling trees, which have a low resistance to visitors' pressures, are given an opportunity to establish themselves. The process of defining terriorial UETs by vegetation, water, relief and fauna is illustrated in Figs. 3, 4 and 5.

5.3.5. Quantitative UETs.

There had been several attempts in the past to express the environmental capacity of the TNP by the maximum number of tourists its area could accommodate without detrimental ecological effects. These attempts were based on estimating the capacity of tourist trails or on defining an "optimum" ratio between the number of tourists and the area of the park and, in general, owing to the arbitary character of indicators and parameters applied, were not successful. In the present approach direct observations indicated that the greatest degradation of the natural environment in the park occurred in places where visitors stop (to look, rest, eat, etc.). Therefore, it was assumed that the joint, *daily* capacity of those places would best reflect the overall quantitative environmental capacity of the TNP. Hence, 120 visitor stopping places, most exposed to the threat of degradation, were first identified. Subsequently, 18 crucial stops (or localities) which primarily influenced the scale of tourist utilization of the park were distinguished. For each of those places the process

of defining quantitative UETs as imposed by vegetation, water, relief and fauna began. Other major elements such as climate, geological structure, soils and morphology were taken into consideration during the evaluation of plant habitats. The specialists carrying out this task endeavoured to determine the earliest time at which changes in the quality of the given element caused by increasing tourism became significant. The resulting number of tourists indicated a quantitative UET.

Some of the basic criteria applied at this stage were: extent of mechanical destruction (treading, erosion, denudation), extent of various sorts of human introductions (foreign species, pollution, litter), or degrees of uniqueness, transformation and resistance. In the process, some restrictions had also to be related to specific time periods. Quantitative and temporal UETs were thus defined. An example for selected localities is shown in Table 1. The principle applied was that the "lowest" of the partial thresholds determines the capacity. Comparison of resulting magnitudes with the existing number of visitors at every locality revealed instantly which places of the park were most exposed to degradation. The final stage was to calculate the environmental carrying capacity of the park, that is, the total number of tourists who could be admitted to its area daily.

This was done by the use of a simulation model which also indicated how to distribute the total number to the 17 entrance points so that the number of tourists reaching particular localities would not exceed the defined quantitative UETs. The signficance of this information to planners and managers is obvious.

6. CONSTRAINTS

The constraints in the development and application of the UET Method fall into two categories: general constraints and constraints encountered in the TNP.

6.1. General constraints

The approach does not require any different data to those which are commonly gathered in studies of this kind. However, to attain the desired ends, uniform ways of handling the data are necessary. An attempt to impose new ways on specialists from other disciplines led to some difficulties. It should be noted, however, that after applying the method, positive comment was usually received and some of the experts volunteered to cooperate in further research or testing.

Another general constraint was the lack of specific methods of carrying out some of the evaluations. For example a particularly difficult question to answer was: "how many people participating in a given type of touristic activity may be admitted at a given time (e.g. daily) to a given locality so that the stress limit of the natural element considered (e.g. vegetation, water, relief, fauna) will not be transgressed?" Where the lack of appropriate methods or readily available data made it impossible to obtain timely results, the use of the Delphi technique (Linstone and Turoff, 1975) had to be suggested in certain fields. Some problems were also encountered in the process of defining degrees of transformation as it is always difficult to obtain reliable information on historical changes in the environment.

6.2. The TNP constraints

The size, intensity and distribution of touristic activities and their environmental impact in the park had not been satisfactorily monitored prior to the study. This was a major difficulty which was only partly overcome by using comparative analyses (areas of similar physiographical conditions but with different intensity or type of use) or the Delphi technique. Hence, it proved impossible to support some of the results with sufficiently firm scientific evidence to enable them to be used fully as a basis for the final proposals of the TNP Plan. For instance, the environmental capacity of the park derived from the quantative UETs and the simulation model indicated that the acceptable daily number of visitors should not exceed 10,000, that is 50% of the existing number. Such drastic reduction of visitors could not be adopted without further evidence, so it was decided to accept the figure only as a long-term target and meanwhile to continue to monitor the environment and develop the method so that successively more reliable estimates of the capacity could be attained. Summing up, the application of the method to the TNP was significantly influenced by the lack of data and by the necessarily short period of time for carrying out the work. This, however, seems to be typical of planning practice where lack of specialist research and expertise, together with time constraints, often determine the reliability of the approach.

7. CONCLUSIONS

The World Conservation Strategy states that "integration of conservation and development can best be achieved through environmental planning and rational use allocation—specifically through ecosystem evaluations, environmental assessments, and a procedure for allocating uses on the basis of such evaluations and assessments . . ." The urgent need to ". . .identify gaps in knowledge . . ." and to encourage ". . . living resource research activities and to relate research to conservation on the ground . . ." is also emphasized.

The UET Method can be seen as a partial response to those recommendations. The method provides an environmentally sound basis for decision making in the planning and management of ecologically sensitive areas by identifying boundary limitations of the environment's capacity to various touristic activities. It also provides some answers to the question of optimum distribution of activities in a given area. These problems are critical to any ecosystem evaluation. Territorial, quantitative and temporal UETs can assist in determining appropriate uses for different ecosystems or living resources and in establishing priority management areas. A new research avenue is also opened up because the approach can be applied to any human activities and to any area. A first step in this direction was in fact completed recently in Poland (Kozlowski and Zadorozna, 1982).

The simplicity and flexibility of the method makes it a good "emergency tool" when quick action is required. This simplicity also makes the method easily understood by non-professionals, an important property since " . . . greater public participation in decisions concerning living resources . . . " is one of the priority requirements of the WCS.

As a supplement to these general remarks it should be pointed out that:

- he method offers a uniform interdisciplinary approach by bringing together evaluations carried out by experts from different disciplines;
- it integrates all the elements and factors which are of significance for a given area or ecosystem;
- by relating existing tourist flows to environmental thresholds it becomes possible to establish where the environmental capacity is already being exceeded and where immediate intervention is needed;
- a built-in flexibility allows use of the approach at various levels of planning and management (e.g. a large national park or a small fishery reserve);
- it contributes to rationalization of data gathering, since once collected the information can easily be updated and the method re-run with new data from field monitoring, thus allowing both planners and managers to be responsive to changing situations and progress in research; and
- it may prevent major environmental blunders in planning and management decision making.

It seems, therefore, that the UET Method can assist in the development of ecosystem and living resource evaluations, in environmental assessments, and in improving the capacity for environmental management, so strongly emphasized by the World Conservation Strategy.

Acknowledgements

This paper is based on the research project commissioned by the US Environmental Protection Agency (EPA), carried out at the Instytut Ksztaltowania Srodowiska (IKS) (Research Institute on Environmental Development) in Poland and recently completed by the interdisciplinary team led by J. Kozlowski (architect/planner) and M. Baranowska-Janota (geographer) as Principal Investigators. The Final Report was published by the EPA (M. Baranowska-Janota and J. Kozlowski, 1981). The team consisted of S. Augustyniak (hydrologist), G. Korzeniak (forester), A. Kulczycki (ecologist), A. Marska (system planner), D. Ptaszycka-Jackowska (lanlandscape architect), A. Rotter (geographer), A. Tomek (ecologist) and B. Zawadowska (biologist). However, this paper does not purport to represent any official position on the problem of defining environmental carrying capacity.

Table 1: Quantitative and Temporal UETs

Locality	Partial quantitative thresholds as imposed by particular elements of the natural environment				Quantitative UETs	Temporal UETs
	Vegetation	Water	Relief	Fauna		
1	2	3	4	5	6	7
1. Exit of the Chocholowska Valley	400	300	2500	300	300	excluding low water periods
2. Huciska clearing	200	300	600	200	200	
3. Surroundings of the hostel in the Chocholowska Valley	150	100	300	100	100	excluding early vegetation period (April, May)
4. Iwanowka clearing	60	60	100	60	60	
5. Iwanowka Pass	35	35	100	0	0	Excluding snow melting periods (to be indicated by weather conditions)
6. Kominiarski Peak	15	15	50	0	0	

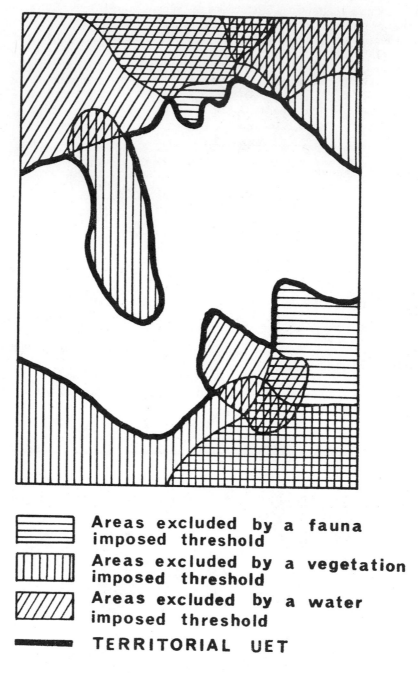

Figure 1. An example of the definition of a combined territorial UET to a given activity.

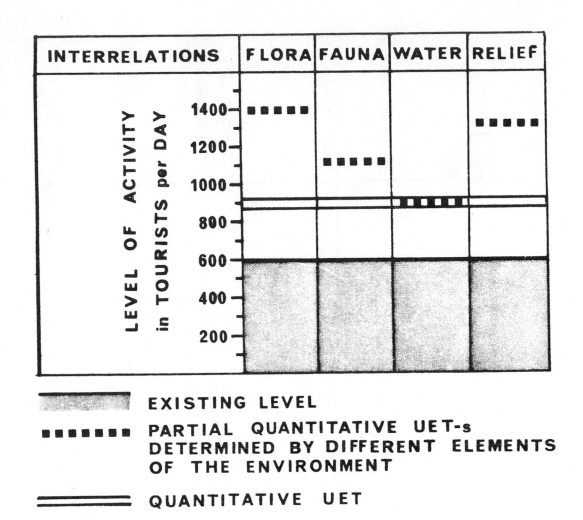

Figure 2. An example of the definition of a quantitative UET to a given activity.

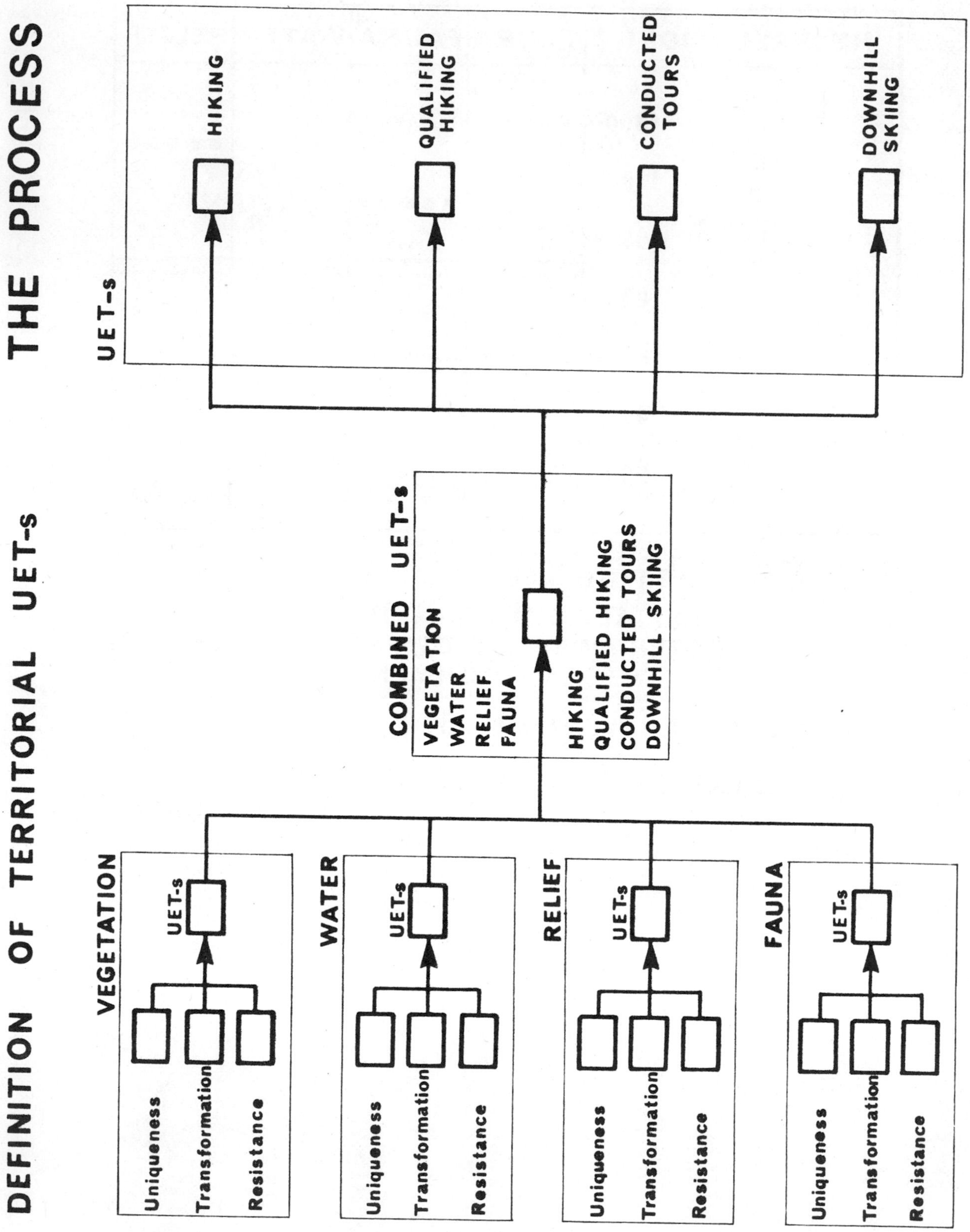
DEFINITION OF TERRITORIAL UET-s THE PROCESS
VEGETATION
Uniqueness
Transformation
Resistance
UET-s
WATER
Uniqueness
Transformation
Resistance
UET-s
RELIEF
Uniqueness
Transformation
Resistance
UET-s
FAUNA
Uniqueness
Transformation
Resistance
UET-s
COMBINED UET-s
VEGETATION
WATER
RELIEF
FAUNA
HIKING
QUALIFIED HIKING
CONDUCTED TOURS
DOWNHILL SKIING
UET-s
HIKING
QUALIFIED HIKING
CONDUCTED TOURS
DOWNHILL SKIING

Figure 3.

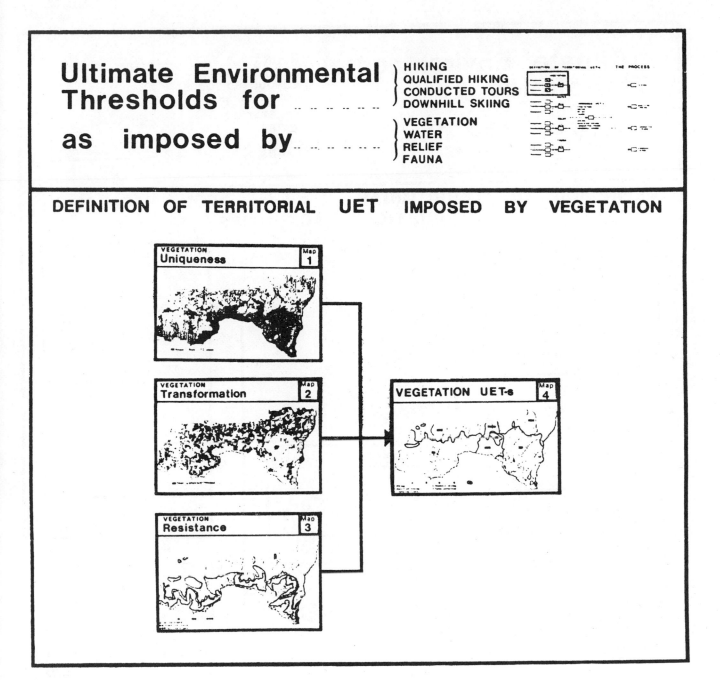

Figure 4.

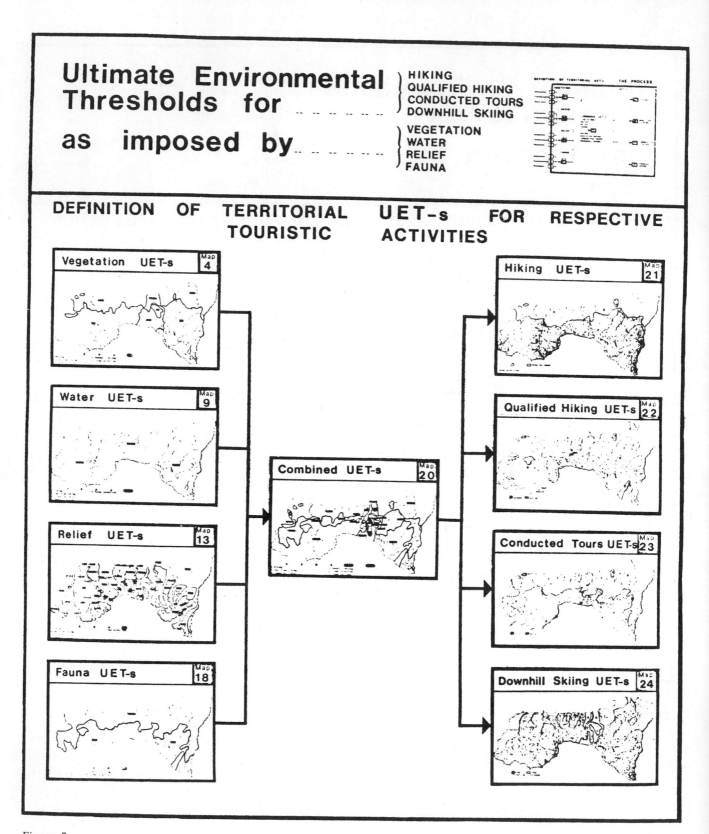

Figure 5.

Development of Nature Reserves and National Parks in the USSR

I.A. Gavva, V.V. Krinitsky and Y. P. Yazan
All-Union Institute of Nature Conservation and Reserves
Ministry of Agriculture
Moscow, USSR

ABSTRACT. *The USSR has had a system of protected areas from the very beginning of the Soviet State; today there are 145 protected areas totalling over 13 million ha. The system has a wide variety of categories and objectives, ranging from strict nature reserves to national parks for recreation and tourism. A number of research programmes are carried out in nature reserves, contributing monitoring information, basic information on species and ecosystems, and information to guide management activities. Despite the successes to date, it is recognized that the protected area system must increase substantially in order to meet the needs of the Soviet people. This expansion is well underway.*

1. INTRODUCTION

In our country, protected areas started to be established from the first days of Soviet Government. Since then, the number of protected natural areas has been steadily rising in the Soviet Union and there has now evolved a system of state nature reserves, national parks, game preserves, partial nature reserves, and nature monuments. There are 145 nature reserves and national parks, occupying an area of over 13 million ha; every year some new nature reserves and national parks come into being in the USSR.

2. NATURE RESERVES AND NATIONAL PARKS

In our country an original concept of nature conservation has been set forth from the very outset, involving the setting up of a system of nature reserves different from national parks. Nature reserves, the strictest form of nature conservation, are, in effect, regional research institutions for nature conservation. They have their own staffs of researchers, including a great many highly skilled specialists. National parks, in contrast, are intended for "recreation and tourism", so there is a dense network of roads, recreation sites, hotels, dining facilities, tourist equipment hire depots, shops, and communication services.

In the USSR, nature reserves are designed to the standardize the monitoring of natural ecological processes in nature ecosystem; to preserve the genetic fund of living organisms peculiar to one or other biogeographic region; and to carry out research work. To be able to perform these tasks the nature reserves enjoy the right of permanent and strict protection; natural resources in nature reserves are exempt from economic uses.

The majority of nature reserves are used for monitoring and baseline research, such as Pechoro-Ilych, Bashkirian, Caucasian, and Central-Forest. Quite a few of them perform the functions of reserves, such as Voronezhskii, Berezinskii, Khopersk, and Kyzyl-Agach. In these nature reserves, alongside their functions as nature standards, steps may be taken to regulate animal numbers by capturing and subsequent resettling of valuable wild animals to other places and feeding of animals and birds in difficult periods of their life cycles. The USSR's nature reserves are universally known for their important contribution to the restoration of the numbers of such extremely valuable game animals as beaver, saiga, sable, elk, and many others; nature reserves have made it possible to preserve numerous species of rare animals, such as goral, sika deer, Bukhara deer, onager, and tiger. Nature reserves are also repositories of rare plants.

There are the so-called minor nature reserves (com-

463

parable to IUCN Category III) securing the conservation of some unique natural features. In the Pitsundo-Myussera nature reserve, for instance, the chief object of conservation is the Pitsunda pine and in the Gekgel reserve, eldar pine. Biocenoses in such nature reserves are, as a rule, incapable of self-regulation, so there is need for management activities aimed at providing favourable conditions for the existence of protected animals and plants, as well as their communities. Some nature reserves, because of their geographical position and a significant recreation pressure, are being converted to national parks; these include Teberda, Issyk-Kul, and part of Stolby.

In the past five years, biosphere reserves have become quite popular. The first series of such nature reserves to be set up in our country were Berezinek, Priosko-Terrasnyi, Caucasian, Repetek, Central-Chernozem, Sary-Chelek and Sikhote-Alin. They have all received Unesco recognition.

3. RESEARCH PROGRAMMES

The research carried out either by the nature reserves staff or by scientists from other institutions on cooperation contracts is quite specific. Research is carried out throughout the year and under conditions excluding man's economic activities; this makes it possible to have a deeper insight into the essence of natural phenomena and to throw light on the quantitative criteria of "norms" and "departure from norms" in the course of natural processes. All research activities in nature reserves can be classified under four headings:

- organization of stationary biogeocenotic observations (observation services) for the progress of natural processes in nature;
- stock-taking of the flora, fauna, and non-living natural objects; mapping and biosurveying of the natural reserve territories;
- elaboration of ecological principles for the conservation of natural ecosystems in nature reserves and of the methods to manage them; and
- studying the ecology of and rare animals and plants in nature reserves as the scientific basis for their conservation and possible economic utilization at specified locations.

Among the particular problems classed under these headings we may note the following:

- working out and identifying quantitative estimation criteria, to serve as indicators of the state of nature (biological monitoring);
- characterization of principal indices of landscape components, biomes and biome subdivisions to determine their reaction to ecological change, as well as the reproductive potential of the animal and plant species inhabiting them;

- working out techniques for a complex evaluation of man's indirect effects on the ecosystems in the nature reserves;
- throwing light on potential dangers for the species (populations), ecosystems, and entire nature reserves; and
- the role of the system of nature reserves in the region, country and particularly its scientific importance.

These problems being solved by scientists in nature reserves are not only important theoretically but they have, moreover, tremendous practical significance, providing us with the scientific guidance needed to preserve, restore, and thoughtfully manage the numbers and structures of valuable animal populations and to make practical use of natural riches in the areas surrounding the reserves.

The Soviet Union's nature reserves have accumulated a wealth of factual material on the way of life, behaviour, daily activities and many other biological features of the animals and plants under study. This material is periodically summarized and made available at meetings sponsored by nature reserves, in scientific papers, and in monographs and textbooks.

The Soviet Union's nature reserves are thus, in effect, the outstanding cases of untapped nature against the background of man-converted landscapes. They perform the role of magnificent monuments emphasizing the creative role of nature, its infallibility, harmony and beauty. Preserving natural wealth, the nature reserves offer a deep insight into the innermost mysteries of life on earth, thus helping man to avoid unnecesary errors. Nature reserves add to natural riches, permitting hunting loads on game animals at the adjoining territories to be increased and thereby providing for a significant economic effect. They popularize the all-important ideas of nature preservation, enabling people to admire nature's beauties, to breathe fresh air, and simultaneously contributing to their education and spiritual enrichment.

4. THE FUTURE OF PROTECTED AREAS IN THE USSR

Nature reserves in the Soviet Union are numerous, and many of them occupy great territories, but the fact is that our country is of unparalleled size. The All-Union Institute of Nature Conservation and Reserves, of the USSR Ministry of Agriculture, is engaged at present in long-term planning of nature reserves in the USSR, to ensure the representation of every natural subdivision of the country. As a result, the number of nature reserves is expected to sharply increase in Eastern Siberia and Kazakhstan, as well as in other Republics in the country.

In the present five-year period, the Institute is continuing its work for further perfection of nature reserve activities. Its major works include:

- the scientifically justified system of nature reserves and national parks in the years to come;
- the ecological and socio-economic justification of the dimensions of protected natural territories;
- standardization of terminology and concepts in the field of nature reserve activities;
- justification of nature reserve regimes (categories) for different natural resources under conservation;
- working out optimal coordination and scientific-methodological guidance for the activities of nature reserves;
- working out effective methods with respect to legal aspects of the conservation of reserve territories; and
- economic aspects of nature conservation measures.

Great importance is being given to nature conservation generally, and nature reserve activities in particular, in many countries of the world. The Soviet Union is engaged in this respect in bilateral cooperation with the countries of the Socialist Alliance, with Britain, the USA, Belgium, France, Sweden, etc. Our Institute also cooperates with other countries, particularly on problems involved in the above-listed scientific areas.

Efforts have been made to set up national parks in the country, but they are yet only seven in number: three in the Baltic republics and one each in Kirghizia, Uzbekistan, Armenia and the Ukraine. Their regime is somewhat different, namely allowing tourism in specified zones. But even in these specific nature-conservation institutions there are stretches under strict reservation where people are not allowed to enter, where animals and plants are allowed free scope, being at the same time rigorously protected.

The recreation problem was formerly not very acute in our country. The country's expanses permitted everyone to engage freely in fishing and hunting, or simply to roam or lie down in unspoiled grass, or to admire the beauty of undistorted landscapes. In the second half of the 20th century, the situation has changed. Living standards have improved, and many people are buying cars, motorcycles, motor and sailing boats; they enjoy much more free time. The call "to nature" has become very popular; and people have become increasingly eager to come in contact with wildlife.

The recreation functions of protected natural areas can be optimally realized in national nature parks and this calls forth the need of organizing a broad system of such forms of nature conservation, which are relatively new to our country.

The Soviet Union with respect to its area, the diversity of natural conditions, and the degree of nature conservation, is unmatched in the world. The moderate experience of national parks in our country suggests our own, home-oriented pathways for organizing the functioning of national parks, which, incidentally, do not contradict international definitions and requirements.

In the zoning of national park territory, alongside stretches of complete reserves, recreation and tourism, there are envisaged territories with national methods of economic activities, land cultivation, traditional handicrafts, domestic and cultural specifications, architectural monuments and minor architectural forms peculiar to local nationalities. Lands allocated for national parks belong, as a rule, to the national park proper, but occasionally there may be several land users. In any case, all economic activities must not be in contradiction with the goals of the national park.

At strict reservation sites, subject to a regime similar to that of nature reserves, scientific observations alone are carried out. At the recreation and tourism areas, usually no camping grounds or tourist facilites are to be found; they are located outside the park boundaries. Movement inside the parks is allowed only by foot along trails or aboard special means of transport.

In the long-term planning of the system of national parks, they should be set up where primordial nature with beautiful landscapes has been preserved, in the first place close to large cities, and in areas with good approach roads.

We in the All-Union Institute of Nature Conservation and Reserves have received more than 110 suggestions for the creation of national parks.

5. CONCLUSION

Nature conservation in our country is considered of national importance. In the past five-year period as much as about 11 billion rubles (US$15.05 billion) were spent to meet its direct requirements. Careful management of nature is an obligation recorded in the country's basic law—the USSR Constitution. This is why reserve activities will be further expanded and improved.

Ecological Monitoring and Biosphere Reserves in the USSR

Y. A. Izrael, F. Y. Rovinsky, and W. A. Gorokhov
USSR State Committee for Hydrometeorology
and Control of the Natural Environment
Moscow, USSR

ABSTRACT. *Information on the state of the environment is a crucial prerequisite to guide the relationship between human society and nature. In the USSR, a new programme on assessing the effects of man on the environment has recently begun to provide the necessary information for management. Monitoring includes observation, assessment, and prediction, integrating observations on a wide range of natural factors. This has considerable applications at the international level as well.*

1. INTRODUCTION

The state of the environment and the state of the biosphere can alter due to natural reasons as well as anthropogenic ones. The use of modern techniques in the utilization of natural resources has led to an increase in living standards accompanied by adverse effects on the natural environment; some effects are developing rapidly and may lead to the irreversible changes. The necessary information on these problems and the timely assessment of the environmental state in the present and in the future are urgent preconditions of an optimum interaction between the human society and nature.

Information on the global background state of the biosphere is of great importance for the evaluation and management of the environment at the national level as well as the basis for the development of an international environmental protection strategy.

This has led to the necessity for a specialized system for observations of the state of the environment in the USSR, called "The Anthropogenic Changes of the Environment State Monitoring System." Hence, monitoring is not a new name for an existing service but the definition of a new system being created for the detec-

tion of the anthropogenic effects on the environment. It is an information system, not management, though it is a necessary part of management.

Anthropogenic effects are often difficult to distinguish, especially at the initial stage when any necessary reaction is likely to be the most efficient. That is why the monitoring system requires detailed information about natural variations and changes of the environment which forms a baseline against which anthropogenic effects can be measured.

Monitoring as an information system with several objectives consists of following elements:

- observation of the environmental state and the factors influencing the environment;
- an assessment of the environmental state and the factors influencing the environment; and
- a prediction of the environmental state and an assessment of the related trends.

One of the basic principles of monitoring is integration. This principle provides observations of air, soil, biota, sea and surface water, and background pollution simultaneously with meteorological, hydrological and biological observations.

2. MONITORING IN THE USSR AND ITS INTERNATIONAL LINKAGES

The creation of a national background monitoring system provides international goals also, because only widely adopted principles of monitoring systems organization and unified methods of observations and analyses are able to ensure the obtaining of comparable data necessary for the assessment of the environmental state both at the global and regional (national) levels. Thus, the information obtained at background stations is the subject of international exchange, as part of the GEMS network.

A network of special stations is being created in the territories of the USSR and other European socialist countries for obtaining information on background environmental pollution. These stations are situated in different geographical zones, in regions remote from local pollution sources and especially in biosphere reserves. In connection with a large scale of anthropogenic effects on the biosphere, the network of stations should embrace all the major geographical zones, because the reaction of biota to the effects of background pollution depends on stability of natural ecosystems, i.e. on their ability to keep up the structural integrity and functional stability of their basic processes.

Division of ecological monitoring into biotic and abiotic monitoring parallels the division of the natural media into living and non-living elements and is further reflected by the major differences in the response of these elements to man-made impacts.

The abiotic programme of background ecological monitoring in Biosphere Reserves in the USSR includes first of all, systematic and integrated observations and measurements for determining of background levels of anthropogenic pollutants in all media, including:

a) atmosphere—suspended particles, lead, cadmium, arsenic, mercury, 3,4-benzpyrene, sulphate, DDT and other organochloride compounds, sulphur dioxide, ozone, nitrogen oxides, carbon dioxide;

b) atmospheric depositions (precipitation, snow cover, dry depositions)—lead, cadmium, arsenic, mercury, 3,4-benzpyrene, sulphate, DDT and other organochloride compounds, main anions and actions recommended for determination at WMO background stations (sulphate, nitrate, chloride *et al*.), pH;

c) water (seas, rivers, lakes)—mercury, lead, cadmium, arsenic, 3,4-benzpyrene, DDT and other organochloride compounds, oil products (in seas), biogenic elements;

d) ground sediments (seas, rivers, lakes)—mercury, lead, cadmium, arsenic, DDT and other organochloride compounds, 3,4-benzpyrene, biogenic elements;

e) soil-- mercury, lead, cadmium, arsenic, DDT and other organochloride compounds, 3,4-benzpyrene, biogenic elements;

f) biota (vegetation, animals)—mercury, lead, cadmium, arsenic, 3,4-benzpyrene, DDT and other organochloride compounds, biogenic elements.

The programme of background observations also provides meteorological and hydrological observations and measurements, characterizing the physical state of natural media, including determination of radiation and thermal balances of the underlying surface and of the atmosphere.

The biotic part of ecological monitoring forms a special observational system, the objectives of which are to develop a modal of the dynamics in the state of the biocenosis based on the observations of biota sensitivity to man-made impacts; the study of the composition and numbers of natural animal and plant populations; and definition of the coefficients of interspecies interactions.

The results of abiotic and biotic monitoring and information analysis related to global pollutant emissions should provide all the parameters needed for developing a model of changes in plant and animal communities exposed to man-made impacts on a global scale. The analysis of these model changes will allow the prediction of changes in the real world as well as the assessment of the level of permissible man-made changes in the state of ecosystems.

To implement Integrated Ecological Monitoring, we should first of all realize the following practical steps:

• establish the priority list of pollutants;
• develop methods for studying pollutant propogation, concentration levels, and the ways of their transformation in various natural compartments; and
• develop the integrated ecological monitoring programme for biosphere reserves and background monitoring stations.

The development of the national monitoring programmes in a number of countries and their implementation within the national biosphere reserve sub-systems, being created under the aegis of Unesco, is of significant practical importance for establishing the Global Environment Monitoring System (GEMS).

First of all, the concept of Global Ecological Monitoring implies the necessity to identify global trends in man-induced changes in the biosphere on the background level of pollution. This implies that the scale of the impact determines not only the priority list of pollutants but also the sites on the earth's surface for performing observations and studies according to the ecological monitoring programme. These speculations provide one of the foundations for creating the biosphere reserves network in a number of countries, particularly the USSR.

Observations, assessment and prediction of the state of the natural environment in biosphere reserves according to the basic principles and objectives of Global Ecological Monitoring should provide the initial information for further determination of the permissible levels of anthropogenic impact on the biosphere and thus play the most important role in the development of measures for the control of environmental quality. Observations and research in biosphere reserves should provide integrated information on the "baseline condition", i.e. nature not exposed to local impacts.

This information, being a constituent part of a country's national system of background observations, naturally makes up a portion of the global information collected within the framework of GEMS. The scope of observations and research in biosphere reserves for backing up Ecological Monitoring as the informational system has not yet been fully defined. The main attention, as is rightly pointed out, should be paid to the biotic components of the ecosystems; these elements are under direct impact from, and most sensitive to, man-made factors.

On the other hand, the need to assess the current state of the natural environment relative to the background level of pollution establishes requirements for the abiotic part of Ecological Monitoring. Clearly, success will be achieved only through a combination of abiotic and biotic monitoring sub-programmes.

The design of the optimum structure of the biosphere reserves faces serious difficulties. A certain gap is observed between practical steps aimed at establishing biosphere reserves and theoretical principles for selecting biosphere reserves; the newly established biosphere reserves frequently do not meet the criteria developed by Unesco experts. Nevertheless, the results obtained in creating the biosphere reserve and background monitoring station network in the USSR, USA and some other countries show that these difficulties can be overcome. The first line of the USSR biosphere reserves includes Berezinsky, Sary-Chelk, Caucasian, Iksko-Terrace, Central-Chernozim, and Sikhote-Allin Reserves.

The programme of Ecological Monitoring in biosphere reserves is well determined by the scope of problems that should be solved in the first instance:

- global background state of the natural environment;
- the observed state of biota and the level of its exposure to man-made impacts;
- forecast of changes in the state of the biosphere; and
- ecosystems according to the predicted trends in the changes in the man-made impacts on the natural environment, and of the global pollution levels in particular.

But any suggestions related to practical realization of the general programme of Global Ecological Monitoring encounter a complex scientific-technological problem inter-related with the development of techniques and the organization of investigations in the sphere of background ecological monitoring. This problem can undoubtedly be solved, but its speedy and most suc-

cessful solution demands on wide international collaboration and cooperation.

It should be noted that abiotic monitoring dominates the currently-implemented monitoring system. It is characterized by a high level of technological and instrumental security, development of analytic techniques and close international cooperation in connection with the problem of long-range pollutant transport, for example.

A number of programmes of multilateral and bilateral cooperation for solving this complex of problems have been approved since the adoption of the integrated programme "Development of Measures for Nature Protection" by CMEA member countries (1971) and the UN Environmental Conference that formulated the "Earthwatch" programme (Stockholm, 1972). Such authoritative international organizations as UNEP, Unesco, WMO, ECE, CMEA, and WHO are responsible for the coordination of these programmes and for their scientific-methodological credibility.

Background observations of natural media pollution in the USSR have been carried out since 1976. They include both systematic (Berezinskyi ad Repetek Biosphere Reserves, "Borovoe" background station) and expeditional observations (the remaining biosphere reserves), which have enabled us identify the annual cycle of a number of anthropogenic substances. Atmospheric concentrations of such substances as sulphur dioxide, lead, arsenic, and cadmium are 2 to 12 times higher in winter than in summer due to their increased emission from energy production and supply systems during the cold period. Along with that, a gradual increase of sulphur dioxide and lead concentrations has been observed for the 1976-80 period.

Geograhical distribution of the priority pollutants in the background regions is not homogeneous. Atmospheric concentrations of sulphur dioxide, heavy metals and 3,4-BaP in the eastern regions are 2 to 3 times higher than in the west, while distribution of DDT and its metabolites is fairly even. Minimum background concentrations have been registered so far in the Caucasian Biosphere Reserves region.

The atmospheric circulation exerts a certain influence on background pollution. Long-term observations at the Borovoe station will allow us to identify some characteristic hypothetical situations that cause an increase in the background concentrations due to air-mass transport from urbanized regions hundreds of kilometres away.

3. CONCLUSIONS

The major effort for the creation of the national system of background monitoring will be directed in the near future at the extension of the network of integrated background monitoring stations, optimization of the programme of observations, study of inter-landscape migration processes, and the development of a programme of biological and ecological research.

The obtained systematic and expedition data on background pollution of natural media do not yet exceed those given in literature. At the same time, these observations indicate rather complex spatial and temporal regularities in distribution of anthropogenic substances at the background level.

The value of these first observations is that the materials will serve as a basis for detection of the long-term tendencies, which reflect the general effect of anthropogenic activities on the background quality of the natural environment.

Protected Areas and Giant Pandas in China

The Ministry of Forestry
Beijing, China

ABSTRACT. *China's most famous animal is the giant panda. Due to a number of factors, the species has become rare and confined to a small part of the mountainous area of the country. In order to help ensure its survival, the Government of China has embarked upon a programme of strict legal protection, the establishment of 10 reserves, scientific research, captive breeding, international cooperation, and publicity and education. Through these efforts, the future of the giant panda has been made far more secure.*

1. INTRODUCTION

China's 9.6 million sq km extend across the temperate, sub-tropical and tropical zones, with a correspondingly complex natural environment and varied climate. Volcanoes, hot-springs, waterfalls and important fossil localities are found in many areas. Its mountains, forests, grasslands, deserts, rivers and lakes are abundant with plants and animals including a large number of endemic species. Blessed with an abundance of nature's wealth, China is now making a serious effort to ensure that nature reserves are established for the benefit of both people and wildlife.

Our government began to plan and establish nature reserves in 1956. By the end of 1981, we had established 85 nature reserves of various types, totalling 2.2 million ha, or 0.23% of our territory. These reserves can be divided into five biomes: forest, desert, wetland, seashore, and island. They can be further classified into four types according to the natural features to be protected, including: (1) natural ecosystems; (2) rare animals; (3) vegetation and rare plants; and (4) natural historical heritage. These natural reserves are of high value internationally, as they are a prime means by which China's natural wealth is being conserved for the benefit of all mankind.

2. THE GIANT PANDA

Of particular international interest is the giant panda *Ailuropoda melanaleuca*, one of the most popular animals in the world and one which is found only in China. Unfortunately, the Panda is also now one of the rarest animals in the world.

This was not always so. Investigations by our palaeontologists over many years and in many parts of the country show that the panda was widely distributed in the Pleistocene (the period of time from roughly two million years ago to 10,000 years ago), with fossils reported from southern China to as far north as Beijing (where it was found at the same fossil site as *Homo erectus pekinensis*, one of man's early ancestors). In the Pleistocene, the panda was found with a number of other species, many of which are now extinct or extirpated from China; these include *Stegodon* (an elephant), *Gigantopithecus* (the largest ape ever known), and the orangutan *Pongo pygmaeus* (now found only on Borneo and Sumatra).

Owing to such factors as low rate of reproduction, change of habitat, change of climate, and other subtle variations of nature, the panda's distribution has now shrunk remarkably; of particular importance was the recent widespread die-off of the bamboo which is so important to their survival. According to our latest information, the panda is now confined only to small areas of Shanxi, Ganshu, and Shichuan provinces.

The giant panda lives in high mountains, coming as low as 1300 m during winter and going as high as

3600 m during summer; its favourite habitat is the bamboo forest found from 2600 to 2850 m, where the mean temperature is 4.35-5.65. In autumn, the panda mainly inhabits in the coniferous forest and during the rest of the year, it lives in broad-leaved mixed forest with a rich undergrowth of bamboo; it particularly favours the bamboo *Sinarundinaria fangiana*.

Generally speaking, the giant panda is solitary except during its mating season Estrous begins in March and lasts until late May or early June, with peak reproduction in April. The panda gives birth to one cub, occasionally two, in the period July to September. Most females nest and give birth in hollow trees or stone caves; the female is always responsible for selecting the site, making the nest, nursing, and looking after cubs.

3. PROTECTING THE PANDA

A number of management measures have been taken to protect the giant panda in China. They are as follows:

3.1. Making protective policies

The giant panda, being classified as a Category I Rare species, is very strictly protected against hunting. If individuals or government organizations wish to capture a giant panda for special purposes, permission must be granted by the Ministry of Forestry. The Chinese Government also has enacted legislation which stipulates that pandas and their derivatives are not allowed to be sold in the markets; anyone who catches a panda or sells a panda and its derivatives without obtaining permission from the proper authorities would be severely punished under the protective legislation.

3.2. The establishment of natural reserves

In order to protect the habitats and breeding grounds of the giant panda, more than ten natural reserves have been designated, with a total area of 550,000 ha. This amounts to 25 percent of the natural reserve area in China at present, a very good indication of the priority which is given to the protection of this species. Sichuan Province has eight natural reserves (Wolong, Fengtongzhai, Wangland, Tangjiahe, Shaozhaizi, Jiuzhaigou, Mabiandafengding, Meigudafengding), Gansu Province has one (Baishuijiang), and Shaanxi Province has one (Foping).

According to the legislation which established these reserves, it is strictly forbidden to reclaim land and fell trees, and to engage in any human activities which are harmful to the habitats of the panda in any part of the natural reserves.

3.3. Scientific research

Relevant scientific research institutes, universities and colleges and the authorities of the natural reserves have been organized to devote their efforts to carry out research activities on the distribution, ecology and population of the giant panda, yielding important information which is then used to guide protective measures. Several observation stations have been built in the places where there is a dense population of pandas and some results have already been achieved on movements and behaviour, food habits and natural propagation of the species.

3.4. Captive breeding

In order to carry on artifical breeding and artificial insemination, a "panda farm" has been built in Wolong Natural Reserve. At the same time, research and application of captive breeding is also in progress in Beijing, Chengdu, Fuchou and other zoos.

3.5. Publicity and education

Publicity and education programmes have been carried out to educate all people, especially those who live near the panda habitat areas. These programmes inform the people of the importance of protecting the panda, explain its uniqueness as a symbol of China, and urge everybody love and protect it.

3.6. International cooperation

The giant panda is not only the precious property of the Chinese people, but it is also a rare and attractive animal loved by people all over the world. Therefore, many countries and international organizations have shown their concern for the protection of the giant panda. The Chinese Government and WWF signed a Protocol for the establishment of a research and conservation centre for the giant panda in 1980. During the last two years, some scientific research results have been achieved thanks to the joint efforts of the Chinese and foreign experts. They are now summing up the scientific research work accomplished in the first stage.

4. CONCLUSION

Under the leadership of the Chinese Government, with the cooperative efforts of relevant scientific research institutes, universities and colleges, authorities of the natural reserves and the broad masses of the people, certain progress has been made in protection of giant pandas. We have full confidence that we can protect this rare national treasure by relying on our own efforts. At the same time, we also welcome cooperation with countries and international organizations which are enthusiastic to support the cause of natural conservation on the basis of equality and mutual benefit; we hope that we can learn from the positive experience from other countries so as to promote the development of nature conservation in China.

The Sherpas of Sagarmatha:
The Effects of a National Park on the Local People

Bruce E. Jefferies
Tongariro National Park, New Zealand

ABSTRACT. *The dramatic increase in tourist trekking in the Himalayan regions of Nepal has created serious impacts on the natural and cultural environment of the Sagarmatha National Park area. Direct field involvement and an alternative approach to park planning and management were key elements of what was a very broad-based, but small scale, effort by the New Zealand Government in cooperating with the Government of Nepal in setting up a national park in the Sagarmatha region of the Himalayas.*

1. INTRODUCTION

Since 1950, when Nepal opened its borders to foreign visitors, the dramatic increase in tourist trekking in the Himalayan regions has caused serious impacts on the natural and cultural environment of the Sagarmatha (Mt. Everest) National Park area. This case study provides a park manager's perspective on the effects of these impacts on the resident population of Sherpas who live within the park boundaries. The effects of this resident group on park values and resources will also be explored.

The soaring number of trekkers in the high Himalayas of Nepal over the last decade has created a booming trade in firewood for some mountain people. But this has occurred at the expense of the forests and the particularly fragile ecosystems of the upper slopes (Eckholm, 1976).

The emphasis given the region since it acquired national park status (in 1976) and was listed as a World Heritage Site (in 1979) has aggravated long-standing problems of forest and shrubland degradation through over-grazing and through excessive firewood and forest litter collection. The difficulties involved in coping with

these problems are diverse, relating heavily to cultural, social and introduced influences. It is necessary to find practical solutions to the conflicts; in Nepal, those solutions must be found which are compatible both with the national park concept and with the survival of the Sherpa people, who have inhabited the region for nearly 500 years (Furer-Haimendorf, 1964; 1975).

2. THE ROOF OF THE WORLD

Sagarmatha National Park, comprising approximately 1113 sq km, is situated in north-eastern Nepal in the Solu-Khumbu District of the Sagarmatha Zone. The park comprises the area known as Khumbu, and includes a number of the best known peaks of the Himalayas, the most significant being Sagarmatha, the world's highest mountain. At lower altitudes, the park includes within its boundaries the homeland of approximately 2,500 Sherpas, although 63 villages and settlements are technically excluded. Further, the areas traditionally used by the Sherpas for grazing and gathering forest products comprise a large proportion of the park.

The Sherpa people are believed to have migrated from an eastern province of Tibet some four centuries ago, and belong to the Nyingmapa sect of Tibetan Buddhism. Today the Sherpas who live in the scattered villages along the valley and tributaries of the Dudh Kosi rely for their livelihood on ranching yak, cattle and other livestock; limited trading with Tibet; agriculture; and, in the last 15 years, tourism. They are employed as guides and porters for mountaineers and trekking tourists, and provide tourists with firewood, food, lodging and other services.

Sagarmatha is one of four national parks in Nepal,

473

the others being Chitwan, Langtang, and Lake Rara. The location of the park is shown in Fig. 1. The natural qualities of the region and the cultural and religious significance of the unique way of life of the Sherpa community make the area an obvious choice for national park and World Heritage status. However, a number of factors, such as the traditional use of the land by the Sherpas, the growth of tourism, and the continuing requirements of major mountaineering expeditions, create conflicts and complex problems in managing the area.

The vegetation of the park comprises sub-alpine and alpine plant communities. The upper limit for forest species ranges from 3,800 m to 4,000 m, depending on localized climatic influences. Sustained cutting of trees has converted considerable areas of forests to open grazing shrublands, leaving remnant forest with fir, pine, birch and rhododenron on more inaccessible slopes. In this extremely high alpine area, vegetation regenerates slowly. For example, a juniper bush may take 60 years to grow to 35 cm above ground level. When juniper is collected for firewood, not only are the branches and foliage collected, but the roots are grubbed from the ground, greatly retarding any regrowth.

3. SOCIAL AND POLITICAL FACTORS

Nepal is listed by the UN among the 25 least developed nations in the world; in this little-developed country the poorest people live in the Himalayan regions. In 1980 the average annual income in the Himalayas was estimated at 782 Nepalese Rupees (US $65), compared with NR 950 in the balance of the country. The National Planning Commission calculated the minimum subsistence level to be NR 2 per day; the high Himalayas has 43 percent of the population living at this subsistence level, the highest proportion in the country (Nepal National Planning Commission, 1978).

The traditional economy in the Sagarmatha National Park region was based on subsistence agriculture supported by trade (Bjonness, 1979). The limited amount of land suitable for agriculture has always been cultivated intensively, but the high altitude and variable weather conditions mean that agricultural output is relatively low. Potatoes, barley and buckwheat are primarily grown for local consumption, and only rarely is there any surplus which can be sold. In some cases animals and their products contribute substantially to the household income, but in general these products only cover the needs of the family.

Until 1959 the most important source of cash income was an active trade with Tibet. Salt and wool were transported from Tibet on yaks over the Nangpa-La pass, in exchange for products like rice, sugar, cattle and nak (yak-cattle hybrid) butter from Nepal and India. But in 1959 the border between Tibet and Nepal was closed, and the traditional trade between India, Nepal and Tibet was severely reduced. This had far-reaching

effects on the Khumbu Sherpas (Furer-Haimendorf, 1964; 1975). Not only was a source of income lost, but there was a movement of Tibetan refugees across the only accessible pass, the Nangpa-La, into Khumbu. These refugees brought with them their livestock—yaks, naks, sheep and goats—which added to the demands on the environment.

The environmental impacts of these external political changes were augmented by the internal political changes in Nepal. Until the mid-1950s there had been traditional constraints on the use of forest products through a system of forest guardians (Shingo-nawa) appointed on a village-by-village basis. But in 1957 the grazing lands and forests of Nepal were nationalized, and in 1963 a new political system called the Panchayat was introduced, which had the effect of democratizing the country, but also of centralizing government decision-making in Kathmandu, 200 km away; Khumbu was isolated by poor communications and limited mail service. Removing influence from local people and placing it in the hands of a remote government (which has only slowly won acceptance from the Sherpas) tended to weaken the traditional restraints on forest utilization, without replacing them by effective new controls imposed by the central government.

4. IMPACT OF TOURISM

To those two new pressures on the environment—an influx of refugees and livestock from Tibet and the loosening of traditional restraints on forest use—a third has been added: a dramatic increase in tourist trekking in the Himalayas (Table 1). In the early 1960s a total of 20 visitors had been recorded in the Khumbu region; in the 1977-78 season an incomplete register showed at least 3,850 trekkers in Sagarmatha National Park (though no real count is made of trekkers who fail to register).

This increase in tourism has had both positive and negative aspects. In recent years tourism and international climbing expeditions have replaced trade with Tibet as a source of cash income for the Sherpas. But the presence of trekkers has negative effects on both the society and the natural resources of the region (Bjonness, 1980). Until the tourist boom, forest resources—and especially fuelwood—were used only for building, cooking, and limited heating. After the influx of the tourists, those resources became a cash crop worth considerable amounts of money.

For example, in 1979 it was estimated that the village of Pangboche (altitude 3,985 m, population 297) generated more than 12 lak rupees (US $91,600) in cash each year from the sale of firewood to expeditions and trekkers in the Upper Khumbu valley. All of this wood is cut from the park forests, with little regard to species, age or site. The villagers have cut most of the forest cover on the western side of the Imja Khola valley and are now cutting in the sensitive forest on the eastern side of the river. It is difficult to control this cutting, in part because selling firewood has probably become essential to the villagers to finance the purchase of high-cost foodstuffs on which, in turn, they have become dependent in part because of the change in their lifestyle fomented by increasing tourism. In addition, the willingness of tourists to pay higher prices has led to a gradual but signficant increase in costs to local people.

Tourism has also had secondary—but important—impacts on the Himalayan environment. Increased wealth from tourism has been used to build larger houses and hotels, both of which rely on increased use of wood for heating and cooking, and thus accelerate the exploitation of forest resources. And within the Sherpa community, financial wealth is usually converted directly into larger herds of yaks, and in some cases into herds of non-traditional animals like sheep and goats, both of which increase the need for grazing. This has had severe impacts on areas close to villages. In general terms, the direct result of increased affluence from tourism has been increased ecological degradation.

5. THE NEW ZEALAND PROJECT

The Sagarmatha region was formally gazetted as a national park on 19 July, 1976 and sometime after the creation of the park the government of New Zealand agreed to assist the Nepalese government in establishing a management programme for the area. The New Zealand Sagarmatha project was a small-scale effort with limited financial resources and personnel. For most of the project period, a project manager resided at Namche Bazar and was involved in the day-to-day management of the park, in support of the Nepalese park warden. Most decisions were made by consensus after discussion with the Nepalese National Parks and Wildlife Conservation Department (NPWCD) in Kathmandu. However, the remoteness of Sagarmatha made close contact with the central office difficult, and at times official interest in the affairs of the park seemed to be limited.

During the initial assessment of the park for possible New Zealand involvement, it was realized that the key to long-term success would be the selection and training of Sherpas for the management of the area. Acceptance of the park by the local people is essential to any management programme, but initially there was (and probably still is) a great deal of suspicion and resentment of the Sagarmatha Park and the regulations for its management—as is the case in many other national parks in developing countries. Training local people for management roles in the park was one method of overcoming this suspicion and resentment, and the overall situation improved substantially when New Zealand-trained Sherpas returned to Khumbu to take up positions within the park's management structure.

Under a formal agreement with the Nepalese government, the responsibility of the New Zealand project was to establish a framework for on-going management of the Sagarmatha site. This involved three main components: the researching and production of a management plan; the training of Nepalese in New Zealand, which was conducted under the Colombo Plan; and the physical construction of facilities within the park.

5.1 The management plan

A considerable amount of study was required to identify effective planning objectives and policies. The first requirement was to gather basic information on tourist trekking by analyzing where it occurred and what impact it had. The second was to elaborate a planning approach capable of handling the problems created by tourism and the accompanying ecological deterioration, with the self-reliance of the local Sherpa population as one of the important factors in any management programme. Specifically the studies examined the activities of tourists within the park and the duration of their stay; the impact of trekking on the natural environment through mapping tourist movements and an analysis of the fuelwood purchased locally; the impact of tourism on the local society; and earlier planning approaches. The results of these studies can be found in Bjonness (1979; 1980; 1981).

The Sagarmatha National Park management plan was evolved in 1979 and accepted by the Nepalese government in 1981. It lists seven major objectives for the park:

1) *Nature Conservation*. To ensure the permanent conservation of viable examples of all the natural communities of flora and fauna occurring in the park, with particular attention to endangered species and their habitats.
2) *Water and Soil Conservation*. To ensure that effective protection and provision of sufficient forest and other vegetative cover on watersheds and catchment areas, to effectively control unnatural erosion and excessive water run-off.
3) *Indigenous Population*. To enable the local population to determine their own lifestyle and progress, and to achieve desirable social and economic development.
4 Religious and Historic Values. To ensure the permanent protection and preservation of buildings and structures of religious and historic significance, and to preserve the cultural and religious heritage of the Sherpas.
5) *Tourism*. To promote tourist and visitor use suitable to the environment and conditions of the park to the extent compatible with the other objectives and in a manner which will provide economic benefit to the local population and to Nepal.
6) *Mountaineering*. To permit continued use of the park's high mountains by competent montaineering expeditions, to the extent compatible with the earlier objectives, and in a manner that

minimizes adverse environmental impact while benefitting the local and national economy and prestige.

7) *Energy*. To ensure that the energy requirements of residents and visitors are provided in a manner that will not deplete or be otherwise detrimental to the natural resources of the park.

A number of special factors affect the management of Sagarmatha. Many of the 2,500 Sherpas resident in Khumbu have legal title to houses, land for agriculture and *yersas* (summer grazing areas), which makes control and management difficult in the areas adjacent to villages (the most susceptible to over-grazing and excessive wood cutting). Park regulations do not apply to the 63 villages within the park boundaries. The topography of the park ranges from 3,000 m at the entrance to 8,848 m at the summit of Sagarmatha, and this presents such a variety of ecological zones that standard management techniques are difficult to implement. The government bureaucracy dealing with tourism is fragmented in a way that makes common policies difficult to achieve. For example, a trekker must first obtain a visa and a trekking permit from the Central Immigration Office, a further permit from the National Parks and Wildlife Conservation Department in the form of an entrance fee collected at main entry points if he wishes to enter Sagarmatha, and a permit from the Nepal Mountaineering Association if he wishes to climb a peak below 6,000 m or an allocation from the Ministry of Tourism for a peak over 6,000 m. And finally, the Sherpas in general have a poor appreciation of natural processes; large yak herds, excessive wood cutting and the collection of forest litter are not seen as actions which contribute to ecological degradation, and many older Sherpas assume that because trees were abundant 500 years ago when their forefathers arrived in Khumbu they will return to the region as a matter of course.

The normal management techniques used in western countries could not be used in Sagarmatha; instead the management approach was directed toward solving the problems which had been obvious to informed visitors to the park for some time. This is the reverse of the usual planning process, which starts with goals and objectives, but the problems in Sagarmatha were too entrenched for this traditional approach.

5.2 Construction of facilities

The New Zealand project built a number of facilities in Sagarmatha park: a trekking lodge at Thyangboche, an important monastery on the main trekking route to the Sagarmatha Base Camp; lodges on the main trekking route at Pheriche and Lobuche; and a comprehensive park headquarters/interpretive centre at Namche Bazar, the administrative and trading centre of the Khumbu area.

It has been argued that these facilities were inap-

propriate for the Khumbu region, but each served a valuable function. The trekking lodge at Thyangboche was constructed as an alternative to large camps in the environmentally and culturally sensitive monastery area. Cooking, heating and lighting are fueled by kerosene and charcoal, providing for the first time a practical demonstration of alternatives to wood. The administrative centre provides an important "pivot point" for park operations, as well as opportunities for making visitors aware of the unique natural and cultural aspects of Sagarmatha park. The trekking lodges also provided an excellent opportunity for contact between the park staff and visitors; it is unfortunate that the NPWCD thought it necessary to contract out their operation to private individuals, since a substantial part of the rationale for constructing these lodges was the opportunity they provided for informing and orienting visitors.

The New Zealand project was also involved in setting up and operating nurseries for reforestation of parts of the park, and this is an excellent example of the educatinal and practical roles the project played. The nurseries provided valuable employment for the Sherpas, and at the same time offered an opportunity to educate them about the processes of ecological deterioration.

5.3 Training

From the first, a major component of the New Zealand project involved training for Sherpas to participate in the management of the park. The training programme had two parts: the local training of personnel in the early stages of the project; and training in New Zealand for local Sherpas and Nepalese. The first of these had only limited success, but the second led to substantial improvement in the operations of the park.

It should also be noted that there are negative aspects to training local people, since they are subject to pressure for special consideration from relatives and friends in the local community. At the same time, the importance of using local people in management roles cannot be ignored.

6. CONCLUSIONS

It was recognized for a considerable period of time that the Sagarmatha National Park Project would not be an unqualified success. The Khumbu region is changing regardless of efforts made to manage land use, ecology and culture, and while the national park concept has slowed the rate of change in some cases, in others it has undoubtedly increased it. One of the unique aspects of Sagarmatha National Park is the necessity of integrating traditional land use practices into national park management planning and implementation. Sagarmatha National Park, perhaps more than any other park in the world, must pay a great deal of attention to the living and cultural requirements of the people who live within its boundaries.

Management planning is not effective without commitment and involvement from the local people. In Sagarmatha, there was no opportunity to approach the management planning phase of the park project in a manner that would consider local input in depth. Consequently, constant efforts must continue to be made to build and develop bonds between residents and park management.

One of the important lessons from the project is that trained local people, who are used to climatic conditions and who understand cultural requirements, are more acceptable to the community. A second is that action should be implemented as close to the resource as possible; advisors, project managers and technicians must be assigned to bases away from centralized offices, and the most important input in the early stages of a park/conservation project should be based on field management. Training, covering a wide sphere of inputs from management to facilities maintenance, is also an important factor in ensuring the future of a project.

One benefit from such projects which is often overlooked is the "spin-off" value to donor countries and their personnel. There is no doubt at all that New Zealand has gained significantly in personnel development from its involvement with the Sagarmatha National Park Project.

During the formative stages of Sagarmatha National Park, ecological conflict and economic dependence made it essential that alternative approaches to park management and planning be considered and implemented. Some of the approaches have been successful and some have failed. The point to note is that a start has been made in protecting this internationally important national park; potentially, Sagarmatha could be established as a model park for this part of Asia.

There are reasons to be optimistic: Sherpas are becoming better educated through Nepalese commitment to education supported by the Himalayan Trust set up by Sir Edmund Hillary, and educated Sherpas are concerned for the environment, and are prepared to change and adapt. One of the attributes of the Sherpa community is its resilience and ability to adapt to changing conditions. Finance from aid institutions to existing Sagarmatha National Park projects, such as the reforestation programme, could be controlled by a local management structure. A possible source of this finance could be the Himalayan Trust.

The New Zealand project in Sagarmatha National Park ended in 1981. It left behind a firm base on which the Nepalese Government can build, or which can be allowed to crumble. This point is important; in the final analysis, only local people and their Governments can make the decisions for the future. It can only be hoped that everyone concerned may be convinced that Sagarmatha National Park merits the deepest commitment and the most positive action possible; the area deserves to be regarded as one of the great national parks of the world.

Acknowledgements

Considerable reference material and many different people have assisted in the preparation of this case study. Of principal note, the following are offered particular thanks: Mr. P.H.C. Lucas, Director General of Lands and Survey, New Zealand; Mr. M. Clarborough, New Zealand Project Manager 1980-1981; I-M. Bjonness, Dept. of Geography, University of Oslo, Norway, who worked with the New Zealand project 1979-1980; Nima Whangchu Sherpa, who trained in New Zealand as part of the New Zealand contribution to Sagarmatha National Park, and who prepared a valuable reference document on firewood use in SNP as part of his diploma in Parks and Recreation qualification from Lincoln College, New Zealand; and my wife, who contributed many valuable comments.

Table 1. Number of Trekkers to the Sagarmatha National Park

1971/72	72/73	73/74	74/75	75/76	76/77	77/78	78/79
	1406	2254	3503	2660 3660*	4254 3550*	3650*	3850*

*Source: Central Immigration Office, Kathmandu, and * data from police check post at Namche Bazar.*

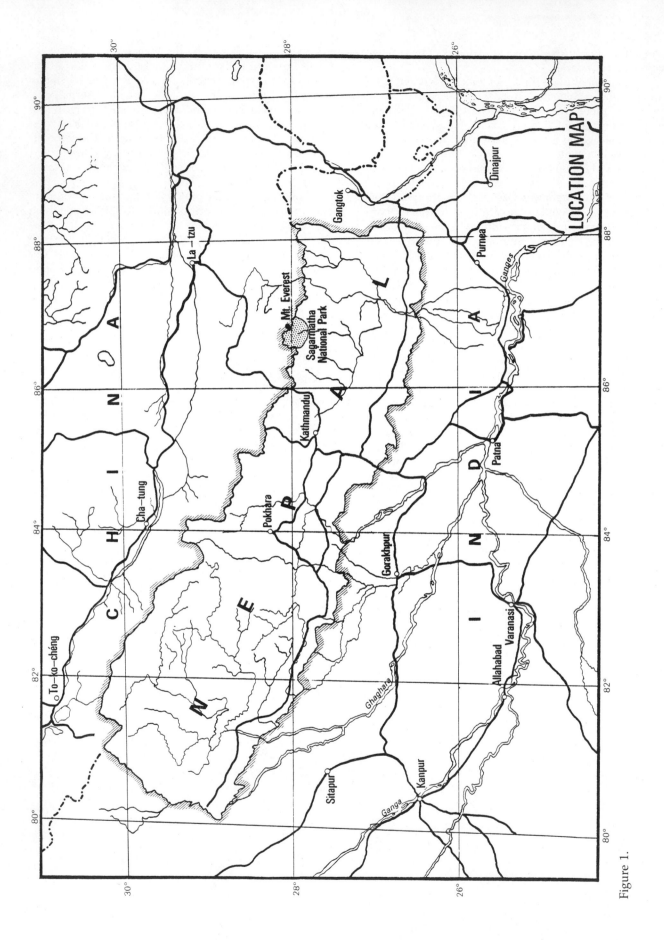

Figure 1.

NATIONAL PARKS, CONSERVATION, AND DEVELOPMENT

Adjustment Between Nature and Human Activity in National Parks in Japan

Masaaki Sakurai
Nature Conservation Bureau
The Environment Agency
Tokyo, Japan

ABSTRACT. *This paper describes the natural and socio-economic characteristics of Japan, outlines the national park system of the country and discusses the present status of protected areas in Japan. It provides a general introduction of the problems faced by national parks, as well as the measures being taken to solve these problems. The importance of national parks for recreation and tourism are given particular attention, along with the problems of land tenure, land ownership, and other land use planning matters of concern in a densely populated country. Some 5% of Japan is currently protected by national parks, and a total 14% of the country is under some form of natural park.*

1. INTRODUCTION

Japan, with her limited land space and excessively dense population, has managed to make diversified utilization of her national land since ancient times. Under such a situation, the Japanese Government has designated any area which it deems appropriate as a "national park", without regard to the forms of land ownership; it has instituted a regulatory zoning system for each region for the control of activities which are aimed at changing natural environment. Naturally, various problems have resulted from this system, and we are striving to solve these problems by several independent approaches. In this case study, however, it is intended to provide a general introduction covering the problems which our national parks are faced with today and the method and measures for their solution, instead of taking up any specific case of a particular national park or any specific problem in a particular region in Japan.

2. BACKGROUND

This section will describe our country's natural and socio-economic characteristics, the outline of the Japanese national park system, and the present status of the national park designated areas.

2.1 Japan's natural and socio-economic characteristics

Japan is an archipelago which consists of four major islands, i.e. Hokkaido, Honshu, Shikoku and Kyushu, and approximately 4000 smaller islands. It is situated along the eastern edge of the Eurasian Continent, extending about 3,000 km from south to north between 24 and 45 degrees north latitude.

Topographically, our national land belongs to the category of the most complex formation in the world, reflecting the effect of the violent orogenic movements in the circumpacific orogenic zone. It is made up of steep mountainous areas, flat terrain scattered between the mountain regions, small alluvial plains, and complex coastlines. The area of mountainous regions is large, forming 63% of the total national land.

Because Japan is situated in the middle latitudes surrounded by seas, the climate is relatively mild, with much rain; but it varies widely by region, and is endowed with rich seasonal variation thanks to its four different seasons. These climatic characteristics have brought about an extremely diverse flora, including sub-arctic conifer forest, temperate deciduous broad-leaved forest, warm temperate evergreen broad-leaved forest, and sub-tropical forest; these floras vary according to latitude and elevation above sea level. It is said that there are about 6,000 different species of higher plants alone.

The total area of our national land is about 378,000 sq km, which is about 0.3% of the total land area of the earth. The population of this limited land area is approximately 117 million, which is equivalent to about 3% of the entire world population. The population density is 310 persons per sq km, making Japan one of the most densely populated countries in the world.

In the aspect of land utilization, forest zones cover 67% of the total land area. The inhabitable space, after deducting all areas of forest, wasteland and water surface zones, is not more than 21% of the land area. The population density in this inhabitable space has reached 1,452 persons per sq km. The gross national product (GNP) per inhabitable space shows an extremely high level at US$12 million per sq km, showing a high concentration in certain limited areas where high density economic and social activities are being conducted.

2.2 Changes in the Japanese post-war socio-economy and the trend of tourist recreation

The Japanese economy and social systems, which underwent devastating chaos by World War II, have made a relatively quick recovery, and the booming business trend beginning in the 1950s has continued to help the Japanese economy enjoy an unprecedented high growth. In fact, the nation's total GNP has climbed during the past 20 years at the annual rate of about 10% — indeed a miraculous phenomenon.

Thanks to this high economic growth, the revenue of our people has steadily increased, thus contributing to the tremendous growth of the people's consumer life. Entering into the 1960s, automobiles have come to find their way into the household of our people in general, and thus motorization has become prevalent. The total number of passenger cars owned as of 1980 was 23.40 million units, or one car per 1.55 families; this is a rate of increase of 48 times during the past 20 years.

By the improvement of productivity, working hours have gradually been reduced, and the 48-hour work week in 1960 was reduced to a 40-hour work week in 1974. Moreover, the system of 2 holidays per week is quickly taking hold as a general practice. The improvement of living standards and increase in free time have contributed to make the people's living more relaxed and affluent so that they can enjoy more leisure time. Because of this, the rate of people's overnight recreation trips has tremendously increased from the 51 million person/times in 1965 to 140 million person/times in 1980.

On the other hand, following the accelerated pace of industrialization, air and water pollution have become hazardous to human life. Likewise, in connection with the progress of the so-called "motorization" and the enormous expansion of networks of roads and highways, largely stimulated by the increasing volume of recreational tours, road construction has come to make inroads into natural scenic areas where tourists converge excessively, thus causing problems of destruction of the very natural environment which attracts the visitors.

Because of this, public opinion calling for anti-pollution and protection of the natural environment has come to be heard loudly, which in turn has invited not only the people's self-reflection on the policy of high perference to economic gains, but also the people's perception of the importance of the role of the national parks in preserving the integrity of our national land, as well as in ensuring our people's good health and affluent living.

Meanwhile, the oil crises which took place in 1973 and 1978 served as a brake to slow down the pace of economic growth. Today, though many of our people believe in maintaining an active and vigorous economic society long into the future, their perception toward the preservation of natural environment and protection of the integrity of nature has not at all dwindled; rather, it has become much more enlightened. For example, according to the "National Survey of Public Opinion Relating to Nature Conservation", conducted by the Prime Minister's Office in 1981, 94% answered that preservation of nature was important.

2.3 National Parks in Japan

The National Parks Law, enacted in 1931, established the national park system in Japan. This Law was amended in 1957 and has been reborn as the Natural Parks Law. The National Park System in our country was modeled after the American system, but there exists a fundamental difference between the two systems: in Japan, a national park is not necessarily limited to only State-owned land but includes private land as well.

The State, for the purpose of protecting and preserving in the long term outstanding natural landscapes which contribute to promoting the health, recreation and culture of the people, may designate a "national park" when it deems that the selected natural landscape sufficiently satisfies the above- described qualifications, irrespective of the form of the ownership of the land. Once so designated by the State, even the owner of the designated land is restricted from taking certain actions without prior authorization by the State. In other words, the owner may be allowed to take certain actions with respect to his land within the national park designated space so long as such action will not disrupt or damage the scenic beauty of the landscape.

This method may not be necessarily ideal for conservation of a national park. But in Japan, where so many people live in a limited small space, it is hardly possible to allow any vast tract of land for the purpose of setting up a national park.

On the other hand, in our country, there is a tradition to highly appreciate the spectacular sight of nature, human activity, and historic structures resulting therefrom, all combined in a harmonious symmetry as

NATIONAL PARKS, CONSERVATION, AND DEVELOPMENT

a beautiful natural landscape. Therefore, this method was both necessary and effective in protecting and preserving the integrity of natural beauty by maintaining the organic combination of nature and man.

The designated area is divided into several zones according to the characteristics of the landscape, and the restrictive measures are applied to different degrees depending on the type of landscape. In making this zoning, careful consideration is given to not only the particulars of landscape, but also its natural state (degree of artificial affects), susceptibility to outside affects (vulnerability to damage), ecological value to wildlife, scientific and academic value, and the importance of its utilization. The zones include areas in which no action other than those necessary for academic and scientific research and for public benefit is permitted, and areas where normal forestry work and fishing are allowed. This type of division of a national park according to the degree of necessity of protection or conservation is called "Protection (Regulation) Scheme". On the other hand, in order to encourage and promote the effective utilization of national parks, there is set up a "Utilization (Facilities) Scheme", to provide and arrange roads, accommodations, camping sites, picnic sites, etc. According to this Utilization Scheme, systematic facilities improvement and utilization are carried out. These two plans combined together are called the "Park Scheme".

The park area and the park scheme are first exposed to careful review and study, taking into consideration the particular nature of the land and social conditions. After review and coordination by related ministries and agencies, the Director General of The Environment Agency takes a decision after seeking the opinion of the Nature Conservation Council, and it is announced in the official gazette.

Today there are 27 national parks in Japan (Fig. 1). The total land area of these 27 parks is 2.02 million ha, about 5% of the total national land area. The annual total of visitors to our national parks was 311 million in 1980, about 2.7 times as many as the total population of Japan. The park which drew the most visitors was the Fuji-Hakone-Izu National Park which is located near Tokyo; 83 million people visit the park each year. There are two other national parks which attract visitors in excess of 30 million annually each, while there are six other national parks each of which attracts more than 10 million visitors annually. The number of visitors to national parks increased year by year during the 1960s and early 1970s. However, since the peak year of 1973, the number of visitors has levelled off.

Several types of national parks in Japan are distinguished as follows:

Shiretoko National Park constitutes a peninsula of volcanic mountain range; *Akan National Park* and *Towada-Hachimantai National Park* have volcanic mountains and lakes; *Daisetsuzan National Park* is the largest in Japan with about 230,000 ha; *Chubu-Sangaku National Park* is a typical mountain park and is called by the name of "the Nippon Alps". All of these are mostly covered by natural vegetation such as the primeval forest and natural grassland, etc., and are very primitive. Besides, more than 85% of each of these park areas is State-owned and well-managed. However, they are not purely for park use and are under the control of the Forestry Agency; they are managed under close coordination between the Environment Agency and the Forestry Agency.

The Nikko National Park, which attracts a great number of tourists from abroad, is rich in natural scenic beauty and artificial splendour and is endowed with the beautiful combination of volcanic mountains, marshes, lakes, water falls and historic structures such as ancient shrines and Buddhist temples, all of which have helped to amplify the attraction and charm of this national park.

The Seto Naikai National Park, one of the first national parks in Japan, offers the familiar landscape of Aegean Sea-like beauty with its calm blue water, numerous small islands seeming to float on the calm surface of the sea, beautiful sand beaches, black-pine groves on the beach side, and terraced fields, all melted together in an exquisitely fascinating composure to create a symmetrical combination of nature and man.

The Aso National Park, world famous for its huge caldera, offers a spectacular sight of a vast grassland which is one of the most important elements of this park's beauty. This splendour of gently undulating green grassland is greatly enhanced by the grazing livestock (cows and horses), which in turn help maintain this vast expanse of pastoral land. In the absence of grazing livestock, this land would turn into a forest land by the work of natural succession.

As described above, there are varied types of national parks in Japan, ranging from those which are characterized by their primitiveness to those which maintain their beauty by application of some artificial means, or those which offer historic structures as one of the major attractions. Therefore, management of those national parks is performed with elaborate care according to their respective particular characteristics.

3. PROBLEMS FACING THE NATIONAL PARKS

This section will introduce various problems which our national parks are faced with, especially those problems arising from the zoning systems.

3.1 Adjustment with land ownership

About 23% of the total land space of the national parks in Japan belongs to private owners; one park has 96% of its land owned by private persons. In order to preserve the integrity of the natural environment in national parks, it is necessary to restrict the scope of private land ownership to a certain extent by providing regulations to restrict forest work and construction, design, and scale of structures to be built within the boundary of the park. On the other hand, ownership of private assets must be respected, so the purpose of national parks and the respect of private land ownership must be properly adjusted to prevent this conflict of interest.

3.2 Adjustment with other utilization of land

The national parks in Japan hold problems of conflicts of interest resulting from overlapping rights established for land utilization. In order to avoid such conflict of interest, efforts must be made for the accommodation of nature conservation with industries, especially such industries as agriculture, forestry, fisheries and quarrying which are dependent on natural resources.

3.3 Adjustment with public utilities

Various kinds of public works dependent upon natural resources, such as hydroelectric power, geothermal power, construction of transmission lines, radio relay stations, water resources development, river improvement projects, and road construction are all undertaken generally on a large scale, and their effect on the natural environment is large. Likewise, from their particular nature, there are frequent cases where these projects are involved or located in the national parks. For this reason, adjustment must be worked out between nature conservation and public utilities.

3.4 Response to socio-economic change

Because of the peculiar nature of the system, the national parks in Japan are vulnerable to socio-economic change, especially along their periphery, and the existing park scheme may become unsuitable to the changing reality. In order to respond to such changes, it is necessary to make adjustments to the park scheme periodically.

3.5 Other problems concerning park management

The rangers who are responsible for the management of the national parks spend much of their working time on procedural jobs such as issuing permits, which amounts to as many as 5,000 cases per year; thus they are unable to spare enough time for the interpretation of nature for visitors. Moreover, the visiting population of national parks in Japan is so high that sometimes visitors excessively converge on a certain area and pose problems of littering, destroying vegetation, and disrupting the quiet environment.

4. SOLVING PROBLEMS

This section will describe some of the adjustments made to solve various problems faced by national parks in Japan.

4.1 Adjustment with land ownership

It is generally accepted that land owners should accept certain restrictions for the sake of the public interest in terms of conservation of nature. In order to encourage such acceptance, there have been provided some preferential measures in favour of land owners, such as a system of land purchase by the State, a system of tax benefits, etc.

4.2 Adjustment for the other utilization of land

The State, in determining a protection scheme for national parks, provides for the zoning of the national parks according to the excellence of landscape, importance of park utilization, situation of land ownership and land utilization, etc. By providing some grading to the restrictive regulations according to zoning, adjustment is made between nature conservation and other utilization of land. The following zoning classification is used:

Special Protection Area: This is an area which offers spectacular sights in a park, and requires strict protection from an ecological standpoint. In this zone, no alteration to the existing natural state is allowed.

Special Area: This is an area which presents excellent scenic beauty, or a specific cultural beauty. In this zone, nature conservation is applied in close coordination with the other utilization of land. Further classification is applied according to the degree of priority for conservation of nature into the following three areas:

1st Class Special Area: This is an area with natural landscapes corresponding to the above described Special Protection Area and requires utmost efforts for conservation of the existing natural landscape.

2nd Class Special Area: This is an area which must be protected and conserved by carefully promoting coordination with agriculture, forestry and fisheries activities.

3rd Class Special Area: This is an area which requires relatively less nature conservation care and where normal agriculture, forestry and fisheries activities are allowed.

Marine Park Area: This is a sea area with beautiful underwater scenery within a national park. In this sea area, no activities which may affect the undersea landscape and its ecology are allowed.

Ordinary Area: This area plays the role of a buffer zone of the Special Area, and where any large-scale development activities which may adversely affect the Special Area are restricted.

NATIONAL PARKS, CONSERVATION, AND DEVELOPMENT

Of other land utilization within a national park, forestry takes the largest area. In our country, it is the general practice to carry out tree planting after timber-felling, or seed trees are left uncut during logging operations so that natural reforestation can occur. In respect of forest management within each national park, the following forestry operations are allowed in the Special Protection Areas and Special Areas, after it has been determined that careful attention will be paid to conservation of the natural environment in close coordination with the Forestry Agency:

Special Protection Area: No felling permitted.

1st Class Special Area: No felling permitted as a rule. However, timber felling deemed to pose no problem to the maintenance of the natural landscape may be allowed using the single cut method, within the limit of less than 10% of the standing volume.

2nd Class Special Area: Only selective cutting is permitted as a rule, but clear cutting of up to 2 ha for each felling zone may be permitted, provided that there will be no problem for the maintenance of the natural landscape.

3rd Class Special Area: No detailed restriction is provided. But forestry operations must be performed, paying careful attention to the maintenance of the natural landscape.

Besides forestry, guidance is provided for each area to restrict such activities as construction of structures, roads, quarrying and mining of rocks and mineral ores, land excavation and filling, picking and gathering plants, and other similar activities. By this guidance, an adjustment between nature conservation and other utilization of land is smoothly performed.

4.3 Adjustment with public utilities

As previously described, those projects of public utilities which are compelled to be located within national parks are mostly on a large scale and their effect to the natural environment is also large. Because of this, when a judgement is required to decide whether to approve any large scale activity within Special Areas, an advisory body is set up by the Director General of the Environment Agency. This "Nature Conservation Council" consists of experts is ecology, biology, landscape-architecture, forestry, botany, zoology, economics, etc., and makes reports and recommendations to the Director General based on its professional and comprehensive viewpoint.

Likewise, in these cases, assessment is made of possible effects of these activities to natural environment as well as for the selection of land sites so that necessary adjustments can be applied to nature conservation.

4.4 Response to socio-economic change

In order to make partial alteration of the existing park scheme to the effects of socio-economic change, a general review of the existing park scheme for each national park is in progress at present. This work is aimed at overhauling the present park scheme and reviewing and reorienting the conservation policy to match the current situation in each park area. When an area has become excessively urbanized, it will be excluded from the national park; on the other hand, if an area located outside of the national park is found to form an integral part of the national park landscape and maintains a satisfactory natural environment, then it may be added to the national park.

After the completion of the review of the park scheme, it is to be subjected to periodic check at five-year intervals so that the scheme can adapt to possible changes in the socio-economic conditions surrounding the national parks.

4.5 Other problems concerning park management

Because of the limited number of rangers and the overloaded permit-issuing job, a problem has arisen in that rangers have little time to pay enough attention to the interpretation of nature for the visitors; in order to cope with this problem, the following measures have been instituted:

- Relating to the restriction of activities by the Natural Parks Law, a part of these easy and simple permit-issuing jobs are entrusted to local prefectural governments. Thus local prefectural governments, city and town offices are extending their cooperation.
- For the guidance of visitors with respect to protection of wildlife, beautification of parks, prevention of accidents, etc., volunteers from the private sector are entrusted with such jobs in the capacity of "Natural Park Guide"; these volunteers now total about 2,000.
- There are several outside organizations which assist and contribute to park management. For instance, the National Parks Association of Japan, is engaged in of studying, researching, and performing public relations for the promotion of national parks, the Nature Conservation Society of Japan is a leader of our nature conservation movement and is contributing to the guidance of visitors by sponsoring nature observation tours, and the Marine Park Centre devotes itself to the activities of studying, researching and performing public relations relating to the marine park areas.

The National Parks Beautification and Management Foundation, which was organized in 1979, uses the revenue from the automobile parking charges collected at various main parking areas of national parks for beautification and cleaning of land areas of national parks and to cover the cost of repair and management of minor facilities as well as for guidance of visitors. There are also some private bodies which undertake cleaning of national parks in various local areas with support from state and local public bodies. These private bodies are organized by national parks concessionnaires who are engaged in transportation, accommodations and so on.

As it is difficult, unlike in the case of a man-built public park, for park administrators themselves alone to effectively control the visiting crowds, there is an effective traffic control which depends on the help of police authorities having jurisdiction over the park area to limit or bar owner-driven automobiles from entering the park area during the peak season whenever there is an over-congestion of visitors. In this case, besides the help of police, cooperation and assistance is provided by local public bodies and from other concerned quarters.

5. OBSTRUCTING FACTORS

Since the oil crisis, the growth of the Japanese economy slowed down to a relatively low level. The idea that effective utilization of land is necessary to revitalize our economic activity has come to take root firmly in the minds of people, and voices calling for the necessity of placing on the first priority list such utility projects as energy resource development—both hydroelectric and nuclear—and construction of roads inside the area of national parks have come to be heard loudly today, making it difficult to counteract these trends by government agencies which are responsible for conservation.

With respect to the Special Protection Areas and the 1st Class Special Areas which constitute the nucleus of our national parks, it may not be so difficult to obtain concensus for the preference of nature conservation, but in respect to the 2nd Class and the 3rd Class Special Areas, it is not so easy to gain such a consensus since the pressure for such development projects is mounting steadily.

By the same token, even for those people who live in the neighbouring area of a national park, the existence of a national park is looked on as a deterrent to the satisfactory economic development in the area because of the small utilization value of the national park land. Therefore, their support for various kinds of development projects is very great, creating a perception gap between the city dwellers who usually have favourable views of nature conservation and the people who favour industrial development.

With respect to the privately owned land within a national park which is especially important for nature conservation, local prefectural governments are allowed to purchase such land. However, land prices have so enormously spiralled up that it has become extremely difficult to negotiate prices with the land owner. When a restriction is applied to the private land beyond the toleration of the land owner, it is provided by law that the State should pay compensation to the land owner for the loss he has incurred by such restriction. But as it is difficult to define accurately what really is the tolerable limit, this legal system has never functioned yet.

As the trend to use a monetary scale for evaluation of value is strong, it has become increasingly difficult to have good understanding of the importance of nature conservation, since assessment of nature in terms of monetary value is difficult.

6. CONCLUSION

As described in the foregoing pages, most of our national land had been already in use in various useful ways for many and carefully thought out purposes when the system of national parks was first instituted in Japan. The state-owned land allocated for the purpose of timber production and land conservation was under the jurisdiction of the Forest Agency. In order to accomplish the objectives of national parks, a zoning system was introduced; although this system may not be perfect for satisfactory management of national parks, more than 5% of the whole national land area has been designated as national park land, and all-out cooperation is being provided by the related administrative agencies, local people, land owners, and the concerned business and industrial quarters for the achievement of the goals of national parks. When the total land area of quasi-national parks and prefectural natural parks is added to the national parks, the entire area of our natural park land reaches as much as 14%. The system of natural parks, designed and managed according to Japan's national priorities, is making a great contribution not only to the conservation of nature, but also to the people's enjoyment of nature.

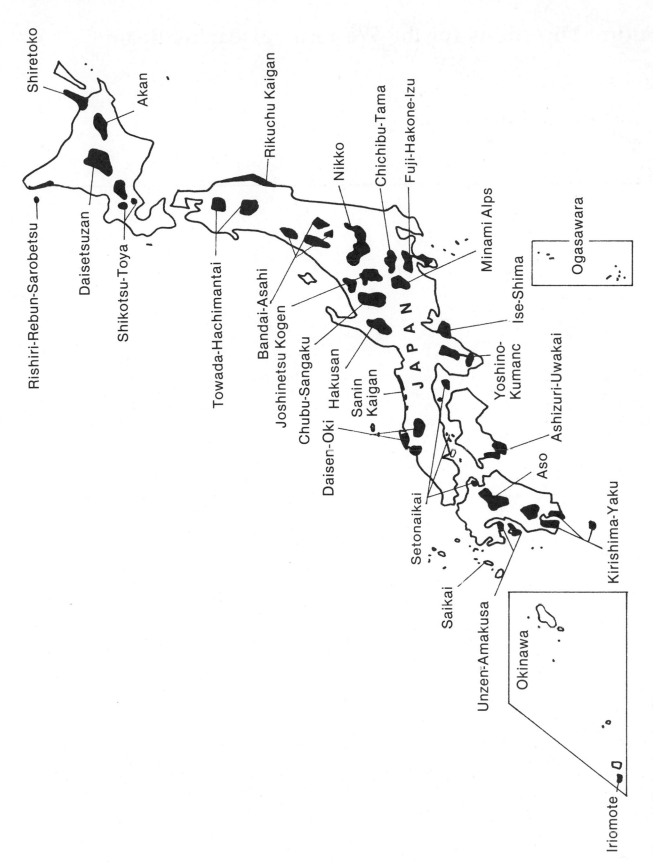

Figure 1. National parks of Japan.

Future Directions for the Western Palaearctic Realm

Mats Segnestam
Executive Director
The Swedish Society for the Conservation of Nature
Stockholm, Sweden

ABSTRACT. *The future of protected area conservation in the Western Palaearctic Realm depends on convincing people of their links with nature. The Western Palaearctic has a long history of human settlement and agricultural development, with the highest proportion of land in agricultural use of any part of the world. This means that there are fewer opportunities to create major virgin parks and protected areas, but there are many opportunities for blending protected areas with compatible sorts of land use. It is, however, clear that while the total area protected has increased more than a hundred-fold during the past 50 years, many biomes are clearly under-represented, especially high mountains and coastal areas. A number of fundamental changes are required in the human perspective of nature, to replace feelings of selfishness and expansionism with feelings of pride and a sense of long-term utilization.*

1. NATURE CONSERVATION AND MAN

Sometimes it seems as though nature conservationists want to ignore man. But of course, that is futile. Nature conservation, area conservation included, begins and ends with man. Man's thoughts and actions, both within protected areas and outside, have a crucial effect on the future of the protected areas. This is true everywhere, and not least in the Western Palaearctic. Man's influence *within* the protected areas of the Western Palaearctic have been discussed and controlled for a long time. In the future a great deal more attention will have to be paid to man's short-term and irrational behaviour in the "everyday landscape" *outside* the protected areas.

In the Western Palaearctic it is the conviction of man's superiority that predominates, the idea that man can rule, control and dispose of other beings on earth—flora and fauna—as he pleases.

Many people refuse to accept the idea of there being any limits to growth, and many do not even ask themselves whether this might be so. Furthermore, there is blind faith in the possibility of solving every conceivable environmental problem with the aid of technology. There is no doubt where the North Americans have derived their Wild West mentality—the conviction that new resources and riches are always waiting to be conquered over the horizon.

In the Western Palaearctic region there is a fundamental lack of understanding of nature conservation in general and of the relationship of nature conservation to development and the limits to growth. There is an equally fundamental lack of understanding about the value of genetic variation. This deficiency is reflected, for example, by a tendency to give priority to the utilization of non-renewable resources at the expense of renewable ones.

How important a part is played by ancient cultural traditions in a region like the Western Palaearctic? It will be a very long time before we acquire thick enough layers of the new cultural varnish of nature conservation-mindedness—a polish which would make it possible for us to accept nature's imposition of limits to the utilization of natural resources and thus bring ourselves to think and plan on a more long-term basis.

One question is whether millenia of evolution have given us a biological heritage, a mental burden, which stands in the way of sensible, long-term and unselfish solutions. Has selfish, extremely short-term survival been given priority to such a degree that today we are unable to see developments in the long term, and unwilling or unable to assume responsibility for tomorrow?

Another question is whether man is capable of understanding in advance the value of genetic variation or whether we will have to make mistakes first. In the latter case, the question is how we can make ourselves avoid the irreversible mistakes.

Too many parts of the world have their version of hell: areas at war, areas of soil destruction, desertification, water shortage, hunger, starvation and death. In some parts of Europe there are antechambers to another kind of hell. We find them in the most intensively industrialized areas, where the world consists of concrete, where all the lakes are artificial, where the environment is polluted, where water is contaminated, where the air is grey and people also grey. What impact does an environment like this have on people's thinking?

2. SOME TRENDS

The Western Palaearctic is a relatively small region with, for the most part, a dense population and with great cultural differences between north, south, east and west. In the following, many of my observations and remarks pertain to the industrial part of the region, which is the oldest industrialized region in the world. Some of the problems I describe are less relevant to the southernmost and southeastern part of the region. The problems there—for example, desertification—are more akin to those usually associated with developing countries in other realms.

Various trends can be discerned in this region. The rapid shift of population to the towns and cities is one example. In parts of northern Europe, for example, 20% of the population lived in the countryside 30 years ago, whereas today over 80% are living in urban communities.

In the Mediterranean area, which has been populated for almost the whole of human history, the pressure from human activities has grown substantially during our own century and has also made itself felt in the marine environment.

The Western Palaearctic has a long history of human settlement and agricultural development. It is the most highly developed agricultural region of any on earth, with a higher proportion of land in agricultural use than any other region. Therefore, there are fewer opportunities to create major virgin parks and protected areas. But on the positive side, there is probably more experience in this region in blending conservation with other considerations; in many countries there are established land-use planning systems and the full range of protected area categories is fairly well exhibited in the region.

In recent decades, agriculture and forestry in large parts of the region have been intensified by means of larger units, increasing mechanization and the use of pesticides and chemical fertilizers. Forestry is based on monocultures and has entered areas not previously exploited.

The great majority of people in the region are still far from understanding the profound implications of the World Conservation Strategy, e.g. roads and towns are still being built with very little restraint on good, fertile soil in many parts of the region, a practice which I would term immoral. This increases the pressure on marginal lands, which are often the only lands still retaining somewhat greater biological diversity.

Industrialization has gathered speed, air and water pollution have grown, and enormous amounts of chemicals have come to be used. The problem of soil and water acidification is one example of an environmental problem which has developed lately and which will have to be solved internationally, since its causes are often located outside the country affected. This is also an example of an environmental problem affecting both protected and unprotected areas.

Exploitation of the sea, including the sea bed, and coastal areas has developed very rapidly in the region.

International tourism in the Western Palaearctic is growing, which is a mixed blessing. The advantages are that more people have learned to appreciate the natural environment of other countries, which means that international pressure for the conservation of areas can be increased, added to which more people are coming to realize, as a result of their travels, how limited the earth is. It is becoming increasingly possible to teach more people more things about the environmental problems of other countries and their connection with environmental issues in one's own country.

The disadvantages are that the natural environment has suffered heavier wear and tear in the areas which remain, and that willingness to reserve areas for recreation in one's own country may decline if it is known or felt that another country within the region has recreation areas to offer.

Developments in the region as I have outlined them have to a great extent been made possible by the availability of large quantities of excessively cheap energy. Directly and indirectly, the extraction and use of this energy cause very great environmental problems, problems which will also affect the protected areas sooner or later in many places.

The rapid deterioration and destruction of the natural environment is very dangerous because people in future will not have anything to make comparisons with.

The pressure of population is growing in parts of the region, but more important are the consumption patterns. Although material abundance is very unevenly distributed, large groups of the population are indulging in conspicuous over-consumption compared to what is possible in other parts of the world and in relation to the long-term supportive capacity of the natural ecosystems. Consequently, the unemployment which prevails in large parts of the region and which is expected to increase, and the political pressure thus generated for an even more intensive exploitation of natural resources, will be important factors influencing future possibilities of protecting areas in the Western Palaearctic.

It should be pointed out here that the region as a

whole has been and still is exploitative towards the rest of the world and many of the problems of developing countries in managing their own protected areas can be traced, directly or indirectly, back to the European cultural influence and economic domination.

3. PROTECTED AREAS IN A WIDER CONTEXT

As I have stressed, human activities have left their mark on the Western Palaearctic over a very long period of time. Exploitation has been highly intensive and is becoming even more so.

The region consists overwhelmingly of man-made landscapes. The question is whether there is any area in the Western Palaearctic which is untouched and which can be preserved in its natural state, considering among other things long-distance air pollution and the exploitation and pollution of the seas.

In a region where the natural environment is so intensively utilized, it is particularly necessary for protected areas to be regarded as part of a pattern of rational land use.

Nature conservation must never be presented solely as a question of protecting certain limited areas. Instead it must be geared to social development and environment protection and must permeate land use. We should put greater emphasis on the World Conservation Strategy (WCS) idea of preserving living processes. An integrated approach is essential, and we should, in accordance with the WCS recommendation, develop national nature conservation and development strategies, which among other things, incorporate land use planning.

We are still thinking too much in terms of protected areas on one hand and the rest of the environment on the other. We must pay more attention to explaining the relationships between protected areas and our surroundings in general. There are no hard and fast boundaries between protected areas and the "everyday landscape". We should have a flexible transition, for example, from ecologically adapted forestry to strictly protected areas. This makes it important for discussions concerning the designation of protected areas to be integrated with the national planning system, and for protected areas not to be regarded as isolated islands. Therefore, we also need to make sure that the protected areas are combined with rules for the utilization of the everyday landscape, for example, arrangements for developing and implementing a conservation approach to agriculture and forestry.

We should, whenever possible, demonstrate the value of protected areas in economic terms. Protected marine areas are potential examples of this kind in the Western Palaearctic. For example, protection of more spawning areas for fish around the North Sea would ensure future income for fishermen.

In order to put further emphasis on the economic value of protected areas, we could very well use them as outdoor laboratories. But this can only be done if the areas are big enough—if the greater part of the protected biotope is left untouched. There is a tendency in some parts of the Western Palaearctic region to underestimate the value of untouched, or relatively untouched, nature and to attach too much importance to the utilization of protected areas as experimental gardens. The undestroyed areas in certain parts of the Soviet Union or northern Scandinavia, for example, are invaluable.

It follows from the above that we need to modernize national legislation in many countries, and this does not only apply to legislation concerning protected areas. It also applies to legislation on energy use, land use planning, forestry, agriculture, etc.

4. PROTECTED AREAS IN A HISTORICAL AND INTERNATIONAL CONTEXT

There is no doubt that the protected areas in the Western Palaearctic region are insufficient. Although the total acreage of protected areas in the Western Palaearctic has increased more than a hundredfold during the past half century, several environments are clearly underrepresented in the intended future network of protected areas. They include high mountain, coastal and marine areas.

In many places the protected areas are still regarded as exploitation reserves. Their protection has been accepted as long as there is no other manifest need for their utilization and only as long as people feel that they can afford to protect them. In many places, "salami tactics" are employed whereby an area originally designated as protected is exploited a little at a time.

It is therefore important that nature conservation should not lose its sense of history: we must have a clear view of historical developments and realize that nature conservation is retreating all the time. When we discuss the existence or otherwise of a protected area in the Western Palaearctic today, this is often a question of compromising on the basis of previous compromises.

Examples of protected areas under heavy pressure from development interests are to be found in every corner of the Western Palaearctic region, in Spain, Switzerland, Turkey, Britain and Sweden, to mention but a few examples.

We have to make it clear that the value of the protected areas is growing rapidly. It is *now* we have to explain the necessity of preserving variation, it is *now* we have to identify and protect areas. The remaining natural or relatively unspoilt habitats are disappearing at appalling speed, and with them a great deal of the remaining genetic diversity.

We should aim high regarding the future network of protected areas. We should not rest content with isolated examples of typical areas. Instead we should also demand the designation of alternative areas similar in character. We can no doubt look forward to certain compromises in the future as well, and so we must now procure for ourselves a margin for such compromises while this is still possible.

We must not confine our efforts in the Western Palaearctic to the protection of wilderness areas. Since the landscape of this region is so intensely influenced by human activities, the preservation of genetic variety is often a matter of preserving the man-made landscape, a landscape in which human influence is of an ancient kind and where modern methods of exploiting natural resources have not yet been introduced.

We must affirm the need for national networks, including a whole variety of systematically selected protected areas. The network created at national level should fit in with a wider regional and national pattern.

Where national networks are concerned, numerous small, local protected areas are an extremely important complement to larger areas, both ecologically and educationally—for the benefit of schools and as a means of selling the idea of nature conservation and protected areas. The diversity of small areas and general nature conservation values have been obscured by the large, glamorous areas.

We should have more interaction at the international level. We should increase international pressure to bring about major conservation measures. The non-governmental organizations have an important part to play here. We should develop international cooperation and international advisory activities so as to make use of the best ideas which have emerged in the various countries. For example, as part of the implementation of conventions, countries should make more use of consultants from other countries in the region, so as to get external advice on their own policy measures concerning the designation of reserves.

We should establish monitoring systems and early warning systems at regional or sub-regional level concerning pollution, species, habitats, development patterns and protected areas.

We need to aim for a clearer view of the economic and scientific importance of biosphere reserves and other protected areas. We can best accomplish this by international cooperation.

We should make full use of the international conventions, which in the Western Palaearctic means above all the Bern and Bonn conventions, as a means of putting pressure on national governments to establish protected areas.

We should develop legislation which will facilitate interventions across national boundaries.

After this plea for greater international cooperation, it is perhaps still appropriate to recall that biological conditions, cultural traditions and the historical development and current role of nature conservation vary a great deal from one part of the Western Palaearctic to another. Consequently we should not aim for excessive uniformity throughout the region. Considering the great cultural, institutional and political differences existing in a region like the Western Palaearctic, one must con-

stantly ask oneself how much work can be devoted to internationally coordinating the designation of protected areas. It is questionable, for example, whether great efforts should be devoted to standardizing the terminology of all countries. It is certainly more important to establish good examples of protected areas designated within a wider framework of land use planning and in surroundings that are managed in accordance with ecological principles. To an international organization like IUCN, it is no doubt also important to work more intensively on a limited selection of countries which are in particular need of international support. Both international knowledge and good examples can then be utilized, for example, with the aid of a "rotating seminar" and sub-regional and bilateral cooperation.

We ought in future to hold more discussions at the sub-regional level concerning protected areas, for example between the countries bordering on the North Sea. The Nordic countries, the Mediterranean countries, the Baltic countries and the Alpine countries, to quote a few examples, have already opened discussions of this kind. The non-governmental organizations can play an important part as pressure groups to bring about sub-regional discussions.

5. BROAD-MINDEDNESS AND FARSIGHTEDNESS

The idea of the necessity of protected areas still needs to be sold to an immense number of people in the Western Palaearctic region. Because of the unawareness now existing of the value of protected areas, the number of such areas is smaller and the protection of those existing is more uncertain than need really be the case.

As has already been made clear, we need to explain more distinctly the different values of protected areas, for example, the value of the marine reserve for baseline data for the measurement of pollution in other areas, for genetic conservation, for fish reproduction, etc. We need, quite simply, to give a better explanation of the sound investment which the designation of protected areas implies.

We must not underrate the need for support for protected areas from the local population. Support of this kind is invaluable for the long-term protection of such areas.

There are top-down and bottom-up approaches to changing people's attitudes. Top-down is government legislation, taxation systems, formal education systems, etc., and bottom-up is community-based initiatives, non-governmental organization activities, etc. We need both, but we do not get the right attitude to conservation just by a set of centrally determined policies. The bottom-up approach is essential; the whole informal system of people's values that come out of the community in which they live will have to be nurtured and encouraged by conservationists much more in the future for lasting commitment to conservation.

In the future we will have to make far more deliberate use of protected areas as a means of selling the nature conservation message, of putting protected areas in a regional context and of explaining every possible international significance that a particular area can have. Information should be addressed both to the indigenous public and to foreign tourists.

The protected areas need to be positioned densely enough for people to "feel at home" in them, to regard these areas as something which really concerns them. A small number of magnificent showpieces will not do, because they will be considered just as exotic as they really are.

We must use the local example as a means of expanding people's views to international level, to make them see the need for measures which are sometimes felt to be an encroachment, to induce them to accept that we have a broader responsibility. This should be possible in large parts of the Western Palaearctic, because resources of education and information ought to be available and because other educational conditions are good enough in many places.

We need to enable people of the future to experience clarity of vision by making more conscious use of the diversity of form and colour in the protected areas. We must not underestimate the importance of concrete examples. Paper descriptions of beautiful scenery and variegated surroundings are no substitute for things which can be smelled, seen, tasted and touched.

We must try to increase people's ability to envisage the future. And induce them to decide what sort of life people ought to be able to lead in future. We must open a discussion concerning the type of development we are to have, and what the monocultural landscape is to look like. Where is the boundary of depletion to be drawn?

We must rapidly educate all those responsible for development and planning, and to try to stop them looking on protected areas as exploitation reserves.

Among other things, we should use satellite techniques and other new mapping techniques to describe what we mean and to indicate the drastic changes undergone by the natural environment in recent decades. (We have to realize that the developers use techniques of this kind to locate new development areas). We need to use these techniques in order to know what is there; to develop conservation action programmes; and to show people in concrete and dramatic pictures what is happening.

We must try to replace feelings of selfishness and expansionism with feelings of pride and a sense of long-term utilization, both among people at the local level and among central policy-makers.

We must preach broad-mindedness.

Chapter 11
The Nearctic Realm

Keynote Address: The Nearctic Realm

Russell E. Dickenson
Director, National Park Service
US Department of the Interior
Washington, D.C., USA

ABSTRACT. *This paper reviews the historical context of the establishment of national parks in Canada, Mexico and the United States, and describes the current park and protected area status in the Nearctic Realm. Mention is made of the value of the World Heritage Convention. In the immediate future, those implementing parks policy in the United States will concentrate on consolidation of existing parks, and must be prepared for intensifying pressures from outside of these areas; Everglades National Park is an example of the various current problems and approaches to address them. A reaffirmation of the basic principle of protection for national parks is called for by the author.*

1. INTRODUCTION

The Nearctic Realm covers the USA, Canada, Greenland, and the highland parts of Mexico and Central America. During this Keynote Address, I shall briefly review the historical context of parks in the realm, review the current situation in terms of protected areas in it, and assess current problems and possible future trends, especially from our own perspective in the USA.

2. HISTORICAL CONTEXT OF PARKS IN THE REALM

The modern-day concept of national parks originated in the Nearctic Realm with the establishment of Yellowstone 110 years ago. As President Ronald Reagan recently pointed out in a statement prepared for IUCN: "Approaches developed in one country may have direct application in others, such as the concept of national parks, wildlife refuges, and other protected areas, which have been pioneered by the United States and are used throughout the world by countries with widely different development levels and political systems". The United States is proud of Yellowstone's role in the worldwide park movement.

Our neighbours to the north and south have kept pace with that first inspiration at Yellowstone. Canada established Banff National Park in 1885, and Glacier and Yoho National Parks in 1886; all three preserve major sections of the Rocky Mountains. Canada also established the world's first National Parks Service in 1911, which preceded that of the United States by 5 years.

The Waterton-Glacier International Peace Park, proclaimed in 1932, sits astride the Canadian-U.S. boundary. It is a symbol and a physical tie in the two nations' friendship and cooperation. On 18 June 1982, I was privileged to be present for the 50th anniversary celebration of the Waterton-Glacier International Peace Park. This great park belongs to the people of Canada and the U.S., but in a real sense, it belongs to the world.

It wasn't until much later that Denmark established the Greenland National Park in 1974. With 70 million ha, this is now the world's largest.

In the southern part of the Realm, Mexico established its first conservation area, Bosque El Chico, in 1898. Today, it is considered the country's first national park. Although a few parks were established in Central America during the 1950s and 1960s, most of that region's parks and reserves were declared during the past decade.

In this historical sketch, I feel that I would be remiss if I did not mention what I consider to be a particularly significant event that has fully come of age since the 1972 World Parks Conference. In 1972, Unesco adopted the Convention Concerning the Protection of the World

Cultural and Natural Heritage. This action responded to the critical need to preserve irreplaceable natural and cultural properties which have special meaning world-wide.

The World Heritage Convention has established a system of international cooperation and assistance to protect natural and cultural properties of outstanding universal value to mankind. The United States was the first nation to ratify the Convention. Of that I am proud. Some 60 other countries throughout the world have now approved the Convention.

On 29 June 1982, Olympic National Park in our state of Washington, was dedicated as the ninth U.S. World Heritage Site. At this time 10 sites have been designated in the U.S. and nine of these are with the National Park System.

3. CURRENT SITUATION IN THE REALM

The Nearctic Realm now includes 308 parks and protected areas with a total area of 138,806,800 ha, according to the most recent figures available from IUCN's Protected Areas Data Unit (PADU) at Kew, England. Of the 22 biogeographical provinces in the Realm, all but the Arctic Archipelago and Greenland Tundra are represented. The Rocky Mountain Province has the highest number of units (44, with nearly 7 million ha) while the Tamaulipan Province has only one area, the Santa Ana National Wildlife Refuge in Texas, with slightly more than 5,000 ha. The Arctic Desert and Icecap Province also includes only one site, the Greenland National Park, but its 70 million ha far exceed the total area set aside in any of the other biogeographical provincess in the world. As Steve Kun from Parks Canada will discuss in more detail, a major new national park has just been established in southwestern Saskatchewan to conserve one of the last remnants of the Grasslands Biogeographic Province in North America.

As points of comparison, the Nearctic has more land devoted to parks and protected areas than any of the other seven of the earth's realms. However, the Palaearctic, Afrotropical, Indomalayan, Australian, and Neotropical realms all surpass the Nearctic in the total number of areas which have been established.

4. PRESENT PROBLEMS AND FUTURE TRENDS

In the Nearctic Realm, we collectively face a wide variety of problems within or adjacent to our parks. These include aesthetic degradation (land development, urban encroachment, insect infestations, timber removal), pollution (acid rain, odors, suspended particulates, hydrocarbon pollutants), physical removal of resources (mineral extraction, poaching, grazing, collection of specimens), exotic encroachment (plants, animals, noise),

physical impact of visitors (campfires, erosion, wildlife harassment, trampling), water quality and quantity changes, and others.

Managers of parks are being tested, as the full range of influences and changes affecting parks, or those likely to affect long term ecological balances, become known. Hundreds of examples exist, but I would like to focus on our experience in Everglades National Park. The proceedings of this Congress will include a detailed case study on Everglades by Superintendent Jack Morehead, and I shall summarize some salient points from it.

Everglades National Park is an area of 5,668 sq km with an altitude range from sea level to 2 m. It is located at the southern tip of the Florida peninsula, including most of the waters of Florida Bay. It is subtropical and the annual rain fall is between 140 cm and 152 cm, 80 percent occurring from May through October. Occasional tropical cyclone depressions deposit up to 50 cm of rain in 24 hours. Approximately 67 percent of the park is subject to yearly inundation.

Five vegetation types predominate: hammocks or tree islands of mature hardwoods; mangrove forests; pinelands (on elevated limestone outcrops); bayheads or strands (in depressions or slight elevations with swamp species such as bald cypress); and sawgrass prairies.

The park was authorized by Congress in 1934 and formally established in 1947. The legislation clearly stated that it was to be permanently reserved as a wilderness and nothing should be undertaken that would interfere with the unique flora and fauna and the essential primitive natural conditions. But since the park was established in 1947 (and before), there have been significant declines of some of the area's most important natural resources.

The park and its rich wildlife resources depend on an immense sheet flow, freshwater system from the north. Extensive manmade alterations over the past 100 years have changed a once unregulated, slow moving sheet flow regime into a complex system of levies, canals and storage impoundments north of and outside the park. These regulate the quantity, quality, and timing of water released to the park.

By the time the park was established in 1947, these arrangements were virtually complete. Most efforts were toward agricultural, urban, and industrial water use. Little consideration had been given to ecological needs. Indeed, in December 1962, other agencies closed the various control structures to the north and virtually all surface water from the north was stopped. They remained closed in 1963, except for one month. Significant long term damage was threatened and the National Park Service strongly protested. This resulted in interim water delivery arrangements, and legislation in 1970 guaranteed 260,000 acre feet annually on a fixed monthly schedule. We feel sure that this is less than the natural historical volume, and of course, the fixed monthly schedule disrupts natural cycles and timing, and the normal drying out period of the marsh system. Our fear is that, in time, such modulation will further reduce natural plant and animal diversity, as well as the number of individuals present of some species.

The dwindling populations of colonial, freshwater wading birds has occurred as a result of several factors, over a considerable period of time. The best estimate available is that up to 2 1/2 million colonial wading birds nested in southern Florida in the 1870 period; extensive commercial hunting, among other things to furnish plumes for hats, in the 1880s and 1890s caused a severe decline. Gradually, new laws, enforcement, and style changes enabled a partial population recovery, but since 1934, there has been a steady decline. Now there are less than 250,000 of the colonial wading birds—10 percent of the number estimated in 1870. Why? The most probable causes of decline after 1934 are a general loss of habitat and disruption of the natural water quantity and schedule. There is a somewhat similar story on the quantity and variety of fish and crustacean populations.

Water is the keystone of the Everglades ecosystems. Ecological needs for water have been considered, but usually political realities have favoured those uses of more immediate benefit to man's comfort and well-being. We are currently involved in an intensive hydrological research and monitoring programme on which to base future decisions. We are working with all agencies and organizations involved to change the water delivery schedule. Our goal: an adequate quantity of water, on a schedule driven by natural rainfall events which may eventually restore a portion of the diversity and quantity of the original Everglades flora and fauna.

Elsewhere, outside of the Everglades in other parts of the continent, additional examples of change include increased development of lands adjacent to parks—that is roads, buildings, and homes. Coal, oil, and gas development in the western United States will likely affect many national parks. Air clarity and quality and water quality and other effects are being currently monitored.

In North America today, we are feeling some of the pangs of reality. The finiteness of our resource base becomes ever clearer. The price of protecting the many unique natural, historic and cultural units in our national park system is eternal vigilance. Change occurs all around us. The tempo quickens each succeeding year.

Isolation which once protected many of the large natural parks is disappearing. No longer are our wilderness parks so remote they are readily accessible only to the few. Parks, in effect, are no longer islands unto themselves alone. Where twenty years ago, we had less than 100 million visits to U.S. National Parks each year, visits now exceed 300 million annually.

We have problems with population growth; land development; pressures for coal, oil and gas; need for new transportation corridors; and a public desire for physical fitness opportunities which brings increasing demands in the back country and the outdoors.

Our goals of preservation and wise use change little. The circumstances under which they must be executed change dramatically. Worldwide, economic conditions drastically alter our park and resource conservation strategies. Thus, a period of rapid expansion of the national parks in the U.S. has now brought us to one of consolidation. Emphasis under current conditions cannot be so much on adding new sites. We now focus available fiscal and personnel resources on better management of existing sites.

We must give priority to the life, health, and safety needs in our parks. We must renew and improve visitor facilities, if not in the parks, closely adjacent to them. We must research critical problems so as to ensure informed judgments in our management. And, we must urge an enlightened use of those adjoining lands and resources to reduce or remove threats such as air pollution, acid rain, water pollution, and so on.

These pressures around the boundaries and within national parks, preserves, and wilderness areas pose severe problems. They intensify questions which cannot be avoided. We must be astute and dedicated professionals if we are to pass these areas and their resources along unspoiled for public use, enjoyment, and inspiration. We must win public support for parks and their principles.

Parks are laboratories where thriving communities show the discerning eye a multitude of examples of efficiency and adaptation. The grand design of nature found there, food production and use, resistence to insects and disease, procreation and natural energy use without man's interference, all have counterparts in human society.

The parks are object lessons for a world of finite resources and infinite needs. There we must recognize the need for and practice the restraint which is vital for our long-term survival. They are places where one can learn that satisfaction is not dependent upon expending resources. These areas promote intensive experience, rather than intensive use. We learn that the joy of an alpine meadow lies not in picking flowers or digging rocks but in leaving them for others to enjoy.

The key trend here, I believe, is not an all-powered central government dictating individual local land-use decisions, but is rather the need for regional planning participated in by all local special interests and local government agencies, including the national park administrator. Enlightened public support for national parks is vital to their future, and I believe that we have that in North America.

A recent period of rapid expansion in the United States park system, both in number of parks and area, drained funds and manpower from pre-existing units. This combined with inflation and weakened economic activity leaves only one current sensible strategy—consolidation of prior gains. Emphasis today is on satisfactorily caring for a high level of public visitation—340 million visits per year—and for correcting sanitation, structural, and other safety problems in existing parks. Some deplore this strategy and call for continued expansion of the system, despite the reality of the budget. I fully expect that when economic conditions improve, we will again address the issue of possible new, worthy, candidate areas for the system. I definitely do not see the National Park System as complete or finished. The System is dynamic. It is held in high regard by most Americans, and I am sure that it will continue to reflect the aspirations, needs, and culture of new generations through continued growth.

Travel and tourism are powerful economic factors which can be used to further park protection. Worldwide, organized travel and tourism organizations depend on natural and cultural destination objectives with strong integrity and appeal. Several U.S. national parks come to mind. Travel and tourism in the U.S. is a $190 billion per year industry, the second largest retail industry in the country. Last year, international travel to the United States totalled 23 million people who spent $12.5 billion. We expect a perceptible increase in foreign and domestic visitation to areas that have been designated as World Heritage Sites as their "world class status" becomes widely recognized. Other countries might also expect the same future trend.

As I see it, there is opportunity for cooperation toward mutual objectives—natural and cultural protection and visitor use, with increased economic benefits to nations, states, and communities.

5. CONCLUSIONS

In closing, I would like to emphasize that national parks, in the last quarter of the 19th century, were intended to be fully protected areas. That principle has become even more important as parks have evolved in the 110 years since Yellowstone.

Parks are held in high esteem by Americans and, I beleve, the world community, because they are not commercially exploited. Natural and historical values are protected.

It is not possible to have a national park with partial protection. It is better to place it in another category if full, traditional national park protection is not possible.

So it is important in this Congress, I suggest, to call for a reaffirmation of basic principles regarding national parks—and what they are—in context to several other categories of protected areas.

We must guard against a dilution of purpose.

Based upon our North American experience, I am convinced that national parks will never be free of the tension inherent between developmental and growth momentum, and that of nature and cultural conservation represented by parks. We must draw on a broadly-based body of public support—globally—assuring parks the highest degree of protection, if we are to keep our word and commitment—the contract—with those who follow us in the 21st century and beyond.

Attempts to Modify Significant Deterioration of a Park's Natural Resources: Everglades National Park

John M. Morehead
Superintendent
Everglades National Park
Homestead, Florida, USA

ABSTRACT. *This case study discusses the dramatic decline of three sorts of natural resources in Everglades National Park: 1) Water (extensive man-made alterations to the natural water flow pattern for the purposes of flood control, land reclamation, and water storage have greatly altered the water regime which is a crucial component of the swamp ecosystems for which the park was established); 2) Birds (the populations of colonial, fresh-water wading birds within the park is a dramatic illustration of a decline of a significant natural resource, set in motion by plume-hunting and maintained by the disturbance of the water regime); and 3) Fish (both commercial and sport fishing have had a severe impact on the fishery resource). The study describes some of the actions which are being taken by park management to mitigate these declines.*

1. INTRODUCTION

This case study discusses the dramatic decline of some significant natural resources of Everglades National Park, and describes some of the actions being taken by park management in an attempt to mitigate and, hopefully, reverse the decline. The study also mentions some of the research and resource monitoring being performed to document resource stability or deterioration and to suggest measures for ecological improvements where needed.

2. ESTABLISHMENT AND PURPOSE OF PARK

Everglades National Park was authorized by Congress in 1934 and established in 1947. The purpose of the park was clearly articulated in the enabling legislation, which stated, "The said area . . . shall be permanently reserved as a wilderness, and no development of the project or plan for the entertainment of visitors shall be undertaken which will interfere with the preservation intact of the unique flora and fauna and the essential primitive natural conditions now prevailing in the area." Subsequent designations, both national and international, have reiterated the 1934 Establishing Act.

In 1976, Everglades was designated as a Biosphere Reserve; in 1978, 5,260 sq km of the park (92.8%) were placed in the National Wilderness Preservation System; and in 1979, the park was designated as a World Heritage Site.

The area receives relatively heavy visitation, with over a million persons recorded annually from 1966 to 1978; over 850,000 in 1979 and 1980; and over 600,000 in 1981 and 1982. The noticeable decline in recent visitation corresponds closely to a similar decline in tourism throughout the Miami/southern Florida region.

3. DECLINING NATURAL RESOURCES

Since the park's establishment, there have been significant declines of some of the area's most important natural resources. Three illustrative examples follow.

3.1. Alteration in water delivery to the park

Extensive man-made alterations to the natural water flow pattern for the purposes of flood control, land reclamation, and water storage have greatly altered the hydrological regime north of Everglades National Park. The once unregulated, slow-moving "sheetflow" regime is now a complex system of levees, canals, water storage impoundments, and water control structures which influence the quantity, quality, and timing of water entering the park (Fig. 2). A review of the history of these alterations is informative.

Before man's intervention, the area generally referred to as the "Everglades" consisted of an immense freshwater drainage system, more than 240 km in length, which flowed unimpeded from the Kissimmee River drainage toward the southwest, across the southern third of Florida and into the Gulf of Mexico (Fig. 1). Rainfall from the northernmost reaches of this system flowed southward into Lake Okeechobee where it was impounded. During wetter years, when the level of Lake Okeechobee rose over 4.6m above mean sea level, water would overflow low points in the lake's banks, contributing surface flow to the larger Everglades marsh to the south. This overflow combined with the rainfall upon the southern portion of the basin, ultimately flowing into a relatively narrow constriction called Shark River Slough.

The completion of a shallow canal, connecting Lake Okeechobee with the Caloosahatchee River in 1883, marked the beginning of significant human impact upon this overall drainageway. As the human population increased in southern Florida in the late 1800s and early 1900s, there was extensive wetland drainage to provide more land for both urban and agricultural development. By the 1930s, the once uninterrupted surface connection between Lake Okeechobee and Florida Bay was completely severed. In several locations, fresh water from the Everglades marsh system was being diverted to the east to be drained into the Atlantic Ocean.

In the 1940s, it became apparent that there was a real need for some form of overall flood control, drainage, and water management in the State. In response, Congress passed the Flood Control Act in 1948 which established the Central and South Florida Flood Control District as the state agency responsible for water management. While the initial concept was to provide flood control and drainage, it soon became obvious that there were also growing, often conflicting, demands for water that made water conservation during the dry season or during years of drought an additional responsibility of the agency. District personnel began the construction of a series of large marsh impoundments, called "water conservation areas", that were intended to store excess water from the rainy season for use in the dry period. At this point, all efforts in water management were being directed toward agricultural, urban, and industrial water use (Fig. 2). Little, if any, consideration was given to ecological needs.

In December 1962, various control structures to the north of the park were closed, and essentially all surface water flow from the north, through Shark River Slough into the park, was stopped. The structures remained closed throughout 1963, and only a minimal opening during one month in 1964 was permitted. This total cut-off of surface flow, plus unusually late rainy seasons in both 1963 and 1964, caused severe drought conditions in a major portion of the park, which threatened to cause significant, long-term ecological damage to the area. In an attempt to remedy this emergency situation, the National Park Service petitioned for surface water delivery guarantees, and a six-year period of negotiations between the Department of the Interior, Department of the Army, and the Central and South Florida Flood Control District followed. Finally, in 1970, Congress passed the Monetary Authorization Act which authorized construction of additional water conveyance facilities and established the current guaranteed minimum deliveries to the park. For Shark Slough, 320,710,000 cu m of water, distributed on a fixed monthly schedule, is now guaranteed annually.

Recent data indicate that from 1941 to 1979, rainfall probably contributed an average of 78 percent of the combined annual inputs of rainfall and surface water entering Shark River Slough. While our understanding of the changes that have occurred in the hydrological regime is hampered by a lack of documentation of historic conditions, we feel that the present water delivery schedule has probably resulted in a reduction of total water quantity and, perhaps more important, has definitely caused a disruption of the natural timing and contrasted volumes of wet versus dry periods. In effect, the existing schedule has reduced the magnitude of both the occasional extremes of high and low water levels of the past, and has severely disrupted the duration and timing of the normal annual drying-out period in the marsh system.

The trend since 1970 has been toward modulation of the normally varied hydroperiod which, in turn, has affected the water-dependent biology. We fear that, in time, such modulation will reduce natural plant and animal diversity and will biologically favour only those few species that happen to be adapted to the modulation. In an ecosystem like the Everglades marsh—one that is not particularly diverse in species to begin with—reduction in population and loss of species can happen dramatically and rapidly. This may already be occurring.

We are currently involved in an extensive hydrological research and monitoring programme specifically designed to provide the data necessary for future management decisions. Information is being gathered on precipitation, water delivery (quantity and timing), conductivity, temperature, flow through the park, innundation periods, levels of innundation, water quality, nutrient and chemical absorption by marsh plants, and effects of water delivery on salinity in the estuary/bay areas of the park. Researchers are working to correlate aspects of hydrology information to biological effects. This analysis will then be used to evaluate proposed water management activities.

We have asked the other agencies involved for their cooperation in developing a revised delivery schedule that can most nearly accommodate the park's ecological needs in consonance with the needs of other system users.

3.2. Decline in the park's bird population

The dwindling populations of colonial, fresh-water wading birds within the park serves as a dramatic illustration of the decline of a significant natural resource. While documentation is largely lacking, the best estimate is that there may have been upwards of 2.5 million colonial wading birds nesting in southern Florida in the 1870 period. These populations were primarily comprised of snowy egrets *Egretta thula*, great egrets *Casmerodius albus*, great blue herons *Ardea herodias*, wood storks *Mycteria americana*, white ibis *Eudocimus albus*, Louisiana herons *Egretta tricolor*, and little blue herons *Egretta caerulea*.

Extensive commercial hunting, especially in the 1880s and 1890s, caused a severe decline in the overall wading bird population as feathers from these species were widely sought by millinery manufacturers. In 1900, Congress passed the Lacey Act, which prohibited interstate traffic of birds or animals killed in violation of state law. The newly formed Audubon Society, hired "wardens" to enforce both the Lacey Act and the state protective regulations that were in effect at the time. Guy Bradley, one of the wardens working the area now included in the park, became so zealous and effective in his enforcement efforts that he was shot and killed by plume hunters in 1905. The commercial plume hunting, the decline in the wading bird populations, and the murder of the Audubon warden were among the primary considerations that led to the eventual establishment of this area as a National Park.

With passing and enforcement of the protective laws against plume hunting, the Everglades wading bird population made a substantial recovery. There were gradual but noticeable increases in bird numbers until approximately 1934, which probably marked the peak of the population recovery. Total population figures, although improved between 1900 and 1934, are not believed to have reached the high numbers observed before plume hunting began.

Since 1934, however, there has been a steady, and perhaps statistically accelerating, decline. It is felt that less than 10 percent of the historical colonial wading bird numbers can now been found in the park. The most probable causes of the decline after 1934 are a general loss of habitat plus the disruption of the natural water quantity and seasonality.

With increased research efforts and improved accuracy of resource monitoring, this continuing decline has been more accurately observed and documented. Since 1967, regional counts have been conducted yearly that provide reliable data. Within the park, a series of monthly surveys were performed between 1978 and 1981 to provide the most accurate statistical information available to date.

Studies to correlate the decline of wading birds to known and predicted hydrological events are now underway. Monitoring of population trends of other bird species is also being conducted. It is encouraging to report that the number of nesting bald eagle *Haliaeetus leucocephalus* pairs in the Florida Bay area of the park— 20 to 25 nesting pairs—has remained rather constant over the past 20 years. In the same area, however, Osprey *Pandion haliaetus*, have declined approximately 58 percent. Again in Florida Bay, the nesting population of brown pelicans *Pelecanus occidentalis* dropped 40 percent from 1977 to 1981.

3.3. Decline of the park fishery

The water area currently included in Everglades National Park historically supported numerous fisheries, both commercial and recreational. The species comprising the bulk of the commercial harvest were striped and white mullet *Mugil cephalus* and *M. curema*, spiny lobster *Panulirus argus*, spotted seatrout *Cynosion nebulosus*, stone crab *Menippe mercenaris*, and, more recently, Florida pompano *Trachinotus carolinus*. The principal fishes of the recreational fishery were gray snapper *Lutjanus griseus*, red drum *Sciaenops ocellata*, spotted seatrout, snook *Centropomus undecimalis*, tarpon *Megalops atlantica*, and bonefish *Albula vulpes*. A few spiny lobsters were also taken by recreational divers in Florida Bay.

In the enabling legislation of the park, the National Park Service was specifically mandated to permit no activities or developments which would detract from the essential wilderness character of the area. Subsequent legislation and designations have underscored the intent of the act to preserve the natural resources. Even before the park was formally established, however, the question of commercial fishing was raised. Commitments were made to the commercial fishermen that have resulted in intense political and personal conflicts, as it appeared to most that fishery resources of the park were declining.

On 28 April 1937, Arno Cammerer, then Director of the NPS, wrote to the Secretary of the Monroe County Fishermen's Association: "With this as a background, commercial fishermen using the waters around the Everglades may expect equally fair treatment. The National Park Service has no intention of imposing regulations relating to commercial and sport fishing other than those contained in Florida state laws or county laws in the event that the latter exist." In a 12 April 1947 telegram, then NPS Director Newton Drury assured Florida Representative Bernie Papy: "You are advised that the longtime NPS policy which contemplates that fishing in National Parks and Monuments shall be done in conformity with state laws and regulations subject to reasonable regulations necessary to protect and perpetutate fish resources will apply to Everglades National Park in keeping with the commitment of former Director Cammerer to Chester Thompson. Commercial fishing will not be prohibited in the proposed park." NPS Director Demaray on 11 May 1951, wrote to Florida's Senator Holland: "You may be assured that we have no intention of deviating from the understanding of commercial fishing in park waters. Actually, the commercial fishing regulations recently issued by the Secretary are designed to implement that understanding through regulating these activities so that the marine resources will be preserved and harvested on a sustained yield basis."

In spite of these apparent assurances, however, the National Park Service did regulate commercial fishing in the park in several important ways. The inland lakes, bays, canals, and rivers were closed to net fishing in 1951. In 1965, more of these inland waters were closed in areas newly added to the park. Also in 1965, crab traps were restricted to certain waters of the park and their use was limited to no closer than 60 m from any key or marked waterway to eliminate hazards to navigation and disturbance to wildlife on the keys.

In the late 1960s and early to mid-1970s, the staff at Everglades National Park began to hear an increasing number of complaints from biologists and long-term fishermen that the fishing in Florida Bay just was not what it used to be. Groups and individuals, particularly the recreation fishermen, began to question whether continued commercial harvest was consistent with Park Service policy, an increased demand for recreational resources, and a declining fishery. As these anecodotal reports of the decline in fishery resources in Florida Bay continued to grow, the National Park Service undertook a program of creel censuses and catch surveys. Using information generated by this program and acting on long-established Park Service policy, the Service in January of 1979 prepared *An Assessment of Fishery Management Options in Everglades National Park. Florida.* The assessment was widely distributed to commercial and recreation fishing interests. In February 1979, four public workshops were held to solicit public advice and comment. The data gathered in these workshops were added to the written comments and analyzed. In September 1979, proposed regulations were published in the Federal Register for public review and four public hearings were held in October 1979. The proposed regulations were designed to reduce pressures on the fishery resources and reallocate these resources among park wildlife, recreational fishermen and commercial fishermen. In March 1980, the final regulations became effective. They contained four major provisions:

- Commercial fishing would be eliminated by 31 December 1985;
- bag limits were established for all species of fish except commercially netted mullet and pompano;
- recreational lobster harvest was eliminated; and
- a 7,500 ha sanctuary was established in northeast Florida Bay for protection of the endangered American crocodile.

The Organized Fishermen of Florida, an umbrella group representing the interests of commercial fishermen, immediately filed an emergency motion for a temporary injunction to prohibit the enforcement of the regulations. This motion was denied in Federal District Court in April 1980, based on the Court's observation that there was no likelihood of success on the merits of the case, that the National Park Service had adequately conducted itself in determining "nonsignificance" in not publishing an Environmental Impact Study, that the regulations are a service to the public, and that the plaintiffs did not demonstrate immediate and irreparable harm.

In April 1981, the National Park Service accepted a rule-making petition from the Organized Fishermen of Florida asking that the Service examine the March 1980 regulations, particularly those relating to commercial fishing. A Federal Register notice, published 17 April 1981, announced a 50-day comment period and two public hearings to be held in South Florida. During the public hearings, individuals and groups essentially restated the positions taken during the earlier public hearings of 1979. The mail received during the comment period was extremely heavy, indicating not only local, but also national interest. The park received only 1,911 public expressions in favor of amending the March 1980 regulations compared with 9,365 expressions supporting the existing regulations.

At the time of this writing, the matter of legal sufficiency of the regulations is still in court. The commercial fishing interests claim that the National Park Service, in light of prior commitments and a lack of conclusive scientific data to statistically quantify a decline in the fishery, must change or retract the regulations. The National Park Service, on the other hand, contends that the opinions of the overwhelming majority of knowledgeable fishermen and biologists provide adequate reason for taking measures to preserve the resource, even though these opinions are not, as yet, backed by adequate statistical data. The apparent drastic changes in the resource dictate that prior commitments, based upon fishery resource conditions that no longer exist, must be changed.

For the past few years, the National Park Service has been continuing the program of creel censuses and catch surveys. While these efforts have provided some useful data on species caught, numbers landed, fishermen hours of effort, catch rate, size, age of fish caught, etc., more detailed data is still lacking. Research has been proposed to investigate two general management questions: have fish populations in the park declined? And if so, what are the causes of the fish population declines?

Depending upon the answers to these first two questions, a second order of research objectives would become: if the decline in fish populations are primarily man-caused, determine what corrective measures can be taken to mitigate the decline, or if the causes of fish population declines are natural, but fishery harvest or practices are aggravating the decline, determine what management measures can be taken to mitigate the decline.

Some of the specific research projects proposed:

- Fish population studies, which include studies on fishery harvest, fish tagging, and larval fish;

- estuary food chain study, including ponk shrimp *Penacus duorarum* study; and
- estuary habitat studies, which include estuary habitat, northeast Florida Bay hydrology, and Buttonwood canal hydrology.

4. CONCLUSIONS AND FUTURE DIRECTIONS

Changes in the volume and timing of water flow into Everglades National Park have caused disruption to the area's ecosystem. Declining populations of several species of birds, declining fish and crustacean populations, changes in bay and estuary salinity, and invasion by exotic plant species all serve as indicators of this ongoing distruption.

While a major research programme is now underway, detailed scientific data to document the extent of the various changes is limited. Lacking such support data, however, opinions of knowledgable persons are so overwhelmingly in agreement that the National Park Service has already taken management action to halt, and hopefully reverse, some of the existing trends.

It is obvious that water is the keystone of the Everglades ecosystem. Surface water flow into the park from the north has now been completely altered by man, and decisions for water release or retention are based upon factors such as flood control, drought prevention, draining land to provide areas for farming or urban development, agricultural water needs, urban water needs, and others. Ecological needs for water have been considered, but usually political realities have favoured those uses which more immediately benefit man's comfort and economic well being.

The National Park Service is now in the process of working with all the other agencies and organizations involved in an effort to change the water delivery schedule for the park. It is hoped tha an adequate quantity of water, delivered on a schedule that is driven by natural rainfall events, will eventually restore a portion of the diversity and quantity of the original Everglades flora and fauna.

NATIONAL PARKS, CONSERVATION, AND DEVELOPMENT

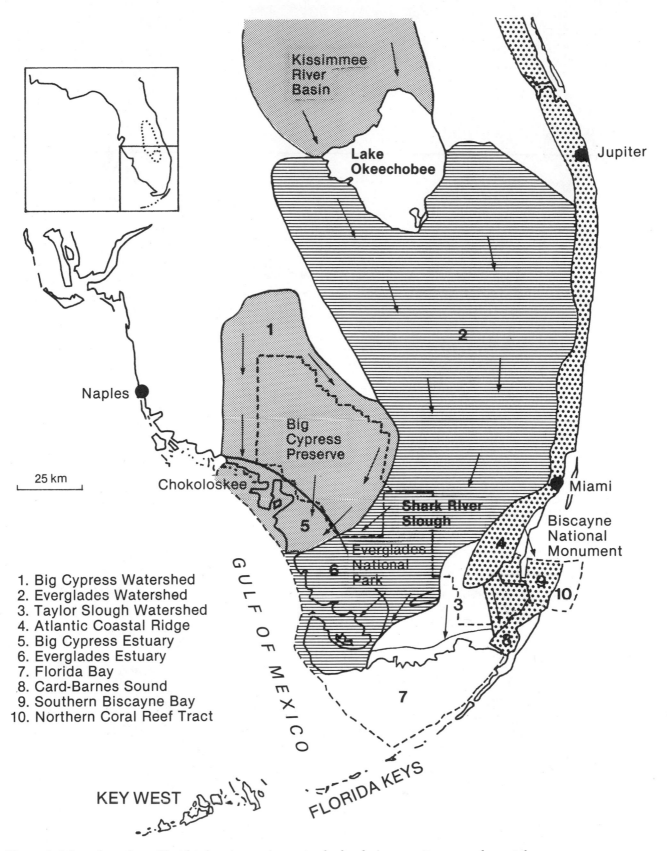

1. Big Cypress Watershed
2. Everglades Watershed
3. Taylor Slough Watershed
4. Atlantic Coastal Ridge
5. Big Cypress Estuary
6. Everglades Estuary
7. Florida Bay
8. Card-Barnes Sound
9. Southern Biscayne Bay
10. Northern Coral Reef Tract

Figure 1. Map of southern Florida showing major watersheds, drainage patterns, and coastal zones.

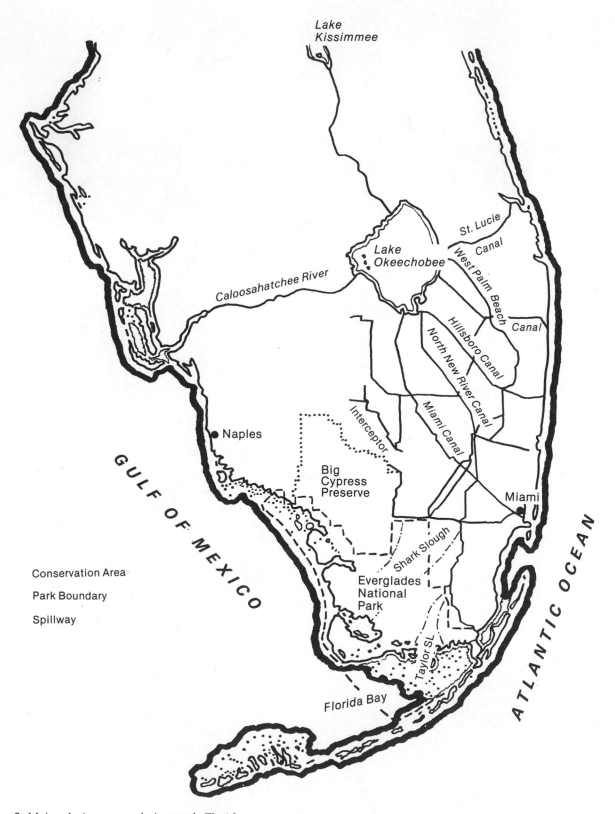

Figure 2. Major drainage canals in south Florida.

Redwood National Park: A Case Study in Preserving a Vanishing Resource

Edgar Wayburn and Michael McCloskey
The Sierra Club
San Francisco, California, USA

Bruce Howard
The Save-the-Redwoods League
San Francisco, California, USA

ABSTRACT. *The establishment by the United States in 1968 of a Redwood National Park and its enlargement in 1978 to its present boundaries focused worldwide attention on a magnificent natural resource, the Coastal Redwood* Sequoia sempervirens. *However, the establishment of this park involved much more, as it happened, than the recognition of the importance of a superb species of tree. It involved unusual economic, political, and social, as well as ecological, aspects, and this particular park effort holds important lessons for park proponents within both government and nongovernmental organizations.*

1. INTRODUCTION

Sequoia sempervirens represents a unique, beautiful, relict flora from the days when dinosaurs roamed the earth. Once these trees grew widely throughout the northern hemisphere, but about a million years ago great climatic changes occurred. Advancing ice sheets altered the growth zone of the redwoods and confined their range to a very limited area along the cool, foggy coast of northern California. Only here on our planet do coastal redwoods remain, making their last stand.

Growing just beyond the reach of wind and salt air from the Pacific Ocean, the belt of redwoods extends from 13 to 50 kilometres inland in an area of steep slopes and unstable soils. The trees reach their greatest size in elevations lower than 610 metres, in regions part lying just a few centimetres below the surface. This incredibly fragile network of roots, no more than 2 m deep, amazingly supports trees ranging to over 110 metres in height, the tallest living things on earth.

The coastal redwood is exceptionally free from fungus diseases and there are few insects which naturally harm it. The trees produce cones and seeds every year. Additionally, the coastal redwood commonly regenerates from stump or root sprouts on logged, injured, or fallen trees, thus giving it advantages over many other species that reproduce only by seed. Redwoods can live for centuries, and trees that were alive at the time of Christ are still standing.

2. HISTORY

California's coastal redwoods survived in a natural state until the white man came to the Pacific Coast. But, as John Muir once said: "As timber, the redwood is too good to live". Coastal redwood soon became prized as a highly versatile as well as long-lsting building material. And by 1900, "by hook or by crook", almost all the redwood-growing land had been acquired as private property. The economy of the redwood region was launched as a single industry subject to drastic periods of boom and bust.

As the population of the United States grew, so did the demand for lumber. Logging technology improved rapidly, which, in turn, increased the volume of timber harvested. Between 1905 and 1929 the average annual cut of coastal redwood was around 1,100 cubic metres. The great depression of the 1930s and World War II lessened the demand until 1947, but from then until the 1960s the cutting of the redwoods reached its peak, exceeding 2.4 million cubic metres a year.

3. PARK EFFORTS

Efforts to preserve the redwoods began almost as soon as the logging. But although periodic studies were made by various facets of government, no material progress in preserving the great trees was made until the first California State Park was established in 1901. Subsequently, the State of California developed an ongoing programme to form Redwood State Parks with the help of the Save-the-Redwoods League.

The first notable effort to establish a Redwood National Park was made by the founders of the Save-the-Redwoods League in 1918. Then Madison Grant outlined the forests which he and other conservationists considered worthy of preservation. These included the Humboldt Redwoods, and those of Redwood Creek (including Prairie Creek), the Klamath River and the Smith River. The League, however, concentrated its efforts on obtaining land or matching funds for the California State Parks, giving priority to acquisition of the great bottom-land groves.

The devastating storms of 1955 and 1964 gave grim evidence that bottom-land groves alone would not preserve the redwoods: in one winter, 600 of the world's greatest trees, supposedly protected, fell in the Humboldt Redwoods State Park. In a region of steep slopes, highly vulnerable to erosion, it was clear that watershed as well as grove protection was needed to preserve the redwood forests.

During this decade, the Sierra Club initiated its campaign for an adequate, protected forest to be acquired by the federal government in a Redwood National Park. By this time, the acreage of virgin redwoods which had been 810,000 ha a century earlier had been reduced to about 121,500 ha. This virgin forest was not, of course, contiguous but was in bits and pieces, some so small they were almost as tall as they were wide. Some 20,250 ha were in 56 State Parks, of which three were particularly noteworthy, containing some of the world's finest redwoods: Jedediah Smith, Prairie Creek and Humboldt State Redwoods. The remaining virgin stands were in private hands. These included magnificent "lawns" of redwoods, over 12,150 ha of them in the Redwood Creek watershed and superb acreage around Mill Creek in the Smith River drainage adjacent to Jedediah Smith State Park.

In the early 1960s, under the urging of the Sierra Club, the National Geographic Society and the Save-the-Redwoods League, the federal government began an earnest appraisal of the potentialities of a Redwood National Park. Studies done by the National Park Service concluded that the greatest possibilities lay in Redwood Creek (where stood the world's tallest trees and several intact watersheds) and in Mill Creek.

Early on, the Save-the-Redwoods League had combined forces with the Sierra Club in the national park effort, but later, the League gave priority to Mill Creek alone (long a dream of the organization) and the Sierra Club chose to fight for a 36,450 ha park on Redwood Creek. To gain a national park in either area, the government would have to buy back the trees and the land on which they stood.

There followed a period of difficult confrontations with the timber industry, arduous negotiations, innumerable further studies, and prolonged political maneouverings. Ultimately, the Congress in 1968 passed an act establishing a 23,490 ha Redwood National Park based largely on Redwood Creek. ($92 million was authorized by the act to achieve the park; the cost would eventually be over $190 million). Even before the bill was signed, it was realized that expansion would be necessary to achieve an ecologically sound redwood protective unit. Thus, after another decade of strenuous debate and litigation, a bill was passed in 1978 enlarging the Redwood National Park to 42,930 ha. (The cost of this may eventually add up to over $360 million; additional claims by lumber companies are still pending).

In all, the Redwood National Park saved 7,954 ha of prime virgin redwood forest; most of the rest of the acreage was cutover land. Within the national park boundaries lay three jewels of the California State Park Redwoods connected by preserved corridors of land and coastland; Jedediah Smith, Del Norte Redwoods, and Prairie Creek State Park. Some 7,833 ha of prime virgin redwood forest is contained in these parks. Thus, the total acreage of virgin forest within the park boundaries is 15,787 ha.

The 1978 park legislation contained some unusual, significant provisions. Funds were provided to mitigate the local economic impact of the park. A programme of rehabilitation was to be developed to restore areas that had been devastated by logging, and eventually to return all of the park to its pristine beauty.

4. COMMENTS ON THE REDWOOD NATIONAL PARK EFFORT

In achieving the Redwood National Park, there were remarkable constraints as well as remarkable gains.

4.1 Constraints

Since the park region was owned privately, it was necessary for the government to buy back private property it had failed to preserve for the public good. The purchase of private lands by a governmental entity can create political disorder; it did so in this case. Polarization of opinion and perceived economic and social impacts also impinged on the original concept of protecting a complete ecological unit.

The pressure of a rapidly disappearing natural resource dictated the absolute need to take major action to preserve at least segments of an invaluable vanishing resource. But, as the park effort escalated, so did the logging of the redwoods. This not only diminished the best chances for a superb park, but drove up the costs of acquisition commensurate with the diminishing resource.

This escalation of the commercial value of redwoods accordingly boosted the monetary value of any land containing large stands of redwood trees. The high cost of acquiring redwood lands was a limiting factor in the size (and shape) of the Redwood National Park. Although a large percentage of the finest redwoods inside the park boundaries lay inside already-acquired state parks, hundreds of millions of dollars were required to gain a national park with fairly adequate buffer areas and corridors necessary to form a contiguous unit. The value of the lands and forests was so great (and was inflating in value at such a rapid rate) that two congressional acts, ten years apart, were required to achieve the present park.

4.2 Gains

Although the Redwood National Park is of a size and shape that is difficult to administer, it forms a contiguous unit containing several forests representative of various areas in the region. And within its boundaries—in state parks as well as within its new acquisitions—it contains some of the world's most magnificent forests.

A remarkable rehabilitation programme has evolved under the National Park Service, which is healing vast areas of wounded land, reducing erosion, and restoring clear-running streams. The ecological benefits of this rehabilitation experiment may well reach beyond the National Park System to other land use areas in the United States and in the rest of the world.

The economic benefits of the rehabilitation programme in the Redwood National Park are helping a local economy which is currently in a period of drastic "bust" in the present housing recession. Unemployment in Humboldt County is now 20 percent; in Del Norte County, 26 percent. However, many laid-off wood workers have found jobs with the Redwood National Park.

The tourism brought in by the establishment of the Redwood National Park has also infused the local economy and given it a broader base which will inevitably become larger and more secure with time. This summer's visitation has increased despite the current recession.

In establishing the Redwood National Park, the American people have demonstrated that they care for the unique natural resource of the coastal redwoods and are willing to pay for its protection. In doing so, they have brought about innovative legislation, established new precedents for park acquisition, and recognized new potentials for the National Park System.

5. ROLE OF THE NONGOVERNMENTAL ORGANIZATIONS

Although a good many nongovernmental organizations provided assistance and support during the final stages of the legislation creating the Redwood Park, the Sierra Club and the Save-the-Redwoods League played significant roles from the very inception of the national park project. These two NGOs represent very different philosophies in the areas of acquisition and methodology in the field of conservation.

The Sierra Club is a broad-based, wide-spread citizens organization with a membership now over 300,000—and growing. It is a volunteer organization with immense grass-roots activity and support. Members are involved locally and nationally, reflecting the Club's local and national priorities and its multi-issue approach to the protection of the environment. The Club works with community and governmental groups and is increasingly effective on the political decision-making level. In the case of the Redwood National Park issue, both volunteer club leaders and staff directed their efforts and, experienced media talents in a campaign to rally national public support to overcome local opposition. This was an effective and successful campaign.

The Save-the-Redwoods League is a self-perpetuating organization which devotes all of its efforts and financial resources to the acquisition of prime examples of redwood forests and redwood lands. All such acquisitions are carried out in close cooperation with the Park Department of the State of California since all these purchases either are formed into state parks or are additions to already existing parks. The League has followed the approach of quiet negotiations with private landowners to achieve an acquisition. In the case of the Redwood National Park, the League had participated in the acquisition of the three state parks which became nuclear parts of the national park and the League contributed one million dollars to buy redwoods which were included in the Redwood National Park.

The impact of these two organizations and their methods of operation were very influential in establishing the Redwood National Park. However, both organizations are dissatisfied that the national park, as it now exists, does not protect complete watersheds. They feel the corridor connecting the state parks with the national parklands is too narrow and too fragile.

The League feels it is essential to acquire complete watershed protection for the nothern section of the park even though much of the redwood land involved has been badly disfigured by commercial development and serious clear-cutting.

6. CONCLUSIONS

Any country concerned with setting up national parks should do so, whenever possible, when public land is available. The buy-back of land which has passed into private ownership can be prohibitively expensive. This kind of park planning calls for vision and prompt action.

The ideal time for establishing a Redwood National Park at minimal cost would have been in the 19th century before the land passed out of public ownership into private hands. The last time to acquire large uncut tracts was in the 1920s. However, the political situation was not propitious until the 1960s, when the costs of acquisition were already exceedingly high and cutting had made severe incursions. National leadership by men of vision at an earlier time could have produced a better park at reasonable costs.

Sound park planning requires as much control as possible of the basic ecological factors affecting the park's resources. Ideally, this will entail acquisition of an entire drainage basin, although the topography in redwood country doesn't always lend itself to this approach. The failure to acquire all of the virgin stands in Redwood Creek in the 1960s resulted in the loss of significant virgin redwood stands and drastically increased problems posed by erosion following logging.

Subsequent expansion of the park in 1978 embraced more ideal boundaries, but resource values were severely compromised by then. Moreover, the costs of virgin redwood land had doubled in the intervening period. While it is true that successive park enactments can revise and improve boundaries for a park, this approach is definitely sub-optimal when the basic resource is being destroyed in the intervening period.

The struggle to expand the Redwood National Park in the 1970s focused on the danger to the existing groves posed by logging in unstable terrain outside of the park, and upslope and upstream of it. By focusing on these problems, the inadequacy of forest practice standards was highlighted. This campaign had secondary benefits of educating the public about the nature and prevalence of such problems and of inducing state authorities to improve standards for logging.

A key innovation in the establishment of the Redwood National Park was the use of a "legislative taking". On the date of the enactment, the lands were transferred from private to public ownership, with the valuation to be determined later by either negotiations or court proceedings. However, the court proceedings have been long delayed by contests from the former owners who have asserted claims far in excess of the government's estimates of fair market value. Three such claims are still in court from the 1978 taking; it took six years to settle claims from the first taking in 1968. It would have been better to have required settlement by a given date to avoid a number of problems arising out of delays: uncertainty affecting the future of the park; accumulating interest on additional payments; and the need to resolve questions of valuation on stale factual records. As fewer and fewer stands of redwood remain to be sold on the market, valuation comes to be more and more conjectural.

In-depth studies should be made to assess the economic impact of establishing a national park in the area directly affected. Funds and/or programmes should be provided to temporarily assist the local economy where necessary. However, care should be exercised so as to avoid the implication that the establishment of the park, and the removal of the forest from timbering operations, is the source of the community's economic problems. These problems really stem from the excessive rate of cut and periodic weaknesses in the housing market.

Closely related to this aspect of establishing a park is the fact that the local people affected economically may strongly oppose the park concept. In such cases, it is necessary to rally national support to counteract local opposition. It is worth noting that the national support was sufficient to overcome local opposition and that the legislative representative from the area failed to oppose enactment of the park.

The economy of local communities around the Redwood National Park was based historically on a single industry—timber. Thus these communities opposed the park, perceiving it as depriving them of their daily bread and butter. They waged a strong campaign in an attempt to sway public opinion to oppose the project. This campaign, in fact, back-fired and rallied further the national interest. Furthermore, in the long run, the Redwood National Park is certain to benefit the local economy. The timber industry is near the end of its resource in the redwood region and the economy must have supplementary bases to keep it going.

Long-range vision and planning are essential to establish a national park. In many cases, the land that requires reforestation, or the land requiring time to recover ecologically, may not meet current park standards. Rehabilitation and restoration, however, may heal the land and return it to its full potential. Thus may future generations benefit greatly.

We have recently visited the Redwood Creek watershed and seen first-hand the rehabilitation programme that is under way. It has been evolving steadily during the past four years and various innovative methods have been tried. Some of these are labour-intensive; others employ large machinery. The efforts are clearly succeeding. The rehabilitated areas have already survived several winters of heavy rainfall. The amount of sediment is being controlled. The devastating road cuts and areas of logging which distorted drainage systems are being obliterated so well that it is difficult to recognize areas which two years ago looked hopelessly disfigured. New redwood growth is coming in and more will follow.

The rehabilitation effort is so encouraging that we believe that there is an excellent chance that the dream of preserving the coastal redwoods will be realized in, perhaps, fifty years, and that in another 300 years, the Redwood Creek forest will stand again as it once stood.

It is extremely doubtful that the great virgin forests of *Sequoia sempervirens* would have been preserved on any significant scale were it not for the efforts of the NGOs. The pressure of these NGOs caused the national

NATIONAL PARKS, CONSERVATION, AND DEVELOPMENT

government to move much faster than it otherwise would have, although their efforts in the 1960s would have been even more effective had they been in greater agreement on the goals to be sought. The involvement of concerned citizens is needed for the preservation of almost any scenic or ecologically valuable resource: it is absolutely essential when the resource has a great and ready monetary value.

The cost of preserving California's coastal redwoods has been dear in terms of dollars and human effort, but how much poorer would the whole world have been without this expenditure?

The Lone Prairie: Protecting Natural Grasslands in Canada

Claude Mondor and Steve Kun
Parks Canada
Ottawa, Quebec, Canada

ABSTRACT. *This case study reviews the nature and extent of natural grasslands in Canada and the impacts of human settlement. It summarizes the conservation measures that were implemented from 1900 to 1950 to protect the faunal elements of the Canadian grasslands from extinction due to habitat destruction and over-hunting. The study highlights the actions taken to resolve the social, economic and political constraints associated with the establishment of a national park in southwestern Saskatchewan to conserve one of the last remnants of the grasslands biogeographic province in North America.*

1. INTRODUCTION

In 1842, some 30 years before Yellowstone would be established as the world's first national park, George Catlin, an American artist and writer, advocated that the entire grasslands region be set aside as a "nation's park" to preserve both the bison and the Indians who depended upon them for their livelihood (Catlin, 1903). As he notes in his memoirs detailing his adventures among the North American plains Indians:

> "And what a splendid contemplation too, when one (who has travelled these realms, and can duly appreciate them) imagines them as they *might* in future be seen, (by some great protecting policy of government) preserved in their pristine beauty and wildness, in a *magnificent park*, where the world could see for ages to come, the native Indian in his classic attire, galloping his wild horse, with sinewy bow, and shield and lance, amid the fleeting herds of elks and buffaloes. What a beautiful and thrilling specimen for America to preserve and hold up to the view of her refined citizens and the world, in

future ages. A *nation's Park*, containing man and beast, in all the wild and freshness of their nature's beauty."

On June 19, 1981, the Government of Canada and the Province of Saskatchewan signed an agreement to establish a 906 sq km national park in the southwestern part of that province to protect one of the last remnants of the grasslands biogeographical province in North America. The creation of Grasslands National Park is particularly important because it marked the conclusion of one more chapter in the 80-year drama to save this important part of Canada's heritage. This case study will outline the extent and nature of natural grasslands in Canada, human impacts on the grassland ecosystem, conservation initiatives to protect elements of this ecosystem, the numerous constraints associated with the recent establishment of Grasslands National Park and the actions that were taken to overcome them.

2. CHARACTERISTICS OF THE CANADIAN GRASSLANDS

In the broadest sense, natural grassland can be considered as an ecosystem in which the dominant plant species are grasses and where aridity is a feature of the environment, for shorter or longer periods. It occupies vast areas of the earth's surface between forest margins on the humid side and the edges of deserts on the arid side. This ecosystem covered approximately 40 percent of the earth's surface before the impact of man and his domesticated animals (Clements and Shelford, 1939); it is found in temperate regions in North America, eastern Europe and northern Asia, northern Australia, and parts of South America and South Africa. Natural grassland has been given various names in various regions, for example, "prairies" and "plains" (North America), "steppe" (USSR), "campos" (Brazil), "llanos" (Venezuela), "pampas" (Argentina), and "veld" (South Africa).

According to Udvardy (1975), the Grasslands Province in the Nearctic Biogeographical Realm is bounded on the west by the foothills of the Rocky Mountains and on the east by the Eastern Forest. It extends northward to the Canadian Taiga and southward to the Gulf of Mexico in central and west Texas and into northeastern Mexico (Fig. 1). Clements and Shelford (1939) subdivided the Grasslands Province into four associations related to sub-climatic conditions. Research by Coupland and Brayshaw (1953) in western Canada resulted in the recognition of a fifth. These five associations include:

1) *Mixed Prairie*: occupying southeastern Alberta and southwestern Saskatchewan and extending southward through the Great Plains, between the Rocky Mountains and the 100th meridian, into northern Texas.
2) *True Prairie*: extending from southern Manitoba southward to central Texas between the Mixed Prairie to the west and the decidious forest (formation) eastward.
3) *Fescue Prairie*: characteristic of the foothills of southwestern Alberta and the grassland portion of the aspen grove region in central Alberta and western Saskatchewan. It also occurs in the elevated plateaux in southern Saskatchewan, Manitoba and Alberta and northern parts of North Dakota and Montana.
4) *Coastal Prairie*: occupying the subtropical climate of the areas bordering the Gulf of Mexico in central and west Texas and into northeastern Mexico.
5 Desert Plains Grassland: occupying the transition zone between desert and forest in Arizona, New Mexico and southward into Mexico.

As shown in Fig. 2, only the first four grassland associations occur in the Canadian portion of the Grasslands Province. At the time of settlement the extent of open grassland was probably in the range of 36 to 40 million ha.

The relative abundance of various graminoid species in the plant cover of any given location is determined by temperature and moisture relationships. Tall species occur in those portions of the landscape where soil moisture is above average, while short grasses tend to dominate in the drier sites. Level to gently-sloping, well-drained terrain supports mid-grasses as dominants.

Because the graminoid flora of the northern Great Plains has developed under much cooler conditions than prevail in many other parts of the earth, some of the more important species are endemic. Of particular note

in this regard is northern wheat grass and short-awned porcupine grass, neither of which are common south of the 49th meridian (Coupland, 1950). Canada also has the most extensive stands of rough fescue in North America (Coupland and Rowe, 1969).

The faunal elements of the Canadian grassland exhibited considerable diversity in pre-settlement times. The major large grazing mammals of this area were the bison *Bison bison*, wapiti *Cervus canadensis*, pronghorn *Antilocapra americana*, mule deer *Odocoileus hemionus*, and white-tailed deer *Odocoileus virginianus*. The black-tailed prairie dog *Cynomys ludovicianus*, swift fox *Vulpes velox*, and black-footed ferret *Mustela nigripes* found their most northern limit in the extreme southern edge of this region. Other vertebrates included over 100 species of birds, comprising galliforms, passerines, shore birds and raptors. At least three species of snakes were common, including the poisonous prairie rattlesnake *Crotalus viridis*.

3. HUMAN IMPACT ON CANADIAN GRASSLANDS

The early activities of European man in the prairie region were associated with the fur trade. By the beginning of the 19th Century, a number of fur trading posts were located along with northern fringe of the open grasslands. The winter collection of furs from the forest region depended on provisions sent to these posts from the grassland region in the form of dried meat procured from hunting. This activity resulted in the decline of populations of bison, pronghorn and elk.

Ranching gained a "foothold" in what is now southern Alberta by the importation of cattle from the United States in the 1870s (Johnston, 1970). Despite major losses due to inexperience, the low cost of land permitted ranching operations to expand rapidly. However, the arrival of the railroad in the early 1880s brought in its first trickle of settlers, which within two decades became a flood. Resulting competition for land, together with severe cattle losses (as occurred in the winter of 1906-07), was so adverse to the success of large ranching enterprises that these rapidly dwindled in number and size. Ranching, as an open-range land use, has survived only in the driest areas of southern Alberta and adjacent southwestern Saskatchewan and in the short growing-season areas of the Rocky Mountain foothills.

Farming for wheat and other grains started in the eastern part of the grassland zone in 1871 and advanced westward with the extension of the transcontinental railway to overtake the ranching activity. It rapidly extended throughout the grassland zone with the development of additional railway lines so that by 1897 the bulk of the Canadian Plains had disappeared past recall. The plough had broken the deep prairie soil and turned its store of riches to the production of wheat. Domestic cattle roamed the range where immense bison and pronghorn herds once grazed.

The area of natural grassland remaining in western Canada is estimated at about 12 million ha, of which one-third is arable (Bowser, 1967). The rate of conversion of native grassland to cultivated land is probably about 50,000 ha per year.

The settlement of the western grasslands has had significant impact upon the grasslands ecosystem. Tillage completely destroys the natural cover of higher plants and greatly modifies the consumer and microbiological components of the system (Coupland, 1973). The reserve of organic matter that has been developed under centuries of natural grassland cover is rapidly broken down. Research at five experimental stations in the northern Great Plains indicates a loss of 35 percent of organic matter and 41 percent of nitrogen after cropping for 34 years (Norum, et al., 1957).

Domestic cattle grazing has probably had more drastic effects on the natural balance of the vegetation than have the natural herbivores. Fencing precludes their roaming from one area to another and there is little natural control of the population as a result of weather factors.

The number of cattle present in three western provinces—Manitoba, Saskatchewan and Alberta—increased from 3.8 million in 1951 to 7.5 million in 1966 (Rasmussen, 1969). Undoubtedly, the natural grassland has absorbed a large proportion of this increased grazing load. Overgrazing results in disappearance of the taller-growing mid-grass species and replacement by short grasses and weedy, unpalatable plants. Eventually the community is invaded by exotic species, also often of unpalatable nature (Johnston, et al., n.d.).

Cultivation and ranching has had serious impacts on the wildlife associated with the grassland ecosystem. The millions of plains bison that roamed the Grasslands province in pre-settlement times were the first species to vanish; only an estimated 1,091 bison remained by 1889 (Hornaday, 1901).

By the turn of the 20th Century, other faunal species that were indigenous to the Plains were reduced to the point of extermination, either by random killing or by the destruction of suitable habitat through tillage. For example, thousands of wapiti or elk, the largest member of the deer family, were slain merely for the sake of their teeth, which were used to fashion "elk-tusk" necklaces. The pronghorn antelope, not actually an antelope but a unique American species that evolved on the western plains, once numbered about 50 million and roamed the plains along with the bison. By 1915, it had been reduced to only a few scattered herds in southwestern Saskatchewan and southeastern Alberta (Rand, 1945). Speed, once its main defence against its natural predators, proved ineffective against high-powered rifles.

The practise of draining or filling-in small water areas (sloughs) located in cultivated areas resulted in a decline in waterfowl production as well (Reuss, 1958). Livestock grazing also affects waterfowl production, since many of these water holes are maintained as watering places for grazing animals, which tramp the vegetation surrounding them and destroy nesting cover.

The introduction of agriculture, on the other hand, increased the abundance of some mammals. Rodents such as the pocket gopher, Richardson's ground squirrel and the black-tailed prairie dog increased greatly with the overgrazing of range lands by cattle and the tillage of virgin prairie. The coyote population also increased to the extent that they apparently became a serious menace to farming through their attacks on sheep and poultry. The increase in numbers of such mammals was only temporary. Extensive poisoning campaigns, gopher-killing contests, systematic hunting and trapping programmes, and bounty systems were initiated by provincial authorites to encourage their total destruction. These programmes were so effective that today only a few small colonies of black-tailed prairie dogs remain in Canada along the Frenchman River in southwestrern Saskatchewan. The black-footed ferret, which depends upon prairie dog burrows for shelter and on the occupants for food, no longer occurs in Canada. It, like the little swift fox, has fallen victim to the traps and poison baits set out for the prairie dogs and coyotes.

4. GRASSLAND CONSERVATION INITIATIVES 1900-1950

After the settlement of the Plains had taken place, people began to look back with concern at the impact on wildlife. Between 1905 to 1915, endeavours to rescue the remnant populations, particularly of bison, elk and pronghorn, from complete extermination were initiated concurrently by the provincial and federal governments.

Provincial efforts to prevent the endangered species from vanishing included amendment of their Game Acts in order to provide for an absolute closed hunting season on the species in question, restrictions on the selling of game, and the initiation of programmes to educate public opinion as to the importance of conserving wildlife resources. Provincial game reserves were also established on the Dominion forest reserves located within the three Prairie Provinces. On most of them, hunting or trapping and the carrying of firearms was prohibited (Hewitt, 1918).

Of the various federal government programmes, the establishment of National Parks under the Dominion Parks Act for the sole purpose of protecting the endangered bison, elk and antelope, was undoubtedly the most important (see Fig. 3).

In 1908, the Government of the Dominion set aside Buffalo National Park, a 440 sq km tract of land (Boudreau, 1908) on the present site of the Canadian Forces Base Wainwright, as a refuge for a small herd of bison purchased by the US Department of the Interior from Michel Don Pablo, a Montana rancher. In six years, the Pablo herd, at the time of purchase the largest bison herd on this continent, increased from 709 to over 2,000 head (Williamson, 1915). By 1922 there were 6,146 bison (Harkin, 1923). The problem now became one of how to dispose of the surplus stock of bison as the capacity of Buffalo National Park had been reached.

Hewitt (1921) suggested that the obvious step was to establish a system of small prairie national parks in other parts of the Prairie Provinces, where small herds could be maintained and viewed by persons interested in their protection. His suggestion met with little success. In the winter of 1923, about 2,000 bison bulls were slaughtered in Buffalo National park and the meat, head and hides were disposed by sale (Harkin, 1925). Slaughtering continued in subsequent years. In addition, surplus stock was transferred to Elk Island National Park, established in 1913 for the preservation of the wapiti, and to Wood Buffalo National Park, created in 1922. The area of Buffalo National Park was gradually expanded to approximately 51,800 ha by 1940. At this time, the lands were declared surplus for national park purposes and transferred to the Department of National Defence for the manoeuvering and training of troops and the use of artillery. Approximately half of the bison herd had been shipped to Wood Buffalo, Elk Island and Riding Mountain National Parks prior to 1940, but the remaining animals were slaughtered when it was discovered that they were infected with tuberculosis (Crerar, 1940).

During the winter of 1906-07, still known as "the hard winter" in southern Alberta and Saskatchewan, the remaining herds of pronghorn antelope almost disappeared from Canada. Between 1912 and 1915 several attempts were made to breed pronghorns in captivity in Buffalo National Park, but met with little or no success (Harkin, 1915). In the spring of 1914, the Northwest Mounted Police notified the Dominion Parks Branch that there was a herd of 42 pronghorns near Foremost, Alberta. No attempt was made to drive and corral the herd, rather the Parks Branch decided to construct an eight-foot high "antelope-proof" fence around the eight sections where the animals were situated. This 21,400 ha tract of land was set aside as Foremost Antelope Reserve in 1915 by Order of the Minister, and declared as Nemiskam National Park in 1922. During this period, the original herd of 42 animals reached approximately 180, apparently one of the most successful attempts to breed antelope in captivity (Harkin, 1924). The success of this venture led to the establishment of two other reserves of similar nature, Wawaskesy National Park, a 15,400 ha area located along the South Saskatchewan River in the present-day Canadian Forces Base-Suffield in Alberta, and Menissawok National Park, a 4400 ha area south of Maple Creek, Saskatchewan (Kezar, 1922). Unlike Nemiskam, however, both Wawaskesy and Menissawok National Parks remained unfenced and undeveloped. After the recovery of the pronghorn antelope over most of its former range, all three parks were declared no longer required for park purposes.

5. THE ESTABLISHMENT OF GRASSLANDS NATIONAL PARK 1950-1981

In 1950, Professor Robert Coupland, an internationally respected grassland ecologist, formed the Committee on Ecology and Preservation of Native Grasslands (Ledingham, 1981). The Committee recognized the vulnerability of the few remnant areas of natural grasslands to destruction by cultivation and to modification of species content by cattle overgrazing. They opposed the recent development of replacing the natural plant cover by tillage and of reseeding to introduced grass species, noting that this practice was exploitive and constituted the greatest danger to the surviving natural grasslands in western Canada (Coupland, 1973). Their attempts to purchase a section (259 ha) of native prairie in the Regina area failed due to lack of purchase funds. Ledingham (1960) emphasized to all Canadians that prairie lands were being monopolized by agriculture and that no effort was being made to save significant areas of grassland in pristine condition.

Between 1957 and 1963, the Saskatchewan Natural History Society (SNHS) attempted to protect a sizeable area of natural grassland by purchasing or leasing provincial Crown lands, but was not successful. They eventually obtained a 33-year lease on a quarter section (65 ha) of land in the Frenchmen River valley in southwestern Saskatchewan in order to protect a large, blacktailed prairie dog colony, one of the few remaining in the Canadian portion of the grasslands region (Stelfox, 1966). When it became evident that they could not achieve their objective on their own, the Saskatchewan Natural History Society passed a resolution in October, 1963, requesting that Parks Canada establish a grasslands national park in the same locality as their Prairie Dog Sanctuary.

A joint federal-provincial study comparing six areas in southern Saskatchewan for establishment as a future national park was conducted two years later (Merrill, 1966). It concluded that the 1,813 sq km area between the Frenchman River and Morgan Creek was the most suitable for national park purposes, as previously suggested by the SNHS (Fig. 4). The Province of Saskatchewan endorsed the findings and asked to enter into negotiations.

In accordance with government procedures, the Federal Minister for the Parks Canada programme obtained Cabinet authority in 1966 to negotiate a federal-provincial agreement setting out the terms and conditions of transfer of administration and control of required lands from the province to the federal government. Subsequent discussions with Saskatchewan revealed their willingness to transfer unleased provincial lands to Canada. However, because the Province envisaged a land assembly cost from $2 to $10 million for the purchase of privately owned lands and to phase-out grazing leases on the remaining Crown lands, they suggested that either the size of the proposed park be substantially reduced or that cattle grazing be permitted.

In an attempt to accommodate provincial concerns, the boundaries of the 1965 grasslands national park proposal were revised (NPSP, 1967) to reduce the park's area by about one-half to 906 sq km (Fig. 4). The new proposal was sent to Saskatchewan in 1967 for consideration. The Province indicated that they were no longer supportive of the proposal, given a clearer view of land costs and because of opposition from ranching and hunting interests. The requirement to transfer mineral rights for the lands in question to the federal government in accordance with the National Parks Act also became a contentious issue as the importance of oil increased, and would eventually delay the creation of a grasslands national park for another 15 years.

Between 1967 and 1972, the federal government made additional concessions in an attempt to resolve the impasse. For example, a new proposal was developed whereby two components—one along the Frenchman River and another including the Killdeer Badlands—would be linked by a parkway (Fig. 4); cattle grazing would be phased out over a given period of time; and, the cost of acquiring park lands would be cost-shared on a 50-50 basis.

In 1972, when it appeared the project might never materialize, an inventory was conducted in order to locate all surviving fragments of native prairie in western Canada. The study revealed some interesting findings (Coupland, 1973). One of the biggest surprises was the number of remnant prairie landscapes that had avoided being ploughed or bulldozed into submission— 13 in Alberta and 8 in Saskatchewan. However, nearly all of these were either affected or endangered by the replacement of natural plant cover by exotic grass species. Others were being scarred by intensive oil and gas exploration programmes and strip mining. All were subject to cattle grazing. The largest and most significant grasslands area, the Suffield Military Reserve in Alberta, was not available for national park purposes. No area would be any less difficult to establish as a "nation's park" than the Val Marie-Killdeer region of southwestern Saskatchewan.

It was also evident that more active negotiation was needed if Canada was to have a suitable grasslands national park in the Val Marie area because: land costs were rising rapidly; as land prices went up, there was increasing pressure to plough under the native grass, thus destroying the basis for the proposed park; the provincial government intended to redistribute leaseholds in smaller, and therefore more numerous ranch units, adding to the complexity, cost and social impact of park establishment (39 ranchers owned or leased land in the proposed park area and eight lived there); and the ranchers were becoming increasingly discontented with the "uncertainty" caused by the absence of a decision.

The first significant step in breaking the deadlock occurred in March, 1975, when the Provincial Minister of Tourism and Renewable Resources and the Federal

Minister of the Department of Indian and Northern Affairs signed a "Memorandum of Intention". This non-binding agreement outlined some of the terms and conditions under which the establishment of the proposed national park would be considered.

As set out in the Memorandum, an independent Hearing Board was created in 1976 to hold public hearings to determine the degree of public support for the proposed national park in the Province. Many naturalists presented pro-park briefs but some agriculturalists, hunters and local ranchers opposed creation of the park. The Hearing Board summarized the submissions as strongly pro-park and recommended the establishment of Grasslands National Park (Beamish, et al., 1976).

In June 1977, Saskatchewan announced approval for the establishment of Grasslands National Park subject to Canada: cost-sharing an oil and gas exploration programme within the park's core areas; acquiring land for park purposes only on a voluntary sale basis; ensuring that neither the Municipal Governments nor the Provincial Government would suffer financially as a result of the national park; and, cost-sharing a study for a tourism and recreation plan for southwestern Saskatchewan and the tourism infrastructure developments identified by the plan.

Although the terms stipulated by the Province set some precedents for federal expenditures in the acquisition of new national parks in Canada, government negotiations were finally completed in 1981. A formal agreement to create Grasslands National Park was signed by both governments on June 19 of that year, thereby assuring that a sample of the grasslands ecosystems would be protected in perpetuity.

6. CONCLUSION

The establishment of national parks in Canada has become more difficult and costly as provincial governments have taken stronger positions with respect to control of their natural resources. Until the 1950s, for example, national parks were created with the provinces turning over to Canada all lands required for park purposes at no cost to the federal government. By the 1960s, a 50-50 cost-sharing in land acquisition was required, including buying third party interests in Crown land. In the past few years, some provinces have suggested that all lands for new national parks, including those owned by the province, should be paid for by the federal government.

The terms negotiated for Grasslands National Park reflect the most assertive phase in provincial attitudes to transfer lands to the Government of Canada for national park purposes. These include:

• cost-sharing of oil and gas exploration prior to park establishment;
• land acquisition by voluntary sale only;
• Canada paying 100% of the cost of buying out

third party interests in provincially owned lands—double the prevous practice of equal cost-sharing;

• Canada paying all owner's disturbance costs, expenses and losses associated with their relocation; and

• the onus rests with the federal government to acquire the park lands whereas in the past, provinces usually undertook this action using their expropriation powers.

Perhaps most significant of all, however, is that the bulk of the park lands will be transferred to Canada over a long period of time. Although the terms of the agreement require the Province of Saskatchewan to transfer to the federal Crown the surface and sub-surface rights of a core area of 18,700 ha by the seventh year of the anniversary date of the agreement, it may take up to 40 years (2021 A.D.) before the balance of 71,900 ha is added to the park.

Will Grasslands National Park achieve its objective? In answering this question, it is important to remember that thousands of people have worked for the preservation of a significant area of grasslands ecosystem. Hopefully, they will continue to work with equal dedication to ensure that both governments will fully respect the intent of the national park agreement and will protect this piece of vanishing prairie.

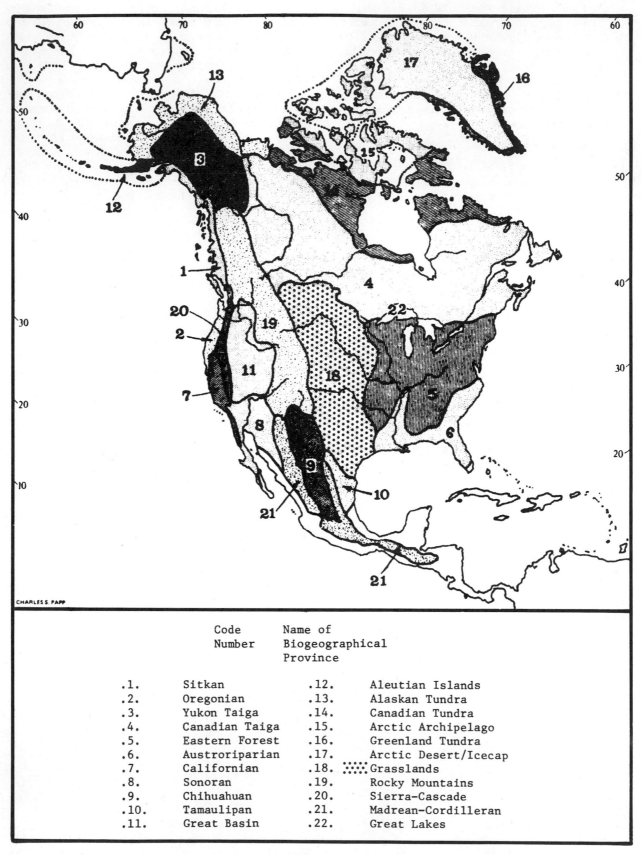

Code Number	Name of Biogeographical Province		
.1.	Sitkan	.12.	Aleutian Islands
.2.	Oregonian	.13.	Alaskan Tundra
.3.	Yukon Taiga	.14.	Canadian Tundra
.4.	Canadian Taiga	.15.	Arctic Archipelago
.5.	Eastern Forest	.16.	Greenland Tundra
.6.	Austroriparian	.17.	Arctic Desert/Icecap
.7.	Californian	.18.	Grasslands
.8.	Sonoran	.19.	Rocky Mountains
.9.	Chihuahuan	.20.	Sierra-Cascade
.10.	Tamaulipan	.21.	Madrean-Cordilleran
.11.	Great Basin	.22.	Great Lakes

Figure 1. Biogeographical provinces of the Nearctic Biogeographical Realm. Source: M. D. F. Udvardy, 1975.

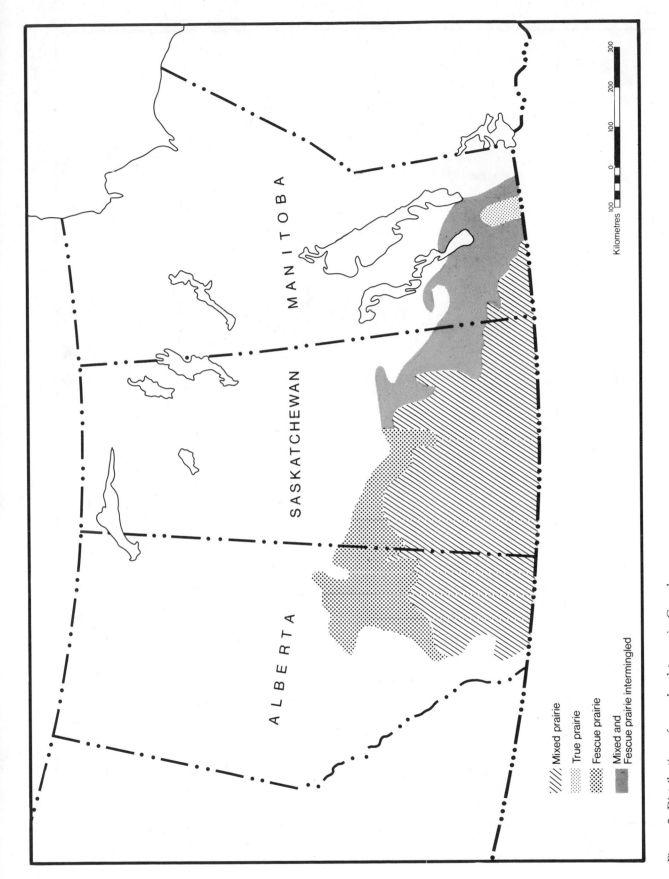

Figure 2. Distribution of grassland types in Canada.

True prairie

Fescue prairie

Mixed and
Fescue prairie intermingled

Mixed prairie

MANITOBA

SASKATCHEWAN

ALBERTA

Kilometres

100   0   100   200   300

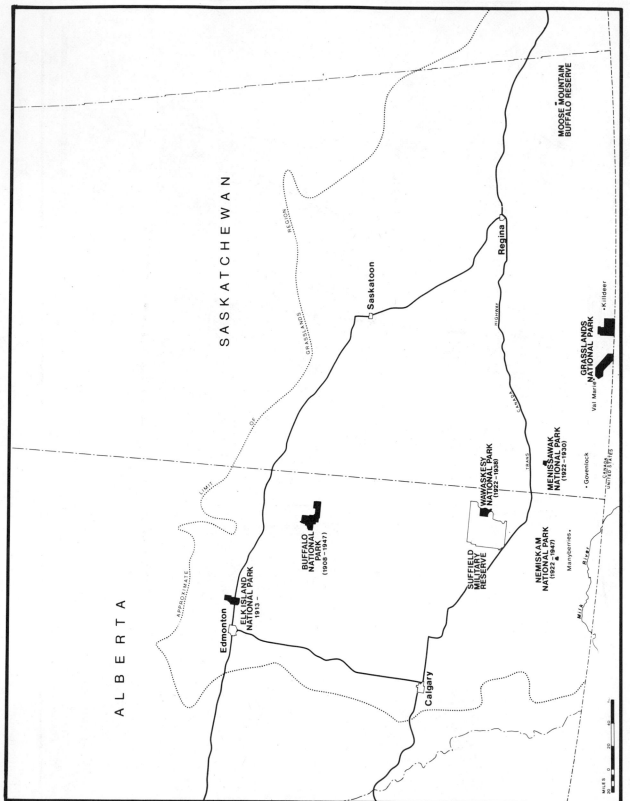

Figure 3. Grassland national parks—yesterday and today.

NATIONAL PARKS, CONSERVATION, AND DEVELOPMENT

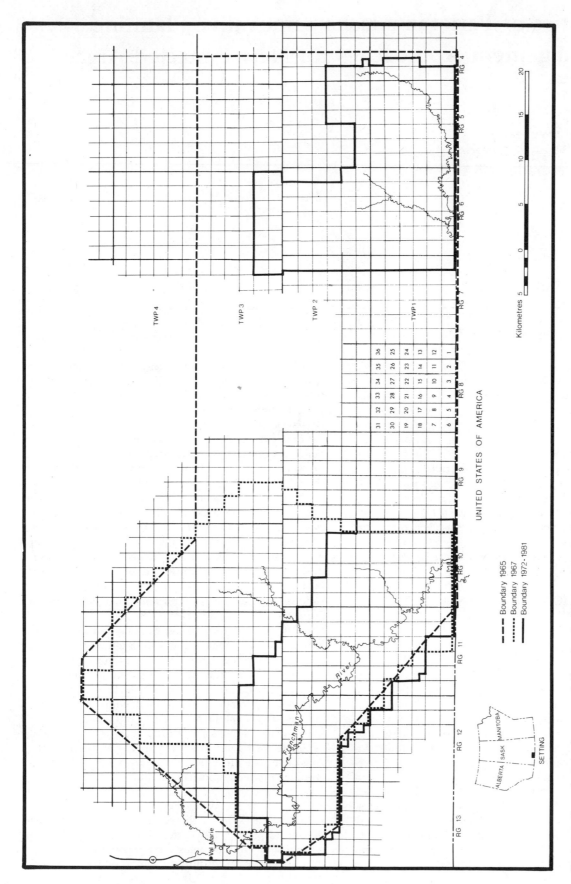

Figure 4. Boundaries of proposed Grasslands National Park 1965–1981.

The Politics of Parks in Alaska: Innovative Planning and Management Approaches for New Protected Areas

Theodore R. Swem
US National Park Service (retired)
Evergreen, Colorado, USA

Robert Cahn
The Audubon Society
Leesburg, Virginia, USA

ABSTRACT. *Passage of the Alaska National Interest Lands Conservation Act (ANILCA) in 1980 constituted a milestone in protection of US National Parks and Protected Areas. In a single piece of legislation, the US Congress gave permanent protection to 41,684,000 ha of land in Alaska, containing some of the world's most spectacular scenery and the nation's most varied and abundant wildlife. The 10-year effort toward passage of the ANILCA featured remarkable cooperation between conservationists, federal government officials and many members of Congress. Special consideration was given to long-term subsistence, cultural and land ownership needs of the native peoples of Alaska; for wildlife protection and ecosystem integrity; and international factors such as worldwide migration of birds and migratory wildlife moving across the Canada-US border.*

1. INTRODUCTION: SIGNIFICANCE OF THE ALASKA LANDS ACT

Passage of the Alaska National Interest Lands Conservation Act (ANILCA) in 1980 constituted a milestone in protection of US National Parks and Protected Areas. In a single piece of legislation, the US Congress gave permanent protection to 41,684,000 ha of land in Alaska, containing some of the world's most spectacular scenery and the nation's most varied and abundant wildlife (Fig. 1). The ANILCA established or added to 60 units, including 5 new National Parks, 10 new National Preserves and 2 new National Monuments. It enlarged and gave better protection to one already-established National Park and 2 National Monuments and then classified the latter as National Parks. It established new units or enlarged 20 areas within the National Wildlife Refuge System and the National Forest System, and created 25 new Wild and Scenic Rivers.

The great size of the areas given permanent protection is important. But of perhaps even greater significance is the way the law was forged over a 10-year period. High among the factors leading to eventual success was the remarkable cooperation between conservationists, federal government officials and many members of Congress, who melded their capabilities and knowledge into an effective partnership. Woven into the fabric of the legislation from the start was a concern for long-term subsistence, cultural and land ownership needs of the native peoples of Alaska. The extensive planning process sought, to as great an extent as possible, to provide for protection of wildlife migration and ecosystem integrity, as well as to take into consideration international factors such as protection of habitat for birds that migrate to all continents, and, in a few locations, for herds of caribou and other wildlife which cross the US-Canada border.

Although not all of the conflicts between preservation and development interests could be resolved satisfactorily, the legislation made numerous concessions to development. Boundaries of the units were drawn so as to provide that 95% of all Alaska lands with proven reserves or geological conditions favourable for oil and gas, as well as all of the Outer Continental Shelf and state-owned submerged lands, would be potentially available for development by private industry. 64% of Alaska lands with favourable hardrock mineral potential would be outside any conservation system unit, and 91% of the state could be open to sport hunting.

As a case study, the passage of the ANILCA provides an epic story of the conflict between those who desired to protect native lifestyles, wildlife and unique natural and cultural areas, and those who wanted to find and develop resources such as oil, gas, hardrock minerals and timber. It is also a story of the way the conservation movement in the United States coalesced as a political force to draw support from thousands of other citizens and a variety of organizations, from church groups to labour unions, to preserve a nation's natural heritage for posterity. And it is a story of how creative planning devised ways to modify protection systems to meet changed requirements.

2. PROFILE OF THE LAND

For many years, protection of the outstanding natural areas and wildlife in Alaska had been a prime but elusive objective for federal government officials and US conservation organizations. By far the largest state (151,760,000 ha), spanning 5 time zones, Alaska has spectacular scenery, the most varied and abundant wildlife and the largest amount of wilderness of any state. Less than 1% of the land has been developed. It includes Mount McKinley, the highest point on the North American Continent, part of the northward-reaching Alaska Range. The Brooks Mountain Range traverses most of the state in a somewhat east-west direction, and the impressive Coastal Range provides a backdrop for southeast Alaska. There are great glaciers, one of which is larger than the state of Rhode Island. Alaska has towering rain forests, more than 3,000,000 lakes, and a coastline half as long as that of the rest of the United States, much of it fjord-like. The mighty Yukon River flows across Alaska for more than 2,200 km, and there are hundreds of wild rivers.

The varied ecosystems provide habitat for an estimated 400,000,000 birds, many migrating to and from North America, South America, Asia, Africa, Australia and Antarctica. Major wildlife species include great herds of caribou, grizzly, brown and polar bears, muskoxen, wolves, wolverines, moose, Dall sheep, mountain goats, seals, sea otters, walruses and whales. And the enormous stocks of fish include salmon, trout, pike, shellfish and grayling.

3. HISTORICAL PERSPECTIVE

Efforts to save distinct areas of Alaska and their wildlife began more than a century ago. Less than 2 years after the United States purchased Alaska from Russia in 1867, Congress enacted legislation to protect seals on the Pribilof Islands. During the next 92 years before Alaska became a state, a number of wildlife refuges were created, mostly to protect migratory birds or marine mammals, and two large national forests were set aside. Mount McKinley National Park was established in 1917, followed by establishment of Katmai and Glacier Bay National Monuments in 1918 and 1925. Almost all of Alaska remained federally-owned public land until statehood.

The 1959 Statehood Act was exceedingly generous to Alaska in comparison to what most other states had been given by the Congress upon entry into the Union. The new state was given the right to select and own almost 1/3 of the land in Alaska, in order to assure it a sound economic base. The state was also given other benefits, the major one being 90% of the royalties and net profits from oil, gas, and minerals produced on the public lands. However, the interests of the natives and the stake of all Americans in protection of natural areas were neglected by Congress in its urgency to pass the Statehood legislation.

3.1 Native peoples' rights

The native peoples—Eskimos, Aleuts and Indians—now constitute about 1/6 of the state's population of 400,000. Prior to the coming of the Russians, they were hunters, fishers and gatherers, and mainly continued this lifestyle until the 1940s. Since then, basic subsistence practices have diminished or changed, depending upon location; these changes have included an increasing substitution of mechanical methods of chase such as motorboat and snowmobile for hand-propelled craft and dog teams, and the increase of the cash economy as a factor in native life. However, the pattern of life for most native people in Alaska at the time of statehood still had much in common with the characteristics of those which ecologist Raymond Dasmann has termed "ecosystem people."

The natives objected to the taking of land by the state, claiming that the Statehood Act did not adequately recognise and protect their aboriginal rights. They claimed that the few acres allowed for each native homesite did not satisy their economic needs or the basic requirements for the subsistence way of life, which was dependent upon large areas for wildlife, fish and plant species, usually far removed from their place of residence. It became obvious that the state could not take ownership of the lands that it had selected until the claims of the native people were settled.

Because of the Federal Government hold on transfer or development of all the land, and growing pressure by oil interests and the State of Alaska to allow development of large petroleum discoveries at Prudhoe Bay on the Arctic coast, Congress finally passed legislation in 1971 addressing native claims. The Native Claims Settlement Act granted natives and their organizations almost US$1,000,000,000 plus the right to select and own 17,807,000 ha of land.

4. PUBLIC INTEREST LANDS PROVISION

At the instigation of conservation groups who made their views known to the Congress, a provision was written into the Settlement Act recognising that the entire American people had a special interest in the allocation of the public (federal) lands in Alaska. Congress directed the Secretary of the Department of the Interior, which has jurisdiction over public lands, to set aside up to 32,376,000 ha for study and possible designation by Congress as national parks or other protected areas.

This opportunity to look at so large an unspoiled area and identify the portions worthy of permanent protection and propose to the Congress how they should be managed had never before been experienced in the US and will never happen again.

4.1 Planning and study period

Conservationists in Alaska and field workers for the Department of Interior's National Park Service (NPS), Fish and Wildlife Service (FWS) and Bureau of Outdoor Recreation (BOR, now a part of NPS) who had studies under way and were considering potential new areas well before enactment of the Native Claims Settlement Act, intensified their effots. An Interagency Planning Group of the Interior Department reviewed agency recommendations and study data and made recommendations for proposed parks, wildlife refuges and wild and scenic rivers. The Planning Group directed preparation of the Environmental Impact Statements (EIS) required by law. A team of more than 50 people from the Interior agencies and the Forest Service, a part of the Department of Agriculture, compiled extensive resource data, assessed alternative boundaries and types of management, identified "areas of ecological concern" outside proposed boundaries and addressed the environmental impacts that would be produced by the various types of management and jurisdictions assigned to the new areas.

In several cases, 2 or 3 of the agencies identified the same areas. The advice of scientists, representatives of native groups and conservationists was sought. In Alaska the "Maps on the Floor Society", an informal group of conservationists, including NPS and FWS experts, met evenings and weekends from 1971 on, to assemble resource data and ideas from all parts of the state in order to determine which areas should be given priority. They formally presented their recommendations to Rogers C.B. Morton, then Secretary of the Interior.

Even with the vast amount of land available, the Interior Department planners found it difficult to include enough land in any one proposal to afford protection to a complete ecosystem, since some species such as caribou, wolves and bear move over extremely large areas. They included entire river drainages wherever possible. And the planners sought to broaden the management policies previously employed and adapt them to the unique circumstances encountered in Alaska.

The end of the study period in December 1973, and the decisions made by Secretary Morton, who outlined proposals for 33,590,000 ha of national parks, wildlife refuges, national forests and wild and scenic rivers, were the first steps leading to the critical series of decisions involved as legislation was shaped and molded.

The recommendations which Secretary Morton sent to Congress were opposed by the State of Alaska and its congressional delegation and by oil and other development interests because development would be prohibited in the large areas to be protected as national parks and wildlife refuges. And the recommendations were opposed by conservation groups as well, because 22% of the new areas were proposed for management by the US Forest Service, and many of the areas were not large enough.

4.2 Degrees of protection given under various designations

Under the US system for managing public lands, the NPS holds the top position in the hierarchy of preservation. Mining and mineral exploration, hunting, logging, or dam building ordinarily are forbidden within national parks, and development of visitor facilities and roads is kept to a minimum.

On FWS refuges, certain mineral leasing activities, such as that for oil development, may be allowed by the Interior Secretary, providing it is compatible with the purpose for which the area was established. Sport hunting is ordinarily permitted on refuges.

The Forest Service, however, encourages logging, roads, oil and other mineral development, as well as hunting. The Bureau of Land Management, which controls all major federal land holdings in Alaska not designated for the park, refuge or forest systems, allows almost all types of resource development. Congress, however, can designate all or part of any federally-owned units as wilderness areas, a designation which prohibits construction of permanent structures, roads and commercial development.

5. GROWTH OF PUBLIC AND CONGRESSIONAL SUPPORT

Neither Secretary Morton's recommendations (submitted to Congress but not supported by Presidents Richard Nixon or Gerald Ford) nor a stronger bill backed by conservation groups, especially the Sierra Club, the Wilderness Society and the National Audubon Society, were seriously considered by Congress over the ensuing 3 years. In 1977, however, a national groundswell of demand for permanent protection of Alaska wildlands began to gather strength.

Major environmental groups from outside the State, allied with conservationists in Alaska, formed an Alaska Coalition, which soon brought more than 50 groups representing organized labour, educators, housewives and all types of citizens throughout the nation into the cause.

Conservation leaders, working with native groups,

prepared legislation calling for 44,516,000 ha to be protected in parks, refuges and wilderness, and included increased protection for rainforest land in Southeastern Alaska which had not been included in the 1972 Morton proposals. A special category entitled "National Preserve", in which large areas would be open to sport hunting but which in all other respects would be managed as if they were national parks, was proposed for a number of the new units or portions of them. The bill was introduced and supported in the House of Representatives by Representatives Morris Udall and John Seiberling and many other congressmen. Newly-elected President Jimmy Carter announced that passage of an Alaska lands protection bill was his highest environmental priority, and the new Secretary of the Interior, Cecil Andrus, prepared legislation for Congress that was only slightly weaker than the Udall bill.

6. CONFLICTING INTERESTS

6.1 Opposition from development interests

Over the ensuing four years, Washington witnessed a heated political battle until the ANILCA was finally passed by the Congress late in 1980. The State of Alaska and its entire congressional delegation, along with oil, hardrock mineral, lumber and other development and business interests, plus hunting advocates, sought to delay or defeat passage of the Udall bill and to pass instead legislation that would put management of much of the lands in the control of federal agencies whose approach allowed multiple use and commercial development, such as the Forest Service and Bureau of Land Management.

The development interests sought to create a public impression that energy resources in these lands were all critically needed by the US, and that the resources were concentrated in the areas being proposed as national park or wildlife refuges. These well-financed lobbying groups (even the State of Alaska spent more than $10,000,000 in promoting its position) were opposed by the better organized and dedicated workers of the Alaska Coalition.

6.2 Counter-attack by conservationists

Many citizens went to Washington to persuade their legislators to support the Udall bill. Others sent their legislators letters and made telephone calls to them. More than 10,000 individuals took an active part in the campaign, which had organizations in each of the 50 states.

To counter the lobbying influence of industry and the State of Alaska, a small group of prominent citizens formed an organization called "Americans for Alaska." Former cabinet members, ambassadors, high military officers, bankers, mayors, heads of labour unions and other civic leaders spent many hours with members of the Congress promoting the need for permanently protecting Alaskan wildlands. Lobbying teams for Americans for Alaska were aided by a former State of Alaska chief petroleum geologist in explaining to members of Congress that only 3 to 5% of the Alaska lands having oil or gas potential would be restricted from exploration and development by the Udall bill.

Meantime, Representative Seiberling had conducted hearings in many locations throughout the United States and found overwhelming support for the Udall bill, except in Alaska, where opinion was evenly divided.

6.3 Crisis averted

The Udall bill was passed with an overwhelming majority when it came to a vote in the House of Representatives in 1978. But Alaska's two senators used parliamentary tactics to prevent action in the US Senate. Thus a crisis approached late in 1978, as the 5-year protection granted by the Native Claims Settlement Act approached its end. Congress ended its session without enacting legislation, and the proposed conservation lands that had been withdrawn from development were about to lose the temporary protection afforded them by the 1973 actions of Secretary Morton.

Before the protection actually terminated, however, President Carter and Secretary Andrus intervened with unexpected executive and secretarial actions which served to protect most of the proposed conservation land until a bill could be passed. Carter, with strong citizen support, used a provision of the 1906 Antiquities Act to designate 17 new national monuments in Alaska, covering proposed additions to the national park, forest and wildlife refuge systems. The designation of these areas as national monuments temporarily prevented any development in the areas or state selection of the land, although Congress could have voted to reverse the presidential action.

7. PASSAGE OF ANILCA

The Senate finally passed a weaker version of the Udall bill late in 1980. But legislation still included almost everything the conservation groups had sought in 1976. Its passage came so late in the legislative year, however, that the House was forced to accept the Senate bill without modification rather than risk having no legislation at all after the inauguration of newly-elected President Ronald Reagan. During his election campaign, Reagan had spoken in opposition to ANILCA because he claimed that it would prevent development of needed energy sources.

8. MAJOR LESSONS LEARNED FROM ANILCA

Sometimes overlooked in the publicity given to the number of new national parks and equivalent reserves created and the large amount of land protected is the fact that important lessons were learned by all concerned and new management procedures were developed during in the 10-year process culminating in passage of the ANILCA.

8.1 Addressing the needs of the native peoples

The NPS and other federal agencies, as well as the Congress and the environmental movement, learned how to deal with rural subsistence use as one purpose of the Act and in such a way that the people could continue their subsistence lifestyle. Hunting to fulfil food needs was allowed for the first time within national parks, and other special considerations were given to native peoples, such as allowing them to live within federally designated areas.

The native peoples were consulted during the planning process. Also, the ANILCA provides that they are to be consulted on management and subsistence practices, and are to be given advance notice and a local public hearing prior to federal agency heads issuing permits for development which might restrict their subsistence activities. The law states that it is the policy of Congress that, "Consistent with sound management principles, and the conservation of healthy populations of fish and wildlife, the utilization of the public lands in Alaska is to cause the least adverse impact on rural residents who depend upon subsistence uses of the resources of such lands . . .''

8.2 Intrinsic values of the land

The planners learned to appreciate land for what it is, rather than trying to change it to meet recreation or energy or other demands of the people. Alaska has the wildest and most remote land in the nation, and through devising special classifications, the government made efforts to perpetuate the land's wildness. As a result, 22,775,000 ha were established as part of the national wilderness system and 33,509,000 ha are scheduled to be studied for possible wilderness classification later. This means that the ordinary standards applied in earlier protected area designations, especially in most national parks—that of giving a priority to providing extensively for visitor accommodations and transportation access— would not be emphasized or perhaps even allowed in Alaska's new national parks. The parkland would have to be used on its own terms and the resources left unchanged for posterity.

9. DISTINCTIVE FEATURES OF ANILCA

9.1 Provision for sport hunting

Instead of excluding from national park boundaries those areas traditionally used by Alaska residents for sport hunting, Congress adopted a new designation, "National Preserve", for 10 new NPS areas, 6 of them adjacent to national parks. In all other ways, national preserves are to be managed as national parks.

9.2 Concessions to resource development

Concessions were also made in some cases for oil, gas, and mineral exploration and development. In setting boundaries for national parks and wildlife refuges, areas with high mineral potential were for the most part excluded. In establishing new national wildlife refuges or additions to existing refuges, provisions were made for the studies of mineral potential and the possibility of development, providing it could be accomplished without harming the habitat.

9.3 Habitat protection

Planners for the new areas set a priority on identifying wildlife habitat needs, especially those connected with migratory bird species and migration routes of large mammals, and tried to satisfy those needs wherever possible. The final results were better than those achieved in the establishment of earlier parks and wildlife refuges, but fell far short of protecting all the needed habitat. The achievement of adequate protection has not been foreclosed for the future, however. For all existing and new wildlife refuges, ANILCA recognized the importance of managing the areas, "to fulfil the international treaty obligations . . . with respect to fish and wildlife and their habitats."

9.4 Unusual protection for valuable forest

Another new step in the ANILCA provisions is the use of the National Monument classification to protect two outstanding areas in the Tongass National Forest, a classification that had not been applied to National Forest lands for almost a half century.

10. THE FUTURE OF ALASKA PARKS AND RESERVES

What does the future hold for the new national parks and equivalent reserves in Alaska?

10.1 Continuing pressure for development

Two comments made on that day in December 1980 when the ANILCA was signed into law indicate the continuing conflict that can be expected in the effort to protect the lands in Alaska.

"We are not finished, we've really just started", said Alaska Senator Ted Stevens, who had led the opposition against the ANILCA and had voted against its passage. "We know that the time will come when those resources now being protected under the new law will be demanded by other Americans."

10.2 Continuing efforts toward more secure protection

"What we have achieved in this legislation, imperfect as it is, marks a great milestone in the history of American conservation, the coming of age of our country's environmental conscience", said Edgar Wayburn, past president of the Sierra Club, who had been working for protection of Alaska wildlands for the past two decades. "The act is not an end, but a beginning. Alaska's superb wildland must have more secure protection. And all concerned Americans will continue to work together until we gain it."

Even though the Alaska lands act is now law, conservationists feel a growing apprehension over its implementation. Under the best of circumstances it would be a tremendous task to implement a 186-page law that deals with such complicated and sensitive issues as the state's land claims and those of Alaska Natives; subsistence hunting and fishing; wilderness preservation; caribou migration; oil and gas leasing; areas open to sport hunting; huge stands of virgin timber open to cutting; and access to remote cabins or mineral claims within or surrounded by vast federal parks or wildlife refuges.

And the circumstances are far from the best. The federal agencies most concerned with putting the pieces together—the NPS and FWS—already are under severe budget and hiring constraints, yet their miniscule Alaska staffs are now faced with the need to develop management plans, conduct studies, and protect almost 38,974,000 ha of additional land in the remotest part of the nation.

10.3 Unfavourable political climate

The political climate has changed drastically under the new Administration. Preservation of park land is out of favour; development of oil and gas is a prime goal of the Reagan Administration.

The first legislative move to reduce the size of national park areas by 4.75 million ha and increase multiple use management areas has already been made through legislation introduced in both the Senate and the House during 1982 by Alaska's Congressional delegation.

10.4 Further studies needed

To carry out ANILCA, it will be necessary to pursue a number of activities and studies. Recommendations are to be submitted to the President on all of the remaining wilderness studies by 1985 and to the Congress by 1987. Baseline studies are needed in several of the areas to supplement research previously carried out, and also to support the management planning and wilderness studies now under way. Also the controversial studies concerning the coastline sector of the Arctic Wildlife Refuge in the eastern Brooks Range of extreme northeast Alaska must be completed.

10.5 Continuing cooperative effort essential

Since subsistence use will continue to be a basic yet controversial issue, studies are needed to monitor it and analyze its impact on resource protection. The native peoples, the state, and the federal government are and will continue to be the largest landowners in Alaska. Although their ownerships have some identity to them, they are mainly intermingled and associated with the ownerships of the others. Since wildlife subsistence users, and even the public do not readily recognize ownership and boundaries, it will become increasingly apparent that the 3 basic categories of owners (the Federal Government, the natives and the State of Alaska) must have more and more dialogue and more and more desire to work closely together to obtain some semblance of regional thinking, planning and management to assure the wisest use of the resources of Alaska for the benefit of all.

The 1980 ANILCA mandated the establishment of an Alaska Land Use Council to encourage and make possible such a coordinated effort. But its success is dependent not upon what comes down from above in the way of direction, but rather upon the recognition at the lowest level of government and among individuals and organizations, of the desirability for such an approach to resolve mutual problems, followed by its extension upward to take fullest advantage of the opportunities provided by the law.

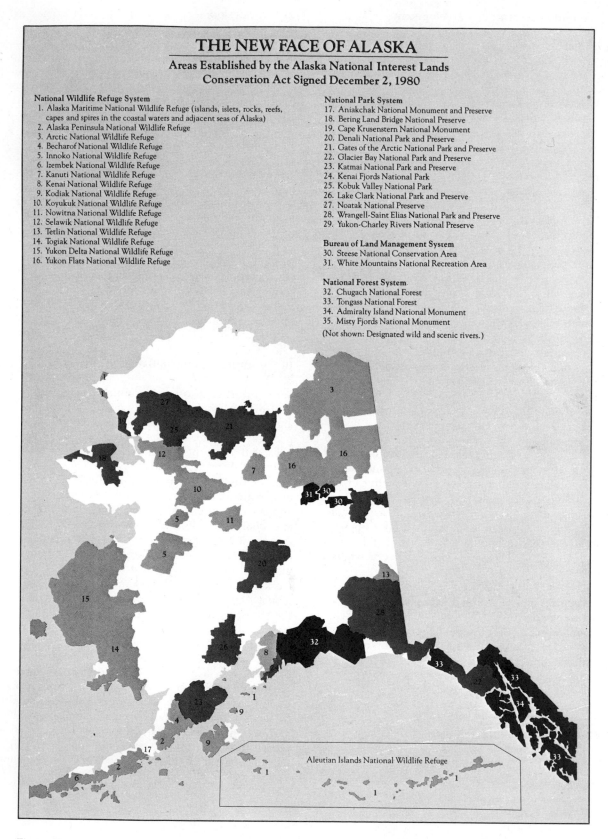

THE NEW FACE OF ALASKA

Areas Established by the Alaska National Interest Lands Conservation Act Signed December 2, 1980

National Wildlife Refuge System
1. Alaska Maritime National Wildlife Refuge (islands, islets, rocks, reefs, capes and spires in the coastal waters and adjacent seas of Alaska)
2. Alaska Peninsula National Wildlife Refuge
3. Arctic National Wildlife Refuge
4. Becharof National Wildlife Refuge
5. Innoko National Wildlife Refuge
6. Izembek National Wildlife Refuge
7. Kanuti National Wildlife Refuge
8. Kenai National Wildlife Refuge
9. Kodiak National Wildlife Refuge
10. Koyukuk National Wildlife Refuge
11. Nowitna National Wildlife Refuge
12. Selawik National Wildlife Refuge
13. Tetlin National Wildlife Refuge
14. Togiak National Wildlife Refuge
15. Yukon Delta National Wildlife Refuge
16. Yukon Flats National Wildlife Refuge

National Park System
17. Aniakchak National Monument and Preserve
18. Bering Land Bridge National Preserve
19. Cape Krusenstern National Monument
20. Denali National Park and Preserve
21. Gates of the Arctic National Park and Preserve
22. Glacier Bay National Park and Preserve
23. Katmai National Park and Preserve
24. Kenai Fjords National Park
25. Kobuk Valley National Park
26. Lake Clark National Park and Preserve
27. Noatak National Preserve
28. Wrangell-Saint Elias National Park and Preserve
29. Yukon-Charley Rivers National Preserve

Bureau of Land Management System
30. Steese National Conservation Area
31. White Mountains National Recreation Area

National Forest System
32. Chugach National Forest
33. Tongass National Forest
34. Admiralty Island National Monument
35. Misty Fjords National Monument

(Not shown: Designated wild and scenic rivers.)

Aleutian Islands National Wildlife Refuge

Figure 1.

NATIONAL PARKS, CONSERVATION, AND DEVELOPMENT

Annex: Alaskan Conservation Units of Great International Significance

Edgar Wayburn
The Sierra Club
San Francisco, California, USA

Alaska is overwhelming on many scores. It is a tremendous country: to see the entire state you would have to travel over 500,000 ha every day for more than a year. It has three formidable mountain ranges, the Brooks Range in the north, the Alaska Range in the centre (which crests in Mt. McKinley, the highest point on the North American continent) and the Coast Range which delineates the state's coastline in the south and southeast. And Alaska has some of the world's most valuable scenic, wildlife and cultural treasures. Fortunately, important areas of Alaska have recently been set aside in protected status to preserve various of these resources. At least five of these areas are of great international significance.

First is the mountain kingdom of the Wrangell-St. Elias Kluane International Park. This includes the Wrangell-St. Elias National Park and Preserve in the United States of 5 million ha and its contiguous counterpart, Kluane National Park in Canada of 3.1 million ha. It embraces Mt. Logan, at 5,852 m the second highest peak in North America, and the even more spectacular Mt. St. Elias, at 5,636 m the third. This unique international park also contains magnificent ice fields and immense glaciers, river glaciers, awesome canyons, such as the Chitistone, and many jewel-like lakes. The vegetation sweeps through every zone from coast to alpine meadow and includes lush rainforests as well as high fields of wild flowers. This is prime country for Dall sheep as well as mountain goats (few places in the world boast both species) and, near the coast, the brown bear is present. One third of the Wrangell-St. Elias park is classified as national preserve, which allows for sport hunting as well as subsistence use.

A second outstanding area is the 7.3 million ha Yukon Delta Wildlife Refuge. This tremendous preserve encompasses the rich deltas of the Yukon and the Kuskokwim rivers. Here are vast wetlands, countless lakes, and ponds, and rivers that wander in ever-changing meanders. Native people have lived within this region for thousands of years, and continue to do so. It is also home to one of the greatest arrays of birds on earth. Here shorebirds, seabirds, ducks, geese and swans rest and nest, and then travel all over the planet to reach their ultimate destinations—in Asia, Europe, to other parts of North America, and even the tip of South America. This wildlife refuge is also a home for pinnipeds which pour onto the shore in incredible numbers.

The third area is one of international archeological importance: this is the Cape Krusenstern National Park, lying north of the Arctic Circle and close to the northwest tip of Alaska. This park embraces and protects segments of the route which early man took in his progress from Asia to the North American continent across the now-drowned Bering Land Bridge. There are twenty-one identified beach ridges along the shore of Cape Krusenstern marking the sites where successive generations of people made their homes in North America. The land is still occupied by Eskimos who lead the same sort of subsistence life, depending upon the sea and the land for their food and shelter, as did their ancestors. Extensive and significant archeological work is in progress here, with the native people being directly involved in the excavations and evaluations.

The sub-Arctic region of Alaska running west of the trans-Alaska oil pipeline comprises a fourth significant newly protected area. The Gates of the Arctic National Park and the Noatak National Preserve together comprise nearly 5.7 million ha. Here there are fewer human settlements than in other national parks. This vast and mountainous region is relatively inaccessible, the only way in being by air. But once there, you can travel through some of the most spectacularly beautiful country on earth. The swift wild rivers are magnificent for kayaking, rafting and canoeing. The great, slow-moving Noatak provides excellent wildlife viewing along with a variety of lovely scenery. Backpackers find good going on alpine tundra (and slow going among the tussocks). This is also prime mountaineering terrain; the Arrigetch Peaks and Mt. Igigpak are outstanding for their rugged beauty and challenging heights.

Alaska's fifth area of international significance is the National Arctic Wildlife Refuge, now almost 7.3 million ha, with a Canadian counterpart of 2.1 million ha. This unique and tremendous protected area provides a vitally important habitat for many Arctic species of wildlife. It is also impressively beautiful, with a great variety of Arctic terrain stretching from the frozen coast to the spectacular mountains of the Brooks Range. Notably, this refuge complex protects almost the entire migration route of the Porcupine caribou herd, along with important calving grounds. This is one of the last great herds remaining in the increasingly pressured Arctic wilderness. Thus the National Wildlfe Refuge represents an

unusual opportunity to preserve a significant population of a species which once roamed over a large part of North America. The south slope of the Brooks Range within this refuge is hospitable for recreationists in the summer, although it can be covered by snow on remarkably short notice. On the northern slope, which descends from sharp peaks and has ribbons of icy rivers, kayaking and rafting can be exciting and enjoyable, albeit extremely chilly. Along with the caribou, polar bear, barren-ground grizzly and Arctic fox are inhabitants of this refuge. They, with the whales which travel the frigid waters of the Beaufort Sea, provide much of the subsistence for the Eskimos who are descendents of the original settlers of this demanding environment; all parts of these animals are put to good use. Subsistence hunting is part of the use of this wildlife refuge, and limited whaling by the Eskimo people occurs at present.

One great problem currently is the fact that oil and gas drilling is proposed for the coastal plains of this refuge. The region to be prospected includes the major calving ground of the caribou, as well as a principal migration route. The U.S. Fish and Wildlife Service is currently conducting a biological study to assess the possible impacts of such drilling.

Living with Exploitation in the Subarctic and Arctic of Canada

J.G. Nelson
Dean
Faculty of Environmental Studies
University of Waterloo
Waterloo, Ontario, Canada

ABSTRACT. *This critical review of exploitation and its effects covers the northern 40% of Canada, some 5 million sq km, and should be of interest to all those concerned with managing economic change and its environmental and social effects in sparsely populated parts of the world. The flora and fauna include many forest, tundra, wetland and ecotonal associations as well as whales, caribou and other animals whose ecology and use pose major challenges to the scientist, policy maker, planner and resource manager. The presence of a number of indigenous human groups complicates matters even further. Environmental management responses to recent development include general land use measures, and the establishment of protected areas of various types.*

1. INTRODUCTION

This case study of exploitation and its effects in Subarctic and Arctic Canada involves a vast, complex area of some 5,000,000 sq km, approximately the northern forty percent of Canada. The flora and fauna include many forest, tundra, wetland and ecotonal associations as well as whales, caribou *Rangifer tarandus*, and other animals whose ecology and use pose major challenges to the scientist, policy maker, planner and resource manager.

The human tapestry of the area is intricate, old, colourful and still being woven. Indigenous people trace their lineage to at least 30,000 years ago in the northern Yukon. The Inuit of the higher latitudes find forerunners in pre-Dorset Arctic hunters of some 5,000 to 6,000 years ago. Europeans entered the area in the 16th Century from both west and east. The introduction of their commercial system in the form of the fur trade, whaling and mining exposed the regional exploitation regimes of the native people to the virtually limitless demands of external markets. The result has been the acculturation and transformation of indigenous culture, and a boom-and-bust pattern in the northern economy. Faunal ranges and populations were drastically reduced by about 1900 when the introduction of game laws, the Migratory Birds Act, and other institutional arrangements combined with changes in taste and technology to allow for the slow and uneven recovery of caribou, musk-ox *Ovibos moschatus* and other fauna. Recent economic and other pressures may, however, have begun to cause new depletions; one example is the Kaminuriak caribou herd which ranges over thousands of square kilometres in northern Manitoba, Saskatchewan and the Northwest Territories (NWT) west of Hudson's Bay.

The present human populations of the NWT and the Yukon Territories (YT), the areas of principal interest in this paper, are about 55,000 and 30,000 respectively. Many of the people can be considered as indigenous, although common use of native languages occurs only among perhaps 600 people in the Yukon and 15,000 in the NWT. Overall the NWT and YT populations are young, with about half of the native people being less than 15 years of age. Both the native people and the European immigrants formerly roamed widely over large areas of this permafrost-rich environment in order to gain a living. Now they are increasingly concentrated in small scattered Subarctic and Arctic mining, trading, administrative and other settlements, whose population is generally in the hundreds. Some urban centres such as Inuvik in the Mackenzie Delta, Frobisher Bay on Southern Baffin Island, and Yellowknife and Whitehorse in the Yukon, are entrepts with populations ranging from 4,000 to 20,000.

The governmental fabric in Subarctic and Arctic Canada has a warp and woof which is very difficult to unravel. Parts of the area are in Manitoba, Saskatchewan and British Columbia provinces where governments are strong within the Canadian federal system in that they largely control land and resources within their jurisdictions. The remainder of the Subarctic and Arctic is in the NWT and YT, which are generally considered to be evolving to provincehood. They do not control their land and resources; they have substantial responsibility for wildlife species, but not habitat. Control over the latter generally resides in the federal government which retains title to more than 95 percent of the area. Federally appointed commissioners are the senior government officials in both territories. They report to the federal Minister of Indian Affairs and Northern Development (DIAND) and ultimately to the federal cabinet. They are advised by Councils or Assemblies which consist of elected members. The Councils or Assemblies can pass ordinances that must be approved by the federal government. The territorial legislative councils also name colleagues to executive groups, whose members frequently carry ministerial-type portfolios.

The local government system basically consists of three types of communities: incorporated urban centres with their own elected council and substantial fiscal and other autonomy; hamlets, with elected councils with limited powers; and unincorporated settlements, frequently homes for indigenous people with virtually no formal fiscal or other government powers. Evolution toward stronger territorial and local government has proceeded further in NWT, where recent elections placed indigenous people in a majority in the Assembly, and where community-based programmes are being more actively promulgated, for example, in tourism and parks. Both territories derive the greater part of their revenue from various types of federal grants inasmuch as the senior government retains most royalty, tax and other powers.

2. EXPLOITATION IN THE LAST 15 YEARS

Given this brief background, attention can now turn to the exploitation and conservation efforts of approximately the last 15 years, when the "oil boom hit the North". Efforts to find petroleum in the Canadian Arctic were initiated in the early 1960s, but it was not until 1968 and the finds at Prudhoe Bay on the north Alaska coast that massive and wide-ranging exploration spread through the sedimentary basins of northern Canada. This activity was accompanied by the continuous development of lead, zinc, gold and other mining, as well as hydro-electric proposals, "road to resources" programmes and other initiatives.

Study of actual mineral occurrence and meso- and mega- projects in Northern Canada shows how extensive the overall exploration and development thrust has been and can be. A number of mines have come onstream in the last decade or so, for example, Nanisivik, a lead-zinc operation in Strathcona Sound, North Baffin Island, or the lead-zinc operations on Little Cornwallis in the high Arctic islands. Many roads, power lines, water diversion projects and other land use changes have been associated with these mineral developments, as well as with exploration for petroleum. Large parts of the Mackenzie Delta are crossed by seismic lines.

Many relatively small and independent land use changes loom large when considered collectively and incrementally. When they are united with long- standing trapping, hunting and other so-called traditional activities, they leave only a few large areas in Subarctic and Arctic Canada as "untrammelled wilderness" or wildlands in the classical sense of the term. These areas are primarily located in large national parks or game reserves or in the very remote and inhospitable high islands, such as Axel Heiberg or Northern Ellesmere Island. In all such areas, however, tourism, park and other activities pose environmental impact and management concerns.

It is the huge development proposals—the mega-projects—that have received the greatest attention among industrialists, government officials, the native people and the public in the last decade. Some of these projects are significantly smaller than others, but still of large magnitude when compared to developments with which we are generally familiar. Mega-projects cost thousands of millions of dollars, depend on massive inputs of technology and labour (although the latter pertains chiefly to the construction stage) and directly and indirectly affect social, economic, biophysical and governmental arrangements over thousands of square kilometres. They generally require massive borrowing, take a decade or more to complete, if that ultimate state indeed ever occurs, and have been proposed in Canada mainly in response to the energy issues arising since the 1973 oil embargo and the rise of OPEC.

There are several outstanding examples: the James Bay Hydro-Electric Project in western Quebec, the Beaufort Sea-Mackenzie Delta petroleum development project in the west Arctic, and the numerous pipelines and tanker routes which are being considered to bring the oil and gas to southern markets.

Although very costly for industry, government and the public, meso- and mega- projects are nevertheless marked by uncertainty as to their technical and economic viability, even without considering the costs of unwanted impacts on society, economy and environment generally. The Beaufort Sea project is a good example. Numerous companies have been involved in exploration in the area since about 1975. Under varying government permit, tax-incentive and other arrangements, thousands of millions of dollars have been spent in dredging and constructing more than forty offshore islands in the shallow Mackenzie delta and offshore waters for petroleum exploration purposes. Additional wells have been developed from drill ships. Modern ice breakers have been built to test prospects of year-round shipping from the delta to east or west coast North American markets. Equipment staging areas, ports, and other support facilities have been developed, notably in existing communities such as Tuktoyatuk and Inuvik. Various pipeline routes have been considered as alternative modes of transport. Indeed, the now famous Justice Berger public inquiry on the first Mackenzie Valley Pipeline proposal was held in part because of an interest in transporting Canadian Beaufort Sea-west Arctic oil to southern markets, although the main goal here was to move Alaskan Prudhoe Bay oil to the United States through Canada.

As of the time of writing, several Beaufort Sea wells have been deemed as promising by industry, but there is no convincing sign yet of the elephant-sized fields that will be needed to pay for costly northern oil to reach market. It costs millions to drill a well. To this must be added the transport and other costs for any discovered oil to reach the consumer. It is worth noting at this point also, that the current global economic downturn, the emergence of a so-called "oil glut", high interest rates in Canada and elsewhere, and the development of a costly Canadian National Energy Policy have all contributed to current serious economic difficulties for petroleum companies operating in the North, notably Dome, a Canadian firm which has financed its Arctic operations in large part through substantial loans.

3. SOME INTERESTS OF NATIVE PEOPLE

Before turning to the land use, resource and environmental management measures that have been developed to control the social and biophysical impacts of exploration in Subarctic and Arctic Canada, some attention should be paid to the so-called "lands claims issue". In the late 1960s and early 1970s when the present northern oil boom began, few treaties had been made with the native people for land and other rights. In the south, such agreements historically have tended to involve a surrender of land ownership claims to the federal government in return for cash payments, some land (usually in so-called reserves), and other concessions. With the appearance of seismic crews in Banks Island and other northern communities, the local residents became concerned about disturbance of trap lines and other means of securing their livelihood. Negotiations have continued since with respect to the control of exploration and development impacts, the interest of the people in participating in new economic enterprises, and the settlement of the so-called land claims.

The Inuit have been divided in their attempt to complete a treaty. The Western Inuit or Inuvialuit came to an agreement-in-principle with the federal negotiators some three years ago, but this has not since been confirmed. The agreement contains provisions similar to those reached in the James Bay area in Quebec in that the Inuvialuit would receive cash and other concessions; own all rights to certain lands, including minerals; and receive certain land use approval and surface mining

rights on other lands, with the remainder being surrendered to the provincial government. In the first two land ownership classes the Inuvialuit would theoretically have considerable control over land use activities which could have adverse impacts on wildlife and other renewable resources.

On the other hand, a principal interest of the Inuit in wildlife is as consumers. As Justice Berger so clearly brought out in his public inquiry on the Mackenzie Valley pipeline, the land is not wilderness to the Inuit, but homeland and habitat. The Inuit generally wish therefore to maintain a productive wildlife and resource basis so they can continue to hunt caribou and other animals indefinitely. This is not to say that all wish a very active hunting and trapping life. Many desire also to share in the benefits of petroleum development or other change if sustainable and sound. They wish to work on oil rigs, in restaurants and other new facilities. They wish also to become increasingly entrepreneurial, to own, invest, and profit from change in the North to an equal, if not greater degree, than migrants from outside the region.

The indigenous people are not generally in favour of arrangements which eliminate all hunting, fishing, and trapping in national parks and related reserves. On the other hand, many of them would restrict mining and other activities from national parks because of the potentially deleterious effect on the wildife that the people wish to harvest. Indeed, in the Inuvialuit or COPE (Committee for Original People's Entitlement) agreement-in-principle there is support for the creation of a 13,000 sq km national wilderness park. The term wilderness is used because, while COPE wants hunting, fishing, joint management and other arrangements, it does not want tourism or other activities of the type often associated with a national park in southern Canada and other parts of the world.

Another aspect of the native wildlife issue is the evidence advanced by government personnel of declines in caribou herds, such as the Kaminuriak, that are purportedly ascribable to native hunting. Other factors are involved, however, and a court case was recently held over the issuance of a land use permit to a uranium company because the Inuit contended that such activity would have a negative effect on caribou populations. Relatively hard positions have been taken by the native people, industry, and some government personnel on such matters. On the other hand, the concept of caribou management boards has recently been developed and such a board will probably be created shortly to manage the Kaminuriak herd throughout its range in Manitoba, Saskatchewan, and the NWT. The Board will have representatives from the native groups and relevant federal and provincial government departments and will maintain data, coordinate studies, and make recommendations for harvest. This initiative is promising but the problems are complex, the jurisdictions and interests numerous, and success uncertain. The national Inuit association, the Inuit Tapirisat of Canada (ITC), currently has taken the position that it will not support the

Kaminuriak caribou management board until Inuit land claims are settled.

4. SOME ENVIRONMENTAL MANAGEMENT RESPONSES TO RECENT DEVELOPMENT

New national parks and caribou management boards are only some of the management responses to growing environmental pressures during the last fifteen years. Such responses can be divided into two broad classes: general land use, resource, and environmental management arrangements; and the establishment of protected areas of various types. The best nomenclature for the latter areas is uncertain. They have been referred to as protected, conservation, wildland, or natural heritage areas.

4.1 General arrangements

The federal government has been the principal agent in introducing several new Acts and sets of regulations, principally in the early to middle 1970s, during the first petroleum rush. Prominent among these are regulations under the Oil and Gas Conservation Act, which deal primarily with safety, pollution control, and other measures at or near the rig and associated facilities; the Arctic Waters Pollution Act, which deals with waste disposal and oil spills by tankers and other ships at sea, for example through the demarcation of shipping corridors; the Inland Waters Act; and the land use regulations promulgated under the Territorial Lands Act. An environmental assessment review programme (EARP) for projects funded or controlled by federal agencies also has been introduced through FEARO, the Federal Environmental Assessment Review Office.

The Inland Waters Act and the land use regulations were introduced with the idea of controlling significant negative impacts of new economic activities but not of preventing development. Both these sets of institutional arrangements have been in place for about a decade and undoubtedly they have made some contribution to protecting the resources and environment upon which other users are dependent. However, many observers consider that they could be improved substantially, particularly the land use regulations.

The EARP process has been heavily criticized during its evolution over the last decade. Some observers have objected to its administrative rather than legal basis and so to some perceived arbitrariness in application of EARP. The process is self-imposed in that the agency decides to undertake screening and an initial Environmental Impact Assessment (EIA). The agency proceeds, if significant environmental effects are anticipated, to a formal EIA. The latter is conducted through FEARO, an agency independent of other federal government units, although reporting to the Minister of Environment. Guidelines are developed, after public and other agency commentary. Public hearings are held on the project. Panels can recommend against a project, but more commonly approve with conditions intended to mitigate unwanted effects.

4.2 Protected, conservation or heritage areas

An array of different types of protected areas has been created in the Canadian north since the early years of this century. Among the earliest were the preserves established in the Arctic primarily to protect the wildlife or game needed for sustenance by the native people, although later the preserves were used as a means of establishing Canadian sovereignty in the Arctic. The first of the preserves was created on Victoria Island in 1919. By 1948 they had increased in number and area to the point where they covered the greater part of the present day NWT and YT. Within the preserves all but native people were prohibited by regulation from hunting, trapping, trading or trafficking without the Commissioner's permission. Certain exceptions were made, for example for prospectors operating under a prospector's license. In 1966, as a result of such factors as pressure for hunting privileges by the increasing number of migrants, the territorial council voted to abolish the largest of the preserves, the Arctic Islands Preserve. Subsequently others were eliminated, so that today only a few relatively small preserves remain, including Peel River on the NWT-YT border and Twin Islands in James Bay.

Game sanctuaries also have been created under the reserve provisions in the territorial game ordinances. The largest of these is the Thelon Game Sanctuary in the central mainland of the NWT. Such sanctuaries cover only a small part of the territories, but are important in that no one, including native people, is legally allowed to hunt within them. They are not rigidly administered however, and the extent of actual hunting is uncertain.

Bird sanctuaries have also been created subsequent to the 1917 Migratory Bird Act, with 15 now existing in the NWT. Management in these sanctuaries is confined to migratory birds, and even here managers are limited in regard to habitat management, inasmuch as the provisions of the Act do not include land ownership. The Canadian Wildlife Service, a federal agency, is responsible for managing the bird sanctuaries. Exploration for minerals and other economic activities is allowable under permit. The conservation effectiveness of the bird sanctuaries is controversial as few evaluations have been undertaken.

The 1973 Canada Wildlife Act is seen as a potential means of securing greater control over birds, their habitat, and other fauna in existing bird sanctuaries, as well indeed as other currently unprotected environmentally significant areas. The Canada Wildlife Act provides for wildlife areas for the purpose of research, conservation, and interpretation. These areas can be purchased, leased or controlled through agreements with other government agencies or private owners, including native people. Only one Canada wildlife area has been created in the NWT and YT to date, in large part because the land is mainly owned by another government agency, DIAND. The interests of native people, industry, and the style of the Canadian Wildlife Service are probably inhibiting factors here as well.

Interest in national parks in Subarctic and Arctic Canada began early in the century. Wood Buffalo National Park was established in 1922 primarily to protect bison (*Bison b. athabascae* and *B. b. bison*). Unlike most Canadian national parks, Wood Buffalo has consistently been managed to provide for some hunting by native people in accordance with conservation controls. In a sense Wood Buffalo is a precursor to agreements that have been proposed for areas under consideration for national parks in the Canadian North today, such as northern Ellesmere Island.

In the 1930s a surge of interest in new national parks occurred in Canada, and park reserves were established in various parts of the country, including Kluane in the southwestern Yukon. No implementation of the Kluane proposal occurred until about 1970, when as a result of growing concern about oil exploration and its effects, pressure developed to create new national parks to protect outstanding natural areas in the North. Three national park reserves were subsequently created in 1972, their final confirmation being dependent on the still unsettled native land claims. The three national park preserves are Kluane, Nahanni in the southern corner of the NWT, and Auyuittuq in southeastern Baffin Island. These parks all exceed 13,000 sq km in area, vast in the eyes of many, but not in terms of northern ecology, where large areas are needed to protect the large ranges of wolves, caribou and other significant animals as well as representative ecosystems. None of the three reserves meet the latter goal for new parks.

In 1979 Parks Canada, the agency responsible for national parks, proposed six new candidate areas in the North: Wager Bay, Bathurst Inlet, Ellesmere Island, Banks Island, the North Yukon, and a Pingo park near Tuktoyatuk on the fringe of the Mackenzie delta. These candidate areas were selected on the basis of inventories of natural features in the North. The inventories aimed at the identification of areas that had sufficient geologic, biologic or other importance to meet designation as Natural Areas of Canadian Significance (NACS). NACS and national parks were to be created in each of the natural regions identified by Parks Canada in the North, as well as other parts of Canada. The natural regions were delimited primarily in accordance with landform and vegetation criteria. NACS and ultimately national parks were to be set aside in each natural region so that samples of the Canadian landscape could be protected in as undisturbed a state as possible for use by recreationists, tourists, scientists and citizens generally. Even given the three existing national parks and the six recently proposed parks, a number of northern natural regions remain unrepresented in the national park system.

In the 1970s, park ordinances were passed by the territorial councils for the creation of territorial parks in the North. Several types of parks were provided for, including small campground or wayside parks, recreation and historic parks, and larger environmental parks. In both the YT and the NWT the parks that have been created are small, for example 48 campgrounds in the Yukon. The establishment of larger parks has been handicapped by industrial concerns, government reluctance to lose possible mineral resources, and the limited budgets provided for park purposes. Another barrier has been the perception that national parks should be the means of creating larger parks in both northern territories. Attitudes against larger parks remain relatively strong in YT today, but appear to be moderating in the NWT where the park role in tourism and associated economic benefits seems to be increasingly appreciated.

Other types of conservation areas are being considered for the Yukon and NWT, including: national landmarks which are designed to protect unique geological or other features usually over relatively small areas; wild and scenic rivers, and coastal and marine parks. A major obstacle to the creation of all 3 types of areas is jurisdictional disagreements among federal and provincial government agencies. Parks Canada has wished to own or directly control such areas where they are judged to be of national significance. However, provincial and territorial governments have seen it as possible to designate areas as of national significance even though owned and controlled by the provincial or territorial rather than the federal government. Other agencies, such as the Department of Fisheries and Oceans, which theoretically could take a leading role in planning and managing marine reserves, have traditionally followed a utilitarian form of resource management in which the emphasis is on sustained resource use rather than preservation of fish and associated ecosystems. Parks Canada is increasingly interested in northern marine parks. However, the implementation of the concept is fraught with interjurisdictional problems, as well as the special management difficulties posed by the fluid nature of the sea and its flora and fauna.

Another type of candidate protected area is the International Biological Programme Site (IBP). More than 100 of these areas were identified by scientists in the ten-year period of the International Biological Programme from 1968-78. In 1976 a special interdepartmental government committee was set up to decide on how to manage them. Six areas were selected for detailed study and in 1981 a proposal was made for one of these, Polar Bear Pass. The proposal provided for multiple use and for management by a committee, without designation under any special conservation legislation. The proposal was criticized as insufficient to protect the Polar Bear Pass area by public groups such as the Canadian Arctic Resources Committee. No proposals for other IBP areas have been forthcoming from government. No ecological site or other comparable legislation like that passed by provinces such as British Columbia or Quebec apparently is being considered for the YT or NWT.

5. CONCLUSIONS

Many conclusions and recommendations have been made during the foregoing discussion so that only a summary of major environmental management needs will be offered at this point.

- More stress should be placed on renewable and aesthetic resource management in planning for development in Subarctic and Arctic Canada. Disproportionate emphasis has been put on mining and non-renewable resource development. A more balanced approach is desirable. This approach should also reflect greater interest in smaller scale development in a regional context, to balance the present strong orientation to costly externally oriented and fiscally risky mega-projects.
- Policies should be re-cast to follow more closely the three basic principles of the World Conservation Strategy, i.e. maintain natural diversity, essential ecological processes, and resource productivity. These principles should be accompanied by a stronger commitment to development in a human ecological context, i.e. paying greater attention to community requirements and preferences through closer work with local people. This is occurring to some degree in national parks planning and in the planning of territorial parks in the NWT. It may also occur more frequently as a result of the development of a new land use planning procedure which is being introduced by the federal government in both territories.
- To begin a more balanced land use and environmental management regime, better methods should be developed for identifying and mapping wildlife calving areas, migration routes, unique or representative flora and fauna and other features and processes which are of special significance to native people and development generally. Without proper management of such environmentally significant areas (ESAs), wildlife and other resources could decline over much larger areas. Landscapes and ecosystems of much value for harvesting, recreation, tourism, research, and conservation could also lessen in quality and social utility. Land use surrounding such ESAs should be mapped in terms of compatibility or incompatability with the special biotic or other characteristics of the ESAs. Acts, agencies and other institutional arrangements should also be analyzed in terms of advantages and disadvantages for managing unwanted impacts of activities in the ESAs and surrounding areas. A coordinated set of protected area types and general land use management arrangements should then be set up, preferably in the context of regional as well as comprehensive planning. A study intended to lead in this direction has been completed for the Yukon by some faculty members and students in the Faculty of Environmental Studies at the University of Waterloo. The study can be improved upon, but is intended as a catalyst for more coordinated and balanced planning and management in the face of the many development proposals of the last decade. As a result of the study it has been recommended that about 25 percent of the Yukon be placed in national and territorial parks, game sanctuaries, Canada Wildlife Areas, and other protected areas.
- Some stress should be placed on the use of conceptual models which show the role of ESAs in more balanced development and environmental management. These conceptual frameworks should show how basic types of land use relate to one another, to management guidelines, and ultimately to the institutional arrangements whereby the system will be managed.
- Better means of describing, analyzing and ultimately of improving land use, resource, and environmental management should also be found. Few normative models of comprehensive management systems exist as a basis for comparing what is, with what should be.
- More stress is needed on finding ways and means of interesting politicians and administrators in the kind of land use, resource and environmental management described in the foregoing recommendations. Perhaps the present economic difficulties, and the abandonment of some of the mega-projects, will create more interest in varied, smaller scale, sustainable development which has strong links with the region as well as the nation and the international community. In the latter regard there has not been sufficient opportunity to discuss MAB (Man and the Biosphere), the World Heritage Convention and other international initiatives in this paper. Some good beginnings have been made in the North however; for example, Kluane National Park (Yukon) and Wrangell-St. Elias Wildlife Sanctuary has been declared an International World Heritage Site. A principal aim of MAB is to promote more effective regional planning around national parks and other protected areas. Hopefully, the concept will soon be implemented in the YT and NWT.

Acknowledgements

This paper is based on knowledge gained during study of and participation in northern development problems during approximately the last 12 years. The study and participation has involved Inuit land claims research, national park and protected areas, coastal and land use issues, pipeline impact assessment, Beaufort Sea development, and study of environmentally significant areas in the YT and currently the NWT. Many people have been colleagues in aspects of their work and I wish especially to thank Carson Templeton, Irving Fox and W. Winston Mair, who were members of the Alaska Highway Pipeline Panel, John Theberge, Terry Fenge, Murray Coolican and Don Gamble of CARC, Al Davidson and his colleagues at Parks Canada, Connie Hunt, Robbie Keith, Bob Scace, Julie Gardner, Sabine Jessen, and all the members of the YESA and NWTESA teams. I also wish to acknowledge the valuable financial help of the University of Waterloo, the Northern Student Training Grant Programme of DIAND, Parks Canada, CARC, and the Canadian Donner Foundation.

Cooperation Between Government and the Private Sector: A North American Example

G. Ray Arnett
Assistant Secretary for Fish and Wildlife and Parks
US Department of the Interior
Washington, D.C., USA

1. INTRODUCTION

As an appointed representative of the present administration, I am primarily concerned with the development and implementation of administration policy as it relates to the management of the national parks and the federal wildlife refuges of the United States. Though the management of these areas is based on laws that go back over 100 years, the administration of these laws is subject to changes in emphasis, primarily as a reflection of the state of society at any given time. In administering these laws, the basic objective must be to use and protect the parks in ways that allow the maintenance of the basic integrity of the resources and of the natural processes that sustain them. The specific means of doing this may vary as long as that primary objective is met.

Today I want to talk briefly about ways in which government and the private sector may work together to achieve that objective, emphasizing what has been done in the United States.

2. THE LEGAL BASIS FOR PRIVATE INVOLVEMENT IN NATIONAL PARKS

In the United States, the parks have always been valued for both visitor use and preservation of natural and scenic resources. The law establishing Yellowstone National Park, the first national park in America, set the theme that has, with variations, been fairly consistent throughout the growth of the national park system of the United States.

In 1916, Yellowstone was ". . . dedicated and set aside as a public park or pleasuring ground for the benefit and enjoyment of the people."

The park was placed under the exclusive control of the Secretary of Interior who was to issue regulations providing for the preservation ". . . from injury or spoliation of all timber, mineral deposits, natural curiosities or wonders within said park and their retention in their natural condition". This language has the effect of banning incompatible lumbering, mining, selling of natural curios, or capitalizing for commercial gain upon the outstanding wonders and vistas of the park (the geysers, Yellowstone Falls, etc.).

However, because the park was to be used by the people, visitor accommodations were anticipated in the Yellowstone Act. Let me quote that section:

"The Secretary may, in his discretion, grant leases for building purposes for terms not exceeding 10 years of small parcels of ground, at such places in said park as shall require the erection of buildings for the accommodation of visitors. All of the proceeds of said leases, and all other revenues that may be derived from any source connected with said park, are to be expended under his direction in the management of the same, and the construction of roads and bridle paths".

This language marks the birth of the concessions operations in the national park sytem. It recognized that certain visitor services could best be provided by private enterprise operating under reasonable regulations. These regulations established by the Secretary and sometimes The Congress have the effect of avoiding operations that are not necessary for the use of the park, or are in poor taste, or designed to unfairly charge the visitor for the services rendered. It also suggests that the money earned by the Government in franchise fees and from other sources within the park, should support, to the extent possible, the operation of the park. While Congress has changed the law regarding the disposition of franchise fees, the idea behind the use of the fees to support park operations is still attractive and receiving renewed attention.

In 1918, less than two years after the National Park Service was established to manage the growing number of parks, Secretary of the Interior, Franklin K. Lane, in a policy directive to National Park Service Director Stephen Mather reaffirmed that parks were to be protected in "essentially their natural state" for the use of the people. He, however, added a third proviso to preservation and use. He stated that: ". . . the national interest must dictate all decisions affecting public or private enterprise in the park."

This line of reasoning was culminated in 1965 when the Congress of the United States passed the Concessions Policy Act. Again, let me quote from that act.

". . . the Congress hereby finds that the preservation of park values requires that such public accommodations, facilities and services as have to be provided within. . . (the national park system) areas should be provided, only under carefully controlled safeguards against unregulated and indiscriminate use, so that heavy visitation will not unduly impair those values, and so that development of such facilities can be limited to locations where the least damage to park values will be caused. It is the policy of the Congress that such development shall be limited to those that are necessary and appropriate for public use and enjoyment of the national park area in which they are located and that are consistent to the highest practicable degree with the preservation and conservation of the areas."

3. CONCESSIONS IN NATIONAL PARKS

The relationship between the National Park Service and park concessioners spans more than a century. Today there are some 520 park concessioners operating in 105 units of the national park system. Their gross receipts totalled $266 million in 1980, with over $5 million in franchise fees being paid to the Treasury of the United States. The gross revenues may be broken down as follows: 23% for food and beverage, 17% for souvenirs, 16% for lodging, and 12% for other services. These services include visitor tours, marinas, boat and canoe rentals, horseback rentals, auto services, etc.

However, in keeping with the language of the Concessions Policy Act, the present National Park Service policy on concessions is that new services will not be provided within the park if they can be adequately provided by the private sector outside of the park boundaries.

When Great Smoky Mountains National Park was established in the 1930s, Secretary of the Interior Ickes agreed in writing with the States of North Carolina and Tennessee that new concession facilities would not be provided in the park, thus leaving to the cities of Cherokee, North Carolina and Gatlinburg, Tennessee and other nearby communities the responsibility for providing food, lodging, automobile services, etc., for millions of annual park visitors.

In addition, the National Park Service adopted a policy statement that campgrounds would not be provided in the parks unless the private sector and others were incapable or unwilling to provide them outside of the parks. In the case of the Great Smoky Mountains National Park alone, there are over 100 private campgrounds outside of park boundaries which have the effect of:

- eliminating costs to the American taxpayers to finance campgrounds within the park;
- providing positive economic incentives to the region; and
- protecting the resources of the park against the provision of unnecessary visitor facilities.

4. OTHER FORMS OF PRIVATE-PUBLIC COOPERATION

Another important area of cooperation between the public and private sectors for protection of parks is private philanthropy. A number of national parks have been largely preserved through private gifts of land. Among these are Acadia National Park in Maine, Great Smoky Mountains National Park in Tennessee and North Carolina, the Virgin Islands National Park in the United States Virgin Islands, and Grand Teton National Park in Wyoming. The Rockefeller family philanthropies alone have contributed tens of thousands of acres of land to the national park system in these and other national parks.

In 1967, the Congress established the National Park Foundation, a charitable and non-profit corporation, to receive private gifts of real and personal property and income or interest therefrom for use by the national park service in carrying out the purposes of the parks. This allows tax deductable gifts from any source to be used anywhere in the national park system—a very useful condition.

Another very important public-private relationship exists between the parks and cooperating associations. These associations are organizations chartered with individual parks or groups of parks that sell interpretive literature usually in park visitor centres. Congress has authorized service employees to work part-time with these non-profit organizations in such things as sales, record keeping, and selection and ordering of literature. The profit from these sales is then available for use in park interpretative programmes.

The Historic Sites Act of 1935 authorizes the Secretary of the Interior to accept donations of historic properties for designation as national historic sites. It also permits the Department to enter into contracts with coporations, associations or individuals for the protection, preservation, maintenance or operation of such sites. Recently the Congress extended that authority to all historic parks, permitting contract operation of these parks by the private sector and others. It also permitted the leasing of historic properties to the private sector for certain approved uses with the revenues from the leases being retained by the National Park Service for historic preservation activities. Elsewhere, tax laws encourage the renovation, repair, and rehabilitation of certified historic properties by the private sector for a variety of purposes, thus adding to their preservation.

Recent tax law also allows tax deductions to individuals who donate an easement for an approved conservation purpose. Regulations to implement the law are still being developed, but the law has the effect of permitting donations of easements that assure the continued use of the property will meet an approved conservation purpose. Such donations need to be consistent with federal, state, or local governmental conservation policy and yield a significant public benefit. This law also has the potential of protecting private lands within park boundaries without cost to the government for acquisition. At the same time it permits continued private uses of such land consistent with the purpose of the park.

Another way in which the national park service and Department of the Interior cooperate with the private sector is through the National Park System Advisory Board. This group of distinguished private citizens, appointed by the Secretary for a specified term of years, adds an important extra viewpoint to the Secretary and Park Director in making major policy decisions affecting the parks. In addition, many recently authorized units of the national park system have their own advisory commissions designed to provide local and regional input to the park superintendent in the formative years of park acquisition and development. Often, these terminate after a given number of years.

Another cost-effective and innovative means of using the private sector in assisting in park operations is through the Volunteers-in-the-Park Act. This law permits volunteers—and there are many of them who are eager to work in a national park—to perform needed services including maintenance activities. The law covers personal liability and provides minimal amounts of federal funds to cover the costs of travel and meals incurred by these volunteers. Such programmes have the potential for significantly stretching the size of the park operating staff and provide low cost and often very professional assistance in interpretation and other services.

The private sector may also assist in the maintenance of historic and cultural landscape. In a fairly large number of historic parks, the National Park Service leases park land to nearby farmers for agricultural uses. This yields several benefits. For the farmers, it increases the size and, hopefully, the profits of his operation. For the National Park Service, it provides a modest income from the leases, but more important, provides for the maintenance of the historic scene at little or no cost. Without the leases, employees would need to be hired to maintain the landscape in its open, historical agricultural condition.

The private sector is used in another very important way. The major cost of maintaining a park system is in operations—the day-to-day activities required to keep roadsides mowed, trash collected, buildings cleaned, roads repaired, etc. Traditionally, this has been done by park employees, and this will continue to be the case, of necessity, in many remote park areas. From the standpoint of achieving park objectives in the most cost-effective manner, however, it is important to look at contracting with the private sector to do this work. While the direct costs may in some cases appear to be roughly equal, the long term or hidden costs of using park employees may suggest a different picture. The activities are largely seasonal, but employee salaries and benefits (such as retirement insurance and sick and annual leave) must be paid all year. In addition, there are costs for park housing, where provided, as well as maintenance facilities and utility costs.

5. CONCLUSIONS

While this paper has dealt only with the public/private relationship in park management within the United States, I suspect that many other nations have developed their own innovative means of using the private sector in park management. In our own experience, we are moving toward an expanded relationship as new authorities on leasing, contracting, volunteerism, and tax law open up new avenues of mutually beneficial cooperation.

If we analyze the types of public/private cooperation involved, we may see that they are applicable in the broadest sense to any park system, regardless of the nation's legal and traditional framework. If one accepts this, then developing the specifics for cooperation is possible. Essentially there are three broad areas of cooperation where the private sector may play a role.

The first and most obvious is where the private sector provides a revenue generating service that is needed or desired by the park visitor. This may include food, lodging, campgrounds, supplies, tours, and rental of services or specialized recreation equipment. Nonprofit groups and volunteers may also provide services for the visitor.

The second relates to hiring the private sector to provide necessary operational services. This may include janitorial services, grounds, road and facility maintenance, and security services, to mention some of the more obvious.

The third way relates to cooperation for the protection and management of park resources. This is a particularly important area to investigate for the future protection of significant landscapes. In the United States, tax law permits benefits to the donor of land for park use, whether it be an outright gift of the land or an interest in the land, permitting certain approved uses to be retained by the donor. Resource protection, particularly for historic properties and landscapes, is also possible by leasing park land or structures for productive uses that are not inconsistent with the purpose of the park. This not only generates income but eliminates or reduces park maintenance costs.

Another variation of landscape protection being looked at in the United States and already in practice in England and in the French regional parks is to establish parks where the majority or a considerable portion of the land remains in private ownership. Such arrangements create new challenges in developing methods to coordinate public use, to protect private property, and to identify appropriate private economic uses. While this may not be particularly applicable to the pristine national parks that preserve outstanding scenic and natural resources, it is perhaps the most effective, and may be the only acceptable means of future protection of cherished national landscapes.

In summary, the world economic picture seems to indicate that prudent and tough-minded management will be required if units of the national park systems are to provide areas of public use and enjoyment, and continue to be adequately maintained in the years ahead. Park managers must increasingly look elsewhere for assistance. With a little forethought and imagination, conditions can be worked out where both government and the private sector benefit from activities of the sort discussed in this paper. What the unit manager must be concerned with is meeting his objectives for public use and park protection in the most efficient and cost-effective way possible. When the private sector can assist in this effort, it should be encouraged to do so. Concessioners have added greatly toward public enjoyment of our national park units, and have assumed responsibilities that have resulted in significant benefit to the national park systems. Private concessioners play an important role in the overall management of our parks and the prudent, innovative park manager will seek ways to encourage greater use of private concessioners in an effort to effect cost savings to the taxpayer, increase the enjoyment of a park experience for the visitor and continue to protect and maintain those units of land and historical sites that comprise the national park system.

Protected Areas for Teaching and Research:
The University of California Experience

Jeffery A. Kennedy
Natural Land and Water Reserves System
University of California
Berkeley, California, USA

ABSTRACT. *California's rapid population growth has resulted in the loss of essential natural habitats long used for teaching and research. This paper outlines the efforts of the University of California to design, develop and administer a system of scientific reserves encompassing over half of California's habitat diversity. Reserves without on-site support facilities are shown to be little-used for teaching and research, regardless of site diversity or proximity to a campus. Small size and encroaching urbanization are the main threats to reserve integrity. As a consequence, reserve management focuses on the compatibility of adjacent land use. Development of a habitat classification scheme is shown to be central to reserve system design, and faunal representation in a habitat-based system is documented for California's native mammals. This case study provides an example of how to design a protected area system to meet teaching and research needs.*

1. INTRODUCTION

Throughout the history of conservation, the world's great universities have played an important role in protected areas management and the training of protected areas personnel. University research programmes develop the theoretical tools, baseline data, and field techniques needed to understand and manage complex ecosystems, while their instructional programmes provide the background education in the natural and social sciences needed by protected areas personnel. Many offer specific curricula in park and resource management. In addition, university public service and extension programmes are a major vehicle for promoting people's understanding of conservation. Clearly, the continued viability of the world's protected areas is intimately dependent on the research findings and educational services provided by its academic institutions.

What is less obvious, perhaps, is the dependence of these same institutions on the "goods and services" provided by protected areas. In the field-oriented natural sciences, there is a limit to what can be learned from a textbook or reproduced in a laboratory. In fields as diverse as botany, geology, ecology, archaeology, ethology, paleontology, wildlife management, genetics, zoology, population biology, and entomology, what is learned in the classroom is only *preparation* for what must ultimately be learned by direct observation in the field. Accessible protected areas which serve as living classrooms and laboratories for field work are essential to a university's teaching and research functions. Protected areas also serve as ecosystem libraries, *in situ* storehouses of genetic diversity, which provide the central data base for all teaching and research in the field sciences.

This case study describes the efforts of the University of California to design, develop, and administer a system of natural reserves encompassing a representative cross-section of California's habitat diversity specifically managed for teaching and research use. The resulting system, the Natural Land and Water Reserves System (NLWRS), is the only reserve system of its size, scope, and diversity in the world that is owned and operated by a university. This case study is presented with the hope that it might provide insight into the ways in which national park and protected area systems might serve comparable needs of the educational institutions of other countries.

To place the NLWRS in world perspective, the State of California includes portions of five biogeographic provinces in the Nearctic Realm; Californian, Oregonian, Sierra-Cascade, Great Basin, and Sonoran (Udvardy, 1975). These provinces in turn encompass a highly diverse mosaic of natural habitats—approximately 390 habitat types (Cheatham, Haller, and Holstein, 1981), primarily determined by the vegetation. This habitat diversity springs in a large part from the diversity of California's physical environment ranging from 32° to 42° north latitude along 1,900 km of Pacific shoreline, California's 42 million ha encompass 10 landform provinces and the lowest and highest points in the continental United States (-86 m and 4,418 me respectively). Regional climates are equally varied with precipitation ranging from 3,050 mm per year in the mixed evergreen forests of the northwest to less than 50 mm per year in the southeastern deserts. Temperatures range from unknown minima in the high mountains (certainly less than -30C in the southeastern deserts). The high degree of biotic diversity and endemism is the direct result of this diversity of the physical environment and a paleo-history of California vegetation which, since the early Eocene, has had tropical, temprate, and arctic floras. As a consequence, the flora is diverse for the temperate zone, with over 7,000 species of vascular plants, roughly a third of which are endemic to the state. A large number of reserves are thus needed to encompass this diversity, and to date, 26 reserves have been established (Fig. 1), totalling 33,865 ha. Two are currently being considered for biosphere reserve designation (Philip L. Boyd Deep Canyon Desert Research Center; Landels-Hill Big Creek Reserve) and one is a prospective addition to an existing biosphere reserve (Santa Cruz Island Reserve).

2. PROBLEM STATEMENT

2.1. Problem definition and documentation

Between 1945 and 1965, California's population grew from 8 million to 18 million, resulting in significant losses of natural habitat to development. (California's population is now approximately 22 million, making it the most populous state in the United States). Included in these habitat losses were field sites long used by the University of California for teaching and research. The loss of 20 sites was documented for just one of its campuses alone, and comparable losses were being experienced by its five other campuses then in existence.

Moreover, even in areas where habitats remained more or less undisturbed, faculty and students were having their field studies repeatedly disrupted by human intervention. Some of it was wilful vandalism of equipment and the taking of study specimens, but much of it was inadvertent disturbance of phenomena and biota under study by conflicting but otherwise legitimate land use such as recreation. The state's natural diversity which had been the wellspring of the University's ex-

cellence in the field-oriented natural sciences was rapidly becoming unavailable for teaching and research use.

2.2. Needs to be met

What was needed was a system of natural reserves, broadly representative of California's natural diversity, to meet the teaching and research needs of the University. Full land ownership was not required so long as long-term protection of the habitats and security of equipment and studies could be ensured. Leases, easements, and cooperative use agreements would be acceptable, subject to certain general requirements. A ten-year term, was deemed to be the minimum acceptable time period for these less-than-fee acquisitions. The ability to provide for support facilities and a minimum level of protection was also identified as an important need: fencing, limited roads and trails for access, storage sheds for field gear, simple shelter for researchers and classes (ranging from primitive campsites through tent platforms and rustic cabins to substantial dormitories), minimum maintenance weather stations, and synoptic collections of biotic and physical elements. So was the ability to regulate user access and manage conflicting reserve uses within the carrying capacity of the site. Since many of these reserves were likely to be small by ecological standards, management of existing land uses *beyond* reserve boundaries would also be an important need. It was recognized that management compromises might be required for those sites which were not fully owned. The reserve system would be available to any qualified student, teacher, or researcher, worldwide.

3. BACKGROUND

3.1. The University of California administration

To better understand the case study which follows, an historical understanding of the University of California's administrative organization will be helpful (University of California, 1974).

The Act establishing the University entrusted its organization and government to a corporate body titled The Regents of the University of California. The Board of Regents was to consist of 24 members, 16 appointed by the State Governor for 16-year terms and 8 *ex officio* members, including the Governor and the Presidents of the University, the Alumni Association, and the State Board of Food and Agriculture, among others. The role of the Legislature was limited to "such . . . control as may be necessary to insure compliance with the terms of the endowments of the University and the security of its funds." The intent of this system of governance was to insulate the University from adverse political influence.

From an initial campus in the San Francisco Bay

Area, which had become California's focus of commerce and culture followig the gold rush of 1848, the University expanded by 1920 to six sites that would eventually become full campuses, each with a Chancellor acting under the President of the University. By 1923, the University of California led the world's universities in enrollment with 14,061 full-time students. In the mid-1950s, local autonomy was granted to the campus Chancellors and in the 1960s, there was massive growth with the addition of three wholly new campuses to meet the needs of California's rapidly growing population. By 1975, enrollment approached 120,000 full-time students at nine campuses, with over 100 research units and affiliated schools.

3.2. Previous attempts to solve the problem

With the loss of field sites becoming steadily apparent in the early 1960s, several individual faculty sought the approval of The Regents to acquire field sites that were important to their department or discipline. All of these individual efforts failed for the same reasons (Norris, 1968): (1) No matter how significant the site or how well-documented the need, each was an isolated proposal, without benefit of a cohesive University-wide plan covering the needs of all the campuses; (2) because there was no plan, The Regents had no way of evaluating how any one acquisition might meet the needs of the state as a whole; (3) similarly, University budget analysts had no way of gaging the cumulative impact of individual acquisitions on the University budget; (4) because of the semi-autonomy ultimately achieved by the individual campuses, there arose certain provincial concerns about the budgeting for a site used by more than one campus (Who could use a given reserve? What happens if one campus gets two reserves and another only one?); (5) perhaps most significant the time was not yet ripe for the reserve concept for, at that time, only a few farsighted ecologists understood the environmental implications of the population explosion California was then experiencing—a broad base of political support had not yet developed.

3.3. Initial actions to create the NLWRS

With an appreciation of why previous efforts to solve the problem had failed an *ad hoc* committee of faculty was formed in 1963. This committee approached the President of the University with a proposal to research and develop a comprehensive, statewide plan to establish a natural reserve system for the entire University. The proposal was accepted and the committee formally appointed. The report of the faculty committee outlined the design and administration of a reserve system, catalogued some 50 sites around the state as potential reserve acquisitions, and formally recommended be created within the University. In January of 1965, The

Regents created the NLWRS and designated seven existing University properties as initial components of the system.

4. ACTIONS AND CONSTRAINTS

4.1. Reserve system design

4.1.1. Habitat classification system. Since a primary goal of the system was to protect a representative cross-section of California's natural diversity, a habitat classification system was needed to guide the acquisition process. Initially, a simplified system of 36 habitat types in eight major categories was developed, based primarily on vegetation and secondarily on landforms. As the system grew, a more sophisticated classification scheme was developed encompassing 178 terrestrial and aquatic habitat types in 10 major categories to provide more specific acquisition guidance (Cheatham and Haller, 1975). This basic classification system was subsequently adopted by the California Natural Diversity Data Base, a joint project of the The Nature Conservancy and the California Department of Fish and Game, and expanded to 390 habitat types in 1982.

4.1.2. Acquisition criteria and reserve classes. Acquisition criteria were developed covering habitat diversity and site significance, degree of disturbance, distance from the campuses, urgency of protection, protection feasibility, legal factors, and cost. An administrative procedure was developed to evaluate prospective acquisition using these criteria. Three classes of reserves were envisioned: near-campus reserves accessible during regularly scheduled class and laboratory sessions to be used for both instruction and student field projects; multipurpose reserves consisting of large, ecologically diverse, relatively pristine natural areas capable of supporting a wide range of teaching and research use from more than one campus (these are the major units of the system); and special habitat reserves featuring less diverse areas which typically focus on special habitats or features such as pygmy forests, vernal pools, typical examples of widespread habitat types, or geologic field mapping sites. It was estimated that approximately 50 reserves would be needed to encompass the state's natural diversity.

4.1.3. Administrative structure and staff. The selection and administration of NLWRS reserves was to be carried out under a University-wide committee of faculty, assisted on each campus by an analagous campus committee. The campus committees were to be responsible for identifying, evaluating, and recommending natural area field sites in support of their faculties' instructional and research programmes. Once acquired, these sites would be assigned to a campus for day-to-day supervision and operation, requiring the appointment of a faculty manager and management advisory committee for each reserve. Part-time secretarial assistance and a small travel and field expense budget were to be available for the campus committee. The committee was to screen acquisition requests in light of the state-wide plan and to develop descriptive literature on the system. This committee would report through the University-wide Dean of Research to the University President and The Regents. Legal aspects of acquisiton were to be handled by the University Treasurer for Real Estate, The Regents, and the General Counsel's office. The Chairman of the committee was to have secretarial support and a small budget to cover the costs of travel, and the development of promotional and descriptive materials. This administrative structure mirrored that of the University as a whole: a University-wide administration coordinating relatively autonomous campus administrations.

4.1.4. Reserve facilities and caretakers.

From the outset, it was recognized that certain minimal facilities would be required for these natural areas to be usable as field sites for teaching and research. It was anticipated that the facilities at the larger multi-purpose reserves would be upgraded ultimately to full biological field station status as their teaching and research use grew. Several reserves, including the Hastings Natural History Reservation, Santa Cruz Island Reserve, and the Boyd Deep Canyon Desert Center, came into the NLWRS with pre-existing field station facilities. Not all reserves were expected to require on-site caretakers, but those that did were to be funded initially at the systemwide level with a two-year phaseover to campus budgetary support.

4.1.5. Programme.

Unlike many biological field stations, the NLWRS as a whole did not have a teaching or research programme itself. Rather, such programmes were to be developed by individual departments, research institutes, and faculty members at each campus. In this regard, the NLWRS was designed to function much like a library—it could emphasize certain types of "collections," but otherwise it was simply available as a passive resource for teaching and research use.

4.2. Acquisition programme

4.2.1. Initial actions.

In the Spring of 1966, the chairman of the new University-wide NLWRS committee spent three months touring the state to identify, evaluate, and prioritize prospective acquisitions. No comprehensive inventory and ranking of California's natural areas or elements of natural diversity was then in existence. Altogether, 76 potential field sites were visited—26 more than initially identified—of which roughly 40 were judged to be desirable additions to the system. From this data base, the University-wide committee chose two or three sites on which to begin negotiating. The negotiation process proved to be long and involved.

4.2.2. Cooperative agreements: public lands.

Aproximately 50 percent of California is in public (non-private) ownership with roughly 45 percent in Federal ownership (National Forests, 20%; Bureau of Land Management, 15%, National Park Service, 4%; Department of Defense, 4%; other, 2%) and 5 percent in state ownership, much of it in the State Parks System. Although most of these lands were limited to high mountain or desert areas, representing a relatively small fraction of California's habitat diversity, they held promise for significant field sites. Initial contacts were somewhat discouraging. Designation of new reserves in other than pre-existing, Federal Research Natural Areas (Federal Committee on Ecological Reserves, 1977) was resisted as an undesired management complication. Although interest was expressed in pursuing cooperative agreements with Federal Research Natural Areas on National Forest Lands, such agreements would not have added much beyond the status quo. Realizing this, the decision was made to concentrate acquisition efforts on sites not then protected by any programme.

4.2.3. Cooperative agreements: University lands.

For similar reasons, it was decided not to pursue cooperative agreements with existing University lands harbouring natural habitats such as experimental forests, fishery research stations, and agricultural experiment stations (Fig. 1). Similar sites were managed by other colleges and universities in California, both public and private. Again, nothing was lost by this course of action beyond a loss of administrative coordination since these sites were still available to the University community. Without protective action, however, important field sites in private ownership *would* be lost.

4.2.4. Private acquisitions.

In the 17 years since its establishment, the NLWRS has added 19 reserves to its initial complement of seven sites. Several were University of California lands, such as the Bodega Marine Reserve, Coal Oil Point Reserve, and the Elliott Chaparral Reserve. Most were either gifts or purchases at less than market value for tax benefits to the seller. A few were use agreements or conservation easements.

4.3. Funding: Constraint on NLWRS development

Adequate funding is essential to the success of any programme, and the NLWRS was fortunate to receive significant funding for acquisitions early in its history. In its first eight years, $575,000 in matching grants from the Ford Foundation generated approximately $1,750,000 for acquisition. Gifts and bargain sales of land significantly extended the purchase power of these funds.

Although funding for acquisitions was adequate, funding for facilities development, maintenance and operation, and staff support lagged far behind. The explanation lies in the historical development of the University. Shortly after the creation of the NLWRS, the University's 100-year history of rapid growth came to an end, as population growth abated, and the economic recession and inflation of the 70s reduced the effective budget of the University. The reserve system was unable to compete with more pressing budgetary needs, significantly retarding the full development of the system (see Section 5.3.)—a graphic example of the interdependence of conservation and economic development.

5. RESULTS AND FUTURE DIRECTIONS

5.1. Acquisitions

In spite of formidable obstacles to adequate budgetary support, the NLWRS has made remarkable progress toward its goal of providing a representative cross-section of California's natural diversity in a system of natural areas managed specifically for teaching and research use.

5.1.1. Habitat and species representation.
The existing system of 26 reserves encompasses 106 of the 178 habitat types identified for the state (Cheatham and Haller, 1975), or 60 percent of the total. Acquisitions have focussed in the southern third of the State where habitat losses due to development have been the greatest and where the greatest number of campuses are found. Largely unrepresented are the characteristic habitat types of the northern and far eastern portions of the State: the North Coast Ranges, the Klamath and Cascade Ranges, the Basin and Range, and Modoc Plateau landform provinces. In addition, there is no representation in the Great Central Valley, although most of the natural habitats there have been lost to agriculture, flood control, and irrigation projects. Several future acquisitions currently being negotiated will fill many of these gaps. Twenty-three of the reserves are fully owned, one is a conservation easement, and two are incorporated by a use agreement, including the largest single reserve, Santa Cruz Island (22,050 ha).

An unconfirmed variable in the acquisition process has been the assumption that faunistic representation is proportional to habitat representation. This assumption has recently been confirmed for California's native, terrestrial mammals. A preliminary mammalian checklist of all NLWRS reserves revealed 65 percent of the state's species, 81 percent of its genera, and 88 percent of its families are encompassed by the 60 percent of the habitat types now represented in the reserve system. The classification scheme appears to be working as intended.

5.1.2. Site selectivity.
Given the initial absence of a comprehensive habitat inventory, several early acquisitions were less-than-optimum in terms of diversity, integrity, protectability, and usability (indeed, two have since been sold or "decommissioned"). But on the whole, the acquisition criteria have maintained system quality.

Over 200 sites have been evaluated for inclusion in the NLWRS, many as gifts, and of these only ten percent have met the criteria for reserve designation.

5.1.3. Cooperation and comparable programmes.
In spite of an early decision to postpone cooperative agreeements on pre-existing protected areas in public ownership (to concentrate instead on unprotected land in private ownership), cooperative agreements have proven to be a valuable tool in expanding the reserve system. For example, the Año Nuevo Island Reserve is owned by the California Department of Parks and Recreation, but under a use agreement the University manages the research programme on the island. Approximately half of the Boyd Deep Canyon Desert Research Center is land owned by the Bureau of Land Management and incorporated into the reserve under a use agreement. Cooperation with the Bureau is likely at the Granite Mountains and Stebbins Cold Canyon Reserves as well. An isolated spring habitat for an endangered desert fish will soon be incorporated into the NLWRS. It will be cooperatively managed as an ecological reserve by the Bureau of Land Management, the California Department of Fish and Game, the Los Angeles Department of Water and Power, and the University of California. The U.S. Forest Service is supporting Federal Research Natural Area designation for the watershed encompassing the James San Jacinto Mountains Reserve, which will provide the basis for future research and management cooperation.

Cooperation with The Nature Conservancy (TNC) has been particularly valued. Santa Cruz Island is owned in part by TNC and the Landels-Hill Big Creek Reserve was a joint project with TNC and the Save-the-Redwoods-League. At least two other TNC-UC cooperative reserves are currently being negotiated. The NLWRS was also intimately involved in the creation of the California Natural Area Coordinating Council and the California Significant Natural Areas Programme, which is a TNC State Natural Heritage Programme administered by the California Department of Fish and Game. These programmes are helping to inventory, prioritize, and protect natural areas and field sites outside the NLWRS.

5.2. Availability and use

The existence of NLWRS reserves has proven invaluable to students and researchers in the field sciences. In southern California, extended class trips can run an ecological transect from the coastal habitats of the Santa Monica Mountains east across the Los Angeles basin, over the Peninsular Ranges, and on to the low and high deserts beyond, visiting six NLWRS reserves, and staying overnight at three of them in the process. Extensions of this transect can be made west to the Channel Islands or north up the east side of the Sierra Nevadas, with overnight accommodations at both sites. Total immersion field ecology classes from several campuses simply cannot function without these reserves.

In the 1979-80 academic year, instructional use accounted for approximately 3,500 users and approximately 48,000 user-hours; in addition research use accounted for approximately 800 users and approximately 56,000 user-hours. The institutions represented included the eight general University campuses, fifteen campuses of the California State University and College system, fourteen other California universities and colleges, and some twenty institutions from outside California. In addition, numerous public agencies, natural history organizations, and individuals have been accommodated as the level of University demand permits.

Over the last ten years, the level of use has doubled as the availability of the reserves has become better known, campsites and other support facilities have been provided, and new reserves have been added. The greatest use has been experienced on the sites having overnight facilities, or at sites which are on or near a general campus.

5.3. Facilities and reserve use

Due to limited funding, provision of adequate facilities has been a major deficiency of the NLWRS. Only seven reserves have on-site laboratory, housing, or other support facilities of biological field station calibre, although five additional sites are close enough to a campus to indirectly benefit from campus support facilities. The balance have minimal improvements primarily limited to fencing, roads, and trails. The implications of this deficiency are significant. There is a direct correlation between the degree of on-site facilities support and the level of site use, irrespective of habitat quality or travel distance from the nearest campus. Ninety percent of the use of the reserve system occurs on the ten reserves with housing and work space facilities. Unless they are on or adjacent to a campus, reserves without basic campgrounds, housing, and secure storage space are little used. Without use, there is little programmatic support for a reserve regardless of habitat quality or other site values. Yet given the difficulty in obtaining maintenance funding, there is an institutional incentive to resist constructing additional facilities since their maintenance cannot be ensured. It is a vicious cycle, and a major problem to be addressed in the future.

5.4. Staffing, management, and protection

A small staff of five in the University-wide office handle the legal, budgetary, administrative, and publications tasks for the system as a whole. Staffing at the campus level ranges from none beyond interested faculty members to part- or full-time support staff in campus-based departments and research institutes. Eight of 26 reserves have paid caretakers and six additional reserves have donors or former landowners living on-site or imme-

diately adjacent, providing modest protection and supervision.

The major threat to the reserves is adverse impacts from adjacent development and the loss of adjacent habitats to that development. Some reserves are becoming habitat islands in a sea of development. To address this problem, the University has developed special consultation rights as an officially designated Trustee Agency in California's environmental impact reporting process. The consultation process allows the NLWRS to evaluate development projects which can result in project modifications and the reduction or elimination of adverse impacts to adjacent NLWRS reserves. Many of our reserves are so small that we have been forced in our protection and management efforts to look routinely beyond reserve boundaries to monitor development which might have adverse impacts on reserve values. Much effort is spent through the consultation process in coordinating the wise development of adjacent lands.

Recent developments in conservation genetics, island biogeography, and reserve design (Gilpin and Diamond, 1980; Frankel and Soul, 1981; Wilcox 1980; Erlich, 1982) clearly indicate that most of the reserves in the NLWRS are much too small to preserve their natural diversity on an ecologically significant time scale. Twenty NLWRS reserves are less than 120 ha in size, although some are adjacent to protected public lands, increasing their effective size substantially. Fortunately, the large multi-purpose NLWRS reserves are relatively well-protected from major disruption. There is an emerging trend in protected areas management to overcome the ecological deficiencies of small size and irregular configuration by enlisting the support of local peoples to protect and manage adjacent habitats (see papers by David Western and Norman Myers). Such local support flows from economic and social benefits derived from the protected area. Unfortunately, the benefits from such small protected areas are either absent or insufficient to counter the economic incentives of urban and suburban development in an industrialized society.

Limited buffer zone preservation is possible, but realistically, such small reserves will ultimately become habitat islands with an associated decline in species diversity. Reserve-based educational extension programmes will be instrumental in preserving the habitat that does remain.

In the final analysis, the primary product or benefit of teaching and research reserves is information—and the understanding of ecosystem functioning that information provides. By studying the decrease in the integrity and diversity of the smaller reserves, we may gain a better understanding of how to manage and preserve larger, more protectable reserves.

5.5. Future directions

Provision of adequate funding for operations, maintenance, management and facilities development is the highest priority need for the NLWRS. A staff fund-raiser has been retained, and efforts to develop a "friends programme" of corporate and individual annual donors has begun. However, the current economic recession, and extensive cutbacks in government funding have made fund-raising more difficult than ever before. The sale of one of our low diversity sites, a gift of the Union Oil Company, is hoped to provide the corpus of a maintenance endowment to meet needs not otherwise funded. Providing funding for critical support facilities will be a high priority for our most important reserves.

Acquisition of new reserves has essentially ceased, save for critical habitat and buffer zone additions to existing reserves and the addition of three new reserves long under negotiation. Future acquisitions, if any, will most likely be limited to habitats in the northern and eastern portions of the state, currently without representation in the NLWRS.

Publications and promotion are another high priority. Currently, only four reserves have published descriptive brochures which identify reserve values and facilities for prospective users. A two-year publications programme has received initial extramural funding to meet the need. A promotional colour movie on the system is nearing completion, and a new descriptive brochure and quarterly newsletter have also been prepared for distribution. Academically, a contribution series has been initiated to catalogue research done on NLWRS reserves, and an intensive field instruction programme drawing students nationwide is being discussed to foster increased awareness and broader use of the system. By fostering the use and understanding of the NLWRS in these ways, we hope to build the political support needed to more successfully compete for funding.

CONCLUSIONS

Natural habitats managed in a system of protected areas are clearly invaluable in supporting the teaching, research, and public service missions of the University of California in the field-oriented natural sciences. Simple protection of habitat has not been sufficient to meet these needs; the provision of adequate on-site support facilities and caretaker supervision is essential, unless the reserves are on or adjacent to a campus. Adequate staffing and funding are, of course, essential to reserve acquisition, facilities development, and maintenance, as well as to habitat protection and management. In keeping with the World Conservation Strategy, a major need exists to demonstrate the importance of educational use of protected areas such as the NLWRS in supporting the conservation of living resources for sustainable development.

Few universities are likely to have the resources or the opportunities to develop a reserve system comparable to the NLWRS. National systems of parks and protected areas, however, may help to meet these needs to the benefit of protected areas, the academic community, and the world at large. Teaching and research are two of society's needs that might be met, at least in part, by the world's national parks. This case study is offered with the hope that it might provide insight into the nature of those needs and the support required to meet them.

University of California
Natural Land and Water Reserves System

NLWRS RESERVES

Berkeley Reserves
1. Bodega Marine Reserve
2. Chickering American River Reserve
3. Hastings Natural History Reservation
4. Pygmy Forest Reserve

Davis Reserves
5. Stebbins Cold Canyon Reserve

Irvine Reserves
6. Burns Piñon Ridge Reserve
7. San Joaquin Freshwater Marsh

Los Angeles Reserves
8. Santa Monica Mountains Reserve Complex

Riverside Reserves
9. Box Springs Reserve
10. Philip L. Boyd Deep Canyon Desert Research Center
11. Etiwanda Wash Reserve
12. Granite Mountains Reserve
13. James San Jacinto Mountains Reserve
14. Motte Rimrock Reserve
15. Sacramento Mountains Reserve

San Diego Reserves
16. Dawson Los Monos Canyon Reserve
17. Elliott Chaparral Reserve
18. Kendall-Frost Mission Bay Marsh Reserve
19. Ryan Oak Glen Reserve
20. Scripps Shoreline-Underwater Reserve

Santa Barbara Reserves
21. Carpinteria Salt Marsh Reserve
22. Coal Oil Point Natural Reserve
23. Santa Cruz Island Reserve
24. Valentine Eastern Sierra Reserve

Santa Cruz Reserves
25. Año Nuevo Island Reserve
26. Landels-Hill Big Creek Reserve

Legend
■ University Campuses
○ NLWRS Reserves
△ Related University Facilities

Related University Facilities
1. Hopland Field Station
2. Sierra Foothill Range Field Station
3. Sagehen Creek Wildlife-Fisheries Research Station
4. White Mountain Research Station
5. Whitaker's Forest Research Station
6. Blodgett Forest Research Station

Figure 1.

Future Directions for the Nearctic Realm

Harold K. Eidsvik
Parks Canada
Ottawa, Canada

ABSTRACT. *The 1980s will be a period of consolidation. The 1970s saw doubling of park and wilderness areas, leaving both budgets and personnel stretched to the maximum. New funding will be scarce as governments attempt to restrain growing deficits, so managers will be cautious about taking on new responsibilities. Professional management capabilities are increasing and this will lead to significant improvements in the planning and scientific management of protected areas. As many future problems are outside protected area boundaries, managers will need to work with external agencies. Significant expansion will occur in protected areas in northern Canada. The protected area system will be intact for the 1992 Congress.*

1. INTRODUCTION

The biogeographic area described as the "Nearctic Realm" includes Greenland (Denmark), Canada, most of the United States and portions of Mexico and Central America. This paper concentrates on the northern portions of the realm. The realm has led the way in contemporary conservation: it produced the world's first national park (Yellowstone 1872); it developed the world's first National Park Service (Canada 1911); and contains the world's largest national park (Greenland National Park, 70 million ha).

National Parks and similar protected areas are a part of the fabric of North American life. They are creations of political systems which have been more or less responsive to the mainstream of the conservation movement.

The United States and the Canadian Park Services employ some 24,000 people and have a 1982 budget of approximately $600 million. In the Nearctic Realm there are some 138 million ha of protected areas (including the 70 million ha Greenland National Park), a vast area three times the size of Malaysia or almost as large as Indonesia. The over 400 parks represent 3.5 percent of the land mass.

Forecasting trends and directions of different governments and levels of government is at best an exercise in speculation and at worst an exercise in mis-information. Nevertheless, some basic elements appear to be consistent:

- The rapid growth of the 1970s in both area and numbers of Parks is not anticipated for the eighties.
- Federal, provincial and state budgets for park organizations are stable but inflation is eroding purchasing power and reducing opportunities for new programmes.
- Local or regional involvement through public participation programmes will continue to be high.
- Within the framework of broad policy statements, decision-making will continue to be decentralized so that parks will reflect regional perspectives.
- As the North American recession deepens, the pressure on governments to utilize protected areas for non-conforming uses will increase. This includes forest and water resources as well as unknown potential mineral resources.

The past has a tremendous influence on the future. To ignore it would be folly. For we cannot bring about change in the future unless we understand the past. In North America there is over 100 years of tradition in park management. This tradition must be respected in looking to the future. At the same time we must remember that the professional tools available to park managers have only been in existence for some twenty years. Here I refer to park systems planning, master planning, island biogeographic theories and so on.

As park managers, we have a responsibility to a large public constituency. We have a responsibility to non-governmental groups which have helped shape political decisions, and we must respond to politicians as a part of the political process.

As professionals we are responsible for the management of protected areas in the full awareness that we live in a rapidly changing world. Natural catastrophies such as volcanic explosions, floods and landslides change natural systems. Technological and social changes influence the way we use or perceive natural areas. We are not charged with preserving static situations, we are charged with managing dynamic systems. To ensure that we pass our heritage on to the next generation in a secure state, we must develop appropriate management techniques to cope with change.

2. SETTING THE STAGE

Four important techniques or methods which are applied to operating our natural areas are preservation, protection, management and integrated planning. Each is appropriate in certain places at certain times. Each of these approaches can achieve our objective of passing on our natural heritage to future generations. This can only be done if we apply the appropriate management techniques at the appropriate time and in the appropriate place.

2.1. Preservation

Preservation as a management technique is appropriate when we have large natural systems operating in response to natural forces. It was appropriate to Yellowstone National Park when it was established in 1872. There were few people in the region; pressures on the natural resources were non-existent. A similar situation still prevails today in much of the Greenland National Park and in portions of the proposed Ellesmere Island National Park in Northern Canada. But preservation is not an appropriate management technique for Yellowstone National Park or Banff National Park today.

2.2. Protection

The need for protection, which I would call phase two of management evolution, led to the establishment of the National Park Service in Canada in 1911 and in the United States in 1916. The establishment of warden or ranger services became necessary when human populations grew in areas surrounding the national parks. There came a need to regulate hunting or poaching and to provide for visitor safety. Protection remains the major responsibility in the management of all protected areas.

Protection services are normally oriented inward, in effect protecting the park *from* the local community rather than *for* the local community.

What is causing a great concern in the Nearctic Realm today is not what is happening inside the parks but what is happening to the 96.5 percent of the land which is not protected. Obviously, with only a small percentage of the land protected, what happens in the surrounding area will have a profound effect on protected areas.

Robert Cahn (1982) writes, "It is the external influences—energy development, urban encroachment, second home construction, air and water pollution and the diversion of water from parkland—that give the greatest cause for alarm. The 1980s surge of development is beating against the parks, which only a few years ago were considered islands of sanctuary."

Today, for example, in contrast to the previous concerns of overuse, we find the spread of acid rain. "In the Adirondack mountains of upstate New York, officially declared ever wild since 1892, more than half the lakes are in critical condition, more than 200 of them devoid of fish. Fish have disappeared completely from at least 140 Canadian Lakes, mainly in Ontario—and scientists fear that as many as 48,000 of Canada's lakes could become fishless over the next decade" (Eckholm, 1982). It is evident that even with extensive areas, large budgets and sophisticated technology, protected area managers can no longer directly control the future of their territories.

Protection as the management philosophy for national parks began to change in the mid-fifties. At this time new techniques and theories in game management and wildland management led to increasing manipulation of natural systems. This was done to achieve specific conservation objectives. The culling or cropping of "over-abundant" local populations of elk or buffalo is an example. During this period there was an increasing awareness that laissez-faire management was not a universal solution if conservation objectives were to be achieved.

2.3. Management

One of the new conservation tools that evolved in the late fifties was zoning. The provisional master plan for Banff National Park in about 1960 applied zoning as a management tool to define wilderness and intensive use areas. The Outdoor Recreation Resources Review Commission in the United States developed a comprehensive zoning system for public lands during the early sixties.

Flowing from zoning as a managment tool was recognition that different parts of a large natural area required different management techniques. Strict nature reserves were identified within national parks to ensure the protection of unique natural features. Roadless areas were identified as were areas for intensive visitor use. The application of these new tools led to master plans or, in today's terminology, management plans. Generally speaking, however, management plans continue to focus inwardly with insufficient attention being paid to the surrounding region.

2.4. Integrated planning

The pressing need in the next decade is to integrate our planning with that of the surrounding region. In other words, we must examine our protected areas and ensure that their role in sustaining development is clearly understood. The contribution of national parks to sustaining development lies in their protection of natural resources such as watersheds to provide clean water, forests for genetic seed stocks, forests to provide wildlife habitat and to ensure soil stability, plants to provide genetic resources, and undisturbed ecosystems to provide research baselines. In addition, national parks can play a vital role in regional and local employment as well as in regional, national and international tourism.

While there is a definite need to integrate the planning of national parks and other protected areas with regional plans, this need is not perceived by managers as being critical in North America. Long-established traditions have fixed a management style in which governments and non-governmental organizations have confidence that the parks can best achieve their objectives under present management regimes. It is therefore unlikely that major changes in management style will occur in North America in the next decade. Integrated planning does not appear to be a feasible approach at this time. There are many reasons for this but certainly federal/provincial/state jurisdictional arrangements are the most critical.

I remain firmly convinced that integrated planning is the best long-term solution to ensure the protection of our natural heritage. I am convinced of this because what is happening outside the parks is having such a great influence on what heppens inside the parks. Similarly, the parks have a tremendous influence on social and economic circumstances of nearby communities.

3. FUTURE DIRECTIONS

3.1. A global perspective

In the next decade, there are few forecasts that can be made with a high degree of accuracy. Most are speculative.

The period we are reviewing at this Congress, 1982 to 1992, is irrelevant in the time scale of natural systems. Yet in the time scale of political systems the decade reflects one or two electoral periods which could be extremely relevant and in the time scale of technology

we could self-destruct. It would be irresponsible, however, to permit these factors to dominate our thinking.

3.2. A technological perspective

Some scientists have seen nature as they orbited the planet. They have seen the power of man and technology, as well as the dominance of nature on our earth. The "Planet Earth" and all its limitations have been brought to our attention through their efforts. Among this group we find those who believe that the future is in human hands and that nature can be manipulated or replaced.

While technologists produce tools capable of bringing about our destruction, they also bring tools for our survival. For example, remote sensing for wildlife and forest management along with radio collars, mini-computers, helicopters, and tranquilizers are all in common usage throughout the realm. Each of these technological innovations contributes to protected area management and will become increasingly important.

Technology also brings increased user pressures through off-track vehicles, light aircraft, balloons, kites, SCUBA equipment, and winter recreation equipment. The impact on natural areas of these visitors remains a concern for many conservationists.

It is difficult if not impossible to speak of technology and conservation without commenting on the potential adverse effects of military programmes. In their best light, military programmes compete with all other elements of government for financial resources. In the Neartic Realm, this budget is $250 thousand million per year. In order to put this in scale, we can look at park budgets, which are comparatively large, but still total less than $1 thousand million. The difficult question conservationists must force politicians to answer is "Do the people want 5 more helicopters for $75 million dollars, or a B-1 bomber for about $60 million dollars or a park system which is not eroded away?" Somehow, park budgets pale into insignificance when compared to military programmes which at their worst will lead to the destruction of all natural systems.

Once potential areas are perceived to have value, then the burden of proof falls on the proponents to prove that the protected area has a higher political value than the competing uses. In the United States, a very strong lobby working within the political system has assured a high profile for conservation values. Questions of social and economic benefits relating to employment and development are central to these debates and demonstrate the difficulty of placing a value on these special areas, whose benefits are largely intangible.

What is required under these circumstances is the planning of protected areas within a much broader concept of land use planning. As Eckholm (1982) states, "Nature Reserves cannot be successfully managed in isolation from society. They must be planned within the context of broader regional developments."

A similar philosophy is pronounced in the World Conservation Strategy, which holds that conservation and development must go hand in hand. As the competition for natural resources becomes more intensive there is increasing evidence that the regional planning route will be followed. The challenge for conservationists lies in building, maintaining and supporting local constituencies who can influence the politics of conservation in the next generation.

3.3. Summary of future directions

If the future were but a projection of the past, most of us in government conservation agencies would welcome a repetition of the decade of the seventies. The world's largest national park was established in Greenland, and in both Canada and the United States explosive growth led to the doubling of the areas within the park system. In fact, globally the seventies were a decade of unsurpassed growth in protected areas.

Looking through the window into the eighties most managers see a period of consolidation. In the United States, Secretary of the Interior James Watt has said, "We will not expand the system until we manage what we have well." In Canada the retrenchment has not been as strongly stated. The expansion of the National Park System has slowed for different reasons. A general downturn of the economy has left all levels of government cautious with respect to new initiatives. Parks Canada looks to new initiatives in northern Canada where there are still significant natural regions not represented in the park system. In relative terms, the investment required to establish these parks are low in comparison to their importance for conservation.

The perspective for the next ten years is therefore one of relative stability. It will be a period where one will see relatively limited acquisition in relation to new parks. At the same time, it will be a period dedicated to improving the management of existing parks with existing budgets. I anticipate that the 1992 World National Parks Congress will look back on a decade which saw:

- An increasiang public awareness of the values of their natural heritage.
- An increasing recognition of protected areas as volatile political issues.
- A shift from protection to management as the underlying philosophy of park administrators.
- No significant shifts in the percentage of land dedicated to protected areas.
- Significant improvements in the management of marine protected areas.
- Continued decentralization of management authority to field managers.

- Increased responsiveness to regional/local advisory groups within the framework of management plans.
- No significant shifts in government expenditures toward conservation programmes.
- An increase in expenditures on resource management.
- A significant improvement in the public and political understanding of the scientific rationale behind the protected areas programmes.
- An increasing public and political understanding of the role of parks as recreation areas and the distinctive role of parks as protected areas.

4. CONCLUSIONS

The past decade has seen a maturing of park systems around the globe—the "Global Society" has arrived. Much can be learned from areas such as Pampa Galeras in Peru, the Great Barrier Reef Marine Park Authority in Australia, the Ngorongoro Conservation Authority in Tanzania and Plitvice National Park in Yugoslavia. Leadership in the conservation world is no longer the eminant domain of the Nearctic Realm.

One hundred plus years of park management experiences have been shared, through the International Seminar, through PARKS Magazine and through personal exchanges. Much remains to be gained from this sharing. Maturing global parks systems now ensure that the sharing could become a two-way process. The parks of the Nearctic Realm are caught in some traditions which require close scrutiny in relation to the parks of other realms. In particular, there is a need to reflect on natural resources management, on relations with adjacent communities, on the protection of marine resources and on the relationships between capital and operational budgets.

The long-term value of parks systems lies in their conservation of genetic resources and as baselines for science. However, with increasing external influences such as acid rain, their value as scientific baselines will decline. With increasingly sophisticated wildlife management techniques their values as refuges will decline, and with increasing tourism their uniqueness as places rarely visited will decline.

If the national parks remain as areas where no resource extraction takes place, then they will become increasingly unique. It is their isolation from our exploitative tendencies which will enhance their value to future generations.

In closing, I would like to say that we in North America look with a great deal of happiness at the achievements of our colleagues around the world and particularly here in Indonesia. We fully anticipate that the next decade will bring innovative ideas from you to us and that we will welcome them and hopefully have the foresight to apply them.

Chapter 12
The Neotropical Realm

Keynote Address: The Neotropical Realm

Gerardo Budowski and Craig MacFarland
Centro Agronomico Tropical de Investigacion y Ensenanza (CATIE)
Turrialba, Costa Rica

ABSTRACT. *The Neotropical Realm has been particularly active over the past decade, both in establishing new areas and in innovative management approaches. The concept of different categories of protected areas is now firmly established in the Neotropical Realm, and management planning is widespread. It is now time to develop more fine-grained systems of assessing protected area coverage at the national or regional level, in order to provide the guidance necessary to further develop protected area systems. Difficulties faced in the Realm include planning and implementation of categories other than national park, planning and implementation of national systems, implementation of management plans, and cooperation between scientists and managers; these difficulties are balanced by an equally impressive set of accomplishments.*

1. INTRODUCTION

The Neotropical Realm extends from the southern subtropical areas of the USA to the southern tip of South America, in "Tierra del Fuego", which is swept by cold Antarctic winds and is anything but tropical or warm.

There is a rich pre-Columbian heritage on conservation in the Neotropical Realm which probably included protected areas, although we understand only a fraction of the past situation. We know that the Incas protected the vicunas in the Andean region, and very possibly their pasture grounds. The decline came under the colonial status and even after independence it was not possible to stop this trend, in spite of some legal moves undertaken in the early 19th century by nobody less than the liberator Simon Bolivar. In Mexico, the Aztecs kept sophisticated semi-natural gardens of medicinal plants. Also, many Amerindian groups, such as the Kuna of Panama, have the practice of establishing natural botanical parks or reserves for the exclusive use by medicine men for the collection of medicinal plants.

There is also some evidence that some of the small rodents were favoured by certain practices, such as protecting trees that produce food, such as *Brosimum* spp. Some trees like the *Ceiba pentandra* in Cuba or animals like the tapir in southern Venezuela were considered taboo, because of their association with human spirits. There are doubtless many other examples.

During the past century natural areas have been receding notably due to a traditional policy of "opening" new areas for agriculture, grazing and colonization, triggered mainly by population growth. This trend has increased over the last 15-20 years, triggered mainly by the very wasteful conversion of tropical forests to pasture, mostly to export lean beef for the hamburger industry in industrialized countries, where it is mixed with germ-fed beef (to meet the legal requirements for maximum permissible fat content). The rate of such conversion during that period reached alarming proportions and continues to grow worse.

Conservation through the official protection of areas of outstanding value probably began in Argentina, through the pioneer efforts of Perito Francisco Moreno in the early 20th century. The first record of a legally protected area was probably in Mexico, in 1898, known as Bosque El Chico Conservation Area, but it does not figure in IUCN's list and like many other protected areas one must assume that it was a well intentioned gesture which has not survived the following decades.

Many of the finest national parks of Argentina were established in the thirties. This included Iguazu, a frontier park created in 1934, which also was established on the Brazilian side in 1939. In Brazil, two national parks, Itatiaia and Serra dos Orgaos, also received legal status in that decade. From then through the decade of the sixties, little by little national parks and protected areas were established in most countries of the realm. For historical and traditional reasons, the emphasis was almost exclusively on national parks and to a small extent on a few other very similar categories (natural monuments, scientific or biological reserves, wildlife sanctuaries). Other management categories were largely ignored as possibilities, indeed many of them had not yet been conceived. Likewise, the process was characterized by the "piecemeal" declaration of individual parks and similar protected areas, usually for highly disparate and varied reasons; it was not conceived of in terms of complete systems or subsystems of wildland management units, either of one or a few categories such as national park, even less so of a broader range of categories covering many types of wildlands management.

One important step which helped to stimulate the declaration of more parks and protected areas as well as broaden the number of different management categories being utilized, was the Convention on Nature Protection in the Western Hemisphere, approved in 1940 and since then ratified by 15 countries (IUCN, 1981).

By far the greatest achievements have taken place in the past 10-15 years, when both the number of legally established areas and the total area included have increased approximately three times. Likewise, the number of different management categories being utilized has increased notably, with categories such as multiple-use management area (national forest or forest reserve), biosphere reserve, water production reserve (hydrological reserve), archeological monument, resource reserve, indigenous or anthropological reserve and national recreation area, becoming ever more widespread throughout the realm during the period. A particularly striking example of this is the case of Central America reported by MacFarland and Morales (1981), where between 1969 and 1981 the number of different management categories went from 6 to 14, the number of wildland units or protected areas from 25 to 149 and the total area protected from 193,500 to 615,000 sq km.

In addition, the concept of planning and implementation of *systems* or networks of parks and protected areas came about in the late sixties (Budowski, 1967; Miller, 1980). And it has been in the last decade, that the first true, but still *very* partial, plans and strategies for national or subregional systems or subsystems of wildlands have been prepared and their implementation begun. Particularly notable have been the efforts in Brazil, Chile, Costa Rica, Dominica, Ecuador, and the Lesser Antilles (Miller, 1980; MacFarland, 1982; Putney, 1981).

The progression from the establishment of individual, scattered national parks to systems/subsystems strategic planning, represents a natural evolution and maturation of the process. It is particularly encouraging to observe the great strides achieved in recent years, which have far out-distanced all previous periods.

2. CURRENT COVERAGE OF PROTECTED AREAS

Table I shows the protected areas (numbers and hectarage covered) by biogeographic provinces for the entire realm, and Table II shows the protected areas by countries. The almost 320 areas represent approximately 450,000 sq km or 1.7% of the total terrestrial area of the realm. However, caution must be used in interpreting this information because it only includes four categories of the 10 basic ones described by IUCN: i.e., 1) Scientific Reserves/Strict Nature Reserves; 2) National Parks; 3) Natural Monument/Natural Landmarks; and 4) Nature Conservation Reserves/Wildlife Sanctuaries. Most countries in the realm have established fairly extensive areas in other categories, particularly notable ones being multiple-use management areas (national forests or forest reserves), watershed protection reserves, resource reserves and anthropological reserves, which, if added to IUCN's inventory, would probably increase the total area covered by at least 2-3 times.

3. WEAKNESSES AND GAPS IN PROTECTED AREAS COVERAGE

It is somewhat difficult to determine the key gaps and weaknesses in the existing biogeographic coverage by parks and protected areas for two main reasons.

First, the IUCN biogeographic classification system (Udvardy, 1975) is of limited usefulness for detailed analysis at the national level, as it is a macro-level system designed for global analysis.

Given that problem, other more objective and finer-scaled classification schemes must be developed and applied in order to be able to determine the adequacy and gaps in protected areas coverage. For example, in all of Central America and at least some South American and Caribbean countries, the Holdridge ecological or life zone classification system is being utilized to determine such coverage and to help in the selection of new wildland management units. That system, of course, has its limitations, but offers the following advantages:

1) It is based on straightforward, clear and easily understood parameters and methods which are used in a standardized manner (i.e. its subjectivity is minimal);
2) the parameters are ones for which information is usually available, being very basic and simple ones: precipitation and temperature;
3) the system is particularly useful in mountain areas where significant changes occur over small distances and areas;
4) it has been used very extensively and is well known throughout the tropical and subtropical Americas;
5) it gives a much better level of descriptive resolution, i.e. a much finer scale, without becoming too bogged down in detail, and still being

easy to utilize with a fairly minimum information base; and,

6) it offers the option, once the basic life zones or bioclimates are mapped, of being able to proceed to greater depth, within the system, to classify and map vegetative associations or ecosystems within each life zone (Holdridge and Tosi, 1972; Tropical Science Center, 1980).

An example of the difference is Costa Rica. According to the IUCN system, the entire country falls within two biogeographic provinces, one of them Cocos Island, and 6 biomes, but with the Holdridge system it consists of 12 life zones and 6 transitions between those zones, some of them easily subdivided into vegetation associations. The system has been applied to 16 countries in the Realm, including all of Central America, most countries in South America, several in the Caribbean, and the eastern U.S., as well as other tropical and subtropical countries. Ideally, the system works best when appropriate field checking is part of the process, but very useful first level life zone maps can be produced in the laboratory from only climatic data. It would not involve much cost and time to produce such first level "laboratory" maps for the rest of the Neotropical Realm's countries or subregions.

Another example of a finer-scaled and -tuned biogeographic classification is the use of "Pleistocene refuges" in the Amazon. More is being learned each year about those areas from which recolonization of vast regions occurred. Their identification is fundamental for the determination of where to establish parks and protected areas, as has been done in Brazil (Jorge Padua, this volume).

The second problem in determining gaps and coverage adequacy is that IUCN's inventory of wildlands or protected areas is still not complete, as mentioned in the previous section. We know (MacFarland and Morales, 1981; Paucar, 1982) that many countries, probably most, in the realm also have established sizeable numbers of protected areas in other categories, particularly categories V-VIII (multiple-use management areas, watershed protection areas, anthropological reserves, etc.), of which only a small fraction has been inventoried in the first round of IUCN monitoring (IUCN, 1982b). As IUCN has recognized, those areas must be included in the inventory process because they (or at least parts of them, depending upon management use zoning and category) protect substantial ecosystems, genetic resources and diversity. That is the case for example in several Central American countries, examples being:

1) Costa Rica where almost 27% of the national territory is in legally declared wildland units of all categories, but only one-third (national parks, biological reserves, wildlife refuges and recreation areas) entered into the IUCN first-round inventory, the other two-thirds being forest reserves, watershed protectorates and Indian re-

serves, which account for approximately 55% of all remaining primary forest in the country; and

2) Belize, where 18.5% of the country is in legally declared wildland units, but only about 1% was covered in the inventory (natural monuments and scientific reserves), the other 99% being in 10 forest reserves.

Thus, until we have both a better biogeographic classification(s), combined with a much more complete inventory, determining gaps and adequacy of coverage will be very provisional. The appropriate studies, for example the overlaying of Holdridge life zone maps for the countries with those of complete inventories of all protected areas or wildland units, has not been done for the vast majority of the realm. In one of the few cases in which it has been done, Costa Rica, a recent study by the Tropical Science Center recommends adding 47 new biological reserves, wildlife refuges, watershed protection zones, forest reserves and national parks, in order to give adequate coverage of terrestrial ecosystems, genetic resources and diversity. The vast majority would be relatively small in size, but in total it would add another 5-6% of the national territory to the wildlands system.

Another word of caution is necessary. As part of completing the inventory of areas, at least some minimal characterization and qualification of the type of management and zoning being applied in those other categories, as well as of the effectiveness of management in them, will be necessary. Since several of those other categories imply more direct uses of natural resources, such qualification will be necessary in order to obtain a first-level idea of effective (as against purely legal) coverage and gaps. Since IUCN will soon begin characterizing the effectiveness of management in the already-inventoried areas, it should be possible to combine the process of improving the biogeographic classification base, completing the wildlands inventory and characterizing effectiveness of management, for all areas. In this entire process it will be very important to keep in mind the very notable potential and need for biosphere reserves (and similar approaches) for protecting key representative "samples" of ecosystems, diversity and genetic resources, as well as for developing new and alternative management technologies for sustained resource use, through experimentation and research.

Despite all of the foregoing, it is already possible to note numerous gaps in the coverage by parks and protected areas using the IUCN classification system and inventory at hand: several biogeographic provinces are not represented at all and at least a dozen others are very poorly represented (Harrison, Miller, and McNeely, this volume; and Dourojeanni, this volume).

Two other general biomes are very poorly covered by protected areas in the realm: the dry (deciduous) forest and the cloud forest. The former is of course most liable to be converted to food or fibre crops and for grazing because, among other factors, the forest can be easily removed by fire. More severe in consequence is the gradual disappearance of cloud forests, in view of their indispensable value as the most efficient water flow protecting device. As sad as it may appear, the value of the cloud forest is not yet sufficiently recognized. How many coastal or freshwater fishermen, for example, recognize that their catch depends on some of these forests or indeed how many scientists are aware of the increased horizontal precipitation from the fog drip that takes place?

Probably the single greatest gap in protected natural areas is in the coastal and marine area of the realm. With the very few exceptions of some scattered protected areas along the coasts of Central and South America and Mexico, this entire portion of the realm has been almost totally ignored. Most of those few protected areas which contain marine and/or coastal resources were established principally because of terrestrial resources, not the marine ones. The establishment, management and development of protected area systems, subsystems and units in the marine and coastal areas is in its infancy compared with progress in the terrestrial part of the realm. The one exception to this general situation is in the Caribbean, particularly the Lesser Antilles, where notable strides in the planning and implementation of marine and coastal protected areas have been made during the past 4-5 years, due to the activities of a number of national resource management agencies and NGOs, the Caribbean Conservation Association and the Eastern Caribbean Natural Areas Management Program or EC-NAMP (Putney, Jackson and Renard, this volume).

Finally, improving the biogeographic classification system, completing the protected areas inventory and characterizing the degree of effective management will go a long way toward providing a more solid base for answering several other key questions concerning parks and protected areas in the realm: have the most appropriate areas been selected as reserves? Are the protected areas of the most appropriate size, shape and distribution? Are they contributing to sustained development? More intensive review at country or subregional level as part of systems and strategy planning will be necessary to more fully answer those questions for the realm.

4. FACTORS WHICH HAVE IMPEDED THE ESTABLISHMENT AND EFFECTIVE MANAGEMENT OF PROTECTED AREAS

As apparently is the case for most other realms, particularly for the ones covering the tropics, there are a number of key factors, which can be summarized as follows (not listed necessarily in order of priority):

- Virtual total lack of planned and implemented subsystems and individual units, other than of national parks and equivalent protected areas; i.e. particularly of multiple use management areas,

anthropological reserves, protected landscapes, biosphere reserves, wildlife refuges and similar categories, and their equivalents in marine zones;
- poorly developed methodologies and technologies for the planning and implementation of those categories and subsystems indicated above, including the research needed to develop those technologies;
- lack of adequately developed methodologies for the strategic planning and implementation of complete national protected area systems, including all potential management categories;
- severe problems with the implementation of systems/subsystems plans and strategies and management plans for individual areas, even when they exist; and, likewise, similar problems with the organization of management agencies to effectively fulfil their responsibilities;
- general lack of clear and explicit government policies which support the establishment, management and development of broad-based national protected areas systems and units, as part of the general development process;
- excessive competition or at least lack of collaboration between institutions involved in the planning and implementation of such systems and units;
- lingering antagonism and lack of collaboration between conservationists and other key disciplines such as foresters, agronomists, engineers and others;
- insufficient quantities of experienced and trained personnel; and
- inadequate funding and similar support.

Each of these could be developed into a full-fledged separate paper, and several have been before. However, let us briefly examine several which have not been so treated:

4.1. Planning and implementation of other management categories

There is very little in the way of experience and developed technologies for the planning and on-the-ground implementation of systems and individual units of virtually all the management categories other than national parks and similar categories such as scientific reserves and natural monuments. The fact that most of the countries in the region have established or are in the process of legally establishing multiple use management areas (forest reserves or national forests), anthropological reserves, biosphere reserves, wildlife refuges and other categories, indicates that the urgent need for such areas has taken hold in many countries and is spreading. The same has even begun in the marine area, beginning with legal establishment of parks and later of marine multiple use areas, fisheries reserves, etc., i.e. the marine equivalents of some of the categories indicated above.

However, the huge gap is between legal establishment and on-the-ground management of such units and subsystems. This is particularly critical in the Neotropical Realm because for almost all of the countries the final decisions on how to allocate virtually all the remaining natural resources are going to be made during the next decade, at most two decades in those few countries favoured by less pressure on their natural resources. Most of these irreversible decisions will have been made and implemented by the time the next World Park Congress convenes.

The critical need therefore is to design, test, improve and then apply on a widespread basis, methodologies for the planning and on-the-ground implementation of those "other" management categories. Although there is always room for improvement, such well-proven methodologies exist, are well-known and are widely used in the realm for national parks and similar categories. However, during the coming decade, without ignoring or leaving behind parks, natural monuments and scientific reserves, which always must form an important part of any well-designed wild areas system, the principal emphasis must shift to those other categories. It must start with pilot, experimental-demonstration cases and then move on to widespread use once the methodologies have been proven. Only if that is done will protected areas systems and units come to be *recognized* as a vital base for sound, sustained development, and in fact be such. If it does not happen, those potential areas will gradually all be destroyed irreversibly, and the parks and similar areas, seen as "green elephants", will follow next.

The foregoing comments apply particularly to the case for multiple use management areas (national forests or forest reserves), biosphere reserves and anthropological reserves, and the equivalents of the first two in marine areas.

The first attempts at solving this problem have begun in the past few years in the realm. In Central America, the first General Management and Development Plans have been developed for multiple use management areas, biosphere reserves, anthropological reserves, wildlife refuges, national recreation areas and archeological monuments (MacFarland et al., 1982). Likewise, the first case of a planning methodology for and a plan and strategy for a national system of forest reserves and equivalent categories is being completed in Costa Rica (MacFarland et al., 1982; Alfaro, 1982). In the Eastern Caribbean, similar pilot programmes are underway, most heavily focussed on the equivalent marine protected areas management categories (Putney, Jackson and Renard, this volume).

An important word of caution in relation to the above: basic and especially applied research is an element that is vital in developing the management technologies needed to implement all of these categories and subsystems. That is particularly true of multiple-

use management areas and biosphere reserves, terrestrial or marine; managing Neotropical wet forests or most wildlife species on a sustainable production basis, for example, is largely an unknown. However, enough *is known* to design and test various schemes in selected habitats and communities and with selected species, in such reserves or protected areas, initially on a limited basis (which will also demonstrate certain use and positive intentions). But, in the Neotropical Realm, with a few scattered exceptions, no one is conducting such experiments yet. The same is true for marine protected areas.

4.2. Strategic planning and implementation of complete national protected areas systems

To date, the development of such systems plans and strategies at national and sub-regional level, and the methodologies to guide their preparation, have been limited in fact to subsystems involving national parks and similar categories. Those experiments have provided very useful lessons and guidelines about such methodologies and how to apply them, but the experience has been necessarily limited by the management categories included.

For most of the same reasons given in the previous subsection, during the next decade it will be critical to design, test, improve and then widely apply methodologies for preparing plans and strategies for *complete* national systems of protected areas, including consideration of *all* management categories. Without such plans and strategies, choices will be made anyway on resource use and allocation, but done so largely in a knowledge vacuum; the results in that case will not be positive and probably downright disastrous in most countries.

Such strategic plans for national systems of protected wild areas, depending on the individual country's situation, could be prepared separately or as a core part of a broader national strategy for management and use of natural and cultural resources. In either case they must feed into the national development planning processes as a core element. Initial steps have been taken to attempt such strategies in several countries of the region: St. Kitts-Nevis, Costa Rica, Nicaragua and Belize.

4.3. Implementation of plans

Most protected areas in the realm are still lacking General Management and Development Plans and most subsystems and systems are *de facto*, having no national plan and strategy. However, this problem will take considerable time to resolve. To prepare such plans, even when proven methodologies exist and when enough trained, experienced national staff is available, takes considerable time and effort and adequate financing. Worst off of all are the agencies in charge of multiple use management areas, anthropological preserves, biosphere reserves and other such categories, because they have no plans and no experienced, trained planners plus there are no methodologies available. The problem therefore, in all these cases, is how to guide management of the areas and subsystems until plans can be prepared for the systems/subsystems and all individual units, which in most cases will take many years to complete.

However, the problem is even more complicated. As shown in the realm by the case of national parks and similar categories, fairly severe problems are encountered by management agencies in implementing both General Management and Development Plans for individual protected areas and systems plans and strategies. There are notable exceptions throughout the realm to both cases (e.g. see Jorge Padua and Ponce and Villa, this volume). Nevertheless, by far the most common situation is that such plans tend to gather dust or at best receive minimal implementation, despite the tremendous national (and frequently international technical cooperation) efforts which go into their preparation.

Added on top of these problems is the general one of relatively poor organization of operations in the management agencies at all levels.

First experimental attempts at solving these problems have been underway in Central America over the past few years. Operational Plans, i.e. short-term (usually annual or bi-annual) detailed plans, have been prepared for entire systems of parks and similar protected areas, for systems of forest reserves and related categories, for many different types of individual protected areas (national parks, forest reserves, scientific reserves, biosphere reserves, watershed protection areas, archeological monuments), and for all central office level technical and administrative departments of some management agencies. By combining all of these, an overall Operational Plan for an entire agency is produced. In almost all of these cases, several rounds of such planning (annual revisions) have been carried out, the plans have been implemented and initial evaluations have been done. The results have been very positive and led to considerably improved management of whole agencies, technical and administrative departments, entire subsystems and all their units, and individual management units. In the last case it has greatly improved establishing priorities and conducting basic or minimum protection and other types of management activities in those numerous cases where a General Management Plan did not exist, and in cases in which such a Plan did exist, its implementation was greatly improved.

More details can be found in MacFarland, Morales, and Barborak, (this volume).

4.4. Lack of cooperation between professions and management agencies

The isolation of planners or managers of protected areas in relation to other professions is an unfortunate stigma that weighs heavily against achievements and has triggered reactions such as competition for "jurisdiction" for funds, and of course for credit in the improvement of quality of life for human populations.

Is this necessary? Can it be avoided? The answers are of course no and yes, respectively. Foresters, for instance, can play an important role in joining the cause of conservation by relieving the pressure on protected areas and cooperate in conservation actions through such action as buffer zones, fuelwood plantations, restoration of degraded lands, by planting nitrogen fixing trees, enhancing traditional systems that combine trees with food plants or cattle (agroforestry). Vice versa, conservationists should cease to criticize indiscriminately many of the wood exploitation schemes, particularly if they are based on plantations—be they exotic or no—that cover lands formerly degraded by faulty agricultural practices. The criticism of *Eucalyptus globulus* in the higher Andes, or for that matter, the billion dollar industry based on pine and eucalyptus plantation in southern Brazil appear counter-productive. Needless to say, the substitution of natural forest by these species should be condemned but not so the reforestation schemes on degraded lands.

5. FACTORS WHICH HAVE ENCOURAGED THE ESTABLISHMENT AND EFFECTIVE MANAGEMENT OF PROTECTED AREAS

Again the list is very long and only a few items are summarized here:

- efficient vigilance by concerned groups;
- promotion of a continuous "presence" such as visiting scientists;
- development of effective leadership;
- outside funding and technical assistance that triggers internal action (FAO, Unesco, IUCN, WWF, etc.);
- high quality publications (and other publicity) such as the series promoted by INCAFO (Spain) in cooperation with local authors;
- successful training programmes;
- recognition of leaders and achievements through awards by outside sources, as an effective tool to back productive people;
- resolutions of the World Conferences on National Parks;
- increasingly enlightened attitudes of large funding or loan agencies; and
- meetings on conservation in the countries or subregions to trigger the setting up of new protected areas.

Again let us illustrate a few cases.

In Costa Rica, which—like many Latin American and Caribbean countries—suffers from acute economic difficulties, the administrators of a wildlife refuge and adjoining National Park (Rafael Lucas Rodriquez and Palo Verde) were ordered by the previous President of the Republic to return a considerable part of the protected area to the owner, who had not yet been compensated for his land. A local conservation organization legally blocked this action by court action, calling it unconstitutional. The court ruled against the President and the integrity of the protected areas was maintained. An efficient vigilance system and enlightened public opinion can take the credit.

In 1972 the 2nd World Congress of National Parks introduced two important suggestions pertaining to international (or frontier) parks and regional systems of national parks and other protected areas (Recommendations No. 6 and 9, respectively). Both led to concrete actions.

In 1979, the Presidents of Panama and Costa Rica formally met along the border to agree on the establishment of the "friendship park" covering over 450,000 ha of forested land along the border, with 6 biomes. The Costa Rican part of that International Park has since been legally declared and basic protection started and the Management Plan for the park and surrounding areas is being prepared in both countries. On the Costa Rican side, the Park forms part of the core area of a contiguous complex of Indian Reserves, Forest (Watershed) Protection Zones and Biological Reserves, which was recently approved as a Biosphere Reserve of some 500,000 ha.

The Resolution on regional systems led to a governmental meeting organized by IUCN in San Jose, Costa Rica, in 1974, with representatives from 6 countries, including for each, representatives of the wildland agencies, tourism organizations, cultural resources and land-use planning agencies. The very detailed resolutions which resulted have been the single most important basis for continuing action-oriented protected areas programmes in Central America since that time.

In the seventies the Central American Bank for Economic Integration has funded the development of two protected areas: Tikal and Poas National Parks. This was not small money; for the improvement of the access road and the construction of the visitation centre of Poas National Park in Costa Rica, for example, $2 million was provided.

Conservation meetings in the countries are often an excellent opportunity to promote the declaration and establishment of new protected areas. The latest is probably the declaration of the 37,000 ha Carlos Botelho Reserve along Brazil's highly vulnerable coastal forest in the State of Sao Paulo, during a Congress on native species on 12 September 1982.

6. A SPECIAL ISSUE: INDIGENOUS POPULATIONS AND PROTECTED AREAS

The literature on this subject is usually a mixture of frustrations, recriminations and failures with no clear solution in sight. The Indian reservation, U.S. style, is not appealing. Complete isolation from other groups appears impossible in the long run. Contact with missionairies, even well-intentioned anthropologists, has its flaws. Clearly for these "ecosystem people" as they have been aptly called by Raymond Dasmann, there seems to be no choice but acculturation, whatever that implies, and many believe that our mission is to make this process as painless as possible.

It may therefore be a pleasant surprise to relate that the Kuna Indians, a group of Amerindians of northeast Panama, have recently decided, partly as a measure to avoid encroachment on their territory by land-hungry colonists, decided that the best solution is to create a large National Park (and probably eventually a Biosphere Reserve) managed and controlled by themselves, with support from the Washington-based Inter-American Foundation, AID and CATIE. The Kunas have asked us to help prepare the management plan and train their people in such things as designing a detailed interpretive plan, carried out by themselves, of the rich heritage of plants and animals as well as landscapes, and of their own culture. They visited us recently in Costa Rica and we hope that this first close cooperation between park planners and Amerindians may set an example that, provided it is successful, could establish a precedent for similar cases elsewhere.

Acknowledgements

This paper was prepared for IUCN's Commission on National Parks and Protected Areas in cooperation with the World Wildlife Fund and Unesco.

Table 1. Number of Protected Areas and Total Area Protected in
each of the 47 Neotropical Provinces of Udvardy (1983)

	Name of Province	Number of Areas	Total Area (hectares)
1	Campechean	3	62,744
2	Panamanian	6	660,902
3	Colombian Coastal	6	860,000
4	Guyanan	25	2,155,122
5	Amazonian	16	13,894,181
6	Madeiran	1	268,150
7	Serro Do Mar	7	181,016
8	Brazilian Rain Forest	14	368,028
9	Brazilian Planalto	2	15,839
10	Valdivian Forest	5	1,685,995
11	Chilean Nothofagus	4	216,014
12	Everglades	15	774,714
13	Sinaloan	5	462,994
14	Guerreran	4	65,511
15	Yucatecan	2	106,970
16	Central American	22	821,425
17	Venezuelan Dry Forest	27	1,125,798
18	Venezuelan Deciduous Forest	12	774,725
19	Equadorian Dry Forest	3	161,300
20	Caatinga	3	236,100
21	Gran Chaco	6	1,294,000
22	Chilean Araucaria Forest	6	153,595
23	Chilean Sclerophyll	3	34,054
24	Pacific Desert	2	360,070
25	Monte	8	1,544,491
26	Patagonian	5	99,793
27	Llanos	3	1,207,000
28	Campos Limpos	3	3,192,000
29	Babacu	1	155,000
30	Campos Cerrados	12	2,518,529
31	Argentinian Pampas	1	
32	Urugayan Pampas	9	37,293
33	Northern Andean	9	913,288
34	Colombian Montane	8	1,397,050
35	Yungas	6	558,092
36	Puna	13	1,215,183
37	Southern Andean	19	4,139,684
38	Bahamas-Bermudean	4	122,540
39	Cuban	4	24,305
40	Greater Antillean	7	220,230
41	Lesser Antillean	16	89,574
42	Revilla Gigedo Island		0
43	Cocos Island	1	3,200
44	Galapagos Islands	1	691,200
45	Fernando De Noronja Island	1	36,249
46	South Trinidade Island		0
47	Lake Titicaca	1	36,180
	TOTAL	331	44,940,128

Note: These figures only include areas of over 1000 ha unless
the area is an island, in which case it is included
whatever the size.

Categories I to V only are included.

Table 2. Protected Areas of the Neotropical Realm (1983)

Country	Number of Areas	Total Area (hectares)
Antigua	2	2,500
Argentina	31	3,458,551
Bahamas	4	122,540
Barbados	1	250
Belize	1	4,144
Bermuda	no information available	
Bolivia	10	4,440,783
Brazil	45	10,799,673
Chile	24	3,061,699
Colombia	30	3,958,750
Costa Rica	19	407,325
Cuba	4	24,305
Dominica	1	6,840
Dominican Republic	5	219,800
Ecuador	9	1,990,200
El Salvador	no information available	
French Guiana	-	
Grenada	-	
Guadeloupe	no information available	
Guatemala	1	57,600
Republic of Guyana	1	11,655
Haiti	no information available	
Honduras	2	400,000
Jamaica	no areas over 1000 ha	
Martinique	1	70,000
Mexico	12	636,475
Montserrat (UK)	no areas over 1000 ha	
Netherlands Antilles	3	13,400
Nicaragua	2	17,300
Panama	6	660,902
Paraguay	7	1,237,538
Peru	18	4,306,499
Puerto Rico	2	430
St Lucia	1	1,600
St Vincent	no information available	
Republic of Suriname	9	582,400
Trinidad and Tobago	12	16,567
Turks and Caicos Islands (UK)	-	
U.S.A. - Florida	15	774,714
Uruguay	7	30,593
Venezuela	36	7,616,711
Virgin Islands (UK)	6	928
Virgin Islands (US)	4	7,456
TOTAL	331	44,940,128

Note: These figures only include areas of over 1000 ha unless the area is an island, in which case it is included whatever the size.

Categories I to V only are included.

They Survive under the Southern Winds: Wildlife Protection in Northern Coastal Patagonia

Ricardo Luti
Director
Centro de Ecologiá y Recursos Naturales Renovables
Universidad Nacional de Córdoba
Córdoba, Argentina

ABSTRACT. *The Valdés Peninsula in Argentina's Chubut Province is an arid terrestrial habitat which supports a surprising diversity of wildlife, accompanied by an exceptional marine fauna which includes seals, elephant seals, penguins, whales, and dolphins. In pre-colonial times, the local people lived in harmony with this harsh-appearing environment, but the massive cultural change which came with the Europeans brought increasing threats to the wildlife. As a result, the provincial authorities developed new ways of conservation, establishing several protected areas. Early problems involving uncontrolled tourism and lack of trained personnel have been overcome, and today the area appears to have stabilized as an important protected area bringing benefits both to people and to wildlife.*

1. INTRODUCTION

Wind-swept and parched under piercing suns, the coastal ecozones of Northern Patagonia offer one of the most striking and wonderful examples of wildlife occupying two worlds: the oceanic waters and the drylands. They provide cases of a number of species mingling and often sharing the resources of both such environments; they present animal and plant forms which either thrive in the saline waters or struggle for survival in the desert.

Primitive man was a component of those ecosystems; but a component who through respect for his fellow creatures, used them wisely and cared for them with hunting habits and weapons that could provide his basic needs without seriously damaging the highly rich biota.

Yet other men came from beyond the ocean. Men who were on a search. Men who did not feel part of the system but masters of it. Men who without properly knowing and understanding it, used and spoiled the natural resources and seriously compromised the survival of many species.

Nevertheless, in the last thirty years conservation and preservation of those environments became a "must" for many Patagonian dwellers as well as for scientists and authorities. In order to succeed in this task, wildlife had to be better understood, so today protection and research go hand in hand.

The extraordinary richness of wildlife on the Patagonian coasts revealed in early surveys proved to be a temptation. For decades, continuous hunting, killing and trapping slaughtered many sea and land species by the thousands without any sort of planning or control. Thus aboriginal predation became civilized depredation.

Wildlife provided hides, pelts, oil, fat, bones and feathers to the new exploiters. There was no mercy for animals which could be regarded as a resource. The killing techniques were varied and some were extremely brutal, such as the clubbing to death of pups and adults among the seals, sea lions, sea elephants and penguins in order to preserve the value of the pelts.

Even today, numerous parched hides of sea mammals from which fat was obtained may be found in many sites. Huge ossuaries may also be frequently seen along the coasts.

By the beginning of the twentieth century the survival of several species was in question; but federal and local authorities as well as some of the Patagonian settlers began to realize the danger, although not much was done to correct the situation until the 1930s when public awareness began to grow and pressure was brought to bear for protective legislation.

But early in the century another stress had been put on the marine wildlife: the exploitation of oil fields, both in continental Patagonia and on the sea shelf. Oil spills began to spread on the ocean surface pushing northwards, into the open sea, or onto the beaches. Wildlife suffered the consequences. Thousands of animals died, their bodies covered with oil, their respiratory systems blocked, their insulation from fur or feathers lost. Then in 1974 a new source of pollution evolved in the Nuevo Gulf from an aluminium smelter near the town of Puerto Madryn, which soon grew from 8,000 to well over 20,000 people.

2. CHUBUT ESTABLISHES PROTECTED AREAS

The impact of human activities on wildlife has thus been serious. Whether by trapping, hunting, fishing, or contamination, man deeply altered the environment as a whole and the animal populations in particular, rendering their rehabilitation slow or difficult. Eventually positive action was taken both by the Federal Government through the Wildlife Direction and by the Government of the Province of Chubut, some of which came under the Pan-American Convention on Wildlife Protection.

National legal action covered the whole of the coastal zone of Patagonia, both marine and terrestrial environments. The provincial offices reinforced those measures for Chubut and provided new ones. Then from 1968, local decisions were taken, the Direction of Tourism of Chubut promoted a law creating the first three Nature Reserves in Peninsula Valds: Punta Loma with its sea lion colony; the sea elephants breeding site at Punta Norte; and Bird Island or Isla de los Pájaros. This marked the beginning of continuous action for wildlife protection, now under the surveillance of the Direction for Conservation of Natural and Cultural Heritage of the province.

Setting an example for the rest of the provinces, Chubut converted San Jos Gulf into a Marine Park and created several Nature Reserves in the following years. Besides the need for protecting wildlife, there was also the intention of promoting tourism, motivating people through intense publicity campaigns by way of newspapers and magazines, brochures, audiovisual sessions, etc., not only within the country but also abroad.

The response to these campaigns came much faster than was expected, way ahead of the logistic and material substructure development that was needed to ensure optimum protection. Thus the protected areas were neither ready nor able to withstand the waves of thousands of visitors that overflowed them.

Notices were often the only sign to people that they were entering a Reserve, since some of them did not have even a ranger for several years; uninformed visitors were only too free to stroll around. In Punta Norte, for instance, the single ranger could not take care of the whole area, a coastal strip several kilometers in length and 500 m wide. People would approach, touch and even mount huge, tame, sea elephants *Mirounga leonina*,

in order to have a picture taken. They would often kick the animals to annoy and infuriate them so as to see the projection of their extraordinary trunks. Weighing up to three and a half tons and moving with a caterpillar motion, the sea elephants are slow and only potentially dangerous. But being shy, a large proportion of them, and particularly the old males, year after year would move to places further away from the tourists' access. Harems of family groups began to scatter along the beach, the unique continental colony becoming partially dispersed.

Sea lion males *Otaria flavescens*, more agile and consequently more dangerous, are capable of attacking people when disturbed during the breeding period; they also became more timid and often swam away at the approach of visitors.

Even in the presence of a ranger or an assistant, it was very difficult to keep people from approaching and bothering the marine mammals. As a result, a wire-net fence had to be stretched along the beach, to keep visitors at a distance. The thoughtless behaviour of visitors, lack of sufficient wildlife information and environmental education concepts transformed a wonderful natural experience into an open but fenced zoo.

Two other Nature Reserves, Punta Pirámides and Punta Loma, host the largest colonies of sea lions on the Peninsula, with up to 1000 animals in the former. Both occupy rocky shelves and very small beaches, all surrounded, isolated and protected by medium-height cliffs. Both make for excellent breeding grounds. The problem that arose during the first few years of the Reserves, which fortunately no longer exists, was people throwing stones at the animals to see them dive from the rocks and swim. For some time this action scared part of the animals away.

Bird Island Reserve, 2 ha of land within the San José Gulf on the northern side of the Peninsula, represents another case. Only 800 m away from the narrow isthmus of the Peninsula, the small island, which can be reached on foot during low tide, was the nesting site of thousands of birds of twelve different species (large sea-gulls, black cormorants, oyster birds, herons, egrets, ducks, etc.). Within a few years only seven species were still nesting on the island and they had reduced populations. The impact of noisy people wandering among the nests, often trying to touch or grab the birds, made many move away.

Both the ranger who was later appointed, and occasional student assistants, had serious problems on several occasions trying to keep visitors away from the higher nesting portion of the island. Scared birds often abandoned their eggs and even chicks, some departing for quieter sites.

The Magellanic penguin *Spheniscus magellanicus* colonies in the Nature Reserves of Punta Tombo and Cabo Dos Bahías-Camarones, both south of the Peninsula, also present an interesting history. Penguins are normally very tame and friendly. It was a delight to walk carefully and slowly through their nesting grounds and to stroll among the animals standing on the beach or wandering around. They would hardly move; curious and unafraid, they would watch people, and often even approach them.

But their misfortune was to have too many visitors all of a sudden, with nobody to protect them. People would grab them, children and dogs would chase them. Afterwards they turned very timid and unless defending their nests or chicks, they would escape into the ocean if people came near them. Cars and other vehicles used to drive across the nesting area, crushing nests, adults and chicks. Tents were set up on the higher edge of the colonies facing the ocean, intercepting the normal walk of the animals towards the sea. Almost every human action severely disturbed the colony.

When the rangers were appointed, and particularly when there were student assistants to help them, things began to improve in the colony. It may thus be said that the first years of all the marine-land reserves were good for tourism but harmful to wildlife.

Perhaps the only exception might be San José Gulf Marine Park, the breeding site of the huge southern right whale *Eubalaena australis*. Apart from scientists, cameramen and tourists would approach the tame whales in boats or small ships during their calving and mating season, but there is little damaging human disturbance at present.

3. MAN AND THE TERRESTRIAL ENVIRONMENT

The Valdés Peninsula, which forms two practically land-locked gulfs, is characterized by tableland forms and scattered low hills. The dry (106 mm average annual rainfall) and windy climate, mild to cold in winter and temperate to warm in summer, is conditioned by both the northern temperate Brazilian and southern cold Malvinas currents. Salt flats are frequent, with one of these occupying the lowest site in Argentina, 48 m below sea level. With immature sandy, stony or rocky soils, vegetation is scarce, with an open canopy; xerophytic shrubs are the most conspicuous plants, with some tough grasses and a few other herbs in between or protected under them. Cushion forms and thorny branches are a common feature. It is indeed a severe environment.

Plants were mainly used by the aboriginal people as forage or fuel. The impact of livestock and the growth of human settlements, both in size and number, badly damaged nature. In addition, plants suffer an early contamination process by gaseous effluvia carried by the wind from the growing city of Puerto Madryn and from the nearby aluminum smelter. Although pollutant residues do not penetrate deep into the soil due to the scarcity of rain, heavy downpours and wind may sweep them into the gulfs through erosion of the upper soil layer. Liquid effluents add their pollutant effects to the waters of Nuevo Gulf.

The animal populations living on the firm land of the major portion of the umbrella-shaped peninsula, as well as on the long and narrow isthmus, have been under pressure from hunters and trappers for centuries. With the increase of human populations, the situation of several species became very seriously menaced. Herds of the largest New World living camelids, the guanaco *Lama guanicoe* used to roam across the peninsula; hide, pelt, wool and meat were precious and Indians used warm guanaco blankets. Since colonization times, populations have been declining, with numbers dropping sharply in the present century. Tenure of the land was a serious problem to tackle since many private ranches were located within the peninsula and even existing laws could not be enforced to protect these animals. Finally, the Tourist Office of Chubut was able to work out a compromise with the landowners resulting in a significant decline in both hunting and poaching, after declaring the whole of the Peninsula a hunting reserve.

The same agreement came to the rescue of the mara *Dolichotis patagonum*, the fascinating large rodent also known as the Patagonian hare, hunted for meat and pelt; of the armadilloes, which make delicious meals and provide their carapace for "charangoes" (small native guitars); skunks, also for the pelt; red and grey foxes (*Dusicyon culpaeus* and *D. griseus*), officially classified as vermin until recent years, when their numbers, especially of the large and beautiful red fox, had dropped to a criticallly low level.

Among the birds no doubt the most interesting is the lesser rhea *Pterocnemia pennata* or "choique". Flightless and with a striking family behaviour, this large animal did not suffer much from the Indians. They used to catch them alive with bolas in order to obtain their long feathers, a permanent temptation. But the animals were released after that with a low percentage of deaths, except for the few which would be roasted and eaten. Even when horses were at hand the status of rhea was not too worrying until recent years. But killing or wounding of the animals plus nest raids to steal the huge eggs impinged severely on the populations.

Delicious, tasty meat has been the reason for the relentless hunting of the elegant crested tinamou *Eudromia elegans*, which gracefully glides through the shrubs.

Today, herds of guanaco, family groups of mara and crested tinamous, troops of lesser rhea and many other species can be seen making a firm comeback. Much is due to the training of personnel and the use of natural science students (mainly biology) as assistants to the rangers and as tourist guides during the vacation periods.

The negative impact of the presence of visitors during the early years of the implementation of the nature reserve system has thus been gradually reduced. Growing awareness of conservation needs by both local authorities and the general public augurs a better future for wildlife in Chubut. A good example of this was the general reaction against a foreign packing plant project for industrializing 50,000 penguins per year from one of the colonies outside the Reserves, without any valid scientific research to back it. Ultimately, authorization was not given by the National Wildlife Division and the project was dropped.

Research is being conducted by the National Patagonia Centre and the National Research Council on population dynamics, migratory habits and behaviour in the broad sense, of several species of both mammals and birds; valuable information has already been gathered, which no doubt will provide useful tools for improving management and protection rules.

Vegetation and soils are also being investigated as well as other environmental components. The National Institute of Industrial Technology is also responsible for basic and applied research concerning the possible use of some renewable natural resources.

There is good communication between the different institutions involved in research, which is evidence of the understanding of the natural processes, a fact which should lead towards an integrated management system with an ecological and conservationist viewpoint.

At present, each Reserve has a permanent Ranger assigned to it, often with some special training. Those which attract more visitors have either permanent or temporary assistants. Surveillance of wildlife well-being has become an important activity during the tourist seasons.

Two Interpretation Centres, two Biological Stations and one Marine Biology Research Laboratory are already functioning, distributed among the coastal reserves. Facilities for rangers, assistants and visitors are gradually being improved and increased. Regulations exist for tourist activities both on land and in the sea, for camping, strolling, swimming, diving and water skiing in the protected zones and for fishing in the surrounding areas.

Legislation concerning sources of contamination has also been considered and improved on in the last few years. In accordance with it and accepting suggestions developed at a national meeting of the Argentine Association of Ecology, held in Puerto Madryn, the aluminium smelter opened an Ecology Bureau for both research on and monitoring of pollution.

The Government, in an effort to protect the San Jos Gulf, declared it a Marine Park with no settlements allowed on the surrounding lands. Consequently, protection of whales and other animals and of Bird Island itself, became more efficient. Furthermore, access to the Peninsula is easy to control; the isthmus being narrow, there is only one entrance road and a Control and Information Post has been set up there.

4. CONCLUSIONS

Chubut's experience teaches several important lessons:

- Good intentions and resolutions by themselves, without immediate and effective implementation, might cause serious damage to the environment, community or species whose protection is desired and high costs might be needed to correct poorly-conceived and premature actions.
- Infrastructure may fulfill a secondary role but training of personnel and logistic support should be guaranteed before offering and opening natural treasures to the public.
- Promotion of scientific research should always come ahead of tourist promotion.
- Although the present success of Chubut is to be encouraged, still more emphasis should be placed on protection and new land and marine areas should be incorporated into the system.
- Concerning Valdés Peninsula, the whole of it should come under full protection in the near future. It represents an extremely valuable geographic and biotic entity which includes dry land, almost land-locked gulfs, a broken coast, cliffs and beaches. It should become a single and fully integrated Nature Reserve, or even better, a National Park. The ecological role, the scientific value and the touristic attraction of such an area would more than justify the enterprise.

A System of National Parks and Biological Reserves in the Brazilian Amazon

Maria Tereza Jorge Padua and Angela Tresinari Bernardes Quintao
Department of National Parks and Equivalent Reserves
Brasilia, D.F., Brazil

ABSTRACT. *This paper describes the programme by which Brazil created seven new conservation units in the Amazon in the past three years, totalling about 7 million ha. It describes the approach that was taken in deciding which of these areas are of highest priority, and in determining the network of areas that is required to conserve centres of diversity and Pleistocene refugia and other sites of biological importance. This methodology is suggested to be of general importance for the design of protected area systems. The next stage in Brazil will be the creation of 30 new protected areas, including a number of management categories which do not yet exist in Brazil.*

1. INTRODUCTION

The publication of "An analysis of Nature Conservation Priorities in the Amazon" (Wetterberg *et al.*, 1976), was a landmark in the planning of a system of national parks and protected areas in the Brazilian Amazon. This document was the main source for the Brazilian System Plan for Conservation Units, which is being carried out in five major stages. The First Stage of the System Plan for Conservation Units (*Jorge Padua et al.* 1979) proposed the establishment of 13 new units for conservation, most of them in the Amazon. Ten of these have already been brought into existence by Presidential Decree, as National Parks and Federal Biological Reserves.

In 1979, there were 2,400,000 ha of land devoted to national parks and biological reserves in Brazil, 0.28% of its entire territory; in the Amazon region in 1979, there was only Tapajo National Park with 1,000,000 ha. With the new additions, there are now some 10,400,000 ha of national parks and biological reserves (1.2% of the national territory), and most of these are in the Amazon region.

The Second Stage (Jorge Padua *et al.*, 1982) of the System Plan calls for 30 new units with new categories of management for Brazil, such as Natural Monument, Wildlife Sanctuary, Parkway, and Natural Park. These new areas, totalling 6,800,000 ha, are to be officially established by means of a Presidential Decree or a law of Congress in the near future.

The successful creation of approximately 7,000,000 ha of national parks and biological reserves in the Amazon in the last two years is due mainly to the planning strategy employed in the various stages of the System Plan for Conservation Units.

The following will give a brief explanation of all the work accomplished in order to achieve the present state of affairs (as of April 1982) and will also include a brief description of the units so far established in the Amazon. In order to facilitate the understanding of this paper, we must clarify that, when we refer to the Amazon, we have in mind the phytogeographical region of Prance (1976) (Figure 1).

2. THE JUSTIFICATIONS FOR THE SYSTEM PLAN FOR CONSERVATION UNITS IN BRAZIL

Influenced by the creation of Yellowstone Park in the United States, in 1872, the Brazilian engineer André Rebouças advocated, in 1876, the establishment of national parks in Brazil as well, suggesting the Island of Bananal and the area of Sete Quedas as logical priorities.

Rebouças did not live to see his suggestion become reality, for neither the Island of Bananal nor Sete Quedas were the first Brazilian national parks; they were only created 80 years after his proposal. In 1937, the National Park of Itatiaia, in Rio de Janeiro, was the first to be established, followed, in 1939, by Iguaçú, in Paraná, and Serra dos Orgãos, also in Rio de Janeiro.

Nearly 20 years passed before other national parks were created. Thus, 1959 witnessed the creation of the parks of Aparados da Serra, in Rio Grande do Sul and Santa Catarina; Araguaia (Island of Bananal), in Goiás; and Ubajara, in Ceará. In 1961, several national parks were created: Emas and Chapada dos Veadeiros, in Goiás; Caparaó, in Minas Gerais and Espríto Santo; Sete Cidades, in Piauí; São Joaquim, in Santa Catarina; Tijuca, in Rio de Janeiro; Monte Pascoal, in Bahia; Braslia, in the Federal District; and Sete Quedas, in Paraná. Ten years later, in 1971, the National Park of Serra da Bocaina, in Rio de Janeiro, was established, followed in 1972 by Serra da Canastra, in Minas Gerais, and in 1974 by Amazónia, in Pará.

As was true of other Latin American countries, the creation of national parks in Brazil, through the 1960s, was justified mainly on the basis of protecting scenic beauty. From a methodological viewpoint, the protection of ecosystems was still precarious. In view of this problem, of the diversity of ecosystems found in the country, and of the limited cultural, scientific, or recreational use of the areas already established, the Brazilian Institute of Forest Development set off in the mid-1970s to elaborate a System Plan for Conservation Units in Brazil, the guidelines of which would be determined by highly relevant scientific criteria.

As a result of the technical-scientific criteria which began to govern the establishment of the new parks called for in the First Stage of the System Plan, many other national parks were created: Pico da Neblina, in the state of Amazonas, Pacaás Novos, in Rondónia, and Serra da Capivara, in Piauí, all in 1979; Jaú, in the state of Amazonas, and Cabo Orange, in the Federal Territory of Amapá, both in 1980; and finally Lençóis Maranhenses, in Maranháo, and Pantanal Matogrossense, in Mato Grosso, both in 1981.

In regard to biological reserves, a few were created in the 1950s: Sooretama, Códrrego do Veado, and Nova Lombardia, all in Espírito Santo, in 1955; and Serra Negra, in Pernambuco, in 1950. Sixteen years elapsed before other biological reserves were set up: Cará-Cará, in Mato Grosso, in 1971; Poço das Antas, in Rio de Janeiro, 1974; Rio Trombetas, in Pará, Atol das Rocas, in the Atlantic Ocean off the coast of Rio Grande do Norte, and Jaru, in Rondónia, all in 1979; and Lago Piratuba, in Amapá, and Una, in Bahia, both in 1980.

There are, therefore, today 24 national parks and 10 biological reserves in Brazil (Fig. 2).

It also became evident that only three categories of conservation units for non-consumptive use of resources (national park, biological reserve, and ecological station) and two for consumptive use (national forest and hunting park) were insufficient to attain the national objectives which needed to be met. A good example is the 32 turtle nesting beaches in Trombetas River, Para; although these nests should be protected, they do not fit the definition of national park or biological reserve. They

would belong, however, to the management category of wildlife sanctuary (IUCN Category IV) which entails objectives similar to those of the biological reserves, but which receives periodical manipulation and protection, and which requires a much smaller area.

The 360 km Transpantaneira Road, of which 176 km have already been built, and which cuts through the "Pantanal Matogrossense", connecting the cities of Poconé and Corumbá, is a good example of a "Parkway", another category introduced in the Second Stage of the System Plan for Conservation Units. Along the marshy borders of the Transpantaneira, there are large concentrations of caimans, birds, capybaras and other animals. The area, which receives a weekly average of 500 visitors, provides a clear picture of the "Complexo do Pantanal" (the "Marsh Complex").

There are still other units which were not included in the Brazilian System Plan: the Roncador Reserve, near Brasilia, which is managed by the Brazilian Foundation of Geography and Statistics; and four areas near Manaus, which are administered for scientific purposes by the Institute of Research of the Amazon—Campina, Experimental Reserve, Egler and Ducke. These units, however, can be regarded as supporting conservation interests.

3. METHODOLOGY USED FOR THE PROPOSAL OF NEW CONSERVATION UNITS IN THE AMAZON

The proposal of new national parks and biological reserves in the Amazon was grounded mainly on "An Analysis of Nature Conservation Priorities in the Amazon", as well as the analysis of nineteen thematic maps, which helped to eliminate all probable incompatibility. In addition, all government departments responsible for any activity in the area were consulted: the National Department of Mineral Research, DNPM; the National Institute of Colonization and Agrarian Reform, INCRA; the National Foundation for the Indians, FUNAI; the Superintendence for the Development of the Amazon, SUDAM; the National Sanitation Department, DNOS; and the RADAMBRASIL Project, among others, as well as the state and municipal governments.

The objectives of "An Analysis of Nature Conservation Priorities in the Amazon" were the following:

- to synthesize the published works of various Amazon specialists into a common format from which biologically significant conservation priorities could be tentatively identified;
- to identify and locate both the existing and the planned conservation units in the Amazon;
- to analyze the potential compatibilities or incompatibilities between the Brazilian programmes of the POLAMAZONIA and the preservation of biologically significant areas;
- to propose an overall outline of a programme for

the preservation of nature in the Amazon, which takes into account the diversity of this region, which permits the identification of priority areas to be preserved, and which is flexible enough to be adapted to future scientific discoveries;

- to make it possible for the public organizations responsible for national parks and equivalent reserves to gain a dynamic, aggressive position from which an Amazon conservation policy could be actively pursued before this option is ruled out by other development projects; and
- to contribute to the development of the System Plan for National Parks.

The document utilized all pertinent scientific literature available at that time, such as the phytogeographic regions, the planned and the existing conservation units, vegetation formations, Pleistocene refugia for birds, lizards, plants and Lepidoptera, development centres of the Brazilian Amazon (the legal Amazon), as well as indications for units of conservation of nature of the RADAMBRASIL project. All this information was transferred to transparent maps, drawn on the same scale, which thus made possible a visual analysis of the approximate relationships among several factors.

Field expeditions were made to up-date evaluation of the areas which displayed high potential to become conservation units.

In regard to vegetation, we tried to identify several general types, according to the Aubreville (1958) and Montoya (1966) structure (FAO, 1976). Wherever possible, the elements corresponding to the aforementioned works were transferred to Figure 3, which, however, is based mainly on Pires (1974). A visit to the centre of one of these formations may reveal that the local situation presents variations, since a vegetation formation consists of several component associations.

Even though approximately 90% of the Amazon consists of tropical rainforest, other types of vegetation contribute to the biological diversity of the area: ''Mata de Cipo'' (Liana Forest), ''Campinas Altas'' (an open forest), ''Mata Seca de Transiçáo'' (a semideciduous forest), ''Igapó'' (mangrove forest), ''Várzea'' forest, ''Cerrado'' (a savanna), grassland of ''Terra Firme'', and ''Várzea'' grassland. In addition, G.T. Prance stated that a bamboo forest had been discovered in the State of Acre in 1976 which has not as yet been charted. The diversity represented by every one of these formations should be protected by a general conservation programme for the Amazon.

The probable existence of Pleistocene refuges in the Amazon, in the tropical rainforest of ''Terra Firme'', were suggested by Haffer (1969, 1974), Vanzolini (1970), Vanzolini and Williams (1970), Prance (1973), Brown (1975, 1976) and Wing (1973). These proposed refuges, especialy where they overlap or merge, are areas which present a high probability of endemic species. Plants or animals are likely to have been genetically isolated in these refuges, which would have served subsequently as centres for the repopulation of the Amazon.

It was possible, by superimposing the maps of the various authorities, to obtain Figure 4, which shows general areas where two or more authors agree upon the existence of Pleistocene refugia. Although this formation is drawn at a gross scale and does not take into account the possibility of recent environmental alterations, it provides an idea of the areas of potential biological importance.

The analysis was carried out in every Phytogeographic Region of the Amazon and priorities were established according to three criteria: first priority was given to those areas which two or more scientists, in independent studies, identified as possible Pleistocene refugia; second priority was given to areas which were likely to represent several vegetation formations and perhaps a refuge; third priority was given to all other parks and reserves of various types, recommended by IBDF, RADAMBRASIL, SEMA, or other sources, as yet not included in the first two categories.

4. MAIN CONCLUSIONS OF THE ''ANALYSIS OF NATURE CONSERVATION PRIORITIES IN THE AMAZON''

- The phytogeographic regions which appeared to have the best coverage were the Atlantic Coast and Jari-Trombetas, as a consequence mainly of the extensive programme of nature conservation in Suriname. There were no Brazilian conservation units in either of the two regions mentioned;
- the Solimés-Amazonas phytogeographic region was the only one which did not have conservation unit coverage, at that stage;
- the Upper Rio Negro and Roraima regions were poorly represented. In the Roraima Region there was only the Brazilian Forest Reserve of Parimá, which represented a transitory management category. In the Upper Rio Negro Region, there was only the Rio Negro Forest Reserve (transitory) in Brazil, and the El Tuparro Faunal Territory in Colombia. There were, however, in these two regions, vast areas which had been recommended for nature conservation by the RADAMBRASIL. The Upper Rio Negro Region encompassed four proposed Venezuelan National Parks and 20 Biological Reserves;
- the analysis of the conservation units according to the vegetation formation showed that at that time the most complete coverage—existing and planned—was in the tropical evergreen rainforest of Terra Firme, which makes up approximately 90% of the area under study. Nevertheless, most of these areas did not meet the priorities established. In fact, neither the National Park of the Amazon (Tapajós) with one million ha, the only Brazilian conservation unit existing in the region

at the time, nor the proposed Rio Negro National Park would be considered as first or even second priority, according to the established criteria;

- the analysis based on vegetation formations also revealed some gaps in Brazil: the "Caatinga" of the Upper Rio Negro; the "Várzea" Grassland of the Upper Rio Xingu and the Atlantic Coast; and the Grassland of "Terra Firme";

- only a few of the existing conservation units, none of which were found in Brazil at that time, co-incided with areas designated priority according to the criteria presented in the document. These conservation units included the following: the Natural Reserves of Kaysergebergte and Taffel-berg in Suriname; the National Park of Caniama in Venezuela; the Isiboro Sécure National Park in Bolivia; the National Park of Sangay in Ecuador; and the national parks of Manu and Tingo Maria in Peru. In addition to these, a new national park, Amacayacu, in Colombia, includes part of one priority area. The study did not include a qualitative evaluation of the protection provided the above-mentioned areas;

- the terminology used to identify conservation units in several nations presented a confusing picture, when viewed regionally. "National park" is a term used by many countries, whereas others use terms such as "Biological Reserve", "Ecological Station", "National Reserve", "Natural Reserve", and "Natural Park". In some cases the objectives of these different categories of management overlap, even within the same country. Where the overlapping categories are created and implemented by separate government organizations within the same country, unnecessary duplication of human and financial resources are often incurred; and

- only in three of the fifteen Brazilian Development Centres of the Amazon (Altamira, Aripuaná, and Juruá-Solomés) were there first priority areas, with high endemic probability according to the analysis of refuges.

From the biological viewpoint, an appropriate goal of conservation in the Amazon would be that of preserving an average of three large samples of each phytogeographic region and three or more smaller ones. The larger samples should have an average of 5,000 km each, including a nucleus of 2,590 sq km and a buffer strip 10 km wide, depending on the local conditions. At least 24 smaller reserves, with about 1,000 sq km each, should also be created for special micro-habitats, such as bird or turtle nesting sites, areas for the concentration of species or for other important natural phenomena such as dunes, waterfalls, and so forth.

5. RESULTS OF THE PUBLIC REVISION

The "Analysis of Nature Conservation Priorities in the Amazon" was widely circulated by IBDF and FAO in both Portuguese and English and public comments were solicited prior to June 1978.

About twenty written responses, both from Brazilians and from foreigners, representing government agencies, research institutes, museums, universities and conservation organizations were received. These were summarized in the document "The 1978 status of Nature Preservation in the Brazilian Amazon" (Wetterberg and Jorge Padua, 1978).

The comments ranged from very brief statements to several-page letters. In some cases, letters were further exchanged in order to clarify points or suggestions. All this mail has been kept in a special file at IBDF for future reference. In general, the comments indicated that, in view of the present state of scientific knowledge about the Amazon, this approach is the most suitable one. *The most important factor is that no all-encompassing strategy was suggested as an alternative.*

After being broadly identified, the potential units for the conservation of nature in the Amazon had to be analyzed in more depth. For this purpose, several new expeditions were made. The trips to the Amazon included an interdisciplinary staff, among whom were scientists who had identified the Pleistocene refuges.

Of the 34 areas visited in the first stage of the System Plan, 13 met the criteria of evaluation and were recommended as national parks and biological reserves. Ten of these areas have already been established as parks or reserves by Presidential Decrees.

Of the 64 areas visited all over Brazil in the second stage of the System Plan, 9 were selected as national parks and biological reserves, in the Amazon, making a total of approximately 6,800,000 ha.

In addition to this system, there is additional basic legislation which limits the use of the renewable natural resources under certain conditions such as, for example, the Forest Code and the Law for the Protection of Fauna. This legislation is particularly effective in areas which are not under any sort of management category or which, due to their meagre dimensions, do not fall into any category.

6. PRESENT SITUATION

Of the 13 areas recommended in the First Stage of the System Plan for Conservation Units, seven have been established in the Brazilian Amazon. Additional areas have been established in neighbouring countries and a composite overview has been published (Wetterberg, Prance and Lovejoy, 1981).

For the Brazilian portion of the Amazon, the Second Stage was released at the time this paper was prepared and, up to the moment of its presentation, obviously no unit had been created yet, but will be in the near future.

It is thus evident that Brazil has taken a giant step forward in the planning of its systems for conservation units, by creating seven new units in the Amazon in the last three years, totalling about 7,000,000 ha. It is also clear, however, that there is still a great deal to do, for the second stage of the Plan was introduced only in April, 1982—and there still remain three stages.

The goal established in "An Analysis of Nature Conservation Priorities in the Amazon", which is endorsed by the government, is that of guaranteeing a minimum of 18,500,000 ha for the Brazilian Amazon in national parks and biological reserves and 5,000,000 ha for the region outside the Amazon, totalling 23,500,000 ha. This implies that about 13 million ha need to be added to the existing 10.4 million ha to complete the system.

It is necessary to implement this system of conservation units, guarantee its integrity, provide the national parks and other protected areas with effective management and control, and prepare them to facilitate scientific research and to receive visitors. We can then feel fairly confident that the natural diversity of Brazil will be conserved for future generations.

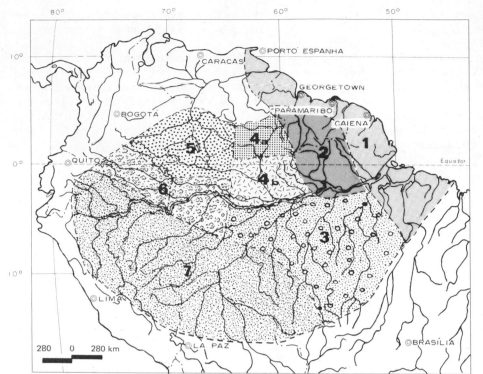

Figure 1. The seven Phytogeographic regions of the Amazon. Source: Padua.

1 Atlantic Coast
2 Jari-Trombetas
3 Xingu-Madeira
4a Roraima
4b Manaus
5 Upper Rio Negro
6 Solimões-Amazonas
7 Southwest

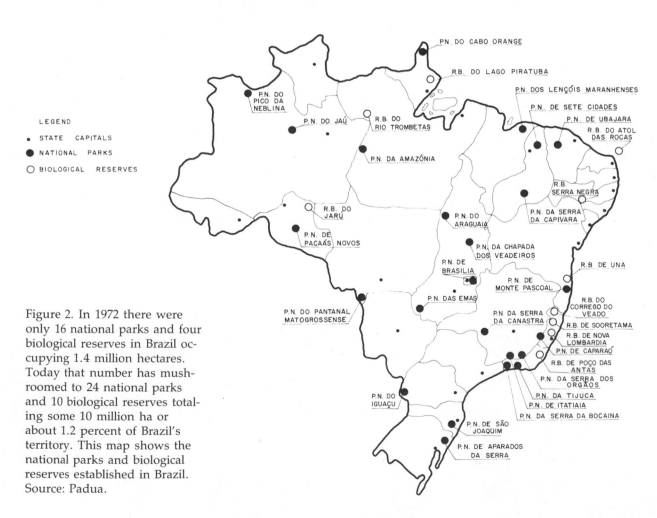

LEGEND
• STATE CAPITALS
● NATIONAL PARKS
○ BIOLOGICAL RESERVES

P.N. DO CABO ORANGE
R.B. DO LAGO PIRATUBA
P.N. DOS LENÇÓIS MARANHENSES
P.N. DE SETE CIDADES
P.N. DE UBAJARA
R.B. DO ATOL DAS ROCAS
P.N. DO PICO DA NEBLINA
P.N. DO JAÚ
R.B. DO RIO TROMBETAS
P.N. DA AMAZÔNIA
R.B. SERRA NEGRA
P.N. DA SERRA DA CAPIVARA
R.B. DO JARÚ
P.N. DO ARAGUAIA
P.N. DE PACAÁS NOVOS
P.N. DA CHAPADA DOS VEADEIROS
P.N. DE BRASILIA
R.B DE UNA
P.N. DAS EMAS
P.N. DE MONTE PASCOAL
P.N. DO PANTANAL MATOGROSSENSE
R.B. DO CORREGO DO VEADO
P.N. DA SERRA DA CANASTRA
R.B. DE SOORETAMA
R.B. DE NOVA LOMBARDIA
P.N. DE CAPARAÓ
R.B. DE POÇO DAS ANTAS
P.N. DA SERRA DOS ORGÃOS
P.N. DA TIJUCA
P.N. DE ITATIAIA
P.N. DA SERRA DA BOCAINA
P.N. DO IGUAÇU
P.N. DE SÃO JOAQUIM
P.N. DE APARADOS DA SERRA

Figure 2. In 1972 there were only 16 national parks and four biological reserves in Brazil occupying 1.4 million hectares. Today that number has mushroomed to 24 national parks and 10 biological reserves totaling some 10 million ha or about 1.2 percent of Brazil's territory. This map shows the national parks and biological reserves established in Brazil. Source: Padua.

NATIONAL PARKS, CONSERVATION, AND DEVELOPMENT

Figure 3. The Amazon has nine major vegetation types. Source: Padua.

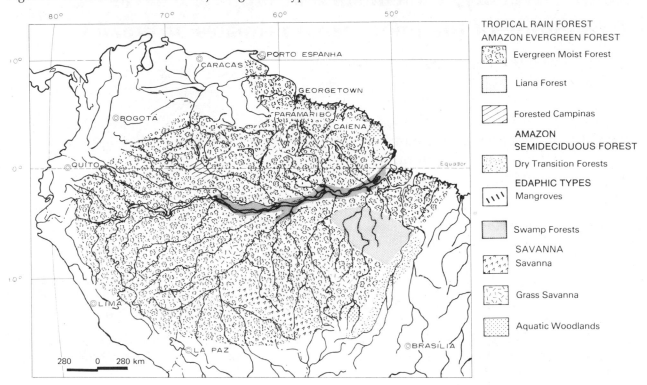

TROPICAL RAIN FOREST
AMAZON EVERGREEN FOREST

Evergreen Moist Forest

Liana Forest

Forested Campinas

AMAZON
SEMIDECIDUOUS FOREST

Dry Transition Forests

EDAPHIC TYPES
Mangroves

Swamp Forests

SAVANNA
Savanna

Grass Savanna

Aquatic Woodlands

Figure 4. General areas recommended for habitat protection include: 1) Bacia do Capim. 2) Oiapoque. 3) Cabo Orange. 4) Cabo Norte. 5) Maraba. 6) Guiana. 7) Ponta do Flechal. 12) Altamira. 9) Caxinduba, 10) Upper Xingu. 11) Jau. 12) Jatapu. 13) Pico da Neblina. 14) Cuxiauaia. 15) Cutiuaia. 16) Loreto. 17) North Napo. 18) Panaua. 19) South Napo. 20) Javari. 21) Huallaga. 22) Serra do Divisor. 23) Ucayali. 24) Inambari. 25) Yungas. 26) Eirunepe. 27) Purus. 28) Marmelos. 29) Serra das Oncas. 30) Parecis. Source: Padua/Parks Magazine, Vol. 6, No. 2, 1981.

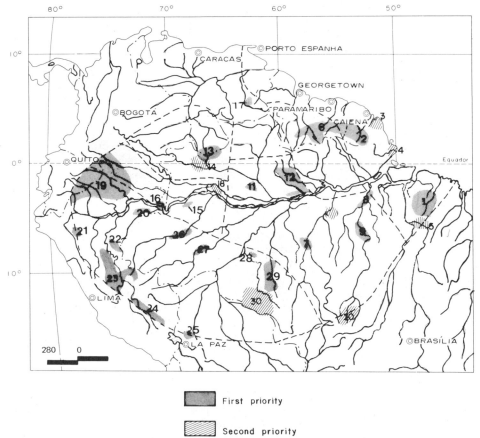

First priority

Second priority

Genetic Diversity, Endemism and Protected Areas: A Case Study of the Endangered Primates of Brazil's Atlantic Forest Region

Admiral Ibsen de Gusmao Camara
Brazilian Conservation Foundation (FBCN)
Rio de Janeiro, Brazil

Russell A. Mittermeier
World Wildlife Fund
Washington, D.C.

ABSTRACT. *The Atlantic forests of eastern Brazil are a unique series of ecosystems quite distinct from Amazonia. These forests contain a large number of unique species of plants and animals, including two genera (Leontopithecus and Brachyteles) of primates. Unfortunately, these genetic resources are under severe pressure from alternative forms of development; local and international efforts in Brazil are concentrating on conserving at least representative samples of the remaining habitats and key species in the Atlantic forests.*

1. INTRODUCTION

The Atlantic forests of eastern Brazil (Fig. 1) are a unique series of ecosystems quite distinct from Amazonia. They originally stretched almost continuously from the state of Rio Grande do Norte at the easternmost tip of South America as far as Rio Grande do Sul, the southernmost Brazilian state, and included some of the finest forests anywhere on earth. However, eastern Brazil, and especially the southeast, was the first part of the country to be heavily colonized, and it is now the most densely-inhabited part of the country and also the agricultural and industrial centre. The result has been forest destruction of incredible proportions, especially in the last 10-20 years of rapid economic development, for lumber and charcoal and to make way for plantations, cattle pasture, and industry. We estimate that only 1 to 5% of the original forest cover remains in the 13 eastern Brazilian states in which Atlantic forest formations are found, and that primary forest that has never been modified by man accounts for well under 1%.

Most of the remaining forests are in a series of federal, state and privately owned parks and reserves in which protection varies from adequate to almost non-existent, and poaching and illegal land encroachment are often serious problems. Only a handful of these protected areas can be considered secure for the future.

Since the Atlantic forests have a long history of independent evolution, they have a high number of endemic plant and animal species. It has been estimated that 53.5% of the tree species of this region are endemic (Mori, *et al.*, 1981) and more than 80% of the primates and many of the birds are as well. Since so little forest remains, the existing protected areas in this region are of paramount importance in ensuring the survival of a wide variety of genetic resources that are unique to Brazil.

In this paper, we will use the primates of the Atlantic forest to illustrate the problems of this region, and the prospects for *in situ* conservation of genetic resources for future populations of Brazilians and for the world at large.

2. THE PRIMATES OF EASTERN BRAZIL

Six genera and at least 19 species and subspecies of nonhumnan primates are found in the Atlantic forest region of eastern Brazil, making this area second only to Amazonia in richness and diversity of primates in South America. The six genera include:

- *Callithrix*, the marmosets, with six species in the region;
- *Leontopithecus*, the lion tamarins, with three species;
- *Callicebus*, the titi monkeys, with one species and three subspecies;

- *Cebus*, the tufted capuchins, with one species and four subspecies;
- *Alouatta*, the howler monkeys, with one species and two subspecies; and
- *Brachyteles*, the muriqui, with one species.

Two of these genera, *Leontopithecus* and *Brachyteles*, are endemic to the Atlantic forest, and a third, *Callithrix*, reaches its greatest diversity there. Of the 19 species and subspecies, 16, or 84%, are endemic. The last three are found mainly in the *cerrado* and *caatinga* formations of central and northeastern Brazil and just extend into the northeastern portion of the Atlantic forest.

Since 1979, conservation-oriented survey work has been conducted on the primates of the Atlantic forest region by a joint survey team composed of personnel from World Wildlife Fund-US, the Zoology Dept. of the Federal University of Minas Gerais and the Rio de Janeiro Primate Center (FEEMA-CPRJ), with the collaboration of the Brazilian Conservation Foundation (FBCN) and funded by World Wildlife Fund-US. This team has investigated the status of eastern Brazilian primates in 25 federal, state and private protected areas, and now has data on 17 of the 19 species and subspecies found there. Their data indicate that fully 13 of these 17 are already endangered and another two are vulnerable, and that several of the endangered species also happen to be representatives of the two endemic primate genera, *Leontopithecus* and *Brachyteles*, so their situation can be taken as indicative of what is happening in the region as a whole (Mittermeirer, *et al.*, 1980; Mittermeier, *et al.*, 1981).

2.1. The golden lion tamarin

One of the most strikingly colored of all mammals, the golden lion tamarin *Leontopithecus rosalia* has always been restricted to the coastal lowlands of the state of Rio de Janeiro. Widespread forest destruction has resulted in the almost total disappearance of its forest habitat, and wild populations of the species have been reduced to extremely precarious levels. The joint survey team has succeeded in locating the golden lion tamarin in only two areas, one the 5,000 ha Poco d'Anta Biological Reserve, which was established in 1974 mainly for the protection of this species, and the other a stretch of forest along the coast to the south of the mouth of the Rio Sao Joao. The latter area has already been divided into lots for beachfront housing developments and appears to be doomed, leaving Poco d'Anta as the only hope for the survival of the golden lion tamarin in the wild.

Unfortunately, the situation in Poco d'Anta is far from satisfactory. The reserve is cut by a railroad and a road, a dam that will flood a portion of it is now being completed, poaching still takes place within its borders, and the guard force of six is not sufficient to patrol the reserve at maximum efficiency. Furthermore, the most

detailed survey (Green, 1980) in the reserve to date has indicated that only about 10% is mature forest and only about 30% is suitable habitat for the lion tamarins. The total population of lion tamarins in the reserve was estimated at about 75 animals.

To remedy this situation, a major programme is currently being developed by the Brazilian Forestry Development (IBDF), which administers the reserve, the Rio de Janeiro Primate Center (CPRJ), which has the only captive colonies of the golden lion tamarin in Brazil, the National Zoo in Washington, D.C., which holds the international studbook for the species, and WWF-US. This programme will include long term research on the Poco d'Anta lion tamarin population, a forest restoration project to increase the amount of suitable habitat in the reserve, and possibly reintroduction of individuals from the highly successful captive colonies. If this programme is launched quickly and if it can achieve its goals, the outlook for this species will be at least a little brighter.

2.2. The muriqui

The muriqui *Brachyteles arachnoides* is the largest South American monkey and the largest mammal endemic to Brazil. It is also the most endangered monkey in the Neotropics, and ranks high on the list of the world's most endangered primates. The joint survey team has thus far been able to document the existence of only about 100 individuals in six small and widely-separated protected areas, and poaching continues to be a threat in several of these. The most important area located to date is a forest on a privately-owned coffee plantation known as Fazenda Montes Clacros, near Caratinga in the state of Minas Gerais. At least 40 muriquis live in this forest, and they constitute what may well be the only large social group of this species left on earth.

The Brazilian Conservation Foundation (FBCN) has initiated a special fund-raising campaign for the muriqui in Brazil, and WWF-US has done the same in the United States. One of the main purposes of these campaigns is to purchase the forest at Fazenda Montes Claros and to develop a reserve and a research and training centre for Brazilian students there. At the same time, these two organizations, together with the Zoology Department of the Federal University of Minas Gerais, have been carrying out an education campaign to increase awareness of the importance of the muriqui to Brazil and to bring about decisive action on its behalf. The education campaign has included lecture tours, both in cities and in the interior, distribution of educational materials (e.g. stickers, t-shirts, calendars, etc.), development of conservation exhibits, and considerable press coverage for the muriqui, especially at Fazenda Montes Claros. A special film, entitled ''Cry of the Muriqui'' has also been produced by the WWF-US Primate Programme, and it is being translated into Portuguese for use on Brazilian television. It includes the first ever wild-shot footage of both the muriqui and the golden lion tamarin, and it will figure prominently in the campaigns.

Given the fact that the muriqui is a spectacular animal and the largest mammal entirely restricted to Brazil, we believe that it could easily become for Brazil what the giant panda is for China. Nonetheless, we must emphasize that this animal is literally on the brink of extinction, and a major international effort will be needed if it is to survive even to the end of the decade.

3. CONCLUSION

It should be clear that the survival of *Leontopithecus* and *Brachyteles* hangs in the balance. Furthermore, since they are unique *genera* and not just unique species, their extinction would represent a substantial loss of diversity not only for Brazil's primate fauna but for the Order Primates as a whole. Consequently, their conservation should be considered a very high priority, both nationally and internationally, and they should be used to

focus attention on the plight on the entire Atlantic forest region.

Fortunately, though the situation for these species and their Atlantic forest habitat must be considered extremely critical, there have been some encouraging signs. The IUCN/SSC Primate Specialist Group has identified the Atlantic forest region as one of the two highest primate conservation priorities in the world, along with the island of Madagascar; WWF-US continues to consider the Atlantic forest one of its major priorities, as it has since 1979; and WWF-International has included the Atlantic forest in its Tropical Forests and Primates Campaign. Within Brazil, the Brazilian Conservation Foundation (FBCN), the Rio de Janeiro Primate Center (FEEMA-CPRJ), and several grass roots conservation organizations in the state of Minas Gerais consider the Atlantic forest their number-one priority, and are increasing their efforts on its behalf. As a result, we hope that it will be possible to save at least a representative cross-section of the faunal and floral diversity of this once magnificent part of Brazil's wildlife heritage.

Figure 1. The original extent of the Atlantic forest region of eastern Brazil.

Inca Technology and Ecodevelopment: Conservation of the Vicunas in Pampa Galeras

Carlos F. Ponce del Prado
Departamento de Manejo Forestal
Universidad Nacional Agraria
La Molina, Lima, Peru

ABSTRACT. *The vicuna was nearly driven to extinction by over-exploitation, but protection has brought about an amazing recovery to the point where vicuna can once again be harvested to bring benefits to local people. This paper describes how the vicuna was saved, and the steps that are planned for the future to both maintain thriving populations of the species and to use the vicuna to bring benefits to local people.*

1. INTRODUCTION

The highlands of Peru cover some 16 million ha, known as "puna." During the rise of the Andean cultures, which culminated in the fabulous Inca Empire, millions of vicunas populated the region. The valuable products they yielded—the finest animal fiber (8-10 microns), meat, skin, and furs—were distributed to bring benefits to both the local people and the imperial Inca government.

The equilibrium between the man and the Andes was destroyed by the conquest of the Spaniards, who looked only on vicuna only as a source of fiber. This exploitation continued until recently, accelerated by human demand until the once-flourishing herds of vicuna had all but disappeared from the puna they once dominated. Peru provided a sad example of human pressure out of control leading to the near-extinction of a valuable species.

The reaction to this perilous situation is the subject of this case study, which is put forward in the hope that our experience will be helpful in other countries which are trying to bring valuable species back from the brink of extinction.

The case study reports on the Pampa Galeras National Reserve in the Ayacucho Department, where, over twenty years, we have developed a technology for vi-cuna management which approaches that of the Incas in managing the vicuna; this involves the maximum use of local people—who still have Inca blood flowing in their veins. The Incas inculcated respect of wildlife by local people through involving them in the process known as "chaco," a sort of round-up that, according to Spanish chroniclers of the 15th century, involved thousands of men.

Of the six species of the Camel family (Camelidae), four are South American and all occur in Peru. The vicuna *Vicugna vicugna* is one of the two species of wild South American camelids; the other is the guanaco *Lama guanicoe*. The llama *Lama glama* and the alpaca *Lama pacos* were obtained after domestication of the guanaco, according to recent interpretations.

During the preColumbian times and especially during the Inca Empire (15th and beginning of 16th centuries), the puna was inhabited by large herds of vicunas and the other camelids. The ancient Peruvians treated the wild species of camelids (vicuna and guanaco) in such a way that they were as useful as the domestic species (llama and alpaca); they argued, according to Garcilaso (1609), that wild species have not been created by the Pachacamac (the Sun God) to be useless.

The domination of the indigenous culture by the European invader led to a disturbance of the relation between the local people and the living resources—the Spaniards had not had centuries to learn how to adapt to the puna and were in any case convinced of their cultural superiority. From the time of conquest, the gradual decline of camelid populations continued until it reached a climax in fairly recent years. In 1957, Karl Koford, in a pioneer work, estimated 250,000 vicunas in all the Peruvian territory; by 1968, Ian Grimwood, for the same range, estimated just 7,500 individuals.

The only explanation for this tragic decline was

illegal commerce of vicuna's products, nourished by very intense poaching.

The alarming diminution was a constant worry of the governments, all the way back to the King of Spain. In this respect, the action of Liberator Simon Bolivar is very significant, who provided in 1825 clear legislation for the protection and rational use of the vicunas. However, as this concern was not reflected in effective field protection, the species continued to decline.

Some 435 years after the fall of the Inca empire and of the rupture between native man and his land, the Peruvian government established in 1967 the Reserva Nacional de Pampa Galeras, with the main objective to protect the last individuals of vicuna (some 600), and to re-establish the rational use of vicuna for the benefit of the Andean communities (which are the most economically disadvantaged in the country).

The puna of Peru, spreading over 12.3% of the country, supports some 2.5 million people, with the subsequent problems of over-population in relation to the available resources. New generations are forced to emigrate to the cities on the coast and in the tropical Amazonian region. It is expected that through new patterns in the use of the living resources of the Andes, new employment opportunities and generation of wealth will occur.

2. BACKGROUND INFORMATION

As was mentioned, the different governments that ruled Peru were conscious about the necessity to stop the diminution of camelid populations and especially of the vicuna. In 1577, the King of Spain signed a royal ordinance forbidding the "hunting of big cattle" including the vicuna among others. Years later, other crown representatives, such as Viceroy Amat y Juniet in 1768, worried about vicuna conservation. This worry continued after the establishment of the Republic and in 1825 a Dictatorial Decree of Simon Bolivar prohibited the killing of vicunas in any numbers and established fines for violators. In 1851, a Supreme Decree forbade the export of alpaca and vicuna "wool" and re-enforced the mentioned Dictatorial Decree. In 1907, regional authorities were directed to enforce the same Dictatorial Decree. Between 1920 and 1926 the textile manufacture with vicuna fibres and the commerce of skin and furs were prohibited and the prohibition of vicuna fibre exportation was reiterated. In 1940, the Congress approved a better-structured law for conservation of vicuna and other wildlife, declaring the special protection of the State over them. These mentioned norms are just some of the nearly two dozen laws protecting the vicuna that were dicated until 1967.

Unfortunately, the decline of vicuna continued because of a growing demand, mainly for the production of high quality textiles abroad and to the lack of law enforcement, especially in the first half of this century. The governmental administration was not totally ignorant of the methods and practices of management of animal populations; guano bird management, including land protection, strict control, and specific regulations, had been carried out since the end of the 19th century. But this experience, possibly the first such management in Latin America, was little recognized by the local governors.

It can be noted that all previous intents to prevent the extinction of the vicuna were in the form of laws on paper without the required enforcement in the field (in spite of having the useful experience of the guano birds).

3. LIMITATIONS AND CONSTRAINTS

When trying to explain the inefficiency of the legal statements, it is possible to identify, among others, the following reasons:

3.1. Political

Insufficient understanding by the high level authorities is evident; there are no clear political guidelines for natural renewable resources conservation, and this is the reason why the wildlife is considered of at most marginal yield.

Lack of information and motiviation in the high political levels prevented effective law enforcement. None of the political parties have a clear position about the socio-economic importance of vicuna and other live resources.

3.2. Legal

The many statutes for the protection of vicuna were very light in the enforcement aspects. Laws were issued without considering the financial aspects of their execution. On the other hand, the national legislation was not co-ordinated with the neighbouring countries which also support vicuna: Argentina, Bolivia and Chile.

3.3. Ecological

The Spanish conquerors imported the cattle species with which they were familiar. Today, "traditional" cattle raising is based on the use of these exotic species, with a very low yield—due to the severe environmental limitations—and the soil is deteriorating because of poor management. Sheep in the puna yield just 4 kg of meat and 1/2 kg of wool per year, while sheep in more appropriate habitats may yield 8 kg of meat and 4.5 kg of wool. Despite the low yields, exotic species are linked in the minds of the people with an image of wealth and success and that means a "better" social status.

The camelids offer a much better ecological and

economic option. The structure of the hooves (with soft pads), the grazing behaviour (nibbling the tops of grasses, permitting a better use of the scantily-distributed high-altitude species of grass), and the physiological adaptation to a severe environment (permitting higher productivity) are all factors which make the camelids the highest-yielding animals of the puna.

3.4. Financial

Budgets of the natural resource managmement agencies are insufficient to carry out optimal management. We can say, without fear of being contradicted, that education, culture and conservation had always received the lowest share of the national budget.

3.5. Socio-cultural

The men of the puna have been exploited by those in power for centuries, yielding an attitude of distrust of any initiative from outside. In this situation, endorsement must be earned by demonstration of real benefits to the people. There is also a problem with superstition; the rural villagers kill a number of newborn vicuna to remove the rennet, which is thought to promote long life when eaten.

3.6. Land tenure

The effective protection of the land is affected by the non-existence, practically, of state lands in the actual and potential areas of vicuna distribution. Most of the lands belong to the communities of countrymen, with illegal private properties developing inside and complicating the figure. For the zoning of lands for vicuna protection, specific agreements with these communities are necessary.

3.7. Scientific

Research about camelids was clearly insufficient and mainly focussed on the general description of species; it was not enough for to start the management of vicuna populations. Very sophisticated research about physiology of domestic camelids, mainly alpaca, was available, but was of little use for vicuna management.

4. THE ACTION

Mindful of the local experience in management of guano birds and the impact of successful recovery programmes in other countries, and supported by political and technical action of Peruvian personalities, the national administration in charge of wildlife management de-

signed an Action Plan for the recovery and subsequent use of vicuna. In general terms, the Plan included the following elements:

- Establishment of a protected area;
- improvement of the national legislation;
- close coordination with the authorities in neighbouring countries who share vicuna habitat;
- international co-ordination to oppose the traffic of vicuna products;
- development of information campaigns at local and national levels;
- research on the management of the species through national institutions such as the National Agrarian University and supported by international technical cooperation;
- personnel training at different levels, with emphasis on field personnel.

4.1. Establishment of the Reserva Nacional de Pampa Galeras

In 1967, after detailed coordination with the Comunidad Campesina de Lucanas (Departmento de Ayacucho), an agreement of specific collaboration was signed whereby the government established the Reserve Nacional de Vicunas en Pampa Galeras, earlier identified by the Servicio Forestal y de Caza, with the aid of National Agrarian University investigators, as the most appropriate vicuna habitat. The agreement signed by the Servicio Forestal y de Caza, representing the state, and the Comunidad Campesian de Lucanas, considered vicuna management as the only use of the 6,500 ha reserve.

The legal document (Resolucion Supreme 157-A), states that the programme of vicuna protection and research must bring economic benefit to the Comunidad Campesina de Lucanas through the participation of local people in the management of these protected areas.

Even before the legal establishment of the Reserve, patrolling of the reserve began, and in July 1965, a two-month training course for rangers was carried out. These personnel not only controlled poaching within the reserve, but also in the 60,000 ha plateau called Pampa Galeras. The poachers were well-supplied and aggressive, so the rangers needed to be armed.

Today, thanks to the experience of controlling 90,000 ha, we know that protection can be accomplished with the establishment of ranger posts—after agreement with landowners—and with rangers enforcing the national protection legislation.

4.2. Improvement of national legislation

The new legislation passed since 1967 provides drastic sanctions to discourage poaching and even more drastic sanctions for those who trade in vicuna products. In this line, Decreto Ley 17816 was promulgated in 1969.

In all the history of vicuna legislation, this Decreto Ley marked a turning point in the attitude of public powers; the punishment of 1 year of prison for each vicuna killed and 3 to 5 years for traders, without liberation on bail, conditional sentence or probation, was a clear declaration of the State's commitment to vicuna conservation.

4.3. International coordination

Realizing that bilateral cooperation is one of the best ways to yield successful results in the protection of natural resources and, particularly, of wildlife, official communications were started between Peru and Bolivia in 1964. In 1969, an agreement between the two governments on conservation of the vicuna was signed and was opened to the adherence of the governments of Argentina and Chile, who signed in 1979 and 1972 respectively.

This agreement has the following measures:

- Prohibition and repression of poaching and trade of fibers, hairs, furs and other products;
- prohibition of export and imports for 10 years;
- the establishment of Reserves and rearing centres;
- periodic meetings of technical and administrative character and the establishment of a permanent information centre; and
- development of education campaigns.

In 1979, the Agreement for the Conservation and Management of the vicuna was subscribed in Lima by representatives of Bolivia, Chile, Ecuador and Peru. This new international agreement recognizes the vicuna as of crucial economic benefit to the Andean people, and endorses the concept of utilization, under strict state control, following the guidelines of wildlife management. Furthermore, the Convenio endorses the previous agreements.

At the international level, Peru subscribed to CITES, which maintains the vicuna as an Appendix I species.

4.4. Training

In the first years of the sixties, the national administration of forest and fauna obtained FAO support for the development of a Faculty of Foresty Science in the Universidad Nacional Agraria, which includes wildlife and national parks in the curriculum, and a School of Forest Technicians.

For field activities, personnel were trained, recruited and retrained, through a special course with a mean length of 10 weeks. From 1965 to the present, 6 couses have been completed; 2 were international.

The Forest Police were formed in 1975 as a specialized branch of the national police; they too receive training in coordination with the forest and fauna administration.

4.5. Extension campaigns

An education campaign designed mainly for the "campesinos" was carried out, notwithstanding the state's economic limitations; this campaign was developed and multiplied through economic and technical international cooperation. Pamphlets, posters, decals, radio programmes, articles in newspapers and a few TV broadcasts were produced and distributed; materials used for local people were primarily of a visual character. High level authorities were also targetted for special attention.

As in many countries, organizations such as WWF, IUCN, the Frankfurt Zoological Society, the Government of Belgium and of the Federal Republic of Germany provided welcome support in this campaign.

4.6. Technical cooperation

The national forest and fauna authority, because of the personnel and budgetary limitations, contacted a number of sources of technical cooperation. In 1965, the Peace Corps of USA helped in the beginning of the field work. The Government of Belgium supported the completion of facilities in the Pampa Galeras Reserve. WWF made an important contribution.

Peru owes a special acknowledgement to the Federal Republic of Germany, which supplied significant technical and economical assistance through the German Agency for Technical Cooperation (GTZ) from 1972 to 1980, providing key momentum to the national programme of vicuna conservation.

Of the 13 ranger posts built betwen 1971 and 1980, 6 were financed by the Frankfurt Zoological Society, 3 by WWF, 1 by Belgium and 3 by the national administration.

5. RESULTS

5.1. Recovery of populations

In 1967, the number of vicuna in the 6500 ha legal zone was 812 individuals, a particularly low level due to a drought. Censuses carried out in the Pampa Galeras Reserve plus the zone of influence (nearly 90,000 ha) from 1974 to 1981 showed the following:

Year	Numbers
1974	10,806
1975	14,151
1976	17,403
1977	20,454
1978	23,001
1979	18,152
1980	18,335
1981	18,356

Following the National Plan for the Utilization of the Vicuna (1976), the total number of vicuna in the entire puna zone has been estimated as follows:

Year	Numbers
1977	45,000
1978	55,500
1979	65,000
1980	72,200
1981	84,000

It appears that success in protecting the vicuna has brought about a new problem: Overpopulation of this endangered species at Pampa Galeras. While absolute protection is needed at the national level, reduction of numbers in Pampa Galeras is imperative. This was one of the major reasons why Peru requested the the vicuna be moved from CITES Appendix I to Appendix II. Unfortunately for the vicuna management programme, the request was refused because of the action of some organizations concerned with vicuna protection, who were misinformed and were uncertain about the success of recovery.

International organizations, notably IUCN, have reviewed the information and field procedures that yielded the above population figures.

5.2. Mixed grazing

In fulfilling the agreement with the Comunidad de Lucanas, the recovery programme also involved grazing by other herbivores. The research conducted has served to correct the idea that lands needed to be set apart exclusively for vicuna protection. Today, we are increasing the productivity of the land through the addition—not just substitution—of benefits produced by the rational use of vicuna. We hope that through time and example, the highland people will resume appropriate treatment of the land through managing native species better adapted to the environment.

5.3. Technical information

After almost 20 years of the vicuna programme, basic research for management has been developed; methods for census, capture, culling and translocation are clearly defined. But education campaigns are still needed, especially at the highest political levels, for prevention of negative reaction to the culling when and where this is needed.

5.4. Field Control

The dramatic recovery of the vicuna population is directly related to the repression of poaching; it is the intention of Peru, in spite of all constraints, that an appropriate vicuna population will be reached, and this requires continuing field control. The ranger work is supported by the cooperation with forest police; when this special branch of the Guardia Civil was designed, the idea was to give it control of the periphery with strategic access to the management areas. However, due to a hastiness in the political decision, all the control was been transferred to Forest Police in 1980.

Experience clearly demonstrates the necessity for the re-establishment of an effective ranger force for the Pampa Galeras region, made up of local people, who due to their birthplace, background and devotion to work, are better able to carry out both technical work with the vicuna and anti-poaching patrols.

5.5. Communal participation

The control, research, training and administrative work was so intense that the coordination with local communities was poorly developed; with the addition of the cultural limitations, the direct participation of local people in the recovery programme was slight. Decreto Ley 22964 (1980) established a system of monetary compensation to the communities and other land owners, for the grazing of vicunas in those lands. This is only one way for the involvement of local people. Participation in the translocation operations is planned, and the maintenance of good relations with the communities will be characteristic of the Pampa Galeras Reserve administration.

5.6. Administrative experience

Different formulae were tested for the improvement of the recovery programme administration. In 1978, the Special Project for the Rational Use of Vicuna was started, endowed with great administrative self-determination and maintaining technical-normative relations with the Ministry of Agriculture, through the General Directorate of Forest and Fauna.

Unfortunately, by a later decision, it lost its power of self-determination and was transferred in January 1981 to the National Institute of Forestry and Fauna. An excess of bureaucracy and centralization in the capital of the Republic is an undesirable characteristic developed during the past few years. An improvement in its tasks must be attained through the decentralization and establishment of regional headquarters in the management areas.

5.7. Management of vicuna population

Since 1977, reduction of numbers was needed because of the carrying capacity had been reached in some areas.

Two ways were used, culling and translocation. The numbers involved in these activities are as follows:

Year	Number
1977	210
1978	400
1979	1558
1980	3012
1981	1467

Translocation from Pampa Galeras was initiated in 1979 with 161 individuals. Estimated cost for translocation is US$ 2,000 per vicuna (capture, transport, ranger post, personnel and maintenance in new places, and compensation to the people in new places).

When research on capture was started, use of tranquilizers and equipment were tested. The fragility of vicuna made this method very risky. Today we imitate the Inca "chaco" technology, which is a kind of large-scale drive into circular yards. Vicunas are driven through sleeves, arranged as the mouth of a funnel.

During the controversy around culling (1979-81), it was suggested to replace the drivers—local people—with helicopters as a way for the improvement of the capture; a test showed that operational costs skyrocketted and the work opportunities for local people were greatly reduced. Today we only support the "chaco," employing local men.

Maintaining translocation as a primary part of the recovery programme, culling is the most effective and rational solution to the local overpopulation problem. Initiated in 1977, without the necessary public opinion preparation as a consequence of an unexpected environmental crisis (drought), the culling received strongest opposition during years 1979, 1980 and 1981.

6. CONCLUSIONS

This brief summary of a wildlife recovery programme so broad and complex as the vicuna programme, is ignoring without doubt many aspects that could be of personal interest to individuals around the world; however, our main conclusions are the following:

- Effective recovery of endangered wildlife is only possible with constant and well equipped patrolling. During the theocratic government of the Incas, vicuna was protected with strong sanctions which included death.
- Recovery of endangered wildlife of high economic value is only possible when local people are involved in all management activities and particularly in the distribution of benefits. In the case of vicuna, 5 centuries after the fall of the Inca empire, we are proposing what had been usual practice of Incas: local responsibilities for the drives (chaco) and proportional distribution of benefits.
- The objectives of the recovery programmes must be totally and widely disseminated, especially if culling is involved.
- When the habitat of the species is shared with other countries, coordination is essential. Poaching and trade are reduced, allowing a better use of funds in the recovery programme (research, etc.).
- Wildlife management requires a non-bureaucratic administration, closely linked to the field activities, and probably a part of the traditional and routine administration of ministries. When a recovery programme spreads over large areas—as in vicuna, over 16 million ha—its regionalization is a necessity.
- If the species gave benefits in the past, the ancient harvest techniques must be analyzed in the light of new technology.

Acknowledgements

This paper was prepared for IUCN's Commission on National Parks and Protected Areas in cooperation with CIDA.

Ecuadorian Strategy for the Conservation of Wildlands and Wildlife

Arturo Ponce Salazar
Departamento de Areas Naturales y Vida silvestre
Quito, Ecuador

ABSTRACT. *After two years of preparatory work, a national strategy for conserving the outstanding natural areas of Ecuador was produced in 1976. The study had three major objectives: in the short-term to identify the best natural areas in the country, to determine the most adequate system of management for each area, and to establish priorities among these areas; in the medium-term, to protect the most important ecosystems in the country and to offer goods and services for urban areas through the administration of protected areas; and in the long-term, to manage the natural areas of the country to provide sustainable goods and services for the benefit of the population without decreasing the natural capital of these areas. The system was based on biogeographic principles, which have been applied along with an assessment of the legal, social, and economic constraints.*

1. INTRODUCTION

1.1. Problems concerning the natural environment in Ecuador

At the beginning of the seventies, Ecuador faced big problems caused by changes to its natural environment. The region situated between the Andes and the coast suffered from the destruction of its original vegetation cover, only small areas of which remain. In the highlands, the felling of trees and the destruction of grasslands by burning inevitably led to erosion; in the plains near the coast, the felling of trees increased the area of desert. In the Amazonas Region, where the ecological conditions are especially fragile, the settlers started to destroy the forests and the building of roads to assist oil production caused other changes to the natural environment. The upper river basins of the cordillera have suffered seriously from traditional practices, like the excessive exploitation of timber. This situation jeopardises the possibility of having new hydroelectric and irrigation projects, which need the fast water currents found in the highlands of the Andes.

Finally, the varied natural character of the different regions had not been used in a rational and efficient way. This variety should be considered a valuable resource for national and international tourism, the planned management of which might result in a source of income for the Government, and also in the enrichment of the lives of our own people.

1.2. Legal aspects of conservation

Action undertaken in Ecuador to conserve the wildlands and their resources started with the declarations of 1936 and 1959, which established the Galapagos Islands National Park. These measures were extended to apply to Ecuador as a whole, by the passing of two fundamental bills. The Law of Protection of Wildlife and Ichthyological Resources (1970) allows for the regulation of hunting and fishing activities, and enables national and international trade in wildlife and wildlife products to be controlled.

The Law of National Parks and Reserves (1971) provides the means to conserve those areas with special scientific, environmental and recreational possibilities, giving the responsibility to the Forestry Service (now National Forestry Programme) to determine the natural monuments, forests, natural areas and other places of special beauty that merit declaration as Reserves or National Parks.

1.3. Technical and administrative aspects

In 1973, the Department of Wildlands and Wildlife was created by the Directorate of Forestry Development. In 1974, the Department was directed to plan a national strategy for the conservation of wildlands and wildlife. It was possible to implement this planning process due to the collaboration of international experts from UNDP/ FAO which produced the Preliminary Strategy for the Conservation of Outstanding Wildlife Areas of Ecuador.

2. FORMULATION OF A NATIONAL STRATEGY FOR CONSERVING OUTSTANDING AREAS

Completed in 1976, the Strategy contained guidelines for management of the most representative of Ecuador's wild areas, for which the following aims have been established:

- In the short term: "to identify the best samples of the natural heritage of the country, to determine the most adequate system of management for each area, and to determine priorities for its legal delcaration, planning and administration".
- In the medium term: "to protect the most important ecosystems of the country, and to offer products and services to the big cities by means of a minimum of administration of the wild areas"
- In the long term: "to manage the wild areas of the country in order to provide permanent products and services which contribute to the benefit of the population and national development without decreasing the natural capital of these areas".

2.1. The studies

The first step was to make an inventory of the most outstanding natural areas in Ecuador, starting with those areas of the country with the least population.

A list was compiled of 60 outstanding areas; others were added later, resulting in a total of 90 areas. Each area has been given a potential designation, as a National Park, Ecological Reserve, Game Reserve, or National Recreation Area. In this way, it was possible to determine a set of essential values for the areas which were included in each kind of administration. Areas of insufficient value were eliminated, reducing the 90 original sites to 39.

In order to determine priorities for the preservation of important wild areas, four basic criteria have been established: representation of each of the biotic provinces; (Udvardy, 1975) representation of the most important coastal environments; inclusion of areas which offer education and recreation services to the big cities; and inclusion of all types of administration: National Parks, Ecological Reserves, Game Reserves and National Recreation Areas.

2.2. Minimum and extended system

Considering the criteria, nine areas were selected for the formation of a Minimum System of Conservation of Wildlands. 20 additional areas were designated part of an Extended System of Conservation. The Minimum System included the following areas:

Parque Nacional Galapagos
Parque Nacional Cotopaxi
Parque Nacional Sangay
Parque Nacional Machililla
Parque Nacional Yasuni
Reserva Ecologica Cotacachi-Cayapas
Reserva Ecologica Manglares-Churute
Reserva de Fauna Cuyabeno
Area Nacional de Recreacion Cajas

In 1979, the following areas were added:

Reserva Ecologica Cayambe-Coca
Reserve Pululahua
Area Nacional de Recreacion el Boliche

At the beginning of 1982, a study of management alternatives for the *Podocarpus* forest were completed, and steps were taken to declare it a National Park.

3. ESTABLISHMENT OF AN ECUADORIAN SYSTEM FOR THE CONSERVATION OF WILDLANDS

The Department of Wildlands and Wildlife has been responsible for developing a Strategy for the conservation of important wildlands in Ecuador. A series of technical and legal steps were undertaken which ensure a high degree of success in the future, especially in relation to the influence of public opinion on the taking of political decisions.

In order to determine the boundaries of the areas, and to obtain a complete knowledge of possible problems related to the ownership of land or, conflict with projects of regional, or national development, visits were made to the different regions, and sectional authorities were interviewed in order to discover exactly which projects might interfere with the management of areas zoned for protection. The most important problem encountered was one of land tenure. In addition there were problems of unplanned settlement and countless cases of illegal appropriation of land. Knowledge of the situation was also obtained by direct contact with the inhabitants of the regions visited.

An awareness programme to increase understanding of the objectives of the planned system of protected areas has been started. Maps have been prepared, showing the boundaries of the areas, some of which may have to be excluded if tenure problems prove insurmountable.

Several results have been achieved. The priority of including in the Strategy the establishment of a system of protected areas "which represent the natural resources and phenonena of the country, and which include a variety of administration systems", has been realised. The wildland areas were legally declared in the Official Register on 20 November 1979.

One of the most important objectives of the Strategy is the integration of planning at the national and regional level by government departments. The National Development Plan 1980-1984, takes into account the Strategy for establishing protected wildland areas.

Finally, on the 22 July 1981, the Ecuadorian House of Representatives passed a new law for the conservation of forests, wildlands and wildlife; Article 69 establishes the ownership of the wildland areas that have come under protection.

4. PRINCIPAL PROBLEMS ENCOUNTERED

The establishment of the system of protected wildland areas was a very complicated task from a technical point of view, and faced many problems.

4.1. During the planning period

Lack of technically experienced personnel delayed the task in Ecuador. To some extent this deficiency was resolved by agreements with universities which collaborated by carrying out basic studies in certain areas. Another difficulty was the lack of coordination between the national institutions and the organizations in charge of development planning; it was difficult to make the authorities aware of the importance of their cooperation.

After completing the strategy and having decided on the implementation of a conservation system for wildlands, various social, political, and economic conflicts arose. Establishing boundaries in selected areas created uneasiness among the population in relation to land to be zoned for protection; landowners, who did not make environmentally sound use of their land, and fearing they might lose it, tried to convince peasants of the uncertain value of defining and setting boundaries to areas.

Important too was the lack of collaboration by national authorities due to their ignorance of the situation, or because they had financial interests in the selected areas. Unfortunately, the regional media did not help to encourage favourable public opinion; on the contrary,

they became a negative force, working against the programme. Contact between the peasants, who have more interest than anyone else in the implementation of the programme, and the teams working towards the implementation is most important.

4.2. During the implementation phase

Without diminishing the importance of the achievements obtained, constraints have been placed on the implementation of the strategy: the budget increase bears no relation to the real requirements of the strategy; the number of professional and technical personnel and guards has been held to a minimum; and the activities of the Administration for Wildlands and Wildlife has been limited by government re-organization.

5. CONCLUSIONS

The present minimum system of natural areas adequately represents the administrative regions and natural areas of the country. Local government, whether provincial or municipal councils, have lately taken special interest in the natural or forest areas around the principal cities, with a view to using them mainly for recreation purposes. The system has been achieved with strong national participation. The time has now come to relate the administration of the natural areas of the country to the national and international tourism programmes, and to the different natural resources of the wildlands.

It is now urgent to link hydroelectric and irrigation projects to protected area conservation. These projects carry a high finanical investment from the State, and there is a need to protect the watersheds and streams, in order to guarantee the durability of the projects.

The preservation of nature, in relation to recreation and education, is an important new trend in Ecuador. The needs of the large urban centres are particularly great, to enable those living in cities to have contact with the natural environment. This will benefit the urban-dwelling population by exposing people to nature's attractions and will help earn influential supporters for the cause of nature conservation.

Acknowledgements

This paper was prepared for IUCN's Commission on National Parks and Protected Areas in cooperation with the United Nations Environment Programme.

Islands for People and Evolution: The Galapagos

José L. Villa
Charles Darwin Research Station
Guayaquil, Ecuador

Arturo Ponce
Ministry of Agriculture
Quito, Ecuador

ABSTRACT. *Located 1,000 km from the South American coast, Ecuador's Galapagos Islands have attracted the attention of naturalists and conservationists since the time of Charles Darwin; national park protection has been extended to 92% of the land area. This paper describes an approach to conservation which unites science, protection, and development in a way which benefits the rather limited human population without destroying the resources upon which development depends. Crucial parts of this programme include the continuing scientific investigation; resource protection, which is aimed particularly at eradicating introduced species; training for students and national park managers; special environmental education programmes directed to the local population; and the development of carefully controlled tourism designed to bring benefits to the local people.*

1. INTRODUCTION

The Galapagos Islands are part of the Republic of Ecuador, located 1,000 km from the South American coast in the Equatorial Pacific. These islands have attracted the attention of naturalists and conservationists for their importance in the study of evolution and island wildlife.

Ninety-two percent of the 8,000 sq km land area is under national park protection. We want to analyze in this paper the important role of this national park through a brief analysis of the results from each of the main services that are offered by this area of high scientific, educational, and recreational value.

2. THE PROBLEMS

There is a tendency in Latin America to orient the management of national parks toward making them valuable elements of the social development process. Some of the parks in this region are not used as intensive recreational areas; their isolation from inhabited areas effectively turn them into inaccessible areas. Such parks do not have the political and economic support necessary for their management since there is no demand for public use and their valuable resources are not actually threatened. Based on the Galapagos example, we suggest that the management of these national parks should be fundamentally oriented toward the achievement of rural development objectives to benefit the human communities living in the surroundings.

The management of a region under environmental conservation brings along a series of political, economic, and social difficulties. National parks are sometimes seen as limitations to human development and not as what they really are: the result of an analysis of the interacting physical, biological, and social elements in the search for the way to make possible the sustained development that people are looking for to improve their living conditions.

The 6,000 inhabitants of the Galapagos claim the right to have economic development, based on the principle of Ecuadorian territorial sovereignty. They claim more attention. But, although they accept their obligation to protect the scientific and educational values of these islands, as part of their natural heritage, they feel that the efforts to conserve the Galapagos Islands bring much more international than national or even local benefits. This is especially due to the overwhelming numbers of foreign visitors that come to see these islands every year and to a lesser degree due to the relative isolation of the islands from mainland Ecuador.

To reinforce their sovereignty, the Government of Ecuador sometimes grants disproportionate amounts of money for development projects which are not of interest, or actively against the interest, of conservation. In this way, tourism and research seem to be the only industries compatible with national park status and of benefit to the local community.

The challenge of orienting the Galapagos National Park management demands the design of a clear image of the future perspective where people are the centre of activities and where it is noticeable that the human community is the first beneficiary of the conservation results.

3. BACKGROUND

The Galapagos Islands are a volcanic formation on the Eastern Pacific formed by 13 major islands and numerous islets and rocks. They were discovered in 1535, and have been part of the Ecuadorian territory since 1832, the year in which people started to colonize, grow various products, and raise cattle.

The islands are located on the equator, between latitudes 89 and 92 degrees E. The climate is tropical oceanic, modified by several converging marine currents, and the natural life reflects these conditions. Fauna is diverse: penguins and sea lions dwell together with cormorants, albatrosses, and frigate birds. Marine vertebrates coming from the American continental seas and even from the Western Pacific flourish together in the islands.

The islands are of recent volcanic origin, about 3 million years old, and were mainly formed by successive accumulation of submarine materials. Living organisms had to reach the archipelago by three natural means: in the sea, with the wind; or being carried by migrating birds. As a result of the isolation from the continent and between the different islands, a major part of its floral and faunal inhabitants have developed into unique species. All of the reptiles, 50% of the resident birds, 32% of the plants, and 24% of the coastal fish, among others, are endemic to the archipelago. To these singularities we should add the extraordinary difference among the creatures from one island to another. It is small wonder that Charles Darwin found in Galapagos the best argument to support his theory on the role of natural selection in the origin of the species.

In the human development aspect, we find many phases of administrative and legal order. From 1832 to 1936, the policy was to reinforce national sovereignty; consequently, human settlement was supported and the exploitation of natural resources encouraged. In 1936, there was a change. A conservation policy was established and the first conservation law was implemented. In 1959, the park jurisdiction was expanded to all the islands and some measures were taken to implement the protection and scientific research programmes.

Since 1973, the islands have been considered as a province of the nation and the concern to maintain their natural state has continued. This interest is expressed in the formulation of the "Management Plan for the Galapagos National Park" (1974), and the "Conservation and Selective Development Plan of The Galapagos Province" (1975).

In this legal and administrative ambit, the conservation and economic development currents were reconciled. The outcome has been positive, with the application of conservation which permits the expansion of opportunities for a better utilization of the natural resources, in the spirit of IUCN's *World Conservation Strategy*.

As a result of applied conservation, there is a conscious approval by the islanders to protect the resources, the establishment of a clear governmental policy to support conservation efforts on the islands, and the improvement of administrative and management mechanisms for the park. Nevertheless, attention is not yet well-balanced due to various factors which influence conservation negatively:

- The conservation policy, although accepted, is not easily understood since the obtained benefits are not measurable;
- there is a lack of trained personnel for the management of the conservation units in the country;
- the traditional practice of taking decisions without the proper public participation still continues;
- the tourist boom with its direct economic benefits makes tour companies powerful units; and
- there is still a lack of interinstitutional coordination in the region.

In 1980, the Galapagos National Institute was established to coordinate activities at central, sectorial, and project levels. This institute, created to give solutions, finds that institutional self-determination creates serious problems for coordination and planning as well as for the establishment of a single directorate for programming.

The management problems can be summarized as follows:

- The induced aspirations of the people are based on continental models;
- the populated areas are taken as isolated elements from the surrounding environment;
- a balanced budget does not exist in order to be assigned to institutions, nor is priority given to the most urgent needs;
- little support is offered to actions dealing with the improvement of human living conditions;
- a master plan for Galapagos development, which will orient the economic activities in coordination with conservation of the ecosystem, does not exist; and
- although scientific research has contributed to many goals in the rescue of species threatened with extinction, there is no truly comprehensive plan for a long-term research strategy.

4. ACTION

The human population since the first colonization has been confined to islands where there is water and it is possible to have ports, grow crops, and raise livestock; given the climatic and soil conditions, the area available for these purposes is small. The Ecuadorian Government decided in 1959 that 90% of the unused land without agricultural potential should be maintained with its natural inhabitants in unaltered conditions. This land was to be used as a place of recreation, scientific investigation, and education. In 1959, the Government turned this land into a national park, which meant the implementation of a rational utilization while maintaining the unique natural resources and generating cultural, economic, and aesthetic assets for the islanders, the Ecuadorians in general, and the whole world.

Parallel to this development and for scientific motives, the Charles Darwin Foundation for the Galapagos Islands was organized in Brussels in 1959. The Ecuadorian Government entrusted to this organization the protection of the insular environment and of the natural species. Since 1964, when the Charles Darwin Research Station was established by the Foundation, scientific research, begun with Darwin's visit in 1835, was deepened and conservation increased. In 1968, when the administrative organization of the national park began to work, intensive conservation programmes and environment recovery plans were developed. The environmental education programmes were improved and coordinated with the applied investigations. At present, there is ideal interinstitutional and international cooperation between the two conservation institutions in the islands: The Galapagos National Park Service and the Charles Darwin Research Station. The continuing support of WWF, IUCN, and Unesco has also been vital.

At present, important factors operate in the islands influencing directly or indirectly, positively or negatively, the environment, including the human population and its activities, the scientific and conservation institutions, and tourism.

By the possession and transformation of land, the introduction of various animals and plants (some of which have turned into harmful plagues to the natural environment) and the increase of the human population and its activities, man has intruded into the insular environment. The economic perspectives were an incentive for tourism to grow; this business may interfere with nature since it is based on the most outstanding natural resources. Facing these two forces, the scientific and conservation authorities try to maintain the natural environment in the best possible condition.

The Galapagos National Park Service, in charge of the park's administration, faces the threats to the insular environment created by the introduction of exotic faunal and floral species. The institution is organized according to the philosophy and policies expressed in the "Protection and Utilization Plan for the Galapagos National Park", a document that establishes objectives, work pro-

gammes, and aspects related to the use of the resource by people, tourists, and scientists. Together with the National Park Service, the Charles Darwin Station carries out investigation work that provides the Park's administration the necessary information and guidelines for the control of introduced species, tourist impact, and other management aspects as well as on the environmental education programme for the people of the islands.

As a result of the natural limitations and the growing knowledge of the surrounding environment, the human population has developed, until now, in harmony with nature; their traditional activities pertaining to farming and animal husbandry, as well as fishing and a few public services, have been reinforced by the conservation movement. Above all, with the development of tourism, new jobs and extra income were generated. Thanks to government interest and the interdisciplinary studies including various Ministeries, the human population, Municipalities, the National Park Service, and the Darwin Station, a "Conservation and Selective Development Plan for the Galapagos Province" was elaborated by the National Planning Committee in 1975. The aim of this plan was to develop the indispensable infrastructure to integrate the population of the islands into the national development process, while maintaining the insular character of the region and trying to conserve the scenic, floristic, and faunistic resources.

On the other hand, tourism has grown within the national park. Policies have been established that limit the capacity of tourist boats, the sites that can be visited, and the number of visitors; the Park Service also trains guides who conduct the tourists around the islands.

The majority of the population, looking at the economic benefit that is obtained by the use of the natural resources and thanks to the educational efforts of the conservation institutions, has understood that the future depends on the balance between proper development and conservation. They realize this policy will guarantee the natural future of the archipelago, the educational and investigative opportunities, the permanence of tourist visits, and the security of being able to connect the chain of primary benefits to the insular population.

5. RESULTS

The national park management was assured with the presentation and approval of the Management Plan. Although its implementation is not complete yet, the results so far are positive. The limited economic resources available for the protection progammes have hindered the implementation of techniques to avoid the introduction of exotic organisms, eradicate rats, cats, dogs, and goats in target areas, and maintain a stable number of park wardens.

To ensure effective conservation policies, there are still several outstanding matters, which can be summarized as follows:

- The incorporation of the marine area of the islands to the park system—in order to accomplish the integral protection of the resources—is still pending;
- a better conception of the legal framework, in accordance with the conditions of the archipelago, is required to provide a more effective mechanism to control the human activities; and
- a comprehensive master plan that limits all the activities of the several institutions is missing. As a result, many errors have occurred: lack of guidelines when there is a demand for the exploitation of certain resources; lack of public participation in the conservation and development aspects; and inefficient inter-institutional coordination.

5.1. Research

The principal result in the scientific research aspect is the establishment of two cooperative institutions, whose nature and relations could be considered as a management pattern. The Charles Darwin Station is a non-governmental independent and international institution; it is in charge of scientific investigation on the islands' ecosystems, especially to support the protection measures. It has a mutual relationship with the Galapagos National Park Service, a national institution with enough power to manage the national park. They maintain close coordination through conceptual, logistic, and financial support.

The investigation and management programmes of Galapagos have had a wide impact on the general public. Information about the islands has been disseminated worldwide and this has led to significant contributions for the protection of the resource and to the realization of the need to find a pattern for human development which prevents the destruction of the resource.

5.2. Protection

The resource protection programme has produced better knowledge of the threats to native fauna populations; in the majority of cases, their preservation has been assured. Giant tortoises have had priority attention: the breeding and repatriation programmes have had very good results. The same can be said about the land iguana programme.

The introduced organism eradication programme, especially for introduced mammals, has met with some success, although it is of long-term duration and high cost. With support from WWF and IUCN, goats and dogs have been eradicated from some small islands. Preparations are being made to eradicate pigs, dogs, and cats; rats may never be eradicated, but efforts are being made to control their effects on the endemic fauna.

5.3. Education

Environmental education is handled by the Charles Darwin Station and involves every investigation programme. Concerning this education programme we should note:

- Opportunities are offered to Ecuadorian university students who use the national park for their field biology studies. An extensive scholarship programme is part of the national park management; to date, more than 100 students have worked on this basis.
- The national park has been considered as an ideal model of training for national park managers. Training courses are held every year and many national and international seminars have taken place.
- A major aspect of the management is the instruction provided to the park "interpreters". The tourist guides receive official training, and as an outcome the visitor is able to understand the conservation image which is the final objective of the park management.
- Special environmental education programmes are directed to the local population. At the beginning, these are oriented to the primary school groups; later they will be directed to other students and the general public.

5.4. Tourism and Recreation

Through a combined system of zoning, marked paths, and regulations, the presence of trained guides and patrolling, the tourism policy has contributed to the protection of islands' resources. The local population's acceptance of the national park has mainly been based on the increase in business and cash flow created by tourism. Tour operators have understood and accepted the controls surprisingly well, due to the mixture of education, greater public participation and the interest of conservationists.

6. CONCLUSION

The Galapagos, given their geographical situation and their peculiar biology, provide an opportunity to shape a model for the entire world, a model uniting science, conservation, and development in a way that would benefit the population without destroying the resources upon which development depends.

Acknowledgements

This paper was prepared for IUCN's Commission on National Parks and Protected Areas in cooperation with the United Nations Environment Programme.

Waterfalls, Hydro-Power, and Water for Industry: Contributions from Canaima National Park, Venezuela

José Rafael Garcia
Director of National Parks
National Parks Institute
Caracas, Venezuela

ABSTRACT. *Canaima National Park is world-famous for Angel Falls, the world's highest. But much less well known is the fact that Canaima provides a crucial service to Venezuela in protecting the watershed of the Caroni Basin, where hydro-electric dams provide electricity to run some of the nation's most important industrial plants. This function is so important that the government tripled the size of the park to 3 million ha, in order to further enhance the watershed protection benefits of the park.*

1. INTRODUCTION

A good number of the world's national parks serve two purposes: to preserve areas of outstanding natural beauty, and to provide areas for the use and conservation of water resources, not only for human consumption or agricultural use, but also for the production of hydro-electric power. Venezuela is a typical example: of its 26 national parks 10 supply important services to the country through conservation of river basins whose waters are of great use to the economic development of the country.

Perhaps the most interesting case is the Guatopo National Park. This park of 100,000 ha and only two hours by car from Caracas, capital of Venezuela, was created in 1958 to preserve the wonderful rainforest. Its value solely in terms of flora and fauna would be sufficient reason for declaring it a National Park. But it was also realized that because of rapid population growth, the capital would come to need the water of river basin which this park possessed. The prediction was correct, and at this moment the park is supplying the metropolitan area with 3,500 litres per second, and in 1985, this figure will be 20,000 litres per second. The most

important thing is that the water from this park is of very high quality, and for this reason, its treatment for human consumption is less expensive.

On the date the park was inaugurated, there were some 4,300 families within the area, working the land and developing small farms; there was also some industrial exploitation of timber. It was decided to move the occupants out of the park. By way of compensation, the non-proprietary residents were paid US$11,700,000, while proprietary residents were given US$4,700,000, a small price to pay for precious water for Caracas.

Another significant example is the Yacamb National Park, which has an area of 14,580 ha and which was inaugurated on 12 June 1962. This park encloses a rainforest of great beauty, as well as important hydrological potential. The rest of the river basin, covering 33,900 ha, was also declared a protected zone. At this moment, a dam is being constructed there to contain the waters of the river basin. By means of a pipe 24.5 km long and 2 m in diameter, the waters from this National Park will be passed to another river basin which, while it has an extremely fertile valley of 30,000 ha, is situated in a zone with a dry climate.

The water transported from this park will be about 9,100 litres per second permanently; 3,000 litres per second will be used for human consumption, while 6,100 litres per second will irrigate the 18,500 ha of the valley.

2. CANAIMA NATIONAL PARK

This park is world famous because it contains the highest waterfall in the world, Angel Falls, which has a free fall of 960 m.

I am sure that many people do not realize that there

are hundreds of other important waterfalls in this park, not the least of which is the Kukenan Falls, with a free fall of 670 m. But the most important aspect of this park is that it occupies an area of 3,000,000 ha, interwoven with rivers, savannahs, and tepuys (tall, vertical-faced, rectilineal mountains), having been increased from its original (June 1962) size of 1,000,000 ha when the Master Plan was completed in 1975.

The Canaima National Park (Fig. 1) forms part of the Caroni river basin, a turbulent dark river, whose hydro-electric potential has been planned to supply electricity to a major industrial zone of Venezuela, in the south of the River Orinoco.

It is important to point out that the Canaima National Park forms one-third of the Caroni basin, which contains some 95,000 sq km; the relation between the area of the park and the basin is highly significant, especially when one considers that in 1985 the river will produce 9,000,000 KW and when the integral hydrological exploitation is indicated, it will produce 20,000,000 KW.

Between 1974 and 1978, US$1,023,000 was invested in hydro-electric projects. The Canaima National Park through this investment, again proved its value as an area of great importance in contributing to the economic development of the country with respect to its hydro-electric potential, without mentioning the other invaluable aspects of the park.

The greatest justification in tripling the area of this park in 1975 was basically that almost all the rivers which drain from the park are within the grand basin of the river Caroni; the eastern river is the basis for the hydro-electrical power for the development of the great industrial development of Guayana.

The newly incorporated areas (2,000,000 ha) have outstanding natural characteristics in their own right, with the most beautiful and spectacular landscapes of the country; waterfalls abound, and the many sensational tepuys constitute the most characteristic orographic formations of the park. These are table-like formations with high plateaux and vertical walls constituted of multicoloured sandstone dating from the Mesozoic era, and constitutes ecological islands where numerous endemic species proliferate.

These tepuys, combined with extensive areas of savannah and forest where fast flowing rivers and spectacular waterfalls intersperse, form the wonderful landscape of this park.

However, the aforementioned contrasts with the ecological fragility of the park; the protective vegetation could easily be damaged, leading to the elimination of the protective forest. This forest would be replaced by the formation of savanna, which would provide a low agricultural production potential and at the same time insufficiently protect the soil against erosion. The powerful laminar erosion would produce sediments which would be carried to the dams, affecting the capacity of the reservoirs and the functioning of the hydro-electric turbines.

What is more, it has been proven in these lands that when forested areas are transformed into savanna, the process is irreversible since the forests live in a precarious balance which depends on the recycling of the organic matter within the same forests. This problem is simply observed in areas where the forest has been destroyed by first cutting down the trees and then burning the residues, or in areas where the forest has been affected by fire. The problem may also be seen by the sides of the motorways which have been constructed, and where by having removed the topsoil, no natural recuperation may be seen even after 20 years.

2.1. Population of the park

The population of the park is 5,000, most of whom are Indians; this population is small in comparison to the park's surface area. Seventy percent of these people are concentrated in 7 villages and the rest are disseminated in other small settlements or family groups.

These people have a diet based on their own permanent agriculture, and on fish and game. The type of agriculture that they practice creates serious problems with the vegetation in that every year they cut new areas of the forest, then burn it (which on many occasions also spreads fires over large areas).

A few years ago, the Venezuela Guyana Corporation began a programme in which they made use of some of the valleys for food production, using simple modern techniques. This programme tends to concentrate the indigenous population within the area, resulting in halting the continual destruction of the forest.

2.2. The Venezuela Guayana Corporation

In 1960, the Venezuela Guayana Corporation was created, which functions as an autonomous institute or parent company. The basic objective in creating this Corporation was exploiting the hydro-electric potential of the River Caroni basin, and to use this potential in the development of a huge industrial zone to the south of the River Orinoco.

This Corporation comprises subsidiary companies and related companies of mixed capital. The subsidiary companies—Siderurgia del Orinoco, Electrificacin del Caron, Ferrominera Orinoco and Bauxiven—exploit hydro-electricity, iron and aluminium. The creation of mixed capital is also foreseen to promote and take advantage of all the industrial potential within the subsidiary companies.

In addition to this industrial development, the surplus electrical energy is transported to other areas of Venezuela, transmission lines will be constructed to carry electricity to the metropolitan area of Caracas.

In conclusion, this important industrial development has involved huge investment, and its overall success will depend on hydro-electric energy. With the recent rise in the cost of petroleum, we can justify not continuing to use it to be burned to turn the turbines of thermoelectric plants; it is estimated that to produce the energy potential of the River Caroni basin, it would be necessary to use 144 million barrels of oil per year. Supposing the price of a barrel is US$30, this would represent an annual saving of some US$4.3 thousand million.

3. CONCLUSIONS

The basic reason behind the development of the Canaima National Park might be justified with reference to the general values of national parks. In the case of this park, the most important attribute is the high quality water, capable of producing hydro-electric power using dams located well outside the national park. As a result of this, the traditional values of the national parks are enhanced in that to conserve the water it is necessary to avoid deterioration of the vegetation and consequently the topsoil, flora and fauna.

Up to this date, the infrastructure for the hydro-electric exploitation of the River Caroni basin has been located in the lower basin, outside the boundaries of the park. It is important to maintain this policy so as to preserve the marvellous landscapes and the integrity of our natural renewable resources.

The case of Canaima and other cases referred to at the beginning of this paper indicate that there can be compatibility in the maintenance of the integrity of the national parks and the exploitation of their water resources potential.

It is helpful to present in numerical terms the economic importance which a natural area may hold, in view of its not being used directly for human habitation, agriculture, cattle-raising and so on. In many cases, these values are more positive for the socio-economic well-being of the country, than when human occupation is allowed in natural areas where the conditions for an adequate standard of living do not exist.

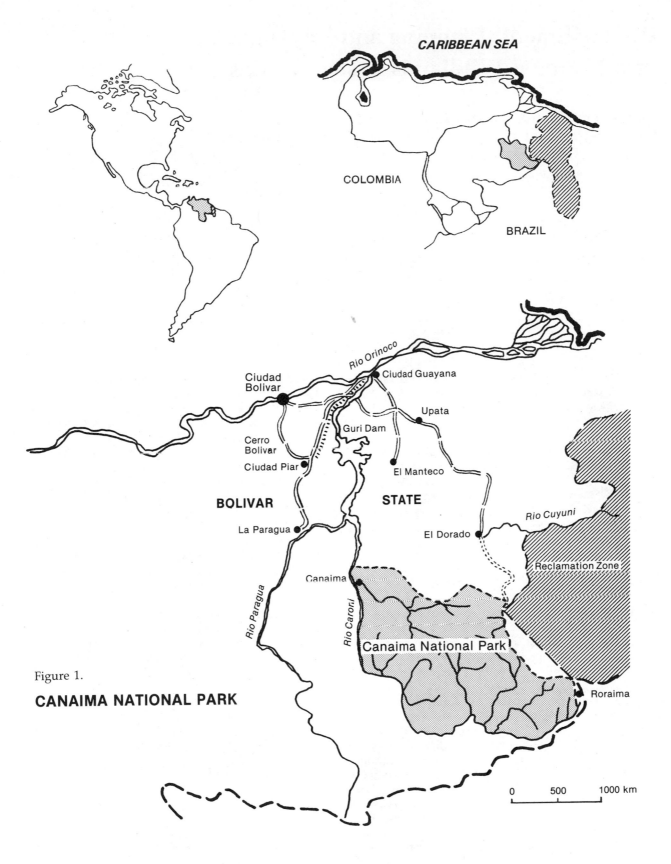

CARIBBEAN SEA

COLOMBIA

BRAZIL

Rio Orinoco

Ciudad Guayana

Ciudad
Bolivar

Upata

Cerro
Bolivar

Guri Dam

Ciudad Piar

El Manteco

BOLIVAR

STATE

Rio Cuyuni

La Paragua

El Dorado

Reclamation Zone

Canaima

Rio Paragua

Rio Caroní

Canaima National Park

Roraima

0   500   1000 km

Figure 1.

CANAIMA NATIONAL PARK

Establishment, Planning and Implementation of a National Wildlands System in Costa Rica

Craig MacFarland, Roger Morales and James R. Barborak
Centro Agronomico Tropical de Investigacion y Ensenanza (CATIE)
Turrialba, Costa Rica

ABSTRACT. *In 1969 five legally established protected areas in three management categories existed in the Costa Rica. None were receiving any protection or management. Between 1970 and 1982, with the creation of the Costa Rican Park Service (CRNPS), General Forest Directorate (DGF) and National Commission for Indian Affairs (CONAI), the situation changed markedly. By 1982, there were 79 legally established wildlands units in nine categories, covering almost 27% of the national territory. Of these, 32 units are receiving "adequate and continuous management," 21 "inadequate and intermittent" management and 26 no management.*

1. INTRODUCTION

From 1950 to 1970, in terms of renewable natural resources allocation and use, Costa Rica was rapidly approaching the condition of a runway train on a steep and curvy downhill grade, with no brakes and no engineer at the controls. The country had begun to irreversibly damage and destroy the very base for long-term sustained development, and was on the brink of even far worse future change.

As a response to these trends, Costa Rica has accomplished a very significant feat over the past 12 years: establishment and partial implementation of a national system of wildlands which is probably the most complex in all of Latin America. By 1982, a total of 79 wildland units had been legally established, covering approximately 27% of the country's total land area. These units are distributed among 9 management categories as follows: 14 National Parks; 10 Biological Reserves; 4 National Recreation Areas; 1 National Archaeological Monument; 1 Biosphere Reserve; 12 Forest Reserves (=

National Forests); 8 Forest Protection Zones (= Watershed Protectorates); 3 Wildlife Refuges; and 26 Indigenous Reserves. Three public institutions are responsible for managing different ones of these categories.

The process of reaching this state has been complex and the management intensity and implementation success with the different management categories and their subsystems by the different institutions has been notably variable; the Costa Rica National Park Service (CRNPS) stands out for its success and dynamism in the establishment, planning, administration and on-the-ground implementation of management, whereas the other institutions have lagged notably behind.

How were the system and/or subsystems designed and planned? What were the strategies and tactics? Did designs, plans, strategies and tactics even exist? What were the key differences in those and other aspects between and among the CRNPS and the other institutions? What key principles and guidelines can be derived from this case study to aid in the solution of such problems in the other countries of Mesoamerica? Can this experience be applied even more broadly to other developing countries in the tropics in South America and even the rest of the world? This paper will attempt to answer all of these questions, except the last one, which is left to the reader to answer.

2. PROBLEM STATEMENT

In 1950, 65% of Costa Rica's national territory was owned by the State, the vast majority of it under forest cover. The other 35% was privately owned, of which one-third was covered by natural forest. By 1970 the land owned by the State and in forests had been reduced to 40%, and the remaining 60%, largely deforested, was privately held. However, this massive reduction in the country's forest cover did not result in any notable increase in cultivated area nor in agricultural production of basic foodstuffs. Instead, *almost all* of that massive change corresponded to an expansion of pastures for very low-density beef cattle grazing, for export, an industry which employs few and enriches even fewer.

By 1970, Costa Rica's total area covered by natural primary forests was only 35%. Almost all of those forests were located in life zones (*sensu* Holdridge) that are marginal or submarginal for agriculture and cattle. Those areas are almost all characterized by having very broken to steep topography and poorly drained, infertile soils very susceptible to erosion.

Given the situation, the following major socioeconomic problems and impacts were visualized for the country in the coming few decades, if there were no change in established trends:

- An increasing shortage of timber and related raw materials, leading ultimately to the collapse of the national forest industry;
- increasing unemployment of the forestry industry's labour force;
- increasing deficiencies in the production of electricity and water, due to the damage to most major watersheds, along with seasonal floods and droughts with extremely negative impacts on agriculture and industry;
- irreversible losses of fauna, flora and recreational opportunities; and
- loss of natural scenic landscapes and other resources which are the base for national and international tourism.

This list obviously could be greatly expanded; the negative socioeconomic, political and cultural ramifications and impacts of such trends are intricate and almost endless.

In marked contrast to this situation, as of 1970 Costa Rica did not have even one protected and managed wildland.

The problem therefore was how to begin from essentially zero and gradually select, establish, plan and implement a protected area system which could counteract the negative environmental trends and thus form part of the solution to the major problems being confronted.

3. CONSTRAINTS

At the end of the 1960's neither the government nor the general public in Costa Rica was conscious of the renewable natural resources problem. That lack of concern was based on widespread belief at both levels that the country still had more than enough resources and that no shortages would develop for a long time, and

that virtually the entire country was suitable for agriculture and livestock. Forested areas were looked upon basically as an impediment to development, a socioeconomic disturbance that should be eliminated. This attitude was backed strongly by a series of laws in which deforestation was considered as an "improvement" to the land.

The principal limitations which impeded the development of a programme to manage renewable natural resources, including establishment and management of wildlands, were the lack of governmental policy on conservation and the absence of institutional mechanisms, financial resources and a legal base of sufficient strength to guide public and private action.

4. ACTION

4.1. Policy and programme

The national programme of protected area establishment and management began with the 1969 Forestry Law, which delineates in general terms a policy designed to solve the problem of natural resource mis-allocation and mis-use by making the State responsible for ensuring the protection, appropriate use, conservation and development of the country's natural resources. The forest heritage is defined as the National Reserves (wildlands without an assigned management category), Forest Reserves, Protection Zones, National Parks, Biological Reserves, as well as any other lands, public or private, which will provide greater economic, social, protective and scenic utility by remaining or being restored to forest cover, than by exploiting them for agriculture, even with advanced technology.

The law established the General Forestry Directorate (DGF) in order to carry out that programme; the DGF started operations in early 1970, four months after the approval of the law, with two Departments: National Parks and Forest Protection.

To orient the first steps by the DGF and its Departments in the wildlands sector, the law established that the Executive Branch of Government, with the DGF's recommendation, would decree in the National Reserves and State, municipal or private lands, those Forest Reserve, Protection Zones, National Parks and Biological Reserves considered necessary to comply with the law. Also, those private lands affected would be obtained by purchase or expropriation. All legally declared wildlands would be inscribed in the Public Register as State-owned "haciendas." Moreover, once created, no part of the National Parks and Biological Reserves could be segregated for other objectives or uses without approval (i.e. a law) of the Legislative Assembly.

In order to advise the Executive Branch on implementing the programme, a National Forestry Council was established by the law, made up of the Minister of Agriculture and Livestock and one representative each of the following institutions: Ministry of Commerce and Industries, ITCO, National Electricity Service (SNE), ICT, University of Costa Rica (UCR) and the National Association of Wood Industrialists.

To cover the costs of the programme, apart from the amounts to be assigned each year from the regular and special annual government budget, the law established the Forestry Fund, to be administered by the DGF directly. That fund is financed by voluntary contributions from many government institutions and any other institutions or persons wishing to donate to it. Also, the Fund can receive all types of goods, property or other donations as well as those from international or bilateral agencies and organizations.

4.2. Special actions which contributed to the national wildlands system

a) In 1969 the Tropical Science Center published the Ecological Map of Costa Rica, which identifies 12 life zones or bioclimates and has been invaluable in helping to select and evaluate potential wildlands.

b) In 1970 the Wildlife Conservation Law was passed, for the first time recognizing wildlife conservation as being in the public interest.

c) In 1970 the FAO Regional Wildlands Project expanded its activities and changed location to the Regional FAO office in Santiago, Chile, with K. Miller continuing as its leader. The Project covered technical assistance, training, research, pilot project development and the preparation and distribution of example methodology manuals and plans, for the selection, establishment, planning and implementation of wildlands and wildlands systems, particularly national parks. The scope of the project was all Latin America, but of necessity it concentrated most heavily in a few countries, including Costa Rica. In a third phase, 1975 to mid-1976, the project's focus was narrowed to Central America and Costa Rica continued to receive substantial technical assistance and training.

d) In 1972 the National Parks Department was elevated to the status of General Subdirectorate and in 1977 it was made a Directorate.

e) In 1972 the first conservation NGO, the Costa Rican Association for the Conservation of Nature (ASCONA) was established to act as a "watchdog" and aid both the public and private sectors in the conservation of natural resources.

f) In 1973 the National Commission for Indian Affairs (CONAI) was created to help promote and guide the protection of the indigenous Reserves and their populations, as a response to increasing pressure for land acquisition by non-Indians.

g) In 1974 the First Central American Regional Meeting on the Conservation of Natural and Cultural Resources was held in San Jos, organized by IUCN and sponsored by FAO, OAS, Unesco, UNEP, WWF and RBF. All countries of the isthmus were represented by official delegates competent in natural resources, tourism, planning and cultural resources. Based on recommendation 7 of the 1972 Second World Conference on National Parks, the meeting proposed a regional system of national parks in which Costa Rica would participate with two pilot national parks (Volcan Pos and Santa Rosa) two international parks (La Amistad, Costa Rica-Panama and Tortuguero, Nicaragua-Costa Rica), and two more proposed parks (Corcovado and Chirripo).

h) In 1975, the FAO Regional Wildlands Project provided technical assistance for the preparation of an extremely important basic document for Costa Rica: *Policies for Wildlands Management*. The major contributions of the study were the recommendation of a set of 11 national objectives for natural resources conservation and a system of 15 wildlands management categories, each with detailed definition, objectives, characteristics and management guidelines.

i) In 1975 the General Directorate of Fisheries Resources and Wildlife was established within the Ministry of Agriculture, but apart from the DGF, thus putting wildlife administration and management in a separate organization.

j) In mid-1976, partially as a continuation of the FAO Regional Wildlands Project, the Regional Wildlands and Watershed Programme (PASC) was established at CATIE, as part of its Renewable Natural Resources Department. It was principally supported in its first few years by RBF, IUCN/WWF and CATIE, the latter having now taken over core funding. The principle objective is to promote ecodevelopment based on natural resource management, including the creation of a regional network of model, experimental-demonstration wildland units of all major management categories. The main elements in the PASC strategy, all carried out with national counterpart teams from the key natural and cultural resources management agencies, include: preparation of national conservation strategies and/or national wildlands systems strategic plans; training and education of national personnel; research on the development of planning and training methodologies and techniques; preparation and distribution of key methodology and training manuals and sample plans; improving communication, collaboration and sharing of human resources between the countries; and obtaining international and bilateral technical and financial aid. PASC's greatest impact, achieved with the active participation of the CRNPS and DGF, has been to train most of the professionals and technicians in the central office staffs and at the level of superintendents of wildlands units.

k) In 1977 the first broad Indian Law was promulgated, establishing that the Indigenous Reserves are inalienable and exclusively for the Indian communities which inhabit them. The law also establishes that the Reserves will be managed by the Indians according to their traditional methods, with advice and collaboration (but not control) from CONAI.

l) In 1979 the CRNPS, with PASC's direct advice and collaboration, began an experimental programme of operational planning for all its management units and central office technical and administrative departments. In 1980, its results were evaluated and the CRNPS permanently adopted the programme. In 1981, via workshops and other training methods for the Forest Reserves Department professionals and the units' superintendents, the operational planning programme was initiated.

m) In 1981 the government, through the CRNPS, contracted the Tropical Science Center to conduct an ecological study and evaluation of the existing system of national parks and equivalent reserves and to recommend new wildland units. The report was recently finished and recommends 47 new Protection Zones, Forest Reserves, Wildlife Refuges, Biological Reserves, National Recreation Areas and National Parks (mostly the first five, only two of the latter).

n) The private National Parks Foundation was established in 1982 and has begun a very active national and international fund-raising programme. It is receiving notable technical assistance from The Nature Conservancy's (USA) International Programme. One of its main activities is to obtain funds for the purchase of private lands inside national parks and other wildlands, which the government can not possibly buy due to the existing economic crisis.

5. CASE STUDIES OF SEVERAL CRNPS AREAS

The following presents examples of the specific actions taken for the selection, establishment, planning and implementation of units managed by CRNPS.

5.1. Cahuita National Park

This small unit (1,100 ha) was the first established legally by CRNPS, in September 1970. A year and a half earlier the Wildlands Management Project at CATIE had prepared a study on the natural and cultural resources of the area, its socioeconomic characteristics and possibilities for tourism. The study recommended protection of the area because it contains the only well-developed coastal coral reef in the country and high scenic beauty and recreational potential. The principal limitations identified were: difficult access (no road); the entire area was in private holdings; a sizeable part of the area was in cocoa and coconut cultivation.

Just after the decree, land tenure and cadastral studies were done. Then the land owners were informed that in a relatively short period they would be compensated. The decree did not include the necessary financing and to date (1982) the owners have not been paid; this has caused serious conflicts with the park's neighbours. The local community has not really accepted the park and its personnel have had to try maintain a conciliatory and pacifist coexistence with the community, varying from very good to very bad in different periods, principally depending on changes of personnel in the park. The conciliatory attitude has included permitting, in sites chosen by the CRNPS, the harvesting of coconuts, artesanal fishing (beyond the reef), installation of a small food and drink concession for tourists in the park, hiring of several local people as permanent rangers, etc.

With the construction of the access road to the park, visitation went from a few hundred/year to more 50,000 in 1981. The park has an administrative- living quarters centre for its personnel, which is also used for visiting scientists and occasional education-interpretive programmes.

Numerous studies on the park's natural and cultural resources, terrestrial and marine, have been done by national university scientists, a Peace Corps marine biologist and others. In 1980 the general Management and Development Plan was prepared as part of regional training workshop on wildlands planning and in 1982 a draft Interpretive-Environmental Education Plan was completed by the Wildlands Management course of PASC, as a practical exercise.

5.2. Tortuguero National Park

The principle objective of establishing this park, in September 1970, was the complete protection from egg extraction along the 20 km of prime nesting beach and from hunting of adults of the green sea turtle *Chelonia mydas*. The establishment was based on recommendations from Dr. Archie Carr, who since 1959 had been studying the species there. Given the Park's inaccessibility and the CRNP's precarious finances, until 1975 the protection of the park (the beach principally) was left to the CCC (Caribbean Conservation Corporation, Dr. Carr's group).

In 1975 by law the park was increased in size and given a budget and the CRNPS's full jurisdiction over the area was rectified. This new law set another positive precedent; because of personal economic interests of a high-placed government member, the President vetoed the law, but the Legislative Assembly over-rode the veto.

5.3. Volcan Poas National Park

The third park established (December 1970), Volcan Poas is an active volcano of great scenic beauty, situated only 57 km (1 hour) from San José and accessible year round by bus or car on a good highway. The area was selected for those reasons, but also because it has great attractiveness for Costa Ricans, especially each March 19th (San José Day) when up to 8,000 persons from the cities of the Meseta Central traditionally visit the volcano. Before its creation, the general Management and Development Plan had been prepared, and it served well to "sell" the project.

In the first years the resident personnel, with assistance from Peace Corps specialists and National Youth Movement (NYM) volunteers, established basic minimum infrastructure and services for visitors and staff. Little by little this was improved until today the park has a complex of interpreted nature trails, a system of guard posts and patrol trails, a large visitor centre with first class educational exhibits, a paved highway into the park, and other infrastructure.

In 1974 at the Regional Central American Meeting on Management of Natural and Cultural Resources, it was selected as the model park for Costa Rica. That same year two FAO specialists and counterparts prepared a revised Management and Development Plan and later that year a preliminary Interpretive Plan, the first of its kind in Costa Rica.

Based on those plans, in 1976 the Central American Bank for Economic Integration (BCIE) approved a loan of $1.8 million, with which the plans have been steadily implemented. This was the first loan by an international or regional bank for development of a national park in Latin America.

Most of the park's 4100 ha belong to the CRNPS, although a few small private lots remain to be purchased. This park has had a tranquil existence because of strong support for it by the local communities and government (tourism, watershed protection for dairy farms and rich vegetable croplands) as well as national ones such as ASCONA and the Biologists Guild.

5.4. Santa Rosa National Park

This park, established in 1971, protects the most important historic site in the country and more than 22,000 ha of tropical dry forest, a type which has almost been eliminated everywhere else in Costa Rica and Central America. In 1966 the historic Casona (main house) and 1000 ha was declared a National Monument and ICT were given the responsibility to manage it. ICT requested technical assistance from the Regional Wildlands Project of IICA (now CATIE) to prepare a man-

agement plan. The Preliminary Management Plan (1968) proposed extension of the area to 11,000 ha to be managed as an Historic National Park. In 1970, the new CRNPS accepted the area from ICT and began to manage it as a National Park. The area had squatters, furtive hunting, and cattle and the historic casona was in extremely bad condition. Thanks to the Minister of Agriculture, the CRNPS was able to obtain a small budget and contracted five rangers and a superintendent and purchase basic equipment, materials and a vehicle. That skeleton staff and volunteers (Peace Corps and National Youth Movement) initiated protection activities and successfully removed most of the squatters. When the Park was formally declared and inaugurated the CRNPS already had been managing it for over a year.

The date of inauguration and legal establishment were carefully chosen to exactly coincide with the 115th anniversary of the Battle of Santa Rosa (20 March), the most important historical date in Costa Rica. The highest government authorities, including the President and First Lady, attended.

Slowly but surely facilities and services were developed for visitors and staff, neighbours and local and regional communities and governments became involved in management and support. The last squatters were removed and the free-running cattle eliminated under agreements with their owners. The Ministry of Culture funded and carried out restoration of the Casona and exhibits were installed. In 1977, 796 more ha of coastal area and in 1979, 11,600 ha of a neighbouring hacienda were expropriated (owned at the time by Nicarguan dictator Anastasio Somoza).

This has been one of the protected areas with the heaviest concentration of foreign and national scientists and much research has been carried out, aiding and supporting appropriate management.

5.5. Manuel Antonio National Park

This small area of only a few hundred hectares contains some of the finest beaches in Costa Rica, areas which had been used for decades by the inhabitants of the nearby (10 km) town of Quepos and the surrounding area as well as many visitors from the Meseta Central, as a recreation area. In 1968 the area was owned by a foreigner who decided to close off both access routes. He installed iron gates which the people of Quepos promptly tore down. He sold the property to another foreigner of like mind: more gates, more conflict. Based on a request by the local community and a journalist, the CRNPS submitted to the local representative to the Legislative Assembly a bill declaring the area a national recreation park. It was immediately presented to the Legislative Assembly and at the same time the Municipality of Quepos held an open public meeting to solicit local opinion on the project. The entire town, including the Association of Small Agriculturists, the Youth Movement and many others at local and national level joined in support of the park's creation. The law passed in 1972. It established a basic budget for the park, required the Executive Branch to expropriate the private holdings, and established an entrance fee of one colon (= $0.12 at that time), one fourth of which would go to the Municipality of Quepos for improvement and maintenance of the road to the park. One more try was made by certain interested parties to have the law rescinded. However, the Local Committee for Development of the Park, set up just after the law was approved, and the CRNPS succeeded in fighting off the move and obtained an emission of government bonds in 1975 to allow the purchase.

At its creation the CRNPS immediately staffed the park and gradually developed minimum recreational and interpretive facilities. In 1981 it received 31,000 visitors.

5.6. Corcovado National Park

Since 1972, the Tropical Science Center (TSC), the Organization for Tropical Studies (OTS), the UCR and many other national, European and U.S. universities and scientists had been fairly intensively studying the ecology, fauna and flora of the Osa Peninsula. Since 1971 a wave of interest arose to establish a large protected area there. The CRNPS was very interested but already had four parks to manage, which absorbed all its scarce human and financial resources. However, in 1975 a series of events developed which put the proposed park in grave danger: a sudden increase in invasion by squatters (most of whom were land speculators) with the associated deforestation; a large mixed national-foreign capital logging firm developed very concrete plans to start a gigantic operation with a consortium of Japanese companies; and hunters began to enter the area in large numbers as word of its spectacular fauna spread. Given the situation, a national and international campaign in coordination with the CRNPS was begun to both build support for its legal declaration and to obtain funds for its establishment and management. The principal movers in this campaign were the TSC, WWF-USA, RARE, the U.S. Nature Conservancy, the Biologists Guild of Costa Rica and IUCN.

As soon as it was declared in October 1975, a Nacional Committee Pro Corcovado National Park was established to coordinate national actions for the immediate taking of possession of the area with proper institutional, legal and financial support. A few weeks later $40,000 was received from The Nature Conservancy and RARE via WWF-USA. To avoid bureaucratic slowdown TSC agreed with CRNPS to handle the administration of that and future donations. With the agreement of the National Committee and the CRNPS, the TSC also assigned one of its staff (a Costan Rican naturalist) as director and the CRNPS assigned all auxilliary personnel.

In sequence the CRNPS and the Park's director carried out the following key activities:

- Contacted the leaders of a small minority political party, but one which has great influence with agricultural workers in general and particularly the squatters in Corcovado (by that time 170 families, or 1500 persons scattered in various parts of the park). That assured that the party would not put obstacles in the way of CRNPS and would cooperate in the relocation of the squatters to new lands;

- various meetings with the President which resulted in: a high-level liason coordinator with direct access to the President and his staff; direct orders to the chief of the Civil Guards air wing to lend all support necessary; direct access to the Executive President of ITCO, so that it would plan and take charge of the relocation and payment to the squatters; and direct access to the Rural Guard Commander to support all those actions and maintain order in the park;

- establishment of two fixed, manned guard posts in strategic positions in relation to the squatters' distribution;

- prohibition of any expansion of agricultural activities and strict control and confiscation of gasoline, chainsaws and arms;

- payment of a half-salary to heads of family during four months prior to the relocation, in order to decrease the pressure to clear more forest for crop planting;

- purchase by ITCO of a large farm on the Peninsula but outside the park, for the relocation;

- payment of the "improvements" and for livestock, and relocation of the squatters; and

- refurbishment of some squatters' houses as permanent guard posts, staff living quarters and basic facilities for researchers.

By 1977, the park had no squatters, 20 rangers (10 from the zone), 4 permanent guard stations wth minimum facilities and radios, 30 horses, 15 km of critical boundaries well-marked and a reconditioned landing strip. It is one of the most important parks in the system, given its size (41,469 ha), extraordinary pristine nature and huge ecological and species diversity. It is rapidly becoming one of the most important research sites in tropical America.

5.7. Braulio Carrillo National Park

This area was declared in April 1978 based on heavy public pressure organized and directed by ASCONA and the CRNPS. The basis was the heavy deforestation that would follow the establishment of a new national highway cutting through the Cordillera Volcanica Central connecting San Jos with the Atlantic coast by a much shorter route. The extremely steep-sloped area included a complex of watersheds with primary forest cover of great importance for the Atlantic lowlands. The TSC in

1975 prepared an important study of the characteristics and potential environmental impact of the road and the colonization wave which would follow it. The park was declared just as road construction started and the CRNPS obtained control in time to prevent colonization.

In 1979 $1.5 million was included within a major USAID loan to Costa Rica for natural resources management, to finance the preparation of the general Management and Development Plan, Interpretive and Environmental Education Plan and other specialized plans, implementation of a National Environmental Education Center and CRNPS Training Center in the park and basic infrastructure for its administration.

To 1982 the CRNPS is managing 27 areas: 14 National Parks, 8 Biological Reserves, 1 National Monument (Arqueological), the National Zoological Park, 3 National Recreation Areas and one Biosphere Reserve (Fig. 1). This accounts for 7.8% of the national territory. Of these, 10 have Management and Development Plans, 3 have Interpretive and Environmental Education Plans and all have an annual Operational Plan. The subsystem receives approximately 600,000 visitors/year (90% nationals, or almost 25% of the country's population). The CRNPS has 450 employees, with 90% in the field.

6. OTHER CATEGORIES OF PROTECTION

6.1. Forest reserves and protection zones

In 1975 the DGF's Forestry Research Department prepared guidelines for the establishment of Forest Reserves and Protection Zones, which in practice have been complied with only partially. These tactical guidelines leave much of the process of selecting potential reserves in local community hands, and management and development planning are not specifically treated.

As the Forest Reserves Department was only created in late 1980, establishment and management has been the responsibility of several different DGF departments, all of which had other priority objectives and functions.

As of 1982, the Department has within its responsibilities 12 Forest Reserves and 8 Protection Zones, totalling 650,959 ha or 12.7% of the national territory. Unfortunately, management of these in every case has been limited to some protection by a few forest guards and a forestry inspector (technical, not professional level) in charge of them. In the entire subsystem there is not one *in situ* administration and most of the inspectors have 2-3 or more units to manage. All decisions are made at central office level. For the vast majority of the units: the boundaries on the ground are neither well-known nor marked; the land tenure situation and actual land use are poorly known; and basic studies are lacking on most resources.

During 1981, the first biannual Operational Plans for all units were completed and their implementation partially initiated; based on those, the first biannual Department Operational Plan was prepared. Two of the principal activities within the latter are:

a) A pilot Management and Development Plan for the Rio Macho Forest Reserve is being prepared to develop, test and improve a planning methodology, which can later be applied to the rest of the Forest Reserves; and

b) A Strategic Plan for the Management and Development of the National System of Forest Reserves and Related Categories is also being developed; it will include the existing subsystem plus potential ones. This will be finished by late 1983 and should give the Department a tool with which to strategically organize and manage the system.

6.2. Wildlife Refuges

The Wildlife Department of the DGF is in charge of managing Wildlife Refuges and conducting research leading to management and rational use of wildlife. Nevertheless, the low budget destined for those purposes, lack of methods and techniques for managing wildlife in the American tropics, lack of a national wildlife conservation plan, and the fact that this department has been moved from one Directorate to another several times in its short life, have been strong limiting factors. Also, the Department is just now for the first time experimenting with the preparation of a biannual Operational Plan.

The Department has three Wildlife Refuges under its responsibility:

Tapanti, actually part of the Rio Macho Forest Reserve; Bolanos Island, a 5 ha marine bird nesting site in the Pacific; and Rafael Lucas Rodriguez Wildlife Refuge, 75,00 ha of wetlands and dry tropical forest, which with Santa Rosa National Park, form most of the protected remaining dry forest in Central America. Only the latter has a Management and Development Plan and initial basic facilities and personnel and a few management activities; it is the first wildlife refuge in Central America with protection and such a plan. No Operational Plan has yet been done.

6.3. Indigenous Reserves

There are 26 Indigenous Reserves with a total of 269,000 ha or 5.2% of the national territory. The basic assumption of these areas is that the natural resources must be well-managed as a basis for sustaining the traditions, culture and life of those inhabitants and thus the nation as a whole. The Reserves are the property of the Indian communities which inhabit them and CONAI is obligated by law to offer advice and technical assistance for their management.

None of those Reserves has a Management and Development Plan nor Operational Plan and they really receive no management except for that carried out by each family on its cultivated fields and fallow areas. Protection is conducted by indigenous guards but their effectiveness is very doubtful as there is no real control or administration.

7. RESULTS

7.1. Management on-the-ground

In 1969, five legally-established wildlands in three management categories existed in the country; none were receiving any protection or management. Between 1970 and 1982, with the creation of the Costa Rican Park Service, General Forest Directorate (DGF) and National Commission for Indian Affairs, the situation changed markedly. By 1982, there were 79 wildlands units (legally established) in nine different categories, covering almost 27% of the national territory. Of these, 32 units are receiving "adequate and continuous management," 21 "inadequate and intermittent" management and 26 no management. Those three intensities of management correspond in their descending order, roughly to the CRNPS, DGF, and, finally, the Indigenous Reserves of which CONAI is the co-responsible agency.

Adequate and continuous management of its areas by the CRNPS can be attributed principally to the following characteristics, in order of importance or priority:

- *In situ* administration (Director and personnel living in the area);
- at least minimum numbers of trained professional and technical personnel;
- minimum necessary infrastructure for staff;
- a mandatory Operational Plan and, in many cases,

a general Management and Development Plan; and
- minimum facilities for visitors or investigators (trails, interpretation, etc.)

The vast majority of the units under the DGF's responsibility qualify for inadequate and intermittent management because of:

- No *in situ* administration;
- no professional level personnel in the areas and the technical ones are inadequately trained;
- lacking the minimum infrastructure for personnel;
- very partial implementation of the Operational Plans which had been prepared for all the areas by 1982; and
- no minimum facilities for visitors or investigators.

For the Indigenous Reserves, all fall within the "no management" category; one could argue that *in situ* administration exists because the Indian leaders live within the reserves, but the only administration is restricted to specific communal matters and not for all the unit. The only administration (and that is not management) occurs long-distance from San Jos and that it by CONAI, with sporadic visits to the areas.

There is a fourth management intensity category which exists which could be termed "efficient management" and which exists in only one unit in the whole national system, Volcan Poas National Park, according to the authors' opinion. With professional and technical personnel in sufficient number (instead of minimum) to protect and maintain the integrity of the area and its resources; adequate (instead of minimum) infrastructure for the staff; excellent general Management and Development Plan, Interpretive and Environmental Educational Plan, and a biannual Operational Plan (revised annually); and adequate (instead of minimum) facilities for visitors or investigators, Volcan Poas provides an example of the level of management which all areas in Costa Rica's system of wildlands should attain if the nation is to earn the full benefits of ecodevelopment.

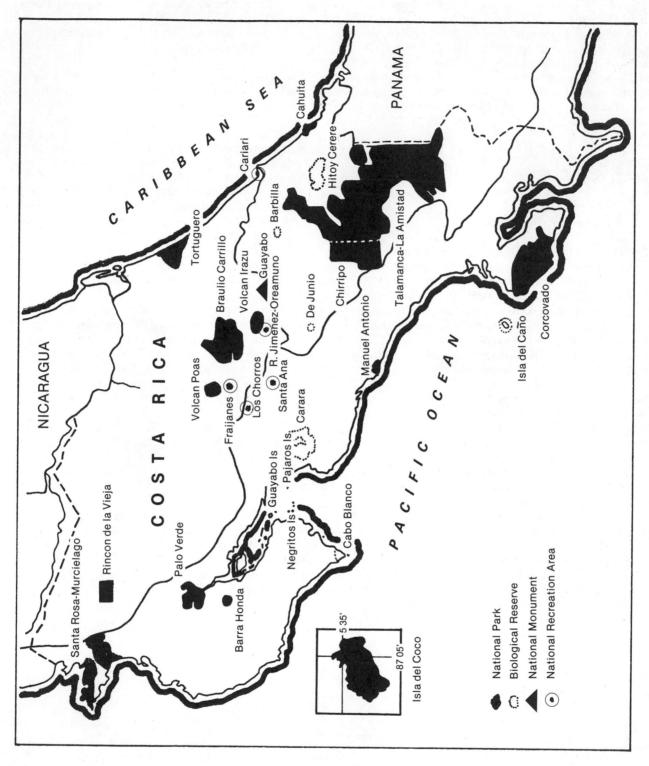

Figure 1. National parks, biological reserves, national monuments, and recreation areas of Costa Rica.

Sea Turtles and National Parks in the Caribbean

Archie F. Carr
Department of Zoology
University of Florida
Gainesville, Florida, USA

ABSTRACT. *Of the threatened and endangered species of the world, marine turtles are among the hardest to shield from further decline. Their intractability as objects of stewardship derives from the complexity of their life-cycles, from the world demand for high-priced sea turtle products, and from collisions with man on ocean beaches, coral reefs and commercial shrimping grounds. This paper reviews the conservation difficulties and opportunities involved in sea turtle conservation in the Caribbean, the need for expanded marine sanctuaries to deal with the problem, and the implications of these efforts for world sea turtle conservation. The valuable genetic resources embodied by sea turtles will best be conserved through a combination of appropriate protected areas, particularly nesting grounds, and management of exploitation wherever the species occur.*

1. INTRODUCTION

As one moves about among conservation agencies and agents one hears on the one hand that the best way to save species from extinction is to create national parks, and on the other hand that management and control of exploitation are what are required. Obviously, both are indispensable—as is also every other device that holds hope of diminishing the losses. If the endangered species is in international commercial demand as sea turtles and spotted cats are, then the fundamental strategy is restriction of international trade. If the chief adverse factor is loss of habitat, then parks and reserves are the principal hope. In the case of the sea turtles, both over-exploitation and habitat degradation are at work, and as seaside populations and development spread, the effects of both are growing. The control that brings the broadest benefit is the creation of parks and sanctuaries, which not only save species but also prevent disruption of the ecologic organization of entire biologic landscapes. An important by-product is public education and good will. The judicious admission of visitors can build essential public support for the exercise.

2. THE SEA TURTLE LIFE CYCLE

There are important gaps in what is known of the ecologic geography of the five genera of marine turtles: *Chelonia* (green turtle), *Eretmochelys* (hawksbill), *Lepidochelys* (ridley), *Caretta* (loggerhead) and *Dermochelys* (leatherback). It is clear, however, that no population of any of them can be given complete protection within a single refuge. However, the genera and species vary markedly in their amenability to protection, because of strong ecologic differences among them, and because each makes drastic seasonal and ontogenetic shifts in its range and habitat; sea turtles share a common basic pattern of such habitat shifting. The young of them all hatch out on land. On leaving the nest they go straight to the sea, where they swim directly away from the shore. For a year or two they are pelagic, perhaps mainly drifting with ocean currents in algal rafts. On reaching weights of around a kilo, the young turtles of six of the eight named species move into inshore waters, and feed in benthic habitats. The yearlings of the olive ridley *Lepidochelys olivacea* and leatherback *Dermochelys coriacea* remain wholly out of sight; nobody appears to have any idea where they are. On approaching maturity, all enter the adult foraging regimen, which varies from the day-night grazing and sleeping routine of the herbivorous green turtle to the as-yet uncharted long-range feeding migrations of the leatherback, loggerhead *Caretta caretta*, and ridleys. There is some evidence that leatherbacks that nest in the Caribbean migrate regularly to waters off New England, and feed on the seasonal bloom of jellyfishes there.

3. ECOLOGIC DIFFERENCES AMONG THE SPECIES

Some marine turtles nest in aggregations, and for these, protection at the breeding place is the most effective conservation measure. However, the species vary markedly in the degree to which they can be helped by sanctuaries. Of the five genera, *Lepidochelys* lends itself to this kind of intervention, because of its tendency to nest at a few restricted localities, and to come ashore there by the thousands on short stretches of beach. These astonishing massings, known in Latin America as "arribadas", are a stirring phenomenon. They occur in only a few places in the world. If, as proposed to the Mexican government (Marquez, 1978), the five *arribada* sites in that country had long ago been declared national parks or sanctuaries, the survival of *Lepidochelys* in Mexico, once the most important breeding ground in the world (with the possible exception of India), would have been ensured. For Kemp's ridley *L. kempi*, the sanctuary status belatedly given its single nesting place, a ten-mile section of the Gulf coast of Mexico in Tamaulipas, just south of the US border, has probably come too late. Forty years ago the *arribadas* there numbered at least 40,000, and probably many more. If a park had been declared there in the early 1940s, *kempi* would today be in good shape. Instead, the *arribada* was wrecked during the 1940s and 1950s, and now the nesting arrivals of a season number only 500 or fewer. This is the most disastrous loss suffered by any species of marine turtle in recent times. A sanctuary could have prevented the loss.

Kemp's ridley does not occur in the Caribbean, though its feeding range comes within a very short distance of the Yucatan Channel, which technically separates the Caribbean and the Gulf of Mexico. A zoogeographic quirk as anomalous as the absence of *kempi* from Caribbean waters is the presence there of *L. olivacea*. It is predominantly a Pacific species but has outlying nesting colonies in West Africa and northeastern South America, and it barely enters the easternmost edges of the Caribbean. In its East Pacific range, where once it was by far the predominant nesting entity, the survival outlook of *olivacea* is not happy. The Pacific coast of Mexico was originally the main reproductive site of the East Pacific population, but the leather trade has destroyed all the *arribadas* there except one in Oaxaca, and that one is being heavily exploited.

The loggerhead and the leatherback are widely, though sparsely, distributed in the Caribbean. Their major American breeding grounds are located elsewhere—those of the loggerhead on the Atlantic coast of the southern United States; those of *Dermochelys* in French Guiana and Suriname. Nevertheless, nesting by both occurs, by separately emerging individuals and by small groups. Loggerheads of all stages of development turn up here and there as foraging visitors, but nowhere in abundance.

The predominant Caribbean turtles are *Chelonia mydas* and *Eretmochelys imbricata*, the green turtle and the hawksbill. Except for the fact that it rarely gathers in large breeding assemblages, the hawksbill appears to be the most amenable of the sea turtles to protection in sanctuaries, because there is less difference in the feeding habits and habitat of the developmental and adult stages. Moreover, hawksbills do not require long reaches of high-energy shore for nesting. They come out on any patch of cove-head beach where there is a little sand suitable for incubation. Because of this open-minded approach to nest-site selection, hawksbills nest far more widely in the Caribbean than any other species. And because the genus is mainly a forager on reefs, the feeding and nesting habitats are often not widely separated. Therefore, practically any littoral marine reserve in the Caribbean might provide protection for an entire local hawksbill population except in its pelagic, posthatchling stage. However, even though some hawksbills may remain in a single area to develop, forage and reproduce, limited information from tag recoveries shows that some individuals do make long migrations. Nevertheless, the species is, on the whole, probably more parochial in its ecology than any other Caribbean turtle, and is thus likely to be an important beneficiary of almost any reef-system or sea beach reserve that is declared in the area.

4. THE SPECIAL PROBLEM OF THE "LOST YEAR"

The difficulty of providing sanctuary for sea turtles of all kinds reaches a peak in the "lost-year" stage of the life cycle. This cryptic interlude is clearly pelagic, and is evidently passed in or near down-wellings or shears between currents, or where water bodies of different densities meet. The linear zones found there are traps for flotsam of all kinds, including the sargassum mats that appear to be an important refuge for young sea turtles. Three species—the Atlantic loggerhead, the Atlantic green turtle, and the Atlantic hawksbill—have repeatedly been found in or associated with sargassum drift. So many sightings of first-year loggerheads in sargassum have now accumulated that their association with the weed-line habitat can no longer be considered conjectural. A weakness in the weed-raft theory is that in the waters off some rookery shores, no sargassum or other rafted flotsam is present. In some, and perhaps all, of these cases, however, shears and concentrations of plankton do occur, and newly emerged hatchlings have been seen feeding in these.

This pelagic stage seems, at first glance, less susceptible to man-made hazards than any other part of the life cycle. Disruptions of the ecology of the seas are multiplying, however. Man's dejecta have spread worldwide and the shearlines are trapping pollutants of all kinds, just as they hold the flotsam rafts that house the little turtles. Moreover, sea turtles are indiscriminate feeders, and the young often ingest the solid wastes— the ubiquitous industrial plastic beads that accumulate in the drift lines and shears, for example. The effects of oil spills on turtles in the weed-lines are disastrous. Liquid oil smears over the eyes and nostrils, and oil pellets choke them or gum their mouths shut when eaten. Hawksbills, green turtles, and large numbers of loggerheads have been found dead or moribund from this cause.

5. SEA TURTLE TAXONOMY AND THE PROBLEMS IT PRESENTS

A somewhat less pressing but fundamentally important problem in deciding how to allocate scarce resources for sea turtle conservation is the elementary state of our understanding of the taxonomy of the group. There are five well-defined genera of marine turtles, and eight species are generally recognized. If all these were as well represented in museum collections as most other vertebrates are, and if large series of specimens of comparable age groups had been studied by up-to-date taxonomic procedures, the number of sea turtle "kinds" bearing scientific names would be far greater. If, as we claim, it is a basic aim of conservation to conserve genetic resources, then just saving the eight currently recognized kinds of sea turtles is obviously not enough.

In the Atlantic system, for example, only one species of the green turtle *Chelonia mydas*, is recognized, with Ascension Island the type locality. However, the species has four big nesting grounds in the Atlantic system, and the turtles that breed there mate and nest virtually nowhere else. After the breeding season they disperse widely; but when the next breeding season comes, they consistently return to the same places to court, copulate and nest again. The mechanisms by which their reproductive journeys are scheduled and guided are completely unknown, but they are surely complex. Each colony must have its own partly imprinted, partly also evolved, set of adaptations for its own specific ecologic regimen. Although evidence of morphologic divergence among these supposed demes has been slow in coming, morphometric, bio-chemical and behavioural differences almost surely exist. Each of the four green turtle breeding colonies is almost certainly a genetically different entity—and to preserve genetic differences is the avowed purpose and obligation of conservation.

These four colonies are all protected, at least on their breeding shores, but they do not embrace the range of diversity in the Atlantic green turtle. On most of the high-energy shores of the Caribbean, diffused or weakly aggregated nesting also occurs. Thus, even if the big breeding colonies are given adequate protection, how do we distribute our concern among the lesser gatherings—each of which is also presumably a genetic deme? When any nesting assemblage, however small, is de-

leted, we have not merely reduced the numbers of individuals in a recognized taxon. Genetic diversity—the commodity we are under obligation to conserve—has also diminished. Quite obviously, there is no prospect of preserving the totality of the genetic resources represented by sea turtles. We have to make a respectable effort anyway, and that will involve setting realistic priorities in allocating the limited conservation resources at our disposal.

There is urgency in those considerations, as far-out as they may seem. But we face losses more jolting than the deletion of local demes. The extirpation of major populations of sea turtles from entire regions, in progress everywhere for centuries, is accelerating; and some of the taxonomically recognized species face extinction. Kemp's ridley may be irretrievably lost. The Mexican black turtle *Chelonia agassizi* seems headed toward a similar fate. Except perhaps in Queensland, the hawksbill is under intolerable pressure from divers, who comb the reefs for snappers, grouper and lobsters, and to whom the inflated prices now being paid for tortoiseshell make it profitable for spear fishermen to ransack the reef systems of the Caribbean—and indeed, of the tropical world. The hawksbill is by far the most clearly endangered species of sea turtle in the Caribbean region.

6. TURTLES AND MARINE PARKS IN THE CARIBBEAN

Up to 20 years ago, almost the only marine parks in existence anywhere were islands or shoreline terrain, usually in places where seabirds nested. During the 1950s, improved diving gear introduced growing numbers of people to the aesthetic and scientific marvels of the submarine environment, particularly the biologic splendour of coral reefs. The idea of the submarine park rapidly took hold. The first reef system to be specially designated an undersea preserve in the Caribbean was Buck Island National Monument in the U.S. Virgin Islands, established in 1961. The beaches there are good nesting grounds, and the extraordinarily beautiful reefs are foraging habitat for hawksbills and young green turtles. More extensive systems of reefs and sea grass flats had earlier been preserved in the Virgin Islands National Park on St. Johns. Since these two preserves were created, marine parks have sprung up around many of the Caribbean islands, and proposals for many more are under study.

The Caribbean parks have been listed by the Eastern Caribbean Natural Area Management Program (1979), and a list of the marine parks of the region appears in Randall (1980). The distribution of nesting beaches and potential foraging and developmental sea turtle habitats in the Lesser Antilles is shown in the atlases of the Eastern Caribbean Natural Area Management Program and further data appear in a West Atlantic Sea Turtle Survey made by the Caribbean Conservation Corporation for the National Marine Fisheries Service (Carr *et* al., 1982) and in a more recent report for the Western Atlantic Turtle Symposium by Fletemeyer (1981).

Marine parks are few in the Greater Antilles. I can find no data on marine preserves in Cuba; there are extensive areas in the Jardines de la Reina, on the south coast of the island, that are worthy of park status. The island of Hispaniola was in times past rich sea turtle country, but the fauna is now much depleted. Haiti apparently is without marine parks, but under the guidance of Jos Ottenwalder, the Dominican Republic has embarked on a vigorous programme of sea turtle conservation, and park status has been proposed for several important areas of nesting and foraging habitat.

Along much of the mainland Caribbean coast marine park development lacks the stimulus provided by the coral reef systems of the islands, but interest in preserving the coastal wilderness and marine littoral is nevertheless slowly growing.

In Mexico, the only protected turtle ground on the Caribbean coast is at Isla Contoy, at the northern tip of Yucatan, where a sanctuary protects the third largest Caribbean nesting colony of *Chelonia*.

In Belize, where the whole magnificent barrier reef is in urgent need of protection, Half Moon Cay National Park has recently been established. The area is described by LaBastille (1982). It seems to me a world obligation to work for park status for extensive sections of this second largest coral reef on earth. Turtle nesting is not heavy there, but the reef system comprises optimal feeding ground for young loggerheads and for hawksbills and green turtles in both developmental and mature stages.

There are no marine preserves in Guatemala. A sanctuary should be declared at Cabo Tres Puntas, where a few nesting loggerheads, leatherbacks, green turtles, and hawksbills are now receiving no protection. In Honduras, approximately 10,000 ha of reefs are embraced by the Bay Islands National Park, but over-exploitation has depleted the once-abundant sea turtle there, and along the entire mainland coast as well. Occasional nesting still occurs in the Miskitia, where a part of the shore is incorporated into the magnificent Rio Platano Biosphere Reserve, the second largest protected area in Central America.

In Nicaragua, the future of the green turtle in the western Caribbean is heavily dependent on the stability of the feeding colony on the tremendous expanse of sea grass flats on Miskito Bank. There is at present no marine park in the area, but a proposal for such a move is under study in Managua.

In Panama, a park in the Cuna Indian country of the San Blas Islands and adjacent coast is proposed. In the past, these islands were famous for the excellent nesting and feeding habitats they provided for hawksbills. Although the turtle population has been drastically thinned out by over-harvesting, the hawksbill still holds on there, and it could be rehabilitated by well-chosen sanctuaries. The most important opportunity for sea turtle conservation in Panama, however, is embodied by the superb spectrum of littoral habitats in the Bocas del Toro area.

In Colombia, where there is an extensive national park system, the marine parks have had setbacks. Construction of a highway between Barranquilla and Santa Marta wrecked the mangrove swamps of Salamanca Park. Dynamiting, spear-fishing and egg poaching have practically destroyed the sea turtle fauna of Corales del Rosario National Park. Tayrona National Park, in which 85 km of beach have been designated a sea turtle sanctuary, is by court edict about to go back into private ownership. The loggerhead nesting beach made known by the research of Kaufmann (1975) lies just outside the limits of Buritaca Park.

In Venezuela, where the first national park in the Caribbean—Henry Pittier—was established in 1937, there are two major opportunities to reinforce the survival outlook of sea turtles. One is presented by Aves Island. The Estacion Cientifica Militar recently established there is scaring off the turtle boats from the Windward Islands that formerly raided the rookery. The other prime turtle habitat in Venezuela is the incomparable Los Roques atoll. This lovely circle of mostly uninhabited islets, 160 km in diameter, is a classic manifestation of atoll physiography—which I had always thought was lacking in the Atlantic system. Los Roques provides optimal nesting, feeding and developmental habitat for the hawksbill. With somewhat closer surveillance than the park guards stationed at the main settlement on Gran Roque are at present able to provide, the atoll could be a vital factor in the effort to slow the decline of the Caribbean hawksbill. A hawksbill hatchery, maintained by the Fundacion Cientifica Los Roques, provides safe incubation for eggs taken from sites where egg hunters regularly operate.

From the standpoint of marine turtle conservation, the most important national park in the Caribbean is Tortuguero National Park in Costa Rica. This area includes 18,947 ha of tropical wet forest and palm swamp, and a 30 km section of the nesting shore of the largest breeding assemblage of *Chelonia* in the Americas.

As delimited, the park has many assets besides its green turtle colony. Hawksbills and leatherbacks also nest there, and the woodlands and waterways of the hinterland are a priceless sample of the diminishing wilderness of the Caribbean lowlands. But the green turtles were the main initial qualification of the area for park designation. Thirty years ago, I decided to try to advance the feeble state of knowledge of sea turtle ecology of that time. I spent two seasons reconnoitering the Caribbean, looking for sites of mass nesting where green turtles could be tagged in great numbers. In 1954, it became clear that the most promising place was Tortuguero—or Turtle Bogue, as it is called in Caribbean English—a 35 km section of the Costa Rican shore between the mouths of the Reventazon and Tortuguero rivers, just south of the Nicaraguan frontier. A tagging camp was promptly established there, and the Caribbean Conservation Corporation has operated this every season since. Returns of tags on Tortuguero beach itself, and hundreds of other recoveries by turtle hunters on distant feeding grounds (see Fig. 1), have outlined the ecologic range of the adult population and revealed the frequency and periodicities of internesting and remigration returns. The Tortuguero population of *Chelonia* has turned out to be by far the largest in the Caribbean, and one of the half-dozen biggest green turtle assemblages in the world. As Fig. 1 shows, the feeding grounds of the colony, though mainly in the Miskito Cays region of Nicaragua, are located at a scattering of sites at various distances north and south of Costa Rica.

The nesting colony shows strong site-fidelity. None of the 26,000 turtles that have been tagged on the 35 km of Tortuguero Beach has ever been found nesting on any other shore. The only other big nesting aggregation of *Chelonia* in the Caribbean is based on Aves Island, a Venezuelan islet in the eastern Caribbean one hundred miles east of Monserrat. Tag-returns accumulated by the Fundacion para la Defensa de la Naturaleza (FUDENA) in Caracas, and by various previous workers, have shown that the Aves turtles reside mainly around the islands of the Lesser Antilles, and that they too are firmly site-fixed on Aves as a breeding ground.

An important early by-product of our Tortuguero research was the governmental attention it attracted to the gross over-exploitation that once went on at the rookery. Before 1956, the whole shore was patrolled by commercial turtlers, and virtually every female turtle that came ashore to nest was either killed for calipee, or rigged with a log buoy and released in the surf, to be picked up by a cruising turtle launch and carried 50 miles down the coast to freezing plants in Puerto Limon. During periods of good weather the slaughter or live export of the nesting turtles was almost complete.

As research at our tagging camp progressed, the activity drew local governmental and international attention to the Tortuguero green turtles, and to the abuse the colony was suffering at the hands of the *"veladores"*, as the turtle turners were called. During the early 1960s, laws were passed prohibiting the killing or molesting of nesting turtles and the taking of eggs. Despite the chronic difficulty of enforcing a law prohibiting the harpooning of turtles close inshore at the nesting beach, and despite strong opposition by the frustrated exploiters in Puerto Limon, Tortuguero is today, after Aves Island, the best-protected sea turtle ground in the Caribbean. The better protection at Aves is due to the presence of the permanent military garrison (Estacion Cientifica Militar) on the island. Needless to say, the garrison was not put there just to protect the turtles, but the protection has come nevertheless.

There can be little doubt that local and governmental reaction to the "scientific presence" at Tortuguero is what saved the green turtle colony from the complete destruction that it faced in the 1950s. Since then, tagging projects have sprung up at important nesting grounds in many other parts of the world; and in nearly every case, the local authorities have been stirred to provide some degree of protection for the turtles involved. At Tortuguero, the most recent development has been the declaration of the beach, together with a broad expanse of forests and waterways behind it, as Tortuguero National Park.

When Tortuguero was declared a national park, it seemed likely, because of its isolation, to remain for a long time a "paper park", little visited by either tourists or Costa Ricans and without proper protection for its timber and wildlife. At that time Mario Boza was generating a perfect jubilee of park-making in Costa Rica— one that has since evoked worldwide astonishment and admiration. Funds have not been sufficient to allow an even development of all the 14 parks that have been declared, and those most likely to bring public support for the park system have naturally received the most attention. Meanwhile, however, Tortuguero has not been neglected. The Park Service has assumed the unenviable job of enforcing the turtle laws, and with financial help from outside sources it has done an effective job on the nesting shore itself. Offshore, however, poaching by the harpooners from Limon, 80 km to the south, continues. By law the turtle canoes are forbidden to approach the nesting beach closer than 3 km. Actually, they come in and spear the female turtles and mating pairs almost within the breaker zone. Little can be done to stop them because no craft suitable for longshore patrolling is available to the Park Service, and the surf is nearly always too strong to launch small boats from the beach.

In spite of that serious leak, exploitation at the Tortuguero breeding ground is much diminished. In 1980, Costa Rica signed the Convention on International Trade in Endangered Species (CITES). Three Nicaraguan packing houses, that had been exporting around 10,000 green turtles a year, were closed, and pressure on the Miskito Cay feeding colony diminished. Today, the survival outlook for the contingent of the Costa Rican nesting colony that resides in Nicaragua is much improved. The same cannot be said of the other group of migrants from the south—from Panama, Colombia and a scattering of more distant places.

7. INTERNATIONAL PARK SYSTEMS AND THEIR BEARING ON SEA TURTLE SURVIVAL

Because of the long-range migrations that marine turtles carry out, effective protection requires international cooperation—not just restriction of international commerce, but also collaboration in creating sanctuaries, or sets of sanctuaries. Although no international sea turtle parks now exist, there are several areas for which such sanctuary systems have been considered, and where they clearly would bring spectacular benefit to sea turtles.

For those of us who for 25 years have worked with the West Caribbean green turtle population at its Costa Rican nesting beach, a reserve in the Miskito Cays feeding grounds in Nicaragua has long been a dream. To this concept, that of a third sea turtle park, in Bocas del Toro Province of Panama has now been added. Marine parks in Nicaragua and Panama would provide vital protection for the species on extensive feeding pastures, in developmental habitats, and at stations along the migratory routes of both the northern and southern contingents of the Tortuguero population. Results of the West Atlantic Sea Turtle Survey of the National Marine Fisheries Service (Carr *et al.*, 1982), and continuing studies by Anne Meylan, indicate that, for sea turtles generally, Chiriqui Lagoon and the Bastimentos area of Panama, are the richest sea turtle territory in the entire Caribbean. Just off this part of the coast, also, the shear along the west side of the Southwest Caribbean Gyre usually swings closest inshore. This shear appears to be the axis of the passive migration route of the entire hatchling production of the Tortuguero nesting ground. The Bocas segment of the shear ought to be closely guarded against pollution—such as may emanate from the operations of the oil pipeline being installed across Panama, with the Caribbean terminal deep within Chiriqui Lagoon.

In a tripartite convention in San Jose, Costa Rica in 1969, Nicaragua and Panama reached an agreement to collaborate in an effort to stabilize and preserve their shared green turtle populations. The Costa Rican nesting shore is now part of a national park. At the World Conference on Sea Turtle Conservation in 1979, Reynaldo Arostegui communicated the interest of his government in developing a national reserve in the Miskito Cays and adjacent coastal area of Nicaragua. In 1980, a group from the United States joined with Nicaraguan representatives in aerial and sea-surface surveys of the proposed reserve area. Since then, perhaps because of unrest in the Miskitia, the project has gone no farther. It is still clearly alive, however, and the question now is whether Panama is motivated to save her share of the resource, along with the biologically rich and aesthetically superb marine landscapes of Bocas del Toro Province. If all this can be accomplished, the resulting trio of sanctuaries will ensure the survival of not just the West Caribbean green turtle, but of magnificent samples of most of the marine ecologic communities of the mainland coast.

Acknowledgements

This paper was prepared for IUCN's Commission on National Parks and Protected Areas in cooperation with the United Nations Environment Programme.

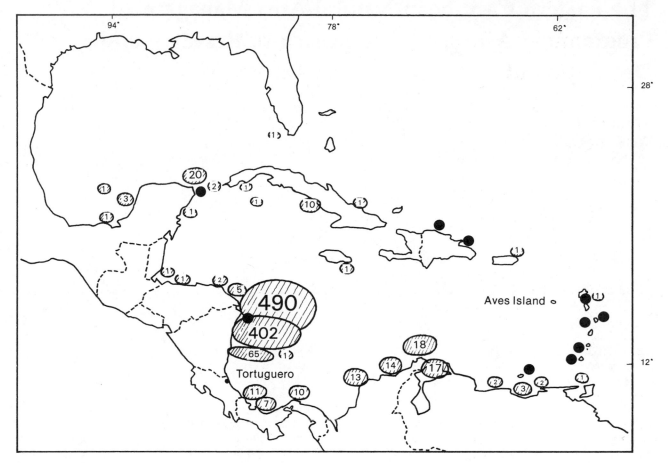

Figure 1.
Foreign recoveries of turtles tagged while nesting at Tortuguero, Costa Rica, 1956–1976. None of the recoveries was made on shore. No Tortuguero turtle has ever been recorded nesting elsewhere. Stars represent recapture localities of turtles tagged while nesting on Aves Island, 1971–1976. Although there have been many recoveries since this figure was first published, these have not materially changed the distribution pattern. (After Carr, Carr, and Meyland, 1978.)

The Eastern Caribbean Natural Area Management Programme: A Regional Approach to Research and Development for Conservation Action

Allen D. Putney, Ivor Jackson, and Yves Renard
West Indies Laboratory
St. Croix, US Virgin Islands

ABSTRACT. *The paper describes the activities of the Eastern Caribbean Natural Area Management Programme (EC-NAMP), a non-governmental endeavour to improve local capacity to manage natural areas critical to development. The programme consists of a series of projects which combine field action, training, and research activities in ways that are mutually reinforcing. The paper presents a series of insights into planning from the bottom up, showing how substantive materials and field demonstration areas can improve the local capacity to manage. As the field projects generate experience, examples, and guidelines, emphasis will shift to broadening the effort to improve the local capacity to manage. In this way, it is expected that the programme will have an increasing impact on the effective and realistic management of natural resources in the region, and provide a documented experience for managers in other parts of the world.*

1. INTRODUCTION

The Eastern Caribbean Natural Area Management Programme (ECNAMP) is a non-governmental endeavour to improve local capacity to manage natural areas critical to development. The programme consists of a series of projects which combine field action, training, and research activities in ways that are mutually reinforcing.

The geographical area of focus is the islands of the Lesser Antilles in the Eastern Caribbean (see Fig. 1). This is a multi-national, small island archipelago characterized by dense populations and limited natural resources.

The case study will detail the reasons for initiating the programme, the way it functions, and some of its successes and failures. We hope to share some experiences and insights that have been gained, especially

with respect to regional systems of national parks and protected areas, integrative methods of programme development, and the full involvement of local people. Although the programme is new and our ignorance often seems overwhelming, it is hoped that the insights that have emerged will stimulate discussions on alternative strategies and approaches, especially when compared to experiences in other parts of the world.

While this study emphasizes action on national parks and protected areas, the programme itself uses an integrative approach to resource management, which covers both ecological and socio-economic aspects of resource use systems, and which uses a variety of management tools. This is necessary when dealing with small islands because of the close inter-relationships and dependencies which predominate within and between the human and natural systems.

2. PROBLEM STATEMENT

Islands by nature are fragile, both in terms of their natural ecological systems and their human social systems. These systems have evolved in relative isolation. When this isolation is removed by air and sea transport links, outside organisms and influences are introduced, and compete with, and sometimes eliminate, the indigenous.

The islands of the Caribbean are particularly under stress. They have some of the densest populations in the western hemisphere and generally are poorly endowed with natural resources. Because of the small size of the islands of the Lesser Antilles, inter-relationships are everywhere evident. What occurs in one part of an island is linked to and has effects on all other parts of the island and its surrounding waters. Thus, the need for effective management of natural areas critical to development is pronounced.

The problems of the islands have been exacerbated by the historic uses to which the resources have been put. The plantation system, monocultures, and dependency on outside resources and economies have been the pattern of resource use from the time European man came to the islands. The natural systems have been severely disrupted by large scale deforestation, and resultant soil erosion and change of micro-climatic conditions, over-exploitation of fish and wildlife stocks, degradation of habitats critical to economically important species, and alteration and pollution of watersheds essential to water production and utilization. The effects on the human societies, especially those caused by the slave and indentured labour systems, have been pervasive and even today are not well understood.

A central and historical problem, then, is one of intensive use of fragile natural ecosystems, often for the benefit of far-distant economies. A long history of this pattern has created significant stress on both the indigenous ecosystems and local societies. The stress is intensified by lack of awareness by governments of the requirements for efficient and sustainable natural resource development; insufficient coordination of management efforts among government, business and local resource user groups; lack of trained resource managers and of institutions in which to train them; and the lack of communication among the islands with respect to natural resource use and management.

At the same time, the small size of the islands involved and the intensive use of their resources provide an opportunity for creating a variety of tools for managing natural resources, especially those found in natural areas, under conditions of stress and competition. The challenge is to determine how protected areas can best contribute to stimulating and sustaining socio-economic development, and how to improve the human capacity to manage. To do this, it is necessary to: determine the role of living natural resources in the development process; learn how to maximize their contribution to society; identify those land and water areas that require particularly careful management as parks or other kinds of protected areas; and create the local capacity to develop and manage adequately these resources. As human populations and resource competition increase worldwide, conditions will more and more approximate the intensive resource use of the islands. Thus whatever can be learned under the stressful conditions of the islands will have increasing application worldwide.

3. BACKGROUND

As shown in Fig. 1, the islands of the Lesser Antilles stretch from east of the islands of the Greater Antilles, near Puerto Rico, to the South American continent near eastern Venezuela. This is a distance of some 750 km, and the marine areas between islands are large compared to their small land mass. The island chain is composed of an inner arc of high volcanic islands with a variety of terrestrial ecosystems and a small marine shelf, and an outer arc composed of low coraline islands with little variety in terms of terrestrial ecosystems, but with significant marine shelf areas.

The socio-economic setting of the region is one of low per capita income, but relatively higher quality of life, in terms of life expectancy and literacy, than in many other developing areas of the world. The disparity among the various social groups is not large when compared to most continental areas. Agriculture, tourism, and fisheries tend to be the leading economic sectors, although the percentage of employment in the public sector is generally quite high.

Historically the plantation system has predominated in agriculture, although this system is tending to decline in importance in many areas. The plantations have produced monocultures for export, especially sugar, coconuts, and bananas. The newer leading economic sectors, especially tourism, are generally in the hands of outside interests. Thus, the historical dependency on and control by outside interests remains to this day.

The utilization of the best agricultural lands by the larger plantations and the increasing use of coastal areas for tourism have had the effect of displacing both small farmers and fishermen from prime areas. In addition, large-scale use of fertilizers and pesticides on the plantations and the pollutants generated by tourism complexes have contaminated water supplies and caused the degradation of many coastal ecosystems. The net result is the shrinking of relatively unaltered natural areas, increasing stress on the natural ecosystems critical to development, and decline in the productivity of traditional agriculture and fisheries.

The historic patterns of development and the colonial past have left the islands deeply divided by language, culture, and economic dependencies. Of the 15 islands or island groups of the Lesser Antilles, 6 are independent countries, 2 are Departments of France, 3 are islands of the Netherlands Antilles, and 4 are dependencies of the United Kingdom. This makes any kind of coordinated action or sharing of infrastructure or human resources extremely difficult.

4. CONSTRAINTS

Given the natural, historical, economic, and insitutional setting, there is a web of constraints to natural resource management in general, and to management of national parks and protected areas in particular. It is often difficult to specifically identify the major constraints to management of natural resources, but many of them appear to be mainly institutional in nature. These include:

- The need to approach management on an island-by-island basis because of the large number of political entities. Each entity requires its own policies, legislation, management infrastructure, and training and education programmes;
- the making of major decisions affecting resource use by outside interests based on foreign criteria and pressures;
- land tenure patterns that limit efficient natural resource utilization;
- structuring of national priorities which tends to undervalue natural resource management and to perpetuate a situation of inadequate funding, staffing, and training; and
- the difficulties of educational and training institutions in developing meaningful and practical curricula oriented to local conditions and environments.

In addition to the institutional constraints, there are severe constraints regarding human resources. Each island is greatly limited in the number of natural resource management personnel that can be trained, hired, and effectively supported. Thus, there are few experienced resource managers, and a poor data base for identifying priorities and initiating effective action.

5. ACTION

For many years, there has been a growing awareness of the few remaining natural areas, the stress on natural ecosystems and local culture, and the aforementioned constraints imposed by the geography and history of the region. This led to the establishment of a non-governmental conservation organization in the region, the Caribbean Conservation Association (CCA), some 15 years ago.

ECNAMP itself was begun in 1977 in response to the concerns of a private U.S.-based foundation, the Rockefeller Brothers Fund (RBF). This foundation had been instrumental in stimulating the Latin American Regional Wildlands Project of the Food and Agriculture Organization, during the early 1970s, and extended this concern to the Eastern Caribbean during the late 1970s. Because of institutional capabilities and key personnel, RBF this time found it useful to support implementation of the Eastern Caribbean programme through a cooperative non-governmental undertaking. This was later dubbed "The Eastern Caribbean Natural Area Management Programme," and linked up the CCA and the School of Natural Resources, University of Michigan, in a common endeavour.

The programme's efforts were initially concentrated on Dominica, an island with an on-going programme for parks and protected areas. As experience in working with the special problems of small islands was gained, the programme was extended to cover the 15 islands, or island groups, of the Lesser Antilles. Greatest emphasis has been placed on natural areas which are critical to development.

Initially the programme was funded in its entirety by the Rockefeller Brothers Fund. That funding base has expanded over the years to include many other sources, especially IUCN, WWF, The Jackson Hole Preserve, Inc., the Canadian International Development Agency, and the Arkville Erpf Fund. Smaller grants have also been received from UNEP and the Caribbean Development Bank. During the past three years, the overall budget for ECNAMP has averaged about US $175,000 per year.

ECNAMP operates through a range of contacts with individuals and institutions. To avoid the drawbacks and overhead expenses of larger institutions, ECNAMP has no permanent staff nor centralized office. This approach is particularly realistic under present circumstances, since most work is funded on a project-by-project basis. It is a particularly cost-effective approach, especially compared to bi-lateral and multi-lateral technical assistance programmes.

Activities are coordinated by a Principal Investigator whose office is located at the West Indies Laboratory of Fairleigh Dickinson University, St. Croix, U.S. Virgin Islands. Three Staff Consultants, each located on a different island, organize and implement activities together with the Principal Investigator. Numerous short term consultants are contracted on a project-by-project basis, and a strong preference is given to individuals from the region. All project activities are carried out jointly with local governmental, or occasionally non-govermental, organizations. Efforts are made to maximize the involvement of local communities. Close working relationships are maintained with a variety of organizations, both inside and outside of the region, which have common objectives.

ECNAMP's working format permits it to evolve to fit in with changing circumstances, be they in terms of personnel, perceived needs and priorities, institutions, or funding possibilities. At present, major areas of programme focus include the identification of regional conservation priorities, assistance in developing local capacity to manage, development of effective methods and approaches for the management of living natural resources, building of public awareness and participation in management, and linking of natural resource use to overall development goals.

5.1. ECNAMP's field activities

The projects being undertaken during 1982 provide an indication of how overall programme goals are translated into action. Several of these projects centre on the development and management of national parks and protected areas. Other projects focus on conservation efforts at the island or regional level, or provide services to cooperating governments or institutions.

5.1.1. Field projects for protected areas have been selected for their suitability for specific experimental themes, local concern for and commitment to the particular area, logistical considerations, and the availability of suitable personnel. All projects, however, include activities which cover all of the elements of the management process (e.g. research, policy and planning, training, education, implementation, and field operations). The major experimental or demonstration themes that have been selected include:

- Methods for identifying and managing a system of national parks and protected areas for small islands;
- evaluation of alternative uses of natural areas critical to development;
- methods for establishing a meaningful process of public participation in the planning and management of protected areas critical to development;
- methods for stimulating social and economic development through national parks and protected areas; and
- new approaches to tourism based on the use of natural and cultural resources and the maximizing of benefits to local people.

5.1.2. Island or regional projects have been initiated in response to particular problems, to develop and disseminate information on a regional basis, or to synthesize the results of field projects. Major areas of effort have focused on:

- A survey of conservation priorities on a regional basis with the production of atlases of graphic information on habitat, environmental, socio-economic, and legal data for each island. Using this information base, regional and local systems of parks and protected areas have been identified and proposed;
- methods for planning and implementing an integrated development approach to marine resources;
- methods for developing island conservation strategies based on user group participation; and
- an assessment of the role of natural areas in the rural production systems of the islands.

5.1.3. A range of service activities promote the dissemination of results of the field and support projects. These include the following:

- Meetings or conferences sponsored by other organizations;
- workshops sponsored by ECNAMP;
- development of publications and articles, especially ones which increase communications between resource users and resource managers;
- use of project areas for demonstration purposes, especially in conjunction with workshops;

- presentations to meetings and lectures at universities;
- consultations or short-term consultancies with other organizations; and
- training and education activities through scholarships, student internships, and workshops.

6. RESULTS

The results that have been obtained from the programme are generally encouraging. The various islands have benefitted from better information about key natural resources, training of personnel involved with the management of natural resources, and management of selected natural areas. The conservation institutions of the region have benefited by an enhanced information base, a more constant presence and service to their membership, and improvement of methods for dealing with the resource management issues of small islands. At the university level, teaching has improved with the experience gained from the field projects and the close collaboration between research and field implementation.

The added knowledge that has been gained contributes to improved management in a variety of ways. In some instances, new data on critical areas have been developed. In other cases, such as with the publication of the Data Atlases for each island, already available data have been compiled and made readily available for decision making. By standardizing the Data Atlas format, it was possible to make regional analyses and comparisons. This supplies critical information for selecting priorities and synthesizing action programmes, and conservation priorities are now more clearly defined at the regional, island, and local levels.

Improved knowledge of the institutions of the region, and of key specialized personnel, has also resulted from programme activities. Thus, with the non-governmental format of ECNAMP and the funding that has been generated, it has been possible at times to share particular individual or institutional capabilities among the islands. Better communication links between the islands have developed. But perhaps the most important output in terms of new knowledge has been the identification of approaches and methods that are applicable to the special setting of small islands.

Another important output from the programme has been the contribution to education and training. Some of the best training has been derived from the close collaboration of ECNAMP consultants with local project participants. Selected individuals have been provided with financial support to pursue university degree programmes or to serve as project interns. Materials for training in the form of case studies and guidelines for management, have been generated from the field projects. These projects also provide potential demonstration areas for future workshops and training exercises, and considerable materials for publications and lectures.

Another important aspect of the programme has been the emphasis on an integrative approach to resource management. This approach has at times caused key personnel to change substantially their perceptions of, and attitudes towards, resource problems or particular management strategies. Integration has been achieved in terms of disciplines and perspectives. For example, the ecological perspective has been integrated with economic, sociological, and cultural perspectives. Scientific and technological knowledge has been combined with traditional and folk knowledge. Projects have often integrated governmental and non-governmental inputs, as well as the knowledge and expertise of the various island, cultural, and language groups.

Although many of the results of the ECNAMP projects have been encouraging, there continue to be several areas of difficulty. The most basic and important problem continues to be the lack of concern on the part of governments, bi-lateral and multi-lateral assistance organizations, and individuals with respect to the conservation of man's biological support systems in general and natural areas critical to development specifically. Thus, the basic receptivity to ECNAMP's programmes must be carefully nurtured in each case. Advisory and Coordinating Committees, which are organized locally for each project, are extremely useful in this respect.

ECNAMP has also had difficulty in finding competent personnel to assist with the promotion of business related to sound resource management. There often seems to be a large gap between the government and conservation organizations on the one hand, and the business community on the other hand. Thus, the goal of integrating good resource management with local business has proved to be elusive.

A similar dilemma has been experienced in relation to the few local universities. They have placed priority on the basic sciences rather than the applied aspects of management. Thus there is neither interest nor travel funds available to relate to the real problems of field activities in natural resource management, either in education or in research. There are recent signs, however, that perceptions may be changing, and that the local universities may be more willing to get involved in applied management activities in the future.

Funding has been an obstacle, not so much in terms of overall availability, but more in terms of specific programme items. Most difficulty has been experienced in funding programme overheads, even though they are quite small compared to most other organizations. Funding projects that aim at synthesizing results of various activities, so that successful approaches can be defined and specific guidelines drawn up, has also been a problem. In general, the longer-term educational outputs seem to be less attractive to donors than the more immediate outputs of environmental management and economic development. Additionally, funding for follow-up projects or for maintaining a relatively constant effort for specific areas over periods longer than a few years has not been easy to secure.

7. CONCLUSIONS

Because of the relative newness of ECNAMP, and the on-going nature of many of the projects, it is perhaps premature to speculate on definitive conclusions. Some initial insights, however, based on only five years of experience, can be tentatively identified.

Overall, the most important insights relate to the basic question of how to select natural areas critical to development and manage them effectively. A more integrative approach to management has evolved, building on experience in Latin America and, more recently, the Caribbean. This approach merges the use of strategic planning with increased emphasis on widespread participation at all project stages. The effect has been to give greater breadth and depth to the research and planning aspect of projects, which in turn smooths the way for realistic implementation. Research, planning, training, and implementation are seen less as distinct project phases and more as fluid elements of a total, non-linear process.

The selection of priorities for the management of natural areas, as carried out by ECNAMP, is based on a variety of criteria. However, we have found that the strategic approach to planning is a useful tool for providing an initial selection of areas. The criteria for establishing priorities may change depending on the focus of the project. Once these criteria are clearly specified, relevant data on the bio-physical and human elements can be gathered, compiled, and presented. These data are then verified and supplemented, as much as possible, through actual field visits. The data are analyzed in their component parts, and then synthesized to enable the selection of action priorities. A further prioritization can be based on other important criteria such as availability of personnel, urgency, local receptivity and interest, etc.

While the strategic approach provides a framework for systematic selection of priorities, it does not of itself provide much guidance for management—it answers the question of "where", but does not guide determination of "what" or "how". The definition of the full range of management objectives for a given area, and of the specific management options available (the "what" and "how" aspects), seem to be best approached through widespread participation. All of the relevant institutions and individuals must participate in the project from the beginning. Consultations after the fact are not adequate. The most meaningful participation is perhaps best initiated at the project planning stage through the formation of a Project Coordinating and Advisory Committee. This committee should consist of interested and committed representatives from relevant government departments, conservation organizations, and resource user groups (e.g. farmers, fishermen, landowners, businessmen, tourism operators, recreationists, educators, and scientists). Often, however, basic groups, such as farmers and fishermen, are reluctant to participate in such committees. A special effort needs to be made to involve them in a meaningful way, and this can many times be accomplished during research activities. Local fishermen and farmers can usually provide detailed information on natural resources and their local uses. This traditional knowledge is often more comprehensive than published scientific information, especially with respect to specific areas.

Perhaps the greatest value obtained from the emphasis on widespread participation is that it establishes an atmosphere conducive to effective implementation. On most of the islands, law enforcement bodies are not able to enforce regulations pertaining to natural resource utilization. In practice, then, regulations tend to be enforced only when there is already consensus at the local level. Conversely, when individuals or groups are not consulted during the early stages of a project, there is quite often active opposition to the implementation of management.

A variety of less comprehensive insights can also be drawn from the experience gained by ECNAMP. Some of the more important include:

- The non-governmental organization has some particular advantages in promoting the establishment and better management of parks and protected areas. Although it tends to receive smaller budgets, it can be significantly more efficient and cost-effective than inter-governmental organizations. It also can maintain a greater degree of flexibility institutionally, administratively, technically, and in response to changing conditions or new insights. It appears that these advantages can only be maintained, however, as long as the programme remains relatively small and personnel are dispersed among field projects.
- The non-governmental organization can promote projects which integrate the inputs of various governmental departments, non-governmental organizations, businessmen, landowners, and local resource users. This creates a realistic working environment for managing natural resources through national parks and protected areas, an important management tool, and it exposes the various groups to, and familiarizes them with, this tool. Too often, it seems that knowledge of protected area management techniques is restricted to a small group of national park enthusiasts, rather than being part of the experience of, and thus available to, a wide range of decision makers.
- While personnel have had to be generalists because of ECNAMP's small size and the dispersed nature of its activities, this has proved to have a variety of practical advantages. It has forced each Project Leader to identify and involve local specialists, both in and out of government, in projects. It has made it possible, and indeed logical, to integrate policy, planning, research, training, and implementation activities so that they become mutually reinforcing parts of a whole. In many cases, these integrative activities have fostered good working relationships that have later carried over to many other activities outside of the immediate project.
- Appreciable project results require long-term involvement in management over a broad range of activities. Short projects with isolated outputs, such as a piece of legislation, a single training session, or a plan for a particular area, usually are not productive in the long run. Such efforts tend to concentrate resources and interest over short periods that cannot be sustained.
- Management of renewable resources in general, and of national parks and protected areas in particular, should: be sustainable ecologically, economically, socially, and culturally; improve the livelihood of the neediest groups at the local level; promote flexibility and the maintenance of multiple options for development; and promote linkages between new leading sectors, such as industry, tourism, or recreation, and traditional resource uses such as farming, hunting, or fishing.
- Most of the already developed technology and natural resource management methods are not applicable to the small island setting. Local solutions need to be sought, documented, and disseminated.
- As far as is practicable, management techniques should respond to the needs of traditional user groups and be implemented at the lowest possible level of social organization (e.g. the family or village level). As resource conflicts arise or manpower constraints dictate, higher levels of social organization will have to be used (e.g. district or national level).
- The local technician is a key element to the success of any management strategy. He should receive priority attention for training and support.
- Training of resource managers is most effective when it is carried out within an institutional and biophysical setting similar to that of the trainee's working environment. Some of the best training takes place, therefore, when it is linked to ongoing field projects in the region.
- Interaction with local people has demonstrated time after time that there is an urgent need to bring conservation awareness and methods into the heart of the governmental, business, and individual planning processes. To do this successfully, it is necessary to de-emphasize the concern for single spectacular species, and shift attention to the maintenance and sustainable use of biophysical and social systems to support development.
- Stimulating the proper utilization of natural resources is just as important as curbing or restraining improper practices. Thus, the positive promotion of desired approaches and development

of appropriate businesses is just as important as establishing regulatory mechanisms.

- Since traditional natural resource utilization techniques have endured during periods of relative stability, they are by definition sustainable as long as conditions of stability remain. Modified techniques are needed when new factors substantially change conditions that prevailed during a period of stability or in response to local perceptions of the need to improve the efficiency of resource utilization. To ensure that the intricacies of traditional methods and attitudes are understood, they should first be described in detail before any management prescriptions are ventured. Indeed, this is a basic part of the participatory emphasis of management, and is the function of research and information dissemination (education) activities.

- Many of the problems encountered by the natural resource manager seem to arise when there is a lack of understanding of both the human and the natural systems, and of the dynamics of the interaction of the two, involved in managing any particular resource. Resource managers tend to have backgrounds in the natural sciences and thus it is often necessary to compensate for the relative lack of knowledge of, and importance attached to, the social sciences.

While the insights derived from ECNAMP are tentative, project activities increasingly provide substantive materials and field demonstration areas for improving local capacity to manage. During its first five years, the programme has concentrated on implementation of field projects. As these projects generate experience, examples, and guidelines, emphasis will shift to broadening the effort to improve local capacity to manage. In this way we hope that the programme will have an increasing impact on the effective and realistic management of natural resources in the region, and provide a documented experience for managers in other parts of the world.

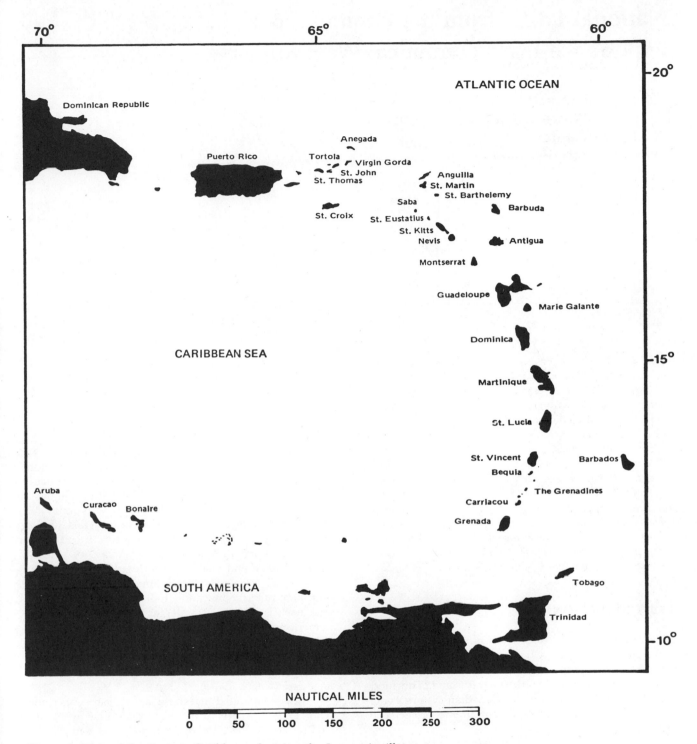

Figure 1. Map of the Eastern Caribbean showing the Lesser Antilles.

National Parks from the Ground Up: Experience from Dominica, West Indies

James W. Thorsell
College of African Wildlife Management
Moshi, Tanzania

ABSTRACT. *This paper describes the development of a new national park in Dominica, a country that previously had no protected areas at all. In establishing the Morne Trois Pitons National Park, 14 coordinated steps are identified: developing local initiative; devloping local public awareness; defining an area of priority interest (the Morne Trois Pitons area); obtaining basic equipment; defining the park boundaries; drafting protected area legislation; preparing interim management guidelines; undertaking a field demonstration project; establishing linkages with tourism and education; preparing the education and interpretative programmes; developing the management capacity; continuing the development of park facilities; establishing a research programme; and ensuring follow-up support. The paper draws conclusions from the Dominica experience and suggests how they might be applied elsewhere.*

1. INTRODUCTION

In 1974 and again in 1978, the Canadian International Development Agency (CIDA) provided grants totalling US $200,000 to assist the Government of Dominica in establishing a national park on the island. The funds were channelled through the Canadian Nature Federation (CNF), whose involvement in the project concluded in 1980.

Looking back, Dominica provides an interesting case study and illustrates some valuable lessons in building a park system from inception to self-sufficiency. It is the purpose of this paper to present the experience gained in the practical implementation of a total park programme. Inasmuch as the project has been judged a success within the region and has acted as a stimulus and model for other islands, the lessons learned should be of wider interest. As Boza noted at the Second World Parks Conference (Elliott, 1974), "There is a notable lack of information on the ways in which developing countries actually set about solving the problems involved in the administration and development of their national parks."

In 1974, Dominica had no parks, no enabling legislation, no management capability, and little public awareness or political support for parks or conservation in general. By 1981, as a result of a multi-faceted 'bootstrap' effort by CNF and others working with Dominica's Forestry and Parks Division (DFPS) there is today an operational national park known as Morne Trois Pitons. It is not a paper park. The infrastructure in place includes a National Park and Protected Areas Act, a headquarters office and visitor centre, marked boundaries, access trails, picnic shelters, numerous environmental education publications, and a trained cadre of staff. The park itself is accepted as integral to the island's development process and now largely operates without outside assistance. Morne Trois Pitons has been placed on the *UN List of National Parks and Equivalent Reserves* (IUCN, 1980a) and has been suggested as a possible World Heritage Site (IUCN, 1981a).

It must be added that these accomplishments came while Dominica faced a period of disruptive events including civil unrest, political turmoil, and natural disasters in the form of Hurricanes David and Allen. Despite these difficulties the parks programme has endured and a post-project audit has concluded that, although there is still work to be completed, the park is essentially operational and effectively managed.

The following discussion outlines the steps in the six-year period of park development and summarizes the factors which contributed to the achievement of project objectives.

2. STEPS IN THE DEVELOPMENT OF THE NATIONAL PARK

The procedure in establishing, developing, and administering an operational national park requires action on a number of different fronts. The following steps can be identified as the key ones in Dominica.

2.1. Support local initiative

Recognition of the unique natural values of the interior of Dominica first came from natural history experts from outside the country. The Director of the island's Forestry Division became sympathetic to these values, and his concern for the environmental damage of a timber harvesting operation reinforced them. This concern led to attendance at the International Seminar on National Parks and Equivalent Reserves, which in turn led to the conception of the idea of a national park in Dominica. Recognizing the assistance that would be required and the international interest in the concept, the Director pursued and invited outside agencies to contribute.

The first lesson is that initiative from the local level, even if it is from only one individual, is a prerequisite for action. One man and a small amount of seed money was enough to launch what was to become Morne Trois Pitons National Park.

2.2. Develop local public awareness

Awareness of national parks and conservation in Dominica in the early 1970s was almost non-existent. To counteract this, a team from the Conservation Foundation prepared a public relations document entitled "A Chance for A Choice". This booklet, a high quality production, presented the potential benefits of a national park on the Island. Distributed widely, the document was very helpful in eliciting interest and receptivity for further work.

A second lesson is that public relations in the early phases of a project conducted by a team of respected outside experts can effectively reinforce efforts being made at the local level.

2.3. Define an area of priority interest

In Dominica, as in most other countries, there will be many candidate sites for selection as national parks. When beginning a park system, all efforts should focus on one area. This strategy allowed a solid programme to be developed in Morne Trois Pitons which subsequently led to consideration for the addition of other areas to the system. The temptation to use the "shotgun approach" rather than the "rifle approach" was thus avoided.

Our third lesson followed from experience gained earlier in Costa Rica: acknowledge limitations and proceed with one key area as a springboard for future additions. (In fact, in 1981, the Dominican Cabinet announced approval in principle to create a second national park at the north end of the Island).

2.4. Obtain basic office and field equipment

To proceed beyond the preliminary paperwork, it was necessary to obtain logistical support to carry out further work. At this point, the first CIDA grant allowed for purchase of a vehicle and appointment of a technical advisor. The Forestry Division provided a visible and accessible office base and the detailed planning work began.

2.5. Define park boundaries

Many national parks throughout the world have been established on lands unsuitable for any other purpose. In the case of Dominica, boundaries of the park were drawn to exclude private lands and lands judged to harbour significant agricultural or forestry potential. Water catchments and lands with high erosion potential were all included in the proposed boundary study, which identified a park area amounting to 8 percent of the land area of the island.

It should also be mentioned that the donation of a significant amount of private land to the park through the Nature Conservancy also affected boundary selection.

The lesson is that when selecting an area for national park establishment, it is important to minimize social and economic disruption. The chances of survival of the proposed Morne Trois Pitons National park were enhanced by boundary definitions using land ownership and agricultural potential criteria. A subsequent rationalization of the boundaries on ecological criteria by Shanks and Putney (1979) confirmed the area selected and provided suggestions for minor adjustments.

2.6. Draft protected area legislation

Once the concept of a national park was publicized and a proposed area defined, the basis for the legal establishment was prepared. Dominica's Parks Act, prepared with help from the Canadian Ministry of Justice, is a broad one, allowing for the creation of national parks, historic sites, and recreational areas. Two alternative acts were presented to the Attorney General, who then presented one to the House of Assembly. The Act was passed unanimously within four months. Action on the parks regulations, however, has taken much longer and only recently have they been presented for gazettement.

The passage of the Parks and Protected Areas Act was the breakthrough that was needed to galvanize further action. Once Dominica had demonstrated its commitment in the area of parks, other agencies came on board and the work began in earnest.

2.7. Prepare interim management guidelines

In Dominica, it was not possible to conduct a full-scale management planning exercise in the early stages of the project. A preliminary plan, however, was prepared outlining the basic objectives and general management guidelines (Thorsell, 1975). This document guided the park in its formative stage but gradually needed updating as conditions changed and as new information became available. A formal management plan for Morne Trois Pitons is now in its final stages of completion.

The lesson here is not to delay action until a sophisticated comprehensive plan can be prepared. A preliminary guideline approach, however, can be useful in identifying the key problem areas. Also, it is preferable for the local staff to prepare this plan for themselves as a staff development exercise.

2.8. Undertake a field demonstration project

Apart from reports, discussion, legislation, and general administrative tasks, a practical on-the-ground recreational facility was provided to physically demonstrate one of the park's attractions. The project selected was a nature trail and picnic shelter development in an easily accessible and attractive area of the park. As a demonstration project, this was done carefully, utilizing local labour. A trail brochure was prepared and an official opening ceremony held, with the Minister and other key officials attending at the site.

The trail has subsequently become a popular facility; virtually every tourist to the Island visits the site and is exposed to the rainforest environment. To our surprise, an equally large visitation by local Dominicans also resulted. Ironically, the gauge of the success of the facility is reflected in the recreation site management input it now requires. The lesson is that a practical, visible, low cost, accessible facility, properly done, generates both local and foreign use, providing immediate public understanding and support for the nature-oriented experiences the park is planned to offer.

2.9. Establish linkages with tourism and education

Once a sample facility was provided and information brochures on the park prepared, these two prime target groups were drawn into the programme. The symbiotic benefits between parks and tourism became immediately apparent and the park has become a strong theme in the promotional literature on the Island's attractions.

Meetings with primary and secondary school teachers indicated that resource materials relevant to the island environment would be enthusiastically received. A special teacher's workshop bringing in environmental education experts from the region was sponsored by DFPS and CNF, further developing the parks/education linkage.

The Dominican experience illustrates that to strengthen local support the involvement of related park user agencies should be cultivated. Integrating the park programme with the Tourism Board and the Education Department created particularly strong linkages that were developed for mutual benefit.

2.10. Prepare education/interpretation programme

The more word of the national park spread, the greater the demand for information became. An interpretive policy guideline paper was prepared (Thorsell, 1978) and a major effort was then directed to this sector. Brochures, magazine articles, trail guides, films, displays, posters, and radio programmes were all used to inform Dominicans and their visitors of the values of the park and the broader island environment. Two 16mm films narrated by the DFPS Director proved to have particularly high impact when shown by park staff at most of the island's schools and villages.

The realization here is that schoolteachers in developing countries are often in great need of resource material about their own environment. Morne Trois Pitons' interpretive programme acted as an effective environmental education catalyst to foster a greater conservation awareness beyond the confines of the park itself. Concomitantly, sales of park publications to tourists have become an ongoing source of revenue.

2.11. Develop management capacity

Building on the original headquarters staff of one, there are now seven professionally competent members of staff who work either full- or part-time on parks responsibilities. At the field level, all Forest Guards and Rangers have been given supplementary training in parks management. Interestingly, there has yet been no evidence of outward mobility of trainees.

A variety of training methods were used, provided in cooperation with WWF-US, Parks Canada, and the ECNAMP programme (Putney, Jackson, and Reynard, this volume). Management capacity in Dominica was thus strengthened by a mix of the following:

- On the job work experience with visiting professionals;
- attendance at International Seminar on National Parks and Equivalent Reserves for four senior staff;
- participation in two regional park planning workshops;
- attendance at regional annual meetings of the Caribbean Conservation Association;

- field attachments with staff at Virgin Island National Park for two senior staff;
- sponsorship of three workshops held locally on the topic of environmental education and park ranger training;
- sponsorship for correspondence courses; and
- provision of reference and study materials for the park library.

No actual counterpart designations were made; rather a cooperative team approach to transfer of knowledge (both directions) was the method that seemed to work best.

The workshops for field level staff were particularly useful as they addressed such practical topics as first aid, search and rescue, chainsaw maintenance, and law enforcement. Training for this level cannot be overlooked as the field staff is responsible for operation of the park on a day-to-day basis.

Our experience in Dominica suggests that training at the local level, using workshops, sponsoring attendance at conferences, study tours, and attachments at other parks combined with knowledge transfer at the working level can effectively supplement long-term education at foreign universities. Further, any training in continental North America must reflect locally appropriate technology considerations; it must recognize the insularity factor, and understand the effects of cross-cultural tourism. Establishing a regional park training school, possibly in conjunction with the University of the West Indies, would be an important step in developing training opportunities at the local level.

2.12. Continue park facility development

While all the above steps were being undertaken, the tasks of managing, protecting and developing Morne Trois Pitons were in progress. Boundary marking, trail construction, and picnic site development were the major facilities provided. Labour from villages near the park was used wherever possible. Some experimenting in materials and design was necessary but three criteria guided all developments: durability in the rainforest environment; local availability of materials; and likelihood of low post-operative maintenance costs.

Our concern was that capital costs for facilities be kept relatively low and that only those structures undeniably essential to the use and operation of the park be provided. The post-project continuation of maintenance by DFPS is a reflection of the rationale of this approach.

2.13. Establish a research programme

Morne Trois Pitons National Park, with its unique rainforest, indigenous fauna, and active volcanic activity, has long attracted international scientific attention. At the same time that research activities were to be encouraged in the park, it was recognized that researchers themselves can cause resource impacts and conflict with other users.

For this reason, the Island Resources Foundation developed a research plan with guidelines for controlling and encouraging proper use by researchers in the park. In addition, research needs were defined, and special facilities and funding sources outlined.

The basic rationale here was that since one of the objectives of the park is to encourage research, it should be planned and managed. Although a research programme has been slow in getting underway, a framework is in place. Perhaps an association with an established university or tropical research institution could be developed to exploit this sector of the park programme.

2.14. Follow-up support

During the early years of the project, an outside professional worked with DFPS on a continuing basis to assist in launching the park. This presence was gradually phased out, the CNF programme concluded and full responsibility for the management of Morne Trois Pitons is now in the hands of DFPS. Post-project follow-up reviews to monitor progress are, however, suggested and should be considered in total project funding (La Bastille, 1975).

Similar to La Bastille's (1973) experience in Central America, occasional return visits by foreign advisors to review progress can add dimension to the effort and act to provide psychological support. This follow-up was not provided for in Dominica but should be a consideration in future projects.

3. CONCLUDING COMMENTS

Beyond the experience gained in achieving each of the previous tasks, there are several general issues relating to the project as a whole that deserve comment.

3.1. Justification of a national park

An important consideration in Dominica was the framework in which the idea of parks was rationalized and presented. In many developing countries the words 'park' and 'environmental protection' strike a negative note to some skeptics in the formative period. It is important, therefore, to treat the park(s) as one element in the total integrated resource management fabric of the country. Parks must be seen to contribute to the total economic development process by providing a flow of multiple benefits including protection of water catchments, prevention of erosion, maintenance of natural systems, environmental education, research, tourism, recreation, and the maintenance of future options.

Within this broader scheme of wildland management, parks can play their most effective role as environmental catalysts. Thus viewed, parks are an indispensible aid in the advancement of resource management and are inescapably associated with a healthy, attractive and, most important, productive environment. As has been noted by Western and Henry (1979), this national economic development motive for parks in developing countries can be the most effective justification for their conservation.

3.2. Developing local relevance and involvement

To assure long-term support, parks must demonstrate that they can be both self-supporting and made relevant to local people. Job creation at the rural level providing visible material benefits is one important element. The involvement of as many segments of the population as possible in the park programme is another.

To develop this involvement is a major challenge for park systems everywhere. But in countries like Dominica, where the conservation movement is in its infancy, aid support may have to extend over a number of years if this is to materialize. From our experience in Dominica, a period of six years was a reasonable time dimension.

3.3. Project administration

As discussed above, the assistance given to Dominica to establish a national parks organization was characterized by:

- The need to work from the ground up—all the fundamental steps were required;
- the strength of local support for the overall objective;
- the practicality of the project and emphasis on accomplishing results on the ground;
- the relatively low level of funding available;
- the mix of input from a variety of individuals and agencies; and
- the on-going and coordinating role of the non-governmental group selected to execute the project.

This last point of administration by an NGO is particularly important as it allowed the extensive flexibility necessary to achieve results without the smothering effects of bureaucracy.

Finally, the cooperative personal relationships between local government officials and visiting experts worked on a peer level and worked well. Too often, projects suffer from personal difficulties between the various individuals involved. Differences and disagreements will, of course, occur but achieving the objective of establishing and effectively managing a national park of international calibre is of such importance that it can override minor differences.

Acknowledgements

The Dominica project was a social product to which many individuals and agencies contributed. First must be recognized Chris Maximea, Director of Forestry and Parks for his vision and continuing commitment to conservation in Dominica. Single-handedly he guided and provided the basis of the park. Second, the park staff at the local level, including Superintendent Colmore Christian, have been most instructive and constructive to all who worked with them.

We all are indebted to CIDA's Non-Governmental Division for sticking with us and allowing CNF to complete the project. CNF's local representative, Penny Honychurch, devoted almost four years of her considerable talents. Other staff provided through CNF were Ted Mosquin, Charlie Harvey, George and Kay Wood, Ruth and Bruce Gordon, and Peggy Heppes.

Parks Canada's cooperation was vital and assured through Harold Eidsvik. Harry Cooper and Roger Hamilton of that agency also did their share. The National Museum's Louis Lemieux and John Whiting made their unique contributions.

Regionally, the long-term input of Dr. Edward S. Towle and the Island Resources Foundation has been and still is assisting in the ecodevelopment of Dominica. Similarly, the Caribbean Conservation Association and Jill Sheppard have always provided support. The follow-up work of Allen Putney and ECNAMP was helpful in the areas of training and expanding the parks programme.

Through the years, the WWF has provided the Dominica Forestry and Parks Division with much needed vehicles and WWF-US has provided scholarships for training. The initial ground work by the Conservation Foundation and by Michael Wright of The Nature Conservancy with the Archbold Estate provided the sparkplug that was needed. Various Peace Corps volunteers also worked ably with their Dominican counterparts.

Future Directions for the Neotropical Realm

Marc J. Dourojeanni
Profesor Principal
Universidad Nacional Agraria
Lima, Peru

ABSTRACT. *The 1970s was a decade of extraordinary achievement for Neotropical protected areas, with the area protected nearly doubling. But there have also been continuing problems, including colonization, highway construction, mining and oil exploitation, water resource development, hunting and fishing, timber extraction, native populations, pollution and other harmful activities outside the boundaries of the areas, and inappropriate (and sometimes insufficient) tourism. Steps required to solve these problems in the coming decade include strengthening environmental consciousness among both the public and government, to complete national protected area system plans, and to link protected area development with rural development. The coming decade will be a difficult period, but will also contain opportunities for protected areas to play a more important role.*

1. INTRODUCTION

In this short essay we will analyse the principal characteristics of national parks and protected areas established in the Neotropical Realm, beginning with the reality of the present and going on to examine the problems which will face these areas in the remainder of this decade. We will examine the sources of pressure that will affect units already established or to be established, and finally we will outline a strategy that might help us to solve some of these difficulties.

2. THE CURRENT DECADE

For Latin America and the Caribbean, this decade is threatened by a period of social unrest as or more important than that which occurred at the beginning of the 19th century, and which ended with independence from the Iberian colonial power. Fueled by the world economic recession, the social tensions already inherent in each nation are starting to erupt, and augur the advent of global changes before the end of the century. It is in this context that we must view the remainder of the present decade when establishing public and private priorities for national parks and protected areas.

The development of national parks and protected areas in the Neotropical Realm can be summarised as follows:

- Initial starts were slow and isolated but increased during the 1960s and particularly in the 1970s, when 50% of all the national parks and other protected areas of the neotropics were created. There now exist about 250 national parks and other protected areas, covering 435,000 sq km.
- In spite of this, by 1980 a mere 1.63% of the Neotropical Realm was designated as protected areas; several of the biogeographic provinces were not represented and at least 12 of them were grossly under-protected. Furthermore, most of the existing conservation units had been established using criteria below the minimum necessary to ensure the maintainance of the species and the ecosystems that they contain.
- Most of the units lack management plans and where such plans do exist they are generally not implemented. Most areas do not have any infrastructure, and many do not have even patrol and surveillance facilities.
- Most of the national parks and other protected areas are not open to visitors and with a few

exceptions, those that are equipped for this purpose receive few visitors.
- The public in general is ignorant about protected areas and reserves, and little governmental help is available in this area.

There are, however, large enough differences between countries with respect to the above points to make any further generalization inopportune.

Given this situation, certain trends can nonetheless be predicted with respect to the remainder of the present decade:

- The number of units will continue to grow, although at a considerably lower rate that in the 1970s. The increase in area protected will, however, come more from an enlargement of the average size of recently- created and new units than from any great increase in units created.
- The ecological make-up of national parks and other protected areas will continue to improve, judging from existing plans for the creation or enlargement of units in most of the countries.
- Undoubtedly, efforts to increase the number of visitors to parks will continue, as will attempts to improve public knowledge and to enlist the help of governments in this form of nature conservation. Notwithstanding, we foresee that the gap between what is desired and what is attained will increase considerably.
- On the other hand, resistance to the establishment of new national parks and reserved areas will no doubt grow and as pressure on those units created in the last two decades increases, it is anticipated that their function as conservation units will be impeded.

Finally, it is probable that by the end of the 1980s national parks and protected areas in the Neotropical Realm will be more representative of ecological diversity than at present, and development and public help will be markedly improved; it is also probable that progress will be slower than in the last decade and that in any case, the global gap between required development and that obtained will be greater than it is today. This situation forebodes still bigger problems for the 1990s.

3. MENACES IN THE FUTURE

Two major sets of problems will be faced in the future: (l) An insufficient number of national parks and protected areas can be established to meet ecological coverage and other needs; and (2) those units already established cannot be adequately maintained. The problems reflect the obvious dilemma of how to most effectively assign the meagre resources available. On the one hand it is obvious that if such places are not protected in time, the opportunity to do so will be lost forever, and on the other hand if the insufficient economic resources must be continually spread over increasingly greater areas, then it will be impossible to consolidate what has already been attained. Nonetheless, this is not an insoluble problem: Economic resources are always available in the national budget if the priority is there. But the problem is that this method of conservation, as many others, does not have a political priority. What has already been attained has been attained in spite of the obstacles.

3.1. Impediments to the establishment of national parks and other protected areas

It is not the purpose of this paper to spell out what is necessary to establish national parks and other conservation units at a regional or national level. It is enough to remember that the biogeographic provinces, the ecosystems that comprise them and the genetic diversity that they contain, are not perfect. For instance, the marine environments of the Atlantic and Pacific oceans, at whatever latitude, are important and must be represented. But there are many terrestrial environments that are not represented, as is the case of Yucatecan Woodlands, Campos Limpos Savanna, and the Bahmas-Bermudan, or which are poorly represented as in the case of Madeiran Rainforest, Serra do Mar Rainforest, Brazilian Planalto Woodlands, Valdivian and Chilean Nothofagus Forest, Guerreran Woodland, Caatinga Dry Forest, Chilean Araucaria and Sclerophyll, Babacu Savanna, Argentinian Savanna, and several others. If more objective judgments were applied, as in the case of Pleistocene refuges or centres of endemism, the actual cover would be more accurately reflected and would indicate that coverage is still very spotty.

An obvious question is what is the ideal percentage of national or regional areas that should be protected. Countries such as Chile and Venezuela already protect about 10% of their national territories, but most countries have protected the minimum at less than the 2%. It would not seem excessive to propose a continental goal of 4%, but that would be very difficult to reach since it implies a doubling of the actual area of national parks and protected areas in Latin America and the Caribbean. Notwithstanding, Peru has built up plans to protect some 7% of its national territory and has made a serious attempt to cover its ecological variety.

The accomplishment of the 4% goal will face the following difficulties:

- Many of the areas that must be protected in the future, i.e. those currently most threatened, are already being exploited for other uses;
- in some countries and environments there is strong reaction against the establishment of national parks and protected areas as a result of unbalanced campaigns and bad publicity. Certain high level Government authorities have declared publicly that

too many conservation units already exist and that the freezing of national territory cannot be permitted to continue; and

- increasingly, governments, while still in favour of nature conservation, support the widespread opinion that new national parks must not be created until the existing ones are properly developed.

3.2. Obstacles to the maintainance of existing national parks and other protected areas

The obstacles to the maintainance of existing conservation units are numerous, and even affect national parks that have been established for a long time; notorious examples have happened in Paraguay and Chile. But it is more frequently the case that the change in use is insidious and takes place in an atmosphere of indifference, or even with the consent of the authorities; this has happened in many countries, among them Peru, Bolivia and Colombia. Sometimes it is not worthwhile to maintain such units. This "erosion" process can also affect only part of a unit and this has been the case, for instance, with one of the principal Argentinian national parks.

Although in the Neotropical context the cases mentioned represent a relatively low percentage, it must be remembered that the limited or zero development of many of the national parks and protected areas stimulates such negative action, and that probably 80% of the units with poor management are threatened by illegal activity.

It is important to analyse the major kinds of pressures that exist against national parks and other protected areas, though these are as varied as the natural resources in them:

3.2.1. Colonization.
This is without doubt the principal source of problems for the units situated in the humid or dry tropics. The parks and other units generally were established in these regions before roads arrived or when free land was still abundant. With time, one of two situations will occur: the rural farmers invade the units in a gradual way; or the state uses the land for agriculture purposes. Both factors can apply in one situation. In Peru, the government has planned the construction of a highway that will cross the Manu National Park, with a view to settlement; in any event, the Park is being gradually destroyed in the highest parts by herdsmen expanding their pastures. Similar problems are well known in almost all the tropical countries and these problems will be worse before the end of the century.

3.2.2. Highways.
The Latin American highways have as their main purpose colonization. But even if the purpose is not that, the results of this activity are unavoidable, because of the national socio-economic situation which predominates. In other cases, there is no risk of colonization but the ill-advised highways increase considerably the difficulties of controlling hunting, illegal collection of wildlife, fires and the destruction of the aesthetic value of the area. Many conservation units in the continent are menaced by new highways due to be built in the next decade.

3.2.3. Mining and oil.
There is great pressure to develop the mineral resources of the units situated in the mountains. In Peru, such is the case in at least four parks and national reserves, among them Huascaran and Paracas. Oil exploration and exploitation already affect the Manu National Park, and now also the Pacaya-Samiria National Reserve. The Peruvian example is only one case, but similar problems occur in Brazil and in many other countries.

3.2.4. Hydraulic infrastructure.
Dams, reservoirs, and other water development activities affect, directly or indirectly, at least 5% of the protected areas of Latin America and the Caribbean.

3.2.5. Hunting, fishing, forestry extraction, collection.
These activities in national parks and other protected areas are, in general, of secondary impact and the pressure created by them will probably diminish. The exception is the growing artisinal and even commercial fishing in parks and marine reserves, including Galapagos and Paracas, among others.

3.2.6. Native populations in the units.
A few protected areas have native populations, more or less primitive, living within their limits. The gradual or inevitable integration of these people into the national economic context creates serious problems for some parks of the Neotropical Realm. In Peru's Manu National Park and its environs, where the forest people are in a pristine state, problems arise as a result of economic activity outside the park, which stimulates migration by other tribes to it. War erupts among the tribes, and there is excessive hunting pressure.

3.2.7. Pollution or generated environment alterations outside the protected area.
There exist some cases in which protected areas are menaced by these problems that at a global level will continue to be secondary during the present decade. Notwithstanding, this is a problem particularly serious for the protected areas in lakes and for those in the marine littoral, including estuaries and mangroves. Also it affects small units situated near the cities.

3.2.8. Visitors and touristic infrastructures.
The lack of tourist infrastructure is not a generalized problem yet, but it is serious in many Argentinian, Brazilian and Costa Rican national parks, among others. It is a difficulty that will fast increase in the next decades because of the necessity to promote the touristic use of parks,

in order to protect them from pressure to use them in a still less compatible way.

The problems that prevent or hinder the administration of the national parks and other protected areas are best envisioned as an interconnected net or chain, with the central problem being the deep lack of understanding at the decision-making levels and among the public of the contributions made to the nation by protected areas. This situation is due to the generalized ignorance of environmental or ecological issues; this lack of comprehension is due partly to the lack of interest, and results in a reduced priority for these issues, which is translated in turn into a priority which is absurdly short of what is required for environmental well-being.

It must be clarified that there is not necesarily a contradiction between the establishment of units and the lack of priority for them. For the public authorities, the creation of a national park is, before anything, another work that reflects a positive light. But the legal action that creates a park does not indicate the budget that its development will require. Besides, the authorities change frequently, and some of them participate consciously and actively in the work, while others have no comprehension of what protected areas are all about.

The insufficient budget given to the administration of nation parks is the key to all the problems. The lack of infrastructure and personel, especially qualified personnel, derives from the lack of control of visitors, public education, research, etc. These lacks lead to the units being considered "abandoned land," so it is understandable that other uses for it are proposed. Also there are few means to orient a public that does not know the parks because they are not visitable; therefore, there is no constituency to defend the areas against external pressures.

As has already been pointed out, it is expected that these problems will increase considerably throughout the present decade, because of the big and growing economic crises and therefore social problems that will attack the continent.

4. WHAT TO DO?

Given the problems described above, and the necessity to manage effectively a significant portion of the remaining natural lands, how can a strategy be developed that can establish priorities for action? The following aspects will be necessary:

- Creation or strengthening of a "conservation conscience" which will influence the decisions that are taken. This is crucial to obtain sufficient resources to carry out the necessary actions to implement the management of protected areas.
- To complete as soon as possible the national system of national parks and other protected areas, in each country. Opposition to the establishment of new areas increases with time, and some op-

portunities are lost forever; a mature tropical forest, for example, cannot be reclaimed from a tapioca patch. It is important to at least have an area declared by law, in advance of any management, rather than to lose the area forever.

- To give proper and timely guidance to the touristic development or public use of most appropriate national parks, in order to demonstrate the socio-economic benefits that such development can bring to regional development.
- To obtain the involvement of international development agencies to help build the necessary infrastructure; such involvement helps to demonstrate to governments that protected areas are considered an international priority.
- To defend with all possible means the integrity of the national parks and other protected areas; even if defeat is inevitable in a given case, the struggle should be sufficiently vigorous to build an aura of respect for such units.
- To give particular attention to the coastal and marine environment in all countries.
- To make a special effort to produce a quantified valuation of the goods and, in particular, of the many services produced by national parks and protected areas in order that they may obtain an adequate priority into the national planning processes.
- To associate, if possible, the establishment and development of the national parks and protected areas to the state programmes of rural development or colonization, among others. Such programmes are of great political, social, and economic importance, so it is the duty of protected area advocates to demonstrate that environmental protection and economic development can reinforce each other.

International technical cooperation can play a decisive role in assisting the development of the national parks and other protected areas of the Neotropical Realm. Multinational and bilateral sources of cooperation at the governmental level can contribute to the basic studies to complete the national systems of parks and protected areas, promote the economic and social aspects of tourism development, and promote the inclusion of environmental components in rural development projects.

In addition, the non-governmental international cooperation sources must intervene decisively to support those in the country promoting the interests of protected areas, providing the ways and means to convince decision-makers to take the appropriate decisions regarding protected areas.

These steps should add to the traditional forms of international technical cooperation, which includes high level training, research, action dealing with specific endangered species, legislation, etc. Notwithstanding the value of such international support, real long-term solutions must be found locally; for example, the low salaries that many governments pay do not allow well-qualified individuals to remain in their positions very long, no matter how dedicated they may be. Therefore, any international assistance must be integrated with local and national efforts to improve the social and economic conditions of the country.

5. CONCLUSIONS

Major and growing problems are foreseen for the national parks and protected areas of Latin America and the Caribbean, but there is a certain optimism. In one way or another, the decades of the 1980's and 1990's will be crucial for the future of protected areas in the Neotropical Realm. These will be decades of both promise and peril, offering an extraordinary opportunity for those involved in the national park and protected areas profession to have a greater influence on the future of this part of the world.

Acknowledgements

This paper was prepared for IUCN's Commission on National Parks and Protected Areas in cooperation with CIDA.

Chapter 13
New Directions
in Protected Area Management

Monitoring Within and Outside Protected Areas

Harvey Croze
GEMS/PAC
United Nations Environment Programme
Nairobi, Kenya

ABSTRACT. *It is no longer possible to "set aside" an area and protect it by police action alone; conservation must be part of the everyday life of populations surrounding protected areas. Management of these areas requires a sound information base which is broader than just the plants and animals in the protected area—we must understand what is happening both inside and outside the boundaries. Monitoring is based on this information base and serves to detect changes and trends and to understand how natural systems work. While each nation will wish to have its own sophisticated monitoring system, it will be some time before such systems can be developed; in the meantime, international efforts may be of significant assistance in helping nations to manage better the biosphere, both within and outside protected areas.*

1. INTRODUCTION: PROTECTED AREAS ARE PART OF THE REAL WORLD

Like man, no protected area is an island unto itself, although many are fast becoming such. Even if the boundaries are fenced, there is inevitable interchange between the area and the surrounding world. And even if the area appears to be a self-contained ecosystem, there will inevitably be trickles of energy and nutrients across the boundaries. More immediately pertinent to the survival of the area is the socio-economic exchange which should take place between the area and the neighbouring people; most of these exchanges are beneficial.

The ecosystem boundary, therefore, is a permeable membrane, and, I believe, most of the interesting discussions and conclusions from this Congress will focus on the concept, maintenance and management of the thin lines which pretend to isolate protected areas from the rest of the world.

Back in the late 1960s, in the Serengeti, that most exciting of ecosystems, we learned (see Norton-Griffiths and Sinclair, 1979) that we had better put some effort into finding out what went on outside the park boundaries, because both the park's animals and the people around the park were having an influence on both sides of the border. Consequently, the Serengeti Ecological Monitoring Programme designed a grid-cell sample frame which included an area outside the park as large as the park itself. In a similar vein, we have heard from D. Western during this congress about the Amboseli monitoring programme which looks at an area of which Amboseli National Park is only some 5% of its surrounding ecosystem. The idea of fuzzy ecosystem boundaries was not surprizing to ecologists, but it certainly has been hard for parks managers, and even harder for politicians, to swallow. Nevertheless, today we routinely monitor within and outside protected areas.

The days are gone when we were able to set aside an area and protect it by local police action alone. Protectionist arguments pale beside the demands of immediate forms of land use tabled by the growing populations on our area's boarders. This simple fact—my second homily of the day—demands that we consider fitting our conservation plans into the land-use activities and aspirations of the surrounding populations. Others will deal with this subject during the Congress. I will dwell on the ineluctable conclusion that the information we collect to serve the management of our protected areas must be broader than that pertaining to just the plants and animals inside the area—we must understand what is happening outside as well as inside.

Our main concerns in protected areas should be to ensure the security of the area, to understand its functioning, and thereby to manage it and use it on a sustained basis. This, my third and last truism, can be

628

illustrated with an even more elementary diagram. There is a closed dependency loop between activities concerned with securing the area, understanding it, managing it and using it. We do not set aside areas by whimsy: we have reasons, which are inevitably expressed in terms of uses. The use, no matter what it is, requires some level of management and ultimately justify the securing. None of this can be done very effectively without understanding how the whole thing works. In this paper, I am going to talk about how to achieve the necessary understanding through ecological monitoring.

2. WHAT IS MONITORING AND WHAT IS IT FOR?

Monitoring is keeping track of things in time: measurements taken in a time-series. It used to connote the notion of control, but it has taken on today a more benign meaning referring to a process of data gathering which should, ultimately, produce enough information to be able to control the situation and manage wisely whatever system we happen to be monitoring.

There are two basic functions of monitoring. One is to detect changes and trends. Since measurements are taken in time, there is the possibility of comparing one time against others. Detection of change, however, requires that sample design be quite rigorous, since reliable detection of change requires a certain measure of precision in the estimates.

The other function of monitoring is to understand how things work. Invariably, to get the most out of our investment, we monitor more than one thing at a time: for example, primary production along with numbers and distribution of herbivores; or the fluctuation of insect populations as well as the behaviour of the bird community. It is not uncommon for an ecological monitoring programme to cover two dozen large mammal species, as much vegetation as can be accommodated, meteorological parameters, and even human socio-economics, given the time, manpower and money. This gives us the raw material for systems analysis; the stuff whereof ecosystem models are made. I use the word "model" advisedly, since most of them are unbelievable; I mean simply any abstraction, no matter how simple, which attempts to express cause and effect. The correlations which continually suggest themselves in multi-species multi-media monitoring, are the best bases for intelligent hunches about how the system works. The hunches have to be tested, naturally.

And—here is the important point—when we begin to get an inkling of how the system works, be it a forest, a national park, or a river, we begin to earn our keep as advisors of environmental managers. We begin to understand where are the pressure points, what is accounting for what, what precipitates the hot spots, in other words, where and how may the managers most

cost-effectively apply their—usually pretty primitive—art.

Without the kind of understanding which ecological monitoring provides, a protected area cannot be properly managed - and that means a protected area will not long survive. We can, indeed, just put a fence around the area, stick up NO TRESPASSING signs, and sit back to let the thing go. Most likely it will tick over for a long time quite happily without interference. But supposing a good land-use planner wants to put the area to some use, perhaps to earn a little revenue to justify its and his existence: use begets security, as I said before. Then he will have to start doing things in the area, such as making roads, providing some water and the odd camp site for the visitors. As soon as that happens, the system begins to be influenced, and, without ecological monitoring, how much it is influenced and to what long term end, is anybody's guess. Not a very sensible background against which to try, for example, to raise a bit of investment capital for development.

3. MONITORING IS GOOD FOR YOU

Not only do we claim to be able to produce the information necessary to manage areas of land, be they protected or not, but we also presume to link our activities to the highest imaginable goal short of nirvana—human welfare.

Consider a so-called "decision tree" which sets, quite arbitrarily, an ultimate goal—the well-being of people—and deduces a series of orderly fields of activity or types of information which are necessary to get to the goal.

In the model, there are at least four systems which are vital to human welfare: communications; education; health; and renewable resources (taken in the broad sense so they can include food and water). Let us concentrate on one of these, and suggest that the optimum use of resources is attained by well-devised, area-specific resource management plans. (I emphasize "area specific", which means relating to particular geographic areas, because it is a key design and planning element which we should always keep in the back of our minds. Decision-makers and land-use planners invariably take their decisions and make their plans first and foremost about particular areas of land, rather than about such un-bankable or inedible things like endangered species and conservation concepts. This means that "environmental scientists" are obliged to present their data analyses in a geographical, areal framework. On the decision tree, we also need the boundaries of ecological zones—nice geographical delimiters—to make sensible Welfare-Optimizing management plans.)

There are a number of different types of resource information which must feed into comprehensive management plans. For any particular area about which we are pressed to make decisions, we need cost-and-benefit information concerning investment in exploitation of mineral and other non-renewable resources, such as fossil water, agriculture and forests, livestock husbandry, and, if we decide to consider it a resource, wildlife and their habitats. Calculation of wildlife and wildland costs and benefits requires knowledge of the supply of wild species and the current and potential forms of utilization, both consumptive and non-consumptive. The types of utilization possible are determined by local demand as well as the supply of the wildlife itself.

Following the diagramme downwards, we start to move away from the conceptual level of disciplines and areas of abstract endeavour down to the world of real wildlife data for environmental assessments. We need descriptive data, such as distributions, numbers and population dynamics. In order to account for the observed state of ecosystems and to understand how they are functioning, we need more details on the nature of basic ecosystem determinants, such as soil, water and primary production.

Finally, at the bottom line, we arrive at the inventory and monitoring methods and techniques which are needed to get particular types of information: aerial photography; satellite imagery analysis; systematic reconnaissance flights (SRF) in low-flying light aircraft; meteorological analysis; radio tracking; and ground studies are all necessary to probe into the intimacies of plants and animals.

You will note that I have not included "genetic resources" and whatever one does with them in the scheme. The reason is this: in most cases, it is not very easy to include a consideration of genetic resources in land-use planning. The rhetoric of genetic resource arguments is doomed to ineffectiveness as it is uttered: "Spare that tree/animal/ecosystem/habitat for it may turn out to be of use one day." It may well, but what a silly thing to say to a politician who has two entrepreneurs and one aid organisation scheming on one side of the area in question, and a burgeoning human population scrabbling at the other. In the face of a panoply of bankable or votable proposals, do we really expect him to take our genetic resource/future generations stuff seriously? If we really believe that those genetic resources will pay off some day, then we had better invest in bringing that will o' the wisp home to roost. Thus we should argue for investment, not in preservation of land *per se*, but in research and development of potential resources and of globally applicable techniques, both of which, just by chance, require rather large outdoor laboratories.

4. HOW TO MONITOR ECOLOGICALLY

Although the ecological monitoring approach works best as a package, it is designed to be applied flexibly at intensities proportional to what can be afforded. Thus, even if funds are short initially, useful work can still be done.

One of the cheapest and most useful things to do is to lay a reference grid over the study area. The grid provides a basis for subsequent description (either by hand or by computer), point referencing, statistical sampling, computerizing and registering different sources and scales of information, for example, a ground survey to an aerial photograph to an earth resources satellite image. The Universal Transverse Mercator (UTM) is a handy world-wide mapping grid to use initially. It has the advantage that large units of 100 by 100 km may be used if the area is very homogeneous or the data particularly coarse. As information improves, the scale can be reduced to 10 by 10 km, one by one km, or even down to tens of meters, all nested within the same geographical referencing framework. Having all the data tied to a standard grid makes repeat observations very easy to compare, and lays the basis for a system of long-term monitoring.

Information on important resource variables related to climate, biota, physical features and human activities are collected systematically over the entire region and then allocated to the grid base. Subsequently, the data, keyed to grid squares, may be further allocated to whatever sub-region appears useful. This approach allows the data themselves to suggest inductively how the region is structured while at the same time allowing the analyst to sub-divide in any fashion he wishes. In this way, also, data collected in a small area can be related to an extensive region and *vice versa* without having to reset the structure of the data base. Monitoring is done in the short term, thus providing information on seasonal movements and variability. Repeated short-term monitoring is, however, the basis of long-term monitoring which establishes trends with time (e.g. animal population changes) and so makes it possible to correlate a number of variables with each other.

Most ecological monitoring practiced today relies on systematic sampling, which has very few disadvantages compared with random sampling, and features considerable advantages—repeatability in time, direct comparability in space, good framework for multi-variate correlations and analysis of variance, ease in re-stratifying the data, possibility of "decomposing" old data bases into a new analytical framework, good display format, and so on. The main disadvantage is that systematic sampling tends to overestimate the variance of the estimates, which is not such a bad thing since it errs on the side of conservatism. In any event, special random samples may be designed if a particularly high degree of precision is required in special cases. (Deeper discussions may be found in Gwynne and Croze 1979; Pennycuick *et al.* 1977; Norton-Griffiths, 1978; UNEP/ILCA, 1981).

If we had world enough and time, many of the best data would be collected from the ground. It is not easy to match the detail of information one can see at arm's length or at one's feet. But, quite simply, there is usually not enough money and time to study protected areas (or any other large area of interest) exclusively from the ground. Nor is ground work always the most efficient, particularly in large areas with rapid seasonal changes:

we miss incredibly revealing views of our protected areas and their surrounds when observations are exclusively earth-bound. If we put our ecologists into aircraft and establish a link to an eye in space, then we can view ecosystems in temporal and spatial perspectives which really have to be seen to be believed, and which are now beginning to be used to justify the rather daunting research and development investments.

The traditional, time-honoured thing to do in a protected area is an ecological inventory: what is there, where and how many or how much? A useful record, a good baseline against which to judge the state of the place in the future. Here again, we may apply the notion of doing what is affordable. One inventory is a good thing; if possible, a number of inventories in a time-series is even better. It is monitoring, in fact.

A typical array of data collected from an ecological monitoring programme looks like this (adapted from Gwynne & Croze, 1979):

"PERMANENT ATTRIBUTES":
  topography/geomorphology
  soils
  drainage
  water holes
  static animal feature (termite mounds, breeding grounds, etc.)

"SEMI-PERMANENT ATTRIBUTES"
  plant physiognomy (cover, vegetation type, etc.)
  plant community composition
  zoogenic features (wallows, salt licks, etc.)
  distribution of non-migratory large animal species
  human settlement (villages, roads, farms, ranches)
  local human economics/land use types

"EPHEMERAL OR SEASONAL ATTRIBUTES"
  rainfall
  insolation
  soil moisture
  evapotranspiration
  plant phenology (greenness)
  plant productivity (biomass, part composition, chemical composition, energy content, etc.)
  distribution of migratory large mammal species
  large mammal productivity (biomass, reproductive state, condition, food offtake, etc.)
  large mammal population structure
  fire
  surface water

Finally, none of the above would be of any use if the information were not returned to the users. This is one of the most important links in the chain of data flow, and the one most often overlooked, in the white-hot frenzy of scientific enquiry. The best solution is probably to invest in educating both decision makers about the utility of ecological data, on the one hand, and technicians and scientists on the necessity of mak-ing the fruits of their labours more palatable, on the other.

Analyses of the data may be done on a largish pocket calculator or a mainframe computer. Neither is entirely satisfying, particularly today when the astounding development of micro-computers will soon make it possible to optimize satisfactorily cost, physical size and data-handling capacity. Thus, we should not be worried by an ambitious data set. Particularly at the outset of the enquiry, as many data as practicable (in terms of cost and analytical possibilities) should be collected, since the more simultaneous data points there are, the greater is the scope for interesting co-variance analyses, and, equally important, the more rational will be subsequent paring down and streamlining of the data set.

5. WHAT GEMS DOES

The Global Environment Monitoring System is a collective effort of the world community to acquire, through monitoring, data necessary for rational management of the environment. Most of GEMS activities in fields of health-related monitoring of pollutants, climate-related monitoring of key components of the world's climate system, and the monitoring of renewable natural resources, are coordinated from the GEMS Programme Activity Centre (PAC), located in UNEP's Nairobi headquarters. It is perhaps necessary to mention that UNEP, including the GEMS PAC, is not "operational" and works mainly through the intermediary of the UN Specialized Agencies and other international bodies such as IUCN, ICSU, etc. If this were not so, the very limited financial resources that UNEP is able to commit to monitoring activities would otherwise be almost entirely absorbed to staff costs. Without crucial operational links to the agencies and their contributions of manpower and resources, it is doubtful whether GEMS would even exist.

If UNEP is not operational, what, one might well ask, does the GEMS PAC do? The well-known, famous "catalytic" role of UNEP does actually have substance. Within GEMS, it means: establishing standard and quality-controlled monitoring activities where none exist, or pulling existing activities into one mutually-compatible global network; it means underwriting environmental assessments to produce information where there are gaps; it means bringing groups of experts together to formulate an approach to an environmental problem; it means enlisting the talent and relevant programme components of the UN Specialized Agencies into common monitoring systems; it means supporting the research and development necessary to devise and test a needed monitoring technique; and it means designing and finding the funds for the implementation of monitoring projects. As it turns out, "to catalyze" is not such an intransitive verb.

I will skip over GEMS activities in health- and climate-related monitoring, and describe briefly the activities in terrestrial renewable resource monitoring: in soils, forests, arid rangelands and endangered species and habitats. All of the activities result in environmental assessment products (analyzed data) which by their nature should be of direct relevance to the management of protected areas.

Very few decisions have ever been made from a soils map. UNEP, FAO and UNESCO decided to work together to produce a new perspective on soils data which would be of use to decision makers. What was needed, it was felt in the mid-1970s, was a picture of the current rates of soil degradation and the immediate risks. The result was a methodology which composited a number of types of soil degradation—wind erosion, water erosion, biological denaturing, salinization, acidification—and expressed them at a scale of 1 to 5 million for Africa north of the equator and the Middle East (UNEP/FAO/UNESCO, 1978). The methods combine remote sensing and field survey with laboratory analyses. According to the UNEP mandate, and, in any event because of limited resources, we cannot do the same for the whole world. So now we promote the approach and hope that national and international agencies will try to test it further, and apply the methodology at whatever scales seem appropriate.

The aim of the GEMS tropical forest cover monitoring project was similar to that of the soils effort—to develop a methodology which would yield products of immediate use to land use planners and managers. So in three West African countries, through FAO, GEMS worked out a suitable combination of satellite and aerial photo interpretation, aerial observations and ground surveys (UNEP/FAO, 1980). It is gratifying to observe that the products of the project are said to be plastering the walls of the Ministry of Planning in Togo as an aid in making decisions about resettling onchocerciasis evacuees. A new tropical forest monitoring project is about to be put in motion in some 13 southeast Asian countries, including, of course, the host country of our Congress.

The other major GEMS activity in the world's forests are the recently completed global assessment of tropical forest resources (UNEP/FAO, 1981 a-d, UNEP, 1982). For the first time, the best data from 76 countries were put into a common format to produce the first of what is hoped will be a continuing series of assessments of the states and rates and causes of decline of the world's forests. In this first assessment, the data were based upon recent published and unpublished local, national and regional reports, spot checked with satellite imagery analysis. They were, obviously, of varying quality. Given the initial heterogenity of data, we are cautious about extrapolations. Nonetheless, the results are intriguing. They suggest, for example, that the global rates of disapppearance may be less than we had suspected before. Although such figures indicate that there is still time to plan on a global scale, we should not become complacent, particularly in the light of the dozen-odd countries which, if current rates continue, will have no forest at all by the end of the century.

Earlier, I talked about the three-tiered, systems-ecology GEMS ecological monitoring strategy which is currently being applied in a large number of arid and semi-arid rangelands. We aim to see established a global network of ecological monitoring units which are attacking serious drylands problems—such as desertification—on a united front. At the moment, we directly support a GEMS demonstration project, implemented by FAO, in the Sahelian region of Senegal, and we contribute to the design or support research and development of methodologies in a number of other projects. In all, some 5% of the world's arid and semi-arid rangelands have been, or are being, or will soon be inventoried and monitored within the GEMS framework—over 2 million sq km altogether, much of which is in or around protected areas. This impressive coverage foretells the day when we will be able to exchange experience and solve common global problems from a shared base of data and experience.

As most of you are certainly aware, the process of monitoring, assessing and cataloguing the status of endangered species has now moved out of the 19th century and become part of today's world. At the request of IUCN and with the mutual agreement of UNEP and IUCN, the activities of the Conservation Monitoring Centre at Cambridge and Kew Gardens are now part of GEMS. We are delighted that the Red Data Book has evolved into a Red Data Base, and proud to have played a modest part in the architecture of the new approach. Soon it will be possible for data on endangered species and their habitats to be registered to the sets of data which are now being used to produce a composite environmental resource picture for decision makers.

Despite what may sound like a rather ambitious programme, we would be the first to admit that we cannot monitor everything; we often concentrate, initially at least, on areas of particular historical or biological interest, such as protected areas and their immediate surroundings. While the monitoring data accumulate, they hopefully, provide useful insights on how to manage the protected areas.

6. WHAT ELSE WE SHOULD DO

We now see quite clearly that national decision-makers urgently need information on the state and trends of critical biosphere components within the lands for which they are responsible in order to make rational land use plans. Surely one of the most important issues in the next few decades must be how governments and society allocate and husband the available living spaces and the living resources within those spaces. Since decisions are made about specific parcels of land rather than concepts, geographical referencing of the biosphere data is crucial (it is not just by chance that we monitor ecologically within a geodetic grid).

At the same time, we have megabytes of information accumulating, for example, from national and international programmes on wildlife, forestry, fisheries, food, populations, pollution. . . all related to the state and trends of the world's life-support systems and the chemical and physical insults we perpetrate on them. In some industrialized countries, the workings of man's habitat and the challenges put to it are already being extensively documented in national geographical information systems.

But what of the rest of the world--where the majority of people live and where poverty is driving people to destroy the natural resource base? We do not know a great deal, but we surely know enough about global ecology to recognize the long-term futility of studying soils, forests, endangered species, oceans or the atmosphere, or indeed man himself, in isolation from the other elements of the biosphere. We also realize that if we isolate one ecosystem from its neighbour, either conceptually or physically, we will get only part of the picture governments need if they are to manage any ecosystem rationally. Yet, so far the only effort to unify and integrate at a global level has been by UNEP and its partners, for example, within the monitoring activities of GEMS and our Regional Seas Programme.

We acknowledge that it will be some time before every nation among us possesses the relatively high technology it requires to inventory, monitor, analyse and understand ecosystem functioning within its protected areas, much less throughout the length and breadth of its own living spaces. Therefore, while encouraging each nation to develop its own capabilities, we believe there is today an urgent need for an international service—perhaps within GEMS—to accumulate, select, examine the quality of, analyze, scale, register, overlay and generally make useful, a wide range of living resources data. Many such data come from protected areas, and their contribution to a global understanding of ecosystem functioning will allow us to manage better the biosphere both within and outside protected areas.

Park Your Genes: Protected Areas as In Situ Genebanks for the Maintenance of Wild Genetic Resources

Robert and Christine Prescott-Allen
PA DATA
Victoria, British Columbia, Canada

ABSTRACT. *Three main points are made in this paper. First, wild genetic resources are valuable. They already make an important contribution to agricultural production. Their potential contribution not only to agriculture but also to aquaculture and silviculture is even greater. Second, as a consequence of the first point, the conservation of wild genetic resources is of great importance for economic and social development. Much of this conservation should be* in situ, *using existing and new protected areas. The use of protected areas as* in situ *genebanks will enhance their socio-economic contribution and strengthen the justification for their support. Third, to develop protected areas into* in situ *genebanks, their planners and managers need to adopt additional criteria for the selection of such areas and additional objectives and measures for management. These are outlined in the section of this paper on basic principles of protected areas as* in situ *genebanks, and a plan is proposed to turn these principles into action.*

1. PREAMBLE: WHAT WE MEAN BY . . .

Wild genetic resource: any heritable characteristic of a wild plant or animal that is of actual or potential use to people. The characteristic may be rapid growth, disease resistance, a pharmacological activity, an environmental adaptation, or the capacity of a timber tree to grow tall and straight: as long as it is or could be of economic or social value and is transmitted genetically, it qualifies as a genetic resource.

Gene: the unit of heredity.

Genotype: a particular combination of genes. Think of all possible genes as a deck of cards; all the cells of an individual plant or animal are dealt a hand of several thousand genes. The geneticist's term for any specific hand is genotype (we are indebted to Ellis and Duffield (n.d.) for this analogy). Except with clonally propagated species, a genotype normally corresponds to an individual.

Gene pool: the total number of different genes within a group of interbreeding plants or animals.

Population: the individuals that make up a particular gene pool.

2. INTRODUCTION

The preservation of genetic diversity (the second objective of the *World Conservation Strategy*) means essentially two things: the preservation of many different species; and the maintenance of the variation within species. Until now, conservationists and the planners and managers of protected areas have concentrated on the first. Now it is time to attend also to the second.

Variation *within* the species needs to be conserved for two reasons. First, genetic variation is essential for species to adapt and survive. This aspect is discussed by Wilcox this volume. Second, variation within species is the raw material of domestication and of the continued survival and improvement of domesticates. Without genetic variation there could be no agriculture, horticulture, silviculture or aquaculture, and hence no sustainable development. The products of this variation are what we call "genetic resources." Those genetic resources that are found in wild plants and animals, and the critical role that protected areas can and should play in their conservation, are the subjects of this paper.

3. THE VALUE OF WILD GENETIC RESOURCES

Many crops have been improved with genes from their wild relatives, several of them substantially. All sugarcanes bred in India are derived from crosses between domesticated *Saccharum officinarum* and wild *S. spontaneum* from Indonesia and southern India. India's sugar industry could not have been established without the acquisition of resistance to red rot from Javan *S. spontaneum*. The vigour and disease resistance obtained from *S. spontaneum* (and to a lesser extent from *S. robustum* from Papua New Guinea) have had a major impact on world sugarcane production, helping to almost double the cane yield and more than double the yield of sugar.

Similarly, cocoa yields have been boosted through the incorporation of vigour and disease resistance from wild and semi-wild *Theobroma cacao* from Peru into cultivars in West Africa, South America and Southeast Asia. In many cocoa producing countries these cultivars are the only officially recognized planting material. Virtually all cultivars of cotton grown in Sudan are resistant to bacterial blight, the resistance being obtained from an African wild cotton *Gossypium anomalum*. *G. thurberi*, which grows wild in Mexico and the USA (Arizona), has increased the fibre strength of several cotton cultivars; and *G. tomentosum* from Hawaii has been an important source of pest resistance for the US crop. Tomato and tobacco, crops worth respectively almost $1 billion and well over $2 billion a year in the USA, could not be grown there without the disease resistance conferred by wild species. Wild tomatoes from Ecuador and Peru have also contributed higher contents of soluble solids, vitamin A and vitamin C, and have helped make the crop suitable for mechanical harvesting.

We have given elsewhere numerous references and examples of the contribution of wild plants to crop improvement (Prescott-Allen and Prescott-Allen, 1981a, 1981b and 1982), but for a final illustration of the value of wild genetic resources for agriculture we cite the rice eaten daily in Indonesia. The crop gets its resistance to blast and grassy stunt virus—two of the four major diseases of rice in Asia (the other two are bacterial blight and tungro virus)—from a wild species, *Oryza nivara*. During the early 1970s, prior to the release of resistant varieties in 1974, grassy stunt epidemics destroyed more than 116,000 ha of rice in Indonesia, India, Sri Lanka, Vietnam and the Philippines. Today, with the widespread use of resistant varieties, the disease has ceased to exist in farmers' fields. Cultivars with *O. nivara* in their pedigree are grown on 30 million ha in India, Nepal, Bangladesh, China and the countries of Southeast Asia. Their economic and social impact has been enormous. Average production per ha in Indonesia has risen to six tons and in some cases to ten tons. Two to three crops a year have become common, and rice production overall has doubled. *Per capita* rice availability has increased from 91 kg in the 1960s to 136 kg today.

Genetic variation within wild species is the major resource of silviculture and aquaculture. Both are in their infancy compared with agriculture, and hence are more concerned with the selection of potential domesticated strains from the wild. The rewards of selecting genetically superior individuals and using them as seed sources and in breeding programmes can be high. Among pines grown in southeastern USA, for example, improvement programmes have produced faster growth (reducing a 25 year rotation by two years), rust resistance, better tree form (especially straightness) and higher wood specific gravity, increasing the dollar/ha value by an estimated 32% (North Carolina State University-Industry Cooperative Tree Improvement Program, 1982). In aquaculture, genetic improvements have increased the growth rate in clams and disease resistance in oysters. With many valuable species, such as penaeid shrimps, the process of domestication has not yet been completed, and fertilized eggs are still obtained from the wild (Glude, 1977).

The lesson of breeding in crops and livestock is that domestication inevitably involves a narrowing of the genetic base. Among the genetic determinants that are soon lost in the course of this narrowing are those controlling pest and disease resistance, and adaptation to changing and marginal environments. The wild relatives of domesticates provide the means for making good these losses. At the same time economic development spurs the search for new potential domesticates among wild plants and animals. The rate of domestication seems to have been roughly constant since the beginnings of agriculture (Simmonds, 1979); if anything, it is now accelerating, not only in the youthful areas of aquaculture and silviculture, but also in agriculture with new crops such as jojoba (*Simmondsia*) and the domestication of insects for pest control and for crop pollination (such as *Megachile* leafcutter bees for the pollination of alfalfa). Both the domestication of new crops and livestock and the improvement of existing ones will bring still greater reliance on wild plants and animals as genetic resources.

4. THE NEED FOR IN SITU GENEBANKS

At present virtually all genebanks (places expressly intended to maintain genes for future use) are *ex situ*. They are seed storage facilities, clonal plantations, seed orchards, rare breed farms, and so on. Why are *in situ* genebanks needed as well? There are at least five reasons.

First, the sheer size of the task. *Ex situ* genebanks are primarily concerned with maintaining domesticated genetic resources. The diversity of wild genetic resources is so great that it seems doubtful that even *ex situ* and *in situ* genebanks combined could safeguard more than a small fraction. That fraction will be very much smaller if *ex situ* genebanks alone must do the job.

Second, the difficulty of maintaining certain species *ex situ*. Some plants and many animals are very difficult to maintain in adequate numbers outside their natural habitats. Tropical trees provide an example: the seeds of many of them have no dormant period and cannot be preserved; their breeding systems are poorly understood; and they require so much space that only a small number of genotypes can be in plantations or botanical gardens. The seeds of several crop species and their wild relatives are "recalcitrant": they cannot be dried (and hence stored) without killing them. They include mango, rubber, filbert, walnut, cinnamon, avocado, coconut, and cocoa (King and Roberts, 1979). A further complication is that many wild species behave differently from the crops to which they are related. It may be quite easy to maintain and regenerate the domesticates but not their wild relatives. Certain sunflower *Helianthus* and peanut *Arachis* species are examples (Beard, 1977; Banks, 1976).

Third, the need for evolutionary continuity. An advantage of *in situ* genebanks is that evolution continues within them. This is especially important for pest and disease resistance. In the wild, resistant species can co-evolve with predators, parasites and pathogens, providing the breeder with a dynamic source of resistance that is lost when the species is transferred to the deep freeze of a long term seed storage facility.

Fourth, *in situ* genebanks can double as living laboratories. Maintenance of a species in its natural habitat allows the breeder to study its ecology and so obtain information that might otherwise be overlooked. Several valuable characteristics of wild tomatoes have been discovered in this way: tolerance of intense tropical moisture and temperatures, tolerance of saline soils, insect resistance, and drought resistance (Rick, 1976).

Fifth, efficient use of existing facilities. National and subnational networks of protected and special management areas already exist throughout the world. The development of these networks into a system of *in situ* genebanks requires rather minor changes (see following sections); and would be a highly cost-effective way of expanding the present system of (largely *ex situ*) genebanks (cheap and easy relative to the return in terms of maintaining a much increased supply of valuable genetic resources and of making them more readily available to breeders and other users). In turn, this additional role for protected areas will enhance their contribution to economic development and strengthen their case for greater support.

5. PROTECTED AREAS AS IN SITU GENEBANKS: BASIC PRINCIPLES

The main users of genetic resources are plant and animal breeders, the people who improve existing crops and livestocks and develop new ones. The tools of their trade are genes and they depend on conservation to maintain the supply of useful genes. For practical reasons, conservationists try to maintain not individual genes but genotypes and gene pools. Hence a system of protected areas that is intended to maintain wild genetic resources

must be designed and managed to maintain particular populations. It is not enough to have a system that safeguards threatened species or maintains ecosystems representative of the nation's biogeographical provinces. Not all populations are equally useful; and useful populations are not distributed evenly throughout the range of the species they comprise. Consequently, it is possible for valuable genotypes to be threatened with extinction even though the species is widespread and abundant.

The following examples illustrate why this is so. The wild rice *Oryza nivara* is a widespread weed in South and Southeast Asia, China and northern Australia. Yet only one accession from Madhya Pradesh in central India carries the gene for resistance to grassy stunt virus that has been so important to the crop; despite extensive screening, no other proven source has been found. The loblolly pine *Pinus taeda* occurs throughout southeastern USA but the only populations that combine fast growth with high resistance to fusiform rust are restricted to a small area in eastern Louisiana. The hoop pine *Araucaria cunninghamii*, indigenous to New Guinea and northeastern Australia, is not threatened as a species but several populations in New Guinea are. New Guinea provenances are both more productive and better adapted to other tropical countries than are provenances from Australia. The owl monkey *Aotus trivirgatus* is the only known nonhuman animal suitable for malaria chemotherapy and immunology studies. It occurs throughout Central and South America but only the rare and dwindling northern Colombian subspecies is of value for this purpose.

What does this mean for the planners and managers of protected areas? For the planner it means the adoption of additional criteria for site selection. For the manager it means the adoption of additional objectives of management.

Current criteria for the selection of sites for genetic or biotic conservation are species and ecosystem oriented. The focus is on threatened or popular species, on unique ecosystems or ecosystems representative of biogeographical provinces, or on combinations of the two. This approach attempts to protect as much diversity as possible without giving preference to any particular species except those that are endangered or recreationally attractive. Essentially it assumes that all species are equally useful (or, by the same token, equally useless).

We need now to ensure that populations of known or likely genetic importance are protected in areas established for that purpose. Unfortunately, studies of the distribution of within-species variation are few and far between. Pending such studies we still have to focus on species rather than populations, but we can begin to identify those species of actual and potential importance as genetic resources, and we can try to maintain as much as possible of the variability within those species.

If a protected area is to become an *in situ* genebank,

then the first move is to adopt conservation of wild genetic resources as a major objective of the area, with provision for designating zones where genetic resource conservation is the primary objective. This is necessary because other objectives can conflict. For example, maintenance of herbivore populations could threaten certain plant populations as a result of grazing pressure, burning programmes and so on. It is also necessary because several required measures will need the authority of a formal, explicit commitment to genetic resource conservation.

Protected areas that fortuitously contain wild genetic resources are valuable but they are not *in situ* genebanks and they are not as valuable as they would be if they were *in situ* genebanks. A protected area becomes an *in situ* genebank when it adopts specific measures to maintain wild genetic resources and gives the users of those resources information on and access to them. These measures include: documentation; habitat management; a permit system for collection of genetic material; and liaison with other organizations.

5.1. Documentation

You cannot use a genebank unless you know what it contains. Many protected areas contain useful species but nobody knows about it because there is no species list. Each protected area intended to be a genebank should have a list of the species it contains. The list should indicate the locations of the species, using map grid references. Names of localities alone are not reliable since they change in the course of time. There should be space for annotating the list with information on ecotypes and, in due course, on genotypes. Ideally, for plants, there should be a herbarium sheet for each species listed (again, giving the precise location); and several sheets if the species is morphologically variable. Many genera are taxonomically confusing and the species within them difficult to identify. Herbarium records serve to validate the species list and can save fruitless trips into the field looking for species that have been misidentified. (There is no need for each protected area to have a herbarium. Arrangements can be made with whatever herbaria exist already.)

5.2. Habitat management

The objective of an *in situ* genebank is not to maintain species diversity, nor to maintain an ecosystem in its "natural" condition, but to maintain wild genetic resources. Some of the species concerned may be adapted to a particular successional stage, in which case that stage should be maintained. An example would be a fire-adapted species like some of the pines. While it may be necessary to set up some protected areas exclusively as *in situ* genebanks, many existing protected and special management areas can be used if zoned for this purpose. It should not be difficult to combine management for genetic resource conservation with other objectives of the area. An outbreeding species like loblolly pine can be logged and still maintained, as long as the best individuals are preserved as seed trees. How the protected area is zoned and how the genebank zone is managed will depend on the adaptations and breeding systems of the species to be maintained and on the nature of the other uses/objectives.

5.3. A permit system for collection of germ material

There are three categories of *ex situ* genebank: a *working* collection, which is not concerned with maintenance of the material but simply with supplying the needs of a particular breeding programme; an *active* collection, which is concerned primarily with evaluation and use and only secondarily with maintenance; and a *base* collection, which is devoted exclusively to maintenance. *In situ* genebanks would be analogous to base collections. Hence they need not be in a position to serve the day-to-day requirements of breeders but rather to ensure the long term survival of the genetic resources they protect. Nevertheless, to enable *in situ* genebanks eventually to be integrated with the system of *ex situ* genebanks it would be desirable for them to provide for the collection of germ material (seed, budwood, etc.) by *bona fide* users: breeders, geneticists, evolutionary biologists, and other genebanks.

5.4. Liaison with other organizations

To be converted quickly and cheaply into *in situ* genebanks, protected areas will need to establish close relationships with other institutions. There should be an arrangement with the nearest appropriate *ex situ* genebank to provide standby storage (whenever needed) of germ material collected in the protected area and to act as a link with the community of germ resource users. There should be an arrangement with the nearest herbarium to house voucher sheets for the protected area's plant species list. An active partnership with universities and colleges would be extremely valuable. Species lists could be compiled and herbarium specimens collected at very low cost if they were done as directed studies and thesis topics, as could more advanced research on the distribution of within-species variation.

6. A PLAN OF ACTION

The following action is needed to establish a global system of *in situ* genebanks:

Stage 1—national level: Make the conservation of wild genetic resources an explicit objective of the national protected area system and provide for the establishment of *in situ* genebanks (both as designated zones of existing and future protected areas and as protected areas established exclusively or primarily as *in situ* gene-banks). This may require a change in the legislation governing existing protected areas, and/or the adoption of new regulations. Because virtually any type of protected area or special management area (e.g. to use the USA as an example, National Parks, National Monuments, National Seashores, National Wilderness Areas, Biosphere Reserves, National Wildlife Refuges, National Forests, National Grasslands, State Parks, Bureau of Land Management lands) is suitable for zoning, it may be desirable to adopt a broad policy—such as a national policy for genetic resource conservation—which could mandate the necessary changes in legislation governing all or most such areas and provide for interagency coordination.

Stage 1—international level: Prepare inventories of wild species and populations of known or likely value as genetic resources. Inventories are needed because without them it is not possible to know what to conserve or where the most important sites for protection are. The inventories should be cross-sectoral, since a given community or ecosystem is likely to include genetic resources of value to more than one sector (for example, a crop relative, a timber tree, and an anadromous fish—of value respectively to agriculture, silviculture, and aquaculture) and it would not be cost-effective to manage the genebank for one sector alone. We suggest that IUCN's Commission on National Parks and Protected Areas (CNPPA) is best equipped to be the lead agency in this major undertaking. The inventories should cover marine as well as land and freshwater species. They could be prepared on a biogeographical realm basis; and could be revised and kept up-to-date through the CNPPA's regular cycle of realm-by-realm meetings. The Protected Areas Data Unit (PADU) would be the ideal vehicle for storing the inventories, particularly because of its integration with the data bases of IUCN's Threatened Plants Committee (TPC) and Species Conservation Monitoring Unit (SCMU). Close liaison would be needed with other international organizations concerned with the conservation of genetic resources, notably FAO, Unesco/MAB, UNEP, and IBPGR (International Board for Plant Genetic Resources).

Stage 2—national and international levels: Make plans for the establishment of *in situ* genebanks. Many species of value as genetic resources probably already occur in protected and special management areas. We do not know, because very few protected areas have species lists and in any case we lack the realm-by-realm inventories of wild genetic resources. As each inventory is prepared it will be possible for national and international agencies to assess the extent to which existing networks of protected areas are maintaining the inventoried species; to determine which zones of which protected areas should be designated as *in situ* genebanks; and to review the gaps that remain and establish priorities for the designation of *in situ* genebanks on sites outside the existing protected area network. It should be emphasized that the establishment of *in situ* genebanks will not necessarily require substantial additions to existing networks; the zoning of already established areas and adoption of the measures outlined in the previous section on basic principles may accomplish much of the task.

Stage 3—national level: Establish *in situ* genebanks. Once the regulatory changes proposed in stage 1 and the plans proposed in stage 2 have been made, the first *in situ* genebanks can be set up. Facilities for documentation will have to be provided but this should have only a very slight impact on budgets and staff allocations as long as there is good cooperation with the nearest university and other suitable institutions. Similarly, the required provisions for habitat management and for the issuing of collection permits are likely to be close enough to current practice to be borne without undue difficulty by the staff and funds already available. At the same time, the development of the protected area network into an effective system of *in situ* genebanks will enhance the social and economic relevance of protected areas, buttress them against encroachment by incompatible land and water uses, and strengthen their case for the budgets necessary for them to fulfill their many functions.

7. CONCLUSION

At present there are only four protected areas in the world (three apparently established and one still in the planning stage) that might qualify as *in situ* genebanks: two in the USSR protecting forage grasses and wild wheat, pistachio, apricot and almond; one in Sri Lanka protecting medicinal plants; and one being planned in India to protect wild citrus and sugarcane (Prescott-Allen and Prescott-Allen, 1981a). Yet *in situ* genebanks could be set up quite easily in many protected areas of all kinds. The need is great and urgent, because wild genetic resources are enormously important economically and socially. Many are disappearing due to habitat loss and other pressures, and *in situ* protection is the prime means of maintaining them.

For protected areas to fulfil this new and vital role will require the same enthusiasm and commitment that the protected areas movement has shown in adopting the goal of adequate protection for ecosystems representative of the various biogeographical provinces. As the 1970s was the decade of biogeographical protection, let the 1980s be the decade of *in situ* genebanks. Let us all work together to "park your genes."

Acknowledgements

This paper was prepared for IUCN's Commission on National Parks and Protected Areas in cooperation with the United Nations Environment Programme.

In Situ Conservation of Genetic Resources: Determinants of Minimum Area Requirements

Bruce A. Wilcox
Department of Biological Sciences
Stanford University
Stanford, California, USA

ABSTRACT. *This paper offers an introduction to the conservation of genetic resources in protected areas, presenting basic concepts of genetics and island biogeography and showing how these can be applied by the protected area manager to real situations on the ground. It focusses on the problem of minimum effective size of protected areas, showing how the process of extinction works in small areas. A method for selecting appropriate "target species" is outlined, along with the methodology for estimating minimum viable populations of the target species. Many of the factors of extinction are caused by man, and therefore can be overcome by more effective management; but more difficult are the chance factors—natural catastrophes, environmental variation, chance demographic events, chance genetic events, and the like—for which the only defense is as large and diverse a population as possible.*

1. INTRODUCTION

Of the wide range of factors that must be taken into account in the selection, establishment and management of protected areas, perhaps none is of greater importance than that relating to minimum area requirements for the preservation of biological diversity. This is because enough areas of adequate size must be established to ensure that the full range of communities, species and genetically distinct populations is "captured" from the outset. It is also because the extent to which certain minimum area criteria are met will determine the capacity of these areas to preserve that range over the long term.

Biologists have long been aware that the size and isolation of natural areas determine in large part the amount of diversity they support. It has only been in the past several years, however, that conservation biologists have recognized as critical the implications of this fact for the conservation of biological diversity. Island biogeography, population ecology and population genetics, which in the past have been largely the domain of the highly specialized academic scientists, are beginning to demonstrate their potential for application to protected area design and management (e.g. Soul and Wilcox, 1980; Frankel and Soul, 1981). For example, the similarity of protected areas and islands, which generally hold far fewer animal and plant species than mainland areas of similar size, has forced a close examination of the possible effects of the imminent isolation facing most protected areas. Similarly, studies of population dynamics and population genetics compel consideration of minimum requirements for long-term survival of isolated plant and animal populations.

The process of adapting basic scientific information to applied needs is slow and difficult, requiring close collaboration of "theoreticians" and "practioners." Furthermore, the level of scientific understanding of nature and biological diversity, although in many respects impressive, would benefit from far more research. Nonetheless, a number of basic principles exist which have direct application to minimum area requirements. The purpose of this paper is to provide an introduction to these principles, to the problem of minimum area requirements, and to provide an overview of general guidelines for their determination in the context of genetic resources.

2. COMPONENTS OF BIOLOGICAL DIVERSITY

Generally speaking, use of the term "biological diversity" requires little or no explanation; but as a resource and an entity serving as a focus of preservation and for the application of scientific theory, a specific definition is required.

2.1. A definition of biological diversity

Biological diversity is the variety of life forms, the ecological roles they perform and the genetic diversity they contain. Since genes are the ultimate source of biological diversity at all levels of biological systems (i.e. molecular, organismal, population, species and ecosystem), "genetic diversity" and "biological diversity" are used interchangeably in some contexts. However, this broad definition of genetic diversity should not be confused with the narrower meaning most often implied by geneticists and conservation biologists, which is simply "the variety of different genes." In fact, genes can be seen simply as the components of biological diversity at the *molecular level* of biological systems. Other components at other levels are the individual organisms at the organismal level, different populations at the population level, different species at the species level and so on.

Studies of ecosystem function show that the levels are interdependent. That is, processess at the community level, for example, influence processess at the genetic level. Therefore preserving genetic diversity, or any other component of biological diversity, requires consideration of all levels. For instance, population genetics as a scientific discipline deals primarily with the problem of how processes at the level of populations (population size and dynamics, dispersal of individuals, natural selection, and chance events) influence processes at the molecular level and vice versa. In fact, most population geneticists are particularly concerned with the problem of how population characteristics influence genetic diversity.

2.2. The focus of conservation: genes, species or ecosystems?

The establishment of a protected area may focus either on preserving some specific type of ecosystem (e.g., Southeast Asian dipterocarp forest) or a particular species (e.g., orang-utan). A protected area may also be established to preserve genetically distinct populations. This includes subspecies, races or varieties (whether or not they have been scientifically named or bear any visibly unique features). Therefore, three different foci of conservation efforts might be distinguished: gene conservation, species conservation and ecosystem conservation.

It is important to realize that preserving ecosystems is not the same as preserving species. Nor is preserving species the same as preserving genes. Since communities are classified according to vegetation structure and the *dominant* plant and animal species, it is quite possible to preserve a community-type and still lose many species. It is also possible to preserve a species and lose genetically distinct populations, although this loss may contribute in the long term to its extinction. Although *in situ* conservation requires that biological diversity be considered as a whole, that is, in the form of intact communities, the types of conservation strategies employed and their outcomes may differ somewhat depending on the focus.

2.3. Genetic diversity as a resource

The implications of genetics to the conservation of biological diversity stem from two unrelated concerns. First, the variety of genes found in nature represent a resource of enormous significance (Myers, 1979; IUCN, 1980). The domestication of plants and animals, which is the basis of the origin, the present existence, and the future of human civilization, is largely the result of artificial selection of organisms with useful genetic traits. Continued genetic improvement of domesticated organisms to improve yields, confer resistance to disease and generally maintain an edge on inevitable environmental change requires that the widest possible range of potentially useful genes be preserved. Of obvious importance are the genes contained in wild relatives of economically important crops (e.g. rice, maize, wheat, etc.), the vast majority of which may remain undiscovered (and most certainly inadequately protected). Even organisms unrelated to any that are currently utilized could have enormous future significance to agriculture, medicine or industry (if they are not exterminated first).

2.4. Genetic variability and species survival

The second reason for protecting genetic diversity is the role it plays in species survival. The term "genetic variability", as used here, is the genetic diversity contained in a single population or a species, which is significant to the "fitness" of individuals and evolutionary potential of populations and species. Geneticists believe, and there is much supporting evidence for their belief, that the genetic variability contained in wild species is essential for their very survival. Some of the reasons for this are discussed below.

3. BIOLOGICAL DIVERSITY AND THE SIZE AND SURROUNDINGS OF PROTECTED AREAS

Perhaps the best way to gain a clear understanding of minimum area requirements is to examine the mechanisms by which biological diversity is diminished through the loss and isolation of habitat area. Although factors other than these can play a critical role (i.e., pesticides, over-harvesting and habitat disturbance), the conversion of natural habitat is unquestionably the major cause of the decline of biological diversity. Indeed, the purpose of establishing protected areas is to exclude certain regions from habitat conversion.

3.1. The process of insularization

The relationship between protected areas and surrounding land is often described as being similar to that of an island and its surrounding waters. For many protected areas the analogy may be extreme. Many forms of land use are not entirely inimical to the support of biological diversity. But for the most part, national parks, game reserves and other protected areas are in almost all cases, or will eventually become, surrounded by land which is modified to one degree or another by humans. The loss or conversion of the surrounding habitat need not be complete to apply the island model.

The process of isolating a biological community, or its components, is called "insularization." By studying this process in natural and experimental systems, researchers have established a number of basic principles pertaining to the effects of insularization on biological diversity. Although many of the details are still in dispute, evidence supporting the general scheme is overwhelming (see Wilcox, 1980 and references therein).

Wilcox distinguished three broad phases occurring in a time sequence to describe the loss of species due to insularization. The following is generally applicable to biological diversity as a whole, and to any of its components.

3.1.1. Sampling principle. A basic principle in ecology and biogeography is the *species-area relationship*. This is the relationship between the size of a parcel of land surveyed and the number of different species recorded on that parcel. As a very general rule, for every 10-fold decrease in the size of a surveyed area, 30 percent fewer species are found. This means that if a protected area is planned to cover some representative fraction of natural habitat, the area will contain an incomplete sample of all species found in the entire region. This can even be true if all habitat types are included (see Diamond, 1980). This principle can be extended to other components of biological diversity. For example, of the species included in the area, an incomplete sample of the genetic diversity contained among all the populations that comprise many of those species will occur within the protected area.

The sampling principle applies most directly to the problem of establishing protected areas. It bears on such questions as: how many, how large and where protected areas should be established. Although there are many possible interpretations of the applicability of this principle to protected area establishment, only two of the more important ones will be discussed.

According to the sampling principle, if protected areas were randomly placed throughout the landscape, a certain amount of diversity would not be captured.

That amount, in terms of the number of species "lost", can theoretically be estimated by the species-area relationship given above.

This problem can be mitigated by taking advantage of the fact that biological diversity is not uniformly distributed. Where adequate biogeographical data exist, "hot spots" of biological diversity can be identified and considered as sites for the establishment of protected areas. Such a strategy is being employed in Brazil, for instance, where distributions of lizards, birds and butterflies are being mapped to determine centres of endemism corresponding to Pleistocene refugia (see Prance, 1981).

The strategic placement of protected areas is therefore necessary in order to capture maximum biological diversity. Yet this can only be done on the basis of biogeographical data, or a biological diversity inventory. Unfortunately, for most regions of the world, data on the distributions of species (and even communities) are insufficient or nonexistent, although inventory programmes for collecting, compiling and managing data (Radford, *et al.*, 1981) are rapidly coming into use.

Since comprehensive surveys of just the species component of biological diversity in even small geographic regions would be impossible from a practical standpoint, the use of "indicator taxa" is recommended (Wilcox, 1982). These are key taxa which (i) are relatively well described taxonomically, (ii) have well-known geographic distributions, (iii) are representative of organisms of major ecological significance, and (iv) can be readily surveyed or censused in the field.

A good example is butterflies. Not only are they one of the best studied invertebrate taxa, but they are representative of perhaps the most numerically abundant and ecologically significant invertebrate groups, the phytophagous (plant-eating) insects. Furthermore, nearly all butterfly species specialize on a narrow range of host-plant taxa, so under most circumstances, the diversity of butterfly species found in an area is a very good indicator of plant species diveristy. In fact, for this and other reasons, the taxa which are more typical of popular conservation efforts (e.g. large mammals and birds) may often be relatively poor indicators of overall diversity.

If there is one most important lesson provided by the sampling principle, it is the following: In the absence of solid information on the distribution of biological diversity, and without a protected area establishment strategy based on that information, even an extensive system of protected areas will fail to capture a significant fraction of biological diversity.

3.1.2. Short-term insularization. The sampling principle describes how a protected area may fail to contain a portion of the entire ensemble of species, and their full range of genetic variability. However, of those species included in the sample, that is, found to occur within the boundaries of the protected area, some frac-

tion will not be self-sustaining as the area becomes increasingly surrounded by modified habitat.

These species are basically of two classes. First, there are those made up of individuals which are more or less evenly dispersed geographically, but are at extremely low population densities (e.g., large carnivores and certain raptorial birds). In such cases, the number of individuals and/or the demographic composition as a closed population is inadequate to maintain stability, and the population will eventually become extinct.

The second class of species are those in which individuals are clumped. That is, they occur at moderate to high densities in local populations, but the populations are widely spaced geographically. This population structure probably characterizes most species. For species in which this pattern is extreme (e.g. migratory birds), the boundaries of a protected area will enclose only a portion of the clump, or the geographic area through which it ranges.

In the above cases, the protected area will either (i) fail to incorporate a sufficient number of individuals to represent a demographically stable unit, or (ii) fail to incorporate a sufficient quantity or range of resources to support such a unit. As far as these species are concerned, the ecosystem which supports them extends beyond the protected area. Once the surrounding habitat is converted, their numbers will begin the decline to extinction.

3.1.3. Long-term insularization.
Many species in protected areas will consist of stable populations, at least over the short term. Yet all species, given enough time, go extinct. In fact, extinction of local populations appears to be relatively common in many organisms. Normally, the loss of local populations through extinction is counter-balanced by their eventual re-establishment by migrants from surviving populations of the same species. However, the reduction in habitat size which accompanies insularization will result in fewer populations to provide this dynamic balance, and population sizes that are smaller than normal (Pickett and Thompson, 1978). The result will be the tendency for a process (extinction of a species) normally occurring on a geological time scale to condense to an ecological time scale.

The long-term effects of insularization could prove to be the most devastating for protected areas. It will therefore be useful to examine the processes involved in more detail. Studies of islands created by the rising sea level in the past several thousand years indicate large losses of species as a result of insularization (Soul *et al*, 1979). Based on these extinction rates, it has been estimated that even the largest protected areas will suffer an attrition of species amounting to as much or more than half their large mammal species in little more than a thousand years. To give a specific prediction, the Serengeti ecosystem, consisting of the Masai Mara Game Reserve in Kenya and Serengeti National Park in Tanzania, would, after 5,000 years as an "island", support only 28 of the 73 large mammal species it currently supports.

The extent to which protected areas will actually exhibit this "faunal collapse" is uncertain. For one thing, the above estimates assume no human intervention, positive or negative. And of course, five thousand years far exceeds the time scale of concern for most governments and other institutions involved in land use planning. However, the best evidence suggests a collapse which is exponential, such that most of the extinctions in the above predictions would occur in less than 1,000 years in larger areas (approximately 10,000 sq km and bigger) and less than one or two hundred years in smaller areas (approximately 5,000 sq km and smaller).

The rationale for considering evidence such as that above, which provides only crude estimates of the possible effects of insularization, is that they can help direct the lines of questioning concerning selection, establishment and management of protected areas.

4. THE EXTINCTION PROCESS

Minimizing the effects of insularization on extinction is clearly a central problem in the selection and management of protected areas. It is therefore useful to examine extinction in detail.

Although extinction is typically perceived an an event (the death of a species or population) it is actually the process leading up to that event which interests conservation biologists. Since conservation biology is a rather new discipline, much remains to be learned about extinction. Nonetheless, the following generalizations can be made.

The extinction process involves the decline in the number of individuals comprising a population (and the collection of populations of a species). (A "population" is a group of interbreeding individuals at a given locality.) The population is the basic unit of survival of a species. It is a dynamic unit in both an ecological and evolutionary sense: its demographic parameters (birth rate, death rate, age structure and population size), and its genetic composition are constantly altered through time due to environmental change.

These ecological and evolutionary responses may or may not be adaptive, that is, enhance the chances of population survival. With reference to extinction, however, we are only interested in those environmental changes and population responses that are negative, that is, which bring about a decline in population sizes or their chances for survival. Frankel and Soulé (1981) list the following factors contributing to extinction (their text should be referred to for further discussion):

1. Biotic Factors

    A. Competition
    B. Predation
    C. Parasitism and Disease

2. Isolation

3. Habitat Alteration

    A. Slow Geologic Change
    B. Climate
    C. Catastrophe
    D. Man

Each of these factors potentially contributes to either an actual decline in population size and/or an increase in its susceptability to decline. Rather than elaborate on each, a very general view of how they operate is provided.

Any factor (natural or human-induced) which brings about a decrease in birth rates or increase in death rates will result in a decline in the size of a population. Under natural conditions, all populations must deal routinely with a myriad of such factors. Typically, these factors do not push a population to extinction because either (i) the factor is density-dependent (its effect becomes less intense as the population size decreases), (ii) the factor is not continuous through time, or (iii) the organisms develop resistance (behaviourially, physiologically or evolutionarily) to the factor.

Under certain circumstances, however, none of these apply, particularly in the case of populations subjected to insularization (it is therefore of little surprise that most recorded extinctions are of island species). Generally when insularization occurs, habitat area becomes reduced in size and isolated the range of sub-habitats over which a species occurs is reduced, and the population structure of the organism is simplified. This overall simplification of a species and its environment provides fewer ecological and evolutionary options; and operation of the above factors largely depends on such options.

5. DETERMINATION OF MINIMUM AREA REQUIREMENTS

Obviously, protected areas should be as large, and contain as much habitat diversity, as possible. But how large and how diverse is enough? Protected areas must not only contain the biological elements being sought for protection, but they must support those elements in perpetuity. This does not mean that intervention through wildlife or habitat management is not an option for the mitigation of problems brought on by insularization. But the cost of such management problems, many of which may even be unmanageable, must be weighed against the expense of setting aside adequate habitat initially.

Ideally, the selection process will involve a choice of several biotically similar areas. The areas may be disjunct or adjoining other protected areas, and have surrounding habitat which is subject to varying degrees of disturbance. Alternatively an established protected area, or system of protected areas, may require an assessment of their design for possible up-grading. The up-grading may involve further land acquisition, trading, easements or other changes in the status of land use of various parcels (Hoose, 1979); and these may be combined with management strategies involving biological intervention.

Regardless of the situation, the general problem is the same: theory from the broad range of scientific disciplines comprising conservation biology must be adapted to a specific set of practical considerations. These involve the legal, social, economic, political and biological conditions characteristic of the locality. Since these conditions vary greatly from place to place, no single formula for the optimal design and management of protected areas to preserve maximum biological diversity exists. Those who are charged with selecting and managing protected areas must therefore equip themselves with a basic understanding of conservation biology, and apply this knowledge on a case-by-case basis.

5.1. Selection of target species

It is possible to apply a protocol for determining minimum area requirements for individual species based on theoretical considerations. For practical reasons (due to the effort involved in collecting and analyzing the required biological data), this can only be done for a few species. However, if minimum area requirements are met for selected species which fulfil certain criteria, adequate survival conditions can be simultaneously assured for many other species in a biota.

The most obvious criteria for selecting such "target species" is that their minimum area requirements be at least as comprehensive as that of the rest of the community. Preserving these species thus will provide a "protective umbrella" for others. In addition to this rationale, species may be chosen because of their ecological significance. A detailed background discussion of how such judgements are made cannot be provided here, but a brief look at some specific criteria for choosing target species candidates under these two general rationales follows.

5.1.1. Umbrella species. Good candidates for target species are species with characteristics normally associated with low population density. Typical examples are species of large body size (e.g., some ungulates), high trophic level (e.g., mammalian carnivores), high metabolic requirements (i.e., mammals and birds as opposed to reptiles and amphibians) (see Eisenberg, 1980 and Wilcox, 1980), patchy distributions (see Diamond, 1980), and species dependent on successional, rare or unpredictable habitats or resources (see Gilbert, 1980; Foster, 1980; Terborgh and Winter, 1980; Terborgh, 1974; and Karr, 1982).

5.1.2. Ecologically significant species. As a result of their central position in the food web of a community, some species may be of such enormous importance that their decline or extinction would cause a cascade of extinctions similar to the faunal collapse scenario described for islands (Section 3.1.3.). Examples are "mobile links" and "keystone mutualists" described by Gilbert (1980). In many communities, but particularly in tropical forests, animals act as agents of pollen and seed dispersal for plants. Bats and birds, for example, are the major seed dispersers in neotropical forests. They act as mobile links between the fruit-bearing trees which support them, and otherwise separate food webs based on the other plants which they support. These other plants depend upon the mobile links for pollination and seed dispersal. The decline in numbers or loss of one or more mobile links in an isolated protected area could result in the extinction of one or more plant species, and along with each of them the numerous host-specific insect species.

More critical yet are keystone mutualists. These are usually plants, particularly trees, providing resources which support large numbers of mobile links. Single, large fruit-bearing tree species may depend on as few as one mobile link for effective seed dispersal, yet they can provide critical support for several other fruit-eating mobile links. The loss of a single keystone mutualist could conceivably cost the survival of hundreds of other species.

5.2. A target species selection procedure

Once target species candidates are selected according to the above general criteria, the list can then be narrowed by following a more specific procedure. One such procedure is at present being developed by the United States Forest Service (Salwasser and Hoekstra, in prep.). It involves scoring species according to features of their population biology and is based on theoretical considerations which are too extensive to be documented in detail here (see Soul and Wilcox, 1980; and Frankel and Soul, 1981). The following test is a modified version of one included in the selection procedure proposed by the Forest Service. Species scoring highest are the most vulnerable to extinction due to the effects of insularization.

1) The estimated number of resident individuals in the protected area is:
   a) less than 2,500 (1 point)
   b) greater than 2,500 (no points)
2) The species is distributed geographically within the protected area in:
   a) local regions associated with specific habitat types (1 point)
   b) a ubiquitous manner throughout many habitat types (no points)

c) localities not separated by habitat barriers (1 point)
d) isolated localities as distinct populations (no points)
3) The average rate of dispersal of potentially reproductive individuals into the protected area from the outside is approximately:
   a) greater than ten percent each generation (1 point)
   b) less than ten percent each generation (no points)
4) The life history characteristics of the species:
   a) provide for only slow population growth under favourable conditions (1 point)
   b) provide for rapid population growth under favourable conditions (no points)
5) The geographic range of the species:
   a) is mainly limited to this protected area (1 point)
   b) includes other protected areas (no points)

Through this type of procedure, a slightly more objective assessment of relative vulnerability to extinction in an existing or proposed protected area can be made. Some of the more specific questions, particularly those involving actual quantitative information (1 and 3) are subject to scientific dispute. Nonetheless, it is doubtful that they will require significant modification as theoretical advances are made. In any case, most of the species-specific data will, in practice, be only very approximate due to the limited precision of most field-collected data, so this procedure is really only meant as a tool for applying general guidelines.

5.3. Target species and protected area selection

The selection of target species can serve several different purposes. Both the general (5.1) and the specific (5.2) components of the procedure provide an evaluation of alternative protected area designs. For example, once several target species candidates are selected according to general guidelines, the group can be subjected, species by species, to the "target species selection procedure" for specific protected area design options. This process is repeated for each design option, in order to find the option producing the lowest score. Although the selection criteria will not cover all possible contingencies (there may be special considerations for certain species and protected area options), it at least provides an objective procedure to assist in the selection of protected areas. It should not be used as a substitute for common sense and at least a rudimentary understanding of population biology.

5.4. Target species and protected area management

The target species selection procedure also provides a basis for protected area management. A sound management policy for established protected areas must include a master plan specifying long-term research and monitoring, and it must anticipate as much as possible, situations where intervention will be required. The development of a management master plan should not be seen as a bureaucratic exercise, but an opportunity to use conservation biology (as well as other disciplines) to ensure maximum protection of biological diversity at minimum expense.

As protected areas become increasingly insular, there undoubtedly will be a need for close observation to detect cases of incipient extinction. Both the species and even the type of intervention required will in many cases be anticipated by a target species selection procedure. The long-term monitoring of such species will provide managers with the opportunity for intervention before they become seriously endangered. An additional benefit of equal importance will be the acquisition of long-term population data. Research based on this information will enhance our understanding of biological diversity and how it can be preserved. In general, then, a management master plan, although inflexible in its main objectives, should continually evolve on the basis of long-term monitoring and research.

6. ESTIMATION OF MINIMUM VIABLE POPULATIONS

A more direct and quantitative approach to determining minimum area requirements for preserving biological diversity builds on the target species concept. This is the estimation of the *minimum viable population* (MVP) for a target species. The MVP is the set of specifications concerning the size and structure of the populations comprising a species that is necessary to provide a margin of safety from extinction. The MVP for a species can be translated into the minimum area requirements by determining the amount and type of habitat that will satisfy the MVP.

The MVP is based on the concept of a population survival threshold. According to theory, there are basic minimal requirements concerning the density, structure and genetics of a population, which ensure its persistance. Determining the MVP involves examining, one-by-one, the factors that threaten a species, and given the population characteristics peculiar to that species, estimating the minimum population criteria needed to resist those threats.

The factors that threaten a species fall into two general categories (Schaffer, 1981): *deterministic* and *stochastic*. Deterministic factors act systematically, by way of some predictable mechanism. Examples are pesticide poisoning, poaching, habitat disturbance and so-on. Stochastic factors (stochastic is the technical term for "chance" or "random") arise from natural accidents. These include *natural catastrophes* such as fires, floods, landslides, droughts etc. Or, they may include less extreme *environmental variation* due to weather, competitors, parasites, predators and diseases.

Two other very important categories of stochastic factors occur due to chance population events. One is *chance demographic events*, which are accidents in the lives of individuals effecting their survival and reproduction. This in turn influences the dynamics of the population as a whole. The other category is *chance genetic events*. These lead to changes in the composition of the gene pool (i.e. the loss, gain or change in the frequency of occurrence of genes). The categories of factors that threaten species can thus be summarized as follows:

I. Deterministic factors
II. Stochastic (chance) factors

    A. Environmental uncertainty

        1. natural catastrophes
        2. environmental variation

    B. Population uncertainty

        1. chance demographic events
        2. chance genetic events.

Although deterministic factors demand strong consideration in protected areas, they are related only indirectly to size, insularity or other habitat area and population features. Alternatively, the influence of stochastic factors is inherently connected with these features. Consider, for example, the contrasting habits of the following two species. The blunt-nosed leopard lizard *Gambelis silus* occurs in limited disjunct patches of arid scrubland separated by farmland in the San Joaquin Valley of California. These patches often support fewer than 100 individuals. The closely related leopard lizard *Gambelia wislizenii* is widespread throughout the western States, in isolated habitat patches in some places, but commonly inhabitating vast stretches of undeveloped scrubland. Both lizards are relatively large, predacious and highly territorial animals occurring at very low population densities, even in optimal habitat. They are ecologically identical except for the degree to which their habitat has been reduced in size, fragmented and isolated. Not surprisingly, the blunt-nosed leopard lizard is currently endangered and the leopard lizard proper is not. However, in spite of its official protected status, the blunt-nosed leopard lizard is unlikely to recover, even if all of the locations of its currently existing populations were protected. The reasons for this should become more clear in the following discussion.

6.1. Environmental uncertainty and estimation of MVPs

Estimating the MVP requires projecting the probability of chance events from information on their past occurrences. This may typically involve as much guesswork as quantitative extrapolation of actual data. The objective is to determine how many individuals, dispersed in what pattern, over which habitats and throughout how extensive a region are necessary to preclude any reasonable likelihood of total extinction due to environmental uncertainty.

Actually environmental catastrophes are required for the survival of some species. Successional habitats are primarily created by chance disturbance. Therefore, the many species in a community which are dependent on such habitats will require protected areas which have been adequately selected to allow for natural catastrophes, or for creating them artificially (refer to Foster, 1980 and Gilbert, 1980 for specific examples; for general discussion see Frankel and Soulé, 1981).

6.2. Population uncertainty and estimation of MVPs

Unlike environmental uncertainty, the influence of population characteristics on a species' resistance to the negative effects of chance population events can be deduced with the aid of theoretical models. For the sake of brevity, only a very superficial discussion of these models and their applications can be provided here.

6.2.1. Quantitative demography and MVPs.
Life table information (age-specific birth rates, death rates, and age structure) can be used to predict the probability of extinction for populations of different sizes. The effects of both chance demographic events and environmental uncertainty can be tested using computer simulation. Using this approach (and arbitrarily defining an extinction probability of 5% over 100 years as the maximum acceptable), Schaffer (1981) estimated the MVP (based on demographic criteria only) for the grizzly bear in North American national parks.

Life table information is usually incomplete or unavailable for all but a few species. Nonetheless, theory from mathematical demography can still be applied to estimate extinction vulnerability for general life history types under specific population and environmental conditions. This is the rationale for question 4 of the target species selection procedure (5.2). (For further explanation, see discussions of "r" and "K" adapted species in any up-to-date ecology text.)

6.2.2. MVP and preserving genetic variability.
The application of genetics in determining minimum area requirements is technically complex and not yet fully developed. Some aspects can nonetheless be reduced to relatively simple criteria. What follows ia a brief discussion of one of those criteria, and how it can be applied to the estimation of MVPs.

Genetic variability plays an important role in the survival of populations. The production, maintenance and loss of genetic variability in a species is determined to a significant degree by population size and structure. Populations of small size and simple structure tend to be more susceptible to the loss of genetic variability than large, geographically dispersed and subdivided populations.

The loss of genetic variability can diminish the chances of survival of a population in two important ways. First, the reduction in genetic variability in a population may lead to *inbreeding depression*. This phenomenon, well known to animal breeders probably for centuries, includes a wide variety symptoms affecting the general viability, reproduction and survival of individuals (see Soulé and Wilcox, 1980; Frankel and Soulé, 1981).

Second, the reduction in genetic variability within and among populations comprising a species amounts to a loss of *evolutionary potential* (Franklin, 1980; Soulé, 1980). This is because genetic variability represents the "raw material" for natural selection. When genes are lost, so too are potentially adaptive traits and future evolutionary options. This includes not only long-term evolutionary chance and even speciation, but also short-term evolutionary adaptation sometimes called microevolution (Dobzhansky, 1970).

Genetic variability is rapidly lost in small populations as a result of genetic drift (random changes in gene frequencies) and inbreeding (breeding among close relatives). On the basis of experimental work and theoretical considerations, 250 is currently accepted as the approximate size threshold for maintaining genetic variability in an "ideal" population (Soulé, in press). To be "ideal", a population must meet certain criteria. Among the most important are (1) the number of reproductive individuals in both sexes is the same (1:1 sex ratio) and (2) the numbers are the same each generation. These conditions are rarely (if ever) fulfilled by natural populations. For instance, many animals are polygynous, with just the dominant males breeding. Since only the individuals that breed successfully contribute to the gene pool of the next generation, the size of a population from a genetic standpoint may be significantly less than its total number of individuals.

To account for this problem, geneticists developed the concept of *effective population size*. This is the theoretical number of individuals based on genetic considerations. A variety of ways to compute this number, usually called *effective population number* (N_e), can be found in the literature. Hartl (1981) provides a most clear discussion with accompanying formulae to calculate N_e or populations that deviate from the 1:1 sex ratio and that fluctuate in size.

The significance of the effect of the population size concept is dramatically demonstrated by the following example (also given by Hartl, 1981). The number of individuals in an isolated colony of the moth *Panaxia dominula* was estimated each year over a twelve-year period. The size of the colony averaged over 7,000 and ranged from 1,300 to 16,000. Based on the year-to-year fluctuations in size, and an estimate of the differences in reproductive success among individuals, N_e was estimated to be as low as 500.

It should be emphasized that N_e, or population size in general, is not the only criterion of importance in determining the MVP of a species, and minimum area requirements. Yet it is a key element and its application is relatively straightforward. The concept of minimum area requirements for the conservation of biological diversity involves such a broad range of complex scientific topics that this brief treatment can only provide a superficial examination of a few; and, of these, even fewer have been chosen for detailed illustration.

The application of scientific theory to the problem of minimum area requirements for protected areas and the genetic diversity they contain, is still very much in the "research and development" stage. The guidelines and suggested protocols presented in this paper must be subjected to experimentation and modification if they are to be sufficiently refined for general use. However, those involved in the selection, establishment and management of national parks and other protected areas must become actively involved in the refining process to ensure its success.

Acknowledgements

This paper was prepared for IUCN's Commission on National Parks and Protected Areas in cooperation with the United Nations Environment Programme.

The Relationship Between Protected Coastal Areas and Marine Fisheries Genetic Resources

William E. Odum
University of Virginia
Charlottesville, Virginia, USA

ABSTRACT. *The fisheries of the world appear to have reached a plateau in total annual catch between 70 and 80 million metric tons, and are unlikely to exceed 100 million tons per year in the future; between 50 and 75 percent of the commercial fish catch comes from species which utilize coastal and estuarine waters. This paper reviews the scientific evidence which indicates a strong connection between critical coastal habitats and fisheries production, discusses the need for protection of these critical habitats and reviews a few examples where protected coastal areas contribute significantly to coastal fisheries. The key to effective habitat preservation for benefit of fisheries genetic resources is to protect the complete sequence of critical habitat types encompassing the entire salinity gradient; the preservation of one type of habitat without consideration of functionally connected habitats may lead to disruptions in life-history cycles and long-term decline in fishery production.*

1. INTRODUCTION

The conventional fisheries of the world appear to have reached a plateau in total annual catch betwen 70 and 80 million metric tons (see the FAO Fisheries Statistics Yearbooks for the years 1970-80) and are not likely to exceed 100 million tons per year in the future (Ryther, 1969). There are many reasons for this apparent approach to some sort of maximum yield; these include, but are not restricted to: the establishment of 200 mile fishing zones; the increased cost of fuel; the full or over-exploitation of most traditional fisheries (e.g. the Peruvian anchovetta); and the pollution, degradation, or loss of critical coastal habitat.

The relative importance of critical habitat loss to the world fisheries catch has not been well documented. There is no doubt that serious alteration of many coastal areas has caused fisheries to decline locally. It is difficult to demonstrate conclusively whether this, in turn, has affected the world fish catch significantly. The circumstantial evidence, however, strongly suggests that this is an important factor and will become even more critical in the future as an expanding world human population generates increasing developmental pressure on coastal regions.

We know that between 50% and 75% of the world commercial fish catch comes from fish and shellfish species which utilize coastal and estuarine waters (FAO, 1980). Further, we know that most of these organisms utilize a variety of critical, shallow-water habitat types (e.g. seagrass beds, coastal marshes, mangrove swamps, mudflats, etc.) during some stage of their life history. Finally, it is increasingly obvious that much of this critical habitat is threatened with serious alteration or destruction. For example, Krishnamurthy and Jeyaseelan (1980) report that most of the mangrove swamps of India have been destroyed or altered to the extent that prawn production has been seriously reduced.

In this paper, I briefly review the scientific evidence which indicates a strong connection between critical coastal habitat and fisheries production. Second, I discuss the need for protection of this critical habitat. Finally, I review a few examples where protected coastal areas contribute significantly to coastal fisheries. Both scientific evidence and examples come largely from the American literature since I have the greatest familiarity with these sources. This basic information, however, should apply in principle to all regions of the world.

2. IMPORTANCE OF COASTAL AND ESTUARINE AREAS TO FISHERIES

The fisheries and shellfish of coastal and estuarine waters fall into two general groups: permanent residents; and non-permanent residents or visitors. Typically, the permanent residents are smaller, feed on smaller items, and may, in fact, function as prey for the visitors (Werme, 1981). The visitor group includes species which visit shallow water and estuaries largely on feeding forays (e.g. mackerel *Scombrus* spp.) and species which use the estuary for extensive periods of their life cycles (e.g. menhaden *Brevoortia* spp.). Since the permanent residents function primarily as forage (exceptions include oysters and scallops), this discussion will concentrate on the species which visit estuaries for a portion of their life cycles. It is this group of estuarine-dependent organisms which provides much of the world's commercial and sport fishery catch.

2.1. A gradient of conditions

Fundamental to an understanding of the life history cycles of the estuarine-dependent species is an appreciation of the biological needs of the organisms and the gradient of physical conditions which exist in estuaries. Typically these organisms, are spawned offshore and move into coastal waters and estuaries as postlarvae or early juveniles. Their two principal needs are food and protection from predation. As they enter the lower portion of the estuary, they encounter a gradient of conditions (Fig. 1) which ranges from near-oceanic salinities at the mouth of the estuary to freshwater at the head. Other factors such as sediment type, oxygen content of the water, and dissolved nutrients may vary along the same gradient (see Odum *et al.*, in press; Morris *et al.*, 1978).

As the postlarvae and juveniles move into the estuary, each species selects an optimal salinity regime and an optimal type of habitat (i.e. mud flats, marshes, sea grass beds, etc.). In general, there is a movement preferentially into low salinity areas first (Wagner, 1973; Chambers, 1980), although this is not the case with all species. The low salinity end of the estuary, encompassing the oligohaline and tidal freshwater zones, offers protection from many predaceous species which are unable to penetrate these regions due to an inability to osmoregulate at such low salinities.

As a result of salinity gradient selection, the juveniles of many species are preferentially scattered along the gradient of salinity (Fig. 2) over distances as great as 100 km or more. Relative position along this gradient may change daily or seasonally in response to variations in freshwater runoff, food availability, or the age of the fish. As the fishes mature, there is a general movement downstream into higher salinity regions of the estuary. For this reason, the highest numbers of postlarval and juvenile fishes are found at the low salinity end of the gradient and the highest biomass at the higher end of the gradient (Wagner, 1973). This pattern reflects the occurrence of large numbers of the very small fishes at the low salinity end and smaller numbers of older, larger juveniles at higher salinities.

2.2. Critical habitat

Coupled with the selection of a preferred salinity regime by postlarval and juvenile fishes and shellfish is the choice of suitable habitat. Each species has characteristic requirements including substrate type, water depth, water clarity, dissolved oxygen content, and type of structure (e.g., mangrove prop roots, marsh grass, or seagrass stems). This means that for each species there exists one or more types of "critical habitat" which are necessary during different stages of the life cycle.

Examples of critical habitat (Fig. 1) include, but are not restricted to: intertidal (low) marshes; high marsh tide pools; mangrove swamps; swamp and marsh creeks; mud and sand flats; passes or openings to the open ocean; open beaches; seagrass beds; macroalgae (e.g. kelp) beds; rocky shores and tide pools; and many types of coral reefs ranging from patch reefs to extensive barrier reefs. Each of these has a characteristic fish and invertebrate fauna made up of resident and visiting species; each performs an important nursery function for specific life history stages of certain species.

2.3. Examples of species use of salinity zones and critical habitat

A clearer picture of the relationship between life histories, position in the salinity gradient, and critical habitat can be gained with several examples. Weinstein *et al.*, (1980) describe the use of the estuary by two fishes, spot *Leiostomus xanthurus*, and croaker *Micropogonias undulatus*. Both fishes move up the estuary as postlarvae into low salinity or tidal freshwater. The croaker generally remain in deeper channels and small tidal rivers while the spot move into shallow water along the fringes of marshes and tidal creeks. As they grow, both species gradually move downstream into higher salinity water where they reside in seagrass beds and other vegetated habitat. Finally, as adults they migrate just beyond the mouth of the estuary to spawn, and the cycle repeats itself.

This is a common type of life history pattern in which the postlarvae and juveniles utilize a variety of low- and medium-salinity zones and move out of the estuary to spawn. In the process they may inhabit as many as 8-10 different types of critical habitat for periods of time ranging from a few hours to many months. On the east coast of the United States, organisms utilizing this life history pattern include: shrimp *Penaeus* spp.; the blue crab *Callinecthes sapidus*; the mullet *Mugil cephalus*; and the Atlantic menhaden *Brevoortia tyrannus*.

The gray snapper *Lutjanus griseus* follows a somewhat different pattern (Stark and Schroeder, 1971). As shown in Figure 3, the young are spawned on the oceanside of coral reefs. After about two weeks the postlarvae move inshore into seagrass beds where they find suitable food (small crustaceans) and protection. When the juveniles reach a length of approximately 70 mm, they move further inshore into the mangrove prop root habitat; they may move upstream into low salinity reaches or remain in relatively high salinity coastal water. As maturing adults they move back to the reef and eventually spawn. After spawning, certain adults remain on the reef and others return to the inshore mangrove prop root habitat. Not only does this species utilize several areas of critical habitat in succession, but they may move back and forth between habitat types on a diurnal basis. For example, the larger juveniles, which have moved to the mangrove prop root habitat, remain among the prop roots only during the daytime and rove through the seagrass beds at night in search of food. As a result, the prop root habitat provides protection and some food, while the grass beds supply the remainder of their food needs.

An example of an entirely different life history pattern is supplied by the striped bass *Morone saxatilis*, an anadromous species. Adult striped bass move upstream into tidal freshwater to spawn. The larvae and young juveniles remain in tidal freshwater before gradually moving downstream to higher salinities. Throughout this period they utilize a variety of habitats including submerged grass beds, marsh edges and creeks, and main river channels.

In these cases and many more, a pattern emerges of multiple habitat usage. No single community can be identified as "the critical habitat." No single salinity zone is of over-riding importance. Instead, the entire freshwater-estuarine-coastal gradient performs an important nursery function.

2.4. Correlations between critical habitat and fishery production

Because of these patterns of life history usage, certain sections of estuarine and coastal waters have far greater densities of fishes and invertebrates than other sections. For example, the shallow waters along the edges of marshes, including tidal creeks, have far more organisms present than nearby deeper water (Weinstein, 1979; Shenker and Dean, 1979; Bozeman and Dean, 1980). Similarly, mangrove swamps support large populations of fishes and invertebrates (see Odum *et al.*, 1982). Day *et al.* (in press) found that fish biomass was 6.8 to 11.5 times greater in shallow water marsh areas compared to adjacent open water.

Following this line of reasoning, it becomes apparent that regions with large expanses of critical habitat should produce greater amounts of fishery organisms than regions with little critical habitat. Consider, for example, the location of many of the world's principal fishing grounds. Commonly, these lie in close proximity to coastal areas with extensive marshes, mangrove swamps, and seagrass beds. In the Gulf of Mexico, the valuable Tortugas shrimp fishery lies adjacent to the mangrove swamps of the Everglades and the seagrass beds of Florida Bay; both areas function as nursery areas for post-larval and juvenile shrimp.

Further north, the rich finfish and shrimp fisheries of Louisianna are located near vast expanses of coastal marshes; Day *et al.* (in press) have shown that the marshes serve as nursery areas for most of the fish and invertebrates caught offshore. Sabins and Truesdale (1974) demonstrated the importance of coastal "passes" or gaps between barrier islands as routes by which these organisms migrate offshore as adults and inshore as postlarvae and juveniles.

In the same region (Louisianna and Texas), Moore *et al.* (1970) found that the greatest populations of fishery organisms occur offshore from areas of high freshwater input (creating a strong salinity gradient as shown in Figure 1) and large areas of coastal wetlands. Turner (1977) found a high correlation between shrimp yield (kg/ha) and intertidal wetland area on a world-wide basis. In the northern Gulf of Mexico, he found that yields of inshore shrimp are directly related to the area of estuarine vegetation.

To summarize, the evidence, although circumstantial, overwhelmingly supports the link between the presence of critical habitat (marshes, mangrove swamps, etc.) and high fishery production.

3. THE NEED TO PROTECT CRITICAL HABITAT

If we accept the premise that critical habitat and fishery production are intimately linked, what happens if the former is removed through some act of man? The answer, once again circumstantial, is that fishery production declines. As an example, Krishnamurthy and Jeyaseelan (1980) report that the prawn production from a partially protected Indian mangrove swamp was estimated to be 110 kg/ha/year; fish production was 150 kg/ha/year. In a nearby estuary where the mangroves were damaged or removed, prawn production was 20 kg/ha/year and fish production 100 kg/ha/year. Odum (1970) reports several cases from Florida in which sport and commercial fisheries declined after destruction or removal of mangrove forests and seagrass beds.

There are many other examples, mostly with circumstantial, *post hoc* data, which indicate that the consequences of critical habitat destruction is a decline in fishery landings. This evidence suggests that protection of critical habitat is essential to maintenance of many coastal fisheries. This is often a challenging task.

One of the great difficulties in attempting to preserve habitat such as marshes, mangroves, and seagrass beds in support of fisheries, is that so many locations and types of habitat are involved. As shown in an earlier

NATIONAL PARKS, CONSERVATION, AND DEVELOPMENT

section of this paper, most species utilize a variety of critical habitats during their life cycle; gray snapper use coral reefs, seagrass beds, and mangroves; striped bass need tidal freshwater channels and marshes along with higher salinity estuarine marshes, rivers and seagrass beds.

Proper management of striped bass may involve preservation, or at least protection, of a salinity gradient which may be in excess of 100 km in length in places such as the Potomac River. Wise management of gray snapper involves habitat many kilometres apart and at varying distances from shore. Individual pieces of critical habitat may lie in different political jurisdictions, even different countries.

4. STRATEGIES FOR PROTECTION AND PRESERVATION

Basically, there are three strategic approaches which can be followed in attempting to manage coastal habitat for fishery resources; each approach is significantly more difficult to implement than its predecessor.

The first and simplest approach is to protect the fishery organisms while they are located in critical habitat and while they exist at key life history stages. For example, in the southeastern United States, most states protect juvenile shrimp (*Penaeus* spp.) while they are within protected estuarine waters adjacent to marshes, mud flats, and mangroves. Shrimp fishing is either severely limited or totally excluded until the shrimp migrate through the passes between barrier islands and move offshore. This not only protects the shrimp while they are too small for effective marketing, but protects seagrass beds, mud flats, and other fragile habitats. Another example of this minimal approach to management is the attempt by the state of Maryland to protect adult migratory striped bass *Morone samatilis* in tidal freshwater during the critical period for spawning. Recent evidence suggests that this has resulted in much higher recruitment of juveniles and may help a long-suffering fishery to partial recovery. These are examples of a management approach which is relatively easy to implement and, may be effective in a limited way, but does not protect the habitat upon which the fishery organisms depend for food and protection.

A second approach is to protect specific types of habitat. For example, in the state of Florida, a large stretch of healthy coral reef was preserved as the John Pennecamp Coral Reef State Park. Destruction of the reef was prohibited along with underwater spear fishing; recreational diving and hook and line fishing were permitted. The result of this action was that the reef remains in a reasonably healthy state and supports a high level of recreational activity. The weakness of the plan is that nearby seagrass beds and mangrove-lined shorelines were not preserved. Since many of the reef fishes use both these habitat types as nursery and feeding areas, their populations were not totally protected.

The third and optimal approach is to protect all habitat types along the salinity gradient shown in Figure 1. This holistic or ecosystem approach has the obvious advantage of encouraging the success of all life history stages and providing a reasonably steady, long-term fishery production. From a pragmatic and political standpoint, it is often impossible to create a preserved area which encompasses such a great area. I feel that this third approach, however, should be the primary objective in the management of coastal habitat for fishery resources.

5. EXAMPLES OF HOLISTIC HABITAT PRESERVATION

The state of Florida provides several useful examples of large-scale, holistic preservation. Although the Pennecamp Coral Reef Park proved to be too restricted in size, subsequent state legislation has provided reasonably strict protection of both seagrass beds and mangrove-lined shorelines throughout the state of Florida. The Everglades National Park was established in south Florida in 1947 and currently encompasses more than 500,000 ha of land and water. Although much of this area is composed of upland plant communities, a significant portion is mangrove, seagrass bed, or coastal marsh. All of these habitat types provide nursery areas for the extensive commercial and sport fisheries which operate in contiguous coastal waters. The great strength of the Everglades National Park is that it includes almost the entire gradient from upland freshwater, through the estuary, and offshore for many kilometres. The nearby Biscayne National Monument similarly includes coastal wetlands and mangroves, seagrass and macroalgae beds, barrier islands and passes, and offshore coral reefs. This means, for example, that the gray snapper *Lutjanus griseus*, which was discussed in an earlier section, is protected (except for hook and line fishing) at all points in its life history (i.e. offshore coral reefs, seagrass beds, and mangrove prop root habitat).

Unfortunately, there are factors which cannot be totally controlled, even in a preserved area as large as the Everglades National Park. For example the watershed draining into the park extends far beyond the park boundaries. This means that activities outside the park, but within the watershed, may have serious effects within the park. For example, irrigation, water diversion, and introduction of pollutants may have negative impacts on the park, but still be beyond the control of park managers. Fish and shrimp populations within the Everglades estuary fluctuate in response to annual patterns of freshwater inflow. Without control of this inflow, it is impossible to completely protect and manage these fishery resources.

The conclusion to be drawn from the Everglades National Park is that no matter how large and seemingly complete a preserved area may appear, there will always be larger scale influences which affect resources within the park. In short, these managed areas are not closed ecosystems and will always be subject to effects from adjacent unmanaged ecosystems.

There is one interesting example in the United States of an attempt to preserve and manage almost all the land and variables affecting a coastal ecosystm. The Apalachicola River and Bay Sanctuary is a joint project by both federal and state (Florida) governments to protect a barrier island, bay, estuary, and river complex (Livingstone, 1981). The sanctuary, consisting of about 80,000 ha, was set aside for a long-term scientific and educational purposes. In addition, this estuarine complex provides between 80% to 90% of the oysters harvested in Florida and functions as a nursery area for many finfish and crabs which are caught in nearby coastal waters. This is certainly an example of holistic preservation since not only coastal habitat is preserved but also bottom-land hardwood forests and freshwater habitat for many kilometres upstream. Unfortunately, not even this sanctuary is complete, since the rivers feeding the Apalachicola estuary originate more than 500 km inland.

Large, holistic preserved areas supporting coastal fisheries are by no means restricted to the United States; a number of examples exist in other parts of the world. In almost all of these cases, a multiplicity of habitat types have been preserved, but all are subject to adverse external influences. It seems that totally holistic habitat preservation is not feasible from a pragmatic and political standpoint; however, attempts to protect and manage complete sets of critical coastal habitat can be successful and are reasonably common.

6. CONCLUSIONS

In this paper I have attempted to demonstrate the connection between different types of coastal habitat and the complex life history stages of most coastal organisms of commercial interest. I have emphasized that preservation of one type of habitat, for example a reef, without thought to functionally connected habitat such as seagrass beds or mangrove forests, may lead to disruptions in life history cycles and long-term declines in fishery production.

The key to effective habitat preservation is to protect the complete sequence of critical habitat types encompassing the entire salinity gradient. Although this is often difficult to accomplish, particularly in areas with dense human populations, there are numerous succcessful examples from many parts of the world. The one step which seems virtually impossible and impractical is to preserve such an extensive tract of land that deleterious external influences are totally excluded.

Acknowledgements

This paper has been prepared for IUCN's Commission on National Parks and Protected Areas in cooperation with the United Nations Environment Programme.

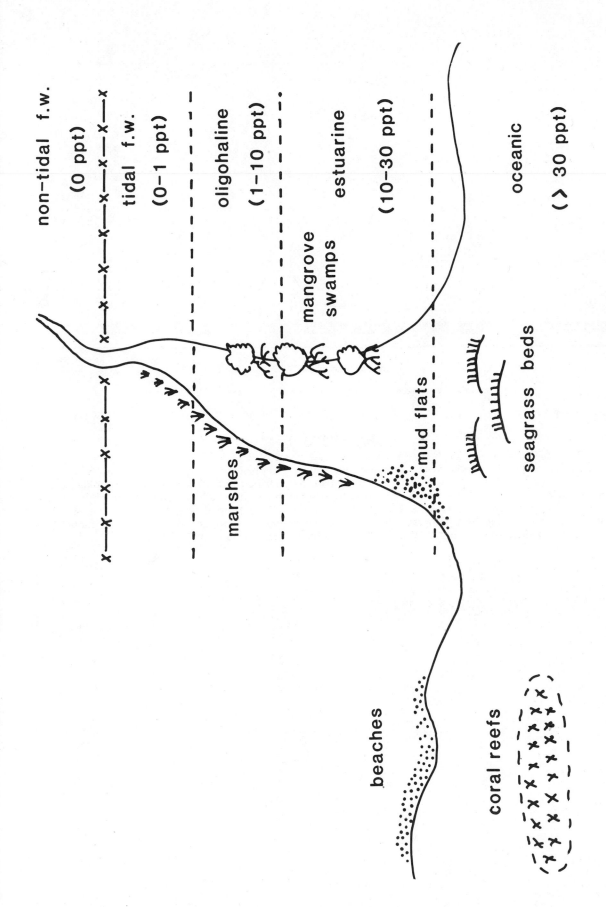

Figure 1. A schematic representation of the salinity gradient from nontidal freshwater to oceanic conditions. Salinity zones are shown in parts per thousand (ppt). Critical habitat types are depicted at characteristic locations.

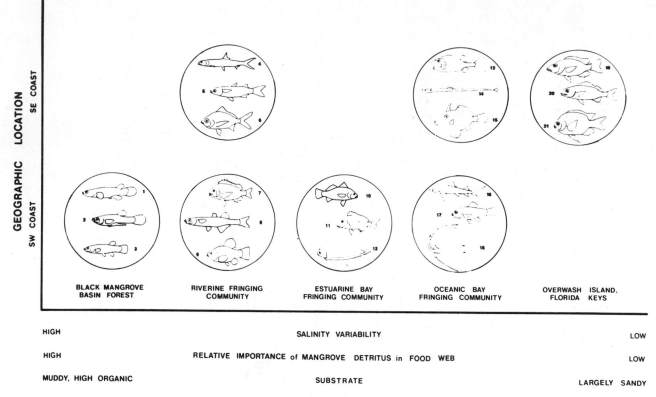

GRADIENTS

Figure 2. Gradient of mangrove-associated fish communities showing representative species from south Florida. 1 = rivulus, 2 = mosquitofish, 3 = marsh killifish, 4 = lady fish, 5 = striped mullet, 6 = yellowfin mokjarra, 7 = juvenile sheepshead, 8 = tidewater silversides, 9 = sheepshead minnow, 10 = silver perch, 11 = pigfish, 12 = blackcheek tonguefish, 13 = scrawled cowfish, 14 = fringed pipefish, 15 = fringed filefish, 16 = lemon shark, 17 = gold spotted killifish, 18 = southern stingray, 19 = juvenile schoolmaster snapper, 20 = juvenile tomtate, 21 = juvenile sergent major. Based on drawing by Carole McIvor published in Odum *et al.* (1982).

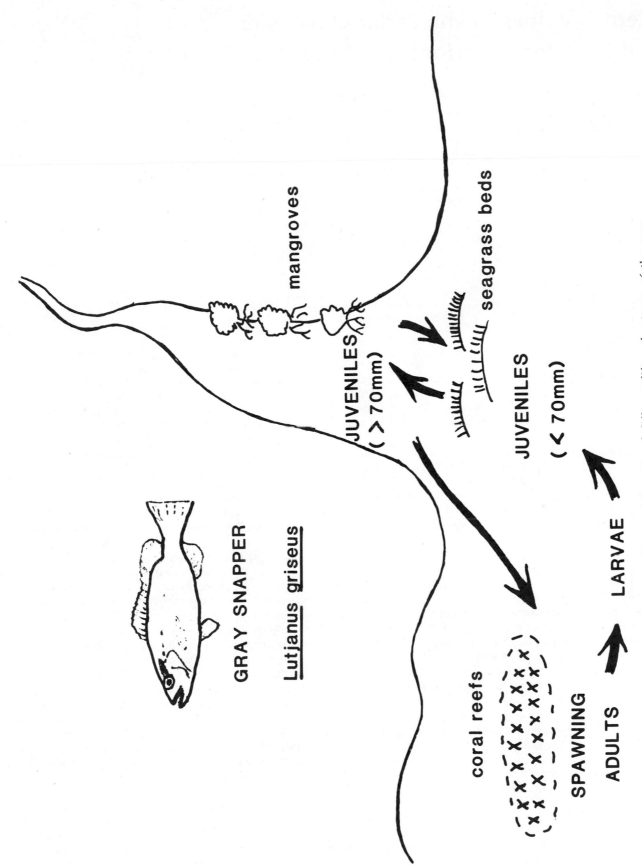

mangroves

seagrass beds

JUVENILES (>70mm)

JUVENILES (<70mm)

coral reefs

SPAWNING

ADULTS

LARVAE

GRAY SNAPPER

Lutjanus griseus

Figure 3. Schematic representation of the salinity gradient and location of different life-cycle stages of the gray snapper, _Lutjanus griseus_. Based on Stark and Schroeder (1971).

Eternal Values of the Parks Movement and the Monday Morning World

Norman Myers
Headington, Oxford, UK

ABSTRACT. *During the coming few years, we must get the parks and protected areas movement established as an accepted phenomenon in a crowded world; if we don't, the end of the century may see us with little of our parks movement left, at least in its present worldwide form. Plainly, the world is running out of space for everybody to do everything they want, but there is growing awareness that wild nature can play an appropriate part in the modern world. In order to accomplish this, protected areas must be coordinated with modern man rather than confront him; far from being considered as "set aside", a park should be viewed as being* brought into *the main arena of human affairs.*

1. INTRODUCTION

The protected area movement, like most things around us, is changing its spots very fast. In fact, faster than some of us may care to think about. During the period between Yellowstone in 1972 and our next meeting in 1992, our movement is likely to be transformed in a dozen different ways. In some observers' eyes, it may be changed beyond recognition.

During the 1980s, we shall designate a lot more protected areas; they may be the last that we shall ever designate. During the same brief phase, we shall likely lose some parks and reserves: let's keep the list as short as we can. Also during the coming few years, we must get our parks movement established as an accepted phenomenon in a crowded world: if we don't, the end of the century may see us with little of our parks movement left, at least in its present worldwide form. Who will bet on a global gathering of this Bali-scale by the time the 2002 meeting comes around?

Plainly the world is running out of space for everybody to do everything they want. This is due not only to increase in human numbers, but to increase in human aspirations—and in the second respect, the developed nations probably play as big a role as the developing nations do in the first. There is simply going to be less survival space for parks and reserves. We have only to look out at the back of our hotels here in Denpasar to get an idea of what much of the world will look like in just another couple of decades. Pressure, pressure on virtually every last corner. Where in Bali could we ever designate a new protected area, at least in the traditional sense? And will the existing reserves not face a rising clamour from land-hungry people? Big problem.

At the same time, millions of citizens around the world seem to be saying that they would like to have more parks and reserves, provided these areas truly meet people's needs. In developed nations and developing nations alike, there is growing awareness that wild nature can play a proper part in our super-modern world. Big opportunity.

Can we match the problem with the opportunity? As our Chinese colleagues would tell us, a time of crisis can be a time for breakthrough. Can we grasp the massive scope that awaits us to take some new initiatives? In short, can we measure up to the challenge that lies ahead of us--a challenge that, however demanding it may appear, should appeal to the pioneer spirit in wilderness enthusiasts?

You will note that I have spoken of "our" parks movement. How about "everybody's" park movement? We here in Bali know what it is all about, we are the converted. How about those who are still unbelievers? If tens of millions approve our cause, and want to see more parks, there are tens of millions more who don't care for us, and even want to see some parks abolished. And there are hundreds of millions who just don't give us a thought, being too preoccupied about tonight's supper. These last people may not agitate to get parks eliminated, but they may quietly go and dig them up for next season's crops. How can we make "our" parks movement into "their" parks movement? Unless we aim to bring many more people under our banner, we can hardly speak to the world through our Bali Declaration and ask all people to make common cause with us. And unless we can get a joint act together with people on every side, what future is there for anybody's parks movement?

Let us look back a moment to the Yellowstone meeting of 1972. Those of us who gathered there recall an occasion that generally proclaimed a philosophy of "the same as before, only more so." More parks along traditional lines, more protection along traditional lines, and all would be well. The guts of the approach was to insulate a series of wildland pockets from human impact.

Ten years later, we can no longer confine ourselves to that tried and trusted approach. True, there is still room for it in certain localities. But in a world where the tide of human activities is reaching out far and wide, we need to expand our erstwhile strategy with some fresh approaches. There is less and less profit in trying to establish islands in the face of the on-rushing tide—a response that becomes more Canute-like with every tick of the clock. How about trying to adapt our islands to the tide? Or even trying to adapt the tide itself to our purposes? Many protected areas are surrounded by a sea of intense human settlement. What scope is there for park people to reach out to the encircling communities, and talk about a better future for both sides?

2. PROTECTED AREAS AND MODERN MAN: CONFRONTATION RATHER THAN COORDINATION

It is that term "sides" that betrays the spirit of the situation. All too often, the park manager has been required to view his charge as an entity that is, by definition, to be protected from the disruptive impact of modern man. Human incursions are permitted only in the form of visitors who do not over-stay their welcome from wild nature.

By adopting a stance of "pristine nature versus contaminating man", policy makers for the parks movement have tended to foster an attitude in park managers and wardens that has not always helped the image of parks in the modern world. According to this attitude, the human communities that live beyond park borders represent a world that is wholly apart from the world within the borders. Not surprisingly, then, these human communities are likely to be indifferent to parks' well-being at best—and at worst, they can even be hostile.

In certain circumstances, park wardens have even been encouraged to view the human throngs outside their gates as somehow antagonistic: hence the tradition in several sectors of the world, and particularly in Africa, to recruit former military persons as park wardens, who thereupon administer their parks as a kind of "campaign" to be waged against an "enemy". As an extreme expression of this management style, many one-time military officers like to organize their rangers as a paramilitary force that primarily pursues poachers in jeeps and helicopters. In January 1981, my wife and I were honoured to attend the Serengeti-Ngorongoro Diamond Jubilee celebrations in northern Tanzania. Impressed as we have been by the Tanzanians' extraordinary record in wildlife conservation, we hardly expected to find that the most prominent and protracted part of the ceremonies would be a goose-stepping parade by rifle-toting rangers. A curious and revealing incident, when Tanzania can offer so many more positive expressions of its park management techniques.

Let us note, moreover, that in certain instances the people living outside the park are indeed opposed to what the park stands for. This adversarial stance arises not only in the developing nations, with their problems of land shortages. It arises also in developed nations, as witness the enduring conflict between Wyoming ranchers and Yellowstone wardens over elk that migrate outside the park and compete with domestic livestock for rangeland grazing; and as witness the current protests by American stock raisers in the environs of several other parks, who want to take up arms against stock-raiding predators that stray out of parks. These bad-blood relationships derive not only from the actual economic costs imposed by a park's existence (losses that could be compensated by park authorities); they sometimes derive from a history of less-than-sensitive attitudes on the part of park managers vis-a-vis the citizenry who inhabit the hinterlands of parks.

Furthermore, the theme of "nature unsullied by man" as a philosophy to underpin the parks movement has promoted a spirit that speaks of "setting aside" a protected area. For sure, protection of wild nature amounts to a special form of land use, and it deserves to be categorized in some way that acknowledges its unique character. But protection of wild nature remains a *use* of land, and a park should not be viewed as somehow detached from the mainstream of everyday life that seeks to put all land on earth to one use or another. Whatever exceptional values are enshrined in a park, and however much these values may contrast with an overly-materialist world outside, a park is not thereby divorced from the way the world normally works. Nor should it be accorded super-special safeguards as if it hovers somewhere between things earthly and things celestial. Far from being considered as "set aside", a park should be viewed as being *brought into* the main arena of human affairs.

This is not a matter of semantics. In this writer's experience across most major regions of the world, no trifling damage has been done to the parks movement through the phrase "setting aside." It looks in the wrong direction altogether, and it has helped to foster the spirit of "us", i.e. the parks supporters, versus "them", i.e. the rest. However appropriate this approach may have been in the early days of the parks movement, when there was need to emphasize the revolutionary nature of designating a patch of wildland as no longer available to conventional forms of land use, it nevertheless remained a form of land use, though an unconventional one. All forms of land use, and especially their administrators, need to maintain good relations with their neighbours. If the neighbours are treated as antagonists, they may start to behave as antagonists.

Something similar applies to the term "protected area" itself. We know what we are protecting an area from (even though the point may not be so valid as is sometimes supposed). But are we so sure what we are protecting the area *for*? And if we are sure, who are the people on whose behalf we are protecting the park? Just the park enthusiasts, who need no persuading of the cause, and who are less than a majority of human populations in those nations of the world where park needs are greatest, viz. the third world nations? If third worlders are not persuaded of the virtues of protected areas, and when they seek for some patch of land where they can sink a digging hoe, they may cast their eyes upon park territories. What if, in traditional style, they tend to view parks as alien enclaves established in their midst?

Parks may be for wild creatures and intact ecosystems and enduring nature. But they are also for people. To underscore the central message: if parks aren't for people, some of them may cease to be parks at all.

In sum, then, protected areas need to shed their air of being something exotic, detached from everyday life. For all that they enshrine special values, even spiritual values in a materialistic world, and for all that they should be specially esteemed for their exceptional values, they also deserve to be perceived as an integral part of the Monday morning world. By extension, they need to be operated along work-a-day lines, with due regard for their "human dimensions".

3. THE SCIENTIST'S VIEW OF PROTECTED AREAS

So much for an expansion of the philosophical approach for the parks movement. Let us now consider how far this fresh approach would match up with the scientist's view of a protected area.

It turns out that the approach makes sound ecological sense. Whatever may have been desired for them, parks can never be "islands." The natural world does not function that way. Across the park's boundary, as across its ecosystem frontier, there are all manner of dynamic fluxes. A rain storm, for instance, takes no more notice of any delimitation than does a flock of birds, or a wild fire, or a herd of wildebeest, or a swarm

of locusts, or a pandemic disease, or a group of caribou (or a gang of poachers). In fact, when we draw a line on a map and declare that within that line is a park, we make a gross intrusion on the landscape: we try to demarcate two separated entities in nature's seamless web of affairs. And let us remember, moreover, that the concept of an ecosystem is a human artifact, and a very crude representation of what the real world is like.

In a scientific sense, then, it is a mistake to suppose that a protected area can be isolated, through park manager's fiat, from its hinterland. Indeed there are various ways in which the hinterland actually supports the protected area. Weather and climate are obvious examples: a protected area needs rain supplies that derive from its surrounding region. Less obviously but hardly less pertinently, a protected area depends on its environs for other supplies of water, in the form of rivers. In Kenya, the Tsavo Park, set in dry bush country, needs all the river flow it can get. But due to over-intensive cultivation in the hinterland, one of the main feeder rivers for the park has become so silted that it dries up for many months of the year (local people are not readily persuaded to look out for Tsavo's welfare, having been told for years that this *national* park could be no object of *local* concern). To this extent, a protected area, like most other tracts of land on earth, represents an exercise in human ecology. However much the parks movement may once have proclaimed otherwise, very few protected areas constitute pristine nature. Their wildlife assemblages, their vegetation patterns, their geophysical landscapes have often become what they are by virtue of man's intervention.

It is ironic that these considerations apply especially in the tropical Third World. Here the land-hungry pressures are greatest, and the park movement is weakest— even though there is often much more of natural value to be safeguarded in the tropics (in terms of species totals, for instance) than in the rest of the world put together. Tropical ecosystems tend to be more dynamic than those elsewhere, and there is greater interplay across their borders. The Grand Canyon and Yosemite can be reasonably well protected by putting a fence around their perimeters, whether on the ground or in people's minds; their principal features, notably the great gorge and El Capitan cliff, are not prone to wander off in search of seasonal grazing. All the more, then, is there need for protected areas in the tropics to be managed in such a way that their needs can mesh with the needs of local people—these people being, for the most part, subsistence peasants who are running short of living space.

4. PROTECTED AREAS AS INTEGRALLY LOCAL ENTITIES

Throughout this appraisal of parks in the late twentieth century, a single conclusion keeps emerging, albeit from different premises. A protected area is an integrally local

NATIONAL PARKS, CONSERVATION, AND DEVELOPMENT

entity. It may be called a national park, and receive legal designation as such, but in all practical senses—ecological, biological, economic, social—it is local factors that determine the "real life" status of the protected area. For all that this observation applies right around the world, it is a key factor in the Third World regions of the tropics.

If, then, local people are intimately involved in a protected area's welfare from the start, and if they can sometimes prove the main determinant in its survival, how can we recruit them in support of our cause? Answer: enable the park to respond to their needs—as they perceive their needs. Again, it is in Third World countries that this consideration is especially crucial. The basic need of many Third Worlders are cash in the pocket and food in the stomach. There is little mileage in lecturing them, however persuasively, about the aesthetic and ethical values of protected areas. Whatever pride a local person may taken in the plaque on a park entrance gate, proclaiming that the park helps to safeguard humankind's great natural heritage, he may also respond that he cannot eat a plaque—and in any case, when is humankind going to do much for him in return?

5. PROTECTED AREAS AND MODERN MAN: COORDINATION RATHER THAN CONFRONTATION

One main way for a protected area to meet local communities' wants, especially in the Third World is, through some form of exploitation of the protected areas' resources. Various forms of exploitation are available. The most acceptable to the parks movement is probably tourism, insofar as it tends to be a non-consumptive form of exploitation. But consumptive forms of exploitation also merit consideration. They can include such activities as relief-season grazing for domestic livestock, commercial fisheries in lakes and dams, even some subsistence hunting. While this writer served as Parks and Wildlife Officer for Africa under the United Nations, he found all these consumptive forms of exploitation practised in one park or another, albeit as covertly as the park managers could arrange them—and these parks enjoyed much better relations with local human communities than did those parks that exemplify a strict "hands off" approach. Let us note, moreover, that consumptive types of exploitation can constitute, through proper regulation, sustainable forms of exploitation, and far from running foul of protected area's long-term interests, they can help to promote its very survival.

True, some park managers will prefer not to countenance exploitation within a protected area itself. But they can still foster it within a "border zone" encircling the protected area. Regrettably, and to the great detriment of the park movement, the border zone strategy has not been fostered with a fraction of the enthusiasm it merits. All too often, park managers have felt more comfortable with the black-and-white ideal of absolute preservationist values holding sway on one side of the line, and alien human activities going their divergent way on the other side of the line. For sure, a multiple-use approach is "messy", insofar as it deals with various shades of grey. But then nature does not operate in black-and-white style. There is nothing so messy as nature, especially the complex nature of the tropics.

While exploitation of a protected area's resources constitutes a sound way for a local community to derive obvious benefits from a protected area, we cannot review the spectrum of exploitation options available, since the scope of this paper is too short. Rather let us focus on the kinds of "cooperative endeavours" that a park manager might envisage with regard to the communities in his area's environs. We could consider an entire "shopping list" of possibilities. But that would require us to look at detailed tactics, and here we must stick with strategy.

Let us sum it up this way. The park manager may well find that he needs to spend as much time dealing with the human communities outside his borders as with the wildland communities inside. He will need to know, for example, the size of these human communities, how fast they are growing, and how large they will become in another 10, 30 and 50 years. He will need to inform himself about their economic status and their future outlook, their land-use traditions, their agricultural lifestyles, their educational hopes, their health programmes, their employment prospects. Above all, he should be in tune with their political aspirations. He should never have to ask local people how they view the park, or rather "their" park, since he should know already. Indeed he should be on network with local people as much as with park headquarters in his country's capital city, perhaps hundreds of kilometres away, and certainly many horizons away in terms of perceptions; and he should meet at least as much with local leaders as with his Parks Director. To do his job he will need to be not only a wildlife scientist and a sound administrator, but he will have to be outstanding at public relations. In fact, he must be something of a salesman. Local people will not buy his message unless he puts it across strongly and surely.

Much of this will mean a departure from the established workstyle of many park managers. The person who tries out this expanded approach will, let us hope, enhance his career. In addition, he should eventually find that he has reduced the chances that the park manager of the 21st century will become a threatened species. When the earth is trying to support twice as many people as now, which is projected to occur within the lifetime of many a park manager starting out on his job today, will there be physical space and community acceptance for protected areas as one of the best human uses we can make of wildlands?

This paper opened by asking whether we shall measure up to the new challenges that await us down the road. Those who wish to speculate on their capacity to tackle the task might consider how they would perform if they were to justify the establishment of a park in the middle of one of the most densely populated localities on earth, the island of Bali. As we look out from our hotel windows, let us ponder on what we would say if we were to make the case to a leading official of the island—or to one of the hotel staffers. Perhaps we would have a pretty good idea of what to say to him. Are we so sure we would know what he would say to us?

Acknowledgements

This paper was prepared for IUCN's Commission on National Parks and Protected Areas in cooperation with the United Nations Environment Programme.

Protecting Wild Genetic Resources for the Future:
The Need for a World Treaty

Cyrille de Klemm
Paris, France

ABSTRACT. *This paper contains an analysis of some of the deficiencies of present treaties dealing with the establishment of protected areas and proposes a world treaty on the conservation of genetic resources of wild species. Details of the proposed legislation are also provided.*

1. INTRODUCTION

It is becoming increasingly evident that as many as one million species may become extinct by the end of this century, and probably countless others thereafter, if no conservation measures are taken in time to stop this irreparable damage. Thus, at a time when remarkable scientific breakthroughs are made in the fields of molecular biology and genetic engineering, the very raw material on which these technologies are based is undergoing an accelerated impoverishment. As a result, future scientific advances, and, as a consequence, future human well-being are being gradually jeopardized.

The realization of the magnitude of the threat is, however, fairly recent. Not long ago, conservationists were mainly concerned with the survival of higher vertebrate species such as mammals and birds, at the most several hundred species. Now tens of thousands of plants and invertebrates are increasingly becoming threatened, mainly through the destruction of their habitats. Moreover, as the destruction of the natural environment accelerates, it becomes more and more obvious that not only should we try to conserve as many species as possible, but that, within each species, the greatest possible degree of genetic variability should be preserved as well, as a safeguard against inbreeding and to provide a broad genetic base for future adaptation to changing conditions, including use by man.

One of the three objectives of the World Conservation Strategy is the preservation of genetic diversity. One way to conserve species is by controlling their overexploitation by means of restrictions on the taking of and trade in protected animals and plants and their products. Since, however, the major threat to the survival of species is the destruction of natural areas, it is clear that the most effective conservation measures consist in the protection of habitats through establishing protected areas for *in situ* preservation. The *in situ* preservation of wild genetic resources, by definition, can be carried out *only* in nature.

The most important scientific justification for protected areas, namely the conservation of genetic resources, is probably the least defendable from a strictly economic point of view because:

(a) economic benefits derived from the use of these resources are only potential whereas immediate development measures for agriculture, forestry and other purposes bring in rapid returns; and

(b) even if some genetic resources could be put to an immediate and highly profitable use, unless they are directly exploited by their country of origin, under the present legal regime of these resources, that country would not be entitled to any share of the benefits thus obtained. As an example, the newly discovered Mexican species of perennial maize may prove of enormous economic value, yet Mexico will get very little if any of the resulting profits.

The most important justifications for protected areas from the point of view of development, such as watershed protection, erosion control, or regulation of water flow, do not necessarily require the protection of genetic resources. As an example, a man-made forest may protect a water-catchment area almost as effectively as a natural forest. Similarly, the destruction of many species in a natural forest (e.g., birds or orchids) will in no obvious way affect its capability to regulate the water flow.

Similarly, it would seem that the preservation of genetic resources would be of little importance for most visitors to protected areas for tourism or recreation; and the areas containing the largest number of species, as tropical rain forests, do not always lend themselves easily to mass tourism especially since animals which live in them may be particularly difficult to observe.

Thus, the most important scientific arguments for the establishment of protected areas have little apparent immediate economic justification, whereas many of the most important arguments with regard to economic development leave out genetic resources.

In view of the perceived low economic profitability of many protected areas it is all the more remarkable that many states have not hesitated to set aside considerable areas of wild lands for conservation. On the other hand it is not surprising that many of the existing protected areas, especially the larger ones, have been established on land which is unsuitable for agricultural development. But where conflicts between conservation and the development of agriculture or forestry arise, such as in tropical rain forests, protected areas are fewer and the creation of new ones more difficult.

Since, in the last analysis, the threat to protected areas is the result of government actions or inaction, the preservation of these areas requires strong legislation and enforcement measures. Without proper economic incentives and justifications, however, this is not easy to achieve. Thus, in spite of the considerable progress achieved in the past years toward the establishment of natural areas for protection, the threat to an increasing number of species becomes more and more manifest as large areas of tropical rain forests and other ecosystems are converted to agricultural or other uses.

The inadequacy of present conservation measures to deal with the situation and the reluctance of governments to take more stringent measures are probably due to a variety of causes. All these causes can, however, be grouped under two major headings: lack of awareness of the importance of the problem; and lack of adequate economic incentives to take the necessary conservation measures. As a result there is also a lack of institutional capacity to manage.

A possible means to increase awareness of governments and decision makers of the importance of wild genetic resources and of the seriousness of the present threats to these resources could be the adoption and broad dissemination of a statement or manifesto signed by the leading scientists of the world, including as many Nobel Prize-winners as possible. Such a statement should be considered as the expression of the consciousness of the scientific community and as a warning of the foreseeable consequences of present practices if they are allowed to continue.

Treaties also can contribute to better awareness of the importance of the problem. They also provide for a commitment on the part of state parties to adopt certain conservation measures and for that reason may constitute a powerful legal weapon in the hands of governments to promote the implementation of such measures in the face of opposition on the part of economic interests. On the other hand, as no financial incentives are provided on an international basis for the conservation of genetic resources, short-term economic interests will often continue to prevail over the long term benefits of conservation.

This paper proposes to review briefly existing treaties dealing with the conservation of wild species, especially as they relate to the establishment of protected areas, to point out certain of their deficiencies and to propose a world treaty on the conservation of genetic resources together with financial incentives to assist in the effectiveness of that treaty.

2. PRESENT TREATIES

Since states exercise their sovereign rights over all natural resources on their territory, they are free to exploit or to destroy the habitat of any species even to the point of causing its extinction. Restrictions to these rights can only be imposed by the conclusion of treaties, i.e. by voluntary contractual agreements.

Treaties providing for the establishment of protected areas have generally been concluded on a regional basis. These are the Convention on Nature Protection and Wildlife Preservation in the Western Hemisphere (Washington 1940), the African Convention on the Conservation of Nature and Natural Resources (Algiers, 1968) which replaces the Convention relative to the Preservation of Flora and Fauna in their Natural State (London, 1933), and the Convention on the Conservaton of European Wildlife and Natural Habitats (Bern, 1979). The latter, however, is mainly devoted to the conservation of species and their habitats. These three treaties are now in force. Other regional agreements include the Agreed Measures for the Conservation of Antarctic Flora and Fauna (Brussels, 1964), the Convention on the Conservation of Nature in the South Pacific (Apia, 1976) and the newly-concluded protocol to the Barcelona Convention concerning Mediterranean Specially Protected Areas (Geneva, 1982). The latter two conventions are not yet in force. In addition, several bilateral or multilateral treaties relating to certain species or groups of species, such as migratory birds, provide for the establishment of protected areas.

At the world level, the Convention on Wetlands of International Importance especially as Waterfowl Habitat (Ramsar, 1971) and the World Heritage Convention (Paris, 1972) have been concluded to safeguard certain areas of particular value and international importance.

Both these conventions are in force. A third global agreement on the conservation of species, the Convention on the Conservation of Migratory Species of Wild Animals (Bonn, 1979), which is not yet in force, refers to the conservation of the habitats of the species listed in its appendices. Finally, reference should also be made to the new Convention on the Law of the Sea. Article 194.5 of that treaty contains a very important provision which makes it an obligation for parties to take measures "to protect and preserve rare or fragile ecosystems as well as the habitat of depleted, threatened or endangered species and other forms of marine life."

Several of the regional seas programmes developed by UNEP have already taken up this obligation even though the new Law of the Sea Treaty is not yet in force. This could lead to the conclusion of a number of specific protocols on the subject of marine protected areas in different regional seas along the lines of the one which has already been signed for the Mediterranean.

In addition to treaties, two international organizations, Unesco and the Council of Europe, have been active in developing international networks of protected areas which, although not founded on an international obligation, enjoy nonetheless a considerable degree of official recognition since they have been established by the governing bodies of these organizations.

The Biosphere Reserves network has been created by Unesco under Project 8 of the Man and Biosphere Programme. The objective of biosphere reserves is the preservation of areas which are representative of all the biogeographical provinces of the world for long-term conservation, monitoring and research. Although it is understood by Unesco that biosphere reserves must have adequate long-term legal protection, this is not a formal requirement and standards of protection vary considerably. In addition, under this Programme a state cannot be prevented from designating inadequate areas or required to remove such areas from the network.

The Council of Europe decided in 1979 to create a European Network of Biogenetic Reserves covering all types of European natural or semi-natural habitats as well as the critical habitats of endangered species. Specialized working groups first determine which are the sites, for each type of ecosystem, which are of truly European importance. Recommendations are then made to member states to designate these sites for the network. Inadequately protected sites may be refused or, if already included, may be excluded from the network.

This paper does not purport to make an analysis of the contents, nor an appraisal of the effectiveness of the conservation treaties listed above. It may, however, be of some value to endeavour to present a few conclusions on some aspects which appear to be of particular importance.

- The regional approach to conservation treaties has been followed because there appeared to be a general consensus among the states of certain regions to conclude them. In principle, the chances of effective implementation are greater when such a consensus exists. On the other hand, this regional approach has resulted in large gaps in geographic coverage, such as Asia, and in considerable differences in the definitions of protected areas, as well as in the content of the conservation obligations of the parties.

- Ideally, there should be a commitment on the part of parties to conservation treaties to conserve certain particular areas of major importance which would be listed in the treaty itself or in an annex. The only agreement which provides for such a commitment is the "Agreed measures for the Conservation of Antarctic Fauna and Flora." As regards the two other conventions which provide for a list of protected areas, the Wetlands Convention and the World Heritage Convention (this also applies to the Biosphere Reserves Network and the European Network of Biogenetic Reserves), states remain free to propose any site they so wish and to withdraw any site from the network when they so wish.

- Enforcement of conservation treaties is particularly difficult. Most treaties, like contracts in private law, are based on reciprocal obligations. As a result, if one of the parties does not comply with the terms of a treaty, the other may retaliate by not discharging their own obligations. In a conservation treaty, however, retaliation is meaningless and self-defeating. Thus, conservation treaties constitute little more than a sum of unilateral commitments the non-performance of which cannot be sanctioned.

- This basic weakness of conservation conventions is compounded by the fact that few of the existing treaties provide for an adequate institutional machinery—a secretariat and a budget. Yet, without such institutions conventions cannot be effectively implemented. An important exception is the World Heritage Convention, which provides for the establishment and financing of a World Heritage Fund and which has a Secretariat provided by Unesco. Even then, however, funds available are far from being sufficient to meet the needs. The only other exception is the European Convention, whose Secretariat is provided by the Council of Europe. As this Convention has only come into force in 1982, it is obviously too early to pass a judgement on the adequacy of the financial means made available to its Secretariat. In view, however, of the present trend toward budgetary restrictions, it is to be expected that finances will, here again, fall short of the needs.

- Under international conventions states seem to be increasingly reluctant to *commit* themselves to establish protected areas. This clearly appears from an analysis of the conventions concluded in the past 10 or 15 years. The obligation to protect wetlands under the Ramsar Convention is so weak that it can hardly be considered as an obligation. The Apia Convention only requires from parties that they "encourage" the creation of protected areas and allows parties, albeit "after the fullest examination," to alter the boundaries of national parks and to authorize exploitation for commercial profit. As to national reserves, the Apia Convention provides that they will remain inviolate but only "as far as practicable." The Bern Convention does not even provide for the establishment of protected areas but merely requires from parties to protect the habitat of the species listed in the Appendices. Finally, the diplomatic conference which adopted the Migratory Species Convention did not accept in the final text any reference to an obligation to create protected areas. References to such an obligation which appeared in an earlier draft were, therefore, deleted.

3. A WORLD TREATY

If the survival of wild species and the maintenance of the genetic resources they contain is a matter of world importance and concern because of their considerable potential value for mankind, no other instrument than a World Treaty will be able to provide a universal recognition of that value as well as the rules that are required to ensure that these resources are available to all nations, that they are adequately safeguarded and that states are compensated for the conservation measures they will be obligated to take.

The idea of a World Treaty on the conservaton of species and ecosystems is not new. It was launched at an international conference in Bern in 1913 and later at the Lake Success Conference in 1949. These attempts, however, remained unsuccessful, possibly because it was felt that conservation conventions would be easier to negotiate and would have a better chance to succeed if they dealt with specific matters, such as trade, wetlands and migratory species or if they related to particular geographic areas.

In view, however, of the present trend towards an ever-increasing rate in the extinction of species, the question arises as to whether the time has come to make a new attempt at the conclusion of a world treaty on the conservation of the world's genetic resources. The basis for such a treaty lies in Principle 2 adopted by the United Nations Conference on the Human Environment (Stockholm, 1972). This principle reads:

"The natural resources of the earth including the air, water, land, flora and fauna and especially representative samples of natural ecosystems must be safeguarded for the benefit of present and future generations through careful planning and management as appropriate."

In addition, Recommendation 38 adopted by that same conference recommends that, "Governments take steps to set aside areas representing ecosystems of international significance for protection under international agreement" and Recommendation 39 proposes that Governments ". . . . agree to an international programme to preserve the world's genetic resources." The first of these two recommendations was never implemented and the second has only been applied to the conservation of cultivated or domesticated races or varieties.

In view of the apparent reluctance of states to commit themselves to a convention on the conservation of natural areas, it would seem preferable to consider the conclusion of a treaty whereby parties would accept the obligation to achieve a certain result, namely the conservation of species and genetic resources, and which would retain a certain degree of flexibility with regard to the means to be employed to reach that objective. Thus, certain states could establish networks of national parks or reserves in the classical sense of these terms, while others might prefer to resort to physical planning techniques or to various forms of incentives or disincentives. In practice a combination of several methods will probably be the most effective, but the degree to which the various conservation instruments available should be used would naturally vary from country to country.

If a new world treaty on the conservation of genetic resources is to succeed, it would seem that some of the basic weaknessess of existing treaties will have to be eliminated. This is particularly true of the absence of true reciprocal obligations and of the lack of adequate machinery and financial means. An essential step towards this objective should be a thorough reappraisal of the present legal regime of species and genetic resources.

Species, as distinct from the individuals which compose them, are scientific abstractions which have no existence in law, no economic value and no owners. The consequence of this is that genetic resources, in other words, all the processes derived from genes which characterize species, are free goods for anyone to use.

But just like industrial processes are used to manufacture industrial products, genetic processes can be used for the production of a variety of goods ranging from new crops to pharmaceutical substances or fuel. Industrial processes have a value and can be owned and patented. So could genetic processes. The failure of legal systems to recognize this possibility is probably the basic reason for the lack of incentives to conserve species.

Indeed, species, that is to say, the full range of the genetic potential embodied in their genes, should be considered as natural productive units, as capital goods, as unique, non-renewable resources. As such, species should be the subject of a legal regime which would be quite different from the one applicable to their individual members.

So far, no legal system has recognized that species

as such have an economic value, nor does it seem that economists have ascribed a value to any particular species. It stands to reason, however, that because of the considerable potential or actual value of some of the processes which are actuated by genes, the value of species may sometimes be very high. A new treaty should, therefore, recognize, as a matter of principle, that species do have a value. The actual calculation of that value will have to be performed by economists with the assistance of biologists. For species which, for the time being, have no anticipated potential value, arbitrary values could be ascribed.

The recognition of the fact that species have an economic value will certainly give rise to claims of ownership and probably to disputes. In view, however, of the universal importance of species for mankind, it would seem that a world treaty should vest the ownership of species in the community of nations. This would enable all states to partake in the benefits accruing from the use of wild genetic resources and would eliminate the risk of seeing certain countries establishing monopolies on the use of these resources when they derive from species of which they are range states. In addition, disputes on ownership would thereby be prevented.

The adoption of such a rule would have three important consequences:

(a) Individual states, while continuing to exercise their jurisdiction over individual members of species on their territory, which they would continue to exploit as appropriate, would nonetheless be under the obligation to maintain sufficient populations of these species to preserve their gene pools. Indeed, they would have a duty of stewardship towards the species under their jurisdiction and that duty should be embodied in the treaty.
(b) Genetic resources of all wild species should be accessible to all nations for research, development or propagation. No State, therefore, should be entitled to deny the use of these resources to any other State.
(c) Equally, there should be an obligation on the part of users of wild genetic resources to pay royalties to the owner of the resources, that is to say, to the world community. The sums thus collected would be used to compensate States that have taken conservation measures to protect species on their territory, to assist in financing conservation measures, and to contribute to the development of these states.

A world organization would have to be set up whose main functions would be to collect royalties and to allocate the sums thus received to member States. Other important functions could include the provision of scientific and technical advice and assistance to member States for the identification of species and ecosystems to be preserved as a matter of priority and for the taking of measures to ensure their conservation, including the establishment and management of protected areas.

If such a treaty were to be concluded, it would, for the first time in a conservation treaty, provide for reciprocal obligations. Indeed, if a party did not discharge its obligations, in particular its duty to preserve the species on its territory, the other parties would have the possibility of retaliating by suspending payments to that state.

Futhermore, the operation of the organization, including, if required, the provision of technical assistance to parties, could be financed by using a portion of the dividends paid in royalties, thus solving the financial problems that have been plaguing other conservation treaties.

It may now be of interest to examine how the system would function in respect of the establishment and maintenance of protected areas, which in most countries will probably remain the major instrument for the conservation of genetic diversity.

The very fact that States would be receiving financial and technical assistance as compensation for the establishment of natural areas will certainly make it easier for them to accept certain constraints. Two precedents demonstrate, indeed, that when States obtain certain advantages from a conservation institution, whether financial or in the form of prestige, they are better prepared to comply with the rules that govern that institution. The first of these examples is the World Heritage Convention, where areas proposed by parties for inclusion on the World Heritage List may be refused by the World Heritage Committee if they are not considered to be of outstanding universal value or if their conservation status is considered inadequate. The second example is the European Diploma which is awarded, at the request of a member State of the Council of Europe, to protected areas of international value which are adequately protected. The award procedure comprises an on-the-spot appraisal of the area concerned. Furthermore, if it appears, after the award has been made, that protection has become inadequate, the diploma may be withdrawn.

It may not, however, be necessary to include in the treaty detailed provisions relating to the identification, selection, establishment, protection and management of protected areas since this may be best left to internal procedures which can be developed subsequently by the governing body of the organization. There should be, nonetheless, a requirement to provide for an obligation to set up protected areas as an important means to achieve the objective of the treaty: the conservation of genetic resources.

Ideally the system should provide, either in the convention itself or in the implementation procedure to be developed after it has come into force, for the following obligations or institutions:

• a system of periodic reviews of the conservation status of genetic resources on the territory of each party (as a precedent, OECD has carried out environmental reviews of certain of its member countries).

- The development of a world inventory of areas worthy of protection because of their international importance. This must obviously be an international task because individual countries lack elements of comparison to determine the value of natural areas on their territory. This appears clearly from the work of the Council of Europe on the identification of areas for the European Network of Biogenetic Reserves.
- The selection of areas for priority conservation and the development of selection criteria.
- A procedure whereby the governing body of the organization could recommend to member States to establish protected areas in the areas thus selected or to safeguard these areas by other measures. States would, of course, remain free not to accept the recommendation if they so choose.
- The right for the governing body to carry out on-the-spot appraisals of protected areas established under the convention, to make recommendations to parties with a view to to improving the protection and management of such areas, and to suspend payments in case of inadequate protection.
- The provision of technical and financial assistance in such fields as research, legal drafting, management, training and all other matters relating to the establishment and management of a network of protected areas.

It is obvious, however, that the conservation of species, and as a result of genetic diversity, requires an integrated approach. The establishment of protected areas will, therefore, often have to be associated to other measures such as restrictions on the taking of and trade in certain species and the development and implementation of appropriate planning measures designed to ensure that there will remain, outside statutory protected areas, enough natural or semi-natural habitats to provide shelter to a variety of wildlife. This is of particular importance since protected areas, if entirely surrounded by developed land, will tend to become ecological islands and will soon become genetically depleted.

It is obvious that each individual country will develop its own approach to planning on the basis of its constitutional and legal system, its customs and traditions and its economic and social requirements. It is not, therefore, possible in a treaty to establish any hard and fast rule with regard to the planning measures that can be taken to ensure the conservation of natural areas and species. On the other hand, a general obligation relating to the necessity of developing appropriate planning legislation and institutions, to be followed by guidance and assistance on the part of the organization, would certainly provide a considerable impetus to conservation.

NATIONAL PARKS, CONSERVATION, AND DEVELOPMENT

The Relationship Between Protected Areas and Indigenous Peoples

Raymond F. Dasmann
University of California
Santa Cruz, California, USA

ABSTRACT. *"Wilderness"—natural areas untouched by man—has always been rare, but only recently have people started drawing lines on maps and preventing people from using resources they have traditionally exploited. But without the support local people, the future of any protected area is insecure, since in their search for the means of their own survival, the temptation to exploit reserved resources may be irresistable. Such support should not be difficult to obtain, provided the proper approach is used; but nature conservation is not to be accomplished only by the establishing of specially protected natural areas—it must be practiced in all places at all times. Guidelines on how to provide for long-term positive interactions between local people and the natural environment are provided.*

1. INTRODUCTION

Perhaps the most difficult problem faced today in our efforts to accomplish conservation of nature is the inability of people to recognize and comprehend the rates at which the world is changing. For as long as people have been on earth there have always been wild areas—the land across the river, the other of the mountain, the frontier. Throughout the human story there has been a backdrop of wilderness before which the acts of civilization were played. There seemed to be always more lands, more timber, more pastures, more wild animals to give substance to the myth of inexhaustible resources.

In the United States, even after most of the country had been settled by Europeans, there were still areas that seemed untamed—wild mountains, southern swamps, deserts. But beyond these were the more magic places, names to excite the adventurous spirits of young people—Africa, the Arctic, the Himalayas, th Amazon,

the really wildest lands. Americans still want to believe that those places are still remote and wild, just as they want to believe that there are "Pacific paradises" that they have not yet spoiled. They are encouraged in this myth by television, with its never-ending wild animal series which hover near "prime viewing time" and occasionally even invade it.

Unfortunately, in those "magic places" for Americans, the people who have always lived there believe the myth also, even though in their latest excursion into the rainforest or the desert they have encountered the villages or the herds of those who had moved in from the other side. People cannot accept the rate of change or the disappearance of natural abundance. It is too fast and it takes place within the lifetimes of adults who spent their growing years in a seemingly changeless land. Nobody before had to worry about taking care of the forest or the wild animals—they took care of themselves, or God watched over them. They had not been human concerns. It is asking much for people to accept that in just five, ten or twenty years all the rules have changed, and that what "always has been" is no longer.

Now we are drawing lines on the map, attempting to separate the wild from the tamed. We designate lands as nature reserves, national parks, or wilderness areas, and we say that these are no longer places where people can live, or take from, or use in any way except the way of the visitor who comes to look, but not to interfere. This is difficult for people who have always lived in wild country and consider themselves part of it.

There may have been areas on earth that were rich and teeming with life but not permanently occupied by people, what we now call wilderness. But it seems more likely that such areas were visited at least seasonally or occasionally by hunting or gathering parties, or were

667

used by the shamans or by young people on a "vision quest." The really barren and lifeless areas of the poles, the most arid deserts, the highest mountains, were not occupied by people, and probably not visited. But they are still pretty much that way today. Most of the land we designate as formal wilderness or set aside in national parks is land passed on to us by people who considered it to be, in part at least, their homeland. We consider it to be of national park quality because they did not treat it the way we have treated land. Too often they have gone, and our legal designations, our wardens and patrols, take their place. Something seems to have gone wrong, somewhere along the way.

We are now attempting to find ways to put things back together, to integrate the conservation of human cultures with the conservation of the natural world. We do this in part to encourage those who have cared for the land in the past to continue to do so, and in part to encourage those who have not cared to begin to take an interest in conservation of nature, to realize that their future is tied in with the future of the natural environment and with the proper use of the lands and resources on which they depend for their livelihood.

We realize that the national parks, nature reserves and other protected areas of the world have most commonly been established without either the advice or consent of the people most likely to be directly affected by their establishment. Without the support, or at worst acceptance, by these people, the future of any protected area cannot be considered secure, since in their search for the means for their own survival the temptation to take wildland resources from the area, or to encroach upon its boundaries, will tend to be irresistable. Furthermore, the prospect for extending any system of protected areas to take in new lands or waters becomes increasingly dim where popular support for protection of nature is lacking.

2. INDIGENOUS PEOPLE

In attempting to work with people who live in or near to areas that have been designated as having protected status by the government of the country concerned, or areas that are considered worthy of some form of legal protection, there is danger that we will confuse ourselves by our own terminology. If we designate some people as "indigenous" and consequently worthy of special consideration, we leave other people in the category of "non-indigenous" and consequently not worthy of special consideration. I do not believe we can risk such a dichotomy, which from the outset establishes two classes of citizens, one with special privileges, and the other presumably to be kicked around as usual.

In one sense there are no indigenous people: all have ancestors who have come from somewhere else. At some time every native group was an invader, an exotic coming from some other place. There are, however, marked differences in how long each of us have

been in a particular place, and the degree to which we have adapted our ways of life to that area. Some can trace their ancestry in a particular area back over centuries, others have just arrived and don't intend to stay. Some are entirely dependent on the resources of a particular area, others come to visit, to trade, or to raid, and have their source of livelihood elsewhere. Attitudes toward land and resources can differ depending on background, tradition and degree of allegiance to a particular living area. There are therefore real differences between people in relation to their response to the need to manage, or protect the resources of an area. These, however, cannot be resolved by a simple native/nonnative dichotomy. Some natives only wish to go somewhere else; some non-natives deeply desire to become natives and to cherish and care for the land they occupy.

In an earlier paper (Dasmann, 1974) I attempted to distinguish *ecosystem people*, as those who live within an ecosystem or several adjacent and related ecosystems and are dependent on those resources for their existence. Such people must over time learn to live within the ecological limitations of their home area if they are to survive. Although individually they may not have a strongly developed ecological consciousness, culturally they are committed to sustainable ways of life that are essentially sound in ecological terms. By contrast, *biosphere people* are those tied in to the *global economy*, whose livelihood is not necessarily dependent on the resources of any one particular ecosystem. I did not intend to set up a dichotomy with this terminology, but rather to indicate the extremes of a cultural continuum. Much of the difficulty encountered in attempting to achieve ecologically sustainable ways of life comes from people who are in transition from one extreme to the other—their cultures have been disrupted or destroyed, and with that their means of working with the natural environment to which their ancestors were adapted, but they have not yet achieved any firm foothold in the global economy.

From the viewpoint of cultural conservation, it is obvious that the ecosystem people are the most likely to be adversely affected by contact with representatives of the more dominant culture, including those who come with the intention of establishing nature reserves. They are also the people who have in the past maintained the ecological conditions that today are favourable to the establishment of nature reserves. However, does this mean that they should be given favoured status? Does their past record of occupancy of the area, including care for the wild species within it, entitle them to remain in place even when the interests of the national government and the international community dictate that nature conservation should be given first priority in that area? If the answer is yes, should this entitlement remain even after they adopt the ways of the dominant society—when automatic weapons replace bows and arrows?

I would suggest that all people who live in an area and consider it to be their home must have similar rights and be given equal consideration when planning for nature reserves or other protected areas. The question to be asked is not whether they are indigenous, but whether their ways of life are compatible with the objectives and goals of conservation. Hunter-gatherers who have traditionally been conservative in their use of wildlife and plant resources and constitute no threat to the future of wild species in that area should be encouraged to remain within a nature reserve and to participate actively in its protection. However, this arrangement can only work so long as their numbers and their resource utilization remain in balance with the productive capacity of the area. As Brownrigg (1982) has pointed out, "protected areas planning must also anticipate population increases and culture change. It is unrealistic to expect a group to atrophy, or worse, to 'return' to some traditional technology long ago discarded in favour of a more modern alternative." Agreement must be reached, however, for population surpluses to be accomodated elsewhere, and for resource utilization, whether traditional or modern in its technology, to remain within prescribed limits. Otherwise the goal of nature conservation is sacrificed.

Hunter-gatherers, fisherfolk, hunter-gardeners, shifting cultivators, and pastoral nomads could in theory all be accommodated within protected areas, providing they agree to the limitations already described. But the same rules must apply to non-traditional people who occupy areas of high priority for nature conservation, including those primarily involved in raising cash crops for export. If their ways of using the land do not conflict with nature conservation priorities, and if they agree to limitations on their numbers and their use of resources, they can equally be welcomed within a protected area and be asked to join in the activities of protecting and managing the reserve.

To say these things is easier than to do them. If the doors of the national parks and reserves are to be opened to some people, perhaps under carefully defined conditions, then what about others who also claim rights to the land or resources of the area? Are those with ownership rights which have been formally recognized by the government to be treated differently from those with traditional rights dating back into the distant past that are not formally recognized? What about those, such as many American Indian nations that once had formal rights, established by treaty, but have lost their land to others or to the government despite these agreements? Furthermore, are we to agree to one set of conditions governing the establishment of protected areas in the non-industrialized world that do not also apply to the industrialized world? Are the Sioux in the Black Hills to be treated differently from the Yanamani in the northern Amazon basin?

What I am recommending is a uniform code for the treatment of people whose cultures or means of livelihood are likely to be affected by the establishment of protected areas. The code can take into account the special problems of endangered peoples, just as wildlife laws become more restrictive when a species is endangered. It must be flexible enough to recognize that some people can be compensated in cash for the lands or resources they may be asked to sacrifice, but that others cannot. Those who cannot are not only those with traditional rights or communal ownership, but all those who closely identify with the land and the natural environment where they live—the new natives on whom the future may depend.

3. NATURE RESERVES AS ISLANDS

Since the work of McArthur and Wilson (1967) there has been increasing interest in the concepts of island biogeography as these apply to the size, shape, and distribution of national parks, nature reserves and other protected areas. The prospect that areas designated for nature conservation may in the future exist as islands surrounded by lands used intensively for the production of food and other necessities for human survival has caused serious concern that these areas may be inadequate to provide for the survival of the species originally contained within them. The basis for this concern has been explored in books by Soul and Wilcox (1980) and Frankel and Soul (1981). To counteract any tendency toward insularization of nature reserves, the Unesco Biosphere Reserve project (Unesco-MAB, 1974) has proposed that such reserves consist of a fully protected core area (strict nature reserve) surrounded by buffer zones which may be used for recreation (national parks) or compatible forms of resource exploitation (managed forests, rangelands, hunting areas, etc.) grading outward to more intensively used areas. Although many designated biosphere reserves do not fit these criteria, those national parks systems that have been reasonably successful for nature conservation, such as those of the United States and Canada, do have *de facto* buffer zones surrounding and often connecting the national parks. These are for the most part federal, state or provincial areas in which use is controlled and managed with a view toward sustainability. Furthermore, even beyond these protected areas the general level of land management is reasonably good, and the common attitude of the human population is at least indifferent and benign, and at best highly favourable to nature conservation. As a result, many towns and cities are *de facto* bird sanctuaries, supporting an unusual abundance and diversity of wild bird species as well as a surprising variety of small mammals.

In those parts of the United States where nature conservation is most successful, it is not the nature areas that are islands, but the human communities. The pattern of human use is such that cities, towns and intensively used rural areas form a pattern of large and small islands connected by transportation corridors, but surrounded by much larger areas within which native vegetation and animal life survive very well.

The future of no country is likely to be secure, and

certainly no system of parks and reserves will survive, if we attempt to set up systems of protected areas—no matter how well distributed—within a system of land use that otherwise is contributing to the degradation of soils, exhausting the productivity of renewable resources, and relying on heavy inputs of agricultural chemicals to compensate for a deteriorating resource base.

In considering the relationships of people to protected areas, therefore, we must look well beyond the boundaries of those areas and work with the local people to create ecologically sustainable systems of land and resource use. Nature reserves must be seen as parts of those systems, not separate from them. Obviously, people must see the opportunity for economic stability in a context of ecological sustainability before they will take a serious interest in protecting the wild environments of protected areas.

Without in any way denying the importance of strict nature reserves, national parks or other closely protected areas, equal attention must be paid to universal rules of land use and nature protection that apply throughout the country. In various calculations of minimum population size needed to maintain the genetic diversity within a wild animal species and minimum area of protected reserve needed to maintain that population, it becomes apparent that we will never have a system of nature reserves or national parks adequate to protect all wild species (Soul and Wilcox, 1980). We must be able to rely on the rational use and management of lands outside the reserves.

The magnificent system of national parks and nature reserves in the state of Alaska is likely to be inadequate to protect wolves and caribou; for those species alone we need virtually the entire state of Alaska. Fortunately we *have* the entire state of Alaska, for the wildlife laws of that state, which apply to all areas, offer—if enforced—the necessary degree of protection. I am proposing therefore that we give attention to rules of land use and nature conservation that apply everywhere and not just to areas within or near protected natural areas. We need to recognize that planet Earth was originally established as a nature reserve, the only one we know of in the entire universe. We need to keep it that way.

4. GENERAL PRINCIPLES OR GUIDELINES

4.1. General principle

The conservation of nature is fundamental to human existence and is the concern of all people everywhere. It is not to be accomplished only by the establishing of specially protected natural areas, but must be practised in all places at all times. All areas must be protected areas to some degree, since even the most heavily ur-

banized areas provide suitable living spaces for many wild species.

4.2. Ownership, tenure and resource use

The rights of land ownership, tenure or resource use do not include the right to land degradation or resource abuse. Recognition of such rights by governments should be dependent upon agreements for reasonable care and stewardship over the land and its resources.

4.3. Protected natural areas

The establishment of protected natural areas intended to provide for the conservation of biotic communities or wild species in surrounding or adjacent areas, but without adequate attention to the interactions between people and the natural environment, can have adverse effects on local economies or cultures. To provide for long-term positive interactions, the following guidelines are potentially useful:

4.3.1. Use of local knowledge. People who have a long history of use or occupancy of areas to be considered for protection also have a familiarity with its species, communities and ecological processes which cannot readily be gained through surveys, inventories or baseline studies by experts from elsewhere. In particular, long-term trends or fluctuations in abundance and distribution of wild species, past influences and changes, values and usefulness for human purposes can be determined most easily from local people. Consultation with these people is essential to gain the knowledge important for both conservation and for the avoidance of conflict.

4.3.2. Local involvement with planning of protected areas. Planning of protected areas should involve those people who are most likely to be directly affected, positively or negatively, by implementation of protected area status. Every effort should be made to achieve the desired conservation objective with minimum disruption of traditional ways of life and maximum benefit to local people. Boundaries of protected areas and regulations governing their protection and use should reflect the actual conservation objectives to be accomplished and the ways in which these can be achieved through local cooperation, rather than attempting to adhere to internationally approved categories. A simple conservation rule that has local adherence and support may accomplish more than a national park that has none.

4.3.3. Local involvement with management and conservation. Insofar as possible, local people should be involved with management and conservation practices within a protected area. All of them, at best, should take an active interest in the protection of that area. At the least, they should provide the guards, wardens, rangers, and labourers.

4.3.4. Use of protected areas to safeguard native cultures. People who have traditionally lived in isolation from the dominant cultures within a country may be protected from unwanted outside interference by establishment of a protected area which includes all of the lands they have traditionally used—giving them the authority to exclude outsiders and to manage the lands as they see fit. Protected natural areas are also useful as buffer zones surrounding the traditional lands of isolated cultures. Outsiders are in this way controlled by the protected area authorities. Neither of these options is intended to exclude interaction or travel on the part of the native group. The reserve boundary or buffer zone has a "one-way screen" keeping out unwanted vistors but not holding people inside who wish to leave.

4.3.5. Economic benefits. Economic benefits derived from a protected area from tourism or other forms of use must be shared with local people according to agreements and contracts reached before the protected area is established. For existing protected areas, renegotiation with local people will be important to give them a greater role in maintaining the protected status of the area.

4.3.6. Definition of "local people". The people directly affected by the establishment of a protected area often include many who are not permanent inhabitants of the area or its vicinity. Other groups may use the area seasonally—migratory hunter-gatherers, nomadic pastoralists, etc. Still others may only use the area occasionally, but those occasions may have great importance in relation to religion, ceremony, or long-term subsistence needs—the area may already be a "reserve" for people who do not live there permanently. All of these people must be considered in reserve planning, conservation, use, and economy.

4.3.7. Planning and development of surrounding areas. Planning or development of protected areas must not be undertaken in isolation from planning and development of the lands surrounding the protected areas to provide a viable and sustainable economic future for the people involved. The principles of agroecology and agroforestry as well as wildlife management should be considered in the planning and development of these areas. The basic principles of ecodevelopment should be applied. The *conservation unit* approach developed by W. J. Lusigi (1978) for Kenya may provide a useful model.

Acknowledgements

This paper was prepared for IUCN's Commission on National Parks and Protected Areas in cooperation with the United Nations Environment Programme.

Global Sharing and Self-Interest in Protected Areas Conservation

David Munro
Sidney, British Columbia, Canada

ABSTRACT. *The establishment and management of protected areas must be considered in the context of the continuing quest for security. Far from being a drawback, this will provide great strength to the protected area movement, as it will relate human self-interest to the establishment of protected areas. A comprehensive, global system of protected areas will materialize only as a result of effective political action which is supported by broadly based public understanding. The cost of such development should be shared broadly.*

1. INTRODUCTION

Today as always the dominating concern of the peoples of the world is security—security from hunger and exposure, security from the impacts of war, riot and insurrection. All of the great issues of the day, and I believe that the establishment and management of protected areas is one of them, must be considered in the context of the continuing quest for security.

The processes by which people draw from their environment secure and continuous supplies of food, water and the materials necessary for clothing and shelter constitute the central theme of economic development. While for the majority of the world's people, life is less nasty, brutish and short than it was a century ago, the course of economic development has been exceedingly uneven in both time and space. Even in the developed countries, significant segments of the population remain inadquately fed and poorly sheltered and in the world as a whole about 450 million people are chronically hungry or malnourished. It is little wonder that economic development preoccupies us all and dominates the political agendas of the world.

The evolution of processes and institutions aimed at the establishment of peaceful and orderly relations among all people—the people of a single, isolated mountain village and the people of the "global village"—has been a main theme of social development, which has also been tragically uneven. We have done little in the course of our history to minimize the incidence or the horror of armed conflict; in fact, we live now under the awesome shadow of a horror that is literally unimaginable. Between 1945 and 1970, over 80 nations were involved in 130 armed conflicts causing millions of deaths, widespread disruption of normal living patterns and inestimable environmental damage. Statistics on the numbers and impact of civil disorders and breaches of the peace within countries are not readily available but it is clear that they are endemic. While political and religious intolerance remain as major causes of armed conflict and civil disturbance, it is quite clear that the incidence of hostility and violence would be reduced if people throughout the world had a greater sense of security about access to resources to meet their basic needs. Security from want and security from war are therefore indivisible.

For some limited purposes it is convenient and useful to consider economic and social development separately as we have just done, but there are vital and obvious relationships between the two, and in considering strategies for problem solving it is helpful if not essential to think of development as a single though very complex process. All social systems, from those based on the unwritten customs of hunter-gatherer societies to those of the highly developed market and centrally-planned economies, embody rules or laws which explicit or implicitly affect the use of resources, the sharing of their products and thereby the effectiveness of economic development. It is clear also that the management and use of resources, indeed of the environment as a whole, is inextricably a part of development.

The *World Conservation Strategy* has convincingly demonstrated the vital nature of the link between conservation (management of human use of the biosphere so that it may yield the greatest sustainable benefit to present generations while maintaining its potential to meet the needs and aspirations of future generations) and development (modification of the biosphere and the application of human, financial, living and non-living resources to satisfy human needs and improve the quality of human life). The significance of the link between conservation and development cannot, as many would like to believe, be diminished by technology; in fact the unwise application of technology has often traded off short-term developmental benefits for longer-term environmental deterioration. Nor can structural changes in economies or societies, whatever other benefits they might yield, minimize the interdependence of conservation and development by one iota.

The interdependence of conservation and development is becoming more crucial day by day. Even though the rate of growth of the world's population has declined, the number of people in the world, particularly in the developing countries, is still increasing and it is almost certain that population growth from 1975 to 2000 will be 50 per cent and that in 2000 there will be more than 6 thousand million human beings. While it will be exceedingly difficult to meet even the basic needs of so many people, the difficulty will be exacerbated if the trend toward extravagant and wasteful consumption of scarce resources continues in the more developed countries and among the privileged classes of the developing countries. Even if there are quite fundamental social and economic adjustments aimed at greater equity in the distribution and enjoyment of resources among the peoples of the world, meeting the needs of more people will mean that greater stresses will inevitably be placed upon natural and modified ecosystems and the need to manage them skilfully and carefully will become even more pressing.

It is as an aspect of land-use planning and land management to promote the security of mankind that the creation and stewardship of protected areas assumes its significance. If by the term "protected areas" we refer to scientific reserves, national parks, resource reserves, eco-development areas, etc., we understand the term to comprise areas in which a variety of management techniques are applied in pursuit of a wide range of goals. On the basis of that understanding, it is clear that protected areas can make a crucially important contribution to development. IUCN's CNPPA has recognized this in developing a broad and flexible concept of protected areas.

Let us review some of the ways in which protected areas can contribute to development. IUCN's report "Categories, Objectives and Criteria for Protected Areas" covers this topic well, relating the benefits to specific objectives of management:

- the maintenance of sample areas of major biota and physiographic features in a natural state is a pre-requisite for science—for the study of ecology and related sciences and therefore for continuing human development;
- the protection of rare and endangered species and their habitats also contributes to meeting the scientific objective, but, in addition, it provides for the maintenance of genetic diversity with all the present benefits that that conveys and it also keeps alive the potential for innovative use of wild species as yet unexploited. For many people it also responds to a deeply felt moral conviction.
- the conservation of outstanding landscapes or other natural features is essential to full development of individual aesthetic sensibilities and may have an economic expression in touristic activities;
- the maintenance of sustainable stocks of renewable resources that are used to meet human needs is a pre-requisite for development that will endure for the long term. It is also the basis for healthy economics today.

The rationale for generously endowed systems of protected areas of all categories throughout the world would seem to be unassailable in theory, but such systems are not widespread. It is necessary to ask why they are not widespread, to identify the impediments to their establishment and to propose the means to overcome those impediments. The general answer to the question, of course, is that an insufficient number of people who can affect the course of events perceives the establishment of such systems to be of value, and therefore the establishment of protected areas is not proposed or, if it is, it is not well supported.

This failure in perception may be a result of ignorance, of simply not understanding the nature of the benefits that protected areas can convey. In such cases the solution is to try harder to spread a comprehensive understanding of protected areas. A considerable effort has been directed to that end but obviously more and better efforts are needed. This Congress is one such exercise in the dissemination of understanding and I hope that its proceedings, particularly those relating to the case studies, are widely distributed, fully and enthusiastically discussed and freely plagiarized. The importance of reference to case studies cannot be overemphasized—papers that describe and interpret what happens on the ground are much more effective than discursive conceptual reviews such as this one.

If a majority of people or, perhaps, a handful of powerful people oppose the establishment of a protected area or a system of protected areas because they feel that their interests will thereby be damaged, the cause may, as suggested, be failure fully to understand the benefits that flow from protected areas but it may also stem from two other roots—an honest difference of view with respect to the best use of land or a wish to pursue short-term gain, be it private or public, at the expense of future benefits.

The question of an honest difference of view requires much more attention than I can give it here. Such differences are everywhere. I mention them, not with any perjorative intent, but simply because they should be kept in mind. Occupational and professional biases condition differing perceptions of land use issues whatever the facts of the case at hand are alleged to be. To give only two examples: a forester may have a thorough understanding of forest ecology, but his bias is towards harvesting a forest crop; the civil engineer and the cement manufacturer undeniably have a vested interest in the construction of dams. These sorts of biases are characteristic of the developed countries, whether they are market oriented or centrally planned, and of the developed sectors of other parts of the world. They are also part of the baggage of the development assistance agencies. But in the traditional sectors of the developing countries, cultural and religious factors provide a fundamentally different basis for differing view points. There are still societies that have little interst in adapting to an economy based on the flow of cash, preferring instead to place a higher value on, for example, livestock or wildlife. By what criteria are we to judge which viewpoint has the greater validity?

What it all comes down to, of course, is a question of land use and the conflicts that surround land-use decisions. Such conflicts relate mainly to the nature of the costs and benefits and how they are distributed. It is important to make the best possible effort to identify and quantify all the costs and benefits associated with a conservation project and to determine who bears the costs and to whom the benefits flow. While this paper is not intended as a guide to cost-benefit analysis, it may be worthwhile to refer to some of the factors that must be taken into account in analysis of proposals to establish a protected area. These are displayed in Table 1.

Two factors complicate what should in theory be a relatively simple calculation. The more important is that some of the benefits are unquantifiable. The other is that many of the beneficiaries, particularly those far from the area concerned, contribute nothing to offset the costs.

Despite the diligent and elaborate attempts of some economists, we remain perplexed by unquantifiables, by the problem of reducing the value of an aesthetic experience to the same terms that are used to evaluate a cubic metre of timber. There is no reason to expect that this problem will ever be solved. This should not be a matter for despair. Economics notwithstanding, value judgements will continue to be determined by consensus and put into effect by political decisions. It is, after all, quite possible to understand something without being able to measure it and describe it in monetary or numerical terms. But it does call for more and better efforts to disseminate understanding and to ensure that non-quantifiable values, including those associated with cultures other than one's own, are given due weight.

To digress only slightly, it is also worth noting that the monetary policies that are currently widespread are less than helpful if not positively destructive in considering future values. When interest rates range from 15 to 20 per cent, we are heavily and ruinously discounting the future. We are saying in effect that we see nothing of any value beyond about five years.

There may be good reasons for high interest rates, but it is time for a thorough consideration of their effects on the future of the environment and natural resources.

The problem of arranging for a fair distribution of the costs of establishing and managing protected areas, a distribution of costs that approximates the distribution of benefits, is also a difficult one, particularly at the international level, but it is by no means totally intractable. There are three means of spreading the burden of costs—considered in their broadest sense.

The most common means, of course, is by the imposition of differential use fees, with higher levels being paid by non-residents. This can be useful and equitable so far as present users are concerned but it ignores the benefits that may accrue in future to currently unidentified segments of the world's population. In any event, it is usually an insufficient measure. Considering the level of fees that is customarily acceptable (that is to say, a level that is not so high as to lead to a net reduction of revenue), user fees can usually be expected to do little more than meet an average level of management costs.

A very limited start has been made in using the second means of sharing the costs of protected areas, by transferring funds or necessary services for the establishment and management of protected areas from the rich to the poor countries through the United Nations system—notably through the technical assistance programs of FAO, Unesco and UNEP with the support of UNDP and using the mechanisms of the World Heritage Convention. As well, the World Bank has provided soft loans for protected area development programmes. The support of the World Wildlife Fund for this sort of activity, notably here in Indonesia, is well known. An extension of this type of development assistance—which can be considered as a necessary investment in the future of mankind—should be considered immediately and thoroughly. I will return to this topic later.

A third possibility for sharing the costs of protected areas is the provision of development assistance for communities that may lose all or part of their income or the means of their subsistence as a result of the establishment of a protected area. Assistance of this sort requires a comprehensive knowledge of the people and resources concerned and it must be planned very carefully. It would be done most effectively, I suggest in the context of the sort of national development planning that is based on a national conservation strategy.

If the sorts of broad cost-benefit considerations just mentioned are taken into account in analyzing a proposal for the establishment and management of protected areas, it is clear that the resulting basis for resolving conflicts in land use and for decision making will be much more useful than the basis provided by analyses that are restricted to quantifiable economic factors and neglect broader global interests. The greater the amount of relevant information available, the greater the extent of common understanding of land use and conservation issues, and the broader the frame of reference for negotiation, the more likely it is that the broadest public interest will be best served by the decision reached. This is why it is essential that information relevant to development of conservation proposals be fully and freely available and that there be adequate provision for and support of public participation in the decision-making process.

A number of conclusions can be drawn from the foregoing. The establishment and management of protected areas is a matter of crucial importance not only to individual countries but also to the world community as a whole. Protected areas give rise to both costs and benefits, some of which can be expressed in monetary terms and some not. If a careful calculation reveals that the benefits exceed the costs in monetary terms alone, or if the balance is tipped in favour of benefits by non-quantifiable benefits that are clearly seen to accrue mainly at present and within the district or country concerned, there should be little difficulty in devising a scheme to ensure equity in the distribution of costs and benefits primarily within the country concerned. If, however, as may quite often be the case, the benefits are seen to be more in the future than in the present and are as likely to be realized by people anywhere in the world as locally, there is a clear case for a more generous level of international cost-sharing than has so far been reached.

A philosophy basic to this argument exists in the concept of the New International Economic Order (NIEO) and is reflected to a limited degree in the UN assistance programmes and the work of WWF referred to earlier. The NIEO emphasizes the principle of global sharing in its call for fuller use of the world's natural resources and for more equitable conditions of trade. But it goes beyond that as a framework for the establishment and management of protected areas by its emphasis on alternative patterns of development ("eco-development") and the use of environmentally sound technologies and by its discouragement of wasteful and irrational use of natural resources. As they evolve, the NIEO and the New International Development Strategy (NIDS), which is intended to be the instrument for its accomplishment, should state more explicitly the vital role of protected areas and the need for global sharing in the cost of establishing a comprehensive world wide system of protected areas. I suggest that this Congress should also reflect that need in its proceedings.

In a time of recession and intermittent armed conflicts, the reiteration of pious hopes for global cooperation might seem foolish and irrelevant were it not possible to look back a bit in history and reassure ourselves that the vision of human progress is not totally insubstantial. Let us consider for a moment how mankind has responded to the plight of the indigent and disadvantaged. For as long as we know, most societies have recognized some moral obligation to help their less fortunate members. In earlier times that obligation was met most often within the family, or simply by sharing among friends, that is to say, by personal charity. Later, in some countries, highly organized private charities and assistance schemes grew up; both costs and benefits were more broadly, though by no means equitably, distributed. Many such schemes still exist, but in a number of countries they have been supplemented if not supplanted by a variety of public welfare and social insurance schemes and more recently we have added programmes for training and development aimed at enhancing the ability of the individual to look after himself. This course of events has been a major element in our pursuit of social justice and it has had an international, intergovernmental dimension, though clearly an insufficient one, since the United Nations was founded. In the long time scale of history, international consciousness of equity, justice and the common interest of humankind has only just begun to emerge. In that perspective there is nothing fanciful or impractical in thinking about a giant leap forward in global sharing of the costs of conservation. For what, after all, is the need more pressing?

Our vision of a comprehensive, global system of protected areas will materialize only as a result of effective political action and despite the admirable initiatives of a few leaders who have been, happily, a bit ahead of their constituencies, effective action will generally be taken only in response to widespread public understanding. The role of governments in developing and using national land-use planning systems and establishing and managing protected areas is, however, not just to respond; governments must lead as well—by disseminating information and understanding and by helping in the founding of a broad consensus for national land management. Collectively, the role of governments, which they must undertake in the context of global development, is to exchange information and technical assistance and to reach agreement on measures for transferring needed financial resources from the affluent to the less fortunate.

The role of the individual and the non-governmental organization, whether professionally oriented or motivated simply by a concern for the welfare of man and the biosphere, is to contribute in every possible way to the formation of a consensus on conservation upon which effective political action can be based.

Acknowledgements

This paper was prepared for IUCN's Commission on National Parks and Protected Areas in cooperation with the United Nations Environment Programme.

Table 1: Factors Relevant to the Establishment of a Protected Area

COSTS	BORNE BY
Land acquisition	Government, donors
Continuing management	Government, donors
Loss of income from extractive use of resources	Local entrepreneur, national or multi-national corporation
Loss of employment opportunity associated with resource use	Local, metropolitan
Loss of products for subsistence	Local
Loss of tax revenue	Governments

BENEFITS	ACCRUING TO
Maintenance of sample areas of major biota	Scientific community, humankind
Maintenance of genetic diversity	Industry, agriculture, humankind
Maintenance of outstanding landscapes, fauna and flora	Local individuals, local communities, tourist and travel operators, governments, humankind
Maintenance of sustainable stocks of resources	Local community, local entrepreneur, national and multi-national corporations
Maintenance of environmental integrity	Local communities and governments, e.g., through the conservation of soil and water
Employment opportunity associated with protected area	Local community
Creation of stable tax base	Governments
User fees	Governments

Chapter 14
Promoting Increased International Support

Keynote Address: The World Conservation Strategy and the Developing World

Ali Murtopo
Minister of Information
Republic of Indonesia

I am pleased to have the privilege of addressing the distinguished delegates to the third World National Parks Congress. It is a great honour for me to share with you the common duty of finding an adequate response to the imminent challenge affecting the whole of mankind, as this matter of nature-conservation obviously is all about.

A number of people have asked me how a Minister of Information fits in a National Parks Congress.

In a developing country like Indonesia, the main responsibilities of a Minister of Information include: nationally, to motivate the people to have a set of attitudes consistent with the common values we uphold; internationally, to solicit and elicit, again through motivation, the appreciation of the international community for the compatability and the consistency of Indonesia's policies and actions with the internationally accepted environmental rules and standards.

Mankind is facing a tremendous challenge as a result of deforestation and other kinds of nature-destroying and nature-polluting activities. The damage done to nature has reached such an alarming proportion that we can say, in all seriousness, that the survival of mankind is at stake. Here we face a a problem for the solution of which the highest degree of motivation is required, nationally as well as internationally. It includes pressures to be brought to bear on governments and peoples the world over to really come to grips with the essentials of what is at stake. This, first and foremost, is a responsibility which cannot escape the attention of a Minister of Information.

I would now like to come down to some specifics. I know that on previous occasions you have already had lengthy and in-depth discussions about the World Conservation Strategy. I know that during the Eighth World Forestry Congress in Jakarta in 1978, a framework of the issues and their solution has been worked out, covering no less than 26 clauses of joint decisions. I am also aware that following almost endless contacts among environmental experts ever since, be they of multilateral, regional or bilateral nature, a comprehensive World Conservation Strategy was published by IUCN, WWF, and UNEP. I was pleased to attend the launch of the World Conservation Strategy in Jakarta in March, 1980. I appreciate the sincere and tireless efforts made in this field by those who are concerned with nature conservation, and I hope that the ideas I set forth here will make a worthy contribution to the implementation of the process.

The statements on environmental conservation which have been made in the course of this Congress have recognized the reality that our planet Earth has its limits, as has been elaborated by the Club of Rome and by the U.N. Conference on the Environment in Stockholm 10 years ago. Three factors are responsible for the limited quality of earth's carrying capacity: the land area cannot substantially expand; the airspace, while it cannot expand either, has to some degree been polluted; the marine area cannot expand.

The peculiarity of the dilemma in this context is that, while on the one hand we see the static nature of Earth, on the other we see the practically unlimited possibilites for the expansion of the human population; this expansion is now proceeding at a rate of about 2% every year.

By the late thirties, earth's population was about 2 billion people; it took scarcely a half century to double the figure to the present 4 billion people. If nothing is done about it, it will take only a quarter century to get this number doubled again to reach the 8 billion mark.

The people living on earth have got to eat and to drink in order to survive; as members of the human race, they are also endowed by their Creator with certain qualities in terms of needs, desires, intellectual capacities, and even the capacity to destroy.

These are qualities which man can develop for the good, but alas, also for the ill of his fellow humans. Man stands on two "legs", the natural "leg" and the cultural "leg"; man possesses the natural instincts to survive the rigours and hardships of life. He eats when he is hungry, he drinks when he is thirsty, he flexes his muscles when attacked, and so on. His cultural "leg" makes him capable of developing his intellectual capacities with a view to satisfying the higher degrees of his wants which include the fuller enjoyment of life, and the fulfilment of his worldly, as well as his spiritual, aspirations. In this latter sphere, he has the capability to make value judgements, to distinguish between the good and the bad.

We have experienced thoughout the history of mankind that the cultural man has been capable of bringing in the fruits of progress and the benefits of development; the same cultural man, however, has also been, and will continue to be, capable of guiding the human race onto the brinks of misery and total annihilation.

Under the circumstances I have described, I think we are in a position to develop a new perception of threat. Not only should we think of threat, as we did in the past, in terms of a military might from outside which is capable of jeopardizing the existence of any sovereign state or group of states; we should also conceive of threat in terms of our inablility to maintain a new balance between the carrying capacities of earth's land, sea and air—which tend to diminish over the years—and the fast rate of population growth.

If the balance is not redressed—and I honestly don't know how—sooner or later, the world will perish.

I conceive this Congress and many other international conferences of its kind as representing the serious efforts we have been undertaking to delay, for as long as possible, the ultimate collapse of our earth. This, I am afraid, is the only choice we have. We can only delay, we cannot prevent the dawn of the day of the ultimate reckoning.

In doing what we are called upon to do, we ought to take a closer look at the crucial problem areas which, to all intents and purposes, make up the necessary ingredients for the implementation of the World Conservation Strategy: the fast rate of population growth; and the declining carrying capacity of earth.

As to the rate of population growth, the global situation presents a striking imbalance in the conditions prevailing in the developed vis a vis the developing countries. About 3.4 billion people, making up 75% of the world's total population, live in 140 developing countries with a share of only 20% of the world's wealth. A total of 1.1 billion people living in the 35 poorest countries have a per capita income percita of less than $300, and a share of the world's wealth amounting to only about 3%. Of the 3.4 billion people, 800 million live in absolute poverty.

The "Great Divide", if we recapitulate, presents the following picture (Newsweek, October 26, 1981):

	Developed countries	Developing countries
Population	1.1 billion	3.4 billion
Per capita GNP	$6,468	$957
Life expectancy	72 years	56 years
Literary rate	99%	52%
Educational expend. p.c.	$286	$18
Military expenditures p.c.	$300	$29
Public health expend. p.c.	$199	$6.50

The very prospect of world population growth in the next decade, in my view, is not encouraging in the light of what we are trying to achieve. In spite of the many successful attempts by the developing countries to reduce the rate of population growth whithin their national boundaries the end result has not made a tangible impact on the severity of the problem as a whole. Whatever successes we have booked in our family planning programmes, they have been offset in many instances by our equally successful efforts to improve health services, and to reduce the mortality rate by an even higher margin.

Thus, the pressures on land resources in developing countries are expected to continue to increase in the foreseeable future. Cultivable land is expected to be rapidly running out, and whatever land is now under cultivation is approaching the limits of its carrying capacity. Deforestation and the concomitant degradation of nature are the logical consequences.

Many people in the developed countries are inclined to lay all the blame for the degradation of nature on the shoulders of the developing world. They have pointed an accusing finger at the traditional methods of land management including shifting cultivaiton, forest fires and so on, claiming that these are to blame for the accelerating process of nature destruction.

We tend to forget that the developed world must shoulder an even bigger share of the blame. The latest products of technological advance have to no little extent been a major source of environmental degradation. The atom bombs which destroyed Hiroshima and Nagasaki to hasten the end of World War II produced an environmental pollution of a dimension we had never known before. Thirty-seven years following the Hiroshima and Nagasaki disasters, the power of technology has been able to parade a series of destructive armaments, including nuclear warhead carrying satellites, which could instantly wipe out all forms of life on earth. I think these distressing phenomena deserve our fullest attention to keep our work in proper perspective.

In all fairness, we have to admit that peoples in the developing countries have the propensity to harm nature, but have been doing so solely for the purpose of satisfying their basic needs including food, energy and housing. Clearing the forest is for them a means to survive.

In the process of development which countries have had to embark upon to improve the standard of living of their peoples, the forests provide the logs for export to earn the badly-needed foreign exchange. In this context, the export drive has been spurred on mainly to meet the increasing needs of peoples in the developed countries to lift up the already high standards of their living conditions. In the process, the developing countries have to pay more for the products imported from in the developed countries than the amount they are receiving from the export of their timber. To make up for the loss, more wood has to be cut for export. And so the cycle goes on and on at the expense of the tropical forest.

I sincerely hope that for the implementation of the World Conservation Strategy, the considerations I have advanced will be taken into account. They provide, in my opinion, the basics on which to approach the new balance with a view to harmonizing the apparent discrepancy between the increasing rate of population growth and the harsh reality of the earth's limits.

The state of the new balance may be decisive in determining how long we can delay the collapse of the earth. This is one reason why I consider your sense of judgement so important, so decisive. It is bound to create history, as it is bound to lay a milestone of human survival.

It is incumbent upon the distinguished ladies and gentlemen at this Congress to choose which alternative is the best under existing circumstances. In family planning terms, for instance, it looks like a choice between less children with higher life expectancy, or more children with lower life expectancy. Or perhaps a third alternative in the sense of more children with better life expectancy may still be feasible.

The point I want to stress here is that, sometimes it is inevitable that we resort to the use of a "who pays for whom" kind of equation. In this context, I welcome the idea underlying the direcion of IUCN's World Conservation Strategy suggested in the phrase "Living Resource Conservation for Sustainable Development." This seems to confirm the same basic premise embodied in the phrase "Forests for People," the theme of the Eighth World Forestry Congress. It clearly recognizes the principle—to be made inherent in National Parks Development—that the welfare of the people in the national territory should be the first guiding principle.

I also welcome the idea that the developed countries share in bearing the costs toward materializing the development of national parks and protected areas within the scope of the World Conservation Strategy.

Nothing is more appropriate and more relevant than such a proposition; it is in the interest of industrialized countries also that they should co-finance the management of national parks and protected areas in the de-

veloping countries. Whether this support should take the form of a 1% survival tax on every imort of timber from developing countries, as suggested by Mr. Charles de Haes, or some kind of import allocations to be fixed every year and to be coupled with more reasonable pricing arrangements, is a matter for further discussion. (The latter form has the advantage that the developing countries will be in a position to plan their timber exports more adequately, and by so doing can improve the management of their forest resources).

However much we value the progress we have been making in the field of nature conservation, I sense that any real overall solution of the problem of human survival requires a much broader, and a much more integrated, global strategy than what we have had so far. It is bad enough to have 4 billion, or 8 billion, people on earth. It is worse that these very people are divided into a category of the rich, and another category of the poor, each pursuing their own self-interests.

In order that the human race can live up to the best expectations of sustaining life on earth for as long as possible, there *must* be the most genuine cooperation, a cooperation in spirit and in deeds, between the rich (now referred to as the North) and the poor (now referred to as the South) to cover *all* spheres of human endeavour.

This should encompass the coordination and integration of global policies in such fields as demography, disarmament, the new international economic order, nature conservation, and so on.

I know that many of these things are outside the purview of this Congress; but, nonetheless, I submit them to your consideration in the hope that they may provoke your favourable response and your appreciation; after all, there is a very close interdependence between the problems in these fields and nature conservation which itself is a problem of a global dimension.

The gist of what I have been saying throughout this address is, basically, on Doomsday, the word we do not like to hear but which we know is now right on our very doorstep. Doomsday in terms of what is revealed in the Holy Scriptures of our religious beliefs, is, of course, beyond the realm of our comprehension. But doomsday as a product of man's own mistakes or ignorance, and even as a product of man's ingenuity, is something we can very well predict and anticipate. It is the latter kind of doomsday which we must avert. We can avert it, if we have the will to do so. To this end we must act in concert and in unison as a human race by galvanizing the very best qualities within ourselves as "cultural men."

UNEP and Protected Areas

Reuben Olembo
Director, Division of Environmental Management
UNEP
Nairobi, Kenya

ABSTRACT. *Within the framework of the World Conservation Strategy and the Charter for Nature, UNEP together with the other members of the Ecosystem Conservation Group, i.e., FAO, Unesco and IUCN, have played an important catalytic role in planning and establishing systems of terrestrial and marine protected areas as well as ensuring that each area is managed effectively. For example, UNEP AND IUCN have undertaken surveys of the distribution of existing terrestrial and marine protected areas at global, regional and national levels and the extent to which they cover representative samples within different natural characteristic ecosystems of the area has been established. On the basis of ths work, recommendations were made for additional areas that should be protected. Training and education activities in national park and wildlife management has been promoted, especially for developing countries and particularly in Africa through UNEP's fellowship assistance to the College of African Wildlife Management in Mweka, Tanzania. Exchange programmes for national park wildlife managers such as international workshops and study tours, have been organized and extension and public information activities undertaken.*

1. INTRODUCTION

Yellowstone National Park, created in 1872, is considered to be the beginning of the establishment of organized protected areas in the world. Viewed in the context of modern ecological thinking, the philosophical arguments which led to Yellowstone could be considered to have been somewhat narrow in concept and limited in scope, but that should not detract from the symbolic significance of Yellowstone's establishment, which may be considered the real beginning of an organized global conservation movement. Few could have foretold that the centennial celebrations of Yellowstone would coincide with a wide-spread upwelling throughout the world of consciousness on environmental issues. As you know, these celebrations perfectly complemented the Conference on the Human Environment held at Stockholm in the same year for the purpose of placing these issues into a sharper focus, thereby leading to the birth of the United Nations Environment Programme and the establishment of a whole new concept in intergovernmental arrangements to deal with pressing global problems. We at UNEP are excited to be at the centre of a large part of the productive new thinking in conservation.

2. UNEP AND CONSERVATION

The subject we have met to discuss is clearly of great developmental interest. The basic approach to modern conservation is not only to discuss parks and other forms of protecting living things and their ecosystems but to understand the function of the living landscape and the interrelationship between living organisms and their environment. A sound utilization and exploitation of water, soils, plants and animals must be predicted upon the long-term maintenance and the rate of renewal of these resources. That is to say, in the development process, we should try to reach a biological balance between the demands for economic sustenance and nature's long-term capacity to satisfy continuously these necessities. This is what is meant by sustained and ecologically sound development.

The matters before you are central to the work of UNEP. Although only 10 years have passed since its creation, UNEP has striven hard to promote conservation of natural terrestrial and marine ecosystms as an integral part and within the context of national economic and social development. Our overall approach is to ensure that resources of the environment are managed and utilized in such a way as not to transgress the limits of the biosphere within which we live.

Neil Armstrong, recounting his experience on the surface of the moon to the World Wildlife Fund International Congress in 1970, said,

". . . . More important, (earth) is the only island we know is a suitable home for man. The importance of protecting and saving that home has never been felt more strongly."

The actual problems of global conservation are vast and complex. This Congress has been dicussing some of them on the basis of biogeographical realms. From a global viewpoint, the major problems must include human population growth, the pollution of the environments including the use of toxic chemicals, erosion through over-exploitation, and the extermination of plant and animal species through overharvesting.

In large parts of the world, erosion is man's greatest and oldest conservation problem, and in recent years, this is increasingly being recognized as the scourge and plunder of successful development, albeit with little and insufficient practical resolve to halt or reverse the process. In its final stages, erosion leads to desertification desertification, which results in ecological degradation with the loss or substantial diminished productivity of land. Because of erosion grazing lands cease to produce palatable pasture; dryland agriculture is abandoned; irrigated fields are abandoned due to salinization, waterlogging and other forms of soil deterioration; and watersheds, vital to the renewal and continuous supply of water, are destroyed. Five years after the world met to discuss these problems at the United Nations Conference on Desertification (organized on behalf of the world community by UNEP), resources to combat this menace are still appallingly insufficient, and in the near future, the picture is bleak. Recently, the Governing Council of UNEP promulgated a World Soils Policy, and the FAO Conference issued a World Soils Charter. Let us hope that the principles contained in these policy statements will be translated into action, and by 1992 when the fourth World National Parks Congress convenes, we will be in better shape.

For centuries, marshes and any land periodically flooded by the sea has been viewed as wasteland, fit only for dumping or reclamation for agricultural, industrial or settlement purposes. While much land has been gained for agricultural purposes, far too frequently such drainage has failed, causing an enormous waste of natural resources and public funds—subsoil water sinks, formerly fertile fields lose their productivity, and fish and game become scarce or disappear completely. The ecological context of such reclamation—the relation between the supply of water and the long-term pro-

ductivity of the soil—and the value of marshes and floodlands for conservation purposes, are often lost sight of.

At the other end of the scale, there is another serious conservation issue: the deterioration of environmental health which arises from polluted air surrounding vast cities and industrial conglomerations and the chemicals used in mechanized agriculture. The pollution of air, water and soil comes from many sources, and man alone is responsible for them except in the case of such natural phenomena as volcanic eruptions. Exhaust fumes from industries, domestic chimney smoke, urban dumps, dangerous gases from all manner of dumped agricultural and industrial chemical wastes, sulphur and radioactive wastes which can be spewed and transported by prevailing winds over long distances—all these are sources of heavy and concentrated environmental pollution and are dangerous not only to man but to all forms of life. It is critical that the conservation movement not only ensures that the industrial society makes an increase of man's economic standards possible but does so without added environmental burdens.

To deal with these and other unmentioned problems, we in UNEP advocate an approach symbolized by the words "environmental planning and management". In its broadest sense, environmental planning is an attempt to balance and harmonize the various enterprises which man, for his benefit, has superimposed upon natural environments. Designed to satisfy one or another of his needs, these enterprises complement one another in terms of economic development, but conflicts and imbalances inherent in all these enterprises must be grasped and eliminated. Integration of all the different aspects of resource development with environmental considerations leads to environmental management.

3. UNEP AND THE WORLD CONSERVATION STRATEGY

It is in this context that right from its inception, UNEP joined IUCN and its two sister organizations of the UN—FAO and Unesco—and the financial involvement of WWF to develop a new appreciation and philosophical framework for conservation activities. The result was the World Conservation Strategy, whose three main principal objectives—the maintenance of essential ecological processes, the preservation of genetic diversity and the ensuring of sustainable use of species and ecosystems—are already familiar to you. With the publication and launch of the World Conservation Strategy in 1980, the conservation movement reached a turning point. For the first time all the nations of the world had common guidelines for planning and initiating conservation action. A major political achievement of the World Conservation Strategy was to move conservation away from its narrow philosophical base which gave us Yellowstone National Park to the centre stage of man's main preoccupation as a monolithic species—development and well-being.

The broadening of this philosophical framework is by no means accidental but a conscious and realistic necessity. Too often the Yellowstone model of conservation was felt (rightly or wrongly) at best a luxury, at worst an impediment to social and economic development. Developing nations, in a hurry to catch the train, argue with justice that they need to clear forested land to meet the land hunger of their people and to satisfy their basic requirements for food; their limited resources might best be spent on direct social welfare programmes, and industrialists complain that strict environmental controls impede basic economic growth. But in making development its central theme, the World Conservation Strategy has provided a means to rationalize conservation goals in terms of real benefits to humanity, and to make it relevant to all and sundry.

In one sense, in adopting this broad framework the World Conservation Strategy follows the Morges Manifesto which led to the establishment of the World Wildlife Fund. In its concluding words the Manifesto stated:

". . . . Mankind's self-respect and mankind's inheritance on this earth will not be preserved by narrow or short-sighted means."

4. UNEP AND PROTECTED AREAS

Within the framework of the World Conservation Strategy and the Charter for Nature, UNEP together with the other members of the Ecosystem Conservation Group, i.e. FAO, Unesco, and IUCN, have played an important catalytic role in planning and extending the systems of terrestrial and marine protected areas, as well as in ensuring that each area is managed effectively. Omitting the related work carried out in the context of the Regional Seas Programme the cost of our joint activities amount to some $28.4 million, of which $11.5 million has been borne by the Fund of UNEP. For example, UNEP and IUCN have undertaken surveys of the distribution of existing terrestrial and marine protected areas at global, regional and national levels, and the extent to which they cover representative samples within different characteristic ecosystems of the areas has been established. On the basis of this work, recommendations have been made for additional areas that should be protected. Consultations have been held with national parks administrators and scientists in the areas concerned, and working conferences for national park officials have been convened to consider the establishment of mechanisms for consultation and cooperation as well as the initiation of follow-up action. Technical advice has been provided on the identification, planning, establishment and effective management of terrestrial and marine protected areas, bearing in mind social and economic conditions in specific regions, and

encouragement has been given for the establishment of an effective network of protected areas.

Effective decision-making in respect of protected areas must be based on accurate inventories which provide a tool for identifying priorities, so within the framework of cooperation between UNEP and IUCN, high priority is given to the UNEP supported IUCN Protected Areas Data Unit (PADU). PADU holds the data upon which Realm-based Directories are based, and is responsible for the preparation, continuous updating and publication of the United Nations List of National Parks and Protected Areas, which includes terrestrial and marine World Heritage Sites, national parks, nature reserves and biosphere reserves. UNEP's programme for protected areas is also implemented through collaboration with and support of the Unesco biosphere reserve programme, an aim of which is the conservation of the natural heritage through conservation of representative ecosystems and the wild species of fauna and flora they contain. By early 1982, 209 biosphere reserves, covering an area of about 120 million ha, had been designated in 55 countries, by 1983 it is expected that there will be about 250 biosphere reserves in some 60 countries.

Other achievements under joint UNEP/IUCN projects include the preparation of a classification of the marine and terrestrial biogeographic provinces of the world which was presented in a biogeographic map with an overlay of protected areas included in the UN List; this world map is on display here at the Congress. Such classifications provide a basis for future expansion of the network of protected areas, and for ascertaining conservation priorities and the adequacy of coverage of terrestrial and marine protected areas worldwide.

UNEP is also giving high priority to marine conservation, and the UNEP/FAO Global Plan of Action for Marine Mammals includes various provisions regarding marine protected areas, including follow-up to the UNEP/IUCN Cetacean Sanctuary Workshop held in Tijuana and the Guerrero Negro in Mexico in 1980.

In implementing Recommendation 1 of the Second World Conference on National Parks (Yellowstone/Grand Teton, 1972), which urged regional groupings of nations to establish mechanisms for collective action to create systems of national parks and other protected areas for the regions concerned, UNEP has taken several steps, under a number of projects, to organize regional meetings on national park coordination under the auspices of UNEP and IUCN. Prior to these meetings visits were made to countries in the various regions to solicit the cooperaton of national parks organizations and to obtain information for assessing the extent to which representative samples of the various types of ecosystems were conserved within each region concerned, or were still inadequately protected under the existing management regimes.

With the assistance of the IUCN Conservtaion Monitoring Centre (CMC) in Cambridge, established with the financial assistance of UNEP and WWF, basic data on species and their habitats are being filed in an interactive data base for use by a wider audience, and should prove a powerful tool for management purposes. CMC participates in the Global Environment Monitoring System (GEMS) with the aim of ensuring a fairly accurate data based on habitats and species, in order to ensure effective and ecologically-sound management measures. Collation of information from many sectors is required in order to produce information useful to planners and managers for the preparation of land use plans which take into account ecosystem structure and function as well as social and economic realities.

A review of the planning and management policies of national parks and other protected areas is being continued by UNEP in collaboration with IUCN; so far reviews have been prepared for the Afrotropical, Neotropical and Nearctic Realms with the assistance of a network of collaborators. However, much remains to be done to improve the quality of information systems on wild animals and plants, protected areas, and legislation, to evaluate the effectiveness of established protected areas and the adequacy of their size, and to provide accurate Directory sheets on each of the areas. Largely thanks to the recommendations and priorities established within the framework of the UNEP and IUCN regional surveys, support for management, provision of equipment and training of personnel has been provided by governments, UNEP, FAO, UNDP, Unesco, WWF, IUCN and other sources.

Training and education activities in national park and wildlife management have been promoted, especially for developing countries and particularly in Africa through UNEP's fellowship assistance to the College of African Wildlife Management in Mweka, Tanzania. Exchange programmes have been organized for national park and wildlife managers, such as international workshops and study tours, and extension and public information activities hav been undertaken. For example, the joint UNEP/FAO regional quarterly bulletin on wildlfie, national parks and wildland conservation ("Tiger Paper") has been issued in the Asia-Pacific region for many years; similar regional publications are about to be launched for Africa and Latin America ("Elephant Paper/Nature et Faune" and "Puma Paper", respectively). Information on parks management on a global scale is being provided through the "PARKS Magazine" by a consortium grouping IUCN, UNEP, FAO, Unesco, WWF, and the Governments of Canada, USA, France, Australia and New Zealand.

In pursuance of the General Principles for Assessment and Control of Marine Pollution contained within the Action Plan for the Human Environment, the Regional Seas Programme was initiated by UNEP in 1974. Subsequent sessions of the Governing Council of UNEP have repeatedly endorsed the regional approach to the control of marine pollution and the management of marine and coastal resources. The Regional Seas Programme at present includes ten regions (Mediterranean, Kuwait Action Plan Region, West and Central Africa, Wider Caribbean, East Asia Seas, South-East Pacific, South-West Pacific, Red Sea and the Gulf of Aden, East Africa, and South-West Atlantic) and has over 120 coastal States participating in it. It is conceived as an action-oriented programme concerned not only with consequences but also with causes of environmental degradation and encompasses a comprehensive approach to combatting environmental problems through the management of marine and coastal areas. The action plans promote the parallel development of legal agreements and of action-oriented programme activities, emphasizing the application of environmentally-sound management practices as the key to safeguarding the marine environment and its resources.

Interaction between conservation experts, park managers and conservation educators is considered an important means of information exchange and transfer of experience. For this reason, and within its limited resources, UNEP has been pleased to use the opportunity presented by regional conferences, seminars, workshops and short-term training arrangements to sponsor participants from developing countries. It is in this context that several participant to this World Congress have been supported from the Fund of UNEP, and UNEP is actively promoting the Conference on Biosphere Reserves to be held in Minsk, USSR, in September 1983.

5. CONCLUSION

In conclusion, I sincerely hope that this meeting will end with strengthened mutual understanding of the needs of cooperative efforts in promoting the objectives of the World Conservation Strategy and a renewed international resolve to increase effective management of worldwide natural habitats and wildlife so as to bring real benefits to those in need.

FAO and Protected Area Management: Where Do We Go from Here?

Gil S. Child
FAO Wildlife and National Parks Officer
Rome, Italy

1. INTRODUCTION

The United Nations Food and Agricultural Organization (FAO) is the United Nations specialized agency whose mandate includes responsibility for executing United Nations-funded projects and programmes in national parks and protected area management. The discharge of this responsibility in response to requests from member countries has led to involvement in a variety of fields at both country and inter-country levels.

The subject areas of programmes will be briefly outlined and a review of their translation into practical activities over the past decade made. An account will then be given of how both the nature of assistance and the modalities of its implementation are likely to evolve over the next decade. It should be observed that most of the trends that are suggested in this latter context are not necessarily peculiar to protected area management, but apply equally to other sectors also.

2. REVIEW OF PAST ASSISTANCE

2.1. Subject areas covered

Relevant projects and activities executed by FAO during the 1970s covered the following main subject areas:

a) *Protected area management*

Here involvement has been at all levels from national systems of protected areas to individual protected areas and sites within them. It has included ecological surveys and resource assessments, identification of areas, planning, establishment, development and management, with all that these terms imply.

b) *Training*
Three broad levels of training have been recognized: higher level (university) for professional staff and researchers; medium level for field managers and wardens; and lower level for rangers, guards, guides and similar categories.

Training projects have included assistance with the establishment and strengthening of training institutions, the provision of fellowships for national personnel to pursue appropriate studies abroad and the funding of study tours to cater for specific requirements.

c) *Institution building*
Advice has been given on the formulation of policies and approaches to nature conservation in general, and national parks and protected areas in particular. The emphasis has been on flexibility and the need to harmonize proposals with local practice, traditions and culture. Assistance with legislation has been provided and a number of countries now have wildlife and national parks laws based on this. It should be pointed out that draft legislative texts have been proposed to meet individual country situations, with inputs from both lawyers and resource managers, and reference to relevant international conventions and norms. The use of model legislation has not been advocated.

Advice and assistance on the creation or strengthening of national organizations responsible for the administration and management of protected areas has been basic to the objectives of several projects. This has resulted in the establishment or upgrading of national park and wildlife administrations in certain countries.

Finally, an important function of FAO Headquarters and regional officers has been the dissemination of information in support of the above.

2.2. Summary of projects

Turning to actual projects that have been executed, there are perhaps two fields where an impact of particular significance to protected area management has been made during the past decade.

The first relates to wildland management, for which planning methodology was developed and tested in the context of regional projects in Latin America, funded by UNDP and Rockefeller Brothers Fund. This pioneering work formed a basis from which many innovations in this field have since been developed and are in use today.

The second was a close association with the training institutions at Mweka and Garoua in Africa, particularly in their early formative stages. Assistance and support was provided to both through FAO/UNDP projects and closely coordinated with help made available by the many other organizations involved. Managers trained at these two colleges now form a nucleus of dedicated staff in many organizations responsible for protected area management throughout the continent.

Table 1 summarizes projects and activities related to protected area management which were executed during the period under review. This shows that some 86 projects, spread over 40 countries and six regional projects, were implemented. It may be interesting to note that over 80 management plans for protected areas in 25 countries were generated by these efforts, besides assistance given in the preparation of proposals and strategies for national systems of protected areas.

Table 2 summarizes the number of fellowships awarded in the protected area and wildlife field annually, from 1975 to the present. More than 100 candidates have received training outside their countries at universities and colleges during this period.

2.3. Structure of projects

The 1970s were the heyday of what might be termed the "classical" project. A large-scale project was headed by a FAO/UNDP Project Manager and staffed by FAO/UNDP experts in appropriate subjects, on assignments. Durations of assignments was measured in years rather than months and additional specialists supported activities on short-term consultancies. Projects were joint undertakings with governments concerned, who pro-

vided a co-manager and counterparts to the various international experts and consultants. Counterparts received on-the-job training and experience from international staff in the course of pursuing project activities and objectives.

In general the international component funded transport, material and equipment, together with external training, while government provided accommodation and other facilities and local support. Unless there were special circumstances, the international budget of a well balanced project would be roughly distributed 30% to personnel, 30% transport, material and equipment, and 30% fellowships and other training, with the remainder covering administrative support.

During this time, the single technical assistance experts of the 1960s had become small-scale projects, usually with most of the above elements. Toward the end of the period under review this situation began to change to what is now perhaps a transition stage, as will be seen below.

Before turning to the future, it should be emphasized that FAO/UNDP projects could only become a reality if *formal requests were made by governments through recognized channels* for them. Furthermore, it is now essentially up to government to decide how UNDP funds programmed for a country should be allocated among the various sectors.

3. FUTURE TRENDS

The World Conservation Strategy and indeed this Congress' theme—"Defining the Role: Protected Areas in Support of Socio-Economic Development"—set the stage for future trends and development. These will in turn influence the content, structure and implementation of assistance efforts.

3.1. Reorientation of project objectives and activities

The overriding consideration which will affect protected areas in much of the developing world for the remainder of this century will be an accelerating pressure for land caused by expanding human populations. The validity of apparently locking up large tracts of land will be increasingly questioned. To meet this challenge, the socio-economic benefits of protected areas and national parks will have to be maximized, particularly those that accrue to people living in their vicinity. In short, more efficient use will have to be made of protected areas and people will have to be seen to benefit from them.

The effect on the technical content of projects is likely to be a shift away from the generalist adviser and the fields of biology, ecology and wildlife towards resource management, resource economics and socio-economics. Planning of areas will become more detailed and refined, while management will be more specific and intensive. Emphasis will be placed on developing strategies, systems and mechanisms that involve and integrate local communities into protected area management. The often-quoted educational, research and genetic resource conservation roles of national parks will have to show tangible results and benefits that can be recognized by society.

Protected area and national parks managers should become less isolated from other resource disciplines and where appropriate, will coordinate their planning and activities with other environmental protection efforts (mountain watersheds, anti-erosion, desertification, etc.). Close cooperation with interested plant and animal geneticists in the area of *in situ* genetic resource conservation should be mutually beneficial. Much concern can be anticipated with the integration of protected areas and national parks into overall land-use planning in the context of rural development. In future management will need to be positive and decisive—the days of endless studies to postpone action are past.

3.2. Training programmes

Training protected area managers can be expected to become much more specific to the evolving requirements of the subject area. The tendency to regard an ecological or wildlife management background as being the most appropriate will disappear. Courses and programmes will increasingly be designed to meet the planning, resource management and socio-economic requirements mentioned above. This is already the trend in Latin America; Asia and Africa can be expected to follow suit.

3.3. Implementation of assistance

Here the trend is already away from the "classical" project summarized above. The title Chief Technical Adviser is replacing Project Manager for the senior FAO staff member on the project. International expert assignments are giving way to national experts where these are available, and projects are being headed by national directors. The accent will increasingly be on supporting local capability to attain national objectives in socio-economic development, where it exists. More use will be made of national and regional institutions. Already, for example, protected area project activities have been sub- contracted to local universities in this context. International expertise will tend to be of a highly

specialized nature and in the form of short term consultancies in support of national experts. The option of government execution is also being pursued and interestingly enough an FAO assisted National Parks project is currently being implemented in this way.

Technical cooperation between developing countries (TCDC) and economic cooperation between developing countries (ECDC) are already a fact. Some wildlife and national park training programmes have already come within the scope of the former. In launching fresh initiatives in training in particular, it is anticipated that a package involving national and regional institutions and TCDC, augmented by short-term international expertise could form a basis for making an impact.

3.4. Funding sources

UNDP has been and still is the main source of financial support for FAO executed national park and protected area projects. Where national financial and economic planning authorities give sufficient priority to the sector in the programming of UNDP resource, future assistance can be assured.

Certain protected area proposals have met the criteria for support from FAO's own Technical Cooperation Programme (TCP) in the past and undoubtedly this will happen again in the future.

Apart from the provision of associate experts, FAO/Government Cooperative Programmes have not supported any projected area management related projects to date. One can only hope that this situation will change in the future.

Trust fund support for national park and protected areas activities has come from the Rockefeller Brothers Fund in Latin America, as mentioned above, and some unilateral Trust Funds in the Near East. More of the latter are to be expected in the future.

4. CONCLUSION

The objectives of assistance to protected area mangement will increasingly become socio-economic and rural development oriented. Technical inputs to projects will change accordingly. The trend in implementation will be more and more towards supporting and augmenting national capability. Protected area management will evolve into a discipline in its own right.

Table 1: FAO Protected Area Related Field Projects and Activities(1) Executed 1972–82(2) by Region

a) *Africa*

No. of countries	No. of Projects	No. Activities[1]
24	31	9
Regional	2	2

b) *Asia*

17	28	6
Regional	2	—

c) *Latin America*

9	3	9
Regional	2	—

Table 2: FAO Executed Protected Area Related Fellowships 1975–82

Year	Africa	Asia	Latin America	Total
1975/76(3)	23	7	4	34[3]
1977	4	2	—	6
1978	1	3	1	5
1979	6	6	—	12
1980	4	9	—	13
1981	2	6	—	8
1982	6	9	1	16
Total:	46	42	6	94

(1) Activity is used to denote protected area related components of projects which also include other disciplines.
(2) Projects which commenced prior to 1972 but were still operational after that date are included.
(3) Figures for two years combined.

How UNESCO's Man and the Biosphere Programme Is Contributing to Human Welfare

Dr. Bernd von Droste zu Hülshoff
Unesco, Division of Ecological Sciences
Paris, France

1. INTRODUCTION

Let me begin with the "evolution" of the concept of ecology as a science and the "co-evolution" of the concept of conservation as an applied filed of ecology. The concept of ecology has evolved considerably since the time of Heckel, who first coined this term in 1869 for the science which studied single species and the conditions that control their lives. This was the time when ecology was simply equated with autecology.

As the concept evolved, ecology came to mean the study of aggregates of mixed organisms called communities, or biocenoses. Synecology was "discovered" as late as 1950, when the ecosystem—the sum of all the plants and animals, plus the physical environment in particular regions—was adopted as a convenient unit for field studies.

A book entitled "The Biosphere" by the Russian, Vernadsky, appeared as early as 1926, but it was only in the 1970's that ecologists paid much attention to the interactions between different ecosystems—natural and man-modified—that make up the biosphere.

2. UNESCO'S MAN AND THE BIOSPHERE PROGRAMME

The Unesco Biosphere Conference in 1968 laid the foundations for the modern Man and the Biosphere concept. The dominant role of man in shaping the biosphere was recognized. Ecology became both a natural science and a human science: a natural science that includes man, and a human science that includes nature. From then on, ecology became a truly holistic science of man and nature, a prerequisite for solving concerete problems of sustainable natural resource use.

What is conservation? It seems that the concept of conservation has followed the same development as the ecological sciences, in a kind of co-evolutionary process. At first, if focussed on the conservation of species; then on the conservation of wild genetic resources and ecosystems; and finally on integrating principles of conservation with the idea of sustainable development which is at the very heart of the World Conservation Strategy. One of the challenges of modern ecological sciences is to identify new and creative ways to merge conservation with development.

The modern definitions of ecological sciences and conservation were integral parts of Unesco's Man and Biosphere Programme (MAB) launched in 1971. Ten years later, in 1981, the validity of the MAB approach was reaffirmed by the 101 MAB National Committees around the world. A new MAB decade was opened under the banner "Ecology in Action", which stressed the need for ecological sciences to apply themselves more to solving concrete problems of sustainable development. Priority was given to the further building up of MAB research networks for tropical and arid regions and human settlements, as well as to the establishment of a coherent worldwide network of biosphere reserves.

At present, there are about 1000 such MAB research projects around the world, in addition to the 215 biosphere reserves in 58 countries, which help provide ecosystem protection and fulfill the role of permanent vast open-air research laboratories. MAB pilot projects also serve for training and experimentation. By encouraging co-operation among research projects, MAB networks help to use scarce manpower and financial resources more efficiently to provide the scientific information needed to deal with pressing problems of land use.

Many of the pilot projects for research and training have been built up as part of the MAB network in the humid tropics. These projects are studying the human use systems through which people manage natural resources. A diverse range of resource management problems, biological and social processes, types of ecosystems and research approaches are studied.

By co-ordinating research and exchanging information within the network, scientists obtain results which can be useful elsewhere in the humid tropical regions. The projects are nationally sponsored, with FAO, UNEP, Unesco, IUCN, ICSU and IUFRO and other international organizations providing some additional support and complementary actions.

Another priority area for MAB is the study of arid land ecosystems. Because dry lands are ecologically very fragile, they require careful management. In the past, human populations were small, and man established a harmonious partnership with nature. Today, with increasing population pressure, arid lands are often used in ways which are ecologically unsound. Overgrazing, for example, can set off a chain of events leading to irreparable soil degradation. To satisfy human needs without damaging the environment, new management systems must be developed for these areas. MAB-IPAL in Kenya is a good example of MAB research efforts on complex land use problems. Scientists and policy-makers are working together to improve herbivore management in marginal areas, while taking account of far-reaching ecological, socio-economic, economic and political dimensions.

3. WHAT ARE THE CHALLENGES OF MAB?

The first challenge of MAB is to identify the proper focus on land-use problems. By focussing a research project on a specific land use problem of common concern, MAB endeavours to achieve a fruitful interaction between the main actors: scientist, decision-makers, resources managers and local populations. The aim is: to deepen understanding of natural and social processes; to provide policy-relevant information; to build up local scientific manpower; to construct bridges between the universality of science and particular needs of national development; and, ultimately, to help provide the foundations for an endogenous development which is rooted in the cultural, social and ecological substrata of a country. Working in isolation, scientists often make proposals which turn out to be impracticable and therefore the research results may fail to make a real impact on decision-making. Interaction and communication among all those concerned by the environment are the keystones for success not only in MAB but also in conservation work.

The second challenge is to achieve a transdisciplinary approach by building bridges between the basic sciences, applied sciences, planning and policy-making. However, the transdisciplinary pyramid with decision-making on the top has weak foundations as long as the crucial fields of basic sciences are neglected. One such field is conservation biology; another one is perception research. The foundation of conservation is extremely weak as long as no major effort is made in the field of conservation science to fill crucial knowledge gaps.

The third challenge is to take into account the different dimensions of land use problems. Space itself has three dimensions. Time and perception add the often missing fourth and fifth dimensions. Together, they make up "Human Use Systems"—the socio-economic and ecological system through which people manage their resources. They are the appropriate units not only of problem-oriented interdisciplinary research but also form the essential context for conservation efforts.

The most critical dimension for conservation is perhaps time. Time scales of concern for proper planning are: genetic conservationist—10,000 years; crop evolutionist—100 years; forester—30-50 years; plant breeder—10 years; politician—next election; hunter/gatherers—1 day to a few weeks. If protected areas are designed without due consideration to the time dimension, they might not fulfill their purpose to maintain species diversity and provide for continuing evolution of species. Thus, we might fail in many cases to fulfill our evolutionary responsibility in the field of genetic resource conservation.

4. BIOSPHERE RESERVES

As mentioned before, a key element of MAB is the international network of biosphere reserves. A biosphere reserve helps us learn how to conserve. Questions as to the optimum size, shape and distribution of nature reserves, and how to allow evolution to continue, still have no definitive answers. Through the research being conducted in biosphere reserves, science can help to find some of the solutions.

A biosphere reserve constitutes a representative example of one of the world's major ecosystems and thus conserves genetically viable plant and animal populations in their natural habitats; provides sites for long-term research on the structure, functioning and dynamics of ecosystems; combines research and monitoring, environmental education, training and demonstration; and seeks the support and participation of the local people, in part through research contributing to their social and economic development. A biosphere reserve is not an enclosed, inaccessible sanctuary. It blends with the surrounding human landscape. Finally, biosphere reserves form an international network linked up with other networks in MAB, thus offering a vast framewrok for comparative research for a continuum reaching from undisturbed natural areas to man-made systems.

The International Biosphere Reserve Congress in Minsk/USSR during September/October 1983 will assess the present state of the international network and draw up future directions for fuller implementation of the biosphere reserve concept worldwide.

The Mexican experience in the two MAB biosphere reserves of Mapimi and La Michilla shows that rational conservation efforts based on scientific research can also stimulate rural development and increase the well-being of local populations. The Mapimi Reserve lies within a semi-desert basin—the Bolson de Mapimi—with grasses, shrubs and cacti and a diverse fauna, all adapted to the harsh arid climate. Before the creation of the reserve, the cattle ranchers found it was more and more difficult to eke out a living from the area's dwindling natural resources. This situation was exemplified by the plight of the giant desert tortoise *Gopherus flavomarginatus*, which provided an easy source of meat but was in danger of extinction.

The central core of La Michilia Reserve is made up of the relatively unmodified, mountainous Cerro Blanco covered in evergreen brush. Pine and oak woodland is typical of the surrounding buffer area. Here, hunting and grazing pressures had wiped out animals such as the black bear *Ursus americanus* and reduced populations of herbivores such as the white-tailed deer *Odocoileus virginianus*. Potentially a rich grazing area, new management systems were urgently required to avoid exhausting the natural resources. Research began in 1976 with intensive field studies to assess the ecological potential of each reserve. This led on to programmes for supplementing and diversifying traditional land use practices, e.g. introducing new forage plants adapted in the area such as the non-spiny prickly pear. A study on white tailed deer in La Michilia has shown that if hunted wisely, this animal is a valuable source of meat and need not compete with cattle for grassland. A desert research laboratory has been built at Mapimi, making possible prolonged scientific investigations and, for the first time, regular collection of weather data. Mexican scientists, together with others from Argentina, France, USA and USSR, have contributed to maintaining a high standard of research and have helped train many young Mexican scientists in the field.

It was quickly realized that if the biosphere reserves were to have a future, the people living in and near them must be assured of making a living. Priority was thus given to developing profitable crops and small labour-intensive industries based on local resources. Experimental strawberry growing at La Michilia has proved highly successful and fruit is now marketed alongside other fresh vegetables, jams and preserves in the major Mexican cities. Basket-making and, cutting and polishing of local semi-precious stones provide further employment. Bee-keeping has been introduced successfully in both reserves and a small industry is being developed in local wood packaging, making crates for transporting fruits and vegetables and bee-keeping equipment. These small-scale efforts have not only raised the living standards of the local people but have helped to relieve agriculture pressure on areas devoted to strict wildlife protection.

5. CONCLUSIONS

Undoubtedly, the Mexican biosphere reserves illustrate how the problems and possibilities of natural resources conservation may differ between the Third World and industrialized countries. The fast rate of population growth in the Third World, together with a rapid rate of destruction of a highly fragile environment creates sooner or later an explosive situation for protected areas. It is true that the record of the past decade is an excellent one for the developing world both in terms of numbers of new reserves and land and water surface set aside for conservation. However, this brand-new "Noah's ark" built for the survival of some of the world's most important genetic resources may sink overnight if protected areas are not decisively contributing to human welfare.

MAB research in biosphere reserves can help to provide a scientific basis for a balanced approach to conservation management which will be of relevance to local human welfare.

Is the best way to protect a natural area to seal it off in a "closed jar" from the outside human world? Sooner or later, such a policy can destroy the area it was intended to protect. Ecological and sociological pressures—both inside and outside—may eventually shatter the reserve.

MAB emphasizes man's partnership with nature. A biosphere reserve is open and interacts with its region. The local people can be its guardians.

Biosphere reserves offer a unique but so far largely unexploited opportunity to involve the international scientific community in a vast effort to improve the scientific basis for natural resource management and conservation. Linked up with other MAB networks, biosphere reserves provide an unmatched worldwide framework for the transfer of scientific knowledge, expertise and techniques for sustainable resource development. To put the biosphere reserve concept fully into practice will be one of the great challenges for the next decade. It is a forward-looking concept of conservation contributing to human welfare.

The Role and Constraints of International Development Agencies in Promoting Effective Management of Protected Areas

Arne Dalfelt
Norwegian Agency for International Development
Oslo, Norway

ABSTRACT. *Although most international aid agencies have policies stating the need to incorporate environmental concerns and conservation in their development programmes, there still exist great differences between these goals and the realities. The role of international aid agencies in promoting protected areas establishment and management is still insignificant. A long list of reasons can be found for this, among them inadequate institutional structures and procedures, lack of ecological conscience in donor agencies, lack of interest and understanding from the recipient part, inadequate planning procedures and more. A solution to these problems must be sought in the creation of public awareness, increased training in environmental conservation, forming organized and intelligent public support and pressure for conservation and using adequate justifications for protection of areas as a vehicle for development. Such arguments should seek to clarify the role of protected areas for the well-being of the poorest segments of the population in the developing countries.*

1. INTRODUCTION

Bilateral and multilateral official aid from the world's western industrialized countries to the underdeveloped or developing countries counted for approximately US $32,000 million in 1980 (DAC, 1981). This figure does not include aid channelled through non-governmental organizations (NGOs). Only a tiny fraction of this amount goes to projects that can be classified as conservation-oriented activities, in spite of increasing evidence throughout the world of environmental deterioration caused in large part by the development process itself.

1.1. Overexploitation

Rapid world population growth and the efforts of Third World countries to provide their population with immediate economic improvement have led to overexploitation of natural resources and passing of the limits of their sustainable use. The results are desertification, dwindling forests and disappearing wildlands, with consequent increased development problems. More and more developing countries are entering a vicious circle in which national efforts to realize fast economic growth leads to increased problems with respect to resource conservation and sustained use of their productive capacities. This in turn leads to increased pressure on the remaining natural resources and so on. The economic and social forces that fuels the development of this vicious circle are so strong that the developing countries in general seem unable to cope with the problems in time to avoid extensive and often irreversible loss of their resource capital.

1.2. Environmental problems

Bilateral aid is very often provided for projects which are intended as measures to cope with environmental or resource problems caused by the above-mentioned deteriorating process. Oddly enough, donor agencies seldom see or fully understand this connection, and therefore rarely attack the root of the problem. And in other cases where the full scope of the problem is clear, they often are unable to solve the problems because of social, economic or political constraints. The overall result is that the world, after almost forty years of large-scale aid programmes transferring considerable funds from the industrialized to the non-industrialized countries, only faces increasing development problems and in some regions even greater threats of famine and human suffering than before the aid programmes started. The complete picture is of course very complex, but there is a slowly awakening awareness that environmental deterioration is a significant and perhaps the major factor causing the negative development problems facing the world today. This "awakening" process is, however, so slow and occurring at such a late stage that many environmentalists question whether it is already too late to avoid the coming of a major environmental disaster that will affect perhaps the whole world.

Speculation around this theme is, however, not the objective of this paper, and the following will focus instead on some of the factors affecting the introduction of more conservation-oriented thinking in most development agencies.

2. THE NATURE AND CONSTRAINTS OF AID ORGANIZATIONS

Aid programmes are political, openly or hidden, and are therefore subject to popular thinking, strategic considerations, economics, pressure groups, religion, fads, bureaucratic preferences and inertia, etc. Stronger involvement of bilateral aid organizations in conservation work therefore depends on how these factors work separately and together.

2.1. Receiver orientation

Among the major factors affecting conservation in aid programmes, perhaps particularly in Scandinavia, is the principle of "receiver-oriented" aid programmes. This means that the recipient country decides, within broad guidelines, the composition of the aid programme. The inevitable result of this is that the programme tends to favour short-term economic exploitation and programmes that aim at conservation and long-term sustained production from the natural resources, not to speak of protected areas, receive much lower priority. Political forces in the recipient country usually have a limited time horizon and are eager to provide their population with fast economic or material benefits, which often increases pressure on wild and marginal lands and wildlife resources.

2.2. Basic human needs

Another factor which should be advantageous to conservation is the stated policy of most donors to give first priority to the provision of basic needs for the poorest section of the population in the receiving countries. It should be advantageous because this policy ideally should lead to projects favouring long-term sustained produc-

tion from all lands according to their producing capacities and in accordance with ecological needs. In practice, however, this often leads to opening up of new lands for food production which in reality often are unsuitable for agriculture, causing serious damage to the resource base.

2.3. Inadequate planning

Inadequately planned and designed aid projects aimed at supporting the poorest segments of the society very often result in a deteriorating situation rather than the opposite. This has been experienced in many cases, for example in potable water drilling projects in arid zones where the pumping has resulted in lowering of the ground water level, thus causing local desertification. Likewise, provision of watering holes for cattle has resulted in increased cattle trampling, erosion and vegetation damage in large areas around the waterholes. Irrigation of agricultural lands in many arid areas has led to salinization problems, land clearing projects for rural development or cattle raising have led to erosion problems or bush encroachment, and ill-planned forestry projects have led to the extermination of plant and animal species, erosion and so on. Industrial aid projects can likewise cause tremendous negative environmental impacts if they are not properly planned from an environmental viewpoint.

2.4. Environmental impact assessments

A major reason for inadequate planning is the rather common reluctance to include environmental impact assessment in aid project planning. This reluctance is only very rarely based on a negative attitude to the concept of ecological analysis. It is rather caused by a fear that environmental impact analysis in project planning represents increased project costs and delays in project implementation. It may also simply be caused by a general lack of knowledge and understanding of ecological processes and interdependence of ecological factors. Very many aid projects simply seek to heal damage caused by natural disasters, without anybody ever questioning the ecological chain of events that led to the disaster, much less addressing the roots of the problems, which may be geographically or temporally distant from the site or time of the damage.

For example, increased frequency of floods in India only very recently has been attributed to deforestation problems in the Himalayas and the secondary effects of sedimentation in the lower riverbeds with consequent raising of river bottom levels. Similarly, reduced coastal fisheries have only recently been seen as a result of use of pesticides in agriculture and industrial pollution in addition to overexploitation.

2.5. Lack of ecological knowledge

It may be understandable that lack of ecological knowledge is a constraint in developing countries, but the reality is that most international aid agencies still have a very limited base of ecological expertise to be used in project planning. Traditionally, international aid agencies are mostly manned by economists, engineers, lawyers, sociologists and production-oriented personnel together with generalists of which few have any adequate training in conservation or ecology. This lack of ecological expertise often results in indifference or even unwillingness to include ecologists in project planning and implementation.

2.6. Intangible values

But even when ecologists are used in project planning they often face difficulties in proving immediate or short-term monetary or economic profits from needed ecological measures. The lack of market prices for conservation values—for example, genetic conservation or improved quality of living as a result of ecological measures in project planning—seems difficult to accept for many aid bureaucrats used to economic anlaysis as a basis for selection of projects.

2.7. Decision making

Ecological analysis and assessment also adds to the complexity of decision making, which is another reason why aid bureaucrats are often slow in accepting the inclusion of conservation and ecological considerations in projects. This adds to the normal phenomenon of governmental bureaucratic inertia whenever new ideas are introduced in an established process of project planning, implementation and evaluation.

2.8. Acceptance of the area protection concept

The concept of area protection seems to create a dilemma in the minds of many people even in the economically developed parts of the world, and it seldom meets with approval before considerable damage has been done to the resources. The establishment of national parks in Scandinavia has, for example, proved to be a complicated political process, meeting considerable individual or organized resistance. Resistance is mainly by people having economic interests in the exploitation of the areas, but may also have other reasons. However, once established and paid for, protected areas often receive overwhelming public moral support for the benefits they provide to recreation, education, science and other fields.

To succeed with the establishment of national parks and reserves, it therefore becomes necessary to have project supporters with statesmanlike vision going far beyond the normal short-sighted economic views of ordinary people. In the context of aid programmes, this becomes necessary at both the recipient and the donor levels, which makes success twice as difficult. However, the establishment of national parks in many developing countries received a head start during the colonial period because the colonial powers were able to ignore any local resistance to the establishment of protected areas. Statesmen with foresight have since been supportive of the creation of protected areas in many countries, but the process becomes increasingly difficult as the population grows, and as resources become more scarce.

2.9. Bilateral aid for area protection

Bilateral aid for the establishment of national parks in third world countries is rather rare. This is caused by the weakness of public supporter groups, but also by the general fact that most of the national parks in these countries were created for the benefit of tourists and a small relatively wealthy elite. The impression that national parks only cater for a selected few seems to be widespread among aid officials. The argument that national parks provide much-needed foreign currency from tourists is given relatively limited weight in project priority selection, and is commonly met with the counter-argument that limited bilateral aid must be reserved for projects directly aimed at providing socio-economic benefits for the poorest section of the local population. A long-term ecological view on national development faces difficulties, and the values of ecosystem or genetic resources conservation is little understood.

Arguments for the creation of national parks and reserves must therefore be found elsewhere. Many areas, particularly in Latin America, include native populations. In such areas very strong arguments can be found for the justification of support from bilateral aid agencies. An estimated 400 million people depend to some extent on the tropical forests for their livelihood, a fact that is not well known, but which represents a powerful argument for area protection. In other areas, important arguments can also be found in watershed protection, provision of energy, and endemic species protection and such arguments must be used to a much larger degree than hitherto.

A prerequisite for support from government aid agencies is that justified requests are channelled through formal procedures and channels in the recipient countries. This means that the proposing or initiating individuals or institutions, for example the Ministry of Environment or the Ministry of Natural Resources in a given country, must be able to get the proposal included among the high priority projects at the national level. These are being presented to potential donors normally by the Ministry of Economic Development or the Treasury or equivalent in the recipient country which has the responsibility to negotiate with donors. Most aid agencies also have other channels that can be used, some of which apply to NGOs, but funds provided outside the formal and normal government channels tend to be limited.

2.10. Country programmes

Most bilateral aid agencies have selected a limited number of countries with which they develop major aid programmes. For these selected countries they agree to provide a predetermined amount of economic aid for the next four to five years on a rolling budgetary basis. This enables the recipient country to plan projects of several years duration.

These country programmes take the bulk of the aid provided, and projects within the country programme are mutually agreed upon in yearly programming sessions. Any projects included in this process will normally receive all the funds necessary for full completion. Support for conservation projects, including protected areas, should be included in these country programmes, but may for reasons explained earlier have to be included as part of other projects aimed at the direct improvement of the socio-economic situation of the poorest people. There are many ways of doing this, for example, adding conservation components into projects which fall under such major headings as rural development, social forestry, watershed management, resources management, etc. Funds provided outside or above the country programmes are more flexible in relation to formalities and restrictions on use but are normally more limited. These funds are however of great interest to conservation work, particularly until public and political support have grown strong enough to ensure the inclusion of conservation activities in the regular programmes.

2.11. Political and public support

Political and public support for protected area establishment and management is essential if increased aid is to be provided for such projects. This is of utmost importance, and public awareness campaigns and public environmental education are thus fundamental in a long-term strategy to provide more governmental economic support for protected areas and conservation in general. Much has already been done over the last ten to twenty years, but public and political conservation awareness and pressure must continue to be built up for still a long time before it becomes sufficient to ensure adequate inclusion in aid programmes. Such conservation pressure must be planned and carried out with care, intelligence and moderation. Set-backs have occurred several times and in several places in the industrial countries with respect to public support, because of unrealistic attitudes and stands taken by over-enthusiastic conser-

vation groups on specific local conservation issues. This has had negative impacts on many established bureaucrats, including officials in aid agencies. And it does not take much to stop a good project in the planning stage, since aid programmes are, like anything else, dependent upon the interests of individuals and groups of people.

3. INTERNATIONAL DEVELOPMENT AGENCIES AND THE PROMOTION OF PROTECTED AREAS

As has been seen from the above, international development agencies have so far not contributed adequately to protected area management for a variety of reasons. There are, however, signs of change in many agencies due to a slowly-awakening awareness of the importance of area and resource conservation and protection. In certain cases this awareness was created by forces outside of the aid agencies. In the United States, environmental groups took the US Agency for International Development to court during the late 1970s because of the Agency's disregard for environmental laws and regulations in their aid programmes. This factor contributed to a significant change in the agency's priority settings.

The environmental consequences of aid projects in the tropics began to surface in the 1960s. Several international meetings dealt with these problems in the latter part of that decade, leading up to the Stockholm Conference in 1972. This Conference meant in many ways a breakthrough for the understanding of the relationship between development and conservation of natural resources. UNEP was formed and the term "ecodevelopment" was introduced, referring to the need to see local and regional development projects in the context of the area's resource base and environmental conditions. The need for intermediate technologies compatible with local social environmental and cultural conditions were gradually accepted. On a wave of worldwide enthusiasm, environmental thinking spread. Slowly, international aid bureaucracies began to move in the right direction, but high population growth, increased food deficits and economic recessions made advances very slow, or even resulted in reductions in environmental projects towards the end of the 1970s. In spite of set-backs, an awareness has been created and along with the continuing and accelerating environmental deterioration in the tropics, bilateral aid agencies will have to move forward on the issue of more ecologically sound projects in the future. The World Conservation Strategy represented a timely climax of the thinking on these issues when launched in 1980, and provided both conservation organizations and development agencies with a written tool for the necessary integration of conservation with development. Most aid giving agencies can today show lists of projects that have been planned and implemented at least to some degree according to ecological criteria, although the list of environmentally damaging projects also continues to grow. Some of the international aid agencies and banks have introduced mechanisms for environmental analysis and impact assessment. The World Bank established an office for environmental questions in the beginning of the 1970s (Goodland, this volume). The International Institute for Environment and Development (IIED) prepared a study in 1977 on how multinational development agencies considered environmental aspects in their work; the results led to a new study of bilateral aid agencies in Canada, West Germany, the Netherlands, Sweden, Great Britain and USA. The study concluded that all the agencies had formulated policy declarations aimed at the consideration of environmental and ecological aspects in their aid programmes, but that there still existed a rather great distance between declared intentions and the realities.

3.1. The US Agency for International Development (AID)

USAID is the world's largest bilateral aid agency. AID is very sensitive to views of the US Congress and this has resulted in a strong environmental commitment for that agency. AID works according to a set of formal regulations dealing with the environment; it also is unique in that it has a comparatively significant staff of environment experts maintaining a dialogue with the aid-receiving countries. This has led to a much better environmental evaluation of projects than in most other aid agencies.

AID also has an overriding policy of aiding the poorest of the poor, but seeks to connect this with environmental considerations to the benefit of these groups. Environmental impact analyses are carried out as a principle for their projects, and environmental profiles are being prepared for many of their counterpart countries. AID has gradually moved into supporting more conservation projects, including reforestation, watershed management, endangered species protection, environmental education, institution building and more. Funds for national parks or protected area management are still rare, although some such projects do exist, for example in Costa Rica and Panama. Recent budgetary cutbacks have also affected these types of projects. The total net flow of official resources from the United States to developing countries and multilateral agencies amounted to US $8,250 million for 1980, or 0.31% of the GNP.

3.2. The Netherlands

The Dutch bilateral aid agency, Directorate General for International Cooperation (DGIC) manages only a limited portion of the total bilateral aid given by the Netherlands. The agency has a very small staff, making environmental analysis of their projects very limited, in spite of the agency's considerable interest in environ-

mental issues which reflects the great interest for such issues in the Dutch parliament and among the public. As a result, the DGIC has established environmental guidelines to be followed in project planning, and draws on tropical ecology expertise in other Dutch institutions. The Dutch National Advisory Council for Development Cooperation prepared a report in 1978 called "Recommendations on Ecology, Aid and Development", which calls for increased efforts in the field of ecology and conservation in Dutch bilateral aid. Funds for projects in protected area establishment and management are still insignificant.

3.3. The Scandinavian countries

Since the 1972 Stockholm Conference, the Scandinavian countries have further developed an environmental awareness and conscience, and all the countries have now included environmental aspects in their aid programmes. Nevertheless, all these countries still have difficulties in living up to their stated goals. The Danish government published their latest report calling for increased environmental attention in aid programmes in August 1982; so far, however, Denmark has implemented very few direct conservation projects, although environmental assessments are carried out for many projects. Finland has only very recently began to include environmental aspects in their projects, although traditionally many of the Finnish projects deals with forest exploitation and water management.

In 1981, Norway issued an official statement at the highest political level which called for increased environmental attention in bilateral and multilateral aid programmes. So far, however, only very few projects can be classified as conservation-oriented, mainly reforestation and watershed management projects. Sweden has for several years had a stated policy concerned with environmental aspects in foreign aid, including a special budget for conservation projects. Sweden has had the most active conservation-oriented programme in Scandinavia, but even so the amount is not impressive compared to the rest of the aid programme. Most of their conservation projects are within reforestation, village forestry and soil and water conservation.

In 1981, a special working group was formed under the auspices of the Nordic Ministerial Council to review and report on the relationship between environment and development, and to recommend on actions necessary to improve the integration of environmental issues in the Nordic aid programmes. The report was delivered in October 1982 and concludes that all the Scandinavian countries aim to give increased attention and support to environmental aspects and projects in their foreign aid programmes. However, the report also states that there are obvious difficulties in putting the aim into practice.

The report recommends that the Nordic aid programmes should be aimed at providing long-lasting improvements to the lives of the poorest segments of the population in the recipient countries. It further states the common responsibility between donors and recipients for the environment, and the need to adhere to the policies of the World Conservation Strategy. It calls for the integration of environmental guidelines in project planning and implementation and recommends the inclusion of environmental aspects in research, training, commercial aid programmes, multilateral aid programmes and contribution to direct conservation projects and institution building. The impact of this report remains to be seen.

4. CONCLUSION

A review of the present situation reveals great differences between the existing broad political goals of more environmental conservation in and for development and the realities of the international aid programmes which are still being planned and executed with little regard to the environment. The role that should be played by the international development agencies in promoting sound management and protection of areas should be far greater than it actually is, if their stated goals of aiding the poorest of the poor on a sustained basis shall ever be a reality. In spite of this, all signs indicate that the next decade will witness an increase in environmental awareness and considerations in aid programmes. Let us hope it will not be too late.

The World Bank, Environment, and Protected Areas

Robert Goodland
Office of Environmental Affairs
The World Bank
Washington, D.C., USA

ABSTRACT. *Environmental criteria (including conservation, pollution control, public and occupational health and safety, and human ecology) are systematically integrated into World Bank projects in the belief that sustainable economic development depends on sound environmental management. Procedures are outlined by which the Bank incorporates necessary environmental safeguards into each stage of the project cycle, from initial identification through final evaluation. The Bank's other environmental functions (including technical assistance and liaison work) also are outlined. Specific Bank projects with significant wildlands conservation components are noted, along with sources of environmental information and guidelines.*

1. INTRODUCTION: THE MEANING OF ENVIRONMENT

The World Bank includes under the rubric "environment" the rational and sustainable development and management of natural resources for the economic improvement and well-being of all peoples, including future generations. The Bank endeavours to ensure that economic development promoted by it does not exceed the regenerative capacities of the affected environment which makes all development—and, in fact, all life—possible. More specifically, environment is taken to mean both the naturally occurring environment as well as that created by human agency (e.g. urban), including public and occupational health and worker safety, and the socio-cultural well-being of peoples affected by the development process.

The Bank's environmental work focusses on the design and implementation of development projects in most of the sectors in which the Bank invests. Some Bank-assisted projects contain a readily identifiable environmental component. For example, the water supply of a large-scale irrigation project in Indonesia is enhanced and its infrastructure protected by conversion of the entire water catchment into a National Park. A significant and growing number of Bank-financed projects are entirely "environmental," for example reforestation, soil conservation, range, wildlife and watershed management, sewage treatment, and pollution control.

"Environment" is described more thoroughly in the Bank's basic publication "The Environment, Public Health and Human Ecology: Considerations for Economic Development" (1982). Two documents—"Environmental ranking of Amazonian development projects in Brazil" (World Bank Reprint Series, 1980) and "Indonesia's environmental progress in economic development", both available from the Bank's Office of Environmental Affairs—outline country-specific examples of environmental progress and indicate the range of environmental concerns in two of our largest clients.

2. TYPES OF ENVIRONMENTAL PROBLEMS

Environmental problems may be divided into three broad categories related to magnitude: global, regional, and local. *Global problems* are often the most threatening and the least apparent. They include persistent biocide residues that through the actions of wind, water, and living carriers, travel far beyond the area where the chemicals were originally applied; the burning of fossil fuels, which affects the carbon dioxide balance and increases oxides of nitrogen and sulphur and the particulate content of the atmosphere; the pollution of the oceans from land sources, oil spills, or dumping from ships on the high seas; and induced changes (e.g., by deforestation) in global climatic patterns.

Regional problems result from geophysical linkages among a group of countries. Typical examples are the effects of river development upstream and downstream, the downstream effects of loss of forested watersheds, the spread of desertification across national borders, and transnational air pollution.

Local problems are confined within national boundaries. These include, for example, accelerated erosion, the extirpation of wildlife habitat and extinction of species, the creation of aesthetic blight, and the eutrophication of water bodies from fertilizer runoff or discharge of domestic sewage.

3. ENVIRONMENTAL CONCERNS IN THE WORLD BANK

Since 1970, when the World Bank established the Office of Environmental Affairs (OEA), the Bank has made environmental, health and socio-cultural concerns an integral part of its economic assistance programmes. In his address that year to the United Nations Economic and Social Council, then World Bank President Robert McNamara emphasized that one challenge facing finance institutions was to devise strategies to help developing countries avoid or mitigate environmental damage that economic projects can cause—without slowing the pace of economic progress. He noted that the costs resulting from adverse environmental change could be enormous, and that a small investment in prevention would be worth many times what would later have to be spent to repair any damage. This point was reaffirmed ten years later by Bank President Clausen, who shortly after taking office in 1981 emphasized: "We are convinced that it is less expensive to incorporate the environmental dimensions into project planning than to ignore them and pay the penalties at some future time."

The Bank's environmental experience has demonstrated that it is feasible to incorporate suitable measures to protect health and environment into development projects. One key has been the Bank's insistence on a pragmatic approach—one tailored to the huge differences prevailing in its 141 member countries. World Bank policy is to integrate environmental aspects totally into the project itself. Each project is approached as having a unique environmental setting. This precludes the application of inflexible environmental regulations to countries with highly differing environmental and economic circumstances.

The Bank views environmental input as fundamental to the good design of projects. Environmental work thus becomes a continuous *process* during development, and not necessarily a discrete component of a project or—even less effective—an add-on. It is not a formal "Environmental Impact Statement" to be filed to comply with legalistic requirements. Environmental criteria are factored into design decisions together with economic and engineering criteria from the earliest stages of the project. In no instance is the monetary cost of environmental and health safeguards (usually no more than 3 to 5 percent of the total project cost) disqualifying.

3.1. General policy

As a general policy, the Bank will not help finance any project that seriously compromises public health or safety, causes severe or irreversible environmental deterioration, or displaces people without adequate provision for resettlement. Project planning or implementation may on occasion fail to anticipate adverse environmental consequences, or the necessary impact projections may be unavailable or inadequate, in which case the Bank attempts to incorporate environmental measures during project implementation.

The problem of managing natural resources and environmental systems is a matter of growing concern, especially in many of the Bank's tropical member countries, since they are inherently more susceptible to the effects of environmental degradation or ecological stress than temperate countries. Since developing countries can ill afford an expensive curative approach to environmental degradation, many are adopting the more efficient preventive management approach (cf., Leonard and Morell, 1981). Developing countries, moreover, tend to have burgeoning populations whose needs for food, fuel, and shelter strain the environment's carrying capacity more than in temperate countries.

Some of these pressures on the environment are:

- Overgrazing and overfishing which damage the food base;
- Lack of water and fuels, or their misuse, contributing to desertification;
- Satisfying the need for fuelwood (as much as one metric ton per family each year), which contributes to deforestation, and thus to erosion, siltation, and floods; and
- Construction of roads, dams, airports, irrigation systems, and power and industrial plants which frequently create new environmental, health and social problems or magnify those already present.

4. ENVIRONMENTAL PROCEDURES OF THE WORLD BANK

The Bank is a strongly project-oriented institution and its projects follow a cycle of well-defined stages. The most relevant in terms of environmental considerations are pre-project work, preparation, appraisal and implementation.

4.1. Pre-project work

A valuable opportunity for environmental improvement lies in economic and sector work. Detailed studies are made of the entire economy of all member countries every two years or so. The resulting "Country Economic Memorandum" is a useful vehicle for subsequently influencing the mix of projects. Similarly, sector reports (e.g. forestry reviews, power surveys, regional studies) can identify environmental and resource opportunities and constraints. Hence discrete projects emanating from such reports will already reflect environmental concerns. Pre-project studies financed by the Bank contain environmental instructions in the terms of reference. This is routine "good operating procedure". Consultants assisting governments with such studies are expected therefore to play an important role in improving environmental management.

4.2. Preparation

Projects are prepared by the potential borrowers (the member governments), often with the help of consultants. A feasibility study often forms the basis of project preparation, which may itself take two or three years. The terms of reference (TORs) for feasibility (and pre-feasibility) studies therefore are valuable opportunities for ensuring consideration of the environmental dimensions, and the Office of Environmental Affairs seeks to ensure that such terms of reference contain comprehensive environmental instructions. Such general terms of reference are designed to provide sufficient scope and freedom for competent environmental specialists to address all relevant issues, but, of necessity, they cannot specify in every case what the issues may be. Similarly, the Bank does not expect all conventional environmental aspects to receive equal attention. It expects the specialist to decide which environmental aspects merit detailed work and which require limited or perhaps no attention.

The Project Brief, an internal Bank document compiled by regional staff during preparations, usually one year before appraisal, specifies measures to minimize environmental costs. The Bank's "Project Preparation Facility" is a source of funds (up to $1 million) which may be used specifically to address unforeseen environmental impacts.

4.3. Appraisal

During the appraisal stage of the project cycle, the Bank comprehensively reviews all aspects—technical, institutional, economic and financial—of the project prepared by the Borrower and lays the foundation for implementing the project and evaluating it when completed. The Bank's appraisal therefore is a decisive point in the project cycle, marking the end of the creative design phase and the start of implementation. Appraisal includes consideration of the possible effects of the project on the environment and on the health and well-being of the people. Measures are specified which will prevent or mitigate any adverse effects stemming from the project.

The appraisal mission prepares a Staff Appraisal Report, a critical document in which OEA is responsible for reviewing all environmental aspects. Although this formal review stage is a useful check, the Bank endeavours to ensure that all major environmental aspects have been addressed before appraisal. Clearly, as the project cycle progresses, environmental improvements become increasingly difficult and less effective.

4.4. Loan negotiations

After appraisal, environmental needs may be discussed during loan negotiations between the Bank and the Borrower. Similarly, the loan agreement may contain legal covenants dealing with environmental aspects, and progress may be required as a condition for effectiveness of the loan, and later for disbursement to begin.

4.5. Implementation

The Bank seeks to ensure that environmental problems will not halt a project after a loan has been invested. Suspending disbursements because of lack of environmental progress would be an extreme measure and would indicate that inadequate environmental measures had been taken earlier on. During the construction and operation of projects, Bank supervision missions, approximately every six months, review environmental progress with the Borrower. The "Project Completion Report" is prepared by the Bank shortly after disbursements have ended, often five or more years after appraisal. This report specifically addresses any environmental, health, sociological or human ecological problems or changes in the project, and is most useful in improving the design of future projects.

4.6. Evaluation

The Bank established a quasi-autonomous Operations Evaluation Department (OED) in 1973 to evaluate the contributions of projects to the socioeconomic development of recipient countries. These post-project evaluations now provide for "environmental post-audits," providing useful feedback information on this aspect of projects' performance.

5. ROLE OF THE OFFICE OF ENVIRONMENTAL AFFAIRS

The principal responsibility of the Office of Environmental Affairs (OEA) is to ensure that environmental aspects of all Bank work are adequately addressed. Most of OEA's time is allocated to the project cycle, particularly the creative design phase from identification, through preparation to appraisal. Thereafter, OEA monitors progress.

The Office of Environmental Affairs staff works with the Bank's Regional Staff, who manage projects directly and who bear the responsibility for all necessary environmental work. Most environmental work is prepared by consultants. OEA assists Regional Staff in finding the type of consulting expertise required, preparing TORs, reviewing consultants' reports and seeing that their recommendations are incorporated into the project. OEA provides project-specific environmental guidelines. OEA assists in deciding how much environmental work is needed on specific projects during preparation, and assists with "quality control" of the results. Since OEA spans all regions, it can note inter-regional differences in environmental progress. Similarly, since OEA deals with all sectors, it works on improving intersectoral (e.g., agriculture vs hydroprojects) development. OEA assists regional staff in incorporating environmental training into both education projects and projects needing permanent environmental input.

OEA also works directly with environmental ministries or agencies of our member governments. Such technical assistance has been particularly productive in improving member countries' capability to monitor environmental aspects of their overall national development programs.

As former Bank President McNamara emphasized, ". . . it is the non-financial assistance of the Bank that is of even greater value than its financial support, indispensable as that is." OEA therefore aims to improve the capacity of member nations to fulfill their own environmental needs. The development of national and sub-national local capabilities is the only long-term solution to environmental management. Recognizing the great importance of environmental planning to the development process, more than 120 member countries have created central environmental agencies. A much larger number of implementing ministries (such as National Power Boards) have their own in-house environmental unit or department. To the fullest extent possible, the Bank works with such agencies, strengthening their role within the development process.

Similarly, OEA encourages the strengthening of non-governmental environmental organizations, and where appropriate, the use of local ecologists or university environmental departments as consultants (cf., Trzyna and Coan, 1976). It assists in starting dialogues between such environmental groups, the implementing ministry and the federal environmental agency. It also encourages Bank missions to work with the environmental agency and encourages their review of TORs and of subsequent recommendations. Where still embryonic, such national environmental agencies may be easily bypassed by the more powerful implementing ministries; OEA tries to ensure they are brought fully into the development process from the earliest stages and responds to requests for environmental institution strengthening. This may take the form of providing counterparts for feasibility studies or environmental reconnaissance, providing longer-term environmental advisers to the ministry, or with training of environmental ministry staff.

6. WILDLAND CONSERVATION IN THE WORLD BANK

The World Bank has assisted with the financing of approximately thirty projects in 21 countries over the last 9 years, which have significant wildland conservation components (listed in Annex 1).

As used here, *wildlands* are defined as national territories of land and water which have been only slightly or not at all modified by modern man, or have been abandoned and have reverted to an almost natural state. Wildlands thus include the full range of natural areas (ecosytems), whether land-based (e.g., forests, woodlands, brushlands, grasslands, deserts), natural inland bodies of water, or coastal marine areas. *Wildland conservation* is used here as the direct protection or enhancement of wildlands and their characteristic plant and animal species. Wildland conservation is therefore a subset of the range of activities that comprise conservation in a broader sense. Within the context of natural resources management, conservation is generally understood to mean the rational and sustainable use of natural resources. In this sense, "conservation" includes valuable activities which reduce pressures to convert intact ecosystems (e.g., timber and fuelwood plantations, erosion control, and intensification of agriculture in already-cultivated areas). "Wildland conservation," however, is here restricted to the management of relatively undisturbed habitat or natural areas, together with their constitutent species. Wildland conservation also may promote the restoration of abandoned, formerly cultivated land, or habitat which has been damaged in some way, in an attempt to recreate the value of the intact ecosystem.

Wildlife conservation was promoted by the Office of Environmental Affairs as soon as it was created in 1970. Malawi's Lengwe National Park was strengthened with Bank assistance in 1973, partly to protect the rare Nyala antelope. The water release schedule of Zambia's Kafue hydroproject was designed to replicate seasonal flooding of the Kafue flats, important grazing land for wildlife including the endemic Lechwe antelope *Kobus leche*. In a rural development project, Mauritius protected the habitat of the endangered Pink Pigeon *Nesoenas mayeri*, also in 1973.

Such conservation components differ greatly in size from 100% of project costs to zero cost but with significant benefit. Kenya's Wildlife and Tourism project (1976) is entirely devoted to wildland conservation. More than $36 million were invested in seven national parks or reserves, supported anti-poaching measures, and provided for wildlife studies and training of personnel. In contrast, manipulation of the Kafue hydroproject water release schedule costs nothing, but important benefits accrue. Similarly in Sudan's Rahad irrigation scheme, the design of a canal was altered to avoid an important wildlife migratory route, yet no additional costs were incurred. The Bank has found that significant benefits to wildlife and to the environment in general can often be obtained by improving the project design at no extra cost. If there is a "typical" wildland conservation component that can be identified and has been costed out separately, then it may cost up to 14% of total project costs (although it is very often less than 1%). Such wildland measures are not always so unambiguous. For example, creation and maintenance of a fire control lane may be included in a project to protect both human settlements and natural forest ecosystem, but may not have a separate cost assigned to it.

One of the most cost-effective measures is expected in Indonesia's 1980 Irrigation XV loan of $54 million. To help protect the watershed catchment area for the Dumoga, Sulawesi, irrigation works, the 2,700 sq km Dumoga National Park was established (Sumardja, Tarmudji and Wind, this volume). This cost less than 1% of the total project cost, mainly to establish and demarcate Park boundaries, develop a management plan, hire needed guards and other personnel, and provide necessary infrastructure and equipment. This relatively small investment in wildland conservation helps protect the Bank's valuable irrigation investment by helping to minimize siltation and the resulting high maintenance costs, and by helping to ensure a steady, year-round flow of water. The Park also preserves much of the rich flora and fauna that is unique to Sulawesi.

The project assisting with protection of the largest land area is in Brazil's Northwest Region Project, approved in 1981. This provides for the protection of more than 15,000 sq km of natural ecosystems, largely rainforest. The environmental component also provides for biotic inventories, research, training of personnel, and monitoring of environmental quality.

Since 1970, the Bank has sought to prevent unnecessary damage to wildlands, either by improving project design or by including wildland components in appropriate projects when the opportunity arises. The Bank affirmed this commitment to wildland conservation by stating, ". . . in countries where there are no adequate natural resources conservation programs and institutions, the Bank will not support projects that might result in disintegration of a habitat not elsewhere represented in the country and not under suitable protection (as in national parks and wildlife reserves)."

This became official policy for forestry projects when it was promulgated in the Forestry Sector Policy Paper of 1978. This policy was reinforced in 1980 when the Bank, together with the Asian Development Bank, InterAmerican Development Bank, African Development Bank, Caribbean Development Bank, The Arab Bank for Economic Development in Africa, Commission of European Communities, Organization of American States, United Nations Development Program and United Nations Environmental Programme, signed the "Declaration of Environmental Policies. . ." Furthermore, the President of the World Bank endorsed the World Conservation Strategy in 1980.

Despite the growing international recognition of wildland conservation as a vital link in sustainable development, the present worldwide investment in wildland conservation is inadequate to enable wildlands to make their fullest possible contribution to economic and social development, for present and future generations. Furthermore, the rate of loss of wildlands is accelerating, as is the rate of extinction and the endangerment of species. Apart from extinctions, the conversion of large areas of forest appears to be worsening local and possibly regional climatic patterns. Recognizing these trends, the Bank is seeking ways to prevent or mitigate the environmental degradation that slows the pace of economic progress in our member nations.

Furthermore, despite the Bank's leadership in supporting wildland conservation, a sub-optimal amount of attention has in the past been devoted to this issue in Bank projects. The Bank is therefore increasing efforts towards the more systematic incorporation of wildland conservation components within appropriate types of Bank projects. The Bank also proposes to undertake a variety of additional activities that directly or indirectly support wildland conservation, in projects and in economic and sector work. Such activities may include assistance to the wildlands, environmental or similar agency in member governments. The development of conservation indicators may be attempted, such as the proportion of wildlands conserved in each nation.

6.1. The role of conservationists

The Bank finances projects prepared by member governments or their consultants. Although the Bank carefully appraises each project before any committments are made, the Bank largely relies on the government for the details of the project, and especially for project quality. A case in point is Indonesia's Irrigation XV project which affects 5 sites thousands of kilometres apart. In such cases, the Bank relies on the government's environmental or wildlife agency to assist the implementing ministry (e.g., Agriculture) in project design. This process can be facilitated if national park personnel become involved in the design phase of the project. Non-governmental organizations can also assist in this regard. Indonesia's Ministry of the Environment is strengthened by over 100 non-governmental environmental societies.

Similarly, biological researchers who may have studied in one particular tract for several years can be alert to development plans and can assist in their improvement.

7. CONCLUSION

This paper demonstrates, in a necessarily abbreviated fashion, the great importance the World Bank attaches to environmental aspects of development projects. The paper indicates where the Bank, the client and consultants are collectively expected to provide the various necessary environmental imputs. This emphasizes the need for developing environmental capability in agencies or firms where it is now lacking, and stresses the growing importance of the environmental units of those government agencies or consulting companies with in-house expertise. Wildland conservation components in Bank-assisted projects are outlined and their increasing importance noted. Finally, environmental terms of reference are designed to provide competent professionals with flexibility to address important aspects and not to waste time and resources on less important matters. This acknowledges the increased responsibility of environmental professionals, and makes the quality of their performance even more critical.

ANNEX 1. PROJECTS WITH WILDLAND CONSERVATION COMPONENTS

EAST AFRICAN REGION (11 projects, 6 countries)

Kenya, Wildlife and Tourism. $36 million wildland component, to develop wildlife-based tourism, including expanded tourist facilities in Amboseli National Park, Marmar Ranch, and Masai Mara, Samburu, Buffalo Springs, and Shaba National Reserves, mitigating adverse environmental impacts of tourism in Lake Turkana National Park, measures to reduce conflicts between wildlife and pastoralists, studies of wildlife and tourism policies, support for Wildlife and Fisheries Training Institute, Wildlife Management Unit, and the Wildlife Clubs of Kenya.

Kenya, Livestock Development II. $3.4 million wildland component, including assistance to Amboseli and Nairobi national parks and Masai Mara Game Reserve.

Kenya, Bura Irrigation Settlement. $.3 million wildland component, including habitat protection and monitoring wildlife populations.

Kenya, Forestry Plantation II. No cost for wildland component, which includes establishment by government of some 7,000 ha of strict nature reserve as a covenant in the Loan and Credit Agreements.

Malawi Shire Valley Agricultural Consolidation. $.13 million wildlife component, to provide continued support for the 15,500 ha Mwabvi Game Reserve and a major proposed extension to the Lengwe National Park.

Malawi Shire Valley Agricultural Development II. $.06 million wildlife component, to strengthen protection of the 13,000 ha Lengwe National Park.

Malawi National Rural Development Program III. $.29 million wildlife component to establish seven new forest reserves.

Mauritius Rural Development. No additional cost for wildland component, which included deletion of 500 ha of native scrub forest from plantation forest development plans due to presence of endangered Pink Pigeon, and establishment of government committee to prevent future conflicts between development plans and endangered species habitats.

Sudan Rahad Irrigation. No additional cost for wildland component, which relocated water supplycanal almost 100 km north so that it would not interfere with wildlife migrations.

Tanzania Tourism Rehabilitation. $.63 million wildland component, including provision of anti-poaching equipment, monitoring of wildlife populations, and a Bank requirement that the government continue to pursue policies consistent with preservation of wildlife resources.

Zambia Kafue Hydroelectric II. No additional cost for wildland component, which includes periodic water releases from the reservoir to replicate the natural seasonal flooding of the Kafue Flats, an important wildlife habitat for the rare and endemic Lechwe antelope.

WEST AFRICAN REGION (1 country, 2 projects)

Ivory Coast Tourism II. Wildland component $2.7 million, to help establish and develop the 19,300 ha Azagny National Park).

Ivory Coast Soubre Hydroelectric. Wildland component $.195 million, to cover the development of a plan to reduce possible increased encroachment pressure on the Tai National Park and the creation of a permanent environmental protection unit within the Energie Electrique de la Cote d'Ivoire to manage the wildland component.

EAST ASIA AND PACIFIC REGION (3 projects, 3 countries)

Indonesia Irrigation XV. $.5 million wildland component, to establish the 270,000 ha Dumoga National Park in

North Sulawesi, designed to protect the watershed for the irrigated lowland crops and to conserve endemic forest plants and animals.

Philippines Watershed Management and Erosion Control. $10.7 for wildland component, including equipment, vehicles and training for natural forest protection.

Thailand Northern Agricultural Development. $.346 million for wildland component, including construction of fire lanes and provision of forest guards to protect 138,000 ha of natural highland forests important for watersheds.

SOUTH ASIA REGION (1 country, 2 projects)

Sri Lanka Tree Crop Diversification (Tea) I. Wildland component $.0192 million, to preserve 2100 ha of steep land in conservation areas.

Sri Lanka Mahaweli Ganga Development III. Wildland component to be specified for implementing a wildlife conservation plan to minimize or mitigate damage to populations of wild elephants and other endangered species affected by the project.

EUROPE, MIDDLE EAST AND NORTH AFRICA REGION (3 countries, 4 projects)

Greece Evros Development. No additional cost for wildland component, which includes establishment of Dadia Native Reserve with 7300 ha strictly protected core zone and 20,700 ha buffer zone, and the cessation of forestry activities which may have threatened the nesting habitat of 22 species of birds of prey, including the endangered Imperial Eagle and Cinereous Vulture.

Morocco Middle Atlas—Central Area—Agricultural Development. Wildland component had no additional cost; it includes the establishment of the 188 ha Sehab Reserve as a scientific "baseline" forest study area, and perhaps as a core area for a future national park.

Turkey South Antalya Tourism Infrastructure. Wildland component $3.4 million, for development of tourist facilities in the Olympus National Park and support for Park staff.

Turkey Northern Forestry. Wildland component $1.8 million, to provide wildlife conservation programme, including restoration of Red and Roe deer to forest areas and national parks.

LATIN AMERICA AND CARIBBEAN REGION (8 countries, 12 projects)

Argentina-Paraguay Yacyreta Hydroelectric. Approximately 1 million wildland component covers relocation of endangered Swamp Deer to natural reserve to be established in Paraguay, and measures to protect riverine forest.

Bolivia Ulla Ulla Development. Wildland component of $.67 million covers population inventories, pasture management research, and anti-poaching measures implemented to conserve the threatened Vicuna.

Brazil Northwest I Agricultural Development and Environmental Protection. $18.72 million wildland component helps to establish and protect the Pacaas Novas National Park and the Guapore and Jaru Biological Reserves, encompassing some 1.5 million ha of natural ecosystems.

Brazil Carajas Iron Ore. $20 million wildland component covers the provision of environmental officers, establishment and management of protected natural areas, biological inventories of areas to be developed, and rehabilitation of mined land. The overall project includes an additional $13.6 million for Amerindian protection.

Brazil Amazonas Agricultural Development. The wildland component of less than 1 million covers the identification and demarcation of 180,000 ha of biological reserves and a larger area of forest reserves.

Brazil Alto Turi Land Settlement. No additional cost for wildland component, which includes preservation of 100,000 ha of natural forest in the project area.

Brazil Maranhao Rural Development. Wildland component of $1.689 million covers the identification and protection of 2 new forest reserves totalling about 100,000 ha and a study to design a strategy for subsequent forest protection and reforestation in the project area.

Colombia Guavio Hydro Power. Wildland component $.3 million covers development of a watershed management plan, including protection of natural forest.

Colombia Upper Magdalena Pilot Watershed Management. $1.9 million wildland to provide field equipment, vehicles, offices, trails, shelters, and operating costs to strengthen protection of natural forest areas, including the Los Nevados and Nevado del Huila national parks.

Costa Rica Highway IV. Wildland component provided by government out of road toll revenues includes modification of road design to minimize environmental impacts, extension of the Braulio Carrillo National Park, and development of park infrastructure.

Honduras Tourism Development. Wildland component of $.189 million covers the development of an environmental control master plan for Roatan Island.

Mexico Baja California Tourism. Wildland component $.29 million covers protection of coastal, marine and desert ecosystems, including research and establishment of fauna protection stations.

Parguay Caazapa Area Development. $.243 million wildland component covers infrastructure for 6,500 ha Caaguazu Forest reserve.

Council of Europe Work on Protected Areas

Division of Environment and Natural Resources
Council of Europe
Strasbourg, France

ABSTRACT. *This paper describes the work of the European Committee for the Conservation of Nature and Natural Resources, mainly centred on the protection and management of the natural heritage. Under the Council of Europe, the Committee has instituted the "European Diploma", which has proven effective in conserving the most representative sites and landscapes in Europe; established the European network of biogenetic reserves, which will enable the genetic heritage of Europe to be conserved; and instituted the Convention on the Conservation of European Wildlife and Natural Habitats (the "Berne Convention"), which is aimed to encourage initiatives concerned with protected areas while stimulating sound management of all natural habitats.*

1. INTRODUCTION

For the past twenty years, the Council of Europe (which comprises 21 member States and has its headquarters in Strasbourg, France) has been the seat of the European Committee for the Conservation of Nature and Natural Resources, whose work is mainly centred on the protection and correct management of the natural heritage. All species of threatened flora and fauna have been systematically and regularly studied, thus enabling "European Red Lists" to be drawn up. Fragile, sensitive and characteristic biotopes of the European continent have also been listed and studied: heathlands, peatlands, alluvial forests, and dry grasslands have all received attention. A long-term project has been the preparation of a "Map of the Vegetation of Europe", which contains much and varied information on the large units of vegetation of the European countryside.

Where protected areas are concerned, especially practical results have been obtained:

- the institution of the European Diploma has proved effective in conserving the most representative sites and landscapes in Europe;
- the setting up of the European network of biogenetic reserves will enable the genetic heritage of our continent to be preserved, as has been shown by the first results obtained; and
- the recent Convention on the Conservation of European Wildlife and Natural Habitats (also known as the Bern Convention) will encourage initiatives concerned with protected areas while stimulating good management of all natural habitats.

2. THE EUROPEAN DIPLOMA

By its Resolution (65) 6, adopted on 6 March 1965, the Committee of Ministers decided to create a "European Diploma" for certain protected natural areas, sites or features.

The Diploma was created to provide a strong incentive to maintain the quality of protection where it already exists and to introduce it where it is still lacking. The regulations (of 1965) for the award of the Diploma state:

"It shall be awarded for a period of five years, and shall be renewable for successive five year periods".

"Any such proposal (necessarily submitted by the government of a member State) shall be accompanied by supporting documents mentioning *inter alia* the international interest of the said area, site or feature, the system of protection already enjoyed and the body responsible for administration of the same."

After the first trials, it was found necessary to amend the regulations and an on-the-spot appraisal must now be carried out both for the first application and for future renewals (Resolution of 19 January 1973). Furthermore, the sites examined are classified in one of the following categories:

- Category A covers nature reserves or sites which have a high ecological value and are strictly protected (IUCN Category I).
- Category B essentially concerns protected landscapes, which are thus open to the public (IUCN Category V).
- Category C associates the social and recreational functions of the area with maintenance of its biological or aesthetic characteristics for the purpose of achieving a first-class environment (IUCN Category VIII).

There is no ranking of these three categories, as the objectives are entirely different.

Moreover, the new regulations state "Should there be notification of the danger of a serious threat to or serious deterioration of the natural area, site or feature concerned, the Secretary-General may appoint an independent expert to assess whether there is in fact any

real danger and to carry out a further on-the-spot appraisal (again accompanied by a member of the Secretariat)" (Article 6.1). This procedure could lead to the withdrawal of the Diploma, the decision being taken by the Committee of Ministers on the proposal of the European Committee.

This modification is very important, as it helps to reinforce the protective status of the Diploma site. The procedure was invoked in 1974 when the Secretary-General of the Council of Europe was warned of the existence of a project for a new high-speed train route between Kln and Frankfurt, which threatened the Siebengebirge Nature Reserve, a Diploma site near Bonn. A special appraisal was carried out, and the project was subsequently mothballed, not only because of this procedure, but also for other reasons, in particular of an economic nature.

The person responsible for each area holding the Diploma prepares, at the end of the year, a detailed report which provides the Secretariat and the European Committee with useful information on the evolution of the situation (fauna, flora, protective measures, infractions, pressure of the public, etc.). Moreover, the managers of the areas meet regularly at Strasbourg, to exchange experiences and to discuss thoroughly some especially thorny problem, such as the effects of tourist pressure, the education of visitors, etc.

To date, i.e. over a period of some 15 years, about 40 applications have been filed by governments and 19 have been approved:

1966	Peak District National Park (United Kingdom)	Category C
1966	Camargue Nature Reserve (France)	Category A
1966	Hautes Fagnes Nature Reserve (Belgium)	Category A
1967	Lüneburg Heath Nature Reserve (FRG)	Category C
1967	Swiss National Park (Switzerland)	Category A
1967	Muddus National Park (Sweden)	Category A
1967	Sarek and Padjelanta National Parks (Sweden)	Category A
1967	Krimml Waterfalls Natural Site (Austria)	Category C
1967	Abruzzi National Park (Italy)	Category B
1969	Wollmatinger Ried Nature Reserve (FRG)	Category A
1970	Boschplaat Nature Reserve (Netherlands)	Category A
1971	Siebengebirge Nature Reserve (FRG)	Category C
1973	Germano-Luxembourg Nature Park (FRG/Luxembourg)	Category C
1976	Vanoise National Park (France)	Category A
1976	Pyrenees National Park (France)	Category A
1976	Kuscenneti National Park (Turkey)	Category A
1978	Weltenburger Enge Nature Reserve (FRG)	Category B
1979	Minsmere Nature Reserve (United Kingdom)	Category A
1979	Samaria National Park (Greece)	Category A

Four applications, from Germany, Ireland and the United Kingdom, are currently being studied.

The European Diploma has been effective. Because of the conditions laid down at the time of renewal, the Council of Europe has in several cases been able to prevent a deterioration of the situation. Thus, for example, in the case of Wollmatinger Ried, extension of the neighbouring airport was abandoned; at Krimml

Falls, projects for developing tourist facilities on the site were adapted to the requirements of the European Committee; in Abruzzi National Park, the financial and staff resources made available to the Park's administration were substantially increased and an overall improvement plan, in conformity with the European Committee's conclusions, is to be drawn up.

It is certain that other sites merit the award of the

Diploma, but it must be remembered that it is a two-edged weapon for the governments concerned. On the one hand, award of the European Diploma enables them to demonstrate the importance they attach to the European dimension of protecting their natural heritage, but on the other they commit themselves more or less permanently to preserving these areas in their natural state. In the majority of countries, withdrawal of the European Diploma would certainly provoke a public outcry, with obvious political repercussions. We have only to imagine withdrawal of the Diploma from the Vanoise or Swiss national parks. It is in fact the extent of public support and the reaction of public opinion which gives the European Diploma its importance. Fortunately, despite the present difficult socio-economic situation, public opinion with regard to natural resources is not weakening. Quite the contrary—in view of the deterioration of these resources it is constantly strengthening.

3. THE EUROPEAN NETWORK OF BIOGENETIC RESERVES

The European Diploma is intended to honour and protect sites which are generally rather large and have a clearly European dimension and significance. During the 1970s the need arose to undertake a parallel, complementary initiative by placing smaller, perhaps more modest, but still interesting, areas under the auspices of the Council of Europe. The European Ministers for the Environment asked the Council of Europe to draw up "a programme for the establishment of a European network of reserves (including frontier areas, where necessary), to conserve representative examples of European flora, fauna and natural areas".

Under the terms of reference conferred by the Committee of Ministers, the European Committee for the Conservation of Nature and Natural Resources has developed a "European network of biogenetic reserves", which has the following characteristics:

- The major purpose of a biogenetic reserve is to maintain the biological balance and effectively conserve one or more land or sea habitats, biocenoses or ecosystems. The reserve must therefore have a legal status giving it effective long-term protection.
- The species of flora and fauna, or the environment as a whole, must satisfy one of the following criteria: typical, unique, rare, or endangered.
- As a result, biogenetic reserves may vary considerably in area. For example, they may just as well be a large expanse of typical Alpine landscape as a stretch of water a few hectares in area sheltering several endangered species of newts and/or varieties of iris. The creation of a buffer zone is strongly recommended in most cases. Ecological research in the reserves is actively encouraged.

A certain similarity can thus be observed between the biogenetic reserves and Unesco's biosphere reserves established under The Man and the Biosphere Programme. There are, however, two appreciable differences: whereas a biogenetic reserve may be justified by the presence of a single (e.g. rare or endangered) animal or plant species, the biosphere reserves have to be representative samples of biogeographical units; and the sole criterion for the creation of biogenetic reserves is their natural genetic wealth or originality, whereas the biosphere reserves take account of human activities.

Resolution (79) 9 sets out two different procedures for forming and extending the network.

1. "Any protected area or part of such area . . . which complies with the main objectives and the principles of . . . Resolution (76) 17 may form part of the . . . network" (Article 1). This procedure has already been adopted by various countries, in particular Italy and France. Its value is that it enables interesting protected areas to be incorporated rapidly into the network.
2. The second procedure is based on a highly methodical approach. The aim is to develop, for each type of biotope and animal or plant species, a sub-network composed of the natural areas that are really the most representative (Article 2). In the case of West European heathlands, for example, the experts have identified a total of 27 areas ("outline list") which they have proposed that the governments concerned include in the "West European heathlands" sub-network. Some of these areas are already designated as nature reserves or are located in a national park, in other words already protected, and their inclusion should not raise any particular difficulties. As far as the other areas are concerned, the countries in question have been invited to take protective measures at the national level so that they can then be added to the sub-network.

This procedure is still in its early stages. As mentioned above, an outline list has been drawn up for heathlands. Similar lists are being drawn up for peatlands, halophilic vegetation and, where animal groups are concerned, amphibians and reptiles. Its disadvantage is that it takes time, but it has the great value of encouraging the formation of sub-networks based on sound ecological considerations. Every list submitted to governments is the result of a comprehensive study of the biotope or group of species in question.

The two procedures described above are therefore complementary, since the first depends mainly on national initiative and the second requires a European approach. Both must be encouraged.

Any government designating a biogenetic reserve gives notice of it to the Secretariat by submitting a descriptive card giving certain information about the area in question (see Annex I) whereby its originality, its importance and, in short, its ecological value can be assessed. This procedure, which is based on very elaborate criteria, reflects the great importance which governments attach to intergovernmental cooperation within the Council of Europe on environmental matters. If the conditions for acceptance are satisfied, the Secretariat informs the government and the area becomes part of the European network. If not, the matter is referred to the European Committee for the Conservation of Nature and Natural Resources, which advises the government concerned on the steps to be taken to ensure conformity.

A list of the biogenetic reserves, giving the characteristics of each area, is drawn up every five years on the basis of the information supplied on the descriptive cards by the authorities responsible.

Resolution (79) 9 also lays down the procedure for withdrawing from the network when, as a result of extensive changes, a biogenetic reserve no longer complies with the objective and principles of Resolution (76) 17.

3.1 Extent of the network

By 31 March 1982, 121 biogenetic reserves had been designated according to the first procedure.

	Number of reserves designated	Total area (ha)
France	31	28,331
Italy	82	51,354
Liechtenstein	1	91
Netherlands	2	46,000
Norway	1	1,555,000
Portugal (provisional)	4	70,000
Greece	4	

Other designations are in progress in several countries, notably Switzerland, according to this same procedure.

Concerning the second procedure, the responsible experts have proposed to five countries that they include particularly interesting sites in the "heathlands" sub-network:

Belgium	4 sites
France	12 sites
Germany	16 sites
Spain	7 sites
United Kingdom	12 sites

The four Belgian sites were already protected and Belgium has integrated them into the sub-network. The other countries are examining the situation, in particular the possibility of creating reserves on sites which are not yet protected.

4. THE CONVENTION ON THE CONSERVATION OF EUROPEAN WILDLIFE AND NATURAL HABITATS (BERNE, 1979)

The Convention has a place in this brief document because, unlike other legal instruments which have similar goals, it deliberately stresses the protection of natural habitats. It is no exaggeration to say that this new legal instrument crowns the twenty years of activity by the Council of Europe as regards nature conservation and will constitute its main course of action for the next ten or twenty years.

The Convention has so far been signed by 19 of the 21 member countries of the Council of Europe, Finland and the European Economic Community; it has been ratified, in chronological order, by: the Netherlands, Liechtenstein, Switzerland, Portugal, Italy, Luxembourg, the European Economic Community, and the United Kingdom. It came into force on 1 June 1982.

The Convention covers the whole of European wildlife, not only threatened species; on the contrary, Contracting Parties undertake to "maintain the population of wild flora and fauna at, or adapt it to, a level which corresponds in particular to ecological, scientific and cultural requirements, while taking account of economic and recreational requirements and the needs of subspecies, varieties or forms at risk locally".

Furthermore, the Convention obliges Contracting Parties to ensure the conservation of the habitats of all wild flora and fauna species. The protection of habitats is of extreme importance for the conservation of wild species, and the text has therefore been drafted in a form that will keep it open for developing cooperation between the Contracting Parties, as for instance in the field of biogenetic reserves.

Obviously, emphasis is given in the Convention to threatened species, migratory and endemic species, habitats of such species and endangered natural habitats. Article 4 deals with habitat protection:

"1. Each Contracting party shall take appropriate and necessary legislative and administrative measures to ensure the conservation of the habitats of the wild flora and fauna species, especially those specified in the Appendices I and II, and the conservation of endangered and natural habitats.

2. The Contracting Parties in their planning and development policies shall have regard to the conservation requirements of the areas protected under the preceding paragraph, so as to avoid or minimize as far as possible any deterioration of such areas."

3. The Contracting Parties undertake to give special attention to the protection of areas that are of importance for the migratory species specified in Appendices II and III and which are appropriately situated in relation to migration routes, as wintering, staging, feeding, breeding or moulting areas."

119 plant species, most from the southern European region, were selected to serve as a first basis for Appendix I, which lists plants which are to be strictly protected; every Contracting Party undertakes to prohibit any deliberate picking, collecting, cutting or uprooting of such plants, as well as possession or sale (as appropriate). The biotopes of these species must be strictly protected and it would therefore be desirable, in some cases, to integrate them into protected areas.

55 species of mammals, 294 species of birds, 34 species of reptiles and 17 species of amphibians (freshwater fish and invertebrates are to be added at a later stage) were included in Appendix II; they will thus benefit from strict protection by the Contracting Parties. To this end, the Contracting Parties undertake to prohibit in particular the deliberate capture, keeping or killing of these species, the damage or destruction of their breeding or resting sites, or deliberate disturbance of them, the destruction, taking or keeping of their eggs, and possession or trade in them. Furthermore, their habitats must also be strictly protected.

Finally, most other mammals, birds, reptiles and amphibians whose conservation status in Europe needs attention are included in Appendix II, which stipulates that any exploitation—hunting included—must be regulated in order to keep the populations out of danger. These regulations include, among others, closed seasons, temporary or local prohibition of exploitation and the appropriate regulation of sale of these animals. Furthermore, if exploitation is allowed, then there is a prohibition of all indiscriminate means of capture and killing, means capable of causing serious disturbance to populations and in particular the means specified in Appendix IV.

It was felt that the aims of the Convention would more easily be achieved if the representatives of the Contracting Parties could invite any state which is not a Contracting Party to send observers to the Committee's meetings, and admit international agencies or bodies, governmental or non-governmental, who wished to do the same. The Standing Committee may further make recommendations to the Contracting Parties concerning measures to be taken for the purposes of the Convention, and to the Committee of Ministers concerning accession by non-member States (see below). It may also, on its own initiative, arrange for meetings of groups of experts. Finally, the Standing Committee may adopt amendments proposed to the substantive provisions, including the appendices.

Although not completely independent, the Standing Committee is thus entrusted with sufficient important powers to keep under review the provisions of the Convention and their application, to carry out research on the conservation status of all species and to adapt the conservation provisions quickly to new situations without having to go through the lengthy decision-making procedure of the Council of Europe. To amend the institutional part of the Convention, approval by the Committee of Ministers of the proposed amendments is required. Non-member States wishing to accede to the Convention may do so and will be invited to accede by the Committee of Ministers at the request of the Standing Committee. An exception was made for Finland, which participated as an observer in the preparation of the Convention and was invited to sign on the same day as the member States and did so.

ANNEX 1. MODEL OF THE DESCRIPTIVE CARD FOR THE EUROPEAN NETWORK OF BIOGENETIC RESERVES

The information given should justify the designation of the area and bear witness to its interest. The various items on the card are not to be completed unless the facts exist and are of an interest warranting the designation.

1. Name of the area:
2. Country (state):
3. Region, county or province:
4. County:
5. Map reference of the centre of the area (topographical map to be attached to the application):
   °N   °East/West
6. Minimum and maximum altitudes:
7. Size of area (terrestrial/aquatic) in hectares:
8. Owner:
9. Name and address of the managing authority:
10. Present protection status:
11. Date legal status granted:
12. Motives for designation:

13. List of predominant characteristics:
14. Measures
    • completed (1)
    • in progress (2)
    • proposed (3)
    for protection, planning, management and restoration:
15. List of the various habitats, biocenoses and ecosystems according to their predominance and description of their physical aspects:
16. List of plant species (including if possible subspecies and varieties) in order of priority:
    • predominant in the biogenetic reserve (1)
    • characteristic of the biotope (2)
    • threatened (rare, vulnerable, in danger) at national level (3)
    • endemic in the biogenetic reserve (4)
    • not native to the biogenetic reserve (5)
17. List of predominant plant associations, stressing the most important species:
18. Indication of aspects of the potential natural vegetation:
19. List of species of fauna (including if possible subspecies and varieties) in order of priority:
    • predominant in the biogenetic reserve (1)
    • characteristic of the biotope (2)
    • threatened (rare, vulnerable, in danger) at national level (3)
    • endemic in the biogenetic reserve (4)
    • migratory in the biogenetic reserve (5)
    • not indigenous to the biogenetic reserve (6)
20. List in order of priority of human activities and their
    • favourable (1)
    • adverse (2)
    • effects on the ecosystem of the biogenetic reserve (agriculture, forestry, hunting and shooting, fishing, mining, recreation, leisure activities, etc.)
21. Types of use to which adjoining territories are put (industry, urbanization, agriculture, forestry, etc.) and repercussions on the biogenetic reserve:
22. Information on the main research programmes and publications:
    • completed (1)
    • in progress (2)
    • proposed (3)

Ten Years Later: The Smithsonian International Experience Since the Second World Parks Conference

Ross Simons
Smithsonian Institution
Washington, D.C., USA

ABSTRACT. *This paper discusses recent programmes of the Smithsonian Institution, including the Nepal-Smithsonian Terai Ecology Project and the Barro Colorado Island in Panama. The paper stresses the importance of conservaton foundations in supporting appropriate activities in developing countries, particularly in developing cooperative programmes. The importance for increasing interchange of information between scientists and resource managers is highlighted and several suggestions are made on how to overcome the barriers.*

1. INTRODUCTION

The Smithsonian Institution's tradition in scientific work abroad dates back to the early 1850s, when naturalists paid by the Institution collected specimens in the West Indies, South America and the North Pacific. These expeditions helped lay the foundation for the National Collections which the Institution, over the years, has nurtured as one of the foremost sources for information on natural history in the world.

Building on its tradition, the Smithsonian continues to play a major role in basic research in biology. Specialists from the National Museum of Natural History, the National Zoological Park and the Smithsonian Tropical Research Institute form the core of the Institution's international programmes, with scientists from the Chesapeake Bay Center for Environmental Studies and the Radiation Biology Laboratory also contributing to the Smithsonian's international environmental programmes.

The Institution has no conscious plan for selecting field sites abroad; individuals or groups of individuals choose their research areas on the basis of their own interests, but in almost all cases, work abroad is devel-oped with a host country counterpart, thus ensuring that objectives of the host country are part of the planning process. It should be stressed that the Smithsonian does not engage in large-scale projects, but typically in projects which engage from 1-5 persons with a budget under $50,000.

The Institution does not have conservation or park management as its primary mission, but rather serves as a biological data collector and repository, from which results can be disseminated to environmental managers. The Smithsonian could be called a "Bureau of Biological Standards", an institution whose collections form an unparalleled baseline data index upon which to judge environmental changes.

The Smithsonian's collections, now numbering over 60 million objects, are regularly used by specialists from throughout the world. These collections aid park managers in identifying flora and fauna found in their jurisdictions, and can be used to document the long-term environmental health of an area, for example, by comparing levels of pesticides found in a specimen 50 years ago against ones recently collected.

In addition to curating the collections, Smithsonian scientists also undertake extensive field research, usually by a single investigator whose particular research interests dictate the field locale. However, of late, considerable emphasis has been placed on multi-investigator, interdisciplinary programmes. Among these efforts is the Smithsonian's International Environmental Sciences Programme. Developed in the early 1970s, with the support of appropriations by the U.S. Congress, the programme focuses on long-term environmental monitoring at selected sites in the tropics. Many of the projects undertaken over the years have been centred in protected areas, including the Galapagos Islands in Ecuador, Guatopo National Park in Venezuela, Chitwan National Park in Nepal, and the Smithsonian's own Barro Colorado Island in Panama. Additional work has been undertaken in the Amazonia region of Brazil and Peru, as well as the highlands around Wau, Papua New Guinea, and the Sinai region of Egypt.

This Programme has yielded significant results in promoting science in general and, more particularly, conservation in these regions. By collecting data over decades, fluctuations or anomalies in the biota of a site can be more easily noted and documented, and the development of a network of sites allows for useful comparisons to be made. An indirect benefit has been the development of relations with the host countries, an improved exchange of information with them and a better appreciation for local conservation measures. The participation of local scientists in these programmes with projects of their own design or in a training capacity has allowed for practical hands-on learning rather than through a mere textbook approach.

Examples of the Institution's experiences at two specific sites, Chitwan National Park in Nepal and Barro Colorado Island in Panama, illustrate of the Smithsonian experience abroad over the past decade.

2. NEPAL

The Nepal-Smithsonian Terai Ecology Project (formerly the Nepal-Smithsonian Tiger Project) originated at the 1969 IUCN General Assembly in New Delhi, when the world's attention was focused on the plight of the tiger and its diminishing habitat. At the Conference, S. Dillon Ripley, Secretary of the Smithsonian, pledged the resources and manpower of the Institution to help save the tiger.

It took nearly 4 years to implement the Institution's pledge. The first step was to determine an appropriate site to undertake the research and the appropriate methodology. It was decided initially to use on tigers radiotelemetry which had been successfully used on grizzly bears and mountain lions for 20 years. This decision proved to be crucial in site selection.

Between 1970 and 1972, scientific teams were sent by the Smithsonian to survey sites in India for long-term tiger monitoring. Various Indian specialists explained their approach to management of tiger populations. They preferred first to delineate reserves for tigers, based on historical patterns; second, to provide the proper gazetting; and last, to provide proper wardening of the selected area. They also maintained that an adequate census of the tiger population was of primary importance and that this census could be accomplished by traditional methods of visual observation and counting pugmarks. This approach has worked very well in India, as shown by the success of Operation Tiger.

The Smithsonian, with its primary interest in research, favoured the use of radio-tracking in its study of tiger populations. A search of the literature indicated that most knowledge of the behaviour of wild populations of tigers came from random observations. The Smithsonian proposed collaring 20 or more tigers, and tracking their movements by radio signals. It was hoped that this method would reveal not only behavioural characteristics, but also reproductive patterns and territorial parameters. It was felt that only after monitoring several generations could one develop a scientifically valid management plan.

During the 1972 Second World Conference on National Parks, the Nepalese delegation fortuitously approached the Institution about developing a programme for the management of tigers in their national parks and reserves. A Nepali with extensive experience in forestry and a candidate for a graduate degree in the U.S. was selected as co-principal investigator, along with a recent American Ph.D. who had radio-tracked mountain lions in Idaho.

In September 1973, the Smithsonian sent a team of scientists to the subcontinent to review potential sites. Two sites were offered in Nepal, one the Karnali Reserve and Chitwan. While early indications seemed to favour Karnali because of previous tiger surveys, agreement was reached on Chitwan because the Nepali Government pledged to make the reserve a national park, which provided the impetus to accumulate the necessary scientific data on which park planners could base their management decisions (see Mishra, this volume).

By undertaking this ambitious and high-risk programme, the Smithsonian hoped to conduct research in an area that was largely closed to scientific studies until the 1950s; to train Nepalis in the latest scientific methods, so that Smithsonian counterparts there would take their place in the world's scientific and conservation community; to help the government to be able to make its own independent decisions on wildlife and park management; and to learn a considerable amount about traditional Nepali techniques in managing wildlife.

In achieving these goals, the programme was successful, with some shortcomings. In terms of scientific data, we achieved far more than we originally envisaged. The project has continually monitored a population of tigers over 3 generations; we now have the most comprehensive data base in existence on tiger reproduction strategies, behaviour and physiology, as well as tiger-prey relationships, yet we are still far from understanding the role vegetation plays in the ecosystem. The ecosystem has one of the highest mammal biomasses in all of the Indian subcontinent and more information is needed on such species as hog deer and chital. Even so, the data generated by this programme has assisted His Majesty's Government (HMG) in reaching decisions to increase the Park size on 2 occasions; the Park now covers 89,400 ha, making it one of the largest on the subcontinent.

The Institution has actively engaged in training Nepali project personnel in modern wildlife techniques, both highly skilled park personnel as well as local *shikaris* (hunters). Two Nepalis achieved Ph.D.'s, two completed Masters, and another is engaged in pre-doctoral work; other park personnel were able to observe the fieldwork for short periods. Eventually, short-courses on site and at the Institution's various facilities in the States would be beneficial to the training of park staff. The existing impediment is not desire, but finance.

Western scientists participating in the project learned much from local personnel. The familiarity of the *shikaris* with Chitwan and their understanding of animal behaviour added considerably to the project's success. However, it has been almost impossible to harness this impressive pool of talent to develop careers in conservation for them; this remains a key issue for the future and one which both the outside institutions working in Nepal and the Nepalis themselves must confront directly.

At the outset of the Tiger Project, the Institution sought to create a permanent mechanism to carry on wildlife research in Chitwan and elsewhere in Nepal—in effect to set up a Dehra Dun for wildlife training on the subcontinent. Such a centre would be of enormous value to Nepal as well as the other neighbouring nations, allowing for the development of a highly skilled cadre of personnel to carry on and adapt techniques previously employed and taught by outsiders.

The Institution is extremely gratified to see that under the patronage of Prince Gyanendra, legislation has been developed for the creation of an international wildlife trust in honour of the late King Mahendra. It is hoped that this legislation will soon be adopted and implemented, giving Nepal a mechanism to carry on long-term wildlife studies with a combination of external and internal support. Such a trust could operate and expand the present Smithsonian facilities in Chitwan into a full-fledged research centre to explore wildlife and park issues throughout the subcontinent. Clearly, this is a major commitment on the part of Nepal and one that they cannot carry on without significant help from the outside. Institutions like the Smithsonian must become major subscribers to the Trust for an extended period, to create an endowment of sufficient size to be self-perpetuating. Nepal must consider ways to raise monies internally for some support; one means may be the imposition of a small tax placed on all visitors coming to Nepal, a portion to be set aside for direct support of the Trust.

The Trust itself must be independent of the national government and should have a significant cross section of international membership but clearly under Nepali control. Like the Charles Darwin Foundation in the Galapagos, the Mahendra Trust should be supportive of the goals and objectives of the Park Service, but not be subservient to it. This allows for better interaction between outside scientific staff and park officials and is a significant factor in raising funds; potential donors seem more inclined to support independent entities than governmental bodies. A great deal of trust and communication is necessary between the Mahendra Trust and National Park officials to avoid problems, but there are successful models which have solved similar potential conflicts.

The future of park management in Nepal is quite bright and the Smithsonian hopes that its modest contribution via the Tiger Project has created a climate for a longer term commitment. The Institution's approach has been a cooperative effort of scientists and park personnel in generating and utilizing scientific data in the creation, extension and maintenance of parks and reserves.

3. BARRO COLORADO ISLAND

Barro Colorado Island (BCI) is in the Panama Canal midway between the Atlantic and Pacific Oceans. The largest island in Gatun Lake, it was created by the damming of the Charges River in 1911 which formed the Canal (see Figures 1 and 2).

The Barro Colorado Island reserve was created in 1923 and was operated for over 2 decades by a consortium of American research institutions. In 1946, the administration of BCI was transferred formally to the Smithsonian. In 1968, BCI became part of the new Smithsonian Tropical Research Institute (STRI), with a research mandate that extends to other parts of the tropics in marine and terrestrial studies.

Since 1946, the island has been maintained as a strict biological reserve (IUCN Category I). While many thousands of scientists have conducted research on the island, no collecting or manipulative studies have been permitted. The Institution maintains a small complex of laboratories and dormitories in a cleared area and has cut some trails but further alterations have not been permitted.

BCI represents the best example of tropical lowland forest in Central America under continuous management and conservation. The Smithsonian, mindful of its obligation, has made substantial efforts to improve the existing support facilities, to provide for proper wardening of the area and to encourage scholars to undertake research. It also maintains an active publications programme, to rapidly transmit the results of its research to a variety of interested audiences.

In recognition of the unique characteristics of BCI, and the scientific and administrative role which the Smithsonian played, the negotiators of the Panama Canal Treaties in 1977 agreed to protect the future status of the Island and to increase the area available for the protection of wildlife. STRI was designated by both governments as the custodian of a new Barro Colorado Island Nature Monument pursuant to Article VI of the Convention on Nature Protection and Wildlife Preservation in the Western Hemisphere.

By increasing the size of BCI Nature Monument from 1,641 ha to 2,193 ha (to include adjacent peninsulas), the landholdings for the Nature Monument roughly doubled from that of BCI proper. This will allow for an additional "buffer zone" to protect BCI proper and additionally provide stepping stones across Gatun Lake for organisms migrating between North and South America.

NATIONAL PARKS, CONSERVATION, AND DEVELOPMENT

BCI has become the first such designated Nature Monument under the Western Hemisphere Treaty. It should be pointed out that this action was one of the first positive steps in implementing the Convention over the last 30 years; prior to this designation, the Convention lay dormant for several decades.

The designation of BCI as a Nature Monument comes at a critical point in the history of environmental affairs in Panama. Increasing attention is being focused on the future viability of the Canal watershed, ensuring its environmental integrity in order to keep the Canal open and properly functioning. Present trends indicate a population growth rate in Panama which will roughly double the number of humans by the year 2000; this projected growth rate is even higher in the area of the watershed.

Although licenses to farm in the Canal area were originally issued to personnel who came to work on the Canal, these licenses were non-transferable, the last having been issued in 1924. Despite this fact, a recent survey indicated over 1,000 farmers were engaged in agricultural pursuits, supporting roughly an additional 4,000 dependents. A major challenge in the immediate future will be how to handle this nettlesome problem, in a way which agriculturists will not lose their livelihood and yet the environmental integrity of the watershed will be preserved and further enhanced.

STRI has addressed its custodianship of BCI in a number of ways. First, proper posting and gazetting of newly acquired lands has been accomplished. Second, the size of the wardening staff has been increased three times in order to increase surveillance against squatters and poachers. Joint patrols have been initiated with Guardia Nacional and RENARE, the Panamanian National Park and Renewable Resource Service. Third, those squatters who currently occupy land in the Nature Monument are being compensated by the Smithsonian for their holdings and are provided relocation assistance. Fourth, a vigorous public education campaign is being launched in cooperation with governmental and non-governmental entities, stressing the importance of the watershed. Fifth, STRI is working in conjunction with RENARE and other entities in the USAID-sponsored programme to protect the watershed. Sixth, STRI is working with RENARE in the development of Parque Soberania located in the Old Pipeline Road area, an area of considerable significance for conservaton in Panama, located contiguous to the Nature Monument boundary to the east. Last, STRI is working with a consortium of Panamanian institutions to develop pilot manipulative studies on the new Nature Monument lands and adjacent areas of the watershed, to explore alternative methods for agriculture in the tropics. The latter project's aim is to dispel the common notion that temperate ideas for agriculture can be easily overlayed on the tropics, and to integrate advances from basic tropical studies for the benefit of tropical development and conservation.

Prior to the assumption of these new responsibilities, the Institution's approach to conservation was largely ancillary, serving as a reference centre to decision-makers in providing scientific knowledge that could be applied for park management and conservation. However, following the Treaty accords, it was thrust into the mainstream of Panamanian environmental considerations.

Since the Treaties, it has been clear that STRI could no longer stand completely apart, as a separate enclave from the issues facing Panama. While heretofore contacts were frequent with many Panamanian institutions, it was necessary to formalize certain relationships. An agreement was concluded with the University of Panama, for the use by Panamanian scholars of STRI facilities, the exchange of results, joint seminars, etc. The building up of a solid scientific infrastructure in Panama with concern for the environment was felt to be a critical factor in developing future environmental and protected area programmes. Additional efforts have been made to solidify existing relationships with RENARE through joint patrols, training and preparation of environmental education materials.

Over the last decade, STRI has witnessed an increasing demand from Central and Latin American entities for training assistance in tropical biology. It has provided a fundamental introduction to research in tropical biology, not only to students, but to park management officials from a number of countries including Panama. Such programmes should be expanded in the future.

To the degree possible, STRI will continue to be responsive to plans for protection of the environment in the Canal area and to bring a respected and authoritative voice to the question of future protected area management in Panama. In addition, utilizing the numerous philanthropic contacts of the Smithsonian, STRI can encourage donations to Panamanian entities to further implement existing park management plans. Efforts will continue in educating the local populace to the problems of the environment in an objective and dispassionate way, recognizing that the future of nature in Panama has been and will continue to be in the hands of the Panamanians.

While STRI's fundamental character as a leading international institution for studies in tropical biology should not change, the efforts of STRI in the protection of the areas embodied by the Canal watershed have helped influence the Government of Panama in directing their attention to environmental problems. But the Government must balance off developmental and social aspirations against environmental concerns. In an age of limited resources, decision-making becomes more critical; the need for competent and objective data must be a critical factor, and STRI will continue to play an important role in Panama and elsewhere as a repository of scientific data and advice.

4. CONSERVATION FOUNDATIONS

Since 1966, the Institution has actively encouraged and supported financially the activities of a series of conservation foundations. The Smithsonian currently serves as the American Secretariat for the Charles Darwin Foundation in the Galapagos, serving as a focal point for contributions to the work of the Darwin Station, providing a logistical and communication base, serving on the Foundation's Board of Directors, and most important, advising on scientific programmes. In addition, many of the Smithsonian's staff are engaged in long-term scientific projects there.

The Institution also is a founding member of the Seychelles Island Foundation which was created to support the on-going work on Aldabra, a biologically significant atoll in the Indian Ocean. The Institution plays a similar role to this Foundation as it does with the Darwin Foundation. The Institution also serves on the Board of Directors of the Wau Ecology Institute in Papua New Guinea, the Organization of Tropical Studies in Costa Rica, and similar organizations which are engaged in preserving significant biological areas and carrying on active research programmes.

The function and proper roles of these foundations are often unknown and misunderstood by outsiders. While some might view these organizations as colonial remnants, they can play a significant role in the future of areas which they are designed to assist. These non-partisan and non-profit organizations enjoy a special sinecure, and, if properly designed, can successfully appeal to donors for conservation and park management projects. A second attribute of such organizations is the ability to draw upon Board members and their own networks for scientific advice. Quite often, these members know of particular experts who could be of value to the host country management officials.

The educational role which these foundations play is also an essential ingredient for success. An increase in public awareness of the biological richness of a particular area and the need for its protection often requires outside stumulus, as internal political and bureaucratic impediments can hamper progress or dampen enthusiasm for park plans. By having organizations freed of these restraints, in effect an "outside environmental conscience", appropriate pressure can lead to action.

Ultimately, all such conservation foundations should be controlled by the host country whose areas are being assisted. However, to maximize the benefits stated above, it is prudent to place several outside organizations on the Board. In regard to financing, every effort should be made from the start to develop an endowment which can sustain the foundation and its research arm as it develops. Ideally, organizations that are asked to join such foundations as Board members should be required to make an initial financial commitment of 5 to 10 years, to ensure a steady source of endowment capital. Host governments, according to circumstances, should provide some measure of financial support; one possible means is by a small tax on visitors to the country, a portion of which could be applied to the foundation.

The creation of conservation foundations must be carefully weighed, in terms of appropriateness to the particular area, the potential interest of the host government and outside donors. Too many similar organizations can only result in destructive competition for a limited philanthropic pool. Perhaps such organizations should be viewed merely as stepping stones to the day wherein host governments can develop the infrastructure and financing to operate their programmes in a self-sufficient manner, a goal that may be a generation away.

5. CONCLUSIONS

While the Smithsonian Institution does not consider its principal mandate as that of conservation and park management, over the last decade through its scientific studies, it has contributed significantly to the activities of national parks and other protected areas throughout the world. The increasing attention being paid to vanishing habitats and species has spurred the Institution to increase its involvement in research and training in the tropics. The ability of the Institution to maintain a significant collection of natural history specimens, coupled with long-term field studies, makes it a valuable resource for those interested in conservation and park management. The experience which the Institution has had in developing its international programmes should be of value to those interested in developing cooperative programmes.

A major problem in developing cooperative programmes is simply informational. Too often a number of institutions have developed programmes for a particular site or the same region without foreknowledge of what other parties were planning. Obviously, this can lead to duplication and overlap, as well as confusion to the host nation. Greater attention should be placed by administrators on sharing information on proposed projects and efforts should be made where possible to integrate activities; institutional rivalries must not impede progress. While it is unrealistic to think that this situation will change overnight, it is an issue which must be confronted.

An additional problem to be examined is the need for increasing interchange between scientists and resource managers. Despite progress over the past decade, some animosity and considerable anxiety remains between these groups. Continued efforts should be made to bring both groups together in formal and informal circumstances, to explore mutual problems. By increasing the dialogue and face-to-face contacts, managers and scientists can begin to alleviate tensions. In addition, development of curricula for both groups should emphasize respective philosophies, methodologies and roles.

As the Smithsonian looks beyond the Bali Congress, it hopes to continue to play a significant role in natural resource protection; increasing awareness on the part of its scientific staff to problems in the tropics dictates an even more concerted effort. As new opportunities arise for cooperation, the Institution is prepared to meet the challenge.

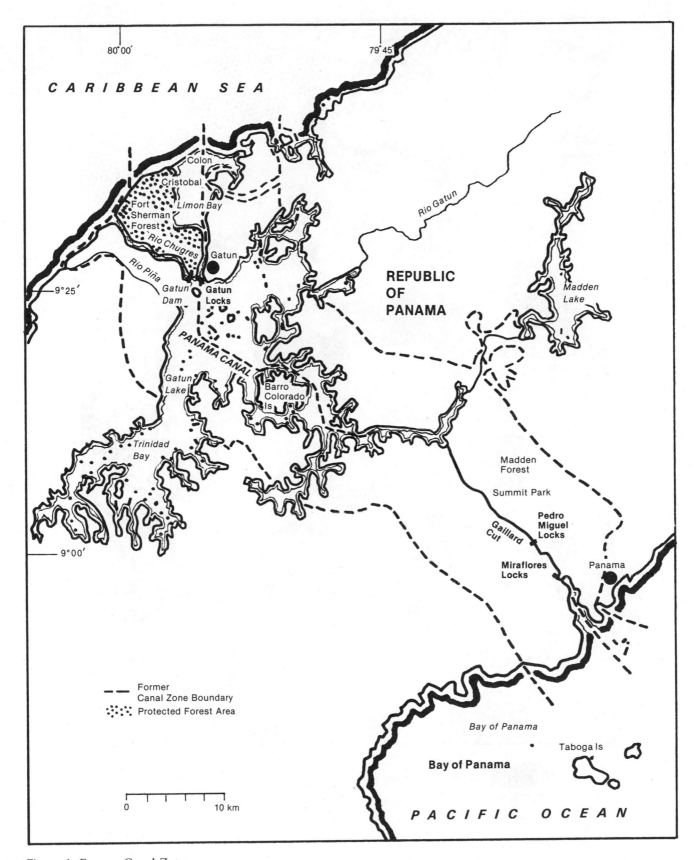

CARIBBEAN SEA

Colon
Cristobal
Fort
Sherman
Forest
Limon Bay
Rio Chugres
Rio Piña
Gatun
Gatun
Dam
**Gatun
Locks**

Rio Gatun

REPUBLIC
OF
PANAMA

*Madden
Lake*

— 9°25'

PANAMA CANAL

*Gatun
Lake*

Barro
Colorado
Is

*Trinidad
Bay*

— 9°00'

Madden
Forest

Summit Park

Gaillard
Cut

**Pedro
Miguel
Locks**

**Miraflores
Locks**

Panama

—— Former
    Canal Zone Boundary
∴∴∴ Protected Forest Area

Bay of Panama

Taboga Is

Bay of Panama

0   10 km

PACIFIC OCEAN

Figure 1. Former Canal Zone.

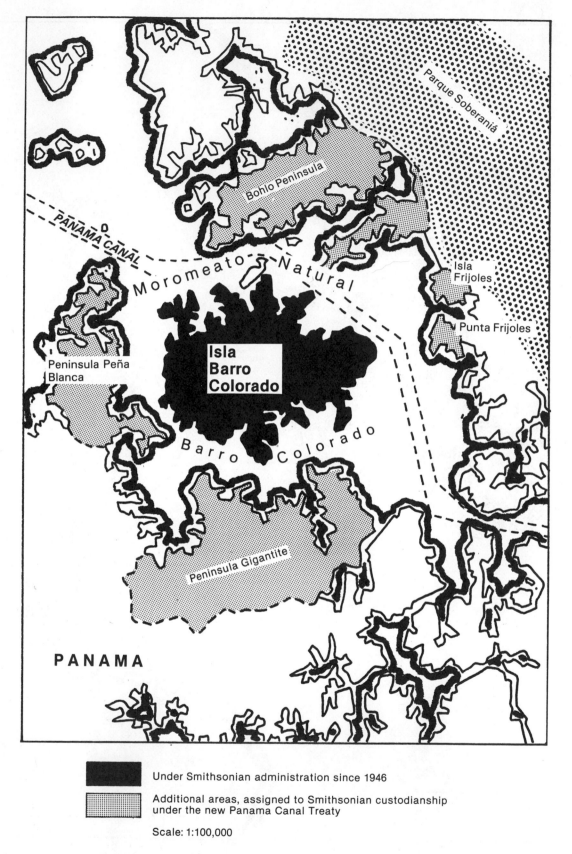

Under Smithsonian administration since 1946

Additional areas, assigned to Smithsonian custodianship under the new Panama Canal Treaty

Scale: 1:100,000

Figure 2. The Barro Colorado Nature Monument.

NATIONAL PARKS, CONSERVATION, AND DEVELOPMENT

Development and Conservation:
Co-Existence through Rational Planning

J. LeRoy Balzer, Ph.D.
Utah International Inc.
San Francisco, California, USA

ABSTRACT. *This paper, written by a representative of industry, covers the planning of resource use with respect to development and conservation. The paper welcomes the World Conservation Strategy and shows how industrial resources, such as technology, labour and capital, can be used to contribute to the process of rational resource planning. All interests, whether managers of protected areas or international developers, must work together to meet the need of defining rates for sustainable resource production and consumption in order to plan areas for preservation, development or maintenance of production. While all interests may not be consistently in agreement, working together is mandatory to obtain the best results for all.*

1. INTRODUCTION

I salute the sponsors of this conference for assembling such a diverse gathering and I join all participants and observers in the hope that, throughout these proceedings, we will better understand our different perspectives and priorities and make progress in achieving mutual goals in the areas of development and conservation—areas which are neither incompatible nor mutually exclusive.

My topic is rational resource planning with respect to development and conservation. I believe that development and conservation can proceed together through the use of rational resource planning.

Today I shall address three aspects of planning:

- The World Conservation Strategy and sustainable development;
- Aspects of sustainable development and planning which are of primary importance to corporations and the mining process; and,

- Suggested uses of industrial resources—technology, labour and capital—as contributions to the process of rational resource planning.

The World Conservation Strategy emphasizes achieving sustainable development with conservation and defines conservation as, and I quote, "The management and human use of the biosphere so that it may yield the greatest sustainable benefit to present generations while maintaining its potential to meet the needs and aspirations of future generations."

As the Director of the Environmental Quality Department for an international mining corporation, I enthusiastically welcome the World Conservation Strategy, the planning potential it brings, and the definition of conservation which lies at the heart of the Strategy.

This definition calls for a balance between conservation and development. Inherent in this balance is the concept of sustainable development. It is through the acceptance of what sustainable development represents that a true balance between development and conservation will be achieved.

Sustainable development calls for an accurate and thorough measurement of natural resource supply and an appropriate and measured allocation of demands upon that supply. We are speaking of the uses of the biosphere here—about the uses of renewable and non-renewable resources.

However, the planning approach to sustainable development must be specific to the kinds of resources for which supply and demand curves are being drawn. When renewable resources are considered, the planning process must focus on the rates at which the biosphere is able to renew itself in order to provide for continuing consumption. When non-renewable resources are considered, the challenge is greater, as the planning process must allow for the tools of capital and technology to develop as sustainers of the biosphere.

Creating a planning process which enables rates of sustainable development for all kinds of natural resources is the ultimate in development and conservation challenges. The art of meeting this challenge is the underlying principle of the World Conservation Strategy, and responsible corporations and governments recognize and accept this.

But all interests, whether managers of parks and wildlife refuges or international developers, must work together to meet the need of defining rates for sustainable resource production and consumption as we proceed to plan areas for preservation, development or maintenance of production. All interests may not be consistently in agreement, but working together is mandatory.

Before discussing sustainable development and rational resource planning as they apply to corporate interests, I would like to mention several marketplace realities which concern development and conservation interests and underscore the planning process.

One of these realities is that conservation usually loses when placed in direct confrontation with development. Conservation does not go very far to pay the rent: development does. Development will always have a very powerful voice because it speaks to the immediate needs of the people of the world. I hasten to add, however, that unconstrained development would have disastrous results for the productivity of the biosphere. And so it is sustainable development which is mandatory for all interests.

I would offer this paradigm regarding sustainable development: one can think of development as "production" and conservation as "maintenance". Development produces the products of the biosphere and conservation assures that the biosphere will be available for production. Societies must produce food, shelter, fuel . . . mainly, from the biosphere. But the biospheric inventory must be allocated with a mix of development and conservation. Sustainable development provides this compromise.

Another reality which faces us is that one quarter of the world's people consume two-thirds of the world's resources, and one half of them consume simply to stay alive. In recognizing this reality, we must also accept that cooperation among divergent interests is mandatory.

The integration of development with conservation in a framework of sustainable development which is brought about by rational resource planning is the goal toward which the World Conservation Strategy and I, as a corporate Environmental Director, aspire.

In discussing aspects of sustainable development and rational land-use planning as they apply to corporate interests, I suggest that corporations and nations, in all stages of development, have similar needs to be met through the planning process. From this perspective, the rational resource planning process should:

1) Directly address the stresses and tensions which arise when questions of conservation and development are debated;
2) be an effective and equitable process which establishes priorities for resource use based upon clearly defined criteria which address the reality of both present and projected needs;
3) accommodate the needs of developing nations whose economies are rapidly expanding due to abundant natural resources that are often in areas suitable for varied uses;
4) encourage professionals representing all interests to work together in open communication;
5) be conducted with the best data and information available for the resource; and, finally,
6) allow policy-makers to make decisions based upon sound scientific information and good public policy.

Regarding these recommended components for a planning process, Utah International has been involved in mineral exploration in Indonesia for several years. We recognize that a country developing as rapidly as Indonesia must consider the best mix of resource uses to meet the nation's economic and conservation objectives.

For a mining company, rational resource planning in a country like Indonesia begins early in the exploration phase and continues throughout the production phase. The exploration phase of a project calls for resource planning to establish both geographic and environmental boundaries within which a company may potentially operate. During the pre-construction phase, feasibility analyses must be conducted to determine if the required project investment can be economically justified by marketplace demand for the product.

This brings me to my third and final point. As systems for planning are established around the world, capabilities of the private sector—technology, capital and labour—should be sought out, since these resources can often contribute susbstantially to the planning and information data base, particularly in remote areas where the developer may be the sole interest to have thoroughly studied the region.

For example, we are at present exploring a 1,260,000 ha concession of land in Kalimantan for potential coal development. Our planning assessment will include the consideration of environmental and social information in conjunction with data on the coal reserves. Much of the large study area will either have no coal or it will fail to meet economic criteria and will be released from development consideration for the foreseeable future.

Through the process of planning and assessment, we expect to develop regional information, perhaps by remote sensing, over much of the study area. The information gathered on lands excluded from development could provide a useful resource inventory for evaluating other land uses.

In the past, the lack of adequate resource data and information has presented significant obstacles to sound planning. In a recent discussion with a former U.S. National Park Service professional who assisted developing countries with park planning, we learned that the entire data base for the evaluation of the proposed Canaima National Park in Venezuela, covering some 2,830,000 ha, consisted, quite remarkably, of a single aerial photograph. My point is that, where it is feasible to do so, resource development corporations can provide baseline information and technology to assist other interests.

International corporations must also be recognized as having the abililty to contribute financial resources to organizations involved in the planning of protected areas. The World Conservation Strategy suggests that industry and raw material users should sponsor the establishment of protected areas for the preservation of unique ecosystems. An example of this corporate involvement can be found in Indonesia, where the forest industry is financing the establishment of a National Park (Eidsvik, 1980).

Numerous and sound ecological reasons exist for establishing selected areas of our world for conservation objectives. The preservation of genetic diversity, the assurance of pristine areas for future generations, and the protection of watersheds are but a few. Humankind has a basic need for things wild and unaffected by man.

As we accept the concept that conservation and sustainable development are inseparable, we must proceed to conduct economic development planning within a framework of conservation and sustainable development. Rational resource planning must provide the guidelines.

In closing, as a member of the industrial community, I espouse the hope for continued cooperation among conservation, development and planning interests and concerns to achieve balanced, global resource uses which no interest, acting solely in behalf of its own concerns, will be able to achieve on its own.

National Parks for Developing Countries

John Blower
UNDP/FAO Nature Conservation and National Parks Project
Rangoon, Burma

ABSTRACT. *Based on experience in Africa and Asia, the author outlines some of the basic problems likely to be faced in planning and establishing national parks and other protected areas in a developing country which is starting from scratch in this particular field. Forms of technical assistance are described, and possible alternatives which may be worth considering for the future are suggested.*

1. INTRODUCTION: THE NEED FOR INTERNATIONAL SUPPORT, PARTICULARLY TO LEAST DEVELOPED COUNTRIES

Of the 118 nations classified by the UN as Developing Countries, less than half have properly constituted national parks. Of these, some possess parks which are among the finest in the world, with well-established professionally staffed organizations to administer them. Such countries are in need of neither external assistance nor advice; on the contrary, with their considerable experience there is much that they could usefully teach others less advanced than themselves in this particular field of resource management. But unfortunately they are in the minority. The majority, especially among the so-called Least Developed Countries, either still have no parks as yet, or merely have areas which, though designated as parks on paper, do not conform to internationally accepted criteria.

This may be due to a variety of reasons: lack of suitable areas or the lack of trained personnel to plan them; political instability and consequent security problems in the remoter areas with the best potential for national parks; lack of recognition on the part of the government concerned of the need for parks; or low priority in comparison with other urgent development needs, such as schools, hospitals, roads or irrigation schemes.

It is all very well to stress the importance of nature conservation and the need for national parks and reserves to such countries, but if we are to achieve any response beyond the ritual lip-service commonly paid to conservation by politicians, we have to understand their problems—and the international community must be prepared to provide effective assistance where needed. It should be accepted that areas which are really worthy of development as national parks are a part of the international heritage as well as of the heritage of the country concerned, and that the poorest countries with a per capita GNP of perhaps less than US$300 a year cannot reasonably be expected to develop parks to the requisite standard without substantial external support.

Based on my experience in Africa and Asia, I shall attempt in this paper to outline some of the basic problems likely to be faced in planning and establishing national parks and other protected areas in a developing country starting from scratch in this particular field. I will also touch briefly on current forms of technical assistance and suggest possible alternatives which may be worth considering for the future.

2. CONVINCING GOVERNMENT PLANNERS AND DECISION MAKERS

Government planners are usually technocrats, often with impressive academic qualifications in economics or political science but even more often ecologically ill-informed, with only the very haziest of ideas about nature conservation, and quite likely to dismiss conservation as an obstacle to economic development. The first task will therefore be to educate the planners themselves, to convince them that resource conservation is a legitimate and indeed an essential development objective in which national parks can play a key role. Needless to say, this is no easy task, particularly for local conservationists at a relatively low level in the government hierarchy. Prophets, as the New Testament reminds us, find little honour in their own country. On the other hand, high level approaches and personal visits by prominent figures in the international conservation field are often very helpful, even though they are occasionally unproductive since people are understandably sensitive about gratuitous advice from outsiders on how to run their country. Study tours by senior officials and political decision-makers to successful national parks in other developing countries can also successfully arouse their interest and demonstrate the possibilities.

3. HOW MANY PARKS?

Having "sold" the idea of national parks, there is then the question of strategy. Should one go ahead and "get all one can" while the going is good? Or concentrate on one or two model parks? It can be argued that if one does not secure all suitable areas when the opportunity offers, one may not have another chance. This is a valid argument, and I personally favour staking a claim on all potential park land even if there is no possibility of developing it for several years. It is always possible to keep land "on ice" in the form of nature reserves or some other category of protected area. I suggest, however, that the temptation to establish too many parks, especially in the initial stages when trained staff and other resources are in short supply, should be avoided. It should also be remembered that as a general principle a small number of large areas provides a sounder basis for conservation of both flora and fauna than a larger number of smaller scattered areas, though this is not to say that smaller areas cannot also play a valuable role in complementing the larger key areas.

Governments are sometimes more ready to allocate budgets for parks than for other conservation areas such as nature reserves in the belief that parks mean tourism and therefore dollars for the Treasury. There is then the temptation to call everything a national park in the interest of a bigger budget allocation. This may lead to degraded or otherwise unsuitable areas being included, or at least to the resources being spread so thin on the ground that their effectiveness is lost. In developing countries as elsewhere it is important to maintain the standards and integrity of national parks, and only truly outstanding areas which meet international criteria should be accepted as this category of protected area. Quality is better than quantity, and it is preferable to start with two or three well-managed parks to serve as models, which can be a source of national pride, than a larger number of badly-managed mediocre ones.

3.1. Need for other categories of protected area

There is also sometimes a tendency to think in terms of national parks to the exclusion of other forms of protected area. Parks are fashionable and, as I have remarked, they are sometimes more successful in attracting financial support than other less-publicized categories of protected areas. But the objective should be to establish a sensible mix which will provide, as far as possible, for all needs and aspirations. Apart from fully protected areas in the form of Strict Nature Reserves or their equivalent, more attention could profitably be given to the development of regional parks administered by state or provincial authorities as distinct from national parks under the central government, in order to encourage local participation in conservation and to foster a sense of local pride and healthy rivalry. Consideration should also be given to multiple-use areas on the line of the National Forests in the United States, which can provide for recreational needs and at the same time allow some degree of economic exploitation (IUCN Category VIII). But while such areas can usefully compliment the parks and reserves wherein conservation is the main goal, they cannot of course provide a substitute for them.

3.2. Danger of over-emphasis on touristic values

Governments, especially in poorer countries, tend understandably to be interested primarily in development projects with prospects of an early economic return, preferably in the form of much-needed foreign exchange. It is therefore natural in endeavouring to "sell" the idea of national parks to a possibly unenthusiastic government to stress their potential as tourist attractions. There are, however, dangers in this since it is likely to lead to the assumption by decision-makers that parks exist primarily for economic gain, with the corollary that if their expectations in this direction are not fulfilled the planners may begin to look for more profitable alternative uses for land. There is also the danger that governments will seek to maximize economic returns from parks through inappropriate developments such as large hotels, highways or golf courses designed to attract more visitors, thus destroying the parks' wilderness values and eventually turning them into areas of which the main objective is mass tourism rather than conservation.

3.3. Constraints on selection of areas

Assuming that one is starting from the very beginning in planning a nation-wide network of parks and reserves, ideally one would follow a model "systems" approach, selecting representative areas covering all major ecosystems based on extensive preliminary surveys. But this is often impracticable because of various constraints. Extensive otherwise highly desirable areas may be ruled out, for example, for security reasons or because they have already been assigned as timber concessions or for other forms of land use. Government decision-makers may also have their own fixed ideas about what and where national parks should be, which may not necessarily coincide with those of the conservationist and parks planner.

The most promising locations will often be in relatively remote sparsely populated areas not readily accessible to people living in the capital city, who, in any case, may prefer artifically landscaped places where they can picnic in comfort to natural wilderness with its wild animals, snakes, malignant spirits and other real or imagined dangers. So while the main objective of the conservationist will be to secure undisturbed and therefore usually relatively remote areas of sufficient extent for effective conservation of ecosystems and endangered species, compromise may be necessary in order to satisfy the wishes of political leaders, and to provide semi-natural areas for the recreational use of urban communities. Fulfilment of such needs, possibly through rehabilitation of ecologically degraded areas near main population centres, may in itself lead to a better appreciation of nature by both government leaders and the public, and thence to an eventual realization of the need to protect natural areas further afield.

4. HOW TO MAKE NATIONAL PARKS WORK

4.1. Parks must be seen to fulfil a real national need

National parks in developing countries inevitably tend to be regarded as something of a luxury, and they can only succeed where they are seen to be fulfilling—by politicians, planners and the public—a real national need. This means, in effect, that they either support an economically important tourist industry, as in several African countries and in Nepal, or that there is a relatively affluent middle class who themselves use the parks for recreational purposes, as in India, Thailand and Indonesia. In this connection it will be found that with increased education, affluence and mobility, attitudes change and young people become more adventurous and more interested in exploring the remoter and less developed parts of their own country, a phenomenon which has been clearly demonstrated in Indonesia in recent years with increasing proliferation of Nature Lovers Clubs, Mountaineering Clubs, Exploration Societies and other organized groups who back-pack into even the most inaccessible areas such as the Snow Mountains of west Irian Jaya. It is this growing appreciation of wilderness for its own sake among young educated people who will become the leaders of the future which offers the best guarantee for the future of national parks in such countries.

4.2. Utilization of existing institutions

Apart from the problem of convincing governments of the need for national parks and possible initial difference of opinion as to what form they should take and where they should be located, the main constraints are likely to be either budgetary or the absence of trained personnel, or, more probably, both. One must therefore make maximum use of existing institutions with relevant expertise such as the Forest Department and local universities, rather than plunge too quickly into the establishment of a separate new national park organization. In most developing countries in the tropics nature conservation was, and in many still is, a responsibility of the Forest Department. This is entirely logical since foresters are or should be trained in practical land management, which is one of the most valuable basic skills needed in planning conservation areas; they also usually know the areas with potential as national parks or nature reserves far better than anyone else. It will therefore usually be preferable in such cases to keep nature conservation and National parks under the Forest Department at least until there is a strong enough cadre of qualified and experienced personnel, including parks planners, ecologists and others, to warrant a separate organization. Even when this point is reached, however, it will still be necessary to maintain close links with the Forest Department on whose continued support and cooperation much will usually depend.

4.3. Legislation

One of the essential prerequisites is appropriate legislation to provide the necessary legal framework for the establishment and subsequent management of the park. In many developing countries in Africa and Asia, conservation of wildlife was originally covered under Forestry legislation, which may provide for establishment of game reserves or sanctuaries, but is unlikely to include national parks. In such cases it is generally impracticable merely to amend the existing law and it is far better to introduce new legislation, either dealing specifically with national parks or in the form of a more general basic Act covering all aspects of nature conservation, including establishment of national parks, with provision under it for more detailed subsidiary regulations dealing with management of parks and other related matters. It is of the greatest importance to get such legislation correct from the start, and to ensure that it is sufficiently comprehensive. It is therefore strongly advisable to obtain the assistance of someone with appropriate expertise in drafting it. If there is no one with the necessary qualifications locally available, it is possible to obtain assistance either from the IUCN Commission on Environmental Policy, Law and Administration, or from the FAO Legislation Branch, both of which have extensive experience in this field and can arrange for short-term consultants to work with the local legal experts in preparing new draft legislation.

4.4. Winning support of local people

Having gained the support of government planners and decision-makers, the most important task is to win the understanding and cooperation of the local people in the vicinity of the proposed parks. This is likely to prove a far more intractable problem. To the small farmer trying to wrest a precarious living from the soil, establishment of a nearby national park is at best irrelevant and likely to be regarded as yet another form of government interference, depriving him of his traditional right to collect forest produce, graze his livestock or hunt, while at the same time attracting swarms of alien camera-clicking tourists and bringing no tangible benefit to him or his family.

No amount of lecturing on conservation needs or the foreign exchange which tourism will bring to the country is likely to make much impression. One can expect only opposition from such people unless strenuous and imaginative efforts are made from the start to involve them in planning and development of the park, and to ensure that their interests are adequately cared for. At the very least, provision must be made for alternative sources of fuelwood and other produce of which they may be deprived through creation of the park. Most of us involved with park planning in developing countries recognize this problem and dutifully include provision in the Master Plan for development of surrounding buffer zones to provide for the needs of the local population. But all too often the budget is inadequate and nothing materializes. It is therefore encouraging to learn that in Indonesia a real start is being made in tackling this problem, with a substantial proposed World Bank project for intensive development of buffer zones and other measures for the benefit of local communities in areas adjoining the parks.

This is an example which could usefully be followed by other international and bilateral development agencies, who too often dismiss requests for assistance in developing national parks as being irrelevant to the real needs of the people and therefore of low priority. But by supporting development of buffer zones, they could both improve the standard of living of the people and ensure effective protection of the natural environment through the park or reserve concerned with its undeniable resulting long-term benefits. It is also an example which one hopes will be followed by the World Bank in other countries, and especially those where the Bank is involved in projects such as large-scale timber exploitation which have a major and potentially harmful impact on the natural environment.

4.5. Creating employment opportunities

Apart from development of buffer zones through agro-forestry schemes and the like, every effort should be made to ensure that local communities benefit through employment as rangers, guards, guides and labourers, rather than bringing people in from other areas. Construction works such as road building should be labour-intensive, even if it takes longer, rather than based on the use of costly equipment which local people are unlikely to have the necessary skills to operate. Buildings should wherever practicable be indigenous in style and materials which will be less costly and more in keeping with the maximum use of local labour. Transportation within the park can sometimes be based on the use of horses, mules or boats, or—in case of mainland Southeast Asia—elephants, which have the advantage of causing less environmental disturbance than motor vehicles and of providing additional employment opportunities. It may also be added that use of animals for travel within the park may in itself prove a considerable attraction to visitors, as has been clearly demonstrated though the very successful use of elephants in the Chitwan National Park in Nepal.

4.6. Involvement of local authorities

In addition to measures to ensure maximum direct benefit to the local people by such policies as I have suggested, it is also important to involve local authorities such as District Councils or their equivalent to the maximum extent possible. They should be involved at all stages from preliminary planning to day-to-day management and should be encouraged to take a proprietary interest in the park as a unique feature of their own district, which attracts visitors from afar and is thus an object of pride and prestige, rather than as a mere imposition of central government. In this connection a parks committee should be set up whose members should include local officials, representatives of communities most affected by the park and of course the Warden or Superintendent in charge of the park itself. If he too can be a local man, so much the better.

In Uganda, in the years before the recent political unrest, half the revenue from the national park entrance fees was paid to the local District Councils to be used for community welfare projects such as improvement of water supplies and building of schools and dispensaries. Though the amounts concerned were not great, this had a very beneficial effect since it provided some compensation for loss of hunting and other rights, and also provided the Councils with a financial stake in the park and some incentive to ensure its success. In particular, it ensured that a serious view was usually taken of poaching offences brought before the local courts. Similar schemes have been operated in Zambia and could be more widely followed elsewhere.

4.7. Communities living within parks

Apart from the population in surrounding areas, there may also be people living within the park boundaries, in demarked enclaves or otherwise. This is a situation best avoided if at all possible since it inevitably leads to all sorts of problems. But sometimes there is no alternative, as in the case of Sagarmatha National Park where it was obviously impossible to remove the Sherpa communities and they had therefore to be integrated into the management of the park. The Sherpas are a relatively advanced and sophisticated people, but there are in Southeast Asia and elsewhere a number of tribal communities, usually forest-dwelling hunter-gatherers living more or less at subsistence level, who live in remote areas where national parks already exist or might be established in the future. Protection of these people and their often unique cultures against too-rapid social change is a legitimate conservation objective and should be given high priority in planning parks in those areas where such communities still survive. They have their own ecological niche, they generally live in harmony with the environment and they can play a useful role in the management of the park. Care should be taken, however, through appropriate zoning and other measures to protect them against excessive exposure to visitors, and to ensure that they are able to pursue their ordinary way of life undisturbed, and without the danger of becoming an undignified tourist spectacle.

I have touched on a few of the problems to be considered in planning and establishing national parks in developing countries. It is by no means an exhaustive list. Many of these countries have already made great advances and have well-established national park systems in which such matters are being taken care of. My remarks are concerned more with those countries not yet in this happy position, and this brings me back to the question of external aid and what forms, assuming it is required, it can most usefully take.

5. EXTERNAL ASSISTANCE

In East and Southeast Asia, the main international agencies involved in nature conservation, wildlife management and national parks during the last 10 to 20 years have been UNDP/FAO and WWF/IUCN. Several national parks in the region bear witness to the fact that this support has produced tangible results. In the field of bilateral assistance the substantial support provided by New Zealand in the development of the Sagarmatha National Park in Nepal has been of particular significance.

What of the future? Such assistance will, I believe, be required for some time to come, at least in those countries which have not yet developed national parks or any kind of national plan for resource conservation. Sooner or later they are likely to realize that they are in danger of missing the boat, and, particularly in those countries at the lower end of the GNP scale, are going to need assistance to catch up, especially in planning, training, legislation, creation of the necessary administrative infrastructure and provision of equipment. In such cases there may be a need for fairly large contributions over several years, such as we have seen in Indonesia, Nepal and elsewhere. But apart from a few isolated cases, the days of large-scale technical assistance projects in this field are probably numbered. Many countries now have National parks and the qualified staff to manage them which, though in some cases short of funds or equipment, are certainly able to stand on their own feet without external support. But nevertheless they may still need occasional support and assistance in certain specialized fields such as interpretive programmes, legislation, the preparation of master plans and the special difficulties to be resolved in the planning of marine parks.

Such needs can best be met by short-term consultancies, preferably employing either suitably qualified people from neighbouring countries or consultants from elsewhere with past experience in the region who could be called on as required. Ideally, if funds were available, the best answer might be a small, specialized team of consultants based within the region with whose problems they would be generally familiar. This team would be available on request, and could also make periodic routine visits to the countries concerned to maintain contact and give advice or assistance if needed. Such a team, which might perhaps be supported by UNEP, could also organize courses and seminars for training/upgrading purposes, either centrally or on a country-by-country basis, and could act as a regional exchange centre for information and ideas.

5.1. Possibilities for greater regional cooperation

Greater cooperation between countries within the region would be of value and should be encouraged. This could, for example, take the form of exchanges of personnel, working attachments to Parks Departments, study tours, liaison visits by management level personnel and periodic mobile seminars involving visits to parks and Reserves, hosted in rotation by the countries concerned—on similar lines to the international annual seminar organized by the University of Michigan, US National Park Service and Parks Canada. Such activities could be funded at least in part under the United Nations Programme for Technical Cooperation between Developing Countries (TCDC). UNDP and the World Wildlife Fund have hitherto been the main sources of non-governmental funding for national parks and related projects, but other possibilities include the World Heritage Fund, for those parks listed as World Heritage Sites, and, as previously mentioned, the World Bank. In the case of such countries as Indonesia which have major natural resource-based industries, it would also seem appropriate that there should be some contribution to conservation projects by the industries concerned, perhaps through a modest tax levied on the export value of the timber, oil, minerals or whatever.

5.2. Long term institutional links

Taking as an example the successful cooperation between New Zealand and Nepal in developing the Sagarmatha National Park, consideratiion should be given to the possibilities of other long-term institutional links between National Parks Services in developed countries and counterparts in countries in a less advanced development stage. Such links could provide opportunities for training, interchange of personnel and the gradual building-up of a close personal relationship between the organizations concerned, to the lasting benefit to both. It would also mean that instead of comparatively short one-off projects with intensive inputs of expertise and equipment for two or three years, followed by a complete break, there could be a much more gradual phasing-out of sustained support and involvement and the continuing possibility of further advice or assistance if and when required. Such support could be funded under bilateral aid programmes or, in the case of Southeast Asia, the Colombo Plan, and need not to be any drain on the usually hard-pressed budget of the parks services involved.

In the industralized countries the lines are already drawn: such protected areas as it is possible to establish are already in existence, and apart from minor adjustments, there is little conservationists can do except to safeguard the *status quo*. It is in developing countries, especially in those of East and Southeast Asia, that great opportunities still exist to create new national parks. Let those of us who are in a position to do so give these countries all the support and encouragement we can, and help them to avoid the mistakes which have been made elsewhere.

The Exchange of Wildlands Technology: A Management Agency Perspective

Gary B. Wetterberg
National Park Service
Washington, D.C., USA

ABSTRACT. *Underlying reasons for increasingly sharing expertise on an agency-to-agency basis are explored along with expected future trends. Both structured cooperative activities (ones under a formal umbrella agreement) and unstructured exchanges are discussed. Various recent examples of agency-to-agency exchanges are given, illustrating a diversity of topics and countries involved.*

1. INTRODUCTION

The promotion of international support for protected areas management is being addressed from various points of view including those of: the global or World Conservation Strategy perspective; national development agencies; private foundations; resource development corporations; and United Nations specialized bodies. This paper presents a management agency perspective on international exchange of wildland technology.

A few definitions are useful in considering the parameters of this point of view. *Wildlands* are "territories of land and water which have been little affected by modern man, or which have been abandoned and are reverting to nature" (Miller, 1980). Put another way, wildlands are those which lie on the least-altered side of a land use continuum which ranges from intensely developed lands to ones which are completely untouched (Schwarz et. al., 1976).

A *Management Agency* in this context is an administrative division or branch of a government which is responsible for the administration and management of parks and protected areas.

Technology, as utilized here, refers to the totality of means employed to achieve conservation objectives. By combination, then, *wildlands technology* refers to the various means used to achieve conservation objectives on those lands which lie on the least utilized and altered end of the land use continuum. Wildlands technology includes such activities as: conservation unit system planning; management planning for individual parks and protected areas; site planning; drafting of environmental legislation; wildland manager training at all levels; environmental interpretation; environmental education; and others.

This paper provides specific examples of agency-to-agency cooperation that have taken place in the recent past in various parts of the world. The examples illustrate a diversity of interests as well as of countries involved, and are meant to stimulate use of the agency-to-agency mechanism for exchange of wildland technology. Of course, it would be impossible to describe comprehensively all current efforts, so only selected illustrative examples have been utilized.

2. INCREASINGLY SHARED TECHNOLOGY

Wildland technology exchange, on an agency-to-agency basis, is becoming increasingly evident. This is partially due to the dramatic increases in establishment of new parks and protected areas in recent years, as well as the institutionalization of management agencies responsible for them. Harrison et. al. (this volume) point out that globally, between 1970 and 1980 alone, nearly twice as many new areas were established than had existed in 1969. Since the first two national parks came into existence in the 1870s, some 120 countries have established more than 2600 areas which are of sufficient status to be included on the *UN List of National Parks and Protected Areas* (IUCN, 1982d).

The personnel of the new or strengthened management agencies have increasing contact through regional and international fora as well as improved and cheaper means of communication. The recent computerization of the global data base through IUCN's Protected Areas Data Unit (PADU) at Kew, England, will soon allow agencies to readily identify counterparts worldwide who face similar problems and may have attempted solutions which are potentially transferable to other countries. The computerized data files, for example, could be manipulated to generate, in a matter of minutes, a list of all agencies managing marine parks containing mangrove ecosystems, or parks containing active volcanic resources. With this information of common interest in hand, even greater agency-to-agency technology exchange may be only a short step behind. However, the means to promote the availability of such information, as well as the linkage between the data base and the agencies which can make use of it, will remain an important function of IUCN's Commission on National Parks and Protected Areas.

By the mid-1990s the rate of establishment of new parks and protected areas will surely decline as the earth's remaining wildlands are allocated to any of a variety of purposes. At the Second World Conference on National Parks, Clawson (1974) identified five stages in the life history of a national park, using examples from various countries to illustrate the pattern: (1) Reservation, (2) Early Management, (3) Rising Public Interest, (4) Park Use Approaches, Reaches or Exceeds Carrying Capacity, and (5) National Parks Become "Crown Jewels". While the stages, and particularly their length, may vary from country to country, this same pattern seems likely as a framework for an eventual completion of park and protected areas *systems* worldwide. As Clawson pointed out, when park systems approach that final level, a consolidation probably will take place. The role of park systems will be to safeguard a nation's unique or representative heritage of biological, historical, or geological areas. Those sites which had been created during the earlier evolutionary stages and which were of less than truly national significance would be annulled or redesignated according to their characteristics.

From an agency perspective this suggests an eventual stabilization of size and an increasingly focused role within management agencies responsible for these areas. Some nations with major land use allocations already generally in place should be approaching this point (for example, the USA, Sweden, Japan, and New Zealand). Periodical internal reorganizations may exist but institutional stability usually predominates. In other countries where many new areas are still being designated, it seems reasonable to expect additional management agency growth and role modifications prior to stabilization (for example, Brazil and Indonesia). Globally, this should occur toward the turn of the century, lagging somewhat behind the slowdown in establishment of new areas. Of course, variations are likely from country to country but the general trend would seem apparent.

In the interim period, sharing of technology between agencies will likely intensify, particularly between those which are relatively stable and those which are still undergoing modifications. Positive exchanges may also very well exist between the dynamic, or still-changing, agencies, especially when both perceive benefits to be gained. However, an intangible "prestige factor" exists which tends to encourage the flow of information from stabilized to dynamic agencies. Furthermore, agencies still at the dynamic stage are less likely than well-established ones to be able to spare personnel from normal operational duties, as well as to possess the credibility necessary to attract supporting funds.

While one frequently imagines the benefits of such exchanges accruing to only the recipient country, Milne (1981) has pointed out that many times these exchanges prove highly beneficial to the donor country too, in terms of cost saving and innovative techniques which may be adopted for use there. He cites, for example, Japanese methods for handling large numbers of visitors, European approaches to park land ownership, and low-cost parking lot construction from Scotland as techniques with possible application in the U.S.

Two types of agency-to-agency technology exchange are reviewed below. The first is "unstructured" in the sense that it is done without a formal umbrella framework, and the second is "structured" exchange, through a regional convention or some other formalized mechanism.

3. UNSTRUCTURED AGENCY LEVEL EXCHANGE

The exchange of wildland technology on an agency-to-agency basis may take place in cooperation with various institutions. Linkages often exist with private foundations, UN agencies, development banks, conservation organizations, industry, and bilateral development agencies. Usually, a management agency in charge of parks and protected areas in a country with a mature system provides technical expertise in response to requests from countries with evolving protected area systems, with expenses covered by any of the above types of institutions.

The following are illustrative examples of agency-to-agency exchanges which have taken place in the past few years (see also Jefferies, this volume and Thorsell, this volume).

3.1 Amazon Countries

The park and wildlife agencies of the Governments of Ecuador and Peru sponsored a 3-week "International Training Course on Protection and Management of Amazon Wildlife" in November 1977 in coordination with the "Intergovernmental Technical Group for the Protection and Management of Amazon Flora and Fauna". The mobile seminar was held in Peru and Ecuador, and 25 park and wildlife managers from 7 Amazonian nations participated. A variety of subjects were addressed including a regional strategy for designating parks and protected areas in the Amazon (Jorge Padua, 1982), management of hunting reserves, Amazon fauna preferred as food for human consumption, and others. Field visits were made to various sites in Peru and Ecuador.

3.2 USA - Tanzania

In 1980-81, the U.S. National Park Service provided assistance in teaching and curriculum development to the College of African Wildlife Management, in Mweka, Tanzania. The project, which was supported in part by the U.S. Agency for International Development, included five two-person teams from the U.S. who travelled to the College and worked in close coordination with resident Tanzanian staff. Teaching materials were developed and some training aids (projectors, mapping equipment, books, and others) were provided. The project covered environmental education/interpretation; park and protected area planning; public communications; and park facility development. A park manual for the course is being drafted which will serve as a textbook and as a reference for field managers. Four faculty members were brought to the United States; they participated in specially designed study tours and in the International Seminar on National Parks and Equivalent Reserves.

3.3 United Kingdom - Barbados

In 1980, the Countryside Commission for England and Wales provided the Government of Barbados with a short-term advisor to assess the possible establishment of a national park on the north and east coast of the island. The report to the Government recommended establishment of Barbados National Park and further technical assistance from the U.K. Since the area involved was generally a "humanized" or man-modified landscape, typical of many of England's protected areas, the conceptual framework for management would have many similarities. In 1982, a follow-up advisor was working for 1 year in Barbados on secondment from the National Parks Authority in England, to establish the institutional framework and policies as well as to train counterpart staff.

4. STRUCTURED AGENCY LEVEL EXCHANGE

In contrast to the unstructured or *ad hoc* examples described above, wildland technology exchange may also take place within a more formalized context. As in the previous examples, linkages often exist between management agencies and various funding institutions. Two examples are reviewed here: The World Heritage Convention and the Western Hemisphere Convention (see also Council of Europe, this volume).

4.1 World Heritage Convention

The Convention Concerning the Protection of the World Cultural and Natural Heritage was adopted by Unesco in 1972. Currently some 64 countries have approved the Convention and 112 natural and cultural properties have formally been recognized as World Heritage Sites. Among other things, the Convention provides for technical assistance to participating countries, and for related financial support through the World Heritage Fund. Such assistance may involve the exchange of wildland technology on an agency-to-agency basis. A few examples include:

- a grant for a Tanzanian to study resource management methods in selected US national parks over a period of six weeks in 1982;
- in-service training of 15 wildlife guards of the Simen Mountains National Park in Ethiopia by experienced graduates of the Mweka College of African Wildlife Management of Tanzania;
- a fellowship for a Zairian conservation official to review management and administration of parks with field level counterparts in Kenya, Canada and the USA for six months in 1982;
- in-service training of an administrator of Panama's Darien National Park with the Costa Rican National Park Service.

4.2 Western Hemisphere Convention

The Convention on Nature Protection and Wildlife Preservation in the Western Hemisphere was drafted in 1940. Its objectives are generally concerned with establishing and managing national parks and other protected areas, as well as fauna preservation. Among other things, the Convention provides for contracting governments to cooperate among themselves in promoting its objectives, to lend assistance to one another, and to enter into agreements, as appropriate, to increase the effectiveness of this cooperation.

The USA, which ratified the Convention in 1941, developed congressional and administrative authorities to facilitate its participation in the mid-1970s. In 1973 the Congress of the United States passed Public Law 93-205, known as the Endangered Species Act. Section 8 of the Act stated that the President shall "designate those agencies which shall act on behalf of and represent the United States in all regards as required by the Western Hemisphere Convention". This was followed by an Executive Order (11911) in 1976 which gave that responsibility to the Secretary of the Interior, and internally it was given to two agencies: the National Park Service (NPS) and the Fish and Wildlife Service (FWS). In 1982, the Endangered Species Act was reauthorized for 3 years, and the pertinent section was strengthened.

While the NPS and FWS carry out various cooperative activities with nations throughout the world, in the discussion that follows, I shall limit comment to NPS exchange with counterpart agencies of the Western Hemisphere, as an example of how an international convention can facilitate inter-agency cooperation.

The NPS frequently receives requests for technical assistance. Such assistance may take any one of three broad forms. The first, and by far the most common, is for written materials. Counterpart agencies may ask for summaries of NPS policies on archeological specimens, concessionaire leases, cave management, fire management, Native American handicraft sales, and others; information on public participation in park planning; design plans for visitor centres; information on occupational health, safety, and industrial hygiene programmes; sign specifications; road and trail standards; or any of a wide variety of topics which can be handled through direct correspondence.

The second form is for custom-designed study tours in the USA. These are always paid by the counterpart government, or a third party, with the NPS providing budget estimates, suggested itineraries, and scheduling meetings with appropriate authorities.

The third form, which is the most glamorous but in reality the least frequently utilized, is direct technical assistance abroad. Again, this is almost always done at no cost to the NPS. Our ability to respond depends, of course, on the availability of technically qualified personnel with the required language fluency. The NPS's primary responsibility is for its own domestic programmes and preference must be given to short-term (up to 6 weeks) assignments in which most costs are paid directly by the recipient government (or UN agencies, development assistance agencies, conservation organizations, or others—as negotiated by the recipient government). Priority is usually given to those types of assistance, such as training, which have the greatest potential for long-term impact and development of self-sufficiency.

In addition, letters of congratulation are frequently sent to appropriate Cabinet level authorities when a new park or protected area is established, a person receives an internationally recognized award for conservation efforts, or a related event occurs such as the 1982 Colombian issue of a commemorative postage stamp for Los Nevados National Park.

The following are several examples which illustrate the three forms of technical assistance.

4.2.1. Argentina. A NPS Landscape Architect, working together with Argentine counterparts, assisted in field surveys and development of a report on landscape assessment, tourism, and national parks in the Salta, Ju-

juy, and Tucuman Provinces as one component of a regional tourism study sponsored by the Inter-American Development Bank.

An Environmental Interpretation Specialist designed and presented a 2-week course for Argentine park personnel at the Ranger Training Center in Nahuel Huapi National Park at San Carlos de Bariloche. The Argentine National Park Service arranged for payment of the international airfare and *per diem* through the New York Zoological Society.

4.2.2. Panama. An architect served as a member of a planning team which prepared the management plan for Soberania National Park as one part of the Watershed Management Project being implemented by the Government of Panama through USAID. The NPS also assisted in developing a study tour of selected U.S. national parks for 15 Panamanian rangers in 1982.

4.2.3. Trinidad and Tobago. Both a Landscape Architect and an Environmental Interpretation Specialist developed site plans and related materials for the implementation of the Caroni Swamp National Park management plan under a project sponsored by the Organization of American States.

The former Superintendent of the Virgin Islands National Park lectured on marine park management while acting as one of the instructors in the Wildland Management Training Workshop in 1979, organized by the Eastern Caribbean Natural Areas Management Program and the Caribbean Conservation Association. Some 20 individuals participated from various Caribbean countries. Associated fieldwork included preparation of a draft management plan for the proposed Buccoo Reef National Park.

4.2.4. Colombia. A working visit to the Blue Ridge Parkway and Grand Canyon National Park was arranged for a Colombian Senator studying questions related to roads and hotels in the U.S. National Park System.

A wide variety of written materials concerning coral reefs, management of national seashores, underwater parks, and public use of underwater resources have been provided to the staff of Los Corales del Rosario National Park. Likewise, information on interpretation of glaciers was sent to the Superintendent of Los Nevados National Park as well as the names of appropriate contacts in both the U.S. and New Zealand.

4.2.5. Ecuador. NPS staff members have served as instructors for park training seminars in Riobamba and Galapagos for both Ecuadorian and regional conservation officers. The Galapagos National Park workshop was partly sponsored by the World Heritage Fund.

In 1982, an employee served for one month on a USAID Forestry Assessment Team, drafting the parks- and wildlife-related proposals for consideration in a 5 year, AID-financed forestry project. Work was carried out in close collaboration with the Ecuadorian Parks Director who served as the advisor's counterpart.

4.2.6. Costa Rica. In 1982, the Director of National Parks in Costa Rica requested a summary of NPS policies on research in the park system, including expenditures, numbers of personnel devoted to research and their organization administratively within the NPS, formal relationships between the NPS and academic institutions, and others.

The NPS has served as a contact point between the Costa Rican NPS and the U.S.'s Potomac Appalachian Trail Club, which has offered to voluntarily assist in trail building and maintenance in Corcovado National Park.

In 1979, a NPS advisor, working with Costa Rican counterparts, drafted a proposed administrative organization for an Interpretive Division of the Costa Rican National Park Service. Interpretive programme outlines were prepared for Cahuita, Irazu, Braulio Carillo, and Volcan Poas National Parks.

The major focal point for wildland technology interchange in Central America is the Wildlands and Watershed Program of the Tropical Agriculture Center of Research and Instruction (CATIE) in Turrialba. NPS assistance has included provision of instructors for two "Central American Mobile Seminars on Planning and Management of Wildlands" and a "Mesoamerican Workshop on Interpretation and Environmental Education". These courses have involved park superintendents, administrators, and field managers from various countries in Central America, South America, and the Caribbean.

4.2.7. Dominican Republic. The National Parks Directorate of the Dominican Republic requested guidance on management and interpretation of limestone cave formations. In response, various materials, including management and interpretive plans, were sent concerning Wind Cave, Carlsbad Caverns, and Mammoth Cave National Parks and Jewel Cave National Monument. A NPS cave restoration specialist corresponded with authorities in the Dominican Republic and provided them with copies of related articles from the Bulletin of the National Speleological Society.

4.2.8. Venezuela. An experienced Urban Park Planner was assigned for one month to assist Venezuelan counterparts in sketching the layout and design of Caracas' Antonio Jose de Sucre Park. In addition, the person served as a guest lecturer at various public meetings, universities, and on national television.

4.2.9. Paraguay. At the request of the U.S. Peace Corps and in cooperation with the Paraguayan Forest Service, USAID, and the USFWS, a 10-day training workshop on wildland and wildlife management was held in Asuncin and Ybycui National Park. The 64 participants from Paraguay, Costa Rica, Ecuador, and the U.S. included U.S. Peace Corps Volunteers working in parks and wildlife in the region as well as their national counterparts.

5. SUMMARY AND CONCLUSIONS

Exchange of wildland management procedures and techniques is increasing between management agencies and will probably grow even more common in the future. This is due to the improved communications between agencies, the increasing realization that potentially adaptable experiences may exist between countries, and the growing pool of common data on parks and protected areas worldwide. Compared to major projects of development assistance agencies or banks, such exchanges are carried out on a small scale and at low costs, sometimes as a component of loan or development projects. Common objectives of protected area managers globally assure the relevance of such exchanges, and benefits often accrue to both the giving and receiving parties. Various examples have been given which illustrate a wide range of interests, as well as of countries involved.

While protected area managers may have similar objectives, technology exchange must be done in a flexible way. Usually, there are no single "right" solutions to management problems; rather, various options, each with its own advantages and disadvantages, exist. Besides language differences, cultural barriers and societal attitudes may often widely separate park and protected area agency counterparts throughout the world. Both donor and recipient agencies should bear these considerations in mind when participating in such exchanges.

The examples presented in this paper have been broadly categorized as structured and unstructured, the former being those which are undertaken as a result of a multinational umbrella agreement or treaty. A treaty mechanism, such as the Western Hemisphere Convention, may be useful in that it can provide for at least a minimum level of continuity through legislatively mandated staff assignments if a country deems it appropriate to do so. Apart from US involvement in agency level exchange of wildland technology through the Western Hemisphere Convention, few other such examples of this type exist at present; even this did not come about until some 30 years after ratification.

National parks and protected areas are now accepted globally as legitimate land use practices by nearly all nations, regardless of political ideology or economic development levels. The time may be appropriate to consider a simple and specific "International Convention on Parks and Protected Areas" which would modernize the somewhat outdated regional treaties, as well as those dealing only with certain ecosystems, and facilitate technological exchanges between countries (see also de Klemm, this volume). Such a convention could be written to meet the evolving needs of the world park community in the 1990s and beyond when designations of new areas cease, management agencies stabilize, and our collective attention focuses on effectively managing the global heritage of resources for which we are responsible.

Chapter 15
The World Heritage Convention

The World Heritage Convention: Introductory Comments

Professor R. Slayter
Chairman
The World Heritage Committee

The World Heritage Convention, for which Unesco is the depository and provides the secretariat, makes a significant innovation in linking together what were traditionally regarded as two quite different fields—the protection of the cultural and the natural heritage. It has also gained international acceptance of the World Heritage concept as ideal that challenges "the spirit," that throughout the world there exist natural and cultural properties and areas of such unique value that they are truly a part of the heritage, not only of the individual nations, but of all mankind.

Furthermore, for the first time, an international legal instrument in the field of conservation provides a permanent framework and financial support for international cooperation in safeguarding the cultural and the natural heritage of mankind through the World Heritage Fund, made up from voluntary and compulsory contributions from State Parties. As of today, the World Heritage List identifies 112 natural and cultural properties fulfilling World Heritage criteria, of which 27 are natural sites and 10 are mixed natural-cultural properties. There is an obvious imbalance* between the number of cultural and natural sites on the World Heritage List which is only partly due to the inherent differences between natural and cultural properties.

It is hoped that IUCN, which has the status of advisory body to the World Heritage Committee, will continue to help Unesco to rectify the imbalance between natural and cultural properties and to achieve the same degree of expertise for natural sites in the World Heritage as is provided for cultural properties.

As an international legal instrument, the Convention, adopted by Unesco's General Conference in 1972, has been quite successful in that it has been already ratified or accepted by 67 States Parties. However, several countries with a wealth of cultural properties and outstanding natural sites have not yet joined the Convention. The World Heritage Committee urges Unesco and IUCN to help achieve better recognition and implementation of the Convention.

The Convention provides States Parties with the possibility of technical cooperation under the World Heritage Fund to preserve their cultural and natural heritage. Cooperation can take a number of forms, such as preparatory assistance, technical cooperation, support to training, and emergency assistance. At present, 13 technical cooperation projects for natural sites are under implementation, 25 fellowships have been awarded for the training of the managers of protected areas and four training courses have received support from the World Heritage Fund. Support is also provided to regional training centres such as the College of Wildlife Management Tanzania. This support consists of teachers' refresher training, fellowships for students from States Parties and purchase of field training equipment.

States Parties wishing to nominate properties for inclusion in the World Heritage List for which they require assistance shoud send their requests through official channels to the Unesco World Heritage Secretariat, Unesco, Paris. The World Heritage Committee decides upon these requests according to its operational guidelines and the resources available under the World Heritage Fund.

It should be recalled that the World Heritage Convention became operationl only five years ago and therefore, quite understandably, has some shortcomings in its activities. However, it is my great pleasure to recognize the excellent supportive work accomplished by IUCN in its successful implementation. Let us continue to work together in further developing the possibilities provided by this innovative legal instrument and let us continue to promote the acceptance of the World Heritage concept, a concept of shared responsibility and international solidarity.

The World Heritage Convention: Protecting Natural and Cultural Wonders of Global Importance— A Slide Presentation

Jeffrey A. McNeely
IUCN Commission on National Parks and Protected Areas
Gland, Switzerland

Some places have special importance for people. They have inspired us by their beauty; given us insights into the history of life on our planet; taught us about the functions of natural ecosystems; informed us about the evolution of our own species and culture; enthralled us with wildlife spectacles; saved species of outstanding universal value; and provided us with examples of how man can live in harmonious balance with his environment. Many such places are so valuable that they form part of the heritage of all mankind.

As the 1960s drew to a close, people around the world became increasingly concerned that important parts of this natural and cultural heritage were in danger of being lost. Poor planning, poor management, and lack of the means to carry out conservation were the main reasons for this dangerous situation.

A new sense of urgency was felt at the international level. Just ten years ago, Unesco began its Man and the Biosphere Programme, the United Nations Environment Programme was started in Stockholm and the 2nd International Conference on National Parks was held in Grand Teton. At each of these major occasions, the idea of a World Heritage Convention was discussed and promoted.

Finally, in November 1972, the Convention for the Protection of the World Cultural and Natural Heritage was adopted by the Unesco General Conference, providing a framework for international cooperation in conserving the world's outstanding natural and cultural properties.

Under the World Heritage Convention, a Committee of member governments is established to decide on sites which have been nominated for the World Heritage List. The Committee also provides technical assistance from the World Heritage Fund. At Nepal's Sagarmatha National Park, for instance, the Fund is supporting solar power development to reduce the consumption of scarce firewood and help save the surrounding forests. Our most valuable resource is people, so the Fund also supports national training programmes and regional institutions such as the College of African Wildlife Management in Tanzania.

The Convention is unique in dealing with both cultural and natural properties. Certain archeological sites or ancient buildings have an impact on history, art or science that transcends political or geographical boundaries; some townsites or groups of buildings are of special significance because of their architecture or place in the landscape; and some sites bear exceptional witness to a civilization which has disappeared. These outstanding works of man are an irreplaceable part of the world's cultural heritage.

Our natural heritage is an equally priceless legacy. Natural sites considered for the World Heritage List include areas which are of superlative natural beauty; sites which illustrate significant geological processes; and natural habitats crucial to the survival of threatened plants and animals. These sites ensure the maintenance of the natural diversity upon which all mankind depends.

This "new" partnership between culture and nature is not really new. It has just been forgotten in the modern rush to industrialize. For most of human history, people have lived as part of nature and even today all of us depend on nature for both its goods—such as forest products—and its services—such as watershed protection or recreation. The World Heritage Convention is a very useful means of reminding us of our link with nature.

A number of sites record man evolving with his environment. The Lower Valley of the Awash in Ethiopia has revealed the most complete skeleton of early pre-man yet known, and a whole family of early humans has been found, providing the earliest evidence of human social behaviour. From a nearby site on the Omo River come the earliest indications of human industry, in the form of stone tools. The use of tools gave man his dominant position in the Animal Kingdom.

At the Willandra Lakes site in Australia is recorded some of the earliest evidence of harvesting fresh-water animals and using grindstones to crush wild grass seeds to flour, showing man's evolving ability to harvest nature's goods. Archeologists have also found the world's earliest cremation burial at Willandra Lakes.

Some of the earliest art was based on nature. Pre-historic painting from Australia's Kakadu National Park and the Vézère Valley in France provides evidence that art originated partly to give hunters a spiritual link with their prey, a link that survives among hunters to the present.

Some sites preserve villages where man flourished on the sustainable bounty of nature. Anthony Island, known as "Skunggwai" to Canada's Haida Indians, was so rich that these non-agricultural people had the leisure time to produce monumental wood-carving unmatched in the world.

Pre-industrial people could also be wasteful. Some American Indian groups centred their life around migrating bison herds, but where conditions allowed, as at Canada's Head-Smashed-In Bison Jump, they killed many more bison than they could use. But the fact that the Jump was used for some 6,000 years indicates that the hunters were in a sort of balance with the available prey.

Not all early human use of the environment was sustainable. Mesa Verde National Park records a long history of increasing human population and cultural sophistication. But suddenly, in the 13th century, settlements on the flat land were abandoned and villages were shifted to cliff caves. Shortly after, Mesa Verde was abandoned, leaving behind a story of cultural complexity and, finally, failure.

From the very earliest periods, man has realized that variety is more than the spice of life: it is the very essence of life. Without the variety of geological formations, climates, and species that contribute to the diversity of ecosystems, without the distinctive contributions of every people, the whole immense tapestry of humanity would have quite a different pattern. The World Heritage Convention recognizes that if any part of our universal heritage is lost, mankind as a whole is the poorer.

Most of us have spent our working lives trying to help conserve natural diversity. The results of our efforts can be seen in some of the existing World Heritage Sites.

Grand Canyon is a rare example of the conflict between two great geological forces: Mountain-building and erosion, revealing a geological record covering two thousand million years.

Nahanni National Park in Canada provides one of the world's great examples of water at work, including almost every distinct category of river or stream that is known.

One of the most spectacular things that happens when water meets rock is illustrated at Mammoth Cave National Park, USA, whose known passages are over twice as long as the next longest cave system.

The grandfather of national parks, Yellowstone is a geologist's paradise, with the world's largest concentration of hot springs and geisers and the largest caldera, clearly illustrating the active evolution of the earth's crust.

Volcanic eruptions at sea created Ecuador's Galapagos Islands. While the landscape is forbidding, it has provided a laboratory for the study of evolution. Giant tortoises vary in physical features from island to island, inspiring Charles Darwin's insights into the process of adaptation to the environment through natural selection, insights which have provided the very foundations upon which modern biology is built.

The culmination of the evolutionary process can be seen at Virunga National Park in Zaire. Ranging from equatorial forest to mountain glaciers, the site may have the greatest diversity of habitats in the world, as well as some of the most interesting plants and animals.

Many World Heritage Sites are of critical importance in conserving major concentrations of wildlife. The great herds of plains animals and their predators in Tanzania's Serengeti National Park provides one of the most remarkable and inspiring wildlife spectacles in the world.

In areas with few large animals, great concentrations of wildfowl still occur, as at Ichkeul National Park in Tunisia, where hundreds of thousands of resident and migratory birds are supported by the highly productive wetlands.

The world's longest coral reef is also a World Heritage Site. Composed of a long series of reefs and islands separated by navigable channels, Australia's Great Barrier Reef is being built by over 400 species of corals, providing a habitat for a host of marine animals.

Only a few of the 38 natural or mixed natural and cultural sites have been mentioned. Eleven more natural sites have been nominated this year, including Southwest Tasmania Wilderness Parks, Lord Howe Island, Rio Platano, Aldabra Nature Reserve, and Selous Game Reserve.

Other areas are certain to be nominated in due course, providing increased protection for important areas and species and illustrating the willingness of governments to undertake the responsibility for maintaining the integrity of their share of the World's Heritage.

But many important areas have not yet been nominated because the States involved have not yet become parties to the World Heritage Convention. A country does not need to be a Party to be doing everything in its power to conserve sites of international importance. But joining the Convention helps to strengthen international solidarity in defense of the heritage of all mankind. By working together to achieve the objectives of the World Heritage Convention, we are all contributing to a better future for humanity.

What the World Heritage Convention Has Meant to Ethiopia

Teshome Ashine
General Manager
Wildlife Conservation Organization
Addis Ababa, Ethiopia

ABSTRACT. *Ethiopia contains a variety of World Heritage Sites, including the natural site of Simen National Park, the mixed cultural/natural sites of the Lower Awash and Lower Omo valleys (where some of the most important human paleontological sites have been found), and the cultural sites of Axum, the rock-hewn churches of Lalibela, and the castles of Gondar. All of these had already been identified by the government of Ethiopia as of outstanding value to the nation. However, the support of World Heritage recognition has been of outstanding benefit to help ensure that the government of Ethiopia is able to implement its management activities.*

1. INTRODUCTION

Ethiopia's World Hertiage Sites consist of both natural and cultural properties. The Simen Mountain National Park is the only natural property while the cultural properties are the rock-cut churches of Lalibella, the Castles of Gondar and the monuments at Axum. Mixed cultural/natural sites are the Lower Valley of the Omo and the Lower Valley of the Awash, where important paleontological and archaeological discoveries have been made; the Awash Valley is the home of the prehistoric creature "Lucy" 3½ million years old, and the Omo valley is where the fossils of another prehistoric being 2½ million years old were found. The Simen Mountain National Park is under the responsibility of the Wildlife Conservation Organization, and the Ministry of Culture is looking after the cultural properties. Even before the inscription of these properties as World Heritage Sites, they were under protection and were being developed. But with the declaration of these areas as World Heritage Sites and the assistance provided by Unesco and other concerned international agencies, their development has gathered momentum.

The importance and significance of the country's heritage is well recognized. In 1975, the Provisional Military Government of Socialist Ethiopia in its economic policy declaration stated, "It should, however, be emphasized that the conservation of wildlife, birdlife, etc., particularly of the rare species and the preservation of the antiquities, will be viewed primarily as national objectives in their own right and not only as a means of attracting foreign visitors. This task of preservation will be actively pursued by the state."

This policy has been put into operation in spite of the many constraints facing the Government in its pursuit of improving the living standard of its people.

Yet the World Heritage inscription itself has helped the people at all levels to better realize the magnitude and importance of all these properties. This has resulted in more concerted attention being paid to their conservation and development. Considering its importance, and in appreciation of the acceptance of the Simen Mountain National Park as a World Heritage Site, Comrade Chairman Mengistu Haile Mariam, Chairman of the Provisional Military Administrative Council of Socialist Ethiopia and Commander in Chief of the Revolutionary Armed Forces, personally visited the park and issued directives for the development of the area.

2. NATURAL PROPERTY: SIMEN MOUNTAIN NATIONAL PARK

2.1. Description

The origin of the Simen Mountains in the northwestern part of the country, can be traced to the beginnings of the geological formation of the earth. Some 25 million years ago a series of volcanic eruptions caused the spreading of the molten rock over an area of 1500 sq km, which later turned into basalt. For millions of years rains ravaged these basalt layers, creating vast sheer escarpments, cliffs and mountain peaks. The great storms eroded the land into canyons 750 m or more deep with the northern escarpment wall extending some 35 km.

These geophysical activities have resulted in a fabulous landscape of awesome 1200 m cliffs, the magnificance of which is seldom found anywhere. The crowning part of it all is the peak, Ras Dashan, rising to some 4,500 m, where snow is quite common. The scenic splendour and serenity of these mountains make this area so unique.

Another outstanding feature of these mountains is the presence of fascinating species of wildlife and birds, endemic to Ethiopia, like the Walia ibex, the gelada baboon and the Simen fox. To preserve and protect these creatures, the Simen Mt. National Park was established here in 1969, as recommended by the two Unesco Commissions headed by Sir Julian Huxley and Dr. Leslie Brown that visited Ethiopia in 1964 and 1965. The park extends over 165 km and is accessible from Debark, a provincial town in the Gondar region, on the Gondar-Asmara highway. A 35 km road connects Debark with the headquarters of the park.

Simen has no roads except this 35 km stretch. Most of the park is interconnected by trails and bridle paths. This is mainly because of the terrain and also to preserve the natural beauty and serenity of the area. Considerable infrastructure has been developed since 1969, consisting of four outposts, administrative buildings, some basic tourist accommodation and residential buildings for the staff. The staff consists of a warden, 30 wildlife guards and 7 supporting administrative staff.

In addition to the endemic species mentioned above, the wildlife includes hamadryas baboon, klipspringer, bushbuck, jackal, hyena, and duiker. The main bird species are lammergeyer, tawny eagle, Egyptian vulture, augur buzzard, thick-billed raven, Verraux's eagle, kestrel, ibis, plover and Lanner falcon.

The vegetation of the Simen forms three horizontal bands. Up to 3,000 m only a few traces of ancient juniper and *Policarpus* forests remain. Above this level up to 3,800 m forests of Giant St. Johns Wort once flourished; few still remain. Above this forest and below the alpine mosses lie superb grasslands dominated by Giant Lobelias.

Prior to the establishment of the Simen Mountain National Park, the wildlife of the area, particularly the endemic species like the Walia ibex, were seriously threatened. Constant poaching had reduced Walias to 100. Burning of shrub cover and the excessive tree cutting had practically denuded the habitat. The wildlife was on the verge of extinction.

In 1969 with the establishment of the park, personnel under a capable warden were deployed here. Over the last few years the needed infrastructure was developed. Four outposts were established. Regular patrols and other preventive measures taken by the park staff drastically reduced the poaching and eliminated much of the habitat destruction. The resettlement of the people occupying the adjacent areas helped in reducing the destruction.

Consequently the habitat recovery was amazing. The number of the wild animals in the region considerably increased; the latest animal counts reveal that the Walia ibex alone is estimated to number today almost 1000. Needless to say, the other species too have simultaneously increased in number.

As a part of the general development envisaged in wildlife conservation, considerable development is planned for the Simen. It includes preparation and implementation of wildlife management plans, in-service training of the basic staff, establishment of more outposts, re-afforestation of the denuded areas of the park and the adjacent region, and soil conservation.

2.2. Constraints in the development of the park and their resolution

2.2.1. Biotic influence. A very major constraint in the development of this park was the presence of a few peasants in the area, eking out a precarious living. Over the years, these people had, through wrong agricultural practices, heavily eroded the land. From the beginning of time, these mountains were covered with alpine forests and shrubs which were denuded in the course of time, making the land almost arid. Thus the people occupying this stretch were living out a miserable existence not even managing subsistence farming; they survived by encroaching into the parkland and killing the endemic animals like the Walia. Although attempts were made to resettle these people in the past, they were not successful.

With the acceptance of the park as a World Heritage Site, the whole perspective of the development of the area underwent a great change. The world acclamation given to this area, through this acceptance, created a national awareness. The Government took strong measures to resettle most of these people in a more congenial land elsewhere with all facilities so that they could pursue a better way of life. The resettlement is continuing. The Simen thus has come into its rightful place in the national scheme of development.

2.2.2. Development of infrastructure. Although national development funds to the tune of some US$400,000 were spent in the past, infrastructure was still needed. The most important need was for a radio communication network to help in fully patrolling the park area and also to keep the various outposts in contact with the park headquarters. Additional field equipment like camping gear, compasses, binoculars, radios and altimeters were badly needed, as were vehicles for patrolling.

With the declaration of this area as a World Heritage Site, requests were made to the World Heritage Committee for assistance which were very graciously accepted after the visit of a Commission to inspect the area. It is a matter of great satisfaction that the infrastructural needs have been met to a very considerable extent.

2.2.3. Training of technical personnel.
Another obstacle in the development of the area was the scarcity of trained personnel, both at the executive and lower levels. With the help of the World Heritage Committee, three fellowships were obtained to the College of African Wildlife Management in Tanzania, one for a post-graduate diploma course and two for diploma courses in wildlife management. The post-graduate holder has returned to take up his duties after completing his studies while the other two are still pursuing their studies.

The Simen National Park has 30 wildlife guards. They have had no worthwhile training and this has somewhat impeded their useful function. This too had to be corrected and a request for assistance was made to the World Heritage Committee, which approved a grant of US$9,000. The training is to be completed before June 1983, and will be given in the local language by the trained staff of the Wildlife Conservation Organization. It will be mostly on the objectives of conservation, field observation and note-taking, identification and census of wild mammals and birds, taxonomic classification, basic principles of soil conservation and habitat preservation, general ecological monitoring and an introduction to the conservation laws of the country.

2.2.4. Preparation of a wildlife management plan.
Now that most of the constraints in the development of the park are being removed, it is felt that a sound wildlife management plan for the area should be developed and implemented. This would need the participation of expatriate experts. A request for assistance in this has been submitted to the World Heritage Committee and is being considered.

The proposal is to hold a seminar in the Simen itself with the expatriate experts and the experts of the Wildlife Conservation Organization participating. Following the seminar, with both the groups collaborating, a wildlife management plan would be formulated and implemented thus ensuring the total conservation and development of the Simen National Park.

3. CULTURAL PROPERTIES

3.1. Axum

The Axumite civilisation flourished in the northern part of Ethiopia from the 5th century B.C. to the 6th century A.D. and was mainly the major facet of the Axumite empire. Although Axum today is only a small township, the obelisks there and the ruins of the ancient temple at nearby Yeha, dating back to the 5th century B.C., remind us of the glories of this ancient civilisation.

In the town of Axum itself there is a stelae field consisting of a standing stelae, a fallen one and other granite monoliths. Excavations conducted here at the beginning of this century recorded some 78 stelae and recent investigations have brought the total up to 119. The stelae are of different dimensions and elaborations with the largest of them, the fallen one, measuring 33 meters. Recent excavations in the stelae field have shown the presence of a complete underground structure consisting of catacombs, tunnels and tombs. The palace of Dengur and the tomb of Kaleb nearby are other culturally important spots.

3.2. The Rock-cut churches of Lalibella

Near the foothills of the 4193 m mountain, Abune Yoseph, in Ethiopia's Wollo Administrative Region, presumably between 10th and 12th century, eleven churches were hewn out of a sloping rock surface of the volcanic red scoria. The construction of these rock-hewn churches is attributed to the Zagwe dynasty that ruled Ethiopia at that time. The most prominent of these kings was Lalibella, after whom these churches are known. But regrettably no historical records remain to tell us of the builders, the unique design and the concentration of so many monuments in one place.

These eleven churches are divided into two main groups of monuments and a lone church, and are interconnected by trenches, tunnels, caves and tombs, creating a labyrinth. Each one of the churches, whether monolithic, freestanding in courtyards or dug out of rock wall, has its own principle of design in the interior and the exterior.

Sometime ago some restoration work of these churches were undertaken. But they were purely cosmetic since no serious study had been undertaken to determine the causes of the decay and deterioration.

3.3. The Castles of Gondar

After the decline of the Axumite civilisation, the capital of the ancient Ethiopian empire shifted to Gondar. The heyday of Gondar was between the 16th and 18th century A.D. which saw the construction of these unique monuments. Out of the total monuments so far discovered, 21 form the World Heritage Site.

3.4. Proposals for the prevention of deterioration, and restoration of all the cultural properties

Since the acceptance of these ancient monuments as World Heritage Sites, a number of proposals have been submitted to prevent their deterioration and to initiate their restoration. This involves 26 monuments in total.

The main obstacle to any such programme is the lack of funds and expertise. Any restoration of this magnitude would need large financial outlays. It is therefore proposed to launch an international campaign to be spread over the next ten years to raise funds for this purpose. A committee at the ministerial level has been formed to organize this campaign and the Director-General of Unesco is to launch it. This campaign is planned to be carried out in close collaboration with Unesco.

Apart from this, under the auspices of Unesco a pilot project was carried out in Gondar for the last three years for restoration work and also to provide some in-service training in restoration. Four years ago a mini-symposium was held at Lalibella to carry out a study of the restoration needed in the rock-cut churches in Lalibella. This too was organized with the assistance of Unesco.

4. CONCLUSION

All the properties in Ethiopia—inscribed in the World Heritage list both cultural and natural—prior to their declaration, were considered by the Ethiopian Government as unique and had been set apart for preservation and development. But their acceptance as World Heritage Sites was indeed a universal acceptance of the significance of these properties.

Although we had made considerable efforts to conserve, develop and restore these properties, we were very much impeded by the lack of expertise, equipment and funds. Since nationally these were not easily available, we had to resort to requesting the help of international agencies like Unesco and IUCN. As mentioned elsewhere, plans have been set afoot to obtain the expertise for the preparation of wildlife management plans and in-service training in the case of the Simen National Park. An international campaign is to be launched shortly to assist in the restoration of our cultural properties, the indentification of which is mostly complete.

Apart from the properties listed as the World Heritage Sites, in Ethiopia there are other natural and cultural properties to be included. Among the 37 conservation areas, there are the Bale Mountain and Abijatta-Shalla Lakes National Parks which, scenically and as centres of wildlife and birdlife concentrations, are very significant; the Abijatta-Shalla Lakes is on the migratory route of thousands of migratory birds from northern Europe and even Asia during the winter.

Equally important are the national parks of Omo, Mago and Gambella. The Omo and Mago are perhaps the last of the unspoiled wilderness in Africa. The Gambella has the largest concentration of wildlife in Ethiopia, with large herds of white-eared kob.

The objectives of the preservation and development of all our World Heritage Sites are the continued educational, scientific and economic benefits of the people of Ethiopia and the world at large as well. With the continued assistance and advice from Unesco, IUCN, WWF and other international agencies involved, we very optimistically remain committed to the achievement of our objectives.

Acknowledgements

This paper was prepared for IUCN's Commission on National Parks and Protected Areas in cooperation with UNESCO.

The Dinosaur World Heritage Site: Responsible Management in Canada

Donn Cline, Ken Erdman, and William Pearce
Alberta Recreation and Parks
Edmonton, Alberta, Canada

1. INTRODUCTION

The Convention Concerning the Protection of the World Cultural and Natural Heritage (1972) is a relatively new international conservation tool. The first four national World Heritage Sites—Nahanni National Park in Canada, Yellowstone National Park in the United States, Simien National Park in Ethiopia, and the Galapagos National Park in Ecuador—were designated in 1978.

In 1979 Dinosaur Provincial Park was added to the list of World Heritage Sites because its fossil features were recognized to be of outstanding value by the World Heritage Committee. For the agency responsible for managing and protecting this exceptional resource, we wish to describe in this paper the responsibilities associated with administering the first World Heritage Site designated that is under provincial or state, rather than national or federal, jurisdiction.

2. SITE VALUE

Dinosaur Provincial Park, as the name implies, has world stature as a fossil resource for the remains of dinosaurs. It appears as exotic badlands stretching fingerlike into a flat topography of prairie grasslands. This network of gulleys, coulees, mesas, and other erosional landforms is stifling hot in summer and barren in winter. Dinosaur remains were first discovered in this part of southeast Alberta in the 1880s, but just after the turn of the century, this landscape witnessed the greatest dinosaur bone rush in the history of paleontology.

The Geological Survey of Canada began collecting in 1912 because of concerned statements to the Federal Minister of the Interior from Alberta about the large-scale removal of dinosaur fossils. The most famous American collector, Barnum Brown, wrote that in four years the American Museum expeditions collected 300 large cases of fossils.

More than 300 recorded specimens of dinosaurs have been removed from a 24-km stretch along the Red Deer valley, including representatives of the major groups of reptiles and associated animals from the Upper Cretaceous period. Scientists suggest that dinosaurs reached their most advanced forms during this time.

Fossil beds have produced whole skeletons, partial remains, fossilized stomach contents, and even skin imprints in the sandstone. The variety has been amazing: a tail club of an armoured dinosaur, most of a hadrosaur skeleton, and the remains of a herd of at least 30 *Centrosaurus* that died en masse have all been unearthed recently.

This heritage allows researchers to trace the prehistoric time frames, reconstruct the fascinating evolution of these life forms, and to learn more about these remarkable creatures that inhabited the tropical deltas and swamps that once existed here on the margin of a warm sea. "Dinosaur Provincial Park represents the most important remaining fragment of the dinosaurian world known to mankind", wrote Dr. Dale Russel, Chief of Paleobiology at the Canadian Naional Museum to the World Heritage Committee.

Today, 30 major museums around the world hold collections from the park and surrounding area. The most notable collections are housed in the National Museum in Ottawa, the Royal Ontario Museum and the American Museum of Natural History. However, through purchase and exchange fossils may also be seen at the British Museum of Natural History, the National Museum of Brazil, the Museo de la Plato in Argentina and many others.

It was not only professional collectors that persuaded the Provincial Government to begin to see the desirability of establishing a park—it had also become fashionable to collect petrified fossil remains from the dinosaur beds and incorporate them into private rock gardens and collections. In 1936, legislation was passed which brought the badlands under provincial protection.

By 1937, a movement had begun to persuade the Provincial Government to establish a badlands park to include the most exotic parts along the river valley. In 1952, the noted paleontologist, Charles Sternberg, was invited by the Alberta Government to direct a survey of the badlands with the idea of establishing a provincial park. He identified the Steveville-Little Sandhill Creek area, where the badlands are concentrated, as the most promising area. The Steveville Dinosaur Provincial Park was established in June, 1955. Exactly 25 years to the month after its creation, Dinosaur Provincial Park was dedicated as a World Heritage Site, thus ensuring international interest in its future protection.

Within the park and adjacent lands are other features of historical and archaeological value that are not related to dinosaur fossils. A stone effigy man, a boulder outline about 50 m in length, is located on the north side of the river. It is suggested that this figure represents the Blackfoot Indian hero, Napi, the Old Man.

A Dream Bed, or Vision Quest Site, was discovered by a park ranger in 1963. It is believed to be the only fasting shelter in Alberta. The dream bed is composed of flat stones set on edge as a wind break. An individual would go to this lonely place in moon-like surroundings and fast until a dream or vision came to him.

River edge habitats represent a fascinating and endangered biological community that stands out in stark contrast to the surrounding grasslands. The badlands themselves are of exceptional beauty and provide habitat for rare species such as the Golden Eagle and the Prairie Falcon. The area is a textbook example of fluvial erosion. In a year, every face of these formations recedes from two to four centimetres, a rate 100 times faster than in the Rocky Mountains. Undoubtedly, there will be new fossil discoveries from this erosion.

3. GUIDELINES FOR MANAGEMENT

As of 1981, there were 85 sites on the World Heritage List. Twenty-five percent are natural areas. The natural areas are under-represented and this must be a concern to us. Natural areas are under great pressure and Dinosaur Provincial Park is no exception.

The year 1979 marked the beginning of an intensive research programme by the Provincial Museum of Alberta in conjunction and cooperation with Alberta Recreation and Parks. Museum crews are working at uncovering and mapping bone beds and other discoveries.

There are pressures on the park because of significant oil and gas reserves located beneath the park and also from pipeline rights-of-way. There is currently a citizen's movement being organized that is demanding expanded and improved camping and recreation facilities within park boundaries. These desired developments are difficult to encompass because of possible impairment of the natural qualities that are under protection.

Obligations of the province are clear. They include identification through comprehensive knowledge of the site, conservation through research, and presentation of the natural resources to visitors. A major new paleontological museum is being planned as a scientific institution with tourist and display intentions in Drumheller, a small city outside of Dinosaur Park.

Research and resource analysis is ongoing. The province is obligated to maintain the site to acceptable standards and is developing master plans that will guide major upgrading or development. Consistent with the World Heritage Convention Directives, the guidelines as outlined by the Government of Alberta in an interim management and visitor use plan are as follows:

- to preserve and manage the paleontological resources of the site;
- to conserve and manage the river habitats, badland environment, native grasslands and critical wildlife habitats of the site;
- to provide interpretive educational programmes that will promote an understanding and awareness of the international significance of the park's resources; and
- to advance mankind's knowledge of the site's resources through scientific research and educational programmes.

At the present time, existing development is generally of a moderate or low scale. There is a small campground, a day use area, an administration area, a viewpoint, onsite exhibits and displays. Most facilities are in a small core area with access provided by a narrow road descending from the prairie flats. The majority of the park lands are natural preserve and restricted areas accessible only by conducted tours.

Interpretation, education and visitor services are in place to play a role within the management and provisions for visitors to a World Heritage Site. A diverse programme of conducted hikes, bus tours, evening programmes, and children's programmes has provided first hand and vicarious experience to approximately 20,000 visitors in each of the past two years. Our approximate gross user figures are 55,000 visitors per annum. Visitor Services Staff are supported by the Rangers and work in conjunction with Alberta Culture.

Another responsibility of management is planning, which is facilitated by an interdisciplinary planning team initiated in 1979. This master planning team develops detailed concept alternatives for review by senior management. The concepts address the issues of resource preservation; visitor use, control, support facilities, recreation opportunities and evaluation; and operation and maintenance.

4. CONCLUSION

Participation by Canada and subsequently by Alberta within the Convention and the inclusion of Canadian sites on the World Heritage List bring both the responsibilities discussed and the following benefits:

- there is international prestige associated with World Heritage Sites;
- there can be substantial tourist traffic and resulting generation of revenues;
- there is the moral protection of the site, the obligation to the international community and the development of local pride and admiration;
- there tends to be increased protection and appropriate development and management; and
- there is the development of a basic understanding of one's own heritage and a developing love for one's own country and heritage.

The World Heritage Convention: Status and Directions

David F. Hales
Samuel Trask Dana Professor
University of Michigan
Ann Arbor, Michigan, USA

ABSTRACT. *This paper examines the nature of the World Heritage Convention, discusses its potential value for the conservation of natural resources of outstanding universal importance, and recommends specific steps which should be taken by a number of actors to increase the effectiveness of its potential contributions.*

1. INTRODUCTION

There are resources, cultural and natural, which serve as bridges between past and future. The importance of these resources to humankind transcends artificial and transitory "boundaries" devised for political reasons, as well as the less artificial but increasingly difficult-to-define human systems known as cultures. These treasures belong not only to the nations within which they are located, and not only to people who live in the latter part of the twentieth century. They belong, most of all, to our children and our children's children.

These thoughts are neither original nor of recent origin. Yet until 1972 they were represented primarily in philosophical rhetoric, although they occasionally made their way into public policy in the form of regional arrangements directed at specifically and narrowly defined classes of resources.

The adoption of the International Convention for the protection of the World Cultural and Natural Heritage (World Heritage Convention) by the Unesco Geneva Conference in 1972 united for the first time the principle of international cooperation with the concepts of international responsibility and stewardship in a permanent framework with legal, administrative, and financial capabilities.

The importance of this development is difficult to overstate, yet the Convention remains largely unknown and certainly underutilized, particularly by those with responsibility for the management, conservation, and protection of natural resources.

In light of this situation, the goals of this paper are threefold: first to demonstrate the importance, relevance, and potential of the World Heritage Convention to those concerned with conservation of nature; second, to identify and describe problems internal to the workings of the Convention which must be addressed before its potential can be fully realized; and third, to suggest measures which can and should be taken, by a variety of actors, to promote the effectiveness and use of an underutilized mechanism.

2. THE WORLD HERITAGE CONVENTION: ITS NATURE, IMPORTANCE, AND POTENTIAL

The World Heritage Convention is an open treaty among nation-states who are members of Unesco. It became enforceable in 1975 when the documents of ratification from the twentieth state were received in its place of repository in Unesco headquarters, Paris, France. (As of December, 1982, 67 nations had ratified the Convention—Appendix I). By ratifying, each nation formally recognizes several principles:

- that each nation holds in trust for the rest of mankind those parts of the World Heritage that are found within its boundaries;
- that each nation has an obligation to support other nations in discharging this trust;

744

- that each nation must exercise the same responsibility to works of nature as to works of humankind; and
- that each nation grants to its co-signatories the right to observe the degree to which it meets its obligations under the Convention (principles adapted in part from Unesco, 1980).

In addition, signatories take upon themselves several specific obligations which focus on the explicit recognition of a duty to identify, protect, and transmit to future generations heritage situated on its own territory. States party to the Convention stipulate the desirability of adopting "general policies" aimed at these goals and agree to take appropriate legal, administrative, scientific, technical, and financial measures if such measure are deemed possible and appropriate. States Parties also agree to keep the public informed about dangers to World Heritage Sites and about preservation measures they are taking.

Equally important, signatories recognize an affirmative obligation to help in the identification and preservation of heritage situated outside of their own territory, and specifically agree "not to take any deliberate measures which might damage directly or indirectly the cultural and natural heritage situated on the territory of other States Parties to this Convention."

The potential inherent in these arrangements for future conservation efforts is significant. The primary actors in the World Heritage Convention are nations. Although the Convention specifically recognizes the sovereignty of its members, and although words such as "appropriate" and "when possible" occur frequently in its text, ratification still entails a significant statement of commitment. Whether or not these commitments are legally enforceable depends substantially on the legal systems in individual states, and remains to be determined. It is also, perhaps, beside the point. These commitments are voluntary pledges backed with national honour, the fulfilment of which can be judged in an international public forum. A powerful force for conservation has been created; its effective use now depends on the skill and wisdom of conservation communities.

The governing mechanism of the Convention is a committee formed of 21 States Parties to the Convention. Each state is to be represented by persons who "possess specialized knowledge concerning cultural or natural heritage." The primary responsibilities of the Committee are to rigorously evaluate sites nominated by member States, and to confer formal recognition as World Heritage Sites upon those which possess "outstanding universal value", and to provide financial and technical resources to nations which need assistance in the protection of Heritage Sites (for types of assistance available from the Committee see Appendix II).

The Committee is also charged with the responsibility of maintaining a list of World Heritage in Danger, comprised of sites formally included on the List of World Heritage which are seriously threatened either by human action or natural causes. Additionally, the Committee is charged with the responsibility of removing recognition as World Heritage Sites from sites which have lost the qualities which led to their inclusion. Implicit in this duty is the responsibility to perodically evaluate the status of sites included in the World Heritage list, a responsibility which the Committee has as yet taken no systematic steps toward fulfilling.

Through the Committee, the Convention offers the conservation incentives of recognition and technical and financial assistance, in return for the specific obligations undertaken by states whose sites are inscribed on the World Heritage List. Here again, the potential value of these mechanisms to conservation is primarily limited only by the skill and wisdom with which they are applied.

The potential of the Convention is not limited to those possibilities already discussed. The authorities granted to the World Heritage Committee also include the ability to financially support public information and education activities related to the purposes of the Convention, the ability to grant training fellowships to individuals directly involved with the management of World Heritage sites as well as to support national and regional training centres, and the ability to contract with non-governmental organizations (primarily IUCN and ICOMOS) for the development of scientific data necessary for the effective functioning of the Committee. The Committee has the authority to engage in fund-raising activities and to accept and expend funds for any of these purposes.

3. FACTORS LIMITING THE REALIZATION OF THE CONVENTION'S POTENTIAL

Although the accomplishments of the Convention to date are quite significant, and certainly praiseworthy, it is more appropriate in the context of this paper to focus on how to increase the opportunities available under its aegis, than to list its successes and give the impression that all is well. The exercise undertaken is one of diagnosis and prescription, not criticism of the patient. It is also worth noting that many of the concerns which are described below derive from the very history which has given the Convention its strength. Many could not have been addressed prior to this time, and none could be addressed had the Convention not been successful so far. Conventions, like babies, must crawl before they can walk, and walk before they can run. This Convention is both precocious and far from recognizing its potential.

At the present time, the World Heritage Convention and the Committee which governs it face issues which can be divided into three main, but somewhat interrelated, categories.

First, there is the need to develop positive and supportive relationships between the two essentially dissimilar conservation/preservation movements, cultural and natural, which are joined in the Convention.

Second, there is a need to address questions of creditability which arise, not from the Convention, but from the way the Committee has developed, or in some instances, not developed, the mechanisms for its implementaion.

And finally, questions of politicization of the Committee, and thus the Convention must be addressed openly and remedied quickly.

3.1. Natural-Cultural Balance

The unprecedented combination of natural and cultural preservation movements, while potentially a great strength of the Convention, underlies many of the practical difficulties which should be addressed.

When the immediate historical lineage of the Convention is considered, it is apparent that its cultural roots are perhaps deeper and certainly more familiar and comfortable to Unesco than are those of nature conservation. Although the Consultative Commission for the International Protection of Nature was legally established by European nations in 1913, with nation-state membership, the outbreak of World War I prevented the meeting of its first General Assembly, and its focus was neither on preserves nor protected areas. The years between World Wars I and II produced no successful movement toward governmental involvement in formal international mechanisms for the protection of natural areas. Although the concept was revived in 1948 in the Constitution of the International Union for the Protection of Nature (Article I(2)) and a manifesto developed at the 1949 IUPN Lake Success Conference, Unesco declined to circulate the document, arguing that the measures called for were impractical.

Perhaps more germane were the efforts of Julian Huxley as Director-General of Unesco to persuade Unesco member-states that the concept of nature conservation was within Unesco's mandate. Although Huxley was able to create some support capacity for non-governmental organizations through Unesco's Division of Natural Sciences Division, as well as set up a committee under the International Council of Museums, which dealt with national parks and nature reserves, Unesco's major interests and resources remained focussed on other functions.

On the cultural side, Unesco had, almost from its beginning, advocated a convention concerning international protection of monuments, groups of buildings, and sites of universal value. Additionally, Unesco has sponsored international campaigns on behalf of Venice, Abu-Simbel, and Borobudur, campaigns which specifically embodied a concept of "world heritage".

On the natural side, the idea of international governmental cooperation re-emerged at a USA "White House Conference" in 1965, and the two trains of thought merged at the UN Conference on the Human Environ-

ment in 1971, resulting in the adoption of the World Heritage Convention by the Unesco General Conference in 1972. Although the merger of two quite different conservation movements was probably crucial to the development of sufficient political support to adopt the convention, the movements clearly retained quite separate identities on a national basis as well as distinct sets of international non-governmental relationships.

With few exceptions, national interest in the Convention was dominated by cultural agencies within each country, and responsibility for Convention activities lodged with Ministries of Culture or their counterparts. As a result, from its very first meeting the World Heritage Committee has primarily consisted of national representatives with cultural, not natural, expertise. Through its first five meetings only five of the twenty-five nations represented on the Committee have sent as delegates or alternate delegates experts in nature conservation.

Although IUCN has, since the third session of the Committee, done an exemplary job of screening natural nominations and making recommendations to the Committee, the Committee's own evaluation of natural sites has often been less than rigorous, and much of the discussion among IUCN and the natural experts on the Committee has not been fully appreciated by the majority of delegates who eventually decide whether or not recognition is merited.

Even though the Committee itself has recognized the need to redress this imbalance since its first session and repeatedly reminded its member states to send delegations representing both cultural and natural expertise, the imbalance continues; at its 1981 meeting in Australia, only two of the 21 delegations to the Committee contained natural experts. It should be clearly noted that the Committee has taken great pains to be fair and evenhanded in its consideration of nominations and in awarding grants for training and technical assistance. In addition, in its Operational Guidelines the Committee has included several provisions to strongly encourage natural-cultural balance. (Appendix III).

The continued domination of convention activities by cultural interests has resulted in a World Heritage list where cultural sites outnumber natural by a ratio of 3:1, and in a failure to maximize the educational impact of the convention. Recognition of this imbalance, and calls for its redress, in no way implies criticism of the active concern and strong support for the Convention from those interested in cultural matters.

The remedy of questions of balance lies primarily in the hands of agencies and organizations within states-parties interested in or responsible for nature conservation, and with the General Conference of States Parties to the Convention.

3.2. Issues of Credibility

In addition to the potential lack of credibility resulting from the under-representation of nature conservation interests and experts on the Committee, several other issues must be addressed if the Covention is to maximize its effectiveness.

Key among these issues is the rigor with which nominations are evaluated. Difficulties arise in three areas: with the criteria against which sites are to be measured; with the degree of compliance with guidelines for content of nominations; and with the Committee's evaluation procedures.

The criteria against which sites are to be measured derive from the Convention itself, and have been subjected to serious deliberation at each session of the Committee, and at most sessions of the Committee's Bureau. They have not, however, been subjected to systematic review in terms of the impact of their application, nor have they been submitted to systematic peer review by scientific experts. While it is apparent that work load and time pressures prevent the Committee from undertaking such reviews at its annual sessions, alternative methods for accomplishing such reviews should be pursued.

With regard to the content of nominations, it is clear from both the Convention and the Operational Guidelines of the Committee that the evaluation of nominations must not only be stringent in terms of the criteria themselves, but also comparative. Paragraph 33(v) of the Operational Guidelines requires that nominations include "a comparative evaluation of properties of the same type or having similar features, which are found in other countries." Enforcement of this provision has been inconsistent. In addition, the Committee has not yet found a feasible means of implementing the provisions in Article II of the Convention, which calls for the preparation of inventories by each state which should include properties which may be nominated in the next five to ten years. Without this management tool, the importance of which was clearly seen in the Convention, the measurement of comparability will remain quite difficult.

The Operational Guidelines also call for nominations to include, in addition to "diagnosis" of the state of preservation/conservation, a discussion of specific preservation/conservation measures the nominating state intends to take, including management plans or proposals for the development of such plans (Paragraph 33(iv)). The same paragraph also calls for discussion of overall development plans for the region in which the site is located so that the state of protection and the adequacy of management plans can be evaluated in the context of potential adverse impacts. In addition, Paragraph 12 of the Guidelines specifies that nominations should include adequate "buffer zones" around sites, and requires both specific delineation and adequate protection of such zones. These provisions have also been inconsistently applied by the Committee in its review of nominations.

Many of these inconsistencies result from the Committee's evaluation procedures which require that the Committee evaluate all nominations during an eight-month period. To be considered during the annual Sep-tember/October Committee Session, nominations must be received by the Unesco Secretariat prior to 1 January. The Secretariat has until 1 April to administratively review the nominations, translate them into the working languages of the Committee and transmit them to either ICOMOS or IUCN for substantive review. ICOMOS and IUCN are also required to complete substantive review by 1 April. In May, the Bureau of the Committee spends less than two days developing their recommendations to the full Committee. The nominations and recommendations are then transmitted to all States Parties to the Convention by 1 August. In September or October the Committee spends less than two days deliberating and acting on all active nominations. In 1981, the Bureau reviewed 46 nominations during its two day session, averaging less than 20 minutes per nomination. The Committee, in 1981, accepted 26 properties to the World Heritage List, averaging less than 30 minutes per nomination. To date, the Committee has received approximately 200 nominations; 112 sites have been inscribed on the World Heritage List; the others have been deferred either for additional information, or indefinitely.

Having described the process, comment seems unnecessary. The expedited procedure, appropriate and manageable during the first few years of the Committee's activities, must be reevaluated and changed if the credibility of the Committee is to be maintained.

An additional major challenge to the credibility of the Committee comes from its lack of procedures to monitor the continuing integrity and protection of the sites it has recognized as having outstanding universal value. Although it is clearly neither desirable nor feasible for the Committee to interpose itself in sovereign matters, it is also clear that the act of nominating commits the nominating state to certain responsibilities, and that the act of designation commits the Committee, on behalf of all parties, to others. While the obligation to protect a site rests clearly with the State in which the site is located, the Committee has no obligation to continue to recognize a site which has not been protected. In fact, the opposite is true; the Committee is obligated to encourage protection through all appropriate means, and to delist a site should the qualities for which it has been recognized be lost.

Most discussions of the issue of monitoring (often because of difficulties in translating the word "monitor") dissolve into debate over perceived negative aspects of such a process, including potential interference with sovereignty and suspicions that advocacy of a monitoring process implies either condescension or mistrust. Such discussion misses the positive aspects of monitoring which are readily apparent to professional natural resource managers. The information transfer inherent in an effective monitoring process, allowing resource managers to share both problems and solutions, would provide both data and incentives conducive to effective stewardship of treasures so valued by nations that they were submitted for recognition.

It is impossible to argue that the need for quiet, mature diplomacy in defense of sites of outstanding universal value has not occurred in the past or will not occur again. The need to address "delisting", either because of natural catastrophe or human action may occur. The lack of monitoring procedures will not forestall these problems, and, in fact, will only make their solution more difficult. The development of monitoring procedures can, however, in a positive way, help avoid serious conflict. That the issue will be difficult to resolve is demonstrated by debate at the 5th Session of the Committee. Continuing efforts to resolve the issue must be encouraged, as a sign that the Committee takes its responsibilities seriously, and as a sign that the Committee is as concerned about heritage resources as it is about politics.

The last "credibility" issue to be addressed here also concerns the Convention's relationship with Unesco, in this case the need to develop a specific, formal relationship between the World Heritage Convention and Committee, and the occasional campaigns which Unesco conducts for the preservation of important resources, primarily cultural. It is in the interest of both Unesco, the Convention, and most important, resources which may become threatened, to develop a means for coordination and mutual support for future campaigns.

It is embarrassing to both the Committee and Unesco when campaigns are conducted for sites which the Unesco Secretariat designates as being of universal importance when those sites have received no recognition from the Committee and are in nations which have not ratified the Convention. The future occurrence of such campaigns will lead to questions concerning Unesco's commitment to the Convention as a workable mechanism for the protection of heritage resources.

3.3. Political Issues

When nations interact, political issues are present. To the great credit of the Committee, and in large measure because nations have largely adhered to their commitment to send resource professionals as delegates to the Committee, many potentially devisive issues are left at the door when the Committee goes into session. It is the clear intent of the Convention that this should be the case; that the focus of the Committee should be on humankind's common heritage and on the protection of resources of universal importance.

Committee procedures already prohibit delegates and observers from speaking on behalf of nominations from their own nations during meetings of the Committee or its Bureau or sub-committees. The Committee has also refused to allow formal presentations by nongovernmental interest groups, and rigidly enforced the procedural aspects of its nomination procedures. In addition to addressing the issues raised earlier in this paper concerning criteria and the substantive content of nominations, two other kinds of subtle but strong political pressures should be addressed.

The first arises from membership in the Bureau, where for practical purposes the majority of inscription decisions are made, of nations which have nominations pending before the Committee. Prohibiting action on nominations from nations represented on the Bureau would not only increase the integrity of the process, but, over a period of years, increase the national representation on the Bureau.

The second pressure arises from Committee consideration of nominations from a nation which is currently hosting its meeting. Rejection or deferral of a nomination, no matter how inadequte, in such circumstances would not only be difficult, but potentially damaging to the Convention. Prohibiting action on nominations from nations who are currently hosting the Committee would save delegates from a very difficult dilemma.

The second category of political issues is far more pernicious. It involves the potential use of the Convention for reasons totally unrelated to resource conservation. The Convention was never intended to be used to resolve questions of sovereignty over disputed territory, nor does its Committee have any legal authority or competence to deal with such disputes. Issues which cannot be resolved by the General Assembly or Security Council of the United Nations are obviously not going to be resolved by the World Heritage Committee, nor will action by the Committee have any practical impact on preserving sites located in disputed territories. The Committee should adopt procedures which prohibit consideration of sites in disputed territories regardless of the source of such nominations unless all countries party to the dispute ratify the Convention and join in the nomination.

The potential for similar situations exists in regard to resources which may be found in the global commons, and the Committee would do well to clearly abjure itself from consideration of such resources at this time.

APPENDIX I: LIST OF STATES PARTIES TO THE WORLD HERITAGE CONVENTION

States	Date*	
Afghanistan	20.03.79	R
Algeria	24.06.74	R
Argentina	23.08.78	Ac
Australia	22.08.74	R
Benin	14.06.82	R
Bolivia	4.10.76	R
Brazil	1.09.77	Ac
Bulgaria	7.03.74	Ac
Burundi	19.05.82	R
Canada	23.07.76	Ac
Central Africa Republic	22.12.80	R
Chile	20.02.80	R
Cyprus	14.08.75	Ac
Costa Rica	23.08.77	R
Cuba	24.03.81	R
Democratic Yemen	7.10.80	Ac
Denmark	25.07.79	R
Egypt	7.02.74	R

States	Date*	
Ecuador	16.06.75	Ac
Ethiopia	6.07.77	R
Federal Republic of Germany	23.08.76	R
France	27.06.75	Ac
Ghana	4.07.75	R
Greece	17.07.81	R
Guatemala	16.01.79	Ac
Guinea	18.03.79	R
Guyana	20.06.77	Ac
Haiti	18.01.80	R
Honduras	8.06.79	R
India	14.11.77	R
Iraq	5.03.74	Ac
Iran	26.02.75	Ac
Italy	23.06.78	R
Ivory Coast	9.01.81	R
Jordan	5.05.75	R
Lebanon	3.02.83	R
Libyan Arab Jamahiriya	13.10.78	R
Malawi	5.01.82	R
Mali	5.04.77	Ac
Malta	14.11.78	Ac
Morocco	28.10.75	R
Mauritania	2.03.81	R
Monaco	7.11.78	R
Mozambique	27.11.82	R
Nepal	20.06.78	Ac
Nicaragua	17.12.79	Ac
Niger	23.12.74	Ac
Nigeria	23.10.74	R
Norway	12.05.77	R
Oman	6.10.81	Ac
Pakistan	23.07.76	R
Panama	3.03.78	R
Peru	24.02.82	R
Poland	29.06.76	R
Portugal	30.09.80	R
Saudi Arabia	7.08.78	Ac
Senegal	13.02.76	R
Seychelles	9.04.80	Ac
Spain	4.05.82	Ac
Sudan	6.06.74	R
Sri Lanka	6.06.80	Ac
Switzerland	17.09.75	R
Syrian Arab Republic	13.08.75	Ac
The Holy See	7.10.82	A
Tunisia	10.03.75	R
United Republic of Cameroon	7.12.82	R
United Republic of Tanzania	2.08.77	R
United States of America	7.12.73	R
Yugoslavia	26.05.75	R
Zaire	23.09.74	R
Zimbabwe	16.08.82	R

*Date of deposit of ratification (R), acceptance (AC)
or accession (A)

APPENDIX II: TECHNICAL COOPERATION

The Convention opens to States Parties possibilities of technical cooperation to support their own efforts to preserve their cultural andd natural heritage. Cooperation can take a number of forms:

- preparatory assistance for the elaboration of nominations to the World Heritage List;
- preparatory assistance for drawing large-scale requests for technical cooperation;
- preparatory assistance for drawing up inventories of cultural and/or natural properties suitable for inclusion in the World Heritage List;
- emergency assistance for properties included in the World Heritage List or potentially suitable for inclusion therein, which are in imminent danger of important damage or destruction;
- conservation measures for properties included in the World Heritage List or considered suitable for inclusion;
- fellowships for training in conservation methods and techniques;
- assistance to national or regional training centres.

This assistance can be provided in a number of ways:

- studies concerning the artistic, scientific and technical problems raised by the protection, conservation, presentation and rehabilitation of the cultural and natural heritage;
- provision of experts, technicians and skilled labour to ensure that the approved work is correctly carried out;
- training of staff and specialists at all levels in the fields concerned;
- supply of equipment which the State concerned does not possess or is not in a position to acquire;
- low-interest or interest-free loans which might be repayable on a long-term basis;
- the granting, in exceptional cases and for special reasons, of non-repayable subsidies.

International assistance on a large-scale should be preceded by detailed scientific, economic and technical studies which draw upon the most advanced techniques of preservation. As a general rule, only part of the cost of work necessary shall be borne by the international community; the contribution of the nation with primary responsibility should be a substantial share of the resources devoted to each programme, unless its resources do not permit this.

APPENDIX III: BALANCE BETWEEN THE CULTURAL AND THE NATURAL HERITAGE IN THE IMPLEMENTATION OF THE CONVENTION

In order to improve the balance between the cultural and natural heritage in the implementationof the Convention, the Committee has recommended that the following measure be taken:

a) Preparatory assistance to States Parties should be granted on a priority basis for:
   (i) the establishment of tentative lists of cultural and natural properties situated in their territories and suitable for inclusion in the World Heritage List;
   (ii) the preparation of nominations of types of properties under-represnted in the World Heritage List.

b) States Parties to the Convention should provide the Secretariat with the name and address of other governmental organization(s) primarily responsible for cultural and natural properties, so that copies of all official corespondence and documents can be sent by the Secretariat to these focal points as appropriate.

c) States Parties to the Convention should convene at regular intervals at the national level a joint meeting of those persons responsible for natural and cultural heritage in order that they may discuss matters pertaining to the implementaton of the Convention. This does not apply to States Parties where one single organization is dealing with both cultural and natural heritage.

d) The Committee, deeply concerned with maintaining a balance in the number of experts from the natural and cultural fields represented on the Bureau, urges that every effort be made in future elections in order to ensure that:
   (i) the chair is not held by persons with expertise in the same field, either cultural or natural, for more than two succeeding years;
   (ii) at least two "cultural" and at least two "natural" experts are present at Bureau meetings to ensure balance and credibility in reviewing nominations to the World Heritage List.

e) States Parties to the Convention should choose as their representatives persons qualified in the field of natural and cultural heritage, thus complying with Article 9, paragraph 3, of the Convention.

Chapter 16
Concluding Session

Closing Address

Dr. Lee M. Talbot
Director General, IUCN

Your Excellencies, distinguished guests, colleagues, and friends—and I emphasize friends:

Because of the abundant hospitality we, who have come here as visitors, have received, we have all come to regard our gracious Indonesian hosts as our friends, and through our close, frank, yet cordial interaction during these two weeks of intensive meetings, we the participants have come to regard each other as friends.

From the standpoint of IUCN, this Congress has been an unqualified success. I say this with assurance for several good reasons. First, many—perhaps most—of you have emphasized to me or to the other organizers that from your standpoints it has been an outstanding success. The quality of the papers and other information provided has been superb. The quality and content of, and most important, the participation in the discussions has been outstanding.

And this deserves some comment. For many, particularly those for whom this is your first international meeting, a large international meeting can be a daunting experience. There is often a feeling a reluctance to speak, particularly if the language is not wholly familiar, and if the audience is large. There is often a feeling that "they"—whoever "they" are, probably the organizers—have their own agenda and do not want interference. There is often a question of whether what I have to say is really important enough to take all the time of all these people.

I hope, and I believe, that all of you have found that regardless of who you are and where you are from, your active participation has been encouraged and welcomed, and that your views have been received with respect and keen interest. These two weeks of meetings have culminated some five years of effort aimed at obtaining views and experiences and expertise from all over the world, and the results clearly show that these efforts have been successful.

This is the World Congress on National Parks, and it is identified as the Third World National Parks Congress. As several speakers have pointed out, there is an interesting, if unintentional, symbolism in the "Third World" terminology. This is the first time this meeting has been held in a developing nation, and the content of our deliberations has showed conclusively that it is in the developing parts of the world—the third world—where the most striking development in parks and protected areas is now happening. As has been emxphasized, in the decade since the last World Conference on National Parks, the area covered by parks and protected areas worldwide has nearly doubled—and most of this has occurred in the developing nations. While the developed nations have talked about the contributions of protected areas to society, in the past few years the developing nations have demonstrated this contribution, and demonstrated it in a variety of innovative and significant ways. In the past few days I have had professionals in park management from many developed nations comment to me that before this meeting they had not realized that there was so much to learn about parks and park management, and they were learning it from the participants here from the Third World.

This Congress has represented a major advance over the previous two meetings. But it is a progression from them, building upon the foundation they laid and affirming it, not relacing or changing it. The IUCN categories of protected areas have been basic to our discussions. There has been no suggestion of change in them; on the contrary, their validity has been strongly affirmed. As has the basic importance of the integrity of categories I to IV—particularly national parks in the original sense—which has been termed the keystone of a protected areas system.

But equally significant, the role of protected areas as an essential component of the development process has been firmly established. But let there be *no question* about this basic concept. By development we mean sustainable development in the sense of the World Conservation Strategy, activities which bring solid and lasting contributions to human welfare. We do *not* mean development in the sense of activities which may bring short term economic gains to some at the expense of long term stability of the ecological and often social systems. And we do not mean inappropriate development activities, such as exploitative ones, in Categories I to IV areas, which would destroy the very values for which the areas were established.

What we have established, however, is that protected areas should be created and maintained in the context of the process of sustainable development. They are and must be seen to be essential contributions to, indeed foundations of, the process which brings lasting benefits to the peoples of a nation and the world. Protected areas are protected *for* people, not *from* people. What has been termed the island mentality of parks is, in most cases, simply inappropriate—ecologically, functionally, socially, and economically. A system of protected areas should be an integral part of the fabric of a people's or a nation's well-being.

Yes, the Congress itself is an unqualified success. We have the Bali Declaration, the Recommendations, the publications are in hand, and they will be available and in your hands soon. We have the friendships and contacts we have built among ourselves during this period. And we have laid the groundwork for a professional organization, and hopefully an internationally recognized profession.

We have laid the foundations for what may be considered a true revolution in the development of protected areas and in the way protected areas are included in the development process. But if all this is to be accomplished, it is up to us to build on these foundations. The success of this Congress will have been a hollow one, if ten years from now we do not look back on a decade of accomplishment consistent with the aims and aspirations we have expressed here.

We must leave this historic meeting with a true and urgent sense of commitment and dedication to turn the aspirations of this Congress into reality.

On behalf of IUCN, I thank you all for your contributions to the Congress, express our hope that you will all do your utmost to make this Congress' plans and objectives a reality, and I pledge that IUCN will do all in its power to assure that in 1992 we will look back on a decade of truly revolutionary accomplishment.

Closing Address

H.E. Professor Soedarsono Hadisapoetro
Minister of Agriculture

In the twelve days since this Congress started, you have gone through intensive deliberations on important subjects of nature and natural resources that concerned all life on our world.

I believe, with your professional thinkings, experiences and observations you have made during the period of the past ten years since the second conference in 1972, have been expressed during the Congress. Now, we step into the beginning of the next ten year period with the list of recommendations and guidelines to be implemented in our development efforts to conserve the nature and natural resources, particularly the national parks.

The Congress has accomplished its task and achieved its objective as stipulated in the Congress programme. For this reason, the Congress is to be congratulated for its success.

The Congress has resulted in two important conclusions, namely:

1) The Bali Declaration, and
2) List of Recommendations of the Congress.

These two products contain formulations of general guidelines, as well as technical and policy guidelines for conservation of nature and natural resources that we are dealing with. The Congress has successfully changed the course of objectives from protection of nature away from man, to a new era placing emphasis on managing nature for the benefits of man. This is important, particularly for developing countries where the development efforts places more emphasis on human needs, because proper management of nature should be part of the development to sustained human welfare.

The Bali Declaration signifies the concencus of determination that the Congress laid down for future undertaking. It comprehensively spells out ways and means of conservation and the need of a global system of protected areas in support of social and economic development which the world requires at present.

Therefore, I appeal to all participants present here to convey this conclusion contained in the Declaration to their respective governments, organizations and institutions for action.

The recommendations which have resulted from this Congress are pertinent to the national programme of protected areas, and urged for their effective implementation. Such implementation of the guidelines require understanding determination and a sense of responsibility of all nations to conserve the natural heritage of our world for future life.

The Directorate of Nature Conservation and Wildlie Management, Department of Agriculture has been a member of IUCN since 1978, and we are in the process of submitting an application for sovereign state membership in IUCN. We are determined to support and to implement the programme of IUCN and the World Conservation Strategy notwithstanding the many faceted constraints.

However, as stated by the Vice President in his opening address, that the benefit of natural resources are equitably shared by developed and developing countries; the responsibility and the expense of safeguarding natural resources for the future should also be equitably shared. We urge, therefore, for generous financial support and the provision of technical assistance from the developed countries and international organizations to the developing countries where the natural heritage of the world are largely found. Conservation and protected areas are not only for the people of a country or a region, but for the whole of mankind.

It is our fervent hope that the guidelines be translated into legislative products, programmes and actions. Joint regional, inter-regional and global programmes be developed and enhanced and a global system of protected areas be promoted for its establishment.

On behalf of the Indonesian Government I would like to congratulate IUCN, through its Director General, for taking the initiative and sponsoring this World National Parks Congress. I hope the choice of Bali as the venue of the Congress was rightly made, not only for its natural and cultural beauty but also for its location that enable you to visit some of our national parks of specific interest.

I hope you have enjoyed your stay in Bali, and whenever possible do please visit other parts of Indonesia and see more of our archipelago. We have a country that consists of many islands, many races of people, many cultures, many languages, many varieties and species of fauna and flora, all of which reflect the richness of the life and the nature we live in. We want to conserve them.

Closing Address

Harold J. Coolidge
Honorary President, IUCN

Indonesia is a truly exotic wonderland full of surprises. One of the greatest of these is the number of you who have come great distances to help formulate a worldwide future programme for protected areas. We have here a suitable third world launching pad to send up our rocket for the next ten years (some say that is too long and it should be five).

You have no idea of the personal satisfaction it gives me to see the worldwide emerging thoughtful interest in "protected areas" that has developed since we sowed the seeds in Seattle 20 years ago. While most of us have now become addicted "paperholics", the Bali declaration, and the carefully worded resolutions will, we hope, carry our message worldwide and thus strengthen the World Conservation Strategy.

I once organized the 10th Pacific Science Congress in Honolulu. I was told that our large attendance was due to the publicity about Waikiki Beach that helped attract so many scientists. The same kind of comment has been said about this Congress in exotic Bali. You all know well how many participants have laboured day after day and night after night in committees to produce our final documents, under the leadership of Lee Talbot, Kenton Miller, and assisted by Jeff McNeely with the splendid programme he put together. Hal Eidsvik's help has been essential. The Indonesian and foreign staffs have done a splendid job.

Anything can happen in Indonesia with its more than 30,000 islands. For example, after the war, the last few Sondaicus rhinos in the forest of Ujong Kulong were threatened by a famous Chinese poacher who decided to make his fortune from their horns. The Japanese guards who had protected these rhinos all through the war were gone, and the young Indonesian Government was too busy then to bother. Happily, a fierce Javan tiger killed the great poacher. Word went out all over Java that anyone entering the rhino forest sanctuary area would surely be killed and eaten. For about two years this tiger myth saved this gravely endangered species. By then new government guards were installed.

In the National Bogor Museum rhino horns from three old mounted rhino specimens were actually stolen, for use as aphrodisiacs. When the curator replaced them with splendid plastic horn replicas, these were stolen three times.

Anything surprising can happen in Indonesia. I ran across a salesman for Dr. Lyon's tooth powder just back from a sales trip in China. He told me that his success there was due to the myth that his bottles contained powdered lion's bones, and that he had no intention of damaging his market by telling people the truth.

I now wish to add my thanks to yours to the Indonesian Government, and especially the Forestry Department for their help to IUCN, and its Parks Commission in making this Congress such a tremendous success, and setting a high standard for our worldwide conservation efforts for the benefit of future generations.

The Bali Action Plan: A Framework for the Future of Protected Areas

Kenton R. Miller
Chairman
IUCN Commission on National Parks and Protected Areas
Gland, Switzerland

ABSTRACT. *This paper summarizes the findings of the third World Congress on National Parks to focus on 10 areas of particular concern: Is the existing worldwide network of terrestrial protected areas sufficient? How can marine, coastal, and freshwater protected areas be included into the worldwide network? How can the ecological and managerial quality of existing protected areas be improved? What can a system of categories of protected areas contribute to conservation goals? How can protected areas be linked with sustainable development? How can the full capacity to manage protected areas be developed? What economic tools are needed to support protected areas? What can monitoring contribute to protected area management? How can international cooperation be promoted? How can a global programme to support protected area management be developed? Based on these 10 key concerns, the Bali Action Plan is presented as the guiding document for promoting and supporting protected areas over the coming decade.*

1. INTRODUCTION

We have spent a productive two weeks together. We have heard a number of papers, participated in workshops and discussions, and visited several protected areas. Our perspective has been one of looking forward, of learning from the past to chart a course for the future which will ensure that wildlands forever remain an important part of the global ecosystem.

We began a fortnight ago with a political perspective. His Excellency the Vice President of Indonesia, Mr. Adam Malik, posed a very realistic framework within which we must all operate, pointing out that protected area conservation cannot be separated from issues of poverty, land hunger, and development. Mr. Peter Thacher, Deputy Executive Director, UNEP, underlined

the urgency of our task by linking protected area conservation with national security; "trees now, or tanks later" left no question about the importance of maintaining natural habitats.

Dr. Lee M. Talbot, Director General of IUCN, provided the philosophical basis for our deliberations by showing how protected areas contribute to the implementation of the World Conservation Strategy's three main objectives: maintaining genetic diversity; conserving life support systems and ecological processes; and ensuring that any use of living resources is sustainable.

Throughout the Congress, we have all been aware that protected areas must become part of the development process. National parks and other reserves must be of real benefit to humanity if they are to survive the increasing demands by people on nature. It should be a matter of considerable satisfaction to all of us gathered here in Bali that this Congress has provided the necessary guidance for a new definition of the role of protected areas in the process of social and economic development.

In summarizing our Congress, I would like to use the papers and discussions to highlight 10 areas of particular concern. From these ten areas we can then develop the Bali Action Plan, which IUCN intends to use for its guidance in promoting and supporting protected areas over the next decade.

2. TEN KEY PROTECTED AREA MANAGEMENT QUESTIONS

I propose to use "management" in a very broad sense, to mean the setting of goals and objectives, the design and choice of means to attain the goals and objectives,

756

the monitoring and evaluating of results, and the process of learning from past experience. By applying a rigorous "management approach" along these lines, the contribution of protected areas to biological conservation and sustainable development can be assured.

2.1 Is the existing worldwide network of terrestrial protected areas sufficient?

We have learned that the worldwide network has been growing at a remarkable and accelerating pace, with some 46 percent of the units and 81 percent of the protected land having been established in the past decade; reports from Alaska, Brazil, and Indonesia illustrated some of the most significant advances. But our goal is to ensure that large samples of all ecosystems are protected, and it is clear that the worldwide network still falls far short of what is needed; a figure of 10 percent of a nation's land area has often been suggested as a guideline for the minimum coverage of protected areas most committed to biological conservation.

The Congress has had before it a large map which indicates an approach to how to assess coverage. Based on a system developed by Professor Miklos Udvardy, University of California, for IUCN, in cooperation with Unesco, UNEP, and the University of Michigan, the map showed the coverage of biogeographic provinces by existing protected areas; an analysis of this coverage has pointed out where the major blanks still exist.

This system has proved useful at a global scale, but it is clear that more precise tools are needed for analysis at the national level. Examples from Brazil, Costa Rica, New Zealand, and Indonesia have provided guidance for such national-level determination of coverage, and the workshop on *Managing Protected Areas* will lead to a manual providing further details on this process.

The difficulties faced in the establishment of new areas was brought home to us very forcefully by the case studies on Redwoods National Park and Grasslands National Park, but the benefits to be earned were illustrated by the Dominica case. One conclusion was very clear: If we expect to add significant new protected areas in the coming decade, our ecological, economic, ethical, and political justifications will need to be very compelling.

2.2 How can marine, coastal, and freshwater protected areas be included into the worldwide network?

Papers on man and mangroves in Malaysia, sea turtles in Sabah and the Caribbean, and the relationship between coastal protected areas and marine fisheries have underlined the significance of coastal and marine ecosystems for mankind. In view of the importance of the coastal zone for human welfare, and of the sea for navigation, food, and other resources, it is anomalous that

coastal and marine protected areas are at such an early stage of development. We have made a major effort at the Congress to place this critical problem into relief.

Professors Hayden, Dolan and Ray, of the University of Virginia, developed for IUCN a system of marine classification for conservation purposes. As part of the cooperative efforts between IUCN, UNEP and the University of Michigan, this system was integrated with the terrestrial biogeographic provinces on the map before us. All known coastal and marine protected areas are shown. The case study on vulnerable marine resources, coastal reserves, and pollution in Southeast Asia showed how the resource mapping technique can be used on a regional level.

A number of nations and regions are making significant progress in coastal and marine conservation. We have heard from Indonesia, Kenya, the Lesser Antilles, and Papua New Guinea in this regard, learning both of progress and of the many real problems which still remain. We heard from the Philippines how one nation is attempting to overcome the complicated institutional barriers to coastal and marine conservation, and we heard from Australia's Great Barrier Reef how a sophisticated zoning procedure is serving the interests of both man and nature. Despite all of these signs of progress, it is clear that there is still a long way to go, particularly in involving marine scientists in conservation issues, promoting cooperation between neighbouring countries, developing concepts of coastal and marine conservation, and overcoming the institutional difficulties involved in the field.

Our three-day workshop on *Managing Coastal and Marine Protected Areas* addressed these difficulties. Drawing on all of the papers presented at the Congress, the workshop will lead to a state-of-the-art manual to be produced by IUCN during 1983; while the manual will not be able to solve all the problems, it will provide a foundation upon which future progress can be based.

2.3 How can the ecological and managerial quality of existing protected areas be improved?

It is clear that many of the existing protected areas were established before ecological principles for protected area design became established, and before it was understood that protected areas can contribute to many development objectives. Further, many areas have been selected and designed with only limited attention to ecological integrity; many protected areas lack control of upstream catchments, contain only certain habitat requirements for featured groups of animals, and adjoin areas which feature land- and water-use practices which are inconsistent with conservation goals. Finally, traditional protected area management can be characterized by its "insular approach"; goals are selected and means implemented within boundaries of designated areas with little or no regard for surrounding lands and peoples. As a result, social and economic conflicts arise along the margins of reserves, and popular awareness and political support for protected area programmes are diminished.

At the Congress, we heard a number of papers about the ecological quality of protected areas, covering such matters as minimum area requirements, the importance of Galapagos for evolution (perhaps the most basic of all ecological processes), the importance of protecting Pleistocene refugia in Brazil, biological principles of protected area design in Papua New Guinea, and designing protected areas to protect endemic species of birds in Hawaii.

It was clear from our discussions that there is a major gap in our knowledge of the protected area estate. The paper on protected areas as *in situ* genebanks for the maintenance of wild genetic resources demonstrated to all of us how fragmentary is our information about the genetic resources contained in the existing protected areas, and how seriously we must work to design new methods of ensuring the ecological integrity of protected areas.

It also became clear that, as society makes increasing demands on the wildland estate, we must greatly improve our standards of management (using the term in its broad sense). The workshop on *Managing Protected Areas* covered this in considerable detail. Management planning was seen as a crucial factor, particularly when area planning can be based on a systems plan which explains to the public and to politicians why, where, and how the protected area system needs to be established. Systems plans, either explicit or implicit, were presented for Indonesia, New Zealand, the United Kingdom, the Mediterranean, the USSR, Costa Rica, Ecuador, and Brazil.

The point was also made that many existing protected areas are under threat, usually by human factors such as fire (Australia), introduced species (Australia, New Zealand, Hawaii), poaching (Botswana), disturbance of the water cycle (Everglades), tourism (Poland; Valdes Peninsula, Argentina)), or encroachment (Atlantic forests of Brazil). One important means for dealing with such threats is to ensure that protected areas are part of regional land-use plans or other arrangements with adjacent lands; we heard a paper developing the general concept, and specific applications were presented from Indonesia, Yugoslavia, Kenya, Japan, and India.

2.4 What can a system of categories of protected areas contribute to conservation goals?

One of the fundamental concepts explored at the Congress was that several different kinds of management categories need to be considered if the growing list of objectives for conservation and development are to be met. National parks alone cannot serve society to meet all its needs from wildland resources. Furthermore, one reason for the increasing challenges to national parks is the absence of other kinds of wildland management regimes established for other purposes.

The case histories presented during the Congress demonstrated the diversity at which countries are already managing their wildlands. Virtually without exception, the *national park* is being retained as the category employed for the careful preservation of sample ecosystems, species, genetic materials and scenery and the provision of services for public education and recreation, research and monitoring. About this fundamental point there was little discussion—only affirmation. However, case after case demonstrated how other approaches could maintain basic ecosystems and preserve genetic diversity while also meeting certain material needs for people. Examples included the provision of timber and firewood, wild meat, water, thatch, grazing, intensive tourism and recreation and the maintenance of cultural landscapes.

A conclusion drawn by the Congress was that the range of management options must now be considered as elements of one, overall effort to conserve nature while dealing openly with the achievement of sustainable social and economic development. Examples showed how by grouping regionally various types of protected areas a wide range of services can be provided on a sustainable basis while at the same time, in the national parks and other more strict reserves, elements and areas of wild nature can be preserved. In fact, with this broader approach, those areas requiring strict protection have a far greater chance of receiving it.

A case study from Australia showed how a national system of protected areas, of various categories, could address a range of national needs, and serve as a tool for environmental planning. A problem lies in the disparity between the general awareness of the national park on the one hand, and the lack of experience with the other categories such as cultured landscape, nature reserve and national forest, on the other. Pilot protected areas for each category need to be established, within each biogeographic realm, to demonstrate to political leaders and local peoples the importance of these alternatives for supporting social and economic development through sustainable approaches to resource management.

2.5 How can protected areas be linked with sustainable development?

For most people in the world, social and economic development is a fundamental right, a prerequisite for human dignity. The World Conservation Strategy showed that sustainable development cannot take place without conservation, and that conservation will fail without sustainable development. The entire Congress was devoted to defining how protected areas can contribute to the process of social and economic development, without any reduction in nature conservation ideals.

Many were concerned early in the discussion that

"development" meant "opening up the national parks to exploitation." But the Congress clearly distinguished between support of local economic and social needs on a long-term basis, and any attempt to physically harvest the last remaining natural core areas in the name of "development"; the last natural reserves of the 1990s will already be relatively few in numbers and biologically small in size, and to further remove the natural capital they contain would reduce their potential value for mankind to insignificance.

Perhaps the most significant role protected areas can play in supporting adjacent lands is to contribute to the sustainability of the development process; stream flows can be ensured, erosion controlled, negative impacts from the reserve (such as large marauding animals) can be controlled, income generated from management activities (tourism, game culling, etc.) can be shared with local communities, and employment can be provided.

Many papers provided illustrations of how protected areas are already contributing to development in non-consumptive ways. Water is particularly dramatic. Cases from Brazil, Malawi, North Sulawesi, Sri Lanka and Venezuela showed that protected areas are providing protection to watersheds, stabilizing riverbanks, and controlling erosion in a cost-effective and economically-important manner; in many of these examples, international development agencies are providing major support, illustrating their conviction that protected areas are contributing to basic human needs, not in spite of their protected status, but *because* of it.

Real benefits are being provided to local people from Chitawan National Park in Nepal, Plitvice National Park in Yugoslavia, the various tiger reserves in India, Amboseli National Park in Kenya, and many others. In the Sahel, protected areas are helping to reclaim the desert. In Zimbabwe, protected areas are providing both meat and real income to local people from the harvest of excess populations of elephants, and in Pampa Galeras, Peru, protection has allowed the once-endangered vicuna to return to productive levels where harvesting for the benefit of local people has become appropriate (based on a system which was practiced by the Incas over 500 years ago).

Of particular significance is the concept that protected areas are important for genetic resource conservation; the needs of the new science of genetic engineering, the importance of wild relatives of domestic plants for breeding purposes, and the contributions of wild animals—as breeding stock or as a harvestable resource in appropriate categories of protected area—were all mentioned. It is clear that genetic resources conservation in protected areas will become increasingly important in the coming years.

Also of considerable concern is the matter of how to utilize the traditional wisdom of societies which live in balance with their local resources, or at least have the knowledge to do so. Case studies from Nepal, Pacific Islands, Papua New Guinea, the Torres Straits, and Yap demonstrated clearly that indigenous people have an important contribution to make to protected area management; conversely, protected areas can also shield such people from unwanted impacts of more powerful societies. But it is also important, as another paper pointed out, to view *all* people living around protected areas as "indigenous people" fully deserving of all consideration in the planning and management of the area.

Finally, and this is perhaps the key point, nature conservation is not to be accomplished only by the "setting aside" of specially protected natural areas—it must be practiced in all places at all times. Taking this view, protected areas can serve as illustrations of how people can live in balance with their environment, with the intention that these illustrations need to be much more widely applied. Ways and means must be found to involve the general public in this effort.

2.6 How can the full capacity to manage protected areas be developed?

Linking protected area conservation with development is a highly complex undertaking, requiring well-trained professionals at all levels; a workshop paper based on an international survey which was answered by about half the countries with protected area systems, estimated that there are now over 100,000 people working in the protected areas of the world. While a few countries have university curricula, even graduate programmes, dealing with protected area management, there is still a major need for training seminars, courses, and workshops at the regional and local levels for protected area managers. Existing regional and national training schools need to be strengthened, and new schools need to be established. Examples presented at the Congress included the College of African Wildlife Management in Tanzania, the Ecole de Faune in Cameroon, and the Conservation Training School in Indonesia.

More specialized seminars are also needed. The "grandfather" of such seminars is the International Seminar on National Parks and Equivalent Reserves, held each year under the sponsorship of the US National Park Service, Parks Canada, and the University of Michigan, with support from IUCN, WWF, Unesco, UNEP, and others. At an International Seminar alumni meeting held at the Congress, it was found that nearly half the Congress participants had attended the seminar, underlining its importance as a universal training and communications effort.

In the future, even more such seminars will need to be held, often concentrating on more restricted subjects and dealing with personnel of all levels. The three-day workshop on *Training Protected Area Personnel* provided a number of guidelines on developing management capacity, which will be published by IUCN in late 1983.

But training is only part of the solution. There remain concerns about the organization of the public and private institutions for managing protected areas. Some organizational forms make it difficult for personnel to have open dialogue on their results and to learn from past experiences. As awareness grows within the responsible agencies and the general public regarding the critical importance of ecologically-sound biological conservation, flexibility will be required to shift emphasis toward scientific nature management.

2.7 What economic tools are needed to support protected areas?

Economic tools, such as cost-benefit analysis, are sometimes used to evaluate the resources found in protected areas. By and large, protected area managers have been poorly prepared to respond to economists who argue that their area should be allocated, for example, to logging. If protected areas are to continue to serve their ecological and humanistic functions, they must be "competitive" at the marketplace. The case study from Plitvice, Yugoslavia, showed one excellent local approach to the problem.

The first step is to ensure that the intangible, non-fiscal values are properly considered by decision-makers. The non-governmental organizations need to be strengthened and encouraged in their lobbying efforts, and the general public needs to be mobilized in support of the ethical, aesthetic, and spiritual values of protected area.

At the same time, it seems wise to develop new economic tools for supporting protected areas. One of the workshop sessions showed that a protected area which is designed and managed without consideration of its potential for use as a centre for human education, employment, research, and enjoyment may be underutililzed; operating a protected area in such a way sows the seeds of potential future disaster. Conversely, by focussing on the ability of a protected area to contribute to human needs in a variety of tangible and quantifiable ways, the resource manager demonstrates that the area is a fundamental link in local, national and international economics. By so doing, the manager increases his ability to obtain the freedom and the resources to maintain the protected area in a manner that both preserves the integrity of the ecosystem and satisfies the needs of the human population.

2.8 What can monitoring contribute to protected area management?

The Congress heard that IUCN has now established a Protected Areas Data Unit, and its first products—the *IUCN Directory of Neotropical Protected Areas* and the *1982 United Nations List of National Parks and Protected Areas*— were displayed. The UNEP Global Environment Monitoring System (GEMS) was explained, and a case study

from the USSR showed one nation's approach to monitoring.

Monitoring is a vital tool for ensuring that protected areas can meet the needs of society. Monitoring provides the basis to compare man's impact upon natural resources outside protected areas with natural sites within parks and reserves. Monitoring serves as a means to study and understand dynamic natural processes, as well as streamflow, animal migration, fire and plant succession. In more specific cases, monitoring is used to follow the response of wildlife to habitat treatments and the recovery of sites after corrective measures are taken in excessively used tourist sites. And, monitoring links wild nature to people by the study of volcanism, earthquakes, hydrological cycles, and other phenomena upon which human well-being often depends.

2.9 How can international cooperation be promoted?

His Excellency the Minister of Information of Indonesia, Mr. Ali Murtopo, made a very convincing case for the responsibility of the international community to contribute the protected areas in the developing world, and Dr. David Munro, past Director General of IUCN, showed that national self-interest and global sharing are intimately inter-related. A number of international cooperation mechanisms have been established, including legal instruments such as the World Heritage Convention, organizations such as UNEP and IUCN, and programmes such as Unesco's Man and the Biosphere Programme.

At the Congress, we heard that international development agencies, which have sometimes been seen as destroyers of nature, have now become strong and effective supporters of protected area management. The World Bank, for example, has xx projects worth some US$ xxx million dealing directly with protected areas and other conservation matters, including training. In addition, private enterprise was represented and showed how industrial resources, such as technology, labour, and capital, can be used to contribute to the process of rational resource planning for the benefit of protected areas. All interests, whether managers of protected areas or international developers, must work together to meet the need of defining rates for sustainable resource production and consumption in order to plan areas for preservation, development or maintenance of production. While all interests may not consistently be in agreement, working together is mandatory to obtain the best results for all.

At the more day-to-day level, papers from FAO, the Smithsonian Institution, international civil servants, and management agencies discussed the underlying reasons for increasingly shared expertise on an agency-to-agency basis and provided a number of examples and guidelines for future cooperation.

2.10 How can a global programme to support protected area management be developed?

It is apparent that all protected areas around the world share problems, concerns, and opportunities. But to ensure practical accomplishments on the ground which take into account relevant cultural and institutional diversity and respond to local needs, a series of regional action plans should be designed and implemented. The IUCN network provides an ideal mechanism for initiating such action programmes, in cooperation with national governments, UNEP, FAO, Unesco, and the World Wildlife Fund.

Further, a communications network involving the global community responsible for or supporting protected areas would ensure the flow of information and support the identify of the protected area profession. The Congress expressed its strong support for the development of such a communications network.

The network could be built upon PARKS Magazine, the International Seminar on National Parks and Equivalent Reserves, and a number of other existing international cooperation mechanisms.

3. THE BALI ACTION PLAN

To provide guidance for the coming critial years, the Congress prepared a series of 20 Recommendations. In addition, working groups from the world's eight biogeographic realms presented reports on priorities for each realm and many of the case studies and other presentations provided examples which should be emulated; the "Future Directions" addresses from each realm were particularly pertinent in providing thoughtful analyses of future trends. Based on this material, the major points of an Action Plan were presented to the closing session of the Congress; further work on the plan was done at the IUCN secretariat subsequently. The resulting Bali Action Plan has now been circulated widely to enlist support and promote projects for implementing the Plan.

The Bali Action Plan recognizes that there are already competent government agencies in most countries whose responsibility is the management of national parks and other sorts of protected areas, and that each of these agencies is already carrying out a programme of work relevant to the needs and priorities of the country involved. However, the 450 professionals attending the Congress also recognized that there was a serious lack of understanding of management tools (biogeography, zoning, monitoring, training procedures, protected area economics, etc.), that budgets are not always allocated to the most important priorities, that management plans are the exception rather than the rule, that relevant information is not flowing as well as it should, that training is lagging far behind needs, and that government officials and the public generally undervalue the role of protected areas in environmentally sound development.

The Bali Action Plan aims to provide guidance and assistance to those agencies which are interested in improving their own management effectiveness in meeting the objectives for which their protected areas were established. Clearly, this is not the work of the IUCN Secretariat alone; it must involve all parts of the Union—State members, Government Agencies, and Non-Governmental Organizations, Commissions and Centres—as well as IUCN's major international partners in conservation: UNEP, Unesco, FAO, and the World Wildlife Fund.

The ten inter-related and mutually-reinforcing objectives of the Bali Action Plan, with a brief summary of necessary activities, are as follows:

Objective 1. TO ESTABLISH BY 1992 A WORLDWIDE NETWORK OF NATIONAL PARKS AND PROTECTED AREAS, TO COVER ALL TERRESTRIAL ECOLOGICAL REGIONS.

Activity 1.1 Develop and make available to all responsible for protected areas, tools and guidelines for the identification and selection of natural areas critical for meeting the objectives of conservation and for supporting development.

Activity 1.2 Promote necessary technical, scientific and financial support for the identification, selection, planning and management of protected areas which fit strategically into the world network.

Activity 1.3 Further develop and distribute a biogeographical classification system for use in the global analysis of protected area coverage.

Activity 1.4 Develop and distribute a more detailed biogeographical classification system with a flexibility of scale which can be used in the analysis of protected area coverage at a variety of regional and national levels.

Activity 1.5 Promote the detailed evaluation at the regional and country level of protected area coverage.

Objective 2. TO INCORPORATE MARINE, COASTAL AND FRESHWATER PROTECTED AREAS INTO THE WORLDWIDE NETWORK.

Activity 2.1 Develop and distribute concepts and tools for the establishment of protected areas in marine, coastal and freshwater environments.

Activity 2.2 Develop a classification system for categories of marine, coastal and freshwater protected areas.

Activity 2.3 Further develop and distribute biogeographical classification systems for marine, coastal and freshwater protected areas, at both the global level and at the regional/national level.

Activity 2.4 Incorporate scientists, managers, administrators and supporters of marine, coastal and freshwater conservation into the protected areas community.

Activity 2.5 Promote the establishment of marine, coastal and freshwater protected areas by all states, including the extension of all currently protected littoral areas into the aquatic environment.

Activity 2.6 Promote cooperation between neighbouring nations sharing resident and migratory species to establish networks of protected areas and other regulations to meet the critical needs of those species, with special priority for threatened and endangered species.

Objective 3. TO IMPROVE THE ECOLOGICAL AND MANAGERIAL QUALITY OF EXISTING PROTECTED AREAS.

Activity 3.1 Develop and make available tools and guidelines for the evaluation of the ecological capacity of protected areas to maintain living resources, and the evaluation of area management to ensure that appropriate measures are being applied.

Activity 3.2 Promote the development of concepts and methods which will lead to scientific principles for management and support the continuous analysis of conservation requirements for each area.

Activity 3.3 Document the living resources contained in protected areas, including preparing and disseminating inventories of wild species and populations of known or likely value as genetic resources.

Activity 3.4 Develop and implement a system of reporting on protected areas under particular threat.

Activity 3.5 Support a systematic approach to the preparation of area and system management plans which provide for management and development to be in accordance with an appropriate range of conservation objectives.

Activity 3.6 Reinforce measures to reduce the external threats to protected areas.

Objective 4. TO DEVELOP THE FULL RANGE OF WILDLAND MANAGEMENT CATEGORIES.

Activity 4.1 Develop and make available the concepts and tools necessary for the design and implementation of each category, in both terrestrial and aquatic habitats.

Activity 4.2 Establish pilot protected areas for each category, within each realm, to demonstrate to political

leaders and local peoples the importance of these alternatives for supporting social and economic development through sustainable approaches to resource management.

Activity 4.3 Include all 10 wildland management categories on the *United Nations List of National Parks and Protected Areas*.

Activity 4.4 Provide for the establishment of *in situ* gene banks.

Objective 5. TO PROMOTE THE LINKAGE BETWEEN PROTECTED AREA MANAGEMENT AND SUSTAINABLE DEVELOPMENT.

Activity 5.1 Develop and make available the tools for the survey of ecological processes, habitat requirements, and other components of protected area integrity to enable managers to critically examine the context for area conservation, and be able to associate conservation with development in adjacent lands.

Activity 5.2 Work with governments and development assistance agencies to achieve the incorporation of protected area considerations and support within development projects.

Activity 5.3 Develop policy guidelines and legal instruments regarding the use of protected areas for research, environmental monitoring and the collection of scientific materials.

Activity 5.4 Develop tools and guidelines for the practical incorporation of new objectives for protected area management of particular relevance to sustainable development, including environmental monitoring and genetic resources conservation.

Activity 5.5 Investigate and utilize the traditional wisdom of communities affected by conservation measures, including implementation of joint management arrangements between protected area authorities and societies which have traditionally managed resources.

Activity 5.6 Carry out research to determine ways to foster appropriate recreation and tourism in protected areas for which tourism has been deemed an objective, and to minimize the adverse impacts of such activities.

Activity 5.7 Develop ways and means of promoting greater public support for protected areas.

Objective 6. TO DEVELOP THE HUMAN CAPACITY TO MANAGE PROTECTED AREAS, ESPECIALLY THROUGH TRAINING.

Activity 6.1 Promote the establishment and recognition of protected area management as a professional career of vital relevance to society.

Activity 6.2 Develop and promote training seminars, courses and workshops at the regional and local levels for protected area managers.

Activity 6.3 Strengthen support to regional and national training schools.

Activity 6.4 Promote the establishment of local, in-service training efforts for all personnel.

Objective 7. TO DEVELOP ECONOMIC TOOLS FOR SUPPORTING PROTECTED AREAS.

Activity 7.1 Develop and distribute tools for the analysis of values, tangible and non-tangible, monetary and non-monetary, associated with protected natural areas.

Activity 7.2 Promote the quantification of values which relate conservation to development, specifically watershed protection but also including genetic resources, pollution control, soil formation, amelioration of climate, provision of recreation and tourism, and others of nature's services.

Activity 7.3 Explore and publish concepts and tools which relate ecology and economics to promote a more consistent perspective for analyzing and explaining the role of protected areas in sustaining development.

Objective 8. TO IMPLEMENT AN EFFECTIVE INVENTORY AND MONITORING SERVICE.

Activity 8.1 Expand and develop the Protected Areas Data Unit (PADU) and related components of the IUCN Conservation Monitoring Center(CMC), to provide information on protected areas, guide the determination of priorities, and support development agencies (both national and international) in relating the design of development projects to critical protected areas.

Activity 8.2 Publish and distribute Realm-based directories and periodic reports to inform and support national and international organizations in their planning activities.

Activity 8.3 Promote arrangements by international organizations, governments, and regional associations of nations for the long-term development and use of data collection systems, such as satellite remote sensing, covering all protected areas.

Activity 8.4 Promote and implement methodology for implementing monitoring systems.

Objective 9. TO IMPLEMENT INTERNATIONAL CO-OPERATION MECHANISMS.

Activity 9.1 Integrate and strengthen ties between protected areas management and the Man and the Biosphere Programme, the Global Environmental Monitoring System, and the World Heritage Convention, to realize the full potential of these instruments for the common objectives of conservation and sustainable development.

Activity 9.2 Encourage and advise all States on the preparation, use, and, where required, updating of international legal instruments which support protected areas.

Activity 9.3 Explore and promote the development of tools and mechanisms for the fair sharing of costs and benefits associated with protected areas management, both among nations and between protected areas and adjacent communities.

Activity 9.4 Explore the potential for new agreements and instruments needed to further strengthen international cooperation, particularly in relationship to genetic resources.

Objective 10. TO DEVELOP AND IMPLEMENT A GLOBAL PROGRAMME TO SUPPORT PROTECTED AREA MANAGEMENT.

Activity 10.1 Design and implement regional action programmes to ensure practical accomplishments close to the ground, taking into account relevant cultural and institutional diversity, and the necessary responsiveness to local needs.

Activity 10.2 Provide technical and scientific guidance through the publication of a series of documents on practical subjects of global concern to protected area management such as those noted in the preceding items.

Activity 10.3 Establish a communications network with the global community responsible for or supporting protected areas to ensure the flow of information and support the identity of the protected area profession.

Activity 10.4 Build the institutional support necessary to carry out these activities as follow up from the Congress.

Activity 10.5 Initiate steps for the celebration of the next World Congress on National Parks in 1992, with intermediate international, regional and national events designed to further the Bali Action Plan.

Activity 10.6 Charge the IUCN to monitor the implementation of this Plan and to report on progress at the next Congress.

4. CONCLUSION

The Bali Action Plan is a revolutionary advance in linking the conservation of protected areas with social and economic development; no matter what the future may hold in store, it is apparent that the natural resources contained in protected areas are a sound investment. The ten objectives of the Bali Action Plan, if broadly supported by governments, conservation organizations and development agencies, and implemented together in a reasonably coherent way, can help ensure that protected area resources are conserved to form an inseparable part of the modern human ecosystem.

In a period of shrinking budgets, global inflation, and widespread pessimism about the future, governments must still find the resources to support their protected areas; many countries, including some with the lowest per capita GNP, are continuing to expand their protected area systems at a rapid rate and will need the appropriate resources to fund this expansion. The Bali Action Plan will help demonstrate to governments and international assistance agencies that the conservation of protected areas should be considered just as important as national defense, education, communication, and public health when priorities for limited budgets are being considered.

With greatly increased responsiblities for helping to ensure that social and economic development meets the real needs of human societies, protected areas can expect to receive a significantly greater amount of support from governments, international development agencies, and local people.

The Bali Action Plan concludes: "Thus, as those professionally involved in protected area planning, management, research and promotion, we go forth from Bali with the *conviction* that the contribution of national parks and protected areas to people and to life on Earth is fundamental if sustainable well-being, ways of life and peace are to be attained; with the *vision* of an emerging enterprise as ambitious and vital as any in the history of humanity; and a *commitment* to solidarity with out children and generations yet unborn, that they shall inherit this unique, small and fragile planet rich in options for determining their own destiny."

RECOMMENDATIONS OF THE WORLD NATIONAL PARKS CONGRESS

PREAMBLE

The Recommendations of the World National Parks Congress, meeting in Bali, Indonesia, October 1982, relate to protected areas which are the subject of the Congress. It is in this field that the participants are expert and can offer advice.

However, the participants recognize that, while protected areas have a central and essential role to play in achieving conservation of living resources, which is a vital ingredient of sustainable development, the selection, establishment, and management of protected areas alone are not sufficient to secure the integration of conservation and development. The other measures are outlined in the World Conservation Strategy.

Moreover, the successful pursuit of the full range of conservation efforts at the national and international levels depends upon progress in related fields. These include raising the living standards of many people in the developing world who are forced by their poverty to over-exploit natural resources, reducing the trend towards over-consumption and waste of resources by the more affluent, controlling pollution, securing a much more rapid and sustained reduction in the rate of population increase, and achieving disarmament.

Nonetheless, protected areas have a vital role to play in the social, economic, cultural, and spiritual progress of humanity. Their importance has too often been neglected in the past. The Declaration of Bali seeks to redress this by securing wider and fuller understanding of the significance of protected areas in the quest for a better way of life. The following Recommendations provide the basis for implementing the intent of the Declaration.

1: INFORMATION ON PROTECTED AREAS

RECALLING Recommendation 14 of the Second Conference on National Parks concerning the importance of undertaking adequate research and investigations on protected areas;

RECOGNIZING that there is a need to identify and summarise existing research on protected areas and to coordinate and facilitate programmes of ecological, sociological, legal, and other relevant types of research;

RECOGNIZING also that a comprehensive and readily available information base covering protected areas, including inventories of the species therein, is essential to a wide range of international organizations, governments, protected area managers, voluntary bodies and individuals;

BEING AWARE of the work of the Conservation Monitoring Centre, with its Protected Areas Data Unit, in collecting, recording and monitoring data on protected areas, on the basis of the Udvardy system of biogeographical realms and IUCN's Categories, Objectives and Criteria for Protected Areas;

The World National Parks Congress, meeting in Bali, Indonesia, in October 1982:

WELCOMES the achievements of the Conservation Monitoring Centre and requests UNEP's continued support of it as part of the Global Environmental Monitoring System;

STRESSES the importance of adequate programmes for research and the recording and monitoring of information, of integrating the variety of monitoring systems within the Conservation Monitoring Centre, and in particular of preparing inventories of species contained in protected areas as a matter of urgency and of communicating these to the Conservation Monitoring Centre;

URGES further that governments and relevant agencies collaborate with IUCN to make the most effective use of the Conservation Monitoring Centre and Environmental Law Centre, and that IUCN and others provide adequate financial support for the further development and coordination of these;

RECOMMENDS that the Udvardy system of biogeographical realms continue to be developed for use on a global scale for the definition and worldwide coverage of protected areas, and that more detailed systems be developed with a flexibility of scale to make them applicable for use at a variety of regional and national levels;

URGES that international organizations, governments, and regional associations of nations promote arrangements for the long-term development and use of data collection systems, such as satellite remote sensing, covering all protected areas;

RECOMMENDS FURTHER that IUCN examine the desirability of including Resource Reserves (Category VI), Anthropological Reserves/Natural Biotic Areas (Category VII), and Multiple Use Areas/Managed Resource Areas (Category VIII) in the United Nations List of National Parks and Protected Areas; and

RECOMMENDS FINALLY that IUCN encourage governments and appropriate agencies to undertake adequate programmes of research, the results of which should be widely disseminated to protected area managers to enable them to predict the consequences of actions within their areas.

2: GLOBAL SYSTEM OF REPRESENTATIVE TERRESTRIAL PROTECTED AREAS

RECALLING Recommendation 1 of the Second World Conference on National Parks concerning the need to widen the coverage of protected areas so as to ensure the conservation of adequate and representative samples of natural biomes and ecosystems throughout the world; and Recommendations 2 and 3 specifically on the conservation of tropical rainforests, and north polar and sub-polar ecosystems;

RECOGNIZING the significant efforts made by governments in the past decade to establish such systems of protected areas;

RECOGNIZING, nevertheless, that established systems of national parks and protected areas are insufficient to accomplish the objectives of conservation, in particular the safeguarding of the world's genetic resources;

REALIZING that the forthcoming decade will probably provide the last opportunity to conserve large samples of relatively undisturbed biomes and ecosystems;

The World National Parks Congress, meeting in Bali, Indonesia, October 1982:

URGES governments to give high priority to the fulfilment of the ecological representativeness of their terrestrial protected area systems by establishing new areas or enlarging existing ones;

AND DRAWS THE ATTENTION of governments to the especially critical situation in the following biomes:

a) Tropical forests: where attention should be given to the conservation of the particularly vulnerable forest systems in South East Asia, the Indian sub-continent (including the Himalayan slopes), East Africa, West Africa, eastern South America, the eastern Andean slopes, Central America, and the islands of the Pacific Ocean, and that these same priorities should also guide IUCN and WWF in their tropical forest programme and campaign;

b) Drylands: Where an urgent international priority is to implement the plan of action to combat desertification adopted by the United Nations in 1977, especially those elements relating to the establishment of protected areas as a means of controlling desertification;

c) Wetlands: where particular emphasis should be placed on wetlands, such as European peatlands, which are subject to rapid reduction;

d) Tundra: where a priority is the establishment of more protected areas in the Eastern Hemisphere.

3: MARINE AND COASTAL PROTECTED AREAS

RECOGNIZING the absolute dependence of the peoples of many nations on food from the sea, and the dependence of sustainable production of food from the sea on protecting the ecological processes and diversity of coastal and marine environments;

RECOGNIZING that the movements of water transmit reproductive products, nutrients, food, and toxic substances, oil spills and other pollutants over large distances regardless of national boundaries;

RECOGNIZING that activities in one State affect the productivity of fisheries in other States, and noting examples from many parts of the world of over-exploitation of stocks of marine life, with the consequent collapse, perhaps irreversibly, of those stocks;

ACKNOWLEDGING the lack of suitably trained or experienced marine resource conservation managers and planners in most parts of the world;

NOTING the limited understanding of ecological processes in the sea, while accelerating human use and pollution threaten the integrity of marine environments;

CONSIDERING the scale of our present lack of knowledge about marine ecosystems in the deep ocean and the rapid pace of discovery of new forms of deep ocean life which have existed for millennia free from interference by those human activities which now threaten the integrity and productivity of marine environments;

The World National Parks Congress, meeting in Bali, Indonesia, October 1982:

RECOMMENDS that coastal nations:

a) Declare as much as possible their territorial seas or other areas of jurisdiction, including islands, as managed areas with appropriate legal status and within these areas establish zones with different degrees of use and protection;
b) Work cooperatively with neighbouring nations sharing resident and migratory species to establish coordinated networks of protected areas and other regulations to meet the critical needs of those species, with special priority for threatened and endangered species;
c) Adhere to the Convention on the Law of the Sea as an important step in ocean conservation;
d) Increase marine research programmes directed at understanding how marine ecosystems function and interrelate, the paths and effects of pollutants, and how to utilize such knowledge in management;
e) Integrate their management of terrestrial, coastal and marine zones as far as the outer edge of the continental shelf by adopting a policy enforceable by law which requires environmental assessment of major economic activities in this combined zone before commitment to such activities is made, with special protection provided for the needs of endangered species;

CALLS UPON IUCN to:

a) Develop as soon as possible an appropriate marine biogeographic classification scheme on global, regional and national levels as a basis for ensuring adequate representation of different marine ecosystems in a wide range of protected areas;
b) Develop as soon as possible a system of categories for marine protected areas to be managed in the open seas, deep oceans and coastal waters analogous to the existing IUCN categories I-X for terrestrial protected areas but adapted to the marine and coastal environment;
c) Develop, in cooperation with countries and international agencies, training programmes for personnel from countries seeking such training;
d) Develop an education programme aimed at a wide audience and focussed on the significance of marine areas, the need for their wise use, and an increased awareness of human relationships to and dependence upon such areas;

CALLS UPON all nations collectively, acting through the Law of the Sea Convention, to establish large sanctuaries in the open ocean in order to further knowledge of those areas beyond the limits of national jurisdiction and to protect the Common Heritage of Mankind; and

RECOMMENDS to governments that all fishery regimes and agreements be reviewed with a view to promoting management on an "ecosystem as a whole" basis, following the model of the Convention on the Conservation of Antarctic Marine Living Resources.

4: ANTARCTICA

RECOGNIZING the great scientific and aesthetic value of the natural ecosystems of the Antarctic Continent and the seas surrounding it and their importance in maintaining the stability of the global marine evironment and atmosphere, and AWARE that the Antarctic provides one of the best places to measure global pollution;

ACKNOWLEDGING the achievements of the Consultative Parties in their stewardship under the Antarctic Treaty in protecting the Antarctic environment from harmful interference;

RECOGNIZING that a mineral regime is now being developed which may lead to the exploration and exploitation of the mineral resources of the region;

CONCERNED that the environmental effects of mineral exploration and exploitation in the Antarctic have been inadequately studied and that mineral resource exploration and exploitation are likely to affect adversely the unique environment of the Antarctic and other ecosystems dependent on the Antarctic environment;

RECALLING that the Second World Conference on National Parks in 1972 recommended that nations party to the Antarctic Treaty should establish the Antarctic Continent and surrounding seas as the first World Park under the auspices of the United Nations, and that other protective designations are being proposed to reflect the unique status of the area;

BELIEVING that, in this second century of the national park movement, the concepts of international parks, reserves and protected areas should be promoted and that the concept of a world park and other appropriate designations should be developed more urgently;

CONSIDERING that Antarctica offers special opportunities for the implementation of these concepts and noting that the 15th General Assembly of IUCN instructed the Council, Commissions and the Director General of IUCN to initiate the preparation of a Conservation Strategy for the Antarctic environment and the Southern Ocean and in particular to seek appropriate forms of designation for the Antarctic environment as a whole and the specific sites within it which merit special attention;

NOTING also that there are appropriate forms of designation which do not imply any change of jurisdiction and that management could be by means of a zoning system providing for a range of uses, but with some uses prohibited in all zones, for example, nuclear testing (which already is prohibited under the Antarctic Treaty);

The World National Parks Congress, meeting in Bali, Indonesia, October 1982:

CONGRATULATES IUCN for its 1981 General Assembly Resolution (15/20) on Antarctica and urges all nations and organizations to work towards its implementation;

RECOMMENDS that the Antarctic Treaty Parties in cooperation with all nations should further enhance the conservation status of the Antarctic environment and foster measures which would:

a) maintain for all time the intrinsic values of the Antarctic environment for mankind and the global ecosystem;

b) ensure that all human activities are compatible with the maintenance of these values;

c) ascribe to the Antarctic environment as a whole an internationally protected area designation which connotes worldwide its unique character and values and the special measures accorded to its planning, management and conservation;

URGES that no minerals regime be brought into operation until such time as full consideration has been given to protecting the Antarctic environment completely from minerals activities and the environmental risks have been fully ascertained and safeguards developed to avoid adverse environmental effects, and thus to maintain the voluntary restriction on mineral development;

URGES FURTHER that the Antarctic Treaty Parties and other interested governments and organizations initiate a comprehensive evaluation of the Antarctic environment and its dependent ecosystems to identify and designate both continental and marine areas to be protected in perpetuity;

URGES the Antarctic Treaty Parties to include advisers from non-governmental organizations interested in the Antarctic environment on national delegations and to pursue policies of open information; and

RECOMMENDS that IUCN seek to establish close working relationships with the scientific organizations which advise the Antarctic Treaty Parties.

5: THE ROLE OF PROTECTED AREAS IN SUSTAINABLE DEVELOPMENT

RECOGNIZING the legitimate aspirations of peoples everywhere to share equitably in the development of the earth's resources and the importance of having such development take place on a sustainable basis;

ACKNOWLEDGING the fact that most materials for development now come from places outside of protected areas and that systems for the sustainable development of these materials must be put into effect;

BUT REALIZING the fundamental role which protected areas can play in assuring the sustainability of the development process, including the provision of a sustained flow of commodities from areas managed for multiple uses and the contributions which parks and nature reserves can make through safeguarding gene pools, protecting watersheds and air quality, fostering

research, affording recreational and educational opportunities, and facilitating appropriate tourism;

RECALLING the wide variety of protective designations which can be used to regulate the use of land and the importance of having designations reflect management objectives;

UNDERSTANDING the critical role which public opinion can play in persuading governments to establish, support, and defend protected areas and the importance of developing domestic constituencies who will promote the well-being of specific areas;

BEING AWARE of the special help which those living in or near protected areas can be in this regard if they feel they share appropriately in the benefits flowing from protected areas, are compensated appropriately for any lost rights, and are taken into account in planning and operations;

REALIZING that protected areas will never be free from threats for inappropriate development; that eternal vigilance is necessary for the broader public interest to prevail; but also realizing that better understanding of the material contributions of such areas can substantially assist in their defence; and

ACCEPTING the need for those who manage protected areas to be increasingly conscious of the larger social context in which the fate of protected areas will be decided;

The World National Parks Congress, meeting in Bali, Indonesia, October 1982:

URGES that nations, in setting aside and managing protected areas make the fullest possible use of the range of protected area categories, Category I through Category VIII recommended by the IUCN;

REAFFIRMS its strong conviction, expressed at the Second World Congress on National Parks in 1972, that national parks and similar reserves (Categories I - III) must be strictly protected against efforts to exploit their natural resources for such purposes as commercial timber cutting, mining, hydroelectric works and other dams and public works, industrial facilities, commercial fishing, sport and commercial hunting, farming and grazing of domestic animals;

CALLS UPON nations to establish more multiple use management areas (Category VIII), and other management regimes of intermediate intensity, around stricter nature reserves so as to prevent them from becoming biologically impoverished islands requests governments and development assistance agencies to assist in providing support for local populations who may be disadvantaged by the establishment or existence of a protected area;

AND IN PARTICULAR CALLS FOR intensified research:

a) on the degree to which gene stocks from national parks and similar reserves (Categories I - III) ought to be made available to plant and animal breeders, pharmaceutical companies, and genetic engineering firms for commercial purposes and whether this can be done without endangering populations with special genetic qualities;

b) on ways to manage soundly tropical forests in multiple use management areas (Category VIII) so as to best maintain species diversity;

c) on ways to evaluate the benefits provided by protected areas to better illustrate their contribution to sustainable development;

d) on ways to foster appropriate recreation and tourism and minimize the adverse impacts of them;

e) in the social sciences to facilitate better understanding of the role of parks in serving human needs;

AND SUGGESTS IN CONCLUSION that those promoting the role of protected areas in sustainable development stress:

a) the contribution which Category I, II, III, VI, and VII areas can make especially in maintaining gene pools of potential importance to nutrition and health;

b) the contribution which Category IV areas can make in providing protein through controlled wildlife cropping;

c) the contribution which Category V areas can make to tourism and recreation; and

d) the contribution which Category VIII areas can make, in countries with tropical forests, to the sustained production of forest products.

6: THREATS TO PROTECTED AREAS

RECOGNIZING that the pressures arising from the needs and demands of local populations around some protected areas threaten the integrity of these areas, for example, through the search for firewood and burning for land clearance;

RECOGNIZING also the continuing problem of degradation of protected areas from road construction and other works, and the need to control the use of vehicles, boats and aircraft affecting such areas;

BEING CONCERNED about the potentially damaging effects on protected areas of exploration for, and exploitation and transportation of minerals, including oil and natural gas;

RECALLING Resolution 13 of the 15th General Assembly of IUCN calling for the protection of representative examples of free flowing rivers from river engineering;

NOTING that various nations have plans to construct dams on wild and scenic rivers impacting on national parks and protected areas, and that, while such schemes may appear attractive in the short-term, they would, if carried out, destroy great natural wonders and other sites of international significance, the long term

value of which in their undisturbed state exceeds the values which would be created by the engineering works;

BEING AWARE of the threat to protected areas from various forms of pollution, and in particular recalling Resolution 14 of the 15th General Assembly of IUCN on the increasing damage being caused to aquatic ecosystems and forests, including those in protected areas, by acid rain and snow;

BEING FURTHER AWARE that the conservation of some species and ecosystems and the integrity of some protected areas is threatened by the presence of introduced species;

The World National Parks Congress, meeting in Bali, Indonesia, October 1982:

CALLS on Governments to initiate measures of sustainable social and economic development which will relieve the pressures of local populations around protected areas on those areas, for example, through the provision of fuelwood plantations;

CALLS FOR the reinforcement of measures to reduce the external threats to protected areas, and in particular, urges governments and relevant agencies to:

a) develop appropriate legislative and administrative mechanisms to ensure that:

• prior impact assessments are undertaken to establish the scale and nature of the consequences of development projects, supported by powers to refuse permission or approval for those inappropriate to their environments;

• appropriate conditions of permission or approval are imposed to safeguard the integrity of the environment where a project is deemed acceptable in principle;

• adequate monitoring is undertaken during construction and operation, with powers of enforcement of the conditions of permission and approval; and

• powers are available to secure suitable restoration on completion of construction and, in the case of temporary works, to secure complete clearance and rehabilitation;

b) reconsider existing proposals,to abandon projects with unacceptable environmental impacts, and to review thoroughly future proposals for the construction of river engineering works within areas of natural, scientific and cultural importance, by exhaustive resource investigation and environmental impact assessments, including the evaluation of options;

c) take action to implement effective measures to eliminate and avoid all forms of pollution which degrade protected areas;

d) devise and implement policies, legislation and regulatory controls to ensure that effective eradication or control measures are undertaken in regard to introduced species in protected areas; and

REQUESTS IUCN to develop and implement a system of reporting on protected areas under particular threat.

7: COMBATING POACHING

RECOGNIZING that poaching is the most important threat to the integrity of some protected areas;

AWARE that any reduction in anti-poaching work could result in the serious loss of wildlife, especially rare and endangered species, in some protected areas;

ALARMED at the increased availability of weapons and the development of techniques of mass killing of wildlife;

AWARE that uncontrolled international trade in wildlife continues to endanger numerous species, and that the Convention on International Trade in Endangered Species of Wild Fauna and Flora (CITES) is the primary tool in attempting to control such trade;

AWARE that anti-poaching personnel often work under difficult and dangerous conditions, and that the survival of wildlife depends on their motivation, discipline and morale;

SENSITIVE to the need for better relationships between protected areas personnel and local populations;

The World National Parks Congress, meeting in Bali, Indonesia, October 1982:

RECOMMENDS that:

a) continued emphasis should be given by governments and conservation aid organizations on strengthening anti-poaching programmes and related training of field staff;

b) adequate funds should be made available to better the social, economic, educational and logistical support to field staff to accomplish their vital tasks;

c) where consistent with management objectives, tangible benefits should accrue to local people from living near protected areas;

d) continued support should be given to CITES, and specifically non-signatory States should be encouraged to join and the enforcement of CITES should be strengthened.

8: ENVIRONMENTAL PLANNING AND PROTECTED AREAS

BEARING in mind that national parks and other protected areas play key roles in the maintenance of essential ecological processes, the preservation of genetic diversity, and the sustainable use of species and ecosystems;

CONVINCED THEREFORE THAT protected areas have an integral place in wise land use and overall environmental planning;

CONCERNED HOWEVER that the ongoing degradation, due to unwise land use in the surrounds of protected areas, is not only adverse to the communities resident in such surrounds but also endangers the security of protected areas;

NOTING that decreasing land productivity and the extension of marginal lands create pressure on protected area resources and increase competition for the remaining natural areas suitable for inclusion in protected areas, and that rehabilitation of appropriate marginal and degraded lands through revegetation and reafforestation can reduce this pressure;

RECOGNIZING THAT the World Conservation Strategy has demonstrated that effective resource management cannot occur when conservation planning and development planning proceed in isolation;

The World National Parks Congress, meeting in Bali, Indonesia, October 1982:

URGES governments and intergovernmental organizations to integrate conservation principles with development planning, for example through the preparation of national conservation strategies, laying particular emphasis on conservation oriented land use;

CALLS ON all levels of governments and intergovernmental organizations to include in regional development plans and human settlement programmes appropriate provisions for the establishment of protected areas complemented by a coordinated system of other conservation and environmental management techniques;

URGES governments and international organizations to promote and support the rehabilitation of degraded lands and the regeneration and recovery of damaged natural areas through reafforestation and other programmes; and

REQUESTS IUCN to prepare manuals with case histories for the guidance of planners, managers, and decision-makers outside the protected area system describing integrated environmental approaches and other techniques for enhancing the security of protected areas.

9: PROTECTED AREAS AND TRADITIONAL SOCIETIES

RECALLING the 15th IUCN General Assembly Recommendation 15/7 on "The Role of Traditional Lifestyles and Local People in Conservation and Development";

RECOGNIZING the global responsibilities which all people share for ensuring the conservation of the biosphere and its varied cultural and natural environments;

ACKNOWLEDGING that traditional societies which have survived to the present in harmony with their environment:

• deserve our respect for their wise stewardship of areas and environments which we now seek to protect;

• are threatened by the alienation or loss to outsiders of rights to land or to particular resources such as timber, fish, and minerals; and

provide instructive examples of environmental management strategies worthy of emulation;

RECOGNIZING FURTHER that many modern technologies are failing because they neglect long-standing, complex and delicate relationships between people and the environment;

The World National Parks Congress, meeting in Bali, Indonesia, October 1982:

REAFFIRMS the rights of traditional societies to social, economic, cultural and spiritual self-determination;

REAFFIRMS further that traditional peoples everywhere have a right to participate in decisions affecting the land and the natural resources on which they depend;

RECOMMENDS that those responsible at every level of protected area research, planning, management and education fully investigate and utilise the traditional wisdom of communities affected by conservation measures;

RECOMMENDS FURTHER the implementation of joint management arrangements between societies which have traditionally managed resources and protected area authorities appropriate to the varied local circumstances; and

REQUESTS that IUCN coordinate and support the interests expressed by its various commissions seeking to study and foster oral traditions associated with ecosystem management of parks and protected areas through appropriate projects.

10: CONSERVATION OF WILD GENETIC RESOURCES

BEARING IN MIND that protected areas have the potential to play key roles in the preservation of the genetic diversity of wild species;

AWARE that wild genetic resources already make an important contribution to agricultural production and provide raw materials for the pharmacological industry and, through breeding, for aquaculture and silviculture;

CONCERNED that wild populations of value as genetic resources are being lost to habitat destruction and other pressures;

CONSCIOUS that the primary means of safeguarding wild genetic resources for present and future use must be *in situ* in protected areas because of their great diversity, the difficulty of maintaining certain of them *ex situ*, and the need to conserve them as populations co-evolving with the ecosystems of which they are a part;

MINDFUL THAT existing networks of protected areas provide the framework for a system of *in situ* gene banks;

The World National Parks Congress, meeting in Bali, Indonesia, October 1982:

CALLS UPON governments and international institutions to:

a) make the conservation of wild genetic resources an explicit objective of protected area systems and provide for the establishment of *in situ* gene banks;

b) review the extent to which wild genetic resources are adequately maintained by existing protected area systems;

c) make and implement plans for the establishment of *in situ* gene banks, including as appropriate the zoning of existing protected areas and the designation of new ones;

REQUESTS that IUCN take a more prominent role in preparing and disseminating inventories of wild species and populations of known or likely value as genetic resources, to assist nations wishing to establish *in situ* gene banks;

REQUESTS that national and international governmental and non-governmental agencies cooperate in the preparation of such inventories, and allocate resources for the establishment of *in situ* gene banks; and

INVITES IUCN to investigate the possible development of international instruments to regulate the commercial exploitation of wild genetic resources.

11: DEVELOPMENT ASSISTANCE AND PROTECTED AREAS

RECALLING Recommendation 17 of the Second World National Parks Conference on Technical and Financial Assistance for National Parks;

STRONGLY ENDORSING the view of the Brandt Commission that "the care of the natural environment is an essential aspect of development";

NOTING with particular pleasure the self-reliance and sense of commitment shown by many developing countries (e.g., our host country, Indonesia) in establishing and providing funds for protected areas;

WELCOMING recent moves by a number of leading multi-lateral and bi-lateral development assistance agencies, with the encouragement of UNEP and others, to adopt and promote the principles of the World Conservation Strategy, and especially the adoption in February 1980 by the main multi-lateral agencies of the Declaration of Environmental Policies and Procedures relating to Economic Development;

WELCOMING also the initiative of IUCN in establishing its Conservation for Development Centre; but

CONCERNED nonetheless that the vital role of protected areas in sustainable development of developing countries, especially for rural populations, is too often disregarded or underestimated in both requests and support for development assistance projects;

The World National Parks Congress, meeting in Bali, Indonesia, October 1982:

CALLS UPON multilateral and bilateral assistance agencies to consider the formal adoption of the following principles to guide their development assistance programmes:

a) that protected areas are an indispensable part of sustainable development, and therefore assistance in the selection, establishment, and management of protected areas is a suitable subject for increased and earmarked development assistance;

b) that support should be provided not only to protected areas as such, but to strengthening the various institutions responsible for them in developing countries;

c) that development projects must scrupulously respect the objectives of protected areas, and accordingly that no such projects should be supported where it has been established that there is a potential adverse impact on protected areas in Categories I to IV;

d) that where, in the national interest, a development project impinges on protected areas in Categories V to VIII, the project must include mitigating or compensating measures, including where appropriate the strengthening of the protected area, e.g., through the addition of more land;

e) that each appropriate development project should include a protected areas component, for example the establishment of a watershed protected area as part of a project for integrated rural development;

REQUESTS IUCN and UNEP, in their continuing dialogue with the development agencies, to promote the adoption by them of such principles; and

URGES governments receiving assistance to give higher priority to conservation projects in their aid requests.

12: MANAGEMENT OF PROTECTED AREAS

RECOGNIZING that the rapid growth in the number of protected areas designated during the past decade has created a corresponding need for effective management;

NOTING that many of these protected areas, especially in developing countries, are under threat of degradation through the lack of effective management;

The World National Parks Congress, meeting in Bali, Indonesia, October 1982:

URGES governments to give high priority to the conservation of all protected areas by:

a) identifying the resources within the protected areas, and the threats to them;

b) preparing management plans which provide for

management and development to be in accordance with an appropriate range of long-term conservation objectives;

c) involving, to the extent feasible, local communities and the wider public in the preparation and implementation of these plans;

d) providing adequate finance and staff even in periods of economic stringency to implement the management plans; and

e) requiring government agencies and private interests to coordinate their activities with the protected areas authorities, so that all activities in the protected area conform with the management plan.

13: PROTECTED AREA PERSONNEL: TRAINING AND COMMUNICATION

RECALLING Recommendations 16 and 18 of the Second World Conference on National Parks, stressing the importance of the exchange of information and of training in the management and operation of protected areas;

NOTING the increasing need for training and development of protected area personnel, especially as increasing work loads are frequently aggravated by staffing constraints resulting from economic considerations;

NOTING ALSO the value of the range of educational opportunities available, particularly regional training schools for protected area personnel in developing countries;

ACKNOWLEDGING the value of the International Seminar on National Parks and Equivalent Reserves which has acted as a catalyst for other regional training seminars and programmes;

RECOGNIZING that, despite its financial difficulties, PARKS Magazine has since 1976 provided an international professional journal essential to training and protected area management, which has met with an enthusiastic reception especially in devleloping countries where there may be a scarcity of such information;

RECOGNIZING with gratitude the continued financial support of IUCN, the U.S. National Park Service, Parks Canada, Unesco, UNEP, WWF and others but noting with concern the persistent difficulties in financing PARKS Magazine for free distribution which has forced discontinuance of the French and Spanish editions;

ACKNOWLEDGING the wish of protected area personnel, as well as other interested people, to share ideas and experience, and to feel a personal sense of identity with park personnel worldwide in a role supportive of IUCN;

The World National Parks Congress meeting in Bali, Indonesia, October 1982:

RECOMMENDS that international, regional, and national agencies continue to support and foster regional strategies of natural resources training and regional training schools in developing countries;

URGES continued support for the International Seminar on National Parks and Equivalent Reserves and other regional and national seminars and training programmes;

FURTHER URGES IUCN to publish PARKS Magazine in three languages as a valuable tool in training and communication and specifically recommends that:

a) no basic changes be made in the present editing and publishing of PARKS Magazine until all options have been investigated; at the same time further effort be made to give the contents the greatest possible international character;

b) IUCN, as the publisher of PARKS Magazine, endeavour to assume greater responsibility for publication and distribution of the journal;

c) consideration be given to setting up a subscription system for individuals and institutions, particularly in developed countries, while maintaining a free distribution list for those directly involved in developing countries;

d) the Editorial Advisory Board assist IUCN in exploring financial sources;

AND FURTHER RECOMMENDS that to enhance communication among protected area personnel and to extend interest and a sense of involvement in the aims of protected areas, IUCN work towards establishing an organization of those involved or interested in national parks and protected areas based on personal membership for whom PARKS Magazine could serve as a channel of communication.

14: DEVELOPMENT OF PUBLIC SUPPORT FOR PROTECTED AREAS

RECALLING Recommendations 19 and 20 of the Second World Conference on National Parks on interpretation and environmental education;

RECOGNIZING that action has been taken to establish interpretive services in protected areas and environmental education programmes of various kinds both within and outside protected areas;

NOTING, nevertheless, concerns expressed at this Congress about increasing pressures from governments, industry, and people on natural systems which warrant protection;

NOTING also the serious economic situation confronting a number of countries which is leading to the deterioration of protected areas to the point of extinction of some species and habitats;

RECOGNIZING that the commitment of governments to establish and manage protected areas is directly related to their perception of community support for such areas;

RECOGNIZING FURTHER that community sup-

port may be gained for national parks and protected areas if communities involved are convinced of their values;

RECOGNIZING also that in many countries voluntary conservation organizations carry out effective programmes to enlist public support for protected areas, particularly at the local level;

The World National Parks Congress, meeting in Bali, Indonesia, October 1982:

RECOMMENDS that governments and relevant agencies take steps to:

a) evaluate the level of public support for protected areas;

b) identify the nature of public concerns about protected areas by consultation and research;

c) develop programmes of interpretation and environmental education, both in the field and by other formal and non-formal educational means, designed to emphasize the social as well as the scientific values of protected areas, giving specific attention to issues of public concern;

d) implement these programmes through means such as curricular elements in schools, short-term conservation courses and study-and-work camps, tree planting campaigns, and providing facilities for youth groups to carry out environmental studies in the field;

e) encourage young people in particular to organize themselves into groups to undertake environmental studies and conservation activities, and support youth exchanges between countries as a means of stimulating international cooperation and understanding of conservation;

f) facilitate greater use of the mass media as an effective way of reaching the public at large;

g) provide appropriate assistance to voluntary conservation organizations for programmes designed to enlist public support for protected areas, and to improve information flows to them.

15: VOLUNTARY ASSISTANCE FOR PROTECTED AREAS

RECOGNIZING that many functions related to the effective management of protected areas throughout the world have been carried out by individual volunteers and voluntary organizations, and that these individuals and organizations have developed a high degree of expertise in many relevant fields;

RECOGNIZING FURTHER that such volunteers and voluntary organizations can render valuable assistance in management in their own countries and overseas;

BEING AWARE that many government agencies responsible for the management of protected areas find it difficult to manage them because of staff shortages caused by adverse economic conditions;

The World National Parks Congress, meeting in Bali, Indonesia, October 1982:

URGES all governments and agencies responsible for management of protected areas to consider the value of assistance available from volunteers and voluntary organizations, and, where appropriate, to take advantage of that assistance, and where possible to give them the necessary financial support;

CALLS upon IUCN and governments to improve information flow to and cooperation with volunteers and voluntary organizations.

16: WORLD HERITAGE CONVENTION

RECALLING the recommendation of the Second World Conference on National Parks on the conservation of the World Heritage;

WELCOMING the inclusion of World Heritage sites as Category X among the protected areas categories accepted by the 14th General Assembly of IUCN in 1978;

CONSIDERING the increasingly important role of the World Heritage Convention in the conservation of natural resources, and in the full and enduring protection of the world's natural and cultural heritage;

NOTING with appreciation that 66 States have now become party to the Convention, and that 112 properties have been inscribed on the World Heritage List, while also recognizing that the Convention has not yet achieved universal coverage nor is the World Heritage List yet fully comprehensive;

CALLING ATTENTION to the range of benefits, including resource protection, and financial, educational, and technical assistance accruing to States joining and participating in the Convention;

COMMENDING the strong commitment to, and energetic participation in, Convention activities by colleagues interested primarily in cultural heritage, which noting the continuing imbalance between natural and cultural experts on delegations to the World Heritage Committee;

COMMENDING the World Heritage Committee and Unesco for the significant successes of the first five years of full operation of the Convention, and recognizing the important roles played by IUCN in these successes; and

RECOGNIZING opportunities to increase the effectiveness of the Convention;

EMPHASIZING the importance of fully protecting sites and properties of outstanding universal value for the benefit of all peoples and so that this heritage may be passed undiminished to future generations;

The World National Parks Congress, meeting in Bali, Indonesia, October 1982:

REITERATES its strong commitment to the principles of the World Heritage Convention;

URGES all States which have not yet done so to become party to the Convention and participate fully in its activities;

RECOMMENDS that States which are Party to the Convention take all necessary steps to ensure that their delegations to the World Heritage Committee include experts in natural areas;

URGES natural heritage authorities within States which are Party to the Convention to become more active in its affairs;

ENCOURAGES States Party to take steps to more actively publicize the importance and activities of the Convention including the development of methods to increase public participation within States Party, pursuant to Articles 17 and 27 of the Convention;

FURTHER URGES Unesco to consider launching international campaigns for natural sites in cooperation with the World Heritage Committee;

STRESSES the importance of maintaining the integrity of World Heritage properties and urges States Party to ensure the fullest application of the Convention respecting protection, conservation, indicative inventories, management plans, progress reports and presentation of properties and to submit indicative inventories and progress reports thereon, and encourages the Committee to continue its efforts to establish procedures to facilitate the development and submission of such reports and inventories; and

ENCOURAGES IUCN to continue its commitment to the development of a sound and comprehensive list of World Heritage Sites.

17: BIOSPHERE RESERVES

WELCOMING the inclusion of biosphere reserves as Category IX among the categories of protected areas accepted by the 14th General Assembly of IUCN in 1978;

CONSIDERING that biosphere reserves are an essential part of the global, regional and national protected areas system;

RECOGNIZING the special contributions which biosphere reserves can make to sustainable development through *in situ* genetic resource conservation, through the involvement of local people in the management of reserves and in surrounding buffer zones, and through scientific research, rational management and monitoring of ecosystems, as well as related education and training;

BELIEVING that there is a need for more and better managed biosphere reserves and that the present shortcomings arise from insufficient understanding of the purposes and characteristics of such reserves, of the criteria and methods for their selection, planning and management, and of the need to develop global, regional and national networks of reserves;

The World National Parks Congress, meeting in Bali, Indonesia in October 1982:

RECOMMENDS that Unesco, in cooperation with governments and international organizations including IUCN, promote an improved understanding of biosphere reserves, and of their selection, planning, and management;

URGES governments and international organizations to give priority to the establishment of networks of biosphere reserves, and also urges the professional groups involved, such as resource managers, conservationists, scientists, and land use planners, to participate in this effort to the full;

RECOMMENDS that particular efforts be made to establish and strengthen biosphere reserves where human pressures have made it difficult to conserve wild plant and animal genetic resources through other means; and in those ecosystems which are poorly represented at present, particularly tropical forests, drylands, and coastal and marine zones; and

ADVISES that the foregoing should be taken into account to the maximum extent possible in the preparations for the International Scientific Biosphere Reserve Congress to be held at Minsk, USSR, in 1983, and should be discussed at that Congress.

18: INTERNATIONAL AGREEMENTS AND PROTECTED AREAS

ENDORSING the importance given in the World Conservation Strategy to the global conventions on the Conservation of Wetlands of International Importance, Especially as Waterfowl Habitats, and on the Conservation of Migratory Species as a means of reinforcing national efforts in respect of protected areas;

CONSIDERING that existing regional conventions for conservation in the Western Hemisphere, Europe, Africa, and the South Pacific, as well as that under development in South East Asia, also reinforce national efforts;

WELCOMING the progress made in the UNEP Regional Seas Programme, and especially the adoption of the protocol for protected areas in the Mediterranean region;

CONCERNED that a draft international agreement on tropical timber, currently under development by the United Nations Conference on Trade and Development (UNCTAD), does not include measures for the conservation and sustainable management of tropical forest systems as an integral part of the exploitation of timber resources;

The World National Parks Congress, meeting in Bali, Indonesia, October 1982:

CALLS on all States, which have not already done so, to become Parties to the global and appropriate regional conventions which support protected areas, to adopt such other conventions as may be required to fill gaps in present coverage;

URGES the States party to the Wetlands Convention to implement speedily the recommendations of the Conference of Parties held in Cagliari, Sardinia, in November 1980;

REQUESTS UNEP to encourage the development and adoption by parties to the various regional seas conventions of protocols on protected areas similar to that already in force in the Mediterranean region;

ADVISES producing and consuming countries of tropical timber that they should postpone final action on the UNCTAD Agreement until adequate conservation measures, including the establishment of protected areas, are incorporated in it, or alternative legal structures have been developed to the same end; and

RECOMMENDS that IUCN use its scientific and legal expertise to encourage and advise all States on the preparation, use, and where required, updating of international legal instruments which support protected areas.

19: FUTURE WORLD CONGRESSES AND MEETINGS ON PROTECTED AREAS

REALIZING the benefits to protected areas of regular gatherings of the nature of the First and Second World Conferences on National Parks and of this World National Parks Congress;

RECOGNIZING the vital role that non-governmental conservation organizations play in shaping public opinion and in developing support for protected areas;

FURTHER RECOGNIZING with gratification the wide spectrum of participation in every aspect of this Congress but considering that a still greater involvement of experts from developing countries is necessary;

NOTING, however, the comparative absence of women participants in this congress in spite of the deep concern of women worldwide for the health of the biosphere, the expertise of women in all fields of nature conservation and all professional nature conservation disciplines;

The World National Parks Congress, meeting in Bali, Indonesia, October 1982:

RECOMMENDS that IUCN consider providing opportunities at more frequent intervals than 10 years for those concerned with protected areas to review the growth of the global system, assess progress, and identify threats which may exist, with consideration being given, therefore, both to holding the next Congress in 10 years time, and also to arranging for an intermediate meeting to be held in 1987 in association with the General Assembly of IUCN expected in that year;

CONSIDERS that those organising a World Congress in 1992 should take into account the suggestions of participants from the Neotropical Realm that this be held in that realm, thereby coinciding with the five hundredth anniversary of Christopher Columbus's voyage to the Americas; and

CALLS UPON those who organise future congresses or meetings on protected areas to provide for adequate participation from non-governmental conservation organisations and similarly to seek to involve women and participants from developing countries more fully.

20: EXPRESSION OF THANKS

RECOGNIZING the complex planning and organization involved in the preparation and running of this World Parks Congress;

VERY MUCH AWARE that members of the Organizing Committee, of cooperating agencies and numerous other persons have worked tirelessly to ensure its success;

GRATEFUL for the excellent facilities available for the Congress and the unique opportunities for participants to enjoy and appreciate the nature and culture of their host country;

The World National Parks Congress, meeting in Bali, Indonesia, October 1982:

RECORDS its warmest appreciation and grateful thanks to the Government and people of Indonesia and Bali in particular for the generous hospitality extended to participants in this Congress;

FURTHER RECORDS its great appreciation to the members of the Organizing Committee and to cooperating agencies and volunteers involved for their outstanding work over the past years and throughout the Congress; and

EXPRESSES its grateful thanks to the numerous persons who have contributed their time and energy to assist the Organizing Committee in the preparation and running of a most successful Congress.

Annexes

I. Participants
II. Awards
III. Bibliography

Annex I.
World National Parks Congress
List of Participants

Mr. Ivor Jackson
Eastern Caribbean Natural Area
Management Program
c/o Antillean Developers Ltd
Jardine Court, St Mary's Street
Antigua

Dr. Ricardo Luti
Director
Centro de Ecologia y Recursos
Naturales Renovables
Universidad National de Cordoba
C.C. 395
5000 Cordoba, Argentina

Ms. Karla Bell
Fund for Animals
P.O. Box 371
Manly N.S.W.
Australia 2095

Mr. Peter Cullen
Principal Lecturer of the Natural
Resources Group
Canberra College of Advanced
Education
P.O. Box 1, Belconnen A.C.T.
Australia

Mr. Bruce W. Davis
Commissioner
Australian Heritage Commission
Dept. of Political Science
University of Tasmania
Box 252C Hobart, Tasmania
Australia, 7001

Mr. Ian Eberhard
Conservation Commission of the
Northern Territory
P.O. Box 38496
Winnellie
Darwin, Australia

Mr. Murray Elliott
Conservation Commission of the
Northern Territory
P.O. Box 38496
Winnellie
Darwin, Australia

Mr. A.M. Fox
35 Beaumont Cres.
The Ridgeway
Queanbeyan
Canberra City, A.C.T. 2601
NSW 26-20 Australia

Mr. Neville Gare
Australian National Parks
& Wildlife Service
P.O. Box 636
Canberra, A.C.T. 2601
Australia

Dewar Wilson Goode
94 Leopold Street
South Yarra
3141 Australia

Dr. R.E. Johannes
CSIRO
Fisheries, Box 20
North Beach
Western Australia
Australia

Mr. Donald A. Johnstone
Director, N.S.W. National Parks
and Wildlife Service
Sydney 2000, N.S.W.
Australia

Mrs. Donald A. Johnstone
c/o above address

Mr. Graeme Kelleher
Chairman, Great Barrier Reef Marine
Park Authority
P.O. Box 791
Canberra City, A.C.T. 2601
Australia

Dr. R.A. Kenchington
Assistant Executive Officer
Great Barrier Reef Marine Park Authority
P.O. Box 1379
Townsville, Qsld. 4810
Australia

Dr. J. Kozlowski
Dept. of Regional and Town Planning
Queensland University
St. Lucia, Brisbane 4067
Australia

Dr. J. Mosley
Director
Australian Conservation Foundation
672B Glenferrie Road
Hawthorn, Vic. 3122
Australia

Dr. P. Ogilvie
National Parks Wildlife Service
P.O. Box 190
Brisbane North Quay
Qsld. 4000
Australia

Mr. Clive W. Price
Head Office, MLC Centre
239 George St.
Brisbane, Qsld 4000
Australia

Mrs. Valerie Price
c/o above address

Dr. D.S. Saunders
Director, National Parks Service
240 Victoria Parade
East Melbourne, Vic. 3002
Australia

Mrs. Saunders
c/o above address

Dr. E.C. Saxon
CSRIO
Box 2111, Alice Springs
N.T. 5750 Australia

Mrs. E.C. Saxon
c/o above address

Mr. John Sibly
Kintore and Geography Dept
South Australia College of
Advanced Education
Adelaide, S.A. 5000
Australia

Mr. J. Sinclair
Fraser Island Defenders Org. Ltd.
P.O. Box 420
Maryborough Q. 4650
Australia

Mr. K.S. Shurcliff
Wildlife Management
South Australia College of
Advanced Education
Conservation Commission of
Northern Territory
Alice Springs, Northern Territory
Australia

Dr. George Stankey
Canberra College of Advanced
Education, P.O. Box 1
Belconnen A.C.T.
Australia 2616

Mrs. George Stankey
c/o above address

Dr. Anthony Start
Box 119, Karratha
Western Australia
Australia 6009

Dr. N. Nigel Wace
Dept. of Biogeography and Geomorphology
Research School of Pacific Studies
The Australian National University
P.O. Box 4, Canberra, A.C.T. 2600
Australia

Mrs. Wace
c/o above address

Mr. Brad Warren
Executive Director
Association for Research
Exploration and Aid
363A Pitt Street
Sydney, 2000
Australia

Mr. Peter Wright
Conservation Commission of the
Northern Territory
P.O. Box 38496
Winnellie
Darwin, Australia

Dr. William Yates
Administrator Christmas Island
Residence of His Honour
the Administrator
Christmas Island
Australia

Mr. Faisal A. Izzeddin
Al-Areen
Wildlife Sanctuary
P.O. Box 5792
Bahrain

Mrs. Faisal A. Izzeddin
c/o above address

Mr. D.D. Mangubo
Dept. of Wildife
National Parks and Tourism
Ministry of Commerce and Industry
P.O. Box 13l
Gaborone, Botswana

Dr. Maria T. Jorge Padua
Diretora do Dept. de Parques Nac.
IBDF
SAIN-Av. L-4
Brasilia-DF., CEP. 70.000
Brazil

Dr. Angela Tresinari Bernardes Q.
Departamento de Parques Nacionais
IBDF
Florestal - IBDG
Ed. Palacio de Desenvolvimento
21 Andar
Brasilia - D.F., Brazil

Admir. Ibsen de Gusmao Camara
Brazilian Conservation Foundation
R. Miranda Valverde 103
Botafogo Cep. 22.821
Rio de Janeiro, R.J.
Brazil

Dr. Walter Emmerich
Agronomist Engineer
Forest Institute
P.O. Box 1322, Sao Paulo
Brazil

Mr. John Blower
c/o FAO Nature Conservation and
National Parks Project, UNDP
P.O. Box 650
Rangoon, Burma

U Kyaw Nyunt Lwin
Director
c/o Rangoon Zoological Gardens
P.O. Box 650
Rangoon, Burma

Lt. Col. Maung Maung
Working People's Settlement Dept.
c/o Rangoon Zoological Gardens
P.O. Box 650
Rangoon, Burma

U Thet Tun
Deputy Director
Nature Conservation and
National Parks Project
c/o Rangoon Zoological Gardens
P.O. Box 650
Rangoon, Burma

U Saw Han
Nature Conservation and
National Parks Project
c/o Rangoon Zoological Gardens
P.O. Box 650
Rangoon, Burma

Ukmin Maung Nyunt
Agriculture and Livestock Breeding
Cadre Training School
c/o Rangoon Zoological Gardens
P.O. Box 650
Rangoon, Burma

U Maung Maung Soe
Agriculture and Livestock Breeding
Training School
c/o Rangoon Zoological Gardens
P.O. Box 650
Rangoon, Burma

Dr. Andrew Allo
School for the Training
of Wildlife Specialists
P.O. Box 271, Garoua
United Republic of Cameroon

Dr. James R. Butler
Dept. of Forest Science
University of Alberta
Edmonton, Alta. T6G 2E6
Canada

Mr. Donn Cline
Assistant Deputy Minister
Alberta Parks and Recreation
10363-108 St.
Edmonton T5J 1L8
Canada

Mr. Ken Erdman
Special Assistant
Alberta Parks & Recreation
Standard Life Centre
10405-Jasper Ave.
Edmonton, Alta. Canada

Ms. Jacqueline Garnett
c/o 1911-128 Street
Surrey, B.C.
Canada

Mr. Clive L. Justice
c/o Justice, Webb and Vincent
Landscape Architects
6435 West Boulevard
Vancouver B.C. V6M 3X6
Canada

Dr. Steve Kun
Director, National Parks
Parks Canada
10 Wellington
Hull, Quebec
Canada

Mrs. Gail Kun
c/o above address

Dr. David Munro
2513 Amherst Avenue
Sydney, B.C.
V8L 2H3, Canada

Dr. G. Nelson
Dean, Faculty of Environment
University of Waterloo
Waterloo, Ontario
Canada

Mr. Robert Prescott-Allen
208-2125 Oak Bay Avenue
Victoira, B.C.
V8R 1E8, Canada

Dr. G. Priddle
Dept. of Geography
University of Waterloo
Waterloo, Ontario
Canada

Dr. Robert C. Scace
Senior Geographer
Reid, Crowther & Partners Limited
P.O. Box 5600, Postal Station 'A'
Calgary, Alta. T2H 1X9
Canada

Dr. G. Scheurholtz
Taisco
P.O. Box 69
Duncan B.C. V9L 3X1
Canada

Mr. Cliff Wallis
615 Deercroft Way S.E.
Calgary, Alta., T2J 5V4
Canada

Mr. C. Wershler
430-15403 Deer Run Drive S.E.
Calgary, Alta., T2J 5V4
Canada

Ing. Ivan Castro Poblete
Executive Director
Nacional Forestal (CONAF)
Corporacim
Av. Bulnes 285, Of. 501
Santiago, Chile

Mrs. Castro
c/o above address

Mr. Cesar Pagliotti Oronazabal
Chief of Nat. Pks Dept.
Forest Service Chile
Av. Bulnes 285 of 401 Santiago
Santiago, Chile

Mr. Li Gui Ling
Deputy Director
Minister of Forestry, NFRRC
Dept. of Forest Policy
Beijing, China

Mr. Yuan Hai Ying
Dept. of Forest Policy
Minister of Forestry
Beijing, China

Mr. Zhang Gui Xin
Dept. of Forest Protection
Minister of Forestry
Beijing, China

Ing. Heliodoro Sanchez
Jefe Division de Parques Nacional
INDERENA
Calle 26 No 13B-47
Bogota, Colombia

Mr. Jim Barborak
Tropical Agr. Research &
Training Centre
Wildlands Management Unit
CATIE, Turrialba, Costa Rica

Dr. Gerardo Budowski
Head
Departamento de Recursos Naturales
and Renovables (CATIE)
Turrialba, Costa Rica

Dr. Craig MacFarland
Head, Wildlands Management Unit
CATIE
Turrialba, Costa Rica

Sr. Roger Morales
Wildlands Management Unit
CATIE
Turrialba, Costa Rica

Maheer Ali
Plant Protection Dept.
Faculty of Agriculture
Assiut University, Egypt

Mr. Teshome Ashine
General Manager
Wildlife Conservation Organization
P.O. Box 386
Addis Ababa, Ethiopia

Mr. Biranda B. Singh
National Trust for Fiji
P.O. Box 2089
Govt. Buildings
SUVA, FIJI

Dr. Matti Helminen
Chief, Office for National Parks
Metsahallitus
Luonnonsuojelualuetoimisto
PL 233, SF-00121
Helsinki 12, Finland

Dr. Michel Batisse
Deputy Assistant Director General
Unesco
Pl. Fontenoy, 7
75700 Paris, France

Prof. Franois Ramade
4 Residence des
Quinconces 91190 GIF
Sur Yvette, France

M. Bernard Salvat
55 rue Buffon
75005 Paris
France

M. Traub
Parc national des Cevennes
48400 Florac
France

Mme Ann Vignier
Min. de l'Environnement
et du cadre de vie
14 Boulevard du General Lclerc
9252 Neuilly-Sur-Seine, Cedex
France

Dr. Bernd von Droste
Division of Ecological Sciences
Unesco
Place de Fontenoy 7
75700 Paris, France

Dr. Hans Bibelrither
Director, Bavarian National Park
8356 Spiegilau
Fed. Rep. of Germany

Dr. Wolfgang E. Burhenne
Adenaueraiiee 214
D5300 Bonn
Fed. Rep. of Germany

Dr. Emmanuel Asibey
Chief Administrator
Ghana Forestry Comm.
P.O. Box M.239
Ministry Post Office
Accra, Ghana

Dr. C. Cassios
Head of National Parks Section
3-5 Hippocratous Street
Athens
Greece

Mr. J.W. Wholey
Assistant Director
for Dir. Agriculture & Fisheries
393 Canton Rd 12th Fl.
Kowloon, Hong Kong

Dr. S.K. Jain
Director
Botanical Survey of India
P.O. Botanic Garden
Howrah-711103, India

Mr. N.D. Jayal
Joint Secretary
Dept. of Environment
Tochology Bhavan
New Mehrauli Raod
New Delhi 110016 India

Pushp Kumar
Conservator of Forests (WL)
Andhia Pradesh
Hyderabad
500004 India

Dr. G.M. Oza
General Education Center
M.S. Univ. of Baroda
Baroda -390-002 India

H.S. Panwar
Director Project Tiger
Ministry of Agriculture
Mastri, Bhavan, New Delhi
India

M.K. Ranjitsinh
Government of Madhya Pradesh
Dept. of Forests
Vallabh Bhavan
Bhopal
India

R.K. Rao
Director
Central Crocodile Institute
Hyderabad
500265, India

Vinod Behari Saharia
Director Wildlife Institute India
Forest Research Institute
Dehradun
248006 India

V.D. Sharma
Conservator of Forests
and Wildlife
Rajasthan
Jaipur, India

Mr. Samar Singh
Government of India
Ministry of Agriculture
& Irrigation
New Delhi - 110 001 India

Mr. Wartono Kadri
Director of Nature Conservation and
Wildlife Management
Department Pertanina
Direktorat Jenderal Kehutanan
Jalan Salemba Raya 16 TlLP
Alamat Kawat
Ditjenkeh, Jakarta Indonesia

Dr. Ronald Petocz
P.O. Box 525
Jayapura
Indonesia

Dr. Soedjarwo
Director General of Industry
Department Pertanina
Direktorat Jenderal Kehutanan
Jalan Salemba Raya 16 TlLP
Alamat Kawat
Ditjenkeh, Jakarta Indonesia

Ms. Jane Blunden
Castle Blunden
Kilkenny
Ireland

Mr. Gilbert Child
Wildlife and National Parks Officer
FAO, Via Della Terme di Casacalla
Rome 00100
Italy

Mr. M.A. Flores Rodas
Assistant Director-General
Forestry Dept., Food and Agriculture Organization of
the United Nations
Via della terme di Caracalla 00100
Rome, Italy

Mr. Francisco Framarin
Gran Paradiso National Park
via delle Rocca 47
10123 Torino, Italy

Dr. Walter Frigo
Stevio National Park
via Monte Braulio 56
23032 Bormio, Italy

Dr. Bartolotti Lucio
Parks Service Dept.
Ministry of Agriculture and
Forests
via Carducci 5
00187 Rome
Italy

Dr. F. Nazzaro
Institute of Zoology
Rome University
Viale dell 'Universita
Rome 32, Italy

Mr. Franco Tassi
Comitato Parchi Nazionali
Vicolo del Curato 6
00l86 Rome, Italy

Mrs. Tassi
c/o above address

Dr. H.H. Roth
Wildlife and National Parks
Adviser to Ivory Coast
04 BP 1240 - Abidjan 04
Ivory Coast

Dr. Osamu Ikenouye
Chairman, Marine Parks Centre of Japan
Toranomon Denke Building
2-8-1 Toranomon
Minato-ku
Tokyo, Japan

Professor Nobua Kumamoto
Visiting Professor to Tulane Law School
Hokkaigakuen University
Asahimachi 4, Sappora
Japan

Susuma Takahashi
Branch Chief of Research in Planning
Natural Parks Planning Division
Nature Conservation Bureau
Environment Agency
3-1-1, Kasumigaseki, Chiyoda-ku
Tokyo, Japan

Ryogo Wakajima
Counselor for Technical Affairs
Planning and Coordination Division
Nature Conservation Bureau
Environment Agency
3-1-1, Kasumigaseki, Chiyode-ku
Tokyo, Japan

Mr. Maher Z. Abu Jafar
The Royal Society for the
Conservation of Nature
P.O. Box 6354
Amman, Jordan

Dr. Harvey Croze
Global Environment Monitoring System
UNEP
P.O. Box 30552
Nairobi, Kenya

Dr. Iain Douglas-Hamilton
African Elephant Specialist Group
P.O. Box 546167
Nairobi, Kenya

Dr. Walter Lusigi
Project Coordinator
Unesco Regional Office for Science and Technology for
   Africa
P.O. Box 30592
Nairobi, Kenya

Dr. Robert Malpas
African Wildlife Leadership
Foundation
P.O. Box 48177
Nairobi, Kenya

Mr. Reuben Olembo
UNEP, P.O. Box 30552
Nairobi
Kenya

Mr. Fred Pertet
Co-Head, Wildlife Planning Unit
Ministry of Environment
and Natural Resources
P.O. Box 42076
Nairobi, Kenya

Mrs. Pertet
c/o above address

Mr. Peter Thacher
Global Environmental Monitoring System
UNEP
P.O. Box 30552
Nairobi, Kenya

Dr. David Western
Animal Research & Conservation
Centre
P.O. Box 48177 Embassy House
Nairobi, Kenya

Mr. Kyongbin Yim
Vice President
The National Parks Association
of Korea
2-97 Cha gjon-dong, Mapo-ku
Seoul 121, Republic of Korea

Park Chil-Sung
The National Parks Association
of Korea
45 Daechi Myon Chune
Yangbun, Chungnam
Republic of Korea

Mr. Oh yo Whan
P.O. Box 177
Dong Daz Moon
Seoul 121, Republic of Korea

Prof. Yongki Kim
Professor of Songkyungkwan University
2-97 Cha gjon-dong, Mapo-ku
Seoul 121, Republic of Korea

Mr. Song Young Han
Local Administrative Officer (Gov't)
2-97 Cha gjon-dong, Mapo-ku
Seoul 121, Republic of Korea

Mr. Shihun Park
President of Korea Landscape Co. Ltd.
2-97 Cha gjon-dong, Mapo-ku
Seoul 121, Republic of Korea

Mr. Kim Sang-soan
Construction Bureau - Director
2-97 Cha gjon-dong
Mapo-ku
Seoul 121, Republic of Korea

Mr. Jangin Moon
Vice President of Korea Nat.
Pk. Assoc. Room 502
Namkang Building 32-2 Mugyodong Jungku
Seoul 121, Republic of Korea

Ms. Samira Omar
Kuwait Institute for
Scientific Research
P.O. Box 24885
Safat, Kuwait

Mr. A.J.E. Estacio
Servicos Florestais E.
Agricolas De Macau
Rua Central 107, Macau

Mr. Joseph Andriamampianina
Direction des eaux et forts
B.P. 175, Universit Madagascar
Antananarivo, Madagascar

Mr. Alfred Kombe (Chief Game Warden)
Dept. of National Parks and Wildlife
P.O. Box 30131
Lilongwe 3, Malawi

Dr. Willie K. Wpato
Secretary for Forestry and Natural
Resources
Private Bag 350
Wilongwe 3, Malawi

Mr. Lamri Ali
National Parks Board
Box 626
Kota Kinabalu, Sabah
Malaysia

Mr. H.J. Shamshuddin Ahmad Buang
Permanent Secretary
Ministry of Forestry
Kementerian Kehutanan
Kuching, Sarawak
Malaysia

Mrs. Buang
c/o above address

Dr. Ong Jin Eong
School of Biological Sciences
Universiti Sains Malaysia
Minden, Penang, Malaysia

Dr. Francis Liew
Deputy Director, Sabah National Parks
P.O. Box 626
Kota Kinabalu
Sabah, Malaysia

Dr. Clive Marsh
Wildlife Officer
Box 1623 Sabah Foundation, Likas Bay
Kota Kinabalu, Malaysia

Dr. Napier Shelton
c/o United States Embassy
AIA Building, 10th floor
Kuala Lumpur
Malaysia

Mr. G.S. de Silva
The Park Warden
P.O. Box 768, Sandakan
Sabah, East Malaysia
Malaysia

Mr. Gurmit Singh
Environmental Protection Society
Malaysia
P.O. Box 382
Jalan Sultan, Petaling Jaya
Selangor Malaysia

Abang Haji Kassim Morshidi
National Parks and Wildlife Office
Jalan Gartac
Kuching, Sarawak
East Malaysia

Mrs. Morshidi
c/o above address

Dr. Anthea Phillips
Park Ecologist
Sabah National Parks
Kinabalu National Park
P.O. Box 626
Kota Kinabalu, Sabah
Malaysia

Ms. Gillian Radcliffe
Bako National Park
National Parks & Wildlife Office
Valan Gartak
Kuching, Sarawak
East Malaysia

Dr. A.W. Owadally
Conservator of Forests
Forestry Service
Curepipe, Mauritius

Mr. Rabi B. Bista, Ecologist
Dept. of National Parks and
Wildlife Conservation
P.O. Box 860
Kathmandu, Nepal

Upreti Biswan
Director General
Dept. National Parks and Wildlife
Conservation
Nepal

Mr. Thirthay Maskay
Senior Warden
P.O. Box 860
Kathmandu, Nepal

Mr. Hemanta R. Mishra
Dept. of National Parks and Wildlife
Conservation
Banesnor
Kathmandu, Nepal

Mr. R.J. Benthem
Vice-Chairman
IUCN Commission on Environmental
Planning
Adam Van Delenstraat 36, 4024 JB
ECK Enwiel, Netherlands

Mr. A. Boer
Head of the Div. on Physical
Planning and Land Use
Dept. of Nature and Landscape-Conserv.
Min. of Culture, Rec. and
Soc. Welfare (CRM)
p/a Sir Winston Churchill Ave 362
2284 JN Rijswijk, Netherlands

Mrs. Boer
c/o above address

Mr. Hans de Iongh
Voorstraat 19
Ysselstein
Netherlands

Mr. C.F. Kleisterlee
Chairman of the Dutch Commission
on National Parks
c/o Min. of Culture, Recreation &
Social Welfare (CRM)
Sir Winston Churchill Ave 362
Rijswijk, Netherlands

Mrs. Kleisterlee
c/o above address

Mr. Eric Newton
Karpata Ecological Center
Bonaire, Netherlands Antilles

Prof. Claus Stortenbeker
Stroocaan 2
Arnhem, Netherlands

Dr. Ing H.D. Van Boheman
Holterchans 11
3432 Ex Nieuwegein
Netherlands

Mr. Tom van 't Hoff
Netherlands Antilles National Parks
Foundation
P.O. Box 154
Bonaire, Netherlands Antilles

Dr. Arthur Dahl
South Pacific Commission
BP 5, Noumea
New Caledonia

Dr. Carolyn Burns, Chairman
Nature Conservation Council
P.O. Box 12-200
Wellington North
New Zealand

Dr. James Clad
91 Ellice Street
Wellington
New Zealand

Hon. Jonathan Elworthy
Minister of Lands
Office of the Minister
Parliament Buildings
Wellington, New Zealand

Mrs. Judith Elworthy
c/o above address

Ms. Julia Gardner
Dept. of Geography
University of Canterbury
Christchurch
New Zealand

Mr. Keith Garratt
Dept. of Lands & Survey
Private Bag
Wellington
New Zealand

Mr. Graham Grant
Sec. to Elworthy
Minister of Lands
Office of the Minister
Wellington, New Zealand

Mr. John Hubbard
c/o Nature Conservation Council
P.O. Box 12-200
Wellington North
New Zealand

Mr. Bruce Jefferies
Chief Ranger
Tongariro National Park
Park Headquarters
Mount Ruatehu
New Zealand

Mr. P.H.C. Lucas
Director-General
Dept. of Lands and Survey
Private Bag
Charles Fergusson Building
Wellington, New Zealand

Dr. Leslie Molloy
New Zealand National Parks and
Reserves Authority
P.O. Box 2593
Wellington
New Zealand

Mr. David A. Thom
Chairman
National Parks & Reserves Authority
P.O. Box 4498
Auckland, New Zealand

Ing. Reynaldo Arostegui
Dept. Aires Silvestre y Fauna
KM 13 1/2 Carretera Norte-Irena
Managua
Nicaragua

Dr. Ibrahim Najada
Director
c/o Direction des Eaux et Forts
B.P. 578, Niamey
Niger

Dr. John Newby
c/o Direction des Eaux et Forts
B.P. 578, Niamey
Niger

Mr. Jan Abrahamsen
Nature Conservation Dept.
Royal Ministry of Environment
Oslo 1, Norway

Mr. Arne Dalfelt
NORAD
P.O. Prose 8142
Oslo 1, Norway

Mr. Olav Gjaerevoll
Professor, Chairman of the
State Council of Nature Conservation
Valentinlysteveien 9, 7000
Trondheim, Norway

Mr. Knut Kvalvagnaes
Norwegian Institute
for Water Research
P.O. Box 333, Blinden
Olso 3, Norway

Mr. Magnar Norderhaug
Ministry of Environment
Oslo-Dep. OSLO 1
Norway

Mr. Olan Saetersdal
Head of Delegation
Nature Conservation Division
Royal Ministry of Environment
Oslo 1, Norway

Mr. Soaud Abdel Aziz Al-Kindy
Council for Conservation
The Palace, P.O. Box 246
Oman

Mr. R.H. Daly
Adviser for Conservation
of the Environment
Sultanate of Oman - Muscat
P.O. Box 246 Oman

Mrs. R.H. Daly
c/o above address

Mr. Ali Salim Hosni
Council for Conservation
P.O. Box 79
Municipality of the Capital
Oman

Mr. Masood Ahmed Mirza
Secretary
National Council for Conservation
of Wildlife
Ministry of Food and Agriculture
Islamabad, Pakistan

Mr. Abdul Latif Rao
Conservator (Wildlife)
National Council for Conservation
of Wildlife in Pakistan
Ministry of Food, Agriculture
and Cooperatives
Pakistan

Dr. Ira Rubinoff
Director
Smithsonian Tropical Research Institute
Balboa, Box 2072
Panama City, Panama

Dr. Peter Eaton
University of Papua New Guinea
Port Moresby
P.O. Box 402 University
Papua New Guinea

Mr. John Mark Genolagani
Marine Biologist
Head of Marine Conservation Programme
National Parks Services
Ministry of Environment & Conservation
P.O. Box 5749
National Capital District
Papua New Guinea

Dr. Navu Kwapena
First Assistant Director (Wildlife)
Dept. of Lands, Surveys and Environment
P.O. Box 2585
Konedobu
Papua New Guinea

Beka Siki
Wau Ecology Institute
P.O. Box 77
Wau, Papua New Guinea

Dr. Marc J. Dourojeanni
Profesor Principal
Departamento de Manejo Forestal
Universidad Nacional Agraria
La Molina, Apartado Postal 456
Lima, Peru

Ing. Carlos Ponce del Prado
Departamento de Manejo Forestal
Universidad Nacional Agraria
La Molina, Apartado Postal 456
Lima, Peru

Dr. Angel C. Alcala
Vice-President
Silliman University
Dumaguetre City
Philippines

Ms. Cecille M. Elum
Head, National Secretariat
Natural Resources Conservation
Office, Manila, Philippines

Mr. Daniele Perrot-Maitre
Resource Economist
National Conservation Strategy
7246 Malugay Street
Makati, Manila
Philippines

Mr. Aniano Poliquit
Head Executive Assistant
Ministry of Natural Resources
Quezon City
Philippines

Mr. Ibarra T.C. Poliquit
Executive Director
Haribon Society, Maicati
Metro Manila, Philippines

Mr. Bruce E. White
Consultant, Haribon Society
Office of the President
National Conservation Strategy
7248 Malugay Street
Makati, Manila, Philippines

Mrs. White
Consultant, Haribon Society
c/o Filipinas Journal
Room 303, Makati Stock Exchange
Ayala Avenue, Makati
Manila, Philippines

Mr. Jose M. Vasconcellos
President
Servico Nacional De Parques
Rue de Lapa 73
Lisbon, Portugal

Dr. Muhammad Al-Kahtani
President
King Faisal University
Eastern Province
P.O. Box 1982, Dammam
Saudi Arabia

Mohammed Ali Melgat
Kingdom of Saudi Arabia
Asir National Park
Saudi Arabia

Ibrahim Ahmed Al-Sayed
General Director of Tourism Dept.
Assir Region, Saudi Arabia

Mr. Andr Dupuy, Directeur
Service des parcs nationaux
B.P. 5135
Dakar Fann, Senegal

Dr. Jose Miguel Gonzalez
c/o Marina 7-2e
Edificio Hamilton
Santa Cruz de Tenerife
Canary Islands, Spain

Don Emilio (Luque) Hernandez
Director General de Urbanismo
c/o Marina 7-2e
Edificio Hamilton
Santa Cruz de Tenerife
Canary Islands, Spain

Dr. Francisco Manuel Rodriguez
Ministerio de Agricultura
Servicio de Agricultura
ICONA Gran via de San Francisco
No. 35, Madrid, Spain

Mr. Don Isidoro Sanchez Garcia
Servicio P. Icona
ICONA Gran Via de San Fransisco
No 35, Madrid, Spain

Mrs. Sanchez
c/o above address

C.V. Jayawardhana
Assistant Director
Dept. of Wildife Conservation
Anagarika Dharmapola Mawatha
Sri Lanka

Malcolm Jensen
Environment Officer
Mahaweli Authority
248 Galle Road
Colombo 4, Sri Lanka

Robert Olivier
Consultant
147 Turret Road
Colombo 7, Sri Lanka

Mr. Krishnepersad Mohadin
Acting Head, Nature Conservation Dept.
Dept. of Development
P.O. Box 436, Paramaribo
Suriname

Mr. Mats Segnestam
Executive Director
The Swedish Society for the
Conservation of Nature
Kungsholms Strand 125
S-112 34 Stockholm
Sweden

Dr. Andrew C. Podzorski
Hilleshog Forest Division
Box 302 S-261 23
Landskrona, Sweden

Dr. Luc Hoffman
WWF
Av. du Mont Blanc
1196 Gland
Switzerland

Miss Maya Hoffman
Augustinergasse 1
Basel 4051, Switzerland

Mr. David Babu
Tanzanian National Parks
P.O. Box 3134
Arusha, Tanzania

Felix A. Lyimo
College of African Wildlife Management
Box 3031
Moshi, Tanzania

Mr. Albert Mongi
Director, Tanzania National Parks
P.O. Box 3134
Arusha, Tanzania

Mr. G.T. Mosha
Acting Principal
College of African Wildlife Management
P.O. Box 3031
Moshi, Tanzania

Dr. James Thorsell
College of African Wildlife Management
Box 3031
Moshi, Tanzania

Suvat Singhapant
Wildlife Conservation Division
Royal Forest Dept
Bangkok, Thailand

Mr. Kasem Snidvongs
Secretary General
National Environment Board
Soi Pracha Sumpun 4
Rama VI Road, Bangkok 4
Thailand

Miss Prapasri Sirijaraya
Faculty of Education
Chulalongkorn Univ.
Phya Thai Road
Bangkok 5, Thailand

Toshiro Kojima
Environmental Legislation
Expect Environmental Coordinating
Unit ESCAP - United Nations Bldg.
Ragadamnern Ave, Bangkok
Thailand

Dr. Reynaldo M. Lesaca
Regional Director
UNEP Regional Officer (Asia & Pacific)
UNEP Building
Rajodamnern Ave
Bangkok, Thailand

Dr. Hédia Baccar
Conseillère cooptée de l'UICN
Attaché de Cabinet
Ministère de l'Agriculture
Tunis, Tunisia

Kacem Slaheddine
Chef du Service de la Chasse
et des Parcs Nationaux
Direction des Forets
Ministere Agriculture
Tunis, Tunisia

Prof. F.I.B. Kayanja
Dept. of Vet. Medicine
Makveve University
P.O. Box 7026
Kampala, Uganda

Acaemician Vladyslov Gorokhov
12 rue Pavlik Morozov
123376 Moscow, USSR

Dr. Ivan A. Gavva
Director All-Union Research
Institute of Nature Conservation
and Reserves
USSR Ministry of Agriculture
142790 P.O. Vllar, Moscow.
USSR

Janet Barber
WWF-UK
Head of Information & Conservation
11-13, Ockford Road
Godalming
United Kingdom

Dr. Morton Boyd
Nature Conservancy Council
12, Hope Terrace
Edinburgh EH9 2AS
United Kingdom

Ms. Catherine Caufield
New Scientist Magazine
London, United Kingdom

Dr. Nigel Collar
Int. Council for Bird Preservation
219C Huntingdon Road
Cambridge, United Kingdom

Dr. J.T. Coppock
Prof of Geography, UIA Edinburgh
High School Yard
Edinburgh EHINP
United Kingdom

Mr. John Foster
Countryside Commission for Scotland
Battleby, Redgorton
Perth PHl 3EW
United Kingdom

Mr. F.P. Gaekwad
c/o Mrs. C. Hill
Flat Sixteen
20 Sloane Gardens
London SW1 W8DJ, U.K.
United Kingdom

Dr. Bryn Hugh Green
Senior Lecturer, Ecology and Conservatio
Wye College, University of London
Ashford, Kent
United Kingdom

Dr. Donald Harding
Dept. of Forestry and Wood Science
University College of North Wales
Bangor, Gwynedd L5Y 2UW
United Kingdom

Mr. Gren Lucas
Deputy Keeper, Herbarium
Royal Botanic Gardens
Kew, Richmond
Surrey, United Kingdom

Mr. Adrian Phillips
Director, Countryside Commission
John Dower House, Crescent Place
Cheltenham, Glos. GL50 3RA
United Kingdom

Mrs. C. Phillips
The Wildfowl Trust
Slimbridge, Glos.
United Kingdom

Mrs. Clare Richards
Assistant Coordinator, Ecoculture
16 Stanley Gardens
London, W.11
United Kingdom

Mr. John Rudge
Nature Conservancy Council
19/20 Belgrave Square
London SWIX 8PY
United Kingdom

Mr. Hugh Synge
Royal Botanic Garden, Kew
Richmond, Surrey
United Kingdom

Mr. Jeffrey D. Tiberi
Park Ranger
Dept. of Agriculture and Fisheries
Botanical Gardens
P.O. Box 834, Hamilton 5
Bermuda

Ms. Sue Wells
Co-compiler Invertebrate RDB
Conservation Monitoring Centre
219c, Huntingdon Road
Cambridge, United Kingdom

Kenneth Anderson
807 Hyde Merrit Rd.
Cheyenne, Wyoming 8007
USA

Mr. G. Ray Arnett
Asst. Secretary of the Interior
Dept. of the Interior
Washington D.C. 20240, USA

Prof. Edward S. Ayensu
Director
Office of Biological Cons.
RM W510, Smithsonian Institution
10th & Constitution
Washington D.C. 20560, USA

Dr. J. Leroy Balzer
Director, Environmental Quality
Utah International
550 California St.
San Francisco, CA. 94104, USA

Mr. James N. Barnes
Executive Director
The Antarctica Project
624 9th St. N.W. 5th Floor
Washington, D.C. 20001, USA

Dr. George Binney
P.O. Box 16
Tumacacori
Arizona 85640, USA

Mr. F. William Burley
Director of Science
The Nature Conservancy International Division
4 East Loudoun Street
Leesburg, VA. 22075, USA

Mr. Robert Cahn
Route 3, Box 316
Leesburg, VA. 22075, USA

Mrs. Pat Cahn
c/o above address

Dr. Archie Carr III
New York Zoological Society
185th St., Southern Building
Bronx, N.Y. 10460, USA

Dr. Harold J. Coolidge
38 Standley Street
Beverly, Mass. 01915, USA

Mrs. Martha A. Coolidge
c/o above address

Bradley R. Cross
Wildland Management Consultant
P.O. Box 1303
Ann Arbor, MI. 48106, USA

Dr. Raymond F. Dasmann
116 Meadow Road
Santa Cruz, CA. 95060, USA

William O. Deshler
4001 Pasadena Drive
Boise, Idaho 83705, USA

Mr. Russel Dickenson
Director
US National Park Service
Dept. of the Interior
Washington D.C. 20240, USA

Mrs. Russel Dickenson
c/o above address

Mr. John Earhart
US Peace Corps
P.O. Box 842
Corona Del Mar, CA. 92625, USA

Mrs. Anne Getty Earhart
c/o above address

Dr. James R. Fazio
Dept. Head and Associate Professor
Dept. of Wildland Recreation Management
College of Forestry, Wildlife and Range Sciences, University of Idaho
Moscow, Idaho 83843, USA

Dr. Nancy Foster
Office of Coastal Zone Management
NOAA
2001 Wisconsin Ave. N.W. Page Bldg 1
Room 336, US Dept. of Commerce
Washington, D.C. 20235, USA

Dr. Robert Goodland
World Bank
1818 H St. N.W.
Washington D.C. 20433, USA

C.R. Gutermuth
2111 Jefferson Davis Highway
Arlington, VA. 22202, USA

Mrs. C.R. Gutermuth
c/o above address

Mr. David Hales
School of Natural Resources
University of Michigan
Ann Arbor, MI. 48109, USA

Mr. Bruce Howard
President
Save-the-Redwoods-League
114 Sansome Street, Room 605
San Francisco, CA. 94104, USA

Mrs. Howard
c/o above address

Mr. Brent Ingram
287 Downey St
San Francisco, CA. 94117, USA

Dr. Jeffery A. Kennedy
Environmental Planner
Natural Land and Water Reserves System
University of California
Berkeley, CA. 94720, USA

Mrs. Barbara J. Lausche
9716 Braddock Road
Silver Spring, Maryland 20903, USA

Mr. Henry P. Little
Western Regional Representative
The Nature Conservancy of Hawaii
1026 Nuuanu Ave., Suite 201
Honolulu, Hawaii 96817, USA

Mr. Michael McCloskey
The Sierra Club
530 Bush St.
San Francisco, CA. 94108, USA

Mrs. Maxine McCloskey
c/o above address

Ms. Lisa McGimsey
The Trust for Public Land
82 2nd St.
San Fransisco, CA. 94105, USA

Ms. K. McNamara
Forestry Adviser for Asia Bureau
USAID - State Dept.
Washington, D.C. 20523, USA

Mr. Guillemere Mann
Nature Conservancy International Program
4 East Loudoun Street
Leesburg, VA 22075, USA

Mr. Robert Milne
Chief, Division of International Affairs
National Park Service
U.S. Dept. of the Interior
Washington D.C. 20240, USA

Dr. Russel Mittermeier
Dept. of Anatomical Sciences
Health Sciences Center
State University of New York
Stony Brook, N.Y. 11794, USA

Mrs. Mittermeier
c/o above address

Dr. Bernard Nietschmann
Dept. of Geography
University of California
501 Earth Sciences Bldg.
Berkeley, CA. 94720, USA

Mrs. Nietschmann
c/o above address

Dr. Francisco V. Palacio
Director
Triniloa Center for Coastal Studies
in Latin America
RSMAS - University of Miami
Virginia Key, Miami, FL. 33149
USA

Mr. Paul C. Pritchard
President
National Parks and Conservation
Association
1701 Eighteenth Str.
N.W. Washington D.C. 20009, USA

Mrs. Pritchard
c/o above address

Dr. Anders G.J. Rhodin
Museum of Comparative Zoology
Harvard University
Cambridge, Mass. 02138, USA

Mrs. Rhodin
c/o above address

Mr. John N. Shores
Wildland Management Center Staff
1407 Morton Ave.
Ann Arbor, MI. 48104, USA

Mr. Zane G. Smith Jr.
Regional Forester
Pacific SW Region
630 Sansome Ave.
San Francisco, CA. USA

Mr. Tom D. Thomas
Director
International Seminar on National Parks
School of Natural Resources
University of Michigan
Ann Arbor, MI. 48109, USA

Dr. Miklos D. F. Udvardy
Dept. of Biology
California State University
6000 Jay Street
Sacramento, CA. 95819, USA

Dr. Edgar Wayburn
Past President of Sierra Club
314 30th Avenue
San Francisco, CA. 94121, USA

Mrs. Peggy Wayburn
c/o above address

Dr. Gary Wetterberg
National Park Service
U.S. Dept. of the Interior
Washington D.C. 20240, USA

Mrs. Wetterberg
c/o above address

Dr. Alan White
Environment & Policy Institute
East-West Center
1777 East-West Road
Honolulu, HI. 96848, USA

Mr. Michael Wright
WWF-US
1601 Connecticut Ave. N.W.
Washington D.C. 20009, USA

Mr. Inoussa Barry
Direction des Parc Nationaux
Reserves de Faune
Ministere de l'Environment
et du Tourisme
B.P. 7044 Ouagadougou
Upper Volta

Mr. Clive Spinage
Senior Wildlife Admin.
UNDP (project 78/008)
B.P. 575
Ouagadougou, Upper Volta

Sra. Cecilia de Blohm
Director - Fundacin para la
Defensa de la Naturaleza (FUDENA)
Apartado 70376
Consejera para Centro y Sudamrica
Apartado 64, Caracas 1010-A
Venezuela

Jesus Delgado
Universidad Nacionales de Los Llanos
Occidentales
Guanare, Estado Portuguesa
Venezuela

Mr. José R. Garcia
Director de Parque Nacionales
Av. Francisco De Miranda
Caracas 1062, Venezuela

Nelson Hernandez Nava
Garrero 28 No 13-11
Barquisimeto
Venezuela

Mr. Miguel Rodriguez
Residencial Venezuela
EDF. Orinoco APTO. 3-D
Bararida, Barquisimeto 3002
Venezuela

Mrs. Elsa Salas de White
Gerente Parque del Oeste
Calle Londres-Resd. el SAman
Aprt 2A las mercedes
Caracas, Venezuela

Powis de Tenbossche
BP 68
Kinshasa
Zaire

Dr. Graham Child
Director, Dept. of National Parks
and Wildlife Management
P.O. Box 8365, Harare
Causeway, Zimbabwe

PRESS

Ms. Sue Arnold
Mr. Graham Bicknell
Australia

Jon Tinker
Kath Adams
John McCormick
Sumi Krishna Chauhan
Earthscan
10 Percy St.
London, W1P 0NR
United Kingdom

STAFF

Mr. Harold Eidsvik
Environment Canada
Parks Canada - LTC Bldg. - 25th floor
Ottawa, K1A 1G2
Canada

Mrs. Malvina Eidsvik
c/o above address

Mr. Bill Henwood
6115-141 Street
Edmonton, Alberta
Canada T6H 4A6

Mr. Richard Herring
Dept. of the Environment
Canadian Forestry Service
Place Vicent Massey, 19th Floor
Ottawa, Ont. KlA OH4
Canada

Ms. Dawna Jones
6115-141 Street
Edmonton, Alberta
Canada T6H 4A6

Ms. Catherine Johnston
51 bis Avenue de Segur
Paris, France

Mr. Cyrille de Klemm
21 rue de Dantzig
75015 Paris, France

Mr. Alan Robinson
National Parks Development Project
c/o PPA
Kotak Pos 320
Denpasar, Bali, Indonesia

Mrs. Karen Robinson
c/o above address

Effendy Sumardja
Senior Policy Officer
Directorate of Nature Conservation
J1 Juanda No. 9
Bogor, Indonesia

Dr. Maarten Bijlveld
Executive Officer
Commission on Ecology
IUCN, 1196 Gland, Switzerland

Mr. Charles de Haes
Director General
World Wildlife Fund
1196 Gland, Switzerland

Mr. Jeffrey McNeely
Executive Officer
Commission on National Parks and Protected Areas,
  CNPPA
IUCN, 1196 Gland
Switzerland

Mr. Daniel Navid
Executive Officer
Commission on Environmental Planning
IUCN, 1196 Gland
Switzerland

Ms. Sue Rallo
Secretary, CNPPA
IUCN, 1196 Gland
Switzerland

Mr. Don Hinrichsen
Editor, AMBIO
The Royal Swedish Academy of Sciences
Box 50005, S-104 05 Stockholm
Sweden

Mr. Robert F. Scott
Executive Officer, SSC
IUCN, 1196 Gland
Switzerland

Ms. Raisa Scriabine
Director, IUCN Public Affairs
1196 Gland, Switzerland

Dr. Lee Talbot, Director General
IUCN, 1196 Gland
Switzerland

Mr. Paul Wachtel
WWF
1196 Gland, Switzerland

Mr. Bernardo Zentilli
IUCN, 1196 Gland
Switzerland

Mr. Jeremy Harrison
Research Officer, PADU
Herbarium, Royal Botanic Gardens
Kew, Richmond, Surrey, TW3 9AE
United Kingdom

Dr. Kenton Miller
Chairman, CNPPA
School of Natural Resources
University of Michigan
Ann Arbor, MI 48109
USA

Mrs. Jean Packard
Editor, PARKS Magazine
4058 Elizabeth Lane
Fairfax, VA. 22032
USA

Annex II.
Awards For Protected Area Professionals

1. INTRODUCTION

We all know people who are doing an outstanding job in managing protected areas. But who else knows these people? While a few prominent individuals receive wide acclaim, a ranger or manager who is performing above and beyond the call of duty is usually recognized only by his immediate superior; seldom is his performance given even national recognition, much less international acclaim.

At the Second World Conference on National Parks, held in Grand Teton National Park in September 1972, a number of international awards were presented, in two categories. International conservation leaders whose work has advanced the national park movement around the world included:

TSUYOSHI TAMURA, Vice President, National Park Association of Japan
HAROLD J. COOLIDGE, Honorary President, IUCN
JEAN-PAUL HARROY, Past Chairman, International Commission on National Parks
JACQUES VERSCHUREN, Director General Zaire National Parks
FRANK FRASER DARLING, Ecologist and Author
ENRIQUE BELTRAN, Director, Mexican Institute of Renewable Natural Resources.

In the second category, the Centennial Commission honoured five younger national park officials in recognition of their leadership and accomplishments in their own countries. They included:

JESUS B. ALVAREX, JR., Philippines
MARIO ANDRÉS BOZA, Costa Rica

ZEKAI BAYER, Turkey
PEREZ M. OLINDO, Kenya
PHAIROT SUVANAKORN, Thailand

2. AWARDS AT THE BALI CONGRESS

A Committee was established at the World National Parks Congress under the Chairmanship of Dr. Emanuel Asibey (Ghana). Members included John Morton-Boyd (Scotland); Angela Quintao (Brazil); Clive Spinage (Central African Republic); Carolyn Burns (New Zealand); Birandra Singh (Fiji); and John Sinclair (Australia). Awards were presented on behalf of the Congress by Dr. Harold Jefferson Coolidge, Honorary President of IUCN, in three categories:

2.1. Special achievement awards

The Committee recognized that there were a few unsung individuals who had made such an important contribution to international protected area conservation that they deserved a special award. These awards, accompanied by a wooden plaque, went to the following:

FRED M. PACKARD (USA). Fred Packard was the US Secretary for the IUCN Commission on National Parks and Protected Areas. He was a loyal friend to all Parks visitors to the US, and was greatly loved because of his interest and cooperation. He established strong ties between the US National Park Service and several sister agencies in other countries. He created the "Parks Valor Award," which has now been re-named the "Fred M. Packard International Parks Merit Award" in his honour. (The award was made posthumously, and was received by his wife, Mrs. Jean Packard).

JEAN-PAUL HARROY (Belgium). Jean-Paul Harroy for many years directed IUCN's National Parks Commission and inspired countries to develop protected natural areas. He built up the world list of national parks, and made it a significant goal which inspired nations to designate areas which would qualify for the list. He remains a dedicated leader in the field of national parks and his influence will be long recognized.

ROBERT I. STANDISH (USA). Bob Standish was the founding editor of PARKS Magazine, the professional journal which unites all those interested in national parks. He built up the magazine from an idea into a reality, tirelessly collecting material from around the world, building up the distribution list, and ensuring that the publication was always of high quality. His retirement from the Editorship of PARKS in 1982 marks the passing of an era.

DR. SOEDJARWO AND HIS STAFF (Indonesia). Soedjarwo is the Indonesian Director General of Forestry, responsible for providing the leadership which has guided one of the most impressive nature conservation efforts anywhere in the tropics. Beginning with a tiny staff and few protected areas, Soedjarwo has built the Directorate of Nature Conservation into a large, well-funded agency with some 11.4 million ha of the world's richest and most diverse natural habitats.

2.2. Special awards for long and distinguished service

The Committee decided that it was appropriate to recognize at the Congress a number of individuals who have had particularly long and distinguished careers. It is hoped that this award would be institutionalized, and made at each subsequent Congress as well. The recipients:

MYLES J. DUNPHY (Australia). Myles Dunphy is recognized for championing the cause of national parks in Australia for most of his life; from 1916 until a few years ago, Mr. Dunphy waged an active campaign for a state-wide system of national parks containing wilderness areas, and completed wilderness parks. His voluntary efforts inspired others and gave impetus for the establishment of a comprehensive system of national parks in New South Wales, Australia. Although ably assisted by others, Dunphy was essentially a "loner", initiating most of the proposals, mapping and describing, publishing and championing the cause of national parks. Mr. Dunphy was a central figure in bushwalking, which spawned the widespread environmental and conservation movement of today. It was largely Mr. Dunphy who forged the connection between bushwalking and concern to preserve the natural environment on which it depends and as the habitat of wildlife.

SIR CHARLES G. CONNELL (UK). Sir Charles Connell is recognized for his effective communication of national parks ideals and objectives to the public. A retired, distinguished Scottish lawyer, since the Second World War Sir Charles has devoted his spare time and energy to nature conservation in Scotland. In his 84th year, he still plays an active part in the business of the Scottish Wildlife Trust which he founded in 1966. The Trust is the only non-government organization in Scotland which caters to the full range of wildlife habitat, currently administering over 60 reserves. He contributed to the drafting of new nature conservation legislation in Britain between 1960 and 1975—a period of great advances with the Countryside Acts, the Nature Conservancy Council Act and Wild Creatures and Rare Plants Act. Sir Charles continues to campaign tirelessly for funds and projects the message of conservation regularly through journals. He is an inspiration to those who have the privilege of carrying on the great work he started.

DR. GEORGE RUHLE (USA). "Doc" Ruhle is recognized for his many services in communicating national parks ideals and objectives to public, and his inspiration to younger national park officers. Dr. Rhule has had 49 years of service with the United States National Parks Service and served as the first naturalist in a number of parks, including Glacier National Park. He has served the international conservation effort in Thailand, South Korea, China and India. Though he has officially retired, he still comes into the office every day and continues to serve as a model for many young conservationists.

FERGUS LOTHIAN (Canada). Fergus Lothian is recognized for his administrative service in the establishment and management of national parks and other protected areas, and for his undaunting efforts to preserve the national parks story of Canada for posterity. Mr. Lothian began work with the Department of the Interior in Canada in 1916. He transferred to the national parks branch in 1924. He worked in Ottawa throughout his career and became assistant Chief of the National Parks Service Division prior to his official retirement in 1966. He has continued to work on contract since then. He now has 58 years of service and has written a four-volume history of Parks Canada. At the age of 82, he continues to go to the office each day to work on volume five.

2.3. The Fred M. Packard International Park Merit Award

Founded as the "Valor Award" to honour parks personnel for acts of unusual courage involving a high degree of personal risk in the face of danger, the award was changed in 1982 to the "Fred M. Packard International Parks Merit Award"—the "Parks Merit Award" for short—to expand its scope and to honour the individual who started the award and established its endowment fund. This is the only award which has the objective of recognizing protected area professionals.

The Committee considered nominations—presented either before or during the Congress—for the

International Parks Merit Award for individuals from each of the world's eight biogeographic realms. A wide range of meritorious accomplishment was considered, including outstanding initiative in developing new programs, in improving relations with surrounding lands, in establishing new areas, in communicating protected area ideals and objectives to the public, and many others.

The Committee also reviewed the previous recipients of the Valor Award:

1980 INSA DIATTA and YANYA DANFA (Senegal). Their inscription read: "Demonstrating exceptional bravery in the face of heavy automatic gunfire, Insa Diatta and Yanya Danfa captured a team of poachers in Niokolo-Koba National Park. In bringing the case to court and prosecuting it successfully, they provided an outstanding example of how appropriate procedures can be used to promote the protection of Senegal's natural resources."

1981 JOSEPH KIOKO (Kenya). The inscription of Kioko's award read: "As warden of Amboseli Game Reserve, Joseph Kioko showed outstanding ability and dedication working with local people to ensure that the reserve was developed into a national park in harmony with the surrounding region, yielding meaningful benefits to the community, the nation and the world."

1981 DECEASED GUARDS OF VIGUNGA NATIONAL PARK (Zaire). The inscription read: "During the turmoil between 1960 and 1967, over twenty rangers gave their lives in the defense of Virunga National Park. Their valor in this critical period ensured the survival of a World Heritage Site for all humanity."

The 1982 Fred M. Packard International Parks Merit Award was presented to the following at Bali:

SGT. MAJ. PETER LOGWE and the Kidepo Valley National Park Ranger Force (Uganda). Sgt. Maj. Logwe is recognized for the team's long record of distinguished service in confronting well-armed aggressive poachers who enter the park locally and also from neighbouring countries. This ranger force has displayed numerous acts of courage, particularly over the past three years. Often outnumbered by better-armed poachers, this force has continually faced fire from automatic rifles, mortars, rocket launchers and machine guns as a result of which eight rangers have been killed in action over the past decade. In addition, in 1980, the force as a whole suffered during the famine which affected Karamoja; two of the rangers' children died of starvation, yet there are no recorded incidents of rangers poaching to feed themselves during that time. Peter Logwe, a ranger since 1969 and leader of the force since 1976, has consistently exposed himself to danger from ambush and exchange of fire.

FATEH SINGH RATHORE (India). Fateh Singh Rathore, the Field Director of Ranthambhor Tiger Reserve is recognized for his conscientious application to duty under adverse circumstances. With outstanding work he achieved effective anti-poaching, control of grazing, fire protection and development of wildfowl habitat through the eradication of water weeds and water conservation. Mr. Rathore was instrumental in bringing about the amicable relocation of a number of villages from the heart of the Tiger Reserve by providing adequate and suitable alternatives to the affected villages. His perseverance and tactful efforts over almost a decade have finally eliminated domestic and commercial grazing from the core area of the Ranthambhor Tiger Reserve in the face of initial opposition and antagonism. This antagonism was expressed most acutely in 1981 when he was seriously injured in a vicious assault by villagers while attempting to discourage their illegal commercial grazing practices. Notwithstanding this, on recovery, Fateh Singh returned to his post with an increased dedication to park values and ideals. Syed Ahmed, driver, Ranthambhor Tiger Reserve, is recognized for his bold and valorous act of shielding and rescuing Fateh Singh Rathore during a vicious assault with lathes and sticks by illegal grazers in the Tiger Reserve in September, 1981. Ahmed shielded Mr. Singh with his own body and was beaten with sticks, for which injuries he was later hospitalized. Without Mr. Ahmed's intervention, the Field Director's serious injuries could well have been fatal.

KEPALA SEKSIS OF INDONESIA (received by Yus Rostandi, Senior Kepala Seksi). The Kepala Seksis (Section Heads = Park Superintendent or Chief Warden) of Indonesia are recognized for the important work which they have carried out in designing and planning Indonesia's system of protected areas, and in the hope that the World National Parks Congress will help to encourage the field personnel of Indonesia's Directorate of Nature Conservation to implement, on the ground, the system which is now so impressive on the map.

SYLVANUS GORIO (Papua New Guinea). Sylvanus Gorio is recognized for his innovative management of parks. As a young graduate he joined the Papua New Guinea National Parks Board in 1968 as a park ranger. He became the first local Director of the Board in 1975. He has developed a system of National Parks and Reserves which has placed Papua New Guinea in the lead of this activity in the Oceanic Realm. He has also been a major figure in developing national parks and protected areas of many countries in the Oceanic Realm.

JAMES PETER STANTON (Australia). Jim Stanton is recognized for his innovative application of resource surveys to the planning of the Queensland park system. Stanton was transferred to the National Parks system of the National Parks and Wildlife Service of Queensland in 1967. With his rare capacity for detailed field work and dedication to the cause of national parks, he carried out the majority of assessments in the wide range of dissimilar Queensland ecosystems, resulting in a rapid growth of the network of Queensland's national parks and protected areas, and proposals to protect representative samples of all major Queensland habitats. He has applied his expertise and dedication to the cause of national parks and protected areas with energy, efficiency and courage, which have resulted in his unparalleled success in helping to extend the national park estate of Queensland.

DR. JOSE RAFAEL GARCIA (Venezuela). José Garcia is recognized for his innovative management of parks. The present Director of the National Parks Directorate of Venezuela, Garcia was appointed the first Director-Superintendent in a National Park in Venezuela in 1952. He has always been a strong advocate and defender of parks and protected areas. His leadership has resulted in the establishment of 26 national parks and 13 natural momuments as well a number of management policies of significance.

MIRAVALDO DE JESUS SIGUARA (Brazil). Miravaldo Siguara is recognized for his conscientious application to duty in the face of adverse circumstances. With very little formal education, Siguara entered the Bahia Forest Service in 1955. He worked hard in the face of grave difficulties and threats to his life for 21 years before he retired in 1981. He rose to the rank of Chief Guard. Through innovative initiative, undaunting courage and drive, with very little support and staff, he succeeded in effectively establishing the Monte Pascoal National Park of Brazil against pressures from loggers and hunters. Upon his official retirement in 1981, his sense of duty and undaunting devotion to national parks service constrained him to turn down a National Indian Foundation's offer of employment. He agreed to continue his hard work in the Una Biological Reserve which is faced with many of the problems and hard living conditions which Siguara overcame to get Monte Pascoal National Parks established.

3. OTHER AWARDS OF SIGNIFICANCE SINCE THE SECOND WORLD CONFERENCE

3.1. The J. Paul Getty Wildlife Conservation Prize

The "Nobel Prize of Conservation," the Getty Prize is awarded each year for outstanding achievement in wildlife and habitat conservation of international significance. The $50,000 prize is administered by WWF-US, with the winner selected by an international jury. Candidates for the Prize are evaluated from a diversity of standpoints, including the conservation of rare or endangered species and their habitats, the conservation of ecosystems, the increase in public awareness of the importance of the natural world, the establishment of conservation legislation, or the foundation of an organization or society of unusual importance to wildlife conservation. In all cases the accomplishment must be pioneering and substantial.

Winners of the Getty Prize

1982 Maria Teresa Jorge Padua and Paulo Nogiero Neto (Brazil)
1981 none
1980 Harold J. Coolidge (USA)
1979 Boonsong Lekagul (Thailand)
1978 Ian R. Grimwood (Kenya)

1977 Salim Ali (India)
1976 Felipe Benavides (Peru)

3.2. World Wildlife Fund Gold Medal

This award is WWF's highest, presented for highly meritorious and strictly personal services to the conservation of wildlife and natural resources. Recipients of the WWF Gold Medal since 1972:

1982 E. Max Nicholson (UK)
1981 Jean-Jacques Petter (France)
1980 George B. Schaller (USA)
1979 Sidney Holt (UK)
1978 Guy Mountfort (UK)
1977 Rudolf Schenkel (Switzerland)
1976 Arjan Singh (India)
1975 Michel Anna (France)
1974 Ann LaBastille (USA)
1973 Archie Carr (USA), José Carvalho (Brazil), Jack Vincent (South Africa)
1972 Andrey G. Bannikov (USSR), Ian R. Grimwood (UK/Kenya), Roger Tory Peterson (USA)

3.3. World Wildlife Fund Members of Honour

Appointed from among persons of great distinction in conservation or fields related to conservation. Among the recipients are the following professionally involved in protected areas:

1981 Wahajuddin A. Kermani (Pakistan)
1980 François Bourliere (France) and Roger Payne (USA)
1979 Harold J. Coolidge (USA)
1978 Eskandar Firouz (Iran), Bernhard Grzimek (FRG)
1976 HRH Prince Gyanendra Bir Bikram Shah (Nepal)
1975 Enrique Beltran (Mexico)

3.4. World Wildlife Fund Award for Conservation Merit

In May 1981, WWF-International instituted a new conservation award to honour people who receive no headlines for their behind-the-scenes work, yet who make substantial contributions and whose work should be recognized. An inscribed scroll is presented to the winner. Recipients of the WWF Award for Conservation Merit who are active in the protected area field include:

1982 Franco Tassi (Italy)
    Romulus Whittaker (India)
    Zahid B. Mirza (Pakistan)
    Abdallah Ben Dhafer (Tunisia)
    Ali Gharbi (Tunisia)
    Mohamed Baraket (Tunisia)

Ramon Coronado (Spain)
Javier Castroviejo (Spain)

1981 Felix Nyahoza (Tanzania)
Sandra Price (USA)

3.5. The Order of the Golden Ark

The Order of the Golden Ark was created by His Royal Highness Prince Bernhard of the Netherlands, Founder-President of World Wildlife Fund, to mark outstanding service to the conservation of wildlife and the natural environment. Those members of the Order who are active in protected area matters include:

1981 John Blower (UK)
M.F. Mörzer-Bruyns (Netherlands)
Marc Dourojeanni (Peru)
André Dupuy (France)
Zafar Futehally (India)

1980 Jesus Alvarez (Philippines)
Boonsong Lekagul (Thailand)
Edward Brewer (UK)

1979 E.O.A. Asibey (Ghana)
Ian Grimwood (Kenya)
Sidney Holt (UK)
A.W. Owadally (Mauritius)
M.K. Ranjitsinh (India)

1978 Raymond Dasmann (USA)
Arjan Singh (India)
George Schaller (USA)
Jacques Verschuren (Belgium)
Yoshimaro Yamashina (Japan)

1976 Gerardo Budowski (Venezuela)
Jean-Paul Harroy (Belgium)
Peter Scott (UK)

1974 Bernhard Grzimek (FRG)
Perez Olindo (Kenya)

1973 Kai Curry-Lindahl (Sweden)
V.L. Serventy (Australia)
Laurence S. Rockefeller (USA)
Felipe Benavides (Peru)

1972 Harold J. Coolidge (USA)
Ira N. Gabrielson (USA)
C.R. Gutermuth (USA)

Annex III.
Bibliography

Acheson, James M. 1981. Anthropology of Fishing. *Ann. Rev. Anthrop.* 10: 275-316.

Afolayan, T.A. 1980. A Synopsis of Wildlife Conservation in Nigeria. *Environ. Conserv.* 7(3):207-212.

African Convention on the Conservation of Nature and Natural Resources 1976. General Secretariat, Organization of African Unity, Addis Abba, Ethiopia.

Ajayi, S.S. 1973. Wildlife Resource Planning and Management. *Nigerian J. For.* 3(2):74-82

Alan, J. Golson & R. Jones (eds.). 1977. *Sunda and Sahul: Prehistoric Studies in Southeast Asia, Melanesia and Australia,* Academic Press, London.

Alexander, P. 1977. Sea tenure in Sri Lanka. *Ethnology* 16: 231-253

AMARU IV. 1980. *The once and future resource managers: A report on the native peoples of Latin America and their roles in modern resource management.* AMARU IV Cooperative, Inc., Washington, D.C.

AMBIO, 1979. Theme issue on Environmental/Development. Vol. III. No. 2-3. Royal Swedish Academy of Sciences.

Andrews, Susan. 1980. *Objectives, Policies and Structure of the Office of Environment and Conservation. In*: Morauta *et al.* (eds.). Monograph 16. Traditional conservation: Implications for Today. IASER. Port Moresby, PNG.

Andriamampianina, J. 1981. Les Reserves Naturelles et la Protection de la Nature a Madagascar, pp. 105-111 *In* Oberle, P. (ed.), *Madagascar, un sanctuaire de la nature.* Lechevalier S.A.R.L., Paris

Anon. 1977. Consideration of a classification of Antarctic and Subantarctic terrestrial, Freshwater and inshore marine benthic ecosystems. *Polar Record* 18: 409-426.

Anon. 1980a. The Nero Syndrome. *Afr. Wild.* 34(4):4.

Anon. 1980b. Facing the Realities. *Afr. Wild.* 34(3):16-18.

Anon. 1980c. *International Trade Statistics of Fisheries Commodities.* NO. 2 STAT.EKS.IM, Direktorat Jenderal Perikanan, Departemen Pertanian, Jakarta; 127pp.

Anon. 1980d. Uganda's elephants face extinction. *IUCN Bull.* 11 (4) : 45.

Anon. 1981. *Fisheries Statistics of Indonesia.* No. 9 Stat. Prod., Direktorat Jenderal Perikanan, Departemen Pertanian, Jakarta; 102pp.

Anon. 1982. Sahara Dust Settles Over Florida. *Washington Post*, p. A7. August 1.

Armstrong, John M. 1972. *The Structure of Management and Planning for the Coastal Zone.* Michigan State University NTIS, pp. 6-8.

ASEAN. 1980. *Report of the ASEAN Workshop on Nature Conservation of th ASEAN Experts on the Environment.* Denpasar, Indonesia, 15-19 September 1980.

Asibey, E.O.A. 1974. Wildlife as a Source of Protein in Africa South of the Sahara. *Biol. Conserv.* 6(1):32-39.

Atkinson, I.A.E. 1961. Conservation of New Zealand soils and vegetation for scientific and educational purposes. *N. Z. Sci. Rev.* 19: 65-73.

Atkinson, I.A.E. 1978. Evidence for effects of rodents on the vertebrate wildlife of New Zealand islands. pp. 7-30 *in* Dingwall, P.R. *et al* (eds.). 1978. *The Ecology and Control of Rodents in New Zealand Nature Reserves.* Department of Lands and Survey, Wellington.

Atkinson, I.A.E., and B.D. Bell. 1973. Offshore and Outlying Islands. pp. 372-392 *in* G.R. Williams (ed.). 1973. *The Natural History of New Zealand.* A.H. and A.W. Reed, Wellington.

Atkinson, I.A.E. and B.D. Bell. 1974. Offshore and Outlying Islands. *Wildlfe Service Publ. 163.* Dept. of Internal Affairs.

Aubreville, A.M. 1958. Nomenclature of African forest formations. CCTA. Second Intern-African Forestry Conference. Pointe-Norte, 3-11 August.

Audiot, Annick. 1982. Les parcs naturels de France et la conservation gntique animale. MS.

Australia, Great Barrier Reef Marine Park Authority. 1979. *The Great Barrier Reef Marine Park Authority.* pamphlet 2pp. Townsville, Queensland.

Australia, House of Representatives Standing Committee on Environment and Conservation. September 1981. *Environmental Protection: Second Report on the Adequacy of Legislative and Administrative Arrangements.* Australian Government Publishing Service, Canberra. pp. vi-99.

Australia, House of Representatives Standing Committee on Environment and Conservation. March 1980. *Management of the Australian Coastal Zone.* Australian Government Publishing Service, Canberra, 86pp.

Australian Academy of Science. 1969. *National Parks and Reserves in Australia.* Aust. Academy of Science, Canberra, pp i-iii and l-45.

Australian Bureau of Statistics. 1981. Projections of the population of Australia 1981 to 1982 (unpublished report).

Australian Conservation Foundation. 1975. Landscape Conservation, Rural Landscape Conservation with particular reference to the rural/urban fringe. Melbourne, Australia. 118pp.

Australian Conservation Foundation. 1978. Aborigines and ACF unite on Land Claims and Aborigines and ACF: The Common Good - statement by ACF and Northern and Central Land Councils. *ACF Newsletter* 10(3): 1-4.

Australian Conservation Foundation. 1980. *The Value of National Parks to the Community.* A.C.F. Hawthorn, Victoria 223pp.

Australian Heritage Commission. 1982. The National Estate in 1981. Australian Government Publishing Service, Canberra, Australia. 225pp.

Australian National Parks and Wildlife Service. 1980. Kakadu National Park. Plan of Management. Canberra, Australia. 410pp.

Australian National Parks and Wildlife Service. 1981. Nature Conservation Reserves in Australia. *Occ. Pap.* 5.

Australian National Parks and Wildlife Service. 1982. Information Paper to CONCOM: Marine Parks and Reserves in Autstralia Outside the Great Barrier Reef Marine Park Region. Council of Nature Conservation Ministers Standing Committee, Canberra. unpublished. 3pp and attachments.

Ayensu, E.S. 1976. International Cooperation Among Conservation-Orientated Botanical Gardens and Institutions, pp. 259-269 in Simmons, J.B. *et al.*, eds., *Conservation of Threatened Plants.* New York and London: Plenum Press.

Ayensu, E.S. 1981. Biology in the Humid Tropics of Africa, pp. 22-36 in Ayensu, E.S. and J. Marton-Lefevre, eds., *Proceedings of the Symposium on the State of Biology in Africa.*

Ayensu, E.S. and J. Marton-Lefevre. 1981. *Proceedings of the Symposium on the State of Biology in Africa.* African

Biosciences Network. Washington, D.C.: ICSU and Unesco.

Bailey, A.M. and J.H. Sorensen. 1962. Subantarctic Campbell Island. Proceedings, Denver Museum of Natural History, Vol. 10.

Bailey, R.G. 1976. *Ecoregions of the United States* (map). USDA Forest Service. Intermountain Region, Ogden, Utah.

Bak, R.P.M. 1975. Ecological aspects of the distribution of reef corals in the Netherlands Antilles. *Bijdr. Dierk.* 45: 181-190.

Banks, D.J. 1976. Peanuts: germplasm resources. *Crop Sci.* 16: 499-502.

Barker, Mary L. 1980. Natural Parks, Conservation, and Agrarian Reform in Peru. *Geogr. Rev.* 70(1): 1-18.

Barth, H. 1858-60. *Travels and Discoveries in North and Central Africa.* London: Longmans & Green.

Basyarudin, H. 1972. Nature Conservation and Wildlife Management in Indonesia. NAS-LIPI Workshop in Natural Resources, Jakarta, Indonesia.

Beamish, J., MacEwen, G. and Richards, H. 1976. *Report of the Public Hearings Board on the proposed Grasslands National Park.* Dept. of Indian and Northern Affairs. Ottawa.

Beard, B.H. 1977. Germplasm resources of oilseed crops - sunflower, soyabeans and flax. *Calif. Agric.* 31: 16-17

Bell, B.D. 1978. The Big South Cape Islands rat irruption. pp. 33-46 in Dingwall, P.R. *et al.* (eds.). 1978. *The Ecology and Control of Rodents in New Zealand Nature Reserves.* Proceedings of a symposium convened by the Department of Lands and Survey, Wellington, 29-30 November 1976. Department of Lands and Survey, Wellington.

Bell, B.D. (ed.). 1981. *Marsupials in New Zealand.* Proceedings of the first symposium on marsupials in New Zealand, Wellington, 9-10 May 1977. Zoology Publications from Victoria University of Wellington, Number 74. 280pp.

Bell, H.V. 1971. *Scient. Amer.* 225: 86-93.

Bellatin, Alfredo. 1963. La comunidad indgena peruana y la programacin de su desarrollo econmico y cultural. *Mensajero Agricola* 158: 6-7.

Bennett, John W. 1976. *The Ecological Transition.* Pergamon Press, New York. 378 pp.

Berger, Justice T.R. 1977. *Northern Frontier Northern Homeland,* The Report of the Mackenzie Valley Pipeline Inquiry, Vols. I and II. Ministry of Supply and Services, Ottawa.

Berlin, B., D.E. Breedlove, and P.H. Raven. 1974. *Principles of Tzeltal Plant Classification: An Introduction to the Botanical Enthnography of a Mayan- Speaking People of Highland Chiapas.* Academic Press, New York.

Berry, A.J. 1972. The natural history of West Malaysian Mangrove Faunas. *Malay. Nat. J.* 25: 135-62.

Berry, M.J., J.F. Laurence, M.J. Makin and A.E. Waddams. 1974. Development potential of the Nawalparasi area of Nepal. Land Resources Study. No. 17. ODA British Embassy, Nepal.

Betancourt, J.A. *et al.* 1979. Honduras' La Tigre: Public Benefits through Conservation. *Parks* 4 (2):

Bezrukov, P.L. and G.N. Baturin, 1979: Phosphorites on the seafloor and their origin. *Mar. Geo.* 31: 317-322.

Bina, R.T., R.S. Jara, E.N. Lorenzo and B.R. de Jesus, Jr. 1978: Mangrove inventory of the Philippines using LANDSAT multi-spectral data and the Image 100 system. *NRMC Res. Monogr.* 2: 1-8.

Bista, D.B. 1967. *People of Nepal.* Department of Publicity, Kathmandu.

Bjonness, I-M. External Economic Dependency and Changing Human Adjustment to Marginal Environment in the High Himalaya - Nepal.

Bjonness, I-M. 1979. Impacts on a High Mountain Ecosystem - Recommendations for Action - Sagarmatha National Park (unpublished).

Bjonness, I-M. 1980. Ecological Conflicts and Ecopnomic dependency on Tourist Trekking in Sagarmatha (Mt. Everest) National Park, Nepal. An alternative approach to park Planning. *Norskgeogr. Tidskr.* 34: 119-138. Oslo ISSN 0029-195.

Björklund, M.I. 1974. Achievements in marine conservation. I. Marine parks. *Environ. Conserv.* 1: 205-223.

Black, Juan, 1974. Galapagos Archipielago de Ecuador. Imprenta Europea, Quito.

Blower, J.H. 1971. The Khumbu National Park. Typed report to the Secretary of Forests HMG/Nepal, Kathmandu.

Blumer, R. 1968. Worms that crock and other mysteries of Karam natural history. *Mankind* 6(12): 621-639.

Blumer, R. and J. Menzies. 1972. Karam classification of Marsupials and rodents *J. Polynesian Society* 81(4) 472-499; 82(1): 86-107.

Bolton, M. 1975. Royal Chitwan National Park Management Plan 1975-1979. FAO, Rome.

Bothe, M. (ed.) 1980. *Trends in Environmental Policy and Law.* IUCN, Gland, Switzerland.

Bottemanne, C.J. 1959. *Principles of Fisheries Development.* Amsterdam: North-Holland. 651pp.

Boudreau, Rodolph. 1908. Certified copy of a report to the Committee of the Privy Council, approved by His Excellency the Governor General on the 7 March, 1908. *Canada Gazette.* Vol. 41, No. 41.

Bourne, W.R.P. 1981. Rats as avian predators. *Atoll Res. Bull.* 255: 69-72.

Bowser, W.E. 1967. Land capability for wheat. *Proceedings of the Canadian Centennial Wheat Symposium.* Western Cooperative Fertilizers Ltd., Calgary, Alberta, pp. 47-60.

Bozeman, E.L. and J.M. Dean. 1980 The abundance of estuarine larval and juvenile fish in a South Carolina creek. *Estuaries* 3: 89-97.

Braanowska, Janota, M. 1977. Zarys metody wyznaczania krancowych przestrzennych progow przyrodniczych dla rozwoju funkcji turystyki. (An outline method for defining ultimate environmental thresh-

olds to devlopment of tourism), *Czlowiek i Srodowisko* 1 (1-2).

Braanowska, Janota, M. and J. Kozlowski. 1981. *Method of Allowing to Identify Ultimate Development Thresholds from the View Point of the Protection of the Natural Environment.* Environmental Protection Agency, Washington, *Final Report* No. EPA 908/5-81-004A. 260 pp.

Brabyn, H. 1976. Protection of the World Heritage, *Parks* 1 (1).

Brandt, R.W. 1976. The Hoabinian of Sumatra: some remarks. *Mod. Quatern. Res. S.E.Asia* 2: 49-52.

Brewster, Barney. 1982. *Antarctica: Wilderness at Risk.* (A.H. & A.W. Reed Ltd., Wellington).

Briggs, J.C., 1975. *Marine Zoogeography.* McGraw-Hill, New York. 475 pp.

British Columbia, Parks and Outdoor Recreation Division. 1982. *Map of Natural Regions and Regional Landscapes for the B.C. Park System.*

Brock, R.E., C. Lewis, and R.C. Wass. 1979. Stability and structure of a fish community on a coral patch reef in Hawaii. *Mar. Biol.* 54: 281-292.

Brotoisworo, E., K.J. Gurmaya, O. Soemarwoto. 1980. Problems of Gunung Tilu Nature Reserve, Conservation Workshop PPA-WWF-FAO, Ciawi, Bogor, 31 Jan.-1 Feb. 1980, 7 pp.

Brown, K.S. Jr. 1975. Geographical patterns of evolution in Neotropical Lepidoptera. Systematics and derivation of known and new Helironiini (Nymphalidae Nymphalinne). *J. Ent.* (B) 44(3): 201-242.

Brown, K.S. Jr. 1976. Geographical patterns of evolution in Neotropical Lepidoptera (Nymphalidae: Ithomiinae and Nymphalinae Heliconiini) Contribucao No. 19, Prog. de Ecologia. Inst. de Biologia. Univ. Estadual de Compina Brazil. Draft manuscript. 31 pp.

Brown, K.S. Jr. 1979. *Ecologia Geográfica e Evolucáo nas Florestas Neotropicais.* Tese Livre Docénicia. Universidade Estadual de Campinas, Ecologia. 265 pp.

Brown, L. 1975. *East African Coasts and Reefs.* Nairobi, Kenya.

Brown, S.G., Brownell, R.L., Erickson, A.W., Hofman, R.J., Llano, G.A. and Mackintosh, N.A. 1974. Antarctic mammals. Antarctic Map Folio Series, Folio 18. American Geographical Society.

Brownrigg, L.A. 1981. Native cultures and protected areas: Management options. pp. 65-77 in *Conserving the Natural Heritage of Latin America and the Caribbean.* IUCN. Gland, Switzerland.

Brusard, Peter F. 1982. The Role of Field Stations in the Preservation of Biological Diversity. *Bioscience* 32(5):327-330.

Bryceson, Ian. 1981. A Review of Some of the Problems of Tropical Marine Conservation with Particular Reference to the Tanzanian Coast. *Biol. Conserv.* 20(3): 163-171.

Bryson, R.A., 1966. Airmasses, streamlines and the Boreal Forest. *Geographical Bulletin* (Canada) 8:228-269.

Budowski, Gerardo. 1960. Tropical savannas, a sequence of forest felling and repeated burnings. *Boletín del Museo de Ciencias Naturales* 6/7 (1-4): 63-87.

Burbridge, P. & Koesoebioino (in press). Coastal zone management in Southeast Asia. In: Chia Lin Sien & C. MacAndrews (eds.). *Frontiers for Development: The Southeast Asian Seas*. Singapore: McGraw-Hill.

Burbridge, P., J.A. Dixon & B. Soewardi. 1981. Forestry and agriculture: Options for resource allocation in choosing lands for transmigration development. *Appl. Geog.* 1: 237-258.

Bureau of Forest Development. 1979. *Overview on Forest Development*. Diliman, Quezon City.

Burhenne, W.E. 1970. The African Convention for the Conservation of Nature and Natural Resources. *Biological Conservation* 2(2):105-114.

Burhenne, W. (ed.). 1974. *International Environmental Law - Multilateral Treaties*. E. Schmidt Verlag, Berlin. (Updated through 1981).

Byrne, John E. 1979. *Literature Review and Synthesis of Information on Pacific Island Ecosystems*. Fish and Wildlife Service, U.S. Department of Interior, Washington, D.C.

Cahn, Robert. 1982. *Christian Science Monitor*. June 14.

California Coastal Commission. n.d. *Coastal Act Policy Handbook*. 12pp.

California Coastal Commission. 1977. *Local Coastal Programs: Addressing Land Use Conflicts*. 2pp.

California Coastal Commission. 1978. *Statewide Interpretive Guidelines*, 13pp

Campbell, A.C. 1973. The National Park and Reserve System in Botswana. *Biol. Conserv.* 5(1):7-14.

Canada (Environment Canada). 1979. *Parks Canada Policy*, 69 pp.

Canada (Indian Affairs and Northern Development). 1972. *National Parks System Planning Manual*. 138 pp.

Canada (Parks Canada). 1979. *A National Marine Park Concept for Canada*. 24pp.

Caoili, A. 1977: Mangrove Resource Allocation and Zonification. *Proc. Nat. Symp. Workshop Mangrove Resource Development*, Paranaque, Rizal.

Carneiro, Robert. 1961. Slash and burn cultivation among the Kuikuru and its implications for cultural development in the Amazon Basin. *In* Johannes Wilbert (ed.), *The evolution of horticultural systems in Native South America: causes and consequences*. Sociedad de Ciencias Naturales La Salle, Caracas.

Carr, Archie. 1967. *So Excellent A Fishe: A Natural History of Sea Turtles*. Natural History Press, Garden City, New York. 248 pp.

Carr, Archie. 1980. Some problems in sea turtle ecology. *Amer. Zool.* 20:489-498.

Carr, Archie, A. Meylan, J. Mortimer, K. Bjorndal, and T. Carr. 1982 *Surveys of sea turtle populations and habitats in the western Atlantic*. NOAA Tech. Mem. NMFS-SEFC 91, 82 pp.

Carr, Archie, M.H. Carr, and A.B. Meylan. 1978. The ecology and migrations of sea turtles of the West Car-

ibbean green turtle colony. *Bull. Amer. Mus. Nat. Hist.* 167, (1):1-46.

Carson, G.L. 1968. Conservation in Sabah, Malaysia. *IUCN Publ.* (N.S.) 10: 495.

Carter, J. 1982. Micronesia: Memoranda put status talks under microscope. *Pacific Island Monthly* 53(5): 29-32

Catlin, George. 1903. *North American Indians: letters and notes on their manners, customs, and conditions*. John Grant, Edinburgh.

Cato, I., I. Olsson & R. Rosenberg. 1980. Recovery and decontamination of estuaries. In. E. Olausson & J. Cato (eds.) *Chemistry and biogeochemistry of estuaries*. Wiley, Chichester. pp. 403-440.

Caughley, G. 1968. Wildlife and Recreation in Trisuli Watershed and other Areas in Nepal. HMG/FAO/UNDP Trisuli Watershed Development Project Report No. 6. FAO, Rome.

Centlivres, P., Gasdre, J., Lourteig, A. 1975. *Culture sur brûlis et evolution du milieu forestier en Amazonie du Nord-Ouest*. Société Suisse d'Ethnologie, Basel.

Chagnon, Napoleon. 1968. The cultural ecology of shifting (pioneering) cultivation among the Yanomamo Indians. *Proc. 7th Ann. Congr. Anthrop. Ethnol.* 9: 249-255.

Chai, P.P.K. 1977. Mangrove forest of Sarawak. Paper presented at Workshop on Mangrove and Estuarine Vegetation Universiti Pertanian Malaysia, Serdang, 10 December 1977.

Chambers, D.G. 1980. An analysis of nekton communities in the upper Barataria Basin, Louisiana. M.S. thesis, Louisiana State University, Baton Rouge, Louisiana.

Chapman, V.J. 1976. *Mangrove Vegetation*. J.C. Cramer, Auckland, New Zealand. 447 pp.

Chase, A. 1981. Dugongs and Indigenous Cultural Systems: Some Introductory Remarks. pp. 112-122. *In* H. Marsh (ed.). 1981. *The Dugong*. Department of Zoology, James Cook University, Townsville, Queensland. 400 pp.

Child, G. 1970. Wildlife Utilization and Management in Botswana. *Biol. Conserv.* 3(1): 18-22.

Child, G.F.T. 1977. Problems and Progress in Nature Conservation in Rhodesia. *Koedoe* (Suppl.) l977: 116-137.

Choudhury, S.R. and Sinha, J.P. 1980. The Kheri Maneaters. *Cheetal* 21 (2) and 21 (3). Dec. 1979 and March 1980.

Christensen, B. 1979. Mangrove forest resources and their management in Asia and the Far East. FAO Regional Office, Bangkok.

Clark, Roger N. 1982. Promises and Pitfalls of the ROS in Resource Management. *Aust. Parks and Rec.* May, 1982. 9-13.

Clark, Roger N., and George H. Stankey. 1977. The Recreation Opportunity Spectrum: A Framework for Planning, Management and Research. *US Dept. Ag. Forest Service, Gen. Tech. Rep.* PNW-98. 32 pp.

Clarke, William C. 1976. Maintenance of agriculture and human habitats within the tropical forest ecosystem. *Human Ecol.* 4 (3): 217-259.

Clawson, M. 1972. Park visitation in the coming decades: problems and opportunities. In: *Second World Conference on National Parks*. Sir Hugh Elliott (ed.), IUCN, Gland, Switzerland. pp. 116-126.

Clements, F.E. and V.E. Shelford. 1939. *Bioecology*. John Wiley and Sons, Inc. New York.

Cobb, S. 1979. Are the Right People Being Trained the Wrong Way? *Wild. News* 14(3), Winter.

Coleman, Neville. 1982. *Underwater 2. The Challenge of tomorrow*. Sea Australia Productions Pty. Ltd., Caringbah, NSW., Australia.

Commonwealth of Australia. 1981. Australian Year Book 1981. Canberra, Australia. 290pp.

Commonwealth Department of Home Affairs and Environment. 1982. Towards a National Conservation Strategy: A Discussion Paper.

Conklin, H.C. 1972. *Folk Classification: A Topically Arranged Bibliography of Contemporary and Background References Through 1981*. Department of Anthropololgy, Yale University, New Haven.

Connell, J.H. 1978. Diversity in tropical rain forests and coral reefs *Science* 199: 1302-1310.

Connor, E., E. McCoy. 1979. The statistics and biology of the species-area relationship. *Am. Naturalist* 113(6): 791-833.

Cooper, Arthur W. 1971. Ecological Considerations. pp. 133-140 in James C. Hite and James M. Stepp (eds.). *Coastal Zone Resource Management*, Preager Publishers, New York.

Cordell, John. 1974. The Lunar-tide Fishing Cycle in Northeastern Brazil. *Ethnology* 13: 379-392.

Cordell, John. 1978. Carrying Capacity Analysis of Fixed-Territorial Fishing. *Ethnology* 17: 1-24.

Cordell, John. (in press). Methods for indigenous fishery conservation. *In: Ecoculture: A strategy for survival*. International Union for Conservation of Nature and Natural Resources.

Corporacion Venezolana de Guayana Informe quincenal. 1974-1978. Caracas, Venezuela.

Corporacion de Turismo de Venezuela. 1974. Parque Nacional Canaima, Plan rector. Ministerio de Agricultura y Cria, Direccion de Recursos Naturales Renovables, Division de Parques Nacionales, National Park Service, US Department of the Interior. Editorial Arte, Caracas.

Costin, A.B. 1970. Ecological Hazards of the Snow Mountains Scheme. *Proc. Ecol. Soc. Aust.* 5: 87-98.

Council of Europe, 1979. Vegetation map of the Council of Europe member states. Nature and Environment Series. Strasbourg.

Coupland, R.T. 1950. Ecology of mixed prairie in Canada. *Ecol. Monogr.* 20: 271-315.

Coupland, R.T. 1972. *Matador Project, operational phase, 1967-72: a summary of progress*. Tech. Rep. No. 1 Univ. of Sak., Sakatoon.

Coupland, R.T. 1973. *A theme study of natural grassland in western Canada*. Report to National and Historic Parks Branch, Canada Dept. of Indian Affairs and Northern Development, Ottawa.

Coupland, R.T. and T.C. Brayshaw. 1953. The fescue grassland in Saskatchewan. *Ecology* 34: 386-405.

Coupland, R.T. and J.S. Rowe. 1969. Natural vegetation of Saskatchewan. *Atlas of Saskatchewan*. (Edited by J.H. Richards and K.I. Fung). University of Saskatchewan, Saskatoon pp. 73-78.

Covarrubias, M. 1937. *Island of Bali*. Cassell, London. 417pp.

Crerar, T.A. 1940. Wainright National Park: Inquiry as to destruction of buffalo, elk, moose and deer. *Dominion of Canada Official Report of Debates House of Commons*. Vol. II, 1940, Ottawa, Printer to the King's Most Excllent Majesty. pp. 1010-1011.

Croft, T. A. 1981. Lake Malawi National park: A Case Study in Conservation Planning. *Parks* 6 (3): 7-11.

Cronan, D.S. 1980. *Underwater minerals*. Academic Press, London, 362 pp.

CSIR, 1982. Proceedings of the Symposium on the Management of Large Mammals in African Conservation Areas (Council for Scientific and Industrial Research, Pretoria.

Cumming, D.H.M. 1975: *A field study of the ecology and behaviour of warthog* Mus. memoir 7. Trustees Nat. Museums & Monuments, Rhodesia: 179 pp.

Cumming, D.H.M. 1981. The management of elephant and other large mammals in Zimbabwe. In *Problems in Management of Locally Abundant Wild Mammals*. pp.91-118. Academic Press.

Curry-Lindahl, K. 1974. Conservation Problems and Progress in Northern and Southern Africa. *Environ. Conserv.* 1(4):263-270.

Curry-Lindahl, K. 1975. Conservation of Arctic fauna and its habitats. *Polar Record* 17: 237-247.

Curry-Lindahl, K. 1980. Zoogeographic subregions of the Pacific Realm as a background for terrestrial ecological reserves., *Environ. Cons.* 7: 67-76, 125-136. Based on a lecture given in 1975 at the 13th Pacific Science Congress.

Curry-Lindahl, K. 1980. Ekologisk kris i u-land. AWE/Gebers, Stockholm, 231S.

Curtis, M.A. 1975. The marine benthos of Arctic and sub-arctic continental shelves. *Polar Record* 17: 595-626.

Dahl, Arthur L., and Ian L. Baumgrat. 1982. The State of the Environment in the South Pacific. pp. 47-71 in *Report of the Conference on the Human Environment in the South Pacific*. South Pacific Commision, Noumea, New Caledonia.

Dahl, Arthur L. 1980. Regional Ecosystems Survey of the South Pacific Area. *South Pacific Commission Technical Paper* 179: 1-99.

Dahl, Arthur R. 1980. *Regional Ecosystems Survey of the South Pacific Area*. Tech. Pap. 19, SPC, New Caledonia.

Dalfelt, A. 1982. A proposal for a tropical moist forest conservation programme for Central America. IUCN, 1982. pp 116.

Dalfelt, A. and M. Norderhaug. 1982. Uhjelp og Okologi. Oslo. pp. 91.

Darling, F.F., and N.D. Eichhorn. 1969. *Man and Nature in the national parks: Reflections on policy.* The Conservation Foundation, Washington, D.C., 2nd edition. 86 pp.

Darling, Sir Frank Fraser. 1980. National Parks . . . a matter of survival, *Parks*, 4, 16

Darlington, P.J. Jr. 1957. *Zoogeography: The Geographical Distribution of Animals.* J. Wiley & Sons, N.Y.

Daryadi, Lukito. 1981. Memori penjelasan serah terima, Direktur Perlindungan dan Pengawetan Alam PPA, Bogor (Indonesia), mimeo, 31 pp.

Dasmann, R.F. 1972. Towards a System for Classifying Natural Regions of the World and their Representation by National Parks. *Biol. Conserv.*, 1972, 4:247-255

Dasmann, Raymond F. 1973. A system for defining and classifying natural regions for purposes of conservation. *IUCN Occasional Paper* 7:1-18.

Dasmann, R.F. 1974. Difficult marginal environments and the traditional societies which exploit them: ecosystems. Symposium on the future of traditional primitive societies. Cambridge, U.K. *Survival International News* 11:11-15.

Dasmann, R.F. 1974. Biotic Provinces of the World. *IUCN Occ. Pap.* 9: 1-57.

Dasmann, R.F. 1974. *Ecological Principles for Economic Development.* J. Wiley & Sons Ltd., London. 252.

Dasmann, R.F. 1975. National Parks, Nature Conservation and 'Future Primitive.' *Ecologist* 6(5):164-167.

Dasmann, R. F. 1980. Ecodevelopment - an ecological perspective. *Tropical ecology and development* 1331-1335. Intern. Soc. Tropical Ecology, Kuala Lumpur.

Davie J.D.S., Saenger P. and Hegerl E. 1981. *First Report on the Gobal Status of Mangrove Ecosystems.* IUCN, Gland, Switzerland.

Davis, G.E. 1981. On the role of underwater parks and sanctuaries in the management of coastal resources in the southeastern United States. *Environ. Conserv.* 8: 67-70.

Day, J.W. Jr., C.S. Hopkinson, and W.H. Conner. (in prep.). Ecological function and control in the Barataria Basin Estuary, Louisiana.

Delogu, O.E. 1974. United States experience with the preparation and analysis of environmental impact statements: The National Environmental Policy Act. *IUCN Environ. Pol. Law Pap.* 7. IUCN, Gland. Switzerland.

Denevan, William. 1971. Campa subsistence in the Gran Pajonal, Eastern Peru. *Geog. Rev.* 61 (4): 496-518.

Dennis, A. 1981: The Paparoa Guide. Native Forest Action Council, Nelson, N.Z.

Department of Home Affairs and Environment. 1972/82 (In press). *Joint Australian Environment Council/Council of Nature Conservation Ministers Report on Environment and Conservation Achievements.* .

Department of Lands and Survey. 1980. Preliminary Reports of the Campbell Island Expedition 1975-76. *Department of Land and Survey Reserves Series* 7, 164 pp.

de Silva, G.S. 1968. Wildlife Conservation in the State of Sabah. IUCN Publ. (N.S.) 20:147-148.

de Silva, G.S. 1969a. Turtle Conservation in Sabah. *Sabah Soc. J.* 5(1):6-26.

de Silva, G.S. 1969b. Marine Turtle Conservation in Sabah. Annual Report. *Res. Bul. F.D.*, 1969 pp. 124-135.

de Silva, G.S. 1969c. Statement on Marine Turtles in the State of Sabah. *IUCN Publ.* 20:75-79.

de Silva, G.S. 1982 (in press). The Leathery Turtle in Sabah. *Borneo Res. Bul.*

di Castri, F., and L. Loope. 1977. Biosphere Reserves: Theory and practice. *Nature and Resources.* 13(1): 2-7.

du Saussey, C. 1980. Transfrontier Parks. *Unasylva* FAO 1980, 32 (127)

Devine, W.T. 1977. A programme to exterminate introduced plants on Raoul Island. *Biological Conservation* 11: 193-207.

DeVos, A. 1969. The Need for Nature Reserves in East Africa. *Biol. Conserv.* 1(2):130-134.

Diamond, J.M. 1975. The island dilemma: lessons of modern biogeographic studies for the design of natural reserves. *Biol. Conserv.* 7: 129-146.

Diamond, J.M. 1980. Patchy distributions of some tropical birds. pp. 57-74 in *Conservation Biology*, M.E. Soule and B.A. Wilcox, eds., Sinauer Associates Sunderland, Ma.

Diamond, J.M. & May, R.H. 1976. Island biogeography and the design of nature reserves. Chapter 9 in R.H. May (ed.), *Theoretical Ecology Principles & Applications.* Oxford, Blackwell Scientific.

Dietrich, G. 1963. *General Oceanography: An Introduction.* Interscience Publishers, New York.

Dingwall, P.R. 1977. The role of science in the planning and management of national parks. *Proceedings of the Seminar on Science in National Parks, Canterbury, August 1976.* N.Z. National Parks Series No. 6, 235-242, Wellington, N.Z.

Dingwall, P.R. 1981. Harry Ell's vision in nature conservation. *Landscape* 10, 23-27.

Division of National Mapping. 1980. Atlas of Australian Resources. Third Series, Vol. 1. Soils and Land Use. Canberra, Australia. 24pp.

Dobzhansky, T. 1970. *Genetics of the Evolutionary Process.* Columbia Univ. Press, New York and London.

Dolan, R., B.P. Hayden, G. Hornberger, J. Zieman, and M. Vincent. 1972. Classification of the coastal environments of the world, Part I, the Americas. Tech. Rept. No. 1, Off. Naval Res. Geography Programs. Univ. Virginia, Charlottesville, Va; pp.163.

Dorst, J. and P. Dandelot. 1970. *A Field Guide to the Larger Mammals of Africa.* Collins, London.

Dorst, Jean. 1974. Parks and Reserves on Islands. pp. 267-276. *In* Sir Hugh Elliott (ed.) 1974. *Second World Conference on National Parks.* IUCN, Gland, Switzerland. 504 pp.

Downes, M.C. 1977. Report of the Consultant on Wildlife Management Programme for Papua New Guinea - 1 Birds of Paradise. Wildlife in Papua New Guinea series 77/23.

Downs, R.E. 1955. Head-hunting in Indonesia. *Bijdr. Taal Land-en Volkenk-Ned.-Indie* 111: 40-70, 280-285.

Dunbar, M.J. 1968. *Ecological developments in polar regions.* Prentice-Hall, Englewood Cliffs, N.J.

Duncan, P. and J. Esser. 1982. The use of fauna and flora as a contribution to environmentally sound development in the Sahel. IUCN, Gland, Switzerland.

Dunlop, Richard C. and Birendra B. Singh. 1978. *A National Parks and Reserves System for Fiji.* The National Trust for Fiji. 117pp.

Dupuy, A.R. 1980. *Conservation de la Nature et Parcs Nationaux au Senegal.* Dakar, Senegal.

Dustan, P. 1977. Besieged reefs of Florida Keys. *Nat. Hist.* 86 (4): 73-76.

Dutch National Advisory Council for Development Cooperation. 1978. *Recommendation on Aid and Development.* Haag, 32 plus Annex.

Dwyer, P.D. 1974. The Price of Protein: five hundred hours of hunting in the New Guinea Highlands. *Oceania* 44: 278-293.

Eastern Caribbean Natural Area Management Program. 1979. *List of parks and protected areas of the Caribbean.* West Indies Laboratory, Christiansted, St. Croix, U.S. Virgin Islands.

Eastern Caribbean Natural Area Management Program. 1980. *Preliminary Data Atlases of the Lesser Antilles.* Caribbean Conservation Association, the University of Michigan and the United Nations Environment Programme. October, 1980.

Eaton, P. and P. Sinclair. 1981. *Wildlife in Papua New Guinea. The Papua New Guinea Environment,* 1981. Division of Wildlife, Konedobu, PNG.

Eckholm, E.P. 1976. *Losing Ground.* W.W. Norton, New York.

Eckholm, Erik. 1982. *Down to Earth,* W.W. Norton and Co., New York.

Ecuador. 1972. Junta Nacional de Planificacion y Coordinacion Economica. Plan Integral de Transformacion y Desarrollo 1973-1977. Quito.

Ecuador. 1977. Recopilacion de Leyes de Parques Nacionales, Reservas y Conservacion de Flora y Fauna Silvestres del Ecuador, 1926-1977. Quito.

Ecuador. 1979. Ministerio de Agricultura y Ganaderia. Estrategian Preliminar Para la Conservacion de Areas Silvestres Sobresalientes del Ecuador. Quito.

Ecuador. 1980. Consejo Nacional de Desarrollo. Plan Nacional de Desarrolla 1980.1984, Segunda Parte, Tomo II. Quito, Marzo 1980.

Ecuador. 1981. Ley Forestal y de Conservacion de Areas Naturales y Vida Silvestre. Quito.

Ehrlich, P.R. 1975. The Population Biology of Coral Reef Fishes. *Ann. Rev. Ecol. Syst.* 6: 211-247.

Ehrlich, Paul R. 1982. Human Carrying Capacity, Extinction, and Nature Reserves. *Bioscience* 32(5):321-326.

Eidsvik, H.K. 1978. Involving the Public in Planning: Canada. *Parks* 3 (1).

Eidsvik, H.K. 1980. National Parks and Other Protected Areas: Some Reflections on the Past and Prescriptions for the Future. *Environ. Conserv.,* Vol. 7, No. 3, Autumn 1980.

Eidsvik, H.K., and K. Erdman. 1980. The World Heritage Convention at Work in Canada: The Dinosaur World Heritage Site. *Parks News* 16 (3): 13-16.

Eisenberg, J.F. 1980. The density and biomass of tropical mammals. pp. 35-55 in *Conservation Biology,* M.E. Soule and B.A. Wilcox, eds., Sinauer Associates, Sunderland, Ma.

Eisner, Thomas. 1982. For Love of Nature: Exploration and Discovery at Biological Field Stations, *Bioscience* 32(5): 321-326.

Ekman, S. 1953. *Zoogeography of the Sea.* London: Sidgwick & Jackson. 417 pp.

Ekman, S. 1953. *Zoogeography of the Sea.* Sidgwick and Jackson, Ltd.

Ellen, R.F. 1978. Nuaulu Settlement and Ecology. *Verh. K. Inst. Taal-Land-en Volkenk.* 83: 1-265.

Elliot, H.F.I. 1972. Island ecosystems and conservation. *J. Mar. Biol. Assoc.* India, 14.

Elliott, M.A. 1981. Distribution and Status of the Dugong in Northern Territory Waters. pp. 57-66 *in* H. Marsh (ed.). 1981. *The Dugong.* Department of Zoology, James Cook University, Townsville, Queensland. 400 pp.

Elliott, Hugh. 1973a. Past, Present and Future Conservation Status of Pacific Islands. pp. 217-227. *In* A.B. Costin and R.H. Groves (eds.). 1973. *Nature Conservation in the Pacific.* Australian National University, Canberra. 337 pp.

Elliott, Hugh. 1973b. Pacific Oceanic Islands Recommended for Designation as Islands of Science. pp. 287-305. *In* South Pacific Commission. 1973. *Regional Symposium on Conservation of Nature - Reefs and Lagoons.* SPC, Noumea, New Caledonia. 314 pp.

Elliott, Hugh (Ed.). 1974. *Second World Conference on National Parks.* IUCN, Morges, Switzerland. 504 pp.

Ellis, G. and J. Duffield. no date. *Better trees for northwest forests.* Forest Genetics Research Foundation.

Eltringham, S.K. & Malpas, R.C. 1980. The decline in elephant numbers in Rwenzori and Kabalega Falls National Parks, Uganda. *Afr. J. Ecol.* 18: 73-86.

Emmerson, D.K. 1980a. The case for maritime perspective in Southeast Asia. *J. Southeast Asian Stud.* 11: 139-145.

Emmerson, D.K. 1980b. Rethinking artisanal fisheries development: western concepts, Asian experiences. *World Bank Staff Working Pap.* 423: 1-97pp.

Endicott, K.M. 1970. *An Analysis of Malay Magic.* Oxford: Clarendon. viii + 188pp.

Energy, Mines and Resources. 1980. *Principal Mineral Areas of Canada.*

England, Natural Environment Research Council. January 1873. *Marine Wildlife Conservation: An assessment of evidence of a threat to marine wildlife and the need for conservation measures.* The NERC publication Series B No. 5.

England, Nature Conservancy Council. 1979. *Nature Conservation in the Marine Environment.*

Environment Canada. 1972. *The Mackenzie Basin*, Proceedings of Intergovernmental Seminar held at Inuvik, N.W.T., June 24-27, 1972. Environment Canada, Ottawa.

Environment Canada. 1981. Ecoregions and Ecodistricts of the Northern Yukon. Environment Canada, Ottawa.

Epler, White-Gilbert. 1972. Galapagos guide. Imprenta Eucropa, Quito.

Epton, N. 1974. *Magic and Mystics of Java*. London: Octagon. 212pp.

Erize, F. et al. 1981. Los Parques Nacionales de la Repblica Argentina. INCAFO, Madrid. 224 pp.

Fabos, J.G. 1979. *Planning the Total Landscape: A Guide to Intelligent Land Use*. Westview Press, Boulder, Colorado.

Falanruw, M.V.C. 1981. Some impacts of land based activities on the marine environment in the Trust Territory of the Pacific Islands and related social factors. Unesco Seminar on Marine and Coastal Processes in the Pacific. 30pp.

Falanruw, M.V.C. 1982. The ecology and management of the fruitbats of Yap. Draft report being processed for publication. 84pp.

Falanruw, M.V.C., *et al.* In prep. The vegetation of Yap. Ongoing work, U.S. Forest Service, Institute of Pacific Islands Forestry.

Falanruw, M.V.C., S. Falanruw and Moon. 1968. The ethnoicthyology of Yap. Unpublished manuscript.

Falanruw, S.C. 1978. Yap Development Planning. *In* Development Planning in the Pacific Sub-Region with Special Reference to Evaluation, Report of a workshop held in Apia, Western Samoa, 15 August-1 September 1977, under the auspices of ESCAP, UNCDPP, and ADPI. Vol. III, pp.4-28.

FAO. 1974. Manejo y Desarrollo Integral de Areas Silvestres. Documento Tecnico de Trabajo No. 4. Proyecto FAO- RLAT/TF-l99. Santiago, Chile.

FAO. 1976a. Nature Conservation in Indonesia. Interim report and action plan.

FAO. 1976b. Report to the Government of Brazil. *A General Programme for Wildlife Management and Conservation in Brazil*. Based on the work of G.B. Wetterberg. Rome, April 1976. UNDP/FAO/BRA/71/545. Technical report 7. (Restricted distribution).

FAO. 1977. Conservation and utilization of wildlife resources, Afghanistan. Interim report. FAO, Rome.

FAO. 1980. The state of food and agriculture 1979. Food and Agriculture Organization, Rome, Italy.

FAO. 1982. Proposed Pulan Seribu Marine National Park. Management Plan 1982-1983. FO/INS/78/061. Field report 31, 48 pp. plus appendix.

FAO/World Wildlife Fund. 1980. Marine management plan, proposed Bali National Park. Special Report, FAO Project INS/78/061. 42 pp.

Farnworth, Edward G., Thomas J. Tidrick, Carl F. Jordan, Webb M. Smaths. 1981. The Value of Natural Ecosystems: An Economic and Ecological Framework. 8 *Environ. Conserv.* 275-282. Winter 1981.

Federal Committee on Ecological Reserves. 1977. *A Directory of Research Natural Areas on Federal Lands of the United States of America*. United States Department of Agriculture, Forest Service, Washington, D.C.

Fenner, Frank (ed.). 1975. *A National System of Ecological Reserves in Australia*. Australian Academy of Science, Canberra ll4pp.

Field, C.R. 1979. Game ranching in Africa. *Appl. Ecol.* 4: 63-101.

Firey, Walter I. 1980. *Man, Mind and Land: A theory of resource use*. Glencoe, Il: The Free Press of Glenco.

Fisher, A.C., J.V. Krutilla, and C.J. Cicchetti. 1972. The Economics of Environmental Preservation: A Theoretical and Empirical Analysis, 62 *American Economic Review* 605-619, September 1972;

Fisher, J., N. Simon, J. Vincent. 1969. *The Red Book*. Collins, London.

Flannery, Kent V., Anne Kirkby, Michael Kirkby, Aubrey Williams. 1967. Farming systems and political growth in Oaxaca. *Science* 158: 445-454.

Fleming, C.A. 1979. The history and future of the preservation ethic. pp. 59-64 *in National Parks of New Zealand*. Proceedings of the Silver Jubilee Conference of the National Parks Authority of New Zealand, Lincoln College, 5-8 July 1978. National Parks Authority of New Zealand, c/o Department of Lands and Survey, Wellington.

Fletemeyer, John. Submitted November, 1981. *Draft of Western Atlantic Turtle Symposium National Report of British Virgin Islands*. IOC Assistant Secretary for IOCARIBE, a/c UNDP, Aptdo. 4540, San Jose, Costa Rica.

Flores Ochoa, Jorge. 1975. Pastores de Alpacas. *Allpanchis* 8: 5-25.

Forbes, H.O. 1885. *A Naturalist's wanderings in the Eastern Archipelago*. London: Sampson Low, Marston, Searle and Rovington. 536 pp.

Forman, S. 1970. *The Raft Fishermen*. Indiana University Press, Bloomington, Indiana. 158 pp.

Forster, R.R. 1973. Planning for man and nature in national parks: Reconciling perpetuation and use. *IUCN Publ. New Ser.* 26: 1-45.

Fosberg, F.R. (ed.) 1965. *Man's Place in the Island Ecosystem*. Bishop Museum Press, Honolulu, Hawaii. 264 pp.

Foster, R.B. 1980. Heterogeneity and disturbance in tropical vegetation. pp. 135-149 in *Conservation Biology*, M.E. Soule and B.A. Wilcox, eds., Sinauer, Sunderland, Ma.

Fox, Allan M. 1980. National Parks as Educational Resources. pp. 107-123. In John Messer and Geoff Mosley (eds.) 1980 *Second National Wilderness Conference*. ACF, Melbourne.

Fox, Allan M. 1981. Interpretive Plan. pp.60-71. In *Norfolk Island Kingston and Arthur's Vale Historic Area Management Plan*. Dept. Home Affairs and Environment, AGPS, Canberra.

Fox, T. 1974. Recreational Requirements and National Parks Systems of Australia. In papers of the Fourth Ministerial Conference on National Parks, Australia (unpublished).

France, Ministry of the Environment. 1979. *Press Back-grounder: Directive on national development governing the protection and development of the coast.* 8pp.

Frankel, O.M. and Michael E. Soul. 1981. *Conservation and Evolution.* Cambridge University Press, New York. 327 pp.

Franklin, I.R. 1980. Evolutionary change in small populations. pp. 75-92. *In* M.E. Soule and B.A. Wilcox, eds. *Conservation Biology* Sinauer Associates, Sunderland, Ma.

Frazer, J.G. 1922. *The Golden Bough.* Macmillan, London. 756 pp.

French, J.R.J. 1980. Australian Forest Policy - A Critical View. *Curr. Affairs Bull.* 57(8): 4-16.

Fryer, G. 1972. Conservation of the Great Lakes of East Africa: A Lesson and a Warning. *Biol. Conserv.* 4(4):256-262.

Fuller, W.A. 1974. Parks and reserves in Polar and Sub-polar regions. pp. 276-291 *In* H. Elliot (ed.). *Second World Conference on National Parks.* IUCN, Gland, Switzerland.

Furer-Haimendorf, C. von. 1964. *The Sherpas of Nepal.* John Murray, London.

Furer-Haimendorf, C. von. 1975. *The Himalayan Traders.* John Murray, London.

Gabriel, B.C. 1978. Mangrove Forests: Problems and Management Strategies. *Likas-Yaman,* 3:1-48.

Gade, Daniel W. 1975. *Plants, man and the land in the Vilcanota Valley of Peru.* W. Junk, The Hague.

Gadgil, M. and V.M. Meher-Homji. 1982. Indo-US binational workshop on conservation and management of biological diversity. (Maps with explanatory notes). Dept. Environment Government of India. Pamphlet.

Galal, S. 1977. The Desert Made by Man. *Nat. Parks Conser. Maga.* 51 (11):11-16.

Gardner, J.E. and J.G. Nelson. 1980. Comparing National Parks and Related Reserve Policy in Hinterland Areas: Alaska, Northern Canada and Northern Australia. *Environ. Conserv.* 7(1):43-50.

Gardner, J.E. and J.G. Nelson. 1981. National Parks and Native Peoples in Northern Canada, Alaska and Northern Australia. *Environ. Conserv.* 8(3):207-212.

Garratt, K.J. 1981. *Sagarmatha National Park Management Plan.* Dept. of Lands & Survey, New Zealand for the National Parks & Wildlife Conservation Office, Kathmandu, Nepal.

Gedney, R.H.; Kapetsky, J.M. and Kuhnhold. 1982. Training on assessment of coastal aquaculture potential in Malaysia. Manila, South China Sea Fisheries Development and Coordinating Programme. SCS/GEN/82/35, January 1982, 62 pp.

Gee, H., J. Fenton, and G. Hodge. 1979. *The South West Book: A Tasmanian Wilderness.* Australian Conservation Foundation, Melbourne, Australia. 307 pp.

Gibb, J.A., and J.E.C. Flux. 1973. Mammals. pp. 334-371 *in* G.R. Williams (ed.). 1973. *The Natural History of New Zealand.* A.H. and A.W. Reed, Wellington.

Gilbert, L.E. 1980. Food web organization and conservation of neotropical diversity. In *Conservation Biology,* M.E. Soule and B.A. Wilcox, eds., Sinauer, Sunderland, Ma.

Gilpin, Michael S. and Jared Diamond. 1980. Subdivision of Nature Reserves and the Maintenance of Species Diversity. *Nature* 285:567-568.

Glick, Dennis. 1982. Ancient Tools for Contemporary Land Use. *Parks* 7(1): 12-15.

Glude, J.B. (ed.). 1977. *NOAA Aquaculture Plan.* US Department of Commerce, Washington D.C.

Goeden, G.B. 1979. Biogeographic theory as a management tool. *Environ. Conserv.* 6(1): 27-32.

Goldstein, Wendy (ed.). 1977. Rain Forests. *Parks Wildlife* 2 (l):1-l07.

Goldstein, Wendy (ed.). 1979. Australia's 100 years of National Parks. *Parks and Wildlife,* 2 (3-4):1-l60.

Golpe Mortal al Parque Tayrona. La Ecologia en Colombia (II). *Cromos* 3367:62-68.

Gomez-Pompa, A., C. Vasquez-Yanes, and S. Guevara. 1972. The Tropical Rain Forest: a nonrenewable resource. *Science,* 177, 762-765.

Gondelles, R., J. Steyermark and J.R. Garcia. 1977. Los Parques Nacionales de Venezuela, Ministerio del Ambiente y de los Recursos Naturales Renovables. Caracas.

Gong, W.K., Ong, J.E., Wong, C.H. and G. Dhanarajan. 1980. Productivity of mangrove trees and its significance in a managed mangrove ecosystem in Malaysia. Paper presented at the Unesco Asian Symposium on Mangrove Environment: Research and Management held at Universiti Malaya, Kuala Lumpur, Malaysia, August 1980.

Gonzalez Ruiz, E.O. 1981. El Guanaco. *Revista Patagnica* 2(2): 30-34, Buenos Aires.

Goreau, Thomas, F., Nora I. Goreau, and Thomas J. Goreau. 1979. Corals and Coral Reefs. *Scient. Amer.* 241(2): 124-136.

Gorio, S. 1978. Papua New Guinea Involves its People in National Park Development. *Parks* 3(2): 12-14.

Gorman, C. 1971. The Hoabinhian and after: subsistence patterns in Southeast Asia during the late Pleistocene and early Recent periods. *Wld. Archeol.* 2: 300-320.

Government of India. 1972. Project Tiger: A planning proposal for preservation of tiger (*Panthera tigris tigris* Linn.) in India. Report of Task Force, Indian Board for Wildlife. 114 pp.

Grant, P.T. & A.M. Mackie. 1977. Drugs from the sea - fact or fantasy? *Nature* 267: 786-788.

Grassle, J.F. & H.L. Sanders. 1973. Life histories and the role of disturbance. *Deep Sea Res.* 20: 643-659.

Green, K. 1980. An assessment of the Poco das Antas Reserve, Brazil, and prospects for survival of the golden lion tamarin, *Leontopithecus rosalia rosalia.* Unpublished report to WWF.

Green, S.W., Gressitt, J.L., Koob, D., Llano, G.A. Rudolph, E.D., Singer, R., Steere, W.C. and Ugolini, F.C. 1967. *Terrestrial life of Antarctica.* Antarctic Map Folio Series No.5. American Geographical Society, N.Y.

Gressitt, L.J. (ed.) 1967. *Entomology of Antarctica.* Antarctic Research Series, Vol. 10, American Geophysical Union, Washington.

Grigg, Richard W. 1979. Coral Reef Ecosystems of the Pacific Islands: Issues and Problems for Future Management and Planning. pp. 6-1 - 6-17. *In* John E. Byrne (ed.). 1979. *Literature Review and Synthesis of Information on Pacific Island Ecosystems*. Fish and Wildlife Service, U.S. Department of Interior, Washington, D.C.

Grimmett, R.E.R. 1956. The challenge to soil science. *Proceedings of the New Zealand Society of Soil Science* 2: 4-11.

Grimwood, I.R. 1974. National parks and wildlife conservation in the Philippines, FAO, Rome.

Groves, Murray. 1977. *Hiri Port Moresby.* Papua. Dept. of Anthro. and Socio., UPNG. Port Moresby, PNG.

Gwynne, M.D. and Croze, H. 1975. East African habitat monitoring proctice: a review of methods and application. Proc. International Livestock Centre for Africa (ILCA) Seminar on *Evaluation and Mapping of Tropical African Rangelands*, Bamako, March 1975:95-142.

Haddon, A.C. (ed.). 1901-1935. *Reports of the Cambridge Anthropological Expedition to Torres Straits.* 6 vols. Cambridge University Press, Cambridge.

Haffer, Jurgen. 1969. Speciation in Amazonian Forest birds. *Science* 3889 (165): 131-137.

Haffer, Jurgen. 1974. *Avian speciation in tropical South America.* Museum of Comparative Zoology, Harvard University. Cambridge, Mass. 390 pp.

Hageman, J. 1855. Aanteekeningen omtrent een gedeelte der Oostkust van Borneo. *Tijdschr. indische Taal- Land-en Volkenk.* 4: 71-106.

Hagen, T. 1969. *Report on the geology of Nepal: Vol. 1. Reconnaissance Survey.* Denkschriften der Schweiz. Naturforsch. Gesellschaff. Basel.

Hales, D. F. 1980. Does the World Heritage Convention Really Work?, *Parks* 4(4):

Halffter, Gonzalo. 1981a. Conservation, development and participations. Paper presented at UNESCO-ICSU Conference-exhibit: Ecology in Practice - Establishing a Scientific basis for Land Management. Paris 22-29 September 1981.

Halffter, G. 1981b. The Mapimi Bioisphere Reserve: Local participation in Conservation & Development. *Ambio* 10 (2-3):

Harcourt, A.H. and K. Curry-Lindahl. 1979. Conservation of the Mountain Gorilla and its Habitat in Rwanda. *Environ. Conserv.* 6(2):143-147.

Harcourt, A.H. 1981. Can Uganda's Gorillas Survive?— A Survey of the Bwindi Forest Reserve. *Biol. Conserv.* 19(4):269-282.

Hardesty, Donald L. 1977. *Ecological Anthropology.* John Wiley and Sons, New York. 310 pp.

Harkin, J.B. 1915. Report of the Commissioner of Dominion National Parks. *Dept. of the Interior Annual Report* for the year ending March 31, 1915. Ottawa. pp. 7-80.

Harkin, J.B. 1923. Canadian National Parks: Report of the Commissioner. *Dept. of the Interior Annual Report* for the year ending March 31, 1922. Ottawa. pp. 7-52.

Harkin, J.B. 1924. Report of the Commissioner of Dominion National Parks. *Dept. of the Interior Annual Report* for the year ending March 31, 1923. Ottawa. pp. 5-36.

Harkin, J.B. 1925. Report of the Commissioner of Canadian National Parks. *Dept. of the Interior Annual Report* for the year ending March 31, 1924. Ottawa. pp. 5-30.

Haron bin Haji Abu Hassan. 1980. A working plan for the Matang Mangroves, Perak, 1980-1989. State Forestry Department, Perka (in preparation).

Harris, David R. 1971. The ecology of swidden cultivation in the Upper Orinoco rainforest, Venezuela. *Geographical Review* 61.

Harrison, T. 1968. Effects of forest clearance on small mammals. In: Conservation in tropical south east Asia. Ed. L.M. Talbot and M.H. Talbot. IUCN, Gland, Switzerland.

Hart, William J. 1966. A systems approach to park planning. *IUCN Publ.* (N.S.) *Suppl. Pap.* 4:1-118.

Hartl, D.L. 1981. *A Primer of Population Genetics,* Sinauer Associates, Sunderland, Ma, l9l pp.

Harwood, Frances. 1976. Myth, Memory, and the Oral Tradition. *American Anthropologist* 78(4): 783-796.

Hayden, B.P., and R. Dolan. 1976. Coastal marine fauna and marine climates of the Americas. *J. Biogeogr.* 3: 71-81.

Hayden, B.P., G.C. Ray, and R. Dolan. (in prep.). A biophysical coastal and marine classification for protected areas. For the International Union for Conservation of Nature and Natural Resources.

Heald, E.J. 1971. The production of organic detritus in a South Florida Estuary. *Sea Grant Tech. Bull. Miami Univ.* 6: 1-110.

Healey, C.J. 1977. Maring Hunters and Traders: The Ecology of an Exploitative, Non-subsistence activity. Department of Anthropology and Sociology, University of Papua New Guinea, Port Moresby. Unpub. doctoral dissertation.

Healy, A.J. 1973. Introduced Vegetation. pp. 170-189 *in* G.R. Williams (ed.). 1973. *The Natural History of New Zealand.* A.H. and A.W. Reed, Wellington.

Heaney, W. 1982. The changing role of bird of paradise plumes in bridewealth in the Wahgi Valley. In: Monograph 16 - Traditional Conservation in Papua New Guinea: Implications for today by Morauta, L., Pernetta, J. and Heaney, W.

Hedgepeth, J.W. 1977. The Antarctic marine ecosystems. *In* Llano, G.A. (ed.). *Adaptations within Antarctic Ecosystems.* Smithsonian Institution, Washington.

Heinsohn, G.E. 1981. Status and Distribution of Dugongs in Queensland. pp. 55-56. *In* H. Marsh (ed.). 1981. *The Dugong.* Department of Zoology, James Cook University, Townsville, Queensland. 400 pp.

Hesse, R., W. C. Allee, and K.P. Schmidt. 1951. *Ecological Animal Geography.* (Second edition). J. Wiley & Sons, Inc.

Hessler, R.R. & H.L. Sanders. 1967. Faunal diversity in the deep sea. *Deep Sea Res.* 14: 65-78.

Hewitt, C. Gordon. 1918. The Conservation of wild life in Canada in 1917: A Review. *Report of the 9th Annual Meeting of the Commission of Conservation Canada.* Ottawa: 118-139.

Hewitt, C. Gordon. 1921. *The Conservation of the Wild Life of Canada.*

Heyligers, P.C. 1975. *Biological and Ecological Aspects Related to the Forestry Operations of the Export Woodchip Industry* - Report of a Working Group set up by the Australian Ministers for the Environment and Conservation and for Agriculture.

Hinchey, M.D. (ed). 1981. Nature Conservation Reserves in Australia (1980), Australian National Parks and Wildlife Service, Occasional Paper 5: 1-51.

HMG. 1968. His Majesty's Government. Soil Survey of Chitwan. Ministry of Forests, Forest Resources Survey. Kathmandu.

Hobart, M. 1978. The path of the soul: the legitimacy of nature in Balinese conceptions. pp.5-28. In: G.B. Milner (ed.), *Natural Symbols in South East Asia.* School of Oriental and African Studies, London.

Hodges, R.G. n.d. *The System of Coastal Management in Victoria: Protection, Control and Financing.* unpublished. 12pp.

Hoffman, R.S. 1974. Terrestrial Vertebrates. pp. 475-568. *In* Ives, J.D. & Barry, R.G. (eds.). *Arctic and Alpine Environments.* Methuen, London.

Hogg, J.T., and Garrett, J.W. *c.* 1976. The eradication of *Pinus contorta.* Waiouru Military Reserve. 11pp.

Holdgate, M.W. & Tinker, J. Oil and other minerals in the Antarctic. The environmental implications of possible mineral exploration or exploitation. Report of the Bellagio Workshop March 1979. SCAR, Cambridge.

Holdgate, M.W. and N.W. Wace. 1961. The Influence of Man on the Floras and Faunas of Southern Islands. *Polar Record* 10: 475-493.

Holdgate, M.W. 1970. Conservation in the Antarctic. pp. 924-945. *In* Holdgate, M.W. (ed.). *Antarctic Ecology.* Academic Press, London and New York.

Holdgate, M.W. 1982. *The World Environment* 1972-82. Tycooly Intern. Publ. Dublin. 637.

Hoose, P.M. 1981. *Building an Ark: Tools for the Preservation of Natural Diversity Through Land Protection.* Island Press, Covelo, Ca, 212 pp

Hornaday, William T. 1901. The destruction of our birds and animals. Reprinted from the *Second Annual Report of the New York Zoological Society.* N.Y. pp. 77-108.

Hudson, B.E.T. 1981. The Dugong Conservation, Management and Public Education Progamme in Papua New Guinea: Working with People to Conserve their Dugong Resources. pp. 123-142. *in* H. Marsh (ed.). 1981. *The Dugong.* Department of Zoology, James Cook University, Townsville, Queensland. 400 pp.

Huff, Don. 1982. Conference Report: Marine Parks Seminar in Hull, Quebec. *Park News* 18(1): 29-31

Hunt, C.D. and A.R. Lucas. 1980. *Environmental Regulation: Its Impact on Major Oil and Gas Projects* - Oil Sands and Arctic. Canadian Institute of Resources Law. University of Calgary, Calgary, Alberta.

Hunt, C.D. 1978. Approaches to Native Land Settlements and Complications for Northern Land Use and Resource Management Policies. *Northern Transitions.* Vol. 2: Second National Workshop on People, Resources and the Environment North of 60°, ed. by R.F. Keith and J.B. Wright, Canadian Arctic Resources Committee, Ottawa, Ontario. pp. 5-41.

Hunt, Constance. 1976. The Development and Decline of Northern Conservation Reserves. *Contact,* 8 (4):30-75.

Huntley, B.J. 1974. Outlines of Wildlife Conservation in Angola. *J. S. African Wildl. Mgmt Assoc.* 4(3):157-166.

Huntley, B.J. 1978. Ecosystem Conservation in Southern Africa, pp. 1333-1384 in Werger, M.J.A., (ed.), *Biogeography and Ecology of Southern Africa.* W. Junk, The Hague.

IBRD. 1981. *Economic Development and Tribal Peoples: Human Ecologic Considerations.* International Bank for Reconstruction and Development (World Bank). Washington, D.C.

Imshaug, H.A. 1972. Need for the conservation of terrestrial vegetation in the subantarctic. pp.229-239 *in* Parker, B.C. (ed.). *Conservation Problems in Antarctica.* Virginia Polytechnic Institute & State University, Blacksburg.

Innes-Brown, M.A. 1972. Analysis of Recreation and Conservation as Functional Concepts of National Parks. Unpublished Thesis, University of New England.

International Federation of Landscape Architects. 1981. Africa—an Environmental Catastrophe. Seminar Proceedings.

International Institute for Environment and Development. 1979. *The Environment and Bilateral Development Aid.* Washington D.C., London. 58.

Island Resources Foundation. 1979. A Research Prospectus for the Dominica National Park Programme. Report to the Canadian Nature Federation.

IUCN. 1967. Liste des nations unies des parcs nationaux et rserves analogues. Ed. J.P. Harroy. IUCN Publ. n.s. 11 Hayez, Brussels.

IUCN. 1969. Proc. X General Assembly, New Delhi. *IUCN Publ.(n.s.) Suppl. Paper* 27. Gland.

IUCN. 1971. United Nations List of National Parks and Equivalent Reserves. *IUCN Publ.* (n.s.) 15:

IUCN. 1972. Proc. XI General Assembly, Banff, Canada. September. *IUCN Publ.* (n.s.) Supplementary Paper 40E. Gland.

IUCN. 1974. United Nations List of National Parks and Equivalent Reserves. *IUCN Publ.* (n.s.) 29. Gland.

IUCN. 1975a. World Directory of National Parks and Other Protected Areas. IUCN. Gland.

IUCN. 1975b. Recommendations of the International Conference of Marine Parks and Reserves. *Suppl. IUCN Bull.* 6(7): 4pp.

IUCN. 1976a. An International Conference on Marine Parks and Reserves. *IUCN Publ.* 37: 1-131.

IUCN. 1976b. *Proceedings of a Regional Meeting on the Creation of a Coordinated System of National parks and Reserves in Eastern Africa.* IUCN, Morges, Switzerland.

IUCN. 1976c. Promotion of the Establishment of Marine Parks and Reserves in the Northern Indian Ocean, including the Red Sea and Persian Gulf. *IUCN Publ.* (n.s.) 35:1-169.

IUCN. 1977. *World Directory of National Parks and Other Protected Areas.* IUCN, Morges, Switzerland.

IUCN. 1978a. *Categories, objectives and criteria for protected areas.* IUCN, Morges, Switzerland. 26 pp.

IUCN. 1978b. *IUCN Red Data Book on Plants.* Unwin Brothers, England.

IUCN. 1979. *The Biosphere Reserve and its Relationship to other Protected Areas.* IUCN, Morges, Switzerland.

IUCN. 1980a. *United Nations List of National Parks and Equivalent Reserves* (Fourth Edition). IUCN, Gland, Switzerland. 121 pp.

IUCN. 1980b. *World Conservation Strategy: Living Resource Conservation for Sustainable Development.* IUCN/UNEP/WWF, Gland, Switzerland. 48 pp.

IUCN. 1980c. *Principles, Criteria and Guidelines for the Selection, Establishment and Management of Mediterranean Marine and Coastal Protected Areas.* Inter-governmental meeting on Mediterranean Specially Protected Areas. Athens, 13-17 October 1980. IUCN, Gland, Switzerland.

IUCN. 1980d. IUCN Red Data Book on Mammalia, Vol. I. IUCN, Gland, Switzerland.

IUCN. 1981a. Conserving the Natural Heritage of Latin America and the Caribbean. IUCN, Gland, Switzerland.

IUCN. 1981b. *Antarctica and the Southern Ocean.* (Inf. Paper No. 1), IUCN, Gland, Switzerland. 20 pp.

IUCN. 1981c. Principles, criteria and guidelines for the selection, establishment and management of Mediterranean marine and coastal protected areas. IUCN, Gland, Switzerland. 39 pp.

IUCN. 1981d. *Draft Action Plan for the Conservation of Nature in the ASEAN Region.* Prepared for the Interim Coordinator ASEAN Expert Group on the Environment by IUCN (first draft 20 February 1981). Gland, Switzerland.

IUCN. 1981e. *The Environmental Law of the Sea: Conclusions and Recommendations.* 42pp.

IUCN. 1982a. *IUCN Directory of Neotropical Protected Areas.* IUCN, Gland, Switzerland. 436 pp.

IUCN. 1982b. *UN List of National Parks and protected areas.* IUCN, Gland, Switzerland. 155 pp.

IUCN. 1982c. *The World's Greatest Natural Areas: An Indicative Inventory of Natural Sites of World Heritage Quality.* IUCN, Gland, Switzerland. 69 pp.

Iverson, R.L., L.K. Coachman, R.T. Cooney, T.S. English, J.J. Goering, G.L. Hunt, Jr., M.C. Macauley, C.P. McRoy, W.S. Reeburgh, and T.E. Whitledge. 1979. Ecological significance of fronts in the south-eastern Bering Sea. pp. 437-465: *Ecological Processes in Coastal and Marine Systems.* R.L. Livington, ed., Plenum Publ. Corp., N.Y., 437-465.

Jackson, Ivor. 1980. Study of Management Alternatives, South-eastern Pensinsula, St. Kitts; Final Project Report. ECNAMP, St. Croix, U.S. Virgin Islands. 48 pp.

Jackson, Ivor. 1981. A System of Marine Parks and Protected Areas for the British Virgin Islands. ECNAMP, St. Croix, U.S. Virgin Islands. 95 pp.

Jennings, J.N. 1972. Some Attributes of Torres Strait. pp. 29-38. *In* D. Walker (ed.). 1972. *Bridge and Barrier: The Natural and Cultural History of Torres Strait.* Research School of Pacific Studies, Australian National University, Canberra. 437 pp.

Jewell, Peter A. and Sidney Holt, (eds.). 1981. Problems in Management of Locally Abundant Wild Animals (Academic Press, New York).

Jochim, Michael A. 1981. *Strategies for Survival: Cultural Behaviour in an Ecological Context.* Academic Press, New York. 233 pp.

Johannes, R.E. 1977. Traditional Law of the Sea in Micronesia. *Micronesia* 13(2): 121-127.

Johannes, R.E. 1978. Traditional marine conservation methods in Oceania and their demise. *Ann. Rev. Ecol. Syst.* 9: 349-364.

Johannes, R.E. 1981. *World of the Lagoon: Fishing and Marine Lore in the Palau District of Micronesia.* University of California Press, Berkeley. 245 pp.

Johannes, R.E. (in press). Implications of traditional marine resource use for coastal fisheries development in Papua New Guinea, with emphasis on Manus. *In*: L. Morauta and J. Pernetta (eds.). *Traditional Conservation in Papua New Guinea: Implications for Today.* Institute of Applied Social and Economic Research, Port Moresby, Papua New Guinea.

Johannes, R.E. & S.B. Betzer. 1975. Introduction: marine communities respond differently to pollution in the tropics than at higher latitudes. pp. 1-12 In: E.J. Ferguson Wood & R.E. Johannes (eds.), *Tropical Marine Pollution.* Elsevier, Amsterdam.

Johnson, B. and R.O. Blake. 1979. *The Environmental and Bilateral Aid.* IIED, London, Washington. 58.

Johnson, H. and J.M. Johnson. 1977. *Environmental Policies in Developing Countries.* Berlin: Erich Schmidt Verlag.

Johnston, A. and Smoliak, S., Forbes, L.M., Campbell, J.A., n.d. Alberta Range Management Guide. *Alberta Dept. of Agriculture, Lands and Forests* Public No. 134/14.

Johnston, A. 1970. A history of the rangelands of western Canada. *Jour. Range Mgt.* 23: 3-8.

Johnston, J.A. 1981. The New Zealand bush: early assessments of vegetation. *New Zealand Science Geographer* 37(1): 19-24.

Johnstone, D. (ed.). 1981. *The Environmental Law of the Sea* IUCN, Gland, Switzerland.

Johnstone, Ian M. 1977. Introductory tropical ecology: A laboratory manual. Dept. of Biol., UPNG. Port Moresby, PNG.

Jones, R. 1981. The Extreme Climatic Place? *In* Henderson, K.R. (ed.) *Hemisphere* 26(1): 54-59.

Jorge Padua, M.T. *et al.* 1979. *Plano do Sistema de Unidades de Conservaao do Brazil.* IBDF, Braslia, 107 pp.

Jorge Padua, M.T. *et al*. 1982. *Plano do Sistema de Unidades de Conservaao do Brazil*. IIa. Etapa. IBDF, Braslia, 173 pp.

Juliano, R.O. 1979. Problems, Issues and Strategies on Fisheries and Aquatic Resources Management in the Philippines. *MNR Quart*. 1:28-35.

Jungius, H. 1976. National Parks, and Indigenous People: A Peruvian Case Study. *Survival Int. Rev*. 2(1): 17-21.

Kapetsky, James M. 1981. Some Considerations for the Management of Coastal Lagoon and Estuarine Fisheries. *FAO Fisheries Technical Paper No. 218*: 1-47.

Karr, J.R. 1982. Population variability and extinction of the avifauna of a tropical land bridge island. *Ecology* 63: 1975-1978.

Kassas, M. 1981. The River Nile Ecological System: A Study Towards an International Programme. *Biol. Conserv*. 4(1):19-25.

Katete, F. 1968. In Laws et al, 1975) p.59.

Kaufmann, Reinhard. 1975. Studies on the loggerhead sea turtle, *Caretta caretta caretta* (Linne) in Colombia, South America. *Herpetologia* 31:323-326.

Kayanja, F.I.B. 1982. Conservation of African mammals in the aftermath of commercial poaching. Third International Theriological Congress, Helsinki, 1982. Proceedings to be published in *Acta Zool. Fennica* (1983).

Kealy, J.W. 1951. The appreciation and preservation of New Zealand forests. *New Zealand Science Review* 9: 39.

Kellert, S.R. 1979. Some objectives for human dimension in wildlife management. Paper presented to the symposium, Human Dimension in Wildlife Management. Yale University School of Forestry. USA.

Kelly, G.C. 1972. Scenic reserves of Canterbury *Biological Survey of Reserves, Report No. 2*. D.S.I.R., Christchurch, 390 pp.

Kennedy, Jeffrey A. (ed.) 1980. *University of California Natural Land and Water Reserves System*. University of California, Berkeley, California. 24 pp.

Kenya National Museum. 1982. Review of Habitat Status of some Important Biotic Communities in Kenya. National Museum, Nairobi, Kenya.

Kessel, S., R. Good, and Porter. 1982. *Computer Modelling in Natural Area Management*. Australian National Parks and Wildlife Service, Canberra.

Ketchum, B.K. (ed.). 1972. *The Waters' Edge: Critical Problems of the Coastal Zone*. The Massachusetts Institute of Technology Press, Cambridge, MA, and London, England.

Kezar, G.G. 1922. *Order-In-Council* P.C. No. 1134. Ref. 109750. Government House at Ottawa.

King, C.M. 1978. Methods of predicting and reducing potential damage by stoats to takahe. pp. 234-244 *in Seminar on the Takahe and its Habitat*. Proceedings of a seminar, Te Anau, 5-6 May 1978. Fiordland National Park Board, Invercargill, New Zealand.

King, M.W., and E.H. Roberts. 1979. *The storage of recalcitrant seeds - achivements and possible approaches*. International Board for Plant Genetic Resources.

Kinloch, B.G. 1963. The Urgent Need for Formalized Training Facilities for Wildlife Management Personnel in the Africa of Today. pp. 208-218 *in* IUCN, 1963. *Conservation of Nature and Natural Resources in Modern African States*. Morges, Switzerland.

Kiss, A.C. 1976. *Survey of Current Developments in International Environmental Law*. IUCN, Gland, Switzerland.

Kist, F.J. 1938. The geo-political and strategic importance of the waterways in the Netherlands Indies. *Bull. Colon. Inst. Amst*. 1: 252-262.

Klee, Gary A. 1976. Traditional Time Reckoning and Resource Utilization. *Micronesica* 12(2): 211-246.

Klee, Gary A. (ed.). 1980. *World Systems of Traditional Resource Management*. Edward Arnold, London. 290 pp.

Koppen, W., 1936. Das geographische System der Klimate, *in* Vol. 3., Handbuch der Klimatologie Gebrden Borntraegar, Berlin.

Kosaki, R.H. 1954. *Konohiki Fishing Rights*. Legislative Reference Bureau, Univ. of Hawaii.

Kozlowski, J. and J. Zadorozna. 1982. Analiza mozliwosci rozwojowych w planowaniu prezestrzennym wojewodztw - zarys metody (Analysis of development possibilities in voivodship planning - outline of the method). *Czlowiek i Srodowisko* 6 (1).

Kozlowski, J. and J.T. Hughes. 1972. *Threshold Analysis - a quantitative planning method*. Architectural Press, London and Halsted Press, New York. 286 pp.

Kozlowski, J. 1975. Krancowe progi w ksztaltowaniu przestrzennym Podtatrza (Ultimate thresholds in planning for Podtarze), *Aura* 5 (3 and 5).

Kozlowski, J. 1977. Environmental Components and Method of their integration into Socio-economic and Physical Planning. *UNEP Occ. Pap*.

Kozlowski, J., M. Janota Braanowska, and D. Ptaszycka-Jackowska. 1979. The Tatry National Park. *Architektura* 383-384 (September - October).

Krishnamurthy, K. and M.J.P. Jeyaseelan. 1980. The impact of the Pichavaram mangrove ecosystem upon coastal natural resources: a case study from southern India. Asian Symposium on mangrove environment: research and management. Kuala Lumpur.

Krisnandhi, S. 1969. The economic development of Indonesia's sea fishing industry. *Bull. Indonesian Econ. Stud*. 5(1): 49-72.

Krutilla, J.V., A.C. Fisher. 1976. *The Economics of Natural Environments*, Resources for the Future, Inc., Washington DC, 1976.

Kula, G.R. 1982. Problems of wildlife management in the Southern Highlands Province. In: Monograph 16. Traditional Conservation in Papua New Guinea: Implications for today by Morauta, L. Pernetta, J. and Heaney, W.)

Kwapena, N. 1980. The ecology and conservation of six species of birds of paradise in Papua New Guinea. M.Sc. dissertation Zoology Department, School of Biological Sciences, University of Sydney, N.S.W. Australia, 1980 - to be published as a book by the Division of Wildlife, Office of Environment and Conservation, Papua New Guinea.

Kwapena, N. 1982. Wildlife Conservation, past and present in the lowlands of Papua New Guinea In: Monograph 16 - Traditional Conservation in PNG: Implications for today by Morauta, L; Pernetta, J. and Heaney, W.).

LaBastille, A. 1973. Effective Techniques for Developing Wildlife Reserves in Developing Countries. *38th N. Am. Wildlife Conf., Proceedings*, p. 89-95.

LaBastille, Anne. 1982. Paradise gained. *Animal Kingdom* 85(4):18-23.

Lacey, Roderick. 1982. *Traditional trade*. In King and Ranck (eds.), 1981. *Papua New Guinea Atlas*. Robert Brown and Assoc., Australia in conjunction with UPNG, PNG.

Lamprey, H.F. 1964. College of African Wildlife Management: A Syllabus. *E.A.Wildl.J.* (2).

Lamprey, H. 1975. Report on the desert encroachment reconnaissance in Northern Sudan. IUCN/UNEP, Morges, Switzerland.

Lamprey, H.F. 1975. *The Distribution of Protected Areas in Relation to the Needs of Biotic Community Conservation in Eastern Africa*. IUCN Occasional Paper No. 16. Morges, Switzerland.

Laurie, W.A. 1978. *The Ecology and Behaviour of the Greater One Horned Rhinoceros*. Ph.D. Dissertation. University of Cambridge, U.K.

Lausche, B.J. 1980. *Guidelines for Protected Areas Legislation*, IUCN, Gland, Switzerland.

Lavers, R.B., and J.A. Mills. 1978. Stoat studies in the Murchison Mountains, Fiordland. pp. 222-233 *in Seminar on the Takahe and its Habitat*. Proceedings of a seminar, Te Anau, 5-6 May 1978. Fiordland National Park Board, Invercargill, New Zealand.

Laws, R.M. 1970. Elephants as agents of habitat and landscape change in East Africa. *Oikos* 21 : 1-15.

Laws, R.M., Parker, I.S.C., Johnstone, R.C.B. 1970. Elephants and habitats in North Bunyoro, Uganda. *E. Afr. Wildl. J.* 8 : 163-180.

Laws, R.M., Parker, I.S.C., Johnstone, R.C.B. 1975. *Elephants and their habitats*. Clarendon Press, London.

Lawson, G.W. 1970. Lessons of the Volta--a New Manmade Lake in Tropical Africa. *Biol. Conserv.* 2(2):90-96.

Lawson, G.W. 1972. The Case for Conservation in Ghana. *Biol. Conserv.* 4(4):292-300.

Le Bar, F.M. (ed.) 1972. *Ethnic groups of Insular Southeast Asia*. Volume 1. Indonesia. Human Relations Area Files, New Haven. 236 pp.

Leacock, Seth. 1962. Economic life of the Maue Indians. *Boletim do Museu Paraense Emilio Goeldi, Antropologia* No. 19.

Lean, Geoffrey. 1982. A Network to Save the Seas: UNEP's Regional Seas Programme. *IUCN Bulletin* 13 (4-5-6): 39.

Ledingham, George F. 1960. In search of grasslands. *Canadian Audubon*. Vol. 20, No. 2: 54-57.

Ledingham, George F. 1981. Acceptance of the J.B. Harkin Conservation Award. *Canadian Plains Research Center Memorandum*. Dec. 16, 1981, University of Regina, Regina, Saskatchewan.

Leh, C.M.U. and A. Sasekumar. 1980. Feeding ecology of prawns in shallow waters adjoining mangrove shores. Paper presented at the Unesco Asian Symposium on Mangrove Environment: Research and Management held at Universiti Malaya, Kuala Lumpur, Malaysia. August 1980.

Leigh, J., Briggs, J., and Hartley W. 1981. *Role of Threatened Australian Plants*. ANPWS, Special publication 7.

Lekagul, Boonsong. 1980. Wildlife and national parks management in the Asia and Pacific region. Background paper for Consultation on wildlife resources for rural development, Hyderabad, India. FAO, Bangkok.

Lembaga Ekologi Unpad. 1980. Rencana Pengelolaan 1980-1985 Cagar Alam Gunung Tilu, Lembaga Ekologi, Unpad, Bandung, 5-76.

Leonard, H.J. and D. Morell. 1981. Emergence of environmental concern in developing countries: a political perspective. *Stanford J. Int. Law* 17(2):281-313.

Leopold, A. 1933. The Conservation Ethic. *In*: G.W. Cox (ed.) 1969. *Readings in Conservation Ecology*. Appleton Century Crofts, New York.

Levine, Barry B. 1981. Abundance and Scarcity in the Caribbean. *Ambio* 10(6): 274-281.

Lévi-Strauss, Claude. 1950. The use of wild plants in tropical South America. *In* J. Steward (ed.), *Handbook of South American Indians*. Bureau of American Ethnology Bulletin No. 143. Washington, D.C.: Smithsonian Institution.

Lévi-Strauss, Claude. 1966. *The Savage Mind*. University of Chicago Press, Chicago. 290 pp.

Liem, D.S. 1975. Wildlife utilization in the proposed Garu Wildlife Management Area, West New Britain; Papua New Guinea. Proc. of the 1975 Waigani Seminar.

Liew, T.C. 1977. Mangrove Forest of Sabah. Paper presented at Workshop on Mangrove and Estuarine Vegetation, Universiti Pertanian Malaysia, Serdang. 10 December 1977.

Linstone, H. and M. Turoff. 1975. *The Delphi Method*. Addison-Wesley Publishing Co. Massachusetts.

Livingston, R.J. 1981. The Apalachicola experiment: research and management. *Oceanus* 23: 14-21.

Lothian, W.F. 1977. *History of Canada's National Parks*. Vol. I, Published by Parks Canada, Ottawa.

Lovejoy, T.E., G.T. Prance, and G.B. Wetterberg. 1981. Conservation Progress in Amazonia: A Structural Review. *Parks* 6 (2): 5-10.

Loyn, R.H., M.A. MacFarlane, E.A. Chesterfield & J.A. Harris. 1980. Forest Utilisation and the Flora and Fauna in Boola Boola State Forest in south-eastern Victoria. Forests Commission, Melbourne, Bulletin 28:1-80.

Lusigi, Walter J. 1978. *Planning human activities on protected natural ecosystems*. Dissertationes Botanicae 48. J. Cramer, Vaduz, Germany. 233pp.

Lusigi, W.J. 1981. New Approaches to Wildlife Conservation in Kenya. *Ambio* 10 (2-3).

MAB. 1980. *Twenty years of Conservation in the Galapagos. Assessments, lessons, and future priorities.* MAB/UNESCO. Quito, Ecuador.

MacArthur, R.H. and E.O. Wilson. 1967. *The Theory of Island Biogeography.* Princeton University Press, Princeton, New Jersey. 203 pp.

MacArthur, R.H. 1972. *Geographical Ecology: Patterns in the Distribution of Species.* Harper and Row, N.Y.

MacKinnon, J. 1981. National Park Development and general topics. National Conservation Plan for Indonesia, Vol VIII, Chapter 42: Buffer Zone Development. FO/INS/78/061 Field Report 19, FAO, Bogor.

MacKinnon, J. 1982. Introduction, evaluation methods and overview of national nature richness. National Conservation Plan for Indonesia, vol. I, FO/INS/78/061. Field Report 34. FAO. 60pp.

Macmillan Company of Australia. 1981. The Heritage of Australia. The Illustrated Register of the National Estate. Melbourne, Australia. 120pp.

Macnae, W. 1974. Mangrove Forests and Fisheries. FAO/UNDP Indian Ocean Programme, Indian Ocean Fishery Commission IOFC/DEV/74/34. Rome. 35 pp.

Macquarie University, Centre for Environmental Studies. 1976. Kur-ring-gai Chase National Park: Preliminary study of its utilization (unpublished).

Majuikan. 1979. Terms of reference for Aquaculture Scheme in Sungai Merbok Estuary, Kedah. 50 pp.

Maldague, Michel. 1981. The Biosphere Reserve concept: its implementation and its potential as a tool for integrated development. Paper presented at UNESCO-ICSU Conference-exhibit: Ecology in Practice—Establishing a Scientific Basis for Land Management. Paris, 22-29 September 1981.

Malinowski, B. 1918. Fishing in the Trobriand Islands. *Man* 18: 87-92.

Malpas, R. (ed.) 1980. Wildlife in Uganda 1980. A Survey. (Typescript 118 pp).

Mangelsdorf, Paul C., Richard S. MacNeish, Gordon Wiley. 1964. Origins of agriculture in Middle America. pp. 427-445. *In* R. Wauchope (ed.), *Handbook of Middle American Indians.* University of Texas Press, Austin..

Margules, C. and M.B. Usher. 1958. *Biol. Conserv.* 21: 79.

Marquez, René. 1978. Natural reserves for the conservation of marine turtles of Mexico. *Fla. Marine Res. Publ.* 33:56-60.

Marsh, H. (ed.). 1981. *The Dugong.* Department of Zoology, James Cook University, Townsville, Queensland. 400 pp.

Marshall, A.J. (ed.). 1966. *The Great Extermination.* Heinemann, London & Melbourne. 221 pp.

Martin, R.B. and R.D. Taylor. 1982: Towards a resolution of wildlife conservation problems in the Sebungwe through regional land use planning. Paper read at *Symposium on the Management of Large Mammals in African Conservation Areas*, Pretoria, 29-30 April, 1982.

Martin, R.B., A. Conway and P. Dix. 1977. *Project Windfall*, Sebungwe Dept. Nat. Parks and Wildl. Mgment, Zimbabwe. Report.

Mason, Leonard. 1954. Relocation of the Bikini Marshallese. Unpublished Ph.D. dissertation. Yale University, New Haven.

May, Robert M. 1978. The Evolution of Ecological Systems. *Scientific American* 239(3): 160-175.

McCay, Bonnie J. 1981. Development Issues in Fisheries as Agrarian Systems. *Culture and Agriculture* No. 11: 1-8.

McClure, H.E. and Hussain Bin Haji Osman. 1968. Nesting of birds in a coconut mangrove habitat in Selangor Malayan Nat. Journal.

McEachern, John and Edward L. Towle. 1974. Ecological Guidelines for Island Development. *IUCN Publications New Series*, No. 30: 1-65.

McHarg, I.L. 1969. *Design with Nature.* Doubleday & Co., New York.

McMillan, George. 1975. *Report on a Tour of Pacific Rim Countries to Study Maritime and Marine Parks and General Coastline Protection.* The Department of Lands and Survey, Wellington, New Zealand. 30pp.

McNeely, J.A. 1975. Wildlife in the Mekong Basin. ESCAP Committee for the coordination of investigations of the Lower Mekong Basin.

McNeely, J.A. 1980. Siberut: Conservation of Indonesia's island paradise. *In*: PARKS Magazine.

Medway, Lord. 1978. The tropical forests as a source of animal genetic resources. *In*: Proceedings of Eighth World Forestry Congress, FAO, Rome.

Meganck, R. and J.M. Goebel. 1979. Shifting Cultivation: Problem for Parks in Latin America. *Parks* 4 (2).

Megitt, M.J. 1958. The Enga of the New Guinea Highlands. *Oceania* 28: 253-330.

Mence, T. 1972. People Who Run National Parks. In Harroy, J.P. ed. *World National Parks Progress and Opportunities*, Hayez, Belgium.

Menzies, R.J., R.Y. George, and G.T. Rowe. 1973. *Abyssal Environment and Ecology of the World Oceans.* J. Wiley & Sons, N.Y.

Merrill, C. 1965. *National Park Potentials in Saskatchewan.* Planning Division Report No. 44. National and Historic Parks Branch. Dept Indian Affairs and Northern Development. Ottawa.

Meurk, C.D. 1977. Alien plants in Campbell Island's Changing Vegetation. *Mauri Ora* Vol. 5.

Meyer, R.L. 1976. Travaux Preparatoire for the Unesco World Heritage Convention. *Earth Law Journal* 2 (1).

Miller, K.R. 1974. Manejo y desarrollo integral de las areas naturales y culturales, Cuba. Informe technico No. 11, proyecto FAO/PNUD/CUB/69/503. Centro de Investigaciones y Capacitacion Forestales. La Habana.

Miller, K.R. 1975. Guidelines for the management and development of national parks and reserves in the American Humid Tropics. Proc. IUCN Meeting on the Use of Ecological Guidelines for Development in the American Humid Tropics, Caracas, 20-22 February 1974. IUCN, Gland. pp.94-105.

Miller, K.R. 1978. Planning National Parks For Eco-development. Univ. of Michigan.

Miller K.R. 1980. Planificacion de Parques Nacionales Para el Ecodesarrollo en Latinoamerica. Madrid, Fundacion para la Ecologia y la Proteccion del Medio Ambiente. 500 pp.

Milne, Robert C. 1981. International Cooperation: Enlightened Self-Interest. *Parks and Recreation* 16(8): 59-62.

Milton, J. and G. Binney. 1980. *Ecological Planning in the Nepalese Terai: A report of conflicts between Wildlife Conservation and Agricultural Land Use in Padampur Panchyat*. Threshold. Washington, D.C.

Ministry of Environment, Norway. 1980. Naturvern i Norge. Nov. 1980, 23. 47.

Mishra, H.R. and B.B. Shah. 1981. *Kingdom of Hope: A review of a decade of Nature Conservation in Nepal.* HMG/Department of National Parks and Wildlife, Kathmandu.

Mishra, H.R. 1974. *Nature Conservation in Nepal. An Introduction to the National Parks and Wildlife Conservation Programe of His Majesty's Government.* Trib. Univ. Press, Kathmandu.

Mishra, H.R. 1981. Wir fingen einen, Morder. Gnade fur den Tiger. *Das Tier*, 6:21 47-51.

Mitchell, B. J. Tinker. 1980. *Antarctica and its Resources.* Int. Instit. Environ. Devel., London.

Mittermeier, R.A., A.F. Coimbra-Filho and I.D. Constable. 1980. Conservation of eastern Brazilian primates—Report for the period 1979/1980. Unpublished report to WWF.

Mittermeier, R.A., A.F. Coimbra-Filho and C. Valle. 1981. Conservation of eastern Brazilian primates—Progress report for 1981. Unpublished report to WWF.

Mock, C.R. 1966. Natural and altered estuarine habitats of penaeid shrimp. *19th Proc. Gulf and Carib. Fish. Inst.:* 86-98.

Molloy, L.F. *et al.* 1980. *Land alone endures: land use and the role of research.* DSIR, Wellington, New Zealand. 286pp.

Mondor, C.A. 1976. The Canadian Plains: The vanishing act. *Nature Canada* 5(2):32-40

Moomaw, J.C. 1960. *A Study of the Plant Ecology of the Coast Region of Kenya, East Africa.* Government Printer, Nairobi, Kenya

Moore, D., H.A. Busher, and L. Trent. 1970. Relative abundance, seasonal distribution and species composition of demersal fishes off Louisianna and Texas, 1962-64. *Cont. Mar. Sci.* 15: 45-70.

Moore, David R. 1979. *Islanders and Aborigines at Cape York.* Australian Institute of Aboriginal Studies, Canberra. 340 pp.

Moran, Emilio F. 1979. *Human Adaptability.* Duxbury, North Scituate, Massachusetts. 404 pp.

Morgan, J. and M.J. Valencia. (eds.) (In press). *Marine Policy Atlas of Southeast Asian Seas.*

Mori, S.A., B.M. Boom and G.T. Prance. 1981. Distribution patterns and conservation of eastern Brazilian coastal forest tree species. *Brittonia* 33 (2): 233-245.

Morris, A.W., R.F.C. Mantoura, A.J. Bale, and R.J.M. Howland. 1978. Very low salinity regions of estuaries: important sites for chemical and biological reactions. *Nature* 274: 678-680.

Moseley, J.J., Thelen K.D. and Miller, K.R. 1974. Planificacion de Parques Nacionales, Guia para la Preparacion de Planes de Manejo para Parques Nacionales. Documento Tecnico de Trabajo No 15, Proyecto FAO-RLAT/TF-l99. Santiago, Chile.

Mosley, J.G. 1967. *Australia-National Parks and Equivalent Reserves* (Map). Aust. Conserv. Found., Canberra

Mosley, J.G. 1978. Regional Parks, National Parks and Wilderness Areas—A Framework for Recreation and Conservation. *Land for Leisure*, pp. 14-24. Royal Australian Institute of Parks and Recreation. Canberra, Australia.

Mueller-Dombois, D. & H. Ellenberg. 1974. *Aims and Methods of vegetation ecology*, John Wiley & Sons, New York. 547 pp.

Muller-Schwarze, D. & Belanger, P. 1978. Man's Impact on antarctic birds. pp.373-383. *In* Parker, B.C. & Holliman, M.E. (eds.). *Environmental impact in Antarctica.* Virginia Polytechnic Institute & State University, Blacksburg.

Mulvaney, D.J. 1969. *The Prehistory of Australia.* Thames and Hudson, London.

Murnyak, D.F. 1981. Censusing the Gorillas in Kahuzi-Biega National Park. *Biol. Conserv.* 21(3): 163-176.

Myers, Norman. 1972. National Parks in Savannah Africa. *Science* 178:1255-1263.

Myers, Norman. 1973. Tsavo National Park, Kenya, and its Elephants: An Interim Appraisal. *Biological Conservation* 5(2): 123-132.

Myers, Norman. 1979. *The Sinking Ark.* Pergamon, Oxford.

Myers, Norman. 1980. The Present Status and Future Prospects of Tropical Moist Forests. *Environmental Conservation* 7(2):101-114.

Myers, Norman. 1981a. A Farewell to Africa. *International Wildlife* 11(6):36-47.

Myers, Norman. 1981b. The two million wildebeest in the Tanzanian pie. *The Guardian* (London). 12 February.

Nachtigal, G. 1981. *Sahara und Sudan.* Berlin: Weidmannsche Buchhandlung, Verlagshandlung Paul Parey.

Nair, M.Y. 1977. An appraisal of the economic potential of mangrove swamps. M.S. Thesis, Universiti Pertanian Malaysia. 134 pp.

National Estate Committee of Inquiry. 1974. Report of the National of the National Estate. Australian Government Publishing Service. Canberra, Australia. 415pp.

National Park Service Planning. 1967. *Prairie National Park (Saskatchewan) boundary proposal.* Dept. of Indian and Northern Affairs. Ottawa. 18 p.

National Parks and Reserves Authority. 1982. New Zealand's National Parks. *National Parks and Reserves Authority Draft General Policy.* July 1982. 45pp plus Appendix A.

NATIONAL PARKS, CONSERVATION, AND DEVELOPMENT

National Parks and Wildlife Service. 1980. *Plan of Management Review, Kosciusko National Park Planning Issue Statement: Fire Management.* New South Wales, Government Printer.

National Parks and Wildlife Service. 1982. *Kosciusko National Park Plan of Management.* Sydney. 162p.

National Parks Authority. 1977. *Seminar on Science in National Parks.* Proceedings of a seminar, Lincoln College, 26-29 August 1976. National Parks authority, Wellington, New Zealand. 373pp.

Native Forests Action Council. 1979: Paparoa National Park. 102pp.

Natural Resources Defence Council, Inc. 1978. *Environment, natural resources and development.* The role of the US Agency for International Development. 31 plus Annex.

Natural Resources Defence Council, Inc. 1980. *Aiding the environment.* Washington D.C. 226 plus annex.

Nature Conservation Council. 1980. *The international significance of New Zealand's indigenous forests.* Information Leaflet No. 19. Nature Conservation Council, Wellington North, and Environmental Council, Wellington. 16pp.

Nature Conservation Council Technical Sub-Committee. 1981. *Integrating Conservation and Development.* A Proposal for a New Zealand Conservation Strategy. Nature Conservation Council, Wellington, New Zealand. 64pp.

Nelson, J.G. 1976. The Future Role of Conservation Reserves in the Arctic. *Contact,* 8(4): 76-116.

Nepal National Planning Commission. 1978. A survey of Employment, Income, Distribution and Consumption Patterns in Nepal. Vol. IV, Kathmandu, Nepal.

NEPC. 1979a. *Philippine Environment Report.* Diliman, Quezon City.

NEPC. 1979b. *Philippine Environmental Law.* Quezon City, Vol. I.

NEPC. 1981a. *Philippine Environmental Law.* Quezon City, Vol. II.

NEPC. 1981b. *Proceedings of the First National Symposium on Coastal Zone Management.* Punta Baluarte, Batangas.

Netting, R.M. 1977. *Cultural Ecology.* Cummings, Menlo Park, California.

N.Z. Forest Service. 1977. *Management policy for New Zealand's indigenous State Forests.* N.Z. Forest Service, Wellington, N.Z., 15 pp.

N.Z. Nature Conservation Council. 1981. *Integrating Conservation and Development: A proposal for a New Zealand Conservation Strategy.* Nature Conservation Council, Wellington, N.Z., 62 pp.

N.Z. Nature Conservation Council. 1981. *The Red Data Book of New Zealand.* Nature Conservation Council, Wellington, N.Z. 175 pp.

Newby, J.E. 1975a. The addax and the scimitar-horned oryx in Niger. IUCN/WWF/UNEP, Morges, Switzerland.

Newby, J.E. 1975b. The addax and the scimitar-horned oryx in Chad. IUCN/WWF/UNEP, Morges, Switzerland.

Newby, J.E. and D.M. Jones. 1980. Ecological Studies in Niger. Zoological Society of London, mimeo.

Newby, J.E. 1980. Can addax and oryx be saved in the Sahel? *Oryx,* XV (3) 264-266.

Newby, J.E. 1981. Action plan for the sahelo-saharan fauna of Africa. *WWF Yearbook* 1980-81. p. 466-474.

Newby, J.E. 1982. Avant-project de classement d'une aire proégée dans l'Aïr et le Ténéré (République du Niger). IUCN/WWF, Gland, Switzerland.

Nicholls, J.L. 1979. The concept of ecological districts, a possible framework for a national biological inventory. *Unpublished paper presented at workshop convened by the N.Z. Commission for the Environment,* Wellington, N.Z.

Nicholls, J.L. 1980. The past and present extent of New Zealand's indigenous forests. *Environmental Conservation* 7(4): 309-310.

Nicolls, W.G. 1981. *Aishihik: The Politics of Hydro Planning in the Yukon.* Canadian Arctic Resources Committee, Ottawa.

Nietschmann, Bernard and Judith Nietschmann. 1981. Good Dugong, Bad Dugong; Bad Turtle, Good Turtle. *Natural History* 90(5): 54-63.

Nietschmann, Bernard. 1972. Hunting and fishing focus among the Miskito Indians, Eastern Nicaragua. *Human Ecology* (1): 41-67.

Nietschmann, Bernard. 1977. The Wind Caller. *Natural History* 86(3): 10-16.

Nooy-Palm, H. 1968. The culture of the Pagai-Islands and Sipora, Mentawai. *Tropical Man* 1: 152-241.

Norris, Kenneth S. 1968. California's Natural Land and Water Reserves System. *Bioscience* 18(5):415-417.

North Carolina State University-Industry Cooperative Tree Improvement Programme. 1982. A report on program objectives, accomplishments and future development efforts. Mimeo.

Norton-Griffiths, M. 1978. *Counting Animals.* (Second Ed.) African Wildlife Leadership Foundation, Nairobi.

Norum, E.B., B.A. Krantz and H.J. Haas. 1957. The Northern Great Plains. In *Soil,* the 1957 United States Dept. of Agriculture Yearbook of Agriculture. p. 498.

Novoa, C. and J.C. Wheeler. In press. Llama and alpaca. In: *Evolution of Domesticated Animals,* ed. I.L. Mason, Longman, London.

Nyahoza, F., 1981. Developments of the College of African Wildlife Management Mweka and her Training Needs. pp. 90-103. *in* IUCN, 1981. *Conserving Africa's Natural Heritage.* Gland, Switzerland.

OAS. 1940. Proceedings of the Convention on Protection of Flora, Fauna and Scenic Natural Beauties of American Countries. Mar del Plata, Argentina.

OAS. 1972-74. Proceedings of the Second and Third International Seminars on Natural Areas and Tourism. Chubut, Argentina.

OAS. 1977. Final Report on Conservation of Marine Mammals and their Ecosystems. Puerto Madryn, Chubut.

OAS. 1978. Final Report on Conservation of Major Terrestrial Ecosystem of the Western Hemisphere. San Jos, Costa Rica.

Obeng, L.E. 1981. Aquatic Ecosystems, pp. 33-64 in Ayensu, E.S. and J. Marton-Lefevre, eds., *Proceedings of the Symposium on the State of Biology in Africa*. African Biosciences Network. Washington, D.C.: ICSU and Unesco.

Odum, H.T. 1971. *Environment, Power and Society*. New York, Wiley.

Odum, W.E. 1970. Insidious alteration of the estuarine environment. *Trans. Am. Fish. Soc.* 99: 837-847.

Odum, W.E. 1971. Pathways of energy flow in South Florida Estuary. *Sea Grant Tech. Bull. Miami Univ.* 7: 1-162.

Odum, W. E. 1976. Ecological Guidelines for Tropical Coastal Development. *IUCN Publ.* (N. S.) 42: 1-60.

Odum, W.E., C.C. McIvor, and T.J. Smith III. 1982. The ecology of the mangroves of south Florida: a community profile. U.S. Fish and Wildlife Service, Office of Biological Programs, Washington, D.C. FWS/OBS-81/24. 144pp.

Odum, W.E., T.J. Smith III, J.K. Hoover, and C.C. McIvor. (in press). Tidal freshwater marshes of the mid-Atlantic coast: a community profile. U.S. Fish and Wildlife Service.

OECD. 1981. Development Cooperation, Paris. 241.

Ogden, J.C. 1976. Some aspects of herbivore-plant relationships on Caribbean reefs and seagrass beds. *Aquat. Bot. 2(2): 103-116.*

Okali, D.U.U. 1981. Forest Resources, pp. 65-92 in Ayensu, E.S. and J. Marton-Lefevre, eds., *Proceedings of the Symposium on the State of Biology in Africa*. African Biosciences Network. Washington, D.C.: ICSU and Unesco.

Ola-Adams, B.A. and D.E. Iyamabo. 1977. Conservation of Natural Vegetation in Nigeria. *Environ. Conserv.* 4(3): 217-226.

Ong, J.E. 1978. The Malaysian Mangrove Environment. Paper presented at the Unesco Regional Seminar on Human Use of the Mangrove Environment and Management Implications. Dacca. Bangladesh, 4-8 December 1978.

Ong, J.E. 1982. Malaysian Mangroves: Their conservation through rational use. Proceedings of the Malaysian Society of Marine Sciences 4th Annual Seminar on The Status and Conservation of Shallow-water Coastal Ecosystems in Malaysia, Penang, 7 March 1981: pp. 5-9.

Ong, J.E.; Gong, W.K.; Wong, C.H. and G. Dhanarajan. 1980a. Contribution of aquatic productivity in a managed mangrove ecosystem in Malaysia. Paper presented at the Unesco Asian Symposium on Mangrove Environment: Research and Management held at Universiti Malaya, Kuala Lumpur, August 1980.

Ong, J.E.; Gong, W.K. and Wong, C.H. 1982. Productivity and nutrient status of litter in a managed mangrove forest. Paper presented at the BIOTROP-Unesco Symposium on Mangrove Forest Ecosystem productivity, Bogor, Indonesia. 20-22 April 1982.

Ong, T.L. 1978. Some aspects of trophic relationships of shallow water fishes (Selangor Coast). Unpublished B.Sc. Hons. Thesis, Universiti Sains Malaysia, Penang. 55 pp.

Oram, Nigel D. 1980. *Some economic aspects of the Hiri trading system of southern coastal Papua.* (unpubl.). Present in Dept. of Linguistics, ANU, Australia.

Oram, Nigel D. 1981. *The history of the Motu-speaking and the Koitabu-speaking peoples according to their own traditions.* In Denoon and Lacey (eds.). Oral tradition in Melanesia. UPNG, Port Moresby. PNG.

Orians, Gordon. 1974. Tropical Population Ecology. pp. 5-65. *In* Edward G. Garnworth and Frank B. Golley (eds.). 1974. *Fragile Ecosystems*. Springer-Verlag, New York. 258 pp.

Orsman, B. 1982. Reprieve from opossum damage for Kapiti Island. *Forest and Bird* 14(2): 18-21.

Ottino, P. and Y. Plessis. *In*: J.M.C. Thomas and L. Bernot (eds.).

Owen, J.S. 1969. Development and Consolidation of Tanzania National Parks. *Biol. Conserv.* 2:156-158.

Oza, G.M. 1978. Indian Wildlife and human civilization. *Indian J. Forestry,* 1 (1): 25-30.

Oza, G.M. & Gaekwad, Fatesinghrao P. 1979. Environmental Deterioration Causing Fears of Food Shortages in India. *Environ. Conserv.* 6 (3): 243-44.

Paijmans, K. 1981. *Vegetation.* In King and Ranck (eds.). Papua New Guinea Atlas. Robert Brown and Assoc., Australia in conjunction with UPNG, PNG.

Palmer, J. and N. Judd. 1981. Campbell Island Archaeological Investigation. (Report to Department of Land and Survey).

Panwar, H.S. 1980. Conservation-oriented development for communities in forested regions of India. *Tropical Ecology and Development.* pp 467-474. Proceedings of the Vth International Symposium on Tropical Ecology, Kuala Lumpur, April, 1979.

Panwar, H.S. (in press). Tiger conservation and communities—socio-economic equations. *International Symposium on Tiger, New Delhi,* 1979. Mimeo. 9 pp.

Park, G.N., and G.Y. Walls. 1978. *Inventory of tall forest stands on lowland plains and terraces in Nelson and Marlborough land districts, New Zealand.* Miscellaneous Publication, Botany Division D.S.I.R., Christchurch, N.Z. 127 pp.

Parker, B.C. (ed.) 1972. *Conservation problems in Antarctica.* Virginia Polytechnic Institute and State University, Blacksburg.

Parks Canada. 1972. *National Parks System Planning Manual.* Information Canada, Ottawa.

Parks Canada. 1975. *A proposed Grasslands National Park —What would it mean?* An information brochure published by the joint Federal-Provincial Committee on the proposed Grasslands National Park. Ottawa.

Parks Canada. 1976. *Natural Areas of Canadian Significance, A Preliminary Study.* Presented at the 15th Federal-Provincial Parks Conference, Regina, Saskatchewan. October 18-22. Ottawa: Information Canada.

NATIONAL PARKS, CONSERVATION, AND DEVELOPMENT

Pearce, D.G. 1982. Westland National Park Economic Impact Study, Department of Lands and Survey/University of Canterbury, 46 pp.

Pearce, William. 1982. Dinosaur Provincial Park—World Heritage Site. Unpublished, a paper presented to the 1982 Interpretation Canada Conference, Banff, Alberta.

Pelzer, Karl. J. 1945. *Pioneer Settlement in the Asiatic Tropics*, American Geographical Society of New York.

Pennycuick, C.J., Sale, J.B., Stanley-Price, M. and Jolly, G.M. 1977. Aerial systematic sampling applied to censuses of large mammal populations in Kenya. *E. Afr. Wildl. J.* 15:139-146.

Pickett, S.T.A. and Thompson, N.J. 1978. Patch dynamics and the design of nature reserves. *Biol. Conserv.* 13:27-37.

Pielou, E.C. 1979. *Biogeography*. J. Wiley & Sons (Wiley-Intersciences), N.Y.

Pires, Joao, M. 1974. Tipos de vegetaao da Amazonia. *Brasil Florestal.* v. 17 pp. 48-58.

Pitelka, F.A., Tomich, P.Q. & Treichel, G.W. 1955. Ecological relations of jaguars and owls as lemming predators near Barrow, Alaska. *Ecol. Monogr.* 25: 85-117.

Polunin, N.V.C. (in press). Marine 'genetic resources' and the potential role of protected areas in conserving them. *Environ. Conserv.*

Ponce Salazar, A. 1981. Parques Nacionales, Reservas Naturales y Vida Silvestre. In Diagnostico de la Situacion del Medio Ambiente en el Ecuador. Fundacion Natura, Quito.

Ponce Salazar, A. and Huber, R. Jr. 1982. Ecuador's Active Conservation Programme. *Parks*, 6 (4): 7-10.

Poore, D. 1976. *Ecological guidelines for development in tropical rainforests.* IUCN, Gland, Switzerland. 39 pp.

Poore, Duncan and Paule Gryn-Ambroes. 1980. *Nature Conservation in Northern and Western Europe.* IUCN, Gland.

Poppleton, F. and H.R. Mishra. 1973. Operation Tiger. A preliminary project for the Conservation of Wildlife in Nepal's Terai. HMG/FAO/UNDP National Parks and Wildlife Conservation Project. Kathmandu.

Prance, G.T. 1973. Phytogeografic support for the theory of Pleistocene forest refuges in the Amazonian Basin; based on evidence from distribution patterns in Caryocaraceae, Chrysobalanceae, Dichapetalaceae and Hecythidaceae. *Acta Amazonica.* 6(1): 5-28.

Prance, G.T. 1976. The Phytogeographic subdivisions of Amazonia and their consequences on the selection of biological reserves. New York Botanical Garden. Bronx, N.Y. USA, 39 pp.

Prance, G.T. 1982. *Biolgical Diversification in the Tropics.* Columbia University Press, New York, 714.

Pranoto, K. 1975. Feasibility studies, Proyek Penyelamtan Banteng dan Jalak Putih Bali. Report Seksi PPA, Bali, Singaraja, pp.8.

Prasad, K. 1982. Legislation and Trade. A paper presented during the Orientation Course in Wildlife Management at Dudhwa National Park, India.

Prescott-Allen, R., and C. Prescott-Allen. 1981. *In situ conservation of crop genetic resources.* IBPGR and IUCN, Rome and Gland.

Prescott-Allen, R., and C. Prescott-Allen. 1982 a. *Wild plants and crop improvement.* World Wildlife Fund (UK), London.

Prescott-Allen, R., and C. Prescott-Allen. 1982 b. *What's Wildlife Worth? Economic contributions of wild plants and animals to developing countries.* Earthscan, IIED, and WWF-US, London and Washington D.C.

Prole, J.H.B. 1967. In *Nairobi City and Region.* W.T.W. Morgan. (ed.). Oxford, Nairobi.

Putney, Allen D. 1979. Towards a Strategy for the Management of Living Natural Resources Critical to Development in the Lesser Antilles. pp. 98-106 *in* William S. Beller (ed.). 1979. *Transactions of the Conference on Environmental Management and Economic Growth in the Smaller Caribbean Islands.* U.S. Government Printing Office, Washington, D.C.

Putney, Allen D. 1980. Overview of Conservation in the Caribbean Region. pp. 460-467. *In* Kenneth Sabot (ed.). 1980. *Transactions of the Forty-fifth North American Wildlife and Natural Resources Conference.* Wildlife Management Institute, Washington, D.C.

Putney, Allen D. 1982. Final Report on a Survey of Conservation Priorities in the Lesser Antilles. EC-NAMP, St. Croix, U.S. Virgin Islands. 38 pp.

PNUD/FAO-ECU. 1971. Plan Maestro Para la Protecction y Uso del Parque Nacional Galapagos. Santiago de Chile, 1974.

Rabanal, H.R. 1977. Mangroves and Their Utilization for Aquaculture. *Phil. J. Fish.* 14(2): 191-203.

Radford, A.E., Otte, K.S., Otte, L.J., Massey, J.R., Whitson, P.D. *et al. Natural Heritage: Classification, Inventory and Information.* University of North Carolina Press, Chapel Hill, 485 pp.

Radway-Allen, K. 1980. *Conservation and management of whales.* Butterworths, London.

Ramsay, G.W. 1978. A review of the effect of rodents on the New Zealand invertebrate fauna. pp. 89-97 *in* Dingwall, P.R. *et al.* (eds.). 1978. *The Ecology and Control of Rodents in New Zealand Nature Reserves.* Proceedings of a symposium convened by the Department of Lands and Survey, Wellington, 29-30 November 1976. Department of Lands and Survey, Wellington.

Ranck, Stephen. 1982. *Recreational Tourism.* In King and Ranck (eds.) Papua New Guinea Atlas. Robert Brown and Assoc., Australia in conjunction with UPNG, PNG.

Rand, A.L. 1945. The 1945 status of the pronghorn antelope, *Antilocapra Americana* (Ord.), in Canada. *Nat. Mus. Can. Bull.* No. 106.

Randall, John E. 1982. Tropical marine sanctuaries and their significance in reef fisheries research. *NOAA Tech. Mem. NMFS SEFC* 80:167-176.

Ranjitsinh, M.K. 1979. Forest destruction in Asia and the south Pacific, *Ambio.* Vol. VIII, No. 5.

Rappaport, R.A. 1967. *Pigs for the Ancestors: Ritual in the Ecology of a New Guinea People.* Yale University Press, New Haven.

Rasmussen, K. 1969. The target for 1980. *Proceedings of the Canadian Forage Crops Symposium.* Western Cooperative Fertilizers Ltd., Calgary, Alberta. pp. 3-17.

Ray, G.C. 1975. A preliminary classification of coastal and marine environments. *IUCN Occ. Pap.* 14: 1-26.

Ray, G.C. 1976. Critical marine habitats. A statement on the nature of marine ecosystems with criteria and guidelines for the description and management of marine parks and reserves. *IUCN Publ.* (N. S.) 37: 75-90.

Ray, G.C., J.R. Clark, N.M. Foster, P.J. Godfrey, B.P. Hayden, S.P. Leatherman, W.E. Odum, J.H. Sather, and W.P. Gregg, Jr. 1981. Interim guidelines for identification and selection of coastal biosphere reserves. Rept. to the Directorate on Biosphere Reserves. U.S. MAB Rept. 8:1-33.

Remmert, H. 1980. *Arctic Animal Ecology.* Springer-Verlag, Berlin, Heidelberg New York.

Renard, Yves. (ed.). 1979. *Perceptions of the Environment, a Selection of Interpretive Essays.* Caribbean Environment, Environmental Studies No. 1. Caribbean Conservation Association, Barbados. 87 pp.

Renard, Yves. 1982. An Interim Report on a Study of the Conservation and Development Requirements for the South-East Coast of Saint Lucia. ECNAMP, St. Croix, U.S. Virgin Islands. 129 pp.

Republic of Kenya. Appraisal of the Wildlife and Tourism Project. International Bank for Reconstruction and Development, Nairobi.

Reuss, Henry S. 1958. *Conservation of wetlands; let's maintain our waterfowl breeding grounds, not drain them.* U.S. Government Printing Office, Washington.

Reynolds, G.W. 1975. Ask John Q Public. *Our Public Lands* 25 (4).

Richards, P.W. 1964. The tropical rainforest. Cambridge University Press, London.

Rick, C.M. 1976. Natural variability in wild species of *Lycopersicon* and its bearing on tomato breeding. *Genetica Agraria* 30: 249-259.

Roberts, B. 1978. International cooperation for antarctic development: the test for the Antarctic Treaty. *Polar Record* 19: 107-120.

Robinson, A., N. Polunin, K. Kvalvagnaes & M. Halim. 1981. Progress in creating a marine reserve system in Indonesia. *Bulletin of Marine Science* 31(3): 774-785.

Robinson, Alan H. 1979. Planning Considerations for preservation and use of the National Seashores. *Coastal Zone Mgmt. J.* 5(9): 5-34.

Roche, M.M. 1981. Securing representative areas of New Zealand's environment: some historical and design perspectives. *N.Z. Geographer* 37(2), 73-77.

Rodenburg, W.F. and R. Palete. 1981. Proposed National Park Dumoga-Bone Management Plan 1980/1981 - 1984-1985. WWF-PPA, Bogor. 77pp. & rev. 10pp.

Rogoff, M.J. 1978. *Statewide computer-based land information systems: an annotated bibliography of an emergent field.* Council of Planning Librarians.

Ross, D.A. 1980. *Opportunities and uses of the ocean.* Springer Verlag, New York. 320 pp.

Ruddle, Kenneth. 1974. *The Yukpa cultivation system: a study of shifting cultivation in Colombia and Venezuela.* University of California Press, Berkeley.

Rugoff, Milton.. 1961. *The Travels of Marco Polo,* The New English Library Ltd, London.

Ryther, J.H. 1969. Photosynthesis and fish production in the sea. *Science* 166: 72-76.

Sabater Pi, J. 1981. Exploitation of gorillas *Gorilla gorilla gorilla* Savage & Wyman 1847 in Rio Muni, Republic of Equatorial Guinea, West Africa. *Biological Conservation* 19(2):131-140.

Sabins, D.S. and F.M. Truesdale. 1974. Diel and seasonal occurrence of immature fishes in a Louisianna tidal pass. *Proc. 28th Ann. Conf. S.E. Assoc. Game and Fish. Comm.* 161-170.

Saenger, P., E.J. Hegerl and J.D.S. Davie. 1981. First report on the global status of mangrove ecosystems. IUCN Working Group on Mangrove Ecosystems. 132 pp.

Sahaya, R.C. 1979. Predators vis-a-vis Prey Densities in Palamau Tiger Reserve. Paper presented to International Symposium on the Tiger, New Delhi, Feb. 1979.

Sahlins, Marshall. 1972. *Stone age economics.* Aldine, Chicago. 348 pp.

Sale, P.F. 1980. The ecology of fishes on coral reefs. *Oceanogr. mar. Biol. Ann. Rev.* 18: 367-421.

Salm, R.V., Y. Abas, & R. Lameanda. 1982. Marine conservation potential of the Togian Islands, Sulawesi. Field Report 37, UNDP/FAO National Parks Development Project FO/INS/78/061, Bogor, Indonesia: iv + 22pp, Appendices, illustr.

Salm, R.V., M. Halim, & T. Soehartono. 1982a. Proposed Pulau Seribu Marine National Park Management Plan (1982-1983). Field Report 31, UNDP/FAO National Parks Development Project FO/INS/78/061, Bogor, Indonesia: vi + 48pp, Appendices, illustr.

Salm, R.V., M. Halim & T. Soehartono. 1982b. *Proposed Pulau Seribu Marine National Park Management Plan* 1982-1983. FO/INS/78/061 Field Report 31, Bogor: vi + 48pp, 2 Appendices, illustr.

Salm, R.V., M. Halim, & A. Abdullah. 1982. Proposed Pulau Seribu Marine National Park: tourism development and conservation progress together. Voluntary Paper, Third World National Parks Congress, Bali.

Salmon, G. 1981: The West Coast: a balanced approach, supplement to *Forest and Bird,* 221, 8pp.

Salvat, B. 1976. Guidelines for the planning and management of marine parks and reserves. *IUCN Publ.,* (N.S.) 37: 75-93..

Salwasser, H.J., and T. Hoekstra. In prep. Application of the Viable Population Concept to National Forest Management under the National Forest Management Act, U.S. Forest Service.

Sankhala, Kailash. 1978. *Tiger: The Story of the Indian Tiger.* Collins, London. 220 pp.

Sasekumar, A. and K.L. Thong. 1980. Predation of mangrove fauna by marine fishes at high tide. Paper presented at the Unesco Asian Symposium on Mangrove

Environment: Research and Management held at Universiti Malaya, Kuala Lumpur, August 1980.

Savoskul, S.S., 1978. Social and cultural dynamics of the peoples of the far north. *Polar Record* 19: 129-152.

Sax, Joseph. 1980. *Mountains Without Handrails.* University of Michigan Press, Ann Arbor.

Sayer, J.A. 1977. Conservation of Large Mammals in the Republic of Mali. *Biol. Conserv.* 12(4):245-263.

Sayer, J.A. 1981. Tourism or Conservation in the National Parks of Benin. *Parks* 5 (4).

Schaffer, M.L. 1981. Minimum population sizes for species conservation. *Biosci.* 31:131-134.

Schelske, C.L. and Odum, H.T. 1961. Mechanisms Maintaining High Productivity in Georgia Estuarines. Proceedings of the 14th Session, Gulf and Caribbean Fisheries Institute, Miami, Florida, pp. 75-80.

Schumacher, E.F. 1974. *Small is Beautiful: A study of economics as if people mattered.* London, Abacus Books.

Schwarz, C.F., Thor, E.C., and G.H. Elsner. 1976. Wildland planning glossary. USDA Forest Service. General Technical Report PSW-13. Pacific Southwest Forest and Range Experiment Station. Berkeley, California. 252 pp.

Scottish Development Department. 1968. *Threshold Analysis Handbook.* Department of Economic and Social Affairs U.N., New York. Document no. ST/ESA/64. Sales No. E. 78. IV.2. 216 pp.

Seidensticker, J. 1976. Ungulate population in Chitwan Valley, Nepal. *Biol. Conserv.* 10: 183-210.

Senger, T. 1974. Park facilities for the Future, in Elliott, Sir Hugh (ed). *Second World Conference on National Parks.* IUCN, Morges, Switzerland.

Shahi, Jai Prakash. 1982. Dudhwa Ke Baghon ko Nar-Bhakshi Kon Bana Raha Hai. *Ravivar*, April, 1982.

Shanks, David and Allen D. Putney. 1979. Dominica Forest and Park System Plan. ECNAMP, St. Croix, U.S. Virgin Islands. 155 pp.

Shannon, R.E. and T.F. Daubert. 1977. Rare II - A Process for the Future. *Journal of Soil & Water Conservation* 34 (2).

Shelley, Collin C. 1981. Aspects of the distribution, reproduction, growth and fishery potential of holothurians (bech-der-mer) in the Papuan coastal Lagoon. UPNG, Port Moresby, PNG.

Shenker, J.M., and J.M. Dean. 1980. The utilization of an intertidal salt marsh creek by larval and juvenile fishes: abundance, diversity, and temporal variation. *Estuaries* 2: 154-163.

Shepard, R. 1969. English reaction to the New Zealand landscape before 1850. *Pacific Viewpoint, Monograph 4,* Wellington N.Z.

Short, R.V. 1976. The introduction of new species of animals for the purpose of domestication. *Symp. Zool. Soc. Lond.* 40:321-333.

SIDA. 1979. *Vatten strategi.* Almenn oversikt. 30.

Simberloff, Daniel. 1982. Big Advantages of Small Refuges. *Nat. Hist.* 91(4): 6-14.

Simberoff, D.S.; L.G. Abele. 1976. Island biogeography theory and conservation practice. Science 191, 285-186.

Simmonds, N.W. 1979. *Principles of crop improvement.* Longman, London.

Simon, N. 1962. *Between the Sunlight and the Thunder.* Collins, London.

Simpson, P. (Comp). 1982. *Ecological regions and districts of New Zealand.* Biological Resources Centre Publication 1, Wellington, New Zealand. 63 pp. (plus maps).

Sinclair, A.E.R. and Norton-Griffiths, M. (eds.) 1979. *Serengeti: Dynamics of an Ecosystem.* University of Chicago Press, Chicago.

Siskind, Janet. 1973. *To hunt in the morning.* Oxford University Press, London.

Skeat, W.W. 1900. *Malay Magic.* MacMillan, London. 685 pp.

Smith, J.L.D. and H.R. Mishra. 1981. Management Recommendations for the Chitwan Tiger Population. The Parsa-Extension and the Bara Hunting Reserve. Smithsonian Institution/World Wildlife Fund Project 1051.

Soegiarto, A. 1979a. The Indonesian marine environment, its problems and management. *BIPT* 23(1): 9-21.

Soegiarto, A. 1979b. Sifat-sifat oseanologi perairan Indonesia sebagai dasar penentuan lokasi suaka alam laut. *Bio Indonesia* No. 6: 41-52.

Soegiarto, A. & Birowo, S. (eds.) 1975. *Atlas Oseanologi Perairan Indonesia dan sekitarnua.* Lembaga Oseanologi Nasional, Jakarta, I: 79.

Soulé, M.E., B.A. Wilcox, and C. Holtby. 1979. Benign neglect: a model of faunal collapse in the game reserves of East Africa. *Biol. Conserv.* 15: 259-272.

Soulé, Michael E. and Bruce A. Wilcox. 1980. *Conservation Biology.* Sinauer, Sunderland, Massachusetts. 395 pp.

South Pacific Commission. 1973. *Regional Symposium on Conservation of Nature - Reefs and Lagoons.* South Pacific Commission, Noumea, New Caledonia. 314 pp.

Specht, R.L. 1981. Conservation of Vegetation Types. pp 393-410 in *Australian Vegetation.* (R.H. Groves, ed.). Cambridge University Press.

Spinage, C.A. 1972. The Ecology and Problems of the Volcano National Park, Rwanda. *Biol. Conserv.* 4(3):194-204.

Spring, C.S. in press. Subsistence Hunting of Marine Turtles in Papua New Guinea. In *Proceedings of the World Conference on Sea Turtle Conservation.* Smithsonian Press, Washington, D.C.

Spring, S. 1977. Bird of Paradise Utilization at the Goroka Show - Wildlife in Papua New Guinea Publication Series 77/5.

Stark, W.A. II and R.E. Schroeder. 1971. Investigations on the gray snapper, *Lutjanus griseus.* Univ. of Miami Press, Miami, Florida. 224 pp.

Stebbins, G.L. & F.J. Ayala. 1981. Is a new evolutionary synthesis necessary? *Science* 213: 967-971.

Steenis, C.G.G.J. van. 1961. *Preservation of Tropical Plants and Vegetation,* Malayan Nature Journal 21st Anniversary, Special Issue.

Steenis, C.G.G.J. van. 1971. Plant conservation in Malesia. *Bull. Jard. Bot. Nat. Belg. Bull. Nat. Plantentuin Belg.* 41: 189-202.

Stein, R.E. Johnson B. 1979. *Banking on the Biosphere.* Environmental procedures and practices of nine multilateral development agencies. 203.

Stelfox, John G. 1966. *An investigation of the current status of prairie dogs (Gynomys ludovicianus ludovicianus Ord) in the Val Marie, Saskatchewan area.* Report to the National and Historic Parks Branch, Ottawa.

Stemmerman, L. F. Proby. 1978. Inventory of wetland vegetation in the Caroline Islands. U.S. Army Corps of Engineers, Pacific Ocean Division, report for contract DACW84-77-C-0062.

Stretton, H. 1976. *Capitalism, socialism and the environment.* Cambridge University Press.

Sumardja, E.A. 1980a. FAO Technical consultation of wildlife resources for rural development, Hyderabad.

Sumardja, E.A., 1980b. What is a national park in Indonesia? *Nature Conservation Workshop PPA-WWF-FAO.* Bogor. 4pp.

Sumardja, Effendy A. 1981. First Five National Parks in Indonesia. *Parks* 8(6): 1-4.

Sumardja, E.A. and McNeely, J.A. 1980. National Parks and Protected Areas of Indonesia: An up-date. *16th Meeting of IUCN/CNPPA.* Perth, Scotland, 54 pp.

Swadling, Pamela. 1980. *Shell fishing and management in Papua New Guinea.* In

Morauta *et al.* (eds.). Mono. 16. Traditional conservation: Implications for today. IASER; Port Moresby, PNG.

Swadling, Pamela. 1981. *The settlement history of the Motu and Koitabu speaking people of the Central Province, Papua New Guinea.* In Denoon and Lacey (eds.). Oral tradition in Melanesia. UPNG and IASER, Port Moresby, PNG.

Swift, J. 1975. Pastoralism and wildlife in dry marginal lands. IUCN, 13th Technical Meeting, Kinshasa, Zaire 7-19 September 1975.

Talbot, Lee. 1979. The Tip of the Iceberg: A biopolitical perspective on the Endangered Species Act. School of Forestry and Environmental Studies. Yale University.

Tamang, K.M. 1979. Population characteristics of the Tiger and its prey. Paper presented to the First International Symposium on the Tiger. New Delhi.

Tamura, T. 1968. The Marine Parks Center of Japan. *Biol. Conserv.*: 89-90.

Tang, H.T.; Haron b. Haji Hassan and Cheah, E.K. 1980. Mangrove Forests of Peninsular Malaysia - a review of management and research objectives and priorities. Paper presented at the Unesco Asian Symposium on Mangrove Environment: Research and Management held at Universiti Malaya, Kuala Lumpur, August 1980.

Telander, Rick. 1981. Riding Herd on Peru's Vicunas. *International Wildlife* 11(3): 36-43.

Temple, S.A. 1981. Applied island biogeography and the conservation of endangered island birds in the Indian Ocean. *Biol. Conserv.* 20(2): 147-161.

Terborgh, J. 1974. Preservation of natural diversity: the problem of extinction prone species. *Biosci.* 24:715-722.

Terborgh, J. and Winter, B. 1980. Some causes of extinction. in *Conservation Biology*, M.E. Soule and B.A. Wilcox, eds., Sinauer Associates, Sunderland, Ma.

Theberge, J.B., J.G. Nelson, and T. Fenge. 1980. *Environmentally Significant Areas of the Yukon Territory.* Canadian Arctic Resources Committee. Ottawa, Ontario.

Thelen, K.D. and Dalfelt, A. 1975. Systems and policies for wildland management and policies and regulations for national parks management. in Costa Rica. Technical Working Document No. CA8(b), Project FAO/UNDP/RLA/72/028. Central American Subregional Office, Guatemala.

Thelen, K.D. and Miller, K.R. 1975. Planificacion de sistemas de areas silvestres, guia para la planificacion de sistemas de areas silvestres con una aplicacion a los parques nacionales de Chile. Documento technico de Trabajo No. 16, proyecto FAO/RLAT/TF-199, Santiago, Chile.

Thilenius, G. (ed.) 1969. 1914-1948. Ergebnisse der Sudsee-Expedition, 1908-1910. Series II-Ethnographie, B. Micronesia. Hamburg.

Thomson, A.P., and J.L. Nicholls. 1973. Scientific reserves in New Zealand indigenous forests. *New Zealand Journal of Forestry* 18: 17-22.

Thong, K.L. and A. Sasekumar. 1980. The trophic relationship of the fish community of the Angsa Bank, Selangor, Malaysia. Paper presented at the Unesco Asian Symposium on Mangrove Environment: Research and Management held at Universiti Malaya, Kuala Lumpur, Malaya. August 1980.

Thorsell, J.W. and F.N. Pertet. 1980. National Parks, Reserves and Protected Areas of Kenya. *Proceedings of the 17th Meeting of IUCN's Commission on National Parks and Protected Areas.* IUCN/UNEP/Unesco/WWF, Gland, Switzerland. pp. 66-72.

Thorsell, J.W. 1975. A National Park on the Island of Dominica. Report to the Canadian Nature Federation.

Thorsell, J.W. 1978. Thinking like an Island: Interpretation in Dominica, West Indies. *The Interpreter*, 10(1).

Thresher, P. 1981. The present value of an Amboseli lion. *World Animal Review* 40:30-33.

Tiger Paper 5, No. 1.27 (January, 1978).

Tolba, M.K. 1982. *Development Without Destruction.* Dublin, Ireland: Tycooly International Publishing Ltd.,

Tolba, M. 1979. *Environmental considerations in the New International Development Strategy.* Stensil. 21 pp.

Tomlinson, D.N.S. 1980. Nature Conservation in Rhodesia: A Review. *Biol. Conserv.* 18(3):159-17.

Tongariro National Park Board. 1980. Tongariro National Park Management Plan.

Train, R. E. 1973. An Idea Whose Time Has Come: World Heritage Trust. *Nature and Resources* 9 (1).

Trewartha, G.T. 1962. *The Earth's problem climates.* London, U.K.

Trewartha, G.T. 1968. *An Introduction to Climate.* McGraw-Hill, N.Y.

Troth, R.G. Successional Role of *Bombax ceiba* in Savannas in Nepal. Project Report. Smithsonian/WWF Tiger Ecology Project, Nepal.

Trotignon, J. 1975. Le status et la conservation de l'addax et de l'oryx et de la faune associée en Mauritanie. IUCN, Morges, Switzerland.

Trzyna, T. and E. Coan. 1976. World directory of environmental organizations. Public Affairs Clearing House (2nd Ed.), Claremont, CA. 258 pp.

Turner, L. and J. Ash. 1975. *The golden hordes: international tourism and the pleasure periphery.* Constable, London.

Turner, R.E. 1977. Intertidal vegetation and commercial yields of Penaeid shrimp. *Trans. Am. Fish. Society* 106: 411-416.

Udvardy, M.D.F. 1975. A Classification of the Biogeographical Provinces of the World. *IUCN Occ. Pap.* 18: 1-48.

Underwood, J.H. 1969. Preliminary investigations of demographic features and ecological variables of a Micronesian island population.

UN Conference on the Human Environment. 1972. Development and Environment. A/Conf. 48/10. 14 plus annex.

U.S. Dept. of the Interior. 1972. National Park Service. *Part Two of the National Park System Plan: Natural History.* 140 pp.

U.S. National Academy of Sciences. 1980. *Firewood Crops: Shrub and Tree Species for Energy production.* National Academy of Sciences, Washington, D.C.

UNEP. 1979. *Development and Environment in the Wider Caribbean Region: A Synthesis.* UNEP/CEPAL Caribbean Environment Programme Meeting of Government Nominated Experts to Review the Draft Action Plan for the Wider Caribbean Region, Caracas, Venezuela. 40 pp.

UNEP. 1980a. *Coastal Ecosystems: A Review.* UNEP, Nairobi, Kenya. 65pp.

UNEP. 1980b. *Genetic Resources: An Overview.* UNEP, Nairobi, Kenya. 132 pp.

UNEP. 1981. Conference of Plenipotentiaries on Cooperation in the Protection and Development of the Marine and Coastal Environment of the West and Central African Region. Final Act UNEP Abidjan, March 1981.

UNEP. 1982. The global assessment of tropical forest resources. GEMS/PAC Information Series No. 3. Nairobi:UNEP.

UNEP/FAO. 1980a. Project pilote sur la surveillance continue de la couverture forestiere tropicale: Togo. UN 32/6.1102-75-005, Rap.Tech.1. FAO:Rome.

UNEP/FAO. 1980b. Project pilote sur la surveillance continue de la couverture forestiere tropicale: Benin. UN 32/6.1102-75-005, Rap.Tech.2. FAO:Rome.

UNEP/FAO. 1980c. Project pilote sur la surveillance continue de la couverture forestiere tropicale: Cameroun. UN 32/6.1102-75-005, Rap.Tech.3. FAO:Rome.

UNEP/FAO. 1980d. Pilot project on the monitoring of tropical forest cover: Benin-Cameroun-Togo. UN 32/6.1102-75-005, Rap.Tech.4. FAO:Rome.

UNEP/FAO. 1981a. Tropical forest resources assessment project (in the framework of GEMS): Forest resources of tropical Africa Part I, Regional synthesis. Rome:FAO (English/French).

UNEP/FAO. 1981b. Tropical forest resources assessment project (in the framework of GEMS): Forest resources of tropical Africa Part II, Country briefs. Rome:FAO (English, French).

UNEP/FAO. 1981c. Tropical forest resources assessment project (in the framework of GEMS): Forest resources of tropical Asia. Rome:FAO.

UNEP/FAO. 1981d. Proyecto ed evaluacion de los recursos forestales tropicales (in el marco del SINU-VIMA): Los recursos forestales de la America tropical. Rome:FAO.

UNEP/FAO, UNESCO. 1979. A provisional methodology for soil degradation assessment. Rome: FAO.

Unesco/FAO. 1970. Vegetation map of the Mediterranean Zone. Arid Zone Research XXX. Paris.

Unesco. 1972. Convention concerning the protection of the world cultural and natural heritage. General Conference, 17th Session, Paris, November 16.

Unesco. 1973. *International Classification and Mapping of Vegetation.* Unesco, Paris.

Unesco. 1980. Operational Guidelines for the Implementation of the World Heritage Convention, WHC/2 Revised October, 1980.

Unesco. 1974. Criteria and Guidelines for the Choice and Establishment of Biosphere Reserves. MAB Rept. Series 22: 1-61. Unesco, Paris.

Unesco/FAO. 1981. Vegetation map of South America. Natural Resources

Research, XVII. Unesco, Paris.

Unesco. 1981. Marine and coastal processes in the Pacific: aspects of coastal zone management. *Unesco Rept. mar. Sci.* 6, 20pp.

United Nations. 1959. Resolution 713 of the 27th session of the Economic and Social Council.

USAID. 1979. Environmental and Natural Resources Management in Developing Countries. A Report to Congress. Washington.

Useem, J. 1946. Economic and human resources, Yap and Palau, West Carolines. United States Commercial Economic Survey, Honolulu. 3 volumes.

US National Park Serice. 1979. Guidelines for the Selection of Biosphere Reserves. Interim Report. Washington, D.C.

Valentine, J.W. 1971. Plate tectonics and shallow marine diversity and endemism, an actualistic model. *Syst. Zool.* 20: 253-264.

Valentine, J.W. 1973. *Evolutionary Palaeoecology of the Marine Biosphere.* Englewood Cliffs: Prentice-Hall. xvi + 512pp.

Valentine, J.W. & E.M. Moores. 1970. Plate-tectonic regulation of faunal diversity and sea-level: a model. *Nature* 228: 657-659.

van der Kroef, J.M. 1954. Dualism and symbolic antithesis in Indonesian Society. *Am. Anth.* 56: 847-862.

van den Hoek, C., A.M. Cortel-Breeman and J.B.W. wanders. 1975. Algal zonation in the fringing reef of Curaao, Netherlands Antilles, in relation to zonation of corals and gorganians. *Aquat. Bot. 1: 269-308.*

van Orsdol, K.G. 1979. Uganda National Parks. *Swara* 2 (4) : 14-16.

Vanzolini, P.E. and E.E. Williams. 1970. South American anoles: the geographic differentation and evolution of the *Anolis Chyrsolepis* species group (Sauri, Iguanidae). *Arq. Zool. S. Paulo* 19: 1-240.

Vanzolini, P.E. 1970. Zoologia sistematica, geografia e a origem das espcies. *Inst. Geografia, Univ. Sao Paulo, Teses e Monogr.* No. 3. 56 pp.

Vermeij, G.J. 1978. *Biogeography and Adaptation.* Cambridge, Mass.: Harvard University.

Vincent, George. 1982. A Report on the Proposed Levera National Park. ECNAMP, St. Croix, U.S. Virgin Islands. 64 pp.

Vogl, R.J. 1979. Some Basic Principles of Grassland Fire Management. *Environmental Management* 3(1): 51-57.

von Someren, G.R.C. 1982. Interview, National Museum of Kenya.

Voss, G.L. 1973. Sickness and death in Florida's coral reefs. *Nat. Hist. 82 (7): 40-47.*

Wace, N.M. and M.W. Holdgate. 1976. Man and nature in the Tristan da Cunha Islands. IUCN, Monograph 6. IUCN, 1196 Gland, Switzerland.

Wace, N.M. 1972. Discussion on the Plant Geography Around Torres Strait. pp. 197-211. *In* D. Walker (ed.). 1972. *Bridge and Barrier: The Natural and Cultural History of Torres Strait.* Research School of Pacific Studies, Australian National University, Canberra. 437 pp.

Wace, N.M. 1979. Oceanic Islands—*World Conservation Strategy*, IUCN, 1196 Gland, Switzerland (unpub.).

Wace, N.M. 1980. Exploitation of the advantages of remoteness and isolation in the economic development of Pacific Islands. In *The Island States of the Pacific and Indian Oceans: anatomy of devleopment.* Development Studies Centre Monograph 23, 87-118. Australian National University, Canberra.

Wagner, P.R. 1973. Seasonal biomass, abundance, and distribution of estuarine dependent fishes in the Caminada Bay system of Louisiana. Ph.D. dissertation, Louisana State University, Baton Rouge, Louisiana.

Waithaman, D. 1974. Tonda Reserve Animal Use Report (Official Ecofile 8-2-4 (2A)). Division of Wildlfe, Environment and Conservation Papua New Guinea.

Walesh, G.W. *et al.* 1977. Land Data Management System for Resource Planning *A.S.C.E. Journal of Water Resources Planning and Management.*

Walker, P.A. 1982. The Australian Resource Information System. Land Use Planning Group Division of Land Research, C.S.I.R.O. Canberra, Australia.

Wallace, A.R. 1880. *Island Life.* MacMillan, London.

Wang, Huen-pu. 1980. Nature conservation in China: The present situation. PARKS Magazine.

Watson, J.G. 1928. Mangrove Forests of the Malay Peninsula. Malay. For. Rec. 6: 1-275.

Watt, K.E.F., L.F. Molloy, C.K. Varshney, D. Weeks, S. Wirosardjono. 1977. *The unsteady state: Environmental problems, growth and culture.* University Press, East-West Center, Honolulu. 287 pp.

Webb, L.J., D. Whitelock & J. Le Gay Brereton (eds.), 1969. *The Last of Lands.* Jacaranda Press, Milton, Queensland. 203 pp.

Weber, W. 1979. Geographic Information Systems (G.I.S.) —A Review and Reflections on the Future Development. *International Yearbook of Cartography XIX.*

Webster, Steven. 1971. An indigenous Quechua community in exploitation of multiple ecological zones. *Revista del Museo Nacional del Peru* 37: 174-183.

Weilbacher, B.F. 1973. Comments on Problems of Conservation and Planning for Their Solution, Session IV. pp. 53-62. *In* South Pacific Commission. 1973. *Regional Symposium on Conservation of Nature—Reefs and Lagoons.* SPC, Noumea, New Caledonia. 314 pp.

Weinstein, M.P. 1979. Shallow marsh habitats as primary nurseries for fish and shellfish, Cape Fear River, North Carolina. *Fish. Bull.* 77: 339-357.

Weinstein, M.P., S.L. Weiss, R.G. Hodson, and L.R. Gerry. 1980. Retention of three taxa of post larval fishes in an intensively flushed tidal estuary, Cape Fear River, N.C. *Fish. Bull.* 78: 419-435.

Weitz, B. 1963: The feeding habits of *Glossina. Bull. Wld. Hlth. Org. 28: 711-729.*

Wendt, Albert. 1978. Reborn to Belong. Paper given at the Seminar on the Role of Museums in Strengthening Indigenous Cultures. Adelaide.

Werme, C.E. 1981. Resource partitioning in a salt marsh fish community. Ph.D. dissertation, Boston University, Boston, Mass. 125 pp.

West, Robert. 1976. Conservation of Coastal Marine Environments. *Rev. Biol. Trop.* 24(Supl. 1). 187-209.

Western Australian Department of Conservation and Environment. 1981. The Darling System, Western Australia. The System 6 Study Report to the Environment Protection Authority. Report No. 8.

Western, D. and D. Sindiyo. 1972. *East African Wildlife Journal* 10(1), pp. 43-57.

Western, D. and W. Henry. 1979. Economics and Conservation in Third World National Parks. *Bioscience,* 29(7):414-418.

Western, D. and J. Ssemakula. 1981. *African Journal of Ecology* 19(1), pp. 7-19.

Western, D. and P. Thresher. 1973. International Bank for Reconstruction and Development. pp. 1-99.

Western, D. 1975. *East African Wildlife Journal* 13(3), pp. 265-286.

Western, D. 1976. A New Approach to Ambolesi. *Parks* 1(2): pp. 1-4.

Western, D. 1982. *Biological Conservation* 24 (2).

Wetterberg, G.B. and Jorge Padua, M.T., Soares de Ca-´tro, C., and Vasconcello, J.M. 1976. Uma Análise de Prioridades em Conservaao da Natureza na Amazonia—PNUD/FAO/IBDF/BRA-45, Srie Tcnica No. 8, 62 pp.

Wetterberg, G.B. and Jorge Padua, M.T. 1978. Preservacao da natureza na Amazonia Brasileira: situaçao em 1978. PNUD/FAO/IBDF/BRA/76/02 Serie Tecnica No. 13. Brasilia. 44 pp.

Wetterberg, G.B., G.T. Prance, and T. Lovejoy. 1981. Conservation progress in Amazonia: a structural review. *PARKS* 6 (2): 5-10.

Wharton, C. 1968. Man, Fire and Wild Cattle in South East Asia. *Proc. of the Tall Timber Fire Ecology Conference*, 8: 107-167.

Whetsell, D. 1980. Tall Grass Prairie National Park: Would It Really be in the Interest of the Public. *Rangelands* 2 (4).

White, F. 1982. The vegetation of Africa. Natural Resources Research XIX. Unesco, Paris. In press.

Wiens, Herold J. 1962. *Atoll Environment and Ecology*. Yale University Press, New Haven. 532 pp.

Wilcox, Bruce A. 1980. Insular Ecology and Conservation. pp. 95-117 *in* Michael E. Soul and Bruce A. Wilcox. *Conservation Biology*. Sinauer, Sunderland, Massachusetts.

Wilcox, Bruce A. 1982. The role of population biology research in the selection and management of biosphere reserves. Proceedings of the US/INDO Workshop on Biological Diversity, Department of Environment, Delhi, India.

Williams, G.R. (ed.). 1973. "Birds". *In: The Natural History of New Zealand*. A.H. and A.W. Reed, Wellington. pp. 304-333.

Williams, G.R. 1979. Two legs (sometimes) good, four legs (always) bad; or a defence of a moderate xenophilia. pp. 65-69 *in National Parks of New Zealand*. Proceedings of the Silver Jubilee Conference of the National Parks Authority of New Zealand, Lincoln College, 5-8 July 1978. National Parks Authority of New Zealand, c/o Department of Lands and Survey, Wellington.

Williams, G.R. and D.R. Given. 1981. *The Red Data Book of New Zealand*. Rare and endangered species of endemic terrestrial vertebrates and vascular plants. Nature Conservation Council, Wellington, New Zealand. 175pp.

Williamson, F.H.H. 1915. Game Preservation in Dominion Parks *Conservation of Fish, Birds and Game*. Proceedings at a meeting of the Commission of Conservation Canada on November 1 and 2, 1915, Ottawa.

Willock, C. 1964. *The Enormous Zoo: A profile of the Uganda National Parks*. Collins, London.

Wilson, Edward O. 1982. The Importance of Biological Field Stations. *Bioscience* 32(5):320.

Wilson, R.T. 1980. Wildlife in Northern Darfur, Sudan: A Review of its Distribution and Status in the Recent Past and Present. *Biol. Conserv.* 17(2):85-101.

Winge, E.N. 1978. Involving the Public in Park Planning: USA. *Parks* 3 (1).

Working Group on Selection and Classification of Protected Areas. 1980. Report to Standing Committee. Council of Nature Conservation Ministers, Australia. 23pp.

World Wildlife Fund. 1982. *Strategy for Training in Natural Resources and Environment*. WWF-US, Washington, D.C., USA. 208 pp. Appendices.

Wynn, G. 1979. Pioneers, politicians and the conservation of forests in early New Zealand. *J. Historical Geography* 5(2): 171-188.

Yap Institute of Natural Science. 1981. Yap almanac calendar. Yap. 16pp.

Yap State Department of Resources and Development. 1980. Statistical yearbook Yap State. 80pp.

Zamora, P. 1981. Conservation and Management Strategies for Philippine Mangroves. *Proc. of the National Conference on the Conservation of Natural Resources*. Manila.